INTERNATIONAL ENCYCLOPEDIA OF PUBLIC POLICY AND ADMINISTRATION

INTERNATIONAL ENCYCLOPEDIA OF PUBLIC POLICY AND ADMINISTRATION

Jay M. Shafritz

EDITOR IN CHIEF

Volume 1: A-C

WestviewPress

A Division of HarperCollinsPublishers

Copyright © 1998 by Westview Press, A Division of HarperCollins Publishers, Inc.

Published in 1998 in the United States of America by Westview Press, 5500 Central Avenue, Boulder, Colorado 80301-2877, and in the United Kingdom by Westview Press, 12 Hid's Copse Road, Cumnor Hill, Oxford OX2 9JJ

Library of Congress Cataloging-in-Publication Data

The international encyclopedia of public policy and administration /
   Jay M. Shafritz, editor in chief.
       p. cm.
    Includes bibliographical references (p.   ) and index.
    Contents: v. 1. A-C – v. 2. D-K – v. 3. L-Q – v. 4. R-Z, index.
    ISBN 0-8133-9973-4 (vol. 1 : hardcover : alk. paper). – ISBN
0-8133-9974-2 (vol. 2 : hardcover : alk. paper). – ISBN
0-8133-9975-0 (vol. 3 : hardcover : alk. paper). – ISBN
0-8133-9976-9 (vol. 4 : hardcover : alk. paper)
    1. Public policy–Encyclopedias.   2. Public administration–
–Encyclopedias.   I. Shafritz, Jay M.
H97.I574   1998
351'.03–dc21   97-34169
                                                                    CIP

The paper used in this publication meets the requirements of the American National Standard for Permanence of Paper for Printed Library Materials Z39.48-1984.

10   9   8   7   6   5   4   3   2   1

Table of Contents

Contributors

Glenn Abney
Georgia State University
Atlanta, Georgia

Guy B. Adams
University of Missouri, Columbia
Columbia, Missouri

Luis F. Aguilar Villanueva
El Colegio de Mexico
Mexico City, Mexico

Abdullah M. Al-Khalaf
Institute of Public Administration
Riyadh, Saudi Arabia

Abdulrahman Abdullah Al-Shakawy
Institute of Public Administration
Riyadh, Saudi Arabia

Mohammed Abdulrahman Al-Tawail
Al-Tawail Management Consulting and Training
Riyadh, Saudi Arabia

Patrice Alexander
Champion International
Roanoke Rapids, North Carolina

Richard M. Alexander
Britannia Royal Naval College, Dartmouth
United Kingdom

John Alford
University of Melbourne
Melbourne, Australia

Leslie R. Alm
Boise State University
Boise, Idaho

Roger Anderson
Bowling Green State University
Bowling Green, Ohio

Clive Archer
Manchester Metropolitan University
Manchester, United Kingdom

David S. Arnold
editor/writer
Falls Church, Virginia

Patricia S. Atkins
National Association of Regional Councils
Washington, D.C.

Gary Baker
University of Missouri, Kansas City
Kansas City, Missouri

Howard Balanoff
Southwest Texas State University
San Marcos, Texas

Danny L. Balfour
Grand Valley State University, Grand Rapids
Grand Rapids, Michigan

Steven Ballard
University of Maine
Orono, Maine

McRae C. Banks
Worcester Polytechnic Institute
Worcester, Massachusetts

Prahlad Kumar Basu
Gyosei International College
Reading, United Kingdom

John Baylis
University of Wales, Aberystwyth
United Kingdom

John F. T. Bayliss
Royal Naval College, Greenwich
United Kingdom

Douglas R. Beach
Beach, Burcke, Helfers & Mittleman
St. Louis, Missouri

Carl J. Bellone
California State University, Hayward
Hayward, California

Jonathan Bendor
Stanford University
Stanford, California

Colin Benjamin
Asia Pacific Development Network
Canberra, Australia

William Bergosh
Bergosh, Buchanan & Associates Ltd.
Kansas City, Missouri

William H. Bergquist
Professional School of Psychology
San Francisco and Sacramento, California

John Bern
University of Wollongong
Wollongong, Australia

Geoffrey R. Berridge
Leicester University
Leicester, United Kingdom

J. B. Billiet
Katholieke Universiteit Leuven
Leuven, Belgium

J. Walton Blackburn
Nebraska Department of Social Services
Lincoln, Nebraska

Stephen R. Block
Denver Option, Inc.
Denver, Colorado

Michael J. Bloom
U. S. Department of the Treasury
Washington, D.C.

Davis B. Bobrow
University of Pittsburgh
Pittsburgh, Pennsylvania

Jean-Luc Bodiguel
Centre De Recherches Administrative, F.N.S.P.
Paris, France

Elizabeth T. Boris
Urban Institute
Washington, D.C.

Jonathan Boston
Victoria University of Wellington
Wellington, New Zealand

Geert Bouckaert
Katholieke Universiteit Leuven
Leuven, Belgium

Tony Bovaird
Aston University
Birmingham, United Kingdom

William M. Bowen
Cleveland State University
Cleveland, Ohio

James S. Bowman
Florida State University
Tallahassee, Florida

Brenda L. Boyd
Rutgers, The State University of New Jersey
Newark, New Jersey

Christopher Brady
Institute of Contemporary History
London, United Kingdom

Guy Braibant
Office of the Prime Minister
Paris, France

Marleen Brans
Katholieke Universiteit Leuven
Leuven, Belgium

Paul M. Brown
attorney
St. Louis, Missouri

Willa Marie Bruce
University of Nebraska, Omaha
Omaha, Nebraska

Jeffrey L. Brudney
University of Georgia
Athens, Georgia

John M. Bryson
University of Minnesota
Minneapolis, Minnesota

Robert Buchanan
Bergosh, Buchanan & Associates Ltd.
Kansas City, Missouri

Beverly S. Bunch
University of Texas, Austin
Austin, Texas

Naomi Caiden
California State University, Los Angeles
Los Angeles, California

Kathe Callahan
Rutgers, The State University of New Jersey
Newark, New Jersey

Guy Callender
University of Technology
Sydney, Australia

David Carnavale
University of Oklahoma
Norman, Oklahoma

Keith Carrington
Rutgers, The State University of New Jersey
Newark, New Jersey

Mary Elizabeth Carroll
San Jose State University
San Jose, California

Stephen Castles
University of Wollongong
Wollongong, Australia

N. Joseph Cayer
Arizona State University
Tempe, Arizona

Paul Chadwick
Communications Law Center
Melbourne, Australia

Tamu Chambers
Russell Sage College
Troy, New York

Hon S. Chan
City University of Hong Kong
Kowloon, Hong Kong

Jeffrey I. Chapman
University of Southern California, Sacramento
Sacramento, California

Richard A. Chapman
University of Durham
Durham, United Kingdom

Douglas L. Christiansen
Purdue University, West Lafayette
West Lafayette, Indiana

Allan J. Cigler
University of Kansas
Lawrence, Kansas

Beverly A. Cigler
Penn State Harrisburg
Middletown, Pennsylvania

Bruce B. Clary
University of Southern Maine
Portland, Maine

Joy A. Clay
University of Memphis
Memphis, Tennessee

Edward J. Clynch
Mississippi State University
Mississippi State, Mississippi

Breena E. Coates
University of Pittsburgh
Pittsburgh, Pennsylvania

Jerrell D. Coggburn
University of South Carolina
Columbia, South Carolina

Michele T. Cole
Neighborhood Legal Services
Pittsburgh, Pennsylvania

Michele Collins
Rutgers, The State University of New Jersey
Newark, New Jersey

Sara Ann Conkling
University of Central Florida
Orlando, Florida

Thomas A. Connelly
attorney
St. Louis, Missouri

Terry L. Cooper
University of Southern California, Los Angeles
Los Angeles, California

Glen Hahn Cope
University of Illinois, Springfield
Springfield, Illinois

David C. Corbett
Flinders University
Adelaide, Australia

Joan Corkery
European Centre for Development Policy Management
Maastricht, Netherlands

Jane Coulter
University of New South Wales
Kensington, Australia

Raymond W. Cox III
Innovations in Management
Sunrise, Florida

Robert A. Cropf
St. Louis University
St. Louis, Missouri

Barbara C. Crosby
University of Minnesota
Minneapolis, Minnesota

Robert B. Cunningham
University of Tennessee, Knoxville
Knoxville, Tennessee

Thomas J. Cuny
Congressional Budget Office (retired)
Washington, D.C.

Dennis M. Daley
North Carolina State University
Raleigh, North Carolina

Glyn Davis
Griffith University
Nathan, Australia

Susan E. Day
University of Central Florida
Orlando, Florida

Patria D. de Lancer
Rutgers, The State University of New Jersey
Newark, New Jersey

Ruth Hoogland DeHoog
University of North Carolina, Greensboro
Greensboro, North Carolina

Joseph DeIorio
Rutgers, The State University of New Jersey
Newark, New Jersey

Herman Deleeck
University of Antwerp
Antwerp, Belgium

Monica G. W. den Boer
European Institute of Public Administration
Maastricht, Netherlands

Robert B. Denhardt
University of Delaware
Newark, Deleware

Michael A. Diamond
University of Missouri, Columbia
Columbia, Missouri

Lisa A. Dicke
University of Utah
Salt Lake City, Utah

Sherry S. Dickerson
Arizona State University
Tempe, Arizona

Robert L. Dilworth
Virginia Commonwealth University
Richmond, Virginia

Mary R. Domahidy
St. Louis University
St. Louis, Missouri

Simon Domberger
University of Sydney
Sydney, Australia

Richard Doyle
Naval Postgraduate School
Monterey, California

Gavin Drewry
University of London
Royal Holloway, United Kingdom

Melvin J. Dubnick
Rutgers, The State University of New Jersey
Newark, New Jersey

Sydney Duncombe
University of Idaho (emeritus)
Moscow, Idaho

William D. Duncombe
Syracuse University
Syracuse, New York

Andrew Dunsire
University of York
York, United Kingdom

M.A. Toni DuPont-Morales
Penn State Harrisburg
Middletown, Pennsylvania

Nicholas M. Economou
Monash University
Melbourne, Australia

Don Edgar
Royal Melbourne Institute of Technology
Melbourne, Australia

Martin Edmonds
Lancaster University
Lancaster, United Kingdom

Damien Ejigiri
Southern University
Baton Rouge, Louisiana

Hassan A. El Tayeb
Ministry of Civil Service
Sultanate of Oman

Robert Elgie
University of Limerick
Limerick, Ireland

David R. Elkins
Cleveland State University
Cleveland, Ohio

Robert H. Elliott
Auburn University
Montgomery, Alabama

John Ernst
Victoria University of Technology
Melbourne, Australia

Kenneth J. Euske
Naval Postgraduate School
Monterey, California

Karen G. Evans
Virginia Polytechnic Institute and State University
Blacksburg, Virginia

Marni Ezra
The American University
Washington, D.C.

Sue R. Faerman
University at Albany, State University of New York
Albany, New York

James A. Fagin
Chaminade University
Honolulu, Hawaii

Ali Farazmand
Florida Atlantic University, Fort Lauderdale
Fort Lauderdale, Florida

Christine Farias
Texas Tech University
Lubbock, Texas

Claire Felbinger
Cleveland State University
Cleveland, Ohio

Fred E. Fiedler
University of Washington
Seattle, Washington

Frank Fischer
Rutgers, The State University of New Jersey
Newark, New Jersey

Patricia S. Florestano
Maryland Higher Education Commission
Crofton, Maryland

Peter Foot
Royal Naval College, Greenwich
United Kingdom

John P. Forrester
University of Missouri, Columbia
Columbia, Missouri

Charles J. Fox
Texas Tech University
Lubbock, Texas

H. George Frederickson
University of Kansas
Lawrence, Kansas

Musaed A. Furayyan
Institute of Public Administration
Riyadh, Saudi Arabia

Vatche Gabrielian
Rutgers, The State University of New Jersey
Newark, New Jersey

Rhonda Galbally
Victorian Health Promotion Foundation
Melbourne, Australia

Ian R. Gardiner
Royal Marines
Portsmouth, United Kingdom

John Garnett
University of Wales, Aberystwyth
United Kingdom

Leo V. Garvin
Garvin & Maloney
St. Louis, Missouri

William R. Gates
Naval Postgraduate School
Monterey, California

Erna Gelles
Bridgewater State College
Bridgewater, Massachusetts

Rolf Gerritsen
University of Canberra
Canberra, Australia

Nicholas A. Giannatasio
University of North Dakota
Grand Forks, North Dakota

Christine Gresham Gibbs
Red Tape, Ltd.
Phoenix, Arizona

Frederick W. Gibson
OppenheimerFunds, Inc.
Denver, Colorado

Jeff Gill
Harvard University
Cambridge, Massachusetts
California Polytechnic State University
San Luis Obispo, California

James F. Gilsinan
St. Louis University
St. Louis, Missouri

George Frederick Goerl
California State University, Hayward
Hayward, California

Deborah D. Goldman
attorney
Bethesda, Maryland

Roger L. Goldman
St. Louis University
St. Louis, Missouri

Robert T. Golembiewski
University of Georgia
Athens, Georgia

Joaquin L. Gonzalez
National University of Singapore
Singapore

Charles T. Goodsell
Virginia Polytechnic Institute and State University
Blacksburg, Virginia

Charles W. Gossett
Georgia Southern University
Statesboro, Georgia

Cole Blease Graham, Jr.
University of South Carolina
Columbia, South Carolina

Richard T. Green
University of Wyoming
Laramie, Wyoming

David E. Greenwood
University of Aberdeen
Scotland, United Kingdom

Frank Gregory
University of Southampton
Southampton, United Kingdom

Jeffery K. Guiler
Robert Morris College
Moon Township, Pennsylvania

James J. Guy
University College of Cape Breton
Nova Scotia, Canada

Mary E. Guy
Florida State University
Tallahassee, Florida

Merl Hackbart
University of Kentucky
Lexington, Kentucky

Lois Haignere
United University Professors
Albany, New York

Steven Haines
Royal Naval Engineering College
Plymouth, United Kingdom

John Halligan
University of Canberra
Canberra, Australia

Ralph S. Hambrick, Jr.
Virginia Commonwealth University
Richmond, Virginia

Alan Hamlin
University of Southampton
Southampton, United Kingdom

Michael M. Harmon
George Washington University
Washington, D.C.

David Kirkwood Hart
Brigham Young University
Provo, Utah

Leonard C. Hawes
University of Utah
Salt Lake City, Utah

Steven W. Hays
University of South Carolina
Columbia, South Carolina

F. Ted Hebert
University of Utah
Salt Lake City, Utah

Jane S. Heide
Heart of America United Way
Kansas City, Missouri

Richard D. Heimovics
University of Missouri, Kansas City
Kansas City, Missouri

April Hejka-Ekins
California State University, Stanislaus
Turlock, California

Gary D. Helfand
University of Hawaii, West Oahu
Pearl City, Hawaii

Nicholas Henry
Georgia Southern University
Statesboro, Georgia

Frederick I. Herzberg
University of Utah
Salt Lake City, Utah

Kent Hibbelin
Bowling Green State University
Bowling Green, Ohio

Abdulrahman A. Higan
Institute of Public Administration
Riyadh, Saudi Arabia

Gregory G. Hildebrandt
Naval Postgraduate School
Monterey, California

W. Bartley Hildreth
Wichita State University
Wichita, Kansas

Graeme A. Hodge
Monash University
Melbourne, Australia

Mihály Hõgye
Budapest University of Economic Sciences
Budapest, Hungary

Randall G. Holcombe
Florida State University
Tallahassee, Florida

Malcolm Holmes
World Bank
Washington, D.C.

Marc Holzer
Rutgers, The State University of New Jersey
Newark, New Jersey

Michael K. Hooper
Penn State Harrisburg
Middletown, Pennsylvania

David J. Houston
University of Tennessee, Knoxville
Knoxville, Tennessee

Michael J. Howard
University of New South Wales
Sydney, Australia

R. Brian Howe
University College of Cape Breton
Nova Scotia, Canada

Christopher Hoyt
University of Missouri, Kansas City
Kansas City, Missouri

Jesse W. Hughes
Old Dominion University
Norfolk, Virginia

Owen E. Hughes
Monash University
Melbourne, Australia

Ralph P. Hummel
University of Oklahoma
Norman, Oklahoma
University of Akron
Akron, Ohio

Albert C. Hyde
Brookings Institution
Washington, D.C.

Warren F. Ilchman
Indiana University Center on Philanthropy
Indianapolis, Indiana

Cynthia Y. Jackson
Michigan State University
East Lansing, Michigan

J. Bruce Jacobs
Monash University
Melbourne, Australia

Rhodri Jeffreys-Jones
University of Edinburgh
Scotland, United Kingdom

Edward T. Jennings
University of Kentucky
Lexington, Kentucky

William Y. Jiang
San Jose State University
San Jose, California

Bob L. Johnson
University of Utah
Salt Lake City, Utah

David A. Johnson
University College of Cape Breton
Nova Scotia, Canada

Judy Johnston
University of Technology
Sydney, Australia

L. R. Jones
Naval Postgraduate School
Monterey, California

Michael Jones
University of Canberra
Canberra, Australia

Alma M. Joseph
Rutgers, The State University of New Jersey
Newark, New Jersey

Philip G. Joyce
Syracuse University
Syracuse, New York

Jamil E. Jreisat
University of South Florida
Tampa, Florida

Jong S. Jun
California State University, Hayward
Hayward, California

Jay D. Jurie
University of Central Florida
Orlando, Florida

Henry D. Kass
Portland State University
Portland, Oregon

Richard C. Kearney
University of Connecticut
Storrs, Connecticut

Kevin P. Kearns
University of Pittsburgh
Pittsburgh, Pennsylvania

Paula S. Kearns
Michigan State University
East Lansing, Michigan

J. Edward Kellough
University of Georgia
Athens, Georgia

Aynsley Kellow
Griffith University
Nathan, Australia

Cornelius M. Kerwin
The American University
Washington, D.C.

Stephan Keukeleire
Katholieke Universiteit Leuven
Leuven, Belgium

Aharon Kfir
Haifa University
Haifa, Israel

Aman Khan
Texas Tech University
Lubbock, Texas

Ines Kilmann
Organizational Design Consultants
Pittsburgh, Pennsylvania

Jae Taik Kim
City University of New York
New York, New York

Cheryl Simrell King
University of Akron
Akron, Ohio

Rosslyn S. Kleeman
George Washington University
Washington, D.C.

Robert R. Klein
Rutgers, The State University of New Jersey
Newark, New Jersey

Donald E. Klingner
Florida International University
Miami, Florida

Charles P. Kofron
Southern Illinois University
Edwardsville, Illinois

Jan Kooiman
Erasmus University
Rotterdam, Netherlands

Dale Krane
University of Nebraska, Omaha
Omaha, Nebraska

Martin Laffin
University of Glamorgan
Wales, United Kingdom

W. Henry Lambright
Syracuse University
Syracuse, New York

Dave Lane
Australian Broadcasting Corporation
Melbourne, Australia

Joseph H. Lane
Hampden-Sydney College
Hampden-Sydney, Virginia

Andrea G. Lange
The American University
Washington, D.C.

Thomas P. Lauth
University of Georgia
Athens, Georgia

Wendell C. Lawther
University of Central Florida
Orlando, Florida

Michael Lee
London School of Economics
London, United Kingdom

Robert D. Lee, Jr.
Pennsylvania State University
University Park, Pennsylvania

Jean-Robert Leguey-Feilleux
St. Louis University
St. Louis, Missouri

Suzanne Leland
University of Kansas
Lawrence, Kansas

Lance T. LeLoup
Washington State University, Pullman
Pullman, Washington

Arthur L. Levine
Baruch College, City University of New York
New York, New York

Elke Loeffler
Research Institute for Public Administration
Speyer, Germany

K. Kim Loutzenhiser
St. Louis University
St. Louis, Missouri

Phillip E. Lowry
University of Nevada, Las Vegas
Las Vegas, Nevada

Jeffrey S. Luke
University of Oregon
Eugene, Oregon

Larry S. Luton
Eastern Washington University
Cheney and Spokane, Washington

Cynthia E. Lynch
Scott Balsdon, Inc.
Baton Rouge, Louisiana

Thomas D. Lynch
Louisiana State University
Baton Rouge, Louisiana

Oliver MacDonagh
Australian Catholic University
Sydney, Australia

Susan A. MacManus
University of South Florida
Tampa, Florida

Graeme Macmillan
Monash University
Melbourne, Australia

Rudolf Maes
Katholieke Universiteit Leuven
Leuven, Belgium

Sarmistha R. Majumdar
Rutgers, The State University of New Jersey
Newark, New Jersey

Pavel Makeyenko
Russian Academy of Sciences
Moscow, Russia

Margaret Mary Malone
Institute of Public Administration
Dublin, Ireland

Bonnie G. Mani
East Carolina University
Greenville, North Carolina

Seymour Z. Mann
City University of New York (emeritus)
New York, New York

Frank Marini
University of Akron (emeritus)
San Diego, California

David E. Marion
Hampden-Sydney College
Hampden-Sydney, Virginia

Arthur I. Marsh
St. Edmund Hall, Oxford University
United Kingdom

Charles E. Marske
St. Louis University
St. Louis, Missouri

Dan J. Martin
Carnegie Mellon University
Pittsburgh, Pennsylvania

Jerry D. Marx
Seton Hall University
South Orange, New Jersey

Reginald C. Mascarenhas
Victoria University of Wellington
Wellington, New Zealand

Kai Masser
Postgraduate School of Administrative Science
Speyer, Germany

Audrey L. Mathews
California State University, San Bernardino
San Bernardino, California

Kay Mathews
University of Kansas
Lawrence, Kansas

Race Mathews
Monash University
Melbourne, Australia

John McAllister
Pennsylvania Department of Labor and Industry
Harrisburg, Pennsylvania

Jerry L. McCaffery
Naval Postgraduate School
Monterey, California

David P. McCaffrey
University at Albany, State University of New York
Albany, New York

Daniel C. McCool
University of Utah
Salt Lake City, Utah

Howard E. McCurdy
The American University
Washington, D.C.

Linda McGuire
Monash University
Melbourne, Australia

John McIlwaine
University College, London
United Kingdom

José Luis Méndez
El Colegio de México
Mexico City, Mexico

Judith A. Merkle
Claremont-McKenna College
Claremont, California

Caroline Meyers
Katholieke Universiteit Leuven
Leuven, Belgium

Roy T. Meyers
University of Maryland, Baltimore County
Catonsville, Maryland

Robert D. Miewald
University of Nebraska, Lincoln
Lincoln, Nebraska

John L. Mikesell
Indiana University, Bloomington
Bloomington, Indiana
Hugh T. Miller
Florida Atlantic University, Palm Beach Gardens
Palm Beach Gardens, Florida
Manfred Miller
Fachhochschule für Öffentliche Verwaltung
Halberstadt, Germany
Rowan Miranda
Municipal Finance Officers Association
Chicago, Illinois
Deborah Mitchell
Australian National University
Canberra, Australia
Jerry Mitchell
Baruch College, City University of New York
New York, New York
Clyde Mitchell-Weaver
University of Pittsburgh
Pittsburgh, Pennsylvania
Patricia Moore
New Jersey Department of Education
Trenton, New Jersey
Douglas F. Morgan
Portland State University
Portland, Oregon
Stephen P. Morgan
California State University, Hayward
Hayward, California
Martin Morlok
Friedrich-Schiller University
Jena, Germany
Wynne Walker Moskop
St. Louis University
St. Louis, Missouri
Dennis C. Muniak
Towson State University
Towson, Maryland
Kim L. Murphree
Center for Trial Insights
Overland Park, Kansas
Vic Murray
University of Victoria
British Columbia, Canada
Bernadette T. Muscat
Penn State Harrisburg
Middletown, Pennsylvania
Katherine C. Naff
San Francisco State University
San Francisco, California
Stuart S. Nagel
University of Illinois, Urbana
Urbana, Illinois

Pernilla M. Neal
Dickinson College
Carlisle, Pennsylvania
Marcia Neave
Monash University
Melbourne, Australia
Dalmas H. Nelson
University of Utah
Salt Lake City, Utah
Lisa S. Nelson
Bowling Green State University
Bowling Green, Ohio
John R. Nethercote
Department of the Senate, Parliament House
Canberra, Australia
Peter Newman
Murdoch University
Perth, Australia
Kenneth L. Nichols
University of Maine
Orono, Maine
John Alan Nicolay
Troy State University
Norfolk, Virginia
Philip Norton
University of Hull
Hull, United Kingdom
Philip Nufrio
Essex County College
Newark, New Jersey
Samuel Nunn
Indiana University, Indianapolis
Indianapolis, Indiana
Kevin O'Connor
Monash University
Melbourne, Australia
Kenneth W. Ogden
Monash University
Melbourne, Australia
Rosemary O'Leary
Indiana University, Bloomington
Bloomington, Indiana
Amalya Oliver-Lumerman
Hebrew University
Jerusalem, Israel
Dorothy Olshfski
Rutgers, The State University of New Jersey
Newark, New Jersey
Deirdre O'Neill
Monash University
Melbourne, Australia
Michael O'Neill
University of San Francisco
San Francisco, California

Derry Ormond
Organization for Economic Cooperation and Development
Paris, France

J. Steven Ott
University of Utah
Salt Lake City, Utah

E. Samuel Overman
University of Colorado, Denver
Denver, Colorado

Alex M. Owen
Monash University
Melbourne, Australia

Susan C Paddock
University of Wisconsin, Madison
Madison, Wisconsin

Michael Paddon
University of New South Wales
Sydney, Australia

Michael A. Pagano
Miami University
Oxford, Ohio

Roberto Papini
International Institute Jacques Maritain
Rome, Italy

Spyros A. Pappas
European Center for Judges and Lawyers
Luxembourg

William H. Park
Royal Naval College, Greenwich
United Kingdom

D. John Pay
Royal Naval College, Greenwich
United Kingdom

Curtis Peet
Bowling Green State University
Bowling Green, Ohio

Shelly Peffer
Cleveland State University
Cleveland, Ohio

William A. Perry
Tennessee State University
Nashville, Tennessee

Rose T. Pfund
University of Hawaii
Honolulu, Hawaii

Bernard T. Pitsvada
George Washington University
Washington, D.C.

Carl Cannon Pohle
attorney
St. Louis, Missouri

John Power
University of Melbourne
Melbourne, Australia

Ross Prizzia
University of Hawaii, West Oahu
Pearl City, Hawaii

Kenneth Pryor
City Manager
Hearne, Texas

Steven Puro
St. Louis University
St. Louis, Missouri

Michael Pusey
University of New South Wales
Sydney, Australia

Charles D. Raab
University of Edinburgh
Scotland, United Kingdom

Hal G. Rainey
University of Georgia
Athens, Georgia

T. Zane Reeves
University of New Mexico
Albuquerque, New Mexico

David O. Renz
University of Missouri, Kansas City
Kansas City, Missouri

Richard D. Rieke
University of Utah
Salt Lake City, Utah

Ann-Marie Rizzo
Tennessee State University
Nashville, Tennessee

Mark D. Robbins
Syracuse University
Syracuse, New York

Roe Roberts
Eastern Washington University
Spokane, Washington

Peter Rodney
barrister
United Kingdom

Debra J. Rog
Vanderbilt University Institute for Public Policy Studies
Washington, D.C.

Bruce D. Rogers
Tennessee State University
Nashville, Tennessee

Judy L. Rogers
Miami University
Oxford, Ohio

Rainer Rohdewold
Lembaga Administrasi Negara
Jakarta, Indonesia

John A. Rohr
Virginia Polytechnic Institute and State University
Blacksburg, Virginia

Barbara S. Romzek
University of Kansas
Lawrence, Kansas

David H. Rosenbloom
The American University
Washington, D.C.

Bernard H. Ross
The American University
Washington, D.C.

Stefan Rossbach
University of Kent
Canterbury, United Kingdom

Hank Rubin
Rubin & Associates
Chicago, Illinois

Irene S. Rubin
Northern Illinois University
De Kalb, Illinois

E.W. Russell
Monash University
Melbourne, Australia

Tanis Janes Salant
University of Arizona
Tucson, Arizona

Cheryl Saunders
University of Melbourne
Melbourne, Australia

Marian Sawer
University of Canberra
Canberra, Australia

Hindy Lauer Schachter
New Jersey Institute of Technology
Newark, New Jersey

Kuno Schedler
University of St. Gallen
Switzerland

Saundra K. Schneider
University of South Carolina
Columbia, South Carolina

Bernard Schwartz
University of Tulsa
Tulsa, Oklahoma

Peregrine Schwartz-Shea
University of Utah
Salt Lake City, Utah

Jacquelyn Thayer Scott
University College of Cape Breton
Nova Scotia, Canada

William G. Scott
University of Washington
Seattle, Washington

Richard B. Scotton
Monash University
Melbourne, Australia

David Scrivener
Keele University
Keele, United Kingdom

Alex S. Sekwat
Tennessee State University
Nashville, Tennessee

Arthur J. Sementelli
Stephen F. Austin State University
Nacogdoches, Texas

Geoffrey Serle
Monash University
Melbourne, Australia

John S. Shaffer
Pennsylvania Department of Corrections
Harrisburg, Pennsylvania

Ira Sharkansky
Hebrew University
Jerusalem, Israel

William J. Shkurti
Ohio State University
Columbus, Ohio

Nicette L. Short
Louisiana State University
Baton Rouge, Louisiana

George Silberbauer
Monash University
Melbourne, Australia

Joseph J. Simeone
St. Louis University
St. Louis, Missouri

Marian Simms
Australian National University
Canberra, Australia

William Simonsen
University of Oregon
Eugene, Oregon

Marshall R. Singer
University of Pittsburgh
Pittsburgh, Pennsylvania

David W. Sink
University of Arkansas, Little Rock
Little Rock, Arkansas

David Sitrin
U.S. Office of Management and Budget
Washington, D.C.

James D. Slack
California State College, Bakersfield
Bakersfield, California

Michael L. R. Smith
Royal Naval College, Greenwich
United Kingdom

John Smyth
Flinders University
Adelaide, Australia

Alvin D. Sokolow
University of California, Davis
Davis, California

Christophe Soulard
European Center for Judges and Lawyers
Luxembourg

Michael W. Spicer
Cleveland State University
Cleveland, Ohio

Brent S. Steel
Washington State University, Vancouver
Vancouver, Washington

James Stever
University of Cincinnati
Cincinnati, Ohio

Jenny Stewart
University of Canberra
Canberra, Australia

Camilla Stivers
Cleveland State University
Cleveland, Ohio

Alan Stone
University of Houston
Houston, Texas

Jeffrey D. Straussman
Syracuse University
Syracuse, New York

Franz Strehl
University of Innsbruck
Innsbruck, Austria

Denise E. Strong
University of New Orleans
New Orleans, Louisiana

James H. Svara
North Carolina State University
Raleigh, North Carolina

Valerie Swigart
University of Pittsburgh
Pittsburgh, Pennsylvania

Ronald D. Sylvia
San Jose State University
San Jose, California

Victoria C. Syme-Taylor
Royal Naval College, Greenwich
United Kingdom

C. E. Teasley III
University of West Florida
Pensacola, Florida

Julian Teicher
Monash University
Melbourne, Australia

Katsuaki L. Terasawa
Naval Postgraduate School
Monterey, California

Larry D. Terry
Cleveland State University
Cleveland, Ohio

A. Robert Thoeny
Tennessee State University
Nashville, Tennessee

Fred Thompson
Willamette University
Salem, Oregon

Michael Thompson
Brigham Young University
Provo, Utah

Kurt Thurmaier
University of Kansas
Lawrence, Kansas

Geoffrey Till
Royal Naval College, Greenwich
United Kingdom

Mary M. Timney
California State University, Hayward
Hayward, California

Terence J. Tipple
Virginia Tech
Falls Church, Virginia
Pinchot Institute for Conservation
Washington, D.C.

Rik Torfs
Katholieke Universiteit Leuven
Leuven, Belgium

John Uhr
Australian National University
Canberra, Australia

Matthew R. H. Uttley
Royal Naval College, Greenwich
United Kingdom

Paul N. Van de Water
Congressional Budget Office
Washington, D.C.

M. Peter van der Hoek
Erasmus University
Rotterdam, Netherlands

Peter J. Van Hook
University of Utah
Salt Lake City, Utah

Paul P. Van Riper
Texas A & M University
College Station, Texas

Jon Van Til
Rutgers, The State University of New Jersey
Camden, New Jersey

Montgomery Van Wart
Iowa State University
Ames, Iowa

Curtis Ventriss
University of Vermont
Burlington, Vermont

Victor H. Vroom
Yale University
New Haven, Connecticut

Gary L. Wamsley
Virginia Polytechnic Institute and State University
Blacksburg, Virginia

James D. Ward
University of New Mexico
Albuquerque, New Mexico

Kenneth F. Warren
St. Louis University
St. Louis, Missouri

Sheilah S. Watson
University of Missouri, Columbia
Columbia, Missouri

William L. Waugh, Jr.
Georgia State University
Atlanta, Georgia

Anthony Webster
Edge Hill College of Higher Education
Ormskirk, United Kingdom

Paul Weiland
Indiana University, Bloomington
Bloomington, Indiana
Harvard Law School
Cambridge, Massachusetts

Lee S. Weinberg
University of Pittsburgh
Pittsburgh, Pennsylvania

Patrick Weller
Griffith University
Nathan, Australia

George Dorian Wendel
St. Louis University
St. Louis, Missouri

Jonathan P. West
University of Miami
Coral Gables, Florida

Roger Wettenhall
University of Canberra
Canberra, Australia

Marcia Lynn Whicker
Rutgers, The State University of New Jersey
Newark, New Jersey

Gordon P. Whitaker
University of North Carolina at Chapel Hill
Chapel Hill, North Carolina

Harvey L. White
University of Pittsburgh
Pittsburgh, Pennsylvania

Richard D. White
Penn State Harrisburg
Middletown, Pennsylvania

Sandra D. Williamson
University of Pittsburgh
Pittsburgh, Pennsylvania

Kenneth Wiltshire
University of Queensland
Brisbane, Australia

Stephanie L. Witt
Boise State University
Boise, Idaho

James F. Wolf
Virginia Polytechnic Institute and State University
Blacksburg, Virginia

Michael A. Wolff
St. Louis University
St. Louis, Missouri

Donald W. Wolfgang
Naval Postgraduate School
Monterey, California

Stephen J. Worrell
Worrell, Griffith, Durreit & Jaynes, P.C.
Glenwood Springs, Colorado

Linda Wouters
Katholieke Universiteit Leuven
Leuven, Belgium

Deil S. Wright
University of North Carolina at Chapel Hill
Chapel Hill, North Carolina

Norman Dale Wright
Brigham Young University
Provo, Utah

James H. Wyllie
University of Aberdeen
Scotland, United Kingdom

Dvora Yanow
California State University, Hayward
Hayward, California

Dennis R. Young
Case Western Reserve University
Cleveland, Ohio

Sharifuddin Zainuddin
University of Malaya
Kuala Lumpur, Malaysia

Ernő Zalai
Budapest University of Economic Sciences
Budapest, Hungary

Spencer Zifcak
Latrobe University
Melbourne, Australia

Richard E. Zody
Virginia Polytechnic Institute and State University
Blacksburg, Virginia

C. Kurt Zorn
Indiana University, Bloomington
Bloomington, Indiana

Foreword

The *International Encyclopedia of Public Policy and Administration (IEPPA)* is a magnificent contribution to the fields of public policy and public administration. Consisting of approximately 900 articles and 2,700 pages, it is a truly comprehensive, all-in-one-place inventory of the concepts, practices, issues, and theories that inform and define contemporary public policymaking, analysis, evaluation, management, and implementation. The *IEPPA* also includes entries on the individuals, commissions, and organizations that have made key contributions to these fields.

Although it is not meant for cover-to-cover reading, those who may read it that way will find that it is an exceptionally high-quality, up-to-date, readable, lucid, and accurate exposition of a tremendous quantum of what is known about public policy and administration. The "International" in the title is completely felicitous—these volumes cross national and cultural borders as well as intellectual ones. The *IEPPA* also covers both policy and administration. This is particularly welcome at a time when the two fields are being pulled in divergent directions by their conceptual frameworks and organization within universities. Although it may be possible to separate policy from administration analytically, in practice they are often thoroughly intertwined. The *IEPPA* will prove invaluable in making each field accessible to specialists in the other, as well as to generalists. In my view, there is no other work that comes even close to bringing together so much knowledge about public policy and administration. The *IEPPA* contains excellent contributions by a phenomenal array of leading scholars. The associate editors, who worked with these contributors, are all outstanding scholars. The result is a work that is authoritative and definitive. It will be the standard work to which one first turns to gain an understanding of the core terms, concepts, constructs, and techniques used by academics, students, and practitioners dealing with public policy and administration.

One could well wish that the *IEPPA* had been published earlier. It certainly would have helped to build knowledge and clarify key concepts at a time when the fields of public policy and administration were rapidly expanding. Nonetheless, the *IEPPA* arrives at a propitious time. The field of public management, in particular, is currently consolidating its knowledge base as a platform for developing better theories and applications. Whether a kind of fin de siècle intellectual housecleaning or a response to the substantial changes that are already upon us, we have been taking stock of what we know and believe, our analytic and conceptual tools, and our inadequacies. This broad effort is reflected in the proliferation of a variety of "handbooks" of various aspects of public management since the late 1980s. It is a sanguine process. New generations of scholars, policymakers, students, and administrative practitioners are inundated with such rapidly growing new knowledge and interpretation that they are at risk of losing touch with the old. Yet the body of thought and practice that developed over the past century with regard to public policy and administration continues to provide knowledge, technique, and insight into central issues that remain highly pertinent. Even reformers, "reinventors," and anarchists need to understand how and why the extant administrative technology developed before expecting to change it successfully.

The *IEPPA* has the great virtue of attending to the past while facing the future. It is an indispensable work that can help equip everyone engaged in the joint enterprise of public policy and administration to deal more effectively with the many challenges that the twenty-first century is certain to bring. If, as in an old sci-fi plot, a public official, manager, or administrator could bring only one book with him or her into the future, the *IEPPA* would surely be it.

Publication of the *IEPPA* is truly a landmark and cause for celebration in the fields of public policy and administration. Editor in Chief Jay Shafritz and his associate editors, Abdullah M. Al-Khalaf, Geert Bouckaert, Beverly A. Cigler, Peter Foot, Arie Halachmi, Richard D. Heimovics, Marc Holzer, Jerry L. McCaffery, J. Steven Ott, David O. Renz, Norma M. Riccucci, E. W. Russell, Larry D. Terry, and Kenneth F. Warren all deserve great thanks for designing, organizing, and seeing the project through.

DAVID H. ROSENBLOOM
Distinguished Professor of Public Administration
The American University
Washington, D.C.

Preface

This Encyclopedia—with 900 articles written by 462 contributors—is intended to be the first truly comprehensive public affairs reference. This four-volume work is designed so that its contents—a combination of historical and descriptive articles, procedural presentations, and interpretive essays—will be of interest to the general reader as well as the specialist. It will serve students, teachers, scholars, journalists, political activists, and the general public as the one indispensable source of readily digestible information about public policy and administration in the modern world.

Contained herein are definitions of the vocabulary of public policy and administration as it is used throughout the world, from the smallest towns to the largest national bureaucracies. And when we say definitions we mean just that: All articles start by defining their topic. So if all the reader is seeking is a quick explanation of the meaning of a concept or practice, he or she need read no further than the first paragraph. The rest of the article will still be there if and when more detailed information is needed.

While some articles are more technical than others, the Encyclopedia is written to be accessible to those who are not experts in the various aspects of public affairs. Nevertheless, the content of the work has not been watered down; the ideas presented are every bit as sophisticated as public policy and administration experts have a right to expect. Writing level is essentially an issue of craftsmanship—not scholarship.

Coverage

The Encyclopedia is a major effort toward the international integration of the literature on public policy and administration—which are two sides of the same coin (policy being the decisionmaking side while administration is the implementation side). Included are articles on all of the core concepts, terms, phrases, and processes of the following aspects of public policy and administration: applied behavioral science, budgeting, comparative public administration, development administration, industrial/organizational psychology, industrial policy, international trade, labor relations, management, nonprofit management, organization theory and behavior, policy analysis, political economy, political science, public administration, public finance, public law, public management, public personnel administration, public policy, and taxation.

Also included are articles on major scholars—such as Kurt Lewin, Dwight Waldo, and Aaron Wildavsky; political leaders who influenced administration—such as Jean Monnet, Franklin D. Roosevelt, and Woodrow Wilson; major public managers—such as J. Edgar Hoover, Robert Moses, and James Webb; historically important committees, commissions and reports—such as the Brownlow Committee, the Glassco Commission, and the Northcote-Trevelyan Report; slang terms—such as crowd out, muddling through, and red tape; significant nongovernmental organizations—such as the Ford Foundation, the International Institute of Administrative Sciences, and the United Way; and major government agencies—such as the Privy Council in the United Kingdom, the Office of Management and Budget in the United States, and the European Parliament.

This Encyclopedia is "international" because it contains extensive coverage of public policy and administration concepts and practices from throughout the world. Indeed, public administration is increasingly an international discipline. While the administrative systems of nation-states were once largely self-contained, today cross-fertilization is the norm. The national marketplace of ideas, wherein policies and techniques once competed, has been replaced by an international marketplace. Thus there are articles on reinventing government in the United States, Thatcherism in the United Kingdom, and the New Zealand model. The reforms discussed in these articles (further elaborated upon by conceptual articles on devolution, managerialism, and market testing, among others) have been widely influential. Different political cultures, let alone differing administrative machinery, require different administrative solutions. Nevertheless, the compelling reason for students of public administration to be fully aware of the wealth of new management ideas and administrative experiments happening in other states is not so much to be able to imitate as to adapt.

In order to provide a sense of the cultural differentiation of the world's administrative regimes, many articles focus on the administrative traditions of a society; for example, the American administrative tradition, the German administrative tradition, and the Islamic administrative tradition. Other articles focus on unique administrative institutions within a state; for example, the Ecole Nationale d'Administration in France, the Federal Reserve System in the United States, and the Prime Minister's Office in Canada. Extensive coverage is also given to the practices and institutions of the European community; for example, directive, pillarization, and subsidiarity.

Finally, because so much of the public's administration is conducted outside of traditional government bureaucracies, extensive coverage has been given to nongovernmental and nonprofit organization management. Thus there are major articles on foundations, voluntary action, and the independent sector, among others.

Format

The Encyclopedia is continuously alphabetized—from ability to pay, to zoning. This organization is especially useful to compare entries that sound similar. It also allows quick comparison of terms with the same root. For example, the entry for "policy" is followed by variants of policy—such as policy analysis, policy leadership, policy studies, and so on. The Encyclopedia follows this format as often as possible, so if the root of a term is known, many of its variants can readily be found. But not all! There are many "policy" articles where the second or third word in the title is policy—such as broadcasting policy, natural resource policy, and transportation policy. To find these and all the other policy issue overviews in this Encyclopedia, you must look in the index in volume 4.

The comprehensive index is an especially useful feature of this Encyclopedia. If the word, phrase, or name that you are seeking is not listed as the title of an article in the table of contents (the alphabetical listing of all articles) in volume 1, then search for it in the index. There you will be referred to every article that deals with it. Even if the term you seek has its own article listed up front, it is still useful to use the index to see which articles give it additional coverage.

The Editorial Team

Although Jay M. Shafritz of the University of Pittsburgh, the Editor in Chief, initiated the Encyclopedia, it was from the beginning very much a team effort. First he consulted extensively with David H. Rosenbloom of The American University in Washington, D.C., and E. W. Russell of Monash University in Australia. Thus they became the "consulting" editors. These three developed the overall design and dimensions of the Encyclopedia. Then they invited 13 other public policy and administration scholars at major institutions to join the team as associate editors. All the editors then sought out the 462 contributors. Each editor was eventually responsible for a few dozen to over a hundred articles. Most editors also wrote articles themselves.

While the relationship between the editor in chief, the editors, and the contributors resembled a traditional hierarchy on paper, there was considerable informal communication among editors, contributors, and the editor in chief. This was highly desirable. Even though the Encyclopedia deals extensively with bureaucracy, one could not be too bureaucratic with its compilers. Indeed, such a varied group of independent minds wouldn't have tolerated it. Thus while the specific articles were funneled through the associate editors before they formally reached the editor in chief, all contributors had direct access as needed.

All articles were reviewed by at least two editors (one editor and the editor in chief). However, because considerable discussion of articles had to take place, particularly for longer articles, many were reviewed by more. Indeed, the editors felt free to call upon experts throughout the world for ad hoc reviews of articles.

The list of articles to be included was determined by a three-step process. First, the editor in chief and the consulting editors developed a list of several hundred entries that was shared with all the associate editors. Second, a negotiating process began during which editors accepted responsibility for entries (meaning responsibility to find someone to write them) and suggested additional entries. Third, as the editors approached contributors, negotiations began anew as contributors had new ideas for entries. All editors had the right to approve the inclusion of entries provided they informed the editor in chief, who acted as a clearing house to avoid duplications. This three-level process was extremely useful in developing the comprehensive list of articles that is this Encyclopedia. The judgments of the various editors and the contributors about what should be included was critical. Thus, the role of the editor in chief was mainly that of coordinator, judge, and, of course, editor. While he conceptualized it, it was the editors and contributors who created it. Any intellectual credit belongs to them. In the final analysis, he was, alas, merely an administrator.

Acknowledgments

The Encyclopedia's greatest debt is to its 462 contributors—scholars and practitioners from 23 countries and 43 of the 50 United States. A complete list of their names and affiliations precedes this preface. The editors thank them for their fine work as well as for their faith in the four-year-long project. It took so long to assemble and edit the articles that some of the faithful even became doubtful. We trust the present four volumes are worth the wait. But that is a judgment readers must make for themselves.

We are also pleased to have the opportunity to publicly thank the many people who in myriad other ways contributed to the completion of this work:

Mosa Abdullah Al-Khalaf, Huda Muhammad Al-Sha'all, Lynn Arts, Harry A. Bailey, Carolyn Ban, Barbara Rose Cramer, Sandy Fitts, Katie Foot, Sarah Foot, Donald Goldstein, Sheila Kelly, Elizabeth Lawrence, Mary Kay Linge, Jean Lyon, Sara McCormick, Pat McCutcheon, Chester Newland, Tom Novack, Daniel Oran, Terry Ott, Nikki Pavlin, Shena Redmond, Rebecca Reno, Alice Russell, Louis Russell, Kelly Saylors, Curtis Schwartz, Joan Schwartz, Luise Shafritz, Annette Chartier Warren, Ken Wright, and Helen Vivian.

A special acknowledgment and heartfelt thanks are due the two people who were more responsible than anyone, other than the editors and authors, for the existence of this work: Mitch Rose of the Mitchell Rose Literary Agency and Leo Wiegman of Westview Press. They made it possible for us to make it possible.

ABILITY TO PAY. A principle derived primarily from public finance theory which asserts that citizens should be taxed at varying levels or rates according to their respective economic strata. More generally, the ability to pay principle is a subset of the larger concept of *equity*, which states that people in equal situations should be taxed equally and people in unequal situations should be taxed unequally.

A Simple Illustration

Professor Jones is opening her morning mail. The first item is a membership renewal notice for a professional association to which she belongs. She observes with some irritation that the association has introduced a new graduated dues schedule based on income. Students pay a flat rate of $30.00; members who earn $20,000-30,000 pay $60.00 in annual dues; those who earn $30,000-40,000 pay $80.00; and so on. As a result of the new graduated schedule, her dues to the association will increase by 35 percent over last year. She briefly considers canceling her membership or underreporting her income (lying). This is one of five associations to which she belongs and her total annual outlay for membership dues is nearly $500.00 and growing. Ultimately she decides to tell the truth and, somewhat grudgingly, writes a check to the association. She makes a mental note to reconsider her decision next year. Professor Jones has, at least temporarily and with some reluctance, accepted one of the operational notions of equity–the ability to pay principle.

The next item of mail is a subscription order for an academic journal. Professor Jones notes that the "institutional subscription rate" is $180.00, but the "individual rate" is only $65.00. She writes a check for the individual rate. Here, Professor Jones has readily and happily accepted another notion of equity–the benefit principle.

The last item in Professor Jones's mailbox is an announcement from the university administration regarding a new policy on photocopying. In an effort to save costs and discourage excessive photocopying, the university copy center will charge professors (or their academic units) differential rates based on consumption. Each academic year, the first 300 pages of photocopying for an individual professor will be charged at the rate of $0.04 per page; the next 300 pages will be charged at $0.05 per page; and so on up to a maximum of $0.09 per page, whereupon there will be a strong economic incentive to use the service of a private photocopying firm. Jones briefly reflects on the impact this policy will have on her, but quickly tosses the notice into the wastebasket, dismissing it as yet another example of bureaucratic micromanagement. Once again, Professor Jones has tacitly accepted a third notion of equity–the consumption principle.

Discussion

These three illustrations are separate but related variants of the same underlying principle of equity–that people in equal circumstances should be treated equally ("horizontal equity") and that people in unequal circumstances should be treated unequally ("vertical equity").

The first example (graduated membership dues) is an example of the ability to pay principle in its purest and most elementary form. The assumption is that members of the professional association who have higher incomes can afford to pay higher dues. While most association members would not recognize it, there also is the implicit, and more controversial, objective of income redistribution among members of the association. Those at the low end of the income scale (such as students and young professionals) receive the full benefit of the association's services at a price that is arguably below fair market value. The more affluent members who pay dues that are well above fair market value are, in effect, subsidizing the membership of the less affluent. Note, however, that the dues schedule, as a proportion of income, remains constant at two-tenths of one percent of the high end of each income bracket (i.e., $60/30,000, $80/$40,000, and so on). This is a modified flat rate approach. It is not a perfect flat rate approach because income levels are divided into brackets. Thus, someone at the low end of the first income bracket ($20,000) pays the same amount ($60) as someone at the high end ($30,000). Consequently, lower-income members within each bracket pay a slightly higher proportion of their total income for membership in the association than higher income members within the bracket. A more sophisticated approach–the one upon which the U.S. personal income tax is based–would assume that people with higher incomes should not only pay more in absolute terms, but also should pay a higher proportion of their income relative to poorer people. The more sophisticated scheme is based on the theory of *marginal utility of income* which says that poorer people are, relatively speaking, more adversely affected by a flat tax than wealthier people even though they still pay far less than the wealthy in an absolute sense. Thus, a $500 tax for a person making only $5,000 is far more burdensome than a $10,000 tax for a person making $100,000 even though both persons pay exactly 10 percent of their income. Concerning the example of Professor Jones and the professional association, one could argue that a person making $30,000 is more adversely affected by a $60 dues payment than a person making $40,000 is by a $80 payment.

The second example (institutional and individual subscription rates) reflects, in part, the ability to pay principle since it is presumed that libraries and other organizations can afford to pay more for academic journals than individual subscribers. More specifically, however, this is an example of the benefit principle, which assumes that people (and institutions) should pay for goods and services according to the benefits they derive from them relative to other users. In this example, it is presumed that an institution like a library derives a larger marginal benefit than the individual subscriber because the value of the subscription is spread among the many potential patrons of the library who will have access to the journal. Thus, according to the benefit principle, the library should pay a higher subscription rate not only because of its ability to pay (relative to the individual subscriber) but also because it derives a higher net benefit. A municipal property tax is, in a way, a type of benefit tax because owners of homes and other real property (unlike renters) receive an indirect financial benefit from many municipal services (e.g., fire and police protection, street maintenance, and so forth) which serve to maintain and sometimes even enhance property values. People who are not property owners, on the other hand, derive only the direct benefits (i.e., safety, convenience) of these services.

The last example (photocopying charges) is based on the consumption principle—yet another variant of the equity concept. A tax or charge on consumption (versus income or savings) presumes that high consumers of scarce goods and services should pay a relatively higher price than low consumers due to the "costs" (often intangible) they impose on society by virtue of their high consumption. There is an implicit punitive philosophy that consumption takes away from the overall well-being of society while savings represent and investment in society. The counterargument is that savings are, in essence, nothing more than a mechanism for delayed consumption. Still, there are many examples where fees or taxes based on consumption are highly appropriate and routinely accepted by the populace. Large trucks, for example, pay a higher fee on tool roads (and also higher taxes, due, in part, to the damage they inflict on the nation's highways). This is an example that actually is a mixture of the consumption and benefit principles because commercial vehicles also derive direct financial benefits from their consumption of a public good. In the area of health care, taxes on tobacco and alcohol are examples of consumption taxes, based on evidence that heavy consumers of these products are more likely to be heavy consumers of health care as well.

The Historical and Political Context

From the field of economics, and with specific reference to taxation, Adam Smith was the first person to clearly articulate the ability to pay and benefit principles. In *The Wealth of Nations* (1776), his seminal treatise on classical economics, Smith said: "The subject of every state ought to contribute towards the support of the government as nearly as possible in proportion to their respective abilities; that is, in proportion to the revenue which they respectively enjoy under the protection of the state" (Book 5, Chapter 2, Part 2).

Ultimately, the definition of equity is a question for politicians and even social philosophers because taxes and user charges are not only a means of generating revenue, but of redistributing income to advance social goals according to a political value system. In fact, the political philosophers of the seventeenth century, such as John Locke and Thomas Hobbes, were among the first to articulate the benefit principle within the context of the contract theory of the state (Musgrave and Musgrave, 1984).

While many people heartily endorse the concept of equity—whether expressed in terms of ability to pay, benefit, or consumption—the implementation of the concept is nearly always controversial. With respect to vertical equity, for example, economists and politicians continue of debate the merits of earned income versus wealth as the basis determining economic strata. How should capital gains be treated? What types of investments (e.g., mortgage interest) should be exempt from income taxes? How should depreciation of capital assets be treated? Is corporate income analogous to individual income as a basis for taxation? These and many other issues related to equity continue to be the source of heated debates in government and academic circles.

Assuming we could agree on the fundamental basis for determining vertical equity, there remain problems with the actual calculation. The question is: how much differently should people of different economic strata be treated to achieve this elusive concept of vertical equity? How should we calculate the relative sacrifice imposed by taxes on people of different economic strata? Even though the notion of progressive taxation (proportional sacrifice) is well established in the United States, there are still efforts among conservatives to introduce a flat-rate income tax in which everyone would be taxed at the same rate. Counterarguments for progressively higher tax rates are based on the social philosophy of income redistribution and the economic theory of declining marginal utility of income.

The debates become even more cloudy when tax policy is viewed as an instrument for stimulating the economy as well as a means for achieving social goals. What tax incentives should be provided for investments in new technologies? What will be the impact on productivity and international competitiveness? Are certain commercial enterprises penalized by tax exemptions granted to nonprofit organizations?

Conclusion

The principle of equity as expressed in ability to pay, benefit, and consumption is a cornerstone of the U.S. tax system and is applied at the federal, state, and local levels. The principle also is applied in many management systems, as illustrated by the choices facing Professor Jones. But, as with most philosophical principles, it encounters controversy in its implementation. If tax systems were designed solely as a means of generating a specific amount of revenue to match a clearly defined set of expenditures, their design would be relatively straightforward. With the added burden, however, of being instruments for income redistribution and catalysts for economic change, the concept of equity ultimately becomes a subjective and value-laden principle more amenable to the calculus of political science than the calculus of economics.

KEVIN P. KEARNS

BIBLIOGRAPHY

Musgrave, Richard A. and Peggy B. Musgrave, 1984. *Public Finance in Theory and Practice.* 4th. ed. New York: McGraw-Hill.

Samuelson, Paul, 1992. *Economics.* 14th ed. New York: McGraw-Hill.

Smith, Adam, 1776. *The Wealth of Nations.* New York: Dutton 1964.

ABSENTEEISM. The absence from work. Absenteeism may be for legitimate reasons such as illness or may be a pattern of personal behavior of an employee. Absenteeism is a major problem for employers because it affects the productivity of the organization. It is a problem in all societies, not just in the United States. Obviously, the employee who is absent from work is not producing. Employers recognize that there are legitimate reasons for employees to be absent. Thus, most provide sick leave and many provide for personal time as well.

Problems arise when employees abuse the leave policy by claiming illness when there is none or by taking excessive leave without pay. In addition to affecting productivity, excessive employee absence leads to increased costs for the employer as more employees are needed to cover for those who are absent all the time. The morale of the rest of the work force also may suffer as they are asked to take responsibility for the work of others.

Absenteeism is often considered an indicator of the health of the organization and lack of employee job satisfaction. It may be a sign of employee withdrawal because of the unpleasantness of the work environment. If, as often is the case, employees habitually are absent on Mondays and Fridays, it also may be a sign of a personal problem of the employee's. These kinds of absences frequently are indicators of substance abuse problems.

To deal with absenteeism problems, employers have attempted to develop positive motivations to encourage employees to avoid using leave time. Most prominent among the approaches has been the practice of permitting employees to receive payouts for unused sick leave at the end of the year. The payouts may be full pay for the time represented by unused leave or may even include a bonus above the unused time. Another option is to allow pay for the unused leave at retirement. Flex time is another approach that may help with absenteeism if the absence from work is due to family obligations such as day care or elder care. In some organizations, options for working at home or by telecommuting are possible when the work is of the type that does not require the physical presence of the employee in the office.

Determining the cause of absenteeism aids employers in devising policies to correct the problem. For example, if problems in finding reliable care for dependents are a major cause, the employer may institute an on-site child care center, subsidize dependent care programs, or permit flexible work hours for the employee.

N. JOSEPH CAYER

BIBLIOGRAPHY

Baumgartel, H. and R. Sobol, 1959. "Background and Organizational Factors in Absenteeism." *Personnel Psychology,* vol. 12 (Autumn) 431–443.

Rogers, Rolf E. and Stephen R. Herting, 1993. "Patterns of Absenteeism Among Government Employees." *Public Personnel Management,* vol. 22, no. 2 (Summer) 215–228.

ABSOLUTE IMMUNITY. An unqualified exemption from judicial proceedings, usually immunizing public officials completely from being sued while functioning in their official capacity. Thus, the protected entities cannot be sued without their consent for their tortious acts even, as Kenneth Warren observes, when committed in flagrant bad faith, with malicious intent, and in violation of the legal rights of their victims (1996, p. 464). Entities protected by absolute immunity can be states, governments and their agencies, or public officials at various levels of governmental activity.

This immunity finds roots in absolute monarchy eventually justified by the concept of sovereignty, first artriculated by the French political theorist Jean Bodin in 1576, and redefined in 1651, in absolute terms by the English philosopher Thomas Hobbes (see **sovereign immunity**). The most extensive use of the legal doctrine of absolute immunity today pertains to foreign institutions.

Foreign Absolute Immunity

The sovereign state can be subject to no other state. To this day, a state cannot be made a defendant in the courts of another state without its consent. absolute immunity is traditionally also extended to foreign heads of state, governments, high government officials, state property, armed forces, and several classes of diplomatic agents.

In *The Schooner Exchange v. McFaddon* (1812), the U.S. Supreme Court showed how absolute this doctrine could be. Two American citizens who claimed to be the owners of the schooner *Exchange* began legal proceedings to recover possession of their vessel (now anchored in the port of Philadelphia as a unit of the French navy), alleging that it was unlawfully held by the French government. The Supreme Court dismissed the case, upholding the absolute immunity of the armed vessel of a foreign state. The question of how the French government obtained possession of the vessel, lawfully or unlawfully, was irrelevant. Today, foreign naval units remain protected by the doctrine of absolute immunity.

Following World War II, however, numerous military units came to be stationed abroad under various collective defense arrangements. To alleviate local friction (frequently resulting from the presence of foreign troops), the states concerned negotiated status-of-forces agreements redefining the immunity of the forces involved, with the host state generally receiving a limited amount of control and jurisdiction. But in the absence of such agreements, immunity remains absolute.

Foreign state property or instrumentalities are also traditionally granted absolute immunity. This practice, however, became a major problem when states came to be extensively engaged in ordinary commercial activity. State-owned merchant vessels or commercial enterprises competed with private concerns, and it made little sense—it was in fact unjust—to give state corporations absolute immunity protection when their private counterparts were liable to normal court action.

Early attempts to limit the scope of this immunity from jurisdiction came in cases arising from the operation of commercial vessels by foreign governments, and were unsuccessful. In *Berizzi Bros. Co. v. S. S. Pesaro* (1926), for example, the U.S. Supreme Court upheld absolute immunity on the ground that it was the sovereign right of a state to engage in commercial activity if it chose this method to add revenue to its treasury. "We know of no international usage which regards the maintenance and advancement of the economic welfare of a people in time of peace as any less a public purpose than the maintenance and training of a naval force" (271 U.S. 562). But a trend eventually developed, leading to a more limited immunity doctrine (see **qualified immunity**).

Today, states are no longer immune from the jurisdiction of foreign courts with regard to their commercial operations, and their commercial property may be levied upon for the satisfaction of judgments against them in connection with their business activities. It must be acknowledged that there is a gray area in which the real purpose of an activity or property (commercial or not) is uncertain. In *Dunlap v. Banco Central del Ecuador* (Sup. Ct., N.Y. County, 1943), immunity was granted because of public functions in procurement of coins for the national currency, though the Ecuadorean government had only five-elevenths ownership in the corporation.

Component organs of a foreign government may be sufficiently identifiable as parts of the governing structure to be granted absolute immunity. But the status of certain agencies in a decentralized system may be uncertain. Are they sufficiently involved in the task of governing the nation to receive absolute immunity? Tass, the Soviet news agency, although established under Soviet law as a corporation, was found sufficiently integrated into the central government as to be immune (*Krajina v. The Tass Agency and Another*, England, Court of Appeal, 1949).

A foreign state's territorial subdivisions will present other difficulties. At what level of territorial decentralization will absolute immunity stop? National governments, particularly the United States and British governments, have long been inclined to advise their courts to give immunity when it served their political purpose. In 1976, Congress enacted the Foreign Sovereign Immunities Act stipulating that State Department suggestions of immunity and support of foreign state claims of immunity would no longer constitute binding determination of immunity. The courts themselves must decide each case on its own merits.

By contrast, diplomatic immunity, for much of its long history, was well-defined and absolute. Foreign representatives were protected even when acting outside their official duties and in violation of the law. In the second half of the twentieth century, however, extensive international negotiations under the aegis of the United Nations led to substantial revision of the law. A more functional approach began to receive international acceptance. Foreign mission personnel are now subdivided into several categories with varying levels of immunity, none of them absolute. The main category of diplomatic agents, however, retains virtually all of its traditionally extensive privileges—that is, nearly absolute, with the exception of some acts performed in the agents' private capacity, for which they are now accountable.

Absolute Immunity of National Origin

Under the influence of English common law, for some 200 years, the United States federal and state governments were protected from tort liability by absolute sovereign immunity. It was argued that lawsuits have a disruptive effect on the governing process and that they are likely to lead government agencies to be overcautious.

As government bureaucracy became larger and more intrusive, pressure mounted to protect the rights of the public and legislation began to be enacted to curb immunity protection. For example, the Tucker Act of 1855 conferred jurisdiction on U.S. district courts to hear claims against the United States concerning contracts; the Federal Tort Claims Act of 1946 allowed, under certain circumstances, suits against the U.S. government for tortious acts committed by its officials; and the 1976 amendment by Congress of Sections 702 and 703 of the Administrative Procedure Act allowed the United States government to be sued for relief other than money damages for the tortious conduct of federal officers.

In 1978, the United States Supreme Court held in *Monell v. Department of Social Services of New York* that local governments could be sued directly under Section 1983 of the Civil Rights Act of 1871, under specified circumstances, thus reversing its earlier stand on the issue. Furthermore, most states, by statute or court decision, proceeded to limit governmental immunity at the state and local levels or even to eliminate it altogether as in *Muskopf v. Corning Hospital District* (1961), in which the California court declared that "the rule of governmental immunity from tort liability . . . must be discarded as mistaken and unjust." Immunity in tort cases "is an anachronism, without rational basis." (359 P2d 458, 460).

As tort action was made possible in one form or another against federal, state, and local government agencies, absolute immunity was nevertheless reintroduced in the form of official immunity (see article on this doctrine). Under common law, public servants did not enjoy immunity for damage done as a result of any act unauthorized by law (an exception being made for judges). But the U.S. Supreme Court in *Spalding v. Vilas* (1896) opened the way to a vast array of absolute immunity privileges when it held that heads of executive departments should be given immunity from civil suits for damage arising from acts done in the performance of their duties. The motive was "wholly immaterial" (161 U.S. 499); public officials remained absolutely immune from damage suits even when acting maliciously with intent to cause harm.

Government administrators came to be viewed as protected by the government's sovereign immunity (*Larson v. Domestic and Foreign Commerce Corp.*, 1949). A further expansion of the absolute immunity of public officials came with *Barr v. Matteo* (1959), when the U.S. Supreme Court extended absolute immunity to virtually all government officials in the performance of their official duties for the sake of vigorous and effective administration in the public interest. The court acknowledged that "there may be occasional instances of actual injustice which will go unre-

dressed, but we think that price a necessary one to pay for the greater good" (360 U.S. 576).

This doctrine was, of course, a formula for evading accountability. As Kenneth Warren notes, it protected irresponsible administrative performance and endangered the constitutional due process rights of private citizens (pp. 464ff.). Not surprisingly, then, efforts were made to set limits to official immunity (see qualified immunity). In 1971, the Supreme Court in its landmark case *Bivens v. Six Unknown Federal Narcotics Agents* restricted the immunity of federal officials by holding that they could be sued for damages when they violated a person's constitutional rights. Interestingly, the court cited *Marbury v. Madison*: "the very essence of civil liberty certainly consists in the right of every individual to claim the protection of the laws whenever he receives an injury" (403 U.S. 388, 396). Section 1983 of the Civil Rights Act of 1871 also provided a foundation for a multiplicity of damage actions against state officials. The trend is now toward the elimination of absolute immunity or its extensive qualification, giving injured individuals a choice in obtaining redress by suing the government or suing the responsible official.

In Britain, much has been done to eliminate absolute immunity altogether. Parliament, however, is almost absolutely sovereign; except for European Union law, it is beyond legal control. The Crown (i.e., the central government) was long considered not subject to the jurisdiction of its own courts, and incapable of being responsible for wrong; but this was overcome, first by the acceptance of liability in practice, then, in 1947, by the enactment of the Crown Proceedings Act, which formally eliminated most of its immunity. The Crown and its servants remain absolutely immune from tort action for acts committed in foreign countries (e.g., acts of violence in foreign affairs); but the aim of the British administrative law system is to subordinate the government to the ordinary law of the land and statutory immunity has been carefully restricted.

The French legal system instituted some governmental liability following the French Revolution (1789) and the demise of the principle that the king could do no wrong. A general principle of state liability was established beyond question with the *Blanco* case, in 1873. The *Feutry* case established in 1908 that the general liability attributed to the state applied also to all public authorities. Absolute immunity remains applicable to the functioning of Parliament and relations between the government and Parliament. Under the act of state doctrine, government action in international relations cannot be called in question in any domestic court. The French state, however, is always subject to the jurisdiction of the French courts in carrying out its obligations under the European Union treaties and in executing the decisions of the European Court of Justice.

More progress has been achieved in curbing absolute immunity in national systems than at the international level. A somewhat recent functional orientation has led to a number of useful restrictions in foreign immunity protection; but nations' perennial fixation on sovereign equality and mutual distrust will doubtless insure the persistence of a substantial amount of absolute immunity protection in international legal practice.

JEAN-ROBERT LEGUEY-FEILLEUX

BIBLIOGRAPHY

Brown, L. Neville and John S. Bell, 1993. *French Administrative Law.* 4th ed. Oxford: Clarendon Press.

Davis, Kenneth Culp and Richard J. Pierce, Jr., 1994. *Administrative Law Treatise.* 3d ed. 3 vols. with 1994 supplement. Boston: Little, Brown.

Henkin, Louis, Richard Crawford Pugh, Oscar Schachter, and Hans Smit, 1993. *International Law.* 3d ed. St. Paul, MN: West Publishing Co.

Jacobini, H. B., 1991. *An Introduction to Comparative Administrative Law.* Dobbs Ferry, NY: Oceana.

Kenner, J. P., 1994. "Prosecutorial Immunity: Removal of the Shield Destroys the Effectiveness of the Sword." *Washburn Law Journal.* vol. 33 (Spring) 402–28.

Mandery, E. J., 1994. "Qualified Immunity or Absolute Immunity? The Moral Hazards of Extending Qualified Immunity to Lower-Level Public Officials." *Harvard Journal of Law and Public Policy,* vol. 17 (Spring) 479–519.

Platz, D. S., 1994. "Buckley v. Fitzsimmons [113 S. Ct. 2606 (1993)]: The Beginning of the End of Absolute Prosecutorial Immunity." *Nova Law Review,* vol. 18 (Spring), 1919–42.

Schwartz, Bernard, 1994. *Administrative Law.* 4th ed. Boston: Little, Brown.

Wade, Sir William and Christopher Forsyth, 1994. *Administrative Law.* Oxford: Clarendon Press.

Warren, Kenneth F., 1996. *Administrative Law in the Political System.* 3d ed. Upper Saddle River, NJ: Prentice-Hall.

ACCOUNTABILITY. A relationship in which an individual or agency is held to answer for performance that involves some delegation of authority to act. Accountability mechanisms are the means established for determining whether the delegated tasks have been performed in a satisfactory manner.

Accountability as a relationship involves one individual or agency being held to answer for performance expected by some significant "other." Although our specific concern here is with accountability as it relates to structures of governance and administration, accountability is a generic form of social relationship found in a variety of contexts. Social psychologists and sociologists regard the need of "having to account to others" as a fundamental means through which individuals adjust to social settings.

Accountability relationships in the public sector have distinct and empirically observable phenomena associated with them. In many instances accountability is associated with democratic administration, but in reality it is as relevant to nondemocratic regimes as it is to those tied to popular rule. And although it is often treated as a secondary factor in public administration, accountability plays a crucial role in shaping and directing the day-to-day operations of government.

Governance Problems and Accountability Issues

Accountability relationships focus the attention of public administrators on particular sets of expectations about their performance. To understand accountability both historically and functionally, we can view it as a sequence of problems facing rulers. These include problems related to (1) delegating tasks and establishing expectations; (2) verifying the performance of those tasks; (3) maintaining the responsiveness of accountable agents; (4) assessing blame for accountable actions; (5) sorting out responsibility among many agents; (6) determining the "master;" and (7) managing under conditions of multiple accountability systems.

Problem of Delegating Tasks and Establishing Expectations

Historically, accountability emerged out of necessity as the tasks of the ruling household became too burdensome for the ruler. Such conditions initially lead to the delegation of tasks to others, and eventually to the granting of authority and discretion to act on behalf of the ruler. With those authorizations come explicit and implicit expectations for the performance of those tasks, and it is in this regard that accountability emerges as a governmental function. Thus, accountability does not necessarily imply the existence of democracy; rather it suggests any form of governance conducted through some delegation of authority.

Once the decision is made to delegate some authority or task to another, several questions must be addressed, including: (a) What tasks should be delegated by the rulers to others? (b) To whom those tasks should be delegated? And (c) how much authority and discretion should these others be given? The answers to those questions have varied from society to society over time. The common thread running through all societies is the development of institutionalized accountability relationships that focus on what is expected of the agent who is given assigned tasks and how the agent's actions are overseen. These relationships are found in tribal societies and ancient empires, in Eastern civilizations and in the West, and in modern democratic regimes as well as totalitarian ones.

What are the measures and means for implementing accountability relationships? This general problem itself has two dimensions, one dealing with the need to verify that expectations are being met, and the other with the desire to maintain the responsiveness of the accountable individual or agency.

Problem of Verification

Verification problems in accountability refer to the measures and means for ascertaining whether one's performance expectations have been met. Solutions to the problem of verification are as diverse as the types of accountability that have emerged over the centuries. Record keeping is an ancient mechanism, as are requirements that those records be submitted for review.

Historically, most of this verification effort has been directed at implementing accountability for public finances. Aristotle, for example, wrote of the need for an office "which receives and audits the accounts of other offices" who handle large sums of public money (*Politics*, VI, viii, para. 16). His comments reflect the assumption that such a verifying function was a necessary part of the design of any government that gives a public official discretion involving the expenditure of significant funds. Broader conceptions of the verification function of accountability have emerged with concern about the legality, effectiveness, and efficiency of public sector operations. As a consequence, the tasks of the modern auditor have expanded greatly to include the techniques of evaluation as well as financial accounting.

Problem of Maintaining Responsiveness

Verification that an official is doing what is expected is one thing, but how does one assure the official will remain responsive to the ruler in such situations? This problem represents the more difficult part of the general issue of implementing accountability, for if improperly solved it can defeat the very purposes for which accountability systems are constructed.

As noted previously, accountability relationships are established as means for carrying out the delegation of tasks and communication of expectations. The very effort to establish such a relationship implies that there is no intention of completely surrendering authority over the task. Rather, there is every indication that the ruler intends to retain ultimate control. Thus, in deferring to an accountable agent, the ruler seeks to maintain some control. Excessive control or overcontrol, however, can be stifling. Too lax control or undercontrol can lead to the abuse of authority or drift. The problem is to design and operate an accountability relationship that focuses on the maintenance of responsiveness to the ruler while allowing for the exercise of needed discretion by the accountable agent.

Here we find a wide range of approaches and mechanisms for resolving an accountability problem. Typically the solution has been found in the development of legal requirements and sanctions, as well as mechanisms of institutionalized oversight. The methods used in ancient Athens would not seem too strange to the rulers of modern democracies. Regular reviews of how officials conducted the city state's business were part of the public agenda, and a general review capped every magistrate's term in office. Accusations brought by auditors and citizens could lead to public trials, with punishments ranging from reprimand and impeachment to imprisonment and death.

Problem of Blame Assessment

Implied in the development of accountability relationships is a dilemma rooted in the possibility that the accountable individual may or may not be causally responsible for any failure in task performance or in meeting established expectations. The dilemma requires that any accountability relationship be capable of dealing with situations wherein causal responsibility for a success or failure is questionable.

The problem of blame assessment is not merely a technical one, for assessing blame is a social action and is therefore sensitive to the cultural context in which it occurs. To better understand the nature of this problem, consider the four types of settings posited in Figure I. The settings are derived by counterposing two factors related to accountability: formal answerability and empirical blameworthiness. Formal answerability refers to whether the accountable actor can be officially called to answer for a failed action. Empirical blameworthiness refers to whether there is an established causal link between the failed action and the official who is being held "to account" for the outcome.

A Type I scenario implies a cultural setting that holds an official accountable only when he or she is found to be both formally answerable and empirically blameworthy. In such a setting the individual being held to account must hold a position where he or she is formally responsible for the action and there is empirical evidence linking the individual to the outcome of interest. In what is perhaps the most famous American example of this, U.S. President Richard Nixon was held accountable for his actions in the Watergate cover-up because he was both formally answerable for the actions of his staff and there was empirical evidence of his involvement in the cover-up. It is likely Nixon would have escaped legal sanction for the actions of his subordinates if the "smoking gun" tape recordings,

FIGURE I. Cultural Settings for Accountability

| | | FORMAL ANSWERABILITY | |
		Yes	No
EMPIRICAL BLAMEWORTHINESS	Yes	I	II
	No	III	IV

which established Nixon's empirical blameworthiness, had not been available as evidence.

Under Type II cultural conditions of accountability, it is possible for an official who is not formally answerable to be called "to account" if there is sufficient evidence (which itself may be culturally determined) that he or she helped cause the performance failure. In such a setting, while a supervisor of a governmental unit may not be explicitly answerable for corruption, poor performance, or even misbehavior by his or her subordinates, charges that the individual was lax in performing oversight duties or training subordinates can result in demands for reprimand or resignation. The widespread practice of holding military officers answerable for an event that occurred "on their watch" represents such an accountability culture. While no formal actions may be taken against the officer as a direct consequence of the event or performance evaluation, notations in a personnel file can mean that promotions or future assignments can be adversely adjusted as an indirect consequence.

Type III cultural settings promote the idea of accountability when an official is answerable even though he or she is not empirically blameworthy. A weak form of this type of accountability is found in the symbolic gestures of many American governmental and corporate leaders when they publicly assume responsibility for a failure or problem. Despite the public humiliation that might result from these mea culpa declarations, those same officials often escape major sanctions (e.g., resignation) by noting that they were not really to blame due to ignorance or the malfeasance of some subordinate. Every so often, however, one hears of a major agency head or corporate official in a similar situation submitting his or her resignation as a matter of honor or obligation. Such a story is more likely to come from Japan, where the culture expects such responses from their top managers. Thus, after a serious jetliner crash in 1985, the head of one company submitted his resignation as a matter of honor. Similarly, the head of another major Japanese firm resigned as a means of apologizing for his firm's legal wrongdoing. In neither case was the resigning official directly or indirectly linked to the episodes in question. Rather, it was a reflection of Japanese cultural commitments to both assume responsibility for the entire organization and to defend one's honor *(giri)* (Benedict, 1946, especially ch. 7).

Finally, Type IV cultural settings of accountability permit someone or some group to be held accountable despite both blamelessness and the lack of formal answerability. This is an accountability system based on scapegoating strategies: the individual or group held "to account" neither caused the outcome nor had any formal answerability for it. Such a cultural setting can be fertile ground for the kind of demonizing nationalism that leads to genocide and "ethnic cleansing." In less nationalistic soil, it can still emerge in the form of generalized bureau-cracy bashing, where the major problems of society and government are laid at the feet of some stereotyped group of civil servants. Organizationally, blame can be assessed on "the workers" or "middle management" or some ambiguous group of outsiders. A fairly common example might be a situation where a local chief of police holds minority community leaders responsible for the police department's inability to lower community crime rates.

There is little doubt that to those nurtured in Western cultures, Type I settings are likely to constitute the ideal among the four alternatives. However, the reality is that at any point in time and place, an accountability relationship will be influenced by its cultural setting. Thus, it would be a mistake to regard the existence of even formal Type I accountability relationship as a bulwark against the inherent biases of these settings. A highly legalistic system of accountability relationships is no guarantee of protection for an innocent person who is "set up" to take the blame for a policy or program failure—especially when the society or organization is ready and willing to accept the accusation.

This was the lesson of the infamous Dreyfus Affair. The sensational events surrounding the arrest, trial, conviction, and sentencing of Captain Alfred Dreyfus in France in 1894 and his retrial in 1899 are well documented. Historians now accept the fact that the French army manufactured evidence that blamed Dreyfus for being a spy. But it is unlikely that a corrupted legal proceeding would have sufficed to convict Dreyfus. The pervasive anti-Semitism that characterized French culture at the end of the nineteenth century was conducive to laying the blame on a Jewish officer to deflect criticism from the army in an effort to bring closure to an otherwise politically sensitive administrative situation. A subsequent bill passed in 1906 restoring Dreyfus to the army and assigning him a promotion and military decorations indicated the official position of the French government that, upon reexamination, there was no evidence of empirical blameworthiness on Dreyfus's part.

Objectively, the problem for the "rulers" is to design accountability relationships so that they can be kept within desired cultural parameters. Such solutions, however, are subject to challenge by others who might find their consequences too narrow or morally reprehensible. An overly legalistic accountability relationship (Type I) might result in allowing some blameworthy individual to escape sanctions, while a Type IV setting (scapegoating) can produce genocidal results, as it did in Hitler's Germany.

Problem of Many-Handed Government

Complicating attempts to deal with the issue of blame assessment is a phenomenon that Dennis Thompson (1987) has termed the problem of "many hands." Modern government is characterized by a proliferation of officials and agencies, and the delegation of authority for particular government policies and programs is often dispersed among several of them. This is especially true in federal systems such as the United States where many social and regulatory programs are implemented through an elaborate array of intergovernmental arrangements. Even if blame assessment is not an issue, accountability relationships must be designed to contend with such situations through mechanisms that were frequently established to deal with simpler forms of authority delegation.

One consequence of this problem is an ongoing effort to reform and reorganize government administration with the intention of making public officials more accountable. Traditional solutions to this problem have involved efforts to consolidate and centralize administrative units dealing with a particular policy or program (e.g., the creation of the U.S. Environmental Protection Agency), while other solutions have involved programmatic budgeting, the use of task forces and similar organizational tools, and the extension of judicial remedies for those who seek redress for specific actions by public officials.

Problem of Multiple Masters

Modernity has also created the problem of multiple masters. The single legitimate source of authority implied in the above prior problems has been replaced by situations where there are multiple claimants on the behavior and actions of public administrators, each with a sufficient degree of legitimacy to warrant attention. Despite attempts by some to posit a single or ultimate master (e.g., the Constitution, the public interest, public opinion, the chief executive, social justice), the real world of accountability reflects the ambiguities and confusion of administrative life in modern democratic states. Pluralist democracies necessarily create a dilemma for those seeking or desiring a unified source of authority. This dilemma is perhaps more familiar to public administrators than any other group involved in democratic governance.

The dilemma posed by this problem has been expressed in a variety of models. The present authors, for example, have posited the existence of at least four accountability systems, each designed to reflect a major—and legitimate—source of expectations for administrative behavior and each reflecting different accountability relationships (see Figure II).

FIGURE II. TYPES OF ACCOUNTABILITY RELATIONSHIPS IN DEMOCRATIC SYSTEMS

		SOURCE OF CONTROL	
		Internal	External
DEGREE OF CONTROL	High	Hierarchical	Legal
	Low	Professional	Political

Hierarchical Accountability. Hierarchical accountability relationships are those most readily recognized by administrators and the general public because these relationships conform to popular conceptions of accountability, including close supervision for compliance with directives. Those favoring hierarchical accountability systems ask administrators to give priority to the expectations of supervisors and other top officials within the organization. Under such a system the administrator may be afforded little discretion and is usually expected to comply with supervisory directives, rules, and standard operating procedures. An example of a hierarchical accountability mechanism is the annual or semi-annual individual performance review, wherein a supervisor reviews and evaluates the performance of a subordinate for compliance with expectations concerning the individual's job accomplishments during that period.

Legal Accountability. Legal accountability relationships emerge from an arena where authorities expect accountable officials to carry out tasks in accordance with constitutional principles, laws, or contractual obligations. The emphasis in this form of accountability is on administrators' obligations in light of the expectations from sources external to the agency or the individual's office. Accountability relationships in this legal category emphasize oversight and monitoring of public officials by individuals external to their office or agency to ascertain whether the obligations have been met. The anticorruption investigations which Italian magistrates conducted throughout the early to mid-1990s into the bribery practices that pervaded the leadership of their government is an example of legal accountability mechanisms at work. Annual financial audits are a more common example of this kind of accountability relationship. In the United States, court review of police arrest procedures is another common example of a legal accountability relationship.

Political Accountability. Political accountability relationships are stressed by those who demand that responsiveness take priority. Under this kind of accountability system, stress is placed on administrators exercising discretion regarding the various expectations they face from external groups or market forces. The relationship of responsiveness to external groups is easiest to observe in the relationship of elected officials to voting constituents. The ballot box represents a straightforward accountability relationship based on responsiveness to citizen voters. Elected officials who are not sufficiently responsive are not reelected.

For administrators, political accountability typically manifests itself in emphases on satisfaction of key stakeholders and clientele-centered management. Popular management reforms of the 1990s, including total quality management and "reinventing government," are examples of management that emphasizes the exercise of discretion with an emphasis on responsiveness to key external groups, with a particular focus on customer satisfaction and citizens as customers. Community-based policing is a law enforcement example of government administration that emphasizes political accountability relationships. Under this form of policing officers shift roles from primarily law enforcers who emphasize arresting suspected criminals to neighborhood public servants who assist citizens in community problem solving. Performance under this responsiveness standard is judged by how satisfied communities are with outcomes, such as the level of crime in their neighborhoods and their perceptions of neighborhood safety, rather than with the number of arrests of criminal suspects.

Professional Accountability. The professional accountability relationships stress the individual responsibility of the administrator above all else as that individual exercises discretion on the job. Administrators operating under professional accountability systems are expected to exercise that discretion in a manner that is consistent with the best professional practices. Underlying this system is the belief that workers granted such discretion will monitor and regulate themselves through adherence to professional norms. The relationship is one of supervisory deference to the expertise of the administrator. An example of professional accountability relationships at work can be seen in the deference granted to engineers in the design of roads and bridges. People without design expertise will defer to engineers' judgment concerning roadbed specifications and load-bearing limits of construction materials. Management practices that emphasize worker participation in decision making exemplify this deference to the discretion of workers based on their specialized knowledge.

The problem with this multiple masters context is that public agencies and public managers find themselves facing more than one set of legitimate accountability expectations simultaneously (Dubnick and Romzek, 1993). While each system by itself might represent a relatively unambiguous set of expectations to guide and assess behavior, their simultaneous application renders accountability one of the great challenges both for government bureaucracies and those who seek to hold them accountable. For managers and agencies in this situation the challenge is deciding how to prioritize and manage these various institutionalized sets of expectations. Their goal is to accommodate as many expectations as possible while avoiding alienation of those actors whose expectations cannot be accommodated sufficiently.

Aggravating this problem for managers and agencies is the shifting nature of the accountability systems and the dynamics among them. Given the complex and frequently contradictory nature of the multiple expectations administrators face, the very process of meeting some expectations may entail failing to meet other expectations. Furthermore,

the very act of giving priority to one set of expectations over another is likely to generate other expectations and conflict.

How does one get effective performance from accountable officials subjected to the problem of multiple masters? Put briefly, for those who hold public administrators accountable, the question is how to overcome the actual and potential deterioration of public services that is likely to develop as a result of the multiple masters problem. At this level, the problem once again may be a matter of how the accountability systems are designed and applied. Depending on how this problem is perceived, proposed and actual solutions have run the range from centralization (to focus the attention of administrators on the priorities of a single master) to market-based strategies such as privatization and contracting out (that focus attention on the desires of multiple masters).

Problems of Managing Under Accountability Systems

Accountability relationships are one of the great challenges for both government bureaucracies and those who seek to hold them accountable. There is a tendency to view accountability as one-way relationships, with the focus on the influence of the controller on the controlled administrator's behavior. In fact, public administrators often play active roles in these accountability relationships, influencing the expectations others have for their performance and the choice of mechanisms under which they will be held to account for that performance.

Modern forms of accountability involve highly complex relationships and they are especially significant for those who must deal with their managerial implications. The combination of the problem of multiple masters and the diverse and often conflicting expectations they are likely to generate presents practitioners with an accountability dilemma. The essence of this dilemma is the inability of "accountable" entities to resolve the problem of many masters and manage the government's business under conditions of multiple accountability relationships and systems. This dilemma is an important issue emerging from the current state of public administration. The management problem posed by accountability relationships is both inescapable and ongoing.

For public administrators, management under this dilemma is a challenge that can be approached in a variety of ways. Under conditions set by the accountability dilemma public managers face role choices ranging from doing nothing or preparing for "damage control" to seizing the initiative and shaping the situations and expectations their agencies might face. We can view those alternatives along a continuum and logically identify four orientations managers can assume vis-à-vis the accountability dilemma: passivity, reaction, adaptation, and strategic control (see Figure III).

FIGURE III. SOLUTIONS TO MANAGERIAL CHALLENGE OF MULTIPLE MASTERS ROLE CHOICE

	Passive	Reactive	Adaptive	Strategic
FOCUS INFLUENCE ON				
Environment	—	—	—	XXX
Situations	—	—	XXX	XXX
Consequences	—	XXX	XXX	XXX

Passivity—ignoring or maintaining an indifferent stance regarding the dilemma—is by definition the absence of a solution to the management problem. Assuming this position subjects the administrators to the whims of political fortune. While such an orientation might be an unwise choice, some administrators may find they have no other option given circumstances that would punish a more active stance.

Reactive managers, in contrast, are those who focus their attention on dealing with the consequences that the accountability dilemma has for themselves and their agencies. Rather than monitoring or taking anticipatory actions in light of changing expectations, reactive managers choose to wait and see what will result from a given situation and deal with the consequences that result. For example, rather than trying to influence their agency's budget allocation, reactive managers take whatever actions are necessary to deal with the consequences of any budget cuts or increases as they occur.

Adaptive managers are likely to assess emerging situations and take anticipatory steps to minimize costly consequences. For example, looking ahead at how the central budget office or the legislature is likely to respond to alternative actions, adaptive managers will select that option that might satisfy or maximize the most positive outcome from the individual's or agency's perspective.

Strategic managers view their job as dealing with agency task environments in order to help shape and direct—even control—the emerging accountability dilemma that their organizations might encounter and to influence likely consequences. Thus, a manager might find it worthwhile to lobby both the budget office and the legislative body in order to instill in them a sense of what they should expect from the agency.

Summary

The reality of administrative dynamics is such that we sometimes lose sight of the fact that accountability involves a number of interrelated and ancient problems. Many of the problems derive from the need for the "ruler" to determine what to delegate and how to hold the authorized agent to account for his or her actions. Others reflect problems derived from the enormous scale and scope of modern governments—problems related to the many hands and many masters that characterize today's political systems.

The fundamental dynamic of accountability remains that of ensuring that public administrators pursue publicly valued goals and satisfy legitimate expectations for performance. As a result of dealing with these problems over time and across different contexts, contemporary accountability relationships are inherently complex, reflecting diverse cultural settings, varied institutional arrangements, and individual role choices. None of those many and various solutions, however, can or should be expected to bring an end to the problems of accountability.

BARBARA S. ROMZEK
MELVIN J. DUBNICK

BIBLIOGRAPHY

Benedict, Ruth, 1946. *The Chrysanthemum and the Sword: Patterns of Japanese Culture.* Boston, MA: Houghton Mifflin.
Burke, John P., 1986. *Bureaucratic Responsibility.* Baltimore, MD: Johns Hopkins University Press.
Dubnick, Melvin and Barbara S. Romzek, 1993. "Accountability and the Centrality of Expectations." In James Perry, ed., *Research in Public Administration.* Greenwich, CT: JAI Press, pp. 37–78.
Finer, Herman, 1941. "Administrative Responsibility and Democratic Government." *Public Administration Review,* vol. 1, pp. 335–350.
Friedrich, Carl J., 1940. "Public Policy and the Nature of Administrative Responsibility." In C. J. Friedrich and E. S. Mason, eds., *Public Policy.* Cambridge: Harvard University Press.
Romzek, Barbara S. and Melvin J. Dubnick, 1987. "Accountability in the Public Service: Lessons from the Challenger Tragedy." *Public Administration Review,* vol. 47, no. 3, pp. 227–239.
Romzek, Barbara S. and Melvin J. Dubnick, 1994. "Issues of Accountability in Flexible Personnel Systems." In Patricia W. Ingraham and Barbara S. Romzek, eds., *New Paradigms for Government: Issues for the Changing Public Service.* San Francisco: Jossey-Bass.
Thompson, Dennis F., 1987. *Political Ethics and Public Office,* Cambridge: Harvard University Press.

ACCOUNTING.

The process of recording, classifying, reporting, and interpreting financial data of an entity.

Accounting is the art of keeping and verifying accounts. Accounts are the books and records of an individual or organization (entity) which are used for purposes of recording the monetary sums resulting from transactions or events. The reports prepared from those accounts are known as financial statements, which are the primary form of accountability for financial resources. A broader definition of accounting in modern society is the process of identifying, measuring, recording, and communicating economic information to users of financial statements in order that they can make informed judgments about an entity. The practice of accounting is often held to be more of an art than a science because of the need to apply judgment in the measurement of transactions for inclusion in the accounts and in the preparation of financial statements from those accounts.

Because the keepers of accounts are required to record many financial transaction in an orderly manner, accounting has long been recognized as a discipline which requires meticulous and careful preparation and the development of logical classifications and systems. This has in turn led to "accounting" being synonymous with ultimate proof, as in "being brought to account" or to "account for oneself."

The Accounting Records

The source and basis of accounting is the accounting record. A record is defined as the state of being recorded or preserved in writing or similar permanent form (such as electronic data). In legal terms, accounting records have been defined in the *Australian Corporations Law 1990* (Part 1.1, clause 9), to mean (a) invoices, receipts, orders for the payment of money, bills of exchange, cheques, promissory notes, vouchers and other documents of prime entry, and (b) such working papers and other documents as are necessary to explain the methods and calculations by which accounts are made up.

The "documents of prime entry" include data files on computers. The maintenance of these records is often referred to as bookkeeping. The earliest examples of accounting records date to the Egyptian, Greek, and Chinese cultures, which developed independent styles and media for recording financial exchanges and wealth. The accepted commencement of modern accounting was the invention of the double entry method—in which for each transaction entries are made to debit one side, credit the other, always keeping the books in balance—by Luca Pacioli, a Franciscan monk writing at the end of the fifteenth century. Ventures commenced reporting profit and losses, and recording assets, liabilities, and equity.

The Structure and Classification of Accounting

The structure of accounting may be viewed in three distinct phases; input (sources of data), processing (the collation, analysis, and synthesis of the data within accounting systems), and output (reporting). The relationship of these phases is summarized in Figure I.

The input or prime entry documents for accounting include evidence of sales (invoices, statements), purchases (order forms, receiving reports), cash payments and receipts

books, salaries and wages, inventory records, journal entries covering non-cash or internal entries for items such as depreciation and amortization of assets, and the distribution of profits (dividends).

The input data is traditionally recorded in the manual books of account, comprising separate books or ledgers called the general or nominal ledger, subsidiary ledgers such as the debtors and creditors ledgers, the journal or day book, and other memorandum records and files. The underlying principle of accounting is that a balance is maintained in the general ledger by making an equal and opposite entry for transactions. For example, when a sale is credited to the sales account of the ledger, the cash or debtors account is debited with an equivalent amount. The books of account are now usually maintained on computers.

Accounting disciplines are usually categorized by objectives, or output (type of reports). *Financial accounting* is concerned with assembling and reporting financial information for external users including equity holders, which enables an entity to satisfy accountability requirements and provide users with information to make decisions about the entity. It is distinguished from *management accounting*, which provides information primarily to management and controllers within an entity for operational decision making. Both financial and management accounting use the same basic information from the accounting records, but differ as to detail and emphasis of their reports. For example, while external financial statements typically disclose a single total amount for sales revenue, management accounting reports would include breakdown of the sales figures between product types, margins, and volumes to enable managers to make key product decisions.

Types of Accounting Transactions

Accounting records are maintained in the books of account under five major transaction categories:

Revenue Accounts. Revenue accounts include all those inflows (or savings in outflows) of future economic benefits or other enhancements which increase the equity of the entity by either increasing assets or decreasing liabilities. This does not include equity contributions by an owner. Transactions and other events which give rise to revenues can include sales, discounts received, fees, commissions, dividends, rent, taxes, grants, and rates. Note that revenue has a wider definition than income, which covers cash or fund receipts only.

Expenditure Accounts. Expense accounts record the consumption or loss of future economic benefits by way of reduction in assets or increases in liabilities leading to a decrease in the equity of the entity. Transactions and other events which give rise to expenditure would be purchases, wages and salaries, depreciation and amortization,

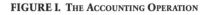

FIGURE I. THE ACCOUNTING OPERATION

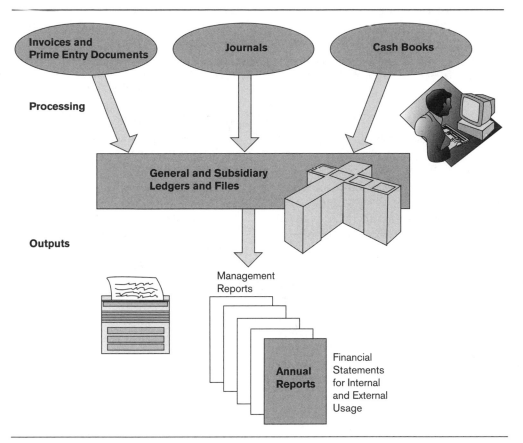

cost of goods sold, cost of services provided, rent, interest, and so forth. Expenditure carries a broader meaning than payment, which is the outflow of cash or funds only.

Asset Accounts. Assets are defined as future economic benefits controlled by an entity as a result of past transactions or other past events. Assets are recorded in the accounts where they will provide some benefit in the future, and can be physical assets such as buildings, plant and equipment; intangible assets such as copyrights, goodwill or licenses; or past expenditures of funds for which benefits are still to be received (prepayments).

Liabilities. Liability accounts record the future sacrifices of economic benefits that the entity is presently obliged to make to other entities as a result of past transactions or other past events. Liabilities include obligations to current creditors for purchases and other services received, borrowings of all forms, past transactions for which the entity is liable (e.g., employee retirement benefits), and services or benefits received in previous reporting periods (accruals).

Equity. Equity accounts record the ownership interests, defined as the residual interest in the assets of the entity after deduction of liabilities. Terms used to describe equity in the private sector include owners' equity, equity capital, capital and reserves, shareholders' funds, and proprietor-

ship. In the public sector equity is referred to variously as public equity, contributed equity, and government equity. Equity is increased by contributions from owners (share raisings, capital raising, grants, and so forth), and excesses of revenues over expenditures for reporting periods, and decreased by distributions to owners and excesses of expenditure over revenues.

Accounting Bases

Accounting records are maintained using the accrual basis whereby items are brought to account as they are earned or incurred (and not as money is received or paid), and included in the reporting periods to which they relate. Other important underlying principles of modern accounting include the reporting entity concept, which identifies the entity (including an economic entity) for purposes of reporting and accountability; the accounting period convention, which requires the entity to classify accounting and reporting into distinct regular periods of time (usually a 12-month period); and the going concern basis, which assumes the entity will continue intact without the need to liquidate or greatly reduce operations.

The measurement of accounting transactions and events in the accounting records can vary between entities, industries, and countries depending on the professional accounting standards and regulations in force. Much effort is being given to standardizing and harmonizing the approach to accounting internationally to aid investors and to promote trade.

Accounting Processes

Accounting systems and methods evolved through many mediums and manual forms until the emergence of computers in the 1960s. The ability to store and retrieve financial data in electronic form has revolutionized bookkeeping and accounting by enabling vast amounts of information to be stored, sorted, calculated, and retrieved quickly, by reducing the error rate, and by eliminating the need for extensive paper trails. This in turn has provided for accountants to concentrate on analyzing and refining data collection and processing systems, and to undertake a more managerial role rather than mundane bookkeeping.

Accounting software packages now undertake much of the processing and checking functions that previously occupied large volumes of clerical staff. Computing combined with telecommunications can eliminate all hard copy from transactions using worldwide systems such as the Electronic Data Interchange (EDI) system. This makes it possible to order goods, arrange delivery, receipt, acknowledge, approve, pay, and update inventory records without using any paper or hard copy documentation.

Functions of Accounting Systems

The functions and processes dependent on good accounting systems include:

- *Planning*: providing the parameters and data for the strategic, corporate, and business planning process essential to survival of entities.
- *Budgeting*: undertaking short- and long-term budgeting for entities, including development of financial and nonfinancial performance measures.
- *Capital expenditure evaluation:* undertaking the analysis for investment proposals.
- *Management control:* production of management accounts and reports.
- *Risk assessment and internal control:* the identification and monitoring of potential areas of loss and exposure for an entity.

Accounting Reports

Financial statements summarize and categorize the data held in the accounting records in order to make the information accessible and sensible to readers. Their basic purpose is to provide those users with information for decision making. General Purpose Financial Reports (GPFR) assume that users require sufficient financial information about an entity to make decisions on the allocation of scarce resources and to satisfy accountability requirements. Specific Purpose Financial Reports (SPFR) are prepared to meet the specific needs of the controlling authority, and therefore do not usually come in a format or contain enough information to be useful in general decision making.

An example of a GPFR would be the annual accounts of a company listed on a stock exchange. These present in a standard format all the financial and nonfinancial information required by regulation and standard-setting bodies to inform users adequately. This includes the earnings/profit and loss statement (or operating statement), a balance sheet (or statement of position), cash flows and supplementary notes giving details of individual balances or transactions, and information about the structure and ownership of the entity.

The objective of GPFR is to provide information on:

Performance. Measuring the performance of the entity in financial and nonfinancial terms. This will be the profit or loss bottom line in a private sector business, or the surplus or deficit disclosed by non-business public sector and not-for profit organizations.

Financial Position. Information about the financial strength or weakness of an entity, its control over resources, capacity for adaptation, and overall solvency is important data for potential investors or creditors.

Financing and Investing Details. Details of sources and applications of funds is relevant to decisions about the allocation of scarce resources.

Compliance. Financial statements often provide assurances that provisions of enabling or regulating legislation have been met, or that the entity has acquitted its obligations to specific grants, minimum requirements, and so forth.

The fundamental objectives of GPFR apply equally to both profit and not-for-profit organizations (such as governments). The format and content of GPFR are determined by professional accounting bodies in their accounting concepts, accounting standards, generally accepted accounting principles (GAAP), and other pronouncements and legislation within each nation and jurisdiction. The International Accounting Standards Committee (IASC) was formed to coordinate, harmonize, and establish international accounting standards; many countries choose to adopt these or at least to ensure their own standards are not incompatible with the IASC requirements.

The public sector has been slow in adopting GAAP, the accrual basis, and GPFR formats for their finances. In most cases this is because governments have traditionally set out the reporting formats and accounting bases under economic rather than professional accounting requirements.

Management accounting is a special branch of accounting which has developed rapidly with the need for management information (see Management, Accounting). Advances in both financial accounting and management accounting have been made through the establishment of national and international accounting research agencies. An example is the contribution made by the Australian Accounting Research Foundation to developing one conceptual framework for both public sector and private sector accounting and reporting standards. As citizens demand greater accountability from their public, private, and not-for-profit sectors, the need for more and better accounting and financial reporting will be at the forefront.

GRAEME MACMILLAN

BIBLIOGRAPHY

Australian Accounting Research Foundation. *Australian Accounting Standards and Concepts. Consensus Statements of the Urgent Issues Group* (Updated frequently). Australian Society of Practising Accountants and Institute of Chartered Accountants Members' Handbooks. (Updated frequently)
Australian Corporations Law, 1990.
Walgenbach, Paul, Ernest Hanson, and Norman Dittrich, 1987. *Principles of Accounting.* 4th edition. Orlando, FL: Harcourt Brace Jovanovich.

ACQUIRED IMMUNODEFICIENCY SYNDROME (AIDS) POLICY.

Governmental responses to the AIDS epidemic. AIDS is a group of physical and mental disorders resulting from a deteriorating immune system. It is caused by the retrovirus, Human Immunodeficiency Virus (HIV). A retrovirus reverses the normal process, known as transcriptase, that builds new body cells. This process involves cells containing deoxyribonucleic acids (DNA), which contain the body's genetic code, and molecules containing ribonucleic acids (RNA), which help to control cellular chemical activities. In the normal transciptase process, RNA acts as the "messenger" among existing DNA as well as between existing and developing DNA. In doing so, RNA transmits the genetic code.

If we assume the body is a house under construction, then DNA performs the function of being the keeper and interpreter of the blueprint as well as the actual bricks out of which the house is built. RNA acts as the messenger that reminds the DNA of what the house should look like (the blueprint) and is also mortar that keeps the bricks in place (controlling cellular chemical activities).

When a virus enters the body, the genetic code triggers an immunal response in the DNA cells. As in the case of an approaching storm upon a house, the RNA messengers remind the DNA that windows and doors need to be latched and also ensures the DNA that the mortar will withstand the wind and keep the bricks from disintegrating.

When a retrovirus enters the body, the process of transcriptase is reversed. The retrovirus captures and engulfs the RNA molecules. Rather than acting as the messengers for DNA, virus-enveloped RNA molecules transmit a unique message to DNA cells. The DNA cells become the messengers for the RNA molecules. In the case of HIV, the message is to ignore that part of the genetic code that triggers immunal responses.

Following the analogy of the approaching storm upon the house, now the DNA are not reminded to close the windows and doors. In fact, DNA messengers encourage other DNA not to take any precautions. Moreover, the RNA mortar used to keep the DNA bricks together no longer wants to "hold" and begins the process of disintegration. As the number of HIV-enveloped RNA molecules grows, the body becomes increasingly convinced that the presence of HIV is desirable and, in fact, a part of the genetic code.

HIV enters the body through blood-to-blood contact with someone who already possesses the retrovirus. Typically it takes four to ten years for HIV to cause sufficient immunal damage to permit the presence of "full-blown" AIDS. A person with "full-blown" AIDS dies from a host of opportunistic diseases and cancers, typically within a two-year period.

The date and source of origin of HIV are unclear. The rampant spread of HIV in the 1970s resulted in a constant increase of people with AIDS in the 1980s. However, samples from a blood bank in Zaire, Africa—blood stored since the 1950s—have tested positive for HIV. The first documented case of HIV/AIDS occurred in tropical Africa in the early 1970s. An infected health care worker probably introduced the retrovirus onto the European continent. In all likelihood, the 1976 bicentennial celebration of the American Revolution, a celebration which brought thousands of people from throughout the world to New York City, was the catalyst for spreading HIV throughout the North American continent. "Jetsetters" helped spread the disease to other parts of the globe. By the late 1980s, the retrovirus had most likely spread to every country in the world. Without comprehensive and routine testing for the HIV antibodies in everyone's blood, there is no way to determine the number of people who are infected with the retrovirus. By the mid-1990s, the number of people infected with HIV was estimated to be well over 1 million in the United States, and 20–50 million throughout the world.

Policy Response to HIV/AIDS

Governmental responses to the HIV/AIDS epidemic have been incremental and disparate, reflecting the nature of American federalism as well as the decentralized, nation-by-nation response throughout the world (see **discrimination, disabilities**). However, two strategies tend to provide a framework through which most HIV/AIDS policies emerge. The first strategy focuses on the medical and public health dimensions of HIV/AIDS. Governments in both the developed and developing worlds have responded by investing resources in basic research to find a cure to HIV. In addition, health care officials have employed two traditional public health approaches in efforts to curtail the spread of HIV: epidemiological tracking and the dissemination of preventative information. More authoritarian governments, such as China and Cuba, have also included a third public health device, quarantining those infected in order to limit further the spread of the disease.

The second strategy views AIDS as a civil rights issue. This is especially the case in Western nations where the HIV retrovirus first struck within the gay community and did so at a time when members of that community were gaining basic civil rights. Hence, governments have also responded by developing policies which protect the rights of the HIV-challenged in a variety of areas, such as privacy and confidentiality, access to adequate health care and treatment, and discrimination in the workplace and other social settings. In the United States, these protections are incorporated in the Americans with Disabilities Act (ADA) and the Vocational Rehabilitation Act (see **discrimination, disabilities**).

Challenges to Effective Responses

These two perspectives, protecting the health of the community and ensuring the civil rights of individuals, make difficult tasks out of developing and implementing governmental responses to the HIV/AIDS epidemic. Together both strategies underscore the tension which often exists whenever values associated with individualism are juxtaposed with values associated with community. Furthermore, the tension between these two strategies illustrates the desire among many people to cast this epidemic in liberal and conservative colors.

For instance, policies that address the civil rights side of the equation are often attacked by political conservatives as being designed to advance the gay lifestyle and encourage premarital sex among heterosexuals. Conservatives point out that a concern for protecting the civil rights of gays in the early years of the epidemic meant delaying the implementation of more effective public health responses, especially the closing of gay bath houses where frequent and unprotected sexual encounters with multiple

and anonymous partners resulted in the explosion of HIV among homosexual and bisexual men. Such sexual practices were considered by the gay community as manifestations of its newly acquired civil rights. From the point of view of conservatives, the content of information about "safer sex" practices is also designed to protect and promote the interests of the gay community because such information often gives only minimal weight to the practice of premarital sexual abstinence.

Policies designed to address health and medical issues, on the other hand, are sometimes attacked by political liberals as being too cautious and time-consuming in the face of an epidemic that requires much more rapid responses. From the liberal point of view, the lethargic nature of the scientific method is most readily apparent in the area of developing effective drugs. Procedures for testing new drugs can easily take up to ten years. Because of the limited number of drugs being tested, moreover, seropositive individuals have only a slight chance of becoming part of an experimental group. Liberals also argue that federal funding in the early years of the epidemic would have been targeted to AIDS research, much more quickly and in much greater levels, if this disease had not been viewed initially as a "gay disease." The fact that AIDS was originally called GRID (Gay-Related Immunodeficiency) did not help the matter.

Funding for HIV/AIDS Policy

In the U.S., federal funding levels in the early 1990s were about $5 billion annually. In 1994, the American people voted in a new majority into both houses of Congress that is much more conservative than all previous Congresses since the outbreak of AIDS. Given the conservative nature of Congress, in conjunction with public demand for a reduction in federal funding, a decline in the level of funding for HIV/AIDS policies is quite likely.

Funding is distributed among four major activities: basic research (35 percent), education and prevention (14 percent), medical care (43 percent), and cash assistance (8 percent). A variety of federal agencies are involved in responding to HIV/AIDS: departments of Health and Human Services, Housing and Urban Development, Labor, Education, Veterans Affairs, and Defense, as well as the Health Care Financing Administration, Social Security Administration, Agency for International Development, and the Equal Employment Opportunity Commission. Within the Department of Health and Human Services, a variety of agencies of the U.S. Public Health Service are involved: the National Institutes of Health, the Alcohol, Drug Abuse, and Mental Health Administration, Centers for Disease Control and Prevention, Food and Drug Administration, Health Resources and Services Administration, the Agency for Health Care Policy and Research, the

Office of the Assistant Secretary for Health, and the Indian Health Service.

Although the fight against HIV/AIDS has not yet produced an effective vaccine or cure, it has provided some insight into the abilities of governments to formulate and implement policy responses to this crisis. Effectiveness seems to increase when responses are coordinated and designed to address the many social ramifications, as well as the medical dimensions, of the disease.

JAMES D. SLACK

BIBLIOGRAPHY

Bayer, Ronald, 1989. *Private Acts, Social Consequences: AIDS and the Politics of Public Health.* New York: The Free Press.

Shilts, Randy, 1988. *And the Band Played On.* New York: Viking Penguin.

Slack, James D., 1995. "The Americans with Disabilities Act and the Workplace: Observations about Management's Responsibilities in AIDS-Related Situations." *Public Administration Review* (July/August).

———, 1992. "Responding to the Global Epidemic of AIDS: Cultural and Political Challenges Facing Governments." *Policy Studies Journal* (Winter).

———, 1991. *AIDS and the Public Work Force.* Tuscaloosa: The University of Alabama Press.

Slack, James D. and Anelia Luna, 1992. "AIDS-Related Documents from 96 American Cities and Counties." *Public Administration Review* (May/June).

Stine, Gerald J., 1993. *Acquired Immune Deficiency Syndrome: Biological, Medical, Social, and Legal Issues.* Englewood Cliffs, NJ: Prentice-Hall.

Strama, Brenda T., ed., 1993. *AIDS and Governmental Liability: State and Local Government Guide to Legislation, Legal Issues, and Liability.* Chicago: The American Bar Association.

ACRONYM. A word formed from the initial letters of a name or phrase. Acronyms provide a shorthand label for referring to frequently used names, titles, or phrases.

The use of acronyms in public administration is a tradition as old as the field itself. Indeed, for novices in the field one of the first hurdles that must be overcome is learning the meanings (and sometimes the pronunciations) of frequently used "alphabet soup" combinations of letters that the many acronyms contribute to the field's jargon or "bureaucratese."

Professional organizations may be given acronymic shorthand labels. The American Society for Public Administration is known as ASPA (pronounced aśpah), the National Academy of Public Administration is NAPA (nápah), the Policy Studies Organization is PSO, the Association for Public Policy Analysis and Management is APPAM (aṕpahm), and the International City/County Management Association is ICMA. ASPA's primary publication, *Public Administration Review,* is known as *PAR* (pahr).

Legislation that is frequently referenced may also be given an acronym. For example, the Comprehensive Employment Training Act is called CETA (seétah), the National Environmental Protection Act is NEPA (neépah), the Racketeer Influenced and Corrupt Organizations Act is RICO (reéco), the Americans with Disabilities Act is ADA, and the Administrative Procedure Act is APA.

Governmental agencies, departments, and organizations often become better known by their acronyms than by their full names. WHO is the World Health Organization, EPA is the Environmental Protection Agency, FDA is the Food and Drug Administration, FAA is the Federal Aviation Administration, OPM is the Office of Personnel Management, OMB is the Office of Management and Budget, COGs are Councils of Government, and BLM is the Bureau of Land Management.

Administrative techniques and management fads are also favored with acronyms. Luther Gulick gave the field POSDCORB (pohsdcorb), a mnemonic device for remembering the key functions of executives–Planning, Organizing, Staffing, Directing, Coordinating, Reporting and Budgeting. Planning, Programming, and Budgeting is known as PPB, Zero-Based Budgeting is ZBB, Management by Objectives is MBO, Organizational Development is OD, Program Evaluation and Review Technique is PERT (pehrt), Total Quality Management is TQM.

Acronyms also have been used to label administrative actions. When people are dismissed from their jobs because their organization or agency is reducing its number of employees, people say they were "RIFed" (Reduction in Force). When a supervisor is passing along information that is vitally important, but agonizingly dull, his or her presentation is said to have a MEGO effect (My Eyes Glaze Over).

New acronyms are constantly being created, so a list could literally fill hundreds of pages and still not include them all. Because the use of acronyms has become so commonplace, and because the use of specific acronyms may be found only within a very limited and specialized area, it is not unusual to find a key to acronyms in the appendix of a technical report. Clearly, acronyms are a central aspect of public administration.

Sometimes acronyms are utilized creatively to catch people's attention. Examples of evocative acronyms include: RAGE (Residents Against Garbage Encroachment), DARE (Drug Abuse Resistance Education), START (Strategic Arms Reduction Talks), and COPS (Community Oriented Police Station). Another creative use is to adopt an acronym that carries a double entendre. For example, CYA refers to a guideline for administrators operating in situations fraught with personal professional danger; one should Cover Your Accountability.

Most often acronyms have represented relatively value-free attempts to shorten the name of something, but their creative utilization has developed into a new twist: the use of attack acronyms. Attack acronyms are verbal weapons used in disputes regarding the advisability of programs, projects, and policies. For example, NIMBY (nihmbee) is a label used to discredit opposition to a proposed land use or project, and stands for the phrase "Not In My Back Yard." Used as a label intended to embarrass people opposed to a particular land use or public works project, NIMBY is generally considered to carry connotations implying that persons so labeled are selfishly and/or shortsightedly opposing a proposed project. When people who live, work, or own property near a proposed project object not to the project itself, but to its location near them, they are often dismissed by public administrators and others in favor of the project as "just a bunch of NIM-BYs." When the opposition becomes especially strident and/or expansive in delimiting their "backyard," as was a group in western Washington State that named itself NOME (Not On My Earth), they might be given an even more dismissive label, BANANA (Build Absolutely Nothing Anytime Not Anywhere).

Those in opposition to the proposed land use, too, have their favorite derisive acronyms; they often label the project a LULU (loo loo), a Locally Unwanted Land Use. Leaky underground storage tanks have been labeled LUSTs. And both proponents and opponents of a project can find occasions to refer to elected officials as NIM-TOOs (Not In My Term Of Office).

LARRY S. LUTON

BIBLIOGRAPHY

Safire, William, 1978. *Safire's Political Dictionary.* New York: Ballantine Books.

ACTION LEARNING.

An approach to management development devised by Professor Reg Revans, by which managers learn in groups through asking questions and solving real problems in the workplace.

Professor Reg Revans first developed his concept of action learning in the British coal industry; since then it has been widely used in public sector organizations as an approach to problem solving and management development. Later applications were in the hospital industry in Britain, in private sector firms such as GEC, and in a variety of government departments and agencies.

Based on the concept that in a turbulent environment, managers need to learn how to take effective action, and that managers are people of action rather than theorists, Revans argued that managers should be placed in a position to learn through taking action, not through making recommendations or analyzing someone else's actions.

Revans argued that managers learned better solving real problems rather than discussing cases, and through formulating questions to be answered rather than being given programmed answers in books and lectures. According to Revans, there are two types of learning, P and Q. P is programmed learning, contained in books and lectures. Q is the learning which comes through inquiry. The latter, being flexible and involving the development of investigative skills, is seen as more useful to practical managers.

Action learning is built around undertaking a project of real significance to an organization. A problem may involve a familiar task in an unfamiliar setting, or an unfamiliar task in a familiar setting.

Action learning emphasizes learning as a social process. Insight is likely to be enhanced if managers work together on solving a problem, and regular joint meetings of the "learning set" or group are undertaken in an atmosphere of mutual self-help. Such meetings are often weekly or fortnightly, and may be facilitated by an adviser to the group.

Action learning can be a powerful process capable of developing managers' skills and solving organizational problems. It can be conducted as a stand-alone approach, or more commonly, integrated with other management improvement programs within the organization.

E. W. RUSSELL

BIBLIOGRAPHY

Foy, N., 1977. "Action Learning Comes to Industry." *Harvard Business Review* (September/October).
Revans, R. W., 1971. *Developing Effective Managers.* New York: Praeger.
———1966. *The Theory of Practice in Management.* London: Macdonald.
Wieland, G. F. and H. E. Leigh, 1971. *Changing Hospitals: A Report on the Hospital Internal Communications Project.* London: Tavistock Publications.

ACTION RESEARCH.

The application of the scientific method modified to solve practical problems. This has evolved as a useful complement to conventional science in those many cases in which individuals or systems of them are involved. The focus is on being rigorously self-reflective about experience so as to permit action planning that leads to desired and desirable changes in the functioning of individuals or human systems. In some countries it is referred to as "participatory research."

Action research, or AR, is an apparently simple notion which has profound relevance. Thus, AR has roots deep in our commitment to intervening in nature to create more desired and desirable lives; and AR has a potential that extends to the heart of our individual and collective existence.

Two emphases support this compound conclusion. The first emphasis describes selected basic features of

Action Research; the second focuses on several concerns about AR.

Action Research Basics

Any list of basic elements risks both overkill and underspecification, depending upon the reader. By way of introduction, however, five features seem necessary to circumscribe AR. It:

- involves a self-reflective inquiry by participants in some collective situation, for example members of an organization, inhabitants of a village, and so on, who are intent on learning about themselves and their collective situation;
- seeks to improve conditions within the experienced situation for example by improving practices in an organization or a profession;
- strives to improve participant skills relevant to what gets done, how, and when in dealing with a shared situation;
- aspires to generate knowledge about practice as well as improvements in it, by solving problems as well as building generalizations that contribute to evolving theoretical frameworks or models that inform practice by involving participants both as subjects as well as objects of research. In short, AR involves "participant observers" as well as "observant participants" in learning about themselves, from themselves; and
- intends a delicate balance: participation and involvement are highly valued, but these can be judiciously informed by available experience and theory.

Even this brief sketch implies that AR differs from "conventional," "straight," or "logical-positivist" science, and a few contrasts sharpen the point. In summary, straight science sharply separates the observer from the observed, emphasizes norms of objectivity and impartiality for the observer, and attributes no capacity for the observed to reflect on its own behavior. Action Research (AR) differs, and basically, as can be illustrated by one substantial contrast. Straight science pays primary attention to whether its generalizations and theories are "correct" or not—that is, whether they mirror some aspects of reality and can be extended to others in a dignified hopscotching toward comprehensiveness. AR is basically concerned with the degrees of participation, involvement, and consensus underlying specific efforts. These conditions improve the chances that reasonable things will be done—in describing an existing state, prescribing a more desired or desirable state, and moving toward that state in self-controlling and self-monitoring ways.

The distinction between straight science and AR is incomplete, however. Thus, consensual processes also play a large role in straight science where, on notable occasions, powerful forces have supported positions which later came to be seen as nonsense, with severe punishments having been meted out to nonconformists while the new learning evolved. Moreover, AR neglects only at its great peril real-world barriers that can frustrate even massive mobilizations of human will.

Action research can deal with a broad range of issues, concerning both local preferences and conditions as well as generalizations from expanding networks of empirical theory. Thus, AR appears under various labels in public agencies and business: Organization Development or OD, Quality of Working Life or QWL, and High Involvement Organizations. Numerous other arenas of application could be enumerated.

Three factors illustrate the powerful motivators to spread AR applications. First, AR at once pre-dates as well as serves the burgeoning idea that broad ranges of people have to be involved in understanding their shared conditions, coping with those conditions and, of paramount importance, coming to progressively improve those conditions. The recognition grows that while institutions such as government and employing organizations can play useful roles, many desired and desirable outcomes are beyond their reach. Hence the growing realization, virtually worldwide, of the central need to empower broad ranges of people: family members as well as citizens of nation-states, marginal farmers as well as professional employees of business and government, and so on. AR constitutes a major vehicle for this empowerment as people learn how to learn from themselves about their condition. Typically, at a minimum, this requires developing appropriate skills and attitudes in response to opportunities for action-taking at low and middle levels of social, political, and economic structures.

Second, AR gains credibility from the "steps" it encompasses, which are both generalizable to a broad range of situations as well as reasonable. Typically, AR involves some client system—often aided by a skilled facilitator or change agent—in progressive action roles:

- sensing a learning opportunity
- contracting between client and facilitator, if relevant
- diagnosing
- data gathering
- data feedback to all stakeholders
- exploration of data
- action planning
- action taking
- evaluation

AR facilitators do not basically act as subject matter experts, in which capacity they might well play the dominant role at each step. Rather, the client system is the expert about most aspects of the local condition, while the facilitator provides skills and perspectives that help the client system mobilize skills and energies. The details can differ broadly, but the characteristic mix is clear in this abstract of an AR application dealing with "river blindness" among inhabitants of an Indian village. Villagers associated the disease with rivers, but a waterborne organism was at fault, and its effects were compounded by reflected sunlight.

This AR application had two goals: raising villager consciousness about the incidence and character of a particular kind of sight impairment, and developing villager skills to act on that heightened consciousness. In a brief outline, approaching the twin goals involved the following steps, among others:

- gaining the support of village elders, all nonliterate, to investigate river blindness;
- contracting with elders to involve newly literate young villagers in a program of remediation and prevention;
- assessing the knowledge base among villagers;
- external experts recommending additions to, or useful changes in, that knowledge base;
- building appropriate attitudes and skills, especially among young villagers but also elders;
- surveying by the young villagers to estimate the local incidence of various stages of river blindness;
- defining local programs of remediation and prevention which, after sanctioning by elders, are implemented by young villagers; and
- assessing effects by young villagers, who reported to elders for fine tuning.

Third, success rates for AR applications are substantial, if not formidable. Measures of success and AR interventions differ widely, but the estimates of success usually fall in the 50–80 percent range (Golembiewski, 1993, pp. 399–406).

Some Concerns About AR

These basics generate a sense of vitality and progress, but they also have encouraged spinoffs that threaten agreements at the AR core. But that is the way of scientific progress. Good ideas provide the foundation from which extensions can be attempted, even though some extensions can be inconsistent with that core, or they may negate it. Consider three basic issues concerning AR's core.

Guiding Values

Just as for all human activities *the* question is: AR for what? One's values—or definitions of the desired and desirable—provide working answers.

AR researchers do not neglect this key question, but they remain far from agreement about the working answer. To illustrate only, some see AR values in limited and pragmatic terms: the goal is to solve some presenting problem without creating other problems, and especially those

which are more formidable than the original problem. Other AR researchers are much more ambitious. They propose to do nothing less than to achieve social justice, as variously defined.

Thus, AR efforts can be distinguished, if approximately, as either emancipatory or as pragmatic. Where one starts, normatively, can make for many differences, even conflicts.

Thus, those committed to emancipatory AR can see their pragmatic cousins as fiddling with trivia while neglecting the burning issues. Similarly, pragmatic AR can view emancipatory AR as promising too much, too soon, and hence as sowing the seeds of their mutual disaster, even if with the best of intentions. This difference in normative stances can be consequential, even crucial.

Viewpoint

Where one stands influences what one sees, and may cause a highly selective perception. So it is with AR, and with important consequences.

To explain, pragmatic AR can incline toward a kind of deliberate nearsightedness, about seeing problem situations in terms of troubleshooting, improving specific relationships, and building local norms.

Emancipatory AR favors the macro view. To paraphrase Robinson (1993), those taking that stance will locate barriers to learning or understanding in the structural features of life: organizational, social, political, and, perhaps primarily, economic barriers. Change in them constitutes the major challenge.

The ideal is clear enough, but practice is uneven. Both the immediate and broader environments are relevant, but they are seldom taken into simultaneous account. For pragmatists, this simultaneity can be viewed as a kind of "paralysis by analysis"—so much to take into account that many useful things get delayed or do not get dealt with. In contrast, emancipatory AR can be critical of those seen as fixating on the proverbial trees while neglecting the forest, and much more beside.

Level of Intervention

Whether one emphasizes remediation or prevention or both, a key question involves the best level of intervention to deal with barriers to inquiry and understanding. At least four such levels can be distinguished:

- improving the relationships between specific individuals and small groups, as in regenerative versus degenerative interaction that takes into account the levels of risk, trust, openness or truth-telling, and public owning of ideas or feelings (Golembiewski, 1993);
- enhancing the problem-solving capacities of individuals, as in double-loop vs. single-loop thinking (Argyris, Putman, and Smith, 1985);
- accumulating comprehensive experience and theory relevant to "learning how to learn"; and

■ institutionalizing a pervasive bias toward self-reflective activity, as in "the learning organization" (Watkins and Marsick, 1993).

Again, the ideal choice of levels—all of the above—is both profoundly correct as well as rare in practice. AR applications usually emphasize one or a few of these levels, and those differences can serve to stimulate progress as well as controversy.

Summary

In sum, AR features and potentialities have attracted much attention and motivated growing applications in many realms of human endeavor. The attractions are robust enough to encourage numerous extensions beyond the AR core, but progress remains incomplete in significant senses. The success rates of AR applications remain substantial, and permit real optimism that the challenging questions illustrated above can be dealt with successfully.

ROBERT T. GOLEMBIEWSKI

BIBLIOGRAPHY

Argyris, Chris, R. Putman, and D. M. Smith, 1985. *Action Science.* San Francisco: Jossey-Bass.

Golembiewski, Robert T., ed., 1993. *Handbook of Organizational Consultation.* New York: Marcel Dekker.

Robinson, Vivianne M. J., 1993. "Current Controversies in Action Research." *Public Administration Quarterly,* vol. 17 (Fall) 263–290.

Susman, Gerald J., and Roger D. Evered, 1978. "An Assessment of the Scientific Merits of Action Research." *Administrative Science Quarterly,* vol. 23 (December) 582–603.

Watkins, Karen, and Victoria J. Marsick, 1993. *Sculpting the Learning Organization.* San Francisco: Jossey-Bass.

ACTION THEORY.

A term that encompasses a broad range of theoretical perspectives in the social sciences in which the principal focus is on the subjective meanings of social actors themselves as the starting point for analysis and theorizing. Rough synonyms for action theory include phenomenology, interpretive theory, and hermeneutics (after the Greek mythological figure Hermes, the interpreter of the gods), although the term may be construed even more broadly to include virtually any theoretical approach in the social sciences that honors the subjectivity of human experience as the primary topic of analysis.

To understand what action theory (or a theory of action) both is and is not, it is advisable to begin with the German historian and sociologist Max Weber's (1978) classic distinction between "behavior" and "action." The former term (later represented by various "behaviorist" psychologies and "behavioral" methodological approaches to doing social science research) refers, in Weber's meaning, to the observable movements of people, independent of any consideration of whether those movements are consciously willed (or "motivated") or simply the result of physical reflex. Behaviorism, as it has evolved during the twentieth century, may now be roughly divided between two, in some respects opposing, camps: (1) the radical behaviorists (perhaps best exemplified by the psychologist B. F. Skinner [1974]) who, in rejecting the scientific validity, and indeed the very existence, of such notions as mind, intention, meaning, and motivation, assert that behavior can be explained deterministically as the product of environmental, albeit often genetically influenced, forces; and (2) the methodological behaviorists, who, while not necessarily rejecting the notions of mind, intention, and so forth, believe that the behaviorists' methodological repertoire of measurement and hypothesis testing is nevertheless warranted by the belief that the meaning or purpose of human activity may be reliably inferred from its detached observation.

Weber defined action, by contrast, as "human behavior when and to the extent that the agent or agents see it as subjectively *meaningful*" (1978, p. 7, emphasis in the original). Following Weber's lead, action theorists are generally agreed that the starting point for analysis is the subjective standpoint of the actors being studied, rather than theories that seek to explain or predict what people say or do in terms of *a priori* schemes of interpretation. Behaviorists and action theorists alike grant a crucial interpretive role for social scientists, but the latter regard the subjectively meaningful interpretations of the research subjects themselves as the principal "data" to be interpreted by social scientists. As suggested by the term "the double hermeneutic," action theorists are, in effect, interpreters of the interpretations of others.

Action theorists' quarrel with behaviorism has taken two general directions. Their disagreement with radical behaviorism chiefly involves a reprise of the ancient philosophical and theological debate over free will versus determinism, that is, whether people may be regarded as intentional agents of their actions, which action theorists answer in the affirmative. (For representative statements of each side of this issue, see Skinner [1974] for the behaviorist position, and Searle [1983] for an argument that satisfies most action theorists.) Action theory's disagreements with methodological behaviorism (sometimes called behavioralism) center mainly on the questions of whether it is logically possible to infer purpose or meaning from behavior in the absence of some knowledge of the human intention that motivates it, and whether as an empirical matter particular inferences about actors' meanings and intentions from observations of their behavior in fact correspond to their actual meanings and intentions.

The many differences in intellectual orientation within the action theory perspective are illustrated by its representation in at least three of the four principal social science paradigms identified by Burrell and Morgan (1979), namely functionalism, interpretivism, and radical humanism. While action theory is most closely allied with the interpretive paradigm, Parsons' (1949) theory of social action, which partly grew out of Weber's sociology, is located squarely within the functionalist paradigm, which is underwritten by many of the same positivistic assumptions and beliefs to which virtually all variants of behaviorism subscribe. Action theorists located within the interpretive paradigm have therefore criticized Parsons and other functionalists who claim to be action theorists for conceiving of action far too deterministically, thus violating Weber's stipulation that action must be understood chiefly in terms of the subjective, and intentional, experience of social actors (Giddens, 1984).

Within American sociology, Berger and Luckmann's *The Social Construction of Reality* (1967) stands as the landmark work in the interpretive paradigm that has informed later developments in action theory in the fields of organization theory and public administration. Although grounded by Weber's claim that the explanation of action must duly account for the subjective viewpoint of social actors, Berger and Luckmann's work owes perhaps a greater debt to the existential phenomenology of Alfred Schutz (1967). Schutz sought to distance the discipline of sociology from the "naturalistic" (or positivistic) assumptions about the social world that had characterized its functionalist mainstream. Using the "face-to-face encounter" as their primary unit of analysis, Berger and Luckmann's own contribution lies chiefly in describing the social world as the ongoing production and reproduction of "objectivations" and "reifications" of subjective—more precisely, inter-subjective—social experience. Through social and institutional relationships, people simultaneously "produce" and are produced by a social world constituted by the artifacts of their experience.

Silverman's *The Theory of Organisations* (1971) builds directly upon the contributions of Schutz and Berger and Luckmann in proposing what he terms the action "frame of reference." Preferring this looser term over "action theory," Silverman's concern is to specify the ground rules for theorizing in the interpretive mode rather than to provide a theory as such, replete with a coherent set of hypotheses susceptible to empirical testing. From Silverman's vantage, in fact, it is doubtful whether the action frame of reference either can or should be expected to produce anything like a general theory of explanation and prediction such as those envisioned by earlier functionalist theorists. He summarizes the principal tenets of his approach as follows:

- The social sciences and the natural sciences deal with entirely different orders of subject matter. While the

canons of rigor and skepticism apply to both, one should not expect their perspective to be the same.
- Sociology is concerned with understanding action rather than with observing behavior. Action arises out of meanings which define social reality.
- Meanings are given to humans by their society. Shared orientations become institutionalized and are experienced by later generations as social facts.
- While society defines humans, humans in turn define society. Particular constellations of meaning are only sustained by continual reaffirmation in everyday actions.
- Through their interaction humans also modify, change, and transform social meanings.
- It follows that explanations of human actions must take account of the meanings which those concerned assign to their acts; the manner in which the everyday world is socially constructed and perceived as real and routine becomes a crucial concern of sociological analysis.
- Positivistic explanations, which assert that action is determined by external and constraining social or nonsocial forces, are inadmissible (pp. 126–127).

In *Action Theory for Public Administration,* Harmon (1981) combines Berger and Luckmann's interpretive perspective with Winter's (1966) "intentionalist" theory of social ethics, the latter mainly influenced by Schutz's interpretive sociology. Building upon Winter's insight that "social ethics translates the discerned regularities with which the social sciences clarify the human project into the practical context of social responsibility," Harmon proposes a normative argument for consensual decision making in public organizations. His argument is essentially a "naturalistic" one, reflecting the belief that the descriptions of social life deriving from interpretivist assumptions about self and society imply the most realistic and defensible bases for moral evaluation. Specifically, the intersubjective nature of the processes by which the social world is produced and reproduced means that consensual decision making, as a formal basis for structuring public organizations, is a natural affirmation of those intersubjective processes. More briefly, the formal requirement of consensus simply institutionalizes intersubjectivity, in contrast with hierarchies, voting, and markets (trading), which institutionalize violations of it.

Action theories located within the interpretive paradigm have been subjected to at least two converging lines of critique—the first, roughly speaking, psychological and the second political—by representatives of what Burrell and Morgan call the radical humanist paradigm. Although the first of these critics are otherwise in agreement with the interpretivists on the centrality of subjectivity in the analysis of social life, Carvath (1977), writing from a

Freudian perspective, and McSwain and White (1987), drawing from the depth psychology of C. G. Jung, have commented on the limitations of interpretivism's almost exclusive emphasis on the sociology of intersubjective experience. Interpretivists, they argue, show insufficient appreciation of the rule of the unconscious, and more generally of theories of the self, that are crucial to explaining the psychological dynamics of subjective experience at the level both of the individual and of social collectivities. Relatedly, the "critical theorists" of the so-called Frankfurt School (Habermas [1971] being the most prominent among them) assert that interpretivist theories conceal a politically conservative bias by offering explanations that tacitly legitimate existing structures of social, political, psychological, and economic domination. In addition to its vital interpretive role, critical theorists argue, social science, including and perhaps especially theories of action, should also perform the emancipatory function of exposing, via continuous critique, the hidden patterns and sources of that domination.

Although much of its literature is highly rarefied and abstract, action theory's ultimate aim is to improve social and organizational practice. To action theorists, however, the meanings of "practice" and "practical" (not to mention "improve") are broader than the instrumental notions of control and efficiency that these words typically connote in the mainstream management and organizational literature. Action theorists regard practical action as also including moral and political considerations, requiring that theorists attend to the interpretive and critical functions that theory may perform as well as its more traditional instrumental one. In addition to its conventional role of enabling systematic explanation and prediction, that is, theory should serve the practical purpose of facilitating, for example in consultant/client relationships, novel redescriptions and understandings of problematic issues confronting organizations, thus revealing heretofore hidden courses of organizational action and approaches to problem solving (Catron and Harmon, 1981). In this regard, it is probably fair to say that action theory, in its more applied incarnation, implicitly underwrites much of contemporary organizational development (OD) practice (White, 1990), as well as what is commonly termed "action research" (Gardner, 1974).

In the years since "action theory" first came into common usage, the range of intellectual thought devoted to explicating the subjectivity of human experience has expanded so greatly that the term has lost much of its ability to demarcate a single coherent theoretical viewpoint. The current ascendance of "postmodernism" in philosophy and social thought, which holds that language is "constitutive" rather than merely descriptive of social life, has further contributed to the mainstream respectability of subjectivity as a, perhaps *the*, core issue in the analysis of social

life. Thus, while action theory's chief assumptions and concerns are more prominent in the discourse of social science than ever before, the term itself appears to be fading from view.

MICHAEL M. HARMON

BIBLIOGRAPHY

Berger, P. L. and T. Luckmann, 1967. *The Social Construction of Reality.* New York: Doubleday.

Burrell, G. and G. Morgan, 1979. *Sociological Paradigms and Organisational Analysis.* London and Portsmouth, NH: Heinemann.

Carvath, D. L., 1977. "The Disembodied Dialectic: A Psychoanalytic Critique of Sociological Relativism." *Theory and Society,* vol. 4, no. 1, 73–102.

Catron, B. L. and M. M. Harmon, 1981. "Action Theory in Practice: Toward Theory Without Conspiracy." *Public Administration Review,* vol. 41, no. 5, 535–541.

Gardner, N., 1974. "Action Training and Research: Something Old and Something New." *Public Administration Review,* vol. 34, no. 2, 106–115.

Giddens, A., 1984. *The Constitution of Society.* Berkeley: University of California Press.

Habermas, J., 1971. *Knowledge and Human Interests,* trans. J. J. Shapiro. Boston: Beacon.

Harmon, M. M., 1981. *Action Theory for Public Administration.* New York: Longman.

McSwain, C. J. and O. F. White, 1987. "The Case for Lying, Cheating, and Stealing–Personal Development as Ethical Guidance for Managers." *Administration & Society,* vol. 18, no. 4, 411–432.

Parsons, T., 1949. *The Structure of Social Action.* Glencoe, IL: Free Press.

Schutz, A., 1967. *The Phenomenology of the Social World.* Evanston, IL: Northwestern.

Searle, J. R., 1983. *Intentionality: An Essay in the Philosophy of Mind.* Cambridge: Cambridge University Press.

Silverman, D., 1971. *The Theory of Organisations.* New York: Basic Books.

Skinner, B. F., 1974. *About Behaviorism.* New York: Knopf.

Weber, M., 1978. *Selections in Translation,* trans. W. C. Runciman. Cambridge: Cambridge University Press.

White, O. F., 1990. "Reframing the Authority-Participation Debate." In G. L. Wamsley *et al.,* eds. *Refounding Public Administration.* Newbury Park, CA: Sage, pp. 182–245.

Winter, G., 1966. *Elements for a Social Ethic: The Role of Social Science in Public Policy.* New York: Macmillan.

ACTIVE LISTENING. A technique for more effective individual or group communication generally associated with five iterated steps: a willingness to listen; concentration on verbal information; attention to nonverbal cues; restatement, or mirroring; and summarization.

Listening does not come naturally to many people. President Lyndon Johnson was aware of this because he had a sign hanging outside his office that declared, "You Ain't Learning Nothin' While You're Talkin'" (Mignon, 1990, p. 308). Many human beings can excel in talking while at the same time remain inept at listening (Stein,

1994, p. ix). Because of this, valuable information, and useful opportunities for individual and organizational enhancement, are often lost. Fortunately, active listening is an easy skill to learn. Impediments to listening are not external disturbances, but poor listening attitudes, and inexperience in reflection and self-awareness. With practice, listening well can become a spontaneous art (Stein, 1994, p. xiv).

An Active Process

As its name implies, active listening involves much more than passive acceptance of sound. First, it is the willingness to listen and be actively engaged in the process. It includes preparation of the internal climate, or a mental willingness to hear, and an external ambiance conducive to the receipt of information—that is, organizational policies and procedures that value and encourage effective communication.

Second, it involves concentrated attention to what is being said. Pitch and cadence are important. Words, phrases, use of metaphor, exclamations, and other patterns must be noted so as to elicit meaning. Strong eye contact becomes essential. Experienced listeners will also concentrate on the speaker's lips. The active listening technique also places emphasis on other nonverbal cues, such as entire body language, pauses and gaps in the conversation, and the gleaning of information from the setting. These nonverbal cues involve "listening with the eyes," not just with the ears. At this stage of the process the listener must be ever vigilant not to overreact to what is being said, and to separate his or her own emotional responses from the words of the speaker. To complete the cycle, the listener must also give nonverbal clues to show that he or she has been listening (Lewis, 1989, pp. 21–22).

Third, it is a restatement. This involves reflecting, understanding, and mirroring back what the speaker has said without interpretive value judgments. Repetition or restatement is also a critical factor in remembering what has been said for later action (Lewis, 1989, p. 21). Since people rarely explain things perfectly the first time, the speaker is afforded a chance to restate his or her earlier position.

Fourth, taking restatement a step further, summarization of what has been said is involved, and comes at the end of the conversation rather than during it. Here the critical details are reviewed and germane ideas are separated from nonessential ones (Lewis, 1989, p. 24).

Active listening begins with the conversation and continues as an ongoing process even when the conversation is concluded. What has been presented in the exchange and summarized needs feedback or action of some sort, because effective listening must transfer what has been heard into action (Mignon, 1990, p. 311).

As a final note on the overall technique, effective listening requires planning, time, and work. It is as much a skill to bring to closure a conversation when the ideas begin to move to redundancy as it is to listen to the ideas being presented.

Applications

The active listening technique has broad application to public administrative situations. It has facilitated union-management relationships. It can be a mediating influence in grievance resolution. It can cement relationships in organizations, restore morale, boost cooperation, and enhance productivity (Mignon, 1990, p. 308).

In the human resources setting, active listening should also be thought of as a skill that can be taught to individuals and groups. It is especially useful to management when new employees enter the workforce, because fresh ideas from heterogeneous networks provide added value to the homogeneity of ideas within the organization.

Effective listening can be used as a methodology as a knowledge-surfacer. It can be useful in qualitative research procedures, in field experiments, on its own or in tandem with other techniques, such as policy analysis or focus group interactions.

All public administrators can benefit by lending their ears to the process of active listening. It is a technique easy to learn, and once learned becomes spontaneous. Remember what Henry David Thoreau once wrote: "The greatest compliment that was ever paid to me was when someone asked me what I thought, and attended to the answer" (Mignon, 1990, p. 310).

BREENA E. COATES

BIBLIOGRAPHY

Bentley, Trevor, 1993. "The Special Skills of Listening." *Management Development Review*, vol. 6, no. 6, 16–18.
Knippen, Jay T. and Thad B. Green, 1994. "How the Manager Can Use Active Listening." *Public Personnel Management*, vol. 23 (Summer), 357–359.
Lewis, David V., 1989. "The Art of Active Listening." *Training and Development Journal*, vol. 43, no. 7, 21–25.
Mignon, Gail, 1990. "Listening Is a Vital Part of the Communication Process." *Journal of Compensation and Benefits*, vol. 5, no. 5, 308–311.
Stein, Howard F., 1994. *Listening Deeply*. Boulder: Westview Press.

ADJUDICATION. A decision, judgment, or procedure leading to a judgment in favor of one side in a dispute. Public administration agencies today, as a result of broad delegation of both rulemaking and order-making powers, have the legal authority to make "laws" or the public policies that govern socioeconomic and political activities in the United States (see **rulemaking**). In fact, scholars estimate that well over 90 percent of the laws that regulate our lives, whether at work or at play, are now made by our public administrators, not by our legislators or our traditional lawmakers. These administrators promulgate public laws or policies through either rulemaking or order-making (adjudication), although frequently a combination of the processes is employed to make and fine-tune agency policies. Agency policies may target the whole society (e.g., general environmental regulations), an entire industry (e.g., passive safety restraints for all automobiles), particular companies or a single company (e.g., safety regulations directed at a specific nuclear power plant), or even an individual (e.g., a termination hearing decision involving a public employee).

Agency policy decisions may grant or deny benefits, for example, permit an industry to operate or not operate under certain conditions; grant or deny a license to a business or an individual; grant or deny a welfare recipient, farmer, or veteran a benefit. Whether benefits are given or taken away, agency actions are ideally supposed to be guided by due process considerations. In agency rulemaking, due process may mean allowing all interested parties ample opportunity to respond to a proposed rule, while in an agency adjudication it may mean allowing a person in a termination hearing sufficient time to examine and respond to allegations of misconduct.

Public administrators make public policies through agency rulemaking and agency adjudications (order-making). Formally, or according to the language of the Administrative Procedure Act (APA), P.L. 404, 60 Stat. 237, Sec. 551(5)(7) (1946), as amended, "'rulemaking' means agency process for formulating, amending, or appealing a rule," while "'adjudication' means agency process for the formulation of an order." While rulemaking is a quasi-legislative process, adjudication is a quasi-judicial process. In technical terms, when a public agency engages in rulemaking the result is a rule. When the agency employs adjudication (order-making), the product is an order. According to the specific language of the APA,

> a rule means the whole or part of an agency statement of general or particular applicability and future effect designed to implement, interpret, or prescribe law or policy or describing the organization, procedure, or practice requirements of an agency and includes the approval or prescription for the future of rates, wages, corporate or financial structures or reorganizations thereof, prices, facilities, appliances, services or allowances therefor or valuations, costs, or accounting, or practices bearing on any of the foregoing.

In contrast, the APA states that an "order means the whole or a part of a final disposition, whether affirmative, negative, injunctive, or declaratory in form, of an agency in a matter other than rule making but including licensing."

When a public agency adjudicates (judges), the agency issues an order that represents a judgment in favor of one party or the other in a dispute. Just as Supreme Court decisions establish policies to be followed (e.g., court-ordered school desegregation), agency orders also set policies and establish precedents that commonly have the impact of laws. The need for agency adjudication arises normally when a dispute touches on a policy area within the regulatory jurisdiction of a particular public agency. The dispute may be between the agency and a private party (e.g., the Federal Communications Commission and a television station), between private outside parties (e.g., two television networks) seeking new policies or policy clarifications affecting operations in their industry, or between an intervenor or "party of interest" in a hearing involving an agency and a regulated company (e.g., an environmental group such as the Union of Concerned Scientists intervening in a licensing hearing involving the Nuclear Regulatory Commission and a utility company).

Adjudications are mostly retrospective in focus. That is, agency adjudicative actions are aimed at trying to settle unresolved past conflicts between specific parties. Because participation is limited only to those parties involved in the agency's adjudicative proceedings, order-making is not supposed to lead to the development of broad public policies for the future. However, despite widespread criticism, some regulatory agencies have preferred to employ order-making to make prospective agency orders of general applicability. When orders play this role, they are made to function more like rules than orders. Critics claim that orders should be restricted in their application so that they are not used simultaneously as retrospective orders and broad prospective rules. That is, critics feel that administrators should not try to use the order-making process to kill two birds with one stone. Order-making is designed to deliberate adjudicative facts, not legislative facts. When an agency is considering adjudicative facts during adjudicative proceedings, either informal or formal, it is concerned with determining who did what to whom and for what reasons in order to settle a dispute between specific parties. Under normal conditions it would be inappropriate during adjudication to entertain legislative facts, which relate only to general public policy considerations but are irrelevant to the specific dispute. (An example of legislative facts is public attitudes toward subsidized housing. An example of a specific dispute about legislative facts is a determination as to whether or not a housing agency illegally denied subsidy payments to a claimant.) The extent of the inappropriateness was made vivid by an insightful Federal Trade Commission comment published many years ago in the *Federal Register:*

> If the tribunal in an adjudicative proceeding is too intent upon fashioning rules for future guidance, the task of rendering a fair result on the record before it may be slighted. Since the task of assessing individual liability on the basis of past practices and the task of fashioning rules of general application for future guidance are different, it

has been argued that a tribunal which seeks to lay down broad rules in deciding individual cases may frequently fail to do complete justice to the parties before it (29 Fed. Reg. 8324, 8367, 1964).

In sum, since administrative orders are supposed to be directed toward parties involved in a controversy, participation excludes the general public, and only adjudicative facts should be seriously entertained. The vast majority of administrative law experts believe that it is foolish under most circumstances to promulgate general public policies through the order-making process.

Differentiating Order-Making from Rulemaking

Definitive guidelines to determine when issues appear appropriate for the adjudicative process simply do not exist. However, a few very rough guidelines that administrative agencies and courts have, generally, endorsed may be helpful. In general, the order-making process (frequently referred to as the case-by-case approach to formulating regulatory policies) is used in lieu of the rulemaking process when (1) the issue in question involves specific parties in a dispute; (2) the matter concerns past behavior and is not future-oriented (although orders set precedents); (3) the issues or problems could not have been reasonably anticipated by the agency; (4) the agency wants to reach only a tentative decision because its administrators lack sufficient knowledge, experience, and confidence at the time in the specific area; and (5) the matter is simply too esoteric, complex, and varied to be resolved by the formulation of a general rule.

It is not always easy to differentiate between order-making and rulemaking, nor is it easy to judge when order-making or rulemaking should be employed to promulgate regulatory policies. The truth is that the legislative rulemaking and judicial order-making functions in administrative agencies are frequently juxtaposed in practice. Adding to the confusion, asserts Edwin J. Madaj, ". . . is the anomaly that formal rulemaking is in many ways more procedurally like an adjudication than an informal adjudication" (1990, p. 445). Trying to differentiate between the two processes often turns out to be a futile academic exercise. For example, when the Federal Trade Commission (FTC) reviews the advertising practices of a certain company, concludes that the practices are deceptive, and orders the company to retract its earlier contentions publicly, is the agency functioning in a purely judicial capacity? The fact is that FTC decisions or orders (such as forcing a company to carry out corrective advertising) almost always shape FTC policy toward certain business practices. In many instances FTC hearing decisions establish rules that businesses dare not overlook. For example, Ford Motor Company would

be foolish to ignore an FTC ruling against Chrysler, an industry competitor. To avoid future and costly complications, the normal procedure is to bring company policies in line with current FTC thinking regarding questionable business practices.

In 1908, in *Parentis v. Atlantic Coast Line Company* (211 U.S. 210), the Supreme Court tried to make a practical distinction between rulemaking activities and order-making activities. The Court said that "the establishment of a rate is the making of a rule for the future, and therefore is an act legislative, not judicial in kind" (at 226). But only a year later the New York Court of Appeals in *People ex rel. Central Park, N. and E. R. R. Company v. Willcox* (194 N.Y. 383) complicated the definitional problem by contradicting the Supreme Court's interpretation of rulemaking. The appeals court contended respectfully that the Supreme Court's definition ran contrary to established judicial authority in New York and added that it was not "convinced that the function of prescribing a rate is necessarily nonjudicial solely because it enforces a rule of conduct for the future" (at 386). Thus, because of the definitional problems, the courts have made a common practice of deciding administrative law cases, especially if the functions are hazy, without ever attempting to differentiate between judicial and legislative activities.

The failure to draw a distinction presents legal problems and causes some confusion because the APA specifies the procedural obligations of administrative agencies under sections of the act labeled "Rulemaking" and "Adjudications." It may be difficult to establish an authoritative position and reach a respected decision based on certain procedural requirements or points of law in the APA if the courts cannot decide which sections of the act to apply, because they are uncertain as to which agency processes are in question.

Two simple tests have been used to try to determine whether agency decisions should have followed rulemaking or order-making processes. Both tests fail as reliable measures, although they should not be discarded as useless since most agencies probably try to comply with the test requirements in general when promulgating policies. The first is the past-future test, which poses the question: Is the agency policy concerned with regulating past or future practices? If the regulatory policy is aimed at controlling future conduct, the policy should have been promulgated through rulemaking procedures. However, if the policy is directed primarily at resolving a dispute involving past behavior, the policy position should have been the consequence of adjudication. The second test, called the specific-general test, seeks essentially to discover whether the promulgated agency policy is directed toward a specific or a general audience. If agency policy is aimed at regulating the activities of no specific parties, but parties in general, the policy should have been generated through rulemaking. If the policy decision is directed toward specific parties (frequently even named parties in a controversy) the policy should have been developed through adjudication.

Unfortunately, however, agency policies almost never tend to be wholly past-specific or future-general in content or application. What compounds this problem further is that agencies have the legal, discretionary authority to decide whether they should employ the rulemaking or order-making approach when making agency policies. Agency discretion is especially well respected by reviewing courts if agency officials take care to rationalize their approach selection as necessary to achieve a particular agency goal. About the only time courts would find an abuse of agency discretion in this matter would be in a situation in which an agency promulgated through adjudication and then applied the new policy in such a way that serious adverse consequences resulted or the retroactive application obviously caused more harm than good (*SEC v. Chenery Corp.*, 332 U. S. 194 [1947]; *NLRB v. Bell Aerospace Co.*, 416 U.S. 267 [1947]; *First Bancorporation v. Board of Governors*, 728 F2d 434 [10th Cir. 1984]; *District Lodge 64 v. NLRB*, 949 F2d 441 [D.C. Cir. 1991]).

For all practical purposes, such agency discretionary power has allowed agencies to ignore the specific-general and past-future tests when making policies, although most agencies do take these tests into account because of external pressures to conform to what is expected. Nevertheless, agency leaders frequently decide to choose either rulemaking or order-making procedures to promulgate agency policies, not because one procedure may be more appropriate, but because one process may be perceived as more convenient by the agency officials. For instance, some agency administrators believe they can control the development of their regulatory policies better if they use the more flexible case-by-case approach, since the courts have generally allowed agencies to change policy directions with each case. On the other hand, the courts have been much more insistent that policies resulting from rulemaking be honored by agencies for the purpose of keeping these policies consistent over time (*Vitarelli v. Seaton*, 359 U.S. 535 [1959]; *Motor Vehicle Mfrs. Assn v. State Farm Mutual*, 463 U.S. 29 [1983]; *South Cent. Terminal Co. v. U.S. Dept. of Energy*, 728 F. Supp. 1083, 1096 [D. Del. 1990]).

KENNETH F. WARREN

BIBLIOGRAPHY

Davis, Kenneth C. and Richard J. Pierce, Jr., 1994. *Administrative Law Treatise.* 3rd ed., vol. I. Boston: Little, Brown and Company.
Kerwin, Cornelius M., 1994. *Rulemaking: How Government Agencies Write Law and Make Policy.* New York: Congressional Quarterly Press.
Madaj, Edwin J., 1990. "Agency Investigations: Adjudications or Rulemaking?" *North Carolina Journal of International Law and Commercial Regulation,* vol. 15.
Warren, Kenneth F., 1996. *Administrative Law in the American System.* 3rd ed. Upper Saddle River, NJ: Prentice Hall.

ADMINISTOCRACY. A term coined by Guy S. Claire (1934) by which he meant a type of government that is created when bureaucrats exercise more governing and decisionmaking powers than do elected officials. In an administocracy bureaucrats make decisions that permit them to simultaneously formulate and implement public policy without having to account to those who are governed in elections. An administocracy results when the powers and responsibilities of governance are primarily in the hands of people who are hired or appointed to government positions.

The early theorists of bureaucracy (Weber, 1947, Goodnow, 1900, Wilson, 1887) assumed that professional bureaucrats would never make public policy, but that they would merely execute the will of elected officials by implementing their policies in an impartial and efficient way. The idea of a nonpartisan, neutral, and compliant administration was the original motivation behind the development of a merit-oriented public service.

Guy S. Claire warned that many democratic government systems have developed–however unwittingly–the characteristics of administocracy. He defined administocracy as an aristocracy of administrators whose personnel are not publicly accountable, but who nevertheless make public policy and exercise the most powerful discretions of government in the implementation of policy. The question of whether a democracy can survive by permitting nonelected and nonresponsible administrators to make decisions affecting the lives of people must be considered by electorates that demand accountability. The question is also posed by public policy analysts who want a comprehensive understanding of the operation of government.

In some states the vast house of bureaucracy has come to have an immense impact on the democratic processes through which public policy is created and implemented. In many states such as Canada and the United States, public administrators often assume the task of initiating public proposals based on the changing needs of their departments and the people they serve. The fact that civil servants may formulate policies that are then passed by a congress or parliament can be a source of concern to any informed public and their elected officials, who grow alarmed when politicians become colonized by administrators. In a democracy it is one thing for administrators to exert influence on the lawmaking process, but quite another for them to formulate the laws that democratically elected officials are mandated to enact.

Public policy that is inspired by the same bureaucrats who implement it is often depicted by political scientists as symptomatic of administocracy. Administration-made policy is as binding as legislated policy but, with the latter, the electorate has some control over policy inputs and outcomes. Legislators are not as permanent a constituency of power in the national and subnational capitals as administrators tend to be. In this regard, members of a congress or parliament come and go but administrators hold their careers as appointed officials over significant periods of time and do not need regular public consent to do their jobs.

For a variety of reasons bureaucrats have a much better chance than elected representatives have of becoming persuasive experts on government matters. On the one hand, public servants with time, experience, and education tend to specialize in their knowledge, whether it be of the environment, issuing passports, transportation policy or whatever. But on the other hand, legislators are expected to expertly deal with all matters in a time frame determined by electoral laws and thus with no guarantees of job security over the long term.

This gives an enormous advantage to public servants over politicians who at best have only a general, partial, and probably shaky knowledge of matters over which they are responsible. Accordingly, the transient, nonpermenant, and most often unspecialized elected representative is in the position of asking the advice of the permanent, full-time, and specialized administrative experts on the relative merits of policies. More often than not, politicians seek and take the advice.

The policy preferences of public servants almost inevitably enter into and affect their advice to their political bosses. When administrators are asked their advice they can hardly avoid making their views known, and when, as often happens, the political representatives and their constituents hold no intense views of their own, the preferences of the public service are likely to become public policy.

Administocracy in the Courts

The characteristics of administocracy may be detected in the ways in which bureaucracies affect policy making. One is adjudication. Many regulatory agencies maintain administrative courts that operate much like regular courts, and whose decisions and awards are enforceable in the regular courts.

Most states have administrative tribunals that grant employees compensation awards. Proponents of administrative courts argue that they possess more specialized knowledge than regular courts and possess the expertise to judge on highly technical questions. But critics of administrative courts doubt the wisdom of giving so much power to administrators. These critics feel that even though the law has empowered an agency or department to regulate in the public interest, the creation of administrative courts means that the legislative branch of government has given administrators a blank check to exercise power.

Administocracy and Policy Implementation

Another characteristic of administocracy is seen as discretionary policy implementation. When a legislature enacts a law the bureaucracy must enforce it, and when the statute is specific, this is a relatively simple procedure. For example, the United States Congress may pass a law requiring that waterways be cleaned of pollution. This law would permit the Environmental Protection Agency (EPA) to do whatever is necessary to achieve this goal. The EPA must then make certain decisions because every waterway cannot be cleaned up at once, and each one entails different ecological as well as political problems.

Deciding how to go about achieving the final goal then becomes the responsibility of public administrators in the bureaucracy. The EPA may decide to hold off for a while on one company while the company installs a water treatment system for waste, but the agency may be more insistent with a second company that is making no attempt at all to deal with waste. These discretionary powers are often unaccountable and beyond the control of politicians and electorates.

Administocracy and Rulemaking

A third potential for extreme administrative power might especially appear in the function of rulemaking. Regulatory agencies and other bureaucratic bodies exercise certain powers of establishing rules and regulations for groups, individuals, organizations and corporations. The rulemaking authority of a bureaucracy can be seen in giving permission to airlines to raise their fares, or to telephone companies to raise their rates, or in requiring cigarette manufacturers to change their advertising strategies so as to inform smokers of the hazards cigarettes pose to their general health.

While most people agree that the public interest is served by such powers, there is the broader question of bureaucratic authority. What happens when an overbearing bureaucracy tries to promote a program that many consider harmful? There is no simple answer, but it is one that societies have to grapple with on a regular basis.

Administocracy and Bureaucratic Advice

Fourth, administocracy can result in the advisory roles of bureaucracies. The growing complexities of modern life have caused legislatures and political executives to rely more and more heavily on the technical expertise of public servants.

A legislature may decide to keep old mines open to maintain the economic viability of a community, but mining experts in a bureaucracy might determine that such mines are unsafe and that they should be closed. Many laws require administrative interpretation, some requiring special expertise. Bureaucrats usually do not have to convince legislators to take their advice; the lawmakers are often only too happy to have the technical assistance of experts. This is yet another way in which bureaucrats influence the formulation of public policy.

The Obscure Lines of Governing

Although democratic constitutions focus on the accountability and regular election of governments, many students of public administration and public policy are aware that the lines between the branches of government have become blurred. The fact that the functions of an administrative agency can overlap the responsibilities of the legislative and judicial branches of government is a significant element to enhancing the powers and authority of the bureaucracy.

In this regard those who study the operations of democracies are apprehensive about the development of a power elite of bureaucrats. The fear is that they will play too dominant a role in the decisions about which they are concerned and over which the public has little or no control. In most parliamentary and congressional systems the decisive power of policy initiative is supposed to be in the hands of executives.

John Kenneth Galbraith (1967) has observed that bureaucracies tend to take on lives on their own—that they can become totally divorced from the world around them. The fear is that bureaucracy will become concerned merely with self-preservation and that it will only attempt to enhance its own position. When this happens a government bureaucracy will become isolated and insulated from the needs of society. In democracies is bureaucracy a master of society or its servant?

Others fear bureaucracy on the grounds that its members are not very representative of the people. Some point to European bureaucracies, which may not reflect the populations they serve in terms of education, race and ethnic composition, wealth, and gender. Both the American and Canadian bureaucracies are largely middle-class but then most North Americans are too, so in these states the public service is somewhat more representative of societies than in some European, Latin American, and African societies. In Canada and the United States governments implement minority hiring practices that are often better than those of private industry. Under pressure from feminists and human rights groups these governments attempt to bring still greater numbers of women and minority group members into their bureaucracies. But in both countries, government bureaucracies are still predominantly white middle-class male preserves that do not accurately represent the social and economic characteristics of the populations they govern.

The term administocracy can be understood as bureaucracy in its uppermost expression and supremacy of power. In the framework of contemporary governments, bureaucracies are gaining greater control of all areas of the governing process: administrative, legislative, and judicial. Bureaucratic control is based on knowledge and technical expertise. Increasingly, legislators rely on bureaucratic minds for advice. Governments are creating more administrative agencies, boards, and tribunals to make and implement their decisions. At almost every level of government an aristocracy of administrators is identifiable.

JAMES J. GUY

BIBLIOGRAPHY

Claire, Guy S., 1934. *Administocracy.* New York: Crowell-Collier.
Galbraith, John Kenneth, 1967. *The New Industrial State.* Boston: Houghton Mifflin.
Goodnow, Frank J., 1900. *Politics and Administration.* New York: Macmillan.
Weber, Max, 1947. *The Theory of Social and Economic Organization.* Glencoe, IL: Free Press.
Wilson, Woodrow, 1887. "The Study of Administration." *Political Science Quarterly,* vol. 2 (June), 197–222.

ADMINISTRATION. The institutions and process by which legislative intentions are realized and subsequent actions recorded for control purposes. In familiar, everyday terms, administration is the "paperwork" side of life. In an army camp or a hospital or a power station, the Administration Block is where they push paper around, as distinct from the real work of the place: soldiering, nursing patients, or generating electricity. Professionals such as doctors, lawyers, and academics similarly tend to distinguish some of what they do—diagnosis and prescription, legal advice and advocacy, or teaching and research—from other things they have to do: writing up reports, filling out forms, making returns, paying bills, keeping accounts, arranging travel, sitting on committees, and so on; they often call the latter "administration."

The Meaning of Administration

Administration as office work, comprising the activities implied in administrative overhead as distinct from the costs of raw materials and shop floor production and so on, is a widespread experience, even within the family, and whether or not it actually involves paper as such. In the context of government or the activities of the state, however, the word has come to have wider connotations: used absolutely, as "the administration" (with or without the capital A), it may be the collective noun for all those holding high executive office, as in "the Clinton Administration"; or it may be the title of a state agency, as in the Food and Drug Administration; or, much more narrowly, it may imply a distinction not between production and overhead, but between the machinery for the authorization of government programs and the machinery for putting them into effect.

The task of writing a generic account of administration is a difficult one precisely because the word has so many legitimate senses. How does administration, whether understood as paperwork or as program implementation, relate to such usages as the nineteenth-century Marxist Friedrich Engels's distinction between "the government of persons and the administration of things"; or as in Letters of Administration in the estate of a deceased person; or as in the old joke which ran: "Method of Administration: place pill in large end of tube provided, insert in horse's mouth, and blow sharply through small end" (the joke is when the horse blows first)? In German and non-Latin languages, the difficulty does not seem to arise. German uses different words for each of the main English senses of "administer." (On the other hand, German cannot distinguish between "policy" and "politics.")

If it were merely that the word has many distinct meanings in English, we might just take note, and have a dictionary handy. But with this word, battle lines are sometimes drawn over its content; work territory is defined, maybe even salary affected, by a verbal usage. A Princeton University professor writing a famous essay about the difference between politics and administration, to combat the "spoils system" in American federal government in the late nineteenth century; a Select Committee of the British parliament arriving at the limits of the competence of the Parliamentary Commissioner for Administration; or a People's Court in Soviet Russia determining whether a misdemeanor before them was an administrative or a criminal offense—these are all examples of live debates where the arguments, to carry the weight they hoped to carry, needed a consensus on the meaning of the key word "administration." At the end of the Vietnam War, peace talks were endangered by the translation of *chanh-quyen* as "administrative" rather than "governmental," giving the American side a false impression of a major concession.

Etymology and Origins

We might seek enlightenment in the etymology of the word. The *Oxford English Dictionary* says the root "minister" is connected to the Latin *minus*, less, in the same way as is *magister* (master) to *magis*, more. A minister is a servant of a master, or the subordinate of a superior, one who helps, assists, or serves, as in the archaic "ministering angel." And of course, one who serves a ruler, and is authorized to act on the ruler's behalf, can be a very powerful person; minister is seen as master.

But even by classical Roman times the word *administrare*, to administer, had acquired most of its various modern senses. In Cicero, used with the dative case, it clearly

meant "to render assistance to." But used with the accusative case, it often meant something like the colloquial English "to run": to run the republic, to run the army, to run the war with the Cimbrians; to carry on, conduct, deal with, take care of; more general than to direct, manage, rule, regulate, or control, but with one or another of those implications. This is a little difficult to reconcile with the root *minus*, unless there is always an implied connotation of running these things for someone, or possibly an implicit contrast, between running the republic and ruling it, between running the army and commanding it, between running the war and initiating it, and the like.

Cicero elsewhere seems to include in the meaning of *administrare* the notion of stewardship. He says the administration of the government, like the office of a trustee, must be conducted for the benefit of those entrusted to one's care, not of those to whom it is entrusted (*De Officis*, in Lepawsky, 1949, p. 89). Note, though, that the one providing care owes the duty of stewardship to whoever entrusted the administration to him or her, not to those cared for.

Cicero also has *administrare leges et judicia*, where "to run" is too weak. It might here mean "serving" the laws and judgments (to the people), though perhaps not quite in the simple sense of "meting out," in which we talk of "administering the chalice" or a pill or the lash (by displacement from administering the sacraments, health care, justice). Better would be "delivering" the laws and judgments, serving their purposes by translating their words into appropriate action; as we would say, carrying them out, implementing or executing them. This is an important understanding for our current concerns.

Even in Latin, therefore, the one word "administer" can mean to serve or dispense, to dispose of authoritatively, to control, to implement, and other senses according to context. The search into etymology and origins may have supplied enlightenment, but not much clarification. Logically, there may always be an implication of subordinate status; but practically, this is often lost (both to client and to administrator) in the power that goes with authorization.

Negations

A second way of arriving at the meaning of a term is to survey what people say it is not. Administration is richly endowed in this respect; the literature of public administration is full of distinctions between administration and something else, as already seen. It is not policymaking; it is not politics; it is not management; nor yet is it executive work, operations, specialist or professional work, and so on.

Not Policymaking. This, as already noted, is the most frequently invoked distinction, given some changes in the terms used. Alexander Hamilton in 1788 noted that although "the administration of government" could comprehend any governmental operation whatever, in its usual sense it was limited to executive details (*The Federalist* No. 72, March 21, 1788). The Princeton professor of political science, Woodrow Wilson, concluded, "The broad plans of governmental action are not administrative; the detailed execution of such plans is administrative" (Wilson, 1887, p. 209).

This distinction, soon to be expressed as that between policies or programs and their administration or execution, became American orthodoxy (see, for example, Goodnow, 1900, p. 11), though the critique was not long in coming (see the survey in Lepawsky, 1949; and Dwight Waldo's authoritative history in *The Administrative State*, 1948). These later analyses showed that the "policy/administration dichotomy," as it came to be called, failed to describe practice—partly because of the necessity of mutual feedback, partly because all decision-making involves discretion, partly because the same people are inevitably concerned in both kinds of action. The *coup de grace* to any analytical distinction between policy-making and administration was given by Paul Appleby's *Policy and Administration* in 1949.

There had been less debate in Britain at this time over this distinction. In the British civil service, the top ranks had come to be known as the "Administrative Class," and their duties were officially defined in 1920 as including those concerned with the formation of policy. Battle lines were drawn rather between what was "administration" and what was "executive" work (given to lower ranks). Yet in the form of a policy/execution dichotomy the idea is the rationale for the recent creation out of central ministries in Britain of a hundred or so Executive Agencies, in the attempt (just as if the American debate had never taken place) to relieve Ministers of accountability for the "executive detail" of services like prisons, national health provision, social security payments, driver licensing and so on, while remaining responsible for "policy." A version of the policy/administration dichotomy is also how the man or woman in any street the world over will explain the difference between the roles of elected representatives and of public officials. It is a wholly necessary myth.

Not Politics. The parallel and sometimes overlapping distinction between politics and administration, succinctly expressed in John Pfiffner's charge that "politics should stick to its policy-determining sphere and leave administration to apply its own technical processes free from the blight of political meddling" (1935, p. 9), is a rather more robust one, since it can more reasonably be equated with the institutional distinction between elected politicians and appointed career public servants or administrators.

There have been many accounts of this distinction. A recent one by Spencer Zifcak (1994, p. 147) suggests that it has three typical faces. First, the *modus operandi* of politi-

cians is to strike bargains and negotiate compromises among various pressure groups: policies are the outcome of the brokering of competing interests. Administrators, on the other hand, are more likely to try to rank preferences, uncover options, anticipate logical consequences, and consider precedents—their stock-in-trade. Second, politicians tend to want to reward friends and punish opponents, and to evaluate changes in terms of votes gained or lost. Administrators, however, learn to adjudicate rival claims by objective and universal criteria as far as feasible, to protect themselves from criticism. Third, politicians are inclined to insist on keeping control even over individual cases, while the administrator's penchant is to delegate and routinize casework to lesser officials, keeping only strategic control.

The specific institutional accommodation (or fudging) of this interface between politicians and officials varies from one country to another. As we have already discovered, it is a mistake to express the difference or role by appealing to the content of terms like administration and politics (even party politics); but in this case (perhaps unlike the previous one), there is a real operational problem to be tackled by constitutional machinery, whatever labels one ties to the phenomenon.

Not Management. As a rule of thumb, it used to be enough to say that government used "administration" where business and industry spoke of "management." Until recent years, the British civil service used "management" to signify responsibilities for control of staff and operations not involving policy work; such jobs went to members of the Executive Class. Some writers, notably Lyndall Urwick (1943), tried to persuade business to adopt this terminology—"administration" for corporate policy and overall coordination, "management" for operational control—but with little success. Instead, the reverse began to happen. In 1969, the term "Administrative Class" was abolished, and nowadays the designation "administrative officer" applies to people at the relatively lowly clerical level. With the reception of "managerialism" under Margaret Thatcher, the top people are now called managers. There has thus been much convergence, both between governmental and business usages, and between American and British usages.

Something of the same sort happened in another respect. There is an explicit confidence in Woodrow Wilson's essay of 1887, as in the later industrial "scientific management" writers (Taylor, 1911; Fayol, 1916), in the existence of universal principles transcending frontiers of time and space, product, and (with care) culture. The British civil service of the turn of the century was highly dubious about such talk of transferability of administrative skills, even from one department to another, though they thought it might be feasible for lower grade clerks. But after the enormous expansions of the early welfare state and of World War I, they turned completely around: a head of the Home Civil Service told a commission of inquiry in 1929 that a member of the Administrative Class who had been running one of these "huge businesses" could run any of them (Sir Warren Fisher, quoted in Dunsire, 1973, p. 33). This theory of "generic administration" has also been regularly under attack, yet survives: it was trenchantly put as late as the first issue of the *Administrative Science Quarterly* (Litchfield, 1956); and, to a degree, it inspires this encyclopedia.

Another conflict that has largely lost its point is the question of whether a good administrator is one who has mastered technical processes, as Pfiffner suggested (and as powerfully exemplified in Luther Gulick's and Lyndall Urwick's *Papers on the Science of Administration* (1937), containing the famous mnemonic POSDCORB for the work of the chief executive; or whether they rather display humane skills for which the preparation is a liberal education and a long apprenticeship on the job, as often suggested in the British literature celebrating the qualities of the elite administrator (e.g., Bridges, 1950). A parallel distinction is between the "generalist" administrator and the "specialist" professional. The administrator, it is said, needs to know how to use specialist advice, but must avoid the blinkered vision and singlemindedness of the "expert"–the good administrator is an expert person, whose prime task is overall vision and coordination. This, however, could be said of any department or organization head, however named, and however trained.

Many of these battles about the proper meanings of terms now have a very dated air, indicating the youth of the discipline. Since about World War II, academic attention has rather been devoted to more positive explorations of administrative processes, in the attempt to improve conventional theories and propound new ones. This new focus began with Herbert Simon's pioneering investigation of administrative decisionmaking (1947), and continued with the development of organization theory in the 1950s and 1960s, implementation theory in the 1970s, rational choice theory in the 1980s, information theory in the 1990s, and all the other branches of inquiry with which a modern administrative scientist must keep up.

Values

Let us then take for granted now, as this proliferation of administrative studies does, a root modern meaning for the term "administration" in the governmental context: the operation of institutions, mechanisms, and procedures for the carrying out, or realization, or implementation, or execution, of government programs and policies. If challenged, we could happily include as well the keeping of records for the evaluation of, and the preparation and formulation of alternatives for, such programs and policies, excluding only their polemic or partisan contention and

authoritative selection, which is by other mechanisms. What are the objectives, the criteria of judgment, the discriminating values of the activity of administration so understood?

Desmond Keeling, himself a very experienced top civil servant, suggested (1972) three outlooks among senior public servants. Some, from the nature of their posits, their training, and their temperments are particularly concerned with legality, conformity to rules and precedents, and mistake avoidance, in the decisions that pass across their desks. These are the "archetypal administrators." Other officials are much more concerned with effectiveness and getting results, albeit with efficient use of resources: these are the "managers." Some finally, think on a broader front, of change in aims and objectives, and the best tactics for negotiating a path towards them with the minimum of disruption and contention in a changing, even hostile, environment. This Keeling calls "diplomacy"; "diplomats" are concerned with the evaluation and development of policy, from the departmental point of view–but also, controversially, where they see themselves obliged by a long tradition to espouse "the public interest," as against the perceived narrower or ephemeral focus of the ruling politicians.

In certain conditions, a single public servant may be obliged to face all these ways in turn, and will often find that a solution that maximizes one of these values is incompatible with maximizing another.

Christopher Hood has given us a slightly different set of "core administrative values" (1991, pp. 10–15). He suggests three stereotyped injunctions for public administrators, which together encompass a large number of administrative doctrines (Hood and Jackson, 1991): "run it like a business" (sigma precepts); "run it like a monastic order" (theta precepts); "run it like the army" (lambda precepts). Sigma precepts relate to economy and parsimony, and enjoin frugality, avoidance of waste, sharp definitions of responsibilities, and tight coupling of aims and evaluations. Theta values relate to rectitude, uprightness, and honesty, and enjoin fairness, equity, and transparency of procedure. Lambda values relate to security and fail-safe assurance, and enjoin resilience, reliability, and robustness, avoiding risk and breakdown, and thus tolerating a measure of overkill and redundancy, overlap of responsibilities, and organizational slack. Again, any particular administrative solution may satisfy two of these sets of values, but is most unlikely to satisfy all three. On these accounts, the ideal values of public service administration in this now usual sense (when contrasted with political partisanship) are "rational" decision making (as it is commonly called), objective, long-term, and universal decision criteria, legality and fairness, routinization wherever feasible, effective and efficient operations, honest and incorrupt dealing, and reliability–but not necessarily all at once. Administration always involves dilemmas of choice, and thus discretion.

You will still find "administration" and its cognates used in its more archaic senses, such as in administering an oath or a small business, or to name the regime of a particular president. It is usually easy to intuit the intended meaning from the context. You will not, nowadays, find many arguments about what administration "really" means, or should mean. We have grown more sophisticated. If in doubt, consider it to have the governmental meaning as suggested at the head of this entry: the institutions, processes, and actions by which legislative intentions are realized; or, more occasionally, by which operations are recorded for control purposes.

ANDREW DUNSIRE

BIBLIOGRAPHY

Appleby, Paul H., 1949. *Policy and Administration*. University, Alabama: University of Alabama Press.

Bridges, Sir Edward, 1950. *Portrait of a Profession: The Rede Lecture*. London: Cambridge University Press.

Dunsire, Andrew, 1973. *Administration: The Word and the Science*. London: Martin Robertson. New York: Halsted Press.

Fayol, Henri, 1916. "Administration Industrielle et Generale." *Bulletin de la Societe de l'Industrie Minerale*, No 3. Translated by Coubrough as *Industrial and General Administration* (Geneva: International Management Institute, 1929); translated by Storrs as *General and Industrial Management* (London: Pitman, 1949).

Goodnow, Frank J., 1900. *Politics and Administration*. New York: The Macmillan Company.

Gulick, Luther and Lyndall F. Urwick, eds., 1937. *Papers on the Science of Administration*. New York: Institute of Public Administration.

Hood, Christopher, 1991. "A Public Management for All Seasons?" *Public Administration*, vol. 69, no. 1, 3–19.

Hood, Christopher and Michael W. Jackson, 1991. *Administrative Argument*. Aldershot, Eng.: Dartmouth.

Keeling, Desmond, 1972. *Management in Government*. London: Allen and Unwin.

Lepawsky, Albert, ed., 1949. *Administration: The Art and Science of Organization and Management*. New York: Alfred A. Knopf.

Litchfield, Edward H., 1956. "Notes on a General Theory of Administration." *Administrative Science Quarterly*, vol. 1, no. 1, 3–29.

Pfiffner, John M., 1935. *Public Administration*. New York: The Ronald Press.

Simon, Herbert A., 1947. *Administrative Behavior: A Study of Decision-Making Processes in Administrative Organization*. New York: The Macmillan Company.

Taylor, Frederick W., 1911. *Principles and Methods of Scientific Management*. New York: Harper Bros.

Urwick, Lyndall F., 1943. *The Elements of Administration*. London: Pitman.

Waldo, Dwight, 1948. *The Administrative State: A Study of the Political Theory of American Public Administration*. New York: The Ronald Press.

Wilson, Woodrow, 1887. "The Study of Administration." *Political Science Quarterly*, vol. 2, 197–222; reprinted 1941, *American Political Science Quarterly*, vol. 56, 481–506.

Zifcak, Spencer, 1994. *New Managerialism: Administrative Reform in Whitehall and Canberra*. Buckingham, Eng., and Bristol, PA: Open University Press.

ADMINISTRATIVE CONSERVATORSHIP.

A normative theory of bureaucratic leadership that gives career civil servants an active and legitimate role in governance. Career administrators are characterized as conservators because of their leadership role in preserving the integrity of public bureaucracies and, in turn, the values of the American constitutional regime.

In the United States, the concept of bureaucratic leadership has been viewed with a degree of skepticism. Such skepticism is due, in part, to Americans' deeply rooted fear of governmental power.

The fear of governmental power can be traced back to the American founders' concern about the arbitrary use of political power. The founders worried that the exercise of substantial discretion by government officials would lead to arbitrariness and, in turn, the inevitable decline of individual freedom. The expansion of the administrative state prompted many scholars of public administration and political science to renew the founders' concern. The growth and expansion of public bureaucracies at the national level in particular, was accompanied by an increase in the delegation of broad discretionary authority and power from the legislature to career civil servants. This increase in authority and power heightened the concerns of many government observers because it was seen as antithetical to democracy (see Lowi, 1979; Schoenbrod, 1993). The enormous power exercised by career civil servants in the so-called fourth branch of government is viewed as incompatible with the constitutional design envisioned by the founders. The founders did not anticipate nor would they approve of a powerful, largely autonomous political institution controlled by nonelected and nonpolitically appointed public officials. Critics argue that the founders were deeply concerned about the possibility of substantial power presiding in one person or institution. This partially explains their preoccupation with need to check the exercise of political power.

The fear of governmental power had an adverse affect on the development of bureaucratic leadership theory. In an attempt to define a legitimate role for public bureaucracies in the American political system and thereby address the so-called bureaucracy/democracy problem, scholars offered prescriptions that rendered bureaucratic leadership a meaningless concept. Career civil servants were cast in a passive role as either subservient technocrats who faithfully followed the commands of elected political officials, or merely referees who regulated the arena in which interest group competition and bargaining occurred (see Burke, 1986). Underpinning each role is the assumption that bureaucrats cannot and should not assume an active leadership role; the U.S. Constitution assigned this function to elected political officials. This image of the career administrator was not seriously challenged until the early 1980s.

In response to the widely publicized "bureaucrat-bashing" of both the Carter (1976–1980) and Reagan (1980–1988) presidencies, academicians, practitioners, and others joined hands to produce a vast and impressive body of literature that defended administrative institutions of government. One line of defense concentrated on establishing an alternative basis upon which to legitimate the role of public administrators in the American political system. In a direct attack on public administration orthodoxy, a band of scholars constructed a persuasive argument that career administrators share with all others a legitimate leadership role in governance (Cook, 1990; Kass and Catron, 1990; Wamsley et al. 1990, 1983; Rohr, 1986). Beginning with the presentation and circulation of the "Blacksburg Manifesto" (Wamsley et al. 1983) at the 1983 annual conference of the American Society of Public Administration (ASPA), supporters of the administrative state sought to refocus the American political dialogue and thereby counter prevailing views that career administrators were a threat to democratic government. Central to this effort was the notion that career administrators, when guided by constitutional principles, help maintain government stability. The theory of administrative conservatorship advances this perspective (Terry, 1995, 1990).

The theory of administrative conservatorship seeks to legitimate the exercise of bureaucratic leadership. Building on the works of Carl J. Friedrich (1972, 1961, 1958), Philip Selznick (1992, 1957), John A. Rohr (1986), and others, the theory of administrative conservatorship depicts career administrators as "conservators" because they have a moral obligation to preserve the integrity of public bureaucracies (Terry, 1995, 1990).

The term "conservator" refers to a guardian, someone who conserves or preserves from injury, violation, or infraction. The term was first given intellectual currency in leadership discussions by Carl J. Friedrich (1961). In an article, "Political Leadership and the Problem of the Charismatic Power," Friedrich uses the term conservator in discussing what he describes as maintaining leadership. According to Friedrich, maintaining leadership "upholds the established order of things." He suggests that the "conservator reinforces old lines of political action which are familiar to all those following him" (p. 21). Friedrich argues that maintaining leadership is "more specifically based on 'authority' if authority is taken to mean the capacity of reasoned elaboration based upon the recognized beliefs and interest of the community" (1961, p. 21). It should be noted that Friedrich's conservator is not the same as Anthony Down's (1967) conserver—the pathetic bureaucratic officials who is "timorous, self-effacing, extremely cautious, plagued by inferior feelings" and afraid of change (p. 97). The conservator is a statesman—one entrusted with preserving the "existing government and its traditional ways of 'getting things done'" (p. 21).

The theory of administrative conservatorship extends Friedrich's concept of maintaining leadership to administrative or bureaucratic leadership. Similar to the political leader who performs the maintaining leadership role, the administrative conservator is concerned with preserving the American political regime and its tradition. The administrative conservator performs this function by preserving the integrity of public bureaucracies. The term "integrity" is central to the theory of administrative conservatorship. When used in organizational analysis, integrity is related to the notion of "distinctive competence:" the special capacities, abilities, and proficiencies possessed by an agency in the performance of particular functions (Selznick, 1957, p. 139). In the context of administrative conservatorship, integrity prefers to the "completeness, wholeness, soundness, and persistence of administrative processes, value commitments, and unifying principles that determine an institution's distinctive competence" (Terry, 1995, p. 27).

The theory of administrative conservatorship prescribes a continuum of leadership roles performed by the conservator. It also offers a variety of prescriptions to assist career administrators in preserving the integrity of public bureaucracies. These prescriptions concentrate on the three primary functions performed by the administrative conservator: conserving mission, conserving values and conserving support.

LARRY D. TERRY

BIBLIOGRAPHY

Burke, John P., 1986. *Bureaucratic Responsibility.* Baltimore: Johns Hopkins University Press.
Cook, Brian, 1990. "The Representative Function of Bureaucracy: Public Administration in a Constitutive Perspective." *Administration & Society,* vol. 23, 403–429.
Downs, Anthony, 1967. *Inside Bureaucracy.* Boston: Little Brown.
Friedrich, Carl J., 1958. "Authority, Reason and Discretion." In Carl J. Friedrich, ed., *Authority: Nomos I.* Cambridge, MA: Harvard Univ. Press, pp. 28–48.
———, 1961. "Political Leadership and the Problem of the Charismatic Power." *The Journal of Politics,* vol. 23, 3–24.
———, 1972. *Tradition and Authority.* New York: Praeger.
Kass, Henry D. and Bayard L. Catron, eds., 1990. *Images and Identities in Public Administration.* Newbury Park: Sage.
Lowi, Theodore, 1979. *The End of Liberalism: The Second Republic of the United States,* 2nd ed. New York: Norton.
Rohr, John, 1986. *To Run a Constitution: The Legitimacy of the Administrative State.* Lawrence: University Press of Kansas.
Schoenbrod, David, 1993. *Power Without Responsibility: How Congress Abuses the People Through Delegation.* New Haven: Yale University Press.
Selznick, Philip, 1957. *Leadership in Administration: A Sociological Interpretation.* Evanston, IL: Row, Peterson.
———, 1992. *The Moral Commonwealth: Social Theory and Promise of Community.* Berkeley: University of California Press.
Terry, Larry D., 1990. "Leadership in the Administrative State: The Concept of Administrative Conservatorship." *Administration & Society,* vol. 21, 395–412.

———, 1995. *Leadership of Public Bureaucracies: The Administrator as Conservator.* Thousand Oaks: Sage Publications.

Wamsley, Gary, Charles T. Goodsell, John Rohr, Orion White, and James Wolf, 1983. "Refocusing the American Political Dialogue." Paper presented at the Annual Conference of the American Society of Public Administration held in New York City, New York.

Wamsley, Gary, Robert Bacher, Charles T. Goodsell, Philip Kronenberg, John Rohr, Camilla Stivers, Orion White, James Wolf, 1990. *Refounding Public Administration.* Newbury Park: Sage Publications.

ADMINISTRATIVE CORPORATISM.

A system of bureaucratic organization in which representatives of interest groups concerned with the work of a particular government agency will be directly incorporated into the executive leadership of that agency.

Administrative corporatism is a variant of corporatist theory and practice and, as such, stands in contrast to pluralist approaches to the nature and working of society and government. Traditional pluralist theory, as expounded by Bentley, Truman and Dahl, holds that society is composed of a host of competitive socioeconomic actors, all seeking to advance their self-interests through interrelationships with other actors in the private sphere and with governments in the public realm. With respect to governmental relations, pluralism holds that there is a clear demarcation between society and the state. Groups exist outside of the state, while seeking to influence policymaking and policy implementation within the state. Similarly, governments exist within the state, distinct and independent from any and all interest groups, though governments, in seeking to advance the public interest, will be called upon to broker the interests of competing groups. Governments will seek to serve the interests of certain groups viewed to be needy, worthy, and important, while downplaying the concerns of other less favorably viewed groups. Group-government relations thus stand at the heart of pluralist theory, but they are relations that occur across the demarcated frontier of the private and the public.

Group-government relations also stand at the heart of corporatism but through a vastly different form of conceptualization and practice. In corporatist theory, as advanced by Lembruch, Schmitter, and Cawson representatives of major, adversarial interest groups concerned with a particular policy field are directly incorporated into government, given at once the power to engage in policymaking and implementation, yet also the responsibility of being called upon to cooperate not only with representatives of government but also those of other competing groups. Corporatism, in theory, is designed to promote better policymaking and administration than is found in pluralist systems, in that government officials and representatives of leading interest groups are brought together

in the expectation that they can collaborate in the development of policy and then cooperate in the implementation and administration of policy. Through such an approach it is hoped that a team dynamic can be developed for addressing the major issues confronting a society and that common interests and aspirations can supersede the competitiveness and adversarialism so prevalent in pluralist systems or organization.

As demonstrated in the works of Lembruch and Schimitter there is much evidence of broad corporatist policymaking and administrative systems within Western Europe, especially in such countries as Austria, Sweden, and Germany. Pluralist and Marxist critics, though, have been quick to argue that not only are corporatist arrangements highly problematical and undemocratic, but that they are basically a European phenomenon, unlikely to find an institutional niche in the pluralist societies of Britain and North America.

The work of Cawson then becomes highly influential. Cawson has arued that corporatist arrangements can exist in a number of manners. The traditional European variant is known as macrocorporatism, in which peak organizations of business and labor collaborate with government in the formation of nationwide macroeconomic policy involving such matters as wage rates, patterns of investment, productivity rates, and research and development policy. Cawson, has also argued, though, that corporatism can exist at the meso, sectoral, or functional administrative level of industrial organization; that is, within particular subnational economic sectors or within particular fields of activity or services important to the efficient and fair operation of an economy. When the focus of analysis shifts from a macroeconomic perspective to a meso-administrative level, Cawson asserts that the potential for corporatist initiatives is greatly increased, especially in societies such as Britain or those of North America. In these traditional pluralist societies, while corporatism may be foreign at the level of macro policymaking, there may be corporatist arrangements within certain sectors of socioeconomic activity subject to administrative regulation.

Through the works of authors such as Cawson, Grant, Self and Coleman, there is evidence of meso-administrative corporatist arrangements in Britain, Canada, Australia, and the United States, not to mention the countries of Western Europe. Such initiatives are most commonly found in the sectors of agricultural and fishery production, land use and residential rental markets, and especially in the fields of labor relations and workers' compensation policy administration. The latter fields, in all of these countries, display classic mescocorporatist arrangements in which governments establish an agency to engage in policymaking and administration with respect to the matters of unionization, collective bargaining, and fair labor practices as well as the assessment of compensation for work-related accidents. In an effort to gain the support of leading interest groups concerned with these fields, governments invite representatives of business and organized labor to directly participate, in a tripartite fashion, in the operation of the agency.

Not only is such involvement designed to bring to the agency a wealth of knowledge and experience, but it seeks to bring the major contending interests together in such a manner that their representatives will be compelled to address the concerns of their opposite numbers as they seek to establish policy and managerial approaches compatible with their own members' long-term interests. Policy and administrative stability is viewed as requiring mutual adjustment gained through mutual understanding and compromise. If such cooperation and collaboration is forthcoming, the policies and administrative decisions emerging through such a process will be clothed in an aura of legitimacy, in that those affected by agency decisions—the particular members of the interests themselves—will be more likely to accept and abide by agency decisions given that these decisions were arrived at with the direct participation of their representatives. Corporatist arrangements aim not only for collaboration in policymaking, but for affective and forthright implementation of decisions once made.

While administrative corporatism can be observed in many Western countries, the existence of such initiatives has not gone unchallenged. Panitch has roundly attacked all forms of corporatism as perpetuating the exploitation of labor, in that corporatist arrangements result in organized labor entering a system of management in which it becomes a minor player coopted and dominated by the combined interests of business and government. In a similar vein Offe has challenged corporatist institutions as representing a threat to democracy, in that administrative corporation results in the transference of policymaking authority away from democratically elected representatives of the people and into the hands of an appointed elite, the majority of whom are not representatives of government. The fear is that public government is replaced by private interest government. And finally, pluralist critics such as Dahl and Brooks attack administrative corporatism on account of its arbitrariness and unfairness to unrepresented interests. The very logic of corporatism extends privilege to those interests deemed significant enough to merit inclusion within the corporatist administration. But how is this decision to be made? By what criteria is socioeconomic importance to be assessed? And what becomes of those interests not accorded incorporation into the corporatist organization? Does the system of incorporation merely replicate an existing and unfair power dynamic in which the already significant witness their position reified to the detriment of all others?

These are powerful criticisms going to the heart of administrative corporatist arrangements in particular, and to the theory of corporatism in general. Advocates of corporatism such as Cawson and Self respond that these challenges can be addressed through the careful organization and management of corporatist arrangements, with the fairness of corporatist initiatives being contingent on the justice which the sponsoring government brings to this task. With proper attention to this dynamic the advocates are adamant that, far from inhibiting democracy and the representation of historically disadvantaged groups, administrative corporatist arrangements can be a significant means to enhancing democracy by bringing hitherto unrepresented socioeconomic interests into the public decisionmaking process. Further, if and when any interest group can demonstrate, in the pluralist forum of public opinion, that it is a force worthy of inclusion into a corporatist form of organization, then eventually governments will respond to this pressure and offer incorporation. In this manner there is the belief that, far from standing in full opposition to pluralism, the working of administrative corporatism will marry certain aspects of pluralist politics to the workings of corporatism.

While the theory and practice of administrative corporatism is controversial and highly contested, the very presence of administrative corporatist forms of organizational throughout most countries in the Western world demonstrates the importance of corporatist theory to understanding the nature of certain types of public sector organizations exhibiting the direct representation of particular interest groups. A pluralist approach alone cannot provide a full account of the power relations found in such organizations. Pluralist theory and practice is not to be dismissed, but to this knowledge must be added an awareness and appreciation of the impact of administrative corporatism to public administration and public policymaking.

DAVID A. JOHNSON

BIBLIOGRAPHY

Bentley, Arthur, 1949. *The Process of Government.* Bloomington: Indiana University Press.

Brooks, Stephen, 1989. *Public Policy in Canada.* Toronto: McClelland and Stewart.

Cawson, Alan, ed., 1986. *Corporatism and Political Theory.* Oxford: Basil Blackwell.

———, 1985. *Organized Interests and the State: Studies in Meso-Corporatism.* London: Sage.

Coleman, William D. and Grace Skogstad, eds., 1990. *Policy Communities and Public Policy in Canada: A Structural Approach.* Mississauga: Copp Clark Pittman.

Dahl, Robert, 1956. *A Preface to Democratic Theory.* Chicago, IL: University of Chicago Press.

Grant, Wyn, ed., 1985. *The Political Economy of Corporatism.* London: Macmillan Publishers Ltd.

Hirst, Paul Q., 1986. *Law, Socialism and Democracy.* London: Allen and Unwin.

Offe, Claus, 1984. *Contradictions of the Welfare State.* Cambridge: MIT Press.

Panitch, Leo, 1979. "Corporatism in Canada." In Richard Schultz, Orest Kruhlak and John Terry, eds., *The Canadian Political Process*, 3rd ed. Toronto: Holt, Rinehart and Winston.

——, 1986. "The Tripartite Experience." In Keith G. Banting, ed., *The State and Economic Interests*. Toronto: University of Toronto Press.

Schmitter, Phillip C., and Gerhard Lembruch, eds., 1982. *Patterns of Corporatist Policy-Making*. London: Sage.

——, 1979. *Trends Toward Corporatist Intermediation*. London: Sage.

Self, Peter, 1985. *Political Theories of Modern Government: Its Role and Reform*. London: Allen and Unwin.

Truman, David, 1964. *The Government Process: Political Interests and Public Opinion*. New York: Knopf.

ADMINISTRATIVE DISCRETION.

The exercise of subjective judgment by administrative officials.

Seemingly no aspect of American public administration engenders more discussion and controversy than the idea of discretion. Yet for most the attitude toward the exercise of discretion must be described as ambiguous and even ambivalent. While few would deny the necessity of the exercise of discretion, there is little agreement on the normative foundation (Bryner, 1987) for that activity. Put most simply, discretion represents the individual judgment as to what activities in an agency are to receive priority. The common assumption is that at any moment in time administrative officials have a choice as to what to do, and that the choice affects the agency and the public.

The fundamental question is whether discretionary decision making by bureaucrats is in and of itself bad. Discretion is problematic from three quite distinct perspectives. First, if discretionary decisions yield nonuniform decisions, do those decisions deny the basic democratic tenet of equality of treatment, and therefore become a threat to democracy itself? For a minority of scholars the problem is reversed. They see bureaucratic norms, which reject the exercise of discretion, as preventing adequate service to citizens in greatest need. The question becomes that of directing or controlling discretion to the service of the ideal of democratic governance, rather than any of the several values of the organization, such as economy, efficiency, or effectiveness. The fear expressed by those who hold this view, including Yates (1982), Gruber (1987), and Hummel (1994) is that the exercise of discretion, when founded on those internal organizational values, can destroy the core of representative democratic government (see also Downs and Larkey, 1986). As Yates argues,

> The public official's fundamental moral obligation in a democracy is to pay increased attention to the definition and treatment of values the more these values are in conflict in a decision. . . . Public officials should provide a . . . thorough value analysis as one of the central justifications of public decisions. Indeed this is how I would define responsibility in bureaucratic decision making. . . . Without that knowledge, it is hard to see how the idea

of democratic control of administration can be anything more than a dangerous fiction (1988, p. 82).

The third viewpoint, which encompasses advocates of privatization such as Butler and Savas and those who have worked for the Heritage Foundation, the Hoover Institute, and other conservative think tanks, sees administrative discretion as destroying politics. Their solution is to radically restrict bureaucratic discretion to have the bureaucrats simply "do as they are told."

The only thing that anyone can agree upon is that discretion must be checked. But how to check discretion is an age-old question. The famous Friedrich-Finer "debate" in the academic journals in 1940 and 1941 addressed this very issue; but then, as now, it was a matter of which side you were on. Few minds were changed. For Carl Friedrich only a check based on professionalism and moral standards was required. Waldo (1984) describes this as the "inner check." The Finer perspective emphasized the external demands of the system of checks and balances, politics, and organizational structure. The central point seems to be that neither perspective is sufficient, though both are necessary components of any approach to bureaucratic accountability and, therefore, control of discretion. As Fesler and Kettl (1991) shape this issue:

> Bureaucratic responsibility has two elements. One is accountability: faithful obedience to the law, to higher officials' directions, and to standards of efficiency and economy. The other is ethical behavior: adherence to moral standards and avoidance even of the appearance of unethical actions. The two elements overlap and are generally compatible, but not always. Morality may call for disobedience to superiors or reporting of superiors' unethical behavior to their superiors, to legislators, or to the public (p. 317).

Perhaps the only way to achieve understanding of the idea of administrative discretion is to break it down into its component parts. The Friedrich-Finer debate shaped the issue as one of individual values versus organizational values. Fesler and Kettl shaped it as one of legal versus ethical behavior. The common thread is that of the dependence on either structural or internal controls. Drawing from this perspective, it is possible to classify administrative discretion based on the control used:

1. legal/constitutional
2. political/democratic
3. managerial/organizational
4. normative/ethical.

Even if administrative discretion cannot be summarized, these four elements can be described. The choices among these elements yield the behavior or perspective on administrative discretion that becomes practice within government agencies. By examining these four components of control of administrative discretion, a fuller view of the parameters of the concept can emerge.

Controls on Administrative Discretion

Legal/Constitutional Control

If one were to examine a text on administrative law the issue of discretion is readily addressed. The focus is on first the source of authority to act, and second on the procedure for exercising discretion (Cooper, 1983, pp. 219–220). The entire process of administrative law and procedure is a mechanism for defining and bounding discretion. Put simply, if the action is within the scope of assignment and is executed following appropriate and approved practice, then discretionary action is permitted. The proper forum for determining whether that action was permissible is the courts. Pierce, Shapiro, and Verkuil (1985) summarize this perspective on administrative law and, by implication, administrative discretion as follows:

> First, the imposition of administratively determined actions is authorized by the legislature through rules that control agency action. Second, the decisional procedures used by the agency must ensure agency compliance with the authorizing legislative directives. Third, judicial review must be available to ensure that an agency will utilize impartial and accurate decision-making procedures and will comply with legislative directives. Fourth, agency decisional processes must facilitate the exercise of such judicial review (pp. 36–37).

In this context discretion is limited by the legislature and second, and more powerfully, by the courts. What is missing is whether the policy produced makes substantive sense. The presumption is that the legislature has fully and completely addressed this concern. Many, but must notably Kenneth Culp Davis, have challenged this view of administrative law for its failure to acknowledge the critical role of discretion in the exercise of the "informal" functions of administration. Davis goes so far as to suggest that justice is impossible without such discretionary actions (1969).

Political Control

The Davis perspective presents a political rather than a procedural question, because the choice is that of "helping" the citizen, or denying that help, by the exercise of discretion. This is a political question, because of the obligation to serve the public that is central to democratic governance. A democratic government is at once responsible and responsive to its citizens. There are three aspects to this question. First is in defining the individual, and potentially idiosyncratic, relationship between the "street level" bureaucrat and the citizen. The "New Public Administration" movement (Marini, 1971) argued that the street level bureaucrat must be an advocate for the poor, the un-

derclass. Decisions at this level should be directed at "helping," not at following organizational norms and policies. This perspective sees little to be gained from controlling discretion. The New Public Administration sought to enhance the scope of discretion. The only limitation was in the adherence to norms of representative government.

Second is in defining the institutional relationship between political officials and administrative agencies. Since the turn of the century mainstream public administration has advocated an adherence to the policies and preferences of the chief executive. The attack on bureaucratic discretion in the 1980s by conservative think tanks and politicians in the U.S. was grounded in the belief that senior bureaucrats were by political preference Democrats, and therefore unwilling to carry out the "mandate" of a Republican president, particularly Ronald Reagan (1980–1988). This view, best epitomized by the Heritage Foundation's *Steering the Elephant,* sought radical privatization as one tool to halt politicized bureaucracy from exercising discretion. This group has all but given up on controlling discretion. The solution is to prohibit it.

Thus in barely a decade two diametrically opposite views on politically motivated discretion sought academic and public support. Between these two extremes resides a third view that bureaucrats have denied the democratic process by imposing bureaucratic structure and barriers (red tape) in the decision process. In other words, it is the unwillingness to exercise discretion that is the problem. It is the Heritage Foundation result (radically limited discretion) but through the rejection of politics, and even democracy, as relevant to the practice of administration. This is the scenario that so concerned German sociologist Max Weber nearly eight decades ago. This perspective is best represented by scholars such as Ralph Hummel who, following the views of Weber, sees bureaucracy as a threat to representative democracy (Hummel, 1994, especially chapter 6). Neither Hummel nor Weber are confident that even the street level bureaucrat has the interests of the citizen at heart.

Managerial Control

This brings us to the third aspect of discretion: discretion as a managerial or organizational problem. The check on discretion here is not a set of statutes and policies, nor a political and ideological outlook, rather it is the norms and standards of the "professional administrator." While some would argue that the profession's emphasis on the status quo is itself a political viewpoint (see, again, Weber and Hummel), the assumption here is that the deference to the three "traditional" branches is not enough. Bureaucrats do not directly challenge those institutions but the reality is that much that goes on day-to-day bears little relationship to the letter of the statute (this was Davis's point). Waldo (1984 p. 40) argued nearly fifteen years ago that the fundamental values of the bureaucrat must be those of American political thought and constitutionalism, but the choice of actions must be grounded in a knowledge of management practices and organization theory to ensure those fundamental values are effectively achieved. Discretion is born of a knowledge of what is possible administratively, not merely what is politically appropriate. The choice of management practices, and the competence to carry them out, thus becomes a component of discretion, because the bureaucrat must choose a course of action. Unlike the rule of law whereby the decision of the courts provided critical guidance, managerial discretion—choosing how to operate a program or agency—has few guidelines or principles, except the lessons of experience or knowledge from the classroom.

Ethical Control

The last aspect of discretion is that derived from the desire to behave ethically. To use the old saying: ethics is about doing what is right, not merely doing it the right way. Discretion may be about choosing to act ethically even when the action has no prior foundation in policy or precedent; it may even require the refusal to follow established policy and procedure. Lest we see ethical behavior as the opposite of rule compliance, it may be easier to define this aspect of discretion as the desire or motivation to act ethically when making public decisions. Stated this way, administrative discretion may in part constitute the responsibility of the administrator to pursue ethical choices regardless of where those choices might lead. The ideal of ethical decision making as an element of policy implementation may produce some unexpected results when combined with other values such as democracy and representative government. The difficult choice (the most critical time for the exercise of discretion) by any public servant is not whether to help someone, but rather the limits of that help. There are inevitably more who seek help than can be served. The difficult choice is to determine, ethically, when to end assistance. One must remember that the longer an official spends on the special case (the nonroutine case) the lengthier the waiting list of those as yet not helped. Worse, this is precisely the situation for which neither bureaucratic routines and policies, nor court rulings, can provide professional guidance.

Challenges and Options

These four problem sets affirm that there is no simple way to define the appropriate limits to discretion. Often this has been cast as the need to protect representative government from the indiscriminate exercise of discretion by nonelected officials. Political writers as diverse as Hamilton and Madison (writing in *Federalist* Paper No. 51) and Max Weber (especially in "Politics as Vocation") have expressed the need to control bureaucratic discretion in the name of representative government. But for all that, it

would appear that one's belief that control is even possible will depend on how one defines the problem. For those who see the issue as predominantly one of administrative process, much is made of legislative and judicial control. For the conservative who sees the issue as one of political ascendancy, the only course of action is to abolish much of the current civil service in order to return most discretion to the hands of political appointees and their elected superiors. For those who see the issue as one of managerial and ethical behavior, there is no way to define discretion; control is achieved only through the application of internalized professional standards and ethical values. It is important to note that in this latter case, discretion is limited by those professional and ethical values and, therefore, not a problem. On the other hand, in the former case discretion is a potentially controllable aspect of administration, and, therefore, something to be shunned. Rather, the focus of attention is on limiting or controlling discretion in the name of democratic representative government. We have come full circle. Douglas Yates, a writer long concerned with whether bureaucracy and democracy are compatible, frames the question thusly, "It is not merely a matter of who guards the guardians—certainly a time-honored question—but more precisely, who regulates or controls the bureaucratic policymakers values and how. . . . Bureaucrats are [after all] in the business of choosing and balancing values routinely—at least whenever they propose policy or interpret statutes" (1988, p. 77).

For many, control of discretion is a serious and almost insurmountable problem for which only radical surgery on bureaucracy itself will suffice. For others it is a matter of self-limitation through proper training, education, and socialization. There is no easy answer here. Clearly, one's attitude toward administrative discretion is tempered by *a priori* attitudes about the power of those internal and external controls available to limit discretion. Those efforts to limit discretion cover the full range from advocacy of greater judicialization of administrative law, to demands for greater specificity in the crafting of statutes and a greater emphasis on ethics training. A few would dismantle the bureaucracy by radical reorganization into nonhierarchical structures, or by attacking the civil service and repoliticizing government agencies.

The more extreme of these views hold some academic and popular currency, but do not seem to have the breadth of support that would give them time for implementation. To the extent that such viewpoints are put into practice, contradictory results may arise. Some organization redesign is likely to occur. Government organizations will be flatter in the future. This would imply that those in the public service closest to the citizenry would be given broader scope. They would be required to exercise more, not less, discretion. The reinventing government movement (Osborne and Gaebler, 1992) would give some managers more latitude (generally those at the top), but it would also encourage careful examination of privatization as an option for carrying out programs. This does not eliminate discretion, but merely shifts it from the public official to the private contractor.

The most likely path will be a greater emphasis on ethics, democratic and participative management, total quality management (TQM), and other management-oriented techniques. This path fits both the academic faith in better education as a cure for problems and the current understandings of best management practice. This is also a concession to the reality that discretion is necessary to the creation of the kind of flexible, responsive, and dynamic organizations that we have come to believe should be the norm.

Until now, the challenge of limiting discretion has been a concern in the United States and, secondarily, in non-Western countries. This has not been an issue in Europe. Because of the emphasis on rule selection (finding the rule that explains the proper course of act), rather than rulemaking, discretionary judgment by bureaucrats is far less a problem. However, to the extent that TQM, participative management, and other such managerial-based techniques are introduced and incorporated into European bureaucracies, changes will occur. These techniques emphasize a flexibility, entrepreneurship, and situation-driven decision making style that is quite different from present practice. Discretionary judgments will become more frequent, and therefore, as in the United States, its limits will become a topic of debate.

RAYMOND W. COX III

BIBLIOGRAPHY

Bryner, G. C., 1987. *Bureaucratic Discretion*. Elmsford, NY: Pergamon Press.
Butler, S. M., 1985. *The Privatization Option*. Washington, D.C.: Heritage Foundation.
Cooper, P., 1983. *Public Law and Public Administration*. Palo Alto: Mayfield Publishing.
Davis, K. C., 1969. *Discretionary Justice*. Baton Rouge: Louisiana State University Press.
Downs, G. W. and P. D. Larkey, 1986. *The Search for Government Efficiency*. New York: Random House.
Fesler, J. W. and D. F. Kettl, 1991. *The Politics of the Administrative Process*. Chatham, NJ: Chatham House.
Finer, H., 1941. "Administrative Responsibility in Democratic Government." *Public Administration Review*, vol. 1. 335–350.
Friedrich, C. J., 1940. "Public Policy and the Nature of Administrative Responsibility." In Friedrich, C. J. and Edward S. Mason, eds. *Public Policy*. Cambridge: Harvard University Press.
Gruber, J. E., 1987. *Controlling Bureaucracies*. Berkeley: University of California Press.
Hummel, R. P., 1994. *The Bureaucratic Experience*, 4th ed. New York: St Martin's Press.
Marini, F., ed., 1971. *Towards a New Public Administration*. Scranton: Chandler Publishing.
Osborne, D. and T. Gaebler, 1992. *Reinventing Government*. Reading, MA: Addison-Wesley.
Pierce, R. J., S. A. Shapiro, and P. R. Verkuil, 1985. *Administrative Law and Process*. Mineola, NY: The Foundation Press.
Rector, Robert and Michael Sanera, eds., 1987. *Steering the Elephant: How Washington Really Works*. New York: Universe Books.
Savas, E. S., 1985. *Privatization: The Key to Better Government*. Chatham, NJ: Chatham House.
Stewart, R., 1975. "The Reformation of American Administrative Law." *Harvard Law Review*, vol. 88.
Waldo, D., 1984. *The Administrative State*, 2nd ed. New York: Holmes and Meier Publishers.
Yates, D., 1982. *Bureaucratic Democracy*. Cambridge: Harvard University Press.
———, 1988. "Hard Choices: Justifying Bureaucratic Decisions." In Moore, ed., *Ethical Insight Ethical Action*. Washington D.C.: International City Management Association.

ADMINISTRATIVE DISINVESTMENT. The reduction or elimination of an agency's administrative capacities. The capacities may include physical equipment and buildings, human resources, and administrative processes. Disinvestment occurs most frequently at times of cutbacks in public support, elimination of programs, reorganizations, and downsizing of organizations.

Introduction

Attention to an agency's capacity to complete its mission tends to surface only after some administrative failure such as the inability of the Federal Emergency Management Agency to respond to a hurricane, the failure of the *Challenger* space shuttle, the breakdown of the postal system in a metropolitan area, or the death of children due to failure of an inspection to catch *E coli* in hamburger meat. Even though partisans disagree about the appropriate level of government effort, most accept that government should possess the capability to undertake politically legitimated public purposes.

Public agencies are vehicles for doing public business. For example, they protect children, assure a safe food supply, bring some measure of safety to financial transactions, or protect individual citizens or whole countries from threats of one kind or another. Agencies resort to a variety of administrative mechanisms to carry out public purposes. They include direct program delivery, indirect delivery through grants and contacts, regulations, or some system of incentives. Each approach demands agencies with skilled workers to participate in complex administrative processes.

Describing Administrative Capacities

Administrative capacities include elements such as office buildings, human capability, equipment, laws, regulations, and money for spending. These things become activated through institutional and administrative processes. A closer look at these elements reveals some dimensions of administrative capacity.

Buildings and Other Physical Aspects of Agencies

The quality of the physical structures, the condition of the transportation fleet, the availability of value-added technological resources such as telecommunication, computers, fax machines, and so forth, all incorporate elements of administrative capacity.

Human Resources

The availability of human skills over long periods of time and the flexibility of resources to meet new requirements represent the human resource dimension of agency capacity. Agencies require technical, program, and governance competencies. First, agencies need employees with the technical skills to be able to define the specific materials for building bridges, to know when harmful bacteria are present in food supplies, or to determine the cause of a plane crash. Second, agencies need program skills to develop and manage the activities and processes that keep the inspection systems effective, that set up review panels for scientific grants, or that coordinate complex public works construction. Third, public organizations demand a work force that understands and is able to work within a democratic constitutional order. Public servants should know when actions may be technically legal but violate established democratic processes or an important constitutional principle, such as the separation of powers doctrine or the Bill of Rights.

Agency Administrative Processes

Agency processes activate other elements of administrative capacity. Physical, technological, and human resources are applied through administrative processes. Such processes come in all forms and range from temporary or ad hoc ones to those that are firmly embedded in the agency's institutional practices. At the most basic level, administrative processes are series of coordinated actions and standard operating procedures that have been created and sustained by agency staffs. Memory, commitment, technical proficiency, and program competency are part of this capacity. These processes contain the keys to solving unusual problems as well as recurring tasks.

Disinvesting in Administrative Capacity

Administrative disinvestment occurs in many of the same ways that cities, states, and national governments disinvest in physical infrastructure. Just as bridges and school roofs rot from delayed attention to maintenance, administrative capacity erodes because of intentional and unintentional neglect. At the most conscious political level, administrative capacity may be reduced because of direct political action. Political changes may bring the elimination of an

agency's ability to provide regulation in a particular industry as a way to achieve a particular political agenda. However, most administrative disinvestment does not result from such explicit political decisions. More frequently, it results from unintended actions, side effects of other political decisions or simply neglect.

When cutbacks occur, for example, equipment and supplies get early attention for elimination. These physical objects support administrative processes.

Signs tell people how to move effectively among buildings, computers and related equipment provide for more effective connection between people and processes, and adequate supplies of pens and forms make the processes work smoothly. While people do learn to do without, there is often a loss of administrative effectiveness, albeit incremental, in the day-to-day workings of an agency. The cumulative effect of these losses can cause diminution of agency capacity.

Downsizing and elimination of middle management levels often have disinvestment outcomes. Middle managers pay attention to administrative systems and processes that aggregate above line supervision and that are missed by top management. They represent the administrative capacity for paying attention to mid-level systems and problems. The middle levels of management provide for continual organizing that permits the systems to function in spite of bulky agencywide policies and the narrower perspectives of those who provide the day-to-day services to clients and customers. Middle managers bring line workers together to look at processes that cross work team functions. The result of this disinvestment in middle level competencies is agencies less able to respond quickly to novel challenges, to improve processes that cut across first line work, and to identify and surmount challenges from the field.

The turmoil and drama during cutback and downsizing periods create additional problems for administrative capacity. Anxiety about being reorganized diverts attention away from maintenance of the many processes that keep public activities functioning. As employees' psychological energies go to addressing uncertainty, maintenance of processes declines, and critical administrative routines suffer from neglect.

Restrictions on communication and travel come as part of most cutback efforts. Travel restrictions, elimination of conferences and meetings, and telephone use are also among the first casualties of a fiscal stress. The resulting damage involves administrative processes that cut across units, not only within an operating unit. Competence for working on tasks that cross organizational boundaries can only be maintained at an effective level through working relationships that come about because of interaction over periods of time. Cuts in travel and other communication opportunities affect interagency administrative processes.

The results of the decline in resources eliminate any cushion for attending to unanticipated challenges and meeting even current demands. In order to keep core services going, agencies often divest themselves of their administrative infrastructure. Agencies cut into their own processes and capacities at the expense of the service. The tools of cutbacks exacerbate disinvestment. Hiring freezes, micromanagement, loss of time by people lead to downward spirals from which agencies take long periods to recover.

Finally, constant reorganization—the perennial answer to political and administrative problems—induces losses of agency capacity. It keeps an agency off balance. Processes, relationships, and institutional memory for dealing with problems get lost with the movement of people and offices from one place to another. Agency staff forget the commonsense ways of doing things and energy goes to the rumor mill rather than to positive processes.

Conclusion

The debate about the role of a competent bureaucracy has focused on the generally understood limitations of bureaucracies in a democratic society. Opponents of public activities often see loss or disinvestment of agency administrative capacity as a necessary way to reduce the role of government. While recognizing the effects of disinvestment, opponents of bureaucratic approaches to public action would accept it as a necessary and sometimes welcome cost. Others would argue that public agencies must develop and maintain crucial administrative capacity for legitimated public activities.

JAMES F. WOLF

BIBLIOGRAPHY

Chandler, Ralph Clark, ed., 1987. *A Centennial History of the American Administrative State.* New York: The Free Press.
Goodsell, Charles T., 1985. *The Case for Bureaucracy: A Public Administration Polemic,* 2d ed., Chatham, N.J.: Chatham House Publishers, Inc.
Kaufman, Herbert, 1976. *Are Government Organizations Immortal?* Washington, D.C.: The Brookings Institution.
Lane, Larry M. and James F. Wolf, 1990. *The Human Resource Crisis in the Public Sector.* Westport, CT: Quorum Books.
March, James G. and Johan P. Olsen, 1989. *Rediscovering Institutions: The Organizational Basis of Politics.* New York: The Free Press.
Rubin, Irene, 1985. *Shrinking the Federal Government: The Effect of Cutbacks on Five Federal Agencies.* New York: Longman.
Tolchin, Susan J. and Martin Tolchin, 1983. *Dismantling America: The Rush to Deregulate.* Boston: Houghton Mifflin Company.

ADMINISTRATIVE FICTION. A work of literature which offers valuable insights on leadership, motivation, decisionmaking, and other organizational concepts related to public organizations (Waldo, 1968), as well as portraying human behaviors pertinent to organizational life. Such unorthodox organizational diagnosis is not new, and can be found in the Bible, Greek theater, and Shakespeare. In the 1960s Dwight Waldo annotated scores of contemporary novels in *The Novelist on Organization and Administration,* and identified three types of fiction directly related to public administration. These included bureaucratic fiction, in which the plot is centered on bureaucratic relationships; administrative fiction, involving decision making within an organization; and the self-explanatory political fiction. Generally, Waldo finds a pessimistic view by scores of authors as to administration's impact on individual values.

In the 1970s, fiction- and science fiction-based collections of readings were used to teach public administration, world history, American history, political science, and politics. Articles such as Howard McCurdy's "Fiction, Phenomenology, and Public Administration," which appeared in *Public Administration Review* in 1973, began to build momentum for an artistic-humanistic approach.

In *Literature in Bureaucracy,* Holzer et al. (1978) presented a conceptual framework for exploring key issues in public administration, ranging from power conflicts to corruption to human factors. Holzer constructed a "Matrix of Concern in Fiction," in which he categorized pessimistic views of bureaucracy's impact on individual values. In Holzer's terms, in an intraorganizational sense bureaucracy not only stifles, but demoralizes or corrupts. In terms of extraorganizational relationships, clients are generally treated as impersonal objects, but may also be the objects of unjust decisions. Holzer also suggests that an individual bureaucrat's reactions to such dysfunctional environments may range over disinterest, impotence, cynicism, and resignation.

Lawrence L. Downey (1987) has noted that fiction can explore conflicts in three predominant areas: legitimization of authority (e.g., *The Caine Mutiny*); relationship of organizations to their external environment (e.g., *Agnes of God*); and relationship of organizations to their internal environment (e.g., *An Officer and a Gentleman*). David A. Gugin (1987) expands on the conflict issue, focusing on fictional treatments of morality and ethics. He places these subjects in two general categories: external and internal. The external category deals with accountability and responsiveness to intent or traditional norms, while the internal subgroup is concerned with individual ethics or morals in conflict with organizationally demanded behavior.

In the 1990s artistic and humanistic perspectives have been further developed. A new journal, *Public Voices,* publishes artistic, humanistic, and reflective expression relevant to the field of public administration; novels and movies are reviewed in each issue. In the management (i.e., business school) context, the "Classic Leadership Cases" project at Hartwick college utilizes writings as diverse as Homer's *Iliad*, Shakespeare's *Henriad*, and Conrad's *Heart of Darkness*. Sheila Puffer's *Managerial Insights from Literature* (1991) draws on such sources as O. Henry, Franz Kafka, George Orwell, James Thurber, Mark Twain, Joan Didion, and Donald Barthelme. The genre and the dialogue continue to grow. Most recently, for example, the volume of essays edited by Charles Goodsell and Nancy Murray, *Public Administration Illuminated and Inspired by the Arts* (1995), examines uses a film, poetry, novels, and aesthetic teachings for the study of such diverse topics as leadership, ethics, and policy making.

"Administrative" issues, especially with regard to leadership, accountability, and personnel management, have been treated in literature since ancient times. Sophocles's *Antigone* and Homer's *Iliad* dealt with issues of leadership and administrative style, discipline, and morale in an organization. Shafritz (1992) traces many insights into management theory to Shakespeare, finding The Bard an invaluable source. Theater productions have provided ample fodder for students of administration throughout the nineteenth and twentieth centuries. For example, the song of the "Modern Major-General" from Gilbert and Sullivan's *HMS Pinafore* is an excellent example of bureaucratic bumbling and pomposity. The Broadway musical *How to Succeed in Business Without Really Trying*, is virtually a textbook on leadership problems and individual opportunities.

Administrative fiction often involves the extraorganizational interaction of agency and client, seeming to view the organization as either impersonal or unjust. Some view bureaucracy as ridiculously insensitive. In Zoschenko's "The Galosh," the trivial task of recovering a lost boot becomes an overly formal runaround; by the time he recovers the boot, the other half of the pair has been lost. In Kishon's "The Jerusalem Golem," a taxpayer whose name is identical to that of a harbor is inadvertently billed for the huge cost of its dredging; unable to get the computer to correct the error, he is also billed for payments toward a debt he cannot pay. In the end, the computer error is not only reversed, but becomes a monthly payment to him which the bureaucracy is just as unwilling and incapable of correcting in its favor.

As social commentary, administrative novels typically pillory the bureaucracy, arguing that little people are oppressed by large organizations. Dickens's "Containing the Whole Science of Government" (*Little Dorrit*) warns us that insensitivity easily shades into injustice. The Circumlocution Office is a bureaucratic jungle that humiliates, frustrates, and overwhelms the individuals it was established to serve. Concerned more with its own perpetuation than with ministering to the public, the Office has become a "politico-diplomatic hocus pocus piece of machinery," the exemplification of "HOW NOT TO DO IT." Form and process have become ends in themselves rather than the

means of providing services to the citizens, who suffer their absence. Similarly, Kosinski's *Cockpit* (1975) relates an incessant shuffling between offices to gain official recognition or authorization, and the special privileges of top level bureaucrats; Kosinski portrays a government which, instead of serving its citizens, serves instead to victimize or even destroy them. And one of Tom Wolfe's themes in the best-selling *Bonfire of the Vanities* is the callous and unthinking behavior of criminal justice officials.

The power of the administrative novel may be gauged by its influence on language. Perhaps Kafka is the most recognized critic of bureaucracy via fiction, even to the extent of the generally accepted adjective "Kafkaesque." He suggests that the impersonal often shades into the unjust, that "objective" rules may reduce individuals to objects, and bureaucrats may become inured to the public's pain. Some of the most depressing anti-client tales are Kafka's, such *The Trial*, in which the character K. is the victim of a seemingly irrational, faceless organization. The novel is about how a little man, an ordinary middle-level bank manager, is suddenly arrested, tried, and executed without any charge. Because the storytelling in the novel exists simultaneously both as a narrative and as an allegory, it is open to different readings by various people. It can be seen as a sociopolitical fable about a ubiquitous and omnipotent power machine, taking place in the real world and creating an atmosphere of alienation dubbed "Kafkaesque" ever after. Or it can be interpreted as a psychological and/or theological novel, where a person is in perpetual trial for his/her sins, regardless of guilt. The frustration with bureaucracy in *The Trial* works not only on the narrative level, but on the visual level as well, as do many novels that become the basis for movies. In the cinema version, Orson Welles has created a depressing surrealistic world full of fear and shadows, where endless gloomy labyrinths and stacks of files on neverending shelves are an organic part of the world, not an exception to it.

The titles of such anti-utopias as Orwell's *1984* and Huxley's *Brave New World*, along with Zamyatin's *We*, graphically portray and reinforce our worst fears of a bureaucratically controlled society in sometimes frightening detail; such scenarios have become shorthand for fears of bureaucratic oppression. Heller's *Catch 22* has also lent its title to the English language as a condition we all fear: a bureaucratic system built on circular reasoning from which there is no escape. In *Catch 22*, a World War II bureaucratic farce which was presented first as a novel and then as a movie, corruption is prevalent, accountability nonexistent, and the treatment of individuals callous. The war's goals are replaced by those of profit and individual comfort. The interests of the illicit M&M Syndicate become more important than military success or soldiers' lives. Similarly, Colonel Cathcart continually increases the number of dangerous missions required by his men, solely for the purpose of enhancing his own reputation. Perhaps the most important theme in the movie, as in the novel, is the ludicrous nature of bureaucratic rules.

In Ken Kesey's 1962 classic *One Flew Over the Cuckoo's Nest* (also an Oscar-winning movie), patient McMurphy disturbs the routine procedures of a mental hospital. Nurse Ratched and other staff serve the controlling needs of the "system." The staff is presented as callous and control-oriented. Nurse Ratched, in particular, is the epitome of a narrow-minded functionary. The crux of the movie is that her authority is challenged by McMurphy's informal power. Her custodial assumptions are in direct conflict with a humanistic orientation toward patient/staff relations. Ultimately, Nurse Ratched and the organization triumph in the harshest terms, and McMurphy's power is negated by subjecting him to the horrible consequences of an irreversible and unnecessary lobotomy–transforming a sane patient into a compliant vegetable.

The literary community is fond of reminding us that bureaucracy can also adversely affect bureaucrats. For instance, in *The Scarlet Letter* Nathaniel Hawthorne's description of "The Custom House" forces the reader, through the author's role of detached insider, to recognize the encroaching listlessness of spirit, the sapping of intellectual vigor and individual initiative. Hawthorne clearly suggests that the loss of "capability for self-support" affects every individual who comes to depend on the public payroll for financial security. His characters symbolize the debilitating effects of a government organization, resulting in an employee's lack of physical or mental vigor. In his poem "Dolor," Roethke (1964) expresses similar feelings of dread, exhaustion and frustration with office work. In the same vein, many British (e.g., W.H. Auden) and American (e.g., Robert Frost) poets express their experiences dealing with bureaucracy; Frederickson and Frederickson (1995) have keenly analyzed the "public" poems of Howard Nemerov.

Overall, fictional public bureaucrats take a beating. Almost without exception writers confirm a pessimistic view of bureaucracy's impact on its clients and even its own employees. Even when we find positive images, they may be overwhelmed, as in the one passage in Steinbeck's *The Grapes of Wrath* which praises an effective federal bureaucracy for protecting its clients in a humane work camp; his overarching theme condemns corrupt local bureaucrats–police in league with banks to evict sharecroppers, and with growers to exploit farm workers. Our society has been presented with, and has bought into, an image of public servants as uncaring and untrustworthy, entangled in red tape, failing to apply the common sense with which average citizens are endowed. The popular view of the public bureaucracy–created in part through the lens of fiction–is that it barely produces intended results, but is profuse in its production of negative and unethical behaviors–stifling, demoralizing, corrupting, impersonal, and unjust.

The administrative novel can be a foil for (re)examining concepts central to public administration. According to Adams and Pugh (1993), Melville's novella, *Billy Budd, Sailor,* focuses on the methods used in arriving at a decision, the characters involved in making it, and the consequences of the decision. Their analysis focuses on the elusive human motives, as well as the complexity and ambiguity, that lie at the heart of decision making. They suggest that the novel, examined in depth, offers powerful opportunities:

In a work such as *Billy Budd* we are presented with a precise and detailed context for the actions depicted in the story. We encounter various perspectives on the problem, and we are allowed to test our own reactions to it. Through the empathetic dimension of literature, we are able not only to feel the agony that sometimes goes into responsible decision making but also to imagine making the decision itself without having to suffer any of the consequences if it goes badly. Because of the nature of a work of literature, we can reflect on the consequences of a given decision as we evaluate the pros and cons of it–a luxury not possible in the workaday world. If we want to engage in speculation "outside of the story," we can make a different decision from that in the story and fabricate a different outcome, writing our own story, as it were.

Administrative literature makes much ado about the process of decision making. It is the principal focus of numerous articles and books that range in approach from the scientific to the anecdotal. Managers are regularly schooled in a variety of rational decision models that posit a logical, systematic, linear process that varies from the comprehensive to the incremental, from the analytical to the political. Emphasis is often given to the objectivization, simplification, and evaluation of reality. With a stress on data collection, hypothesis building, and analysis as precursors to choice based on rational self-interest, the models may sometimes appear artificial, parsimonious, and dehumanizing. There is a challenge in helping students approach administrative choices with a better understanding and perhaps a greater capacity for imagination and creativity while engaged in the process of decision making. It is our belief that literature provides one means of responding to this challenge.

We are interested specifically in what literature can offer in attempts to understand the process of decision making. Can literature suggest an alternative to the familiar models for decision making? Does it widen or alter our perspectives as we face day-to-day problems or critical issues? One thing that is immediately apparent is that, whereas management theory frequently looks to models or to frames in its approach to decision making, literature has as one of its major characteristics a refusal to simplify. Literature resists categorization and exploits ambiguity; it asks question instead of proposing answers; it muddles the political and decisional (as well as the moral and ethical) waters instead of charting channels for safe navigation or clearing a path. If clarity and rationality are the usual objectives in decision making, what then can we learn from the study of literature as it applies to decision making?

Administrative fiction has been a central concern of writers throughout the world. In many cases, because of censored social science and restricted political discourse, these works of fiction played very important roles in shaping public perceptions and attitudes. Authors from Eastern Europe have openly or in a disguised form criticized bureaucratic inefficiencies and political corruption in their novels, plays, and pamphlets. For example, administrative fiction has long been an element of Russian literature, very often the most influential critique aimed at ills of the society. Of all Russian writers, Nikolai Gogol is the one who is most obvious as a source for (insightful) administrative commentary in Russian fiction. Although his works date back to the middle of the nineteenth century, the bureaucratic world Gogol depicts in his stories and plays is the familiar world of red tape, abusive clerks, impersonal and intimidating executives.

Gogol's *The Inspector General* (a.k.a. *The Government Inspector*) is a play based on a classic plot of mistaken identity. The corrupted officials of provincial town N. expect an incognito government inspector from the capital, St. Petersburg. Because of their corrupt practices and dismal performance, they so dread the inspection that they mistake a young man with manners, who stays at the local inn and refuses to pay, for the expected inspector. This young man–Khlestakov–in reality is a penniless nonentity, who uses the opportunity and "borrows" money from the mayor, accepts the mayor's servile hospitality, takes bribes both from local bureaucrats and the local populace, flirts simultaneously with the mayor's wife and daughter, and narrowly escapes before being exposed. It is important to note that Khlestakov does not manipulate local officials to get what he wants (as a matter of fact, he wants nothing but a little money to pay for the inn and have a dinner), but is manipulated and elevated by them.

Gogol's *The Overcoat* is a sad story of a poor little clerk who longs for one only thing in his life: a new overcoat, which in his eyes will not only warm him up, but upgrade his status as well. When he is robbed of his coat, the hero dies from dread and cold.

The tradition of critical examination of bureaucracy in Russia was continued in the works of such famous writers as Chekhov, Saltykov-Shchedrin, and others. Chekhov's *The Death of a Chinovnik (Bureaucrat),* for example, told the story of a little bureaucrat who sneezed at a superior in a theater, and was so afraid of the imagined consequences that he died

from fear and dread. The line of bureaucratic criticism became weaker, but did not die, after the Bolshevik Revolution in 1917. For example, Mayakovsky launched a savage attack on Soviet bureaucracy in his play *The Bedbug* (1968), wherein a futuristic Communist bureaucracy was portrayed as having nothing human left to offer.

In an essay on "Literature and Public Administration Ethics," Frank Marini supports the use of literature:

> By reading imaginative literature, our students may gain not only a knowledge of what we consider key issues for our field but also an empathetic grasp or vicarious experience of these issues. The literature can focus issues and at the same time allow students to identify personally with fictional characters who have confronted similar issues. . . . It permits an analytical perspective from a safe distance: the subjects are, after all, not real people (though they may seem familiar enough); their problems may be our problems–but we know that our analysis of them is not a matter of somebody's life or death. More important than the safe analytical nature of literature is its affective quality: literature helps us feel the dilemma of an administrator responsible for upholding policy while confronted with questions of compassion, exception, human considerations, and specific circumstances, the frustrations of someone caught in bureaucratic red tape, etc. Out of the analysis and vicarious experience offered by literature, we enjoy a widened perspective arising out of our imaginative experience of people in different situations. At its best, literature can alter our world view (1992, p. 113).

The messages in novels, stories and plays should not be dismissed just because they are predominantly negative. Fiction can play a role in changing expectations of performance in the public sector. It has been also argued that narratives of people in organization–"the stories people tell"–are an important source of insight for our understanding of organizations and management theories (Hummel 1991). Bureaucracy's critics–writers, as well as those in other, associated media: reporters, artists, and directors–are a societal asset insofar as they have assumed the responsibility for persistently addressing the full and subtle range of ethical issues within public organizations. They are warning us that public bureaucracies are often dysfunctional; enervating and inefficient; the antithesis of creativity; cancers in our social fabric. Novelists and others portray the clean, well-lit buildings which house our bureaucracies as some of the most dangerous places in our society. And because entertainment is a palatable conveyor of criticism, the messages in novels (as well as cartoons, movies, and other forms of artistic expression) may be especially effective in generating a dialogue within a bureaucracy, or between bureaucrats and clients. The "foil" might be a novel, or a movie based upon a novel, which portrays government as corruptly suppressing the truth. A dialogue between bureaucrats, knowledgeable critics, and citizens could illuminate the implicit solutions suggested by authors–problem-solving approaches which puzzle the public sector and may account for its failure to respond to critics. Government too often fails to untangle red tape, to eliminate waste, to treat its clients and employees humanely. From the perspectives of the public and their novelist surrogates, avoidable human tragedies are all too routine. Messages that bureaucracy stifles productivity cannot be dismissed as simplistic, for many social science theories are grounded in the same assumptions.

The same tensions that novelists underscore–bureaucratic control versus individual initiative–have been resurfacing for decades. They have staying power because the problems of bureaucracy are still unsolved, because the organizational sciences have not been able to change most organizations, because bureaucracy is still perceived as violating the public trust. But novels and short stories offer as yet unexploited means for drawing attention to our most basic organizational concerns, and sometimes they underscore the same models that students of government also recommend.

MARC HOLZER AND VATCHE GABRIELIAN

BIBLIOGRAPHY

Adams, Elsie B. and Darrel L. Pugh, 1993. "Decision Making and Melville's 'Billy Budd, Sailor.'" *Public Voices*, vol. 1, no. 1 (Fall 1993) 59–74.
Downey, Lawrence, 1987. "The Use of Selected Fiction in Teaching Public Administration." Paper presented at the first national conference on Public Administration, the Arts, and the Humanities, the New School for Social Research, New York City.
Frederickson, Ronald Q. and H. George Frederickson, 1995. "The Public Poems of Howard Nemerov." *Public Voices*, vol. 1, no. 3 (Winter 1995) 7–22.
Goodsell, Charles and Nancy Murray, eds., 1995. *Public Administration Illuminated and Inspired by the Arts*. Wesport, CT: Praeger.
Gugin, David, 1987. "Bureaucratic Decision Making and Bureaucratic Ethics: An Argument for the Novel." Paper presented at the annual meeting of the American Society for Public Administration, Boston.
Hawthorne, Nathaniel, 1978. *The Scarlet Letter*. Preface, "The Custom House," reprinted in Holzer, Marc, Kenneth Morris and William Ludwin, eds., 1978. *Literature in Bureaucracy*. Wayne, NJ: Avery Publishing Group.
Holzer, Marc, 1993. "Creative Insights into Public Service: Building an Ethical Dialogue." *Public Voices*, vol. 1, no. 1 (Fall 1993) 9–22.
Holzer, Marc, Kenneth Morris and William Ludwin, eds., 1978. *Literature in Bureaucracy*. Wayne, NJ: Avery Publishing Group.
Hummel, Ralph, 1991. "Stories Managers Tell: Why They Are as Valid as Science." *Public Administration Review*, vol. 51, no. 1 (January/February).
Kafka, Franz, 1954. *The Trial*. New York: Penguin Books.
Kesey, Ken, 1962. *One Flew Over the Cuckoo's Nest*. New York: Viking.
Kosinski, Jerzy, 1975. *Cockpit*. New York: Bantam Books, Inc.
Marini, Frank, 1992. "Literature and Public Administration Ethics." *American Review of Public Administration*, vol. 22 (June 1992) 111–125.
Mayakovsky, Vladimir, 1968. "The Bedbug." In *The Complete Plays of Vladimir Mayakovsky*. New York: Clarion Book.
McCurdy, Howard E., 1973. "Fiction, Phenomenology and Public Administration." *Public Administration Review*, vol. 33, no. 1 (January/February) 52–60.
Orwell, George, 1949. *1984*. New York: Harcourt, Brace.
Puffer, Sheila, 1991. *Managerial Insights from Literature*. Boston: PWS-Kent.
Shafritz, Jay M., 1992. *Shakespeare on Management*. New York: Birch Lane Press.
Steinbeck, John, 1939. *The Grapes of Wrath*. New York: Viking Press.
Waldo, Dwight, 1968. *The Novelist on Organization and Administration: An Inquiry into the Relationship Between Two Worlds*. Berkeley: University of California Press.
Zamyatin, Eugene, 1924. *We*. New York: E.P. Dutton.

ADMINISTRATIVE LAW.

That branch of the law that controls the administrative operations of government. Its primary purpose is to keep governmental powers within their legal bounds and to protect individuals against the abuse of such powers. In the American conception, administrative law is concerned with powers and remedies and answers the following questions: (1) What powers may be vested in administrative agencies? (2) What are the limits of those powers? (3) What are the ways in which agencies are kept within those limits?

In answering these questions, administrative law deals with the delegation of powers to administrative agencies; the manner in which those powers must be exercised (emphasizing almost exclusively the procedural requirements imposed on agencies); and judicial review of administrative action. These form the three basic divisions of administrative law: (1) delegation of powers, (2) administrative procedure, and (3) judicial review. This article presents an overview of these three subjects, focusing on the federal system as contrasted with state or local agencies, which have similar principles applicable to them.

Delegation of Powers

Administrative power is as old as the American government itself. The very first session of the First Congress enacted three statutes conferring important administrative powers. Well before the setting up of the Interstate Commerce Commission (ICC) in 1887–the date usually considered the beginning of American administrative law–agencies were established which possessed the rulemaking and/or adjudicatory powers that are usually considered to be characteristic of the administrative agency. Modern

American administrative law, nevertheless, may be said to start with the ICC, the archetype of the contemporary administrative agency. It has served as the model for a whole host of federal and state agencies that were vested with delegated powers patterned after those conferred upon the first federal regulatory commission.

Conscious use of the law to regulate society has required the creation of an ever-growing administrative bureaucracy. The ICC has spawned a progeny that has threatened to exhaust the alphabet in the use of initials to characterize the new bodies. Nor has the expansion of administrative power been limited to ICC-type economic regulation. A trend toward extension into areas of social welfare began with the Social Security Act of 1935. Disability benefits, welfare, aid to dependent children, health care, and a growing list of social services have since come under the guardianship of the administrative process.

During the past quarter century, a new generation of administrative agencies has also been created. These agencies have been a direct product of the increased concern with consumer and environmental protection that has so changed American public law in recent years. The leading agencies among this newer breed are the Environmental Protection Agency, the Occupational Safety and Health Administration, and the Consumer Product Safety Commission.

These agencies promote social, rather than economic, goals. They issue regulations to protect public health and safety and the environment. Virtually every economic activity is affected in some way by federal health, safety, and environmental regulations. In fact, the traditional area of economic regulation is now dwarfed by the growing fields of social health and welfare and environmental concern.

The first prime task of administrative law was to legitimize the vast delegations of power that had been made to administrative agencies, particularly at the time of President Franklin D. Roosevelt's New Deal. Two 1935 decisions of the Supreme Court struck down the most important early New Deal statute on the ground that it contained excessive delegations of power because the authority granted under it was not restricted by what the courts call a defined standard.

The requirement of a defined standard in enabling legislation was imposed by the courts in order to ensure against excessive delegations. The delegation of power must be limited, either by legislative prescription of ends and means, or even of details, or by limitations upon the area of the power delegated. The statute must, in other words, contain a framework within which the administrative action must operate; in the Supreme Court's recent words, it must lay down an "intelligible principle" to which the agency is directed to conform. The "intelligible principle" serves the function of ensuring that fundamental policy decisions will be made, not by some appointed officials, but by the body directly responsible to the people,

the legislature. If there is no guideline in the statute to limit delegations of power, the administrative agency is being given a blank check to make law in the delegated area of authority. In such a case, it is the agency, rather than Congress, that is the primary legislator.

Despite these considerations, it must be conceded that, during the past half century, the courts have moved away from the strict view that laws delegating power must be invalidated unless they contain limiting standards. The 1935 cases are the only ones in which delegations have been invalidated by the Supreme Court. Since then, delegations have been uniformly upheld by the federal courts. Broad delegations have been the characteristic Congressional responses to the endemic crises of the contemporary society. As new crises have arisen, the tendency has been to deal with them by delegating broad power to the executive. When inflation threatens to get out of hand, Congress gives the president power to stabilize prices, rents, and wages. Though there is nothing in the statute beside the bare delegation of stabilization power, the courts rush to sustain the grant, reading into the statute an implied standard which Congress did not bother to put into the statute. When an energy crisis or some other emergency arises, the unchallenged solution is to confer vast chunks of authority on the president, with no attention given to the need to guide or limit the power delegated. The result is that the principle that the Constitution limits Congress in delegating its legislative authority is essentially nugatory, for the courts now require little of Congress when it vests power in administrative agencies.

There has, however, been a countervailing tendency which should be noted. American judges themselves have begun to express dissatisfaction with the trend toward wholesale delegations unrestrained by defined standards. Thus, in a 1993 case, a federal judge declared, "A jurisprudence which allows Congress to implicdly delegate its criminal lawmaking authority to a regulatory agency . . . so long as Congress provides an 'intelligible principle' to guide that agency—is enough to make any judge pause and question what has happened. Deferent and minimal judicial review of Congress's transfer of its . . . lawmaking function to other bodies, in other branches, calls into question the vitality of the tripartite system established by our Constitution."

In 1974, the Supreme Court itself repeated the rule that a delegation of power must be accompanied by discernible standards. And in 1980 and 1981, then Justice, now Chief Justice, William Rehnquist stated that he would rule that the law at issue was invalid because it contained an excessive delegation of legislative power. Some of the most distinguished judges, speaking off the bench, have called for revival of meaningful limitations on delegation of power. It is true that these judicial statements have not yet had effect on case law. But they are significant, as an indication of judicial dissatisfaction which may foreshadow a movement back to the days of enforcement of the defined standards requirement.

Mention should also be made of renewed legislative efforts to control the exercise of delegated powers. The most significant legislative technique developed in this connection was what come to be called the "legislative veto"–exercised through statutory provisions empowering one or both houses of Congress to disapprove agency action by passage of an annulling resolution. The technique is derived from the practice of "laying" delegated legislation before Parliament, subject to annulment by resolution of either house, which has long been an established feature of English administrative law. However, in a 1983 case, the Supreme Court decided that the "legislative veto" technique violates the constitutional requirement of separation of powers.

Administrative Procedure

American administrative law has been based upon Justice Frankfurter's oft-quoted assertion that "the history of liberty has largely been the history of the observance of procedural safeguards." Our system, more than any other, has emphasized administrative procedure (the procedural requirements imposed upon administrative agencies). The starting point in such emphasis has been the constitutional demand of due process. But our law has gone far beyond the constitutional minimum. Building upon the due process foundation, the law has constructed an imposing edifice of formal procedure. The consequence has been a virtual judicialization of American agencies; from the establishment of the Interstate Commerce Commission to the present, much of American administrative process has been set in a modified judicial mold.

One must, however, note that application of the due process requirement in specific cases depends upon the function being exercised by the given administrative agency. In particular, the crucial dividing line is that between rulemaking and adjudication. Rule-making is the administrative equivalent of the legislative process of enacting a statute, under which agencies announce the standards that will apply in the future; compliance with them is as mandatory as compliance with a statute. Agencies engaged in rulemaking are, as a general proposition, no more subject to constitutional procedural requirements than is the legislature engaged in enacting a statute. This means that agencies are freed from the necessity of imitating courts when they are functioning as sublegislatures; except for specific statutory requirements, the procedure to be followed in rulemaking is largely a matter for the agency concerned. Unless a statute requires otherwise, a rule or regulation will normally not be invalid because of agency failure to hold a hearing or to consult or otherwise seek, before promulgation, the views of those affected.

However, the federal Administrative Procedure Act (APA) (a statute enacted by Congress in 1946 that imposes general procedural requirements on all federal administrtive agencies) does impose procedural requirements upon rulemaking. In general, it may be said that the APA provides for a system of antecedent publicity before agencies may engage in substantive rulemaking. General notice of any proposed rulemaking must be published in the *Federal Register* (the official publication in which federal administrative regulations are published). The agency must then afford interested persons the opportunity to participate in the rulemaking process through submission of written data, views, or arguments, with the opportunity to present them orally in some, but not most cases, with all relevant matter so presented to be considered by the agency.

Rulemaking under the APA is often called "notice-and-comment" rulemaking. The APA does not mandate anything like a formal hearing prior to rulemaking. All that it requires is that the agency publish the notice of proposed rulemaking and give interested persons an "opportunity" to participate. The purpose is to work a democratization of the rulemaking process without destroying its flexibility by imposing procedural requirements that are too onerous. It may be true, as Justice Jackson pointed out in a famous opinion, that most people have neither the time nor the interest to read the "voluminous and dull" *Federal Register*. But those subject to administrative authority tend to be members of trade, business, professional, or other organizations interested in the subject areas of a particular agency, who regularly scan the *Register* for relevant notices of proposed rulemaking and then, after alerting their members, send in materials supporting the organization's view to the agency concerned.

If the general principle governing rulemaking is that due process does not require formal procedures before regulations are promulgated, the constitutional principle governing administrative adjudications is the opposite one. The requirement of due process has been interpreted as requiring a formal adversary hearing–what has come to be called an evidentiary hearing–before administrative decisions which adversely affect private individuals may be made. It is with regard to adjudicatory decisions that the American administrative process has, as already noted, been set largely in the judicial mold.

This means that before an administrative decision which adversely affects an individual may be made, that person has a right to an evidentiary hearing, which means a hearing closely approximating a judicial trial. Included in that right is the right to:

1. notice, including an adequate formulation of the subjects and issues involved in the case;
2. present evidence (both testimonial and documentary) and argument;

3. rebut adverse evidence, through cross-examination and other appropriate means;

4. appear with counsel;

5. have the decision based only upon evidence introduced into the record of the hearing;

6. have a complete record, which consists of a transcript of the testimony and arguments, together with the documentary evidence and all other papers filed in the proceeding; and

7. have the agency explain the basis for its decision—an important means of assuring agency adherence to the law, within the broad discretion given on fact, policy, and even legal issues.

Some observers have criticized the requirement of a full hearing with a formal record before administrative adjudications. How can administration be carried on effectively if every administrative decision that affects private rights must be preceded by a trial-type hearing? This question was addressed to the present writer when he testified in 1956 before the Franks Committee investigating administrative law in Britain. Does not the right to a full hearing "tend to gum up the administrative works?"—this was the query asked by a British barrister.

The answer given was a negative one: ". . . in our experience the rights which individuals have are not insisted upon in every case. . . . It does not happen in that way for various reasons, in part the question of expense, in part the fact that there is no point really at issue and therefore no point in going through the formality of a hearing. I have seen the figures in some agencies, and in none of them are full rights insisted upon in more than five percent of the cases. That is what makes the thing workable."

The individual's right to a full hearing does not mean that a full "day in court" must automatically be held in connection with every trifling dispute with which an agency has to deal. If the right to a formal hearing were insisted upon in every case where it exists, it would virtually paralyze administration. But the fact is that the right is asserted in only a very small percentage of the cases. The leading official study of American administrative law noted that hearings were held in less than five percent of the cases disposed of by federal regulatory agencies. In nonregulatory agencies the percentage of hearings is even smaller. During the 1992 fiscal year, the Department of Health and Human Services processed over 100 million claims; in that period some 250,000 HHS hearings were held.

The constitutional right to due process gives the individual affected a right to an evidentiary hearing. Like other constitutional rights, the right to be heard can be waived. The vast bulk of agency decisions are made without resort to formal proceedings, because the right is waived most of the time.

Three important developments with regard to adjudicatory procedure should be noted. The first is the extension of the right to an evidentiary hearing from the older field of regulatory administration to the burgeoning benefactory apparatus of the welfare state. Before 1970, the latter was still beyond the due process boundary, since there was a constitutional right to procedural safeguards only in cases where the administrative decision adversely affected the individual in his *rights*. If the individual was being given something by government to which he had no preexisting "right," he was being given a mere "privilege" and was "not entitled to protection under the due process clause."

All this was changed by the landmark decision in *Goldberg v. Kelly,* 397 U.S. 254 (1970), which held that public assistance payments to an individual might not be terminated without affording that person an opportunity for an evidentiary hearing. The Court specifically rejected the rule that there was no right to a hearing because public assistance was a mere "privilege." "The constitutional challenge," declared the Court, "cannot be answered by an argument that public assistance benefits are a 'privilege' and not a 'right.'" It is no longer accurate to think of welfare benefits as only privileges. "Such benefits are a matter of statutory entitlement for persons qualified to receive them." In this sense, they are "more like 'property' than a 'gratuity.'"

The same reasoning applies to other cases involving social welfare benefits, particularly those under the Social Security Act—the federal statute which provides for extensive programs of Old Age, Survivors, and Disability Insurance, as well as Aid to Families with Dependent Children, Supplemental Security Income, and other social welfare programs. The Supreme Court has, however, held more recently that, with regard to some of these federal benefactory programs, not involving dire need, the required evidentiary hearing may be held after the payments to the individual concerned have been terminated by the agency concerned.

Secondly, the Supreme Court has recently been following a cost-benefit approach to the question of the particular procedures to be required in an administrative proceeding. The Court has indicated that that question is to be determined under a tripartite test that requires the balancing of: (a) the private interests affected; (b) the risk of an erroneous determination through the process accorded and the probable value of added procedural safeguards; and (c) the public interest and administrative burdens, including costs that the additional procedures would involve.

The Court has used the cost-benefit test to decide that the exclusionary rule (which bars the admission of illegally seized evidence in a criminal trial) does not apply in an administrative hearing to determine whether an alien should be deported. The Court's analysis concludes that the costs involved in applying the rule in such an administrative proceeding far exceed the benefits to be secured from excluding the evidence in the given case. The decision has been criticized as reducing basic rights to the level of the counting house, but it has been followed by other courts.

The third important development with regard to adjudicatory procedure concerns the important changes made in the processes of hearing and decision in federal agencies by the Administrative Procedure Act. Unlike the first two, which are based on the Constitution, and thus apply to state agencies also, the APA is limited to federal entities, although most states have similar laws applicable to their agencies. The APA set up within each agency a corps of independent hearing officers originally called hearing examiners. These examiners, who were given powers comparable to those of judges in the courts, were to preside over evidentiary hearings. Under APA, examiners were empowered to issue initial decisions, which became the decisions of the agencies concerned unless those decisions were appealed.

What the APA did was to set up within each agency the equivalent of first-instance and appellate tribunals. The first-instance level was to be at the hearing stage, before an independent hearing official vested with the power to make a decision, subject to appeal to the agency heads, who were thus relegated to the apellate level. More recently, there has been a further judicialization of the trial level. The hearing officers provided under the APA have envolved into an administrative judiciary, endowed with authority to make binding decisions (subject to appeals to the agency heads) in adjudicatory proceedings. In 1978, Congress confirmed this development by a statute which expressly changed the title of APA hearing examiners to administrative law judges.

The evolution of hearing officers under the APA, culminating in their judicial status as administrative law judges, has set the pattern for the developing system of administrative justice. In particular, we can project a continuing increase in the size of the administrative judicial corps. When the APA provisions went into effect, the federal agencies employed 197 examiners. In 1992, there were over 1,200 ALJs in thirty federal agencies; over 70 percent (850) were in the Social Security Administration, reflecting the impact of that agency's mass justice upon the administrative process. Only the fiscal squeeze of recent years has prevented the number from rising substantially higher. The Social Security Administration alone projects an administrative law judge corps of well over 1,000 in the next decade. In the next century, we can predict that there may well be a federal administrative judiciary running into the thousands and administrative law judges in ever-increasing numbers dispensing both regulatory justice and the mass justice of an expanding welfare state.

Judicial Review

Judicial review is the balance wheel of administrative law. It enables practical effect to be given to the basic theory upon which administrative power is based. As the Supreme Court has explained it, "When Congress passes an Act empowering administrative agencies to carry on governmental activities, the power of those agencies is circumscribed by the authority granted." The responsibility of enforcing the limits of statutory grants of authority is a judicial function: when an agency oversteps its legal bounds, the courts will intervene. Without judicial review, statutory limits would, to paraphrase Thomas Hobbes, be naught but empty words.

The overriding principle with regard to judicial review is that in favor of the availability of review. Judicial review of administrative action is the rule and nonreviewability an exception which must be demonstrated. In federal administrative law, the original English common law system of review has been superseded by an elaborate statutory system. Federal statutes creating administrative agencies generally provide for judicial review of the acts of those agencies. But the mere failure of Congress to provide specifically by statute for judicial review is no evidence of intent to withhold review.

On the contrary, the omission of review provisions by the legislature gives an administrative agency no immunity from the normal judicial scrutiny of the legality of its actions. The Supreme Court has stated that "judicial review of a final agency action by an aggrieved person will not be cut off unless there is persuasive reason to believe that such was the purpose of Congress." Mere legislative silence is not such "persuasive reason"; it indicates only that the legislature intended to leave the individual to the general review remedies available in American administrative law: the nonstatutory remedies derived from English law, as well as that under the federal Administrative Procedure Act, since there is a general provision for judicial review in the APA. To hold otherwise would be contrary to the *ultra vires* theory upon which the American system is based, under which administrative power is limited to the authority granted by statute.

A similar result is reached even when a statute contains a provision which appears to prohibit judicial review. Thus, judicial review is available despite the fact that a statute provides that the challenged administrative decision "shall be final." This is the approach that is normally followed.

Indeed, interpretation of such a provision to prohibit all judicial review might raise a difficult constitutional question. In the oft-quoted words of Justice D. Brandeis, "The supremacy of law demands that there shall be an opportunity to have some court decide . . . whether the proceedings in which the facts were adjudicated was conducted regularly." In American administrative law, where an administrative order impinges directly upon personal or property rights, there is a constitutional right of judicial review. The Constitution does not permit the legislature to shield administrative agencies from all judicial scrutiny.

As far as the scope of judicial review is concerned, all systems of administrative law make a basic distinction between questions of law and questions of fact. The former are for the judge, the latter for the administrator. Hence, there is full review of questions of law, but only limited review of questions of fact. In American administrative law the scope of review of facts is limited by the so-called substantial evidence rule. Under it, the reviewing court looks only to see whether the administrative finding of fact is supported by substantial evidence, that is, such evidence as a reasonable mind might accept as adequate to support a conclusion. There is broader review of agency decisions on questions of law. But the so-called Chevron doctrine, announced by the Supreme Court in 1984, narrows judicial review of administrative interpretations of statutes. Under Chevron, the administrative agency, not the reviewing court, has the primary role in statutory interpretation. Chevron requires the courts to give effect to a reasonable administration interpretation of a statute even if the court would have interpreted the statute differently. For a more detailed analysis, see scope of review.

Freedom of Information

Mention should also be made of the Freedom of Information Act (FOIA) enacted by Congress in 1966. Before then, the people's "right to know" was a journalistic slogan rather than a legal right. The 1966 statute changed this since it gave any person, with no showing of any specific need, a legally enforceable right of access to government files and documents. The FOIA effects a profound alteration in the position of the citizen vis-à-vis government. No longer is the individual seeking information from an administrative agency a mere suppliant. In signing the new law, the president said, with pardonable inaccuracy, that it entitled Americans to "all the information that the security of the nation permits."

This is not the place for a detailed analysis of the Freedom of Information Act. Some understanding of its basic thrust is, however, essential to those interested in administrative law. Under the key FOIA provision, on request for identifiable records, each federal agency shall make the records promptly available to any person. If they are not so made available, the federal district courts are given jurisdiction to enjoin the agency from withholding records and to order the production of records improperly withheld from complainant. In the court action, the normal rules governing actions against agencies give way in two vital respects. The normal rules are (1) that agency acts have a presumption of validity, and the individual challenging them has the burden of proving their invalidity and (2) that the scope

of review of challenged agency action is limited. Under the key provision of the FOIA, (1) the court shall determine the matter *de novo,* and (2) the burden is on the agency to sustain its action in withholding information.

This means that the complainant does not have to overcome any presumption in favor of the correctness of the agency's action. All a complainant must allege in an action under the FOIA is that he made a request for identifiable records which the agency turned down. The burden then shifts to the agency to justify its refusal. It can normally meet this burden only by showing that the records involved fall within one of the nine exceptions excluded from the statute. Disclosure is made the general rule, and only information specifically exempted by the act may now be withheld. Where the records called for in a given complaint do not come within the exceptions, the court must order their production—there is no residual discretion to withhold beyond that given by Congress.

BERNARD SCHWARTZ

BIBLIOGRAPHY

Davis, Kenneth C. and Richard J. Pierce, Jr., 1994. *Administrative Law Treatise,* 3d ed. Boston: Little Brown.
Koch, Charles H., Jr., 1985. *Administrative Law and Practice.* St. Paul, MN: West Publishing Co.
Schwartz, Bernard, 1991. *Administrative Law,* 3d ed. Boston: Little Brown.
Warren, Kenneth F., 1996. *Administrative Law in the Political System,* 3d ed. Englewood Cliffs, NJ: Prentice Hall.

ADMINISTRATIVE LAW JUDGE.

A federal or state judicial officer designated by federal or state law to hear and determine adjudicatory claims or disputes involving federal or state administrative law. Generally the term "administrative law judge" refers to federal hearing officers who hear and decide claims or disputes arising in the various administrative agencies of the United States. Many departments of the federal government have such "judges" to adjudicate claims or disputes concerning federal administrative law. State administrative law judges hear and decide cases such as claims under the workers' compensation laws. The administrative law judges in the federal system resolve issues that arise in the administrative agencies and independent regulatory agencies.

Administrative law judges are not positions created by the U.S. Constitution but are akin to a United States District Judge in the federal judicial system, and are created by statute or regulation to hear and decide issues.

Originally called "hearing officers" or "hearing examiners," the modern administrative law judge is "functionally comparable" to the trial judge. The process of federal agency adjudication is structured presently to guarantee that the administrative law judge employs independent judgment in weighing the evidence, free from the pressures of the parties and other agency officials. When the head of the agency approves the decision of the administrative law judge, that decision is final for purposes of judicial review.

There are some 30 federal departments and agencies that have some 1,200 administrative law judges. By far, the Social Security Administration has the most judges who hear and determine the thousands of claims filed under the Social Security Act.

Administrative law judges in the federal system are selected only after rigorous testing, written and oral, and long legal experience. An agency selects its judges from a register of eligible candidates after a comprehensive screening examination, rating process, and selection by the Office of Personnel Management.

Once chosen and employed as a federal officer, the administrative law judge may not perform investigative or prosecutorial functions inconsistent with judicial responsibility. The administrative law judge presides over an adjudicatory hearing and assures that the parties are given due process and treated fairly and impartially. The judges preside at administrative agency hearings and have broad adjudicative powers.

Administrative law judges are authorized and appointed by federal administrative agencies pursuant to the Administrative Procedure Act, adopted by Congress and signed by President Truman in 1946. Under that act, hearings before administrative agencies are to be conducted by a federal administrative law judge, and such judge has powers to administer oaths, rule on relevant evidence, regulate the course of the hearing, make or recommend decisions, and make findings of fact and conclusions of law.

A decision by a federal administrative law judge, when made final by the head of the department, is, under the Administrative Procedure Act, subject to limited judicial review. The federal judiciary may set aside the agency action for various reasons including a decision which is not supported by substantial evidence.

The following federal agencies employ administrative law judges:

Agriculture Department
Commerce Department
Commodity Futures Trading Commission
Education Department
Environmental Protection Agency
Federal Communications Commission
Federal Energy Regulatory Commission
Federal Labor Relations Authority
Federal Maritime Commission
Federal Mine Safety and Health Review Commission
Federal Trade Commission
Health and Human Services Department
Food and Drug Administration
Departmental Appeals Board
Social Security Administration
Housing and Urban Development Department
Interior Department

Justice Department
Drug Enforcement Administration
Immigration Review
Labor Department
Merit Systems Protection Board
National Labor Relations Board
National Transportation Safety Board
Nuclear Regulatory Commission
Occupational Safety and Health Review Commission
Securities and Exchange Commission
Small Business Administration
Transportation Department
Office of the Secretary
U.S. Coast Guard
U.S. International Trade Commission
U.S. Postal Service

JOSEPH J. SIMEONE

BIBLIOGRAPHY

Davis, Kenneth C. and Richard J. Pierce, Jr., 1994. *Administrative Law Treatise,* 3rd ed. vol. 1. Boston: Little, Brown.
Warren, Kenneth F., 1997. *Administrative Law in the American System,* 3rd ed., abridged. Upper Saddle River, NJ: Prentice Hall.

ADMINISTRATIVE MODERNIZATION IN AFRICAN DEVELOPING COUNTRIES.

The two-step process of conflict and compromise, involving the imposition of colonial institutions on native institutions, and then the modification of those colonial systems upon the achievement of independence for those countries.

Background

Administrative modernization in African developing countries began with (1) the African administrative tradition, the native-grown administration which was basically driven by village values, mores, and customs, followed by (2) the colonial administration which was essentially a European administration modified to suit the colonized areas, and (3) the hodgepodge administration models—a mixture of the African-grown administration and the European style which have emerged since the gaining of independence by African countries and other developing countries. Accordingly, this article is organized into three sections. The first section defines and discusses briefly the African administrative tradition that provides the foundation upon which modernization has been built. The second section reviews colonial administration; and the third and final part discusses the types of administrations which have evolved since the 1960s when most of the African and other developing countries gained their independence.

In the African administrative tradition, social and quasipolitical structures were set up in a hierarchical manner. The administrative structure consisted of the following units: the family, clan, and village. The family unit was the base unit and served as the foundation upon which the rest of the administrative structures depended.

Each unit had well-defined functions as well as the role expected of the leadership in each unit. For example, in the family unit, the husband was the administrator in such matters as family finance, discipline, education, and apprenticeship. However, he deferred to the eldest man in the family, who was the overall administrator in such matters as land sharing and in settling disputes among brothers or issues concerning the role of women.

In the clan unit, which encompasses several families who are related, a leader was appointed the head of the clan. The leader of the clan was chosen based on his respect for elders, his accomplishments in wrestling, excellent farming skills, and a display of native intelligence.

In the village unit, the leadership was provided by a chief who was either appointed by the village or inherited the title and its functions. It was the duty of a village chief to ensure that law and order were strictly enforced, customs and mores preserved for generations to come. Infractions of customs and traditions were swiftly addressed and offenders punished according to the severity of infraction. While there were no written rules or regulations that governed the administrative tradition, the village customs, values, and mores were all the rules needed to keep the administration functioning efficiently. As a result of the hierarchial structure of the administrative tradition, each unit was expected to resolve a problem that was within its bounds and only when it could not resolve a problem was that issue referred to the next higher unit. For example, a family problem must be first addressed in the family unit. If a family could not resolve the issue, the next unit to which the problem was referred to was the clan unit. If for any reason the clan unit was unable to resolve the problem, which was rare, it was then referred to the village chief, who consulted with the village elders and the heads of each clan to resolve the issue.

All issues were addressed based on the village values, customs, and mores. The African administrative tradition viewed from the perspective of modern administration may seem primitive and authoritarian, but upon close examination, the village administration exhibited traces of democratic principles, albeit informal ones. The African administrative tradition operated on village values, customs, and community mores until the advent of colonialism. As Chinua Achebe (1959) in his book *Things Fall Apart* craftily and arrestingly portrayed, things began falling apart when the African administrative tradition was replaced by the colonial administration.

The Colonial Administration

The first assault on the native administration came from early Christian missionaries. The missionaries attacked the customs and traditions of the natives, describing them as primitive and ungodly. For example, in the African administrative tradition, land disputes were settled by one person swearing on an oracle claiming that he owned the land. Once a family member swore on an oracle against another family member the dispute was settled. The two families who participated in the oracle swearing were forbidden to eat together until after several years, when a certain rite was performed by a village priest if both family members were still alive. It was against this background that the missionaries preached that the native gods and oracles were false gods. When Okonkwo, the village chief in *Things Fall Apart*, saw that his village customs and traditions were being assaulted, he fought back by destroying the newly constructed missionary church house. What Okonkwo, the village chief, did not realize in time was that the missionary—in addition to bringing new religion which was completely at odds with the native religion—was also accompanied by a new government.

Under this new government, most of the functions that were performed by village chiefs and elders were taken over by District Commissioners who built court houses where they judged cases and sentenced people to prison. Okonkwo was jailed for weeks for destroying the church building. The imprisonment of Okonkwo shocked the village to the core and they never quite recovered from the shock. Gradually it dawned on the village people that their native-grown administration was irrevocably changed. Disputes, criminal cases, and the like, which before the arrival of the missionaries and the colonial government were settled by chiefs and clan heads, were now settled by District Commissioners. Instead of clan heads, carrying messages to the village people, the District Commissioners appointed police constables who arrested people and carried messages to the people affected. Instead of relying on customs and traditions as the basis for law and order in the community, education and religion were introduced to attenuate the influence of customs and traditions.

Gradually, the native administration was replaced by colonial administration, which relied on District Commissioners as the chief administrators, and the chiefs were assigned subservient roles and functions. The most modernizing factor as always was education. The colonial government, in order to ensure a successful and lasting campaign, began investing in education and soon some of the natives were trained in the ways of European administration.

The model of colonial administration consisted of district Commissioners, District officers, police constables, tax collectors, and civil servants. In the civil service, the highest ranking officer was the permanent secretary, who reported to the District Commissioner. Civil servants were told that they were the servants of the people and were expected to serve the people. But this was in name only, for the civil servants instead of treating the public as the masters treated the public as servants and themselves as masters. This is the legacy of the colonial administration that most of the African countries inherited. This model of administration consisting of a pyramidal structure has remained one of the models of administrations which many African countries have practiced even after gaining their independence. The next section examines the administrations which have evolved since most African countries gained their independence.

Post-Independence Administration

There is no definitive theory or theories which can summarize the models of administrations that have evolved since most African countries gained their independence. Rather, evidence points to a hodgepodge of models of administrations comprising half-copied European models mixed with structures of native-grown administration.

Most of the developing countries, upon the attainment of independence, retained the administrative structures that were setup during the colonial administration. However, as time progressed, the type of political and governmental machinery that has developed is one that is dominated by self-seeking elites and privileged classes (Mehmet, 1978). In addition, the government was and is still divided along tribal or ethnic lines.

As a result of this type of administration—divided along tribal lines led by self-seeking elites—the normal social institutions such as the legal system, and the bureaucracy, and the educational system that ordinarily would serve the public serve only those who have the means and access to the system. For example, as articulated by Ozay Mehmet, "the new industrialists are typically the wealthy and privileged families with kinship links to politicians and officials controlling the decision making process" (1978, p. 25).

There are two main distinguishing features of this type of administration. The first is the tribal nature of the administrative structures. Once the political system was controlled by a certain tribe, all key administrative positions were held by persons from the ruling tribe. Appointments were made regardless of training backgrounds and qualifications. The only relevant qualification was belonging to the tribe that was in power. Additionally, appointees and other bureaucrats made sure that most of the services were channelled to their tribes.

The second aspect of the tribal administration was its urban focus. Most developments were in the urban areas at the expense of rural areas. This concentration of services in the urban areas may partly explain why the movement of rural people to urban areas continues.

This model of administration, in which only the privileged had access to a system which operated along tribal lines, held sway for most of the developing countries until the late 1970s when another form of administration evolved: the military administration.

By the late 1970s, it had become clear that the military had emerged as a competing political organization in developing countries. This is because by the end of the 1970s nearly all developing counties had at least one military administration. Some countries at this time had experienced more than three military administrations. By the 1980s Nigeria had experienced more military administrations than any other country in Africa.

The structure of the military administrations can be summarized in two categories. In the first category, the military completely monopolizes the political arena and rules by fiat. Here the military rules as it sees fit and ignores the rules governing normal institutions such as the judicial, the bureaucracy, and the governance system. The military effects these changes by first setting up a military supreme council, which replaces the executive branch of the government and assumes absolute authority over any other ruling body, including the judicial branch. Usually, the supreme military council, consisting of the military leader and several highly placed military heads, sets policies by fiat or decrees. New policies are executed by other military officers serving at the regional and local levels who are appointed by the supreme council.

At the regional and local levels, the military officers appoint hand-picked bureaucrats who serve at their pleasure in managing the bureaucracies under the direction of the military heads. Only those services deemed necessary by the military leaders are provided.

The judicial system also serves at the pleasure of the military. Because the judicial system dispenses justice according to the dictates of the military establishment, the judicial system is one of the most corrupt institutions in developing countries. As Kilson's 1992 article in *The Economist* pointed out, Nigeria, like most other developing countries, has many fine lawyers, but the judiciary is tainted by trials settled with bribes. The bureaucracy is not different from the judicial system. The level of services provided by bureaucrats to the citizenry and the community is also contingent upon the level of bribery offered.

The other type of military administration is the quasi-military-democratic administrative structure. In this model, the military appoints some civilians as tokens to serve in the supreme military council. The inclusion of token civilians in the military ruling council offers the appearance of a military administration functioning under democratic values and institutions. Scholars have dubbed this type of model military-democratic governance, which is at best an oxymoron. A military administration that rules by decrees cannot by any stretch of imagination be a democratic system of governance, the number of civilians involved notwithstanding. The outcomes of the military form of administrations have been disastrous to say the least, both politically and economically. As Barber B. Conable, president of the World Bank put it, in 1990: "In the 30 years since most African countries gained independence, the region's living standards have declined, and its infrastructure has decayed. Great expectations have been betrayed, leaving sub-Sahara Africa one of the poorest areas in the world (p. 3)."

The many years of a wealth-grabbing, autocratic client state relationships that have prevailed in most developing countries have resulted in the marginalization of basic institutions necessary for stability, growth, and democracy. More importantly, this has turned the continent into a battle ground of contending dooms such as overpopulation, poverty, starvation, corruption, and vanishing resources (Kilson, 1992).

As a consequence of the failure of the military administrations in developing countries, citizens in most of these countries have begun to demand the establishment of democratic institutions that will truly serve the people—ones that will have nothing to do with any form of military administrations. The military as a modernizing factor in administration is begging for a change. A new administrative order is needed in developing countries.

DAMIEN EJIGIRI

BIBLIOGRAPHY

Achebe, Chinua, 1959. *Things Fall Apart*. Greenwich, CT: Fauxett Crest.
Conable, Barber, 1990. "Reflections on Africa: The priority of Sub-Sahara Africa in Economic Development." Addresses to the Bretton Woods Committee Conference on Africa's Finance and Development Crisis, Washington, D.C., April 25.
Finkle, Jason and Richard Gable, 1966. *Political Development and Social Change*. New York: John Wiley and Sons, Inc.
Grugler, Joseph and William Flannagan, 1978. *Urbanization and Social Change in West Africa*. Cambridge, London, New York: Cambridge University Press.
Kilson, Martin, 1992. "Thinking about African Re-democratization." Discussion paper prepared for Colloquium on the Economics of Political Liberation in Africa, Harvard University.
———, 1993. *The Economist*, (Aug. 21–27).
Mehmet, Ozay, 1978. *Economic Planning and Social Justice in Developing Countries*. New York: St. Martin's Press.

ADMINISTRATIVE MORALITY.

Recognizing that one is a fiduciary of the public trust and responsibly serving the public interest with honesty, fairness, and integrity while overseeing the operations of government.

Administrative morality in public administration is a difficult concept to define. "Administrative" refers to those persons who occupy positions of authority within government. They perform the duties identified by Gulick in his 1937 report for the Brownlow Commission as POSDCORB: planning, organizing, staffing, directing, coordinating, reporting and budgeting. They may perform these functions at the executive, managerial, or supervisory levels. They may be political appointees, career civil servants, or simply persons who earn their living in federal, state, or local governments and in not-for-profit organizations. Administrators are those who carry on the business of government by ensuring that equitable and legitimate services are delivered efficiently and fairly. They are often called bureaucrats because they work in a bureaucracy.

"Morality" refers to both character and behavior. It is a term that captures who one is, as well as what one does. Moral administrators are honest and honorable. They can tell right from wrong. They serve the public interest with integrity and justice. They put the interest of the government and citizens above their own personal interest. They have an inner core of strength which enables them to make difficult decisions, and they live their commitment to uphold the law of their land.

John Rohr, an American scholar, says that administrative morality is a function of the regime, that is, of the fundamental political order of a country. In his book *Ethics for Bureaucrats* (1989), Rohr argues that unless an administrator believes in the value and morality of the underlying political order of his or her country, issues of administrative morality are impossible to address. One cannot retain personal morality while enforcing laws or implementing programs of a fundamentally immoral regime.

The concept of administrative morality implies that private virtue extends to public virtue. Dennis Thompson, in his discussion of "Integrity in the Public Service" (1992), explains, "Personal ethics originates in face to face relations among individuals, and it aims to make people morally better. Political ethics arises from the need to set standards for impersonal relations among people who may never meet, and it seeks only to make public policy better by making public officials more accountable." In other words, administrative morality requires both good character and just behavior. It is the opposite of administrative corruption, which is the abuse of one's governmental role to promote one's private advantage.

Origin and Subsequent History

Administrative morality has been a topic of discussion for more than twenty centuries. This brief description of its history is not meant to be comprehensive, but illustrative. In China, Confucius (c. 500 B.C.E.) taught that those who enter public service must have high moral virtue, seek after knowledge, and have a propensity toward action which maintains justice and peace. In the Judaic-Christian tradition, humankind is asked to love mercy, do justice, and walk humbly with their deity. The fourth century (B.C.E.)

philosopher Aristotle provided a framework for understanding morality that continues to influence thinking about administrative morality today.

Aristotle's vision of morality is described by Glenn Tinder in *Political Thinking: The Perennial Questions* (1991): "living well is not doing just as one pleases but depends on understanding and adhering to a pattern of life that is valid for all human beings; discovery of this pattern requires unusual insight as well as the gradual development of tradition; most people, therefore, need society to provide moral illumination and structure for their lives; government is the principal agent of society and thus is properly involved in the fulfillment of society's moral responsibilities" (p. 176).

How, then does the moral administrator act in his or her role as "principal agent"? Tinder explains, "Moreover the moral responsibilities of government should be carried out less through coercion than through example, through education, and through the respect, rather than fear, inspired by the laws" (p. 176).

Justice is an important theme through the centuries of discussion about administrative morality, although, historically, scholars have not agreed on what is meant by justice. For Aristotle in the fourth century justice meant distribution in accordance with merit. For Marxist philosophers, justice means distribution in accordance with need.

In her book *Six Theories of Justice* Lebacqz (1986) captures the complexity when she raises these questions: "Does justice require maximizing utility, benefiting the least advantaged, accepting the consequences of choice, honoring human dignity, treating equally, or liberating the poor and oppressed?" These questions remain critical as one explores the definition of administrative morality, for, indeed, the moral administrator must "do justice and act with benevolence and integrity" (Denhardt, 1991).

The founders of the United States were convinced that humankind are creatures of self-interest, and determined that the only way that administrative morality could be ensured was thorough a constitutional system of checks and balances. James Madison, who has been called the philosopher of the U.S. Constitution, explained in *Federalist* No. 51, "If men were angels, no government would be necessary. . . . In framing a government which is to be administered by men over men, the great difficulty lies in this: you must first enable the government to control the governed; and in the next place oblige it to control itself."

Professional and scholarly discussion of administrative morality in the field of public administration began in the United States in the late nineteenth century. In a reaction to populist government the earliest scholars, namely Eaton (1880) and Wilson (1887), cast administrative morality in terms of efficiency and productivity. Terry Cooper, in his introductory chapter to the *Handbook of Administrative Ethics* (1994), explains, "Although the Progressives were

concerned about the unfairness of unequal treatment of the citizenry based on willingness to lend support to a political machine, they were even more disturbed by the inefficiency of these informal governments. . . . One comes away with the impression that the more serious defect in machine government was thought to be its inefficiency rather than its lack of justice or liberty. Ethical conduct (administrative morality) for the Progressives was efficient action. " (p. 4).

Thus, the origin and history of a concern with administrative morality stretches through the centuries. Although neither serious scholars nor practicing administrators have come to a firm agreement on what is meant by the term, they do agree that it is necessary for good government. They also agree that it somehow entails an element of justice, and that it is both a part of the fiber of the administrator and the results of administrative actions. What they're not as certain about is how to ensure administrative morality.

Underlying Theoretical Framework

In this latter part of the twentieth century, there is not yet an underlying theoretical framework of administrative morality. Rather there is a conglomerate group of scholars, each investigating and theorizing about some small part of what it means to be a moral administrator, or how a government or a citizenry encourages administrative morality, or how administrative morality can be taught, encouraged, or enforced. Today's scholarly divergence is rooted in what has come to be known as the "Friedrich-Finer debate."

Begun in the late 1930s, the debate was summarized by Finer (1941) as follows: "My chief difference with Professor Friedrich was and is my insistence upon distinguishing responsibility as an arrangement of correction and punishment even up to dismissal both of politicians and officials, while he believed and believes in reliance upon responsibility as a sense of responsibility, largely unsanctioned, except by deference or loyalty to professional standards."

This debate has continued in one form or another through the years. In 1995, it has become a part of two large frameworks which Brent Wall (1991) calls the "bureaucratic ethos" and the "democratic ethos." Within the bureaucratic ethos paradigm, the public administrator is viewed as a technocrat who is employed to follow directions, and who requires control mechanisms to insure responsible moral conduct. Administrative morality here is couched in terms of technical expertise and efficient government service. Within this paradigm, public administrators are viewed as functionaries, not critically responsible humans. Their authority is predicated upon Weber's *zwerkrationale:* legal rational authority. In this set of assumptions, administrative morality emerges from a system of legitimation rather than a system of values. Here the moral dilemma is how to enforce the rules—what is known as how to get administrators to "do the thing right."

The democratic ethos, on the other hand, places administrative morality in a societal framework, where the moral administrator is described in relation to regime values, citizenship, serving the public interest, and commitment to social equity. The democratic ethos calls for responsive and responsible decisionmakers who are able to define the ethical dimensions of a problem, and to identify and respond to an ethic of public service. Those who argue for a democratic ethos in administrative ethics suggest that no public servant is insulated from politics, and that simply following the rules may be an inadequate moral response. Within the philosophy of a democratic ethos lies the recognition that a public administrator may be required to choose between two equally legal possibilities, and must, therefore determine "to do the right thing."

The horns of the dilemma can be captured in the current concerns worldwide about controlling corruption in government. The bureaucratic functionary carrying out carefully prescribed technical responsibilities will have little opportunity to act corruptly, to counter, or even to report corruption of political officials. Bureaucracy is predicated upon control by laws and sanctions. The bureaucrat whose behavior must be controlled is seen as a technocrat, not a moral actor. As the nineteenth century philosopher de Tocqueville pointed out, it takes moral effort to probe for personal insight. An emphasis on following the rules diminishes the ability to make moral judgments.

On the other hand, the public administrator who is a responsible citizen first is not so easily controllable. This administrator exercises discretion, rather than blind obedience. For an administrator seeking to "do the right thing," John Rohr (1988) suggests that the moral problem is "how to exercise his discretionary powers in a responsible manner even though he is not formally accountable to the electorate" (p. 170). Here, administrative morality requires integrity, which has been characterized by Dobel (1990) as "regime accountability, personal responsibility, and prudence." Such integrity may mean that the public employee is less controllable, but more responsible.

The ideological difference between controlled behavior and socially responsible behavior is captured in what's known as the ethical "low" and "high" roads. The "low road" is reactive and negative. It emphasizes compliance, and can result in adherence to the letter of the law while the intent of the law goes unaddressed. The "low road" focuses on prohibiting wrongdoing and requires elaborate rules with strict enforcement procedures. Here administrative morality can be described as obedience and compliance.

The "high road" is an affirmative strategy that expects administrative discretion, encourages ethical behavior, and deters, rather than merely detects, problems. The "high road" is proactive and affirming. It is the road of people

with high standards. Here administrative morality can be described as responsible, responsive behavior at its best.

What kinds of administrators are able to take the high road? They were first described by Stephen Bailey in a 1964 article in *Public Administration Review*. Bailey identified three mental attitudes and three moral qualities necessary for administrative morality. Public servants, he said, must have the qualities of optimism, courage, and fairness tempered by charity. These qualities will interact to enable the administrator to overcome the inadequate information, ambiguity, and indecision that are inherent in the government workplace. Bailey's description of administrative morality is the foundation upon which the current discussion of virtue and ethics are based.

Clearly there is disagreement about how to describe administrative morality and how to ensure it. As Jos (1990) noted, "Public administration's attempts to develop an account of the morally responsible administrator now span 50 years, and while the effort has been worthwhile, the results have been disappointing."

Current Practice in the United States

According to John Rohr (1989) in his study of administrative ethics in four countries:

> Ethics in American public administration falls conveniently into two major categories—the legally enforceable and the aspirational. The first deals almost exclusively with financial irregularities in such matters as bribery, conflict of interest, and financial disclosure. For the most part, these questions are governed more by statutory construction than by constitutional principle. The second category goes beyond legal obligation and looks for practical ways in which civil servants might operationalize their oath to uphold the constitution of the United States (p. 505).

Current practice in the United States can be illustrated by the results of recent surveys. Patrick Dobel's (1990) survey of U.S. government employees indicates that 22.4 percent of the respondents believe that public organizations follow the "low road," with "a reactive, legalistic, blame-punishment approach that focuses on discouraging and detecting unethical behavior among public employees." The "high road" was much less evident in this survey, with only 7 percent of the respondents reporting that their organizations utilize "proactive, human-development, problem-solving approaches that focus on encouraging ethical behavior and deterring unethical behavior." Notably, 63.9 percent of the respondents believed that "most organizations have no consistent approach."

A survey of members of the American Society for Public Administration (Bowman, 1990) yielded similar results, with 7 percent of the respondents reporting that their organizations utilize a "high road" to ethics, while nearly one-fourth report a "low road" approach (p. 347).

The most comprehensive collection of empirical research on current practices in regard to administrative morality in the Unites States is contained in Frederickson (1993), *Ethics and Public Administration*. Cooper's (1994) *Handbook of Administrative Ethics* provides extensive discussions about administrative morality by the most distinguished scholars in the field.

Variations of Practice

Variations occur in how persons in different countries name their concern with administrative morality. In the United States, most scholars refer to "administrative ethics," while in many other countries the emphasis is on "controlling corruption." Ethics and corruption are, of course, opposites of one another. Ethical people act rightly. Corrupt people deviate from norms of good and appropriate behavior. The difference in terminology, however, reflects a profound difference in underlying assumptions about the nature of humankind. Those who seek to control corruption most surely expect malpractice, and strive to prevent it. Those who reflect upon *administrative morality* expect responsible behavior, and endeavor to encourage it.

What is called administrative morality may also vary according to culture and regime values. Cooper's (1994) *Handbook of Administrative Ethics* contains a section called "Administrative Ethics in Other Cultures," which describes the different practices in China, Canada, France, the United Kingdom, the United States, Zimbabwe, and Australia.

In a survey of municipal clerks in Australia, Canada, Cyprus, Great Britain, Israel, Malaysia, Netherlands, New Zealand, Switzerland, South Africa, and the United States, Bruce (1994) found few statistically significant differences between the responses of persons in the United States and persons in the other countries. In cities where respondents reported that "most people employed in my city are ethical," certain conditions exist. These include: government-provided education and guidelines about what is legal and what is not, organizational sanctions which define punishment for corrupt behavior, a municipal code which clearly defines expected standards, and citizens who would be outraged if those standards were violated in their government.

This survey indicates that administrative morality is more likely to occur in a climate where government employees have high personal standards, where supervisors encourage truth, and where employees regularly come together to discuss ethical problems. These are statistically interrelated activities that represent ethical "high road" conditions. These activities emerge from assumptions that public employees exhibit responsible behavior when encouraged to do so. They support Dobel's (1990) argument

in his "Integrity in the Public Service" that no one approach to encouraging administrative morality is sufficient.

WILLA MARIE BRUCE

BIBLIOGRAPHY

Bailey, Stephen, 1964. "Ethics and the Public Service." *Public Administration Review*, vol. 24, 234–243.

Bowman, James, 1990. "Ethics in Government: A National Survey of Public Administrators." *Public Administration Review*, vol. 50, no. 3, 345–353.

Bruce, Willa, 1994. "Controlling Corruption in Municipal Governments Around the Globe." In Urie Berlinsky, A. Friedberg, B. Wemer, eds., *Corruption in a Changing World: Comparisons, Theories, and Controlling Strategies*. Jerusalem: Israel Chen Press (Moshe) Ltd.

Cooper, Terry, 1994. *Handbook of Administrative Ethics*. New York: Marcel Dekker.

Denhardt, K., 1991. "Unearthing the Moral Foundations of Public Administration: Honor, Benevolence, and Justice." In James S. Bowman, ed., *Ethical Frontiers in Public Management*. San Francisco: Jossey-Bass.

Dobel, J. Patrick, 1990. "Integrity in the Public Service." *Public Administration Review*,(May/June) 354–366.

Eaton, Dorman B., 1880. *Civil Service in Great Britain*. New York: Harper Bros.

Finer, Herman, 1941. "Administrative Responsibility in Democratic Government," *Public Administration Review*, vol. 1 (Autumn).

Frederickson, H. George, 1993. *Ethics and Public Administration*. Armonk, NY: M. E. Sharpe.

Friedrich, Carl, 1940. "Public Policy and the Nature of Administrative Responsibility." In E. S. Mason and C. T. Friedrich, eds., *Public Policy*. Cambridge: Harvard University Press.

Gulick, Luther and Lyndoll Urwick, eds., 1937. *Papers on the Service of Public Administration*. New York: Institute of Public Administration.

Jos, Philip H. 1990. "Administrative Responsibility Revisited: Moral Consensus and Moral Autonomy." *Administration and Society*, vol. 22, no. 2 (August) 228–248.

Lebacqz, Karen, 1986. *Perspectives from Philosophical and Theological Ethics*. Minneapolis: Augsburg Publishing House.

Pugh, Darrell, 1991. "The Origins of Ethical Framework in Public Administration." In James S. Bowman, ed., *Ethical Frontiers in Public Management*. San Francisco: Jossey-Bass, pp. 9–33.

Rohr, John, 1988. "Bureaucratic Morality in the United States." *International Political Science Review*, vol. 9, no. 3, 167–178.

———, 1989. *Ethics for Bureaucrats*, 2nd ed. New York: Marcel Dekker.

Thompson, Dennis F., 1992. "Three Paradoxes in Government Ethics." *The Public Manager* (Summer) 57–60.

Tinder, Glenn, 1991. *Political Thinking: The Perennial Questions*, 5th ed. New York: HarperCollins.

Wall, Brent, 1991. "Assessing Ethics Theories from a Democratic Viewpoint." In James Bowman, ed., *Ethical Frontiers in Public Management*. San Francisco: Jossey-Bass, pp. 135–157.

Wilson, Woodrow, 1887. "The Study of Administration." *Political Science Quarterly*, vol. 2 (June).

ADMINISTRATIVE NATURAL JUSTICE.

A concept respecting due process found in the theory and practice of administrative law in those societies with a British parliamentary heritage.

Administrative natural justice refers to a set of formal rules of procedure to be followed by quasi-judicial administrative decision-makers in their exercise of state power. Bureaucratic entities such as parole boards, immigration and refugee boards, welfare boards and occupational licensing authorities, for example, all exercise powers which blend judicial with executive decision making. As they engage in such regulatory work, which can directly affect the rights and interests of individuals and corporations, these bodies need not operate strictly like courts but, for justice to be done and to be seen to be done, British administrative law has developed certain rules of just procedure. The rules of natural justice as developed in Britain and the Commonwealth have their counterparts in the rules of "due process" in the United States and the "*principes generaux du droit*" found in the "*droit administratif*" of France.

Administrative natural justice in the British systems is rooted to two main rules: "*audi alteram partem*"–"hear the other side"–and "*nemo judex in sua causa debet esse*"–"no man can be a judge in his own case." These rules have formed a principled foundation for a twofold body of legal procedures that structure quasi-judicial administration. First, a person to be affected by a quasi-judicial administrative decision must be made aware of the case affecting his or her rights or interests, and be given an opportunity to address the issue. Second, the decisionmakers in the case must be free from any conflict of interest which could offer the reasonable apprehension of bias.

In actual practice these rules have been interpreted and elaborated by British, Canadian, and Australian courts as providing, under certain circumstances, for such legal and administrative requirements as: adequate notice of a hearing; the right to an oral hearing; the right to examination and cross-examination of evidence and argument; the right to counsel in legally complicated matters; the right to reasonable adjournment (continuance in American parlance); and the right to written reasons for judgment. With respect to bias the courts have held that a decisionmaker should have no pecuniary interest in the given matter in dispute as well as no close personal relationship with any of the contending parties. Further, there should be no institutional bias as resulting from the decisionmaking agency blending the functions of fact-finding and prosecution with that of adjudication, nor should there be the apprehension of attitudinal bias as witnessed through decisionmakers possessing preconceived understandings and attitudes to the particular issues in dispute.

A breach of these rules will be grounds for judicial review of the impugned decision, with the courts having the power either to quash a decision which they believe was arrived at unfairly, or to remand the matter to the original decisionmaker for fair reconsideration. It is important to note, however, that the application of the general rules of natural justice to particular cases will vary with the given decision-making institution and the nature of the decision being made. The courts have stipulated that the rules of natural justice are neither absolute nor need they be necessarily universal in their application. In Canadian administrative law, for example, workers' compensation boards with high volume caseloads are not obligated to produce lengthy, formal written reasons for routine decisions. Similarly, in Britain, labor relations board restrictions on the participation of legal counsel have been upheld as a means toward promoting informality, expeditiousness, and economy in labor law proceedings. In applying the general rules of natural justice to particular institutions and types of decisions, the courts have demonstrated a predisposition to establish a set of specific procedures which will provide for reasonably fair and just decisionmaking given the set circumstances.

In comparing the British concept of natural justice with the American one of due process, certain interesting similarities and differences emerge. The rules of due process in the United States display a marked relationship to natural justice, given that both concepts share the same purpose in establishing procedures through which quasi-judicial administrative power can be exercised in a fair manner. The major difference between the two systems is to be found in the much greater degree of codification of the rules of due process found in the United States. Through the development of the Administrative Procedure Act (APA), dating from 1946, the U.S. federal government has established a set of statutory procedural rights and obligations applicable to all federal regulatory agencies. The APA, in turn, has had substantial influence in the development of procedure within state and local authorities.

As the U.S. has moved quite strongly in the direction of codification, certain jurisdictions within the British heritage have themselves come to be influenced by this approach, also moving to codify certain of the rules of natural justice. This dynamic is witnessed most notably with the Australian Commonwealth government and with the provincial government of Ontario in Canada. As these developments occur one witnesses the rules and practice of natural justice evolving, as they have evolved for the past century; in turn, one witnesses an important demonstration affect from one jurisdiction to another. As these liberal democracies have all developed elaborate systems of quasi-judicial administrative decisionmaking, it is not surprising to see them learning from the experiences of one another respecting the manners in which such governmental power can be structured and controlled.

DAVID A. JOHNSON

BIBLIOGRAPHY

Brown, L., Neville, and John S. Bell, 1993. *French Administrative Law*, 4th ed. Oxford: Clarendon Press.

Carter, Leif H., and Christine B. Harrington, 1991. *Administrative Law: Cases and Comments,* 2nd ed. New York: Harper Collins.
Jones, David P., and Anne de Villars, 1994. *Principles of Administrative Law.* Toronto: Carswell.
Wade, Henry W., 1994. *Administrative Law,* 7th ed. Oxford: Clarendon Press.

ADMINISTRATIVE POLICIES. The rules of procedure and behavior that govern the relationships among organizational personnel and between the organization and those outside the organization.

In the classic bureaucracy described by German sociologist Max Weber (1946), the lifeblood of the organization is the policies and procedures that define the relationship among the individuals within that organization. Administrative policies define the direction and style of operation of the organization. Most often these policies are communicated through a manual or rule book, which defines and delimits the actions of organizational members. The extent of rule compliance by those organizational members is one of the characteristics by which Weber classified hierarchy. It is through the "authority" of policy that control and coordination are achieved in such organizations. According to Gulick (1937) the establishment and perfection of the "structure of authority between the director and the ultimate work divisions . . . is the central concern of the theory of organization" (p. 7).

Policy is not merely a matter of structuring work. Gulick goes on to admonish us:

Any large and complicated enterprise would be incapable of effective operation if reliance for coordination were placed in organization alone. Organization alone is necessary; in a large enterprise it is essential, but it does not take the place of a dominant central idea as the foundation of action and self-coordination in the daily operation of all of the parts of the enterprise (p. 37).

Administrative policy must both address the structure of the organization and define the purpose for the existence of that organization. Both of these matters will be discussed below, though it must be stated at the outset that for most of this century Gulick's warning that structure was not sufficient was lost. The all too easy assumption that purpose was defined in legislation and thus external to most public organizations left the issue of the structure and method of coordination as the only topic of discussion and analysis. This meant that administrative policy existed for the purpose of affirming the hierarchy. Leonard White, who wrote the first American textbook on public administration in 1926, could still write in the 1950s,

All large-scale organizations follow the same pattern, which in essence consist in the universal application of the superior-subordinate relationship. . . . Every position in the organization finds its appropriate place in the hierarchy, designated by a distinctive title, the incumbent

possessing authority to give orders to subordinates and bearing responsibility to receive and obey orders from superiors. Authority is the capacity to make decisions that are accepted by a subordinate as a guide to behavior, irrespective of his own judgment as to the merits of that decision. . . . The lines of authority and responsibility flow along the path of hierarchy. . . . The functions of the hierarchy are numerous. It is the channel of command. It is the principle channel of communication, downward and upward, along which flow information, advice, specific instructions, warnings and commendations. It is the channel for the delegation of authority. It establishes a sequence of related centers for decision making. . . . (1954, pp. 35–36).

Rules, policies, structures are created to distinguish between the authority of the superior and the subordinate. The perspective is inevitably top down and, therefore, the policies which create the hierarchy are negative. They are prepared for the purpose of telling the subordinate what he or she cannot do (this is not necessarily the norm in Europe). The goal of such rules is, according to Weber, to eliminate discretionary action. The effective organization is one in which decisions (problems) flow upward, while specifically defined actions are undertaken by subordinates. The scope of those actions is delimited in advance. Situations outside the normal course of events (nonroutine) are defined as problems and are sent upward for a decision on who will act and how to act. In this way the goals of the organization are not derived from formal mandates, but rather emerge as a set of constraints defining acceptable performance (Allison, 1971, p. 82). Allison discusses the implications of this reliance on fixed policies, or as he describes them, standard operating procedures:

SOPS constitute routines for dealing with standard situations. Routines allow large numbers of ordinary individuals to deal with numerous instances day after day, without much thought. But this regularized capacity for adequate performance is purchased at the price of standardization. If the SOPS are appropriate, average performance . . . is better than it would be if each instance were approached individually (given fixed talent timing and resource constraints). But specific instances that . . . do not have "standard" characteristics are often handled sluggishly or inappropriately (p. 89).

Administrative policies when viewed as a matter of structure and coordination emerge as potential problems, not the path to efficiency. Structuring the organization becomes a source of stagnation and ineffectiveness when confronted by situations which are not routine.

It is this failure to adjust to change or new circumstances that limits the value of reliance on routines and policies. Many have observed the phenomenon whereby rule compliance becomes the objective of the organization. When such a means-end inversion occurs, then bringing circumstances into conformance with policy, rather than flexibility of policy, becomes the proper behavior. In another context Wallace Sayre described this as "the triumph of technique over purpose" (1948).

It should also be noted that the resistance to change that is assumed to be characteristic of bureaucracy and bureaucrats can be explained by this reliance (overreliance?) on policies. Allison well chronicles the dilemma of the policy-bound organization; as long as things do not change, reliance on policy routines improves organization performance, but when confronted with new situations or demands for change those policy routines become an impediment to performance.

The problem is the emphasis on policies to knit together an organizational structure with little or no regard for Gulick's second mandate of the need for a dominant central idea. It is the failure to ask the question "why are we here?" or more likely failure to ask the question anew, that prevents the organization from focusing on organizational policies to implement goals, rather than merely to define the structure and work relationships. This instrumental view of administrative policy limits the potential effect of those policies. The result is that administrative policies and rules are regarded as a double-edged sword. Charles Perrow, a long-time student of organizational behavior, captures this ambivalence as follows:

> Rules do a lot of things in organizations; they protect as well as restrict; coordinate as well as block; channel effort as well as limit it; permit universalism as well as provide sanctuary for the inept; maintain stability as well as retard change; permit diversity as well as restrict it. They constitute the organizational memory and the means for change. As such rules in themselves are neither good nor bad, nor even that important (1973, p. 30).

The Importance of Mission

Of great importance is the central purpose or mission of the agency. As stated earlier, the all too easy assumption that the mission and purpose was received full-blown and complete from the political side of government (either by statute from the legislature or orders from the chief executive) prevented this aspect of policy from being fully explored in practice. With the emergence of the ideas associated with organizational development, leadership theory, strategic management and, most recently, total quality management (TQM), a greater emphasis on and concern for the core mission of the agency has evolved over the last three decades. The early work of James D. Thompson (1967) on dominant coalitions and organizational dynamics of change set the stage for a re-emergence of mission-focused policy as a basis for defining the organization. Fred Fiedler's (1967) contingency view of management im-

plied a leadership style that tried to help the organization adapt to the environment as it experienced that environment. Not only was flexibility of management called for, but increasingly the goals and tasks of the organization had to be shaped to respond. Administrative policy was about facilitating change, not dictating a routine.

In the late 1970s a number of ideas such as transformational leadership (Tichy and Ulrich, 1989), strategic management, and total quality management helped reinforce the idea that the managers must facilitate the defining of a vision/mission for the organization. The manager who can transform an organization must have the "ability to help the organization develop a vision of what it can be, to mobilize the organization to accept and work toward achieving the new vision, and to institutionalize the changes that must last over time" (Tichy and Ulrich, p. 344). It is this vision/mission that would be the normative foundation for organization change. Bryson (1988) suggests six questions must be answered to complete a mission statement.

1. Who are we?
2. In general, what are the basic social and political needs we exist to fill or the social and political problems we exist to address?
3. In general, what do we want to do to recognize or anticipate and respond to these needs or problems?
4. How should we respond to our key stakeholders?
5. What is our philosophy and what are our core values?
6. What makes us distinctive or unique? (p. 105).

With the foundation of a well-defined mission it is through tools such as strategic management and TQM that change occurs. The new administrative policy is directed at taking advantage of these tools. The "institutionalization" process is what truly transforms the organization. This is not all that far removed from Gulick's point about the central dominant idea.

From this perspective the role and purpose of administrative policy is more attuned to the culture of the organization, rather than its structure and work patterns. The common thread is in the interaction and interrelationships among workers and between workers and those outside the organization. Mission- or vision-oriented policy has more to do with the tone and style of the organization than it does the formal relationships of authority and command.

This is not an inconsequential distinction. Certainly those who have studied bureaucracies in non-Western and developing nations learned long ago that the appearance of hierarchy and bureaucratic arrangements often belies very different practices within (Peters, 1984, p. 41). It is not the influence of traditional culture that we are describing here, but rather the conscious choice of policy to reshape the dominant culture of the organization, but the effects are the same. These are policies which define the norms of behavior as well as the ideological norm of members. In the latter case it is consciously chosen policy, but the lesson is the same: that the socially constructed definition of how people should interact can be more powerful than the authority structure that defines formal relationships. At a minimum it would seem that such policies, to the extent that they reflect dominant culture, are more controlling of behavior than the bureaucratic rules for structuring work.

This is not to suggest that "transformational" administrative policy is inevitably at odds with policies for structuring work. But one obvious difference, at least in this context, is the tendency for structuring policies to be limiting and restrictive, and for transforming mission-facilitating policies to be directed toward freeing people to operate on their own initiative (this is certainly not a hard and fast rule—an organizational culture may be just as authoritarian, forbidding and restrictive as those resulting from policies for structuring work).

A sidebar on this perspective is to think in terms of the phenomenon of the formal and informal organization. The success of the organization is often attributable to the workings of the informal organization; it is the way to cut red tape and get things done. There is a connection between the formal and informal organization and the two types of administrative policy described here. It could be speculated that the visioning, mission-directed transformation processes of strategic management and TQM are attempts to codify, if not formalize, the informal organization. They are certainly efforts toward "deconstructing" the formal organization, and toward capturing the energy and influence of the informal organization.

To summarize, administrative policies have two purposes. First is to define the structure of the organization and to establish the lines of authority within that structure. The more hierarchical and bureaucratic, the greater the reliance on universal and impersonal rules to define structure and authority. It is, after all, this idea of rule domination that sets the hierarchy apart as an organization type. Nonhierarchical organizations use policy to structure relationships as well, but those policies may carry less influence over work patterns than in a hierarchy. The second purpose is to define the mission and culture of the organization. It is not unusual for these policies to be "unwritten" rules of conduct. Studies in comparative administration suggest that some type of worker-defined or socially defined set of norms develops in organizations, as in the case of the "sala-" administrations defined by Fred Riggs. The informal organization first noted in the Hawthorne studies of the 1920s and 1930s represents a second version of this type of policy. In the last two decades leadership theory and management theory have come to emphasize practices which require formal administrative policy directed at defining organizational culture. The origins of this notion are in Gulick's mandate for a dominant central idea as a prerequisite of organizing. The management perspective and philosophy here assumes that "organizing" is a perpetual task (see, for example, the work of Karl Weick) and therefore defining the dominant central idea, now called visioning, is a task returned to repeatedly by the organization. Administrative policies must be directed toward facilitating change. Flexibility and adaptability, not routinization, are behind such policies.

RAYMOND W. COX III

BIBLIOGRAPHY

Allison, Graham T., 1971. *Essence of Decision.* Boston: Little, Brown & Co.
Bryson, John M., 1988. *Strategic Planning for Public and Nonprofit Organizations.* San Francisco: Jossey-Bass Publishers.
Fiedler, Fred, 1967. *A Theory of Leadership Effectiveness.* New York: McGraw Hill.
Gulick, Luther, 1937. "Notes on the Theory of Organization." In Lester Gulick and Lyndall Urwick, eds. *Papers on the Science of Administration.* New York: Institute of Public Administration.
Perrow, Charles, 1973. *Complex Organizations,* 2nd ed. Glenview, IL: Scott, Foresman & Co.
Peters, B. Guy, 1984. *The Politics of Bureaucracy,* 2nd ed. New York: Longman.
Riggs, Fred W., 1964. *Administration in Developing Countries: The Theory of Prismatic Society.* Boston: Houghton Mifflin.
Sayre, Wallace, 1948. "The Triumph of Technique over Purpose." *Public Administration Review,* vol. 8, no. 2.
Thompson, James D., 1967. *Organizations in Action.* New York: McGraw Hill.
Tichy, Noel and David Ulrich, 1989. "The Leadership Challenge: A Call for the Transformational Leader." In Otto, ed., *Classic Readings in Organization Behavior.* Belmont, CA: Wadsworth, pp. 344–355.
Weber, Max, 1946. *From Max Weber.* New York: Oxford University Press.
Weick, Karl, 1979. *The Social Psychology of Organizing,* 2nd ed. Reading, MA: Addison-Wesley.
White, Leonard D., 1954. *Introduction to the Study of Public Administration,* 4th ed. New York: Macmillan Co.

ADMINISTRATIVE PRAXIS. Organizational endeavors undertaken with a critical consciousness on the part of managers. The concept of praxis has been embraced by many venerated philosophers and social theorists. Because of its impact on the traditions of political and administrative thought, praxis has become an intrinsically important term in administrative theory. Because the idea of praxis is an elusive concept, to appreciate the concept fully it must be approached in a number of different but compatible ways.

The term *praxis* is often used interchangeably with *practice,* as both imply action. The word practice has a limited meaning in English that praxis does not. Practice is habitual action repeatedly performed so that one may acquire skill. Praxis, like practice, concerns human activity that produces certain outcomes or objects. This activity is, however, not viewed in the narrow, "practical" sense. As Vazquez (1977) points out, "All praxis is activity, but all activity is not praxis" (p. 149). Praxis is an old term to which administrative action has given new life. The ancient Greeks define it as "practical activity," "action," or "doing." For Aristotle, praxis meant a special kind of human activity devoted to "political life," as contrasted with contemplation or abstract reasoning (*theoria*). In his analysis, theory implied intellectual activities of thinking, abstracting, and reflecting, whereas political life as practical activity praxis implied the performing of an activity that has moral significance (Lobkowicz, 1967; Joachim, 1951). Whereas Aristotle related praxis exclusively to politics, Marx broadened praxis to include all activities that contribute to the humanization of the person (Markovic, 1974). Marx was concerned with consequences of action, "with altering the material conditions of life, with making the world a better place. That better place was for him one where human activity is at last everywhere fully human. The goal of revolutionary praxis is to liberate human activity from the forces that debase it, to realize a condition wherein the life of noble actions is available to each person because of the noble acts of every other person" (Allan, 1990, p. 4).

The praxis of human action is extensively used in existentialism, phenomenology, critical theory, classic political theory, Marxist theory, ethnomethodology, hermeneutics, and postmodern ideas. Although praxis inquiry is emphasized differently by different philosophers and social theorists, there is a common concern with understanding human activity from the subject's point of view (in contrast to emphasizing activity that is a biological or natural act influenced by a passive, uncritical consciousness).

Practice is different from praxis in that practice takes place without an individual employing any type of critical consciousness. Praxis, on the other hand, is always an activity developed by an individual and directed at an object that is shaped as such by the means of the transformation. It requires a reflexive, critical consciousness to discover and create future possibilities. Thus, praxis is defined as human activity in which an individual uses a reflexive consciousness and social praxis involving communicative action to transform his or her reality over time (June, 1994, pp. 91–103).

In praxis, action requires critical consciousness. Individual praxis is different from the behavior of animals. Animals are unable to think critically or reflexively about the external environment and their own behavior. Robots can perform various productive works, but their activities are programmed by humans. Both animals and robots may be efficient in adapting to the physical environment as well as performing productive activity, but they have no praxis because they do not exercise critical consciousness. Only humans, as conscious beings, are able to relate to themselves and the world reflexively, that is, to reflect, analyze, foresee, and decide their course of action.

Praxis can also arise out of social processes involving the sharing of mutual interests. As such, it is social activity in which individuals collaborate critically and reflectively with other actors in order to accomplish collective purposes. Thus, social praxis involves an intersubjective praxis—a form of discourse embedded within a web of meanings that the actors experience personally in relationship with others. Habermas's (1973, 1981) contribution to the understanding of the social conception of human action is most insightful in describing intersubjective action. According to Habermas, practical interest is the foundation of social practice: communication and the establishment of mutual relationships between individuals. Practical interest refers to those aspects of knowledge and action concerned with establishing a shared understanding in intersubjective situations in order to achieve community and mutuality. Thus dialogue and use of language are the basic social means of practical action. For example, a manager may attempt to promote meaningful social relationships with his or her employees through communicative action.

Whereas social praxis is activity in which the subjects are engaged individually and collectively in changing social reality, an organizational praxis is action in which individuals attempt to transform organizational and individual reality and to create newly constituted intersubjective reality, involving "the creation not only of new objects but also of new needs and potentialities" (Crocker, 1977, p. 18). Through the process of self-reflection and reasoning, the individual can evaluate knowledge and interest critically and can transform them through meaningful change. The act of reflexive self-inquiry changes the consciousness of the individual. In changing his or her consciousness, the individual becomes involved in the process of changing the organizational reality.

In the context of changing organizations, the individual becomes a transformer of reality when he or she perceives the contradictions between individual freedom and organizational control and takes on the responsibility of resolving these contradictions. In changing dehumanizing conditions, the individual exercises an emancipating praxis within the context of the organization. Through reflection and action (praxis), the individual has the possibility of transforming the organization and redesigning it in order to satisfy shared needs.

Praxis and the Public Manager

Public managers are often viewed as people who are mostly concerned with "practical" results that satisfy basic utilitarian needs. "Practical" implies a nonphilosophical and uncritical approach to activity; in other words, practical managers are committed to sensible performance of their role as defined by the organization. They are less interested in philosophical and normative discourse that deals with purpose, conflicting interests, and ethical consequences of their action. Their role performance is generally oriented toward the efficient accomplishment of tangible results.

Because many activities that people perform in organizations are repetitive in nature and do not require much thought, even though they may be cumbersome and depersonalizing, some people feel comfortable with what they do. Much of the literature on administrative theory has emphasized the necessity for improving the performance behavior of employees by expecting them to master standardized procedures for conducting repetitive activities. Employees are expected to become efficient in applying procedures and rules through short-term training and the socialization process of working with others in the organization. Many theorists and practicing administrators assume that through the practice of applying new knowledge (or theories) to the improvement of their organizations, organizations can achieve a high degree of objectivity and consequently can increase productivity and efficiency.

In contrast, others may be critically aware of the inadequacies and undesirable consequences of their actions, often imposed on them by the people above them in the workplace. What is important about the latter case is critical and reflexive consciousness exercised by a conscious administrator, as opposed to habitual performance of everyday activities. Praxis-oriented administrators will be more sensitive to and aware of the moral consequences of their acts. They will be more concerned with the feelings of their clients and the promotion of the public good.

According to Habermas (1981), praxis expresses itself as a communicative action in which individuals interact with one another, relating themselves to the objective world (i.e., administrative organization). In order to transform the object, the individual engages in praxis to establish intersubjectivity through communicative action. In other words, the meaningful construction of intersubjective understanding is possible only when managers and other organizational members engage in intersubjective praxis; that is, each subject tunes into the consciousness of the other by trying to understand and share in the other's experiences and ideas through authentic and critical dialogue.

Furthermore, to be praxis-oriented one can begin by simply asking what is required in having a relationship that persists over time. Each party to that relationship must have a continuing identity; that is, each party must perceive himself or herself as acting and engaging in dialogue with the other party. Praxis discourse allows administrators to understand the meanings of actions that are grounded in everyday experiences in the workplace, realizing the dialectical possibility of resolving various contradictions between two opposing intellectual traditions: the positivistic versus the interpretive epistemology and organizational goals versus individual needs.

JONG S. JUN

BIBLIOGRAPHY

Allan, G., 1990. *The Realization of the Future*. Albany, NY: State University of New York Press.
Bernstein, Richard J., 1971. *Praxis and Action*. Philadelphia: University of Pennsylvania Press.
Crocker, D. A., 1977. "Markovic's Concept of Praxis as Norm." *Inquiry*, vol. 20, 1–43.
Dewey, John, 1929. *The Quest for Certainty: A Study of the Relation of Knowledge and Action*. New York: Capricorn Books.
Freire, P., 1970. *Education for Critical Consciousness*. New York: The Seabury Press.
Habermas, Jurgen, 1981. *The Theory of Communicative Actions*, vol. 1. Trans. by Thomas McCarthy. Boston: Beacon Press.
———, 1973. *Theory and Practice*. Boston: Beacon Press.
Joachim, H. H., 1951. *Aristotle: The Nicomachean Ethics: A Commentary*. Oxford, U.K.: Clarendon Press.
Jun, Jong S., 1994. *Philosophy of Administration*. Seoul: Daeyoung Moonhwa International.
Lobkowicz, Nicholas, 1967. *Theory and Practice*. Notre Dame: University of Notre Dame Press.
Markovic, Mihailo, 1974. *From Affluence to Praxis: Philosophy and Social Criticism*. Ann Arbor: The University of Michigan Press.
Vazquez, Adolfo Sanchez, 1977. *The Philosophy of Praxis*. London: Merlin Press.

ADMINISTRATIVE PROCEDURE ACTS.

Legislation establishing procedural standards governing how governmental agencies must perform their business. The focus of administrative law today is the administrative process itself—the procedures that administrative agencies must follow in exercising their powers. This is a natural reflection of growing concern with the procedural aspects of administrative action. This concern is a recent development. Earlier in the century administrative law was divided into the subjects of powers and remedies. Delegation of authority and judicial review alone were stressed. More recently there has come the realization that of equal, if not greater, importance is the exercise of administrative power. With this realization has come the emphasis on procedural safeguards to ensure the proper exercise of administrative authority—an emphasis that found legislative articulation in the federal Administrative Procedure Act (APA) of 1946, a law laying down the basic procedures that must be followed by federal agencies.

The APA is now the foundation of federal administrative law. It is printed in its codified form in Title 5, United States Code. For the student of administrative law, understanding of the APA provisions is as important as understanding of the Uniform Commercial Code provisions is for students of commercial law.

Administrative procedure legislation has also been enacted in the states. The state laws have, in the main, been based upon the Model State Administrative Procedure Act approved by the American Bar Association and the National Conference of Commissioners on Uniform State Laws in 1946. A Revised Model State Act was approved in 1961, and a new Model Act in 1981. Though acceptance of the Model Act was slow at first (with only five states adopting it by 1959), the act now serves as the basis of administrative procedure legislation in 27 states and the District of Columbia. In addition, three states have enacted APAs based upon the 1981 revision and 20 others have also enacted administrative procedure legislation.

Both the federal APA and the comparable state statutes are based upon the fundamental distinction between administrative rulemaking and adjudication (or, to use the term in most state APAs, "contested cases"). They normally require only a notice–and–comment procedure prior to rulemaking, though some contain hearing requirements (e.g., Iowa, Massachusetts, Minnesota, Ohio, and Wisconsin). As far as adjudication is concerned, the procedure acts prescribe basic procedural requirements, such as evidence, burden of proof, decision procedure, and hearing officers. The federal APA and some state acts provide for independent administrative law judges (ALJs) to preside at administrative hearings. These ALJs are empowered to make to make initial decisions in cases before them. Twelve state APAs provide for a central pool of ALJs who are assigned to different agency hearings as they are needed. Most state APAs, however, do not contain provisions for independent hearing officers; in these states hearings are presided over by members of the agency staff.

BERNARD SCHWARTZ

BIBLIOGRAPHY

Schwartz, Bernard, 1954. "The Administrative Procedure Act in Operation." *New York University Law Review,* vol. 29 (June) 1173–1264.
———, 1953. "The Model State Administrative Procedure Act–Analysis and Critique." *Rutgers Law Review,* vol. 7 (Spring) 431–458.

ADMINISTRATIVE SEARCHES AND SEIZURES.

Searches, often called inspections, carried out by an administrative agency for a regulatory purpose, sometimes leading to the official taking of property and/or the arrest and administrative detention of a person or persons.

Background

The Fourth Amendment is clearly one of the most important constitutional amendments because it protects individuals "in their persons, houses, papers, and effects, against unreasonable searches and seizures." The amendment specifically prohibits search warrants from being issued except "upon probable cause, supported by oath or affirmation, and particularly describing the place to be searched, and the persons or things to be seized."

Despite its critical relevance to the preservation of individual liberties, this amendment has always been diffi-

cult to interpret and apply in practice. What constitutes an unreasonable search and seizure has not always been easy to determine. Generally, the courts have ruled that the particular circumstances surrounding the search and seizure determine the reasonableness of the search and seizure. For example, warrantless searches and seizures have been allowed by the courts when it could be demonstrated that circumstances made it unfeasible to obtain a warrant. Consequently, the constitutionality of certain search and seizure tactics has often been decided on a case-to-case basis, creating great uncertainty in search and seizure law. But one thing is certain: evidence obtained through illegal searches and seizures cannot normally be used in federal or state courts, although such evidence may be used for questioning witnesses before grand juries. But do Fourth Amendment privacy protections apply to administrative searches and seizures which involve noncriminal matters?

Historically, the prevalent attitude has been that certain Bill of Rights guarantees, such as Fourth Amendment rights, should only apply to criminal procedures, not to civil procedures. For example, Fourth Amendment safeguards have not been applied customarily to deportation proceedings involving the Immigration and Naturalization Service, because such proceedings are considered civil and not criminal proceedings protected by the Bill of Rights. It was apparently not considered necessary to apply Fourth Amendment protections, as well as other Bill of Rights safeguards, to civil cases because the penalties for civil offenses were not perceived as severe enough to warrant elaborate Bill of Rights protections for individuals. Besides, it was maintained that the state could not afford to absorb the extra administrative costs for such protections and that the extension of such safeguards would make efficient and effective administration impossible.

But it would be patently naive to hold that administrative actions cannot result in the severe deprivation of a person's personal liberties since Congress, as well as state legislatures, has delegated to administrators the power to inflict grave punishments upon individuals or corporate persons without providing them with the benefit of independent judicial judgment. Consequently, concerned observers have begun to question very seriously how fair it is to deny persons constitutional due process protections in certain situations just because the proceedings are labeled "civil" instead of "criminal" (Wright, 1984, pp. 1129–1146). In his concluding comment on "administrative bail," for instance, Bernard Schwartz (1991) asserted: "What the present law means is that the constitutional right to bail can be denied a man in jail by the simple device of providing a 'not criminal' label for the techniques used to incarcerate. Imprisonment awaiting determination of whether that imprisonment is justifiable has precisely the same evil consequences to an individual whatever legalistic label is used to describe his plight" (p. 107).

Administrative Seizures, Arrest, and Detention

Is it possible in this civilized and free democratic country to be arrested and imprisoned for relatively long periods of time, sometimes for many months, without ever stepping into a courtroom? Shocking as it is, the answer is yes. In *Wong Wing v. United States*, 163 U.S. 228 (1896), the Supreme Court held that persons cannot be imprisoned as a *punishment* unless they are first given a criminal trial, according to constitutional requirements, and sentenced by a judicial tribunal. Such a due process safeguard has always been considered essential to any society which cherishes liberty. According to Bernard Schwartz, "the absence of nonjudicial powers of imprisonment sharply distinguishes our legal system from those we disparagingly describe as totalitarian" (1991, pp. 98–99). However, it is crucial to point out that the court in *Wong Wing* ruled explicitly that in America persons can be apprehended and sent to jail as long as the incarceration is not done with the intent to punish. In this immigration case, the Court reasoned that immigration administrators can legitimately detain or confine persons temporarily in order to carry out effectively their congressionally mandated legislative functions (at 235).

Thus, Congress has delegated to administrators the power to arrest and temporarily imprison persons who have not been accused of or convicted of any criminal wrongdoing. But why should Congress want to give administrators the discretionary authority to arrest and imprison noncriminals? In some cases the administrative power to seize and confine persons appears quite reasonable and necessary in order to protect the larger interests of society; but in other situations the power seems to permit administrators to exploit and punish innocent persons in a patently unreasonable way.

On the reasonable side, it seems sensible that public health administrators, to protect the public health, should have the authority to apprehend and confine those who pose a dangerous health threat to a community. In *Ex parte Hardcastle*, 208 S.W. 531 (Tex., 1919), the court asserted that it makes good sense to uphold laws which call for the confinement of those who have been exposed to or are carriers of infectious diseases, even if the laws call for the confinement of such persons without the benefit of a judicial proceeding. Obviously, to protect the general welfare by preventing the spread of a contagious disease, public officials would have to possess powers to enable them to act quickly to stop such individuals from walking freely in the community. For example, the recent AIDS crisis has caused some to recommend the radical step of rounding up and confining those with AIDS to stop the spread of the deadly disease. This suggestion has created much controversy. In fact, early in President Bill Clinton's administration numerous Haitian refugees were detained at Guantanamo Bay Naval Base against their will for long periods

of time with U.S. authorities refusing to grant them parole because they had tested HIV-positive. Was this action fair to the refugees? A U.S. district court thought not, ruling that Attorney General Reno and other federal officials had abused their discretion by refusing to grant these Haitian refugees parole simply because they had tested HIV-positive (*Haitian Centers Council, Inc. v. Sale*, 823 F.Supp. 1028 [E.D. N.Y. 1993]). But were Attorney General Reno and the other federal authorities just trying to promote America's public health and safety?

The vital questions seem to be: When do seizures and confinements become unreasonable and unjustified, even in light of administrative efforts to promote the public interest? How much should the individual be expected to suffer for the good of the public welfare? The public has an interest in a public prosecutor's ability to prosecute a murder case successfully. Therefore, it may be in the interest of the prosecutor to hold a key material witness to a murder in jail until the trial. But how long should the prosecutor be allowed to detain the witness—days, weeks, many months? Continued postponements of trial dates have been known to push trial dates back for months, possibly delaying the trial's outcome for more than a year. Can any society in good conscience hold a material witness, guilty of no crime, in jail for such a long period of time? Should an INS administrator be permitted to seize and incarcerate for months, without benefit of bail, an illegal alien whose deportability is being determined by the INS? Are not such administrative arrests and detentions flatly contrary to the spirit of the Fourth Amendment, however technically legal they may be in the eyes of the courts? Is not a legal system rather strange if it provides more due process protections from arrests and imprisonment to those accused of violent crimes than to those accused of no criminal conduct at all?

Abel v. United States, 362 U.S. 217 (1960), is an excellent case for conveying the potential dangers behind the use of administrative arrests and detentions. Specifically, the case serves to demonstrate how an administrative official, with power granted by Congress, can work with law enforcement officers to undermine Fourth Amendment safeguards. Abel was a Soviet spy whom the FBI believed was engaged in espionage activities against the United States. Upon learning about his whereabouts, the FBI wanted to arrest him at his hotel, but FBI officers lacked enough evidence against him to satisfy the probable cause requirement needed before a judge would be willing to sign an arrest warrant. To circumvent the constitutional red tape, those FBI agents sought the assistance of INS officials. Having been told by the FBI that Abel was an illegal alien, the district director of the INS made out an arrest warrant. Both FBI and INS officers then went to Abel's hotel with the administrative arrest warrant to make the arrest. This FBI-INS cooperative effort allowed the FBI to obtain an arrest which the FBI alone would not have been able to make if it had to uphold Fourth Amendment due process restrictions. After the arrest, Abel was placed in solitary confinement for five weeks at a detention camp. It was not until criminal charges were finally filed against him that the judicial branch was brought into his case.

The Court in *Abel* had to decide whether the administrative procedures leading to the arrest and imprisonment of Abel were lawful under the Fourth Amendment. Specifically, Abel had charged that the arrest was unconstitutional because the arrest warrant did not satisfy the Fourth Amendment's warrant requirements. However, the court upheld the constitutionality of such "standard" INS arrest procedures (at 233).

From the very beginning this decision attracted heated protests from liberal critics who believed that the ruling sanctioned actions against individuals which the constitutional framers, in writing the Fourth Amendment, definitely wanted to prevent. In a dissent to *Abel* Justice William J. Brennan argued that the Fourth Amendment was written to prevent such violations of a person's basic rights. Brennan made the point that under this administrative arrest, where no judicial voice was heard, the INS never had to justify any of its actions to an independent judge. Clearly, he maintained, some judicial control over such administrative actions are needed to preserve constitutional due process requirements (at 248–256). In his dissent Justice William O. Douglas remarked: "How much more convenient it is for the police to find a way around those specific requirements of the Fourth Amendment! What a hindrance it is to work laboriously through constitutional procedures! How much easier to go to another official in the same department! The administrative officer can give a warrant" without having to show "probable cause to a magistrate" (at 246).

However, not all lower courts have always followed the controversial *Abel* holding. For example, in 1994 in *Alexander v. City and County of San Francisco*, 29 F3d 1355, the Ninth Circuit Court ruled that an administrative search warrant obtained by health inspectors to check for health code violations did not authorize police officers to enter a home to arrest the occupant, which actually led to police killing the occupant. The court stressed that prior cases, including ironically *Abel*, ". . . make it very clear that an administrative search may not be converted into an instrument which serves the very different needs of law enforcement officials. If it could, then all of the protections traditionally afforded against intrusions by the police would evaporate, to be replaced by the much weaker barriers erected between citizens and other governmental agencies. It is because the mission of those agencies are less potently hostile to a citizen's interests than are the missions of the police that the barriers may be weak as they are and still not jeopardize Fourth Amendment guarantees" (at 1361).

Three years after *Abel*, in *United States v. Alvarado*, 321 F2d 336 (2d Cir., 1963), the court upheld the constitutionality of an administrative arrest during which immigration authorities took even greater liberties with the Fourth Amendment. This time, acting according to statute, they arrested an alien without first obtaining an administrative warrant. In *Abel*, at least an administrative warrant was obtained before the arrest was made. Admittedly, the administrative warrant, as contrasted with a regular judicial warrant, does not go very far in protecting an individual under the Fourth Amendment. Nevertheless, some reasons must be given to show cause for deportability before the administrative warrant can be signed by an administrative officer. Allowing persons to be searched and seized, without any cause being given to anyone before the seizure takes place, appears only to encourage dangerous administrative abuses and strip the Fourth Amendment of its practical utility for individuals.

What, then, is the real significance of *Abel* and *Alvarado* in light of the Fourth Amendment? The Fourth Amendment, to reiterate, guarantees essentially that persons cannot be subjected to "unreasonable searches and seizures." If searches and seizures were to be carried out, the constitutional framers required probable cause to be established before search and seizure warrants would be issued, presumably by an independent judicial officer. These quite simple constitutional procedures seemed to provide the necessary safeguards to ensure that if searches and seizures were executed, they would be kept within reasonable bounds, consistent with the concept of limited government. The Fourth Amendment emphasizes that its provisions "shall not be violated," and nothing in the amendment suggests that its provisions cannot be violated by law enforcement officers but can be violated by other governmental administrators—regardless of how the courts have interpreted the applicability of the Fourth Amendment.

Circumstances dictate that some reasonable exceptions occasionally should be tolerated in any laws, but it does appear that the courts went unwisely and too far in *Abel* and *Alvarado*. The courts in *Abel* and *Alvarado* permitted law enforcement officers (FBI and U.S. customs officials respectively) to achieve their search, seizure, and confinement objectives by calling upon INS agents to do the job that they were not able to do legally under the constitutional restrictions of the Fourth Amendment. With the information obtained from the administrative searches, the FBI and customs officials were then able to build criminal cases against Abel and Alvarado. Justice Douglas believed such underhanded and tricky governmental actions defeat the noble purpose of the Fourth Amendment, and that the facts of the *Abel* case suggest clearly "that the FBI agents wore the mask of INS to do what otherwise they could not have done. They did what they could do only if they had gone to a judicial officer pursuant to the requirements of the Fourth Amendment" (*Abel v. U.S.*, at 245). Brennan's dissent stated that such official trickery serves too well to remind the law enforcement officers that they can make their jobs easier by employing the same tactics to escape the commands of the Fourth Amendment (*Abel v. U.S.*, at 248–256).

The *Abel* and *Alvarado* holdings conflict with the separation of powers doctrine in that the courts in both cases allowed administrators to act as arresting officers, prosecutors, and judges. Specifically, the courts accepted as constitutional a situation in which officials from the same agency were allowed to: (1) decide whether sufficient probable cause existed to justify the issuance of an arrest warrant; (2) issue the arrest warrant itself; (3) carry out the arrest; (4) conduct a general search of the premises to obtain damaging evidence to be used in a criminal trial; and (5) determine whether the arrested person should be confined. Adding further to the consolidation of administrative power under these circumstances, a prior case had upheld a statute giving such administrative officials the powers to determine whether bail should be given and, if so, at what amount over $500. Ironically, the courts have allowed such a concentration of power in the hands of administrators because the Fourth and Eighth Amendments were not perceived to be applicable to such administrative actions but were held to be applicable to police actions against suspected criminals. But regardless of the labels given to these state actions taken against persons, Bernard Schwartz (1991) concluded that they "can scarcely conceal the reality of individuals being deprived of liberty without the essential safeguards contemplated by the Bill of Rights" (p. 107).

Today, many legal scholars believe that the United states has gone too far in employing various rationales to deprive persons of their fundamental constitutional due process rights. In a criminal case that has considerable relevance to administrative law, a divided Supreme Court in 1987, in *United States v. Salerno*, 107 S.Ct. 2095, upheld the constitutionality of the Bail Reform Act of 1984, 18 U.S.C., Section 3142 (e), which permits courts to order pretrial detention of persons charged with serious crimes if it is felt, after a pretrial hearing, that they would pose a threat to the community. The Salerno holding immediately drew harsh criticism from liberal groups (for example, the American Civil Liberties Union) as well as the three dissenting justices in the case (Justices Marshall, Brennan, and Stevens). Justice Marshall started his dissent by addressing the potential tyrannical character of the Bail Reform Act: "This case brings before the Court for the first time a statute in which Congress declares that a person innocent of any crime may be jailed indefinitely . . . if the government shows to the satisfaction of a judge that the accused is likely to commit crimes, unrelated to the pending charges, at any time in the future. Such statutes,

consistent with the usages of tyranny and the excesses of what bitter experience teaches us to call the police state, have long been thought incompatible with the fundamental human rights protected by our Constitution" (at 2105–2106).

Justice Marshall objected vigorously to what he felt was the Court's absurd and destructive distinction between regulatory and punitive legislation, even though a similar distinction and application of the distinction had been made long ago in *Wong Wing*. To Marshall, the distinction made by the majority could allow constitutional guarantees to be taken away by the state, under the administrative or regulatory rationale, any time the state felt that certain persons may in the future commit acts that would pose a danger to society. Marshall concluded: "The majority's technique for infringing this right (due process) is simple: merely redefine any measure which is claimed to be punishment as 'regulation,' and, magically, the Constitution no longer prohibits its imposition" (at 2108). The blatant point that Marshall is making—and it has clear implications for administrative law—is that it is dangerous to uphold laws or regulations, especially when basic constitutional rights are at stake, on the premise that they serve a legitimate regulatory goal of making the community safer. Such could lead to the destruction of our cherished constitutional liberties since virtually all statutes and rules could be justified on such "regulatory interest" grounds.

However, possibly responding to the harsh criticisms it received for its Salerno decision, the Supreme Court in *Foucha v. Louisiana*, 112 S.Ct. 1780 (1992) softened the clout of *Salerno* by stating: "It was emphasized in *Salerno* that the detention we found constitutionally permissible was strictly limited in duration. . . . Here, in contrast, the state asserts that because Foucha once committed a criminal act and now has an antisocial personality that sometimes leads to aggressive conduct, a disorder for which there is no effective treatment, he may be held indefinitely. This rationale would permit the state to hold indefinitely any other insanity acquittee not mentally ill who could be shown to have a personality disorder that may lead to criminal conduct. . . . Freedom from physical restraint being a fundamental right, the state must have a particularly convincing reason, which it has not put forward, for such discrimination against insanity acquittees who are no longer mentally ill" (at 1787–1788).

Searches

From the perspective of administrative law, probably the most serious threat to the guarantees of individual liberty under the Fourth Amendment is posed by the power of administrative officials to employ their discretionary authority to have arrested and imprisoned, in the absence of judicial intervention, persons not charged with any criminal misconduct. Fortunately, however, administrative arrests (seizures) and detentions are relatively uncommon. But administrative searches are very common. For example, at the peak of its regulatory prowess, in fiscal year 1976, the Occupational Safety and Health Administration conducted 90,369 workplace inspections. Typically, administrative searches are used to inspect premises (for example, a person's house or a company's plant), documents (for example, a person's tax receipts or a corporation's records), and regulated operations (for example, how a chemical manufacturer complies with federal standards in disposing of its toxic wastes). Such administrative inspections may also present challenges to the right to privacy under the Fourth Amendment.

Why have Congress and state legislatures given administrators the authority to carry out administrative inspections? The reasons should appear quite obvious. Max Weber acknowledged in his scholarly writing on public bureaucracy that the real strength of bureaucratic organizations resides in the information they collect, store, and use. To function properly, administrative agencies must be able to obtain vital information which can help them perform their assigned regulatory activities. Or in the words of some renowned administrative law scholars, at least in one sense "administrative agencies do not differ from other institutions: their effectiveness is determined by the information they can acquire" (Robinson, Gellhorn, and Bruff, 1980, p. 487). Bernard Schwartz (1991) points out that "information is the fuel without which the administrative engine could not operate; the old saw that knowledge is power has the widest application in administrative law" (p. 110).

Actually, agencies can obtain most of the information they seek without much difficulty. In fact, much of the data they need can be found by simply referring to their own records, files elsewhere in the governmental bureaucracy, governmental publications, and other readily accessible data sources. Agency staffs can also obtain information through normal research processes which do not involve any direct investigations into the private affairs of individuals and businesses. And even if agency administrators feel that they must obtain certain information from persons and businesses, most times such private parties cooperate rather cheerfully, freely disclosing to these governmental officials what they want to know.

There are occasions, however, when individuals and businesses believe that requests for information, frequently in the form of physical administrative inspections, encroach too far upon their right to privacy as protected by the Fourth Amendment. When such resistance occurs, administrators can compel private parties to disclose to them the information they want, sometimes by forcing them to submit to administrative inspections, as long as statutes permit such investigations. Almost all agencies do possess such statutory power. Actually, to protect the administrative investigatory function from possible impotence, virtu-

ally all agencies have been given the weapon of the administrative subpoena. It was established in *Cudahy Packing Co. v. Holland,* 315 U.S. 357, 363 (1942), that the administrative subpoena can be employed coercively to subpoena records and witnesses.

Before discussing the applicability of the Fourth Amendment to administrative searches and inspections, some remarks should be made regarding the government's authority to demand that persons and businesses keep certain records and present specific reports of activities which are needed to assist the government in its efforts to promote the public interest.

Fourth Amendment Limitations on Administrative Inspections

In a genuinely free society (of course, within the limits of what is necessary to maintain socioeconomic and political stability), persons should be protected from unreasonable encroachments upon their personal privacy, whether the intention of the state's search is to uncover criminal evidence or to discover code violations in a person's home or business. Although heated arguments still persist over whether administrative inspections should be restricted by Fourth Amendment provisions, it is clear that personal liberties cannot survive in a nation if governmental officials show wanton disrespect for a person's right to privacy. It is therefore obvious that if personal privacy rights are to be protected, no governmental officials can be allowed to intrude at their discretion into a person's private life, whether the public officials be FBI agents or OSHA inspectors. The Court in United *States v. Martinez-Fuerte,* 428 U.S. 543, 569 (1976), made the point that limits must restrict official intrusions into the private affairs of others or administrative tyranny will surely result. As the Court emphasized in *Wolf v. Colorado,* 338 U.S. 25, 27 (1949), protection against arbitrary invasions of a person's privacy is fundamental to the preservation of a free society; it is at the core of the Fourth Amendment. To permit any public administrator to exercise unconfined, unstructured, and unchecked discretion in the area the Fourth Amendment was written to guard is to place the liberty of everyone and every business at the absolute discretion of any administrator who has an interest in anyone's personal or business affairs. Such a situation would surely spell the end of freedom. Justice William O. Douglas conveyed this point succinctly in his dissent in *New York v. United States,* 342 U.S. 882, 884 (1951): "Absolute discretion, like corruption, marks the beginning of the end of liberty." And in *California v. Hodari D.,* 111 S.Ct. 1547, 1561 (1991), dissenting Justices Stevens and Marshall, criticizing the Court majority's lack of respect for the Fourth Amendment's protective rights, warned, quoting Justice Brandeis, that our constitutional framers conferred upon us "... the right to be let alone—the most comprehensive of rights and the right most valued by civilized men. To protect that right, every unjustifiable intrusion by the government upon the privacy of the individual, whatever the means employed, must be deemed a violation of the Fourth Amendment." It should not be overlooked that totalitarian governments retain their position of dominance over their citizenry by allowing their state officers to exercise shockingly broad discretionary powers to spy on persons and business operations, as well as to search and seize individuals and their property. Because personal freedom poses a threat to the survival of totalitarian regimes, governmental laws are typically aimed at destroying individual liberties (for example, freedom of speech, freedom of the press, and the right to be free from unreasonable searches and seizures). In police states, very few, if any, searches and seizures are perceived by governmental authorities as unreasonable. The right to privacy carries little meaning in such regimes, where state rights are considered far superior to individual rights. In reflecting upon the character of totalitarian states, Ronald Bacigal (1978) concluded: "Unchecked power to search and seize is crucial to the maintenance of a totalitarian state." In sharp contrast, he found that democratic nations have adopted prohibitions against unreasonable searches and seizures in an attempt to keep the government from becoming oppressive and the people free: "Strict controls on the government's power to search and seize inhibit the enforcement of oppressive laws, and serve as a bulwark against totalitarian government" (p. 559).

The causes of tyranny were well known and publicized by the founders of our nation. A reading of the *Federalist Papers* would convince anyone of this. The colonists, under British rule, had become quite sensitive to the abuses and excesses of governmental power. As a matter of historical fact, it was largely the reactions by the colonists to oppressive British rule that caused the American Revolution. It is in this context that Justice Felix Frankfurter exclaimed in his dissent to *United States v. Rabinowitz,* 339 U.S. 56, 69 (1950), that the drafting of the Fourth Amendment's "unreasonable searches and seizures" provision must be understood. The precise intent of the constitutional framers in including the Fourth Amendment in the Constitution cannot be known for sure as no records were kept, but the Supreme Court, in *Chimel v. California,* 395 U.S. 752–763 (1969), contended that credible historians have acknowledged that the Bill of Rights' authors, who had suffered at the hands of oppressive British governors, wanted future generations of Americans protected against arbitrary intrusions into their private affairs by any governmental officials.

But how have the courts applied the Fourth Amendment to administrative searches, which mostly involve inspections aimed at discovering whether persons and businesses are complying with various agency regulations in the areas of health (including perceived moral health),

safety, and welfare? Because the regulatory activities of the emerging administrative state are relatively new to the American scene, well-established law on how the Fourth Amendment should be applied to administrative intrusions into the private practices of individuals and businesses has not yet developed. Opinions on how the Fourth Amendment should apply to administrative searches have varied greatly from court to court and even within the same courts. In 1971 in *Wyman v. James,* 400 U.S. 309, for example, the Supreme Court said essentially that administrative inspections were not searches restricted by the Fourth Amendment since they are not intended to produce evidence which could be used in criminal prosecutions. However, two decades earlier, in *Rabinowitz,* the Supreme Court recognized that search and seizure standards must be applied to administrative officials to prevent capricious and malicious administrative behavior.

Administrative search law is very complex and involves administrative searches of all kinds, some requiring administrative search warrants. As a general rule, warrants are not required when the businesses or concerns are historically and pervasively regulated (pawn and gun shops); statutes authorize inspections (mines, nuclear power plants); a special danger is posed to the public health and safety (restaurants, transportation services); a heightened state interest exists (gambling establishments); and no reasonable expectation of privacy exists. Generally, administrative search warrants are required when these above conditions do not exist and where individuals and businesses have a reasonable expectation of privacy.

Recent court decisions in administrative search law have tended to expand the power of the administrative state by ruling in favor of rather intrusive searches, thus reducing the expectation of privacy (*Dow Chemical Co. v. United States,* 106 S.Ct. 1819 [1986]; and *Florida v. Riley,* 109 S.Ct. 693 [1989]). Both decisions upheld "high-tech" aerial searches, even though dissenting Justices Brennan, Marshall, and Stevens (Justice Blackmun wrote a separate dissenting opinion) thought such searches could sanction George Orwell's dreaded vision of Big Brother watching us. Many scholars argue that *Dow Chemical* and *Riley* unfortunately sanction high-tech warrantless searches that can be classified as nonintimate and nondetailed. Although this involved a helicopter police search, *Riley* has implications for warrantless administrative searches because the courts apply less strict Fourth Amendment restrictions when administrative searches are involved.

Lisa Steele (1991) is very concerned that new technologies will allow invasive, "intimate" warrantless searches, given general judicial sympathy for such searches, and such will bring ". . . Orwell's vision closer to reality" (p. 302). Since the *Dow Chemical* rulings federal, state, and local governments have been experimenting with various new technologies that have allowed "Big Brother" to get a better peek at what businesses and citizens are doing. For example, sophisticated radar equipment can produce high-resolution radar images (reflections) by sending a high energy pulse at objects in homes and businesses or within the "curtilage" of these homes and businesses. Infrared sensors have been used to detect infrared light and heat through the walls of homes and businesses, while aerial searches of "open fields" within the "curtilage" of private homes and businesses can be conducted from space by high-tech satellite equipment.

Unfortunately, in recent years courts have used all sorts of rationales, some patently absurd, to justify high-tech governmental searches. Often, courts have argued that such searches are reasonable and the person or place being searched had no reasonable expectation of privacy because the high-tech equipment "only assisted" or "materially enhanced" the natural senses or that the equipment used is "widely available commercially" or that the searched party did not do enough to guarantee privacy such as stopping detectable heat losses from a structure or that the person did too much to guarantee privacy, thus creating reasonable suspicion to justify a search warrant or that the searched party "knew or should have known that he was observable" even if the observation was made from a distance high in the sky. Steele concludes that the courts should carefully examine the implications of such high-tech searches on our Fourth Amendment privacy rights.

KENNETH F. WARREN

BIBLIOGRAPHY

Bacigal, Ronald J., 1978. "Some Observations and Proposals on the Nature of the Fourth Amendment." *George Washington Law Review,* vol. 46 (May).

Robinson, Glen O., Ernest Gellhorn, and Harold H. Bruff, 1980. *The Administrative Process,* 2nd ed. St. Paul, MN: West Publishing Company.

Schwarz, Bernard, 1991. *Administrative Law,* 3rd ed. Boston: Little, Brown, and Company.

Steele, Lisa J. 1991. "The View From on High: Satellite Remote Sensing Technology and the Fourth Amendment." *High Tech Law Journal,* vol. 6 (Fall).

Warren, Kenneth F., 1996. *Administrative Law in the American System,* 3rd ed. Upper Saddle River, NJ: Prentice Hall.

Wright, Ronald F., 1984. "The Civil and Criminal Methodologies of the Fourth Amendment." *The Yale Law Review,* vol. 93 (May).

ADMINISTRATIVE STATE. A term usually found as the administrative state (TAS), originating in the 1940s and used most commonly to characterize the expanding structures and functions of the administrative mechanism of modern governments. Specific emphases differ widely, but most typically the term connotes great size and complexity, and some recent usage implies such institutional power and discretion as to threaten constitutional arrangements. The term has thus far been confined almost entirely to the public administration literature of the United States and Canada.

Early recognition of the emergence of the TAS concept has frequently been associated with Woodrow Wilson's oft-quoted statement in his famous 1887 essay on "The Study of Administration": "It is getting to be harder to run a constitution than to frame one." The situation today is still much as suggested by the late Arthur W. Macmahon, distinguished Columbia University political scientist, in his 1948 combined review of the first two books bearing the words "the administrative state" in their titles: the term is "so profoundly suggestive, so near to cliche" (p. 203). Nevertheless the phrase has the advantage of connoting a neutrality notably lacking in the competing and currently far more popular terms of bureaucracy or bureaucratic state.

Though well-known in public administration and political science circles for half a century, the TAS phrase is still infrequently used. It has never been a reference topic in printed periodical or book indexes, nor is it a Library of Congress "controlled vocabulary term" (official subject heading). Apparently, this entry is the first in any dictionary of either political science or public administration. A search of 25 or so current textbooks in public administration has revealed only one specifically discussing TAS, and then for barely two pages compared to more than 30 devoted to bureaucracy (Fesler and Kettl, 1991, pp. 1–3).

Origin

The first use of TAS as a key phrase seems to have occurred in an article by the late Joseph Rosenfarb (1904–55), New York lawyer, labor relations specialist, and author who published an article in the February 1945 issue of the *North Carolina Law Review* titled "The Administrative State: Compulsives in Labor Relations" (pp. 89–106). Here he concludes that in the modern state, "it will be in the realm of public administration that the main emphasis will be placed. Hence we are on the threshold of what should be called the administrative state" (p. 104). In a prefatory note he adds, "This article constitutes a portion of a forthcoming book on the nature and functions of the modern state. It will bear the title of this article: 'The Administrative State'" (p. 89).

He and the well-known political scientist and public administration analyst Dwight Waldo then both published volumes in 1948 carrying the TAS phrase in their titles. Waldo's book, his first major work, was based on his doctoral dissertation and published while he was an assistant professor of political science at the University of California, Berkeley. Rosenfarb's work was his third. Titled *Freedom and the Administrative State,* his volume, never widely read, has been essentially forgotten. This may be in part because of an incredible error by, presumably, both *Public Administration Review* and Macmahon in the joint review noted above. Inexplicably, Rosenfarb is cited throughout the review as "Goldfrab." Not once is the author identified by his correct name. Perceptive and well-argued, Rosenfarb's book deserves better, for it is typical of a popular and influential approach to governmental reform in the period between the world wars.

Rosenfarb (1948) begins with an extensive analysis of underlying U.S. political reasons for an increasing reliance on governmental regulation and administration. Legislatures can no longer draft laws that are self-executing, he observes, and the adversarial and nonexpert judicial process is ill adapted to decision making about highly technical and complex issues. Then, in one of the early recognitions of the special relevance of independent regulatory commissions to the integration and power of U.S. public administration, he posits: "Only the administrative bureau or tribunal combining the . . . executive, legislative and judicial processes could perform the tasks entrusted to modern government" (p. 206). Like many who lived through the great economic, social, and political crises of the 1920s and 1930s on through World War II, Rosenfarb was responding by advocacy of a centralized state which, though democratic in traditional terms and fully supportive of private enterprise, would be firmly committed in the name of equity to governmental intervention, central planning, and an integrated administrative system. Thus "will administration gain in importance and lend its character to the whole state" (p. 206). "The administrative state," he concludes, "incorporates the principle that to be good it is not enough for government to be strong, but without being strong it cannot be good" (p. 229). Such an approach (often termed "liberal" in the U.S. today) to the welfare state has dominated democratic theory and practice worldwide for much of the last half century. It was under such auspices that the initial concept of TAS was born.

Waldo has never claimed invention of TAS as a phrase. "It was simply in the air," he has said (telephone interview, January 26, 1995). His 1948 volume, *The Administrative State*, is, as advertised in its subtitle, *A Study of the Political Theory of American Public Administration*. Covering the literature of the previous half century, the work analyzes an extraordinary range of published material and, republished in 1984, has remained a classic for which there is as yet no sequel. Beyond its title, the book contains no further reference to TAS. Indeed, Waldo apparently never pursued the matter elsewhere except when, very briefly twice in the 1980s, he has argued that "a strong case can be made that 'administrative state' is a redundant expression: that a state by its nature is administrative else it is not a state" (1984, p. 191).

By implication Waldo's 1948 administrative state equates to modern public administration as practiced at all levels of U.S. government. In his joint review Macmahon concludes that Waldo's "striking contribution is to show the historical frame of the assumptions of half a century of writing about public administration" (1948, p. 204). For Waldo that frame is essentially a turn-of-the-century Pro-

gressivism vacillating between the views and methods of those who looked forward, like Rosenfarb, to a planned and administered society and those who were committed to "the old liberal faith in an underlying harmony, which by natural and inevitable processes produced the greatest possible good if the necessary institutional and social reforms are made as a result of more pragmatic and much less doctrinaire considerations" (p. 17).

These "two dissimilar but not inconsistent books," as Macmahon characterized them (1948, p. 203), brought TAS into the lexicon of public affairs, but only subliminally. During the next three and a half decades a bare half dozen relevant works appear, and only one in the 22 years between 1957 and 1979. Most of the more comprehensive treatments of TAS appeared before 1970, though there has been a modest revival of interest in aspects of TAS since the middle 1980s, which marked both the republication of Waldo's book and the centennial of Wilson's 1887 essay on administration.

As can be seen here, the concept has, however, interested a number of the best known authors in political science and public administration, commencing with Waldo. They do not, however, comprise anything like a school of thought or otherwise cohesive group except that most have been more or less associated with public administration. Even the few who have dealt with TAS in any full sense diverge greatly in basic themes—Waldo, say, compared to Rosenfarb. For most TAS is one of several concerns rather than "the" concern. Moreover, for none of the authors cited here does TAS provide a theme for more than one effort.

Other General Works

Other authors of the more comprehensive treatments of TAS include Marshall E. Dimock (1951), Fritz Morstein Marx (1957), and, especially, Emmette S. Redford (1969).

Attracted by the TAS concept "which has recently come into wide use" (Dimock, 1951, p. viii) and familiar with both Rosenfarb's and Waldo's writings on the subject (his first footnote cites them both, p. 1), the late Marshall Dimock in his *Free Enterprise and the Administrative State* defined TAS as "the political state when it has taken on heavy responsibilities . . . especially those that deal with economic life. The administrative state is the civil service state. . . . Administration threatens to overshadow policy making and politics. It is an interventionist state" (1951, pp. viii–ix). However, Dimock is unique among TAS analysts in an equal concern about a steady drift toward private economic concentration in the U.S. "If we are to steer clear of either extreme of collectivism," he writes, "monopolistic capitalism on the one hand or state collectivism on the other, we must think more clearly than we have about the philosophy of the state, the economy, and the individual and their juxtaposition in public policy and administration" (p. 167). Remedies are to be sought in the maintenance of economic competition and industrial efficiency, bolstered by effective government regulation, so that there is freedom of management to manage. "The chief role of government should be stabilization, not detailed control" (p. 166). Underneath all this there must be on the part of both government and business a concept of service in the name of humanity.

Marx's *The Administrative State* (1957) is best described by its subtitle, *An Introduction to Bureaucracy*. One of the first general studies of bureaucracy, it is unique among the works cited here because it is largely comparative. There is little specific reference to the United States in this second volume of "The Chicago Library of Comparative Politics." Even the definition of TAS is relegated to a footnote (p. 2): TAS "should be thought of not as a state devoid of legislative and judicial organs but as a state in which administrative organizations and operations are particularly prominent, at least in their quantitative aspects." Throughout, Marx makes no effort to distinguish TAS from bureaucracy in general, with major headings distinctly Weberian—for example, "Bureaucracy as Structure," "Bureaucracy as Indictment," and "The Requirement of Rationality." Though the texts of Dimock and Marx have little in common, their underlying conclusions are similar in one important respect: their mutual concern that the proper focus of TAS be upon the welfare of humanity. "The men of the top cadre must shift their attention from watching 'processes' to measuring their impact," Marx writes, "from 'getting things done' to giving each citizen his due, from the technology of administration to its effect upon the general public, from utility to ethics" (p. 187).

The relationship of TAS to democracy has provided a subtheme in several works, but Emmette Redford's *Democracy in the Administrative State* was the first—and remains almost the sole—effort under the TAS category to consider this critical relationship in rigorous depth. "My purpose in this book," he says, "is to reconcile the two" (1969, p. 4).

Redford writes only about the U.S. experience with TAS, which he defines as "a political-administrative system which focuses its controls and renders its services through administrative structures but includes also the interaction of political structures through which these are sustained, directed, and limited" (p. 4). Administration can be democratic if it follows the canons of a democratic morality which derives from three interrelated ideals. First, "man is, for man, the ultimate measure of all human values. This is the individualistic foundation ... the ideal of individual realization" (p. 6). Second, "all men have worth deserving social recognition ... This is the equalitarian component" (p. 6). Third, personal worth (liberty) "is most fully protected by the action of those whose worth is assumed" (p. 6). That is, there must be universal political participation.

In considering TAS he recognizes the growing program specialization and fractionalization within TAS but sees these as bridged by participative mechanisms. Participation through aiming at majority votes is much less important for attainment of the democratic ideal than a system promoting "the inclusiveness of the representation of interests in the interactive process among decision makers" (p. 44). As the subject of administration, citizens must be treated humanely and with due process. This means a right to know what is going on, a right of access and to be heard, a right to a fair forum, and a right of appeal; and there must be special provisions for the poor. The duties for public employees of TAS to perform should be in exchange for material and psychic rewards and not so absorbing that there is no privacy.

Redford sees TAS continuing to expand "because politicians see that people have interests that can be fulfilled only by public policy and public administration" (p. 182). The public and private sectors are interlocked in a kind of public-private analog to federalism. An escape from TAS "would not mean escape from the administered society" (p. 180). His solutions lie in the realms of political understanding and pragmatic political choice, based on the concepts of democratic morality and citizenship as outlined above, rather than in proposals for system or constitutional change.

There are procedural problems that affect the workability of TAS, such as effective representation of both urban and rural poor, too much administrative secrecy, and threats to individual privacy. There are also basic political considerations. Interaction processes take place at any or all of three political levels; micropolitical, subsystem, or macropolitical. The worst problems, Redford has concluded, derive from the latter—from presidential overload and, especially, from the growing inability of Congress to act with either unity or dispatch.

TAS and Congress

Here Redford's views converge with those of three other TAS analysts who, unlike Redford, are mainly interested in TAS as a foil to help explain Congress's interests and how it functions. These are James McGregor Burns, who published his first major political work, *Congress on Trial: The Legislative Process and the Administrative State,* in 1949; and Lawrence C. Dodd and Richard L. Schott, whose *Congress and the Administrative State* appeared in 1979. The former is predictive and the latter confirmative, with Redford in between.

With no reference to the works of either Rosenfarb or Waldo, issued a year earlier, Burns devotes all of two long paragraphs to TAS. Its assumptions are "that our elaborate administrative apparatus is here to stay; that it must be at the service of the great mass of the voters; that it must be given direction and purposefulness; that it is a rather delicate mechanism and cannot stand too much tampering." The legislator who has created TAS, he observes, is "uneasy at the sight of this looming bureaucracy." The great danger to TAS lies, Burns argues, "in the centrifugal tendencies of a Congress which could seek to turn the administrative system to its individualistic purposes, with the result that "the bureaucracy degenerates into a jumble of clashing principalities separately responsible to every group except a majority of voters" (quotes from pp. 115–116). This concludes Burns on TAS, but the clear implication is that the danger is imminent.

Some 30 years later Dodd and Schott affirmed that the danger had arrived. The decentralization of Congress into subcommittee government has meant that the executive branch is now "best characterized as agency or bureau government rather than presidential government in the true sense of the word" (1979, p. 323). They are also convinced "that Congress faces a serious problem in monitoring and influencing the administrative state under existing institutional and constitutional arrangements" (p. 357). Unquestionably created by Congress, often for compassionate reasons, TAS has taken on, they conclude, "a life of its own and has matured to a point where its muscle and brawn can be turned against its creator" (p. 2).

The Legitimacy Question

The Dodd and Schott study symbolizes the disenchantment with TAS that first surfaced in national politics under President Richard Nixon. Since then criticism of TAS has continued unabated, rising to a shrill crescendo during and following the mid-term elections of 1994. Much of this literature is found under headings other than TAS, such as bureaucracy, reinventing government, and deregulation. This critical view developed late in the literature of TAS, and most pointedly in John Marini's 1992 study, *The Politics of Budget Controls: Congress, the Presidency, and the Growth of the Administrative State*.

Factually, Marini's political analysis (1992) of the congressional-TAS relationship is in the Burns, Redford, Dodd and Schott tradition, but pushed a step further: the presidency—especially through Wilson, Franklin D. Roosevelt, and Johnson—pushed for TAS, with Congress often opposed. After TAS was a reality "Congress became its greatest benefactor and defender" and the presidency, from the time of Nixon, its most implacable foe (p. 12).

Preferentially, however, Marini, along with many others of the growing anti-bureaucratic school, rests much of his anti-TAS position on a presumption of illegitimacy. That is, so the argument runs in brief, the U.S. TAS is the result of a turn-of-the-century Progressive centralizing thrust to create "an engine of compassion" (p. 10). While this "did not violate in any way the letter of the Constitu-

tion" (p. 183), it has been subversive of such fundamental U.S. constitutional principles as "limited government, separation of powers, and American federalism" (p. 185). Hence, the legitimacy of TAS "rests uneasily within the structure of American constitutionalism" (p. 184).

The principal response to Marini's illegitimacy argument of 1992 has been in print since 1986, when John A. Rohr published his *To Run a Constitution: The Legitimacy of the Administrative State*. Marini cites Rohr's study, but never confronts it directly. Rohr, of course, was aiming his defense of TAS's legitimacy at a number of prior critics writing under other key terms, notably "bureaucratic state."

"When I speak of the 'administrative state,'" Rohr has written, "I mean the political order that came into its own during the New Deal and still dominates our politics. . . . Its hallmark is the expert agency tasked with important governing functions through loosely drawn statutes . . . (it is) in reality the welfare/warfare state we know so well" (1986, p. xi). His legitimacy argument is complex. However, he has expressed its essence as follows: TAS "is a plausible expression of the constitutional order envisioned in the great public argument at the founding of the Republic" (p. 181). That is, TAS is in accord with the theory and practice of the Federalists, who won the argument and set both political and administrative precedents.

A Canadian View

The one totally foreign volume about TAS—*The Administrative State in Canada* (Dwivedi, 1982), essays in honor of the distinguished public administration scholar then retiring from Queens University, J.E. Hodgetts, edited by O.P. Dwivedi—was of course, being Canadian, not very foreign. About the nature of the Canadian TAS, the essays mirror the U.S. literature, stressing the "Janus-like image" (p. 5) of "social servant and state juggernaut" (p. 7). Moreover, "the administrative state has had to reconcile the inherent tensions between the efficiency objectives of management science with its centralist bias, and the responsive and participatory traditions of (Canadian) political science with its decentralist bias" (p. 233). However, the introductory essay by V.S. Wilson of Carleton and Dwivedi of Guelph stresses two important differences between the TAS system of Canada and that of the United States. First, they point out that the creation of a central TAS was essential for the formation of a united Canada, given its extraordinarily decentralized settlement. The second difference is "a rather philosophical one: Americans possess a trait of debating contemporary issues in terms of fundamental principles . . . we in Canada are much more pragmatic." Public administrative matters do not provide "important aspects of constitutionalism in Canada" (p. 4).

The decade between 1985 and 1995 has seen two other types of TAS literature: one in the form of several studies relating to TAS in terms of single issues, and the other via two multi-issue symposia.

Single Issue Studies

Jerry L. Mashaw's *Due Process in the Administrative State* (1985) emphasizes and analyzes in great legal detail the increasing tendency of TAS to produce a "quasi-judicial model for administrative decision making" (p. 35). There has been much discussion of the judicialization of administrative procedure on the model of a civil trial, but few opinions as considered and thoroughly argued as those of Mashaw. He seeks a balance between the full constitutionalizing (judicialization) of due process and related procedures and the full exclusion of lawyers and court formality from TAS processes (pp. 267–271). This is the closest there is to a study of TAS-judicial relationships.

Intergovernmental Relations in the American Administrative State by David M. Welborn, and Jesse Burkhead (1989) defines TAS as "the complex of bureaucratic structures and processes through which the bulk of governmental business is conducted" (p. 1). The TAS emphases here are twofold: first, as the U.S. TAS became much more intergovernmental in character between 1930 and the 1960s, the effect was an "enlarged scope and penetration of national power" (p. 1). Then as interest groups became central actors, the result was the current exceedingly complex pattern of decentralized, subgovernment politics involving both vertical as well as horizontal relationships among federal, state, and local political and administrative units.

Also in 1989, Richard W. Waterman wrote *Presidential Influence and the Administrative State*. This is the only study thus far to relate entirely to TAS and the presidency. Waterman's primary interest, however, is in the administrative presidency. He concludes that in directing agencies the president can "usefully employ some of the techniques of the administrative presidency . . . especially the president's appointment power" but also that "presidents must seek to persuade key elements within their own executive branch . . . in much the same manner as a president must bargain and compromise with Congress" (p. 2).

Managing Leviathan: Environmental Politics and the Administrative State, edited by Robert Paehlke and Douglas Torgerson (1990), has been published under the auspices of Canada's Trent University, but four of the nine authors are from the U.S. Their focus is in terms of the international environmental movement, with the main thesis stressing that environmental administration departs from conventional public administration in several respects. Initially, by questioning assumptions about human domination of nature and the environment through the classical structures of government and the private sector, they question the morality of the TAS type of control system. Further, and contrary to TAS, environmental administration (EA)

departs from conventional administration, public and private, in at least five other ways. EA issues are hard to compartmentalize for they involve a "pervasive complex of problems" (p. 292). Problem boundaries are open and, for the most part, unclear. With a slogan of "think globally, act locally" (p. 293) EA has a clear decentralized thrust. It is antitechnocratic in that, while it draws heavily on experts, their findings sooner or later have to be put in the simpler political contexts of everyday living. Finally, any EA decision or action system must, in light of the preceding, remain unusually flexible. The primary solution is to make TAS (Leviathan here) more open and participatory. In this respect the collective authors have something in common with Redford, whose TAS work they cite in their first footnote.

Bicentennial Symposia

The 1985–95 decade also saw the publication of two major symposia relating to TAS, both prompted by the bicentennial of the U.S. Constitution, which coincided with the centennial of Woodrow Wilson's famous 1887 essay on "The Study of Administration." *The American Constitution and the Administrative State* (1989), edited by Richard J. Stillman II, is best described by its subtitle, *Constitutionalism in the Late 20th Century*, for only two of 13 essays build on prior TAS literature. Stillman's own "Introduction" stresses the conjunction of events—notably the formation of the first independent regulatory commission, the Interstate Commerce Commission, in 1887—which made the late nineteenth century so important in the development of TAS. Lawrence J. O'Toole, Jr.'s "Doctrines and Developments: Separation of Powers, the Politics-Administration Dichotomy, and the Rise of the Administrative State" supplements Rohr's prior treatment of the separation of powers through, especially, case histories of relevant legislation such as the Pendleton Act of 1883. As Stillman says, the remaining essays help to fill a void in the bicentennial literature "by studying critical problems at the interstices of the Constitution and administration which have thus far been dealt with in only a few books" (p. 9). In this Stillman is correct, but the result is a collection of fragments. For example, Chester Newland on "Public Executives" and Kenneth L. Kraemer and John L. King on "Computers and the Constitution" are revealing, but they are unconnected and the relation to TAS unclear.

A Centennial History of the American Administrative State (1987) edited by Ralph Clark Chandler, is similar. That is, only three of 17 chapters deal precisely with TAS. However, the introductory chapter by Paul P. Van Riper, on "The American Administrative State: Wilson and the Founders," is unique in its formulation of an operational definition for TAS. Somewhat expanded from a 1983 version in *Public Administration Review*, the article brings together ten criteria. Six come from Max Weber: classical organization, recruitment by merit, rational decision making, rule of law, written procedures and records, and a well-developed money economy. Four others derive from other sources: a base in quantitative techniques; supporting technology, especially in communications; enforcement of responsibility and ethical standards; and all of these in a well-developed system. Based on this generic definition, Van Riper concludes that the U.S. has met these criteria twice: first, under the Federalist and Jeffersonian Republican regimes, with Alexander Hamilton as the central figure; and second, commencing in the late nineteenth century, with the civil service reformers and President Theodore Roosevelt as initial driving forces, and ending with President Lyndon Johnson's Great Society legislation.

Van Riper sees each TAS with tendencies toward self-destruction. The fatal flaw in the first U.S. TAS lay in a "widespread perception of its elitism" (p. 25); that of the second in widespread evidence of overload and development into the kind of overpowering and totally absorbing bureaucratic state portrayed by Ralph P. Hummel in *The Bureaucratic Experience* (1982). That is, Van Riper's approach is secondarily distinguished by a cyclical view of the rise and decline of two TAS systems in the U.S. through time.

Rohr's essay on "The Administrative State and Constitutional Principles" is a summary reformulation of his 1986 work noted above. "A Century of the Intergovernmental Administrative State" by Deil S. Wright stresses three developments, beginning with the end of the dual federalism in the late nineteenth century. This was followed by a century of developing intergovernmental relations (IGR), a term not in broad use until the 1950s. The third focus represents the essay's most distinctive contribution to the TAS concept. This describes what Wright terms intergovernmental management (IGM), the new (to government) kinds of entrepreneurial skills required to maneuver among three levels of government and a myriad of federal and state grant-in-aid programs.

The remaining chapters in the Chandler symposium resemble those in the Stillman volume. All concern important matters in U.S. public administration, but the result is still somewhat disconnected. However, by providing an editorial introduction to all contributions, Chandler improves the unity of the volume.

Conclusion

Both of these last two studies illustrate the inherent difficulty in coming to grips with the TAS concept. Unlike the term "bureaucratic state," for example, which can be anchored to Max Weber's brief essay, there is no such reference point for TAS. Redford's study is the closest there is. Is TAS the regulatory state, the welfare state, the socialist Leviathan, just another bureaucratic state, or, as we say, "all of the above"?

On the other hand, the very looseness of the TAS terminology permits one to define as the situation requires, with no violation of one or another norm, for there are none. Moreover, TAS is a relatively neutral term, carrying with it none of the intellectual baggage of, for example, Weber, Hummel, or Karl Marx, not to mention a host of derogatory connotations that hover around "bureaucracy." The fact that this encyclopedia is the first of its kind to include TAS as a subject heading is suggestive of its intellectual future.

PAUL P. VAN RIPER

BIBLIOGRAPHY

Burns, James McGregor, 1949. *Congress on Trial*. New York: Harper.

Chandler, Ralph Clark, ed., 1987. *A Centennial History of the American Administrative State*. New York: The Free Press.

Dimock, Marshall E., 1951. *Free Enterprise and the Administrative State*. Birmingham: University of Alabama Press.

Dodd, Lawrence C. and Richard L. Schott, 1979. *Congress and the Administrative State*. New York: John Wiley and Sons.

Dwivedi, O. P., ed. 1982. *The Administrative State in Canada*. Toronto: University of Toronto Press.

Fesler, James W. and Donald W. Kettl, 1991. *The Politics of the Administrative Process*. Chatham, NJ: Chatham House.

Hummel, Ralph, 1982. *The Bureaucratic Experience*. New York: St. Martin's Press.

Mashaw, Jerry L., 1985. *Due Process in the Administrative State*. New Haven, CT: Yale University Press.

Macmahon, Arthur W., 1948. "The Administrative State." *Public Administration Review*, vol. 8 (Summer) 203–211.

Marini, John, 1992. *The Politics of Budget Control: Congress, the Presidency and the Growth of the Administrative State*. Washington, D.C.: Crane Russak.

Marx, Fritz Morstein, 1957. *The Administrative State: An Introduction to Bureaucracy*. Chicago: University of Chicago Press.

Paehlke, Robert and Douglas Torgerson, eds., 1990. *Managing Leviathan: Environmental Politics and the Administrative State*. Peterborough, Ont.: Broadview Press.

Redford, Emette S., 1969. *Democracy in the Administrative State*. New York: Oxford University Press.

Rohr, John A., 1986. *To Run a Constitution: The Legitimacy of the Administrative State*. Lawrence: University Press of Kansas.

Rosenfarb, Joseph, 1945. "The Administrative State: Compulsives in Labor Relations." *North Carolina Law Review*, vol. 23 (February) 89–106.

———, 1948. *Freedom and the Administrative State*. New York: Harper Bros.

Stillman II, Richard J. ed., 1989. *The American Constitution and the Administrative State: Constitutionalism in the Late 20th Century*. Lanham, MD: University Press of America.

Waldo, Dwight, 1948. *The Administrative State*. New York: Ronald Press Co.

———, 1984. "Communications." *Public Administration Review* (March/April) 191–192.

Waterman, Richard W., 1989. *Presidential Influence and the Administrative State*. Knoxville, TN: University of Tennessee Press.

Welborn, David M. and Jesse Burkhead, 1989. *Intergovernmental Relations in the American Administrative State*. Austin, TX: University of Texas Press.

Wilson, Woodrow, 1887. "The Study of Administration."
Political Science Quarterly, vol. 2 (June).

ADVERSARY SYSTEM.

System of justice wherein the opposing sides have the opportunity to prove their case by presenting evidence and challenging each other's view of fact or law before an impartial third party. "Adverse" means to be opposed, resistant, or contrary to a proceeding, claim, or application. In civil law, *adversus* means against. To have an adversary is to have an opponent such as a litigant-opponent as an opposing party in an action or writ.

Historical Background

The Anglo-American system of justice, modeled on the English system, is generally based on the right to trial by one's peers as set forth in the Magna Carta or great charter signed in 1215. The American court system is an adversarial system wherein the defense and the prosecution are adversaries with the judge serving as a referee. The adversarial process is one of opposites locked in opposition rather than a cooperative process. The assumption underlying an adversary system is that all disputes have at least two sides and that the "truth" is often found somewhere between the two versions presented by the opposing parties. The ideal adversarial process is one wherein the prosecution and the defense represent and debate the merits of their positions, to the best of their ability, introducing relevant evidence to support their positions whereby the facts surrounding the dispute will emerge and the truth will be discovered.

In an adversarial system, the process of discovery is more important than the discovery itself, for an adversarial process underscores abiding by the "rules of the game" and ensuring the rights of the accused. This suggests that due process of the law, as initially addressed in the Magna Carta and further established in the Fourth, Fifth, Sixth, and Fourteenth Amendments, is absolutely essential to the successful enactment of an adversarial process. The adversarial process must be bound by procedures that allow it to proceed in a fair and equitable manner so the adversaries have an equal opportunity to prove their assertion of guilt or innocence.

Given the considerable resources the state can deploy in opposition to a defendant, not only is the defendant entitled to legal defense, but the prosecution must present its case "beyond a reasonable doubt." In addition, the defendant is afforded constitutional protections against double jeopardy, self-incrimination, and other practices that would deprive the defendant of "life, liberty, and property without due process of law." These extensive protections for the defendant partially reflect the founding fathers' concern that a powerful government could tyrannically impose its will on individuals.

Defining Characteristics

Prior to the Magna Carta as well as in parts of the world today, an inquisitorial process rather than an adversarial process is apparent. With an inquisitorial process all parties, including the police and the courts, cooperate at all stages in the process. The investigation, review of evidence, and questioning of the accused as well as determination of guilt are all joint and cooperative endeavors. This approach conceptualizes the "truth" as objective, as a reality that exists "out there in the world" awaiting discovery. With the defendant a passive bystander, all other participants in the inquisitorial process are involved in a cooperative search for the truth. This approach assumes that a unified, cooperative approach among all participants can best insure that the innocence or guilt of the defendant is properly revealed.

Although the American court system in characterized as an adversarial system, examples of inquisitorial processes can be seen. The grand jury system is an example of one aspect of the American system of justice that incorporates significant dimensions of an inquisitorial process. A grand jury is called to establish whether or not there is "probable cause" based on sufficient evidence to prosecute a defendant. A grand jury is typically called by the prosecuting attorney. The prosecutor makes a one-sided presentation to the grand jury based on evidence and testimony carefully selected by the prosecution. The defendant is not present during the grand jury session and cannot be represented by counsel. The prosecutor must convince a majority of the jurors that probable cause exists to prosecute.

Although the grand jury cannot establish the guilt or innocence of a defendant, the decision on whether or not to prosecute is a critical step in the legal system. The underlying philosophy of the grand jury is that a closed, nonadversarial process is appropriate to establish the sufficiency of evidence for prosecution. The absence of important due process safeguards underscores the inquisitorial character of the grand jury system.

Despite the high ideals of the American court system to dispense justice through a fair, equitable, and thorough search for the truth, the actual operations of many courts fall far short of the ideals. Anyone who has witnessed a small claims court or a traffic court in action has likely witnessed something other than an adversarial process, bound by constitutional safeguards. The actual operation of many of these courts might more aptly be described as examples of a dispositional process. In a similar fashion, administrative law proceedings are often nonadversarial in nature. Administrative law hearings are typically rather informal. No right to counsel is guaranteed and therefore, no attorneys are present during the proceedings.

The typical lower criminal court where minor criminal violations are adjudicated is also an example of a dispositional process. A tremendous number of cases are regularly processed in a very limited amount of time. The guilt or innocence of the accused is seldom contested. The major concern is with efficiency, with routinely and swiftly disposing of a large number of cases. Mass-produced "justice" often results in the actual court proceeding taking less time on the average than routine police encounters with citizens in the field. Given the fact that the overwhelming majority of criminal cases are heard in lower courts, the image of the Anglo-American system of justice as an adversarial process may be more myth than reality.

The combative give-and-take between highly trained adversaries—one representing the defendant, the other the state—is seldom seen in the typical American courtroom. This is especially so when a court-appointed or public defender is involved. Burdened by heavy caseloads which contribute to the impersonal quality of justice, and lack of funding for expert witnesses, trained investigators, and sophisticated defense strategies, public defenders are often ill-equipped to confront the extensive legal resources of the state. Not surprisingly, the overwhelming majority of criminal defendants whose cases are heard in American courts are convicted. This is typical of all criminal courts in America, but especially so in lower criminal courts. The proportion of criminal cases resolved by a guilty plea is enormous, a clear majority in many court systems.

The drama of the adversarial process, of defense and prosecuting attorneys locked in legal combat, is seldom fully played out in the courtrooms of America. Given the legal resources necessary, few cases could properly be characterized as truly adversarial in nature. The swift disposition of cases, not a protracted adversarial process, comes to be seen as normal and to be expected.

In contrast to the adversarial process, the assumption underlying the dispositional process is that the decision to arrest, like the decision to prosecute, is not arrived at either randomly or haphazardly. The defendant is assumed to be guilty, either in the case as charged or certainly of some other crime or crimes they have previously committed, heretofore having successfully avoided arrest and/or prosecution. Rather than being concerned with determining guilt or innocence, the primary concern is to ascertain the most efficient means to settle cases. To minimize the amount of time and other resources necessary to dispose of cases requires collaboration between the prosecuting attorneys, the judges and, to whatever extent they are involved, the defense attorneys.

The role of the prosecutor is crucial in determining whether our system of justice is primarily adversarial, inquisitorial, or dispositional in character. The prosecutor occupies the central law enforcement position and is expected to prosecute individuals accused of a crime. The prosecutor is also an officer of the court, however, and must be concerned with seeking justice and protecting the due process rights of the accused. Most assuredly, the prosecutor is also a political figure held accountable by the public. The difficulties in balancing the often conflicting demands associated with this position are indeed challenging. How is a prosecutor to be effective, as measured by conviction rates (an important political goal); just, as in not prosecuting either the innocent or those cases with mitigating circumstances; and punitive, as in wholeheartedly prosecuting all cases? Faced with these inherently contradictory demands, prosecutors have tended to emphasize the goal of effectiveness as evident during election campaigns. This goal can be more readily measured and communicated to the public.

If an adversarial system is consistent with an emphasis on due process protections of the accused, a dispositional system is consistent with an emphasis on crime control. Recent trends in America have clearly shown that the increasing fear of crime has worked in favor of an emphasis on crime control rather than on due process protections. Certain advantages of the adversarial process incorporate a number of important safeguards into the American system of justice however. An adversarial system establishes a means for openly and thoroughly examining the evidence and relevant facts in a case. It protects the rights of the accused by concentrating that responsibility in the hands of a specific individual: the defense attorney, an expert qualified to represent the accused. It provides an important system of checks and balances whereby power is distributed among the various participants in our system of justice, particularly the prosecutor, the defense attorney, and the judge or jury.

CHARLES E. MARSKE

BIBLIOGRAPHY

Thomas, Charles W., and John R. Hepburn, 1983. *Crime, Criminal Law, and Criminology.* Dubuque, Iowa: W. C. Brown.

ADVERSE IMPACT.

Also known as "disparate impact"; instances where supposedly neutral employment or other practices have a disproportionately negative effect on racial or ethnic minorities, women, or other protected groups. An example would be height and weight requirements for jobs in law enforcement that operate to disqualify many more women than men. When the negative impact on members of protected classes becomes significantly large it is assumed to be prima facie evidence of discrimination (see **discrimination, gender; discrimination, racial**).

In the United States, agencies enforcing equal employment opportunity law issued the *Uniform Guidelines for Employee Selection* in 1978, in which adverse impact is defined as occurring when the selection rate for members of protected classes is less than 80 percent of the rate for the most frequently selected group. Adverse impact can also be determined from a comparison of the utilization of a protected group in an organization's work force to the percentage of the relevant qualified labor force consisting of members of that same group. When the two percentages are significantly different, discrimination may be suspected.

Development of the Concept of Adverse Impact

The doctrine of adverse or disparate impact was first articulated by the United States Supreme Court in the landmark case *Griggs et al. v. Duke Power Company* in 1971 (401 U.S. 424). Prior to passage of the Civil Rights Act of 1964, Duke Power Company hired African Americans only for its lowest paying positions as physical laborers. Following the effective date of the 1964 civil rights law, the company permitted blacks to apply for any jobs open but required a high school diploma or a passing score on a standardized intelligence test for jobs other than those at the lowest level. These new requirements had the effect of keeping African Americans out of all but the lowest jobs so that the segregation that had existed under the earlier openly discriminatory policy continued. The Court ruled that because the company could not show the new job requirements were in any way related to job performance and because the requirements operated to exclude most black applicants, the company's employment practices were illegal.

The outcome of the *Griggs* case added significantly to the effect of laws prohibiting discrimination. It was clear following passage of the 1964 Civil Rights Act that intentional discrimination (disparate treatment in the Court's idiom) would be prohibited, but the *Griggs* ruling and the concept of adverse or disparate impact that came from it indicated that nonintentional discrimination was equally offensive. Adverse impact analysis was intended to prevent practices that are facially neutral and even neutral in intent from operating to restrict opportunities for minorities, women, and others.

The Burden of Proof

Following the standard set out in *Griggs,* practices having an adverse effect on protected groups must be shown to serve a business necessity if they are to be permitted. When adverse impact cases come to court, minority or female plaintiffs must first provide evidence of an appropriate statistical disparity. Once that is demonstrated, the burden shifts to the respondent organization to articulate a nondiscriminatory reason for the practice or practices producing the disparity; that is, the organization must show how the practice or practices challenged serve business purposes. If this defense is made, the burden shifts back to the plaintiffs to show that the respondent's argument is merely a pretext for discrimination in that other nondiscriminatory practices exist that would equally serve the business necessity articulated.

As an example, an employment examination procedure might be challenged because it disproportionately screens out minority applicants. If the employer can demonstrate that the examination is a valid instrument for predicting subsequent job performance (i.e., it serves a business necessity), then the exam could be allowed to stand despite the disparity, unless minority employees could demonstrate that another equally valid procedure would not produce the disparate selection rate. It is in large part because of the decision in the *Griggs* case and the notion of adverse impact that employment examination validity has become one of the more important human resource management issues of the past two decades.

In a controversial 1989 decision, however, the *Griggs* decision was essentially overturned by the Supreme Court in *Wards Cove Packing Company, Inc. v. Atonio* (490 U.S. 642). Following *Wards Cove,* the burden of proof was to remain with employees at all times in adverse impact cases. It became necessary that employees prove employment practices producing an adverse impact were selected by the employer precisely because of their discriminatory effect. Thus, the distinction between adverse impact and disparate treatment that had previously hinged on the issue of an employer's intent to discriminate no longer existed. Civil rights advocates saw this as a major setback and efforts were mounted in Congress to respond to the Court's decision. Those efforts culminated in the Civil Rights Act of 1991, which reinstated standards for adverse or disparate impact analysis as they had been originally articulated in 1971 in *Griggs.*

Adverse Impact and Affirmative Action

Because evidence of a statistical disparity may be used as the basis for legal challenges to employment practices, it has been argued that the concept of adverse impact has added impetus to affirmative action (see **affirmative action**). In other words, employers and others may be more likely to engage in affirmative action to avoid, to the fullest extent possible, the kinds of statistical disparities that give rise to law suits based on adverse impact analysis. A good defense against charges of discrimination brought by minority plaintiffs, it is reasoned, is to have a well-integrated work force. Proponents of affirmative action regard this as another important outcome of the *Griggs* decision and the Civil Rights Act of 1991.

J. Edward Kellough

Bibliography

Questel, Lynn K., 1989. *Federal Laws Prohibiting Employment Discrimination.* Athens: Carl Vinson Institute of Government, The University of Georgia.

Riley, Dennis D., 1993. *Public Personnel Administration.* New York: HarperCollins College Publishers.

ADVOCACY.   The active support of or the pleading for a cause. The term encompasses at least three different kinds of activity: legal representation, interest group lobbying, and ideological persuasion. Open, democratic, heterogenous societies encourage all three types of activity as a means of influencing government policy. The United States, with governmental structures that are simultaneously complex and porous, supports large cadres of lawyers, lobbyists, and pundits whose primary work is that of advocacy. The complexity of government requires this infrastructure of advocates to equalize the relationship between citizens and the bureaucracy. Government's porousness means that influence can be exerted at many different levels, thus further encouraging advocacy as an essential means of policy development.

While it is often said that the United States is a government of laws and not of people, this bromide glosses over the exceedingly complex relationship among the processes of lawmaking, implementing, and advocacy. When Congress passes a law such as Social Security, the Clean Air Act, or Medicare, it often does so at the behest of interest groups who believe that the law will benefit either their constituents specifically or all citizens generally. Indeed, legislation is often written by an interest group and submitted by a friendly member of a legislative body who advocates the group's cause.

Awareness of the need for government action in a particular area can come about through the efforts of those who "sound the alarm" that a problem exists and will get worse without some policy initiative. Advocacy is therefore an essential element in both the recognition of a problem and the crafting of a solution or law to ameliorate it.

But the passage of a law does not ordinarily provide a detailed blueprint for how the law is to be carried out. That responsibility is left to the agency in whose policy area the law falls. If, for example, a law is passed dealing with childhood education, the U.S. Department of Education would be responsible for determining how benefits are distributed, under what conditions, and for how long. Thus, the laws passed by Congress are often followed by detailed sets of regulations formulated and promulgated by various governmental agencies. This agency rulemaking function provides another opportunity for advocacy, as those whose activity will be affected by the rules seek to avoid onerous regulatory burdens while those who will be helped seek to maximize the law's intent.

Of course, an individual can run afoul of either a substantive law or the regulations formulated to implement it. In the former case, the individual would need an advocate to plead in court. Advocacy in the latter instance would be in front of an agency's administrative tribunal.

Because advocacy is such an integral part of our processes of government, advocacy itself has become increasingly institutionalized. As noted, lawyers, lobbyists, and pundits form a professional core of advocates who ply their trade in venues that often require knowledge not available to the ordinary citizen. Certain groups, therefore, occupy a more advantageous position when attempting to influence government or agency policy than does either the individual citizen acting alone or less well-established entities. Four characteristics are increasingly associated with successful advocacy.

First, effective advocacy is conditioned by the degree of organization of those who seek to affect the legislative or rule making process. The more organization, the more likely a successful advocacy. Second, access to resources for employing lobbyists or legal counsel affects the success of an advocacy effort. In general, the more resources available for supporting or pleading a cause, the more successful that effort will be. Third, governmental processes tend to favor groups that are stable. Since both advocates and rulemakers labor under the constraints of imperfect knowledge and technology, many successes from an advocacy process are shortlived. The unanticipated results of a new rule, law, or policy require adjustments and continued advocacy. In a complex environment problems are not so much "solved" as managed. Finally, groups that are able to capture the mass media can mobilize public opinion and help form the general perception of what constitutes an appropriate problem and solution. A dramatic event, therefore, will often be the catalyst for an intense advocacy effort.

The characteristics increasingly associated with successful advocacy have caused many to question whether the ordinary citizen is any longer able to influence government or enjoy equal protection before its laws. If, for example, those with organization and access to resource are better able to influence the workings of government, are lawmakers only listening to the rich and powerful, the denizens of "Gucci Gulch?" Such a view oversimplifies the process, since most Americans are probably represented in one way or another by a group that has both the organization and the resources to have at least some influence on the course of policy deliberations. *Public Interest Profiles* (1988–89) describes 250 influential public interest and public policy organizations ranging from the National Association of Manufacturers, which represents over 80 percent of the manufacturing interests in the United States, through the American Association of Retired Persons with 28 million members, to a variety of religious group lobbies including the National Council of Churches, the United States Catholic Conference, and the American Jewish Congress. There are groups representing Arab-Americans, the homeless, people against drunk driving, and those interested in eliminating the abuse of farm animals. The volume lists 32 groups devoted to environmental causes alone. The Foundation for Public Affairs, which produced this listing, monitors over 2,500 public interest/public policy groups active at the national level. The problem then may be less one of an elite advocacy structure than of an apathetic population increasingly willing to leave advocacy to a committed core of individuals.

The answer to the question of equal access to advocates becomes more complicated when one considers issues of legal representation before courts or governmental agencies. Here it is much less certain that individuals are able to equally advocate before various tribunals. At this level, it appears that resources, organization, and stability are clearly determinative of a favorable outcome. There are a number of reasons for this. First, the law treats corporations as individuals. Thus, General Motors and the neighbor next door are each individual entities in the eyes of the law. General Motors, though, has greater access to both the legal and monetary resources necessary to pursue an issue to a favorable conclusion. Indeed, the capacity of large corporations to engage in protracted litigation may even discourage government agencies from vigorously pursuing their every rule infraction. Since public bureaucracies are evaluated on both efficiency and effectiveness, it may not make sense to use scarce resources in pursuit of a single multilayered corporate violator, when a large number of smaller violators can be processed within agency budget constraints. Finally, our legal and administrative systems reflect a cultural bias against the more marginal in society, whether individuals or groups. Lack of resources, stability, and organization are often considered to be indicative of a certain moral laxity, and thus such individuals or groups are more easily viewed as blameworthy.

Although those with organization and resources are in a better position to obtain the services of professional advocates such as lobbyists and lawyers, the access to pundits may be becoming easier. Many of these advocates operate in an increasingly democratized media environment that includes public access cable television and talk radio. This phenomenon is now recognized and cultivated by the established political structure. More people can therefore sound the alarm about problems real or imagined, capturing the attention and allegiance of public opinion. What is unknown is whether the complexity of many public issues can be sufficiently articulated in a forum that lends itself to the expression of simple problem statements and solutions. One thing is certain, however. In the United States, with over 630,000 licensed lawyers, many thousands of interests groups at the local, state, and national levels, and an expanding media forum for public discussion and debate, advocacy will remain an important element of both the culture and its governmental processes.

JAMES F. GILSINAN

BIBLIOGRAPHY

Black, Henry Campbell, 1968. *Black's Law Dictionary*. St. Paul, MN: West Publishing Co.

Foundation for Public Affairs, 1988. *Public Interest Profiles*. Washington, D.C.: Congressional Quarterly.

Gilsinan, James F., 1990. *Criminology and Public Policy: An Introduction*. Englewood Cliffs, NJ: Prentice Hall.

Stillman II, Richard J., 1991. *Preface to Public Administration: A Search for Themes and Direction*. New York: St. Martin's Press.

ADVOCACY ORGANIZATIONS.

Nonprofit organizations that organize under section 501(c)(4) status of the IRS code to engage principally in the promotion of a cause or the dissemination of information directed toward the purpose(s) of the organization, including lobbying efforts to influence policy or legislation. Advocacy organizations include social welfare organizations as "action" organizations defined by the IRS. By advocacy we mean the identification and purposeful pronouncement of concerns, needs, or agenda of clientele served by a nonprofit organization.

Advocacy and Advocacy Organization

It is important to distinguish between advocacy as an activity engaged in by nonprofit organizations in general from advocacy as a type of nonprofit organization. Actually, all types of organization and almost all nonprofits engage in advocacy activity in one form or another. Advocacy activity can include public education (or public relations) about an issue or cause, such as attempts to inform and/or change public attitudes about the abilities and rights of the mentally retarded or those with AIDS. Often advocacy activity means gaining legislative support for the cause of the organization. The target may be a legislative body or government official, whether city council, county government, school board, state legislature, or the U.S. Congress. These efforts are also called lobbying.

There are many ways in which voluntary, nonprofit organizations lobby to affect public policy. For example, the objective may be a new piece of legislation that causes the redirection or creation of programs or the attempt to influence tax policy changes or administrative reform. Advocacy activity also may include pursuit of or reinterpretation of a judicial decision through litigation or an effort to influence administrative regulation and deregulation although, technically, these last two examples of activities are not considered lobbying.

In some respects, advocacy by nonprofit organizations may differ little from the lobbying efforts of profit-making organizations that seek to influence legislation, regulations, and other factors that may affect them as contractors for the delivery of a public service. A major difference is that the board or other members of a nonprofit agency do not derive profit from governance of the organization. This "nondistribution constraint" is a rationale offered by supporters of nonprofit advocacy who argue that nonprofits speak for a noncommercial and ofttimes unrepresented public interest. Some public or population is the intended beneficiary rather than a special economic or commercial interest.

Limitations on Advocacy

The pursuit of public interest by nonprofits has limitations defined by the law. Restrictions are placed on the extent to which some nonprofits may promote themselves or their cause by legislative advocacy. Briefly, "charitable" non-profits, those tax exempt under Section 501(c)(3) of the Internal Revenue Code, are organized for specific public benefit purposes. These are the only U.S. nonprofit organizations that are both exempt from federal income taxes and to which contributions by taxpayers may be deducted. Presently, the law is clear about the legality and extent of lobbying and advocacy activity by 501(c)(3) nonprofit organizations. In 1976, legislation explained and expanded the amount of lobbying these nonprofits can conduct. In 1990, the Internal Revenue Service clarified the regulations that support both the spirit and the intent of the 1976 law (Smucker, 1994).

The 1976 lobbying law and the promulgated regulations define lobbying simply as the expenditure of money by the nonprofit organization to attempt to influence legislation. If there is no expenditure by the organization for lobbying, there is technically no lobbying. For example, if a 501(c)(3) volunteer is reimbursed by the nonprofit for out-of-pocket expenditures, these funds count as lobbying expenses. But personal advocacy before any body of government by volunteers or nonsalaried members of a non-profit organization that incurs no costs to the organization is not subject to these limitations. Many successful 501(c)(3) organizations develop skillful no-cost public relations efforts that build grassroots community awareness beyond their members and generate political support for positions. These include activities such as encouraging news media to comment on the group's position or publish favorable supporting editorials. A nonprofit has the potential of substantial lobbying power in its capability to enlist as many of its volunteer members as possible in support of its lobbying efforts. However, a 501(c)(4) organization, like its cousin under 501(c)(3), would lose its tax-exempt status if it became involved directly or indirectly in a political compaign involving a candidate for public office.

Other kinds of advocacy activities not considered lobbying and permitted without limit include communications to members about legislation and making available "nonpartisan analysis, study or research" about a particular issue. Responding to written requests from a legislative body for technical advice about pending legislation and the discussion of broad social, economic, and other policy issues when there is no discussion of specific legislative actions are also permitted (Smucker, 1994). These activities are the subject of debate in Congress and could be modified with new legislation.

Smucker (1994) summarizes the many details in the 1976 law and the regulations promulgated in 1990. In brief, the law and regulations establish specific spending ceilings for advocacy activities based upon on a sliding scale of percentages of the charity's budget for the year (20 percent of the first $500,000 and ending at 5 percent of expenditures over $1.5 million with a maximum ceiling of $1 million a year, as described in IRC 501(h).) Details of the application of laws that govern the tax-exempt status of these organizations are complex and can require legal counsel. Nonetheless, Smucker (1994) believes the 1976 lobbying law provides extraordinarily generous limits and 501(c)(3) organizations should not be put off by the sometimes complex information regarding the law.

The public interest conception of advocacy has its critics. At question is who determines the public's interests? Interests in a democracy are diverse and one person's public good may not be that of another. Recent arguments directed at the public interest conception of advocacy contend that the nonprofit sector has a liberal political bias toward those on the margins of society. Politically conservative critics believe this bias supports the continuation of a welfare policy that has not been especially successful nor always in the general public interest.

Private foundations do not come under the 1976 law and thus are prohibited from making expenditures for lobbying purposes. The foundation may, without tax liabilities, make a general purpose grant to a public charity that lobbies.

"Action" or Advocacy Organizations

Nonprofit organizations with special intent to lobby extensively choose to organize under Section 501 (c)(4) tax status and trade away the tax-deductibility of donations for the opportunity to engage in much more substantial attempts to influence legislation. It is these organizations which we consider truly advocacy organizations, what IRS regulations call "action" organizations. (Some large 501(c)(3) organizations have established "sister" 501(c)(4) organizations—contributions to which are not tax deductible as charitable gifts—to carry out their legislative advocacy.)

Illustrations of organizations that have chosen to organize as 501(c)(4) are considered by our definition as advocacy organizations. Examples include the Sierra Club and the National Rifle Association. Usually advocacy organizations seek to address broad social concerns or social movements rather than just the outcomes of benefit only to their members. They are often at the focus of extensive public debate and controversy about their cause or concerns.

The Conscience of a Nation

In summary, the *raison d'être* of nonprofit organizations is their mission or cause. Voluntary nonprofit organizations have dual roles of "case" (provision of social services) and "cause" (advocacy of social action) on behalf of their clients and mission. Advocacy gives "cause" a voice; "case" transforms the "cause" into action. As O'Neill (1989) reminds us, advocacy by nonprofit organizations represents the "conscience of a nation." In fact, O'Connell (1989) has called the role of advocacy "the quintessential function of the voluntary, nonprofit sector."

Congress has placed limits on the use of tax-deductible dollars for advocacy activity (lobbying) and because all contributions to 501(c)(3) organizations are tax-deductible charitable contributions, these groups face the strictest limitations in advocacy activities. None of the limitations apply to personal advocacy by volunteers, whose voices when heard operates at the heart of our democracy. As volunteer members of nonprofit organizations and citizens of our democracy, all are granted freedom to speak out and address the policies and actions of government and other established organizations, and thus to work to transform the political agenda and help carry out major social reforms.

RICHARD D. HEIMOVICS

BIBLIOGRAPHY

Henton, Douglas C. and Steve A. Waldron, 1983. "The Role of the Independent Sector in Governance Reform." In *Working Papers for the Spring Research Forum: Since the Filer Commission*. Washington, D.C.: Independent Sector.

O'Connell, Brian, 1976. "The Contribution of Voluntary Agencies in Developing Social Policies." New York: Council of Jewish Federations.

O'Neill, Michael, 1989. *The Third America*. San Francisco: Jossey-Bass Publishers.

Smucker, Bob, 1994. "Nonprofit Lobbying." In Robert Herman and Associates, ed., *The Handbook of Nonprofit Leadership and Management*. San Francisco: Jossey-Bass Publishers.

AFFIRMATIVE ACTION. Policies designed usually to enhance educational or employment prospects for racial and ethnic minorities and women who, because of discrimination, have been or currently are denied equal opportunity (see **discrimination, gender; discrimination, racial; equal employment opportunity**). In the United States, these policies were first utilized in the 1960s. Executive Order 10925, for example, issued by President John F. Kennedy in 1961, required federal government contractors to "take affirmative action to ensure that applicants are employed and that employees are treated during employment without regard to their race, creed, color, or national origin." Kennedy's order also required federal departments and agencies to take "affirmative steps to realize the national policy of nondiscrimination in government employment. President Lyndon B. Johnson's Executive Order 11246 of 1965 reasserted affirmative

action requirements of the Kennedy order applicable to government contractors.

Permutations of Affirmative Action

Specific programmatic efforts characterized as affirmative action related to employment usually begin with an employer's review and assessment of minority and female employment patterns. The purpose of the assessment is to identify jobs or positions where minorities and women are underrepresented (see **affirmative action plan**). Employers can then scrutinize personnel policies and possibly eliminate or modify those that have the effect of disproportionately screening out targeted groups, provided that suitable alternative policies are available. Efforts are also undertaken to actively recruit additional minority and female employees into the organization and to establish programs through which minorities and women in lower-level positions can develop skills sufficient to enable them to move up the organizational hierarchy.

Affirmative action contrasts sharply with previous equal employment opportunity strategies dating back to the 1940s. Early EEO policy consisted largely of statements prohibiting discrimination and programs through which individual complaints of discrimination could be investigated. Under that system, the employer reacted to instances of discrimination only after they were brought to the employer's attention by individual victims. Because many individuals were hesitant to register complaints, especially when laboring in discriminatory situations, policies limited to complaint processing and official pronouncements prohibiting discrimination proved to be of limited utility. Affirmative action is intended to the supplement those strategies by requiring the employer to act in a positive fashion to curtail and overcome the effects of discrimination directed against minorities and women.

Approaches to affirmative action such as the expansion of recruitment activities to include women and minorities, programs intended to enhance the upward mobility of lower-level workers, and efforts to remove institutional barriers to the employment of disadvantaged groups have been widely accepted and are relatively noncontroversial. Such policies, integral to most equal employment opportunity programs, are consistent with nondiscriminatory principles. Nondiscrimination requires, for example, that recruitment efforts include attempts to attract women and minorities to the organization rather than simply relying on strategies that intentionally or unintentionally exclude those groups.

In the early 1970s, however, numerical goals and timetables for minority and female employment began to appear in affirmative action plans. Numerical goals are targets for the representation of women and minorities in an organization's work force. Timetables are dates or time frames within which goals are planned to be accomplished. Although goals and timetables require no employer to hire or promote employees who do not possess requisite qualifications, they do allow for the consideration of race, ethnicity, and gender in employment decisions and are sometimes erroneously referred to as quotas. A 1971 memorandum to federal agency and department heads by Robert Hampton, Chairman of the United States Civil Service Commission, sought to distinguish goals from quotas by indicating that a goal is an objective an organization attempts to accomplish in a timely fashion within the context of merit, while a quota implies that employment is restricted to members of particular groups or that a specified number of members of those groups are to be employed without regard to merit principles (see **goals and quotas**).

The primary impetus for development of goals and timetables as an approach to affirmative action came from the slow rate of progress of minorities and women under earlier affirmative approaches. The use of goals and timetables represented a significant policy change. Because goals are formulated on the basis of race, ethnicity, or gender and efforts to achieve them include preferences extended to minorities or women when such individuals possess the necessary qualifications and it can be shown that those groups have been disadvantaged by past or current discrimination, selection policies no longer remain neutral. As might be expected, considerable controversy and, hence, judicial activity have resulted from affirmative action in this form. In fact, the debate over numerical strategies for affirmative action has risen to such a level that many people think only of goals and timetables or quotas when affirmative action is considered. Some argue that the limited preferences such policies provide for women and minorities constitute reverse discrimination (see **reverse discrimination**).

Justifications for Affirmative Action

How are race-, ethnicity-, and gender-conscious policies such as goals and timetables justified given that other policies, such as the Civil Rights Act of 1964 in the United States, prohibit discrimination? Frequently, the justification rests in part on a concept known as compensatory justice. This is the notion that groups such as minorities or women, who have historically suffered discrimination and have been denied opportunity as a result, should be given certain limited advantages to compensate for the past. Opponents of affirmative action counter that while the compensatory argument may hold for identifiable victims of discrimination it should not be applied to groups since some group members may not have suffered discriminatory treatment. Arguments for race-, ethnicity-, and gender-conscious affirmative action, however, are also usually

justified in more utilitarian terms in that they work to integrate society, reduce income inequalities, further distributive justice, and promote efficiency by ensuring that the talents of all individuals are utilized. In government employment, it is also suggested that when the work force is more representative of the people, it may be more responsive to the people's needs (see **representative bureaucracy**).

In the United States, the legality of race- and gender-conscious affirmative action has been upheld by the Supreme Court when certain conditions have been met. For example, when challenged on statutory grounds under provisions of the Civil Rights act of 1964 prohibiting discrimination, affirmative action has been permitted when it is designed to address a manifest racial or gender imbalance in traditionally segregated job categories, it is constructed as a temporary strategy, and it does not unnecessarily trammel the rights of nonminority males (see *United Steelworkers of America v. Weber*, 443 U.S. 193 [1979] and *Johnson v. Transportation Agency, Santa Clara County, California*, 480 U.S. 616 [1987]). Government programs, however, may also be challenged on constitutional bases. When affirmative action by a government employer is challenged under equal protection provisions of the Constitution that limit the government's ability to draw distinctions among its citizens, those programs are subjected to a rigorous review generally known as strict scrutiny. To achieve constitutional legitimacy under strict scrutiny, racial classifications incorporated into affirmative action programs must serve a compelling governmental interest (such as correcting past discrimination by the government employer involved) and must be narrowly tailored to meet that interest in that they are the least intrusive means available to achieve the government's objective (see *City of Richmond v. J.A. Croson Company*, 488 U.S. 469 [1989] and *Adarand Constructors v. Peña* 115 s.ct. 2097 [1995]).

Impact of Affirmative Action

Since affirmative action came into use, minorities and women have gained access to many types of positions previously denied to them, but progress has not been rapid. Furthermore, it is difficult to know how much of that progress can be attributed directly to affirmative action programs and how much may have occurred as a result of broader societal change. An examination of federal government employment trends in the United States shows that minorities and women steadily increased their representation in the ranks of the civil service since the early 1960s, but the rate of increase was exceedingly slow, especially for minorities, and today both groups remain underrepresented in higher-level positions. Still, many observers see affirmative action as an important aspect of equal employment opportunity policy, and it remains a potent symbol of our resolve to counter discrimination directed against women and minorities.

Affirmative Action in Other Contexts

Although affirmative action most often focuses on equal employment opportunity, the policy is applied in other settings as well. For example, colleges and universities receiving government financing have implemented affirmative action programs for minority admissions. Governments also often set aside a percentage of their contracting business for the benefit of minority-owned enterprises, and the United States government has even developed an affirmative action program for the distribution of commercial radio and television broadcast licenses. In addition, racial and ethnic minorities and women are not the only groups targeted for affirmative action. Affirmative action plans developed by federal agencies and contractors in the United States must also include provisions pertaining to persons with handicaps.

The phenomenon of affirmative action is international as well. There are programs in place in several countries in addition to the United States, particularly in nations with noted racial, ethnic, or class divisions. India, for example, has a well-developed system of preferences or "reservations" for members of lower Hindu castes and other disadvantaged classes seeking government employment. Bangladesh offers similar preferences in public employment to citizens from disadvantaged sections or regions and to women to help make the government work force more representative. Pakistan has also developed quotas for government employment of ethnic minorities. Britain has implemented affirmative action programs to benefit women and ethnic or racial minorities focusing on training and other positive actions short of actual preferences. Affirmative action has also been implemented in other countries of Western Europe and in Canada.

Affirmative action has proved to be one of the most contentious public policies of the late twentieth century. Fundamentally, it is concerned with the redistribution of opportunity from those who have enjoyed historic advantages to those who have historically suffered discrimination. Affirmative action in some form is likely to endure until the time is reached when minorities and women are no longer disproportionately excluded from positions of power and prestige.

J. EDWARD KELLOUGH

BIBLIOGRAPHY

Greene, Kathanne W., 1989. *Affirmative Action and Principles of Justice*. New York: Greenwood.
Kellough, J. Edward, 1989. *Federal Equal Employment Opportunity Policy and Numerical Goals and Timetables: An Impact Assessment*. New York: Praeger Publishers.
Kellough, J. Edward, 1991. "The Supreme Court, Affirmative Action, and Public Management: Where Do We Stand Today?" *American Review of Public Administration*, vol. 21 (September) 255–269.
Livingston, John C., 1979. *Fair Game? Inequality and Affirmative Action*. San Francisco: W. H. Freeman and Company.
Ratner, Ronnie Steinberg, 1980. *Equal Employment Policy For Women: Strategies for Implementation in the United States, Canada, and Western Europe*. Philadelphia: Temple University Press.
Sowell, Thomas, 1990. *Preferential Policies: An International Perspective*. New York: William Morrow.
Taylor, Bron Raymond, 1991. *Affirmative Action at Work: Law, Politics, and Ethics*. Pittsburgh: University of Pittsburgh Press.
Tummala, Krishna K., 1989. *Equity in Public Employment Across Nations*. New York: University Press of America.

AFFIRMATIVE ACTION PLAN. A written document outlining strategies for affirmative action, usually designed to enhance employment prospects for racial and ethnic minorities and women. An affirmative action plan sets out in detail efforts that an organization intends to undertake to overcome past and current discrimination against targeted groups (see **discrimination, gender; discrimination, racial; equal employment opportunity**). Affirmative action plans typically include the following components:

Program Analysis. A review of the structure of the organization's equal employment opportunity (EEO) program and the resources allocated to the program. This review will address questions such as whether there are a sufficient number of EEO staff people in place and whether the EEO staff have access to top management and supervisors. The extent to which the EEO staff, such as complaint investigators and affirmative action officers, receive adequate training in EEO and personnel management should be determined. Additional questions might include whether other resources allocated to the program are adequate and whether supervisory and management personnel receive adequate training regarding EEO responsibilities.

Utilization Analysis. An examination of current employment patterns to determine the level of utilization within the organization of members of targeted groups, including minorities and women. This part of the plan should assess the current level of representation of minorities and women in various grades and occupations in the organization's work force. Current work force utilization should then be compared to the previous year's work force. Gains made in the employment of targeted groups should be noted and an assessment of the extent to which minorities, women, and other targeted groups remain underrepresented in any occupations or grade levels should be undertaken.

Underrepresentation can be determined by comparing the proportion of the relevant labor force comprised of members of minority groups and women to the organization's employment of minorities and women.

Problem Identification. Identification of aspects of the employment process that pose problems for or barriers to the employment of targeted groups. A critical assessment of the organization's personnel policies and procedures should be included in this part of the affirmative action plan. Care should be taken to determine whether qualification requirements are set appropriately or whether they may be artificially high and thus operate to the disadvantage of targeted groups. Attention should also be addressed to questions of whether recruitment efforts effectively reach minorities, women, and others. Also, systems should be in place for collecting information on current employee skills and training needs, and upward mobility and training programs should operate to ensure that all employees are able to reach their fullest potential. The analysis should determine if promotions and separations are conducted in a nondiscriminatory fashion.

Action Items. A statement of program objectives designed to overcome barriers to the employment of targeted groups. This aspect of the affirmative action plan should clearly identify specific and measurable objectives for enhancing employment prospects for minorities, women, and others. Problems identified with the development of qualifications, the design of recruitment efforts, and the functioning of upward mobility programs should all be addressed. Responsibility for correcting problems should be assigned to specific individuals with the authority required to make necessary changes.

Numerical Goals and Timetables. Numerical objectives may be developed for the employment of minorities and women in occupational categories where those groups are underrepresented. These objectives and the timetables or schedules proposed for their accomplishment should help to guide recruitment, upward mobility, and other efforts in the organization to facilitate the employment of targeted groups. Goals should be set based on projected job openings and the estimated availability of qualified women and minorities in the relevant labor markets. The Supreme Court has placed significant limitations on this approach to affirmative action.

J. EDWARD KELLOUGH

BIBLIOGRAPHY

Shafritz, Jay M., Norma M. Riccucci, David H. Rosenbloom, and Albert C. Hyde, 1992. *Personnel Management in Government: Politics and Process,* 4th ed. New York: Marcel Dekker.

United States Equal Employment Opportunity Commission, 1987. *Instructions for the Development and Submission of Federal Affirmative Employment Multi-year Program Plans: EEO Management Directive 714.* Washington, D.C.: Government Printing Office.

AFL-CIO (AMERICAN FEDERATION OF LABOR-CONGRESS OF INDUSTRIAL ORGANIZATIONS).

A voluntary federation of national and international labor unions operating in the United States. The AFL-CIO is not a union, but rather a "union of unions" that established the federation to represent them in developing and pursuing broad national and sometimes international policies and to coordinate their various activities.

History

The AFL-CIO developed in 1881 in Pittsburgh as a federation for skilled craft workers; it was formally established in 1886. Twenty-five national craft union affiliates selected Samuel Gompers, head of the Cigar Makers Union, as their first president. Gompers soon made the AFL a powerful actor in the American economic system. Under his leadership and guiding philosophy of "business unionism," the AFL grew steadily and survived the Great Depression. Problems developed after Gompers's death because of a leadership gap and, most importantly, the AFL's continuing refusal to permit nonskilled, noncraft workers and their unions to join the organization. This posture eventually provoked a secession movement led by John L. Lewis of the United Mine Workers, who sought to bring mass production workers within the federation. Lewis's Congress of Industrial Organizations (CIO) was highly successful in organizing industrial workers in the automobile and steel industries, leading the AFL to eventually compete for industrial workers as well. After years of organizational warfare between the organizations, they merged in 1955 as "the united house of labor," with 16 million members.

Most of the largest American labor unions are AFL-CIO affiliates, including, in the public sector, the American Federation of Teachers, the American Federation of State, County, and Municipal Employees, the Service Employees International Union, the International Association of Fire Fighters, the American Postal Workers Union, the National Association of Letter Carriers, and the American Federation of Government Employees. Controversy has erupted from time to time with predominately private-sector union affiliates such as the Teamsters, which was expelled from the Federation in 1957 for corruption, but readmitted in 1987.

Structure

The AFL-CIO is at the apex of the U.S. labor union structure. Eighty percent of all union members in the United States belong to AFL-CIO unions. Each affiliate union is autonomous in conducting its own affairs and its relationship with employers. Any national union can join the AFL-CIO if it accepts the federation's principles and obligations. The federation is governed through biennial conventions, and led by a president [for many years George Meany (1955–1979); Lane Kirkland as of 1997], a secretary-treasurer, and 33 vice presidents. These individuals, all of whom are elected, constitute the Executive Council, which governs between conventions. A General Board, comprised of the Executive Council and the principal officers of each affiliate union, meets at least annually to determine policy questions referred to it by the Council.

Standing committees include: legislation, civil rights, international affairs, political education, education, social security, community services, economic policy, research, housing, public relations, safety, occupational health, and organization and field services. Groups of affiliates with related problems are coordinated by departments of the AFL-CIO (e.g., maritime trades, metal trades, public employees). These departments are essentially subfederations with their own constitutions and officers.

Functions

The Committee on Political Education (COPE), formed at the time of the merger in 1955, extends AFL-CIO influence in electoral politics and educates members on political issues and candidates; prepares public policy reports; conducts voter registration drives; and contributes campaign moneys to candidates.

In addition to the COPE activities described above, the AFL-CIO conducts political lobbying at the national and state levels, especially for issues such as worker health and safety, labor rights, minimum wage, and social security. In 1994 the federation conducted a strong but losing campaign against the North American Free Trade Agreement (NAFTA). It also assists affiliates in organizing new members and gaining bargaining rights and status, and helps resolve interunion disputes over organizing and other matters.

The AFL-CIO is normally allied with the Democratic Party in its political activities and candidate endorsements. An exception was in 1972, when the federation endorsed Richard Nixon over George McGovern for president.

In 1991, the AFL-CIO began an associate membership program, the National Association of Working Americans, to broaden participation to the general public.

The AFL-CIO is largely responsible for instituting collective bargaining as the method of preference for resolving wages, benefits, and terms of employment with management.

RICHARD C. KEARNEY

AFRICAN ADMINISTRATIVE TRADITION.

An administrative tradition that is a native-grown administration, guided by strict adherence to village values, customs, and mores under the leadership of village chiefs, elders, age groups, clan leaders, and family heads. Customs and mores are the unwritten rules and laws which guide every aspect of the African administrative tradition.

The African administrative tradition is basically organized around the following units: families, hamlets, kindreds, villages, districts and provinces/regions (see Figure I). In each unit, there is a quasi-political structure for dealing with administrative, developmental, civil, criminal, ceremonial, disciplinary, and burial issues. In all the units, however, culture and strict social mores dictate the code of conduct in addressing all issues whether social, religious, or economic. Thus these six basic units provide the basis for understanding the African administrative tradition. In order to appreciate the role and significance of culture and social mores in the African administrative structures, a generic definition of culture from the African point of view is offered.

African culture expresses itself in such social forms as common customs, morals, ethics, and religion, and in material objects such as musical instruments, household utensils and food (Mbiti, 1990). The traditional African mores are clearly defined and rigidly observed.

For example, custom dictates and demands that the elderly be addressed with the utmost respect and be deferred to whenever a judgement call is demanded in certain matters. Social mores also defined the roles of various groups in the community. The roles of women were traditionally strictly consigned to domestic matters and women were expected at all times to support and obey their husbands. No such reciprocity was expected or demanded from men to women.

The basic unit of the African administrative tradition is the family. The word family has always had a broader meaning in Africa than it was ever had in other parts of the world. In the African traditional society, family included parents, children, grandparents, uncles, aunts, brothers and sisters who had their own children, and other immediate families (Mbiti, 1990). The household was the smallest unit of a family, consisting of children, parents, and sometimes grandparents. While a husband was the chief administrator of a household unit in such matters as family budget, feeding, labor, education, and discipline, the oldest man in the family circle served as the overall administrator, preside over family land disputes, and offered counseling. In organizational terms, the family unit was the basic block that supported all other units.

The hamlet was a broader extension of the family unit. The hamlet included many uncles, brothers and their wives and children, and the children's children and grandparents with filial relation to the first family unit. A hamlet was led by a spokesman, in effect the administrator, who was unanimously appointed by male members in the hamlet of a hamlet. His duties and responsibilities included arranging meetings (1) to settle disputes among family mem-

FIGURE I. AFRICAN ADMINISTRATIVE STRUCTURES AND ORGANIZATION

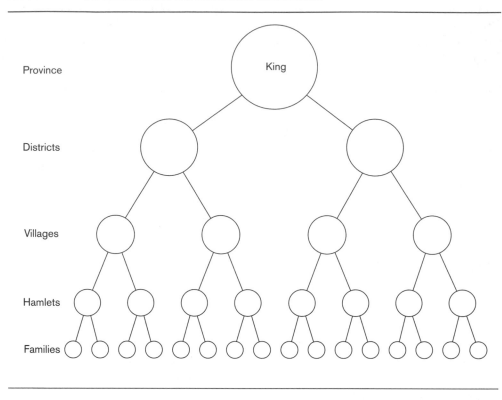

bers and (2) to plan and develop strategy for maintaining progress among children in various families. Such plans often included teaching and developing good farming skills or learning an appropriate trade. If any of these tasks involved expenses that were beyond a family household's income, it was the duty of the spokesman to arrange a meeting to decide how to levy a certain amount amongst males over 20 years of age in each family unit. No administrative duties were assigned to anyone under 20. This is because males under 20 were under community apprenticeship studying village values, customs, and tradition and therefore they were not yet considered mature enough to assume any village or community leadership.

From the hamlet, a bigger organizational structure emerged: the kindred. The kindred consisted of larger hamlets, relatives and bigger families who were connected in one form or another. The kindred was a bigger family circle than the hamlets, and functioned like a hamlet except that it handled bigger issues.

The kindred, like the hamlet, had a spokesman who was always appointed by the elders in the group. Appointment of a spokesperson was based on certain qualities such as the person's accomplishments, respect for elders, seniority, level of intelligence displayed before the elders, and the

degree of prowess in farming and other physically demanding activities. The administrative functions of a spokesman in the kindred were limited to addressing issues that concerned relatives and family groups, as well as developmental issues for the kindred. Larger community issues and problems were addressed at the village level.

Most villages had their local chiefs. In some villages, the title of chief passed on from one generation to another. Village chiefs had their administrative functions clearly spelled out by the village. The duties included maintaining law and order, dispensing justice as fairly as possible, ensuring that customs were preserved, and when necessary going to war if the interest of the village were threatened or violated. While village chiefs had no aides who were officially or publicly appointed to assist them, the various leaders in family units and kindreds served as aides. If for instance, a custom were violated by someone in a village, it was the duty of the chief to summon the village and determine the appropriate punishment. The village meeting was arranged by the chief sending out one of the spokespersons to go out late in the evening or at down using a drum to announce a meeting. Whenever the villagers heard the drum, everyone knew what it signified and responded accordingly. Women were not invited unless it was an issue that concerned women. Women had their own meetings and leaders who addressed women's issues. However, issues that could not be resolved by women were referred to the men for resolution.

During a village meeting each kindred was represented either by the eldest or a spokesman of the family or the kindred. Once a decision was taken and approved by the chief, it was implemented to the fullest. Here, one observes an informal democratic process in place because the chief never took any weighty decision without consulting the elders and the village people whom he ruled.

The administrative structures became a little complex at the district level. Here the key administrative functionaries were the paramount chiefs and chiefs who received their marching orders from the provincial leader or king. Of course, it must be remembered that certain tribes or communities in Africa had no kings; for example, the Ibo people never recognized or had a king. The highest ruler was a chief who ruled by consensus of elders in the community. At the provincial level, the king was an equivalent of a commander-in-chief of a nation. He had his own army and could go to war at will. Usually his wishes were carred out by chiefs who transmitted his messages to the villages and families. In some parts of Africa, some chiefs were dictatorial; in other parts there were some quasi-democratic institutions that existed, such as the councils of village elders and age group associations.

The councils of village elders were the leaders of thought who deliberated with the chiefs before any rules were made. On the other hand, age groups addressed issues that did not concern the whole village, but issues that mattered to them. When any age group failed to resolve an issue it was the duty of that age group to refer the matter to their immediate senior age group; if this group did not resolve the problem, it was finally referred to the village chiefs, who would call a meeting of the council of village leaders. These institutions were in place until the colonization of Africa and the subsequent changes that occurred.

Long before the advent of colonization, most of Africa was rural, with few trading centers. These trading centers served as the hub of major economic activities. As observed by Josef Gugler and William G. Flanagan (1978), "During Europe's Dark Ages and Renaissance, the Western Sudan below the Sahara was the scene of rivalries among empires that at times surpassed in wealth and strength the European counterparts to which they were linked indirectly by a web of trade in gold" (p. 5).

Three powerful empires existed long before colonization—the Ghana, Mali, and Songhay empires. The maintenance and control of these empires provided classic examples of the administrative structures that existed long before colonization. Each empire had several trading centers and towns along trade routes that were fiercely guarded. These centers were the hubs of economic activi-

ties that provided most of the wealth that supported the empires. In order to ensure that trading centers were not disrupted, several administrative structures were instituted by the ruler of each empire. For example, each empire had a standing army that was ready to go to war if the sources of wealth to that empire were threatened or attacked. The power of an empire, according to Gugler and Flangan (1978) "was based on the institution of market inspection to ensure honest dealings, and the creation of decentralized administration in which most chief office holders were either from rich families or were married into royal families" (p. 10). Thus in each empire the following administrative positions existed: paramount chiefs who presided over provinces; area chiefs who presided over towns and villages; market inspectors appointed by area chiefs who ensured orderliness and peach in the trading centers and kept watch for intruders or potential invaders.

At the provincial level, a paramount chief constituted a decision body called the traditional council of chiefs and elders, made up of all chiefs in the districts and villages. It was this body that decided on weighty issues such as tax, trading, and other provincial problems. Whatever was decided by the traditional council of chiefs was transmitted to the villages via the chiefs. At the villages, the council of village elders and a clan leaders, the kindred leader, and the family leaders constituted the local ruling body. In all, one sees administrative structures that smacked of a democratic process with democratic institutions, albeit not as sophisticated as the modern institutions, of today. The significant thing about these structures is that they provided the basis upon which modernization of African administrative structures was erected, although the colonization of Africa marked the beginning of disintegration of the administrative tradition in Africa.

For example, once Africa was completely colonized, the position of paramount chiefs who presided over provinces was changed to District Commissioners and the positions of chiefs in town were replaced by District Officers, while the chiefs were relegated to addressing rural issues and problems which the Europeans were least interested in. In the colonial administration, the rural areas were not considered important except insofar as they had something to offer to the urban trading centers. This apparent neglect of rural areas and selective development of certain urban areas explains why most African rural areas remained underdeveloped. It also explains why African urban areas have had much attraction for those in the hinterland. Worse still, it explains why the urban areas remain heavily congested and underdeveloped, because only a few areas were developed with minimum facilities. Over time, millions of rural people have migrated to the cities searching for a better economic life. The urban facilities even during the colonial administrative were inadequate to support the urban population and have remained so, years after the termination of colonial administration.

The few administrative structures that were instituted during the colonial administration—which were designed to serve the colonial interest—have to a large degree remained with little modification. In some instances the structures have been abused since most African countries became independent. The number of coups that have occurred in Africa since independence attest to the lack of political stability and need for improved administrative structures.

In summary, the African administrative tradition represented a historical brand of village administration that was guided by village mores, customs, and tradition. This system of administration, though not as sophisticated as modern administration, has much to offer today. Because it was an administration that was solely based on moral principles, village values, community mores, and customs, it comes close to being the purest form of administration that was ever practiced. In today's brand of administration characterized by greed and ethnocentrism, devoid of moral values, it may be worthwhile for the modern administrator to reexamine some of the precepts that governed the African administrative tradition. And for the African countries struggling to develop democratic institutions, a review of the African administrative tradition should be required reading.

DAMIEN EJIGIRI

BIBLIOGRAPHY

Abimbola, W., 1976. *An Exposition of Ifa Literary Corpus, Ibadan.* Oxford: Oxford University Press.
Ajay, J. F. and S. Robert, 1964. *Yoruba Warfare in the Nineteenth Century.* Cambridge, Eng.: Cambridge University Press.
Awolalu, J. O., 1973. "Yoruba Sacrificial Practice." *Journal of Religion in Africa* 5(2) 81–93.
Gugler, J. and W. Flanagan, 1978. *Urbanization and Social Change in West Africa.* Oxford: Oxford University Press.
Field, M. J., 1956. *Theories of Primitive Religion.* London/New York: Oxford Press.
———, 1960. *Search for Security.* London/New York: Oxford Press.
Mbiti, S., 1990. *African Religions and Philosophy,* 2nd ed. London: Oxford Press.

AGENCY. An administrative subdivision or unit of government (also called a board, bureau, commission, department, organization, office, and so forth) having the primary purpose of executing governmental functions and laws. Public administrators work in a great variety of administrative agencies. Public agencies vary in size, location, complexity of functions, and goals. Most public administrators, as common sense would dictate, are probably in agencies which reflect their particular skills, especially since the agencies have been created to handle a specific area of concern in society, such as housing, transportation, energy, or health. Thus, one would expect to find administrators with training and experience in housing matters in the U.S. Department of Housing and Urban Development (HUD), while one would expect to find a disproportionate number of energy experts working in the U.S. Department of Energy (DOE).

Public agencies also vary according to their prescribed statutory status in the administrative system. An agency's defined legal status plays a major role in determining the extent of political power the agency can probably wield as it interacts with other political actors in its environment. Essentially, there are three basic types of public agencies, although their legal distinctions are commonly blurred: (1) independent regulatory agencies; (2) quasi-independent regulatory agencies; and (3) executive (cabinet) departments.

Independent Regulatory Commissions

Although interest group theorists present credible arguments for the position that no true independent governmental agencies exist, there are nevertheless in the U.S. administrative system public agencies commonly known as independent regulatory commissions or boards. These commissions perform powerful regulatory functions in American society; yet they exist outside the executive departments and beyond the jurisdiction of the president. Congress has given commissioners in these agencies great quasi-legislative and quasi-judicial powers. They are supposed to employ these powers to create rules and orders deemed necessary to regulate specific industries. They have also been granted limited powers to determine whether the regulated have complied with the rules and orders and to punish violators, usually through fines, revocation of licenses, failure to renew permits, and so on. Because the actions (rules, orders, and penalties) of these commissioners may result in the loss of, say, the right to operate a business, those caught in the regulatory embrace of independent regulatory commissions frequently perceive their power to be awesome. The first independent regulatory commission, the Interstate Commerce Commission, was established in 1887, about one hundred years after the founding of the United States. Other such agencies were created later, including the Federal Trade Commission (FTC), Federal Power Commission (since 1977 the Federal Energy Regulatory Commission), Securities and Exchange Commission (SEC), Federal Communications Commission (FCC), National Labor Relations Board (NLRB), Federal Reserve Board (the Fed), Federal Maritime Commission, and Consumer Product Safety Commission.

Actually, these independent regulatory agencies were created in response to the feedback from the sociopolitical environment, which placed imposing demands on Congress to create bodies of administrative experts able to deal with the varied and complex problems which plagued modern technological society. As the decades passed, it became obvious that Congress no longer had the time, patience, or special talents to regulate all of the vital activities necessary to preserve social order and prosperity in American society. Nor did the courts have the capability to settle all of the disputes between parties and agencies that emerged inevitably as a natural consequence of public policy implementation efforts.

To prevent politics from interfering with the legislative and judicial judgments of these administrative experts, certain structural and procedural precautionary measures were taken by Congress in the creation of these agencies to help protect them from outside contaminative and disruptive political pressures. All independent regulatory commissions are multiheaded and usually consist of five to seven members, although there are exceptions to the general rule. For example, the Interstate Commerce Commission has eleven commissioners. All independent regulatory commissioners are appointed by the president with the consent of the Senate, but they cannot be removed except for cause (malfeasance, misfeasance, or nonfeasance). To help insulate commissioners from inappropriate White House meddling into their business affairs, the courts have ruled against presidents who have tried, without proper cause, to remove such commissioners. Political reasons are inadequate grounds for removal.

To further add to their structural independence, the president must appoint these commissioners to fixed terms, and these fixed terms are staggered to prevent any single president from appointing too many people to the commissions. One further check—the rule that no more than the simple majority of a commission may consist of members of the same political party—has kept presidents from stacking independent commissions with appointments in their favor. The role partisan politics can play in commission decision making is thus minimized.

But such independence from viable political controls has caused many critics to refer to this independent regulatory commission system as the headless fourth branch of government, and critics feel that such structure makes centralized administrative planning and coordination of policy virtually impossible. Systems theory would suggest that, although the independent commissions are not immune from external environmental pressures, external influences could, nevertheless, be minimized by their particular structural arrangement. Independent regulatory commissions are never so independent that they are not subject to budgetary controls placed upon them by the president and Congress, by public disclosures of their performance, by verbal reprimands by governmental and civic leaders, by investigations by Congress, and by other systemic demands to which they must respond. For example, because of the wide publicity given to General Accounting Office reports (GAO in the investigatory arm of Congress), critical GAO reports can be quite damaging to the image of any independent regulatory commission, thus tending to destroy any illusion independent regulatory commissioners may have of their actual independence from environmental forces.

Quasi-Independent Regulatory Agencies

Many writers who focus attention on administrative structure make no distinction between independent and quasi-independent regulatory agencies, especially since no distinction is made formally in the U.S. *Government Manual*. However, a practical distinction does exist. The first independent regulatory commission, the Interstate Commerce Commission, which was established in 1887, best exemplifies the purest independent regulatory agency. The ICC is structurally independent, not even attached structurally to the Department of Commerce, and it is also rather well protected from outside interference by statute. But not all so-called independent regulatory agencies and commissions are so structurally or statutorily independent; thus their independent status is somewhat compromised. For example, the Federal Aviation Agency was created as an independent regulatory commission to promote the airline industry and regulate air safety. Yet a number of experts believe that the FAA's regulatory independence is compromised to some extent because it is housed in the Department of Transportation and is therefore under that department's sphere of influence. Other agencies, such as the Environmental Protection Agency (EPA) and the Food and Drug Administration (FDA), were created as independent agencies with vast adjudicative powers, as is typical for the model independent regulatory commission. However, the EPA and FDA, like several other agencies, find that their regulatory independence is more imagined than real since Congress saw fit to place them within the executive branch: their leaders are not protected by statute from removal by the president. Nevertheless, the courts have slammed the door shut on presidents who have tried to meddle with administrative officials who perform quasi-judicial functions in such agencies, regardless of whether they are specifically protected by statute from presidential intrusion (*Wiener v. United States*, 357 U.S. 349 [1958]).

Executive Departments

According to some public administration scholars, it is frequently very difficult to separate a quasi-independent regulatory agency's operational status from that of a regular executive department's, although executive departments are generally regarded as less powerful in a political sense, possibly because they are under the day-to-day watchful eye and control of the president. Presidential supervision over executive departments tends to make them considerably less independent than either independent regulatory commissions or quasi-independent regulatory commissions.

Essentially, cabinet departments (such executive departments as the Department of Defense, Department of Transportation, Department of Health and Human Services, and Department of Energy) have been created as administrative agencies to assist the president in refining and implementing those public policies enacted by Congress. In contrast, independent regulatory and quasi-independent regulatory agencies play a more traditional regulatory role, thereby relying more heavily upon the standard regulatory tools of rulemaking and order-making.

Other Public Agencies

In addition to working in independent regulatory agencies and executive departments at the federal or state levels, public administrators are also found in other governmental offices, government-supported corporations, and private agencies and corporations working under government contract.

Other governmental offices can range from relatively well-known and important ones, such as the Small Business Administration and the National Science Foundation, to obscure and relatively inconsequential ones (for example, the American Battle Monuments Commission and the Renegotiation Board). These agencies, commissions, and boards were created as a response to special and narrow demands placed on government; and they normally function with very limited staffs and budgets, especially as compared to such giant government agencies as the U.S. Department of Defense (DOD).

The Federal Crop Insurance Corporation, the Federal National Mortgage Association, the Tennessee Valley Authority, the Smithsonian Institution, the U.S. Postal Service, and the National Railroad Passenger Corporation (Amtrak) provide examples of federal government corporations that are totally or partially owned by government and yet sell goods and services (mail delivery, electric power, bank deposit insurance, transportation service) much like private businesses. Government corporations also exist at the state level, where they are frequently called authorities. These authorities must often operate turnpikes, harbors, and airports.

Before 1945 government corporations possessed a great deal of independence and flexibility and functioned practically like any business. However, increasing concern during the 1930s about the unaccountable democratic character of such corporations as the Tennessee Valley Authority (TVA) led to the 1945 passage of the Government Corporation Control Act. Essentially, this act gives government corporations policy direction and fiscal control. Specifically, the act subjects these agencies to the usual congressional investigations and budgetary checks, such as audits, and to civil service statutes. For administrative purposes, some of these corporations are attached loosely to major departments, and their governing boards are staffed by persons appointed by the president.

The government corporations that provide goods and services at both the federal and state levels frequently cannot break even at the relatively low rate they charge (rates which private businesses, incidentally, would regard as too low to make a healthy profit). But because the goods and services provided are considered by the government to be vital to the promotion of the public welfare, they are usually supported in part by governmental subsidies. The challenge, in regard to government corporations, is to find the correct balance between granting these corporations the flexibility necessary for quick and wise business decisions in a rapidly changing environment and maintaining safeguards essential to preserving their democratically responsible character.

Such institutions as Gallaudet College, Howard University, and the American Printing House for the Blind are regarded as federally aided corporations. They function as private institutions, their boards of directors and personnel free from governmental intervention. However, because they are funded by tax dollars, they must be considered quasi-public agencies that must comply with numerous procedural due process restrictions required of the more traditional governmental agencies.

But it is difficult today to judge just which organizations or agencies are purely private. The role of government expands as increasing demands are placed upon government; with it grows government pervasiveness. It appears that there are few, if any, sizable organizations left in America today which do not have to comply with required governmental procedures of some kind; equal opportunity employment requirements are frequently cited examples. Actually, some scholars argue that most of us today work for governemnts, at least indirectly. Should those who work for private corporations, universities, and the like consider themselves quasi-governmental employees? Maybe not, but the fact is that Harvard University, IBM, McDonnell Douglas, General Motors, and other such organizations must enter into certain quid pro quo agreements with government as a condition for receiving governmental contracts, grants, loans, and subsidies. Ideally, the arrangements are mutually beneficial. While the government obtains such necessary supplementary goods and services as airplanes, scientific information, transportation service, and trained future leaders, the private organizations benefit financially, and in many cases receive the added benefit of prestige. Nevertheless, the bottom line is that in order to do business with government, these "private" agencies must play by government's rules, many of which entail following elaborate procedures related to fair employment practices, work safety, use of human subjects in research, and so on. Completing compliance and various data forms to demonstrate that proper procedures are in fact being followed normally occupies a great deal of time, so much time that some "private" managers have seriously questioned whether playing ball with government is really worth it.

KENNETH F. WARREN

BIBLIOGRAPHY

Davis, Kenneth C. and Richard J. Pierce, Jr., 1994. *Administrative Law Treatise,* 3rd ed., vol. 1. Boston: Little, Brown and Company.

Warren, Kenneth F., 1996. *Administrative Law in the American System,* 3rd ed. Upper Saddle River, NJ: Prentice Hall.

AGENCY BUDGET SUCCESS. Agency achievement of monetary and organizational goals through annual participation in the budget process; also known as agency strategies.

Budgeting involves a yearly interaction between agencies, who make claims on resources, and central executives and legislators, who assess these requests and authorize spending. Agency budget success extends beyond the unidimensional standard of increasing this year's budget over last year's budget. Receiving more dollars signifies success. However, governmental units also want to maintain good relationships with other actors in the budget process, preserve agency stability, and operate during the spending year with budget management flexibility.

The Budget Base

As Aaron Wildavsky points out in *The Politics of the Budgetary Process* (1992), agency budget proposals include last year's budget, known as the base, and a request for new money, known as the increment. Benchmarks of agency budget success include "short term success"– the percentage of the current request funded–and "long term success"–the percentage increase in the base. Money added to last year's base usually represents a permanent budget expansion. Unless revenue downturns occur, budget reviewers accept budget bases as given and concentrate on increments or request for new money. During periods of fiscal scarcity, budget reviewers revisit the base and make cuts. In this environment, protecting existing money becomes an important indicator of budget success.

The definition of the base affects budget changes from year to year. Traditionally, an agency's base consists of the dollars appropriated last year, and many governments still use last year's appropriation. However, some governments, including the United States federal government, view the "current services" baseline as the base. The baseline includes the money necessary to continue current activities. Thus, it encompasses the last appropriation plus additional resources needed to cover cost increases tied to inflation, such as escalations in utility costs. When coupled with a practice of taking the base as given, a current services baseline often favors the existing division of the budget pie among agencies. If revenues grow 4 percent, but every budget automatically increases by 3 percent to maintain current services, the "new money" increment equates to only 1 percent. As a result, budget reviewers lose flexibility to cover agency requests for new and expanded activities, and agencies find it difficult to increase their budget beyond the baseline.

The Dance for Dollars

Agency Asking Environments

The ability of agencies to increase their base depends on their asking environment. Spenders find it easier to secure new money during periods of revenue growth and tougher when dollars decline. In addition, institutional and political factors enhance or detract from each agency's ability to increase its budget in good revenue times and to mitigate cuts during revenue downturns.

Revenues. Agencies push for budget increases when a growing economy produces meaningful growth in government revenues. William Niskanen in *Bureaucracy and Representative Government* (1971) suggests that administrators strive to maximize their agency's budget. Lance T. LeLoup and William B. Moreland in *Public Administration Review* (1978) present evidence verifying the efficacy of pushing for large increments. Agencies receive the biggest escalations when they ask for enormous percentage increases over their base. Budget reviewers cut away much of the requested new money, but aggressive agencies still end with a greater percentage increase over last year's budget than units with more moderate requests. LeLoup and Moreland argue that budgeters should ask for as much new money as can be defended. They note, however, that the agency's asking environment may restrict budget requests. Most budget scholars agree with Aaron Wildavsky's observation in *Politics of the Budgetary Process* (1992): Administrators function as budget satisfiers and only ask for an amount that will be viewed as credible by budget reviewers. Agency assertiveness cannot succeed without growing revenues and favorable circumstances created by institutional wedges and political support.

During the last two decades, shrinking revenues affected agency asking environments in America and around the world. As Allen Schick points out in *Public Administration Review* (1986), agency advocacy of budget increases causes an upward drift of spending. Peter Aucoin (1991) in *The Budget-Maximizing Bureaucrat: Appraisals and Evidence* reports that central executives in industrialized democracies use several techniques to limit agency budget growth. These persons cap total spending and divide resources among program areas. They freeze hiring and tighten eligibility requirements for entitlement programs. They use comprehensive financial control systems to identify slack resources for cuts in future years. In addition, commissions from the private sector conduct external reviews of agency spending to catalog potential costs savings. Several governments with declining money keep spending in check by adopting target or fixed ceiling budgeting. Before agencies submit budget requests, executives assign targets or ceilings that specify a dollar limit for each agency's budget proposal. Ceilings often fall below current available dollars. The assignment of a budget ceiling leads to the pre-approval phase of budgeting described by Schick in *Public Administration Review* (1988). Agency success depends on negotiating an acceptable ceiling before preparing their detailed budget proposal.

Individual Agency Characteristics. Most budget scholars recognize that budget outcomes result from a multitude of factors. Wildavsky reviews United States federal budgeting and Abney and Lauth study American state budgeting in *Public Budgeting and Financial Management* (1993). These authors suggest that individual agency characteristics influence budget success. Spenders realize that they need to consider the hand dealt them when developing a budget request.

Institutional forces affect budget success. Agencies with mandatory "entitlement" programs driven by formulas find it easier to claim additional resources than units whose level of funding depends on the discretion of the executive and legislators. For example, statutory minimum foundation program formulas increase elementary and secondary education budgets in American states. Medicare's formula leads to expanded United States federal spending. In other instances, agencies develop formulas on their own and use them to compute budget requests. Proposals built on voluntary formulas stress that the requested increment is based on "neutral" scientific data. Agencies targeted by court orders, such as corrections departments mandated to reduce prison overcrowding, use these decrees to extract additional resources. In federal systems, state or local agencies capable of attracting federal money leverage budget increases with the lure of national dollars. These units often argue that more matching money is required to retain federally subsidized programs. Many governments also add activities to attract more federal funds. For example, American states add discretionary Medicaid services because of a favourable federal match. Agencies with increased workloads make claims on resources that organizations with static or declining client demands cannot justify. The agency's place in the organization also may affect its ability to obtain budget increases. In American states, agencies

that report directly to the budget-writing chief executives may receive better treatment in the executive unified budget proposal than units reporting to boards or independently elected officials. The executive budget often shapes the distribution of resources approved by the legislature.

Political support from the executive, key legislators, well-placed interest groups, and the public also influences an agency's ability to increase spending. Agencies with missions valued by the executive and key legislators fare better than units with low priority programs. If possible, agencies shape their budget requests to fit executive and legislative priorities. For instance, if these elected officials emphasize economic development, public schools and universities stress their contribution to this goal. Even low priority agencies may find angles to enhance their support. Thus, welfare agencies who submit budgets to fiscal conservatives find it useful to emphasize efforts to collect court-ordered support payments from parents separated from their children. These agencies argue that money from "deadbeat dads" enables families to leave the welfare rolls.

Agencies also make an effort to show that they follow the intent of the legislature. Wildavsky suggests that United States congressional appropriation subcommittees closely monitor conformity with their wishes, and Abney and Lauth find the same pattern in American state legislatures. Programs that deliver services in many legislative districts find it easier to build coalitions in support of budget increases. Occasionally, spenders justify budget increases based on a "legislative mandate" passed in previous sessions. Their budget requests point out that statutes obligate them to ask for more money.

Agencies develop ties with clients and cultivate positive relationships. They encourage these persons to convey positive information to executives and legislators. Agencies with politically effective recipients or "clients" may experience greater success than units with less influential supporters. For example, the beneficiaries of economic development programs enjoy more political leverage than mental patients in government hospitals. Occasionally, client groups carry out mass demonstrations to show that persons feel strongly about maintaining or increasing budget support for programs. From time to time, general public support of agency programs makes it easier to secure more money. The National Aeronautics and Space Administration's "man on the moon" program enjoyed widespread public support and concomitant budget success. The budgets of American criminal justice agencies at all levels of government benefit from the public's fear of crime.

Building a Compelling Case. Abney and Lauth as well as Wildavsky find that agency success also depends on making a compelling case that programs effectively address societal needs. As Wildavsky points out, successful agencies cite tangible achievements and avoid excessive and unverified claims. Agencies often use social indicators and other data to display the need for expanding existing programs and for starting new ones. For example, a public health department might cite the number of persons requiring immunizations and lay out the consequences for society if adequate funds are not forthcoming. Agencies use data to show attainment of program objectives. However, evidence suggests that positive reactions from clients carry more weight than data. As Abney and Lauth point out, budget reviewers use data to highlight failures while ignoring statistical information that supports success.

Maintaining Relationships with Other Budget Players

Wildavsky, as well as Sydney Duncombe and Richard Kinney, in *Public Budgeting and Finance* (1987), stress the importance of agency credibility with budget reviewers. Clearly, respected agencies find it easier to get items included in the executive budgets and appropriation bills. Duncombe and Kinney persuasively argue that agency administrators stress the importance of maintaining relationships with persons with whom they will deal in future years. Most view this factor as more important than maximizing the current year budget increase. Credibility takes years to develop, but it fades quickly when budget reviewers perceive that agency administrators mislead them. For example, making the case that a crisis exists may result in a budget increase. If reviewers later sense that no emergency occurred, however, the agency suffers in future budget cycles. Loss of confidence may result in budget cuts without regard to the "merits" of the program.

Wildavsky points to the reciprocal relationships that exist between agencies advocating more spending and analysts who act as guardians of the public purse. Executive and legislative budget analysts expect agencies to advocate and make cases for spending increases. Analysts realize policy and political considerations accompany spending requests. Failure to address issues percolating from agencies may lead to policy and political repercussions for their political superiors. At the same time, agencies cultivate relationships with executive and legislative budget analysts. An examiner converted to a program advocate enhances the chances of agencies receiving budget increases. The views of analysts carry weight when executives and legislators review budget requests.

Executives also provide active support for budgets of highly regarded agencies during the legislative session. In jurisdictions with line item vetoes, a good relationship with the executive also produces benefits. These respected units may argue successfully against a veto of money added to the executive budget recommendation by the legislature.

Preserving Agency Stability

A budget that preserves agency stability also signifies agency success. During periods of fiscal austerity, budget proposals emphasize that the new money requested only provides enough additional resources to deliver existing services. Even during periods of revenue growth, agencies often do not fight for every available new dollar. Some increases may accompany unwanted new programs or transferred programs from other agencies that do not contribute to the agency's objectives. Large budget increases also may be difficult to digest and use effectively. If new or massive program expansions lead to disgruntled citizens, the negative reactions could cause difficulty in future years. Generally, agencies pursue what Bias and Dion in *The Budget Maximizing Bureaucrat: Appraisals and Evidence* (1991) call a budget boosting strategy. That is, units seek stable yearly growth instead of massive increases. Agencies also realize that long-term benefits accrue from operating as a team player. Asking for a huge increase could maximize dollars, but budget analysts may resent the need to make major cuts. The executive may view aggressiveness as a sign of not participating on the team. Relationships with other agencies may suffer as well.

Budget Management Flexibility

Agencies also view retaining budget flexibility during the spending year as budget success. Spenders need the ability to deal with emergencies by moving money. When budgeted resources cannot cover service demands in high priority programs, they want the flexibility to move money from low priority programs. Clearly spenders prefer freedom to make budget changes on their own. Nevertheless, agency administrators with good reputations work effectively within a system that gives executives or a small group of legislators authority to approve changes during the spending year.

Agencies also lobby for appropriation bills that provide maximum flexibility during the spending year. Agency executives prefer lump sum appropriations, with no spending restrictions, or object classification appropriations that distribute money among major categories, such as personnel and equipment. Budgeters dislike detailed program and line item appropriations since these formats limit budget management flexibility.

When governments operate with budget ceilings, agency administrators need managerial discretion over resources. Central executives often guard against cuts in service by mandating that agencies maintain or increase levels of output. In effect, spending units must take steps to improve productivity, a process that often requires an internal reallocation of resources. Agencies also strive to retain cost savings for their other programs and resist returning money created by economies to the treasury.

EDWARD J. CLYNCH

BIBLIOGRAPHY

Abney, Glen and Thomas P. Lauth, 1993. "Determinants of State Agency Budget Success." *Public Budgeting and Financial Management*, vol. 5, no. 1, 37–65.

Aucoin, Peter, 1991. "The Politics of Management of Restraint Budgeting." In A. Bias and S. Dion, eds., *The Budget Maximizing Bureaucrat: Appraisals and Evidence*. Pittsburgh: University of Pittsburgh Press.

Bias, A. and S. Dion, eds., 1991. *The Budget Maximizing Bureaucrat: Appraisals and Evidence*. Pittsburgh: University of Pittsburgh Press.

Duncombe, Sydney and Richard Kinney, 1987. "Agency Budget Success: How It Is Defined by Budget Officials in Five Western States." *Public Budgeting and Finance*, vol. 7 (Spring) 24–37.

Gosling James J., 1985. "Patterns of Influence and Choice in the Wisconsin Budgetary Process." *Legislative Studies Quarterly*, vol. 10 (November) 457–482.

LeLoup, Lance T. and William B. Moreland, 1978. "Agency Strategies and Executive Review: The Hidden Politics of Budgeting." *Public Administrative Review*, vol. 38 (May/June) 232–239.

McCaffery, Jerry, 1984. "Canada's Envelope Budget: A Strategic Management System." *Public Administration Review*, vol. 44 (July/August) 373–383.

Niskanen, William A., 1971. *Bureaucracy and Representative Government*. Chicago: Aldine-Atherton.

Rubin, Irene S., 1991. "Budgeting for Our Times: Target Based Budgeting." *Public Budgeting and Finance*, vol. 11 (Spring) 6–14.

Schick, Allen, 1986. "Macro-Budgetary Theory Adaptations to Fiscal Stress in Industrialized Democracies." *Public Administration Review*, vol. 46 (March/April) 124–134.

———, 1988, "Micro-Budgetary Theory Adaptations to Fiscal Stress in Industrialized Democracies." *Public Administration Review* (January/February) 523–533.

Sigelman, Lee, 1986. "The Bureaucrat as Budget Maximizer: An Assumption Examined." *Public Budgeting and Finance*, vol. 6, (Spring) 50–70.

Thompson, Joel, 1987. "Agency Requests, Gubernatorial Support, and Budget Success in Stage Legislatures Revisited." *Journal of Politics*, vol. 49 (August) 756–779.

Wildavsky, Aaron, 1992. *The New Politics of the Budgetary Process*, 2nd ed. New York: HarperCollins Publishers.

AGENCY MISSION.

A brief statement which defines the primary purpose for which a public sector agency exists.

The notion of mission, from at least the Middle Ages, has related to religious, diplomatic, political, and military practices of sending individuals or groups of people to preach, convert, negotiate, or fight in relation to specific beliefs, ideas, or actions. Generically, mission can apply to an individual's life purpose or specific vocation. As the concept of mission has evolved, so one emphasis has also shifted from an individual to an organizational focus.

A more contemporary idea of mission has developed from private sector business practice, which, in turn, was based on the ancient military concept of strategy, and mission, in warfare. In this context, the mission statement defines the core business activities of an organization. It is the private sector, organizational definition of mission that the public sector has adopted.

The conceptual and theoretical basis for an organizational mission is found in strategic planning and strategic management literature. More recently, the literature on quality management and quality service, and transformational leadership, has also included the concept of mission. But why do public sector agencies need to grapple with the notion of mission?

In the last decade, at least, there has been an increasing imperative for governments to respond to global fiscal pressures. As resources have diminished so governments and public sector managers around the world have been forced to reduce, or refine, program and service provision. The question: "What business are we in?" has become increasingly more important for whole public sectors and agencies within.

The articulation of agency missions across a public sector provides governments with some basis for determining which programs and services they want to provide. The extent to which a government believes in individualist, or collectivist, responsibilities of the state in terms of its citizens will, to a large extent, determine which businesses governments want to be in.

Agency mission statements are also important in determining the actual machinery of government as the post-bureaucratic model, or managerialist paradigm as it is popularly referred to, often splits the policy and operational roles of agencies. In this sense, commercial agencies of government that compete in defined markets may be separated from their policy agencies, which do not compete in a market and are financed entirely by government budget allocations.

The move towards privatization, contracting out, and user-pays policies has placed pressure on public managers to define the business of the agency. In this way, programs and services no longer consistent with government priorities may be dropped, privatized, or contracted out. From an economic perspective, neoclassical thinking suggests that government should only be involved in the provision of essential services, such as national defense, policing, foreign diplomacy, or the provision of care for people unable, by way of mental disability, to care for themselves.

In the case of monopolistic government-owned enterprises, government may create a simulated, internal market environment by establishing regional businesses, or a series of different businesses, so that entities can be set up to compete. In this context, the development of an agency mission statement is essential.

Mission statements are critical for agencies across the sector, not just for the commercial activities of governments. In a sense, for the noncommercial agencies of government the identification and articulation of a mission statement is more difficult and less clear-cut than for the commercial arm of government. For a noncommercial agency, defining a mission statement may challenge tradition and a particular mind-set and force the agency to rethink the business that it should be in, given the prevailing circumstances. The diversity of some agency operations, too, makes the articulation of a mission statement quite difficult. In recent years, as public sectors have become more focused on the needs of customers, agency mission statements are often now couched in customer service terms.

The practical consideration of an agency mission will usually take place within a strategic planning framework of some kind, involving collaborative decision making among senior executives, possibly other staff, and/or external constituents. A range of determinants based largely on private sector practice will typically be considered in terms of where and for what purpose organizational resources will be allocated. For example, the major customers; main products, programs or services; the operating or geographical domain and scope of operations; and the distinctive competence or competitive advantage of the organization.

For the public sector, additional considerations for developing an agency mission include the specific enabling legislation, policies, or operating mandates; the key constituents, or beneficiaries of the programs and services; the value-added component which makes the agency's programs or services essential and indispensable; and the staff's role in terms of organizational achievement. An agency's mission or its operations do not necessarily have to be confined in the long term, as a strategic objective of an organization may involve the redefinition of core business through revised or new legislative or policy mandates of government.

Developing an agency mission is not always easy and there are a number of potential pitfalls if not done well. Sometimes mission statements are developed through brainstorming processes which may not involve systematic analysis of the core elements of a mission statement, as the literature suggests. In this case, discussion about the agency mission may revolve around semantics rather than the substance of the agency's core business activities. Furthermore, gaining commitment to the agency mission requires strong and sensitive leadership and effective communication with all constituents.

Involvement of some kind in the development of the agency mission statement is important for all staff if the leadership is going to facilitate "buy-in" and commitment over time to implementing the mission. When staff are involved it is also critical to manage expectations in terms of what their involvement might produce. Executive managers who include staff input in the developmental process and then do not reflect that input in the final statement may create a negative response towards the commitment process.

The way the agency mission is presented to staff can also influence the level of commitment to implementation. Displaying an agency mission statement in public places can have both positive and negative effects. If, for example, the agency mission is just posted publicly without any involvement of staff or explanation to them, the level of commitment is likely to be low. On the other hand, if staff have participated in the process and have been kept informed, their level of commitment may be significantly increased.

The content and format of an agency mission are also important. The mission statement, of itself, may be a short, simple sentence defining the core business activities of the agency. The statement may be qualified or supported with additional statements that outline in more detail aspects of the programs and services; the key beneficiaries and customers; the organizational vision (that is, the best possible outcome in ideal circumstances); the organizational operating philosophy, values and beliefs; the desired organizational culture; and the contribution staff will make to the implementation of the mission. Organizational goals and strategies and performance monitoring information may also be included.

One confusing aspect of defining an agency mission statement is that some public sector organizations use the same management terms to denote different aspects of management. On the other hand, some terminology is used interchangeably to mean the same thing. One prime example in which this occurs is between mission and vision statements. Sometimes a mission statement will encompass a vision statement as well, but only be referred to in the documentation as the vision, or vice versa. Terminology is critical, and therefore needs to be agreed to at the beginning of any process designed to develop an agency mission statement, or the like.

Agency mission statements have both internal and external purpose and an agency mission statement needs to be meaningful for its audience. In the public sector the "audience" may comprise diverse, pluralist interests both within and external to that agency. The mission may be published in a glossy document made available to the public that may include a statement of mission as part of an overall strategic plan, or statement of strategic intent. The agency mission may also be published within annual reports of public sector agencies.

If published outside the organization, the agency mission can communicate to external constituents in broad but precise terms what the agency does, where it operates, for whom it exists, community consultation opportunities, and issues of equity and access. The agency mission in this context is a public statement that may influence the way external constituents perceive the public image of the agency.

At the main interface between the internal and external constituents, agency mission statements may be displayed in public areas such as counters. While missions displayed in this manner, have a public focus, they are also designed to provide staff with a corporate view. Internally, the agency mission provides direction for all staff so that they understand and can contribute to organizational achievement in a manner consistent with the agency's specific mission.

Equally important, an agency mission, and particularly the process of analysis required to develop it, is a foundation for other critical managerial activities. For example, the process of identifying the distinctive competencies of the organization—the technologies and skills the organization requires to undertake its business—can suggest a human resource management strategy and initiatives.

Consideration of the agency mission can indicate certain recruitment, training and development, and work force planning strategies. The questions to be asked include: If this is our mission, what competencies does this agency collectively need to possess to carry out its core business activities? Do we have them now? Who do we need to recruit to ensure that we possess these capabilities? How do we train and develop our staff? What kind of work force planning do we require to maintain, or enhance, our distinctive competence? Information technology as a technological competence relating to agency needs may also be part of this analysis.

Identification of the key constituents or customers is a key step but the analysis needs to go further, especially when considering the parameters of program and service provision. What do our customers want, need, or expect from the agency? How may constituents' expectations be managed? Will constituents' expectations conflict with the legislative and policy frameworks of government? Do we serve a powerful interest group at the expense of less powerful but equally important groups in the community? What should the scope of our operations be? Whom should we serve? Where will we locate our offices? How can we spread our resources across a broad geographical area? Is there any opportunity for partnership or strategic alliance to enhance service provision, or to provide economies of scale?

Overall, articulation of an agency mission suggests a resource allocation strategy. Concern for the value-added component also assists the agency to consider what useful or essential role it plays in the community. What would happen if the agency did not exist? Which organizations might fill the void? What needs to be done by the agency to ensure continuing viability?

In summary, it is apparent that the formulation, articulation, and implementation of an agency mission is a critical aspect of public management. By defining the fundamental purpose and focusing on its core activities, a public sector agency can make the best use of limited resources in the interest of its citizens.

JUDY JOHNSTON

BIBLIOGRAPHY

Ansoff, I., 1987. *Corporate Strategy*. London: Penguin.
Bowman, C., 1990. *The Essence of Strategic Management*. NY: Prentice Hall.
Bowman, C. and D. Asch, 1987. *Strategic Management*. Houndmills: Macmillan.
Bryson, J., 1988a. "A Strategic Planning Process for Public and Non-profit Organizations." *Long Range Planning*, vol. 21, no. 1.
———, 1988b. "Strategic Planning: Big Wins and Small Wins." *Public Money and Management* (Autumn).
——— 1988c. *Strategic Planning for Nonprofit Organizations*. San Francisco: Jossey Bass.
Chaffee, E., 1985. "The Concept of Strategy: From Business to Higher Education." In J. C. Smart, ed. *Handbook of Theory and Research*, vol. 1. New York: Agathon Press.
David, F., 1991. *Concepts of Strategic Management*, 3rd ed. New York: Macmillan.
Foster, T., ed., 1993. *101 Great Mission Statements*. London: Kogan Page.
Hendry, J., G. Johnson and J. Newton, eds., 1993. *Strategic Thinking*. Chichester: John Wiley.
Hunger, J. and T. Wheelan, 1993. *Strategic Management*. Reading, MA: Addison-Wesley.
Koteen, J., 1989. *Strategic Management in Public and Non-Profit Organizations*. New York: Praeger.
Lewis, G., A. Morkel and G. Hubbard, 1993. *Australian Strategic Management*. New York: Prentice Hall.
Mintzberg, H., 1989. *Mintzberg on Management*. New York: The Free Press.
———, 1991. *The Rise and Fall of Strategic Planning*. New York: The Free Press.
Mintzberg, H. and J. Quinn, 1991. *The Strategy Process*, 2nd ed. Englewood Cliffs, NJ: Prentice Hall.
Nutt, P. and R. Backoff, 1992. *Strategic Management of Public and Third Sector Organizations*. San Francisco: Jossey-Bass.
Tregoe, B. and J. Zimmerman, 1980. *Top Management Strategy*. New York: Simon and Schuster.
Viljoen, J., 1991. *Strategic Management*. Melbourne: Longman.

AGENCY THEORY. A view of organizations as sets of contracts between buyers and sellers of services. The buyer is termed the "principal" and the seller the "agent." The contract specifies what each must do. Typically, the principal pays the agent a salary, wage, or fee. Additionally, the principal may provide physical, technological, and staff support to the agent in the form of work space, tools and devices (telephones, computers), secretaries, and other assistants. The agent, in return, must carry out the directives of the principal.

Principals and agents are assumed to be motivated by self-interest. Their purposes and objectives are not identical. Consequently, there may be tensions and conflicts between how principals want the work to be done and how the agents do it. When the agent does not conform perfectly to the principal's directives, the agent is said to be "shirking." Agency theory views shirking as endemic and pandemic in organizations because agents often have more information about their work than do the principals. The principal may respond to information asymmetry in several ways. Strict hierarchy and accounting procedures can be adopted. Incentives can be provided to induce the agents to conform more fully to the principal's directives. Socialization and leadership may be emphasized.

As with traditional bureaucratic theory, agency theory focuses on control and authority. However, it does not view bureaucratic subordinates as powerless cogs in an organizational machine. Rather, control of administrative performance runs both from the top down and the bottom up. Further, the concept of organization is disaggregated into individual contracts between principals and agents. The overall organization takes its form through the interconnections among these contracts. The whole contractual package can be viewed as a macroagreement, such as a collectively bargained employment contract or, more abstractly, an employer's personnel system.

According to agency theory, organizational behavior is the outcome of the individual actions of agents and principals. Consequently, agency theory does not easily accept organizations as units of analysis. To get around this problem, principal-agent models may treat administrative agencies as homogeneous, singular entities (agents). In this fashion, it becomes possible to study legislative-agency interactions from a principal-agent perspective.

Agency theory makes important contributions to understanding administrative behavior. It suggests that the greatest challenge facing management both internally and externally is to develop a commitment to trust and good faith between the principals and agents in producing mutually beneficial outcomes for the organization as a whole. In most employment situations, both the principals' and the agents' interests must be recognized in order to reduce shirking. Intensification of hierarchical control, as prescribed by bureaucratic theory, is not universally appropriate.

Contemporary agency theory also has some serious limitations. Principal-agency models, which are intended to clarify relationships and incentive structures, are currently too simple to capture the full complexity of administrative behavior. In practice, there may be multiple principals, as under the separation of powers in the United States. Principals, such as legislatures, may not have sufficiently clear intent to specify precisely what the agent should do. The U.S. Congress has been notoriously fragmented in using its committees and subcommittees to oversee and control administrative action. Positing that agencies are coherent entities motivated by a few interests, such as maximizing their budgets or slack, actually violates the fundamental assumption of agency theory—that organizations comprise contracts among individual principals and agents with differing self-interests. Viewing principals and agents as motivated solely by individual self-interest (methodological individualism) ignores the social dimensions of work and the findings of the human relations approach to analyzing organizations. Further, principal-agent models typically ignore employment law, though legal constraints on principals and the distribution of liabilities for agents' harmful actions are of obvious importance (see **respondeat superior**).

HON S. CHAN AND DAVID H. ROSENBLOOM

BIBLIOGRAPHY

Bendor, Jonathan, 1990. "Formal Models of Bureaucracy: A Review." In Naomi B. Lynn and Aaron Wildavsky, eds., *Public Administration: The State of the Discipline.* Chatham, NJ: Chatham House.
Gill, Jeff, 1995. "Formal Models of Legislative/Administrative Interaction." *Public Administration Review*, vol. 55 (January/February), 99–106.

AL-FARABI, ABU AL-NASSAR MOHAMMED (872–950).

An Islamic philosopher best known for his work on the ideal state and society, which he based on three principles: cooperation, happiness, and an organized hierarchy of leadership.

Abu Al-Nassar Mohammed Al-Farabi was born in Turkestan and got his first education in Iraq. An Islamic philosopher who wrote several books in philosophy, Arabic arts, and Islam, he is best known for his book about the ideal state in which he described the principles of the ideal society and the characteristics of the ideal leader. Al-Farabi provided three principles of the ideal society. The first principle is total cooperation between its people. He states that all individuals work to satisfy certain needs that they cannot satisfy by themselves without the cooperation of others. All people depend on others to satisfy their needs and thus the existence of such a relation requires total cooperation. The second principle is that the overall goal of the ideal society should be achieving happiness for all the citizens. Happiness, Al-Farabi contends, cannot be achieved without total cooperation. Finally, the ideal society should be organized hierarchically where the highest level of the hierarchy is reserved to the leader of the society. The lowest level of the hierarchy is reserved to the people who serve others but do not expect to be served. The factors that determine the level of any individual are the person's skills, knowledge, and abilities. Any other factors should not be considered in deciding the level in which an individual can be.

Al-Farabi's ideal state must also have an ideal leader who must have natural as well as acquired traits. The natural traits that the ideal leader must have are: (1) physical capacity and competence; (2) imagination and conception; (3) sharp memory; (4) intelligence and comprehension; (5) eloquence and good speaking abilities; (6) devotion to knowledge and eagerness to benefit from knowledge; (7) lack of greediness; (8) honesty and sincerity; (9) generosity and highmindedness; (10) lack of interest in wealth and high interest in the society's affairs; (11) commitment to justice and equity; and (12) strength and energy. In addition to natural traits, the ideal leader must acquire six traits. The ideal leader must acquire wisdom, knowledge, analytical skills, vision, physical fitness, and awareness and consciousness of other civilizations. Even though Al-Farabi strongly emphasized these traits and their importance for the ideal society, he acknowledged that people who have all these traits are rare to find.

The political and social environment in which Al-Farabi lived and wrote most of his work had its influence on Al-Farabi's writing and thinking. At his time, during the Abbasyah Caliphate (750–1258), the Islamic state was weak and the Abbasyah caliphs were corrupt. The principles of the ideal society were a response to an Islamic society that did not have any of these principles at the time Al-Farabi wrote. Similarly, the traits of the ideal leader were Al-Farabi's effort to reform the practice of the Abbasyah caliphs, who lacked most of these traits. Al-Farabi was also influenced by the writings of the Greek philosophers. At age 80, Al-Farabi died in Damascus, leaving behind his significant work about the ideal state and the policies of civilization.

ABDULLAH M. AL-KHALAF

AL-GHAZALI, ABU HAMED MOHAMMED AHMAD (1058–1111).
An Islamic philosopher whose writings on politics, ethics, and administration were major contributions to Islamic scholarly literature.

Abu Hamed Mohammed Ahmad Al-Ghazali was born in Ghazalah, Persia, and spent his first years traveling between Persia and Iraq studying Islam and philosophy. He taught in Baghdad, where he wrote most of his well-known books in Islam, philosophy, politics, ethics, and administration. Two of his books are considered to be great contributions to the Islamic library. The first of these is *Al-Falsafah wa al-Alhlaq (Philosophy and Ethics)* and the second one is *Al-Tubr al-Masbuk fe Nasihat al-Muluk (Kings' Advice)*. These books were written during the second Abbasyah Caliphate, which had great impact on Al-Ghazali and his writings. His political and administrative thought reflected the political and social environment at that time. He witnessed the collapse of the Islamic state and observed the behavior and practice of the corrupt Abbasyah Caliphs. His book *Kings' Advice* was a response to that environ-

ment. It contains an extensive discussion of justice and equity supported by verses from the Holy Qura'an. He provided ten principles of justice and equity derived from the Holy Qura'an that he viewed as requirements for successful leadership. He provided these principles in a form of a letter to the sultan (king):

1. Know the importance of leadership and the importance of justice and equity to leadership. It is a blessing to be a king only if you serve justice and equity; otherwise, it is a curse because you will be held accountable in front of Allah in the day of judgment. If justice and equity do not overweight your interests and desires, you will be one of the Allah's enemies.
2. Associate with the objective scholars to whom the truth is more important than your satisfaction, and avoid the ones who try to earn your satisfaction in order to gain financial benefits.
3. It is not enough to serve justice and equity, but you must command your employees and servants to do so as well. It is your responsibility to make sure that they serve justice and equity.
4. Avoid being egotistical and authoritative to gain citizens' support and commitment.
5. Do not like for your people what you do not like for yourself. Be one of the people so you can feel what they feel and see their problems.
6. Know that Allah prefers satisfying people's needs to spending your time in extra prayers.
7. Do not let your desires control you and the luxury life prevent you from serving justice and equity. If your goal is to satisfy your desires, you will not have time for your people.
8. Since you can be compassionate, gentle, and kind to your people, do not be harsh and mean. If you do, you will lose support and power.
9. Concentrate on gaining citizens' satisfaction to gain their support and commitment, not on forcing them to obey with rancor.
10. Do not seek the satisfaction of anyone if it conflicts with any of the principles of Islam. You should always be controlled by the principles of Islam. Know that satisfying Allah is far more important than satisfying the people.

ABDULLAH M. AL-KHALAF

AL-MARWARDI, ABU AL-HASSAN ALI BIN HABEEB AL-BASRI (957–1058).
One of the greatest scholars of religion, politics, and administrative affairs in the Islamic world, and a pioneer in the fields of public administration and policy.

Abu Al-Hassan Ali bin Habeeb Al-Basri Al-Mawardi was born in Al-Basrah, Iraq, and got his first education in Al-Basrah, then moved to Baghdad, Iraq, where he continued his education. He is considered one of the greatest Islamic scholars, not just in religious matters but also in political and administrative affairs.

During his lifetime the Islamic world, of which Baghdad was then the capital, was governed by the Abbasyah Caliphate, the Islamic political system from 750 to 1258. Since this political system became corrupt, Al-Mawardi and other Islamic scholars were not spared from corruption. However, though corrupt, Al-Mawardi was aware of what was happening and started to write about this political and administrative situation.

The main objectives of his writings were to provide consultation and guidelines to the leadership, composed of the caliph, governors, and other members of the government. The guidelines were developed to remind those in charge of how things had to be run in accordance with the governing principles as cited in the Holy Qura'an and Sunnah. He then wrote several books in this matter. Among them are *Adab Al-Donia Wa Al-Deen, Al-Ahkam Al-Sultaniah, Al-Wazarah,* and *Al-Hawi Al-Kabeer. Al-Ahkam Al-Sultaniah (King's Governing Rules)* is a systematic study of the essentials of the Islamic government administration. In this book, he discussed the following subjects:

The Islamic State. Al-Mawardi pointed out that an Islamic state is different from a non-Islamic state because it is based upon coherence between the religion (Islam) and the politics (the way people should live together). In Islam authority emerges from the people.

The Presidency of the State. He referred to this position as "caliphate" or "imamah," which means the presidency of the state. He believed that the task of the leader was to protect Islam, defend it, and take of the Muslim's affairs. He also developed the characteristic duties and condition of both caliph and caliphate.

Ministry. Al-Mawardi discussed types of ministries that should exist in an Islamic state depending on whether the minister participated in making decisions or just implementing them.

Bureaus. Al-Mawardi discussed the politico-administrative organization of an Islamic state with centralized and decentralized bureaus regarding the military, labor, and finance.

Control and Supervision. To deal effectively and efficiently with the problem of corruption, Al-Mawardi thought that control and supervision should be part of the politico-administrative organization of an Islamic state, involving all those responsible. He discussed the characteristics of a supervisor (faith in Islam, honesty, competence, and community orientation). He placed the politico-administrative control under the *Nadher Al-Madhaleem,* whose role was to handle grievances at different levels.

Local Government. To Al-Mawardi, the size of the Islamic state should dictate the best, most efficient way of governing, with sharing of responsibilities between the central government and the regional politico-administrative authority. This, in turn, caused Al-Mawardi to talk about local governments (emirates). He then classified these local governments into two types, namely general local governments and special local governments. The difference was that in the general local governments, the prince (governor) had a wide authority in all regional politico-administrative affairs (such as judicial, military, and financial matters). On the other hand, in special local governments, the governor had only limited authority. For example, he was not entrusted either to collect funds or interfere with the judiciary or military matters.

Thus, from reading the works of Al-Mawardi, especially his book *Al-Ahkam Al-Sultaniah,* one may conclude that he was one of the pioneers in the field of public policy and administration through his views and suggestions concerning ways to run government affairs and to deal with the problems of corruption and abuse of power by those in positions of responsibility.

ABDULRAHMAN A. HIGAN

ALCOHOLISM.

ALCOHOLISM. A pattern of pathological alcohol use; impairment in social or occupational functioning due to alcohol (see **employee assistance program**).

Alcoholism is a costly problem with various implications for public administrators. Managers in public agencies need to be concerned for employees' health, and the absenteeism and lower productivity of alcoholic employees. Policy makers, implementers, and analysts need accurate data to analyze the cost effectiveness of Medicare, Medicaid, and other health insurance payments for treatment of alcoholism and related health problems. Reaching consensus on the definition of alcoholism, the extent of the problem, and cost-effective alternatives for treatment complicate the tasks of those involved in this policy process.

Defining the Disease

It is difficult to calculate the number of alcoholics with precision due to the stigma attached to the disease and the consequential denial by the patient, the family, and the physician. While alcoholism was considered a moral or legal problem some doctors refused to treat those with the disease (Mendelson and Mello, 1985). These problems were ameliorated in 1956 when the American Medical Association declared that alcoholism is a disease and a medical responsibility. The American Medical Association's 1956 decision reflected that alcohol abuse can result in addiction, and physical dependence upon and tolerance for alcohol's effects, a medical problem.

Several definitions of alcoholism have evolved. The World Health Organization's (WHOs) definition of alcohol type drug dependence stresses cultural criteria: an individual's consumption exceeds the limits that are accepted by his or her culture; an individual consumes alcohol at times that are not considered appropriate by his or her culture; or an individual consumes alcohol to the extent that social relationships or health are impaired. While the WHO definition bases a diagnosis of drug dependence of the alcohol type on cultural criteria, which could vary from country to country, the American Psychiatric Association's (APA) definition is based on factors related to alcohol's effect on social and occupational function, and damage to personal health. The APA criteria relate to more objective factors, such as addiction, tolerance, and physical dependence, which would be apparent in alcoholism's late stage. APA makes a distinction between alcohol abuse and alcohol dependence, the latter term referring to alcoholism. Alcohol abusers use alcohol for at least a month in a way that deviates from healthy or normal use and impairs social or occupational functioning. Some characteristic patterns of alcohol use by abusers are: the inability to cut down or stop drinking; the need to use alcohol daily; repeated attempts to reduce or control drinking by abstaining from alcohol for a period of time or by limiting drinking to certain times of the day; blackouts; occasionally drinking a fifth of spirits or the equivalent in beer or wine; continually drinking even when drinking worsens physical disorders; and drinking nonbeverage alcohol. Some signs of social and occupational impairment include: absenteeism; violent behavior, traffic accidents, or arrests while intoxicated; job loss; or difficulties with family members or friends. Alcoholism or alcohol dependence includes the characteristics associated with alcohol abuse, and either tolerance or withdrawal. Tolerance is the need for more alcohol to achieve a given effect,or decreased effect of a given amount of alcohol. Withdrawal describes symptoms which are associated with stopping or decreasing drinking. Shaking in the morning or malaise that can be alleviated by drinking are signs of withdrawal. While the APA's criteria for diagnosing alcoholism relate to late stages of the disease, the National Council on Alcoholism (NCA) outlines three criteria that can be used in the early and late stages of the disease; physiological; clinical; and, behavioral, psychological, and attitudinal (Mendelson and Mello, 1985).

The Extent of the Problem

Alcoholism is prevalent. According to one estimate, 10 to 15 million people in the United States have major alcohol-related problems that indirectly effect another 35 million people, such as family, friends, and coworkers (Mendelson and Mello, 1985). France, Ireland, Scotland, England, and Finland also have high alcoholism rates. Italians, Chinese, and Jews have low rates, as U.S. subcultures, and the Italians also have low rates in their own countries. Explanations for the variation in rates of alcoholism relate to theories about cultural norms, the influences of parents and peers, and social and personal influences. What are customs related to alcohol, drinking, and drunkenness? What are the values, sanctions, and attitudes with respect to drinking? What behaviors do families teach children? Does the family drink only with meals, or do they often drink between meals? Do parents set examples of moderate drinking? Is abstinence socially acceptable (O'Connor, 1978)?

Alcoholism is costly. In 1988 alcoholism cost the U.S. economy $27.4 billion in productivity losses alone. Problem drinkers are absent 3.8 to 8.3 times as often and file 5 times as many workers' compensation claims as other employees. Productivity losses are not the only costs. Add the costs of absenteeism, treatment of the illness and support costs for treatment, premature death, road accidents, crime, social welfare program administration, destruction of property by fire, time spent caring for family members, and law enforcement to the productivity costs, and the economic cost of alcoholism totals $85.8 billion each year (U.S. DHHS, 1990).

Treatment Alternatives, Costs, and Effectiveness

Ninety percent of the Fortune 500 companies in the United States have implemented employee assistance programs (EAPs) to reduce the costs of alcoholism (see **employee assistance programs, stress**). The average cost per employee for an EAP ranges from $12 to $20 per year and generates from $5 to $16 in savings for each dollar invested. The Hughes Act (Public Law 91–616), Office of Personnel Management (OPM) regulations, and Public Law 93–282 encourage federal agencies to establish EAPs. In the 1970s state and local government entities also began to implement programs.

Two federally funded programs in the U.S., Medicare and Medicaid, provide funds to treat alcoholism, so policy makers are concerned with providing effective prevention and treatment at the least cost. Medicare provides benefits to those over 65 years of age, and will reimburse hospitalization expenses for treatment of alcoholism as a psychiatric disorder. Medicaid will reimburse for the medical expenses of low-income individuals and families. Medicare and Medicaid programs emphasize inpatient treatment even though studies of the effectiveness of inpatient and outpatient treatment programs suggest that both may be effective and inpatient medically based treatment is more expensive (Mendelson and Mello, 1985).

Two U.S. laws, the Family and Medical Leave Act (FMLA) and the Americans with Disabilities Act (ADA), affect employers' rights and responsibilities with alcoholic employees. Under the FMLA employers may provide up to 12 weeks of unpaid leave to alcoholics for rehabilitation. The ADA protects otherwise qualified employees with physical or mental disabilities from discrimination. For example, an employer could be guilty of discrimination for failing to select a rehabilitated employee who is qualified and capable of performing the duties of a position. Such legislation provides incentives for employers to support alcohol rehabilitation programs for their employees and employer-sponsored programs have high success rates because the perceived risk of job loss represents high stakes. If success is measured by rehabilitation, not just job retention, company programs achieve approximately 50 percent, state hospital programs achieve 20 percent, and police-court inebriates achieve 10 percent success rates (Schramm, 1977).

Summary

Alcoholism is a disease with high costs to organizations, to employees, and to families of those with the disease. Alcoholism drains the economy in the United States and in other countries where the disease is prevalent. Having approached consensus on a definition and having recognized the costs, those involved in the policy process can address the need for cost-effective treatment for alcoholism and related health problems.

BONNIE G. MANI

BIBLIOGRAPHY

Mendelson, Jack H., and Nancy K. Mello, eds., 1985. *The Diagnosis and Treatment of Alcoholism,* 2nd ed. New York: McGraw-Hill Book Company. Diagnostic criteria described by Mendelson and Mello are consistent with those stated in the American Psychiatric Association's *Diagnostic and Statistical Manual of Mental Disorders,* 4th ed., published in 1994.
O'Connor, Joyce, 1978. *The Young Drinkers: A Cross-National Study of Social and Cultural Influences.* London: Tavistock Publications.
Schramm, Carl J., ed., 1977. *Alcoholism and Its Treatment in Industry.* Baltimore: The John Hopkins University Press.
U.S. Department of Health and Human Services, 1990. *The Economic Costs of Alcohol and Drug Abuse and Mental Illness: 1985* (DHHS Publication No. ADM 90-1694). San Francisco: Institute for Health & Aging, University of California.

ALIENATION. A malaise affecting people in society and within organizations that is characterized by five states of mind and related behavior—powerlessness, meaninglessness, normlessness, isolation, and self-estrangement (Seeman, 1959).

The Multifaceted Nature of the Concept

Alienation is a concept that arouses a great deal of controversy in scholarly circles. There is no one precise meaning of the term, although most would agree it signifies in one form or other the notions of isolation, separation, and "otherness." Furthermore, alienation can equally refer to estrangement from others, dissociation from the self, or both. Nor is alienation restricted to negative sense; it can also be a neutral term. The fact that it is open to such a wide variety of explanations has been a problem for social science research: "The evasiveness and pervasiveness of the term is sometimes the despair of scientists. Some are overwhelmed and even shocked by the vagueness of alienation and the number of meanings it may have. Its popularity stands in indirect proportion to its precision" (Feuerlicht, 1975, p. 10).

To glean meaning from the many understandings about alienation within the context of public administration, one needs to briefly review the major scholarly thinking about it. Alienation addresses the fundamental problems of human existence, such as the nature of the true self. Theologians believe that humans became alienated when they separated themselves from God. The French philosopher Jean-Jacques Rousseau and his followers taught that estrangement for humans started as soon as they separated from his "natural" physical condition. The German philosopher G.W.F. Hegel described alienation as self-estrangement from the harmonious and interactive development of personality, citizenship, and knowledge. The concept of anomie was developed by the French sociologist Emil Durkheim who explained it as alienation from society. Sigmund Freud used the concept of alienation to explain psychological states of mind (Feuerlicht, 1975, pp. 18–36).

Alienation was a concept so overused in the 1960s that by 1972 its obituary was being forecasted (Lee, 1972, p. 121). Scholars criticized the seemingly endless interpretations of alienation, preferring to replace it with substitutes such as oppression, malaise, reification, or nonparticipation. However, despite the belief that alienation as a theory was used up and finished, it lived on. In fact, those who criticized it often found that they could not do without it (Feuerlicht, 1975, pp. 11–12).

Alienation in the Public Workplace

For public administration, the term alienation derives most meaning from the works of Karl Marx, Max Weber, and Melvin Seeman. Marx found alienation to be an economic concept that began with the division of labor. Separation from the tools of production and the products of one's labor, from peers, and even from the self is the genesis of estrangement in Marxist thought (Marx, 1963). Max Weber described alienation as relating to norms and structures in bureaus that inevitably restrict the leverage the organization has in dealing with its individual participants (Weber, 1946). Building upon Marx's concept, work alienation was described by Taylor as an unavoidable price to pay for achieving efficiency in industrial production (Oldenquist and Rosner, 1991, p. 11). Melvin Seeman's empirical research operationalized the concept into the five categories: powerlessness, meaninglessness, normlessness, isolation, and self-estrangement.

Social scientists who view the concept from Marxist, Weberian, or Taylorist perspectives see alienation arising from specific organization behavior. They content that because capitalists must maximize productivity to maximize profit, they create a number of workplace situations that often lead to estrangement. First, tasks are fragmented so that workers can be used as interchangeable parts; fragmented jobs requiring repetition and speed-up of work for maximum efficiency and profit bring with them an increasing sense of powerlessness and estrangement within the employee (Oldenquist and Rosner, 1991, p. 194). Second, by dividing and segmenting the working class, groups can be managed more effectively and this can discourage worker uprisings (Marx, 1963); it is this very division that reduces group solidarity and promotes meaninglessness (Seeman, 1959). Unsatisfying jobs—those jobs that do not fulfill the psychological needs of the working person for involvement, meaning, achievement, recognition, autonomy and self-actualization (Guyer and Heinz, 1992, pp. 125–152)—generate alienation. Such jobs are generally rank-and-file positions and service jobs. Workplace alienation, thus, can arise from a number of different factors.

The Future of Alienation

Despite heavy criticism of it in the 1970s, in recent times this concept has experienced a resurgence of interest within public administration. This is due to the vast expansion of low-paying service jobs in the United States in both the public and private sectors, which come with inadequate benefits, or no benefits at all. Management today is in a cost-conscious mode that frequently requires workers to do more work in less time so that profit can be maximized. The decline of working conditions and the inevitable decrease in employee standards of living has again resulted in alienation of the workforce, manifested through

levels of stress, burnout, substance abuse, and other mental health problems.

BREENA E. COATES

BIBLIOGRAPHY

Feuerlicht, Ignace, 1975. *Alienation: From the Past to the Future.* Westport, CT: Greenwood Press.
Guyer, Felix, and Walter R. Heinz, 1992. *Alienation, Society, and the Individual: Continuity and Change in Theory and Research.* New Brunswick: Transaction Publishers.
Lee, Alfred M., 1972. "An Obituary for Alienation." *Social Problems,* vol. 20, p. 121.
Marx, Karl, 1963. *Early Writings.* ed. and trans. by T. B. Bottomore. London: A. Watts Publishers.
Oldenquist, Andrew and Menachem Rosner, eds., 1991. *Alienation, Community and Work.* Westport, CT: Greenwood Press.
Seeman, Melvin, 1959. "On the Meaning of Alienation." *American Sociological Review,* vol. 24, pp. 783–791.
Weber, Max, 1946. *From Max Weber: Essays in Sociology,* Hans H. Gerth and C. Wright Mills, eds. New York: Oxford University Press.

ALTERNATIVE DISPUTE RESOLUTION.

A collective phrase embracing a variety of processes for the resolution of disputes outside (or as an alternative to) the usual judicial process in courts of law. The dispute resolution processes usually included under this term are negotiation, mediation, settlement conference, early neutral evaluation, mini-trial, summary jury trial, mediation-arbitration (med-arb), and arbitration. Negotiation, mediation, and arbitration are the most prominent processes.

Definitions

Negotiation is a process in which disputants communicate directly with each other or through professional negotiators, whom they have retained, about issues on which they disagree in order to generate a mutually acceptable resolution.

Mediation involves a skilled neutral person (the mediator) who facilitates the negotiation among disputing parties so as to help them negotiate a mutually satisfactory agreement. The mediator or mediators do not judge the issues or suggest decisions. The mediator manages the communication process so the disputing parties can create their own agreement.

A settlement conference involves a skilled neutral party (usually an attorney) who hears arguments from disputing parties in order to do an informal assessment or advise the parties on the law and precedents relating to their dispute and then suggest a settlement.

Early neutral evaluation involves an evaluator (usually an attorney) chosen by disputing parties or appointed by a judge to assist in narrowing the issues in dispute, facilitate case planning and management, and help in developing a settlement where that is possible.

A mini-trial is a process in which a neutral party and representatives of all disputing parties with settlement authority hear arguments and evidence relating to issues in dispute and then conduct settlement negotiations.

A summary jury trial involves a group of people selected by parties in dispute to be representatives of the prospective trial jury. The people (now acting as a focus group) hear summary presentations of arguments and evidence on a complex case and then deliberate on and decide the issues. Their decision may or may not be binding.

Mediation-arbitration (med-arb) is a process in which parties in dispute agree in advance to work first with a mediator to assist their negotiation in the search of a mutually acceptable resolution. They further agree in advance that if they are unable to generate a resolution through mediation, they will submit their arguments and evidence to another person who, acting as an arbitrator, will decide the case.

Arbitration involves one or more persons with special training in dispute resolution and with expertise in the subject of a dispute, who in a private hearing receive and consider arguments, evidence, and testimony provided by the disputants, and who then issue a binding or nonbinding decision. Arbitration employs many of the procedures found in litigation, but in an informal proceeding with significantly relaxed rules.

Origin and History

The methods currently considered to be alternative dispute resolution (ADR) processes have been practiced, in one form or another, since the earliest moments of civilization. Homer describes ancient Greeks turning to an arbitrator, and mediation has long been communitarian practice in China. Family elders, respected community members, and religious leaders have served in many ways to work out disputes, short of violence.

It has been in the last half of the twentieth century, however, that ADR has been institutionalized in the West, identified in a formal, public, way as part of society's remedies for those in dispute. World War II left the United States with a daunting collection of unresolved labor-management disputes. Labor had strong membership and the power to strike, and they were determined to participate in the coming prosperity. But a series of major strikes in essential industries might have damaged the prosperity. Some method was needed to work out labor-management problems without disempowering labor unions or utilizing crippling strikes. Arbitration was the method used, and it remains a major process in labor-management relations.

The decade of the 1960s produced a new array of disputes arising from protests against the Vietnam War, discrimination against people of color, women, and other oppressed groups, exploitation of the environment, and unsafe working conditions. U.S. federal laws such as the Civil Rights Act of 1964 gave the force of law to the resolution of these disputes, but the judicial system was unprepared to handle the increased caseload. Because of the uneven distribution of wealth and vital cultural resources, there was concern that many were unable to access the legal system.

To meet these needs, neighborhood mediation centers were established to bring justice closer to the people and to provide less costly and less adversarial methods of working out conflict. Professionals from the labor management field provided guidance to the new dispute resolution providers, and public and private funds supported free and low-cost mediation. From this start, there has been a geometrical growth in mediation centers, along with the emergence of professional mediators, who are employed in a wide range of disputes such as family and divorce cases, commercial disagreements, real estate contract disputes, franchise conflict, consumer complaints, insurance settlements, and medical malpractice.

Underlying Theoretical Framework

The early emphasis on ADR came from efforts to handle the excessive burden on the courts and, at the same time, to offer a resolution system that was closer to the people, quicker, and less costly, and which could resolve conflicts without destroying human relationships. With newly legitimized grievances ranging from race, sex, and disability discrimination through consumer protection and environmental protection and reaching into the entire workplace, community, and our ways of doing business, the courts had neither the physical capability nor the proper methods to resolve these complaints. The American Bar Association (ABA) appointed a special committee on the resolution of minor disputes in 1971, hoping to find a way to divert away from the courts disputes that did not truly require formal, adversarial proceedings. That committee became a standing committee of the ABA and was, in 1993, included as a full-fledged section of the ABA.

The premise that ADR lowers court caseloads is no longer seen as a principal rationale for ADR. It has been impossible to demonstrate a significant reduction in caseload as a result of ADR. However, almost 90 percent of the cases scheduled for trial are settled before they actually go to court, and ADR methods can expedite these out-of-court settlements by providing a range of possible methods and techniques for settlement.

Current Practice in the United States

In the years from 1975 to 1995, ADR matured in a variety of ways. The growth of community mediation centers has continued. They offer mediation services for virtually any dispute. Mediation is the involvement of an impartial third party in an existing dispute between two or more parties in which the mediator engages in negotiation, both procedurally and substantively, for the purposes of facilitating communication between the parties and promoting resolution of conflict through the development of an agreement that is acceptable to the disputants without the imposition of an agreement from the mediator.

When people are unable to come to an agreement on their own, it is often helpful to find another person who has the respect of all the disputants, someone who can (1) set an atmosphere that is conducive to agreement; (2) assist the disputants in communicating by gathering information from each side and releasing it to the other side when it will assist agreement; (3) help the disputants clarify their objectives for solution; (4) break the common log jam that comes from excessive or unrealistic expectations; (5) turn attention toward an integrative solution; (6) manage to keep the disputants talking together; and (7) crystalize the rationale on which an agreement can be made and implemented.

Mediators, then, are not simply neutral third parties. They may take an active or interventionist role. People who seek mediation may have already tried negotiation and failed, or they may be going to a mediator as a first step prior to consulting attorneys. So the mediator actively serves to facilitate the process of information exchange among disputants.

Successful mediators know how to interrupt and intervene in the communication among the disputants in order to structure the process of mediation by using such tactics as (1) identifying and enforcing communication rules, such as who speaks when and for how long; (2) ending the discussion; (3) setting and enforcing an agenda; (4) setting roles, such as who has what task; and (5) giving orienting information, such as background knowledge.

A mediator can also intervene to reframe the disputants' statements by (1) suggesting alternatives; (2) restating and clarifying what has been said; (3) noting and reinforcing points of agreement; and (4) being a good listener.

Mediators can, in addition, expand the information resources by (1) seeking opinions and evaluations from disputants; (2) seeking proposals of offers; (3) requesting clarification of proposals; and (4) asking disputants to explain themselves more clearly.

Research to date concludes that the most effective mediators provide insight by identifying issues, translating themes into proposals, and focusing on the points of agreement.

Arbitration has outgrown its focus on labor-management problems to become the resolution method of choice for many organizational settings. Organizations such as the American Arbitration Association (AAA) help business and professional groups include arbitration clauses in their contracts. When taking out an insurance policy, going to a new health care provider, purchasing a home or an expensive consumer product, contracting for a construction project, or accepting a new job, people find with increasing frequency a clause such as this: "Any disputes arising out of the conditions of this contract will be submitted to arbitration following the rules of the American Arbitration Association."

U.S. courts have taken the position that such an agreement is binding on the parties, and they will not allow them to circumvent arbitration in order to go to the courts. The United States government and most of the individual states have laws identifying arbitration as a legitimate dispute resolution method that is supported and encouraged as an alternative to the courts.

When a dispute arises, the parties follow the dictates of their arbitration agreement. They make contact with the arbitration provider to arrange a hearing. The provider will charge a fee for this service proportionate to the amount of money involved in the dispute. A list of qualified arbitrators will be supplied to all parties to the dispute. Arbitrators are selected first because they have at least ten years of experience in the area of the dispute such as labor-management, commercial, or construction. Arbitrators must also become qualified by taking training in how to conduct an arbitration.

The disputing parties will be allowed to strike any of the prospective arbitrators whom they feel would be unlikely to render a fair and impartial decision. The arbitrators will decline an appointment if they have any relationship that would, or would appear, to compromise their neutrality. Once an arbitrator agreeable to all parties is selected (frequently arbitrators work in panels of three), the arbitrator will take control of the process.

The arbitrator will set the time and place of the hearing, conduct a preliminary conference to identify and narrow the issues, explain procedures, and handle any motions. Arbitrators are empowered to issue subpoenas to compel the attendance of those chosen to provide testimony at the hearing, and witnesses can be placed under oath by the arbitrator.

At the hearing, the arbitrator will identify the issues in dispute and the parties present. It is common that attorneys will represent the parties, but it is not required. Anyone may be selected as an advocate. The party bearing the burden of proof (usually called the plaintiff) will be invited to make an opening statement, followed by that of the opponent. The plaintiff will then call witnesses who will provide the testimony and evidence in support of the case. The opponent will be invited to cross-examine all witnesses.

When the plaintiff's case is complete, the opponent (usually called the defendant) will call witnesses and the plaintiff will be allowed to cross-examine them. When all witnesses have been heard and cross-examined, the plaintiff will give a summary argument, followed by the defendant. The plaintiff may choose to reserve the right to make a rebuttal argument following the defendant.

The arbitrator will adjourn the hearing when this process is complete. Unlike judges in courts, the arbitrator may keep the hearing open to receive additional written argument and evidence.

How is an arbitration different from a trial at law? The arbitrator can set the degree of formality of the hearing, and may choose an informal procedure in which everyone sits at a table and speaks conversationally. Arbitrators have the freedom to receive evidence such as hearsay that would be inadmissible in court, and their decisions are not subject to appeal unless an argument can be made that the arbitrator was unfair or behaved improperly. Although arbitrators are usually paid and adversaries usually hire lawyers to represent them, the overall costs of arbitration are well below those of a trial. This comes from the speed with which arbitrations can be set up and completed, thereby reducing lawyer's costs, and the absence of discovery procedures such as taking depositions from prospective witnesses, which can be enormously expensive.

LEONARD C. HAWES AND RICHARD D. RIEKE

BIBLIOGRAPHY

Axelrod, R., 1970. *Conflict of Interest: A Theory of Divergent Goals with Applications to Politics.* Markham.
Blake, R. R. and J. S. Mouton, 1984. *Solving Costly Organizational Conflicts.* Jossey-Bass.
Bush, R. A. B. and J. Folger, 1994. *The Promise of Mediation: Responding to Conflict Through Empowerment and Recognition.* Jossey-Bass.
Cahn, D. D., Ed., 1990. *Conflict in Intimate Relations.* Guilford.
Coser, L., 1956. *The Functions of Social Conflict.* The Free Press.
Deutsch, M., 1977. *The Resolution of Conflict: Constructive and Destructive Processes.* Yale University Press.
Fisher, R. and W. Ury, 1981. *Getting to Yes: Negotiating Agreement Without Giving In,* 2nd. ed. Houghton Mifflin.
Grimshaw, A. D., Ed., 1990. *Conflict Talk: Sociolinguisitic Investigations of Arguments in Conversations.* Cambridge University Press.
Haynes, J. M. and G. L. Haynes, 1989. *Mediating Divorce.* Jossey-Bass.
Horowitz, D. L., 1985. *Ethnic Groups in Conflict.* University of California Press.
Kritek, P. B., 1994. *Negotiation at an Uneven Table: Developing Moral Courage in Resolving Our Conflicts.* Jossey-Bass.
Moore, C. W., 1987. *The Mediation Process: Practical Strategies for Resolving Conflict.* Jossey-Bass.
Ozawa, C. P., 1991. *Recasting Science: Consensual Procedures in Public Policy Making.* Westview Press.
Pruitt, C. and C. Snyder, Eds., 1969. *Theory and Research on the Causes of War.* Prentice-Hall.
Rieke, R. and K. Stutman, 1990. *Communication in Legal Advocacy.* University of South Carolina Press.
Schelling, T. C., 1963. *Strategy of Conflict.* Galaxy Books.
Susskind, L., L. Bacow and M. Wheeler, 1983. *Resolving Environmental Regulatory Disputes.* Schenkman Publishing.
Umbreit, M. S., 1994. *Victim Meets Offender: The Impact of Restorative Justice and Mediation.* Criminal Justice Press.

ALTERNATIVE FUND. A charitable fund-raising organization established as an alternative to United Way to support social causes excluded, or not well-supported, by the United Way system. Most such funds focus on particular areas of charitable giving and community concern and most operate at the local level. Examples include Black United Funds, Combined Health Appeals, International Service Agencies, National Voluntary Health Agencies, and various other social action funds, united arts funds, environmental federations, and women's funds. In 1994, an estimated 183 such funds existed, collecting more than $ 260 million in contributions compared to more than $ 3 billion for United Way (Bothwell, 1994).

The emergence of alternative funds, beginning in the 1950s and firmly taking root in the 1970s, is best understood in the context of the history and rationale for United Way and the tensions associated with that system. According to Brilliant (1990), efforts to coordinate charitable community fund-raising began in earnest in the U.S. in the years following the Civil War when social needs burgeoned, charities proliferated, and concerns arose over the efficient coordination and allocation of charitable funding. Early efforts in Buffalo, Denver, and Cleveland led to the contemporary model of a professionally staffed organization, led by business and other community leaders, raising charitable funds through an annual campaign for distribution in a coordinated fashion among community charities. The movement of such community fund-raising organizations spread rapidly throughout the country in the early part of the twentieth century.

During the first half of the twentieth century, the community fund-raising movement was influenced in its structure and operations by a number of key developments (Brilliant, 1990). Led by the YMCA and the Red Cross, national federated agencies formed and began to conduct their own fund-raising campaigns to support their local affiliates. During World War I, the War Chest movement, which was designed to mobilize charitable resources on behalf of war-related charitable services, introduced two new concepts: (a) the inclusion of some of the national federated agencies into community fund-raising drives, and (b) appeal to the general public for contributions, not just to businesses and wealthy givers. Some War

Chest campaigns operated in concert with existing community fund-raising organizations, and after the war many of these organizations adopted the name Community Chest and incorporated aspects of the War Chest model.

Another important development for the community federated charity movement was the introduction of payroll deduction schemes (Brilliant, 1990). This began with corporate sector labor agreements in the early 1940s that allowed for union dues to be deducted from paychecks, and accelerated with the introduction of compulsory withholding of income taxes by the federal government in 1943. The new venue for soliciting contributions for charitable causes in communities became the labor forces of large business corporations, as well as federal and state government work forces. Brilliant (1990) describes a seminal event in 1947 that began to transform the community fund-raising (Community Chest) movement into the modern United Way:

> ... a meeting held by Henry Ford II on July 15, 1947, for the purpose of launching the United Health and Welfare Fund of the State of Michigan ... marked the official birth of what would become the United Fund, a federation created to resolve the problems caused by increasing numbers of independent fund-raising appeals and competition from the burgeoning health agencies. ... And it signaled a new direction of the chest movement, away from concentration on people in their local community, and door-to-door fund-raising, to a more aggressive complex and interlocking role with national agencies, labor, and the world of work.
>
> The basic elements of the United Fund concept were not new: workplace solicitation; corporate support; labor involvement; an attempt at inclusiveness, including national agencies; and even payroll deduction had happened before. But the combination of all these elements resulted in a new gestalt, which included formalization of limited access to the workplace (p. 29).

An equally important event was the institution in 1956 of workplace solicitation of federal employees, expanding a practice that had begun in 1931 when President Hoover allowed Community Chest and Red Cross chapters to solicit federal workers in their communities (Glaser, 1994). The Kennedy administration consolidated the federal workplace program into what became known as the Combined Federal Campaign (CFC), which originally permitted United Way and three other federations to participate in an annual federal fund drive.

These seeds of the modern United Fund contain within them tensions that led in subsequent decades to the formation of the alternative funds. First, they created monopolies over fund solicitation, particularly in the corporate workplace, which would be problematic for new groups trying to gain access to the system. Second, while

the United Fund was meant to be inclusive, it was controlled by mainstream business, labor and community interests, and hence subject to resisting the inclusion of unpopular causes or fringe groups. Third, in order to accommodate major national charities such as the Red Cross, the YMCA, or the Girls Scouts and Boy Scouts, which were capable of effective fund-raising on their own, united funds had to assure that the shares of proceeds to these traditional groups would be maintained, hence limiting United Way flexibility to respond to new groups, causes and needs.

While the United Way movement thrived in the decades following World War II, the foregoing structural characteristics, combined with many diverse social pressures to accommodate new charitable causes and organizations, eventually spawned efforts to open the system to greater competition and choice and to the formation of alternative funds. Two seminal organizations provided models for the development of alternative funds around the country: the Commerce and Industry Combined Health Appeal (CICHA) established in Baltimore in 1959 was the progenitor of other Combined Health Appeals—federations of the local chapters of major national health agencies such as the American Cancer Society and the Muscular Dystrophy Association; and the Brotherhood Crusade formed in Los Angeles in 1969 following the Watts riots provided the model for the formation of Black United Funds—community funds that solicit for charities in the African American community not adequately supported by United Way. These and other funds eventually successfully challenge United Way's exclusive access to workplace solicitation (Brilliant, 1990).

In 1980, the alternative fund movement received an important boost when the federal government allowed local charities that were not members of United Way to participate in the CFC (Glaser, 1994). The number of charities participating in the CFC grew from 33 in 1980 to 785 in 1992, while United Way's share of revenues declined from 69 percent to 35 percent over this period (Glaser, 1994). Over the same period, employee contributions raised by alternative funds overall rose from $35 million to approximately $250 million, and by 1993 more than 10 percent of Fortune 500 companies had opened their workplace giving programs to United Way alternatives (Bothwell, 1994).

The United Way system has responded to the competition represented by alternative funds in a number of ways, including initial resistance, various modes of collaboration and accommodation, and most notably by redesigning its own practices to allow for "donor option" or "donor choice" in the designation of contributed funds. In the 1990s, for a variety of reasons, contributions to United Way began to stagnate while alternative funds continue to grow and proliferate. While United Way adapts to the new environment of competition for workplace contributions, the phenomenon of competition itself is raising an old issue in a new form for employers and for the alternative funds themselves: How can charitable fund-raising in the workplace by many competing funds be coordinated and organized in a manner that is efficient in terms of fund-raising costs, and tolerable to the organizations whose employees are being solicited?

DENNIS R. YOUNG

BIBLIOGRAPHY

Bothwell, Robert O., 1994. "Federated Giving: Recent History, Current Issues." Draft report, National Committee for Responsive Philanthropy.
Brilliant, Eleanor L., 1990. *The United Way: Dilemmas of Organized Charity.* New York: Columbia University Press.
Glaser, John S., 1994. *The United Way Scandal.* New York: John Wiley & Sons.

AMERICAN ASSOCIATION OF FUND-RAISING COUNSEL, INC. (AAFRC).

A trade association of fund-raising consulting firms.

The American Association of Fund-Raising Counsel, Inc. was founded in 1935 to advance philanthropic causes and ensure the ethical practice of fund-raising professionals. Early organizational leadership recognized that the field of fund-raising was so mistrusted and misunderstood that a Fair Practice Code had to be the first order of business. These standards have recently been renamed "the Standards of Membership and Professional Practice."

With headquarters in New York City, AAFRC is the primary source of detailed information summarizing the national state of philanthropy through its annual publications, *Giving USA* and *Giving USA Update.* The Association is also a leader in providing the field with data on state fund-raising laws and legislative developments affecting philanthropy.

Membership in AAFRC is limited to firms recommended by current member firms. There are other requirements confirming the applicant firms' long-term success, professional credentials, and adherence to professional practices that meet the Standards of Membership and Professional Practice espoused by the Association.

The organization boasts 23 member firms, and is funded through membership dues based on professional fee billings. Celebrating its fiftieth anniversary in 1985, the Association announced the founding of the AAFRC Trust for Philanthropy. This special fund will endeavor to "advance research, education and public awareness of philanthropy."

AAFRC is located at 25 West 43rd Street, Suite 820, New York, NY 10036 (telephone: 212-354-5799).

WILLIAM BERGOSH AND
ROBERT W. BUCHANAN

BIBLIOGRAPHY

Kaplan, Ann E., ed., 1994. *Giving USA 1994: The Annual Report on Philanthropy for the Year 1993.* New York: AAFRC Trust for Philanthropy.

AMERICAN ADMINISTRATIVE TRADITION.

The administrative cultures and management practices of governments within the United States.

The tradition of public administration in the United States is the griffin in the globe's menagerie of national managerial traditions: mythical and improbable, but fierce in demeanor and capable of occasional flight. To phrase it more prosaically, the core of the American public administrative tradition may be reduced to a single word: constraint.

A tradition is not, we should note, the same thing as a profession, that is, a largely self-regulating practice and self-aware field of study. "Tradition" is, to borrow a definition from *Webster's,* "Belief, habit, practice, principle, handed down verbally from one generation to another, or acquired by each successive generation from the example preceding it" (p. 1574). Compared to a profession, a tradition is more visceral than intellectual, more cultural than practical, more grassroots than grand, more encompassing than specializing.

As the title of this encyclopedia indicates, we shall focus on the American administrative tradition as it is found in the public sector, not in the private sector. Whereas "constraint" is the watchword in explaining the American tradition of public administration, it is not a term that comes readily to mind in describing the national tradition of business administration; in the private sector, "aggression" is perhaps the appropriate moniker of the American administrative tradition. It is difficult, after all, to conceive of the shrewd, daring, and rapacious "robber barons"–the flamboyant tycoons of the nineteenth century who founded the American corporate state–as being associated with any administrative tradition of constraint. The tradition of administering governments differs dramatically from the tradition of administering businesses in the United States.

All national traditions are shaped by strong and deep undercurrents peculiar to the national culture. When cultural currents are recognized and articulated by intellectuals, a society's brawn and brain unite in powerful forms. Traditions are born. Nowhere is this combination more evident than in the American tradition of public administration. We shall consider, first, those cultural characteristics that seem unique to the United States, and, second, the intellectualization of those characteristics by the nation's early political thinkers.

Origins: Cultural Underpinnings of the American Tradition of Public Administration

There seems to be an unshakable faith among scholars that the characteristics of a people stem from the thoughts of their great thinkers, and a corresponding skepticism towards the notion that the great thoughts of these thinkers derive from the characteristics of the people in whose midst they think. We tilt toward the latter bias.

In the eighteenth century when the republic was being founded, Americans were, by and large, revolutionary yet rational, enlightened but often uneducated, anti-authoritarian but cautious—and (despite the genius of the U.S. Constitution) occasionally fumbling in establishing democratic institutions. These cultural characteristics have since evolved into new forms, but forms that would still be quite recognizable as basic American traits to a citizen of the United States living 200 years ago.

Understanding one's own culture, as Alexis de Tocqueville taught Americans, is best done with help from observers who are not of the culture which they observe. We shall rely on just such observers, and, more to the point, concentrate on those analysts who focus on the hub of any culture's administrative tradition: the administrative organizations in which that tradition manifests itself.

One such observer is, like de Tocqueville, French. Michel Crozier identified what he believed to be the core characteristics of the American administrative organization that derived directly from the American national culture: division of labor and due process of law.

American organizations are dominated by their specialized and splintering divisions of labor and their obsequiousness in observing due process of law, and these twin cultural factors produce organizational pathologies unique to American bureaucracies. Functional specialization results in an abnormally high number of jurisdictional disputes among and within American organizations, while Americans' passion for due process of law produces a plethora of impersonal bureaucratic rules that are designed to protect the individual from injustices, but which also are obstacles to organized action. Both cultural traits tend to magnify the role of lawyers, or any official who is in a position to interpret organizational rules, jurisdictions, and prerogatives, and this aspect often impedes change in American organizations.

In Crozier's view, American organizations, on the whole, tend to protect the rights of individuals more effectively, are better attuned to reality, are characterized by more cooperation, and are generally more open than are those of other nations. But the existence of many centers of authority in American organizations, and the difficulties that must be surmounted in coordinating them, pose problems of change for American organizations. Although American organizations are likely more open to innova-

tion than are others, "Willful individuals can block the intentions of whole communities for a long time; numerous routines develop around local positions of influence; the feeble are not protected so well against the strong; and generally, a large number of vicious circles will protect and reinforce local conservatism" (p. 236).

A Hollander, Geert Hofstede, places the organizational pathologies unique to the American administrative tradition in comparative and systematic perspective. By analyzing the common cultural manifestations of managers in the offices of an American-based multinational corporation in over 40 nations, Hofstede identified five fundamental dimensions of national culture: power distance, uncertainty avoidance, individualism-collectivism, masculinity-femininity, and long-term/short-term orientation. Specific national cultures can be any combination of these. Without indulging in an extended description of each of these dimensions, we shall attempt to synopsize how they pertain to the American administrative tradition.

The United States is a small power distance country (that is, its citizens value equality); a weak uncertainty avoidance nation (in fact, it is well below average, indicating high risk-taking propensities and tolerance for dissent, among other characteristics); exceptionally individualistic as a society; well above average as a masculine culture; and has a short-term orientation.

Relying on these characteristics, Hofstede describes the United States (and the other English-speaking nations) as an "achievement motivation culture," which relates to a hierarchy of human needs that places personal achievement near the top and security near the bottom. But other cultures have different motivations. Some cultures, for example, may be masculine (like the United States) but also have strong needs to avoid uncertainty (such as Italy, Japan, and Mexico). These nations are "security-motivated cultures," or cultures which turn the pecking order of values found in the United States upside down; security-motivated cultures place security near the top of the pyramid of human needs, and personal achievement near the bottom.

Other nations may, like the United States, have weak uncertainty avoidance qualities, but are feminine cultures (a combination found in all the Scandinavian nations), and still others may be polar opposites of the United States, being feminine societies that have strong uncertainty avoidance needs (a combination found in Israel and Thailand). These are "social motivation cultures," or cultures that place a high premium on the quality of social life. In the case of the Scandinavian countries, a propensity to take risks is combined with a commitment to society's well-being; in Israel and Thailand, a need for security is combined with a commitment to social health.

Individualism, masculinity, a sense of fairness, a preference for equality, and low needs for security number prominently among those national traits that distinguish American culture from others, and which have had a particular salience in the formation of the American administrative tradition. But it is in the public sector where these cultural characteristics have had their greatest impact on that tradition.

Articulations: Early and Influential Expressions of the American Tradition of Public Administration

At least three early and highly influential articulations of these uniquely American cultural characteristics placed them squarely in the tradition of American public administration that was beginning to gel in the eighteenth century: the Articles of Confederation, the first state constitutions, and the debates and writings of the nation's founders, especially Alexander Hamilton and Thomas Jefferson.

The Articles of Confederation—which, from 1791 to 1789, provided the first framework for the new nation—were as emblematic of the early Americans' fondness for managerial mish-mash as they were evidentiary of Americans' insistence on administrative constraint. The relatively scant attention paid in the Articles to such notions as matching accountability with authority and specialized divisions of public labor (notably in the Articles' disinclination to distinguish legislative responsibilities from executive responsibilities in the government's structure) no doubt was the product not only of a grassroots revulsion with princely prerogatives, but equally of the nation's early political thinkers wrestling with the dilemma of how to organize something truly new: big democracy. Because the nation's first charter had to account for a vast territory and a large population, it somehow needed to be devised so that it could transcend the only governmental form that democracy had ever used before, the town meeting. Unfortunately, the Articles of Confederation did not meet this historic challenge.

The state governments reigned supreme under the Articles. Congress was really a convention of ambassadors from the states, rather than an assembly of legislators. The Articles of Confederation did set up a rudimentary national civil service, but it was a bizarre bureaucratic beast that had no authority to act on its own or enforce much of anything. The national civil service, consisting of the Departments of Foreign Affairs, War, and Treasury, and an existing Post Office Department, reported directly to committees of the Continental Congress. There was no national chief executive; in fact, the first draft of the Articles of Confederation, written in 1776, was rejected by the Second Continental Congress on the specific grounds that it had proposed an overly empowered executive.

When Daniel Shays ignited his ill-conceived rebellion in 1786, the new nation's political leaders discovered that no arm of "American government," such as it was, had been authorized or organized to put down the disturbance, and eventually that chore fell to the Massachusetts state militia. At least one petulant English observer foresaw the impossibility, as demonstrated by Shays's Rebellion, of his former colonies ever founding a government worthy of the name, and he attributed this failure to Americans' fixation on a weak executive: "As to the future grandeur of America, and its being a rising empire under one head, whether Republican or Monarchial, it is one of the idlest and most visionary notions that was ever conceived even by writers of romance" (Josiah Tucker, as quoted in Smith, 1980, p. 82).

At about the same time that the Articles of Confederation were being written, the states were busily drafting their own constitutions. Eleven of the 13 states adopted constitutions between 1776 and 1780. Connecticut and Rhode Island did not write their constitutions until well into the next century, and instead retained their charters, which had been granted to them by England in the 1600s. This was because these charters actually created genuine republics within those states, including reasonably authoritative chief executives and legislators who were elected by the people, and the only emendation that was required was the elimination of references in the charters to the king.

The eleven states that adopted constitutions were notably aggressive in limiting the powers of the chief executive. Only New York's constitution (with Massachusetts's running a distant second) provided a reasonably strong executive, and this comparatively exceptional power vested in New York's governor seems to have been attributable to the unique combination of John Jay, Robert Livingston, and Gouverneur Morris—New Yorkers who had a heavy hand in drafting their state's constitution, and all of whom were unusually able men who believed in the utility of a relatively central authority.

The remaining constitutions stipulated that the chief executive was to be appointed by the legislature or the courts, and all of them, in turn, severely restricted their chief executives' appointment powers. With only two exceptions, Massachusetts and New York, the governors in all of the 11 states amounted to little more than a military commander, and all executive and most judicial powers—as well as legislative authority—were placed firmly within the legislatures. With the exceptions of New York and arguably Massachusetts, states determinedly ignored the notion that their governments and people might benefit from the presence of an empowered executive. In fact, 10 of the 13 original states had gubernatorial terms of only a single year.

Perhaps even more ominous from the viewpoint of both effective and democratic government was the fact that the drafters of state constitutions in most of the states simply did not conceive that there were distinctions between branches and even functions of government. Making laws and making them work were one and the same, and this blurring of basic governmental responsibilities, which appear so separate and distinct to us today, may have been at least a partial product of the tradition established by the English shire. The shires were largely the creation of the masterful medieval manager, King Edgar the Peaceful (959–975), some 800 years before the American Revolution. They served as subunits of his majesty's government, and were based on the premise that the king's delegate, the shire-reeve (now called the sheriff), could make, manage, and have a loud voice in the adjudication of the laws within the bounds of his (that is, the sheriffs) shire. That all of the states were influenced by King Edgar's administrative creativity during the Dark Ages of Europe is indisputable; each of the 13 states had adopted England's use of shires in the form of countries well before the Revolution.

This confusion of governmental function and governmental branch, as evidenced in most of the states' first constitutions (or, more accurately, this innocent ignorance about the benefits of matching function with structure), still continues in the United States in its most vivid form in the nation's 3,043 county governments. American counties and their citizens always have displayed a structural and attitudinal ambivalence as to whether they were free-standing local governments or administrative arms of state governments. One standard dictionary of American history notes that American counties "have been maintained here through three centuries with surprisingly little modification" (Anderson, 1962, p. 237).

It might appear to some that the absence of authority granted by the Articles of Confederation to the national government, and the virtual absence of authority provided by the great majority of the original state constitutions to elected or appointed state administrators, were Rousseauan testaments to true, populist, and "natural" democracy. Hardly. Passing few people (about 6 percent) were allowed to vote on anything or anyone in any of the states, and only three states (Massachusetts, New Hampshire, and New York) permitted their chief executives to even be elected independently by those few people who were qualified to vote. In only one state, Massachusetts, were the people permitted to ratify their own state's constitution by popular vote. Democracy was not only new—it was distrusted.

Layering and striating all of this early American activity in drafting confederations and constitutions was the massive brilliance of the early American political elite, but particularly that of Hamilton and Jefferson.

Hamilton displayed throughout his writings on government a strong interest in the administrative apparatus of the state. A friend of Hamilton's reported that Hamilton was contemplating a "full investigation of the history and science of civil government and how practical results of various modifications of it upon the freedom and happiness of mankind . . . and to engage the assistance of others in the enterprise" (Kent, 1898, pp. 327–328).

Interestingly, in light of the later thinking of early twentieth century contributors to a theory of public administration, Hamilton never bought in to the idea that there were "principles of administration." Consider a sample of this view provided by the illustrious Leonard D. White, who wrote in 1936 (at the height of the "principles of administration" movement) that a principle of administration "is as useful a guide to action in the public administration of Russia as of Great Britain, of Irak as of the United States" (p. 25). Hamilton would have quickly dismissed such bombast, noting that efficient public administration "must be fitted to a nation, as much as a coat to the individual; and consequently, that what may be good to Philadelphia may be bad to Paris, and ridiculous at Petersburg" (Syrett and Cooke, 1961–1979, vol. 22, p. 404).

As these differing perspectives imply, Hamilton's approach to public administration was above all practical. Hamilton therefore extolled a strong chief executive in the public sector, equating a strong executive with the "energy" needed to make a government function: "A feeble executive [by contrast] implies a feeble execution of the government. A feeble execution is but another phrase for a bad execution; and a government ill executed . . . must be, in practice, a bad government" (1961, "No. 70," p. 423). Things, in sum, had to get done.

But, even more than a strong chief executive, Hamilton advocated a very strong bureaucracy. Hamilton urged that department heads be paid exceptionally well, that they possess substantial powers, and that their tenure in office should extend beyond that of the chief executive who appointed them. In fact, Hamilton felt that a brief tenure of bureaucrats in high office would "occasion a disgraceful and ruinous mutability in the administration of the government" (1961, "No. 72," p. 436). Compare Hamilton's views with what has happened in the United States today, in which the average tenure of an undersecretary or assistant secretary in the federal government averages 22 months (Heclo, 1977, p. 103), and in which fully one-third of the political appointees in the federal Senior Executive Service change jobs or leave government every year (Ingraham, 1987, p. 429).

One logically would infer from such realities of the federal condition that Hamilton's views did not have a lasting impact on the early formulation of the American administrative tradition, and one would be right. Hamilton's notions on how public administration ought to work were in direct contradiction to the ideas and ideals of Jefferson, whose influence on the American administrative tradition was far more pervasive than was Hamilton's.

In stark contrast to Hamilton, who embraced a dynamic government, Jefferson disdained the very idea of it. Jefferson wrote to James Madison, "I am not a friend to a very energetic government. It is always oppressive. It places the government more at their ease, at the expense of the people" (Bowen, 1966, p. 105). As president (1801–1809), Jefferson practiced what he preached—he remains the only president who never vetoed an act of Congress.

Jefferson celebrated and, to be blunt, romanticized, the ideals of localist, yeoman democracy as the core of the American political experiment. Lynton Keith Caldwell suggests that, because of Jefferson's abiding belief in the perfectibility of the common man and woman, it followed that the best government was the most participatory government, and the most participatory government was "no friend to bureaucracy, to professionalism in public administration . . . or to the administrative state as a shaper and director of national development" (1990, p. 482). Jefferson's "profound distrust of bureaucracy" (p. 483) is in part responsible for the "presidential tendency" to be "proactive in relation to foreign affairs and reactive in relation to domestic issues where power must be shared with Congress. Thus, America today has a powerful, costly, and energetic executive who intervenes abroad on numerous occasions but who often seems politically incapable of rational, informed forecasting or planning for the nation's future" (p. 484).

Of Hamilton, Paul Van Riper has written, "If anyone deserves a title as *the* founder of the American administrative state . . . it is not Wilson, Easton, or Ely but Alexander Hamilton" (1983, p. 480). Perhaps. But Hamilton, brilliant thought he was, nonetheless rejected as intellectually tenuous and administratively debilitating many of the basic cultural values of his new nation as they pertained to the conduct of public administration. Van Riper may well be correct in his identification of Hamilton as the founder of the profession of public administration in the United States. But it is to Jefferson that credit must be given as the founder of the tradition of American public administration. It was Jefferson who, by his eloquent articulation of what he believed to be the transcendent goodness of the average American, gave intellectual credence to those currents in the American political culture that have resulted in the lasting American tradition of constrained public management. It is a tradition against which Hamilton's professional and academic progeny still war.

By the end of the eighteenth century, as a result of the nation's founders putting into words (whether as civic charters or as philosophic ramblings) what they saw as their fledgling nation's deepest character—and the reality of that character itself—the American social contract was given recognizable form.

A social contract is an agreement, often more understood than expressed, between the citizens and the state that defines and limits the duties and responsibilities of each. For example, although there is a richer variety of apparent social contracts in Africa than in most continents, Aidan W. Southall describes early African governmental structures as "half enlarged household, half embryonic state" (1953, p. 195), emphasizing the familial nature of the African social contract. In Asia, a foundation of Confucian philosophy has supported a social contract which, in many nations, legitimizes the head of both government and society as a highly authoritative, compassionate, and wise father figure. And in Europe, the contract is a covenant, subject to adjustment, in which those who govern and those who are governed are seen as equal partners. Not so in the United States, where the social contract is a consequence of revolution; all power is held by the people, and is delegated by them (if they wish) to their government. Government is very much a "servant" of the citizenry in every sense of the word, and this uniquely American social contract is partly responsible for the constraint that permeates the American tradition of public administration.

Attenuations: The Legacy of Limited Public Administration in the United States

A tradition of administrative constraint—some would say of governmental gridlock—is especially evident at the federal level. That gridlock is, undeniably, at least partly the result of different parties controlling different branches of the federal government throughout much of the twentieth century, as well as a conservative strain in the American polity which passionately holds that gridlock is good because government is not—a conservatism that obtains some of its nourishment from Jefferson's belief in human perfectibility. But gridlock also is a consequence of the inevitable undermining of administrative action that accompanies such cultural dimensions as a people's deep commitment to a person's right to due process of law (an arduous and time-consuming effort), functional specialization (with its unavoidable battles over jurisdictional turf), and highly individualistic and masculine values (guaranteeing *mano a mano* confrontations among agencies, branches, and levels of government, when more collective and feminine values likely would achieve more concrete results in a public context).

Nearly a generation ago, the distinguished and politically sophisticated Washington insider Lloyd Cutler, in his capacity as then-counsel to the president, bemoaned his government's seeming inability to act: "Under the U.S. Constitution, it is not now feasible to 'form a government.' The separation of powers . . . whatever its merits in 1973, has become a structure that almost guarantees stalemate today" (1980, p. 127), and argued for a new constitutional convention that would amount to a wholesale rewriting of the Constitution along parliamentary lines. (Shades of

Hamilton!) Cutler described the problem, but mistakenly ascribed its cause to what is really a symptom; the American tendency to govern by gridlock is less a consequence of an outdated Constitution, and more the product of a still-vigorous political culture which wrote it. Scrapping the Constitution, as Cutler advocates, will not change the reality of an administrative and political tradition in which frustration is the only constant.

The subnational governments display their own tradition of constrained public administration. They are less reflective of governmental gridlock (although the states and localities have their share, too), and more expressive of the dilemmas endemic to the uniquely American administrative tradition of the feeble public executive. The intellectual and practical connections between the first spindly structures of American public administration erected in the eighteenth century, and the contemporary executive role in American subnational governments, but especially local governments, are unusually clear and direct.

More than 67 percent of American municipalities and over 23 percent of counties (Renner and De Santis, 1993, pp. xiv, 67) hire city managers or chief administrative officers who typically have large powers, and who usually report not to the elected chief executives of these governments, but to their legislative bodies, such as city councils or county commissions, which have the sole authority to hire and fire them. As a result of the growing popularity of this long-dominant practice among local governments, the majority of elected local chief executives have few powers.

Only 26 percent of American mayors have the sole authority to appoint municipal department heads (Renner and De Santis, 1993, p. 67), and mayors have "input" in the dismissal of department heads in less than 28 percent of cities and towns. Only nine out of a hundred mayors in the United States are responsible for preparing the agenda for the city council (Anderson, 1989, p. 28).

In more than half (52 percent) of all American cities and towns with populations of 2,500 or more, well over 90 percent of the mayors cannot veto legislation passed by the council or commission; astonishingly, over four-fifths of the mayors in the 41 percent of municipalities that use the mayor-council plan, which ostensibly is the "strong executive" form of American local government, have no veto power (Adrian, 1988, p. 10).

Counties have even weaker chief executives. Only 8 percent of chief executive officers in American counties have a veto power. Fifty-eight percent of these executives have terms of only a single year, and only 22 percent are elected directly by county voters—a much lower proportion than in municipalities, where the overwhelming majority of mayors are elected directly by the people (De Santis, 1989, pp. 60–61). It is in county governments where the original American administrative values, as reflected in those first state constitutions, still flourish most verdantly.

The American tradition of public administration is orthodox in that it reflects the dimensions of the culture in which it is embedded. But it is unique in that it is a tradition in which administrative constraint, symbolized by gridlock and executive limitations, is the overriding feature.

The emblem of the American tradition of public administration is not the same as that of the nation—the eagle. The emblem of American public administration is the improbable griffin.

NICHOLAS HENRY

BIBLIOGRAPHY

Adrian, Charles R., 1988. "Forms of City Government in American History." In *The Municipal Year Book, 1988.* Washington, D.C.: International City Management Association, pp. 3–11.

Anderson, Eric, 1989. "Two Major Forms of Government: Two Types of Professional Management." In *The Municipal Year Book, 1989,* Washington, D.C.: International City Management Association, pp. 26–32.

Anderson, Wayne, ed., 1962. "County Government." *Concise Dictionary of American History.* New York: Charles Scribner's Sons.

Bowen, Catherine Drinker, 1966. *Miracle at Philadelphia.* Boston: Little, Brown.

Caldwell, Lynton K., 1990. "The Administrative Republic: The Contrasting Legacies of Hamilton and Jefferson." *Public Administration Quarterly,* vol. 13 (Winter) 470–493.

Crozier, Michel, 1964. *The Bureaucratic Phenomenon.* Chicago: University of Chicago Press.

Cutler, Lloyd N., 1980. "To Form a Government." *Foreign Affairs,* vol. 59 (Fall) 126–143.

De Santis, Victor S., 1989. "County Government: A Centry of Change." In *The Municipal Year Book, 1989.* Washington, D.C.: International City Management Association, pp. 55–84.

Hamilton, Alexander, 1961. "No. 70" and "No. 72." In Clinton Rossiter, ed., *The Federalist Papers.* New York: New American Library, pp. 423–431 and pp. 435–440.

Heclo, Hugh, 1977. *A Government of Strangers: Executive Politics in Washington.* Washington, D.C.: Brookings Institution.

Hosftede, Geert, 1980. *Culture's Consequences: International Differences in Work-Related Values.* Beverly Hills, CA: Sage.

Ingraham, Patricia W., 1987. "Building Bridges or Burning Them? The President, the Appointees, and the Bureaucracy." *Public Administration Review,* vol. 47 (September/October) 425–435.

"Introduction," 1993. In *The Municipal Year Book, 1993.* Washington, D.C.: International City Management Association, pp. ix–xv.

Kent, William, 1898. *Memoirs and Letters of James Kent.* Boston: Little, Brown.

Renner, Tari and Victor S. De Santis, 1993. "Contemporary Patterns and Trends in Municipal Government Structures." *The Municipal Year Book, 1993.* Washington, D.C.: International City Management Association, pp. 57–69.

Smith, Page, 1980. *The Constitution: A Documentary and Narrative History.* New York: Morrow Quill Paperbacks.

Southall, Aidan W., 1953. *Alur Society: A Study in Processes and Types of Domination.* Cambridge: Cambridge University Press.

Syrett, Harold and Jacob E. Cooke, eds., 1961–1979. *The Papers of Alexander Hamilton,* 26 vols. New York: Columbia University Press.

Van Riper, Paul P., 1983. "The American Administrative State: Wilson and the Founders–An Unorthodox View." *Public Administration Review,* vol. 43 (November/December) 477–490.

White, Leonard D., 1936. "The Meaning of Principles of Public Administration." In John M. Gaus, Leonard D. White and Marshall E. Dimock, eds., *The Frontiers of Public Administration.* Chicago: University of Chicago Press, pp.13–25.

ANNEXATION. The means by which general-purpose local governments expand their territory. The opposite of annexation is detachment, the removal of an area from a jurisdiction. Land being annexed into a municipality may be detached from another jurisdiction, such as a township, or it may come under additional jurisdiction, as when county land is annexed by a city but also remains part of the county. In some cases undeveloped land is annexed in anticipation of future development, and in other cases, annexation consolidates already developed land into the already served and taxed area of the municipality.

Origin and Subsequent History

Annexation dates back to the early 1800s and continues to be very common. In the past, developers could build just outside the municipal boundaries and then leave it to the buyers to seek annexation and access to the accompanying municipal service. This practice often caused problems because of substandard construction or poor infrastructure connections, leading to major expenses for the local government.

Municipalities have become more sophisticated and now often negotiate annexation agreements with developers prior to construction. This often involves negotiating some concessions in municipal planning requirements in exchange for open space set-asides, higher quality infrastructure, and other concessions from the developer.

Underlying Theoretical Framework

The usual purpose of annexation is twofold: to be able to extend municipal services to areas not previously served and to increase the tax base of the local government. Because of the financial benefits commonly associated with annexation, municipalities often aggressively annex to avoid becoming landlocked by surrounding suburbs and conceding sources of revenue. Annexation often brings in more revenue than the cost of the additional services that must be provided, allowing lower tax rates. Annexation may also extend a municipality's regulatory power, except in cases where the municipality already has some extraterritorial jurisdiction granted by the state.

Annexation laws vary from state to state, particularly in terms of what kind of approval is needed for the annexation to occur. Approval may be required by any combination of voters in the municipality, by the area to be annexed, or by judicial, quasi-legislative, or legislative bodies. In all cases, the annexing municipalities have veto power. Permissive annexation laws are sometimes accompanied by laws allowing municipalities to prohibit incorporation of another municipality within a certain distance of the existing municipality's boundaries.

Where annexation laws are permissive, metropolitan regions are likely to develop less-fragmented urban structures, with a lower number of municipalities per county. Annexation may therefore contribute to economies of scale, areawide coordination, and equalization of needs and resources. Some argue that one larger government is more visible and therefore more accountable than several smaller governments. Others argue the opposite, that the competition among smaller governments leads to greater efficiency.

Municipal annexation policies aim to accommodate a community's reasonable growth needs. In particular, the power to annex is important, unless other municipalities not inclined to limit growth are available to annex the same land. Annexation increases the likelihood of development, so refusing to annex is one way to help protect sensitive lands such as wetlands.

Current Practice in the United States

Annexations are often initiated by developers who wish to have municipal services extended to their projects. Typically, a petition signed by majority of the property owners in the area to be annexed is required to initiate the process. In Ohio, for example, the sponsors file this petition with the clerks of the county and the township or townships involved. The legal map, or plat, is surveyed and verified, and public hearings are held. Approval must be granted by the county commissioners, who forward their decision to the property owners in the annexed area, the township(s), and the municipality. The municipality's governing council has veto power. If the municipal council approves, the decision is filed with the county auditor and the secretary of state's office.

Annexations are also initiated by municipalities. New property, no matter how it is zoned, can generate revenues if the property tax is available. Where the sales tax is directly available, municipalities will seek to annex potential commercial property. In high-growth areas, municipalities may compete in annexing territory to control and benefit from future growth. Such annexation "wars" extend municipal boundaries far beyond current needs. Annexation may itself attract development and in-migration. Once territory is annexed, the municipality loses some of its authority to prevent development.

Although they are often numerous, most annexations only add small acreages and populations to the municipality. Assessments of the costs and benefits of annexation to municipalities and to the areas to be annexed require the municipality to forecast growth, costs of services and attendant personnel, supplies, and equipment, and the probable impact on each revenue source. Calculations may change depending on whether the projections are short-term or long-term. Residents of the annexed area will likely encounter new taxes, but may benefit from lower insurance rates, larger state and federal tax deductions, and lower service rates. Costs and benefits will vary according to the intergovernmental service and taxing context specific to the area. Nationwide and regional trends in funding and service coordination will also affect the fiscal impact of annexations.

Variations in States, Regions, and Cultures

In the United States, the northeast region and Hawaii are the only areas where annexation has not played an important role in municipal growth. This is because these states require legislative approval of any annexation action, which is the most restrictive type of annexation statute. In Vermont and New York, only villages are allowed to annex territory; there are no provisions for city annexation.

Variations in state laws governing municipal taxes may lead to different patterns of annexation effort. Permission for municipalities to receive directly a portion of sales tax revenue stimulates annexation, as do property tax rate-increase limits. In states that allow counties or special districts to provide municipal services, the attractions of being annexed are reduced for property owners.

Annexation approval schemes vary widely among the states. Only Idaho, Nebraska, and North Carolina allow a unilateral municipal annexation decision. All others require some combination of approval from the voters, the annexed area, quasi-legislative or legislative bodies, or a court. Restrictive annexation laws are associated with a high number of local governments per county, as in California, New Jersey, Illinois, and Pennsylvania. In some areas, the Justice Department must also review annexations for their conformity to the Voting Rights Act of 1965.

LISA S. NELSON

BIBLIOGRAPHY

Coe, Charles K., 1983. "Costs and Benefits of Municipal Annexation." *State and Local Government Review* 15:44–47.
Institute for Environmental Education, 1993. *Common Groundwork: A Practical Guide to Protecting Rural and Urban Land.*
Cleveland: Western Reserve Resource Conservation and Development Council.
Kelly, Eric Damian, 1993. *Managing Community Growth: Policies, Techniques, and Impacts.* Westport: Praeger.
Liner, Gaines H., 1993. "Institutional Constraints and Annexation Activity in the U.S. in the 1970s." *Urban Studies*, vol. 30, no. 8: 1371–1380.
MacNeill, Norman A., and Daniel A. Nissenbaum, 1986. *Annexation Agreements.* ICMA Management Information Service Report, vol. 18, no. 3, March: 1–21.

ANNUAL CAMPAIGN. Fund-raising efforts during a calendar or fiscal year to acquire operating funds for a nonprofit organization.

Historically, charitable organizations have always had annual campaigns, although early efforts were ongoing and, perhaps, were not defined as being "annual," or even "campaigns." Still, the basic premise was present—an organized effort to acquire gifts to continue day-to-day operations.

In modern development programs, the annual campaign has taken on the appearance of a mini capital campaign. These campaigns emphasize prospect evaluation, donor options to identify with specific needs and programs, major gift strategies, and even opportunities to be part of a larger capital campaign effort. Many hospital and university capital campaigns roll annual funding needs into the fund-raising goal and justify the strategy on the basis of being able to concentrate on major giving without having to worry about doing the more labor-intensive annual campaign.

It is important for nonprofit organizations to define clearly the differences between their annual campaign and other fund-raising endeavors, particularly the capital campaign. They must also articulate the "place" of the annual campaign when describing all of the sources of gift and grant income, that is, where the annual campaign fits in their overall development goals.

Usually, it is apparent that the annual campaign is in place to raise the difference between all other sources of income and the amount needed to fulfill the requirements of the annual operating budget—the "life blood" of the organization. George A. Brakely, Jr., in his "Tested Ways to Successful Fund-Raising," illustrated the importance of the annual campaign as a "living endowment." His example shows that annual fund-raising resulting in unrestricted or budget-applicable gifts totaling $500,000 would be equal to investment income of an endowment of $10 million.

All organizations holding annual campaigns seek one or more of the following: direct gifts, memberships, or fulfillment (gifts related to premiums). Using annual campaigns, they generally seek to maximize participation and raise the sights of donors. It is generally conceded that 50 percent of the year's donors will renew their contributions at the same level and that an additional 15 percent will increase their gift.

The methodologies of annual campaigns are comprehensive and share many of the same facets of the capital campaign. They can be structured with

- chairpersons and committee leadership;
- a predetermined goal based on a combination of actual need and perceived feasibility;
- orchestrated publicity, including a published case statement rationalizing the need for support;
- a sequential solicitation format;
- a challenge to donors to match a lead gift;
- certain gift clubs commensurate with the size of the donor's gift
- a clearly defined pledge period;
- alternative ways of participation through usable gifts in kind;
- approaches to both corporations and foundations;
- major gift strategies; or
- some effort at encouraging donors employed at matching gift companies (and those who are directors of such firms) to seek matching gifts from these corporations.

Annual campaigns, however, differ from capital campaigns in several respects.

- Annual campaigns are confined to a period between a starting date and an ending date, usually within one year.
- Annual campaigns seek gifts from individuals that will come from their current income rather than from assets.
- Annual campaigns are seldom targeted to fund either endowments or capital assets, like new or renovated buildings.
- The pledge period generally does not extend beyond a year.
- Annual campaigns do not recognize major gifts by permitting donors to attach their names to specific items of the campaign.
- The potential giving-level of leadership is generally higher in the capital campaign setting.
- Capital campaigns usually do not entail organized phone-a-thons, or constituency-wide direct mail appeals.
- Foundations are not usually a major source of annual funds, except those few that are dedicated to a specific nonprofit organization, or those that provide grants to operations.
- Annual campaigns are usually staffed by development professionals who have less experience than those who staff capital campaigns, planned giving programs, and other major gift efforts—except in those smaller nonprofit organizations the cannot afford or do not require more-experienced assistance.

Nonprofit organizations often depict the fund-raising mix using a pyramid, with annual campaigns as the foundation for all of the other methods. Here is a typical example:

planned giving
capital campaign
special gift or project
annual campaign

Another way for one to look at where the annual campaign fits in the development process is to examine what might constitute the typical "donor lifetime"–the duration of the relationship with the nonprofit organization. Here is an example of the progression a donor might experience with a nonprofit organization that does a good job of bringing the donor along at an ever-increasing level of commitment of support for that organization.

planned gift
capital campaign gift
special gift or project support
renewals upgrade
acquisition gift annual campaign

Whether the annual campaign is seen as the foundation for nonprofit support or as the doorway to major giving, it is still the most basic of fund-raising activities in any nonprofit organization. It is the annual campaign that enables it to continue its day-to-day programs by supporting current operations and identifying new donors.

WILLIAM BERGOSH AND
ROBERT W. BUCHANAN

ANTITRUST. Generally describes that body of federal and various state laws designed to protect trade and commerce in the United States from unlawful restraints, price discrimination, price-fixing, and monopolies. Prior to the enactment of the antitrust laws, the U.S. government took a laissez-faire attitude toward business in general. By 1890, however, the Sherman Anti Trust Act put an end to that attitude, and the act continues to embody, for the most part, the federal law on the subject.

The Sherman Anti Trust Act was enacted by Congress to end great aggregations of control and power, and thereby to protect individual citizens who are helpless in the face of such overwhelming control. The idea was to organize industry in smaller units that could effectively compete with each other and thus promote free enterprise. The principal purpose of the act was to secure equality of opportunity and to protect the public against evils commonly incident to monopolies and abnormal contracts that tend to suppress competition.

The statute was enacted for several more specific reasons. It protects trade and commerce among the states and foreign nations from unlawful restraints and monopolies; it maintains free competition in commerce in the public interest; it protects against abusive or coercive influences of monopolistic forces; it prevents undue interference with the right of freedom of trade; and it prevents restraints to free competition in business and commercial transactions that may tend to limit production, raise prices, or otherwise control any given market to the detriment of the consumer.

The act provides for a public as well as a private remedy for violations. Monopolies or combinations in restraint of trade or commerce are criminally punishable. In addition, there is a civil right of action for triple damages to those who are injured by monopolistic oppression. The statute does not inhibit the intelligent conduct of business nor force every type of business into the common mold, however. It does not police intermediate transportation of goods and property, and it does not provide remedies for wrongs actionable under state law. Finally, it does not compel competition, and it does not necessarily render illegal ordinary contracts or combinations of manufacturers or merchants and traders that promote advantages and meaningful operations.

The antitrust laws do, however, broadly condemn all contracts, combinations and conspiracies that restrain the free and natural flow of trade in intermediate commerce or commerce with foreign nations, or that restrain the liberty of any given merchant to engage in trade. More specifically, Section 1 of the act makes illegal combinations of restraint of interstate trade or commerce. Section 2 makes illegal combinations or conspiracies to monopolize or attempt to monopolize interstate trade and commerce. The second section essentially supplements the first and ensures that the public policy embodied in the first section cannot be evaded or frustrated. Whether a combination or a conspiracy violates the act is a wholly legal, rather than an economic, question.

Under the act, condemned are contracts entered into for the purpose of eliminating competition that exists; contracts preventing development of new competition; combinations effectively excluding or attempting to exclude outsiders from a market; or agreements of combinations that directly restrain the manufacture, purchase, and sale or exchange of goods. The act is not only limited to combinations to price-fix, limit production, or bring about deterioration in quality, although these are key prohibitions of the act.

Of course, direct control of prices of articles moving in interstate commerce, no matter how achieved, is forbidden by the antitrust laws. Under the act, fixed prices mean agreed prices, and it matters not whether they are set at a minimum or a maximum, whether a formula is used, or whether the price is fixed at the going market price. In addition, economic benefit will not excuse price-fixing.

In order to constitute a violation of the law, the union of two or more persons and minds to accomplish some purpose in violation of the act is necessary. Whereas unlawful agreement is necessary under the act, no formal agreement is required, and the agreement may be tacit as well as expressed. The conspiracy may be implied from a course of dealing. Also, the act condemns every means, no matter how clever, to accomplish a forbidden conspiracy. If the end that is sought violates the spirit of the act, the measures are immaterial. In addition, a specific intent to restrain commerce or create a monopoly is not required; persons so combining or contracting will be presumed to have intended to do so by the nature of the consequences of their agreements. The law cannot be evaded by good nature or intent.

Essentially, the antitrust laws assert that law can and should control marketplace conditions, assuming that it is in the public interest for government to exercise substantial indirect control over the economy. It is interesting to note, however, that the U.S. antitrust laws contrast sharply with those of most other countries, which tolerate or even encourage cartels and other business combinations. It is also of interest that our government's enforcement of the antitrust laws has varied over the years. Nevertheless, the antitrust laws remain in full force and effect and are an important fixture in the American economy.

CARL CANNON POHLE

BIBLIOGRAPHY

Black, Henry Campbell, 1983. *Black's Law Dictionary*. 5th ed. St. Paul, MN: West.
Corpus Juris Secundum: A Complete Restatement of the Entire American Law as Developed by All Reported Cases, 1658 to Date. St. Paul, MN: West.

APPLIED BEHAVIORAL SCIENCE (ABS).

The application of social science to solve specific social problems. There has always been a certain degree of tension between the arcane world of the scientist and the everyday lives of common people. In the broadest sense, ABS is an effort to bridge that gap.

In scientific research a distinction is often made between "applied" and "basic" research. Basic behavioral research focuses on elemental characteristics of human nature. For example, a study of systemic incentives in human behavior would be considered basic research. In contrast, applied research is much more discrete in focus; it is concerned with specific problems in need of immediate solution. A study of how to increase caseload efficiency in an agency is an example of applied research. There is, of couse, an important relationship between the two: basic research provides the theoretical and empirical building blocks that permit researchers to develop techniques and concepts for applied research. However, there is no strict dichotomy between the two, but rather a continuum.

The foundation for contemporary behavioral science was developed around the turn of the century, primarily in Germany, England, and the United States, and was based principally on pioneering work in psychology, sociology, and anthropology. The modern usage of the term "behavioralism" was developed in the 1950s at the University of Chicago, at other universities and at the Ford Foundation. These institutions wanted to avoid the term "social science" because, in the McCarthy era, it might be confused with socialism, which would greatly reduce any possibility of funding or political support. Charles Merriam's call for a "science of politics," Herbert Simon's *Administrative Behavior* (1947), and Harold Lasswell's concept of policy science (1951) had a significant impact on the development of behavioralist thought at the time. Today the terms "social science" and "behavioral science" are sometimes used interchangeably, but the former is usually regarded as somewhat more inclusive than the latter.

When the concept of behavioral science was still relatively fresh, Bernard Berelson (1963) identified its principal objective: "The ultimate end is to understand, explain, and predict human behavior in the same sense in which scientists understand, explain, and predict the behavior of physical forces or biological factors" (p. 3). Such an interpretation might be viewed as naive and presumptuous today, but in the 1960s behavioral science was seen as just another way to make science serve humanity.

Behavioral science has had a dramatic impact on the discipline of political science. Following World War II the discipline was transformed by a new emphasis on behavioralism. Somit and Tanenhaus, in *The Development of Political Science* (1967), argue that behavioralism "may be treated, if only metaphorically, as an attempt to move political science from a pre-paradigmatic (or, literally, nonscientific) condition to a paradigmatic stage" (p. 175). However, the behavioral trend was not viewed with favor by many political scientists; the resulting debate over the relative merits of the behavioral approach consumed two decades. And although the basic tenets of behavioral science are still much in evidence, most political scientists in the late 1990s speak of the "post-behavioral era." Perhaps the most direct lineage of applied behavioral science in political science and public administration is policy science, which grew out of the same realm of thought at the University of Chicago.

The contemporary concept of applied behavioral science is still not clearly delineated. However, five common, fundamental elements can be identified.

First, ABS is interdisciplinary. It has developed over time in a variety of disciplines, and continues to transcend academic boundaries. This is in part because the objective of ABS is not academic recognition in and of itself, but resolution of a significant societal problem.

Second, ABS is data-driven. ABS researchers tend to focus on phenomena that are observable and verifiable. There is a rigorous adherence to quantitative technique, but in recent years social scientists have begun to accept qualitative research as a viable alternative research strategy.

Third, ABS is theoretically driven. The assumption of behavioral scientists is that data cannot be properly interpreted without good theory. Hence ABS is based on verifiable theoretical constructs.

Fourth, contemporary ABS is concerned with relevance. In its earliest formulations, behavioralism assumed a preference for "pure" research that avoided the normative minefields of prescriptive research. But subsequent practitioners have altered this perception. In essence, the "applied" element of ABS was added later. Today many scholars assume a prescriptive orientation to ABS.

And finally, there is a predominant theme in ABS that the ultimate purpose of such research is to improve the condition of humankind. Thus, it is an effort to use the tenets of science to increase our understanding of ourselves, and in so doing, improve our quality of life.

DANIEL C. MCCOOL

BIBLIOGRAPHY

Berelson, Bernard, ed., 1963. *The Behavioral Sciences Today.* New York: Basic Books.
Fisher, Donald, 1993. *Fundamental Development of the Social Sciences.* Ann Arbor: University of Michigan Press.
Lasswell, Harold D. and David Lerner, eds., 1951. *The Policy Sciences.* Stanford, CA: Stanford University Press.
Ripley, Randall B., 1985. *Policy Analysis in Political Science.* Chicago: Nelson-Hall.
Simon, Herbert A., 1947. *Administrative Behavior.* New York: Macmillan.
Somit, Albert, and Joseph Tanenhaus, 1967. *The Development of Political Science: From Burgess to Behavioralism.* Boston: Allyn & Bacon.

APPRENTICE. A full-time employee who receives training in all aspects of a skilled trade, taking from one to six years. On-the-job training and formal instruction are applied to prepare apprentices for occupations requiring a wide and varied range of skills and knowledge. High school or vocational education school is usually a prerequisite for entry into an apprenticeship program today. Upon completion of the apprenticeship, the individual attains journey worker status. Among the skilled trades offering apprenticeship programs are electrical, tool and die making, and printing.

Apprenticeship programs are administered by the union, by the employer, or jointly through an apprenticeship committee composed of labor and management representatives, sometimes joined by representatives of associations or government agencies. These committees may determine the need for apprentices in a given locality and establish standards for education, training, and experience. In the U.S. private sector, apprenticeship programs are administered by the Bureau of Apprenticeship and Training, which promulgates standards on instructions, job duties, safely, and equal employment opportunity. The Apprenticeship Act of 1937 (29 *USC* 50) authorized the U.S. Secretary of Labor to formulate and promote the labor standards needed to safeguard the welfare of apprentices and to cooperate with the states in promoting these standards. Some unions in the United States have been accused of discriminating against certain types of people in their apprenticeship programs, particularly African Americans, Hispanics, and women.

Apprenticeships are one of the oldest forms of learning. In the United States, apprenticeships were adopted in the colonies from the British tradition. Children were "bound out" by their parents to a master under a written, legal contract, which usually ended when the apprentice reached the age of 21 years. The master provided his household's amenities, including bedding, food, and clothing, and taught the apprentice his trade. The apprentice agreed not to reveal his master's secrets. Usually, the apprentice did not receive wages. Today, apprenticeship agreements spell out the length of the arrangement, a wage scale, work processes to be taught, instruction on subjects related to the trade, and other provisions.

It has been estimated that 340,000 individuals are registered in apprenticeship programs in the United States, in some 770 occupations.

RICHARD C. KEARNEY

APPROPRIATE TECHNOLOGY.

Any device or work arrangement that reduces the effort or cost involved in producing a product and that enhances an individual's self-reliance and self-determination. Development is considered an ongoing, evolving mental process more than an economic condition. E. F. Schumacher's 1973 book, *Small Is Beautiful,* has served as a foundation for the appropriate technology movement, and his ideas have attracted a small, dedicated band of followers around the world. The movement encourages small-scale, craft enterprises that are environmentally sensitive. In producing to meet societal needs, an individual entrepreneur or small community collective selects tools and materials readily available within the country and techniques of production and organizational arrangements compatible with local social practices. Appropriate technology does not dictate a set of techniques, because techniques must be adapted to place and need. Appropriate technology places human needs at the center of developmental change.

The movement occupies a middle ground between, on the one hand, unchanging, traditional practices and social organization, and, on the other hand, large-scale producers who treat workers as expendable cogs in an impersonal ma-

chine. Appropriate technology seeks changes compatible with the local environment and supportive of individuals taking control over the forces in that environment. Individual and *communal values* take priority over organizational values.

Core values of innovation, education, small-scale technologies, economic viability, and environmental sensitivity drive the movement. The relative importance among these values differs according to one's situation. Appropriate technology advocates who are working in developing nations emphasize labor intensive, low-capital ventures having widespread local application; ventures that educate people about the advantages of an approach to development that minimizes imported technologies. Solar water heaters, water purification processes, bio-gas conversion, and inexpensive small motors are among their projects.

Appropriate technology in developed nations concentrates on conserving energy and minimizing environmental degradation. Entrepreneurs seek niche markets that large-scale producers have overlooked or have not met because they lack sensitivity to local conditions. Microbreweries using ecologically sound technologies and pesticide-free grains and growers using composting techniques and raising organically grown vegetables are among their success stories. Appropriate technology fights large-scale technology throughout the world. The principle is to put people first and to let the technology emerge naturally: Development is *human development*. The appropriate technology literature differs concerning developing and developed countries, thus I discuss these applications separately.

Developing Nations

Developing nations generally have an appreciation of their traditions, an abundance of labor, and a shortage of capital. To be culturally sensitive, projects are labor-intensive with low capital demands. Appropriate technology aims for an upgrading of the techniques of production, while at the same time involving local people, insofar as possible, in the design, manufacture, operation, and maintenance of the technology. By involving local people, an innovative frame of mind is encouraged. Improved living conditions result from adhering to the values of participation and innovation. Each policy or project should be cost-effective, individually growth-producing, and respectful of people.

Food, housing, and health are targets for improvement in production processes, for each of these issue areas directly affects both people and the environment. Food should be healthful and its production should minimally disturb the environment, housing should meet needs rather than wants, and health policy should emphasize prevention rather than cure. Needs are locally determined and locally met: gas from animal wastes; electricity from windmills; water purification, irrigation, and draining; sanitation; housing construction; heating and cooking stoves and solar cookers and water heaters; improved methods of harvesting, separating, drying, storing, and milling grain, and of extracting oil from various fruits and seeds and processing sweeteners into sugar. All of these activities strive for simple technologies, improved processes, and easily repaired machines.

Advanced technology has less power for social development than does appropriate technology. Multinational firms import advanced technology, and these foreign enterprises negotiate with large-scale, established, local economic and political forces. Multinational firms locate in developing nations to take advantage of low-cost labor. By maintaining traditional relationships, the multinational firm reinforces local cultural expectations while providing a wage slightly above the local going rate. This wage strategy minimizes demands for developmental change and enhances the corporate image of the multinational.

Appropriate technology supporters argue that capital-intensive projects in developing countries often employ expatriate labor, involve technologies that are not supported by the local economy (such as computers and other products with complicated production and repair processes), and do not meet the local needs for *employment* or education. Capital-intensive technologies demand substantial resources and do not meet the long-term development interests of the nation. The local jobs created by these large-scale projects often require unskilled rather than skilled labor, thereby minimally upgrading local human resources. Product design, tool manufacture, and equipment repair are often reserved for the home base in the developed country.

Obstacles to Appropriate Technology in Developing Countries

A significant obstacle to adopting appropriate technology in developing countries is the presence of multinational firms. Although multinationals inhibit developmental change, they provide governments of developing nations immediate economic and political benefits that are difficult to resist. Thus, multinationals collude with local governments, with the result of hampering efforts to develop appropriate technology and its attendant social effects.

Free trade policies benefit the multinational, which exports its efficiently produced goods; and the cheap imports brought by free trade benefit the low-income consumers. A problem arises in the host country if the multinational closes its production facility, which may happen for any of the following reasons: (1) the multinational finds another location with cheaper labor, (2) the raw material from the

host country is exhausted, (3) world supply of the product expands to render the production facility inefficient, or (4) production or consumer preferences change to lower the demand for the product.

From the government's perspective, allowing the multinational firm to enter the local market is preferable to creating a government-owned or government-subsidized local large-scale enterprise. Allowing the multinational to absorb the risk protects the developing nation from heavy indebtedness should changes in world supply, price, or consumer preference render the facility inefficient. For example, Algeria invested heavily in government-owned enterprises that incorporated large-scale imported technologies and skilled expatriate labor, anticipating that oil revenues would pay for the investments. When the world oil price dropped by two-thirds, Algeria was faced with heavy debts, which forced closure of many industries and resulted in high unemployment and consequent political instability. Expatriate labor was a political liability, yet necessary to keep the oil sector in operation. Had Algeria granted operation licenses to multinational firms and encouraged local appropriate technology, it would likely have weathered the oil revenue crisis.

From a political perspective, a nation's leadership is usually satisfied with multinational relationships. The large-scale firm's demand for low-wage labor soaks up some unemployment without raising local political demands. The expatriate multinational managers have no connections with local political aspirants, and any foreigners who dabble in politics are quickly expelled from the country. By encouraging self-improvement and participation, appropriate technology incubates social forces that assert themselves into the political arena, thereby placing demands on the political system. Because these new political forces are locally based, reflect local concerns, and are dispersed, they cannot be easily controlled and may challenge the national leadership.

For example, local, small-scale industry may petition for tax benefits or import controls on competing items. Proponents of appropriate technology argue that these tax advantages are necessary to encourage risk-taking, entrepreneurial behavior, and to attract capital from the traditional investments of land and buildings (which provide minimal multiplier effect) into productive enterprises. Successful entrepreneurs are likely to extend their challenge into the political realm, demanding a role in national decisionmaking. The smaller and more diverse the entrepreneurs, the more difficult to control. Large-scale local producers may be co-opted because they are few; widely dispersed small-scale producers are less easily controlled.

Economics impacts politics, and national elites in developing countries often fear the political implications of a vibrant appropriate technology movement. If in seeking to control the movement, governments inhibit free expression and entrepreneurial behavior, the drive for development is hampered.

Macrolevel obstacles to the growth of appropriate technology include the difficulty of obtaining credit, a free trade mentality, and a bias against small-scale production. Available credit indicates a positive affect by the government toward the philosophy of appropriate technology, but governments generally favor large-scale investors, either for political reasons or because large investors are presumed to have a stronger influence on the nation's economic growth. Government willingness to eliminate tariffs on products that are produced locally is a disincentive to local producers. Appropriate technology proponents argue that most developed countries protected their infant industries and that developing countries should be afforded the same opportunity. The absence of support from the government through loans and import restrictions make appropriate technology development more risky.

Large-scale enterprises, particularly multinational firms, have an important, sometimes subtle, impact on innovation. The depressing effect on local entrepreneurial activity can be seen in the following example from tourism in Egypt. Western tourists have always been attracted to Luxor, Egypt, located up the Nile River from Cairo, for Luxor is the center of pharaonic history and a world-class touristic site. Until recently, tourists would generally reach Luxor by train or plane and stay in hotels there. This system provided considerable local employment: for guides, horse cart and taxi drivers, street vendors, and for people who staff curio shops, hotels, and restaurants. Tourists integrated smoothly with the local economy.

Then, Western hotel chains built in Cairo. These multinational corporations began to organize tours to Luxor, often by Nile steamers, which travel by river and dock away from downtown areas. Tourists are whisked from the ships to historic sites by bus, and souvenirs are available shipboard. Within Luxor, independent small entrepreneurs (owners of taxis and horse carts and guides) as well as locally owned souvenir shops, restaurants, and hotels have difficulty surviving, because the large-scale operations are controlled and directed from Cairo. Small operators find it difficult to compete, not because of price but because they cannot gain access. Profits from the Luxor tourist business are predominantly earned by large corporations; large-scale business has driven out small-scale business. This shift from small to large is not based on price but came about because the system was effectively structured to eliminate competition. Large-scale economic and political structures combine to hamper individual growth, innovation, and development.

An important microlevel obstacle to appropriate technology is a cultural value system that takes a relaxed attitude toward technical detail and personal responsibility. Machines require maintenance, and if they are cooperatively owned maintenance may be neglected. People must come to assume responsibility for the consequences of their actions and pay the price for inaction. Experts from the West can demonstrate the product or process and work with locals, but the locals must take responsibility if the appropriate technology process is to take root. The foreign expert must be sensitive to involve the locals sufficiently through the whole project so that "ownership" and its obligations are well understood.

Appropriate technology is not a term that magically transforms poor and rural areas into vibrant centers of entrepreneurial activity. Like any change, successful appropriate technology projects face an uphill battle against entrenched local interests, an inefficient economic system, and an apathetic social system. Achieving progress against these odds requires a confluence of economic need, outside support, and luck. Even in the United States 80 percent of businesses fail, and these ventures have the advantages of social support and substantial information regarding risks. Appropriate technology will likely always have an uphill battle as a change agent.

Appropriate Technology in Developed Nations

Proponents of appropriate technology in developed nations have an agenda emphasizing a holistic concern for earth and people, both present and future. In their view, the developed nations treat natural resources carelessly. Citizens of industrialized Western nations constitute 20 percent of the world's population and consume two-thirds of the world's goods and services. This profligacy threatens the quality of our present life and the very existence of life in years to come.

Driven by the law of supply and demand, entrepreneurs often market what will sell, with little consideration for value or the societal impact of uncosted "free" goods, such as air and water quality. Not only does manufacturing incur negative side effects, but disposing of finished products once they have been used is an expense to be borne by society. The failure to consider disposal as a cost factor in the manufacturing process skews productive advantage to the industrial polluter and works to the disadvantage of smaller environmentally sensitive producers.

Appropriate technology seeks to minimize environmental degradation by converting the mind-sets and behaviors of people in the developed countries to more environmentally responsible behavior, to develop an environmental conscience. Future generations need the cooperation of the people of the United States if their lives are to be fulfilling, and we may improve their life chances if we adhere to the credo that "less is more," that quality is more important than quantity.

These values are held by "green" parties in multiparty political systems and among small segments of parties in political systems in which two parties dominate. Although environmental and appropriate technology groups have had the opportunity to communicate their message to citizens, political support for these movements has been relatively weak. Few ordinary citizens would oppose political participation, self-help, holistic medicine, organic gardening, or personal growth, yet these are not priority issues for most people. The dramatic oil price rises of the 1970s brought on the pursuit of alternative energy sources, fuel-efficient cars, and environmental concerns, and the appropriate technology movement flourished. Recently, as oil prices have dropped and as economic growth has resumed in the West and continued its rapid rise in East Asia, citizens have relegated appropriate technology to a secondary concern.

Conclusion

The appropriate technology movement is a way of thinking about how people should relate to the planet and to each other: in harmony with nature rather than exploitive of nature, using technologies that minimally disturb the ecology, and using creative talents continually to improve the human condition.

Appropriate technology may be seen by onlookers as either old-fashioned or no different from neocolonialism and as a threat to the existing political balance. However, the appropriate technology movement acts as a conscience of the international community. Its principles of innovation, small-scale technology, and participation challenge both authoritarian regimes in developing countries and environmentally insensitive big business.

Because human beings do not seem able to maintain their intensity on the issue of community participation, and moneyed international interests readily collude with authoritarian and democratic regimes alike, the appropriate technology movement may never dominate a nation's economics and politics. Nevertheless, there are pockets of dedication to these principles including interested individuals around the world and institutions such as the Center for International Cooperation and Appropriate Technology of Delft University the MeMo Movement, both in The Netherlands; the Intermediate Technology Grouping in Great Britain; the Socially Appropriate Technology Information System (SATIS); and various appropriate technology groups throughout Asia, Africa, and South America. With their support these ideas of small-scale technology appropriate to the time and place will likely endure.

ROBERT B. CUNNINGHAM

BIBLIOGRAPHY

Boes, Jan, and Wim Ravesteijn, eds., 1989. *Appropriate Technology in Industrialized Countries.* Delft, The Netherlands: Delft University Press.

International Labour Organization, 1978. *Appropriate Technology for Employment Creation in the Food Processing and Drink Industries of Developing Countries.* Geneva, Switzerland: International Labour Office.
Jequier, Nicolas, ed., 1976. *Appropriate Technology: Problems and Promises.* Paris: Development Center of the OECD.
Madu, C., 1992. *Strategic Planning in Technology Transfer to Less Developed Countries.* New York: Quorum Books.
Riedijk, Willem, ed., 1982. *Appropriate Technology for Developing Countries.* Delft, The Netherlands: Delft University Press.
Schumacher, E. F., 1973. *Small Is Beautiful.* New York: Harper & Row.

ARAB ADMINISTRATIVE DEVELOPMENT ORGANIZATION (ARADO).

An organizational entity within the Arab League established to consolidate Arabic administrative systems and to promote national administrative development in the Arab world.

In 1969 ARADO was established as one of the Arab League specialized organizations, reflecting the Arab League's and its members' interest in administrative development since 1956. In 1956 the Arab League Council realized the need for administrative development and decided to hold conferences in administrative sciences on a regular basis.

In 1957 the first Arabian Administrative Sciences Conference was held in Damascus, Syria. Three years later, the second conference was held in Rabat, Morocco, where its members recommended the establishment of an organization specializing in the advancement in and development of administrative sciences in the Arab countries. In 1961 the Arab League Council endorsed the recommendation, and the board of trustees of the Arab Administrative Sciences Organization (ARASO) held its first meeting on January 1, 1969. In 1982 the name of the organization was changed to Arab Administrative Development Organization (ARADO). ARADO is located in Cairo, Egypt.

The overall goal of ARADO as stated in its charter is to contribute to and work toward achieving administrative development in the Arab World in a way that assists in consolidating the Arabic administrative systems and serves the accomplishment of a total national development. The charter states that ARADO can achieve its goal through: (1) developing a national strategy for administrative development in the Arabic World that is compatible with the national strategies for administrative development in the Arab countries, in coordinating with the specialized organizations in the Arab League, specialized Arabic organizations, and administrative development agencies and organizations in the Arab countries; (2) providing assistance and support to administrative development agencies and organizations in the Arab countries, contributing to the development of these agencies and organizations, and improving the performance of their employees; (3) improving the effectiveness of Arabic administrative agencies and their work forces, particularly top management; (4) exchanging expertise in administrative development and academic institutions; (5) developing modern Arabic administrative concepts and spreading knowledge and administrative ideas in the Arab World; (6) coordinating and cooperating with international administrative organizations; (7) consolidating the administrative terms and their use in the Arab World; (8) manifesting the role of effective management in achieving administrative, economic, and social development; and (9) assisting the Arab countries that have not yet used Arabic as their official language.

The administrative system and structure of ARADO comprises the broad of trustees, the executive council, and the executive body. The highest authority is the board of trustees, consisting of the representatives of the Arab countries in the Arab League. The second level is the seven-member executive council, elected for two-year terms by the board of trustees. It meets twice a year. The executive council's role is to assist the board of trustees in performing its work. It develops the policies and strategies of the organizations and it oversees their implementation. The third level, the executive body, is headed by the director general of ARADO, who is elected by the board of trustees for four years, based on the recommendation of the executive council.

To carry out its responsibilities, ARADO has four major departments: training, research and studies, information and documentation, and consultation. Since its establishment, ARADO has conducted a large number of studies, published many books, trained a significant number of trainees (in more than forty training programs), and has provided consultations to agencies and organizations in Arab countries. ARADO publishes a quarterly journal, *Arabic Journal for Administration,* that is devoted to administrative development issues in the Arab World.

ABDULLAH M. AL-KHALAF

ARBITRARY AND CAPRICIOUS BEHAVIOR.

An exercise of legal authority with an unequal hand, such that discrimination occurs between persons or classes of persons in similar circumstances. It includes actions that are not guided by laws, principles, or rules but that are taken impulsively, according to whim. Ideally, in the advanced legal and governmental systems in the world rule of law governance, which contrasts sharply to arbitrary and capricious rule (made infamous historically by the whimsical behavior of ruthless monarchs who served "above the law") has replaced arbitrary and capricious governmental rule.

A typical example of arbitrary and capricious behavior is a case wherein a statute, law, or regulation is abused by the discretionary authority conferred upon an administrative agency or board. For instance, in the United States in the nineteenth century, the city of San Francisco adopted an ordinance to regulate hand laundries. The ordinance was established for the public safety purpose of protecting against the spread of fires, which were used to heat water in the predominantly wooden-structured laundries. In the process of enforcing the law, an uneven hand was applied such that Chinese hand laundries were shut down and non-Chinese hand laundries were allowed to remain in business, even though there was no difference in the nature or scope of the Asian and non-Asian laundries. The exercise of legal authority thus discriminated against a class of equal members in an arbitrary and capricious manner.

Arbitrary and capricious behavior can also encompass an abuse of discretion. This situation occurs when an activity, which is regulated or controlled according to specific regulations, is unevenly applied. If two applicants, are in full compliance with all of the elements of a regulation, but one is denied licensing while the other is approved, this exercise of the legal authority would constitute an abuse of discretion. There is no rational basis for denying the request of the one applicant who has fully complied with all the elements of the regulation.

Any public body possessing discretionary authority is subject to review according to the arbitrary and capricious standard. This standard was developed under the law to ensure that there was equal application and protection of the power of public bodies. Due process and equal protection have been denied by the arbitrary and capricious use of the discretionary authority granted to an administrative body. Agencies or courts possessing the power to review the actions of administrative agencies will always measure the agency's conduct, in part, using the arbitrary and capricious standard. If the exercise of the discretionary authority by the administrative body is fair, even-handed, and equally applied, the administrative body's actions will withstand the arbitrary and capricious test of reasonableness.

THOMAS A. CONNELLY

BIBLIOGRAPHY

Strauss, Peter L. et al., 1995. *Gellhorn and Byse's Administrative Law: Cases and Comments,* 9th ed. Westbury, NY: Foundation Press. Chaps. 3 and 8.
Warren, Kenneth F., 1996. *Administrative Law in the Political System,* 3d ed. Upper Saddle River, NJ: Prentice-Hall. Chap. 8.

ARCHIVES.

Documents selected from the totality of the records created by an organization for permanent preservation because of their enduring value; or, agencies actually responsible for organizing the collection and preservation of such documents. The use of the term "document" is merely a convenience to cover a wide range of physical formats, from clay tablets in the ancient world to data held in electronic form in the modern; it includes pictorial and audio material. The term "archives" can also be used to refer to the agencies collecting and preserving the documents, such as the Archives de France, a system that includes both the central and departmental archives services in France.

Public and "Private" Archives

Two main types of archival sources can be identified. First, "public archives," are institutions that collect, preserve, and make these documents accessible. They are public bodies whose role is to maintain the collections of the various units of a country's administrative structure that exist at different levels. Legislation enacted at the appropriate levels attempts to ensure the existence of mechanisms whereby the records of administrative bodies are properly maintained. Appropriate categories and individual documents, when their current use is finished, are regularly transferred to the designated archival office for permanent retention. This often results in the pattern of a single central office and a network of independent local agencies: in the U.S., the National Archives together with the state archives; in the United Kingdom, the Public Record Office and the county record offices.

"Private archives" include those of business, societies, educational establishments, religious organizations and other institutions, as well as personal and family papers. In many cases these will not have been retained by the creating body but will have found their way into a variety of private and public repositories, including universities, museums, and public libraries. Attempts to keep track of the scatter of such collections has led to the creation of bodies such as the National Register of Archives in the U.K. in 1945 and the continuing publication (since 1962) of the *National Union Catalog of Manuscript Collections* in the United States.

The Modern Concept of Archives

The development of the modern concept of the state archives can be dated from the end of the eighteenth century. The triumph of French republicanism in 1789 led to the founding of the Archives Nationales in France in that year. The enactment of systematic archival legislation during the years of the French Revolution (1789–1796) marked a move away from the view that archives existed solely for the benefit of the sovereign or head of state or of their institutional creators. The late-eighteenth-century idea was to separate older historical records on a consis-

tent basis from current records, recognize the rights of public access to the former category, and see to the appointment of archivists as a help to those wishing to consult the records rather than solely as a support for those creating them.

The establishment of opportunities for training of archivists at the École des Chartes in Paris from 1821 meant that France continued to take a leading role in developing a central core of basic archival principles during the nineteenth century—a role reflected in such terms as "respect du fonds" (all documents produced by a single office of government being kept together as an unique unit), which are still used today. During the Nineteenth century a number of European countries followed the French model, and central state archives were either created newly or were developed out of existing archival traditions. In the U.K. the Public Record Office was established by Act of Parliament in 1838. Although the United States had had an Historical Manuscripts Commission and a Public Archives Commission since the 1890s, with the roles of locating and publishing documents of historical value, it was not until 1934 that the National Archives was established.

Developments Post-1945

In the period after World War II a long-running source of professional debate has been the relationship between "records management," that is, the concern with documents that are still in current or semicurrent use, and "archives," the concern with those records selected for permanent retention. Professional associations and associated literature have grown up associated with both activities. At one level the arguments can be seen to be polarized in the views of two individuals. Sir Hilary Jenkinson of the Public Record Office in the U.K., in his classic *Manual of Archive Administration* (1922, 1937, rev. ed. 1965), made no mention of records management and saw the role of the archive repository as being to retain rather than to select. By contrast, T. R. Schellenberg of the U.S. National Archives, in his equally seminal *Modern Archives: Principles and Techniques* (1956) laid greatest emphasis on the principles of records management and on the archivist's role as having ultimate responsibility for the selection of modern records for retention.

In most countries it is probably true to say that the debate is now largely resolved. The development of the "lifecycle" concept—whereby records management is seen as a management skill based upon the principle of appraisal, and the application of standards, criteria, and judgment to individual items or categories of records in order to determine what should be retained in the short term, what should be destroyed, and what transferred to archives—has been able to involve both records managers and archivists in establishing the standards whereby each document's progress through the cycle can be monitored.

Standards

Much recent professional debate has centered around standards for archival description and the challenge of coping with records in electronic format. Once again, for the former there has been a cultural divide, with a number of countries working on their own standards. This has led to the production of (among others) the Society of American Archivists' *Archives, Personal Papers, and Manuscripts (APPO)* (2d ed. 1989); the British *Manual of Archival Description (MAD).* (2d ed. 1989), and the Canadian *Rules for Archival Description (RAD)* (1992). The need to reconcile these standards led the International Council on Archives to appoint the Ad Hoc Commission on Descriptive Standards in 1989. It is too early to tell whether the publication by the Commission of *ISAD (G): General International Standard Archival Description* in 1994 will prove to be universally acceptable.

Electronic Records

Electronic data present particular problems for the archivist; especially, ensuring that the principles of appraisal can be properly applied to the electronic medium and resolving the technical difficulties of preserving the records selected. With the relatively short shelf-life of much existing electronic media, there is the requirement for regular conversion to new formats. Software dependence relating to the environment of creation requires decisions on whether only the contents of the file or also the relevant software and hardware need to be preserved.

International Activity

The postwar world has also seen considerable developments in archival activity in the countries of the developing world, often associated with post-independence national information plans. Important roles in promoting this activity have been played by the United Nations Educational, Scientific, and Cultural Organization (UNESCO) and by the International Council on Archives (ICA), founded in 1950, often working in concert. Numerous advisory missions have been funded by UNESCO to advise on the creation or consolidation of records centeres, national archives, and training programs.

Since 1979 UNESCO activity has been largely focussed through its RAMP (Records and Archive Management Program), one of whose most valuable functions has been its extensive publications program, concentrating on the production of standards and guidelines for the whole range of archival activities from legislation to preservation. The ICA has a number of standing committees to consider aspects such as education, training, reprography, and terminology. Additionally, it has fostered the formation of re-

gional branches, which can consider particular local problems and possible local cooperative solutions.

Some branches, such as that for East and Southern Africa (ESARBICA) have managed to sustain continuous productive activity over a number of years with regular conferences and publications. Others, such as those for the Caribbean and West Africa, have found that the problems of distance, differing traditions of record-keeping, and lack of finances have allowed only sporadic activity. The work of the ICA, and indeed a perspective on archives around the world, can be followed through its journal *Archivum* (1951) and its *Bulletin* (1973).

As well as concerns for developing standards and procedures for current archival practice, the ICA has also recognized the needs of scholars in newly developing countries by sponsoring the "Guides to the Sources of the History of Nations." The first three series for Latin America, Africa, and Asia and Oceania have together yielded over fifty volumes (between 1962 and 1995) listing relevant materials in European countries and North America. They have now been joined by parallel series listing the holdings of record offices located within those continents themselves.

Another organization of growing importance is the Association of Commonwealth Archivists and Records Managers (ACARM). In addition to holding conferences and publishing a newsletter, the organization has been responsible for organizing workshops in a number of Commonwealth regions, focusing particularly on the need for established records management programs and the creation of records centers.

Public Archives and the Rights of the Citizen

Although much of the professional activity surrounding the management of records and archives is scholarly and devoted to the support of the conditions for documentary research for cultural purposes, the integrity of public archives remains fundamental to the protection of democratic political rights and the rights of individual citizens alike. The integrity of public records systems as potential evidence provides an important component of public accountability since major misdemeanors rarely go undocumented, while individual rights, from compensation and property rights to the very status of citizen itself, are universally supported by a system of public records on which all must rely. The cultural task of the archivist, however significant, is matched by a task of equal gravity as custodian of the records that evidence the rights and property of the state itself, its rulers, and its citizens. For such reasons, the rules governing archives and a measure of independence in the status of the Keeper of Archives are often afforded constitutional or legal protection in the apparatus of states.

JOHN MCILWAINE

BIBLIOGRAPHY

Australian Society of Archivists, 1993. *Keeping Archives.* 2d ed. Ed. J. Ellis. Port Melbourne, Australia: Thorpe.

Bradsher, J. G., ed., 1988. *Managing Archives and Archival Institutions.* London: Mansell.

Cook, M., 1993. *Information Management and Archival Data.* London: Library Association.

International Council on Archives. 1984. *Dictionary of Archival Terminology.* Munich: Saur.

Rhoads, J. B., 1983. *The Role of Archives and Records Management in National Information Systems: A RAMP Study.* Paris: UNESCO.

Schellenberg, T. R., 1965. *The Management of Archives.* New York: Columbia University Press.

Significant journals include: *American Archivist* (Society of American Archivists, 1938–), *Archivaria* (Association of Canadian Archivists, 1975/76–), *Archives* (British Records Association, 1949–), *Archives and Manuscripts* (Australian Society of Archivists, 1955–), *Journal of the Society of Archivists* (U.K., 1955–), *Records Management Quarterly* (Association of Records Managers and Administrators, U.S., 1967–).

ARGYRIS, CHRIS (1923–).

Both disciple and critic of the human relations model. He is best known for formulating the concept of "double loop" thinking. As a human relations disciple, Argyris's values are rooted in the belief that organizations must seek ways to integrate themselves with their employees (Argyris 1990). As a critic, Argyris (1957, 1973a, 1973b) believed that the more popular human relations practices tended to overmanipulate and control people. Argyris came to believe that T groups and "organization development" ideas lacked precision as to how to improve the quality of life within organizations.

Argyris (1965, 1990)—as does his peer Warren Bennis (1993)—sees innovation and creativity as the key to individual and organizational change. Bennis and Argyris can be considered the behavioral sciences' early pioneers on innovation and creativity.

In his *Public Administration Review* article, "Some Limits of Rational Man Organizational Theory," Argyris sought to describe a problem-solving and decision making process in organizations that could move them "from X to Y." In Argyris's view, the "traditional administrative theorists create views of organizations . . . and organization structures . . . that lead to entropy" (1973a, p. 255). Argyris called for a more rigorous examination of the human variables of "growth and self-actualization" in the study of the human system.

This position embroiled Argyris in debate with Nobel laureate Herbert Simon. Their argument centered around the values of human relations principles versus rational-man theory. Argyris described rational-man theory (Allison 1971; Simon 1957; March and Simon 1958) as limited in its view of man: "[I] plead . . . to the rational-man theorists to consider more seriously the variable found in the behavioral science research focusing on human realization and growth within organizations" (1973a, p. 254). Argyris believed that if these theories could not be enlarged to adopt a more encompassing view of man, "organizations will not be able to continue their remarkable accomplishments" (1973b, p. 355). Simon accused Argyris of being antistructure, and in his view, reasoning was a "shackle of freedom." Argyris responded that it is the design and administrative components of organizations that "are the shackle[s]." He encouraged the rational-man theorists to address this challenge by helping to build a new paradigm of organizational change. "They needn't have much to say on the subject if they would integrate their work with ours" (1973b, p. 356). Argyris believed, "If history is any guide, the ultimate direction will be to develop administrative theory that integrates both of these points of view" (1973a, p. 253).

Arygris's debate with Simon best illustrates public administration's paradigm dilemma. According to Jeffrey Pfeffer (1992), the fields of organizational science, such as public administration, have failed to reach consensus in both method and empiricism. "One might have thought . . . that progress would have been made in evaluating the relative usefulness of these different theoretical foci, and winnowing down the avenues to be explored. . . . however, if anything the field is more fragmented and diverse than it has been" (p. 608). Unlike the natural sciences, where new paradigms generally evolve out of older ones, public administration and the organizational sciences continue to function in a climate of paradigmmatic tension.

With the publication of *Reasoning, Learning, and Action* (1982), Argyris attempted to ease these paradigmmatic tensions. Its central premise is that the organization's human potential is best achieved by breaking an institution's bureaucratic barriers. Eliminating such barriers will increase the organization's decisionmaking and problemsolving capacities.

Argyris characterized the bureaucratic culture as "entropic" (i.e., single-loop mentality). Single-loop thinking renders organizations incapable of reexamining their programs, goals, and processes. In contrast, "double-loop" learning allows the individual to break out of the stifling bureaucratic culture and enhance individual capacity to solve problems. "Double-loop" learning occurs when the individual examines his behavior against his original values and assumptions. Double-loop learning allows managers and employees to break out of the "structure," it enhances an individual's capacity to solve problems. In his most recent work (1993a and 1993b), Argyris explains and illustrates how double-loop thinking can help the organization of the 1990s manage in an environment of chaos and change.

Double-loop learning can redirect the focus of today's public organization. It can help the public organization grow and adapt in response to the pressures brought on by cutbacks and downsizing. Chris Argyris's learning paradigm has influenced other writers who echo the "learning and action" formula. These writers see the need for today's organizations to function as "learning systems" as they undergo structural change. Like Argyris, they believe that higher-level thinking will allow an organization to renew and grow ad infinitum (if growth is one of their objectives).

Public organization in the late 1990s is now faced with the choice: Does it grow, or continue to decline? To meet this challenge, according to Oakley and Krug, the "scales of life" need to shift within organizations: a redirection in focus. Public organizations need to move consciously away from the "scales of life," which are put in place by the various establishments of society (parents, schools, church, employers) that focus on what is being done "wrong" rather than what is being done "right." Chris Argyris's learning paradigm seeks to help organizations move to constructive thoughts instead of negative ones.

PHILIP NUFRIO

BIBLIOGRAPHY

Allison, Graham T., 1971. *Essence of Decision*. New York: Little, Brown & Co.
Argyris, Chris 1957. *Personality and Organizations*. New York: Harper & Bros.
———, 1964, Rev., 1990. *Integrating the Individual and the Organization*. New York: Wiley.
———, 1965. *Organizations and Innovation*. Homewood, IL: Richard D. Irwin.
———, 1973a. "Some Limits of Rational Man Organizational Theory." *Public Administration Review*. vol. 33: 253–267.
———, 1973b. "Organizational Man: Rational and Self-Rationalizing." *Public Administration Review*. vol. 33: 354–357.
———, 1982. *Reasoning, Learning, and Action*. San Francisco: Jossey-Bass.
———, 1990. *Overcoming Organization Defenses*. Wellesey, MA: Allyn Bacon.
———, 1993a. *Knowledge for Action: A Guide to Overcoming Barriers to Organizational Change*. San Francisco: Jossey-Bass.
———, 1993b. *On Organizational Learning*. Reading, MA: Addison-Wesley.
Bennis, Warren, 1993. *Beyond Bureaucracy: Essays on the Development and Evolution of Human Organization*. New York: Jossey-Bass.
March, James G., and Herbert Simon, 1958. *Organizations*. New York: Wiley.
Pfeffer, Jeffrey, 1992. "Barriers to the Advance of Organizational Science: Paradigm Development as a Dependent Variable," *Academy of Management Review*, vol. 18, no. 4: 599–620.
Simon, Herbert A., 1945. Re. 1947, 1957. *Administrative Behavior: A Study of Decision Making Process in Administrative Organizations*. New York: Free Press.

ARTS ADMINISTRATION (ARTS MANAGEMENT).

The application of the five traditional management functions—planning, organizing, staffing, supervising, and controlling—to the facilitation of the production of the performing or visual arts and the presentation of the artists' work to audiences. The administration and facilitation of the creative process and its communication to an audience is common to both public, nonprofit arts organizations (nonprofit theaters, symphony orchestras, opera companies, dance companies, museums, public broadcasting, and performing arts centers) and private, commercial, for-profit artistic entities (e.g., commercial theater, "popular" music, private galleries, film, television, radio, and video).

History of Arts Administration

Evidence of artistic expression—performance and visual—can be found in the oldest of prehistoric site excavations; whether these events and drawings were managed in any real way is pure speculation. It can be safely argued, however, that the earliest organized and managed performances were religious rituals, and that these events were administered and controlled by the leaders of these various religious sects. These early "arts administrators" controlled all aspects of the "performances" in question: aesthetics, financing, and accessibility to the "audience". A more formal and perhaps less sectarian form of arts administration took root when the Greeks began their state-sponsored festivals in the sixth century (B.C.E.). In Athens, a principal magistrate (*archon eponymous*) organized and managed the play festivals that were financed by wealthy Athenians (*choregoi*). The Romans produced their state-sponsored arts festivals in much the same manner, but here city magistrates approved and coordinated festival activities while the day-to-day management fell to the *domini* who, as managers, handled all of the necessary festival arrangements.

During the Dark Ages, organized production activity, financial support, and facilities for festivals and other official performance events virtually disappeared. Artists survived almost exclusively by touring. For traveling troupes, management of the operation was the responsibility of one of the performers; thus was born the *actor-manager*. Touring companies led by an actor-manager were common not only in Europe but throughout the world.

In the Middle Ages, religious organizations once again asserted their role in the arts and arts administration throughout officially sanctioned performances. As in the past, management control of the performances was centralized within the Church itself. These Church-sponsored events quickly evolved into public festivals and pageants, losing their direct liturgical content, and they became more popular as broad entertainment. By the 1300s, the Church lost all control over expanding performances;

management and sponsorship was handled by medieval trade guilds, where a member of the guild served as producer or manager, a person known as the *manager-director*. As the pageants grew in size and complexity, the management system evolved into separate roles for the director and the manager. The guild member retained artistic control but *pageant master* contracted the actors, scheduled rehearsals, and oversaw all phases of production.

The explosion of theater, opera and ballet activity during the Renaissance led to further professionalism and expansion of arts administration. A new and more vital function of arts managers during this period was solicitation of financial support—from the Church, the monarchies, and shareholders. While church and state support was pure subsidy, with no expectation of a return on the investment, the shareholders received a portion of the profits. Finance management quickly became an important management function.

Western arts activity (and arts management) followed the European settlers to the Americas. The first commercial theater company in the Western Hemisphere was founded in 1599 in Peru by Francisco Perez de Robles. Lewis Hallam established the first North American theater company in 1752 in Williamsburg, Virginia. By the middle of the Nineteenth century, the rail system in the United States helped establish an elaborate network of touring theater companies. Troupes of actors—each with an established and recognizable "star"—would go from town to town, performing in front of sets owned by local theaters. Under this system of *combination companies*, few permanent theater companies existed. As a result of this transience, the touring companies were at the mercy of and dominated by booking agents and producers. One of the most notorious was the Theatrical Syndicate, an agency that was formed when three New York booking offices merged. The other major art forms—classical music, opera, and visual art—did not suffer from as much centralized control and went on to a far more secure life in large American cities at the turn of the century.

As mass-entertainment technology evolved during the first half of the twentieth century, the traditional live and visual arts experienced significant competition from radio, film, and television. In the United States, museums and music, dance, and theater organizations struggled to make ends meet, primarily through the support of wealthy patrons. Government subsidization of the arts, a common and major source of financial support for arts organizations in most other societies around the globe, was not part of the United States system until September 16, 1965, when the United States authorized the creation of the National Endowment for the Arts (NEA). The NEA's leadership in funding nonprofit arts organizations led to a renaissance of U.S. arts activity; over 500 nonprofit arts organizations have been established since the mid-1960s.

Arts Administration in Practice

In an arts organization, the primary management functions of planning, organizing, staffing, supervising, and controlling are utilized in support of the administration and coordination of what Stephen Langley (*Theatre Management in America: Principle and Practice*, 1980) refers to as the four basic elements of a performance or exhibition:

- the creative raw material (the idea, the script, the scenario),
- a person or persons to interpret the material (actor, singer, dancer, painter, sculptor),
- a place to present the material (theatre, barn, church, hall, courtyard), and
- an audience to witness the performance or view the work of art.

Facilitating the synthesis of these four elements into performances or exhibitions is most commonly divided among five management departments: strategic planning, finance management, fund-raising, marketing, and facility or physical plant management. All of this activity is undertaken in support of the art for which the company or institution was created: visual art, performance art, music, dance, or theater. In addition to the administration of these five departments, significant management activity takes place in managing the artistic process: the development of a theater piece, a ballet, or an opera; or the presentation of a symphony, a painting, or a piece of sculpture. However, when most people in the arts industry talk of arts management, they are referring primarily to the purely administrative functions of an arts organization, not the management practices involved in producing the artistic work.

Currently, arts administration is practiced in two distinct but related spheres of activity: nonprofit, or public sector, arts organizations and commercial, or private sector and entertainment companies. Both systems utilize the four management functions and five operating departments, with some variation depending on the size, scale, and scope of an individual institution's operations.

The Public, or Nonprofit, Arts Sector

The primary mission of a nonprofit arts organization is the development of quality artistic expression and the distribution of that art to the widest possible audience. Monetary profit is not the motive. Most nonprofit arts organizations begin with a plan for producing or presenting their art; theirs is a product-oriented approach in which the goal is to produce or present the best work possible. The organization is sensitive to the demands of the market (the audience), but the marketing process is directed toward bringing people to a product already created, not modifying the product (the art) to meet the demand of the audience. Complicating the management process is the second goal—

accessibility to a wide audience—which dictates an admissions price below both the fair market value of the work and the actual total cost of producing or presenting the art. Rather than attempt to find the point of equilibrium between supply and demand, prices are set at artificially low levels to encourage the broadest possible participation. The difference between the total cost of the art and what a company generates in earned income (ticket sales, admissions, concession revenue, or other related income) is called the *earnings gap*; arts managers attempt to fill this gap through contributed income (cash and in-kind donations from individuals, businesses, private foundations, and/or governmental agencies). This balance of earned and contributed income varies depending on the arts discipline, ranging from no earned income at all and 100 percent contributed income (free museums or other free arts activities) to 70 percent earned and 30 percent contributed income (large nonprofit theater companies).

In most countries, nonprofit arts institutions are incorporated or organized under laws that exempt them from various federal, state, and municipal taxes, given the fact that their missions serve a public purpose or provide for the betterment of the community. They are not privately held businesses but public institutions, much like libraries, public universities, or public hospitals. In many ways, these nonprofit arts organizations are similar to the state-sponsored festivals of Ancient Greece and Rome. Because of this nonprofit, tax-exempt status, surpluses of income over expenses must be reinvested into the companies rather than distributed to individuals or other entities.

A nonprofit arts institution is governed by a board of directors (sometimes referred to as a board of trustees) comprising individuals from the communities or constituencies the organization serves. These directors, who serve without compensation, may be selected because of the expertise they bring to the organization (legal, banking, marketing, etc.) or as representatives of specific constituencies (geographic, ethnic, or professional). The board governs the company on behalf of the community at large, in the public trust; its members are legally responsible for any and all action taken by the organization.

The board, in turn, hires one or two people to administer the artistic and management operations of the institution—the top management team. Though the board holds *ultimate* control of a nonprofit organization, the executive staff maintains *immediate* or day-to-day control. The board *governs*, setting broad policy and direction; the staff *manages*, fulfilling those goals and handling the ongoing operations of the organization. Together, the board and top management staff are responsible for an organization's strategic planning, the first of six management departments. In most nonprofit arts organizations, the selection, planning, and development of performances or the collection and exhibition of visual art work falls under the control of a chief artistic officer, someone in residence at the

institution who oversees the artistic operations of the company. The chief artistic officer might be known as an artistic director, music director, choreographer, or curator. Planning and administration of the management functions in support of the art are traditionally handled by a chief executive officer, whose title might be managing director, executive director, or general manager. In traditionally structured organizations, these two individuals may be considered equals—both reporting to the board of trustees for their particular area of responsibility (Figure I). In other instances, one executive may report to the other, who in turn is solely accountable to the board for the entire operation (Figure II). In yet other situations, one person may serve as both chief artistic officer and chief executive officer, and may be known as the general director, producing director, or other broad title (Figure III).

Just below the executive staff in the traditionally structured institutions is the second layer of administration in most nonprofit arts organizations—middle management—who control the remaining four management departments: finance management, fund-raising, marketing, and facility or physical plant management (Figure IV). These managers take the strategic and programs plans formulated by the top management team and develop and administer the day-to-day plans that fulfill the broad institutional goals and objectives.

The Private, For-Profit Arts Sector

Unlike their nonprofit counterparts, private sector arts organizations are owned by individuals or shareholders—people who invest time, energy, and money in an organization, hoping for a financial return, a cash profit. Like any private enterprise in any industry or field, these companies are not exempt from taxes and do not receive tax-deductible contributions from the sources of donations to nonprofit organizations. The mission of a for-profit arts organization is like that of any other private firm: the gener-

FIGURE I. A Version of the Traditional Hierarchial Structure in which both the Chief Artistic Officer and Chief Executive Officer Report to the Governing Board.

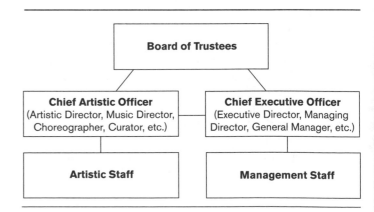

FIGURE II. Two Versions of the Traditional Hierarchial Structure in which Accountability and Responsibility to the Governing Board is Held by Only One Chief Officer.

FIGURE III. A Version of the Traditional Hierarchial Structure in which Chief Artistic and Chief Executive Duties and Responsibilities are Structured Under One Individual.

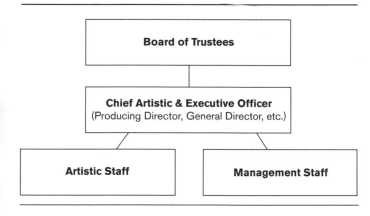

ation of cash profits for its owners and investors. Here, management is market-oriented: finding or creating a demand and then satisfying that demand. The art produced need only be good enough to generate enough sales to result in a cash profit; costs are kept as low as possible, spending enough to maintain an acceptable level of quality—acceptable defined as motivating people to purchase the product. In addition, private-sector managers actively seek the equilibrium point between supply and demand, pushing up prices are far as they can without experiencing a drop in gross revenue.

The private, for-profit structure is virtually unheard of in the dance field; this also is true of the symphony orchestra and opera communities (though nearly the entire balance of the music industry today is operated on a for-profit basis). The film industry is almost exclusively for-profit, though many film houses that show small "art" films or revivals of classic commercial films are nonprofit organiza-

tions. The television and radio industries contain both private broadcast or cable operations and public or nonprofit operations. Private, for-profit galleries are quite common, however. Probably the most widely known of the private-sector arts is the commercial theater, best embodied in the Broadway theater industry in the United States.

Commercial theater operations may be managed under a corporate structure, with a board of directors reporting to shareholders, but it is most commonly structured as a *limited partnership*. One or more producers serve as the general partner(s), supported by the investments of their limited partners. As managers, producers maintain both ultimate and immediate control of a commercial theater venture, hiring all other staff and overseeing every aspect of the production. Middle management functions may be carried out by staff members in the producers' or general partners' offices, or by independent contractors.

Variations on the Traditional Corporate Model

Recently, the nonprofit arts industry has experienced some significant organizational stresses: (1) decreased contributed income from nearly all sources, as a result of increased demand from other public sector agencies or drastic changes in economic structures, situations or systems (Russia, Great Britain, Germany); (2) increased competition for trustees and volunteers, as a result of the ever-enlarging pool of nonprofit organizations and a flat—some say declining—supply of people willing to commit to volunteer leadership positions; and (3) steadily increasing costs due to the labor-intensive nature of the performing arts.

Nello McDaniel and George Thorn of Arts Action Research (New York City) have called for serious rethinking of administrative structures and systems in nonprofit

FIGURE IV. THE TRADITIONAL HIERARCHIAL STRUCTURE: A TYPICAL TABLE OF ORGANIZATION (ADMINISTRATIVE SIDE ONLY) IN AN ARTS ORGANIZATION.

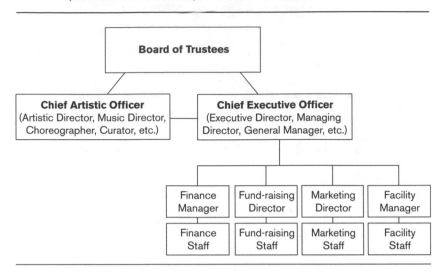

FIGURE V. THE McDANIEL/THORN VISUALIZATION OF A PROFESSIONAL/VOLUNTEER UNIVERSE IN AN ARTS ORGANIZATION.

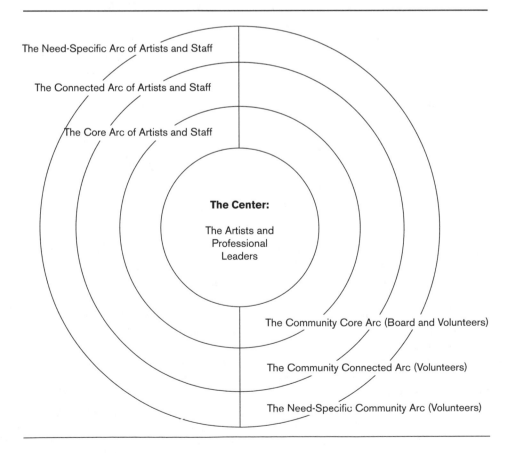

arts organizations. McDaniel and Thorn believe that the traditional corporate model (Figure IV) is no longer appropriate for arts organizations if they hope to survive in the twenty-first century, much less operate in efficient and effective ways. McDaniel and Thorn do not, however, recommend a new corporate model. They urge arts organizations to take a holistic approach to the development of organizational structures and cultures, an approach that places the artists, artistic process, and professional leaders at the center of organization (Figure V). At the core are people closely involved in a company's work. In a ring around these two circles is the connected arc, representing, according to McDaniel and Thorn, "those people who have an ongoing relationship with the center, but only on an as-needed basis." The final circle is the need-specific arc, representing the individuals who perform or serve on an as-needed basis but are not interested in a long-term relationship with the institution. This series of four concentric circles is not an administrative structure but a way of thinking about how people can relate to and work with and in support of an institution's artistic mission. Thorn and McDaniel believe that a holistic culture and structure will emerge from this visualization and orientation.

This holistic approach can be applied to the board and volunteers as well as the staff. The community core will correspond to the professional core, with a shared belief in the work at the center of the organization and its contribution to the community. The second circle, the Connected Community Arc, comprises people who are willing and able to undertake specific tasks, but this organization may not be their top priority, though they do maintain a continuing relationship with the company. The final arc represents the Need-Specific Community, in which individuals are called upon to assist the company on a short-term basis for a very specific task (e.g., construction project, computerization, legal services, etc.).

Professional Training and Development

As nonprofit arts organizations flourish and become more established and sophisticated in the second half of the twentieth century, management opportunities also have flourished and become more professional. Until recently, it was not uncommon for a member of an orchestra, an acting company, or a dance troupe to undertake management responsibilities, as that individual could not or would no longer perform as an artist. The increased demand for professionalism, combined with the current challenges in managing arts organizations, has resulted in arts administration as a viable, independent professional career track. Dozens of service organizations—in all disciplines and at all levels of professionalism—assist arts managers in developing and refining management skills. In addition, formal graduate-level degree programs in arts administration are available on all continents at over 35 colleges or universities. Hundreds of undergraduate schools offer courses or full programs of study in this area as well.

DAN J. MARTIN

BIBLIOGRAPHY

Langley, Stephen, 1980. *Theatre Management in America: Principle and Practice*. Rev. ed. New York: Drama Book Publishers.
Langley, Stephen, and James Abruzzo, 1990. *Jobs in Arts and Media Management: What They Are and How to Get One*. New York: ACA Books.
McDaniel, Nello, and George Thorn, 1994. *Arts Boards: Creating a New Community Equation*. New York: Arts Action Issues.
———, 1993. *Toward a New Arts Order: Process, Power, Change*. New York: Arts Action Issues.
Shore, Harvey, 1987. *Arts Administration and Management*. Westport, CT: Greenwood Press.

ASPIRATIONAL MANAGEMENT. A form of participatory organizational design that places people at the heart of organizational structure and success. It uses the shared values of the organizational members to develop the learning capacity of the organization and to guide the evolution of its culture.

Introduction

Aspirational management is an approach for making organizations work better. It is based on the principle that many organizations must become learning organizations that is, ones that know how to acquire and use information rapidly and are flexible, adaptive, and responsive to their environments. Aspirational management requires the development of shared values and a clear vision of the direction and future of the organization to improve its learning capacity. Hence it is the relationships among the members of the organization that not only result in a shared vision but also ultimately determine the quality of the organization.

Aspirational management and creating learning organizations through the use of values and aspirations originated in the private sector. Robert Haas created the term "aspirational management" in reference to the fundamental cultural transformations within the Levi Strauss Company (Howard 1990, p. 144). Haas stated that such transformations require that each member of the organization articulate both what kind of person he or she wants to be and his or her desired legacy. Similarly, R. Stayer (1990) found that organizational performance begins with the expectations and hopes of the worker. Jim Collins and Jerry Porras (1994) discovered that aspirational management is a common cultural characteristic of the most successful companies. Several authors discuss the critical importance of "mutual aspirations" (Kouzes and Posner 1987, p. 128) and "living the values" if organizations are to improve continuously (DePree 1989, Block 1987).

This entry characterizes the assumptions and context for the development of aspirational management and identifies conditions under which aspirational management is most likely to be successful. It characterizes four components of aspirational management: the aspirations statement, living the values, creating a continuous learning capacity, and team-centered evaluation and reward systems. It concludes with an introduction to implementing aspirational management in the public organization.

The Context in Public Administration

Aspirational management proposes a transformation of organizational cultures. Specifically, it leads organizations away from structured, hierarchical, and mechanical forms of organizational design and toward open, interactive, and "self-organizing" forms of organizations. As such, it has strong roots in the literature on organizational culture (see especially Morgan 1988; Belasco 1990; and Block 1987) and literature relating organizational form to decisionmaking and policy impact (see Archibald 1970; Ballard et al. 1991).

Three primary assumptions are at the heart of aspirational management. First, it is based on the belief that information resources are accessible, understandable, and broadly usable throughout the organization (see Cleveland 1985). This is in sharp contrast to traditional assumptions that information is controllable and, typically, best used only by top management. Second, aspirational management assumes that participatory, open, and interactive organizational communication is more suited to developing a learning environment than hierarchical reliance on structures, line and staff relationships, competitive personnel systems, and top-down communication. Third, aspirational management assumes that responsiveness to customers, adaption to external conditions, and social responsibility will continue to place increasing demands on the organization and will require rapid learning and adaption at all levels of the organization.

Organizational culture transformations, as they relate to aspirational management, are summarized in Figure I. Aspirational management leads organizations away from conventional forms and structures toward self-organizing organizations. Two fundamental differences exist between conventional and self-organizing organizations. First, self-organizing organizations place primary value in people as the basis of organizational functioning and success. This contrasts sharply with conventional organizations which assume people must be controlled and managed in order to perform according to minimum standards. For conventional organizations, it is assumed that failure results from bad people; for self-organizing organizations, people are the source of growth, learning environmental responsiveness, and adaptability.

FIGURE I. ORGANIZATIONAL CULTURE TRANSFORMATIONS

Conventional Organization (disappearing bureaucracy)

Profits (or turf protection), career advancement, and authority determine organizational change.

The individual self-perspective depends on position (job description) and ascribed status.

Communications is one-way, top down.

Learning is undervalued, individually and organizationally.

Failure results from bad people.

Organizational improvement occurs by identifying the "right models," new management techniques, or aggressive leaders.

We learn from success.

Social responsibility is minimized.

Decisionmaking is centralized, controlled, and vertical. Leadership is equated with position in the hierarchy.

Reward systems are formal, highly structured, and competitive.

Self-Organizing Organization (emerging adhocracy)

People, values, and customer satisfaction make the organization.

Self-perspective depends on competencies and capacity to influence the organization's product.

Communication is unrestricted, multiple, open, lateral, and fast.

Learning is central to survival; it is continuous for the individual, the team, and the organization.

Failure results from nonadaptive systems.

Improvement occurs as core organizational competencies advance, as participation improves, and as the customer/environment is better understood.

We learn from failures and from continuous feedback systems.

The organization is, mobile, destructured, lean, and open. Roles flexible and temporary.

Social responsibility is central to long-term success.

Decisionmaking is team-oriented, complex, open, horizontal. Leadership roves among team members, based on expertise.

Reward systems are routine, open, shared, timely, ad hoc, informal, and noncompetitive.

Adopted from Ballard (1991); Rogers (1992); Harris (1980); and Senge (1990).

Second, the two approaches have very different perspectives regarding stability and change. The conventional paradigm hopes for or tries to impose stability, environmental control, routine behaviors, formal communication mechanisms, and formal reward and evaluation systems. Self-organizing organizations assume high degrees of ambiguity in the external environment and, therefore, within the organization. In the conventional model, structure is imposed by those in control and is assumed to be the best way to achieve organizational goals; in the new models, structure emerges as organizational members continually create and recreate their organizations in response to the environments in which they function. As new organizational cultures are created, communication is necessarily more open and lateral; learning (individual, group, and organizational) needs to be fast and continual; roles are flexible and leadership is shared; and the evaluation systems are routine, informal, open, shared and non-competitive (Morgan 1986; Senge 1990; Ballard et al. 1991).

Aspirational management is related to total quality management (TQM), human relations approaches to organizations, and empowerment theories. Among its primary similarities with these approaches are its assumptions about the inevitability of change, complexity, and partial chaos; attention to the customer; lack of reliance on formal structure and roles; and emphasis on holistic organizational systems. However, aspirational management is more democratic and egalitarian than TQM because of its emphasis on transformational leadership and the capacity of individual members and teams. It is more accepting of risk, error, and learning from experience, and it is internally noncompetitive (see Rogers and Ballard 1995). It places organizational culture at the center of successful change (Collins and Poras 1994); thus, it can be contrasted with approaches to organizational change that emphasize the management skills of leadership (Levin and Sanger 1994).

The Content of Aspirational Management

Aspirational management consists of four elements: an aspirations statement, the will to "live the values," a commitment to creating a capacity for continuous learning, and designing team-oriented evaluation and reward systems. Each are described below.

The Aspirations Statement

An aspirations statement represents for organization members "what they want for the organization; what kind of person they want to be in the work place and what kind of legacy they want to leave behind" (Haas, as quoted in Howard 1990, p. 144). The aspirations statement includes both vision and core values. A vision is the future we want to create for our organization. Core values speak to our beliefs and ethics, how we want to interact with our clients or cutomers, how we want to treat each other and how we want to influence society (Block 1987). Levi Strauss & Company captures these elements of vision and core values in its aspirations statement:

> We all want a company that our people are proud of and committed to, where all employees have an opportunity to contribute, learn, grow, and advance based on merit, not politics or background. We want our people to feel respected, treated fairly, listened to, and involved. Above all, we want satisfaction from accomplishments and friendships, balanced personal and professional lives, and to have fun in our endeavors.

When we describe the kind of Levi Strauss & Co. we want in the future, what we are talking about is building on the foundation we have inherited: affirming the best of our company's traditions, closing gaps that may exist between principles and practices, and updating some of our values to reflect contemporary circumstances (Howard 1990, p. 135).

The aspirations statement of Levi Strauss & Company represents not only the kind of organizational community they want but also how they want the company to do business. A compelling aspirations statement captures both of these elements—a commitment to a quality product or service as well as to the processes for accomplishing the work (Block 1987).

If organization members are to own the aspirations, then building the statement is a task that includes each organization member (Senge 1990). The statement is derived from individual visions, and ultimately weaves these personal aspirations into a shared vision of the organization. People seek to be connected to one another in an undertaking that they view to be worthwhile. Shared aspirations for the organization and each other provide that common sense of worth and significance (Block 1987; Howard 1990; Senge 1990; Stayer 1990). To achieve the commitment of staff rather than only their compliance, each organizational member should be given the opportunity to express his or her own vision and to help build the integrated organizational vision. This process is less likely to succeed if the group accepts the vision of one member—usually that of the manager. Thus, commitment to shared aspirations emerges from a participatory and dynamic process (Senge 1990).

The purpose of identifying the shared values of organization members and of capturing those values in a statement of aspirations is that staffs come to share congruent images of what the organization is about and where it is going. These values then become internal controls for member behavior. Rather than the manager enforcing rules, staffs monitor their own behavior, using the aspirations as the parameters for what is "right." "In a more volatile and dynamic business environment, the controls have to be conceptual. They can't be human anymore . . . values provide a common language for aligning a company's leadership and its people" (Howard 1990, p. 134). Gareth Morgan (1988) also described how shared aspirations can serve as internal controls:

> When people have a good sense of what their organization stands for and where it is going, they can determine the course and appropriateness of their behavior and judge whether a particular innovation will resonate with broader aims. . . . Employees can develop an instinctive feel for what is appropriate. Or as one executive put it, they can arrive at a situation where "You don't have to be

told 'Here are the bounds.' You know! You can feel it. It's there" (p. 48).

Colleges and universities that operate on an honor code regarding academic honesty, some religiously affiliated colleges, and various groups within universities, such as bands, research teams, and so forth, are examples of groups that use values as a way to bond members together and to influence individual and group decisionmaking. A potential pitfall here is that the values become an ideology—imposing a set of beliefs without regard to differences among people. Including all voices in creating the aspirations by which an organization operates and continually reviewing the statement for its appropriateness to the current context and membership are important aspects of making an aspirations statement a meaningful and ethical approach to decisionmaking. Of course, this becomes increasingly difficult with larger organizations.

The result of an organization that operates from a set of internal controls, as represented in the aspirations statement, is an organization of self-directed teams and individuals. Using the aspirations as a guide, organization members individually and collectively evaluate what they do and how they do it in light of their shared values rather than waiting for the manager to tell them when and how to do their work (DePree 1989; Howard 1990; Stayer 1990). Clearly, self-directed individuals and teams need something different from the manager than the old "command and control" role (Peters 1992). What does the manager in the new organizational culture do? He or she embodies the aspirations and models this way of being in the organization. The second aspect of aspirational managment, "living the values," outlines new roles for the manager.

Living the Values

Emerging organizational cultures (as described in Figure I), which spawn flattened decisionmaking structures, participation, and shared leadership, call for new approaches to management and supervision. "With the props of hierarchy removed, managers will have to coordinate through the development of shared values and shared understanding and find the right balance between delegation and control" (Morgan 1988, p. 8). If public organizations can adopt a set of aspirations as their guide for behavior and decisionmaking, then the role of the supervisor requires re-examination. Increasingly, supervisors are asked to find ways of helping, overseeing, and working with members, rather than controlling them. Thus, "management" begins to focus on empowerment—building the capacity of its people to take the initiative, to make decisions, to "do the right things" in light of their shared aspirations.

For the aspirations statement to guide the behavior of staffs and to become the basis for internalized controls, managers will work with them to help them understand how to participate effectively in this new, more participa-

tory, organizational culture. Just because the aspirations statement has been adopted does not mean that staffs, either individually or in teams, know how to function autonomously in the organization. First, the employees must believe that the supervisor really will give up control and allow them the responsibility to take initiative and make decisions based on the aspirations. Second, they must believe that they have the required skills to assume this wider responsibility for their actions. Often, even though they want more responsibility, staffs have been conditioned to question their own capabilities. Thus the supervisor's role becomes one of coach, career counselor, team player, teacher, and philosopher rather than cop, naysayer and pronouncer (Stayer 1990, p. 80). Supervisors spend their time reinforcing the aspirations, building people's ability to operate this way in the organization, and reminding them in the process of their common purposes and dreams.

The key to making the transition from authority vested in the manager to authority resting in shared aspirations is that the actions of the manager must be consistent with the aspirations statement. Student affairs organizations that adopt an aspirational approach require supervisors who model the kind of behavior that the aspirations promote. Aspirational managers personify what the organization is trying to achieve—an empowered staff that can take reposibility for their jobs and each other and a commitment to offering quality service to students and to the institution. Employees must be able to rely on the supervisor's word and know that once they have been given autonomy, the supervisor will not revert to the old command-and-control style in midstream. "Yo-yo empowerment" will destroy the concept of shared decisionmaking and collaboration. Maintaining or regaining the commitment of the staff will be difficult if their supervisor vacillates between empowerment and control (Kiechel 1992, p. 157). The aspirations will become nothing but a sham. People will not put values into practice if their supervisors do not (Howard 1990).

This shift away from traditional management techniques poses a challenging task for managers as well as for some staff:

This role for the manager is much tougher [than traditional command and control] because you can't rely on your title and obedience to get things done. You have to negotiate goals rather than set them. You have to accept decisions that may be different than your own. You have to be willing to take your ego out of it. That doesn't mean abdication. Managers still have to make decisions, serve as counselors and coaches, be there when things get sticky and help sort out the tangles (Howard 1990, p. 136).

This transformation occurs in fits and starts. Despite the best of intentions, supervisors will sometimes revert to old ways. Gaps may occur between their newly adopted principles and their practices. How supervisors or managers handle this lapse is the key to keeping the investment in creating an aspirational community on track. If a supervisor makes a mistake–for example, by taking control of an issue or problem that is more appropriately the responsibility of an individual or team–admitting the error and working as a team to fix it will go a long way toward rebuilding relationships with the staff. Supervisors who admit their mistakes also let organization members know that failure facilitates growth. Empowerment of staffs is enhanced when they perceive this "failure safety net" (Plunkett and Fournier 1991, p. 47). They are more willing to take the risks of trying the new behaviors required of them in aspirational organizations when they see their supervisor doing so too (Howard 1990).

Continuous Learning

Organizations that have successfully implemented aspirational management approaches teach us that continual education and training are the foundation of staff empowerment (Peters 1992; Stayer 1990; Howard 1990). Just as supervisors take on new roles in this managerial approach, so do the employees. As previously discussed, self-organizing organizations rely less on hierarchical structures to define roles, responsibilities, and functions. Instead, they increase the capacity of people to create the structures, roles, and responsibilities that are responsive to current environmental conditions. As these conditions change, employees reorganize themselves in order to meet the new demands facing the organization.

Shared aspirations guide organizational members through these continual changes. The values expressed in the aspirations provide direction on how and where change occurs, who will take leadership at any given moment, and which functions will remain and which will be modified or eliminated. Organization members and teams are active participants in making these decisions rather than only the supervisor or manager.

Clearly, the ambiguity and uncertainty posed by new organizational cultures require something very different from staffs than the conventional organizational culture. Rather than following the directives of the supervisor, they are asked to take the initiative and to use their creativity in resolving organizational problems. This presupposes, of course, that staffs believe that they have the authority and competency to take on decisionmaking responsibilities reserved in the past for the manager. "The majority of employees resist 'being empowered' in the initial stages because they lack the prerequisite competencies to comprehend the concept and participate in the process" (Giddens 1990, p. 15). Hence education, training, and development are particularly important in the early stages of implementing an aspirational management approach. In addition, managers as well as staffs should understand that it will take longer for some to be comfortable with these new roles than it will for others.

In a report for the U.S. Department of Labor, Giddens (1990) identified ten competency categories for employees who are empowered to participate in the decisionmaking processes of their organization as individuals and as members of self-directed work teams. These include: self-awareness; growth-orientation; a commitment to empowerment; interpersonal competency; group leadership and membership skills; a commitment to group productivity; ability to link self and group to the system; interdependence; an ability to interact with the environment; and a commitment to enhancing society. The themes that emanate from this list of competencies for empowered organization members include effective communication skills, personal development, group and interpersonal skills, collaborative approaches, and the ability to understand the "big picture" of the organization as it relates to its environment.

Finally, in self-organizing organizations that operate around a set of aspirations, managers and staffs engage in double-loop learning. Double-loop learning is a process by which organization members reflect on how well they have achieved their purposes and also whether those purposes themselves remain relevant and appropriate. It requires of managers and staffs alike an ability to remain open to changes in the environment and an ability to challenge operating assumptions in a most fundamental way (Morgan 1986).

Team-Centered Evaluation

Evaluation and reward systems are a critical component of self-managing teams. However, emerging concepts of self-organizing organizations place much different emphasis on the purpose and conduct of evaluation than do traditional organizational concepts. Evaluation and reward systems are traditionally viewed to be most appropriate as a final component of an organizational change process or as a summary review of performance over a given time period. Indeed, traditional concepts of evaluation in hierarchical organizations view it to be an after-the-fact process for determining whether goals have been met. Frequently, evaluation viewed in this manner establishes the incentive structure for individual behavior; members behave according to the incentives established in the evaluation system.

Yet, it has become increasingly clear that evaluation and reward systems structured in this manner are bad for morale, make collaborative processes more difficult, and frequently provide untimely feedback regarding organizational performance (Wheatley 1993; Ballard et al. 1991). If reward systems punish failed attempts, risk-aversion behaviors will become commonplace. If reward systems focus primarily on individual achievement, individuals will have a powerful incentive to ignore the organizational consequences of their actions. Because these tendencies can become pathological, some suggest that evaluation systems be eliminated (Deming 1986).

Even among less radical thinkers than Deming, widespread agreement exists that traditional reward systems structured to be consistent with hierarchical organizations fail (Walton 1991; Senge 1990). They fail because they embody the command-and-control philosophy that requires bosses, status discrepancies, annual evaluations, and few connections between individual behavior and organizational success. Traditional systems also fail because they foster competitiveness among employees rather than the team-oriented, collaborative processes necessary for learning organizations.

Appropriate reward systems can be created if they are clearly tied to statements of aspirations and to the learning capacity of individuals and groups. This requires a rethinking of how and when evaluation occurs. Several characteristics of useful evaluations may be identified:

- They may be team-driven rather than individually centered. Individual actions make sense only with respect to the success of the group or the organization.
- Evaluations may be invisible and informal. Useful evaluations occur routinely; they are behavior specific, ad hoc, and on-the-spot rather than at predetermined times.
- They may be product, process, or service-driven rather than driven by needs for individual advancement. Thus, the quality of learning, usually measured by one's team, is more important than simple quantitative measures of individual performance.
- Evaluations may also be oriented toward training and development needs. They should ask the question, "what needs to happen to learn better and faster" rather than questions related to salaries and promotions.

These characteristics suggest that reward systems should not be modeled on those that exist in other organizations or that had previously been in place. They should be directly linked to the vision of the organization and be developed in a participatory environment.

How do we develop such systems? First, we should realize that structural changes in an organizational system are usually long-term processes. Second, given the informal nature of useful evaluation systems, the process of creation will probably be very dynamic. In essence, evaluation systems will change as the organization learns and as members become more and more comfortable with providing immediate, team-oriented feedback.

Even though successful evaluations require broad participation throughout the organization, managers assume a critical role in developing the atmosphere in which such systems can be developed. Managers should begin by understanding that members must feel secure in their new evaluation roles. Managers are not necessarily better evaluators than other organizational members, but they can play a positive role through such means as recognition, appreciation, communication, involvement, and solicitation of ideas. Even the most severe barriers to empowered teams, such as pay inequities, can be reduced by showing sincere effort to do as much as possible to overcome them.

Conditions for Using Aspirational Management

Aspirational management proposes a fundamental transformation of the values and culture of the organization. Hence the first condition for considering its use is the long-term commitment of the organization to a new culture. In significant contrast to many management innovations, successful implementation of aspirational management cannot be expected in the short-term; in fact, the desired outcome itself (learning capacity, adaptability, etc.) is extremely difficult to measure or determine. Thus the appropriate analogy is that of beginning a long journey without a precise destination in mind. The process of changing the culture to one that is self-organizing is the primary outcome.

The second condition is a clear understanding that the existing organizational culture, structure, or design is simply inadequate to deal with future needs. Most often, this occurs because of a crisis of significant external demands for organizational change. Such conditions are easy to identify in the public sector, for example, fiscal distress, rapidly changing policy goals, alienation and cynicism in the public, and increasing competition and privatization. Even though it is obviously difficult to give up existing organizational paradigms for one that is somewhat unknown, the external pressures on public organizations, nevertheless, are making this transition more and more feasible.

A third condition is that the organization must be committed to being responsive to its clients or customers. The importance of this condition is that it is frequently the starting point or the catalyst for organizational learning; organizations that continuously interact, respect, and listen to their customers are ones that understand their inadequacies well and make commitments to addressing them (Walton 1991; Carr and Littan 1990). Typically, this is more difficult in the public and non-profit sectors than in the private sector. Yet many public agencies must be able to satisfy their customers if they are to survive, let alone succeed. To take just one example, the significant trend toward privatization is clearly related to dissatisfaction with the ability of public agencies to be responsive to citizen needs (National Governor's Association 1993).

A fourth condition for adopting aspirational management is that the organization must value its people. This goes well beyond the traditional debate among theory X, Y, and Z. Rather, it is the extent to which the organization believes that people (not organizational structure or leadership) make the difference and the organization's willingness to invest in this resource. Investment includes training and development to ensure the necessary skills and knowledge. But it goes well beyond this to include the members' psychological attachment to the organization (esteem, respect, sense of well-being), as well as their level of empowerment to make decisions or errors, to be creative, and to try new things. Aspirational management requires that all four of these conditions be present (Collins and Poras 1994). They are equally important, and together they create the conditions necessary to begin the very difficult transition toward a new culture.

Conclusion

When and how can aspirational management be implemented in public organizations? One general answer to this question, which bears repeating, is that no models or formulas exist that can be easily transferred from other organizations. Although the characteristics of aspirational management are common across a diversity of organizations (Ballard et al. 1991), these characteristics and the specifics of implementation will require skillful adaptation to the particular context of the institution.

A second answer logically follows from the first–implementation must be determined and driven from within the organization (Schmidt and Finnigan 1992). The conditions for success *can be* controlled from within the organization; they depend on the relationships among members (Wheatley 1993). Indeed, success appears to have much more to do with the degree and breadth of organizational commitment than it does with external factors. Further, success does not appear to depend on who starts the organizational change process–leadership, members of the organization, or pressures from events such as financial crises (Ballard et al. 1991).

What does appear to be critical is the philosophy by which aspirational management is pursued. Simply stated, successful implementation requires holistic, long-term, and courageous approaches. Aspirational management is holistic in that all four primary characteristics must be pursued—an aspirations statement, commitment to living the values, commitment to learning and development, and restructuring reward and evaluation systems. Aspirational management is long-term and courageous in that many of these components cannot be accomplished in the short-term and in that they may never be "completed." In essence, the process is a product, too. As one CEO put it, "Yet another thing I've learned is that the cause of excitement . . . is not change itself but the process used in producing change.

Learning and responsibility are invigorating and aspirations make our hearts beat" (Stayer 1990, p. 83).

STEVEN BALLARD AND JUDY L. ROGERS
[Excerpts reprinted with permission of the National Association of Student Personnel Administration.]

BIBLIOGRAPHY

Archibald, K. A., 1970. "Three Views of the Expert's Role in Policymaking." *Policy Sciences,* 1: 73–86.

Ballard, Steven, C. Massingill, C. Morris, W. Nesbit, B. J. Nicoletti, C. Spruce, and J. Talbot, 1993. "Total Quality Education for Public Schools: Linking Customers to Communities." *Policy Papers,* 93–03. Orono, ME: Margaret Chase Smith Center for Public Policy.

Ballard, Steven, T. Walton, T. Torragrossa, and M. Benner, 1991. "High Performance Organizations: Implications for Change in the Public Sector." *Policy Papers,* 91–01. Orono, ME.: Margaret Chase Smith Center for Public Policy.

Belasco, James, 1990. *Teaching the Elephant to Dance: Empowering Change in Your Organization.* New York: Crown Publishers.

Block, Peter, 1987. "Creating a Vision of Greatness: The First Step Toward Empowerment." *The Empowered Manager,* 99–129. San Francisco: Jossey-Bass.

Carr, David K., and Ian D. Littan, 1990. *Excellence in Government: Total Quality Management in the 1990s.* Arlington, VA: Coopers and Lybrand.

Cleveland, Harlan, 1985. "The Twilight of Hierarchy: Speculations on the Global Information Society." *Public Administration Review* 20 (January-February): 185–195.

Collins, Jim, and Jerry Poras, 1994. *Built to Last: Successful Habits of Visionary Companies.* New York: Harper & Row.

Deming, W. E., 1986. *Out of the Crisis.* Cambridge, MA: Center for Advanced Engineering Study, Massachusetts Institute of Technology.

DePree, Max, 1989. *Leadership Is an Art.* New York: Dell.

Giddens, P., 1990. *"Recommendations for Basic Skills Required for Empowerment."* Unpublished report to the Secretary's Commission on Achieving Necessary Skills, U.S. Department of Labor.

Harris, P., 1980. "Innovating with High Achievers." *Training and Development Journal* 34 (10), 45–50.

Howard, R., 1990. "Values Make the Company: An Interview with Robert Haas." *Harvard Business Review* 68 (5): 133–144.

Kiechel, III, W., 1992. "When Management Regresses." *Fortune* (March): 157–159.

Kouzes, J., and B. Posner, 1987. *The Leadership Challenge.* San Francisco, Jossey-Bass.

Levin, Martin A., and Mary Byrna Sanger, 1994. *Making Government Work: How Entrepreneurial Executives Turn Bright ideas Into Real Results.* San Francisco: Jossey-Bass.

Morgan, Gareth, 1986. *Images of Organization.* Beverly Hills: Sage.

———, 1988. *Riding the Waves of Change.* San Francisco: Jossey-Bass.

National Governor's Association, 1993. *An Action Agenda to Redesign State Government.* Washington, D.C.: NGA.

Peters, T. 1992. *Liberation Management: Necessary Disorganization for the Nanosecond Nineties.* New York: Alfred A. Knopf.

Plunkett, L. and R. Fournier, 1991. *Participative Management: Implementing Empowerment.* New York: Wiley.

Rogers, Judy. 1990. "Emerging Leadership Models: Implications for Public Policy Education." In R. Carriker and R. Hildreth (eds.), *Increasing Understanding of Public Problems and Policies, 1990*. Oak Brook, IL: Farm Foundation.

———, 1992. "Leadership Development for the 90s: Incorporating Emergent Paradigm Perspectives." *NASPA Journal* 29 (4): 243–252.

Rogers, Judy, and Steven Ballard, 1995. "Aspirational Management: Building Effective organizations Through Shared Values." *NASPA Journal* 32 (3), 162–178.

Schmidt, W., and J. Finnigan, 1992. *The Race Without a Finish Line: America's Quest for Total Quality*. San Francisco: Jossey-Bass.

Senge, P., 1990. *The Fifth Discipline : The Art and Practice of the Learning Organization*. New York: Doubleday.

Stayer, R., 1990. "How I Learned to Let My Workers Lead." *Harvard Business Review* 68 (6): 66–83.

Walton, M., 1991. *Deming Management at Work*. New York: Harper & Row.

Wheatley, Margaret, 1993. *Leadership and the New Science*. New York: Barrett-Koehler.

ASSESSMENT CENTER.

A process, not a place; it is a formal procedure incorporating both group and individual exercises for determining the participant's knowledge, skill, and ability, or how well the participant performs tasks that are important for the job under consideration. It differs from other techniques because it uses multiple behavioral exercises to evaluate behavior. The exercises simulate to the extent practical the actual circumstances encountered on the job.

The assessment center is one of the most commonly used promotion tests in the public sector today. As of 1992, over 60 percent of cities of 50,000 or more population use the assessment center, especially for law enforcement and fire service positions (Lowry 1994).

The current assessment center process was first described by Bray in his pioneering studies for the AT&T corporation (Bray et al. 1974). Although there have been studies that question the validity of the assessment center (for example, Sackett 1987), there is an overwhelming body of evidence that supports the validity of the method (for example, Thornton and Byham 1982; and Thornton 1992).

In addition to the demonstrated validity of the assessment center, there has been no reported evidence of improper bias. Cultural diversity in organizations is enhanced by using the assessment center method. In a recent survey of over one hundred users of the assessment center in public sector organizations, more than 90 percent of the respondents reported that assessment center participants who were selected for promotion performed satisfactorily or better in their new jobs. No respondents reported any adverse impact or other evidence of improper bias (Lowry 1994).

Assessment centers are widely accepted by management and participants and their unions. Managers are impressed by the relevance of the exercises to the real world within their organizations. Participants and their unions generally see assessment centers as a fair and true test of their ability to do the job.

Organizations using the assessment center realize several important benefits. The first such benefit is the valid prediction of managerial potential provided by a properly conducted assessment center. The next benefit accrues to the participants. They receive feedback about their specific strengths and weaknesses and their ability to do relevant tasks. Another, less obvious, benefit is the positive effect of assessor training. Management personnel who receive training as assessors and who participate in the evaluation process refine their own skills. Many organizations train more of their management personnel to be assessors than they will every need just because they see this as an important and effective way of improving management skills. Other benefits of the assessment center process include the early identification of management talent and the diagnosis of training needs.

There is one reported disadvantage to the assessment center—the cost (Lowry 1994). It is estimated that the average cost per candidate in a properly conducted assessment center is approximately $350. On one hand, compared with written tests or even oral interviews, this cost appears high to many public sector managers. On the other hand, senior law enforcement and fire service managers report that the perception of fairness and relevance has resulted in a much more satisfied department and has reduced the number of formal complaints and grievances filed by unsuccessful candidates for promotion.

The Assessment Center Process

There is general agreement among researchers and practitioners that assessment centers must have several distinct and essential elements to ensure their validity. These elements are extracted in part from "Guidelines and Ethical Considerations for Assessment Center Operations," authored by the Task Force on Assessment Center Guidelines (1989):

1. It is necessary to first identify the tasks, dimensions, attributes, characteristics, qualities, skills, abilities, motivations, or knowledge that are necessary for effective job performance. This identification is done through a job analysis that also identifies what should be evaluated by the assessment center. Because the job analysis is central to the validity of the assessment center, it is recommended that it be conducted by a professional.
2. Judges (assessors) observe behaviors and classify these behaviors into some meaningful and relevant categories such as tasks, dimensions, etc.
3. The assessment center must be designed to provide information for evaluating the categories previously determined by the job analysis.

4. More than one assessment technique must be used. These can include tests and simulations, among other things. The assessment techniques must provide reliable, objective, and relevant behavioral information for the organization in question.

5. The techniques must allow for multiple opportunities to observe the participant's behavior related to each category being assessed.

6. More than one assessor must evaluate each participant. Information about the participant may be collected and used from peers and self-assessment. Assessors must not know the participant, except in a casual way, and must have never supervised the participant. Age, ethnicity, gender, and functional expertise must be considered in the selection of assessors.

7. Provide enough training so the assessors can consistently evaluate behaviors to arrive at reliable and accurate judgments. The following are considered minimum training goals:
   a. Knowledge of the organization and job.
   b. Knowledge of the assessment techniques and the relevant categories to be evaluated.
   c. Knowledge of expected typical behaviors, and examples of effective and ineffective performance.
   d. Demonstrated ability to record and classify behaviors, and knowledge of the forms used in the center.
   e. Knowledge of the process for evaluation and rating and how integration is to be accomplished.
   f. Knowledge of the rules for dissemination of results, how feedback is to be given, and the use the organization will make of the final results.
   g. Knowledge and practice in the roles to be played by the assessors and role players in the various exercises.

The assessors must prepare some form of report or record of the observations made in each exercise in preparation for the integration process.

The integration of behaviors must be based on a pooling of information from the assessors (integrating discussion), or through a validated statistical integration process. It should be noted that the simple averaging of scores by assessors, with no pooling of information, does not constitute a valid assessment cent

Participants must be informed of the process that is to be used. Feedback about their performance in the center must be made available. Prior training of participants in the process is useful to reduce their anxieties.

Conducting the Assessment Center

The validity of an assessment center is directly related to the way the center is conducted. Failure to follow the previously mentioned guidelines can influence the results and perhaps invalidate the process. This section provides details on the proper way to conduct a valid assessment center.

Prior to the actual conduct of the center, certain essential processes must take place. These include job analysis, developing the exercises, selecting the assessors, and training the assessors and participants. These steps are described below.

Job Analysis

The process begins with a properly conducted job analysis. It should be performed by a professional trained in job analysis procedures. The analysis must be based on the *Uniform Guidelines for Employee Selection Procedures* (Equal Employment Opportunity Commission [EEOC] et al. 1978). Persons knowledgeable of the job under test should be used to provide specific information about the tasks performed and the requisite knowledge, skills, and abilities for effective performance of the job. These persons are referred to as Subject Matter Experts (SMEs). The final product of the job analysis should be a rank-ordered list of tasks arrayed in the order of their importance, and for certain types of assessment centers, a list of the important performance dimensions.

The original assessment center model—described fully by G. C. Thornton in *Assessment Centers in Human Resource Management* (1992)—used performance dimensions as the primary basis for the scores in the assessment center. This "Dimension-Specific" assessment center typically includes constructs such as leadership, planning and organizing, decisionmaking, and judgment, and other skills and abilities, such as oral and written communications.

As the assessment center evolves, new approaches are being used. For example, there is a trend away from the use of some or all performance dimensions. They have been shown to be difficult to define and measure. Leadership is an example of a construct that has not been fully and completely defined. This has led to the use of "Task-Specific" assessment centers. In this type of assessment center no performance dimensions are identified or evaluated. The assessors evaluate only how well the participant performs the elements of one or more job related tasks. They no longer need to attempt to sort out or evaluate performance dimensions. The reliability and validity results from these centers thus far are at least as high as those reported for Dimension-Specific centers (Lowry 1993a).

Developing the Exercises

The job analysis will reveal, among other things, the requisite performance dimensions and the principal tasks performed by the incumbents in the position. The exercises are developed with the aid of the SMEs to give participants the opportunity to perform simulations of the actual tasks. The exercises should be based on the most important tasks the incumbent performs on entry to the job.

The exercises used in assessment centers usually include simulated work activities. The activities might include requirements to respond orally or in writing to requests for information or to present solutions to problems; to interact with peers, subordinates, or superiors; and to respond to operational situations. The use of the SMEs in the development of the exercises ensures the relevancy of the exercises—a critical element of a properly conducted assessment center.

Selecting the Assessors

In most assessment centers, the assessors will observe the participants in one or more exercises. During each exercise, they will record the behaviors, and ultimately record scores for the related performance dimensions, for the elements associated with tasks, or for all of these. (Assessor selection criteria are described in the Task Force's "Guidelines" 1989, and in Lowry 1939b).

In many regions, assessors are "swapped" between organizations, thus reducing the costs of the assessment center. Generally, assessors should come from equivalent organizations and be in the same or higher-level positions as the job under consideration. For first-level supervision jobs, for example, police sergeant or fire officer I, nontechnical, often referred to as "civilian," assessors should generally not be used, unless they have had specific experience in these positions in equivalent organizations, or they can be trained to make judgments concerning the technical aspects that will be evaluated. For middle-management and especially for senior-management positions, civilian assessors are generally appropriate.

Nontechnically qualified assessors can do an effective job in nontechnical exercises. However, they can have difficulty in technical exercises unless the evaluation criteria are exhaustive and the assessors are thoroughly trained. The same rule applies for any assessor: exhaustive evaluation criteria, and careful, complete training.

Training

The assessors and participants must be trained. Contrasted with the private sector where organizations frequently employ full-time assessors, public sector assessors are often doing it for the first time. Assessor training involves how to observe, record, classify, and evaluate behaviors, and the forms and procedures to be followed. The "Guidelines" (Task Force 1989) stress the importance of training and suggest minimum requirements. In Dimension-Specific centers care must be taken to ensure the assessors are fully aware of the definitions of the performance dimensions and have the opportunity to classify multiple behaviors into the proper dimension. The training required for Task-Specific centres is often less than that for Dimension-Specific centers. This is because it is not necessary to train assessors to classify behaviors into performance dimensions.

Participant training should be ongoing process to develop and improve relevant knowledge, skills, and abilities. There is no way to "cram" immediately before an assessment center. Rather, potential participants should seek on-the-job training opportunities and education and training to improve their managerial and supervisory skills. The participant who has taken advantage of these opportunities will be better prepared for the assessment center.

Participant orientation should take place immediately prior to the center to acquaint the participants with the process that will be used, the assessors, the rules that will be followed, and the scheduled time and place for the exercises. It is suggested that participants be given a complete written description of the assessment center process that will be used, at least eight weeks before the center.

What the Assessors Do

The assessors in any properly conducted assessment center will invariably observe, record, classify, and evaluate behaviors. In Dimension-Specific centers the classification process is more extensive than in Task-Specific centers. There are some other differences in the way various assessment centers are conducted, and these will be addressed.

Observing, Recording, Classifying, and Evaluating Behaviors

The assessors will observe the participants and record their behaviors on special observation checklists. These checklists include the important elements of the task to be performed in the exercise, specific performance dimensions to be evaluated in the exercise, or both. On written materials submitted for evaluation, the material itself constitutes the observations. The assessors will, therefore, "mark-up" the written material to identify the important behaviors and the specific task elements or performance dimensions associated with the behavior.

After each exercise, the assessors will highlight the most important and relevant behaviors. In Dimension-Specific centers the assessors will classify the observed behavior and match it with one or more performance dimensions, for example, leadership. In Task-Specific centers the assessors will match the behavior with one or more task elements, for example, "Made the candidate feel at ease?"

The assessors will give the participant an initial score for each performance dimension or task element. In Task-Specific centers, an initial score is given for the overall exercise; this is not always required in Dimension-Specific centers. The assessors will share their observations with the other assessors in an integration discussion before giving final scores. The integration discussion is not required, but it is seen as desirable by assessors.

The integration discussion may be held after each exercise (my preferred way) or when all the exercises are completed. The conduct of the integration discussion has been examined. There is a real possibility that one or more assessors can improperly influence or be influenced by other assessors. Therefore, during the integration discussion no evaluative comments should be made, nor should assessors ever divulge their scores. Tests have shown that these simple procedures reduce the amount of improper influence on assessor scores (Lowry 1991, 1992).

Participant Strengths and Weaknesses

The next step is extremely important. It provides the basis for the feedback to the participants on how well they did in the assessment center. After each exercise, each assessor will list the most important strengths and weaknesses of each participant. It is important that the assessors list specific behaviors that illustrate what they determine to be the participant's most important strengths and weaknesses. These evaluative statements will be provided to the participants without attribution to the assessor.

Scoring

After all the behaviors have been described by the assessors, and the strengths and weaknesses have been listed, they enter a final score for the items on the checklist—task elements, performance dimensions, or both. In some centers, an overall score will be provided for each exercise. Typically, in Dimension-Specific centers the score for each performance dimension is determined during an integration discussion after all the exercises are completed.

The final score for the participant should be based on the weights assigned (if any) to the various performance dimensions, task elements, or exercises. The decision on how to arrive at the final score should be validated and should represent a sound statistical process. One technique that has been used is a simple arithmetic average of the weighted or unweighted scores.

Feedback

The results of the assessment center must be given to the participants. Feedback can be provided in a face-to-face session between the center administrator and the participant. Another technique is to give the participant a written report that summarizes the strengths and weaknesses reported by the assessor, as well as the scores. Regardless of which form is used, feedback is essential. No assessment center should be considered complete without feedback. The participants and assessors should be given the opportunity to express their views about the process. In some cases, participants are asked to comment on the relevancy and fairness of the center. Assessors are often asked to give general comments on participant weaknesses as a form of training-needs analysis.

Conclusion

A properly conducted assessment center is a powerful and effective tool for selecting personnel for hire and promotion. It is also useful for diagnosing training and development needs. The magic words are "properly conducted." The information provided here will help one better understand what a properly designed and conducted assessment center looks like. It will also help if one is either a participant or assessor.

PHILLIP E. LOWRY

BIBLIOGRAPHY

Bray, D. W., R. J. Campbell, D. L. Grant, 1974. *Formative Years in Business: A Long-Term Study of Managerial Lives.* New York: Wiley.

Equal Employment Opportunity Commission (EEOC), Civil Service Commission, Department of Labor, and Department of Justice, 1978. "Adoption by Four Agencies of Uniform Guidelines on Employee Selection Procedures." *Federal Register* 43: 38290–38315.

Lowry, P. E., 1991. "The Assessment Center: Reducing Interassessor Influence." *Public Personnel Management,* vol. 20 (Spring): 19–26.

———,1992. "The Assessment Center: Effects of Varying Consensus Procedures." *Public Personnel Management,* vol. 21 (Summer): 171–184.

———,1993a. "The Assessment Center Process: Assessing Leadership in the Public Sector." Paper presented to the 1993 Annual Meeting of the International Personnel Management Association Assessment Council, Sacramento, CA, June 21, 1993, and subsequently accepted for publication in *Public Personnel Management.*

———, 1993b. "The Assessment Center: An Examination of the Effects of Assessor Characteristics on Assessor Scores." Public Personnel Management, vol. 22 (Fall): 487–501.

———, 1994. "A Survey of the Assessment Center Process in the Public Sector." Paper presented to the 1994 Annual Meeting of the International Personnel Management Association Assessment Council, Charleston, SC, June 29, 1994.

Sackett, P. R., 1987. "Assessment Centers and Content Validity: Some Neglected Issues." *Personnel Psychology,* vol. 40: 13–25.

Society of Industrial and Organizational Psychology, Inc., 1987. *Principles for the Validation and Use of Personnel Selection Procedures.* 3d ed. College Park, MD: Society of Industrial and Organizational Psychology.

Task Force on Assessment Center Guidelines, 1989. "Guidelines and Ethical Considerations for Assessment Center Operations." *Public Personnel Management,* vol. 18 (Winter): 457–70.

Thornton, G. C., 1992. *Assessment Centers in Human Resource Management.* Reading: Addison-Wesley.

Thornton, G. C., III, and W. C. Byham, 1982. Assessment Centers and Managerial Performance. New York: Academic Press.

ASSOCIATION FOR RESEARCH ON NON-PROFIT ORGANIZATIONS AND VOLUNTARY ACTION (ARNOVA).

An association made up of scholars and practitioners representing over twenty disciplines, who are engaged in philanthropic and nonprofit studies, founded originally in 1971 as the Association of Voluntary Action Scholars (AVAS). By the mid-1990s, the membership represented scholars and practitioners from over fifteen nations.

As a 501(c)(3) organization (tax-exempt charity under the Internal Revenue Code), ARNOVA has officers, board members, and a growing general membership of scholars and practitioners. The association is self-defined in its membership literature as "the only independent multi-disciplinary scholarly association with a primary commitment to promoting research on the wide variety and forms of philanthropic, voluntary and nonprofit sector activities." Similar to other professional organizations, ARNOVA encourages research and its dissemination by providing a forum through which scholars and practitioners, working in academic and applied settings across disciplines, can interact and benefit from the experiences and expertise of their diverse colleagues.

ARNOVA sponsors an annual conference and has spawned regional colloquiums. Its members share research through open forums and roundtable discussions, interdisciplinary workshops, and panels in which new and ongoing research is presented, critiqued, and compared to the general theory in the field. Membership in the organization offers informal networking opportunities for members seeking an ongoing dynamic interaction on research works in progress. With the availability of Internet capacity, these opportunities are growing.

The benefits of ARNOVA membership include conference participation as well as subscriptions to the ARNOVA-sponsored journals *Nonprofit and Voluntary Sector Quarterly, Citizen Participation and Voluntary Action Abstracts;* and *ARNOVA News;* as well as special publications such as the *Annual Conference Proceedings* in which abstracts of conference papers appear. Membership also provides discounts on related publications, and timely announcements of related conferences and research opportunities.

Over the years the association has become more institutionalized. This is reflected by awards presented annually to honor members' work and scholarship. These include recognition at the annual conference for the year's outstanding article published in *Nonprofit and Voluntary Sector Quarterly;* for the year's outstanding Ph.D. dissertation; for distinguished book; for distinguished contributions to research; and a service award. Volunteer committees review nominations and works nominated for the specific awards, and membership on the association's various committees is sought annually through requests in *ARNOVA News.*

In December 1994 the organization's executive office moved to Indiana. For information, contact ARNOVA at 550 West North Street, Suite 301, Indianapolis, Indiana 46202.

ERNA GELLES

ASSOCIATION MANAGEMENT.

The administration of democratically governed private, nonprofit organizations that serve the collective needs of their individual or organizational members. According to David Knoke, these "collective action organizations": "(1) seek nonmarket solutions to particular individual or group problems; (2) maintain formal criteria for membership on a voluntary basis; (3) may employ persons under the authority of organizational leaders; and (4) provide formally democratic procedures to involve members in policy decisions" (1990:7).

Association management is a subspeciality of the more general field of nonprofit organization management. Though several dozen universities offer specialized graduate programs in the management of nonprofit organizations, only a few universities, including George Washington University, the University of Maryland, and De Paul University, have had courses of study specifically addressed to association management. The American Society of Association Executives (ASAE) also offers a variety of courses on this subject throughout the United States (Dunlop 1989).

Associations may be roughly classified into four major types, according to whether their members are organizations or individuals, and the sectors of the economy in which their members operate:

1. business trade associations, such as the National Association of Manufacturers, whose members are profit-making businesses;
2. business trade associations, such as the National Association of Realtors, whose members are individual business people;
3. professional associations, such as the American Dental Association or the American Economic Association, whose members are individual professional workers; and
4. philanthropic associations, such as the American Symphony Orchestra League or the Jewish Community Centers Association, whose members are private, nonprofit organizations.

Although these constitute the major categories, there are various other types of associations that fall outside these classes or fall between the categories. For example, the National League of Cities consists of members that are public sector organizations. Labor unions in which membership is voluntary qualify as associations, constituting another category. Finally, associations that attract a mix of individual and organizational members, such as the Child Welfare League of America, fall between the stipulated categories. Knoke (1993) estimates that a third of business trade associations have both organizational and individual members.

Even though all associations are nonprofit and hence exempt from corporate income tax, they are classified under various federal income tax categories, depending on their purposes. These classifications include business leagues [501(c)(6)], social welfare advocacy organizations [501(c)(4)], and charitable organizations [501(c)(3)]. Only the charitable organizations are eligible to receive contributions deductible from personal or corporate income taxes.

Salamon (1992) estimated that there are almost 60,000 nonprofit business and professional associations operating in the United States. However, association management as a career focuses on the minority of these organizations that have substantial budgets and employ significant numbers of paid staff. Knoke (1993) found that roughly three-quarters of the 3,500 national business trade associations that he analyzed have budgets less than $250,000.

The management of associations requires a set of competencies somewhat atypical of management elsewhere in the nonprofit sector or in other parts of the economy. For example, except for charitable and social welfare advocacy organizations, associations do not engage substantially in charitable fund-raising, and even charitable associations will often leave the development of these resources to their local organizational members. Overall, the distinctive character of association management reflects the democratic and membership-driven nature of these organizations. In particular, association managers must commonly be:

- able to facilitate processes of democratic governance, including voting procedures; membership meetings; working with elected officers, volunteer boards, and committees; and other aspects of organizational democracy;
- skillful in marketing the organization to potential new members;
- adept in quality management and sensitive to retaining membership by responding to member needs, including the provision of useful and strategic information and other service benefits;
- skillful in managing controversial operational or policy issues that may divide the membership and undermine organizational unity;
- sophisticated in media relations so as to enhance the standing of the association's membership and promote its positions in the public arena;

- adept in government relations in order to advocate effectively for membership positions on public policy;
- skillful in identifying and educating members to important public issues, trends, and other developments affecting their fields;
- skilled in defining and supervising research on issues of interest to members;
- able to negotiate with contractors, public bodies, and other external parties in order to provide desired services and benefits to members and promote policies beneficial to them;
- able to supervise staff effectively and oversee contractors that provide education, technical assistance, information, and other services to members;
- competent as financial managers in order to ensure the fiscal integrity of their associations; and
- entrepreneurial, exploring new ways to serve members and developing new sources of income in order to expand member benefits or keep membership dues within acceptable limits.

The relative emphases on these different talents varies with the particular association. Smaller associations, for example, depend more heavily on revenue from member dues (Knoke 1993) and hence place greater reliance on management's ability to retain and expand membership. Social welfare advocacy associations may be more focused on public policy, and professional associations may be more concerned with direct member benefits. Larger associations draw on sales revenues more heavily and thus are more likely to emphasize managers' entrepreneurial and marketing talents. Associations with larger memberships, staffs and budgets, or more widely dispersed chapters and branches, will require more fine-tuned bureaucratic, marketing, and political skills to cope with these challenging circumstances.

Associations also differ in the degree to which their agendas and activities are directed by professional staff versus volunteer members. Dunlop (1989) found that associations are becoming more staff-driven over time and that associations with organizational members tend to be more staff-driven than those with individual members. Dunlop attributes the secular trend toward staff dominance to growing staff professionalization and organizational growth and diversification. The balancing of staff strength and volunteer activism has become an important issue in association management as associations demand stronger management and enterprising behavior to cope with an increasingly competitive environment, yet need to remain highly responsive to their memberships. More generally, this issue reflects the inherent tensions in associations between bureaucracy and democratic decision-making. In Knoke's words: "The trick for many organizations is to walk the fine line between democratic paralysis and bureaucratic arrogation" (1990, p. 230).

In national charitable and social welfare associations whose members are local nonprofit organizations, the structural issue involves not only democratic versus bureaucratic decisionmaking but also the nature of the relationship between organizational members and the central association. In particular, Young (1989) identified three major structures among national nonprofit associations: the trade association form, the federal form, and the corporate form. Oster (1992), however, observed the similarity of some national charitable associations to business franchise operations. This range of structures reflects a spectrum of control by which national associations influence their local organizational members and vice versa. That spectrum runs from very loose central control and highly autonomous organizational members (trade association structure), to shared national and local control (the federal structure), to strong central direction (corporate structure), suggesting that the challenges to association managers may be especially diverse in the philanthropic sector.

Since colonial times, associations have been a significant aspect of American public and commercial life (Hall 1992). They have grown increasingly important in recent times, as the political economy has become more diversified and complex and as public policy has become more pervasive, leading many more groups to organize to promote their collective interests (Knoke 1993). In the aggregate, associations now spend more than $60 billion annually and employ more than a half million people (Dunlop 1989). The specialized field of association management has emerged as a result of these developments.

DENNIS R. YOUNG

BIBLIOGRAPHY

Dunlop, James J., 1989. *Leading the Association,* Washington, D.C.: American Society of Association Executives.
Hall, Peter D., 1992. *Inventing the Nonprofit Sector.* Baltimore: Johns Hopkins University Press.
Knoke, David, 1990. *Organizing for Collective Action.* New York: Aldine de Gruyter.
———, 1993. "Trade Associations in the American Political Economy," Chap. 5 in David C. Hammack and Dennis R. Young (eds.), *Nonprofit Organizations in a Market Economy,* San Francisco: Jossey-Bass.
Oster, Sharon M., 1992. "Nonprofit Organizations as Franchise Operations." *Nonprofit Management and Leadership* 2: 223–238.
Salamon, Lester M., 1992. *America's Nonprofit Sector.* New York: Foundation Center.
Young, Dennis R., 1989. "Local Autonomy in a Franchise Age." *Nonprofit and Voluntary Sector Quarterly,* vol. 18, no. 2: 101–117.

ASYMMETRICAL FEDERALISM.
A form of federal organization in which the constituent subnational, geopolitical entities that comprise the country—states,

provinces, cantons—are accorded differing jurisdictional powers either under the formal constitution or through informal constitutional practice.

The traditional understanding of federalism as advanced by Kenneth Wheare (1963), and as generally witnessed in the world's federations, is that the constitution will make provision for the national government to possess a certain range of distinct jurisdictional powers and, likewise, that the subnational governments will equally possess a range of different or concurrent powers. The division of powers so organized will assure that all policy fields are assigned to one of the two orders of government and that the various subnational entities are accorded an equality of powers among themselves. One state, for example, is to possess a range of powers equivalent to those held by every other state.

Asymmetrical federal arrangements deviate from this federalist norm by allowing for the differential constitutional treatment of subnational governments. Asymmetrical federal arrangements give priority to certain sociopolitical realities of regional exceptionalism over the principle of regional equality. In theory, the practice of asymmetry can result in particular states or provinces possessing constitutional jurisdiction over certain policy fields, such as immigration and communications, while in other states or provinces possessing such fields would fall under the jurisdiction of the national government. The logic of this dynamic is that certain subregional entities within the broader federation have special interests or cultural affiliations that make them so distinct from the other subregional members that such special treatment is required to satisfy the political and cultural needs of the affected entity such that it can comfortably coexist with the other constituent members of the federation.

Although asymmetrical federalism is highly problematic, the difficulties associated with the theory and practice of the concept have not prevented various federal states from experimenting with this form of federal organization.

Canadian history and current constitutional practice offer some fascinating examples of asymmetry. The Constitution Act of 1867 stipulates that both French and English are official languages in the legislature and courts of Quebec; no similar provisions extend to the other provinces of "English" Canada. The Constitution further provides for the provinces of Ontario, New Brunswick, and Nova Scotia, but no others, to transfer jurisdiction over civil law to the federal government. Though this power lies dormant, never having been exercised, it remains a part of the formal Constitution. A similar form of asymmetry, however, was practiced in Canada for some six decades in the late nineteenth and early twentieth centuries. Whereas provinces possess general jurisdiction over natural resources, the three prairie provinces of Manitoba, Saskatchewan, and Alberta were prevented, by the federal government, from exercising such authority until a constitutional amendment of 1930 placed them on an equal footing with their sister provinces. Finally, from 1965, the government of Quebec has exercised its constitutional powers to opt out of a federal national pension plan program; Quebec administers its own similar program.

Given this history of asymmetry, it is not surprising to witness significant political interest being shown in Canada in the late 1980s and early 1990s in the concept of asymmetry as a mechanism to resolve certain of Canada's constitutional dilemmas. One of these concerns the manner in which the province of Quebec can be entrenched within the Canadian federation while recognizing its distinct cultural identity and political interests, while also maintaining a strong national government. In the round of megaconstitutional negotiations in the early 1990s, resulting in the failed Charlottetown Accord, there was serious attention given to proposed reforms that would have witnessed the Government of Quebec being granted jurisdiction over matters of culture, communications, immigration, and trade, though such matters would have remained federal areas of responsibility in the remainder of the country.

Australia, likewise, has made some significant use of the asymmetrical model by means of intergovernmental administrative agreements. The Australian Constitution makes allowance for the creative balancing of jurisdictional responsibilities between the federal Commonwealth government and the government of some or all of the states. Although there are numerous differential revenue arrangements between the Commonwealth and the states, forms of asymmetry are most clearly observed in the field of natural resource development—particularly river management and hydroelectric power generation.

Under the Australian Constitution of 1900 the states are given jurisdiction over principal utilities, water and power, and the Commonwealth has authority over trade and commerce and navigation; both spheres of government thus have jurisdictional capacities with respect to river management. In the River Murray project, involving the Commonwealth government and those of New South Wales, Victoria and South Australia, the federal government has relinquished its authority over the Murray River to a management commission dominated by representatives from the above listed states. In contrast, in the Snowy Mountain development system, these roles have been reversed, with New South Wales and Victoria accepting Commonwealth primacy in the establishment and management of the Snowy River redirection and harnessing plan. Even though these arrangements were very much contingent upon the political will and financial power of the given governments at particular points in time, they have resulted in differential treatment among the states with respect to the policy field of river management.

The Australian experience illustrates the administrative flexibility permitted through asymmetrical arrange-

ments, but it is India that demonstrates how central national power can be enshrined and promoted through asymmetry. Under the Indian Constitution, notwithstanding the division of powers between the national Union government and the states, the Union government is given jurisdictional authority to assume administrative control in any state by a declaration (under broadly specified conditions) of "President's Rule." Further, the Union government has the power to declare a national emergency in one or more states, effectively terminating the authority of the given state government. Although such emergency powers are found in the constitutions of other democratic federal states, such as Canada and Australia, the Indian case is interesting because of the extent of the differential manner in which these special powers have been used.

President's Rule has been used in numerous instances in a number of India's states during the last forty years, such as: Punjab, 1951, 1988; Andhra, 1954; Kerala, 1960, 1964; Orissa, 1961; Kashmir, 1991; Tamil Nadu, 1988; Uttar Pradesh, 1993. In turn, direct emergency power was declared nationwide during the 1975–1977 period by then-primeminister Indira Gandhi, to deal with an alleged threatening insurrection. Under the first set of circumstances what was witnessed is particular states losing their constitutional guarantees of self-government while other states continue to enjoy their powers of constitutional autonomy; under the second circumstance all states were equally disadvantaged by the emergency declaration, though it is to be noted that such Union power can be applied selectively against particular states.

Other examples of asymmetry in certain other countries can be briefly mentioned. The Malaysian Constitution of the early 1960s treated Singapore significantly differently from the other Malaysian states, prompting political dissatisfaction, ultimately leading to the rupture of Singapore from the Malaysian federal union. Even now the Malaysian constitution makes special jurisdictional provisions for the Borneo states of Sarawak and Sabah by which these entities are granted greater powers than the other "mainland" Malaysian states.

This Malaysian approach to asymmetry, in turn, replicates the differential state powers found in the constitution of the Federation of Rhodesia and Nyasaland, 1953–1963; the latter case is another example of asymmetry leading to constitutional collapse.

Despite this checkered history of asymmetry, the current development of the European Union may witness the entrenchment of asymmetrical jurisdictional power arrangements for the member states, as particular states, such as Britain and Denmark, insist on special status for particular legislative fields. The British government, for example, is currently opposed to the application of the European Social Charter to the fields of British labor relations and social welfare policy.

It is interesting to observe that the United States has not experimented with constitutional asymmetry. Although U.S. federal grants-in-aid of particular socioeconomic projects in the United States allow for differences in policies and administration within the states, such federal initiatives do not establish constitutional asymmetry because the states retain their full and equal constitutional powers. Asymmetry connotes differential constitutional powers among subnational governments, not simple policy and administrative differences between such entities.

As the foregoing review of asymmetrical arrangements illustrates, some countries have experimented with asymmetry, but most have not done so to any great degree. Despite the appeal that asymmetry has for acknowledging the unique nature of particular subnational entities of federal states, the logic of asymmetry poses certain major problems.

Asymmetry is often perceived as providing for "special status" for particular regional entities. This special status may be viewed as being unnecessarily beneficial and supportive of a regional government and society, giving rise to political jealousies in other regions not so advantaged. Or it may be viewed as being unnecessarily harsh and detrimental to a particular region, giving rise to a feeling of political discrimination within the region so affected. The former case reflects the arguments often raised against asymmetry in Canada, and the latter reflects opinions often expressed in India. In both cases, asymmetrical constitutional arrangements are subject to criticism on the grounds that asymmetry challenges the fundamental federal principle of the equality of the constituent political entities composing the federal state. When this equality principle is vitiated still other tensions arise.

As asymmetry entails different states or provinces possessing differential jurisdictional powers, this also means that the jurisdictional powers of the federal national government differs throughout the regions. In some areas a particular field of jurisdiction will fall under national authority, but in other regions the same field will be a matter of state or provincial responsibility. The result is a fracturing of national authority, what certain Canadian analysts have referred to as "checkerboard federalism." The fear is that asymmetrical arrangements, though designed to demonstrate sensitivity to particular regions and their socioeconomic concerns, may simply enhance the process of regional particularization to the point of promoting and legitimating secessionist ideas. This approach can be taken in assessing the separation of Singapore from Malaysia.

Asymmetrical arrangements also raise a difficult constitutional law issue with respect to representation in the federal parliament or congress. In the Canadian case, for example, public pension plan policy is a matter of federal jurisdiction, except in quebec where it falls under provincial jurisdiction. Should the members of Parliament from Quebec, however, have a right to vote on federal pension plan policy and legislation as it affects the rest of Canada? It is theoretically possible that the Quebec caucus of the federal Parliament may prove to be the deciding voting bloc with respect to this policy initiative. Should they have the right to exercise such legislative authority when the Parliament in which they sit does not possess legislative jurisdiction within their province?

If one answers this question in the negative, however, one is stipulating that, for certain matters, particular groups of elected representatives must absent themselves from the legislative process, which can have the direct effect of altering the balance of power within the legislature. Within a parliamentary system, what happens if a government loses its majority if it loses a certain bloc of ministers of parliament from a particular region? Does the government fall, or do the rules of parliamentary procedure and confidence have to be redrawn?

These are fundamental questions that go to the heart of the logic of asymmetry and that have never been adequately resolved. In Canada, Australia, and India, these questions have simply been ignored, likely on account of their complexity. In the early Malaysian Constitution, Singapore was compelled to lose parliamentary representation because of its "special status" through asymmetry; this loss of representation quickly became a point of tension between Singapore and Malaya, precipitating the separation of the two.

Asymmetry thus stands as a fascinating variation of the theme of federalism. Given the differential nature of subnational societies in federal states, there can be interest shown by political leaderships in the development of asymmetrical distributions of jurisdictional powers. The very complexities and problems attendant with such arrangements, however, stand as testament to why asymmetry remains as a minor element in federal constitutional design.

DAVID A. JOHNSON

BIBLIOGRAPHY

Brass, Paul R., 1994. *The Politics of India Since Independence*. 2d ed. Cambridge: Cambridge University Press.

Burgess, Michael, and Alain-G. Gagnon, eds., 1993. *Comparative Federalism and Federation: Competing Traditions and Future Directions*. London: Harvester Wheatsheaf.

Hanks, P. J., 1991. *Constitutional Law in Australia*. Sydney: Butterworths.

Hogg, Peter, 1992. *Constitutional Law of Canada*. 3d ed. Toronto: Carswell.

Milne, David, 1991. "Equality or Asymmetry: Why Choose?" In Ronald L. Watts and Douglas M. Brown, eds., *Options for a New Canada*. Toronto: University of Toronto Press.

Seidle, F. Leslie, ed., 1994. *Seeking a New Canadian Partnership: Asymmetrical and Confederal Options.* Ottawa: Institute for Research on Public Policy.
Wheare, Kenneth C., 1963. *Federal Government.* London: Oxford University Press.

AT-RISK POPULATIONS.

The concept of "at risk" applied to organizational theory; refers to dangers that may lead to high rates of "death" among organizations or organizational populations. Similar to the way individuals are pruned to higher death risks based on physical or environmental factors, organizations or organizational populations characterized by identified risk factors are considered to be at higher odds for death. The following sections explain the connection between organizational populations and biological populations, organizational and environmental characteristics determining risk factors, and methodological, conceptual, and theoretical problems associated with the study of organizational populations at risk.

Organizational Populations Versus Biological Populations

Organizational populations are at a constant risk of death. Quantitative-historical studies of organizational populations can identify organizational and environmental characteristics of risk and thus contribute to the understanding and strategy development directed to avoid these risks.

The study of organizational populations at risk has emerged from the biological theories of population ecology (Hawley 1955). These biological theories aimed to explain why we observe so many different kinds of biological species (e.g., animals). The answer to this question was that all of the different species exist in order to allow for ecological selection. In this process the environment selects out the species that were chosen to survive, and extinguishes the species that do not fit the environmental constraints, and thus fail to survive.

The organizational ecologists replicated this question in the context of organizational populations by asking "Why are there so many kinds of organizations?" (Hannan and Freeman 1977, p. 939). This assertion has a "fact" format, but critics believe that it is not clear whether an observation into populations of organizations supports it. C. Perrow (1986, pp. 212–213) argued that there are very few organizations that are of the same kind in the major industries. There is not much variation among units (species-wise), but historical data show that the large corporations—the conglomerates—rarely die. In addition, the theory does not apply to public sector organizations that are not selected by efficiency and adaptation criteria but rather by

"value" to society. For example, schools, fire stations, and libraries do not become "extinct" when they fail to adjust to environmental needs, but continue to exist as a result of their contribution to society, which is beyond economic criteria per se.

Another problem in the transformation of the biological theory to the organizational one is in the nature of the environment. On one hand, the biological environment consist of various species, foods, and other survival resources over which the competition determines the odds for survival. Organizations, on the other hand, operate in environments that are composed mainly by human actions. These actions constitute the grounds for politics, power, legitimacy, and support processes, which makes the issues of adaptability, competition, and selection far more complex than they are among biological species. Despite the higher complexity of organizational environments, organizations are capable of influencing their environments more than are biological species. Large organizations such as General Electric, General Motors, or the federal government not only adapt to environmental constraints but also act on influencing their environment (Weick 1979).

The population ecologists of organizations argue that the variations in organizational forms are due to environmental selection rather than adaptation (Aldrich and Pfeffer 1976). According to this view, organizations do not learn enough about changes in the environment and thus fail to adjust their structures and technology to what is needed for adaptation and survival in the changing environment. (It should be noted that, in contrast to this approach, other organizational theorists [for example, Thompson 1967] argue that boundary-spanning units in the organization are directed to gather the needed information on the environment in order to ensure organizational adaptation.)

According to M. T. Hannan and J. Freeman (1977: p. 931) there are four major internal constraints that prevent organizations from change and encourage structural inertia (inability to change organizational structure to respond or adapt to environmental demands requiring change). These internal constraints include: (1) investment in capital equipment and specialized personnel that are not easily transferable to new tasks or functions; (2) limitations in information processing regarding activities and units within the organization; (3) hardships in changing the political balance within organizations; and (4) internal forces directed to sustaining traditions and institutionalized procedures and norms.

In addition there are four external pressures toward inertia. They include: (1) legal and fiscal barriers to enter or exit product markets; (2) lack of information about the environment needed for conducting organizational change; (3) avoiding risks to organizational assets, such as legitimacy due to changes in the organization, will violate the existing claims for legitimacy; and (4) discrepancies between individual and collective rationality. (Collective rationality in choosing the optimal strategy is problematic since a strategy that is rational for a single decisionmaker may not be rational if adopted by a group of decisionmakers.)

The major question exerted from the population ecology theory is "What are the criteria for the environmental selection process?" This question is important for two reasons when the discussion switches to organizational populations: First, it is scientifically interesting to detect the underlying procedures of the selection process, the nature of "at-risk" populations, and their characteristics. Second, the knowledge gained from scientific study of organizational populations can be adapted by organizational strategists and applied toward acquiring a better organizational fit with environmental constraints so that populations at risk can avoid death.

Population theories of organizations deal mainly with risks of death; however, some recent theories have applied the concept of risk to other organizational phenomena such as "births" (Zucker, Darby, and Brewer 1994, Hannan and Freeman 1987), or "inter organizational alliances formation" (Oliver 1993). By doing so, these studies switch the focus from the end side of organizational death to other stages in the "life cycle," while using the concept of at risk to identify other stages or processes of organizational populations. However, due to the limited number of studies in these categories and different assumptions and hypotheses raised in these studies, they are excluded from this discussion.

Organizational Features of Populations at Risk

The concept of "liability of newness" was coined by Stinchcomb (1965, pp. 148–150). This concept refers to the fact that, as a rule, a higher proportion of young organizations suffer from death.

Young Organizations

Stinchcomb offers four major reasons for this phenomena. First, new types of organizations involve new roles, which cannot be taught by predecessors or through communication but require a decisionmaking process and specialized skilled individuals who would invest in education. For example, a manager in a new organization needs to generate rules and procedures that did not exist before and are a result of a skilled decisionmaking process. Second, inventing new roles and matching them to the structure and relations in the organization is timely, generates conflicts, and generates temporary inefficiency. Communication channels are not clear, standard social routines are not established yet,

and personal responsibilities for doing the job are not developed. Third, the fact that new organizations rely on relations among strangers means that trust-based exchanges are not yet developed. This lack in interpersonal trust reduces kinship loyalty and thus efficiency. Fourth, new organizations have not yet established stable ties to the clients of their products or services. These ties are one of the crucial resources directly related to organizational survival.

Studies of organizational populations provide empirical evidence to the risk associated with newness. The mortality rate of organizations starts high and drops steeply with age. This pattern was found in newspaper organizations (Carroll and Delacroix 1982), voluntary social service organizations (Singh, Tucker, and House 1986), and in labor unions and semiconductor firms (Freeman, Carroll, and Hannan 1983). In addition to the liability of newness, some populations suffer from a "liability of adolescence." This liability results from the fact that most organizations have enough initial resources to survive the early stages of their life cycle, and since no sufficient amount of negative information about their performance exists at early stages, rational decisionmakers will not abandon the organization at early stages. Only when the initial resources are exhausted and negative information regarding organizational performance becomes available do organizations risk a higher death rate (Bruderl and Schussler 1990, pp. 533–535).

Small Organizations

Organizational size may be associated with age, but the arguments regarding the risks that small organizational populations confront are different. Larger organizations have advantages over small organizations in raising capital; they face better tax conditions and government regulations and can compete better for qualified personnel (Aldrich and Auster 1986). Studies have found that larger organizations have a lower and later risk pick for death than do smaller organizations (Bruderl and Schussler 1990). In the public sector, smaller agencies may have a smaller client base, which is associated with limited resources and thus a higher risk for death.

Changing Versus Inert Organizations

The ecological literature is somewhat contradictory in its discussion of the relations between structural inertia and risk of organizational death. Structural inertia of organizations refers to continuous stability of the organizational form, technology, procedures, and routines.

At the developing stages of the population ecology paradigm, organizational inertia was considered one of the major risk factors that led to lower adaptation to environmental changes, and thus to selection (e.g., organizational death) (Hannan and Freeman 1977; Stinchcomb 1965). In a later development, Hannan and Freeman (1984, p. 149) suggested that inertia may also be an outcome of environmental selection, and in fact can act as a "protective mechanism" in reducing the risk of organizational death.

Inert organizations enjoy a high level of perceived reliability, since they have the capacity to "produce collective products of a given quality repeatedly." Inert organization are also highly accountable, since they follow norms that are perceived as rational. These two features, reliability and accountability, increase the survival chances of organizations.

Legitimate Organizations

Organizations gain legitimacy when their actions are endorsed by powerful external collective actors and when they establish strong ties to external constituencies (Singh, Tucker, and House 1986, p. 176). Legitimacy is a measure of organizational status, controlled by external entities (Pfeffer and Salancik 1978). It represents a strong match between the values of societies and organizational actions (Meyer and Rowan 1977). Increased organizational legitimacy is considered to be highly related to organizational survival. J. V. Singh, D. J. Tucker, and R. J. House (1986) have studied voluntary social service organizational populations and found that the acquisition of external legitimacy corresponds to a significant reduction in the hazard of organizational death. Organizations that do not gain legitimacy over time experience a constant risk of death, which does not decline with organizational increasing age (Singh, Tucker, and House 1986, p. 189). This finding is consistent with the liability of newness described previously, since it is very hard for young organizations to acquire external legitimation at a young age. It also provides support to the arguments presented by Stinchcomb (1965).

Environmental Features of Populations at Risk

Increased environmental competition means that there is stronger demand for resources compared to their availability. Such a condition may result from either a reduction in resources or an increase in the demand for them.

Competition

In general, competition is a risk to organizational survival and requires adjustments to the changing environment. Strategies for reducing the effects of competition involve issues such as transaction cost (Williamson 1981, 1985); strategy selection (Porter 1980), resource dependency (Pfeffer and Salancik 1978), and networking (Baum and Oliver 1991), which are beyond the scope of this issue.

Density

According to Hannan and Freeman (1988) density of organizational populations captures both legitimating and competitive forces. The pattern of the relations between density and mortality is not linear, but nonmonotonic, having the form of an inverted U. Their argument states that at early stages of development of new organizational forms, the growth of the population legitimates the organizational form and decreases the mortality rate. However, as density increases, the competitive pressures become stronger than the legitimizing forces, and an increase of organizational mortality is evident. In their study of newspaper populations, Hannan and Freeman (1988) argued that increased density led to an increase in the legitimacy of the new form. However, at a later stage, density increased competition, which led to a higher mortality rate. Although the argument of density dependence has a strong logical basis and empirical data has supported it (Carroll and Hannan 1989), problems related to the specification and measurement of legitimacy still need to be resolved (Zucker 1989).

Niches

Niche-width theory (Hannan and Freeman 1977) defines the uniqueness of the organization and the space it captures within a specific "organizational field" (DiMaggio and Powell 1983). It specifies whether and under what conditions specialist or generalist strategies of organizations provide them with survival advantages. Freeman and Hannan (1983, pp. 1126–1129) predicted that when the environment acts irregularly and "patchy," the specialist strategy will reduce organizational mortality rate. This will occur regardless of environmental variability, since it will allow for short rough times; whereas in stable environments, specialist strategy is better for lower levels of environmental variability and generalist strategy fits higher levels of environmental variability. In other words, simple environments are better for specialized organizations, while in complex and unpredicted environments generalist organizations have better survival odds since their wider range of specialization allows them to reduce the overall risks.

Issues in Conducting Organizational Population Analysis

The study of organizational populations at risk is based mainly on populations of organizations at the level of analysis rather than on single organizations.

Levels of Analysis

Populations are composed by many organizations that share the same or similar characteristics in terms of structure, goal, or product. Various studies have focused on populations of newspapers, day care centers, schools, colleges, insurance companies, and wineries. Defining a population of an organization is not a simple issue, and it becomes more complex and less precise when the data come from secondary historical sources.

What does it mean to be similar in some respects? A newspaper organization can be defined in many different ways—it can include or exclude weekly papers, periodicals, professional journals, or political pamphlets. Even if it includes daily papers only, they may be published in different languages, have a local or a national distribution, or be directed to segmented reader populations (e.g., specialists) or to the general population (e.g., generalists), which would mean that they are operating in different environments and that they confront different constraints.

These definition problems make the question of "what constitutes an organizational population?" hard to answer. The biological language provides some help. Hannan and Freeman (1977, p. 935) borrowed from biological theories that define species by their genetic structures and propose to define populations based on their "blueprint for organizational action, for transforming inputs into outputs." B. McKelvey (1982) defined populations as sharing the same elements of dominant competence, which are the "technical core" of the organization, the technical and managerial activities that transform "inputs into those outputs critical to the population's survival" (p. 174).

Not all population ecologists agree on the importance of classification of organizations. B. McKelvey and H. E. Aldrich (1983, p. 125) argued for a "theoretically grounded empirical taxonomy" that would identify organizational populations. They indicated that this will prevent hasty definitions of populations and allow for systematic analysis. Hannan and Freeman favor a more flexible definition that would allow researchers to define their populations based on the focus of their intended analysis. Thus newspaper populations may include all kinds of newspapers in one study and only daily papers in another. This definition flexibility will allow more creative research, but will reduce the comparability of the findings across organizational populations.

Statistical Methods

The study of organizational populations at risk uses several complex statistical methods. The leading method is "event history analysis," which uses "at-risk" events (such as organizational death or birth) as the dependent variable. Statistical programs such as RATE (Tuma 1980) or SAS logistic regressions (Yamaguchi 1991) are used to specify the independent variables that aim to explain organizational death or birth.

Researchers of population ecology are using these models to determine the hazard rate of organizational mortality or birth. This hazard function tests for probability that an organization will die or survive depending on other variables specified in the statistical model. Such variables include firm age, size, industry, legal status,

product orientation, and others—all depend on the theoretical model proposed by the study. Organizational data sets used for this purpose are very large and represent long historical periods, thus the results can offer both longitudinal (historical comparison) or cross-sectional (horizontal comparison) of subpopulations of organizations and their differential impact on organizational mortality probabilities.

Criticism of Population Ecology Theories

The criticism of population ecology focuses on three major issues: problems of defining variables, problems of specifying populations, and problems in adequacy between hypotheses and empirical analyses. These criticisms are related to the problem of falsification, which was raised by K. Popper (1956). Popper argued that scientific theories can never be proven as "true," but they have to be falsifiable. This means that theories have to include clear guidelines as to how and when they can be rejected by empirical findings. As theories "survive" continuous empirical tests, they are corroborated and thus are considered closer to being true. In the following section, I review the major criticisms of the population ecology of organizations theory.

Problems of Defining Organizational Death. Organizational death is not a simple concept, and its measurement is complex. What is the point of time is which an organization is declared "dead?" Is it when it lays off all of its employees? When it closes its gates? or When it informs the economic community that it is closing down? Is a merger with another organization considered death, or does a name-change reflect death? Each of these definitions can be considered "death"; however, they may occur at different times, and, therefore, may generate different results in the statistical analysis. Inadequacy in defining and measuring organizational death leads to problems of generalization, in which it may be hard to compare across studies and systematically corroborate the theory. In addition, there are problems in comparing organizational death across different types of organizational forms. In this context we can ask, Is a death of a business organization similar to the death of a public agency? Not only are these two organizational deaths different in nature, but they should also be explained by different models and independent variables.

Problems of Defining Populations. How does one define an organizational population? There are two answers to this question. The first (Hannan and Freeman 1977) states that the definition of the boundaries of any studied population is mainly a decision of the researcher. In contrast, McKelvey and Aldrich (1983) argue for a systematic empirical taxonomy for defining populations (see "levels of analysis" section). Due to the variations in the definitions of populations' boundaries, empirical findings of studies should be interpreted within the context of the population, and with careful attention to the characteristics of that population.

Adequacy between Theory and Tests. C. Perrow (1986, p. 209) criticized the population ecology theory on the grounds of its inability to be sufficient to explain biological theories. Biological species exist in ecological settings, which determines their ability to adapt and thus their ability to survive. These adaptation process are lengthy, to the degree that it would take centuries for fish to learn to walk. Organizations, however, can react much faster to changes in the environment since they are social rather than biological systems. Weick (1979) argued that organizations are active in enacting their environment and do not "wait" for the environment to "select" them out. Thus, by assuming similarities between the biological and the social theories, the empirical tests fail to check for adaptability efforts. It is obvious that organizations may be selected out by their environment by failing to adapt properly to the changing environment, regardless of their efforts. However, the theory does not provide the tools for accounting for efforts to adapt. Another criticism of the theory is that it avoids tautological arguments (Campbell 1969; Aldrich and Pfeffer 1976). Critics have argued that since organizations that do not match environmental constraints fail, the surviving organizations are, by definition, suited. Since the differences in survival rates or patterns can be detected only retrospectively, this may lead to a circular argument, such as "Bureaucratic structures were selected by a process favoring bureaucratic organizations."

AMALYA OLIVER-LUMERMAN

BIBLIOGRAPHY

Aldrich, H. E., and E. Auster, 1986. "Even Dwarfs Started Small: Liability of Size and Age and Their Strategic Implications." In Barry M. Staw and L. L. Cummings (eds.), *Research In Organizational Behavior*, 8:165–198. Greenwich, CT: JAI Press.

Aldrich, H. E., and J. Pfeffer, 1976. "Environments of Organizations." *Annual Review of Sociology*, 2: 79–105.

Baum, J. A. C., and C. Oliver, 1991. "Institutional Linkages and Organizational Mortality." *Administrative Science Quarterly* 36:187–218.

Bruderl, J., and R. Schussler, 1990. "Organizational Mortality: The Liability of Newness and Adolescence." *Administrative Science Quarterly* 35:530–547.

Campbell, D. T., 1969. "Variation and Selective Retention in Socio-Cultural Evolution." *General Systems* 16:69–85.

Carroll G. R., 1984. "Organizational Ecology." *Annual Review of Sociology* 10:71-93.

Carroll, G. R., and J. Delacroix, 1982. "Organizational Mortality in the Newspaper Industries of Argentina and Ireland: An Ecological Approach." *Administrative Science Quarterly* 27:169–198.

Carroll, G. R., and M. T. Hannan, 1989. "Density Dependence and the Evolution of Newspaper Organizations." *American Sociological Review* 54:524–541.

Freeman, J., G. R. Carroll, and M. T. Hannan, 1983. "The Liability of Newness: Age Dependence in Organizational Death Rates." *American Sociological Review* 48:692–710.

Hannan, M. T., and J. Freeman, 1977. "The Population Ecology of Organizations." *American Journal of Sociology* 88: 1116–1145.

———, 1984 "Structural Inertia and Organizational Change." *American Sociological Review* 49:149–64.

———, 1987. "The Ecology of Organizational Founding: American Labor Unions: 1836–1985." *American Journal of Sociology* 92:910–943.

———, 1988. "Density Dependence in the Growth of Organizational Populations." In Glenn Carroll, *Ecological Models of Organizations*. Cambridge: Harvard University Press.

Hawley, A. H. 1955. *Human Ecology: A Theory of Community Structure*. New York: Ronald.

McKelvey, B. 1982. *Organizational Systematics: Taxonomy, Classification, Evolution*. Berkeley: University of California Press.

McKelvey, W., and H. E. Aldrich, 1983. "Populations, Natural Selection, and Applied Organizational Science." *Administrative Science Quarterly* 28:101–128.

Meyer, J. W., and B. Rowan, 1977. "Institutionalized Organizations: Formal Structure as Myth and Ceremony." *American Journal of Sociology* 83:340–363.

Oliver, A. L., 1993. "New Biotechnology Firms—A Multilevel Analysis of Interorganizational Relations in an Emerging Industry: Bringing Process into Structure." Unpublished dissertation, UCLA.

Perrow, C. 1986. *Complex Organizations: A Critical Essay*. 3d ed. New York: Random House.

Pfeffer, J., and G. R. Salancik, 1978. *The External Control of Organizations*. New York: Harper & Row.

Popper, K. 1956. *The Logic of Scientific Discovery*.

Porter, M. E., 1980. *Competitive Strategy: Techniques for Analyzing Industry and Competitiors*. New York: Free Press.

Singh, J. V., D. J. Tucker, and R. J. House, 1986. "Organizational Legitimacy and the Liability of Newness." *Administrative Science Quarterly* 31:171–193.

Stinchcomb, A. L., 1965. "Social Structure and Organizations. "In J. G. March, (ed.), *Handbook of Organizations*, 153–193. Chicago: Rand-McNally.

Thompson, J. D., 1967. *Organizations in Action*. New York: McGraw-Hill.

Tuma, N., 1980. *Invoking RATE*. 2d ed. Menlo Park, CA: SRI International.

Weick, Karl, E., 1979. *The Social Psychology of Organizing*. 2d ed. Reading, MA.: Addison-Wesley.

Williamson, O. E., 1981. "The Economics of Organization: The Transaction Cost Approach." *American Journal of Sociology* 87:548–577.

———, 1985. *The Economic Institutions of Capitalism*. New York: Free Press.

Yamaguchi, K., 1991. *Event History Analysis*. Vol. 28 of Applied Social Research Method Series, Newbury Park, CA: Sage Publications.

Zucker, L., 1989. "Combining Institutional Theory and Population Ecology: No Legitimacy, No History." *American Sociological Review* 54(4):542–545.

Zucker, L. G., M. Darby, and M. Brewer, 1994. *Intellectual Capital and the Birth of U.S. Biotechnology Enterprise*. Working Paper, National Bureau of Economic Research, Cambridge, MA.

AUDIT. A systematic examination of accounts or program activities, so as to ascertain their accuracy; a means of verifying the detailed transactions underlying any item in a record.

Dictionary definitions emphasize the auditor's roots in financial control. This is still a central feature of governmental audit. As will be noted below, however, audit has moved beyond financial records to a more general concern with program activities. The auditing that will be at the focus of this entry is *external* or *independent* auditing. This is distinguished from *internal* audit, typically conducted by personnel responsible to the head of an administrative unit. External audit is meant to be independent of the administrative or executive agencies whose activities are reviewed. In many countries, the external auditor is attached to the legislature. In order to bolster its independence, the budget of the audit body may escape the control of the executive budget unit, and its personnel may be outside the general civil service.

External audit has become a significant element in the processes of program evaluation, policy implementation, and political accountability. It has attracted more attention than internal audit from scholars concerned with public policy and administration.

A Long History

The *Book of Kings* reports a financial problem with the construction of Solomon's temple. Solomon had to transfer a number of Galilean towns to Hiram of Tyre in order to settle his debts (1 Kings 9:11). The Israelite kings may not have employed auditors as we know them, but they tolerated shrill criticism by prophets. In periods that are dated from 1000 B.C.E. to 587 B.C.E., Nathan was the critic of King David, Elijah and Micaiah of King Ahab, and Jeremiah of Kings Jehoiakim and Zedekiah.

Chinese auditing occurred as early as the Zhou Dynasty in 1100 B.C.E. A predecessor of the United Kingdom's National Audit Office left a record from the twelfth century C.E. of a sentiment that many auditors still share: "The highest skill at the Exchequer does not lie in calculations, but in judgments of all kinds."

The modern history of the U.S. General Accounting Office (GAO) resembles that of numerous other national auditors. Indeed, the GAO has assumed a leadership position among auditors by propagating its conceptions and techniques in the international associations and journals of governmental auditing. Established in 1921 as an organization responsible to congress, the GAO assumed functions that had been conducted in the executive branch by a unit of the Treasury Department. The principal work of the early GAO and its predecessor was the auditing of financial records, checking vouchers against items in appropriations bills that authorized outlays for particular purposes. An important point in the history of government

auditing was the move to sampling vouchers, rather than the examination of each payment. Later auditors began moving outward from a concern with financial records to a concern with the substance of governmental activities. Until now, however, some national auditors continue with the traditional emphasis of finance, with little or no concern for program issues.

Like other auditors, the GAO has concerned itself with the criticism of problems, or negative findings about programs. Auditors generally let some other body praise those program details that perform well.

A prominent figure in the history of auditing is Elmer Staats, Comptroller General of the United States from 1966 to 1981. He expanded the hiring of auditors with training beyond the fields of accounting and law to graduates of social sciences, natural science, and engineering. During the 1970s Staats popularized the concept of *three E*s as the focus of audit: Efficiency, Economy, and Effectiveness.

The Focus of Auditing

The focus of governmental audit has moved in several directions, some of them controversial. Following the theme of Statts's *three E*s, auditing now deals with issues of equality, equity, the environment, ethics, and electronic technology, as well as evaluation and econometric analyses of program impacts. New trends in government, like privatization and the activities of multinational organizations, have attracted the attention of auditors. The labels *operational auditing, effectiveness auditing, performance auditing, performance review, value for money auditing, system-oriented auditing,* and *program evaluation* appear in audit reports. Though some scholars identify these activities with Staats's concern with effectiveness, economy, or efficiency, others identify nuances that distinguish one audit approach from another. The mix of terminology is apparent in the following sentence taken from a publication of the Swedish National Audit Bureau: "The main task of the Swedish National Audit Bureau's Performance Audit Division is to initiate the examination and promotion of effectiveness and efficiency in Sweden's governmental administration."

It is also possible to distinguish between the audit of accomplishments in the short run (what some call *outputs* or *program results);* and accomplishments in the long run (what some call *outcomes* or *implications*).

Although those who speak for certain audit bodies claim that they review only the administration of policy and not the contents of policy itself, some of their organizations report on major policy options while they are awaiting government decisions. The GAO has employed the term *forward-looking audits* to cover reviews of social and economic problems that, in the view of auditors, have not attracted adequate concern from policymakers.

What all of these approaches have in common is the concern of auditors to go beyond their traditional examinations of financial reports or agency compliance with the law. They emphasize an audit of program accomplishments.

In order to support its extensive inquiries, the GAO offers its staff in-house courses in research methods, statistics, and computer science that resemble the programs of social science faculties at respectable universities. Among the sophisticated audit reports of the GAO are:

- a review of education reforms that found indicators for gains in pupil achievement not isolated from the effects of programs to teach testing skills;
- a study of freight trucking that identified some variables useful in predicting high levels of risk from road accidents; and
- a study of fatality rates associated with certain types of passenger vehicles that controlled for numerous variables dealing with traits of drivers, road conditions, and weather.

The Auditor's Structure and Mandate

Numerous audit bodies are headed by a single individual. Others are led by a board or commission, and the German audit body is headed by a body of judges who act like a court in making key decisions about audits. Consistent with principles of independence, head auditor(s) are likely to be appointed for lengthy terms, with extraordinary provisions for removal prior to the expiration of the term. The United States Comptroller General serves for 15 years.

Government auditors typically operate under a law that defines the organizational structure of the audit body, its relationship to the executive and legislative branches, procedures for obtaining funding and personnel, and topics that auditors must examine, may examine, or must not examine. Various audit bodies are explicitly enabled or denied the right to examine the activities of public enterprises and local authorities. Some may examine only those enterprises where the government owns more than one-half of the shares, or has contributed more than one-half of the capital. Some audit bodies are denied the right to examine or assess the goals of government policy. The *three Es* have found their way into a number of laws defining the jurisdictions of state auditors. A typical act enables the auditor to examine the legality of actions undertaken by governmental bodies, as well as the accuracy and completeness of their financial records and the extent to which they have operated in an efficient, economic, and effective manner.

Charting the auditor's jurisdiction is not always simple because laws establishing some bodies may explicitly exclude them from the general statute dealing with the government auditor. Israel's State Comptroller is unusual in having a legal mandate to determine whether audited bodies have operated in a "morally irreproachable manner." This recalls the location of the auditor's head office, only a few kilometers from the place where the prophet Jeremiah directed his shrill criticism against the establishment of his day for its moral shortcomings. The State Comptroller has reprimanded ranking politicians for their patronage activities. It has gone beyond the edges of government, per se, to censure individual citizens who have contributed to more than one political party in violation of what the auditor identifies as appropriate political morals.

In point of fact, the explicit metes and bounds of the auditor's jurisdiction may be less important than the personnel resources at the auditor's disposal and the auditor's decisions as to priorities. Much of what the Israeli State Comptroller has examined under the heading of moral integrity could also have been reached under the headings of legality, economy, efficiency, or effectiveness. Even where audit bodies are denied the right to criticize government policy, they may come so close to that concept (e.g., by examining major program activities that are integrally related to policy goals) as to render the prohibition insignificant.

As auditors have entered issues of special sensitivity, they have become involved in disputes as to "how far should the auditor go?" The Israeli State Comptroller has provoked outbursts from ranking policymakers by reports that expressed opposition to military campaigns. A negative report about weapons research and development reached the Cabinet's table shortly before a vote was scheduled on the continuation of the program. That report may have affected the decision, by a majority of one, to cancel it. The audit produced an outburst against the auditor from the prime minister, who was on the losing side of the vote.

Numerous government auditors tread cautiously in the field of public higher education, perhaps out of respect for the concept of academic freedom and institutional independence. The typical audit in this field concerns issues of institutional administration or equipment acquisition, rather than academic programs. There have been notable exceptions. One report by the UK's National Audit Office (NAO) examined the allocation of resources to specific programs of instruction and research against the criteria of fields said to be important for the national economy. Another report criticized a program to encourage early retirements because it produced staff reductions in those areas (e.g., science and engineering) where the auditor concluded there was a demonstrated need for more teaching. It did not reduce staff numbers in the humanities where, according to the NAO, there were surplus staff and programs. A report of the Swedish National Audit Bureau criticized the suitability of certain courses in programs of architectural education. A report about nine graduate programs at the University of Lund examined the decisions of department heads, the distribution of resources among different categories of students, and outcomes in terms of doctoral dissertations actually completed. The conclusions identified "good" and "bad" departments, recommended restrictions on the number of students in certain programs and the termination of students who prove to be unproductive.

Characteristically, auditors have few if any tangible powers to order that certain activities go forward or desist. The weight of audit reports lies in their prestige and their power to persuade other officials, or the public at large, that officials have erred.

Auditors in some countries have struggled with professional norms concerned with the revelation of wrongdoing against political pressures to support the incumbent regime. The Philippines Commission on Audit produced several incisive criticisms of prominent programs and individuals during the final years of the Marcos regime. Some of these reports were made available for the public at large, while others were provided only to ranking officials. The Commission on Audit also financed research by Filipino scholars, whose papers were delivered at academic conferences. One paper dealt with overt and covert motives for creating government companies and described the tricks used by political insiders to siphon resources from them. Another paper hinted at current problems by describing how a previous generation of Filipino elites had made themselves rich at the state's expense.

The present Comptroller of the United States, Charles A. Bowsher, has argued that there is much work for government auditors that is not on the frontier of their activities. Significant economic and social damage can result from the lack of attention to routine issues of management in established programs. According to Bowsher, the auditor can use the classic principles of public administration to remind key officials about the importance of orderly budgeting, personnel management, program planning, and monitoring.

As auditors have moved into sensitive areas, they have encountered challenges to their activities. One of the individuals criticized by the Israeli State Comptroller for contributing to two political parties appeared on television. He defended his legal and moral rights and questioned the State Comptroller's right to criticize lawful activities that he pursued as a private citizen. He explained that he wanted to assure postelection access for his points of view in an election that seemed likely to be closely contested between the major parties.

A classic book on auditing written by E. Leslie Normanton emphasizes the auditor's role of independence. To the extent that auditors criticize ranking politicians, the goals of government policy, or the failure of policymakers to address social problems, the audit body may lose the capacity to review the activities associated with those politicians or policies in a way that will be seen as objective and above the political fray. Like other key personalities in policymaking and administration, the auditor is well served by political skills and sensitivity. This includes knowing what

to examine, how to present the findings, and how to defend audit activities against other participants in policymaking who attack the auditor for reports that are perceived as interfering in politics or policymaking.

IRA SHARKANSKY

BIBLIOGRAPHY

Brown, Richard E., Thomas P. Gallagher, and Meredith C. Williams, eds. 1982. *Auditing Performance in Government: Concepts and Cases.* New York: Wiley.

Friedberg, Asher, Benjamin Geist, Nissim Mizrahi, and Ira Sharkansky, eds., 1991. *State Audit and Accountability: A Book of Readings.* Jerusalem: Israeli State Comptroller.

Mosher, Frederick C., 1979. *The GAO: The Quest for Accountability in American Government.* Boulder: Westview Press.

Normanton, E. Leslie, 1966. *The Accountability and Audit of Governments: A Comparative Study.* Manchester, England: Manchester University Press.

Sinclair, Sonja, 1979. *Cordial But Not Cosy: A History of the Office of the Auditor General.* Toronto: Maclelland and Stewart.

AUDITOR GENERAL. An office created by parliament in Westminster systems to undertake the external audit of public moneys, to provide independent assurance on public sector financial reports and assess the efficiency and probity of public sector resource usage.

Title of Auditor General

Auditor General refers to the office of the chief public auditor of the realm under Westminster systems of Parliament, and is sometimes joined with the title of Comptroller as in "Comptroller and Auditor General" of the United Kingdom. The title was established with the British Exchequer and Audit Departments Act of 1866, although the functions and practices of having a chief government auditor predated the legislation in the position of "Comptroller of the Exchequer." The position has become synonymous with public auditing, and is retained by British Commonwealth countries and former colonies even though the titles and structure of the public audit offices have been modernized and streamlined to match contemporary government accounting practices. For example, the British public audit is now undertaken by the National Audit Office, of which the Auditor General is the chief officer, reporting directly to Parliament and to the people. Equivalent titles and structures exist for the function of public auditing in the United States, the European Community (Courts of Auditors), Africa, and many Asian countries. The public auditors now meet and issue auditing standards internationally under the auspices of the International Organisation of Supreme Audit Institutions (INTOSAI).

History of Public Auditing

Public auditing can be defined as an independent assurance that the citizens' resources are being properly managed and accounted for. It is fundamental to the accountability of governments, with a long and ancient tradition that predates the beginnings of commerce. There are references to public auditing in the early civilizations of the Egyptians, the Hebrews, the Greeks, and the Romans. Aristotle in *The Politics* states that "to protect the treasury from being defrauded, let all public money be issued openly in front of the whole city, and let copies of the accounts be deposited in the various wards."

The British system of audit commenced with the Norman invasion. The City of London was subject to audit in 1298, with a dictum that "if a chamberlain, bailiff or other servant failed to account, the auditors could testify and have him arrested under a statute made in 1285". Henry VII (1485–1509) personally undertook audits by regularly inspecting and initialing accounts submitted by the Treasurer of the Chamber. Henry VIII appointed "General-Surveyors" in place of the office of the Exchequer to record his wealth. Medieval audit bodies continued in many countries until around the close of the eighteenth century when the finances of the monarchs were finally separated from their subjects, and parliaments started appointing auditors to represent the people. In France this separation occurred when the office of the Premier President in the Chambre ended with the guillotining of the last de Nicolia. The British Exchequer was replaced by Audit Commissioners in 1832, and the office of Comptroller and Auditor General was established in 1866.

Role and Scope of Public Auditing

The role and scope of public auditing has changed and expanded in line with increased size and complexity of government activities. For example, the auditing authority of the U.S. Congress is the General Accounting Office (GAO), headed by the comptroller general of the United States. The GAO examines the finances of most of the federal government agencies, with the wide ambit of investigating the receipt, disbursement, and application of public funds. This examination has been expanded by the legislature progressively to cover not only accounting systems and transactions but, increasingly, the efficiency and effectiveness of expenditure, incorporating analysis of program management and policy decisions by the executive branch.

Most Auditors General have extended their traditional activities of ensuring compliance with regulations of government revenue collections and expenditures to include reviews of the efficiency, economy, and effectiveness of public resources. They usually stop short of commenting on matters of policy, which is the prerogative of the elected government. The distinction between operational and policy issues is, however, often unclear, particularly in politically sensitive financial areas such as public debt, new program initiatives, and justification of capital investments.

Independence

Independence is a critical characteristic for the successful functioning of the Auditor General's role. Under Westminster principles, the Auditor General reports directly to Parliament and is separate from the executive arm of government. The person who holds the office in bicameral systems can only be removed by both houses of Parliament agreeing to the dismissal. Other issues of independence involve sufficient resourcing of the office, an open and fair system of appointment, and a medium- to long-term appointment (7 to 15 years), which spans electoral terms. A continuing area of debate is the inevitable friction created between the Auditor General and the executive government, and the degree to which the role of auditing can be positive in supporting the financial and managerial reforms taken by many governments—or whether it should be confined to being an observer and commentator only.

Common Issues and Challenges for Auditors General

The common issues and challenges that Auditors General face internationally include the monitoring of the privatization process in all forms, dealing with "fiscal stress" created by the lack of revenue and increased demands for expenditure, monitoring and measuring deficits, debt levels, changing technology, greater accountability expectations from citizens, and, most important, the introduction of generally accepted accounting and reporting principles by every level of government (see **accounting**). Where accrual accounting is introduced into government entities for the first time, the auditors are required to give audit opinions on asset and liability values rather than the simple cash statements. Difficulties in implementing accrual accounting and maintaining basic accounting records and registers, the shortage of skilled accountants, deficiencies in accounting standards relating to public entities, massive restructuring of economies, and the greater need for relevant financial information are all placing pressure on Auditors General.

The role of INTOSAI is to provide international auditing and accounting standards related to government reporting, and information sharing among members, leading to a global awareness of the importance of auditing public institutions. The benefits of this cooperation at an international level have been to strengthen the independence of Auditors General through the implementation of international standards of practice and to compare experiences in facing similar problems.

GRAEME MACMILLAN

BIBLIOGRAPHY

International Journal of Government Accounting, various issues.
Irish, Ronald, 1966. *Auditing.* Melbourne, Australia: Law Book Company Limited.
Normanton, E. L. 1966. *The Accountability and Audit of Governments.* Manchester, England: University Press.
Reports of the Australian National Audit Office and the office of the Victorian Auditor General.

AUSTRALIAN ADMINISTRATIVE TRADITION.

The culture, practices and evolving history of public management in Australia since European settlement. Australian administrative tradition is characterized by an early interventionist role for the state, organizational innovation, and an enduring commitment to a nonpartisan, career public service.

Administrative traditions follow function, and Australian practice has evolved with a changing role and identity for the public sector. In its first phase, the bureaucracy was military, concerned with running penal colonies. As a civil society emerged, the public sector kept much of its directive rule-bound character, but developed distinctive organizational configurations. This long-term pattern began to change in the 1980s, as a new "managerial" public sector emphasised value for money and customer service.

Origins

Australia was claimed for the British Crown in the late eighteenth century and settled by convicts and marines in 1788. The original European colony has been described as the "original Gulag," a harsh and repressive regime in a strange and distant land. Authority centered in the office of governor and was enforced by troops. Convict labor created buildings, roads, farms, and barracks, under military supervision. The small number of free settlers was overshadowed by the economic contribution of the public sector, and state provision of many services remained a defining characteristic of Australian administration.

This tradition of public provision reflected prevailing economic realities. With a small, scattered European population and the high costs of importing materials and machinery, private undertakings were unlikely to succeed. After the subdivision of the original colony in the mid-

nineteenth century into several separate colonies, each with its own Parliament, colonial governments tended to take responsibility, therefore, for utilities such as railways, roads, and ports. Later, they would provide gas and electricity and mail and telephone services. Colonies sponsored immigration and funded settlement of new parts of the continent, usually at tragic cost for the indigenous peoples. Governments regulated industry and labor, and used tariffs to protect local industry.

The state, in sum, was always interventionist. Much of its efforts went into creating the conditions for a private sector and for civil society, and both remained heavily influenced by public sector values.

Indeed, some commentators still characterize Australia as a legally based society in which democratic norms have been abrogated by rule-bound, judicially defined behavior. Certainly, the active and large public sector required by pioneering colonies exhibited a strong emphasis on procedure and probity, on administration through precedent. Timeliness and responsiveness were considered less important than correctness, and authority was heavily structured around hierarchy. Although Australians complimented each other for their egalitarian nature, they favored public administration, which was largely concerned with regulation, offering little scope for personal flexibility or innovation.

Colonial Administration

Though it is easy to criticize colonial administration as concerned with input rather than results, a distinctive and successful pattern of public administration emerged in colonial Australia. This was characterized by a separation of state activities between government departments, under ministers, and free-standing statutory authorities responsible to Parliament. Such corporations were controled by eminent, and sometimes expert, boards and provided much public infrastructure. One colonial politician described the strong Australian attachment to statutory authorities as a means to "keep the railways out of politics, and politics out of the railways." Statutory authorities allowed planning of public provision without the intrusion of vested political and economic interests and reinforced the ideal of a public sector separate from crude ministerial controls.

Other distinctive institutions kept colonial politicians from controling personnel decisions in the core public service. By the late 1880s colonies began creating public service boards to control intake and promotion within the government service. For the next century these boards would administer complex entrance exams, personnel rules, and elaborate appeals systems designed to ensure an independent, professional, nonpartisan public sector. They would oversee the slow shift to a truly merit-based public service.

Observers divide on how successfully Australians created an administrative tradition up to the task of supplying those services that, in other nations, might be left to the market. The two most famous judgments are contradictory. In *Australia,* W. K. Hancock (1930) argued that the distinctive Australian version of "state socialism," was flawed, not least because it was unable to recruit administrators capable of unraveling and understanding economics. The public sector was rule-bound and hierarchical, distrusting the resplendent talent of the highly educated. An emphasis on recruitment at sixteen years of age and promotion through seniority discouraged university graduates from joining. In a celebrated passage, Hancock suggested, "Democratic sentiment applauds the sound argument that every office boy should have a chance to become a manager, and perverts it into a practical rule that no-one shall become managers who has not been an office boy" (p. 142).

Yet in an equally influential assessment, A. F. Davies (1958) argued that "the characteristic talent of Australians . . . is for bureaucracy." This talent, suggested Davies, runs counter to cherished self-image yet has been exercised on a massive scale to produce, in this century, "a national government machine . . . thoroughly professional at the core" (p. 3).

The difference in time between quotations is important. Hancock was reflecting on an extended period of "Australian paternalism," as he termed it, when colonies embarked on "economic adventures" designed to open up the nation by providing infrastructure beyond the resources of the private sector. Hancock felt many of these enterprises misjudged, though he blamed politicians rather than administrators for embarking on public works without "trained economic forethought." He wrote when the Commonwealth public service was still small and under construction. It would make its mark only during World War II, when the demands of total mobilization and challenges of postwar reconstruction drew talented administrators, including many with economics qualifications, to the new national capital in Canberra.

When Davies wrote, at the end of the 1950s, he could look back on the achievements of those new recruits, now senior managers. Australia had successfully established a prosperous postwar society, well serviced with basic utilities and experimenting with public sector provision of university, science, and medical research. The public sector had supplied wondrous technical achievements, such as the Snowy Mountains River Scheme, and long-running unique institutions, including an arbitration system with commissioners regulating labor disputes in the interest of economic growth and social harmony. Regulation and protection of industry appeared to ensure domestic manufacturing, and all political parties had learned to live with a mixed economy, which assumed a major role for public provision. The sector was seen as honest, capable, and reliable.

The Managerialist Challenge

Contemporary commentators now portray the 1950s as a time of comforting illusions. Policies implemented by the public sector, notably tariff protection of local industry, turned out to be counterproductive. Prosperity faltered in the 1970s, and the public sector was blamed for consuming too much of the national product. From 1975 cutbacks in the federal service, and stagnation—with occasional forays into incompetence and corruption—at state level, eroded the confidence and capacity of public administrators.

The impetus for change to Australian public administration arose in this period, but not until the 1980s did major innovation appear. A new mood surfaced first in the Australian states and then, soon after the 1983 election of the Hawke Labor government, in the Commonwealth. By the time academics had found a label for the movement—the derisive "managerialism"—it had already transformed administrative practice.

Managerialism began with the critique that much work done by the public sector was inappropriate. The effort put into detailed regulation was no longer required. Economic growth would follow from freeing up industrial and financial sectors, not from continued state intervention. As governments began to deregulate, the old skills of the public sector had to replaced by a new, entrepreneurial approach. The leading exponent of change, Michael Keating, first Secretary of the Department of Finance, and then of the Department of the Prime Minister and Cabinet, talked of "letting the managers manage." Public sectors should remove their traditional personnel and financial control mechanisms, replacing them with objectives, corporate plans, and transparent budgets. The public sector should get out of areas that could be as well performed by business. The public sector should be smaller, smarter, and cost effective.

For those leading the change, the 1980s and 1990s were the most exciting period since the beginnings of the Commonwealth service in 1901. The whole repertoire of modern public sector management techniques, from contracting out to performance pay, was being introduced. Core public service numbers fell dramatically as large utilities were made autonomous statutory authorities or, increasingly, sold off to the private sector.

For critics, the same period was one almost of vandalism. A proud and capable public sector was being dismantled by people committed to models drawn from the discipline of economics—Hancock's revenge—as economics graduates came to dominate central agencies and define program objectives. One sociologist referred to the "end of the nation-building state," arguing that the shared values across political parties and the bureaucracy that had shaped modern Australia were being replaced by a mean-spirited concern with bottom lines. The "economic rationalists," with their reliance on private sector techniques, were held to blame for the loss of a coherent, integrated state. In such accounts the "thoroughly professional" national government machine became a key social institution, its dismemberment a politically fraught exercise in short-term gain.

Assessing Modern Australian Public Sector Traditions

There is little doubt the managerialist revolution has fundamentally altered public sector practice in Australia, and so the traditions that characterize local public administration. Viewed as a set of institutions, the public sector is smaller and more clearly split into a few core agencies and a large number of business enterprises still, but perhaps only temporarily, under government ownership. Within core agencies, new management practices stress devolution of responsibility, clarification of objectives, and appraisal of performance. Public sector managers are expected to operate within a budget. They are held to account for performance, though the old rules of probity and ethical behavior still apply. The traditional institutions of control, such as Public Service Boards, have disappeared, and rhetoric now stresses risk-taking in search of economies, effectiveness, and client focus. Hierarchies have been flattened, teamwork is expected, and quality has become a central concern.

The roles of public servants are also changing. In 1939 some 75 percent of Commonwealth public servants delivered transport or communications services. All of these functions, and their staffs, have now been transferred to corporations or the private sector. Those public employees who remain are more likely to perform policy work, or to oversee private contractors delivering public-funded services. Even in portfolios such as defense, private companies now run military bases and service military equipment.

Those who remain in public positions are more likely to be female and from non-English-speaking families than their predecessors, though equal opportunity in public employment remains an objective rather than a reality; few state or Commonwealth agencies have yet worked up to a woman chief executive.

The long-term implications of managerialism are less clear. Michael Keating has argued that management reform improves the capacity and responsiveness of the public sector, but not its fundamental objective of service to the government of the day. His critics charge that the instrumental values underpinning managerialist techniques will, after two centuries of successful leadership, remove the capacity of the state to drive national development. Since tradition follows function, managerialism will encourage different patterns of behavior within public administration. A less interventionist state requires less self-confident administrators, and fewer professionals. Alternately, policy skills will become more important, as will evaluation expertise. Both favor university graduates, a now almost-mandatory qualification for public sector managers. Better policy skills can only be a benefit, though in the responsible government model that guides Australia it is the capacity of the political elite rather than their bureaucratic advisers that ultimately sets the character of public actions.

GLYN DAVIS

BIBLIOGRAPHY

Considine, M., 1988. "The Corporate Management Framework As Administrative Science: A Critique." *Australian Journal of Public Administration* 47 (1): 4–18.
Davies, A. F. 1958. *Australian Democracy: An Introduction to the Political System.* London: Longman.
Halligan, J., and J. Power, 1992. *Political Management in the 1990s.* Melbourne, Australia: Oxford University Press.
Hancock, W. K., 1930. *Australia.* London: Ernest Benn.
Painter, M., 1987. *Steering the Modern State.* Sydney, Australia: University of Sydney Press.
Parker, R. S., 1993. *The Administrative Vocation.* Sydney, Australia: Hale and Iremonger.

AUTHORITY. Synonymous with power, authority is the power to control, command, or influence a person or a group of persons, a situation, a decision, or the use of resources. Authority can refere to the power or right given to a government, court, agency or person; or to the person or body of persons who exercise the power. Also, authority can refer to the decree, statute, court rule, or judicial decision that is issued by a person, a body of persons, or a court exercising authority. For example, until the time of Marcus Aurelius, the Roman emperor, the emperor exercised his supreme judicial power in person. In the later Roman Empire, this power was transferred to a council called the consistory, composed largely of jurists, who acted in the name of the emperor, and whose judgments were of equal authority with his rulings. The judgments issued by the consistory were known as *decreta*. It is from *decreta* that the modern word "decree" is derived. Like the consistory, these decrees had the same authority as the personal authority of the emperor.

Authority can refer to the direct power to control, command, or determine that a government, agency, or person has—or to the indirect power that is derived from influence, persuasion, character, ability, or station. Indirect power is often unofficial power. The term "de facto" is used to describe this type of power. De facto power is power that is exercised or possessed in spite of the absence of legal authority.

Authority can be ascribed power or achieved power. Ascribed authority consists of those powers that one obtains because of rank, position, or law. For example, a supervisor has certain power to regulate the conditions of work of a subordinate employee. These powers include both reward and punishment powers. Achieved authority consists of those powers that one obtains because of ability, character, information, or association.

In the United States the highest authority granted by law is the Constitution. In descending order of authority are (1) treaties with foreign powers and acts of Congress, (2) state constitutions, (3) state statutory law, and (4) common law.

Origin and History

"Authority" first appeared as a Middle English word in the early-to-mid 1200s. It was derived from Old French and can be traced back to Latin origins. The wearing of a signet ring in ancient Egypt indicated that one had authority to exercise certain powers. This personal power could be transferred to a written decree. The authenticity of the decree would be indicated by making an impression of the signet ring upon the decree. This practice of marking the authenticity of a decree by an impression from a signet ring of a person with the personal authority to issue such a decree was a common practice throughout history. Contemporary practice still dictates that certain official documents have some symbolic mark to indicate the authenticity of the document; however, the impression of the signet ring to indicate authenticity has been replaced by the embossed seal.

In the Roman Empire the wearing of certain rings indicated one's authority or power and was a practice regulated by law. For example, in the later Roman Empire a gold ring indicated that one was freeborn; a silver ring indicated that one was a freed slave; and, an iron ring indicated that one was a slave.

In both ancient and contemporary societies in Africa positions of authority or power are indicated by the carrying of a fly wisp, mace, or stool. For example, men of authority or "elders" of certain tribes carried three-legged stools approximately 14 inches high. These stools indicated the power of the elder to listen to disputes among members of the tribe and to dictate a solution or settlement to the dispute similar to the power granted to a judge. To indicate that the elder was speaking in an authoritative manner, he would sit upon his "judgment seat" while listening to the parties and rendering his decree.

In South Pacific island and South American tribes it was a common practice to indicate one's authority or power within the tribe by the use of tattoos. Tattoos upon one's body, including the face, indicated one's rank or position in the tribe. Thus, chiefs and other high leaders were frequently decorated with extensive tattoos to indicate their power and rank.

One of the more significant discussions of authority is the topic of sovereignty; the authority a nation exercises over its own citizens. Sovereignty or authority over the citizens of a nation can be derived from (1) the use of force, (2) heirship, or (3) a rational-legal model. In both ancient and contemporary societies there are numerous examples of persons using force to take control of governments. War is an extreme example of such force. When governmental authority is seized by use of force, sovereignty is often in direct opposition to freedom of political expression by the people.

Early Teutonic kings were elected, but this practice ended with primogeniture. The monarchy passed from parent to firstborn children, and under the influence of Christianity the kings of England and Europe were crowned and anointed by ecclesiastical authority. This practice is known as the divine right of kings. It posits that underlying the passing of authority from one monarch to another by heirship is the premise that the monarch is selected by a higher divine authority; thus, creating an obligation for the citizens of the nation to accept the authority of the monarch. This method of establishing the authority of the monarch is much more peaceful than seizing control of the government by force, but it frequently results in a similar state of totalitarianism. Early English and French monarchs, for example, believed that all authority was derived from the Crown, including any authority delegated to Parliament or other political parties. Thus it was believed that in the presence of the monarch this delegated authority ceased to exist. A remnant of this philosophy was seen to be practiced until recently in that the monarch of England was not subject to taxation. The doctrine of the divine right of kings ended in England with the Revolution of 1688 (also known as the Glorious Revolution) and in France with the French Revolution (1789). Today primogeniture is a secular basis for authority with the power of the monarch limited by constitution, legislation, or custom to such powers as: appointments to office, approval or rejection of legislative measures, granting of clemency and pardon, and negotiation of treaties.

Theoretical Framework

Democratic forms of government derive their power from rational-legal models of authority. For example, *Robert's Rules of Order*, not the President is the authority for regulating parliamentary procedures in the U.S. House of Representatives. The explicit agreement to regulate the conduct of members and the consideration of bills before the House is based upon reason and law. The adoption by the House of Representatives of a set of rules to govern behavior reflects the belief that is paralleled in the federal government that authority is neither inherent nor residual, but rests on grants of authority vested by the Constitution.

The origins of the philosophy of limited governmental authority can be attributed to the concept of the social contract. Thomas Hobbes, a seventeenth-century English philosopher, said that individuals accept a common superior power to protect themselves from their own brutish instincts and to make possible the satisfaction of certain human desires. In return for these benefits, it is necessary that the citizens grant to the government certain authority over them. In other words, for the common good, citizens give up some individual liberties, rights, and freedoms. John Locke argued, however, that sovereignty remained vested in the people. Locke said that governments were trustees and that such governments could be legitimately overthrown if they failed to discharge their functions to the people. Locke argued that governmental authority is limited and revocable. Locke's arguments regarding the revocability of governmental authority were to become the foundation for the Declaration of Independence and the revolution against England's rule of the American colonies.

After the successful overthrow of England, the colonies established a new government based upon constitutional authority. Because the new government was a form of federalism in which several political authorities claimed simultaneous loyalties of the citizens of the nation, that is, the federal government, the state government, the county, and the municipal government, the question arose as to which political authority had ultimate claim to sovereignty.

The philosophy of nullification argued that the states were the ultimate source of sovereignty. The government formed immediately following the Revolutionary War adopted the Articles of Confederation as the document defining the power of the government. This document strongly affirmed the principle of nullification.

The thirteen states were considered to be a group of freely associated states with the power to recognize or ignore in accordance with their best interests the actions of the federal government. The result was a weak and limited federal government. The extent of this weakness is illustrated by the fact that the Articles of Confederation did not provide for a federal court. Without such a forum, citizens with legal grievances against each other but who were from different states had no neutral, authoritative agent to resolve such disputes. However, the constitution adopted following the Constitutional Convention provided for a strong federal government with certain general and specific authority over the states. In the course of history, the authority of the federal government increased and the power of the state and local government decreased.

It is interesting to note that with respect to the membership of the United States in the United Nations the same argument regarding the principle of nullification is a major concern. Most member nations, including the United States, accept the authority of the UN over them as limited and revocable. Article 94 of the *United Nations Charter* established the International Court of Justice. Unlike the authority of federal courts over the states, the UN has argued that the authority of the International Court over the United States is valid only if the United States chooses to recognize and comply with such authority. In 1985, President Ronald Reagan formally rejected the policy of automatic compliance with decisions by the United Nations International Court of Justice. (Other major countries that also endorse the principle of nullification of World Court decisions are China, France, Germany, Italy, and countries of the former Soviet Union.)

The Constitution provides for the orderly revocation of grants of power to individuals elected or appointed to office, including federal judges who are appointed for a life term, through the process of impeachment. Using this procedure even the President of the United States can be removed from office under Article I, Section 3 of the Constitution. In more than 200 years only two presidents have come precariously close to removal by impeachment. In 1868, President Andrew Johnson was spared removal from office when the Senate was not able to obtain a two-thirds majority on the vote to impeach him. Congress had attempted to remove him from office for defying the authority of Congress and violating the Tenure of Office Act. In 1974, the House of Representatives Judiciary Committee voted to impeach President Richard M. Nixon for obstructing justice, abusing his constitutional authority, and failing to obey House of Representatives subpoenas in connection with what became known as "Watergate." President Nixon resigned from office and no action was taken on the recommendation. Providing for similar powers to the citizens of the state and municipal governments, state and municipal officials may be removed from office by the process of recall.

The Constitution provides that federal courts have authority over state courts. Using a writ of certiorari, a federal court can require that the record of the proceedings in a state court be sent to the federal court for review. The United States Supreme Court has the same authority over the federal district courts. State constitutions provide for similar authority of the state's supreme court over lower state courts.

In the United States, police powers of state, county, and municipal law enforcement agencies are based upon general legislative authority. State and municipal law enforcement agents are said to have common law arrest powers. These powers are limited only by express provisions contained in the United States Constitution or the state's constitution. Federal law enforcement agencies and federal courts are limited to statutory powers; do not have common law powers. Federal law enforcement agents cannot exercise arrest authority unless a power is specifically authorized by legislation or the Constitution. This provision limits the scope of authority of federal law enforcement agents. Though this authority is limited to statutory powers, it is interesting to note that federal agents' geographical authority is superior to that of state, county, and municipal law enforcement agents. Unless specifically provided by mutual aid agreements, state, county, and municipal law enforcement agents are limited to the exercise of their powers within the political boundaries of the state, county, or municipality, respectively.

The chief administrator of federal law enforcement agencies is appointed by the President with the approval of the Senate. The title of most chief administrators is "director." The chief administrator of state law enforcement agencies is appointed by the governor, and the title of most state chief administrators is also "director." The chief administrator of municipal law enforcement agencies is appointed by the mayor, city council, or a board of police commissioners, and the most common title given to this administrator is "chief of police."

The only *elected* chief administrator of a law enforcement agency is the head of the county sheriff's office. This agency was one of the original law enforcement agencies utilized from the founding of the nation. The office was adopted from England. In the United States, the office of the sheriff was made an elected position to invest the power of the office in the people and not the monarch in an effort to prevent tyranny. The chief administrator's title is "sheriff" and his or her second in command is commonly called the "undersheriff."

Because of the fear of a strong central government by the founders of the United States, the authority of the police was invested in numerous fragmented, semiautonomous law enforcement agencies. The results of this decision is a law enforcement system with overlaying, fragmented authority. Even though a centralized federal law enforcement system having authority over state, county and municipal law enforcement agencies would provide for better efficiency, fear of abuse of authority has resulted in strong resistance to such a centralized law enforcement system in the United States.

Current Practice

Although Congress and the executive branch of the government have great authority in prorogating and enforcing laws, the exercise of this authority is not without accountability and responsibility. For example, in 1935, Congress provided that it was necessary to give notice to the public of the intent to enact a federal regulation, and all federal regulations must be published in the *Federal Register*. A regulation that is not published in the *Federal Register* is not binding upon persons who are unaware of its existence. All federal regulations must be codified and published in a compilation called the *Code of Federal Regulations*. The trend appears to be toward making government more accountable for the authority that it exercises.

All public agencies have a hierarchical model of authority. This pyramid-shaped organizational model invests the greatest authority in the person at the top and lesser degrees of authority as one descends the organizational chart. In those public agencies where employees wear uniforms, the authority of the individual is usually indicated by his or her uniform or by symbolic decorations placed upon that uniform. In the Air Force, Army, and Marines the highest rank is general and the lowest is private. (The highest rank in the Navy is admiral and the lowest rank is seaman.) Silver stars worn on the shoulder straps and collar lapel indicate the rank of general. Though the rank of general was officially created in the United Stated by Congress in 1799, the rank was unofficially ascribed to George Washington in the American Revolution. Prior to World War II there had only been five generals in the United States: Washington, Ulysses S. Grant, William T. Sherman, Philip H. Sheridan, and John J. Pershing. The scarcity of generals ended with World War II.

Authority within these military organizations is divided into two major divisions, enlisted personnel and officers. The hierarchical authority of the enlisted personnel is designated by the classification E–1, E–2, E–3, and so on, where E–1 is the lowest rank and E–9 is the highest rank. Officers are classified by a similar system in which O–1 is the lowest rank and O–9 is the highest rank. There are titles and uniform decorations indicating rank for each classification, that is, private, sergeant, lieutenant, captain, major, and so forth.

Police and correctional agencies use a model of authority similar to military organizations. In justice administration agencies the most commonly used names in designating the hierarchy of authority from least to maximum is police officer, sergeant, lieutenant, captain, and major. Police and correctional agencies do not use the ranks of general or private. Ranks below the chief administrator but above major are frequently identified as assistant chief, deputy chief, undersheriff, or other title. To further identify the authority of the employee, frequently there is a change in the uniform for those ranks of sergeant and below and those of lieutenant and above. To indicate their authority as supervisors persons of the rank of lieutenant and above wear military style shirts, which are white; whereas employees of a lower rank wear colored shirts. The most common colors in police and correctional agencies are blue, dark blue, and tan.

Non–law enforcement state, county, and municipal employees use the same hierarchical model of authority, but do not military style uniforms or use military titles to indicate rank.

Contemporary practice demonstrates an emphasis upon Lock's philosophy of social contracts in which authority is vested in the people. In such management practices as community-based policing and community-based school management, public agencies are acknowledging that their authority is derived ultimately from a grant of power to them by the citizens. Even private organizations acknowledge this philosophy. Current management theories for private organizations emphasize the empowering of employees to make decisions at the line-level without approval from higher management. Advocates such as Tom Peters in *Liberation Management* (1992) indicate that one of the most efficient and productive methods of management involve increasing the authority of the line employee.

JAMES A. FAGIN

BIBLIOGRAPHY

Chang, D. H. and J. A. Fagin, 1985. *Introduction to Criminal Justice.* Lake Geneva, WI: Farley Court of Publishers.

Cox, R. W., S. J. Buck, and B. N. Morgan, 1994. *Public Administration in Theory and Practice.* Englewood Cliffs, NJ: Prentice-Hall.

Fagin, J. A., 1990. "Security Management Policy for the Personal Computer Environment" (pp. 69–93). In Frank Schmalleger, ed. *Computers in Criminal Justice.* Bristol, IN: Wyndham Hall Press.

Frederickson, H. G., ed., 1995. *Ideal and Practice in Council-Manager Government.* Washington, D.C.: International City/County Management Association.

Newell, C., ed., 1993. *The Effective Local Government Manager.* 2d ed. Washington, D.C.: International City/County Management Association.

Peters, T., 1987. *Thriving on Chaos.* New York: Knopf.

———, 1992. *Liberation Management.* New York: Knopf.

Robert, H. M., 1981. *Robert's Rules of Order.* New York.: Scott, Foresman, and Company.

Swanson, C. R., L. Territo, and R. W. Taylor, 1993. *Police Administration* 3d ed. New York: Macmillan.

B

BACKBENCHER. A nonministerial member of a parliamentary assembly. The term is characteristically British in origin and usage and is used to distinguish the majority of elected members of a parliament from "frontbenchers," that is, those who sit on the front or ministerial benches, or "treasury" benches, as they are often termed, in reference to their primary responsibility for controling public expenditure. Frontbenchers occupy their prominent spot in recognition of their executive status as cabinet or junior ministers.

The term "private member" is the traditional description of a backbencher, used by way of contrast to government member or minister. Private members' business is that category of parliamentary business that is not sponsored by the government of the day, and it allows backbenchers to raise for parliamentary consideration items of local interest, representing particular constituents, or of wider community interest where the national parties have yet to declare a firm policy. The standard academic analysis of backbenchers' influence tends to focus on their capacity to use opportunities for private members' business, or their contribution to the business of the House through participation on parliamentary committees. This latter activity lends itself to studies of backbench specialization, where members might build up a profile of expertise on a defined span of policy or administrative matters through their committee assignments (Judge 1981: pp. 186–203).

There are no set parliamentary rules through which backbenchers become frontbenchers; mechanisms of appointment vary with the conventions of different political parties. The rise to executive office is usually associated with support for the chief or prime minister, who either personally or through party ballot arranges for a selection of frontbenchers from the pool of parliamentarians. Leading members of an opposition party or coalition of opposition parties are now termed "opposition frontbenchers" (or "shadow ministers"), in contrast to "opposition backbenchers." Analysts claim that the alliance between the two frontbenches is stronger than the separation between executive government and the legislature: Backbenchers alone have a vested interest in seeking "to hold, or redress, the Executive-Legislative balance in favour of the legislature," (Reid 1966: pp. 25–27).

Backbenchers' institutional interests are not necessarily aligned with those of either set of frontbenchers; their situations are common, regardless of party. Even though the two frontbenches struggle over the reins of government, backbenchers struggle to get access to even basic information about ministerial and bureaucratic performance. Not that they can be taken for granted. Party leaders appreciate the latent power of the backbench, which can bring down even serving prime ministers, like Margaret Thatcher in Britain and Robert Hawke in Australia. Research on "backbench revolt" indicates that even ministries with strong parliamentary majorities can expect to have government legislative proposals defeated or substantially amended by disaffected backbenchers (see, e.g., Norton 1993: pp. 80–83). Some parliamentary parties, as in Canada, are extending their leadership selection process to incorporate conventions of extraparliamentary membership, which effectively frees the parliamentary leadership from immediate dependence on the backbench.

Backbenchers face their own selection uncertainties and must retain the confidence of party preselection officials in their own electorate. The proliferation of local members of parliament's "surgeries" illustrates the abiding concern with community consultation, which can understandably displace competing parliamentary duties. Carefully managed, local party and electorate confidence can give backbenchers a sphere of independence against parliamentary leaders.

The balance of power, however, rests with the frontbench leadership, which exercises two kinds of discipline over backbenchers. First, it can make or break chances of promotion to ministerial or shadow ministerial positions. Even in large parliaments like that in Britain, a quarter to a third of a governing party's members are likely to hold some form of ministerial office. Given the turnover at the top, chances are that by playing it safe a backbencher will secure a ministerial promotion. Even in those parties in which the parliamentary party elects the ministry, the leaders still retain power over portfolio selection, so unwelcome arrivals can be allocated unwelcome ministerial tasks.

Second, the leadership has "the party whips" at their disposal, tasked with marshaling the backbench along ministerially desired debating and voting lines. The British term "lobby fodder" accurately describes the whip's perspective on the backbench. Free, or "unwhipped" votes by which backbenchers may make up their own minds are increasingly rare in parties intent on obtaining or retaining government.

Opportunities available to private members to promote their own interests are limited by competing demands of party frontbenchers. Government backbenchers might play an important part in putting politically convenient parliamentary questions to ministers, but opposition backbenchers face competing interests from their own shadow frontbench. The test case of backbenchers' influence concerns their ability to initiate or amend legislation. United Kingdom figures suggest that government backbenchers are almost twice as likely to achieve legislative amendments as are opposition backbenchers (Norton 1993: p. 83). More latitude and perhaps greater real control is found in internal party meetings, where backbenchers can openly speak their minds.

Backbenchers tend to find their parliamentary hours consumed by committee duties, on party as well as parliamentary committees. Only the latter have considerable powers of public inquiry, protected by parliamentary privilege. Backbench committees for the scrutiny of government administration are among the growth industries of contemporary parliaments. Cynics suggest that they are a clever device invented by political executives to keep the backbench busy and out of harm's way; and some supporting evidence comes from the fact that "oversight" committees do tend to refrain from the hard grind of legislative examination, which might be regarded as the core business of a legislature.

Hope of improvement rests more with backbench will rather than institutional reform. For Westminster-derived parliaments, the public accounts committee, which investigates public service inefficiencies, stands out as one of the model backbench forums, even to the point of reserving the chair for an opposition backbencher, very much the exception to the rule. Opposition backbencher Harold Wilson, later to be Labour prime minister, used his post as chair to prepare for ministerial advancement by presiding over "the only blood sport which is sanctioned by Parliament," (Reid 1966: pp. 105–106). Toleration of such bodies is a test of a frontbench's support for the spirit of the parliamentary backbencher. A fitting UK symbol of the initiative of the backbench is the private member's bill, which effected the 1983 reorganization of the National Audit Office, over the resistance of the government of the day.

JOHN UHR

BIBLIOGRAPHY

Herman, V., ed. 1972. *The Backbencher and Parliament*. London: Macmillan.

Judge, D., 1981. *Backbench Specialisation in the House of Commons*. London: Heinemann.

Norton, P., 1993. *Does Parliament Matter?* Hemel Hempstead, England: Harvester Wheatsheaf.

Reid, G., 1966. *The Politics of Financial Control*. London: Hutchinson.

Richards, P. G., 1972. *The Backbenchers*. London: Faber and Faber.

BALANCED BUDGET REQUIREMENT.

A constitutional or statutory provision requiring a budget in which receipts equal outlays. A balanced budget is a symbol of responsible fiscal policies, sound financial management, and overall good government. Most cities and nearly all states have balanced budget requirements, even though such requirements are not always what they appear to be. The federal government does not have a balanced budget requirement. However, growing concerns in recent years over the persistence of federal deficits and the magnitude of the federal debt have increased the likelihood that a constitutional amendment requiring the federal budget to be balanced will be passed by Congress and sent to the states for possible ratification.

State and Local Requirements

State and local governments typically have balanced budget requirements, but such requirements do not prevent deficits. Deficits are possible because of which budget must be balanced and when it must be balanced.

Forty-nine states, excluding Vermont, have balanced budget requirements. In 35 states the requirement is part of the constitution and in 13 states the requirement is statutory. The U.S. General Accounting Office reports that in Wyoming a balanced budget is neither a constitutional nor a statutory requirement but a requirement in practice.

Which budgets must be balanced? Balanced budget requirements usually extend to the general fund (including trust or other special funds) but do not extend to capital budgets, which are used to fund capital improvements and are financed by the issuance of state debt. State and local governments typically have limits on their capacity to issue debt, expressed as dollar limits or as a percentage of revenue collections or tax base. However, when determining if the budget is in balance, annual principal and interest payments, but not outstanding debt, are taken into account.

When must the budget be balanced? When the governor presents it to the legislature? When the legislature enacts it? At the conclusion of the fiscal year? Answers to these questions vary among the states. Governors in 43 states are required to propose balanced budgets, in 36 states the budget enacted by the legislature must be balanced, and 39 states require a balanced budget at the end of the fiscal year—although 11 of these states permit a deficit to be carried over to the next fiscal year.

States do not have provisions for automatic spending reductions if the proposed or enacted budget is not in balance, but unlike the President of the United States, state governors generally have power to achieve balance during the fiscal year by reducing spending. The National Conference of State Legislatures reports that in many states the governor has unlimited power to reduce spending, in some states gubernatorial power is limited to across-the-board reductions, and in a few states the governor must consult with the legislature before making midyear reductions. Sometimes the appearance of balance is achieved through smoke and mirrors and end-of-year balance is achieved through gimmicks. To achieve the appearance of balance without the necessity of revenue increases or spending reductions, selected expenditures might be shifted off-budget, revenue estimates might deliberately be overestimated and expenditure estimates deliberately underestimated, and pension fund liabilities might temporarily be unfunded. End-of-year balance might be achieved by use of reserves from a rainy-day fund, interfund borrowing, deferring payments until the following year, or by such accounting gimmicks as closing the books for expenditures at the end of the fiscal year (e.g., June 30) and keeping the books open for receipts until perhaps "June 35."

Requirements that local government budgets be balanced are found in state constitutions, state statutes, and local charters. Similar to state practices, many local budgets are required to be balanced upon submission, some also are required to be balanced when adopted, and some also are required to be balanced at the end of the year. Carol Lewis reported that more than four-fifths of the 100 largest U.S. cities balance upon submission and/or adoption.

In addition to constitutional or statutory requirements, state and local governments seek to balance their budgets because investment rating services, such as Moody's and Standard & Poor's, regard budgets with fund balances as evidence of sound financial management practices and credit worthiness. Balanced budgets at the state and local level also are achieved because the norm of "balance" is enforced by professional practice and public expectations.

Proposed Federal Balanced Budget Amendment

During the 50-year period fiscal year (FY) 1947–FY 1996, presidents have proposed balanced budgets to Congress only eight times. The last time the federal fiscal year ended with the budget in balance was 1969. In 1985 Congress passed the Balanced Budget and Emergency Deficit Control Act (also known as the Gramm-Rudman-Hollings Act), which established declining deficit targets aimed at balancing the budget in FY 1991. In 1987 Congress revised that law and adopted higher deficit targets aimed at balancing the budget in 1993.

Dissatisfaction with the performance of Gramm-Rudman-Hollings led to passage of the Budget Enforcement Act (1990), which focused balanced budget efforts more on limiting discretionary spending than on annual deficit reduction targets and established pay-as-you-go rules for revenue reductions and increases in entitlement programs. Even though, beginning in 1993, the deficit declined for three consecutive years, annual deficits in excess of $200 billion and a national debt rapidly approaching $5 trillion have been cited by proponents of a balanced budget amendment as evidence that Congress is unable and unwilling to balance the federal budget: unable, because of spending increases required by entitlement programs, and unwilling, because of spending increases enhancing the political future of individual members. Opponents of a balanced budget amendment contend that it will hinder the federal government's ability to respond to downturns in the economy through countercyclical taxing and spending policies, and spending cuts required to achieve balance will fall disproportionately on social service programs.

The most recent version of a balanced budget amendment to the U.S. Constitution calls for a proposed budget transmitted by the President to Congress in which total outlays must not exceed total receipts. Congress may provide for excess outlays over receipts by a three-fifths vote of each House. Congress may waive the balanced budget requirement for any fiscal year in which a declaration of war is in effect or the United States is engaged in a military conflict that causes an imminent and serious threat to national security and is so declared by a majority of each House. Total receipts shall include all receipts, except those derived from borrowing, and total outlays shall include all outlays, except those for repayment of debt principal.

Debate over a constitutional amendment requiring the federal budget to be balanced is not simply a controversy over financial management, it also is a philosophical debate between conservatives and liberals over the size and role of the federal government. It is a debate over the extent to which the federal government should be responsible for seeking to improve inflation and unemployment conditions through taxing and spending policies, over the scope of Medicare, Social Security and welfare policies, over the benefits and burdens of federal tax policy, and over the assignment of functions among the levels of government in the federal system. It is about politics as well as finance.

THOMAS P. LAUTH

BIBLIOGRAPHY

Albritton, Robert and Ellen Drain, 1987. "Balanced Budgets and State Surpluses: The Politics of Budgeting in Illinois." *Public Administration Review*, vol. 47 (March-April): 135–142.

Hutchison, Tony and Kathy James, 1988. *Legislative Budget Procedures in the Fifty States: A Guide to Appropriations and Budget Processes* (especially 92–95). Denver: National Conference of State Legislatures.

Lewis, Carol W., 1994. "Budgetary Balance: The Norm, Concept, and Practice in Large U.S. Cities," *Public Administration Review*, vol. 54 (November-December): 515–524.

Rubin, Irene S., 1993. *The Politics of Public Budgeting: Getting and Spending, Borrowing and Balancing* (especially 164–206). 2d. ed. Chatham, New Jersey: Chatham House.

Savage, James D., 1988. *Balanced Budgets and American Politics.* Ithaca: Cornell University Press.

U.S. General Accounting Office, 1993. *Balanced Budget Requirements: State Experiences and Implications for the Federal Government* (March): 1–48. Washington, D.C.

BALANCING TEST. Concept utilized by courts in resolving cases, which involves a weighing of the significance of the rights and interests of the respective parties. The concept is often used by trial courts when they are called upon to grant equitable relief, such as in the form of an injunction prohibiting one party from doing an act or allowing a party to do an act, which activity cannot be adequately addressed by an action at law. In ruling on an injunction, courts will attempt to balance the equities between the parties by considering the relative hardship likely to result to either of the parties if the injunction is granted or denied. The overall goal of the court is to fashion an order that will least inconvenience either party and yet assure the prevailing party appropriate relief.

The general concept has gained significant notoriety from its use by appellate courts in United States constitutional law cases. Although the concept has been applied to cases involving almost every constitutionally guaranteed right, it is most often used in First Amendment or freedom of speech cases and Fourth Amendment cases involving administrative searches.

Application of the balancing test emerged when certain factions of the Supreme Court began to accept that the constitutionally guaranteed right of free speech was not absolute at all times and under all circumstances. This led to an attempt to balance First Amendment rights against other interests and gave rise to a significant debate concerning which intrusions or restraints placed upon freedom of speech are constitutionally permissible. Those supporting a balancing test approach are often opposed by those supporting an "absolutist" approach, which holds certain constitutionally protected rights as absolute and not subject to compromise or restriction.

Theoretically, the test is applied to the facts in a case in an attempt to strike a balance between individual free speech interests and societal and governmental interests. In order to restrain free speech, the balancing test must result in a conclusion that there is a superior governmental interest that outweighs individual rights of free speech and to which such individual rights must yield.

In generally applying the balancing test, the Supreme Court has over time evolved certain standards or specific tests that have been applied in free speech cases. For example, utilizing the bad tendency test, the Supreme Court allowed legislative prohibitions against free speech if such speech had a tendency to lead to substantial evil—such as that which may run counter to the public welfare, or that which tends to corrupt public morals, incite crime, or disturb the peace.

This test later gave way to the clear and present danger test, which set forth the standard that the state would not limit free speech based solely upon the dangerous tendency of words alone. The abridgement of the right of free speech could only be justified in cases in which there was a reasonable apprehension of danger resulting from the speech involved.

Later, the clear and present danger test was modified somewhat with what came to be known as the ad hoc balancing test. This test required a case-by-case analysis and a weighing of the individual interests versus societal interests before free speech could be restricted.

At about the same time and in another case, the Court used the rationale that came to be known as the redeeming social value test. The standard espoused in this test held that free speech was not within the confines of the First Amendment and therefore not protected if such speech was utterly without redeeming social importance. It is expected that new and different standards will slowly evolve over time as different issues come before the Court and as the makeup of the Supreme Court itself changes.

The Constitution of the United States places on the Supreme Court the duty to say where an individual's freedom ends and the State's power begins and the balancing test standards derived therefrom are a response to this duty and are the tools used to draw the often fine line between these competing interests.

STEPHEN J. WORRELL

BIBLIOGRAPHY

16A American Jurisprudence. 2d. ed. 1949. "Constitutional Law," §506.
27 American Jurisprudence. 2d. ed. 1966. "Equity," §106.
Hill, Louise L., 1993. Lawyer Advertising. Westport, CN: Quorum Books.
Restatement of the Law. 2d. ed. 1979. "Torts," §941.

BARNARD, CHESTER I. (1886–1961).

Chief executive officer of New Jersey Bell Telephone Company and president of the Rockefeller Foundation, distinguished for his behavioral approach to organization theory and for his book, The Functions of the Executive (1938a), one of the most enduring classics in the literature of twentieth-century management.

Barnard's Early Life

Barnard's birthdate of November 7, 1886, coincided with the dawn of Progressivism in administration, signaled by Henry Towne's 1886 speech to the American Society of Mechanical Engineers and Woodrow Wilson's article, "The Study of Administration," which appeared in 1887 in the Political Science Quarterly. Towne and Wilson argued for the Progressive reform of administrative practices in both voluntary and public organizations. In retrospect, their appeals, occurring close to the time when Barnard was born, seemed to be a most fortuitous coincidence. By 1938, when Barnard published The Functions of the Executive, America had modernized in ways that were to a certain extent consistent with Progressive principles. Few in those days understood as well as Barnard did, the consequences that such modernization had for those professional managers who were responsible for changing and improving the performance of America's private and public institutions.

Barnard was born in Malden, Massachusetts, and soon after his birth his family moved to Cliftondale, where he attended the local public grammar school. Barnard graduated at the age of fifteen and had to provide for his own living. He moved to nearby Boston, where he learned and practiced the trade of piano tuner for two years. But Barnard decided that he was destined for better things in life and that this ambition required more education. So he applied and was admitted to Mt. Hermon, a trade and college preparatory school, founded by the famous evangelist, Dwight Lyman Moody. Through a work-study program, poor but deserving boys were given the opportunity to advance their job skills or to move on to college.

Barnard chose the college preparatory curriculum, which he followed for two and one-half years as a resident student. He left Mt. Hermon without taking a diploma because he had already passed the entrance examination and was accepted to Harvard College. He entered the college in 1906 as a member of the fabled class of 1910, which included T. S. Eliot and Walter Lippman. Barnard did not receive a Harvard degree, having left the university in 1909 with some requirements unsatisfied.

He took a position in the statistics department at American Telephone and Telegraph company (AT&T), which his boyhood friend, Walter Gifford, had just established. The statistics department had a broadly defined information-gathering and distributing function. Barnard's first task was to collect and analyze foreign telephone rates and services. His knowledge of several European languages and his analytical skills were well suited to this job. Barnard was quickly promoted to "commercial engineer" and served for a short time in 1917 with the War Industries Board as a technical adviser to the rate commission of the U.S. Telephone Administration. This was Barnard's first important public service appointment in a long career that included many other such assignments over and above his regular duties at AT&T.

Barnard's greatest accomplishment as a commercial engineer came when he successfully presented the case before the Colorado Public Service Commission in 1918 for a major rate increase for the Mountain States Telephone and Telegraph Company. He was rewarded in 1922 for his exemplary staff work with his first line-management job. He was made vice-president and general manager of Pennsylvania Bell Telephone Company, a position that he held for five years.

AT&T's top corporate management decided in 1927 to create a new operating division, the New Jersey Bell Telephone Company (NJBT). Already by 1925, Walter Gifford had been promoted to president of AT&T. Not neglectful of his old friend Barnard, Gifford made him the chief executive officer (CEO) of NJBT. Thus began Barnard's twenty years as head of this company, a tenure that ran concurrently with Walter Gifford's presidency. Both men retired from the Bell System in 1947, with Gifford being AT&T's longest-serving CEO and Barnard's 38-year corporate mentor.

Given AT&T's favored status as a regulated monopoly, company policy encouraged its executives to engage in public service commensurate with the level of their organizational position. Barnard accepted these extra-company responsibilities with a vengeance. His next major service assignment came in 1931 when in the darkest depression days he took charge of the New Jersey Emergency Relief Administration. For his work with this state agency, the New Jersey Exchange Club awarded him its medal for exemplary service. Barnard, proud of these achievements, wrote them up as a "case-study," detailing how he had handled the Trenton "riot" of the unemployed. Barnard presented his case at several Harvard University venues, including the Graduate School of Business Administration.

Government and Foundation Service

As early as 1940 the federal government tried to entice Barnard to Washington, D.C., to help with war preparations. He resisted these overtures for a time but finally in 1941 he accepted the position of Assistant Secretary of the Treasury under Henry Morgenthau, Jr. Barnard went to Washington with many other corporate "dollar-a-year" men, but lasted just six weeks. He returned to Newark and NJBT thoroughly disgusted with Morgenthau and the whole Washington environment, which he believed was dominated by the "reds."

The second time Barnard left NJBT was in spring 1942 to assume the presidency of the United Service Organizations (USO), a nonprofit corporation that provided welfare and recreational services for the armed forces. He gave the USO his full-time attention for a year, returning to NJBT in 1943. He continued to run the USO in absentia until 1945. When he finally stepped down at the war's end President Harry Truman awarded him the Medal of Merit for his service.

Retiring "early" after thirty-eight years with AT&T, Barnard, now sixty-one, was not ready to abandon public life. Already a member of the Rockefeller Foundation's board of trustees, to which he was appointed in 1942, Barnard was named the foundation's new president upon the retirement in 1948 of Raymond B. Fosdick. Considering his age, and the foundation's policy of retiring its officers at sixty-five, Barnard's appointment was viewed as interim and transitional: a steady and experienced administrative hand to guide the foundation through the difficult postwar years. As foundation president, Barnard, for a brief time, came close to the center of American establishment power through his connections with John J. Rockefeller, Jr., John J. McCloy, John Foster Dulles, and Dean Rusk.

While still at the Rockefeller Foundation, Barnard joined the National Science Board (NSB) as one of its charter members, and after six months, when James Conant stepped down as chair, Barnard was appointed to that position in his place. He headed the NSB between 1952 and 1955, which were critical years, because it was then that the NSB formulated policies that guided the National Science Foundation (NSF) during its formative period. In 1956, after six years with the NSB, four as chair, Barnard retired yet again, this time permanently from all major service activities. He died five years later, on June 7, 1961, a few months short of his seventy-fifth birthday.

Intellectual Heritage

Barnard's extensive and varied career as a professional manager should not excite too much wonder. Many other highly placed people of his time moved with similar alacrity among important positions in government, education, philanthropy, and business. Barnard's remarkable legacy to management, and the thing that set him apart from his contemporaries, was his published and archival canon of written works, the most important of which is *The Functions of the Executive* (1938a). Barnard's intellectual enterprise, in its most global aspect, was to legitimize the new American managerial class that had arisen during the two decades between the wars. Although not altogether successful with this undertaking, he did produce many rich concepts that are now commonplace in administration's lexicon. A brief review of his most important contributions to organization and management theory follows in this order: systems theory, cooperation, ethics and moral behavior, decisionmaking, bounded rationality, consent theory of authority, zone of indifference, informal organization, communication, and logical and nonlogical behavior.

Some of Barnard's ideas cannot be understood apart from his connection with Harvard University and its Graduate School of Business Administration after he became a highly placed executive with AT&T. Elton Mayo, Lawrence J. Henderson, Richard Cabot, Wallace B. Donham, Alfred North Whitehead, and many other Harvard luminaries of the 1930s were among his acquaintances. Indeed, A. Lawrence Lowell, president of Harvard University and these named individuals arranged for Barnard to give a series of lectures, the Lowell lectures, on the subject of management and then encouraged him to write the book based on these lectures that became his magnum opus.

Barnard and the members of his Harvard circle had significant influence on each other's thinking. Lawrence J. Henderson, a famous biochemist and the intellectual focal point of his circle, had become a convert to the sociological theories of the Italian economist Vilfredo Pareto. At the heart of Pareto's massive work, *The Mind and Society* (1916, 1923), was the notion of systems theory that deeply impressed Henderson. However, it was left to Barnard to *introduce management* to the idea of organizations as open, "living," systems. Nevertheless, because of Henderson, Paretian concepts permeated the Harvard Business School throughout the 1930s. These ideas, in fact, became the framework for Fritz Roethlisberger's and William Dickson's book about the Hawthorne studies, titled *Management and the Worker* (1939). This book, using a Paretian theoretical foundation, inspired the human relations movement in management that emerged after World War II.

Cooperation, in Barnard's thinking, was equal to systems in conceptual importance. From his perspective, cooperation had the most desirable characteristics of social action because it produced outcomes that were always greater than the sum of individual contributions. From this cooperative "gestalt," surpluses were created that, when distributed equitably, caused the material and psychological satisfactions to emerge that were necessary to elicit from people the behaviors required for the efficient and effective performance of organizations.

Barnard, for the first time in administrative literature, discussed extensively questions about management's *moral* behavior and the complexity of executive moral *responsibility*. He believed that moral integrity in managers was essential since they had to be moral exemplars for others in an organization. They were required to resolve conflicts of moral codes and, ultimately, they had to inculcate morals in others that would coincide with the values of management and the organization. Barnard was acknowledged as management's first moral philosopher because of his Chapter 17 in *The Functions of the Executive* (1938a). That reputation carried over to his years at the Rockefeller Foundation, where he was engaged in a debate over the role that the foundation should play in reconstructing the nation's values after World War II.

Barnard's concept of decisionmaking was easily his most influential, mainly because it inspired Herbert Simon's work on this subject, which Simon pursued in his book *Administrative Behavior* (1947). Simon's ideas, particularly about individual decisionmaking, bore a marked resemblance to Barnard's. For his part, Barnard's two-fold theory of decisionmaking was traceable directly to John R. Commons' labyrinthian book *Institutional Economics* (1934). Barnard, following Commons, compared individual to organizational decisionmaking. On one hand, individual decisions were the results of transactions or exchanges of resources between two persons, one with resources at his or her command and one without—a kind of primitive resource dependency theory. On the other hand, organizational decisionmaking, discussed by Barnard as the theory of opportunism, was a rational process whereby management selected the "strategic factors" for use that contributed the most to organizational performance.

Closely associated with decisionmaking at the organizational level, but especially so at the individual level, was the concept of bounded rationality, usually attributed to Herbert Simon. However, Barnard's similar notion of "limited choice" seemed to be his own invention, several years ahead of Simon. It referred to the condition of human physical, social, and psychological limitations that prevented individuals from maximizing their utilities. Limited choice and bounded rationality meant essentially the same thing. Barnard based his arguments for cooperation on limited choice, whereas Simon's concept of "satisficing" rested on bounded rationality.

The consent theory of authority was the central component in Barnard's approach to formal organizations. Following the political scientist Roberto Michels (1915, 1949), Barnard argued that authority rested with subordinates in hierarchical structures. If they did not follow orders, then, argued Barnard, how could it be said that their superiors had authority over them? Thus authority only existed when it was legitimized by those who were subject to it, and the act of legitimation occurred when subordinates obeyed the orders they received from their bosses or supervisors.

This hypothesized relationship between orders and legitimate authority led Barnard to frame his well-known concept of the "zone of indifference." The zone of indifference was a desirable condition wherein the orders received by subordinates were what they expected to receive. Therefore, high compliance and, by definition, high legitimacy for the source of those orders resulted. Of course, Barnard also allowed for less-desirable states, orders that fell into zones of unacceptability and neutrality. This latter zone is often confused with the zone of indifference, but that is a serious misreading of Barnard's concept.

It was obvious to Barnard that it was in management's interest to increase the number of orders falling within the zone of indifference. To do so, Barnard thought the behavioral sciences could assist managers by showing them how to manipulate employees' attitudes and, consequently, their perception of the work situation. Thus, management did not have to be a passive player in the authority game. Rather the behavioral sciences seemed to demonstrate, to Barnard's satisfaction, that managers could actively intervene in employees' cognitive processes to engineer their perceptions in order to achieve their consent to higher authorities.

Those spontaneous groupings and associations of people that arose in formal organizations have been called "informal organizations." Barnard acknowledged their presence and held them to be natural and necessary for formal organizations. Although Barnard's treatment of the informal organization was perhaps the least satisfying among his many fruitful ideas, it was insightful nonetheless. For example, he felt that formal organizations grew out of spontaneous groupings of people and also that the informal organization legitimized management authority by its collective acceptance of orders. Finally, Barnard argued that group pressure was useful for keeping rebellious indi-

viduals in line. Therefore, the management implications of the informal organization were evident. As managers had to gain access to the individual's psyche in order to shape attitudes, they also had to manipulate group culture and norms so as to make them compatible with formal organizational values.

Communication was the vehicle for transmitting management's rational orders to employees concerning organizational requirements as well as the means by which people expressed their nonlogical personal interests, attitudes, and aspirations. Both aspects of communication were essential in organizational life, and Barnard highlighted them in his book. As a result, communication became one of the best known Barnardian concepts.

But he was not alone in recognizing the importance of this subject. Among his contemporaries at Harvard, Roethlisberger, Mayo, and others emphasized the notion of logical and nonlogical language as being the communication counterparts of logical and nonlogical behavior. They were convinced by the data accumulating from the interview program of the Hawthorne studies that what employees said logically was not what they felt emotionally. Managers had, therefore, to look behind words in order to get at the true reasons for behavior that more often than not arose from nonlogical attitudes, sentiments, and feelings.

Interestingly, the inspiration for this insight did not come from psychologists or psychiatrists but from the redoubtable Pareto, who framed it in terms of "residues and derivations." Residues were subjective, socially created values, norms, symbols, myths, and attitudes that were at the core of individuals' behavior, which people often explained away by giving objective and logical reasons for acting in one way or another. Pareto called these logical disguises derivations, and believed that the relationship between residues and derivations was the source of and explanation for most human behavior. These Paretian notions had powerful analytical values for the Hawthorne researchers, particularly during the interview phase of the program, and their influence on Barnard is evident as well, especially in the Appendix of his book, which he titled "The Mind in Everyday Affairs."

Despite the rich and varied nature of Barnard's organizational concepts, he himself was not satisfied with the framework into which he placed them. Management, he felt, needed an entirely new epistemology that transcended the standard, positive science orthodoxy driving social science research. To advance in this direction, Barnard wanted the social sciences to borrow from the physical sciences methods for the measurement of sense data. However, they should add to this elements of social subjectivism. Furthermore, the social sciences had to work on the connections between sense data and subjectivism, and it was in this regard that Barnard felt they were most deficient.

In the end, Barnard wanted a concrete science of behavior that supported the efforts of administrators in concrete management situations. Of necessity, this new social science had to be integrated, drawing upon history, biosocial facts, and sociology for concepts and data. In short, social science needed a systems epistemology that integrated knowledge from all those sciences that were concerned with behavior. Barnard's book and the architecture of his thought approached organization and administration in this way.

The Functions of the Executive (1938a) has had its fiftieth anniversary, achieving the status of a classic in administrative thought. It is one of the most widely cited sources in management literature, as well as the inspiration for a wealth of critical commentary, theory building, and empirical research. If anything, Barnard's reputation as a thinker in the field of management has risen in the last ten years, and this augers well for the continuation of Barnardian scholarship in the future.

WILLIAM G. SCOTT

BIBLIOGRAPHY

Barnard, Chester I., 1938a. *The Functions of the Executive.* Cambridge: Harvard University Press.
———,1938b. *Organization and Management: Selected Papers.* Cambridge: Harvard University Press.
Commons, John R., 1934. *Institutional Economics: Its Place in Political Economy.* Madison: University of Wisconsin Press.
Michels, Roberto, 1915, 1949. *Political Parties.* Glenco, IL: Free Press.
Pareto, Vilfredo, 1916, 1923. *The Mind and Society.* New York: Harcourt Brace Jovanovich.
Roethlisberger, Fritz J., and William J. Dickson, 1939. *Management and the Worker.* Cambridge: Harvard University Press.
Ryan, Lori V., and William G. Scott, 1995. "Ethics and Organizational Reflection: The Rockefeller Foundation and Postwar 'Moral Deficits,' 1942–1954." *Academy of Management Review,* 20 (2), (April): 438–461.
Scott, William G., 1992. *Chester I. Barnard and the Guardians of the Managerial State.* Lawrence: University Press of Kansas.
Simon, Herbert A., 1947. *Administrative Behavior.* New York: Macmillan.
Williamson, Oliver E., (ed.), 1990. *Organization Theory from Chester Barnard to the Present and Beyond.* New York: Oxford University Press.
Wilson, Woodrow, 1887. "The Study of Administration." *Political Science Quarterly,* vol. 2 (June).
Wolf, William B., 1973. *Conversations With Chester I. Barnard.* ILR Paperback No. 12. Ithaca, NY: Cornell University, School of Industrial and Labor Relations.

BATTERED WOMEN'S MOVEMENT.

The collective efforts of organizations, services, networks, and reform activities serving abused women and their children, also referred to as the shelter or refuge movement. The battered women's movement is a worldwide social movement founded by feminist and grassroots activists to protect abused women and their children and end violence by men against women. It emerged from the women's movements of the 1960s, first in Britain and later in the United States, followed by Canada and Australia, as groups of women, working together to provide refuge and shelter to other women who sought safety from domestic violence, translated personal experiences into political action.

The British Experience

In Britain, efforts on behalf of battered women first coalesced as a social movement with the work of Erin Pizzey. In 1971, Pizzey, working with a small group of local women, founded Chiswick Women's Aid, the first refuge for battered women in England. At any one point in time, it housed dozens of women and their children who were fleeing violence at home but had nowhere to go and no legal recourse.

The common law doctrine of coverture, which defined a woman's condition during marriage, gave a husband the right to "chastise" his wife. In England, a husband's absolute power of chastisement was not abolished until 1829. Domestic chastisement—wife-beating—was legal in most U.S. states until the 1870s. It remains accepted practice in many countries today.

Chiswick Women's Aid provided visibility for the issue and evidence in support of needed services. But it was Pizzey herself who is credited with successfully publicizing what traditionally had been primarily a family matter, its privacy protected by existing social structures and the legal system.

By 1974, other shelters and refuges had been established by Women's Aid groups in England, Scotland, and Wales. In that year, a coalition of these shelters formed the National Women's Aid Federation (NWAF), which espoused the formation of a democratic, egalitarian organization to further the movement. NWAF's decision alienated Pizzey, who wanted to keep control centralized in Chiswick Women's Aid.

The U.S. Movement

Different approaches and conflicting principles also affected the development of the battered women's movement in the United States. Safe places and programs for abused women, such as Haven House in California and Rainbow Retreat in Arizona, both affiliated with Al-Anon (serving spouses of alcoholics), existed in the early 1960s, as did organizations run by religious groups and the Salvation Army. But it was the work of feminist and grassroots activists, as well as of battered women themselves, that mobilized the necessary support and government involvement to enable the movement to gain momentum.

Patterned after the anti-rape movement of the 1970s, which had successfully built networks of political activists and organizations around a single issue, the American battered women's movement established statewide systems of shelters and services to influence policymakers and to secure funding.

The work of movement activists in Britain had helped to create public awareness of the issue in the United States. By the time Women's Advocates in Minnesota and Transition House in Boston opened in the mid-1970s, the most pressing problem facing the American movement was the struggle for funding.

The first U.S. shelters relied on collective, non-hierarchical organizational structures to empower women to work on their own behalf. As the movement spread and new shelters opened, differences in philosophy and political assumptions (often reflecting the communities they served) were evident in the organization of the shelters themselves. Those based on egalitarian, participatory organization models encountered more difficulty in attracting financial support than those with more traditional, hierarchical structures.

Adding to the difficulty in building external support in some areas was a general antipathy toward professionals in the movement. This anti-professionalism was based on the negative experiences battered women had with professionals in the legal, medical, and social work fields who objectified them as "cases" and "clients" and viewed them in terms of then-prevailing victim provocation theories, that is, as having "caused" the abuse.

In the United States, however, shelters were able to fashion hybrid organizational structures that combined democratic principles with sufficient hierarchy to satisfy funders. By 1978, the National Coalition Against Domestic Violence (NCADV) had been established. Prior to that, state coalitions had been developed to foster a range of services, including shelter, individual counseling and group support sessions, children's programs, and empowerment training.

The success of the battered women's movement in expanding such services has caused some to argue that it is no longer a social movement that seeks liberation, equality, women's empowerment, and, ultimately, the end of male violence against women, but rather it has become a collection of government co-opted social service agencies. At the same time, others maintain that the U.S. and British experiences have transformed women's lives and influenced similar actions internationally. Nonetheless, concerns about the effects of increasing formalization and professionalization on the battered women's movement remain, particularly in the United States.

Legislation

In Britain, permanent housing for battered women, in addition to temporary refuge, has been from the outset a key element of the movement's agenda, based on a belief that there cannot be safety without a place to live. Although housing coalitions in England and Scotland obtained legislation giving battered women a legal right to housing apart from the abuser, these statutes are not uniformly enforced. In the United States, there is no comparable legislation. Instead, state legislatures have enacted protection from abuse statutes that provide for the exclusion of the abuser from the home, giving the battered women exclusive possession for defined periods of time.

The Movement's Spread

The tensions within the movement and between a shelter's philosophy and its ability to gain support are not unique to British and American shelters. As the battered women's movement spread to other countries, as activists traveled abroad to provide information and assistance in opening new shelters, and as international conferences (such as the International Conference on Battered Women, held in Amsterdam in 1978, and the 1988 International Women's Conference in Wales) gave women from all parts of the world a forum to discuss the issue, differences in political orientation, feminist tradition, and culture became apparent. These differences would shape their respective programs in different ways. For example, in the United States and Britain, among others, where the issue is no longer a private matter, the focus is now on reforming the criminal justice system. In many third world countries, where wives are possessions, efforts are concentrated on finding ways to provide refuge while working to change women's position in society.

MICHELE T. COLE

BIBLIOGRAPHY

Dobash, R. Emerson, and Russell P. Dobash. 1992. *Women, Violence and Social Change.* London: Routledge.

Heise, Lori, 1989. "Crimes of Gender." *World Watch,* March-April: 12–21.

Lindgren, J. Ralph, and Nadine Taub, 1988. *The Law of Sex Discrimination.* St. Paul, MN: West Publishing.

Pharr, Susanne, 1990. "The Battered Women's Movement: A Brief Retrospective—and a Call for Action." *Transformation,* Vol. 5, no. 5:1–3.

Pizzey, Erin, 1977. *Scream Quietly or the Neighbors Will Hear.* Short Hills, NJ: Ridley Enslow Publishers.

Schecter, Susan, 1982. *Women and Male Violence: The Visions and Struggles of the Battered Women's Movement.* Boston: South End Press.

Walker, Lenore E., 1979. *The Battered Woman.* New York: Harper & Row.

BENEFIT-COST ANALYSIS. A set of systematic procedures for valuing the provision of certain goods and services. Every economic agent, whether it be a household, a firm, or a government, attempts to maximize some defined goals or objectives subject to the resources available to it. A household tries to maximize utility from the consumption of goods and services; a firm tries to maximize profits or minimize losses; and a government aims at maximizing the welfare of its citizens. In order for government programs or projects to result in maximum welfare, it is often necessary to determine the extent to which the benefits resulting from these activities outweigh their costs before decisions can be made to undertake them. This is not an easy task since it involves the entire society and requires, at least in theory, the maximization of a social welfare function that is hard to define in precise measurable terms. Nevertheless, benefit-cost analysis (BCA) remains the single most important decision tool for allocating the scarce resources of a society.

When a government undertakes a policy or provides certain goods or services, it frequently results in the private sector having more of some scarce goods and less of others. BCA offers systematic procedures for valuing these goods; but it is not a panacea for every single social and economic question. It provides no easy solutions, especially when trying to evaluate intangibles like national security or control of environmental pollution, but it ensures consistent decisionmaking that focuses on the appropriate issues. This entry presents a broad overview of the concept of BCA, discusses the economic rationale that provides the framework for doing BCA, and recommends the appropriate decision rule(s) for selecting the best alternative.

Background and Development

Benefit-cost analysis is not a new concept. It was first popularized by Jules Dupit, a ninteenth-century French economist, then by Italian social scientist Vilfredo Pareto, and later in the 1940s by the British economists Nicholas Kaldor and John Hicks. In the United States, it achieved statutory authority with the passage of two major pieces of legislation early this century, the River and Harbor Act of 1902 and the Flood Control Act of 1936. The Flood Control Act was, in fact, the first to enunciate the familiar standard that applies to all benefit-cost analyses—that for a project to be selected, the benefits must exceed the costs—but the act gave no specific guidance on how to define the benefits and costs.

In the 1950s, the report of the Interagency Committee on Water Resources, known as the *Green Book,* tried to bring economic analysis to bear on evaluation decisions. In 1952, the Bureau of Budget (BOB) adopted its own set of criteria for appraising river-development techniques. With the advent of President Lyndon B. Johnson's Great Society Programs in the mid-1960s, BCA formally entered the political arena. During this period, government expenditures on defense, agriculture, health, and education were increasing at a fast pace, and some form of budgetary planning was desperately needed for weighing the benefits and costs of these programs and for setting priorities. Benefit-cost analysis and the adoption of the now famous Planning, Programming, and Budgeting System (PPBS) in 1965, first, by the Defense Department and then by other federal agencies provided that planning. In 1977, twelve years after the formal adoption of PPBS by the federal government, the Office of Management and Budget (OMB) adopted another budget system, called Zero-based Budgeting (ZBB), that incorporated some of the logic of benefit-cost analysis into budgetary decisions. Although PPBS did not have a good record of success, it did lay out the foundations for spreading the benefits of BCA at all levels of government. To this day, it remains one of the most viable techniques for evaluating government projects and programs.

The Basic Conceptual Framework

All benefit-cost analyses begin with a clear statement of goals and objectives. For the private sector, these objectives are usually stated in terms of the financial accounts by which the manager of a firm or business is expected to pursue the interests of its owners and the shareholders. The managers are expected to undertake measures that would maximize the flow of income received over time by the shareholders. Similarly, there are situations in the public sector in which public managers can model their behavior in the same manner as the private sector. The model of private firms applicable to public agencies depends on the type of goods and services these agencies provide. On one hand, public agencies that provide public goods and services for sale can and often do function like privately owned firms, using the conventional price mechanism and other behavioral rules of market operations. On the other hand, public agencies that provide goods and services that cannot be sold to consumers in a businesslike manner, such as national security, must base their decisions on the level of provision and the objectives underlying that provision rather than on the financial criterion alone. In other words, it is not the financial but the social objective that must be the foremost determining factor in making public decisions.

This, however, creates an interesting measurement problem. If the objectives of a project, whether they are social or financial or both, are relevant to the calculation of benefits and costs, then one must ask how these are defined, measured, and valued. The objective of BCA from a public sector perspective is to maximize social welfare, but, as noted earlier, it is not quite so simple to accurately define and measure social welfare. From an operational point of view, however, one needs to consider some criteria by which it is possible to determine the extent to which an accepted project would lead not to maximization, in the conventional sense of the term, but to an improvement in social welfare, assuming one at least has a tacit understanding of what social welfare is.

The interpretation and measurement of social objectives in terms of social welfare have led to two schools of thought—one based on the traditional decisionmaking approach and the other the Paretian approach. According to the former, a social objective is one pursued by someone who is responsible for making decisions that affect the society in the aggregate and one who is also accountable to the public for those decisions. From this point of view, benefit-cost analysis is a process of appraising decision problems as viewed by the decisionmaker or a group of decisionmakers who hold the same view of the society and how its welfare is measured. This situation is more consistent with financial decisionmaking in the private sector. According to the latter, BCA must be based on a set of normative considerations as to what the social objectives ought to be. The underlying notion here is that these objectives can be obtained from a consensus on value judgments of the individuals who make up the society. The proponents of this approach maintain that social objectives should be statements of consensus based on ethical judgments (and a body of such judgments can be found in mainstream welfare economics). The Paretian doctrine, which is the standard-bearer of this approach, simply states that situation A is preferred to situation B if at least one person is better off and no one is worse off. Allocations based on such arguments are considered to be more efficient than any other criteria acceptable to the decisionmakers. Since no one is worse off, the decisionmaker does not have to make interpersonal judgments, thus making it possible to operationalize the approach in some measurable way. Therefore, it makes sense to suggest that, from a Paretian point of view, social welfare involves both economic efficiency and distributional justice.

The basic value judgment on which the Paretian approach rests is ceteris paribus, or, everything else remaining the same, which simply means that an increase in economic efficiency is good if it does not result in a decrease in distributional justice. For instance, if a project or a policy is expected to cause a decrease in economic efficiency, then in order to support it, it would be necessary to show that the decrease in efficiency is outweighed by an improvement along some other dimension of social welfare, such as distributional consideration. However, even though many consider the Paretian approach to be superior to the conventional decisionmaking approach (since it identifies increases or decreases in social welfare), it is impossible to measure every single aspect and value judgment that must go into defining social welfare. Moreover, it is impossible to find a situation in which a particular policy or program leaves no one worse off.

What happens then to those who lose or are made worse off? The Paretian approach allows for a system of side payments from winners to losers, thereby reducing the individual gains while eliminating the losses. In other words, the Pareto improvement criterion makes sure that those who gain are willing to compensate those who lose so that no one will be worse off than they were before, but in the aggregate the society as a whole will be better off. An example that is frequently used by economists should help clarify this. Suppose a government has a policy that reduces taxes on imported goods, which makes most consumers better off since they can buy these goods at a lower price. Although it benefits the consumers, it hurts the domestic producers, who suffer from a shrinking market for their goods. In other words, the system leaves the producers worse off. In a situation such as this, the policymakers can adopt the Kaldor-Hicks principle—according to which the gainers from the policy could compensate the losers and still be better off. The assumption is that the changes in people's welfare can be measured in monetary terms by their "willingness to pay" for the benefits they receive and by the "willingness to accept" compensation by those who lose. These benefits and costs borne by individuals can be aggregated into "social benefits" and "social costs" such that a decision could be accepted only if the social benefits exceed the social costs, that is, if the net social benefit is positive. Therefore, in any choice situation, the fundamental principle is to select the policy or alternative that produces the greatest net benefit or the greatest net social benefit.

Calculating Benefits and Costs

The central problem in any benefit-cost analysis is the valuation of benefits and costs for any project, public or private. But, as noted earlier, the actual valuation becomes more complex for public projects because of the nature of goods and services a government provides and because of the difficulty in measuring social welfare, even with the Pareto improvement criterion. From an operational point of view, one could use the private sector experience as a starting point.

Let us look at a simple problem involving two mutually exclusive projects, X and Y. The real benefits and costs of project X are Bx and C_x and those for project Y are B_y and C_y, respectively. The benefits and costs of each project are realized over time, given by t. To determine whether both projects are admissible and which one is preferable, one can compute the net return by simply subtracting the benefits from the costs of each project. A project is admissible only if its net return is positive, that is, if the benefits exceed the costs. If both projects are admissible, the firm should choose the project with higher net return. But most projects involve a stream of real benefits and returns that occur over time rather than instantaneously. Let us say that Project X has a stream of net returns, some of which may be negative, such that

$$(B_0^x - C_0^x), (B_1^x - C_1^x), (B_2^x - C_2^x), \ldots, (B_t^x - C_t^x).$$

Similarly, Project Y generates streams of costs and benefits B^y and C^y over t' years, where t and t' may not be the same period.

$$(B_0^y - C_0^y), (B_1^y - C_1^y), (B_2^y - C_2^y), \ldots, (B_t^y - C_t^y).$$

For n such projects, one only needs to calculate the differences in the benefits and costs over time and the same expression would apply in each case.

Net Present Value

The above expressions, although correct, raise an interesting issue in the sense that one cannot easily compare the dollar amounts from different time periods because the value of money, called the *time value of money*, does not remain the same over time. In reality, it decreases as time goes by. Inflation, if nothing else, contributes to this general decline in the value of money. The problem can be easily resolved by using a simple concept, called the *present value*, or *PV.* The present value of money is the maximum amount one would be willing to pay today for the right to receive an amount in the future. To put it simply, it is the current worth of a future stream of money, that is, benefits and costs.

Suppose an amount, P, invested today (in the late 1990s) at an interest rate, r, of 5 percent produces $100 next year, the present value of this $100 in today's term is $95.24 = P/(1 + r) = P[1/(1 + r)] = \$100[1/(1 + 0.05)]$. The present value of $100 two years from now in today's term is $90.70 = \$100[1/(1 + 0.05)]^2$, and so on. In general, when the interest rate is r, the present value of a future stream of money in t years is $\$V(1 + r)j$, where V is the value of money at any future point in time and j is the jth period for $j = 1, 2, 3, \ldots, t$. Thus even without inflation, a dollar in the future is worth less than a dollar today and, as such, it must be discounted by an amount equal to the interest rate. The rate at which future returns are discounted to present value is called the *discount rate* and $1(1 + r)$ is called the *discount factor.* We can easily expand this notion to show the present value of a future stream of benefits and costs and their differences over time in the following manner:

$$NPV = \sum_{j=0}^{t} \frac{(Bj - Cj)}{(1 + r)^j}$$

where j extends from 0 to t, r is the rate of discount or interest rate, and *NPV,* called *net present value,* is the difference between the sum of discounted streams of benefits and costs. As a general rule, when comparing n mutually exclusive projects, the one with the highest net present value is the one that should be selected.

Internal Rate of Return

Instead of assuming a value of r a priori and computing the present value on the basis of this, one can try to use an alternative rate, called the *internal rate of return*, or IRR. An internal rate of return is the rate at which the net present value of a discounted stream of benefits and costs is zero, and can be expressed as follows:

$$IRR = \sum_{j=0}^{t} \frac{Bj}{(1 + i)^j} - \sum_{j=0}^{t} \frac{Cj}{(1 + i)^j} = 0$$

where i is the discount rate instead of r. The IRR can be easily compared with the opportunity cost of capital or discount rate to see whether a project has positive net benefits. If $i > r$, the present value of the project is greater than zero and the project should be undertaken; otherwise, it should be rejected. For example, if a project has a return of 4 percent on its investment, but another has 3 percent, obviously the one with the higher return should be undertaken.

Project selection based on IRR could be misleading. Consider again two projects, X and Y, where Project X requires an initial expenditure of $100 and yields $110 a year from now, so that its rate of return is 10 percent. Project Y requires $1,000 today and yields $1,080 in a year, generating a rate of return of 8 percent. Assume that neither project can be duplicated and also that one can borrow and lend freely at 7 percent rate of interest. Thus if one has to use IRR, Project X should be preferred to Project Y since it has a return of $3 ($10 minus $7 in interest costs on an initial investment of $100), which is closer to 0 even though Project Y earns a much higher return ($10 = $80 minus $70 in interest costs on the initial investment of $1,000). Although, theoretically, Project X should be selected if one has to go by IRR; in reality, Project Y should be preferred since it has a much higher return for the same period. Therefore, when projects are of different sizes, on one hand, the internal rate of return does not always serve as an ideal guide. On the other hand, the net present value provides a more realistic scenario in terms of the actual situation.

Looking at the same example, we can see that NPV for Project X is much lower at $2.80 (that is, $-100 + 110/1.07 = 2.8$) than for Project Y which is $9.40 (that is, $-1,000 + 1080/1.07 = 9.346$). Using net present value as the decision rule, one should obviously select Project X, as the case should be.

Benefit-Cost Ratio

A third measure is the benefit-cost ratio, B:C. A benefit-cost ratio can be simply defined as the return on a dollar's worth of investment and can be expressed as $\Sigma_{B_j}/\Sigma_{C_j}$. For a project to be admissible, it is necessary that a project's benefit-cost ratio be greater than one. Application of this rule always gives correct guidance because B/C > 1 implies that B − C > 0, which is equivalent to the present value criterion for admissibility. However, the benefit-cost ratio is not always useful to compare admissible projects.

Consider a community that is considering two methods of disposing of toxic wastes. Method I is a toxic waste dump that produces benefits worth $250 million and costs the community $100 million, thus producing a benefit-cost ratio of 2.5. Method II involves sending the wastes to another community and produces benefits worth $200 million at a cost of $100 million with a benefit-cost ratio of 2. Obviously, method I is preferred since it has a higher B-C ratio. However, if one could add an additional constraint to the scenario by incorporating, say, the costs of seepage-induced crop damage of $40 million in the calculation for method I, the benefit-cost ratio would be ($250 − $40)/$100 = 2.1, which would still be higher than method II and the toxic waste dump should be preferred. Forty million dollars can also be considered as an increase in cost, in which case the BCR would be 1.79 ($250/$140). In sum, both IRR and B:C can lead to incorrect decisions depending on how one calculates benefits and costs, what is included in these calculations, the rate one uses for discounting, the size of projects being compared, and so on.

Public Sector Discount Rate

It is important to recognize that the way the public sector computes its costs, benefits, and discount rates is somewhat different from the private sector. The discount rate used by a private firm usually reflects the rate of return on alternative investment(s). The general understanding here is that the opportunity cost of funds to a firm produces the correct value of 'r', which is not necessarily true for the public sector. There are several reasons that explain why.

Cost of Borrowing Capital

Assume that a government investment project has no bearing on the overall portion of national output devoted to investment and consumption. So a dollar of public investment exactly displaces a dollar of private investment and the benefit-cost problem is simply that of achieving the optimal allocation of this fixed pool of resources devoted to investment. For efficiency to be achieved, private and public investment should be equally profitable. Hence both private and public investment evaluators should use the same investment decision rules. As a general rule, private investors invest up to the point where the gross before-tax rate of return on investment equals the before-tax rate of interest on private securities and, therefore, theoretically at least, it should be used as a standard for public investment. Since the before-tax rate of return measures the marginal productivity of private capital, it also represents the opportunity cost of having these same funds devoted to public investment.

However, the same investment opportunities may not be equally available for public and private investors. Public and private projects may yield different streams of secondary (private) investments, and many public investment projects may be financed by taxes that could ultimately reduce private consumption, thus raising an interesting question: Can the before-tax private market interest rate be viewed as the opportunity cost of public sector capital?

The private market rate of interest is a price that operates in financial markets by equating the demand for saving with that of investment. It shows how private consumers balance the present versus the future. But there are externalities in the market that might require correction of this price. For instance, if society provides for future generations, then the social discount rate will be below the private rate, since for most public investments the benefits come well after the costs, raise the net present value of the public investment project, and stimulate more government investment. When the supply of funds devoted to investment is variable, it is not appropriate to use the before-tax market interest rate. The existence of externalities and the influence of government fiscal and monetary policies could lead to higher interest rates and lower amounts of public investment. Though the private rate applied to public sector ensures optimal allocation of a fixed pool of investment funds, it does not ensure that it is of the right size.

Average or Weighted Average Cost of Capital

Since funds come from both private investment and private consumption, an average or weighted-average approach should be used. For that portion of the public investment financed by reducing private investment, the before-tax return on private investment gives the appropriate marginal opportunity cost. But for that portion financed out of private consumption, the after-tax return on consumer saving gives the relevant marginal cost. According to this rule, r', the weighted average cost of capital is expressed as

$$r' = sr + (1 - s)r_c(1 - t)$$

where s equals the proportion of the resource cost of the public investment coming from private investment, r equals the before-tax interest rate faced by investors, and $r_c(1 - t)$ equals the after-tax rate of return faced by consumers. The weighted-average rate, though useful, has some drawbacks. The existence of market imperfections such as financial regulations and taxes greatly diminish the attractiveness of after-tax rate of return to savers, and any average based on it as a standard for discounting is not necessarily accurate. So, instead of trying to arrive at the right private discount rate, one can try to use an alternative, known as the *social rate of time preference*.

Social Rate of Time Preference

This measures the valuation that society places on consumption that is foregone in the present. There exists for society a collective rate of time preference that relates the value of net benefits received at some future time to the value of an equivalent net benefit available today. This collective rate of time preference is the market rate of interest represented by long-term government securities. In equilibrium, the collective rate of time preference, as measured by the market rate of interest on riskless securities, will be equal to the marginal rate of return on private capital, which represents the opportunity cost of capital. If this equality does not hold, society will want to increase or decrease its savings until the collective rate of time preference just equals the marginal rate of return on invested capital after allowance for risk. The social discount rate determined in this manner is the appropriate rate to use in evaluating public projects. In a democratic society in which public decisions reflect the collective social will, the level of taxation for financing public projects should reflect the collective or social rate of preference for present over future consumption of public goods.

To find the social rate of discount from private rates of time preference, we must relate the aggregate value of net benefits enjoyed by all individuals at some future point in time to the aggregate value of an equivalent amount of net benefits that these individuals would enjoy today. In order to do this, we need to make several assumptions about individual preferences for private and public goods and services. For instance, one can argue that the social rate of discount should be determined by the government on the basis of social objectives. This would provide a rate at which the individual discounts his or her own future consumption, but his or her social rate of discount is based on the assumption that his or her sacrifice of present consumption is accompanied by the sacrifices of all others in the society. Therefore, individuals may have a social rate of discount that is lower than their private rate of discount.

Alternatively, one could look at the economy's optimal combination of investment and saving. The economy's growth rate can be used as a measure of the optimal social discount rate. As an economy saves and accumulates capital; the marginal benefits of capital accumulation are given by the marginal product of capital, or 'r'. The marginal cost is the stock of capital that must be maintained at the rate k for any level of capital intensity (also known as capital-labor ratio). Hence society should save until $r = k$ and the true social discount rate becomes k. For the United States, k has averaged about 3.5 percent since World War II, slightly below the before-tax real investment rate (r) of about 4 percent. But for underdeveloped countries where the capital-labor ratio is much lower, the disparity between r and k and the importance for discounting would be much greater. Therefore, when the size of the pool of funds devoted to public investment is fixed and public investment clearly displaces private investment, the before-tax investment rate of return, r, appears to be the proper social discount rate. When the size of the pool is not fixed, r appears to become irrelevant and some other social rate of time preference appears to become relevant. If the private rate exceeds the social rate, it may be better to invest in the private sector at the rate of r.

When r and k differ, it may be appropriate to use the social rate of time preference, k as the proper discount rate for public projects. But the quantity to be discounted is the entire stream of consumption goods resulting from a project. Hence, if a government project really does displace private investment that would have yielded r, the lost consumption stream is computed on the basis of r and then discounted at rate k. This implies that the high-yielding private investment that really is displaced by the government investment is considered an opportunity cost of the project, and private investment that is not displaced is not considered an opportunity cost.

Related Issues

From a private sector point of view, the computation of benefits and costs is relatively straightforward. The benefits from a project are the revenues received, the costs are the firm's payments for inputs, and both are measured by market prices. The evaluation problem is more complicated for the government because social benefits and costs may not be reflected in market prices. The benefit-cost analysis may vary depending upon whether the local, state, or federal government is the decisionmaker. Even within a government the values assigned to different levels of benefits and costs will vary depending on their composition and how individuals view them. However, for BCA to be useful to decisionmakers, it should accurately reflect their values. There are several ways in which this could be achieved.

Use of Market Price

The price of a good reflects the marginal social costs of its production and its marginal value to consumers. If the government uses inputs and/or produces outputs that are traded in private markets, then market prices should be used for valuation. But there are imperfections in real-world markets that create monopolies, externalities, and uncertainty; hence, prices do not always reflect true marginal social costs and benefits. Therefore, market prices may not always accurately reflect the benefits and costs of a public project.

Use of Shadow Price

Since the prices of goods in imperfect markets generally do not reflect their marginal social costs, one can use *shadow prices* to replace market prices. The shadow price of a commodity is its underlying social marginal cost. Though market prices in imperfect markets are different from shadow prices, in some cases market prices can be used to estimate the shadow prices. The relevant shadow price depends on how the economy responds to government interventions. Let us look at three specific situations: (1) monopoly, (2) taxes, and (3) unemployment.

Monopoly. Suppose a public project uses a monopolistically produced input such that the price is above marginal cost. The question then is: Should the government value the input at its market price or at its marginal production cost? The answer would depend on the impact of the government purchase on the market. If the production of inputs is expected to increase by the exact amount used by the project, on one hand, the social opportunity cost would be the value of the resources used in the extra production. On the other hand, if there is no additional production of inputs, the use of these inputs by the government would come at the expense of private consumers, whose value of the input is measured by the demand price. If some combination of the two responses is expected, a weighted average of price and marginal cost would be appropriate.

Taxes. If an input is subject to a sales tax, the price received by the producer of the input is less than the price paid by the purchaser. This is because some portion of the purchase price goes to the tax collector. If that is the case, should the purchaser's or the producer's price be used by the government to value an input (that is subject to sales tax)? If production is expected to expand, then the producer's supply price is appropriate. If production is expected to stay constant, the purchaser's price should be used. For a combination of responses, a weighted average is required.

Unemployment. Cost-benefit analysis assumes that all resources are fully employed. But a public project may involve hiring workers who are currently involuntarily unemployed. Because hiring an unemployed worker does not lower output elsewhere in the economy, the wage the worker is paid does not represent an opportunity cost. The worker only forgoes leisure when hired, the value of which is low if unemployment is involuntary. If the government is running its stabilization policy to maintain a constant rate of employment, hiring an unemployed worker may mean reducing employment and output elsewhere in the economy, and the social cost of the worker is his or her wage. Even if the worker is involuntarily unemployed when the project begins, he or she will not continue to be so during the entire duration of the project. It is a problem of forecasting an individual's future employment prospects. Therefore, pricing of unemployed resources is a problem. In the absence of a major depression, valuation of unemployed labor at the going wage is probably a good approximation for practical purposes.

Effects of Price Changes

Private firms are small relative to the economy and hence do not have to be concerned that changes in the amount they produce will affect the market price of their product.

But public sector projects can be so large that they induce changes in market prices. For example, a government irrigation project could lower the marginal cost of agricultural production so much that the market price of food falls. But if the market price changes, how should the additional amount of food be valued? At its original price? At its price after the project? Or, at some price in between? In other words, what are the social costs and benefits of changing the price?

The economic tool for answering these questions is consumer surplus, the amount by which the sum that individuals would have been willing to pay exceeds the sum they actually have to pay. Changes in consumers' surplus are measures of the effects on the welfare of individuals of changes in the prices of goods they consume. If there are changes in the prices of factor services, such as labor and material, this would lead to changes in producer surplus.

Therefore, a price change could have direct and indirect effects on both consumer and producer welfare. For example, if a mass transit railway that operates across a major city is closed, there will be changes in the demands for other goods. The demand for cars, bicycles, and local bus services would increase and the demand for housing near former railway stations would decrease. Any of these changes might in turn cause changes in market prices. A decrease in the demand for housing near railway stations would cause a fall in prices of such houses. These indirect effects cause great problems for benefit-cost analysis. It is often difficult to predict such indirect effects that are caused by a project or even to identify them after a project has been undertaken. Again, when dealing with indirect effects in BCA, there is the danger of double counting, that is, counting a single element of benefit or cost more than once in the analysis. Also, deciding when an indirect effect is a benefit or a cost that is independent of the direct effects of a project is difficult. The point that is being made here is that in applying BCA, one must be aware of the existence of these problems and the alternatives that could be realistically pursued.

Summary and Conclusion

In this entry we summarized the principal elements of benefit-cost analysis with an emphasis on the differences between private and public sector project appraisals. We analyzed the various tools and concerns related to BCA and discussed the relative advantages and disadvantages, including a discussion of the inappropriateness of market rate of interest as well as the problems in selecting an appropriate social rate of discount.

The technique of benefit-cost analysis has been refined over the years, but it still poses considerable problems when applied to real-world situations. The introduction of the Planning, Programming, and Budgeting System, although a move in the right direction, did not quite produce any major changes in the way in which a government selects its projects. There are also practical difficulties in implementing BCA, especially when there is no consensus as to what the objectives of a government are, or how they are defined, measured, and interpreted. These are more complex and fundamental questions that need to be addressed at a different level and from a different perspective; they are beyond the scope of conventional decision tools, including benefit-cost analysis. Despite this, benefit-cost analysis remains the single most important tool for making rational decisions in a world of limited resources.

AMAN KHAN AND CHRISTINE FARIAS

BENTHAM, JEREMY (1748–1832).

The English utilitarian philosopher who held that self-interest is the prime motivator, and that government should do the greatest good for the greatest number.

Early Years

Bentham, the son of a middle-class attorney, was born in London on February 15, 1748. Considered a child prodigy, he was reading history at age three, began studying Latin at four, and graduated from Queen's College, Oxford, in 1763 at the age of fifteen. He studied law in London because his ambitious father had high hopes for him to become a judge. Bentham, however, soon became disillusioned with the law and chose instead to dedicate his life to challenging the political, legal, and social issues of his time.

Bentham's father died in 1792, leaving him a substantial inheritance, thus Jeremy was able to pursue his intellectual musings without the burden of working for a living. According to an early biographer, John Bowring (1843), Bentham was described by his contemporaries as "jovial, amiable and pleasant" and, "the most affable man in existence, perfectly good-humoured, bearing and forbearing, deeply read, deeply learned, eminently a reasoner, yet simple as a child."

He was known to be temperamentally lazy with respect to getting his writings printed. Most of his ideas were written in thousands of pages of unpublished manuscripts that he disseminated to a small, but committed, group of like-minded followers (the Benthamites). Many of his works were edited by others and were not published until after his death. He was, nonetheless, an influential prolific author on a wide range of subjects, including law, utilitarian government, public ethics, economics, and prison reform.

Law

Bentham's essay, "Comment on the Commentaries" (1775), was a critique of William Blackstone's *Commentaries on the Laws of England*. It is generally believed that this writing marked the beginning of Bentham's philosophic radicalism. The language and style of this early work is clear and concise—much different from his later works.

Bentham's lasting contribution to legal theory, *Of Laws in General*, was not published until 1945, and was only published in its entirety in 1968. Although unpublished during his lifetime, his legal reform writings and ideas were widely discussed and shared by his contemporaries. His ambition was to construct a complete set of laws that could be applied internationally. He traveled widely, visiting the influential thinkers and legal theorists of Western Europe. He had disciples in England, France, Spain, Portugal, Greece, and the Americas.

Bentham's Common Law theory had two main components: (1) justice; and (2) utility. He believed that justice sets a fixed and inflexible standard; justice is clear, determinate, easy to discover and to observe. Although justice provides regularity and stability, utility provides the flexibility necessary to ensure equity amidst constantly changing circumstances. He extended his legal concept of justice and utility to government in general.

Utilitarian Government

Bentham developed a concept of utilitarian theory that accommodated the liberal values of liberty, equality, and personal inviolability. In his first book, *A Fragment on Government* (1776), he outlined the four basic concerns of a good utilitarian government: (1) security; (2) subsistence; (3) abundance; and (4) equality. Security, Bentham argued, is the most important source of utility because it is a necessary condition for human survival. He maintained that government should be expected to provide both security and basic subsistence. He understood that a lack of subsistence leads to starvation and anarchy. He considered basic subsistence to be an entitlement. In times of abundance, government should ensure that any excess in community resources is distributed equitably. Government, according to Bentham, must always strive to provide "the greatest good for the greatest number" (*A Fragment on Government*, 1776). He recognized, however, that different public officials had different concepts of what constituted "the greatest good." He knew that these decisions were based on value judgments influenced by public ethics.

Public Ethics

One of Bentham's best known early works, *An Introduction to the Principles of Morals and Legislation* (1780), established his fundamental ideas about public ethics. He was concerned with the business of public administration and the ethics of public office. Bentham recognized that the "ruling few" have an obligation to the "subject many." He argued for a "codification" of civil and penal law. He believed that the public must be critically aware of the actions of their political leaders, to ensure that decisions are made in the best interest of the community. For this reason, he argued for a formal system of checks and balances under the scrutiny of publicity and public opinion. While pondering these ethical issues, he recognized and considered the influence of law, utilitarian government, and public ethics on the economy.

Economics

While in Russia visiting his brother, Samuel Bentham (1757–1831), an engineer and general in the Russian armed forces, Bentham wrote his first essay in economics, "Defence of Usury" (1787). This work showed him to be a believer in the economic principles set forth by Adam Smith in *The Wealth of Nations* (1776). His critique was that Adam Smith did not follow the logic of his own principles. Bentham believed that every person is the best judge of what is best for him- or herself. Government and laws should not hinder anyone in pursuit of his or her own best interest. He argued that there is no reason not to follow this utilitarian doctrine in economic and financial applications.

Bentham's later works on economics were adaptations of the laissez-faire principle. In his essay, "Manual of Political Economy" (1793), he attempted to provide a comprehensive list of what the government should and should not do—and the list of what the state should not do is much longer. One thing that he thought the state should do is to protect the disadvantaged. Bentham became interested in the deplorable conditions of European prisons and he set out on a crusade to reform them.

Prison Reform

Bentham collaborated with his brother, Samuel, to reform the prisons of Western Europe. He recommended that criminal penalties be fixed that would impose an amount of pain just in excess of the pleasure that might be derived from the criminal act. He looked upon punishment as a deterrent; and he is credited with the familiar phrase "the punishment should fit the crime" (*View of the Hard Labour Bill*, 1778). He argued for imprisonment as a substitute for corporal punishment.

As a result of his demands for prison perform, Bentham was commissioned to design a model prison for England in 1799. Fifty-three acres of land were transferred to him, upon which he was to erect his ideal design. Bentham's "Panopticon" prison design (first conceived in 1784) was a round structure with the cells on the outside walls and staff living quarters in the center. The idea was to "maximise" observation into the cells by the prison "inspector" (*Panopticon*, 1791). According to John Bowring (1843), the advantage of the Panopticon design is that, "to be incessantly under the eyes of the inspector is to lose in effect the power to do evil and almost the thought of wanting to do it."

Bentham touted his design as a one-stop reformatory for the social ills of the time. He claimed that the Panopticon design could be used for "punishing the incorrigible, guarding the insane, reforming the vicious, confining the suspected, employing the idle, maintaining the helpless, curing the sick, instructing the willing in any branch of industry, or training the rising race in the path of education: in a word, whether it be applied to the purposes of perpetual prisons in the room of death, or prisons for confinement before trial, or penitentiary-houses, or houses of correction, or workhouses, or manufactories, or mad-houses, or hospitals, or schools" (*Panoptican*, 1791). He hoped that his design would serve as a social laboratory where experiments could be performed in a controlled setting.

A Panopticon prison was built in St. Petersburg, Russia, in the early 1800s; however, it burned down in 1818. The Panopticon prison design was adopted in the United States in the construction of the Virginia State Prison in Richmond, Virginia, in 1800, and at the first Western State Penitentiary in Pitttsburgh, Pennsylvania, in 1826. Ultimately, Bentham's model prison design was doomed to failure. When he designed it, the penal philosophy was one of solitary confinement without labor. Shortly thereafter, penal philosophy changed to solitary confinement at hard labor. The Panopiticon cells were simply too small for work. Besides, during the day, the natural exterior light shining through the cells made it difficult for the staff in the center to see into the cells. Ventilation and air circulation were constant problems. By 1833, the original Western State Penitentiary was razed after less than seven years in operation.

Bentham's Panopticon prison project was never built on the original proposed site in England. He battled for years with William Pitt, the First Lord of the Treasury, to receive compensation for his work. Bowring (1843) noted that it was Pitt's hope to see Bentham "die broken-hearted, like a rat in a hole." Bentham was quite distraught. William Wilberforce, the contemporary Christian philanthropist and opponent of slavery said, "Never was any one worse used than Bentham. I have seen the tears run down the cheeks of that strong-minded man, through vexation at the pressing importunity of creditors and the insolence of official underlings, when day after day he was begging at the Treasury for what was indeed a mere matter of right. How indignant did I often feel, when I saw him thus treated by men infinitely his inferiors!" (Halevy, 1928). Pitt's successor in office finally paid Bentham 23,000 British pounds for his work in 1813.

Assessment

Throughout his writings on law, utilitarian government, public ethics, economics, and prison reform, Bentham weaved the common thread of utilitarian philosophy. More than just a philosopher, however, he was an articulate, outspoken critic of public and political institutions. He may rightfully be considered as the progenitor of the administrative legal tradition. On one hand, critics have suggested that his concepts were too broad, oversimple, or ambiguous. They point out that his elaborate arguments are sometimes founded on insufficient and ambiguous premises. Advocates, on the other hand, recognize Bentham's limitations in historical context. It has been said that he was a visionary born 150 years too soon (Blaug, 1991).

Bentham labored well into his seventies on the task of codifying law. He disciplined himself to write fifteen folio pages every day, and he continued to produce an inexhaustable series of reform proposals until his death. His small house was only a few hundred yards away from the Houses of Parliament. He frequently entertained members of Parliament and he significantly influenced thinking in both Houses.

In 1824, Bentham and his friends founded the *Westminster Review* to ensure that their political reform ideas were considered along with the ideas proffered by the Whigs in the *Edinburgh Review*, and the Tories in the *Quarterly Review*. He is recognized for coining the terms "international," "codify," "minimise," and "maximise" (Blaug, 1991). His wide travels convinced him of the need for shared legal concepts among nations. He labored greatly to codify his concept of international law, and was frustrated by the realization that political differences hindered his dream from a practical perspective. His fundamental utilitarian convictions were always directed at minimizing expenses and maximizing results. His cogent ideas contributed to the reform of English administrative law, and he is given credit for the 1829 Metropolitan Police Act, the 1833 Education Act, the 1833 Factory Act, the Poor Act of 1834, the 1840 Railway Regulation Act, and the 1848 Public Health Act (Blaug, 1991).

Bentham died in London on June 6, 1832, at the age of eighty-four, without finishing his comprehensive book *Constitutional Code* (begun in 1822), wherein he synthesized his earlier writings and established the foundation of classic liberal political thought. In his will, he provided for a significant bequest to University College, London (an institution he helped to found in 1827), subject to the condition that his remains would be permanently displayed at the college—he so wanted to spend eternity with his students! Upon his death, and in accordance with his own instructions, his friend Southwood Smith pronounced the funeral oration over his body, which was then dissected in the presence of his friends. The skeleton was reconstructed, fitted with a wax head of his likeness (his real head was mummified), dressed in his own clothes, and set upright in a glass case. University College continues to honor his request to be forevermore on display; thus Bentham's remains remain one of London's minor tourist attractions.

JOHN S. SHAFFER

BIBLIOGRAPHY

Barnes, Harry Elmer, and Negley K. Teeters, 1947. *New Horizons in Criminology.* New York: Prentice-Hall.

Bentham Works Cited: Many of Bentham's works were not published until well after they were originally written. The dates below indicate the year(s) that Bentham actually wrote the pieces, not necessarily the dates that they were published.

Bentham, Jeremy, 1775. "Comment on the Commentaries."
——, 1776. *A Fragment on Government.* Edited by F. C. Montague. Oxford: Clarendon. (Reprinted in 1891 and 1951.)
——, 1778. *View of the Hard Labour Bill.*
——, 1780. *An Introduction to the Principles of Morals and Legislation.* London: Pickering.
——, 1787. "Defense of Usury."
——, 1791. *Panopticon.*
——, 1793. "Manual of Political Economy."
——, 1822–1830. *Constitutional Code.*
——, 1830. *Of Law in General.*
Blaug, Mark, ed., 1991. *Henry Thorton, Jeremy Bentham, James Lauderdale, and Simonde De Sismondi.* Cambridge: University Press.
Bowring, John, ed., 1838–1843. *The Works of Jeremy Bentham.* Eleven vols. Edinburgh: William Tait. (Reprinted in 1962 by Russell and Russell in a limited edition.)
Halevy, Elie, 1928. *The Growth of Philosophic Radicalism.* Translated by Mary Morrris. London: Faber and Faber.
Kelly, Paul Joseph, 1990. *Utilitarianism and Distributive Justice: Jeremy Bentham and the Civil Law.* New York: Oxford University Press.
Postema, Gerald J., 1986. *Bentham and the Common Law Traditon.* New York: Oxford University Press.
Smith, Adam, 1776. *The Wealth of Nations.* New York: Modern Library, 1937.

BEST PRACTICES. The selective observation of exemplary programs across different contexts in order to identify innovative practices in public management that can be transferred and adopted to other contexts.

A long and rich history exists in the field of public administration of relying on practice and experience, the observation of the day-to-day workings of organizations and managers, in order to develop new principles for reform. Frederick Taylor and Frank Gilbreth studied the movements of iron workers and brick layers to discover the "one best way" of performing specific tasks. Fritz Roethlisberger and Elton Mayo interviewed and observed factory workers at the Hawthorne Electrical Plant and unwittingly uncovered the behavioral side to management. Herbert Simon studied municipal employees to understand administrative behavior and decisionmaking. Henry Mintzberg chronicled the day-to-day activities of managers to develop theories of management. Peters and Waterman examined the organizational characteristics of leading American firms to promote a model for organizational excellence. The common thread among these examples was the desire to improve the existing practices by observing the practice and behaviors of individuals and organizations.

More recently the desire to identify the best way of doing something in the public sector, whether it be educating children or paving roads, has resulted in the establishment of numerous awards programs that recognize government innovation. The most prominent of these is the Ford Foundation's Innovation in State and Local Government Awards Program which was established in 1985, and is administered by the Kennedy School of Government at Harvard University.

Each year the Innovation Program receives well over one thousand applications. A national committee reviews all the applications and selects twenty-five semi-finalists, of which ten receive major awards, "on the basis of the creativity involved in the innovation, the significance of the problem it undertakes to solve, the program's value to the clients who benefit from it, and its transferability to other jurisdictions." (*1992 Innovations:* p. 16–19)

The Exemplary State and Local Awards Program (EXSL, 1992) provides evidence of tangible accomplishments through productive public management: enhanced efficiency, capacity and quality-of-life outcomes throughout the public sector. Sponsored by the National Center for Public Productivity, since 1989 EXSL has received well over two thousand nominations, and one hundred and forty awardees have been selected through a peer review process by the Section on Management Science and Policy Analysis of the American Society for Public Administration. Awards are made to projects and programs that produce significant cost savings, measurable increases in quality and productivity, and improvements in the effectiveness of government services. Programs chosen are highly rated on: program outputs, impact on quality of life of population served, cost effectiveness, client support/satisfaction, innovative nature, obstacles or encumbrances which had to be overcome, nature of the problem which was addressed, degree of difficulty, and transferability or ability to serve as a model for other programs.

EXSL programs address society's most difficult-to-solve problems such as providing no-cost medical care for the indigent, unclogging court calendars, installing pollution and flood controls, expanding the supply of decent housing, increasing critical services to senior citizens, and rehabilitating youthful and older offenders.

Hard evidence that "government works" can be found in these national awards programs as well as in state, county, and municipal awards programs. Each year thousands of projects are nominated for formal recognition by dozens of associations of their peers, such as the National League of Cities, the U.S. Conference of Mayors, the American Society for Public Administration, the League of California Cities, and the International Personnel Management Association. After rigorous, objective scrutiny hundreds receive awards as models of problem solving and revitalization. They have accomplished what government's critics demand: entrepreneurial actions by public servants to improve public services and save public tax dollars. These successes in federal, state and local agencies are directly counter to assumptions that public servants care little about operational efficiency and effectiveness.

Despite the stereotypes and the broad range of services which we call upon its members to provide, the public sector is often innovative, entrepreneurial and savvy—using state-of-the-art methods to improve efficiency and quality, to achieve outcomes as promised. As Osborne and Gaebler conclude in *Reinventing Government* (1992), "we were astounded by the degree of change taking place . . . public sector institutions—from state and local governments to school districts to the Pentagon—are transforming the bureaucratic models they have inherited from the past, making government more flexible, creative, and entrepreneurial" (1992, p. xxii).

There has been and continues to be a great deal of work within the public management community as to how to improve the processes of service delivery. There are many examples of innovation within the public sector, many productive applications of knowledge, many confirmations of more efficient and higher quality services. *Reinventing Government* is just the latest rediscovery of that work.

At the state level, for example, New York State's Management and Productivity program has saved hundreds of millions of dollars since 1982 (Cuomo, 1991; New York State Office of Management and Productivity, 1991), $134 million in 1991 alone. Recent initiatives:

- Produce substantial recurring savings, particularly in the areas of welfare, Medicaid and reductions of administrative burdens on agencies.
- Encourage employee involvement in efforts to save funds and improve services.
- Enhance accountability for the effective operation of state programs.
- Assist local governments through a variety of technical assistance and savings projects.
- Apply new information systems and energy conservation technologies to reduce costs and improve services.

At the county level, Streib and Waugh (1991) have found considerable confidence in the administrative and political capacities of counties to design, implement, finance, and manage effective programs. Los Angeles County's Productivity Improvement Program has achieved millions of dollars in savings and national recognition (Carr, 1991; Dobbs 1992). The program is driven by management support, employee participation and recognition, open communication, financial incentives, networking and an overall commitment to the twin goals of efficiency and effectiveness.

At the local level, Ammons (1991) has identified thirty-five jurisdictions and thirty-nine officials as reputational leaders in local government productivity and innovation. The Local Government Information Network (LOGIN) contains a database of over forty thousand cases of innovative, entrepreneurial accomplishment at the state, county and municipal levels.

Public sector awards programs include: All-American Cities, National Civic League; Awards of Merit, *American City and County* magazine; Celebrating Innovations in Local Democracy Awards, National League of Cities; City Livability Awards, U.S. Conference of Mayors; Davis Productivity Awards, State of Florida; Downtown Development Awards, *Downtown Idea Exchange* Magazine; Energy Innovations Awards, Department of Energy; Exemplary State and Local Awards Program (EXSL); Ford Foundation's Innovations Project at Harvard's Kennedy School; Helen Putnam Awards, League of California Cities; Historic Preservation Awards, Advisory Council on Historic Preservation; Innovative Financing Awards, Federal Highway Administration; National Association of Counties; Outstanding Program Awards, American Society for Public Administration, various chapters and sections; Privatization Council Achievement Awards; New York City Productivity Forum; Productivity Awards, New York State; Public Employees Roundtable; Records Management Awards, International Institute of Municipal Clerks; Recycling Awards, U.S. Conference of Mayors/Heinz Recycling Awards, Environmental Protection Administration; Urban Land Institute Awards for Excellence; International City Management Association; American Public Works Association; Government Finance Officers Association; International Personnel Management Association.

Conclusion

Successful problem solving projects—award winning or routine—are not the simple "common sense" solutions typically posed by politicians, voters, corporate critics and the media: "cut the fat" or "cutback management," "economize" or "privatize," "work harder" or "work smarter," "businesslike management" or "Japanese management." If only such straightforward adages were what public organizations needed then government's efficiency would not be at issue. But simple prescriptions are not very useful. They are based upon popular misperceptions of public management. They are contrary to the complex problem-solving processes governments (or private organizations of comparable size) require in order to address our society's most difficult-to-solve problems such as crime, pollution, or homelessness. Rather, the provision and improvement of services, in government *or in the most profitable private sector firms,* is complex and requires hard, detailed work.

Best Practices Abstracts

The following abstracts are examples of best practices which won awards from both the Exemplary State and Local Awards Program and the Innovation in State and Local Government Awards Program.

Competition with Privatization, Phoenix, Arizona

Summary

The Department of Public Works of the City of Phoenix, Arizona has established a program which utilizes a non-traditional approach to competing with private industry. **"Competition with Privatization"** is used to increase productivity and significantly cut agency costs.

Text

"Competition with Privatization" is a unique approach to providing the highest level of municipal service to the taxpayer, at the lowest possible cost. The City of Phoenix was faced with growing budget problems, and was increasingly awarding municipal contracts to private organizations. In response, the Department of Public Works sought to enhance the competitive atmosphere in which it operates through increased technology, labor-management cooperation, innovative practices and community involvement and support. The focus of the program was on solid waste collection, which impacts every household and provides citizens a means to evaluate municipal services on a first-hand basis. The program's primary objective was to win back City sanitation contracts and to save city revenues. In 1989, savings and cost-avoidance totaled approximately $1.2 million dollars, and the Sanitation Department was recognized as second only to Fire among all City departments and services. The program has also engendered improved employee moral and labor-management relations, which has resulted in productivity enhancements, innovations (e.g. using retread tires) and participation in the competitive bidding process by department employees. "Competition with Privatization" allows government services to compete with private industry on equal footing, as no decision to contract out is made prior to the call for private bids. Therefore, municipal agencies are encouraged to compete with private firms, rather than take a "do nothing" approach to providing services to the public. The Phoenix program encourages participative management, and cooperation between unions and the City, in a combined effort to win back lucrative contracts for the City. At present, the City of Phoenix has earned back all contracts that were previously lost to private contractors.

Housing Vermont,
State of Vermont

Summary

"Housing Vermont" is a statewide, nonprofit corporation created by the Vermont Housing Agency in 1988 to preserve and/or develop affordable rental housing for its citizens. The program was also established to foster innovative relationships between public and private interests in Vermont, in response to the need for affordable housing.

Text

This program primarily serves low- and moderate-income families in Vermont, who will most benefit from affordable rental housing. The development effort was made possible by the formation of "Housing Vermont" which deviates from other similar development projects. An important and innovative component is the Vermont Equity Fund, an investment vehicle designed to give corporate investors an opportunity for relatively low-risk investments in housing. "Housing Vermont" encourages private corporations to invest in affordable housing in exchange for Low Income Housing Tax Credits, whose value has been increased by at least 30 percent over a traditional syndication through the efforts of the issuer. The Equity Fund is the first investment vehicle of its kind supported by a state housing finance agency. Within its first two years of operation, "Housing Vermont" has seen through the completion of 700 units of perpetually affordable housing, representing a highly effective partnership between public and private interests. The program has also committed an additional $4.9 million of equity towards the creation of 328 units of housing in three developments of mixed income, senior and family housing. There also exists a commitment to rehabilitate a significant stock of existing housing in Vermont which is at risk of being converted to market rents. "Housing Vermont" also acts as a developer, which translates into significant cost savings for each project undertaken. As an arm of the Vermont Housing Finance Agency, "Housing Vermont" is a statewide public entity, yet because it functions at the operational level, it has more flexibility and independence than a traditional state agency. With some legal and administrative hurdles to overcome, "Housing Vermont" is a program likely to be successful in other large municipalities or at the state level. It stresses local involvement in the issue of affordable housing, the assurance of perpetual affordability and a commitment to work closely with private interests and developers.

Electronic Benefit System,
Ramsey County, Minnesota

Summary

The "Electronic Benefit System (EBS)" program of Ramsey County, Minnesota enhances the delivery of public assistance benefits through the existing network of Automated Teller Machines (ATM) located throughout the County.

Text

Retention of a depository bank had been a long-term problem in Ramsey County, with area banks asserting that public assistance clients congested their lobbies and necessitated additional personnel during the period in which they cashed their benefits checks. As a result, in 1987 Ramsey County launched a pilot program, which issued clients' benefits electronically, offering withdrawal through a network of ATMs. Currently there are 11,000 clients receiving checks through this electronic system, representing over $4.5 million monthly in AFDC, Refugee Assistance, General Assistance and Minnesota Supplemental Assistance. Clients are able to access their benefits through three ATM networks, and thus do not have to worry about benefits being lost or stolen. Through surveys, clients indicate that the EBS program is more convenient than receiving a check, and they are better able to manage their money as they do not have to withdraw all of the benefits at once. The EBS program serves 88 percent of the potential clientele, and there are strong indications that client support and satisfaction are high. Eligibility workers determine whether EBS is appropriate for new enrollees, and alternative delivery is arranged for people with handicaps who do not have access to an ATM. This program eliminates the need for thousands of paper transactions, as checks are no longer issued to the majority of the County's public assistance clients. There is strong public support as well, as the EBS program is no costlier than the old method of check issuance. It is anticipated that food stamps will be added to the electronic system in the near future, and from that, the County hopes to realize actual program cost savings.

Medicaid Waiver Project,
State of Tennessee

Summary

"Medicaid Waiver Project: Home and Community Based Services for Mentally Retarded Adults," was established in 1986 and addressed the need to provide additional long-term community care to mentally retarded adults 18 years of age and older, at costs less than those associated with institutionalization.

Text

The State of Tennessee developed the waiver project to provide three services: case management—assessing, coordinating, locating and monitoring services to the client; day and residential rehabilitation services—training clients to develop skills for community living; and respite care services—providing short term care to therapeutic foster care clients to relieve the regular foster care provider. To date, the waiver project has served a total enrollment of over 1,000 clients, supported by three respite care providers, 22 therapeutic foster care homes and 29 community agencies. The waiver project has proven cost-effective throughout the first two years of operation, by saving $8 million dollars in Medicaid costs for 1987 and 1988. The costs associated with institutionalized care are $94 dollars per day, as opposed to $39 dollars per day for the waiver project, in 1987. The 1988 figures also bear out the cost savings, at a rate of $98 dollars per day (institutional care), versus $43 dollars per day (community-based care). The project also established a complaint handling system to report any problems associated with the community-based providers, with no substantial complaints registered. Representatives of mental health advocacy groups have stated that the quality of care in the project met their standards, especially in light of the significant cost savings, and the ability to keep clients in the community. The waiver project was funded by the federal government through Medicaid, and administered at the state level by the Medicaid Bureau of the Department of Health and Environment. Community-based services were managed by the Department of Mental Health and Mental Retardation.

Statewide Long-Term Improved Management (SLIM) Program, State of Arizona

Summary

The "**Statewide Long-Term Improved Management Program**" is an effort to streamline state government while improving the quality of services delivered by using a variety of management techniques, including Total Quality Management. Working in conjunction with state employees, a report was delivered to the Governor detailing over 300 recommendations for improving services within the 12 agencies examined.

Text

The Governor of Arizona (Symington) believed that state services could be delivered at a higher quality and at a lower cost if quality management principles were infused into the culture of government. In order to review the 12 largest agencies within the Executive Branch, a steering committee in cooperation with teams of state employees

and a cadre of outside consultants evaluated what was taking place within each of the 12 agencies selected. These teams of employees analyzed the processes used to deliver services, organizational structures, areas of duplication and/or overlap, areas for potential privatization, spans of control, layering of management, cost of management, cost of quality, and resource utilization. Working with agency management, this process produced recommendations which then moved into the implementation phase. Implementation of recommendations was completed by "empowered" agency employee teams, facilitated by a member from the SLIM Team. This process includes production of detailed plans, measurements for continuous improvement, costs to implement, enhancements to the original recommendation, and a recording of savings from final implementation.

MARC HOLZER AND
KATHE CALLAHAN

BIBLIOGRAPHY

"1992 Innovations in State and Local Government." *The Ford Foundation Report.* Fall 1992, vol. 23, no. 3: 16–19.
American Society for Public Administration, Washington, D.C. National and chapter awards programs.
Ammons, David N., 1991. "Reputational Leaders in Local Government Productivity and Innovation." *Public Productivity and Management Review,* 15 (1): 19–43.
Carr, Cathy. 1991. "Los Angeles County Productivity Managers Network: An Alternative to Traditional Productivity Program Management." *Public Productivity and Management Review,* 15 (1): 47–59.
Cuomo, Mario M., 1991. "Productivity Initiatives in New York State Government." *Public Productivity and Management Review,* 15 (2): 109–112.
Dobbs, Matti F., 1992. "Los Angeles County Productivity Study." Unpublished manuscript.
EXSL (Exemplary State and Local Awards Program), 1996. Newark, N.J.: National Center for Public Productivity, Rutgers University.
Local Govrnment Information Network, (LOGIN). St. Paul, MN: Norris Institute.
National Center for Public Productivity. Newark, New Jersey: Rutgers, The State University of New Jersey, Campus at Newark.
New York State Office of Management and Productivity, 1991. MAP Annual Report. Albany, New York.
Osborne, David and Ted Gaebler, 1992. *Reinventing Government.* Reading, Massachusetts: Addison-Wesley.
Overman, E. Sam and Kathy Boyd, 1994. "Best Practice Research and Postbureaucratic Reform." *Journal of Public Administration Research and Theory,* 4 (1): 67–83.
Streib, Gregory and William L. Waugh, Jr., 1991. "Administrative Capacity and the Barriers to Effective County Management." *Public Productivity and Management Review,* 15 (1): 61–70.

THE BEVERIDGE REPORT. The report, *Social Insurance and Allied Services,* published in 1942 under the direction of British economist William Beveridge (1879–1963) which proposed the "cradle-to-the-grave" social programs adopted by the United Kingdom after 1945. It provided both the intellectual and policy basis of universal welfare provision that was both a major feature of political consensus in postwar Britain and an example for many European Social Democratic parties after 1945.

Attempts at British social welfare reforms in the first half of the century look piecemeal and selective when contrasted with the vision and commitment represented by the bipartisan support of the Welfare State. The experience of World War II—notably the hazards of bombing and the necessity for rationing—gave rise to a popular willingness to accept greater direction from government planning than had been the norm prior to 1939. The influence of wartime conditions allowed a cross-party consensus to develop over the need for improved welfare policies. The condition of innercity children evacuated to more prosperous areas shocked public opinion and moved the government to take positive steps to eradicate this sort of poverty. Cheap or free school meals and milk were made available to all children and not just to those who were defined as poor. Free milk, orange juice, and cod liver oil were provided for all expectant mothers and for children under five years. Thus, prior to the publication of the report, some moves had already been made toward accepting the principle of universal welfare provision.

The focus for political, economic and academic discussion on postwar social planning was Beveridge's report itself. It appeared in December 1942 at a time when ultimate victory in Europe could be foreseen but also at a moment when new incentives had to be found to maintain the war effort. Sir William Beveridge (himself a liberal academic) went beyond the original terms of reference in his reports and called for a general attack on what he called the "five giants on the road to reconstruction": disease, ignorance, squalor, idleness, and want. In particular, he stated that no satisfactory scheme of social security could be devised unless there were family allowances, comprehensive health and rehabilitation services, and the avoidance of mass unemployment.

The report was extremely popular with the general public. As a result, the all-party, wartime government felt compelled to commit itself to the arguments of the report, if only in principle. On one hand, the widespread support for universal social insurance may have been the product of a society made more generous by the experience of war. On the other hand, altruism does not fully explain the strength of support that was apparent. The fact that so many people were either serving in the armed forces or employed in munitions industries, and were thus directly concerned about their postwar employment, was a contributing factor. (Given the post-1918 experience of just these groups, the anxiety was fully justified.) Similarly, the associated prospect of universal health insurance was naturally attractive to people who had been finding the cost of private health insurance a burden. And the memory of the Great Depression was never far away. Such personal self-interest suggests why key lobby groups were also generally in favor of Beveridge's ideas. The evidence presented to his committee showed that hardly any trade unions opposed extensions of national insurance; even witnesses from the business sector generally favored more intervention by the state in matters where national efficiency was the criterion. Wartime, in short, seemed to have created new attitudes about what the state could achieve.

The Implementation of the Beveridge Report

Prewar social surveys had shown that the cost of bringing up children was a frequent cause of "want" and thus there was pressure for the existence of state allowances for each child. Beveridge was sympathetic to arguments that this would cure poverty and reverse the fall in the birth rate, but he also saw family allowances as a means of maintaining work incentives. Unemployment relief took family size into account, whereas wages did not, so unless allowances were paid to people in work a person might be better off if unemployed. This seems to have been the argument that convinced the government. The 1945 Family Allowances Bill was introduced, providing for payment of allowances, without a means test for the second and subsequent child. However, whereas Beveridge had recommended in his report a subsistence level of 8 shillings a week, adjusted for inflation as required, the actual allowances brought in were fixed at 5 shillings a week, thereby releasing government from an obligation to raise allowances with the cost of living.

The heart of the Beveridge Report was the proposed amalgamation of all existing state insurance and pension schemes into one, providing subsistence benefits whenever an insured person's earnings were interrupted. Though the wartime government was never fully committed to the idea of such subsistence, the 1944 White Paper, *Social Insurance,* generally followed Beveridge's proposals for the expansion of national insurance.

The government did agree with the Beveridge assumptions about "disease" as a social ill and that there should be a comprehensive health service available to all, without any conditions of insurance contributions. However, it proved to be impossible during the war for the details of such a service to be agreed upon, either between political parties or with the interest groups involved, especially the medical profession. Nevertheless, war itself had already increased the state's role in health care. Greatly exaggerated prewar estimates of casualties in air raids had led to the provision of 80,000 Emergency Hospital beds, compared with 78,000 beds in voluntary hospitals and 320,000 in local authority hospitals. Moreover, the Emergency Hospital Service gradually extended its operations from war casualties to treatment of sick people transferred from innercity hospitals and then to other evacuees. In discussions between 1943 and 1945 on a future national health service, however, both Conservative ministers and the British Medical Association showed themselves to be determined to safeguard private practice and the independence of the voluntary hospitals. The 1944 White Paper, *A National Health Service*, left much undecided and was avowedly only a consultative document; postwar developments under the Attlee Labor government brought the proposals to fruition.

The 1944 Education Act sought to attack Beveridge's concern with "ignorance." The minister primarily concerned with the implementation of the act was the Conservative member of the Cabinet, R. A. Butler. The 1944 act raised the school-leaving age to 15 and required the completion of earlier schemes for the reorganization of the elementary schools into primary and secondary age-based streams. Fee-paying was abolished in all local authority secondary schools, but not in the 200 or so direct-grant grammar schools. Butler was anxious to retain the distinctive character of the latter, partly to avoid too sharp a contrast between the state sector and what the British term "public schools," the latter being largely for the well-to-do. However, the real implementation of these reforms would rest on the future allocation of resources to the education sector by postwar governments.

After 1942, William Beveridge turned his attention to the giant "idleness" and, by 1944, his strictly unofficial "report," *Full Employment in a Free Society*, was nearly ready for publication. The government was determined to preempt Beveridge's proposals and hurried out its White Paper, *Employment Policy*. In it, the government avoided a commitment to full employment and instead accepted the maintenance of a high and stable level of employment as just one of its primary responsibilities. No legislation was proposed on the grounds that employment could not be created by government alone. It was not until after 1945 that Britain elected a series of governments committed to Keynesian demand management methods of economic regulation, which, among other things, assumed that government was directly responsible for employment levels.

The Beveridge Report in Postwar Britain

The financial pressures that were exerted on the postwar governments resulted in a continuing review as to how the welfare reforms were to be sustained. As the cost of these reforms increased during the 1960s and 1970s, criticism was expressed at the spiraling cost that this kind of state responsibility entailed. After election victory in 1979, the Conservative government became committed to the idea of examining how the burden of these reforms could be passed back to the private sector. The system of benefit payments to those who are unemployed or otherwise disadvantaged in some way was subject to review.

As for the National Health Service, perhaps the most significant reform that came out of Beveridge's proposals,

it too is being restructured under the premise that demand-led, universal free health care is not something that governments are able to provide. The electorate is once again persuaded to take advantage of a growing private health care sector.

In sum, the sort of society that Beveridge was considering while writing his original report has changed remarkably and thus the concept of a "welfare state" appears to many as old fashioned and paternalistic.

VICTORIA C. SYME-TAYLOR

BIBLIOGRAPHY

Beveridge, W., 1944. *Full Employment in a Free Society*. London: George Allen and Unwin.
———, 1942. *Social Insurance and Allied Services*. New York: Macmillan.
Cairncross, A., 1985. *Years of Recovery: British Economic Policy 1945–1951*. London: Methuen.
Fraser, D., 1973. *The Evolution of the British Welfare State*. London: Macmillan.
Harris, J., 1977. *William Beveridge: A Biography*. Oxford: Oxford University Press.
Peden, G., 1985. *British Economic and Social Policy: Lloyd George to Margaret Thatcher*. London: Philip Allan.
Thane, P., 1982. *The Foundation of the Welfare State*. London: Longman.

BIENNIAL BUDGETING.

A system of budgeting in which one or more of the following recurring budgetary activities are carried out each two years instead of each year: executive submission, legislative consideration, appropriations, or authorizations.

Biennial budgeting by a governmental entity refers to the practice of budgeting for a two-year period as opposed to a one-year period. Most national governments, including the United States, budget for a one-year period. Some subnational (state and local) governments budget for a two-year period, and a biennial budget has been discussed and proposed for the U.S. government as recently as 1994. The frequency of the budgeting process is usually reported in reviews of state budgetary practices (Fisher 1988; Howard 1973; Lee and Johnson 1989; Lynch 1990; Mikesell 1986; Schick 1971). This frequency (annual or biennial) is called budget periodicity and denotes the quality of being recurrent at regular intervals. For state governments, the budget interval is a one-year (annual periodicity) or a two-year (biennial periodicity) period.

A distinction is made between budget cycle and budget periodicity because much of the discussion of budgetary processes has focused on the phases of the budget cycle: planning, preparation, execution, and evaluation. The budget cycle typically lasts two or three times as long as the budgetary period itself. An annual budget, for example, is in the planning stages well before the fiscal year in which it is to be executed has begun, and it is evaluated at some time after the execution phase has been completed. Budget cycles overlap; several phases can be observed at any point in time. The budget of a prior year can be evaluated while future year budgets are being planned and prepared and the current year budget is being executed. Budget periodicity, however, refers only to the length of time for which the budget document is binding, typically one or two years.

Origin

Currently, 31 states budget annually and 19 budget biennially (see Table I), but this has not always been the case. In 1940, forty-four states employed biennial budgets. At that time, only four states (New Jersey, New York, Rhode Island, and South Carolina) had annual legislative sessions, which precluded the possibility of annual budgets for all but those four states. The frequency of legislative sessions appears to have been an important, and sometimes deciding, factor in the history of budget periodicity.

By 1965, 21 states had begun to conduct annual legislative sessions. The professionalization of state legislatures and increased legislative staffs usually accompanied the changes to an annual legislative session. Twenty of the annual legislature states were also budgeting annually, with only Alaska continuing to budget biennially in the presence of annual legislative sessions. The additional time and effort required for budgeting motivated the changes to annual budgeting. In each of these cases, the move to annual budgets was made simultaneously with the decision to

TABLE I. State Budget Periodicity in 1990

Annual Budget		Biennial Budget	
Alabama	Massachusetts	Arkansas[b]	New Hampshire
Alaska	Michigan	Hawaii	N. Carolina[a, b]
Arizona	Mississippi	Indiana	N. Dakota[a, b]
California	Missouri	Kentucky[b]	Ohio
Colorado	New Jersey	Maine	Oregon[a, b]
Connecticut	New Mexico	Minnesota	Texas[a, b]
Delaware	New York	Montana[b]	Virginia
Florida	Oklahoma	Nebraska	Washington[a]
Georgia	Pennsylvania	Nevada[b]	Wisconsin
Idaho	Rhode Island		Wyoming[a]
Illinois	S. Carolina		
Iowa	S. Dakota		
Kansas	Tennessee		
Louisiana	Utah		
Maryland	Vermont		
	West Virginia		

Notes: [a] adopt a single budget for the biennium,
  [b] no allowance for off-year adjustments.

Sources: Compiled from various sources.

TABLE II. Recent Changes in Budget Periodicity

Biennial to Annual	Annual to Biennial
South Dakota (1964)	Georgia (1971)
New Mexico (1966)	Hawaii (1971)
Oklahoma (1968)	Iowa (1974)
Utah (1969)	North Carolina (1975)
Illinois (1970)	Minnesota (1975)
Tennessee (1970)	Indiana (1978)
Connecticut (1971)	Florida (1978)
Iowa (1971)	
Mississippi (1971)	
Missouri (1971)	
Nebraska (1972)	
Minnesota (1973)	
North Carolina (1973)	
Georgia (1974)	
Indiana (1975)	
Alabama (1976)	

Source: *The Book of the States*, various issues.

conduct annual legislative sessions. Half of the states that held annual legislative sessions restricted the additional off-year session to fiscal and budgetary matters.

By 1971, five more states had begun to conduct annual legislative sessions: Idaho, Iowa, Mississippi, Oklahoma, and Utah. Mississippi, Oklahoma, and Utah began to adopt annual budgets at the same time. Idaho and Iowa continued to budget biennially in the presence of annual legislative sessions—the first two states to change the frequency of legislative sessions without changing budget periodicity. Georgia, which had budgeted annually in the past, returned to biennial budgeting. This was the first indication that the frequency of legislative sessions need not coincide with budgetary frequency, with Idaho, Iowa, and Georgia as the innovators.

Initially, states tended to adopt annual budgets as a matter of course when their legislatures began to meet annually, but more recent history has not repeated this pattern. Forty-two states now conduct annual legislative sessions, representing an almost complete turnaround from the 1940s, when only four state legislatures met annually. Not a single state has reverted to biennial legislative sessions after the change to annual sessions was initiated, but the recent history of budget periodicity has been more tumultuous. Just since 1969 there have been 19 alterations in state budget periodicity (see Table II). Seven states changed from biennial to annual periodicity. Four other states changed from biennial to annual, but have since returned to biennial budget periodicity. One state changed from annual to biennial, and yet another changed from biennial to annual, back to biennial and finally returned to annual.

Hawaii abandoned annual budgets in 1971, opting for biennial budgeting. Reportedly, legislators believed that they could devote more time to systematic administrative program reviews and evaluations during the course of the second session. Connecticut changed from biennial to annual budgeting in 1971, at the same time that the legislature began meeting annually, limiting the second session to budgetary and fiscal matters. Though the reported motivations for these two changes were the same, they resulted in opposite budget periodicity choices. In the late 1980s and 1990s, several states have reconsidered the budget periodicity question as part of overarching governmental and budgeting reform.

Current Practice

Historically, the overall trend in budget periodicity has been away from biennial and toward annual, like the overall trend in the frequency of legislative sessions. The history of budget periodicity has not exactly mirrored that of legislative sessions. No state has returned to a biennial legislature after a change to annual legislative sessions has been adopted. Annual budgets do not evoke the same loyalty though; some states revert to biennial budgets after experimenting with annual ones, others never adopt annual budgets at all. Despite the overall trend toward annual budgeting, state differences in budget periodicity persist.

To strike a balance between flexibility and continuity, some biennial budget states adopt two one-year budgets every other year (Arkansas, Hawaii, Indiana, Kentucky, Maine, Minnesota, Montana, Nebraska, Nevada, New Hampshire, Ohio, Virginia, Wisconsin). Of these, the budget document for the second year cannot be altered in Arkansas, Kentucky, Montana, and Nevada, with only Montana having a provision for annual supplemental appropriations to cover revenue shortages. Hawaii, Indiana, Maine, Minnesota, Nebraska, New Hampshire, Ohio, Virginia, and Wisconsin all allow for modifications or reforms in the nonbudget year of the biennium. Such modifications are not automatic, as they would be in annual budget states. The appropriate majority of the legislature must agree to consider the modification, which might require a special legislative session, a supplemental appropriation, or both. Although two one-year budgets might seem equivalent to annual budgeting, the organizational costs of budgetary revisions are much higher in biennial budget states than in annual ones.

Other biennial budget states adopt a single budget for the biennium (North Carolina, North Dakota, Oregon, Texas, Washington, Wyoming). Of these, some states have provisions for off-year adjustments to the original budget (North Carolina, Washington, Wyoming); but North Dakota, Oregon, and Texas do not. The Oregon legislature has the power to call itself into special session and to set the agenda for that session; North Dakota and Texas cannot. Even among states that can adjust the original document, the costs of modifications are higher than in annual budget states, where budgetary changes occur as a matter of course.

Theoretical Framework

What constitutes the optimal budget periodicity choice for a state government? Roy Meyers (1988) of the Congressional Budget Office has posed this question. He suggests that the budget period should be short enough to allow for responsiveness to the prevailing political mood and economic conditions. It should also be long enough not to require the constant attention of budget-makers, and to permit some degree of continuity in public policy implementation. Obviously, monthly budgets would allow for almost total control over spending, but they would be repetitive, unwieldy, and would lead to much policy uncertainty. Five-year budgets would drastically reduce the workload for budgetary decisionmakers, but would be extremely susceptible to fluctuations in the environment and inflexible to changing political priorities.

Comparisons of annual and biennial budgets are not so clear-cut. Annual budgets are more flexible than biennial budgets, since adjustments can be made more frequently in response to economic and political fluctuations. Biennial budgets provide additional certainty for funded programs and policies, although they are susceptible to the uncertainty of more remote revenue and expenditure forecasts. Which periodicity choice is "better" might depend on the particular political and economic conditions of the state at a particular point in time. No single budget periodicity choice has prevailed and persisted over time at the state level.

Most of the extant budget periodicity literature consists primarily of survey responses collected from state budget officials. (See, for an example, Yondorf 1987. Kearns 1994 summarizes several surveys.) These surveys provide valuable insights regarding factors that are thought to contribute to a particular state's choice of budget periodicity. The responses came from elite actors in state or federal budget offices, operating in both executive and legislative capacities. Annual budgeting and biennial budgeting each have proponents and detractors in the executive and legislative branches. These individuals may have had vested interests in the budgeting process and might have had reason to support or disclaim the status quo accordingly.

Arguments in favor of annual budgeting include: the increased time for legislative consideration of the budget; the enhanced control that legislators have to manipulate intergovernmental transfers and to oversee agency activity; the increased accuracy of revenue estimates; the reduced power of the executive branch for discretionary spending; and the elimination of many special sessions and supplemental appropriations. Some budgetmakers prefer biennial budgeting because they believe that budgets, preparation costs, and overall expenditures are all lower, and that the opportunity exists for more long-term planning, program evaluation, and legislative deliberation of spending decisions. These views are more thoroughly discussed in the review of survey results later.

Frequency of Legislative Sessions

Many states changed to annual budget periods when the change to annual legislative sessions was made. The professionalization of state legislatures is thought to have contributed to the move to annual budget periods. The increased role of the legislature in budgetary tasks has also been cited. Annual legislative sessions and larger and more sophisticated legislative staffs have equipped state legislatures to deal with the additional workload of annual budgets. Some state officials expressly report that the motivation for annual budgets was "to make the budget cycle correspond with a change to annual meetings of the legislature."

Increased State Spending

The General Accounting Office (GAO) reports a direct correlation between state spending and state budget periodicity. Only two of the ten top-spending states continue to use biennial budget periods (Ohio and North Carolina) in the presence of annual legislative sessions. Moreover, biennial budget states account for 38 percent of the states, but only 28 percent of state expenditures. Annual budget states account for 62 percent of the states and 72 percent of state expenditures. This disproportion has led some analysts to conclude that the decision to budget annually is a result of the growth in demand for state spending.

Complexity

The budgetary task confronting state legislatures has increased in both size and complexity over time. As state governments undertake to deliver more goods and services to their citizenry, the budget process is complicated accordingly. The complexity of the budgeting process influenced many states to approach the task more frequently. Annual budgeting gives the legislature more opportunities to scrutinize the budget and the various agency requests for funding increases.

Forecast Accuracy

Accuracy of revenue forecasts was the reported motivation of some budget players who preferred annual to biennial budget periods. The reduction in the uncertainty of revenue forecasts for the second year of the biennium appealed to many survey respondents. Since most state legislatures confront a balanced budget requirement, accurate forecasts of revenues and expenditures are a necessity.

Other economic fluctuations can also be dealt with more effectively with an annual budget period, reducing the need for special legislative sessions. Increased reliance on individual income taxes has rendered states more vulnerable to economic fluctuations, and made forecasts more unreliable. Proponents of biennial budgets stress the opportunity for oversight and program evaluation. Biennial budget periodicity might allow for more long-range planning, but according to some survey respondents, such planning and oversight is at the cost of accurate revenue forecasts.

Intergovernmental Transfers

The effect of increased intergovernmental transfers on state budgetary processes has been assessed. David M. Hedge (1983) concludes that "the effective implementation of federal programs has become increasingly dependent on the willingness and ability of state officials to comply with federal directives and requirements." In an increasingly complex federalist system, annual budgets allow for the more frequent adjustments that might be necessary to qualify for some types of intergovernmental aid. Texas A&M researchers Wiggins and Hamm concur; based on interviews with officials in five states, their study found that federal funding "encourages" annual budgeting.

Executive-Legislative Conflict

Annual budget periods give the executive branch less discretion in expenditure decisions. To compensate for the uncertainty of the revenues in the second year of the biennium, biennial budget states appropriate to broader budget areas, maintain discretionary funds, or allow the executive branch a certain level of expenditure discretion. Not surprisingly, executive and legislative survey respondents tend to disagree on the need for such measures. As the chronology of budget periodicity reveals, annual budgets have been used at times when the legislative majority and governor were from differing political party affiliations. The GAO reports that some of the responses to their survey indicate that annual budgets improve legislative control over budgetary matters.

Survey results offer mixed findings of whether "extra" time is available for the evaluation of existing programs or the development of longer-term plans. Proponents claim that biennial budgeting allows more time for planning and oversight. Opponents claim that the work will fill the time allotted to it, and weigh the forecasting difficulties associated with biennial budgeting. Kearns (1994) has considered the question of why some states budget for a one-year period while others budget for a two-year period, using statistical analyses of the political and economic factors that have been thought to contribute to a state's propensity to budget annually or biennially.

Survey findings detect little or no perceived expenditure impacts from the budget period itself. Some respondents indicated that biennial budget states spend less than annual budget states. Others perceived that the budget period itself does not account for any expenditure differential among the states. In states that have experienced changes in budget periodicity (from annual to biennial or from biennial to annual), no perceived change in spending has been reported. Risk-averse budget decisionmakers are thought to budget less for the second year of a biennial budget period than they would if the budget were prepared annually. Supposedly, this is due to the increased uncertainty that accompanies revenue forecasts and expenditure projections for the more remote time period. Such risk-avoiding behavior is conventionally believed to result in lower spending in biennial budget states than in annual budget states.

Kearns (1994) shows that when the effects of state budget periodicity are isolated, biennial budget states spend more per capita than do annual budget states. This disparity is attributed to the preference by interest groups for the certainty of a second-year appropriation to the frequency of opportunities to appeal for wealth transfers to their group. Budget periodicity has not been considered specifically in the expansive interest group literature, but Crain, Schughart, and Tollison (1988) contend that enforcement mechanisms give assurance to the agreements struck between lobbyists and legislators. Biennial budget periodicity qualifies as such an enforcement mechanism; any deal that is made is binding for two full years. Biennial budgeting gives assurance to lobbyists and the interest groups they represent that the political favors obtained in biennial budget states are more durable than those obtained in annual budget states. More durable budgetary legislation is valued by special interest groups because of the tenuous (i.e., noninstitutionalized) connection between interest groups and budgetary decisionmakers.

Variations

The U.S. experience with biennial budgeting has been at the state level, but the complexity and enormity of the national budget process has motivated discussion of biennial budget for the federal government. The U.S. Congress's *National Performance Review* (1993) called for the institutionalization of biennial budgets and appropriations for the federal government: "We should not have to enact a budget every year. Twenty states adopt budgets for two years. They retain the power to make small adjustments in off years if revenues or expenditures deviate widely from forecasts. As a result, their governors and legislatures have much more time to evaluate programs and develop longer-term plans."

Most observers agree that biennial budgeting would increase the already considerable discretion that the executive branch has over implementation of the budget. Con-

gress does have some monitoring capability over the executive branch's implementation, and proponents of the biennial budget claim that biennial budgeting would increase the monitoring capabilities of Congress making the off-year available for planning and monitoring pursuits. In every state in which biennial budgeting is used, some mechanism enhancing executive discretion has accompanied the biennial budget. Survey results are mixed as to whether the additional year really allows for more planning and oversight.

The idea of biennial budgeting has been around for some time. Then-Congressman Leon Panetta introduced the first biennial budgeting bill in 1977, and dozens have been offered since. Panetta introduced HR 9077, which envisioned a two-year budget process for the U.S. Congress. Year one would have been devoted to oversight, with year two devoted to resolution and appropriation. Panetta's appointment as Director of the Office of Management and Budget early in the Clinton administration brought biennial budgeting to the fore of the budgeting reform movement.

Comprehensive biennial budgeting has yet to be passed by Congress, although the federal government has had some experience with budget plans that cover two years or more. In 1987, the President and Congress drafted a budget plan for fiscal years 1988 and 1989 that set spending levels for major categories, enabling Congress to enact all 13 appropriations bills on time for the first time since 1977. In addition, Congress directed the Department of Defense (DOD) to submit a biennial budget for fiscal 1988 and 1989 in order to give Congress more time for broad policy oversight. At the time, Congress asserted that a biennial budget would improve Defense Department management and congressional oversight. A biennial defense budget was thought to be an important step toward complete biennial budgeting. But while administrations continue to submit biennial budgets for DOD, Congress continued to appropriate on an annual basis, apparently reluctant to relinquish second-period control.

Recall that some states chose to budget annually because the related tasks had become more complex and required the more frequent attention of the legislators. Proponents of a biennial budget for the federal government claim that the budgetary task is so complex and unwieldy that it cannot be dealt with effectively in a single year. The sheer bulk of the federal budget suggests that the problems confronting federal budget-makers are vastly different from those associated with the budgets of the individual states. Yet the state experience is still considered by many to be a laboratory of sorts for federal policy, including budget periodicity.

According to a GAO (1987) study, "Trends and experiences in state government can provide useful information to federal decision-makers as they consider the various biennial budget proposals." Congressional Budget Office analysts concur, observing that "arguments for and against federal biennial budgeting often proceed by analogy with budgeting in the states. This is particularly true in the Congress because many Representatives and Senators have had experience as state legislators or governors and would like to try at the federal level the procedures that they are familiar with at home."

PAULA S. KEARNS

BIBLIOGRAPHY

Fisher, Ronald C., 1988. "The Budget Process." In *State and Local Public Finance*. Glenview, IL: Scott, Foresman and Company.

General Accounting Office, 1987. *Budget Issues: Current Status and Recent Trends of State Biennial and Annual Budgeting.* Accounting and Financial Management Division of the General Accounting Office, Washington, D.C.: Government Printing Office (GPO).

Higgins, Richard G., 1988. "Biennial Budgeting for the Federal Government?" *Public Administration Review,* 48: 938–940.

Howard, Kenneth S., 1973. *Changing State Budgeting.* Lexington, KY: Council of State Governments.

Kearns, Paula S., 1994. "State Budget Periodicity: An Analysis of the Determinants and the Effect on State Spending." *Journal of Policy Analysis and Management,* 13: 331–362.

Lee, Robert D., Jr., and Ronald W. Johnson, 1989. *Public Budgeting Systems,* 4th ed. Rockville, MD: Aspen Publishers.

Lynch, Thomas D., 1990. *Public Budgeting in America.* Englewood Cliffs, NJ: Prentice-Hall.

Meyers, Roy T., 1988. "Biennial Budgeting by the U.S. Congress," *Public Budgeting & Finance,* 8: 21–32.

Mikesell, John L., 1986. *Fiscal Administration Analysis and Applications for the Public Sector.* Chicago IL: Dorsey Press.

Proposals for a Biennial Budget, 1983. Washington, D.C.: American Enterprise Institute for Public Policy Research.

Schick, Allen, 1971. *Budget Innovation in the States,* 1971. Washington, D.C.: Brookings Institution.

U.S. Congress House Committee on Government Operations, 1993. *National Performance Review.* Washington, D.C.: GPO.

Yondorf, Barbara, 1987. *Annual Versus Biennial Budgeting: The Arguments, the Evidence.* Denver: National Conference of State Legislatures.

BILL OF ATTAINDER.

A legislative declaration of the punishment of individuals, without the safeguards associated with a judicial trial. Bills of attainder are prohibited by Article I, Sections 9 and 10 of the U.S. Constitution.

Because the framers of the Constitution were familiar with oppressive uses of attainment by the English Parliament and American state legislatures, they voted unanimously, and with little debate, to prevent both Congress and state legislatures from enacting them. During the American Revolution, several states vindictively passed bills of attainder against Tories. The New York legislature, for instance, attainted a former governor on the grounds that he had "voluntarily been adherent" to King George III. At the Constitutional Convention, critics such as Alexander Hamilton feared that popular passions would be too quick to use attainment to infringe on the liberty of any persons the people found obnoxious.

In early modern England, bills of attainder were not always viewed so negatively. From the mid-fifteenth century through the eighteenth century, when they began to die out, these legislative judgments were a recognized means for ridding either the monarch or the Commons of powerful ministers who offended them. They applied only in capital cases such as treason. In noncapital cases, the comparable legislative judgment was a bill of pains and penalties. According to Blackstone's *Commentaries* (1769), upon a legislative judgment of death, or outlawry in cases where the individual had fled, the individual was attainted, "stained, or blackened," beyond the point of redeeming reputation or credit. In addition to death, attainment involved forfeiture of estate and "corruption of blood," which disinherited not only the attainted person, but also his or her heirs.

Montesquieu, writing in 1748, defended bills of attainder on the grounds that circumstances sometimes require that individuals be deprived of liberty "in order to preserve it for the whole community." In addition to the example of England, he cited legislative punishment of too-powerful individuals in the ancient republics of Athens and Rome.

Even Thomas Jefferson defended attainment as a remedy in certain kinds of cases. In 1778, at the request of Virginia Governor Patrick Henry, he drafted for the Virginia Assembly a bill of attainder against an infamous Tory, Josiah Phillips, who with several others, was known to have committed murders and destroyed property. Jefferson still defended the attainment of Phillips 37 years later, in a letter written to L. H. Girardin in 1815. "The occasion and proper office of a bill of attainder is this," he wrote:

> When a person charged with a crime withdraws from justice, or resists it by force . . . no other means of bringing him to trial or punishment being practicable, a special act is passed by the legislature. . . . This prescribes to him a sufficient time to appear and submit to a trial by his peers; declares that his refusal to appear shall be taken as a confession of guilt.

U.S. Supreme Court interpretations of the Article I prohibition against bills of attainder have never recognized this justification. In fact, with their prohibition in the U.S. Constitution, these bills joined a growing body of practices that were considered to violate natural rights. U.S. Supreme Court interpretations in constitutional adjudication contributed to this development.

Although a bill of attainder originally covered only criminal proceedings against designated individuals and in capital cases, the Supreme Court has extended the constitutional prohibition considerably. Taking the view that the framers of the Constitution intended to prohibit all extrajudicial determinations of guilt and punishment, in accordance with the doctrine of separation of powers, the Court has, over time, broadened the prohibition to cover noncapital cases, civil proceedings, and classes or groups of unspecified individuals. This broadening has occurred in response to legislative acts that did not fall within the conventional definition of a bill of attainder but that seemed to the Court to violate the principles of justice that the framers intended the prohibition to uphold. That is, these acts of the legislature, in some way, restricted or punished individuals without a trial.

The first step in broadening the definition of bill of attainder came in *Fletcher v. Peck* (1810), when Chief Justice John Marshall interpreted the prohibition against bills of attainder to include bills of pains and penalties. In two 1867 cases, *Cummings v. Missouri* and *Ex parte Garland,* the Court struck down state and federal laws that effectively prevented persons who had rebelled against the Union from working in certain professions because they could not honestly take an oath that they had never been disloyal. This ruling cast disqualification from office as punishment within the meaning of a bill of attainder. In *United States v. Lovett* (1946), the Court followed the same approach to invalidate a law that denied salary to three federal employees named as subversives by the House Committee on Un-American Activities. Finally, in *United States v. Brown* (1965), the Court struck down a section of the Labor-Management Reporting and Disclosure Act of 1959, which made it a crime for members of the Communist Party to serve as officers or employees of labor unions. For the Court, the problem was that the law did not articulate a general rule that persons who commit certain specified acts are "likely to initiate political strikes" and then leave "to courts and juries the job of deciding what persons have committed the specified acts or possessed the specified characteristics." Instead it designated "in no uncertain terms the persons who possess the feared characteristics and therefore cannot hold union office without incurring criminal liability." That punishment of a group of persons without due process of law made the statute an unconstitutional bill of attainder.

An absolute prohibition against bills of attainder can be upheld against the will of the legislature only in the type of democratic political system that relies on a written constitution and judicial guardians to protect individual rights from majoritarian elements. In more majoritarian parliamentary systems, any rights associated with higher law sources, such as England's unwritten constitution or Israel's Basic Laws, can be restricted by ordinary legislation.

WYNNE WALKER MOSKOP

BIBLIOGRAPHY

Blackstone, William, 1769. *Commentaries on the Laws of England,* Vol. 4. London.
Chafee, Zechariah, 1956. *Three Human Rights in the Constitution of 1797.* Lawrence: University of Kansas Press.
United States v. Brown, 1965. 381 U.S. 437.

THE BILL OF RIGHTS.

The first ten amendments added to the Constitution of the United States, setting forth several basic substantive and procedural rights and protections of persons against arbitrary governmental action. The Bill of Rights was originally a listing of individual rights and protections against the new national government, which was created by the Constitution of 1787. The Bill of Rights arose out of the politics surrounding the making and ratification of the new Constitution; fears about the powers of the proposed national government forced backers of the Constitution to promise to include amendments setting forth individual rights, thereby guaranteeing the Constitution's ratification by the states. The First Congress (which was established when the Constitution was ratified) proposed the amendments in 1789 and the new states adopted them in 1791, more than two years after the ratification of the Constitution.

The theoretical concept of a Bill of Rights involved a listing of fundamental individual liberties possessed by persons before the formation of government and against which government could not transgress. This concept and many of the particular rights so guaranteed had roots in British history back to the Magna Carta, the list of rights that the nobles forced King John to accept in 1215. It received fuller expression in the Bill of Rights of 1689, a culmination of the puritan revolution in the late seventeenth century, a time when Britain's American colonies were developing their own early governments.

The extent of the acceptance of the concept of a Bill of Rights is indicated by its adoption in many state constitutions during and after the Revolutionary War, while the former British colonies were governed under the Articles of Confederation. States that adopted Bills of Rights in their new constitutions in the Revolutionary period were New Hampshire, Vermont, Massachusetts, Pennsylvania, Delaware, Maryland, Virginia, and North Carolina. Andrew C. McLaughlin (1935) noted that these Bills of Rights

accept the theory that government rests on consent and exists for the protection of rights. The Virginia Bill of Rights, largely the work of George Mason, contains the same philosophy as the Declaration of Independence and it was passed in the state before the Declaration was passed. It announces the doctrine of "inherent" rights of the people and the doctrine that all power is derived power. It then outlines in a masterly way the principles upon which free government rests. Associated with the announcement of the fundamental principle that power springs from the people and that people have the right to alter and abolish government are certain other declarations of secondary rather than primary importance; they are of service in maintaining the more elementary and fundamental rights. The announcement of religious liberty in the Virginia Bill is especially significant as an indication of the liberalizing effect of the Revolutionary movement. The first and most elementary principle of bills of rights is that men possessed rights before government was formed. Human rights are supposed to have existed before the establishment of government or state. (p. 115)

A further indication of the acceptance of the principle that there are individual rights protected against governmental action is indicated by a listing of individual rights by the Congress of the Confederation in the ordinance adopted for the governance of the Northwest Territory on July 13, 1787, while the Constitutional Convention was meeting in Philadelphia. The Continental Congress declared that a far-ranging list of rights "shall be considered as articles of compact between the original States and the people and States in the said territory and forever remain unalterable, unless by common consent" (Corwin 1953); some of these rights are as follows:

Art. 1. No person, demeaning himself in a peaceful and orderly manner, shall ever be molested on account of his mode of worship or religious sentiments, in the said territory.

Art. 2. The inhabitants of the said territory shall always be entitled to the benefits of the writ of *habeas corpus,* and of the trial by jury; of a proportionate representation of the people in the legislature; and of judicial proceedings according to the course of the common law. All persons shall be bailable, unless for capital offenses, where the proof shall be or the presumption great. All fines shall be moderate; and no cruel or unusual punishments shall be inflicted. No man shall be deprived of his liberty or property, but by the judgement of his peers or the law of the land; and, should the public exigencies make it necessary, for the common preservation, to take any person's property, or demand his particular services, full compensation shall be made for the same. And, in the just preservation of rights and property, it is understood and declared, that no law ought ever be made, or have force in the said territory, that shall, in any manner whatever, interfere with or affect private contracts or engagements, *bona fide,* and without fraud, previously formed.

Art. 3. Religion, morality, and knowledge, being necessary to good government and the happiness of mankind, schools and the means of education shall forever be encouraged.

Art. 6. There shall be neither slavery nor involuntary servitude in the said territory, otherwise than in the punishment of crimes whereof the party shall have been duly convicted.

Meanwhile, at the Constitutional Convention many controversies lay in the path of reaching consensus on a new constitution. Fundamental to these controversies were the sometimes differing traditions of life, politics, and government under thirteen separate colonies for more than 100 years of British rule. There had been a short period of united purpose among the colonies during the Revolutionary War, 1775–1783. Unity was more severely tested during the postwar period to 1787 as the loose confederation of thirteen new states existed under the Articles of Confederation.

The inadequacies of the national government of the Confederation quickly became apparent, and the movement toward a stronger national government resulted in the call for a constitutional convention in 1787. But fundamental and often divisive questions had to be addressed in the process of constitution-making: How strong should a new national government be? Did the people or the states possess ultimate sovereignty? How were governmental powers to be divided between states and national government? How permanent was the union? Could states withdraw if they believed that the basic compact had been broken? What was the status of slavery? Finally, should the constitution guarantee the individual rights of citizens against government? If so, would the basic protections be those usually associated with a Bill of Rights, whether that of England of the late seventeenth century, those of the revolutionary state charters after 1776, or those that the Continental Congress had guaranteed in the ordinance of the Northwest Territory in the summer of 1787 while these debates were taking place at the Constitutional Convention?

Almost any proposal at the Constitutional Convention could be controversial, therefore it is not surprising that, whether the issue was the power of the new national government or the guaranties that the small states would not be overwhelmed by the large, a call for a Bill of Rights in the Constitution would emerge, as either a fundamental issue or as a tactical ploy.

Anti-Federalists had argued the need for a Bill of Rights to protect against an arbitrary central government during the Constitutional Convention and the ratifying debates. It was the Federalists at the Convention, most particularly Alexander Hamilton, who in the *Federalist Papers* and in the state ratifying conventions argued that previous bills of rights were aimed at the possible abridgements of liberties by kings and princes and would not be necessary in a government based on the power of the people. Nevertheless, it finally became politically necessary to promise a Bill of Rights to gain ratification.

To fulfill this promise after ratification of the new Constitution James Madison, in the early days of the First Congress, introduced a list of amendments drawn from 124 amendments that had been proposed by the states. Of these, 17 were accepted by the House of Representatives, 15 by the Senate, and 12 became the compromise version of both houses of Congress (Corwin 1953: 750). Ten of the twelve amendments became part of the federal Constitution when Virginia's legislature became the eleventh state to ratify on December 15, 1791, thus becoming the three-fourths majority required. (The legislatures of Connecticut, Georgia, and Massachusetts were not recorded as ratifying.) In the newly adopted Bill of Rights, it was only the national government, as embodied in congressional powers, against which the protections would be erected.

Thus it was clearly the national government that the framers of the First Amendment had in mind when they wrote, "Congress shall make no law respecting an establishment of a religion or prohibiting the free exercise thereof; or abridging the freedom of speech, or of the press; or the right of the people peaceably to assemble, and to petition the Government for a redress of grievances." Indeed the Senate had specifically rejected one of Madison's proposed amendments, which read: "The equal rights of conscience, the freedom of speech or of the press, and the right of trial by jury in criminal cases shall not be infringed by any State." Nevertheless, for the next century the Supreme Court would be urged to apply the Bill of Rights to the states as well. The initial test of this proposition came in *Barron v. Baltimore* (7 Pet. 243) in 1833, when Chief Justice John Marshall ruled that the Bill of Rights could not be applied to the states. But as Edward S. Corwin (1953) observed:

> Nevertheless the enduring vitality of natural law concepts encouraged renewed appeals for judicial protection [against the states]. Expressions such as the statement of Justice Miller in *Citizens Savings and Loan Association v. Topeka* that "It must be conceded that there are rights in every free government beyond the control of the States [20 Wall 655, 669 (1875)]" probably account for the fact reported by Charles Warren that "In at least twenty cases between 1877 and 1907, the Court was required to rule upon this point and to reaffirm Marshall's decision of 1833."

With the adoption of the Fourteenth Amendment in 1867, new lines of argumentation opened for those who wished to gain the protections of the Bill of Rights against actions by state governments. Even if it was intended primarily to protect the newly freed slaves, the Fourteenth Amendment provided that "no State shall make or enforce any law which shall abridge the privileges or immunities of citizens of the United States; nor shall any State deprive any person of life, liberty or property without due process of law; nor deny to any person within its jurisdiction the equal protection of the laws."

As early as 1873, the Supreme Court, in the *Slaughter House Cases* (83 U.S. 36), rejected the contention that the privileges and immunities clause of the Fourteenth Amendment included the privileges and immunities of citizens under the U.S. Constitution, including the right to do business free from arbitrary governmental interference. This decision closed for several decades the avenue for the incorporation of the entire Bill of Rights through the privileges and immunities clause of the Fourteenth Amendment. In subsequent years, however, Justice Harlan, Justices Brewer and Field, and a minority of four justices, with Justice Black as a spokesperson in 1947 in *Adamson v. California* (332 U.S. 46) urged that the history of the Fourteenth Amendment seemed clearly to establish that its authors intended to apply all of the privileges and protections of the Bill of Rights through the medium of the first section of the Fourteenth Amendment.

Historical and theoretical arguments about whether the Bill of Rights was intended by its framers to be applied to the states were eventually circumvented by "incremental selective incorporation." This approach gradually extended the more fundamental protections of the Bill of Rights to citizens against the states through the due process clause of the Fourteenth Amendment. What became selective incorporation was described in 1908 when the Court said in *Twining v. New Jersey* (211 U.S. 78, 99), "It is possible that some of the personal rights safeguarded by the first eight amendments against National action may also be safeguarded against state action because a denial of them would be a denial of due process of law. If this is so, it is not because those rights are enumerated in the first eight amendments but because they are of such nature that they are included in the conception of due process of law." By 1925, in *Gitlow v. New York* (268 U.S. 652, 666) the Court had progressed to saying, "For present purposes we may and do assume that freedom of speech and of the press—which are protected by the First Amendment from abridgement by Congress—are among the fundamental personal rights and liberties protected by the due process clause of the Fourteenth Amendment from impairment by the States."

In 1932, in *Powell v. Alabama* (287 U.S. 45, 68) the Court extended selective incorporation to the right to counsel, finding such to be of "fundamental character." Two years later Justice Benjamin Cardozo provided a classic description of the test of whether a particular right under the Bill of Rights was fundamental, justifying incorporation through the due process clause of the Fourteenth

Amendment. Cardozo said that such would occur when the questioned state procedure "offends some principle of justice so rooted in the traditions and conscience of our people as to be ranked as fundamental" (*Snyder v. Massachusetts*, 291 U.S. 97, 105 [1934]). Cardozo added in *Palko v. Connecticut* (302 U.S. 319, 325 [1937]) that certain applications of selective incorporation were "implicit in the concept of ordered liberty."

The process of selective incorporation proceeded to the point that it could be said by the early 1970s that whether the Supreme Court had ruled provisions of the Bill of Rights to have been incorporated or absorbed by the Fourteenth Amendment and applied to the states, or whether the Court had declared them to be such fundamental liberties as to deserve application to the states, virtually all of the basic rights and protections of the first eight amendments were now protections against both federal and state governments by identical standards (*Constitution of the U.S.* 1973: 905–906). Such basic protections and the ruling cases concerning their application to the states were set forth in the same words in both the 1973 and 1987 editions of the *Constitution of the United States* as follows:

The following list does not attempt to distinguish between those Bill of Rights provisions which have been held to have themselves been incorporated or absorbed by the Fourteenth Amendment and those provisions which the Court indicated at the time were applicable against the States because they were fundamental and not merely because they were named in the Bill of Rights. Whichever formulation was originally used, the former is now the one used by the Court. *Duncan v. Louisiana*, 391 U.S. 145, 148 (1968).

First Amendment:

- Religion–Free exercise: *Hamilton v. Regents,* 293 U.S. 245, 262 (1934); *Cantwell v. Connecticut,* 310 U.S. 296, 300, 303 (1940). Establishment: *Everson v. Board of Education,* 330 U.S. 1,3,7,8 (1947); *Illinois ex rel. McCollum v. Board of Education,* 333 U.S. 203 (1948).
- Speech–*Gitlow v. New York,* 268 U.S. 652, 666 (1925); *Fiske v. Kansas,* 274 U.S. 380 (1927); *Stromberg v. California,* 283 U.S. 359 (1931).
- Press–*Near v. Minnesota ex rel. Olsen,* 283 U.S. 697, 701 (1931).
- Assembly–*DeJonge v. Oregon,* 299 U.S. 353 (1937).
- Petition–*DeJonge v. Oregon, supra,* 364, 365; *Hague v. C.I.O.,* 307 U.S. 296 (1939); *Bridges v. California,* 314 U.S. 252 (1941).

Fourth Amendment:

- Search and seizure–*Wolf v. Colorado,* 338 U.S. 25 (1949); *Mapp v. Ohio,* 367 U.S. 643 (1961).

Fifth Amendment:

- Double jeopardy–*Benton v. Maryland,* 395 U.S. 784 (1969); *Ashe v. Swenson,* 397 U.S. 436 (1970), (collateral estoppel).
- Self incrimination–*Malloy v. Hogan,* 378 U.S. 1 (1964); *Griffin v. California,* 380 U.S. 609 (1965).
- Just compensation–*Chicago, B. & Q. Railroad v. City of Chicago,* 166 U.S. 226 (1897).

Sixth Amendment:

- Speedy trial–*Klopfer v. North Carolina,* 386 U.S. 213 (1967).
- Public trial–*In re Oliver,* 333 U.S. 257 (1948).
- Jury trial–*Duncan v. Louisiana,* 391 U.S. 145 (1968).
- Impartial jury–*Irvin v. Dowd,* 366 U.S. 717 (1961); *Turner v. Louisiana,* 397 U.S. 466 (1965).
- Notice of charges–*In re Oliver,* 333 U.S. 257 (1948).
- Confrontation–*Pointer v. Texas,* 380 U.S. 400 (1965); *Douglas v. Alabama,* 380 U.S. 415 (1965).
- Compulsory process–*Washington v. Texas,* 388 U.S. 14 (1967).
- Counsel–*Powell v. Alabama,* 287 U.S. 45 (1932); *Gideon v. Wainwright,* 372 U.S. 335 (1963).

Eighth Amendment:

- Cruel and unusual punishment–*Louisiana ex rel. Francis v. Resweber,* 329 U.S. 459 (1947); *Robinson v. California,* 370 U.S. 660 (1962).

Provisions not applied are:
Second Amendment:

- Right to keep and bear arms–*Cf. United States v. Cruikshank,* 92 U.S. 542, 553 (1876); *Presser v. Illinois,* 116 U.S. 252, 265 (1886).

Third Amendment:

- Quarter troops in homes–No cases.

Fifth Amendment:

- Grand jury indictment–*Hurtado v. California,* 110 U.S. 516 (1884).

Seventh Amendment:

- Jury trial in civil cases in which the value of controversy exceeds $20–*Cf Adamson v. California,* 332 U.S. 46, 64–65 (1947), (Justice Frankfurter concurring); See *Minneapolis & St. L.R. Co. v. Bombolis,* 241 U.S. 211 (1916).

Eighth Amendment:

- Bail–But see *Schlib v. Kuebel,* 404 U.S. 357, 365 (1971).

- Excessive fines—But see *Tate v. Short*, 401 U.S. 395 (1971) (Utilize equal protection to prevent automatic jailing of indigents when others can pay a fine and avoid jail).

In a work such as this encyclopedia, which is intended for public administrators, a few of the protections of the Bill of Rights that are of particular importance for public administrators or for the citizens they serve should be noted. Obviously public administrators have an obligation to protect all constitutional rights of U.S. citizens when an occasion arises.

Of particular importance is the guarantee that citizens cannot be deprived of life, liberty, or property without due process of law, guaranteed against federal action by the Fifth Amendment and against state action by the Fourteenth Amendment. Moreover, there are both substantive and procedural rights that administrative law authorities consider to be particularly associated with the administrative process, though because of space limitations only a few such rights can be illustrated here.

An example of a substantive right being of special interest to public administrators can be seen in the treatment of political patronage—the centuries-old tradition that the electoral victor had also won the right to the political spoils by being able to reward his or her followers with political jobs. This patronage system had been the target of the good government movement, which won the adoption of the merit system on the federal level in 1883 when the Pendleton Act established the right to be considered for federal employment without regard to political affiliation. In a series of cases that began with *Elrod v. Burns* (427 U.S. 347, [1976]) and ended with *Rutan v. Republican Party of Illinois* (497 U.S. 62, [1990]), which significantly reiterated *Branti v. Finkel* (445 U.S. 507, [1980]) the Supreme Court ruled that a political patronage system that required allegiance to, work for, contribution to, and sponsorship by a political party sponsor would inevitably tend to force patronage employees to compromise their true beliefs and therefore must be forbidden.

In terms of procedural due process it can be said that since the Bill of Rights guarantees citizens wide-ranging protections against unwarranted governmental intrusions into their lives, public administrators are limited by what the Court has ruled to be arbitrary invasions and violations of protected rights and liberties.

Nonetheless, to guarantee these protections, as in the Fourth Amendment's protections of individuals "in their persons, houses, papers and effects against unreasonable searches and seizures," illustrates the complexities of such protections. What is an unreasonable search and seizure is a perennial question, often calling for new interpretations as new technologies arise (e.g., computer-based data systems and high-tech infrared sensor aerial searches). As Kenneth F. Warren (1996) has pointed out,

the constitutionality of certain search and seizure tactics has often been decided on a case-to-case basis, creating great uncertainty in search and seizure law. But one thing is certain: evidence obtained through illegal searches and seizures cannot normally be used in federal or state courts, although such evidence may be used for questioning witnesses before grand juries. (p. 513)

Warren further noted that the greater question for administrative law arises from the historically prevailing principle that certain protections of the Bill of Rights, such as those of the Fourth Amendment, apply only to criminal and not civil procedures. The matter is compounded in its application: In a complex field such as the administration of the immigration and naturalization laws, to be returned to a country of origin will be argued by the departed alien to be a criminal penalty. But the courts have consistently regarded such as a civil proceeding necessary for the effective administration of the Immigration and Naturalization Service's laws and regulations. (*Abel v. United States*, 362 U.S. 217 [1960]); *United States v. Alvarado* (321 F. 2d 336 [2d Cir., 1963]).

GEORGE DORIAN WENDEL

BIBLIOGRAPHY

Corwin, Edward S., ed., 1953. *The Constitution of the United States; Analysis and Interpretation.* Washington, D.C.: Government Printing Office.
McLaughlin, Andrew C., 1935. *A Constitutional History of the United States.* New York: Appleton-Century-Crofts.
United States Constitution, 1973. Washington, D.C.: GPO.
Warren, Kenneth F., 1996. *Administrative Law in the Political System.* 3d ed. Upper Saddle River, NJ: Prentice Hall.

BISMARCK, OTTO VON (1815–1898).

The conservative chancellor who created the modern German state and who is known for his authoritarian personality and for his compulsory state-organized system of social insurance, set up to solve problems in the German Empire that arose from industrialization.

Bismarck was a conservative German politician in the turbulent period characterized by industrialization, by the beginning of liberal parliamentarian democracy, and by the formation of nation-states in Europe. As chancellor of the German Empire, he created (1881–1889) a system of legal social insurances, as such the first in Europe.

His political career began in the Prussian assembly (1847) and as Prussian delegate in the new Bundestag in Frankfurt (1851). In 1862 he was called to the office of minister-president of Prussia. In a period of heavy internal and international conflicts, Bismarck sustained the Prussian monarchy of Wilhelm I against the pressure of the parlementarian majority.

After the military victory over Austria (1866), Prussia became the first power within the German Confederation

(*Deutsche Bund*). After the historical military victory over France (1870), the (Second) German Empire was created as a federal-unionist state, with Wilhelm I as *Kaiser* and Bismarck as *Reichskanzler.*

In foreign politics, Bismarck aimed to maintain the German-Prussian hegemony in Europe, and to isolate France. Internally he used all his forces to combat the opposition, the Catholic Zentrumpartei (*Kulturkampf*, 1872–1879) as well the beginning social democracy (*Sozialistengesetz*, law against socialism, 1878–1890). After an electoral defeat, and because of differences of opinion with the young emperor Wilhelm II, he was dismissed in 1890.

Bismarck was an authoritarian personality, with strong conservative-monarchical ideas; his actions, however, were characterized by realism and pragmatism. The combination of these elements make him a unique historical figure, although his realizations in many fields remained too closely related to his person.

In Germany, as in other European countries, liberal social policy was limited to modest encouragement of a lot of local private initiatives of self-help. In fact, they were the very starting points of what became, in the second half of that century, the social organizations, such as friendly societies, pension funds, and trade unions. Indeed, the heavy social problems caused by industrialization, especially during the economic recession of the 1870s, incited government to promote systematically and subsidize these private and primitive initiatives of social insurance, always organized on the basis of voluntary membership.

In the same period, by way of parlementarian discussions and voting, a legislation of labor protection was created in the United Kingdom, France, and Belgium. Bismarck preferred another way, however, not of intervening in the labor relations, but of reforming the social structure and improving the living conditions by the introduction of a comprehensive and compulsory state-organized system of social insurances. This system was announced in the *Kaiserliche Botschaft* of 1881, followed by the bills on insurance to cover sick payments (1883), industrial accident insurance (1884), and an invalidity and old age pension scheme (1889).

Essential in Bismarck's social insurance system was that it was compulsory, that it was linked to the wage-labor contract, and that it was financed by obligatory contributions by three partners: employers, employees, and the state. In this way, Bismarck aimed at institutional cooperation between the two classes of capitalists and wage-earners, while at the same time emphasizing the responsibility of the state. Nevertheless, in the administration of social insurance, the role of the state was limited because the numerous existing mutual organizations (*Hilfkassen*) were integrated into the new system, which implied that employers and employees were involved. This uniform system was introduced in all the regions of the new Reich. The basic structure still exists today in Germany; it gradually came to existence in other continental European countries, fitting in with already existing forms of subsidized self-help. Accordingly, this type of social insurance is called "Bismarckian."

The uniqueness of Bismarck's initiative was that in opposition to the liberal ideas of nonintervention of the state in social affairs shared by the bourgeoisie and the industrialists, he introduced at an early stage an obligatory insurance as a fundamental social reform in favor of the workers. He had also a particular political purpose, namely to take the wind out of the sails of the rising social and political opposition. The socialist labor movement came to organize itself (Gotha program of 1875), clerical circles (Catholic as well as Protestant) promoted local social initiatives, and there was a growing scientific interest for *Sozial Reform* (*Katheder-Sozialismus*).

Bismarck wanted especially to eliminate the growing social-democratic party, which was considered a danger to the state. By means of a state-organized system of social insurance he intended to integrate the industry workers into the newly formed German Reich, the industrial superpower and unified state. He called social insurance "the Red Cross posts behind the capitalist front." His social policy was part of his personal paternalist and authoritarian state concept.

The evaluation of Bismarck's legislation remains ambiguous. He had created a system of which the characteristics are still applicable in the 1990s. The social advantages of it were real, but remained limited to a relatively small category, mainly consisting of the better-off factory workers. The spirit of the legislation was state-authoritarian, but the political advantage of this was weakened largely by the struggle against the confessional organizations and especially against the socialists, as well as by the lack of social arrangements in other fields of social policy. All this had contributed to the dismissal of Bismarck in 1890, whereafter he withdrew in bitterness.

In reforms introduced by government and Reichstag in the period after Bismarck, the emphasis on power politics and discipline diminished, and more stress was laid on the social advantages of the insurance system.

In the standard theory about social security a distinction is made between two structurally different types of social security systems: the Bismarckian or continental, and the Beveridgean or Anglo-Saxon system. The former includes obligatory social insurances connected with labor performance, organized by profession and financed by contributions of employers and employees, with benefits proportional to wages. Where social insurance is work-connected, social partners (organizations of employers and employees) play an important role by their institutional participation in policymaking and administration. The so-called Beveridgean type of social security, on the contrary, provides a national system of social insurance, financed by general taxation, with flat rate benefits on a minimal level.

In this model, supplementary income is to be insured on the free market by occupational or private insurances; and the social partners are not directly involved in decision-making and administration.

HERMAN DELEECK

BIBLIOGRAPHY

Köhler P. A., and Zacher H. F. (herausgeb.), 1981. *Ein Jahrhundert Sozialversicherung in Deutschland, Frankreich, Grosz Britannien, Oesterreich, und der Schweiz.* Berlin: Duncker Humblot.

Mommsen, W. J., ed. 1981. *The Emergence of the Welfare State in Britain and in Germany.* London: Croom Helm Ltd.

Zöllner, Detlev, 1981. *Ein Jahrhundert Sozialversicherung in Deutschland.* Berlin: Duncker Humblot.

BLACKSBURG MANIFESTO. A document written by Gary L. Wamsley, Charles T. Goodsell, James F. Wolf, John A. Rohr, and Orion F. White of the Center for Public Administration and Policy, Virginia Polytechnic Institute and State University at Blacksburg, Virginia. The *Blacksburg Manifesto* presents a prescription for a constitutionally based and legitimate public administration that plays a key role in governance as well as management. This unique document arose out of its authors' discussion at a faculty retreat in 1982, comparing their views about the nature of public administration and what had been happening to it under the Carter and Reagan administrations. Much to their surprise, instead of discovering areas of disagreement, the authors found a shared institutional understanding of public administration and concern for its legitimacy, which marked them as heirs of the intellectual heritage of such traditionalists as Norton Long, Paul Appleby, Emmette Redford, Phillip Selznick, and Dwight Waldo.

The *Blacksburg Manifesto* is perhaps the only comprehensive and explicitly normative view in the current dialogue about public administration. It was introduced in a panel at the annual convention of the American Society for Public Administration (ASPA) in 1983. The concepts composing the *Manifesto* were first printed in the Public Administration. Theory Network's non-journal *Dialogue* in 1984. Revised versions were included in Ralph Clark Chandler (1987), and in Larry B. Hill, (1992). In 1990, the *Manifesto*'s authors, with additional sections written by Philip S. Kronenberg, Camilla M. Stivers, and Robert N. Bacher, expanded on the concepts of the original *Manifesto* in *Refounding Public Administration* (Womsley et al. 1990). During the period since the introduction of its key concepts, and largely as response to these concepts, the dialogue about public administration's role and legitimacy has been enlarged and lively.

The *Blacksburg Manifesto* is a response not only to bureaucrat bashing, to increasingly inept presidential transitions, and to the antigovernment tone of partisan politics but also to the suffocating hold of behavioralism and positivism in the social sciences and to the lack of an institutional grounding for public administration in the Minnowbrook perspective. Its foundational premise is that the turn-of-the-century "founding" of public administration as a self-conscious field was actually a misfounding–a misapplication of the tenets of managerial or administrative science onto government. The authors contend that it is this misfounding that has, in large part, left the field open to questions of legitimacy and has exposed public servants to an ever-increasing barrage of bureaucrat bashing (see **bureaucrat bashing**). The *Manifesto* proposes a refounding of public administration in the normative concepts of governance and constitutionalism and suggests that such a refounding will lead to recognition of the legitimate role of public administration in the governance of America.

The basic concepts of this refounded public administration include the public administrator as a constitutional officer, bound by oath to apply constitutional principles to the practice of public administration and deriving legitimate authority from the principled debate of the American founding period (see Rohr 1986). Questions of authority in a democratic state are always problematic. The Blacksburg perspective sees authority as intimately connected with effective participation–the two are necessary conditions for each other. The *Manifesto* envisions the public administrator uniquely placed in the policy process, first, to search for the public interest–not necessarily a substantively defined public interest, but rather the public interest as an ideal and a process; and second, to guide policy in the direction that is indicated by that search. The *Manifesto*'s authors regard public administration as a vocation–a calling to service of one's fellow citizens–a moral enterprise, as contrasted with the mere management of public agencies. They envision an active, empowered citizenry as partners in the governance process.

These facets of public administration are brought together in the "Agency"–a social construct of intended rationality and intended community, which is a center of social learning, technical expertise, and *phronesis,* or practical wisdom. The Agency is, therefore, the focal point for public dialogue and the development of policy directions that not only reflect constitutional principles and values but that are also appropriate and workable.

Public administrators, then, are agential leaders whose authority is derived from their civic virtue, their sense of vocation, and their experience in administration. They operate as agents–special citizens acting for all citizens, with all citizens, and by authority from citizens. Their pursuit, in conjunction with an empowered citizenry, of the public interest leads to the highest form of government–rule by all in relationship.

Above all other considerations, The *Blacksburg Manifesto* has invigorated the discourse about the purposes and legitimacy of U.S. public administration. In an era of increased reliance on privatization and as notions of "reinventing government" capture the national agenda, there is an even more pressing need to explore the meaning and significance of citizenship, public service, public administration, and governance in the United States.

KAREN G. EVANS AND GARY L. WAMSLEY

BIBLIOGRAPHY

Chandler, Ralph Clark, ed., 1987. *A Centennial History of the American Administration State*. New York: Free Press.
Hill, Larry B., ed., 1992. *The State of Public Bureaucracy*. Armonk, NY: M. E. Sharpe.
Rohr, John A., 1986. *To Run a Constitution*. Lawrence: University Press of Kansas.
Wamsley, Gary L., et al. 1990. *Refounding Public Administration*. Newbury Park, CA: Sage Publications.

BOARD OF DIRECTORS.

People vested with the legal responsibility to govern and control the affairs of organizations. Accountability for any nonprofit organization ultimately rests with its board of directors (sometimes called board of trustees). Although the board may delegate management authority to a paid staff person, known as the executive director, the board can never be relieved of its legal and fiduciary responsibilities. Governing board members are stewards of the public interest and have a burden of responsibility to use and preserve the organization's assets for advancing a beneficial mission.

Board membership is an admirable act of citizenship for those who are willing to accept a significant amount of volunteering. These special people are generally not compensated for their board service, and they must balance their board obligations with personal demands of work, family responsibilities, and other community activities. This commitment to community service is tied to a long history of voluntary action, with roots that precede the founding of the United States. The innate desire to help is said to be a unique quality in America, a democratic attribute that influences the modern nonprofit board of directors.

Because of the board's legal responsibilities, personal limitations on directors' time, and the daily involvement of the executive director, there is often confusion between the board and staff over roles, responsibilities, turf, and expectations for performance. The board and executive director must clearly understand their mutual expectations if they are to develop a healthy governing body.

Why Have a Board?

Of the many reasons for having a board of directors, legal necessity is primary. In some states, only one board member is required for incorporating an organization, but most states require at least three or more individuals to serve as directors of a governing board. The Internal Revenue Service also requires nonprofit organizations seeking or maintaining recognition for tax-exempt purposes to have governing boards of directors. Members of governing boards are expected to engage willingly in board activities, without receiving any benefit of the organization's assets or earnings.

Aside from the legal necessities, the most practical reasons for having a board of directors are to ensure that the organization is effectively managed and is working toward the achievement of a mission that has a public purpose. Few nonprofit organizations have the resources to employ the personnel with the expertise that is necessary to accomplish their organizational activities. The collective wisdom of the board of directors can serve as a bank of skilled and knowledgeable resources to provide support, advice, and counsel. It has been widely proposed that board members should comprise the three Ws; individuals who are willing to "work," some with "wisdom," and others with "wealth."

Why Would Someone Want to Serve on a Board?

Each person has his or her own reason for voluntary board service; however, one of the most often-stated is to serve one's community. Volunteering as a board member is an honor and a fundamental privilege of a free people.

There are many reasons for joining or for staying on a board. For example, board participation may be an expectation of one's employer. It may provide an opportunity for gaining or maintaining social status in the community, satisfy socializing needs, lead to new knowledge and skills, and enhance one's résumé. For some people, voluntary board service satisfies religious convictions based on a belief in the organization's cause or mission; or is based on personal experience of a problem (such as a disease or tragedy) that is addressed by the work and mission of the organization.

The Board's Relationship with Its Executive Director

The board's motivation for hiring an executive director is to have expert help with managing the organization and to provide the support necessary to achieve the organization's mission, goals, and objectives. The executive director can also assist each board member with fulfilling his or her personal board commitments.

Various authors have described their ideas about the ideal working relationship between the board and executive director. Two governance models prevail. One model builds on the traditional view that the executive director is employed as a subordinate to the board. The working relationship is characterized by distinct and separate roles for the board and executive director, with the board directing, supervising, and limiting the director's activities as the board sees fit.

The other governance model builds on ideas of partnership and collegiality between the executive director and board of directors. This model acknowledges that the board of directors has clearly defined legal responsibilities. However, the model differs from traditional approaches in a fundamental way: The executive director takes an active role in assisting with or coordinating the participation of board members in fulfilling their governance commitment. This form of board management makes full use of the executive director's distinctive management and leadership skills. Consequently, the quality of the board's performance is a direct result of the executive director's ability to steer and promote productive interaction among board members. The executive director can call upon board managers to intervene when necessary in either the internal or external environment of the organization.

Who Is in Charge of Making Policy?

Prescriptions for effective board practice often state that the board is legally responsible for making policy and the staff is responsible for carrying it out. Though this division of labor is technically correct, it is inaccurate in its practice. The staffs of nonprofit organizations have a significant level of influence on the creation of policy. Since they are closest to the operations and programs of the agency, they may know when a new policy would provide the guidance needed to get the job done. Thus, staff input is almost always required to create new policies. In addition, the staff often shapes the policy by drafting proposed policy statements.

In effective nonprofit organizations, the staff's point of view on matters of policy development is considered an integral part of governance. Often, effective organizations are those in which the board adopts policy with input of the staff, and the staff implement policy with the advice, counsel, and support of the board.

What Are the Major Areas of Board Responsibility?

There are at least nine major areas of board responsibility; namely, to

1. determine the organization's mission;
2. set policies and adopt plans for the organization's operations;
3. approve the budget, establish fiscal policies and financial controls, and monitor financial position of the organization;

4. provide adequate resources for the organization through establishment of resource-development goals and commitment to fund-raising through giving and soliciting;
5. develop organizational visibility through networking and linkage to the community;
6. ensure that the organization's corporate and governance documents are updated and secured, and all reports are filed as required;
7. recruit and select new board members and provide them with an orientation to the board's business;
8. recruit, hire, evaluate, reward, or terminate, if necessary, the executive director of the organization; and
9. protect and preserve the organization's nonprofit tax-exempt status.

The Role of Board Officers

The officers of the board of directors have a responsibility to set the tone for organizational leadership. The duties of the president (chairperson), vice-president, treasurer, and secretary are described in the organization's bylaws.

President

In most nonprofit organizations the title and position of president refers to the highest level volunteer who also serves as chairperson of the organization. However, in some nonprofit organizations a corporate model of governance is followed, therefore, the title of "president" replaces the more commonly used title of "executive director." If the president is also the paid chief executive, the position usually allows for participation as a board member. In this instance, the role of chairperson is handled by the chief volunteer.

The volunteer president or chairperson is responsible for the activities of the board and for assigning board committee chairs, unless assignments are automatically spelled out in the bylaws. The chair is responsible for monitoring the work of the board and evaluating the board's performance. The chair presides at and calls special meetings of the board and sets the direction for organizational goal setting. This volunteer position requires a great deal of time commitment and responsibility.

Vice-President

In the absence of the volunteer president, the vice-president usually assumes the duties of president and the responsibility for chairing board meetings. Often, the role of vice-president entails chairing a major committee of the board. In some organizations, the vice-president automatically becomes president-elect, a succession plan that may not be effective in all organizations. The position of president should be earned by leadership performance, commitment to the mission, and proven governance abilities.

Service as vice-president does not assure that the individual would be a suitable president and board chair.

Secretary

The board secretary has the obligation to protect the organization's corporate documents, such as the bylaws, the articles of incorporation, board and committee minutes, and important correspondence.

Many individuals try to avoid election to the office of secretary because of the myth that the board secretary must take the minutes of the board and executive committee meetings. The board secretary does not have to write the minutes, but he or she is responsible for ensuring that the minutes are taken and accurately reflect the business meetings of the board and executive committee. To accomplish this assignment, the board secretary may want to take the minutes or rotate the responsibility. In some organizations a paid staff person takes the minutes. In this case, the secretary might review a draft before it is circulated to the full board. Upon becoming official annals of the organization, the board minutes should be signed and dated by the board secretary. In organizations that rely on parliamentary rules and procedures (such as *Robert's Rules of Order,* Newly Revised), the board secretary is required to become familiar with the meeting procedures and may have to make procedural rulings.

Treasurer

The treasurer should not be expected to do the bookkeeping and accounting for the organization. Instead, the treasurer is responsible for making sure that the organization's finances are properly accounted for and excess revenues are wisely invested. If a finance committee exists, the treasurer often serves as its chairperson. On behalf of the board, the treasurer ensures that financial controls are in place and tested on a periodic basis. The treasurer also participates in the selection and recommendation of an auditing firm. The treasurer reports on the financial statements at board meetings, executive committee meetings, and, if applicable, at annual meetings of the organization. Although an accountant or banker is often recruited to serve as the treasurer, the position does not necessarily require a professional background in accounting or finance. The treasurer should understand finances and be able to articulate the financial issues of the board.

The Board's Role in Fund-Raising

The board must play a fundamental role in raising money and resources. Board members also have the personal responsibility of making financial contributions in addition to giving their voluntary time to the organization. Instituting a policy that requires board members to contribute is sometimes employed. Whether boards approach the issue with timidity or fervently debate it they cannot escape one of their primary responsibilities, which is to ensure that their organizations have adequate funding to accomplish their missions. Therefore, time cannot be a substitute for a cash gift; both are required of board members.

How much a board member should contribute is another issue. Boards that establish minimum contribution levels are likely to exclude the participation of individuals from certain economic backgrounds. Boards that are more open to diversity across socioeconomic lines will generally suggest that the amount of individual contributions be guided by personal and financial circumstances. In this way, even board members with limited funds can be financial contributors.

Unanimous giving among the board sets the right tone for fund-raising. It enhances the credibility of the organization when it seeks contributions from others. Unanimous-board-giving practices have even become an expectation among many funders. Their view is that board members should be giving before they begin asking. If board members do not give, why should anyone else?

Issues of board-giving can be greatly minimized if the expectation is addressed in the recruitment phase of board membership. When board prospects accept positions on the board, they know what is expected.

Giving is only one part of the board member's obligation; the other part is to assist in planning and solicitation activities. Collectively, the board can identify a pool of potential contributors. Friends, business associates, relatives, and vendors are among likely prospects. Some board members shy away from verbally asking for money, but they may be able to write letters or at least sign letters that have been drafted for them by staff.

Some organizations find it helpful to have training on the board's role in fund-raising. This enables the board to identify and resolve their issue of participation. In addition, training and role-playing in a safe environment may assist in building confidence before attempting the "real thing."

Board Composition

Determining the composition of a board of directors is claimed by some to be a blend of science and art. The "scientific" components involve an application of psychology and sociology of human behavior, especially applying knowledge of motivational factors that influence joining and participation. Additionally, knowledge of group theory, concepts, and methods is helpful for understanding the process of uniting people of diverse backgrounds, personalities, and experiences into a board of directors. Group dynamics can also be used to explain the developmental phases that boards go through to weld them into effective decisionmaking groups.

Board composition should not be the result of opening the door to just anyone who is willing to serve but should result from purposeful recruitment strategies. Prospective board members, for example, should be familiarized with the organization's purpose, mission, vision, goals, and objectives, as well as board duties, responsibilities, and the organization's expectations. When this type of information is properly conveyed to the prospect, it becomes easier for board recruiters to judge whether an individual's reactions are favorable or unfavorable. These reactions can be used to determine which individuals are not likely to make a strong commitment to board service. Additionally, with this information board prospects may decide to self-select out of the recruitment process.

The task of filling vacancies on the board should be approached carefully and should result in a board composition that is able to advance the organization's mission. There are two preparatory steps to actively recruiting the right person. The initial step is to acknowledge that organizations go through different stages of development similar to the various life cycles experienced by individuals. Various maturational stages lead to differing organizational issues and needs. Assessing which phase an organization is in is useful not only to prepare the organization for change but also to determine the leadership qualities required of potential board members. Matching an organization's life cycle to the requisite skills of a board member could lead to more effective and purposeful organizational outcomes.

A second step is to conduct a thorough demographic inventory of board composition, which will reveal the board's weakest representational areas. Inventory results will show a compositional balance or imbalance in such variables as gender, age range, ethnicity, socioeconomic status, political party affiliation, educational level, professional or vocational interests, knowledge of consumer issues, and location of primary residence. Information of this type can be valuable to organizations especially seeking to create a diverse board.

As suggested, the composition of a board can contribute to the level of ease or difficulty with which an organization is governed and managed. A board composed of individuals with similar socioeconomic backgrounds or other familiar traits may reach consensus more often, but it is less likely to formulate challenging ideas or seek out policy reforms. Compared to homogeneous boards, those that reflect diversity among their members are likely to experience greater participatory challenges. Even though diversity is an enriching quality in a board, its members must contend with differing values, mores, and interpretations of community information and beliefs.

The Executive Director as Board Member

Some nonprofit organizations use a corporate model of governance structure in which the position of executive director is transformed from staff to member of the board as its president–chief executive officer (CEO).

The model of corporate governance may not be an appropriate structure for all nonprofit organizations. It is used by larger and more complex institutions that rely on a strong CEO. Regardless of size, the CEO as staff and board member must be wary of conflicts of interest and must avoid participating in discussions or decisionmaking that will lead to personal benefits. Critics of nonprofit organizations using corporate models suggest that the CEOs have no choice but to use the knowledge they have acquired in managing the day-to-day operations. This knowledge is often used to influence the direction of the board and organization.

There is a dearth of comparative research on the benefits and disadvantages of corporate models as compared to traditional models in use by nonprofit organizations. Consequently, it is impossible to suggest that any one model will lead to success.

Board Recruitment and Orientation

Preconditions of board recruitment include identifying the governance needs of organizations in (life cycle) transition and discovering the characteristics and qualities to be found in new board members. There are many variables to consider in sizing up a board prospect, including:

1. an individual's ability to create a vision, problem-solve, and facilitate conflict resolution;
2. an individual's commitment of time to participate fully;
3. enthusiasm for the organization's mission, vision, goals, and values;
4. a person's skills and experience in such areas as public policy analysis and fund-raising, or expertise in program service delivery; and
5. diversity factors.

Once a profile is developed that describes the ideal board member, the recruitment task can formally begin. On the basis of expediency, many nonprofit organizations make the mistake of ignoring the profile and recruiting the friends of board members. Sometimes, individuals are invited to become prospective board members for the simple reason that they are alive and seem agreeable to serving! Serious problems may occur when attempts have not been made to match the needs of the organization with the ideal board member. Locating someone who matches the profile and agrees to serve, however, is not a guarantee of board success. In fact, most governance problems seem to stem from the recruitment process. Though using a profile can increase the likelihood of finding the right person, a perfect match does not guarantee that problems will not arise, such as, nonattendance at board meetings, lack of participation in board committees, an unwillingness to contribute financially, or interfering or trying to micromanage the day-to-day operations of the organization.

Finding a board prospect who fits the profile is, indeed, a critical part of the assignment, as is fully informing the prospect about specific board duties. The lack of knowledge about the expectations for board member role and governance responsibilities will directly contribute to organizational confusion, ineffectiveness, and a breach in a board member's commitment. Since each organization's board of directors has a different mission and focus for its work, even the seasoned board member who joins a new board should receive a briefing on the organization, its expectations of board members, and board responsibilities. It is imperative to seek an agreement to serve only after the board prospect understands the parameters of board service.

Many organizations assume that an agreement to serve on the board is the equivalent of making a commitment to the various board duties and responsibilities. Organizations that recruit in this fashion may find that board members stop attending meetings and are unresponsive to the needs of the organization.

Board members should never learn what is expected of them after the fact. An invitation to the prospective member to observe a board meeting and an introduction to other members can be beneficial to all.

Organizations sometimes give prospects a board-prospecting packet, which may contain some or all of the following: a history of the organization; board job-descriptions; a copy of the articles of incorporation and bylaws; a copy of the organization's purpose or mission statement; an organizational chart; and a description of program services, with a list of committees and duties of each. This packet may also include a roster of the current board, with work affiliations, addresses, and phone numbers; dates of future meetings and special events; an annual report and organization brochures, newsletters, or related materials; and a copy of a recent auditor's financial report, annual budget, and financial statements.

It may also be helpful for the organization's board to assign a veteran member to assist the prospect in "learning the ropes." The availability of a support person may encourage the board prospect to join a concerned board of directors. The veteran could serve as a resource person during the recruitment phase and then as a mentor or helper during the transition period following induction.

How Many Board Members?

There is no formula for determining the appropriate size of an organization's board of directors. The size of the board must be tailored to suit the needs of the organization.

One helpful way to determine board size is an organizational life-cycle analysis, referred to previously as a prerequisite to board recruitment. Organizations and their boards experience various developmental stages, all of which can influence the number and type of skilled board members that are needed. Sometimes board size is a result of tradition and cannot be explained rationally. Final board size can also result from trial and error, reflect the board practices of other nonprofit organizations in the community, or simply be the result of not finding replacements after individuals complete their terms of office or quit.

Large- and small-sized boards have both advantages and disadvantages. Some organizations tinker with the size of their board in the belief it will help achieve a quorum more consistently, (that is, the minimum number of individuals who must be present at board meetings to officially transact board business). Despite these attempts, group size has no actual bearing on boards achieving quorums on a regular basis; quorum issues are problems of commitment, not board size.

The number of people on a board can be a factor that influences how board members comport themselves. Large boards are generally unwieldy because it is difficult to pay attention to so many people. Because the larger group will find it more difficult to become cohesive and familiar with the cohort, it may tend to be more formal in its board conduct and meetings. Organizations that are just starting out, or those in need of a boost in financial resources, may be better served by a larger board of 20 to 25 individuals. In this case, the larger the number of board members the greater the chances of reaching out to potential donors.

On one hand, smaller boards are limited in accomplishing supportive activities such as fund-raising. On the other hand, a smaller group may have to rely on its creativity, such as developing a fund-raising plan for implementation by a committee of staff, board members, and other community volunteers. Organizations that do not rely heavily on the board alone for fund-raising or other supportive activities might be better served by a board of no more than ten members. The smaller group would have more of an opportunity to become cohesive; learn experientially how to mesh effectively their collective wisdom, advice, and counsel; reach decisions through consensus; and it would have no need to use controling, parliamentary procedures for conducting board meetings.

Board Liability

Though nonprofit boards of directors are infrequently sued, the risk of liability is nevertheless a legitimate concern for volunteer board members. Financial losses associated with a lawsuit can be devastating to an organization and its board members. The quality and manner in which boards make decisions or fail to make decisions can result in a legal challenge that tests whether they have met or failed in their responsibilities as stewards of public interest.

Board members and prospective members are often comforted by the knowledge that the nonprofit organization has purchased a director's and officers' (D&O)

liability insurance policy. Concerns about lawsuits have caused a rising demand for this type of insurance, and consequently, premium costs vary widely.

A factor that affects the cost of D&O insurance is the nature of the organization's work, whether it is, for example, a direct service health care agency or an organization that promotes the arts. Features and exclusions may also differ greatly from one policy to another and affect the price and value of the policy.

Indemnification refers to the organization ensuring that it will pay the reasonable costs associated with liability suits, such as judgments and settlements against its board members. This practice is sometimes compelled by state law. In other situations it may be an optional practice of the board. In either event, the organization's bylaws outline the extent of indemnification. Indemnification cannot, however, be exercised when the organization brings a suit against its own board members. In practice, indemnification is a form of self-insurance and assumes that the organization has the funds to pay legal costs. Given the resources of some nonprofit organizations, this assumption may not be valid.

In addition to indemnification and D&O liability insurance coverage, a board of directors can purchase various liability insurance policies, including, but not limited to, the following specialty policies: general liability, employees' liability, malpractice, automobile, and fiduciary.

To encourage board and other voluntary service in community organizations, all 50 states have passed volunteer protection laws. The extent of protection varies among the states, and this form of legislation has largely been untested in the courts.

Volunteer protection laws and the varieties of liability insurance premiums are not the only ways boards can protect themselves. The most effective form of protection is limiting risk by adhering to effective governance practices. There are three standards of conduct that should guide the board member, as follows:

- *Duty of care:* imposes an obligation that all board members discharge their duties with the care that an ordinarily prudent person would exercise under similar circumstances. This includes being diligent, attending meetings, and becoming acquainted with issues before reaching a decision.
- *Duty of loyalty:* requires that each board member act primarily in the best interest of the organization and not in his or her own personal best interest or in the interest of individuals at the expense of the organization.
- *Duty of obedience:* imposes an obligation that board members will act in conformity with all laws in addition to acting in accordance with the organization's mission.

For the voluntary members of boards of directors, acting prudently, lawfully, and in the best interests of the organization can, in part, be achieved by adhering to the following six responsible board practices:

1. *Becoming an active board member.* Board members who are familiar with the organization's mission and purpose are generally able to make better decisions for the organization. Members may wish to review the mission annually to serve as a reminder that the board uses the mission statement as its guide in decision-making.
2. *Attending all meetings.* Being absent from meetings will not necessarily excuse a board member from responsibilities for decisions reached by those in attendance. In fact, a member's absence from meetings increases potential risks for the entire board because it is making decisions without the benefit of the views of all of its members.
3. *Insisting on having sound financial management tools and control systems.* Board members need to learn how to read and use financial statements and audit reports to understand and monitor the organization's fiscal health. They also need to understand that their decisions have a financial impact on the organization.
4. *Speaking up.* Members should not remain silent when they disagree with a decision or an opinion expressed by others. Additionally, board members should ask questions when the organization's goals and objectives are not being met.
5. *Identifying conflicts of interest.* Board members need to avoid participating in discussions or decisionmaking when they have conflicts of interest. Even the perception of a conflict of interest must be avoided, if possible. If they are faced with an actual conflict or even the perception of one, board members must inform the other directors of the situation and excuse themselves from participation in related areas of decisionmaking or transactions.
6. *Staffing.* In addition to its having personnel policy guidelines for the executive director, the board must be certain that these personnel policies are adequate and updated to reflect all applicable mandates of law.

In summary, minimizing the risk of board liability requires an active and involved board of directors.

Dismissal of Board Members

Terminating a member from the board of directors for nonattendance at board meetings or lack of follow through on assignments that are required for the board's decision-making purposes, for example, is a delicate procedure. Unfortunately, there are times when it becomes necessary to discharge board members because their actions create liability risks.

The chairperson of the board has the responsibility to request resignations from board members. The executive director plays a supportive role to the board chair and board member in what for all can be emotionally trying and embarrassing. Asking someone to leave the board may be a tough assignment, but it does not have to escalate into a major problem.

Sometimes a board member's conduct fails to meet expectations, and there may be legitimate reasons for this. Work-related responsibilities or family illness or crisis may prevent an individual from following through on board commitments. A member's personal problems may give the board a reason to offer that individual a leave of absence or to provide a graceful exit for a person under a great deal of stress. A stressed board member may even experience a sense of relief in no longer feeling burdened by board responsibilities. In some situations, inviting the outgoing governing board member to serve on the advisory board instead of completely severing his or her board ties may especially be warranted for maintaining important community relationships.

Confidence and sensitivity should be used when approaching the board member with the idea of resignation. A board member should be given every consideration to effect a smooth departure. Ultimately, the member's "saving face" is important for maintaining relationships at this level of community involvement.

To prevent the need for board dismissals or to support the actions of the board chair when a dismissal is called for, the board should adopt a principle stating that its work and organizational mission are too important to allow for unnecessary liability risks associated with uncommitted board members. The board can do some prevention work by adopting a bylaw passage and job description that reflect standards for board member conduct and participation. Of course, some organizations have rules of this type but choose not to enforce them. For a member to violate or ignore such bylaw provisions suggests poor judgment and raises the liability risks of the board.

How Often Should the Board Meet?

A board is generally required to meet at least once a year. In practice, some hold meetings once a month, every other month, or once each calendar quarter. Frequency of board meetings and the duration of each meeting should reflect the culture of the organization and the type of strategic issues requiring board attention. Dealing with planning and policy issues, threats of litigation or bad publicity, and concerns of financial obligations are reasons for a board to meet more frequently. Organizations that are new in their development, or in process of managing significant changes, as compared with an organization in a steady state, would also benefit from meeting more frequently.

A board of directors may request that the board meet more often because it has not completed its meeting agenda. This may be a symptom of unsatisfactory meeting management skills or the need for longer meetings, rather than the need to meet more often.

Effective meetings are focused, to the point, and stick to the agenda. Meetings can be effective when board members come prepared, having studied the agenda and the issues prior to the meeting. Board members who get sidetracked, have side conversations, come late, or leave early may be indicating commitment problems, which are not solved by increasing or decreasing the number of meetings.

Boards which continually experience time troubles with their meetings should first be attentive to time management techniques rather than to increasing the number of meetings. For example, the agenda should be mailed out at least a week to ten days in advance. Agenda items should be allocated realistic time frames for discussion and taking action, in addition to time designated for the routine review of minutes, financial reports, and progress reports on the implementation of the organization's strategic plans.

Newly identified obstacles are not always solved during board meetings. Instead of reacting to unfinished issues and business with more board meetings, attempts should first be made to streamline the review of issues by assigning the task to an appropriate standing or ad hoc committee. In this way, the committees can try to remedy issues or bring their findings and recommendations back to the board or executive committee without monopolizing the board's time and agenda.

How Long Should a Board Member Serve?

The solution to a member's length of service that is practiced by many organizations is to stagger the expiring terms of office. Rotations of three-year terms, for example, would mean that each member serves for three years, but, at the end of each year, obligations would end for one-third of the members. This system gives the board ample time to evaluate the performance of board members, to determine whether they should be invited back for another term. Additionally, the experience base accumulated by outgoing board members is information these members use to decide whether they would like to be reelected for another three-year term.

Some organizations also place a limit on the number of consecutive terms a person may serve. After reaching the maximum number of consecutive terms of service, the board member would automatically leave the board. A board member who rotated off could be elected again after a year or more, when consecutive service would not be an issue. After reaching the allowable service limit, an individual could also continue to support the organization's cause in some other capacity, such as on a committee or advisory board.

It is important that all board member terms do not expire at the same time. Without some overlapping representation from members of the board, the organization would lose its important history and continuity of policy development and strategic direction. Veteran board members bring a maturity and depth of understanding about the issues the organization faces, and when the board adds a group of newer members it brings enthusiasm and fresh ideas to the board's governing role.

How Are Governing Boards, Advisory Boards, and Honorary Boards Different?

When one is referring to the term "board of directors" or "board of trustees," the reference is to a *governing board*, a grouping of individuals who have assumed a legal responsibility for an organization's existence. These people make policy and are responsible for how money is generated and spent, toward the accomplishment of a mission that can be beneficial to the general public or to a segment of the population.

Advisory boards, however, do not bear the legal burdens of governing boards. An advisory board exists to assist the governing board or the executive director in examining issues and recommendations. Recommendations that result from the work of an advisory board do not have to be accepted or followed by the governing board.

Honorary boards are usually composed of individuals who are well-known because of some measure of celebrity or prominence in the community. Honorary boards do not necessarily meet. In fact, some individuals agree to serve as honorary members because they do not have the time or inclination to attend meetings. Individuals serving in this honorary capacity lend credibility to an organization by allowing the use of their prominent names in brochures and on letterheads.

Sometimes, members of honorary boards and advisory boards are enlisted to assist in organizational fund-raising activities. The visibility and credibility of the honorary or advisory member sends a signal to the community that the organization is worthy of financial support.

Types of Committees

Committees are categorized as either standing committees or ad hoc committees. Ad hoc (or special) committees, on one hand, have a life-span equal to the completion of the committee's assignment. Standing committees, on the other hand, are part of the permanent governance structure of an organization with duties and responsibilities described in bylaws. Standing committees may include executive, finance, bylaws, fund-raising, public relations, nominating, personnel, planning, and policy committees, or any other committee that the organization believes should exist indefinitely to aid in governance. Seven of the most common standing committees are described as follows:

1. The *executive committee* functions in place of the full board and handles routine and crisis matters between full board meetings. Empowered to make decisions for the organization, the executive committee is usually composed of the organization's officers. Depending on the size of the organization's board of directors, composition of the executive committee could include committee chairs or other selected leaders among the board. The executive committee is usually chaired by the board's volunteer president or chairperson.

2. The *finance committee* is responsible for monitoring the organization's finances and financial controls and attending to audit requirements. Typical functions for the finance committee are to oversee organizational investments and to work with the executive director to develop an annual budget.

3. The *nominations committee* is responsible for identifying and recruiting appropriate candidates for board positions and bringing forward its recommendations to the full board. This committee sometimes has the responsibility for planning board development activities and board retreats.

4. The *personnel committee* is usually responsible for recommending policies to guide the supervision of staff. In some organizations, this committee may have the responsibility for overseeing the search for an executive director and then for her or his performance evaluation. Members of this committee may need to acquaint themselves with personnel laws and regulations that regulate labor practices.

5. The *program committee* is responsible for monitoring the organization's service delivery system and may assist in evaluating client services. This committee is often responsible for keeping track of community trends that might affect the organization's short-term and long-term objectives. In complex organizations with multiple services, there may be subcommittees that are responsible for monitoring each of the organization's program services.

6. The *resource development committee* is responsible for examining alternate methods of fund-raising and for establishing annual fund-raising goals. This committee often is active in the solicitation of gifts or participation in special events. In addition to raising money, it may solicit in-kind contributions.

7. The *public relations* or *community relations committee* has the responsibility for developing good relations with the larger community and with important community groups. The committee examines opportunities to participate in community events that will bring visibility to the organization. It may oversee the writing of press releases and may develop relationships with media professionals.

Participants appointed to standing or ad hoc committees do not need to be members of the board of directors. Committee members may include staff, volunteers, representatives from community agencies, and consumers of service. Committee chairs are usually appointed by the board's chairperson.

What Are the Advantages and Disadvantages of Boards' Assignment of Work to Committees?

Advantages to boards of using committees include shared leadership and decisionmaking responsibility. If committee members follow through on their assignments, it is possible that more work will be completed in less time. Based on the composition of committees, there is the potential for a wider range of views, which enhances problemsolving. Committees can also provide some continuity to the work of the organization should the paid staff change.

Committee activity is not all positive, however. Some suggest that committees waste time in accomplishing work that could have been handled more efficiently by one individual. In order to satisfy the concerns of committee members, there is also a tendency for committee members to compromise and dilute the strength of a decision or proposed outcome.

Committee activity is not all negative. Some assignments are handled better in committees than by one individual. In order to reduce the chances of stirring up controversy, assignments that have multiple parts or deal with sensitive and "political" issues are handled better by a committee, especially a committee that comprises individuals with a range of viewpoints.

STEPHEN R. BLOCK

BIBLIOGRAPHY

Block, Stephen R., and Jeffrey W. Pryor, 1991. *Improving Nonprofit Management Practice: A Handbook for Community-Based Organizations.* Rockville, MD: OSAP/Public Health Service, U.S. Dept. of Health and Human Services.

Carver, John, 1990. *Boards That Make a Difference.* San Francisco: Jossey-Bass.

Chait, Richard P., and Barbara E. Taylor, 1989. "Charting the Territory of Nonprofit Boards." *Harvard Business Review* (Jan.-Feb.): 44–54.

Conrad, William, and William E. Glenn, 1976. *The Effective Voluntary Board of Directors.* Chicago: Swallow Press.

Drucker, Peter F., 1989. "What Business Can Learn from Nonprofits." *Harvard Business Review* (Sept.-Oct.): 88–93.

———, 1990. "Lessons for Successful Nonprofit Governance." *Nonprofit Management and Leadership,* vol. 1, no. 1 (Fall): 7–14.

Hadden, Elaine M., and Blaire A. French, 1987. *Nonprofit Organizations: Rights and Liabilities for Members, Directors and Officers.* Wilmette, IL: Callaghan & Co.

Herman, Robert Dean, and Stephen R. Block, 1990. "The Board's Crucial Role in Fund Raising,": 222–241. In Jon Van Til, et al., *Critical Issues in American Philanthropy.* San Francisco: Jossey-Bass.

Herman, Robert Dean, and Richard D. Heimovics, 1991. *Executive Leadership in Nonprofit Organizations.* San Francisco: Jossey-Bass.

Herman, Robert Dean, and Jon Van Til, eds., 1989. *Nonprofit Boards of Directors: Analyses and Applications,* New Brunswick, NJ: Transaction Publishers.

Kurtz, Daniel L., 1988. *Board Liability* New York: Moyer Bell.

Middleton, Melissa, 1987. "Nonprofit Boards of Directors: Beyond the Governance Function,": 141–153. In Walter W. Powell, ed., *The Nonprofit Sector: A Research Handbook,* New Haven, CT: Yale University Press.

O'Connell, Brian, 1985. *The Board Members Book.* New York: The Foundation Center.

O' Houle, Cyril, 1989. *Governing Boards.* San Francisco: Jossey-Bass.

Saidel, Judith R., 1993. "The Board Role in Relation to Government: Alternative Models,": 32–51. In Dennis R. Young, Robert M. Hollister, and Virginia A. Hodgkinson, eds., *Governing, Leading, and Managing Nonprofit Organizations.* San Francisco: Jossey-Bass.

BOUNDARYLESS.

BOUNDARYLESS. The ways in which organizations delineate themselves internally and with their external environment, with a goal of minimizing constraints to flexibility imposed by boundaries, whether functional, political, psychological, hierarchical, multicultural, or related to professional specialization.

Origination of the Term

The term "boundaryless" came to prominence in the 1990s and is likely to remain an important way of defining modern organizations, whether public or private. It has its roots in the rapid evolution of organizations to less-bureaucratic configurations, including the "delayering" or "flattening" of organizations. The Quality Movement, best typified by Total Quality Management, has also been a key ingredient in promoting boundarylessness as a precept. General Electric (GE) Corporation has been the most notable exponent of boundaryless operations. The Academy of Management Annual Conference of 1993 had boundarylessness as its main theme, another indication of the growing significance assigned to boundaryless forms of management.

Traditional Interpretation

In a traditional sense, boundaries have been expressed in three ways. The first relates to the lateral or horizontal dimension of an organization, namely the demarcation between functional components of the organization. The second is the hierarchical or vertical dimension; and the third pertains to the boundary between the internal organization and its environmental domain. Such boundaries have been traditionally discussed in terms of boundary-spanning, boundary permeability, even boundary management. The focus tended to be on the functionality of boundaries from the standpoint of work specialization and organization of the enterprise. From a structural viewpoint, a fourth boundary dimension can be identified. It is the diagonal interaction that can occur across lateral and horizontal boundaries between entities of the organization, or with external organizations. Such interaction is common in Japanese companies. It is less common in Western companies.

Impetus for Change

The rigidity of traditional boundaries has been increasingly called into question because of the dynamics of environmental change, globalization of business, need to respond rapidly to markets, management by process (which cuts across boundaries), the inherent need to speed up communication processes, the move to more participative forms of management, emphasis on cross-functional teams, a belief in empowering employees, and a variety of themes related to the perceived need to transform organizations culturally.

New Thinking

There has been a shift away from traditional interpretations, which are structurally centered, to an address of other forms of boundaries. This new focus is on the more subtle and hard-to-map boundaries such as the psychological, leadership, historical, and political aspects of an organization. The history of the International Business Machines (IBM) Corporation suggests a culture that imposes psychological barriers to action that are as real as functional boundaries. As an article by Larry Hirschhorn and Thomas Gilmore (1992) suggested: "These new boundaries are more psychological than organizational. They aren't drawn on a company's organizational chart but in the minds of its managers and employees." They went on to say that "because these new boundaries are so different from the traditional kind, they tend to be invisible to most managers."

Because this reinterpretation of boundaries tends to be embedded in the organizational psyche, modification of boundaries to meet such ends as increased flexibility can be difficult to achieve. There must first be an awareness of the "boundaries" and their cultural foundations. The focus turns to mental models rather than the lines and boxes on the organizational chart. It also requires an opening up of communication. One common boundary can be a communications impasse between the executive level and rank and file, best characterized by inattention to the ideas of line workers by supervisors.

Boundarylessness Is Relative

Even the most ardent advocates of boundarylessness understand that it is a relative term. Some semblance of boundaries are required for identification with a group and for discharge of the management function. To dissolve boundaries totally, whether traditional or nontraditional, can lead to disorientation and organizational breakdown. Kenwyn K. Smith and David N. Berg (1987) pointed out that "without boundaries there is fusion" (p. 103). Discernment and the ability to diagram relationships is lost. Because there are multiple boundaries, there can be wide variability in the amount of boundarylessness viewed as appropriate. Free-flowing communication across "borders" is now often encouraged. The advent of interoffice communication via E-mail helps create fluidity of communication. Rather than use rules and procedural prescriptions to govern interaction, values become the determiners of what is appropriate organizational behavior. At GE, for example, the bounding values are speed, simplicity, and self-confidence. As long as those overarching prerequisites are honored, there is great latitude permitted. There is *also* great emphasis at GE on operating in a boundaryless fashion.

The degree of boundarylessness can be viewed as falling at some point on a rather wide spectrum—a continuum from almost total unfettered boundary passage to one that is subject to specific constraints. Some of the constraints will be grounded in the need to create and sustain competitive advantage. One example would be the extent to which the organization is willing to offer information to competitors. Even in this area, the degree of boundarylessness may not be transparent. For example, Baxter Healthcare, with over 100,000 products being marketed in over 100 countries, regularly shares information and provides training to competitors if their products serve to round out Baxter's product line.

Margaret Wheatley (1992) has pointed out that boundaries are necessary. "They make it possible to know the difference between one thing and another" (p. 28). In the end, it is a case of variable relationships that define where an organization lies with regard to the multiple dimensions involved. There is also paradox involved, because some boundaries may be largely dissolved or blurred, whereas other dimensions maintain considerable force. As Ralph O. Stacey (1992) outlined, "The tightness or looseness of boundaries around a network system is determined by the manner in which managers, especially those at the top . . . intervene to use their power" (p. 181). Boundaries that relate to a given dimension (e.g., hierarchy) can also look different when viewed from different vantage points in an organization. Stacey suggested that "for the managers' subordinates the boundaries are too tight, but for the managers themselves, the boundaries have been removed" (p. 181).

The Global Factor

The complexity of dealing with boundaries and striving for relative boundarylessness has increased as companies have become more multinational. Some cultures have been steeped in bureaucratic structures and formalism. They do not adapt easily to more fluid ways of doing business, with traditional hierarchical levels bypassed in the interest of expediency. For example, bypassing traditional lines of authority may be condoned in Sweden, whereas it may tend to be viewed negatively in Italy. In China, it might represent a basic breach of integrity. This type of situation complicates the issue of boundarylessness, since what is viewed as stifling and excessively bureaucratic in one culture may be the comfortable modus operandi in another. The implications are that certain forms of boundarylessness will tend to run cross-grain to certain national cultures, suggesting that any move to a boundaryless form of management in multicultural settings will require intensive effort in preparing the organizational culture for such change.

The GE Example

GE is the second-largest of the Fortune 500 companies (1995) and has long been a trendsetter in terms of management practices. No company has gone further to adopt a boundaryless mentality than GE. The corporation, under the leadership of Jack Welch (Chief Executive Officer since 1981), has three core management techniques it now employs to gain competitive advantage: work-outs, best practices, and process-mapping.

The work-out approach involves empowerment and unlocking of the organization in order to change. Welch indicates that "with work-out and boundarylessness, we're trying to differentiate GE competitively by raising as much intellectual and creative capital from our work force as we possibly can." (Tichy and Sherman 1993b). Welch goes on to define boundarylessness as "the breaking down of barriers that divide employees—such as hierarchy, job function and geography—and that distance companies from suppliers and customers." To Welch, boundarylessness is a matter of openness, trust, and sharing of ideas. These can be very difficult commodities to acquire in organizations that are as large, complex, and international as GE. Therefore, it is the work-out methodology that is used, in the words of Welch, to "Jimmy the locks" that keep employees out of the decisionmaking process (Stewart 1991: 41).

The work-out methodology was created in 1988. Work-outs can be configured in a variety of ways, but commonly involve 25-to-50 individuals for about three days. The group is further divided into subgroups of eight-to-ten people. Group composition can be confined to a natural team or drawn from a variety of sources (e.g., customers,

multiple organizations, more than one hierarchical level). The groups work on issues that are either assigned to them or are developed through group activity. (Many of the early work-outs at GE addressed removal of bureaucratic encumbrances.) The finale on the third day involves presentation of group proposals to the top manager. No more than five minutes are spent on a given proposal. What distinguishes the process is that top management must make decisions on the spot, with any denials explained. It places leader credibility on the line. The work-outs at GE represent a means of dislodging long-entrenched thought patterns and bringing about major change in the corporate culture. By GE's mixing individuals cross-organizationally and interspersing customers with its workforce, boundarylessness is encouraged. Communication networks are activated that extend across lateral boundaries. Leaders can find it necessary to adopt a much less authoritative style in working with employees.

As Noel Tichy and Stratford Sherman relate in their book about GE (1993a: p. 21), boundarylessness is Welch's concept of integrating all the constituencies inside and outside the company. "This is the value that underlies GE's increasingly supple organizational style. A boundaryless organization should break down the internal barriers of hierarchy, geography, and function, while nudging the company into closer partnership with its customers and suppliers" (p. 62). Within GE, the work-out is the lever of choice in achieving this end.

The Public Sector

There has been a tendency to cordon off the public sector when addressing management theories. The public sector can be dismissed as different because it is theoretically not as sensitive to market forces and issues of profitability as is the private sector. However, this argument has a particularly hollow ring in the 1990s, as public and private systems continue to blur and interdependencies grow. Privately and publicly run organizations are becoming more and more interwoven and more boundaryless, one to another. Privatization of services in the public sector is another factor. There has been talk of public bureaucracies being established devoid of a specific mission, competing with the private sector to provide whatever municipal services may be required. This concept is a step beyond what has been commonplace in the private sector in that it envisions a boundaryless instrumentality at inception.

The public sector (and the segments that compose it) is marked by a veritable crazy quilt of overlapping and congruent jurisdictions delivering similar or analogous services. It is easy to see how boundarylessness as a concept can upgrade quality-of-service delivery in the public sector. However, it will require reorientation of political boundaries and selective convergence of federal, state, county, and municipal systems in order to pool capital and increase capacitization in relation to customer needs. This is already well advanced in some U.S. communities (e.g., New York City). As Wheatley (1992) states, "The challenge for us is to see beyond the innumerable fragments to the whole, stepping back far enough to appreciate how things move and change, as a coherent entity" (p. 41).

Relationship to Chaos Theory

The essence of chaos theory is "order without predictability" (Wheatley 1992: 123). It teaches, in effect, that if a system is allowed to play itself out long enough, it will find its way to some form of order. In other words, rather than compartmentalize systems, we can achieve equivalent or better results at times by simply allowing the system to seek its own natural shape—often a more practical shape than that which can be derived from predetermined boundaries and tight controls. This, in turn, relates to an opening up of psychological boundaries in allowing the human spirit to seek creative solutions to problems. In the end, boundarylessness requires trust in the self-regulation properties of organizations within the parameters of shared values and vision.

ROBERT L. DILWORTH

BIBLIOGRAPHY

Hamel, Gary, and C. K. Prahalad, 1994. *Competing for the Future.* Boston: Harvard Business School Press.
Hastings, Colin, 1993. *The New Organization.* London: McGraw-Hill.
Hirschhorn, Larry, and Thomas Gilmore, 1992. "The New Boundaries of the 'Boundaryless' Company." *Harvard Business Review* (May-June).
Schein, Edgar H., 1992. *Organizational Culture and Leadership.* 2d. ed. San Francisco: Jossey-Bass.
Smith, Kenwyn K., and David N. Berg, 1987. *Paradoxes of Group Life.* San Francisco: Jossey-Bass.
Stacey, Ralph D., 1992. *Managing the Unknowable: Strategic Boundaries Between Order and Chaos in Organizations.* San Francisco: Jossey-Bass.
Stewart, Thomas A., 1991. "GE, Keeps Those Ideas Coming." *Fortune* (Aug.).
Tichy, Noel M., and Stratford Sherman, 1993a. *Control Your Destiny or Someone Else Will.* New York: Doubleday.
———, 1993b. "Jack Welch's Lessons for Success." *Fortune* (Jan.).
Wheatley, Margaret J., 1992. *Leadership and the New Science,* San Francisco: Berrett-Koehler.

BRAINSTORMING. A formal system for promoting group creativity and generating options for action.

Though the term "brainstorming" is often used to describe any process in which a group meets for a freewheeling session to come up with new ideas and approaches, the term strictly refers to a formal system for idea-generation devised by Alex Osborn and set out in his 1953 book. Osborn was writing in the context of the Madison Avenue advertising world and its appetite for new ideas, however zany, but his brainstorming technique can play a useful part in the policy development process, and related techniques have often formed part of government training programs.

Osborn's Principles

Osborn prescribed a formal system for brainstorming, designed to provide order and structure, shelter fragile ideas, protect creativity from the tyranny of "group-think," and ensure a prolific output of options.

His system requires a chairperson, who guides the group of ten-to-fifteen people through the process. An initial task is to state, and then restate, the problem. The process of restating the problem can be invaluable in gaining insight into the issues to be brainstormed. The group then brainstorms one or more of the restatements. This is achieved by strictly observing four principles, which must be displayed before the group. These principles are: (1) suspend judgment; (2) freewheel; (3) pursue quantity; and (4) cross-fertilize.

The group pursues idea-generation for a fixed period of about thirty minutes, during which some 80 ideas may typically be generated. If the flow of ideas dries up, the group may take a break and restart, expecting perhaps 20 further ideas in a second round. The ideas may be written on blackboards, or on note cards or adhesive paper slips that can be resorted under topics during the evaluation process.

A subgroup then sorts the ideas and evaluates them against agreed criteria (e.g., cost, practicality, impact, etc.). Sometimes this process takes place several days after the original session. The most useful ideas are placed on a short list for further action or consideration.

Usefulness of Brainstorming

Brainstorming is a technique for application in "idea-deficient" situations. If a group observes its rules, they can draw ideas from the whole of a group (not just the confident members). Also the tendency to be excessively critical can be offset, and an antidote is provided to group-think and tunnel vision. However, the generation of ideas in this way is not a substitute for more comprehensive problem-solving and analytical techniques, which are needed in most complex situations.

Related Techniques

Brainstorming is closely related to other group problem solving techniques, such as William J. Gordon's technique "synectics," and the Delphi technique, both of which provide more scope for individual thought to coexist with group processes. It is also linked to creativity training. Many similar ideas are to be found in the writings of Edward de Bono (1970), such as "lateral thinking," and in his promotion of tools for idea-generation techniques, such as the "think tank" idea-generator, based on random word association.

Conclusion

The formal structure of Osborn's brainstorming allows it to produce prolific ideas, to allow the suspension of judgment, and to shelter the unexpected while delivering results in a very economical time frame. Provided its limitations are understood, it is a technique that can add process and ensure results, thus providing an attractive alternative to unstructured "brainstorming," where rules and outcomes are unclear, and time and energy are wasted.

E. W. RUSSELL

BIBLIOGRAPHY

Bono, Edward de, 1970. *Lateral Thinking.* London: Ward Lock.
Evans, James R., 1991. *Creative Thinking in the Decision and Management Sciences.* Cincinnatti: South Western.
Haefale, John W., 1962. *Creativity and Innovation.* New York: Van Nostrand Reinhold.
Osborn, Alex F., 1953. *Applied Imagination.* New York: Scribner's.

THE BRITISH ADMINISTRATIVE TRADITION TO 1914.

The management practice and organization culture of the British prior to World War I. Although by 1914 the British system of civil administration was widely admired and copied, this was far from the case during the eighteenth century. Then, British politics and government, like those of many of its European neighbors, were enmeshed in nepotism, patronage, and chronic inefficiency. The nineteenth century reforms of the public service transformed this system through successive inquiries, reforming statutes and other administrative reforms. On the way, principles such as open competition for entry, the ministerial department, Treasury Department financial control, and the systematic scrutiny of expenditure by the Auditor-General became firmly established; they were to become lasting foundations of the public institutions of many countries. To understand the full significance of these governmental changes, we must look back to the last stages of the ancien régime.

The eighteenth-century form of politics, which depended on patronage to secure day-to-day majorities in the House of Commons, was in ruins by the 1820s. The evils of the nineteenth century did not take the same form as the evils of the eighteenth. The old type of sinecure, the open sale or inheritance of offices and the making of profit

from office had virtually disappeared. But the root cause of these abuses, the recruitment of the civil service through political patronage, remained. The peculiar direction that this took in the early nineteenth century was the systematization of patronage for all the lower branches of the civil service, and the vesting of patronage in individual private members of parliament rather than in the government as such. By the closing years of the Napoleonic wars the parliamentary managers (or whips) were already complaining of these tendencies, which were probably the consequence of the new type of politics based on legislative policies and programs rather than the fruits of office.

However, even if no government in office after the passage of the Reform Act of 1832, (which cleansed the electoral system) could any longer base its existence on bought support, the system of civil service recruitment originally designed to serve this end remained to serve others: namely, provision for the families, friends, and clients of Ministers of Parliament (MPs) and private members (still a highly intermarried and interconnected class), as did the satisfaction of the MP's sense of power and their capacity to exercise cheap benevolence. This civil service system also nurtured the buccaneering type of parliamentarian, (especially that of a borough member who used his influence to build up his individual support). Thus patronage had tended to box the compass in its political effects. It now bolstered aristocratic influence rather than ministries, and personal rather than party policies. It was a prop for social privilege and a clog on the emergent independent electorate and opinion.

What of the public service that was recruited? Sir Charles Trevelyan, permanent secretary of the Treasury, produced a terrible indictment in 1849, which was to be repeated in his and Stafford Northcote's report on the civil service of 1853. This *Report on the Organisation of the Civil Service* (1854) found that "admission into the civil service is indeed eagerly sought after, but it is for the unambitious and the indolent or incapable that it is chiefly desired" (p. 4). It was the last refuge, not of scoundrels exactly, but of those who had failed in other professions or were delicate in health or undistinguished in intellect, yet sufficiently fortunate as to have a string that could be pulled on their behalf. There was no examination whatever for some departments; for the rest, it was a mere formality. The Treasury made one attempt in 1840 to ensure that the clerks for the main departments should at least know the principles of double-entry bookkeeping, but their circular had been ignored by most offices and was soon neglected by the remainder. There was, moreover, no lower age limit for the service, so that a boy could make the rounds of many jobs before coming at last to what Trevelyan caustically named his "secure asylum."

The consequence was a general undifferentiated mass of mediocrity, with the corollary that work degenerated into meaningless routine and promotion into a mechanical movement according to seniority. The vicious circle was complete. Of course, there were exceptions to the rule. The regular methods of recruitment did occasionally throw up men of marked ability; Anthony Trollope, the novelist, at the Post Office, for example, or Thomas F. Elliott and Charles Murdoch at the Colonial Office. But such men were comparatively rare.

Needless to say, even early nineteenth-century England could not be governed solely by routiners and ancient methods. There was some innovation prior to the reforms of the 1850s, but the vast new social problems, energy of ideas, and political developments all demanded fresh expedients. The two most important of these expedients were the filling of leading positions in the service by men from other walks of life and a new race of executive officers. As to the former, almost all the great Victorian civil servants were recruited from outside the Civil Service, including Trevelyan himself, and James Kay Shuttleworth, James Stephen, Edwin Chadwick, John Simon, Nassau Senior, Joshua Jebb, Sir John Burgoyne, Herman Merivale, Henry Taylor, William Farr, Southwood Smith. Some were lawyers; others were physicians, dons, businessmen, chemists, or engineers. So far, so good: The practice of recruiting from outside the system did produce chief administrators of the highest class. But it also produced crusading, war-lording, and empire-building within the service, and to a grievous extent, exorbitance and excursions into politics. The very system bred "statesmen in disguise" while depressing the ordinary service. Once again a vicious circle operated. "The permanent Civil Servants are habitually superseded because they are inefficient and they are inefficient because they are habitually superseded."

To a lesser extent the same weaknesses were discernible in the second expedient, the new field administrators, inspectors, assistant commissioners, surveyors, engineers and, medical officers, working directly under a new type of board. They, too, were almost invariably recruited from outside, from the ranks of half-pay semi-redundant naval and army officers, physicians, chemists, surveyors, engineers, and barristers. Again the practice did supply, as the regular service certainly could not have done, the sudden demand for scores of men of initiative, inventiveness, and professional or quasi-professional training for the new fields of state action, labor, poor law, public health and police regulation. Though it would be difficult to over emphasize these peoples' individual merits, the new model, in the circumstances of the time, had its limitations.

First, it did nothing to improve the old civil establishment. The inspectorates (to use the most convenient corporate term) were concentrated in the novel fields of state activity. In a sense, the innovation resembled the eighteenth-century device of the improvement commission, whereby new ad hoc agencies were tagged on to an unreformed system without regard to consistency or coordination. Second, the ill-defined status of the inspectors aggravated the exaggerated and often injurious degree of administrative independence that marked many of the new ventures of the 1830s. The history of the Poor Law administration (by which the improverished were organized and made to work) between 1834 and 1847 provides many examples of this weakness. Third, a supreme merit of the new order was that it vested the power to make appointments in a central board, not the political head of a department or minister in Parliament. A further incidental advantage was that the very nature of the new branches of administration often demanded subordinates with some measure of technical qualifications, medical, engineering or chemical, thus ipso facto guaranteeing a certain competence. But who was to guard the guardians? How were the central boards themselves to be removed from the hands of the political families?

When it came, the reform of the civil service was promoted by middleclass radicals rather than by utilitarian or other high theoretical pressures. It is significant that the first major external move came from William E. Gladstone, as Chancellor of the Exchequer under Lord Aberdeen's Coalition Government (1853–1855). What were his objects in setting up the Northcote-Trevelyan inquiry into the civil service in 1853? First, to reduce the cost of administration: Gladstone expected that reform would produce efficiency and business methods in government, which would automatically produce many savings. Here, of course, he was at one with the middleclass reformers of the 1830s. Their demand for the abolition of sinecures and the reduction of the number of offices, and at least part of their opposition to the creation of new departments, sprang from their simple passion to save money and to get good value from what was still being spent. A second purpose was to reduce the extent of state activity, at least to rationalize, consolidate, and simplify existing state activity and eliminate overlapping. This attitude rested on the premise that state spending (to use Gladstone's own terms) was inherently "sterile" as against the "fructification" that money underwent in the pockets of citizens.

Gladstone was also inspired by the idea of formal civil equality, which powerfully impelled middleclass radicals. The civil service (even more than the universities and almost as much as the armed services, which were also under attack) was a stronghold of the aristocracy. Gladstone's fellow conspirator, Trevelyan, complained that the old established political families habitually grew fat on the public patronage. Gladstone thoroughly agreed. Finally, Gladstone himself described his efforts as his contribution to parliamentary reform. "Parliamentary" may sound like a surprising adjective, but it was in fact most apt. Administrative reform was a logical follow-through to the Reform Act of 1832. The maintenance of the patronage system counteracted the representative principle in politics, bolstered client politics, and negated the placing of a portion of political power in middleclass hands, which the Reform Act had seemed to promise.

Thus the prime aim of Gladstonian reform was not to produce a "modern" type of administration or even an "efficient" administration in the mechanical sense, although, of course, such a reform was a necessary preliminary if either of the two were to be absolutely established. Gladstone's aims were rather those of fiscal, civil, and political reform, according to the traditions established earlier in the century by Sir Robert Peel and his followers, and the "Manchester School" of reformers. Though Trevelyan fully shared these principles, he cast them in his own particular mold. His own further objectives were the control of the entire public service by the Treasury and the use of open competition for recruitment and promotion, and reward and punishment. Trevelyan was ever a Treasury man, profoundly disturbed by the weakness of its control of public finance in the first half of the nineteenth century. Step-by-step in the years 1849 to 1854, he and his Treasury assistants virtually secured the desired powers by establishing a more modern system of forward accounting and budgeting and the need to win antecedent Treasury consent for all possible public spending. The Audit Act of 1866 capped these developments by facilitating direction and checks from the center.

As to the more general reform, Trevelyan's opportunity came in 1853, essentially through Gladstone, who provided the indispensable link with high politics. From the start the new chancellor eagerly accepted Trevelyan's specific aims, entry by merit, promotion by merit, dismissal for incompetence, and division of the service into intellectual and mechanical grades, and Gladstone's former secretary, Northcote, rounded off the connection. In March 1853 Trevelyan and Northcote were commissioned to undertake an official inquiry into the Board of Trade, and this was followed up by inquiries into seven other departments.

But now another factor entered the equation. Gladstone was concurrently involved in two Royal Commissions, on the condition of Oxford University and the state of the public schools; and Northcote himself sat on the Oxford Commission as well as on that of the reorganization of the civil service. Mysteriously, the three movements began to intertwine. In particular, the Oxford reformers, especially Benjamin Jowett of Balliol, took a hand in the reform of the public service. In concrete terms, this intermingling of university, public school, and administrative reform produced not only the proposal of a permanent commission of examiners for all appointments to the civil service, a revolutionary and far-reaching step in the long term—but also and still more important, the grounding of the civil service of the future upon a caste drawn from the reformed public schools and universities and judged by the curricula of these institutions. More or less simultaneously

the domination of classics and mathematics in these curricula was confirmed, and the public schools began to increase rapidly in number.

In certain ways this imposed interconnection of school, university, and administrative reform seems quite perverse. But there is good reason to suspect that nothing less was aimed at than the exclusive preservation of the vital sphere of civil administration for the educated upper- and upper-middle classes. "In an age when the shadow of democracy was already looming on the horizon," wrote Asa Briggs in *Victorian People* (1955) "men like . . . Jowett and Trevelyan realized the need for plentiful supply of informed gentlemen" (p. 169). How far the antidemocratic purpose (if such it was) of administrative reorganization was realized I shall not attempt to say. But certainly a link between the higher civil service and a humanities education of the type provided by the older universities was forged. It was to endure for a century, at least.

The major recommendation of the Northcote-Trevelyan Report was the abolition of patronage in all forms. Instead, the civil service should be entered only through competitive examinations, conducted periodically by an independent board; there should be an age limit for candidates and a strict period of probation for the successful; as well as a division in the service, with corresponding examinations and scales, between the "mechanical and the intellectual type of labour." The objects of the reform were listed as, first, reduction in numbers and greater efficiency of operation; second, considerable saving; and third, the raising of the standards of the public schools and universities. Open competition and promotion by merit within the service were expected to increase its prestige sufficiently to have a marked effect on public school and university teaching. Underlying all is much of the old middleclass competitive principle. The best was to be secured by rewarding energy and intelligence, with the corollary of destroying security for the unfit. It was in its own way a rather simple application of the open labor market concept to the field of professional government.

The Whigs, although ostensibly the progressive party, were reluctant to act on the report: its cousinhood had long treated the highmost civil service as its own peculiar province. Something had to be done, however, in the light of the devastating findings. But it was done by an executive measure—an Order in Council of May 21, 1855—not by statute. This procedure not only bypassed the House of Commons and thus forestalled the radicals but also reemphasized the old idea that the civil service was a subject for the royal prerogative, that it belonged to the executive and not the political domain. The order gave the shadow of reform without the substance. It set up a permanent commission of three to conduct examinations for what it called "junior situations in the civil Establishment;" and for these posts it required a certificate from the commission as to the candidate's age, health, character, and ability to carry out the relevant duties. But it neither insisted on competition for posts nor interfered in any way with the rights of nomination of political patronage.

It was not until Gladstone returned to the Exchequer in 1860 that the next blow was struck. A select committee secured by him in that year found that although a few abuses had been checked since 1855, on the whole the new examinations were "a delusion to the public and a fertile source of abuse," and that the immense numbers rejected by the commission at the preliminary stage showed how irresponsible nominators had always been. Open competition, the committee continued, was the answer. But it could not recommend it unreservedly because of vested interests. Instead it put forward a compromise. Candidates were still to be nominated, but within this closed group, competition for places was to be open and determined by written examination. The compromise gradually bore some fruit until, during Gladstone's first administration, the decisive step in reform was taken with the famous Order in Council of June 4, 1870. This order swept away the nomination system and rendered competition full and open. It was, however, more limited than is commonly supposed. One major qualification was that it applied only to certain specified departments; another, that even in those departments various specific offices were exempt. On the other hand, the War Office Act of 1870 marked an extension of the new principles to yet another field.

Before Gladstone left office in 1874 the next step in the reforming process had been taken with the appointment of the Playfair Commission, a second general review of the Northcote-Trevelyan type. Sir Lyon Playfair, by now a stock scientific and educational adviser to governments, was a typical Gladstonian Liberal, and his commission's report inevitably stressed how much remained to be done before Trevelyanism reigned supreme. During the following decade the competitive system was so extended that its cumulative effects began at last to tell, and the division between the grades was also biting in. It had taken more than twenty years to displace the old order over the majority of the public service.

Yet again under Gladstone's aegis, another assault on the remnants of the ancien régime was launched with the establishment of the Ridley Commission (a renewal, in effect, of the Playfair) in 1886. After its report and the subsequent implementation, only a small area of the service remained outside the ring. Only the Foreign Office, the more senior posts in the other ministries and ministerial secretaries were still exempt. Even these final redoubts fell after the MacDonnell Commission of 1912, which represented the ultimate and universal triumph of orthodox Gladstonian Liberalism in this field. All was now swept into the arena of competition.

Thus like the decline of Crown influence three-quarters of a century earlier, the decline of patronage in the civil service was a gradual process, stretching over 50 years. Again like the earlier process, it is impossible to state precisely when the decline in patronage reached such a point that the new order predominated quantitatively. But just as somewhere in the decade 1800 to 1810 crown influence ceased to be an effective part of the general political system, so also somewhere in the decade 1875 to 1885 the center of gravity shifted within the public service and the products and fruits of patronage ceased to be the preponderant element within the system. Of course, the two movements were related.

Very broadly, they may be regarded as manifestations of the same radical reforming tendency. Trevelyanism aimed at formal civil equality in the sense of opening careers to talent (or what was so regarded in terms of the preordained tests); at contributing toward the destruction of the traditional political and social power structure; at rationalization, quantification, and uniformity; at effective controls of both public labor and public expenditure; and at establishing ministerial accountability more firmly. All this was in the mainstream of British radicalism.

Such a drive was conceived of by many as both democratic and egalitarian in tendency, although the motives the principal authors of the reform, Trevelyan and Gladstone, were rather, in the first case, power-hunger, efficiency, and economy, and, in the second, the ethics of the public good and private self-fulfillment through duty. But the democracy applied only to the upper one-tenth of society, and the equality was circumscribed by a syllabus based on a set "humane" and "gentlemanly" interpretation of education.

The merits of the reformed public service need no emphasis. It is not a myth, but the simple truth that its integrity, laboriousness, devotion to the common interest, and general level of intelligence rendered it a pattern for many other governments, especially within but also outside the British Empire. At the same time, the social and economic costs of such a system may have been very high. The Gladstonian assumptions that public expenditure tended to be the enemy of social reform, that it was the chancellor's business to ensure that it absorbed as small a portion of the national income as practicable, and that, unless jealously overseen, departments would spend more than they needed, were all inimical to state action. Treasury control not only facilitated the achievement of these objectives but also produced an official climate hostile to new ideas, fresh undertakings, administrative experiment, and forward or creative planning. Treasury conservatism applied even in its own parish: There was no major innovation in public finance from 1850 until the introduction of PAYE (the regular deduction of income tax from pay checks, known as Pay As You Earn) in 1940.

Moreover, the higher civil service, in ordinary times, tended to be drawn from a very narrow band of society in educational as well as class terms, to say nothing of the virtual absence of women from these echelons before World War I. Its recruits were almost without exception lacking in scientific, mechanical, technological, or commercial training or experience. Scarcely any were men who had earlier practised another profession. The Oxford and Cambridge general and humanities type of man predominated. The novice tended to be stereotyped despite the boasts that the gymnasia of classics and mathematics fitted one for almost any subsequent occupation. On the contrary, the cumulative consequence was excessive formalism, rigidity, and timorousness and a sort of "lay priesthood" raised from initiation to respect the "order."

Hence the critical importance of the waves of new energy, exterior experience, and experimental dispositions infused into the service by the success of certain social reforming agitations of the years 1890–1910, as well as by the two World Wars. As with the innovations of 1830 to 1850, they set loose in the public domain a host of mature men, often used to commanding and deciding, to thinking in other fashions and creating things anew.

OLIVER MACDONAGH

BIBLIOGRAPHY

Briggs, Asa, 1955. *Victorian People.* Chicago: Universtiy of Chicago Press.
Cohen, E. W., 1941. *The Growth of the British Civil Service.* London.
Dicey, A. V., 1905. *Lectures upon the Relation Between Law and Public Opinion in England During the Nineteenth Century.* London.
Fourth Report, Royal Commission on the Civil Service. 1914. [Cd 7338] xvi.
Hart, J., 1960. "Sir Charles Trevelyan at the Treasury." *English Historical Review.* lxxv.
Hughes, E., 1949. "Sir Charles Trevelyan and Civil Service Reform 1853–55," Parts I and II *English Historical Review,* lxiv.
Hume, L. J., 1981. *Bentham and Bureaucracy.* Cambridge: Cambridge University Press.
MacDonagh, O., 1977. *Early Victorian Government 1830–1870* (especially chap. 11). New York: Holmes & Meier.
McDowell, R. B., 1964. *The Irish Administration 1801–1914.* Westport, CT: Greenwood Press.
McLeod, R. M., ed., 1988. *Government and Expertise.* Cambridge: Allen & Unwin.
Parris, H., 1969. *Constitutional Bureaucracy: The Development of British Administration since the Eighteenth Century.* London.
Report of the Civil Inquiry Commission. Parliamentary Papers (hereafter cited as P.P.) 1875. [c. 1113] and [c. 1226] xxiii.
Report of the Select Committee on Civil Service Appointments. P.P. 1860. [440] ix.
Report on the Organisation of the Civil Service. 1854. [1713] xxvii.
Roseveare, H., 1969. *The Treasury, 1660–1870: The Foundations of Control.* New York: Barnes & Noble.

BRITISH ADMINISTRATIVE TRADITION FROM 1914. The management practices and organizational culture in Britain from 1914 to the present time.

British Administrative System in 1914

The British Empire was at the zenith of its power in 1914, with a policy and administrative apparatus "on which the sun never set," extending to every continent and corner of the globe. As well as providing domestic administration within the United Kingdom, Britain, through the Colonial Office, and the India Office ran or influenced a multitude of additional administrative systems in some 60 dependencies around the globe–many having comprehensive systems of governor, parliament, and representative assemblies or Privy Councils, Executive Councils, or Legislative Councils; others incorporating distinctive local administrative roles, such as that of *custos* in Jamaica or district commissioner in Ceylon. Yet throughout the whole ran threads of administrative coherence and commonality– ranging from fundamental institutions like those of Auditor-General, Registrar General, and Surveyor General to the most routine administrative concepts, such as the annual single-number registry system for office filing, as ubiquitous in the empire as the red coats of ceremonial detachments of troops. In many respects, the British administrative system stood in 1914 at the culmination of nineteenth-century development: the ultimate realization of Empire and greatness.

Impact of World War I

Through its devastating social and economic impacts and the new aspirations and values to which it gave rise, World War I is often seen as marking the commencement of twentieth-century arrangements, in Britain, not least in administration and policymaking. During the war, Britain had to contest with the military might of its opponents, but it also had to face domestically, the impact of the 1916 Irish Easter Rising, and internationally, the impact of the Revolution of 1917 in Russia. The peace principles of Versailles in 1919, with their emphasis on self-determination, pointed to the path Britain's colonies would successively take. But the need to overcome problems of employment, housing, and structural change in industry emerged as challenges at home that would be critical for British administration in the coming decades.

Administrative and Constitutional Developments

Total war had disrupted the British administrative system to the point at which it was recognized, by 1917, that a fresh reconsideration of the role and structure of government in postwar reconstruction should take place. The appointment of the Committee on the Machinery of Government, chaired by Viscount Haldane, marked Britain's intent to design new structures on a rational basis for the postwar world. The inclusion among the committee members of Beatrice Webb, Fabian socialist and reformer of public administration, signaled the value attached to a planned outcome.

The Ottawa Conference

The principles of self-determination after World War I, and the part played in the war by troops contributed by nations of the British Empire, led to moves toward greater self-determination for some nations within the Empire. Imperial conferences of 1926 and 1930 led to the 1931 Statute of Westminster, by which a number of nations within the Empire were accorded the new status of "British Dominion," conferring substantial independence and self-determination under the British crown. The three characteristics of such dominions (for example, Australia, New Zealand, Canada, South Africa, the Irish Free State, and, until 1934, Newfoundland) were that they were territorial communities outside Great Britain that shared allegiance to the British Crown, that they were to be viewed as equal in status to Great Britain and thus to one another, and that they were "in free association" in a "British Commonwealth of Nations." They were subject to some constitutional limitations and links, however, for example, the retention in some dominions of the right of appeal from the highest dominion court to the Privy Council in London, the retention of the imperial honors system, and the retention of governors and governors-general appointed by the Crown and holding certain "reserve powers" of uncertain extent.

Depression and Steps Toward War

The 1930s depression impacted Britain heavily and the early thirties were marked by very high unemployment and poverty, epitomized by the famous 1931 march of miners from Jarrow in Yorkshire to London. During this period economic orthodoxy was severely challenged by left-wing thought. However, the most significant development in economic thinking at this time was the appearance in 1936 of John Maynard Keynes's *General Theory of Employment, Interest and Money,* the seminal influence of which was to transform the machinery of state in Britain and much of the world over the ensuing fifteen years. Keynes's ideas concerning the positive role of the state in stimulating demand and his ideas in relation to an international monetary order were seen internationally as profound and were formative in establishing British institutions in the 1940s.

World War II

World War II had a revolutionary impact on British systems of administration and policy, involving the conscription by the state of virtually all wealth and resources and all knowledge and manpower in the interests of national survival in total war. Manufacturing, transportation, science, and information all became subject to the directives of ministries whose purpose was to achieve maximum efficiency in the war effort. Prodigious technological developments resulted during this period—not only as to new methods of rapidly constructing munitions, ships, tanks, and trucks but also at the forefront of communications technology, in radar, code-breaking, and in the development of electronic signals, which laid important foundations for the emergence of computer science at the end of the decade.

The Welfare State

Toward the end of World War II, as victory came in sight, British public administration reached another profound milestone as planners began to consider the nature of the society that should be created in the peace; and as the concept of a welfare state that would care for the citizen "from the cradle to the grave" was developed. The Beveridge Report of 1942 was seminal in the articulation of this concept; which would involve the most comprehensive provision for the needs of the citizen in relation to housing, welfare, employment, and health yet developed. The vision and institutional structure then forged was to serve Britain for 40 years, shaping aspirations and assumptions as well as guaranteeing the material basis of the life of its citizens.

Parallel developments in other spheres were as breathtaking, and included the introduction of new institutions internationally in the political and economic sphere (the United Nations, the World Bank, the International Monetary Fund, and many others), as well as the nationalization domestically of many formerly private industries, coal, steel, and railways among them. The nature of the British state as it emerged from World War II had been transformed.

The Nationalized Industries

The public corporation as a structural entity for operating and managing government-owned public utilities had been pioneered in Britain's Australian and New Zealand colonies from the 1880s, but in 1909, with the creation of the Port of London Authority, the concept spread to England and was championed in the 1929 and 1945 Labour governments by Herbert Morrison. Particularly in the period from 1945, under the government of Clement Attlee, the role of the public corporation in Britain was extended to a number of nationalized heavy industries, including railways and coal and steel production, in addition to the traditional areas of water and power generation. The public corporation model sought to balance commercial freedom with public purpose and responsibility, and though these corporations often succeeded in obtaining that balance, they also often failed; ministerial intervention on political grounds often adversely affected their performances. Although during the 1960s and 1970s select committees proposed various means for enhancing the management of these industries, by 1979 a conservative administration had been elected that through privatization, set about the task of returning these industries to the private sector. "Re-privatisation" had indeed been the term first applied to this task by management theorist Peter Drucker, whose ideas were adopted by the Thatcher government.

Decolonization

Among the colonies of the British Empire, the aspirations of justice and self-determination implied by the peace after World War II rekindled nationalist aspirations. Led by the extraordinary accession to independence of the Indian subcontinent in 1947, after 200 years of colonization by Britain, the following 15 years were to see most significant nations within the former British Empire granted independence, or at least self-government. The new entity of the Commonwealth of Nations was brought into being as a community of free nations, with little of the former political significance of empire. The British administrative tradition at this point was radically transformed: No longer was it the most widely dispersed administrative framework in the world; it became instead an administrative tradition or inheritance. As an inheritance, it continues to shape the institutions and administrative practices of many former British colonies, but as a historic and conditional tradition rather than as the prevailing enforced code. Reflecting this, the narrow "British Commonwealth of Nations" made up of the dominions recognized by the Statute of Westminster evolved into a looser Commonwealth of Nations, which included a number of republics with their own heads of state.

Civil Service Developments

The British civil service retained in essence the domestic structure that had developed in the later nineteenth century. Modernization was aided by significant public service inquiries, however, such as the 1966 Fulton Report, which examined the structure, recruitment, training, and management of the civil service. Its main recommendations included better use of professional specialists; the scrapping of excessive vertical divisions in classification; a questioning of the traditional preponderance of the Oxbridge elite in the civil service; the development of specifically management skills among civil servants; and a lessening of Treasury domination. Techniques and concepts such as "hiving off" agencies and establishing "accountable man-

agement" flowed from the report, though in the end its impact on the traditional civil service was less marked than its authors had hoped for.

Britain's Economic Decline and Turn to Europe

In 1973, an important new dimension was added to British public policy and administration when Britain joined the European Economic Community (EEC), which promised free access to the markets of Europe and other benefits that seemed called for by Britain's economic decline relative to its former status and to that of emerging economies. As the EEC developed into the European Community (EC) and headed toward closer political and monetary union, both the British Parliament and the British Civil Service ceased to be supreme in a number of important areas of policy and administration. At each stage of this evolution, traditionalists contested the perceived surrender of sovereignty, often instancing examples of bureaucratic pettiness from Brussels to support their contentions. However, the color of the last quarter of the twentieth century in public administration in Britain was marked by two great themes, the growing emergence of the European Community–level of public policy and administration externally, and the winding back of state apparatus internally.

Thatcher Years

The Conservative government of Margaret Thatcher from 1979 marked a sharp swing to the right ideologically, and government structures and programs established in the preceding period of the welfare state were severely cut. Privatization policies in the 15 years after Thatcher's accession saw virtually all major public corporations and nationalized industries returned to the private sector, with the exception of the Post Office. The coal, steel, automotive, air, road and, eventually, rail, transport, electricity, gas, and water industries were all privatized by a variety of techniques, including floats and trade sales. The task of championing the public interest was devolved to a new type of administrative body in the specialized regulatory offices set up to supervise many categories of privatized industry—signified by strange acronyms such as OFGAS (the gas industry regulator), OFWAT (the water industry regulator); OFFER (the electricity industry regulator) and so on. How well the public interest is served by this new structure is a matter of conjecture.

Apart from major public administration reform in relation to public enterprise, the final period of the Thatcher government saw a serious attempt to reform central departmental government. The Ibbs Report of 1988 led to the Next Steps programs, and many former departmental functions were devolved to highly focused, performance-oriented "executive agencies."

Contemporary Overview

By the mid-1990s the task of privatization in Britain's public sector was substantially complete, and central government departments had also been significantly slimmed and commercialized. One of the last significant colonies, Hong Kong, was reunited with China in 1997, and there were hopes that a solution to centuries of turmoil in Ireland might be in sight. With European monetary union closer, the incorporation of many aspects of British administration into wider European systems was proceeding. The Monarchy itself was under some pressure, with the Queen agreeing to pay income tax and open discussion as to the constitutional function of the Monarchy on the national agenda. Despite the rate of change in public administration and public policy in Britain in the preceding years, many questioned the cost of the changes in terms of reduced social equality and democratic accountability; whether the abandonment of the welfare state was too high a price to pay for economic revival and the approbation of financial markets. Reassessment of this balance currently forms an important theme in British national debate.

E. W. RUSSELL

BIBLIOGRAPHY

Commonwealth Secretariat, 1994, *The Commonwealth Yearbook.* London.
Flynn, N. 1993. *Public Sector Management.* Hemel Hempstead, England: Harvester Wheatsheaf
Greenwood J. and D. Wilson, 1989. *Public Administration in Britain Today.* London: Allen and Unwin.
Keynes, John Maynard, 1936. *The General Theory of Employment, Interest and Money.* London: Macmillan.
Metcalfe, L., and S. Richards, 1990. *Improving Public Management,* Newberry Park, CA: Sage.
Wheare, K. C., 1949. *The Statute of Westminster and Dominion Status.* New York: Oxford University Press.

BROADCASTING POLICY.

Policy having to do with broadcasting, or the dissemination of sound and pictures by wireless or wired technologies from a central point to a dispersed audience with appropriate receiving equipment.

As the century closed, broadcasting as a strand of public policy remained as politically, culturally, and diplomatically sensitive as it had been since its origins in the 1920s. But it would no longer be a discrete strand, nor stay readily within the control of national governments. Technology wove broadcasting into other, traditionally separate, policy strands. The public interests that purpose-built broadcasting laws previously served were being left to market forces or covered by a quilt of diverse government policies, including antitrust and copyright laws, arts funding, privatization strategies, and trade agreements.

Technological change so affected broadcasting from the 1970s that its very definition was in flux by the late 1990s. Even though the "appropriate receiving equipment" for audiences was still usually a radio or television, the video cassette recorder had moved control over the time of viewing from the broadcaster to the recipient. The set-top decoder allowed the broadcaster to require that the audience pay to view, as in theaters. No longer did broadcasters merely disseminate free programming so as to attract viewers to advertisers. Interactivity meant that the dissemination could no longer be defined as "one-way," to differentiate it from the telephone. Earlier definitions of broadcasting as "wireless" were confounded by the growth of cable services into much more than a retransmission method in urban areas where signals over the airwaves were poorly received. As their subscriber numbers grew, the cable networks began to rival the traditional over-the-air TV networks and to challenge the telephone companies. Cable was casting broadly its programs and its influence. The massive capacities of fiber optics to create what was popularly called the "information superhighway" arrived in a cable, not over the air, although wireless technologies would also play a role.

End of Scarcity

The involvement of public administrators in broadcasting stemmed from the need for the state to control use of the radio frequency spectrum, a finite public resource. Unless space on the airwaves was centrally apportioned, interference would reduce its utility to all.

It suited governments of all types to control access to broadcasting because of the power that first radio then, especially, television were perceived to wield. Evidence of the potential abounded: deft use of radio by Hitler, Churchill, and Roosevelt before and during World War II; influence of TV coverage of the Vietnam War on public opinion in the United States; glimpses via TV of life beyond the Iron Curtain as a factor in the collapse of the Soviet bloc, then the Soviet Union; gradual "dumbing down" of electoral politics in the democracies to conform to the "visual grammar" of television, which had evolved principally to advertise and entertain.

In democracies, technical scarcity provided a justification for oligopolies and content regulation that sat uneasily with professed commitments to market forces and freedom of expression. In the United States, the Federal Communications Commission applied to broadcasters a "fairness doctrine" which would have been constitutionally impossible to impose on the American press. Australia's broadcasting regulators required of commercial operators that specific quotas of locally made programming be put to air. In Britain, commercial broadcasting was tightly limited, thereby maintaining the ascendancy of the publicly funded BBC. France and Germany were among the many European countries that restricted entry into broadcasting to the advantage of the state-controlled broadcasters.

A side effect of such policies was the growth of concentrated media power among the few commercial broadcasting licensees. In some countries, policymakers tried to restrict the potential for abuse of such power by limiting by law the number of broadcasting outlets any one entity could own or control. Others restricted cross-ownership in the same market of television and newspapers, or of television and radio, or of newspapers and radio. The unique cultural and political role of broadcasting meant that most countries prevented foreign control, a policy that further strengthened the positions of the largest domestic media organizations by excluding foreign competitors of comparable financial strength and technical expertise.

By the mid-1990s most of the policies previously outlined were dissolving under the combined pressures of technological change, globalization of markets, and the growth of economic activity based on information, in particular financial services and audio-visual products.

Delivery systems had grown in channel capacity and spread of coverage through the expansion around the globe of direct broadcasting by satellite. In developed nations—and in privileged enclaves in developing ones—scarcity of broadcasting delivery systems was turning to glut through terrestrial microwave systems (Multipoint Distribution Services, or MDS), cables of enormous capacity, and the adaptation of the humble copper-wire telephone line to carry video (Asymmetric Digital Subscriber Line, or ADSL). Digital technology permitted words, numbers, sounds and pictures to be rendered in a common binary form, greatly compressed and disseminated at economically feasible rates via a delivery system best suited to the location of the audience. It was confidently predicted that audiences would grow with the spread of the delivery networks and access to the relevant receiving equipment such as reception dishes, set-top decoders, personal computers, and modems. New hybrid consumer appliances began to appear, combining features of a telephone, radio, TV, and computer.

These technological changes promoted a convergence of the previously separate industries of broadcasting, publishing, computing, film, and telecommunications. Mergers and alliances among some of the largest corporations quickly followed, of which the combination of Time-Warner and Turner Broadcasting (controller of CNN), of Disney and U.S. television network Capital Cities/ABC, Inc., and of Rupert Murdoch's News Corporation and MCI, the second-largest U.S. telecommunications carrier, were three of the most formidable. Convergence was self-reinforcing as the new larger entities invested in consumer applications for the technologies and marketed them vigorously via their media outlets.

Governments had lost several of the landmarks that had previously guided broadcasting policymaking. Scarcity was ending, and with it one justification for licensing and content regulation. Broadcasting was no longer an industry separated by technology from other media such as print, so the days of industry-specific rules such as cross-media ownership limits seemed numbered. Technical limits to the geographic reach of a broadcaster were disappearing, raising doubts about the rationale and enforceability of the broadcasting policies of every sovereign state.

These changes coincided with a strong preference in public policymaking in favor of the market and against government-directed solutions. Deregulation and privatization were strong themes, especially after the break-up of the Soviet bloc, and broadcasting policy was not immune. Portions of the radio frequency spectrum, a public resource previously licensed, began to be sold at auction. Content regulations began to be eased on the basis that market forces would ensure that the public interest in diversity was safeguarded.

The difficulty for policymakers was that the existing concentration, tolerated during the age of scarcity, gave existing media players a considerable advantage over would-be entrants. The alliances that were spurred by convergence gave the strongest existing corporations even greater strength. They tended to exploit the new technologies first and best and so maintain ascendancy. In Australia, for example, the nascent pay TV industry was by 1995 dominated by two joint ventures: Foxtel, comprising the nation's dominant newspaper publisher (News Corporation) and telecommunications provider (Telstra); and Optus Vision, made up of the owner of the strongest TV network and most major magazines (Kerry Packer) with Continental Cablevision and the country's second telecommunications carrier (Optus, in which major shareholders were Bell South and Cable and Wireless).

Legislators in the United States, Europe, and Australia were urged to ease limits in domestic law that restricted the growth of media corporations so that "homegrown" organizations could become stronger for the competition in the global marketplace. The U.S. Telecommunications Act, signed into law by President Clinton in February 1996, embodied this logic by deregulating, in particular, the previous exclusion of cable TV operators and telephone companies from each other's markets.

From the United Kingdom came proposals to ease cross-ownership limits and replace them with a single limit on any one group's "share of voice" of all media combined. The core difficulty was to determine the "exchange rate" or common denominator in which the influence and effects of every medium could be rendered and each group's share of the total voice calculated. Competition policy and antitrust law were suggested as a suitable, generic form of regulation to prevent the ills of concentration that media-specific regulation had previously tackled. However, desire to compete globally produced simultaneous pressure to ease competition law domestically so that a country's corporations generally, not just its media organizations, could grow large enough for the international marketplace.

Local Identity in a Global Market

Policymakers faced "television without frontiers," the title of a 1989 European Union directive. A global market encouraged global products and most of them came from the United States. Governments in other countries came under domestic pressure on political and cultural grounds. Some were concerned that the freer flow of information, and of American-style democracy, would unsettle their own political environments. Others feared the effect of a consumerist, permissive screen culture on their own religious, social, and cultural mores. For instance, "Asian values" were said to be at risk. Policy responses varied widely. Some attempted to ban or restrict public access to satellite dishes (Saudi Arabia, China) or to certain programming on satellite services originating offshore (Singapore, which also tried to censor the Internet). Others fashioned policies that required the provision of a fixed minimum proportion of local content (Australia). Countries supplemented Hollywood's output by subsidizing local production through arts policies, by requiring domestic commercial broadcasters to provide it, and by making local content a special responsibility of public broadcasters.

Broadcasting became interwoven with trade policy. The Uruguay Round of negotiations of the General Agreement on Tariffs and Trade (GATT), aimed at liberalizing world trade, incorporated trade in services for the first time, partly at the urging of a United States frustrated at barriers to its film and television exports, especially those protecting European markets. But an alliance of smaller countries, led by France, ensured that the GATT retained, on cultural grounds, exceptions for domestic policies that discriminated against foreign programming.

The global picture of broadcasting policy and culture was complex. Sometimes, the transnational broadcasters voluntarily censored in order to ensure smooth access to the growing middleclasses of the rapidly developing economies of Malaysia, Indonesia and, above all, China. For example, Rupert Murdoch's Star TV dropped the BBC World Service from its northern beam after China objected to its content. In countries with a sufficiently large number of potential viewers for programs in particular languages, for instance Hindi and Mandarin, the transnationals commissioned and broadcast them or acquired interests in local broadcasters who did so. Non-English global networks developed, in particular Spanish programming through Mexico's Televisa.

Uncertain Role of Public Broadcasters

The confluence of diminishing technological scarcity and a surge of faith in market solutions had a powerful impact on public broadcasters. The United States was atypical in the early years of broadcasting in not building a potent, government-funded broadcasting network to match its national commercial networks. In the UK, Australia, and Canada such public broadcasters usually predated commercial operators, growing large alongside them and developing widespread infrastructure, programming expertise, and audience reach. Although mostly free of advertising and funded from the public purse or by a license fee imposed on viewers by law, the public broadcasting corporations of the UK, Australia, and Canada were formally independent of the government of the day. Actual independence depended on the attitudes and interplay of government ministers and public broadcasting's directors. In many countries broadcasting was entirely state-owned and independence was curtailed with varying degrees of severity.

The 1980s and 1990s brought great change. In Eastern Europe, political change saw the privatization of former state broadcasters or the introduction of commercial competitors that changed the environment in which the state broadcaster functioned. Technology created pressure for more commercial broadcasters in Western Europe. Greater competitive pressure for advertising revenue in the mass market and the advent of pay TV led to market fragmentation. Commercial operators coveted the often relatively better-educated, better-resourced section of the public who preferred the programming offered by the public broadcasters. Governments in Britain, Canada, and Australia wondered whether the end of scarcity meant the state no longer needed to fund so large a public broadcaster. The Republican-dominated United States Congress reconsidered its endowments to the arts, on which much independent public broadcasting relied. Inevitable grievances among politicians of varied ideological complexions about the news and current affairs coverage of the public broadcaster fueled a desire for change, but was not the only cause of the policy rethink.

Challenged to justify their state funding and noncommercial status in the media environment of the mid-1990s, public broadcasters argued in part that they could help to preserve local culture during globalization and contribute to the diversity of news and information sources necessary to the proper functioning of a democracy.

Special Factors in Broadcasting Policymaking

A constant element in broadcasting policy in elective democracies is the fact that media organizations are perceived by political decisionmakers to have potential influence over voters and therefore over the outcome of elections. Evidence for this influence varies but it is the perception that counts. It gives the lobbying efforts of the industry added force during the shaping of broadcasting policy.

The nexus between media and government was most strikingly demonstrated in Italy in 1994 when Silvio Berlusconi, owner of the country's largest communications group, Fininvest, became prime minister after an election campaign in which he received the strong backing of his own media outlets.

The interrelationship of media and government and its implications for democracy seemed particularly relevant not just to the older democracies, but also to the rebuilding of civil society and democratic institutions in countries emerging from military or one-party rule in Eastern Europe and Latin America, countries showing signs of doing so in Asia, and in the special case of South Africa after the transition to majority rule in 1994. The issue of course subsumes broadcasting policy but is also peculiarly relevant to it. It was debated in academic literature and among policymakers, in particular international agencies, but received less attention in the mainstream mass media, an indication of the power of the media to influence, by omission, what is neglected by public policy as much as to influence, by emphasis, what is discussed, if not what is determined.

PAUL CHADWICK

BIBLIOGRAPHY

Cunningham, Stuart, and Sinclair, John, eds., 1994. "Global Media Games," theme issue of *Media Information Australia,* no. 71 (February).

Department of National Heritage, UK, 1995. *Media Ownership: The Government's Proposals.* London: HMSO, Cm 2872 (May).

Keane, John, 1991. *The Media and Democracy.* London: Polity Press.

MacLeod, Vicki, ed., 1996. *Media Ownership and Control in the Age of Convergence.* London: International Institute of Communications, Global Report Series.

Pool, Ithiel de Sola, 1983. *Technologies of Freedom: On Free Speech in an Electronic Age.* Cambridge, MA: Harvard University Press.

———, (posthumous; Eli M. Noam, ed.), 1990. *Technologies Without Boundaries: On Telecommunications in a Global Age.* Cambridge, MA: Harvard University Press.

Postman, Neil, 1985. *Amusing Ourselves to Death: Public Discourse in the Age of Show Business.* New York: Viking Penguin.

BROWNLOW COMMISSION.

A three-member committee appointed by President Franklin D. Roosevelt to study the problem of government organization and management and to make recommendations for its improvement, also known as the President's Committee on Administrative Management. Its members consisted of Louis Brownlow, chairman, Charles E. Merriam, and Luther Gulick.

Since the turn of the century government had grown in size and scope as had the American economy. Moreover, with the Great Depression of the early 1930s government's responsibility and complexity increased as new programs were implemented to aid the American people through the economic crisis of the Depression. However, despite this increased responsibility and complexity there was no change in the structure of government to handle these new tasks and challenges; government was becoming increasingly inefficient and ineffective and government was on the brink of its own crisis. President Roosevelt, in a message to Congress accompanying the report of the Brownlow Commission, said of the problem: "Our struggle now is against confusion, against ineffectiveness, against waste, against inefficiency. This battle, too, must be won, unless it is to be said that in our generation national self-government broke down and was frittered away in bad management."

On January 8, 1937, the Brownlow Commission submitted to President Roosevelt its recommendations for change in the administrative management and structure of government to improve its efficiency and efficacy. These recommendations focused on six areas: The White House staff, personnel management, fiscal management, planning management, administrative reorganization of the government and accountability of the Executive to Congress.

The White House Staff

On the issue of the White House staff the commission recommended an increase in the President's immediate staff. Given the increased workload of the President there needed to be a staff to assist him to gather information from and disseminate information to the administrative and managerial agencies as necessary. This staff would be designed to improve the efficiency and efficacy of communication. The commission also recommended an increase in the general office staff and the establishment of a fund so that the President could purchase the time of experts as necessary to assist in the endeavors of the government.

Personnel Management

The second major issue addressed by the report of the Brownlow Commission was in the area of personnel management. As stated by the commission as a preface to its recommendations in this area: "Personnel administration lies at the very core of administrative management. The effective conduct of the work of the Government depends upon the men and women who serve it. Improved plans for government organization and management are of little value unless simultaneous recognition is given to the need for attracting, retaining, and developing human capacity in the public service" (President's Committee, 1937; 7).

The improvement of personnel management required three major components. The first of these components was the extension of the merit system to include almost all employees. The second called for the reorganization of the Civil Service Commission as a central personnel agency of government, to be called the Civil Service Administration. This Civil Service Administration would have an administrator who advises the President in all personnel issues and a Civil Service Board of seven members to be appointed by the President that would be responsible for issues related to the merit system. The third recommendation of the Brownlow Commission was to improve the classification and compensation system. The government, because of its low salary structure, was beginning to lose administrators, managers, and other employees to the higher-paying private sector.

Fiscal Management

Although the Bureau of the Budget had been created sixteen years prior to the recommendation of the Brownlow Commission, there was still work to be done in the area of financial management. The commission recommended that the director of the Bureau of the Budget should concentrate on "matters of fiscal policy and planning not routine duties." In addition the Bureau of the Budget should supervise the "preparation and execution of the budget" (President's Committee, 1937: 19). The Commission also recommended that the United States Information Service should be within the Bureau of the Budget for coordination purposes.

Moreover, the Brownlow Commission made additional recommendations to change the structure of the positions of the Comptroller General (and the title of that position to Auditor General) and the Secretary of Treasury to coordinate the accounting practices of government and to yield better information for both Congress and the President in fiscal matters.

Planning Management

The recommendations in this area consisted of the creation of a planning board of five members to be appointed by the President. This board would, like many existing state boards at that time, be responsible for planning the use of national resources across the needs of the nation. This board would be called the National Resources Board.

Administrative Reorganization of the Government of the United States

It is in this section and on this issue that the Brownlow Commission made its most sweeping recommendations. In an attempt to reduce the number of agencies that reported to the President, the commission made recommendations in five areas: a plan of reorganization, Executive responsibility for efficient organization, departmental organization, Independent Regulatory Commissions, and government corporations. These recommendations included the creation of the Department of Social Welfare and a Department of Public Works, the increased accountability of the President to Congress through the development of independent auditing procedures, changes in the scope and responsibility of the divisions of government, and the consolidation of the many existing departments of government into 12 major departments. The twelve departments recommended by the commission were: Department of State, Department of Treasury, Department of War, Department of Justice, Post Office Department, Department of the Navy, Department of Conservation, Department of Agriculture, Department of Labor, Department of Commerce, Department of Social Welfare, and Department of Public Works.

On the issue of Independent Regulatory Commissions the report suggested that these commissions be brought within the jurisdiction of specific departments so as not to conflict with the authority of or effective management of the Executive Branch of Government (President's Committee, 1937: 37). The proliferation of commissions preceding the release of the report had served to fragment the authority and ability of government to address policy effectively.

Finally with respect to government corporations, the commission endorsed their use but cautioned that these too should be placed under "special supervisory agencies to give continuous and careful scrutiny to their affairs" (President's Committee, 1937: 41).

Accountability of the Executive to the Congress

Finally, the commission recommended the improvement of the accountability of the Executive to Congress through an audit of fiscal and other activities. In addition, the report recommended the creation of separate committees of the Congress for "investigational activities, [to] hold hearings, and consider legislation and appropriations" (President's Committee, 1937: 43). The creation of these fiscal monitoring committees was also to be complemented by the creation of other committees to "keep currently informed of the three managerial agencies dealing with the budget, personnel, and planning which we recommend should be set up directly under the President, [that] would go far toward lessening the evil effects of the present lack of coordination" (President's Committee, 1937: 44).

The Brownlow Commission report and its recommendations served to illustrate the many inefficiencies and lack of efficacy of the government as it was structured in 1937. Their plan of reorganization served to decrease the fragmentation and improve the level and type of communication within the federal government. This report and the implementation of some of its recommendations served as the basis of a modern government equipped and structured to deal with the increasing needs and complexity of the growing American society.

MICHELE COLLINS

BIBLIOGRAPHY

Fesler, James W., 1987. "The Brownlow Committee Fifty Years Later." *Public Administration Review*, vol. 47 (July–August).

Karl, Barry D., 1963. *Executive Reorganization and Reform in the New Deal.* Cambridge, MA: Harvard University Press.

President's Committee on Administrative Management, 1937. *Administrative Management in the Government of the United States.* Washington, D.C.: U.S. Government Printing Office.

BUDGET ADJUSTMENTS, CITY.

Decisions made by city officials in response to a changing fiscal environment for purposes of enhancing their city's situation.

Background

Increased consumer demands for public services, stagnating or declining revenues, additional mandated responsibilities from state and federal governments, military base closures, declining state aid, and many other factors conspire in a multitude of ways to put pressure on city budgets. Some general factors affecting city budgeting over the past decade or more include the decline in federal aid to cities since 1978 and the 1990–1992 national and global recession. Other more particularistic factors have had differential impacts on cities in the early 1990s, according to reports from the National Governors' Association and National Association of State Budget Officers. These include the decline in the high-tech industries in California and Massachusetts, cutbacks in state aid to cities in New York, Alaska, Nebraska, North Dakota, and California, and restrictive legal changes in the treatment of cities by their states, such as the elimination of state sales tax exemptions on purchases by Minnesota's municipalities.

Cities are adaptive organizations; they both respond to changes in their environments and mold their environments to their own needs. Even so, as Harold Wolman (1983) argued, conscious fiscal decisions reflect cities' responsiveness and adaptation to change. And because each city is a unique organization, one city's response to change may not be the same as another's. As the fiscal environment changes, one city may raise tax rates, another

may cut spending, and yet a third may use its reserves from earlier years to shore up its service-delivery responsibilities.

Official responses to environmental change can assume a variety of hues, ranging from the most visible from the vantage point of the consumer-taxpayer (e.g., cutting services and raising taxes) to the fairly invisible (namely, freezing municipal hiring and postponing capital spending) to the creative (e.g., contracting-out and "load-shedding," which sometimes give the illusion of reducing taxes). These decisions are not made lightly. In general, the most politically acceptable response to an environmental change is to do nothing; that is to say, it is the preferred state in the political world to do nothing in the expectation that the environment will revert to its prechange condition and the fiscal pressure on the budget will be relieved. From this perspective, fiscal decisions are made then, in a deliberative fashion and only after the do-nothing option has been found untenable. Moreover, because purposive fiscal policy actions are taken in a political arena and exposed to public scrutiny, these decisions are taken after extensive political and fiscal analyses.

The three questions I address here are: (1) What specific revenue and expenditure actions–referred to as "fiscal policy actions"–have cities taken during the study period (1986–1993)? (2) When and under what conditions are conscious decisions on fiscal policy actions taken? And (3), do fiscal policy actions close the gap between the predicted (budgeted) revenue-expenditure imbalance and the actual gap? Because it is assumed that disruptions to a city's revenue-expenditure equilibrium precipitate fiscal action, one must rely on two measures of a city's fiscal environment, an imbalance measure and an ending balance measure.

Methodology and Data

All cities with populations greater than 50,000 are sent surveys on their fiscal conditions in the spring of each year (since 1986) by the National League of Cities. These fiscal data cover both an expansionary period (1985–1989, 1993) and a recessionary or very slow growth period (1990–1992). Questionnaires are mailed annually to approximately 536 cities. The 1987 response rate was 41.9 percent, in 1988 it was 33.9 percent, in 1989 it was 48.9 percent, in 1990 46.2 percent, in 1991 42.9 percent, in 1992 51.4 percent, in 1993 51.1 percent, and in 1994 the response rate was 50.6 percent. This rate tends to be higher for the larger cities than for smaller cities. In 1994, for example, 45 of the 51 largest cities, or 88.2 percent, responded (including New York City, Los Angeles, Chicago, Detroit, and Philadelphia) as did 85 of 147 cities, or 57.8 percent, in the medium-sized city category (100,000–299,999 population).

The survey asks for financial information about the city's General Fund (revenues, expenditures, ending balances, revenue composition) and for adopted fiscal policy *actions* (not proposals) taken in the previous 12 months.

The survey is sent to chief fiscal officers and requests actual data for the previous two fiscal years and budgeted (or estimated) data for the current fiscal year. The General Fund is considered by Leo Herbert, Larry Killough, and Alan Steiss (1984) as "the most important fund in governmental accounting" through which most major "operations of the governmental unit are conducted." It is the only accounting entity common to most cities. The General Fund finances those general operations of the city that generally do not have special or dedicated revenue sources. Consequently, although the survey is not comprehensive of all city finances and funds, it does request data on the most significant and universal city fund. The General Fund is the largest fund, accounting for approximately half of total city budgets.

Two measures of city fiscal conditions are calculated for this study. The first is an ending balance measure. It is calculated as General Fund ending balances as a percentage of expenditures and is a cumulative measure of a city's fiscal health. It accounts for prior-year surpluses that are carried over to the next fiscal year and used to finance general operations of the city. Due to state-imposed budget balancing requirements for most cities, a city's ending balance should never drop below zero.

The second is a measure of imbalance, and it compares the General Fund's current-year revenues with current-year expenditures. This measures a city's fiscal conditions for a specific fiscal year and does not measure a city's cumulative fiscal condition. It is measured as current-year revenues minus current-year expenditures, divided by current-year expenditures. For example, a city with $10 million in expenditures and $11 million in revenues would be rated at +10 percent.

Fiscal Policy Actions

The most visible and, according to surveys conducted by the U.S. Advisory Commission on Intergovernmental Relations (ACIR), one of the least-favored forms of raising public revenue is the ad valorem tax on real estate, or the property tax. When people were asked to identify which of four taxes is the worst (the property tax, the state income tax, the federal income tax, or the sales tax), the clear winner for nearly two decades has been the property tax. Yet, most city officials are barred statutorily or constitutionally from tapping into the other, less-offensive revenue sources by their states. And for other municipalities, as a result of the tax and expenditure limitation movement that started in earnest with the passage of Proposition 13 in California in 1978 and Proposition 2-1/2 in Massachusetts two years later, even the property tax is off limits (especially for cities in California and Massachusetts.)

Revenue Actions

Nevertheless, a substantial number of municipalities raise the property tax rate each year, according to data presented in Figure I. In fact, between 1987 and 1990, more than one-third of all responding cities reported that the property tax rate had been increased—and that figure includes in the denominator a large number of California cities that cannot constitutionally raise the property tax rate. The proportion of cities taking this action since 1990 has dropped to under one-third, as property tax activism, along with tax activism more generally, has begun to diminish.

Cities that have the authority to raise other (nonproperty) tax rates and that have, in fact, raised those other tax rates since 1986 amount to approximately the same proportion of cities that have raised the property tax rate during the same period. Cities with a local-option sales tax authority increase their sales tax rate very infrequently; on average, less than 10 percent of cities with this option actually raised the sales tax rate each year. Likewise, cities with a local-option income tax authority tended not to raise that tax rate between 1986 and 1993. More cities, however, did raise "other" tax rates (e.g., inventory, license) during the study period, from a high of about 25 percent of all cities in 1987 to a low of just under 15 percent in 1991 and 1992. And the percentage of cities that adopted a new tax increased from the 10-to-15 percent range between 1986 and 1989 to nearly 20 percent in 1990, before falling back under 10 percent in 1992 and 1993.

These trends suggest that, even though general taxes (especially the property tax) are not politically popular, city officials do not shrink from their fiscal responsibility of funding city services with sufficient revenues. Nevertheless, a comparison of the trends for general tax increases in Figure I with the trends for fees and charges in Figure II during the same period demonstrates that even as cities have frequently returned to broad-based general taxes as a means of shoring up their budgets, by far the most common revenue-generating action for the past decade has been in the area of user charges and fees. The percentages of cities that have adopted new fees, raised existing fees, or raised or implemented new development or impact fees has been substantial over the decade.

Figure III presents the trends for all three of these revenue-related actions. Unlike the apparent reluctance to increase tax rates, cities are not timorous about raising user charges and fees, especially between 1986 and 1990 when over three-fourths of all cities raised fees on at least one city activity. Moreover, during this time period, cities have been exceptionally active in identifying programs and activities for which a user fee would be appropriate. In fact, nearly as many cities implemented new fees (that is, charged for services that heretofore most likely had been provided through general tax revenue) as raised their property tax rates. Approximately one in every three cities for each year between 1986 and 1993 identified a new activity on which a fee could be charged. Although the number of cities that have found new activities on which to attach a fee has slowly been declining, it is still quite substantial.

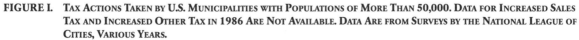

FIGURE I. Tax Actions Taken by U.S. Municipalities with Populations of More Than 50,000. Data for Increased Sales Tax and Increased Other Tax in 1986 Are Not Available. Data Are from Surveys by the National League of Cities, Various Years.

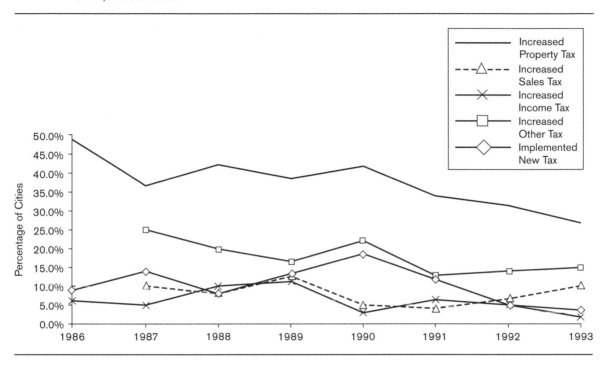

FIGURE II. Fee Actions Taken by U.S. Municipalities with Populations of More Than 50,000. Data for Raised Impact Fees in 1986 Are Not Available. Data Are from Surveys by the National League of Cities, Various Years.

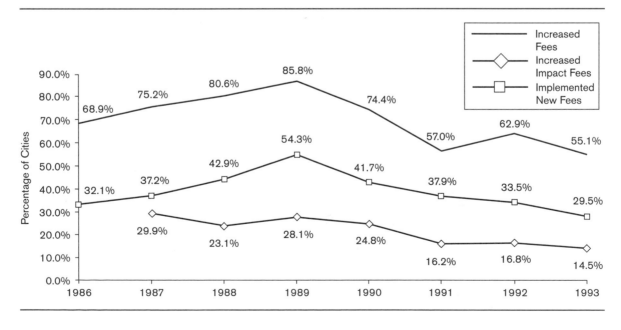

FIGURE III. FEE OR TAX ACTIONS TAKEN BY U.S. MUNICIPALITIES WITH POPULATIONS OF MORE THAN 50,000. DATA ARE FROM SURVEYS BY THE NATIONAL LEAGUE OF CITIES, VARIOUS YEARS.

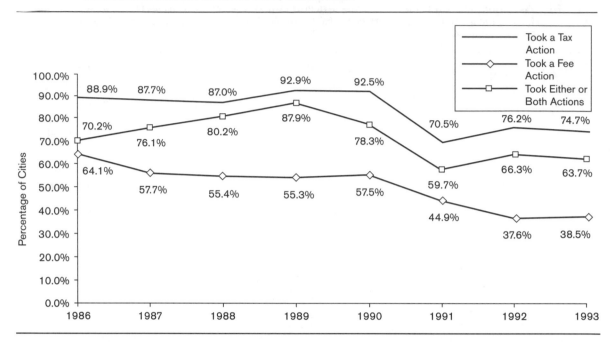

FIGURE IV. EXPENDITURE ACTIONS TAKEN BY U.S. MUNICIPALITIES WITH POPULATIONS OF MORE THAN 50,000. DATA ARE FROM SURVEYS BY THE NATIONAL LEAGUE OF CITIES, VARIOUS YEARS.

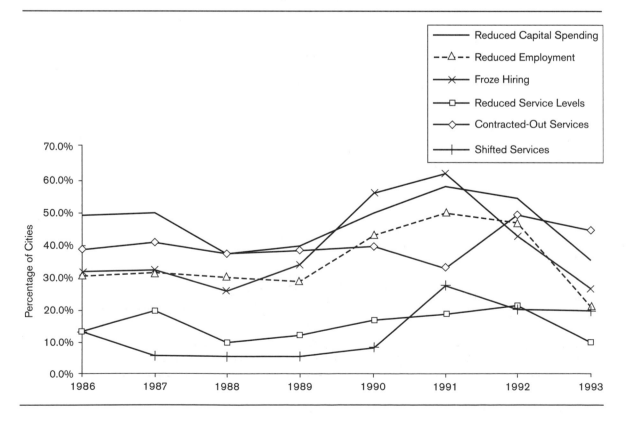

Finally, the adoption of impact and development fees (and raising those fees) during the 1980s was part of a greater national trend toward innovative financing of city infrastructure activities. This form of financing infrastructure appears to be waning in the 1990s as the percentage of cities that have either adopted or raised impact or development fees has been reduced to approximately half its earlier rate.

Expenditure Actions

On the spending side of the ledger, actions taken by municipalities include not just the typical reductions in city services and cutbacks in municipal employment but also the sharing of the costs of service provision with other governments. This division of expenditures in turn reduces a city's direct costs and its contracting-out, which shifts the costs elsewhere. Since 1986, the most frequently chosen expenditure action has been the option to "reduce actual levels of capital spending" (Figure IV). Capital spending on infrastructure is more sensitive to shifts in the underlying economy than almost any other spending category. Cities find it more expedient to postpone street resurfacing or streetlight replacement or other major capital outlays than to postpone or cut back in other areas. Once the underlying economic condition improves, these capital projects can be reinstated. The trend for capital spending reductions shows the largest number of cities cutting back on capital spending in 1990, 1991, and 1992, at a time that corresponds with the height of the recession.

It should also be noted that the relatively high percentage of cities that invariably choose this expenditure option suggests that cities may consistently exaggerate their capital spending plans for the fiscal year, in full knowledge that some of those approved projects will be postponed until a later date. Data on capital budgets for 1993 and 1994 were collected. Respondents were asked to supply information on the size of appropriations for their city's capital budgets and then to compare the appropriated capital budget with a realistic estimate of how much they expected their city would actually spend during the fiscal year. The realistic amounts were approximately one-third less than the budgeted amounts, suggesting that capital budgets are routinely overestimated—a conclusion also reached in annual city fiscal studies undertaken by the Municipal Finance Officers Association for the Joint Economic Committee of Congress in the late 1970s and early 1980s (U.S. Cong. Joint Economic Committee 1983).

Expenditure actions that are more closely aligned with public perception of cutbacks are actual reductions in service—an action that has been taken quite infrequently according to survey respondents—and freezing or reducing city employment. Actual reductions in service levels is an action that has been taken by 10 to 20 percent of all municipalities over the study period. It should be noted that there was a slight upward trend during the recessionary years of 1990–92, and then in 1993 the trend returns to the prerecessionary norm. Freezing and reducing city employment levels appears to be more volatile than other expenditure actions. Employment freezes, which remained around the 30 percent mark for the first four years of the survey, surged to over 50 percent in 1990 and 1991, before dropping back to normal levels in 1993. Actual reduction in municipal employment followed a similar path. Between 1986 and 1989, approximately 30 percent of all cities reduced their payroll. Between 1990 and 1992, nearly half of all municipalities reduced employment. In 1993, the percentage of cities that had cut their workforce dropped back to prerecession levels.

The last two categories, contracting-out—which has become an increasingly popular option—and shifting service delivery costs through interlocal agreements, have been identified by a small, but significant, number of cities. At first, the trend for these two options was not expected to be as high as that for the other expenditure actions because the survey asked if the city had contracted out a *new* service during the past fiscal year or if the city had entered into *another* interlocal agreement in addition to existing ones. In other words, once a city had decided to contract-out for, say, garbage collection services, it would not identify this option in any future surveys. Likewise, once an interlocal agreement for, say, emergency medical services, had been signed, the city would not identify this option in future surveys. Nevertheless, both of these options appear to be relied on fairly consistently over the course of the study period.

Contracting-out city services is an activity that has enjoyed fairly stable popularity over the study period, increasing from approximately 35 to 40 percent of all cities between 1986 and 1991 to nearly half of all cities in 1992 and 1993. Indeed, contracting-out was the second expenditure action of choice for the first four years of the study period, slightly behind "reductions in actual levels of capital spending," and by 1993 it had become the most frequently mentioned expenditure action.

Finally, the survey between 1986 and 1990 asked if cities were "shifting costs" of service delivery to other governments, a question that evoked a very low affirmative response. The question was amended in 1991 and asked if cities initiated "interlocal agreements" for the purpose of reducing costs or improving operating efficiencies. Once the question was altered, nearly one-in-four cities answered that indeed interlocal agreements were initiated during each of the subsequent three years.

Triggering Revenue and Expenditure Actions

Cities as social organizations exist within a changing environment. They adapt to changes in that external environment as well as to changes in consumer preferences within the internal environment. Cities seek an equilibrium position in which revenue and expenditure patterns meet the demands of the citizenry within a constrained budget. In a study of urban economic development projects, Michael Pagano and Ann Bowman (1995) found that shifts in the external or internal environment stimulated searching for a mechanism to reestablish the ex ante equilibrium. For cities, this search for policy options, or what Richard Cyert and James March (1963) refer to as "problemistic search," consists principally of identifying revenue or expenditure actions. The timing of the search for these expenditure and revenue actions is the focus of the next section.

One-Year Fiscal Problems

News of fiscal and economic catastrophes carries with it the need to do something in response. The 1978 property tax limitations in California sounded the call to action for California's cities, as did the post–cold war downsizing of the defense industry, which is so prominent in California's economic health. The economic recession of 1990–1991 resulted in cities' cries of desperation that were nearly as loud as those emanating from city halls when Congress did not reauthorize the general revenue sharing legislation for fiscal year 1987. And the public clamor over the excessive costs of federal (and state) mandates on city budgets have placed this new budget item high on city "hit lists." The implication of this kind of dire news, such as that conveyed by the previous illustrations, is that cities must respond immediately and decisively in order to reestablish the ex ante equilibrium between service levels and fiscal support.

Yet, projected budgetary difficulties for any one year as a consequence of lost revenues or onerous costs may not trigger a problemistic search. That is, these external "shocks" to the annual city budget preparation process would manifest themselves in either diminished levels of projected revenues (e.g., in response to tax limitations or defense industry cutbacks) or higher levels of projected expenditures (e.g., mandate burdens), or both. In either case, revenues and expenditures would be out of alignment, and one would expect that expenditures might even be projected to exceed revenues for the current fiscal year. The question here, then, is whether this one-year revenue-expenditure imbalance triggers a problemistic search.

Empirical data from cities' approved budgets were collected in year *t* and compared to fiscal policy actions actually taken during that year (these latter data were collected from surveys administered in year *t* + 1). Because the hypothesis is that a revenue-expenditure imbalance will induce a city to take some fiscal policy action, the probit statistical technique was employed. The probit model posits that a city will or will not take a specific tax, fee, or expenditure action (the dependent dummy variable) when confronted with a budgeted imbalance (the independent variable). Only one statistically significant finding from this analysis for seven years (1987–1993) could be ascertained

TABLE. I DOES THE CURRENT-YEAR FISCAL IMBALANCE PRECIPITATE FISCAL POLICY ACTIVISM?

	Current-Year Fiscal Imbalance
1987	Contracted out (.055) (+)
1988	–
1989	Implemented new fee (.064) (−)
	Reduced capital spending (.044) (−)
1990	–
1991	–
1992	Raised impact fee (.089) (−)
1993	Reduced capital spending (.063) (−)

NOTE: Significance levels follow the fiscal policy action. Although social science standards usually identify the .05 level as reasonable, this table also includes relationships that are significant at the .10 level. The plus and minus signs in the next set of parentheses refer to the direction of the relationship. Excluded are cities with expenditures over $1 billion.
SOURCE: Data received from surveys sent to all cities with a population over 50,000 by the National League of Cities, 1987 through 1993.

(Table I). (Note: Revenue actions include increasing the property, or any other tax rate: implementing a new tax; implementing new fees; raising or imposing development or impact fees; or raising user fees on existing services. Expenditure actions include reduction in service: actual reductions in capital spending; reducing the growth rate of operating spending; municipal hiring freezes or cutbacks; contracting-out; and sharing the costs of service provision through interlocal agreements.) Of all the possible revenue and expenditure actions only in 1989 could the imbalance measure be statistically associated with an action and that action was actual reduction in capital spending.

In other words, cities with budgeted negative imbalances in 1989 were likely to have reduced their actual levels of capital spending. Other than that fiscal policy action, no other revenue or expenditure action was found to be significant at the .05 level of significance.

If, however the significance level is raised to .10, the following fiscal policy actions are found to be important: In 1989 cities that were budgeted to be in a negative imbalance implemented new fees; in 1992, these negative imbalance cities tended to raise impact fees again and in 1993, these tended to reduce actual levels of capital spending. A counterintuitive (and unexplained) finding is that cities that budgeted for a positive imbalance (revenues exceeded expenditures by more than 5 percent) in 1987 tended to contract-out city services.

In general, then, it appears that over the seven year-study period, the degree to which cities budgeted for revenue-expenditure imbalances was useful in predicting the selection of a specific revenue or expenditure action in only a few circumstances.

Cumulative Fiscal Problems

Cities may be able to weather the one-year budgeted revenue-expenditure imbalance by "cautious budgeting" (that

TABLE II. Do Declining Ending Balances Precipitate Fiscal Policy Activism?

	Ending Balance Per Capita	Ending Balance as a Percentage of Expenditure
1987	Raised impact fee (.06) (+)	Reduced operating growth (.08) (−)
	Reduced operating growth (.01) (−)	Reduced employment (.02) (−)
	Reduced employment (.09) (−)	Froze employment (.005) (−)
	Froze employment (.001) (−)	
1988	Reduced services (.08) (−)	Increased fees (.09) (−)
		Reduced services (.02) (−)
1989	Reduced services (.11) (−)	Reduced services (.01) (−)
	Contracted out (.05) (−)	Contracted out (.10) (−)
	Interlocal agreement (.09) (−)	
1990	Implemented new tax (.05) (−)	Implemented new tax (.01) (−)
		Reduced services (.04) (−)
1991	Increased other tax (.04) (+)	Increased other tax (.07) (+)
	Increased fees (.01) (−)	Contracted out (.03) (−)
	Interlocal agreement (.03) (−)	Interlocal agreement (.06) (−)
1992	Reduced capital spending (.08) (+)	Raised impact fees (.02) (+)
	Reduced services (.06) (+)	
1993	Raised sales tax (.10) (−)	−
	Reduced operating growth (.02) (+)	

NOTE: Significance levels follow the fiscal policy action. Although social science standards usually identify the .05 level as reasonable, this table also includes relationships that are significant at the .10 level. The minus and plus signs in the next set of parentheses refer to the direction of the relationship. Excluded are cities with expenditures over $1 billion.

SOURCE: Data received from surveys sent to all cities with a population over 50,000 by the National League of Cities, 1987 through 1993.

is, deliberately overprojecting expenditures and underprojecting revenues) in order to forestall the decision of taking any fiscal policy action. A second question, then, is whether cities' revenue or expenditure activism changes as their cumulative fiscal conditions deteriorate. In other words, if cities position themselves to survive a fiscal shock to their budgets in any one year, what is the level of revenue-expenditure imbalance that can be tolerated by any city before it must make wholesale budgetary changes in response to those shocks? Do cities wait until they have no savings left before they take fiscal action or do they identify a benchmark imbalance point that triggers fiscal action? To address this issue, two cumulative measures are employed. One measure is defined as the ending balance as a percentage of expenditures; the other is per capita ending balance. Again, probit analysis was employed in order to ascertain whether or not a statistically significant relationship existed between the fiscal policy action a city actually took and its predicted ending balance as a percentage of expenditures or its ending balance per capita.

Results from the probit analysis show that, except for one year (1992), at least one revenue or expenditure action was associated with a budgeted decline in city ending balances, measured on a per capita basis (Table II, first column). In 1987, cities that predicted ending balances would decline took the fiscal policy actions of reducing the growth rate of operating spending, reducing city employment, and freezing city employment levels; however, the

only fiscal policy action significant at the acceptable .05 level was the decline in the growth rate of operating spending. In 1988, city services were reduced as per capita ending balances were budgeted to decline, although this action was not significant at the .05 level. In 1989, city service reductions, contracting-out, and interlocal agreements were significant (only contracting-out was significant at the .05 level). In 1990, cities that were budgeting for smaller ending balances per capita tended to implement new taxes. In 1991, increased fees and interlocal agreements were significant at the .05 level. And in 1993, raising the sales tax rate was significant at the .098 level. One fiscal policy action in 1987 (raising impact fees), in 1991 (increasing other tax rates), and in 1993 (reducing the growth rate in operating spending) and two fiscal policy actions in 1992 (reducing capital spending and reducing service levels) were significant, but in the wrong (counterintuitive) direction.

With the independent variable now defined as budgeted ending balances as a percentage of expenditures (Table II, second column), certain revenue and expenditure actions were found to be significant, except for two years (1992 and 1993). In 1987, of the three significant expenditure actions (reducing operating growth rate, reducing employment, freezing employment), only the latter two were significant at the .05 level. In 1988, of the two factors, only service reduction was significant at the .05 level, a finding that was duplicated in the next year as well. In 1990, service level reduction and implementing a new tax

TABLE III. Do Current-Year Imbalances or Declining Ending Balances Predict "Aggregate" Revenue or Expenditure Actions?

	Ending Balance Per Capita	Ending Balance as a Percentage of Expenditure	Imbalance
1987	Expenditure (.086) (−)	−	−
1988	Expenditure (.056) (+)	Revenue, fees only (.074) (−)	−
1989	Revenue, taxes only (.022) (+)	Expenditure (.013) (−)	
1990	−	−	−
1991	Revenue, fees only (.016) (−)	−	−
1992	−	−	−
1993	−	−	Revenue (.073) (+)

NOTE: Significance levels follow the fiscal policy action. Although social science standards usually identify the .05 level as reasonable, this table also includes relationships that are significant at the .10 level. The minus and plus signs in the next set of parentheses refer to the direction of the relationship. Excluded are cities with expenditures over $1 billion.

SOURCE: Data received from surveys sent to all cities with a population over 50,000 by the National League of Cities, 1987 through 1993.

were found to be significant. In 1991, contracting-out was significant and, in 1992, raising impact fees was significant, although the sign was wrong.

Finally, in order to ascertain whether or not any fiscal policy action was significant in addressing the revenue-expenditure imbalance, all specific revenue actions (raising property taxes, raising income taxes, raising fee levels, etc.) were collapsed into one aggregate variable called a "revenue action" and, likewise, all specific expenditure actions (reducing employment, reducing service levels, interlocal agreements, etc.) were collapsed into another aggregate variable called an "expenditure action." These new dependent variables were regressed against the same three independent variables (revenue-expenditure imbalances, ending balances per capita, and ending balances as a percentage of expenditures) in order to examine whether either a revenue or an expenditure action is more likely to be caused by a worsening of values in any of the independent variables (Table III). For four of the years the coefficient was in the predicted direction and only two were significant at the .05 level. That is, cities with comparatively low budgeted ending balances as a percentage of expenditures were likely to adopt an expenditure action in 1989, and cities with comparatively low budgeted per capita ending balances were likely to enact fee increases in 1991.

Making a Difference

The final question I set out to address is whether fiscal policy actions close the gap between the predicted (budgeted) revenue-expenditure imbalance and the actual gap. A separate analysis I conducted on "rebudgeting outcomes" concludes that a combination of both conservative budget preparation and fiscal policy activism have the desired effect of not only keeping service levels fairly even but also of maintaining generally stable ending balances as a percentage of expenditures. In other words, fiscal activism does help close the gap between the budgeted revenue-

expenditure imbalance and the actual gap. This issue was also addressed in part in the preceding sections. Therefore, by referring to the earlier tables and figures, several general, and tentative, conclusions might be drawn from this preliminary analysis.

First, as Figures I through IV clearly demonstrate, in general, cities are active in finding ways to hold down expenditures and maintain or increase revenues, regardless of their fiscal condition. Approximately nine in ten U.S. cities took at least one revenue or expenditure action between 1986 and 1990. Since then, the proportion of cities that were classified as having taken at least one fiscal policy action has declined, but only marginally, to approximately three in four cities.

Second, no specific fiscal policy action (at the aggregate level) seems to explain the shoring up of the revenue-expenditure imbalance (Table III); in other words, except for declining ending balances in 1989 and 1991, which triggered an expenditure and a revenue (fee) action, respectively, empirical evidence does not unequivocally support the notion that fiscal stress triggers a revenue or expenditure response. Nevertheless, the statistical significance of *specific* revenue or expenditure actions is suggestive (Table II), although by no means conclusive. For example, as ending balances as a percentage of expenditures decline, reducing city service levels was more likely to be selected as an appropriate fiscal policy option for three of the seven years in the study. Further, cost-cutting measures (contracting-out and interlocal agreements) were policy actions that cities took in response to deteriorating ending balances.

Neither of these broad sets of actions should be misconstrued. When ending balances decline or revenue-expenditure imbalances occur, cities are making fiscal policy adjustments. This analysis only suggests that those cities experiencing fiscal difficulty are, in many cases, no more likely to make fiscal policy adjustments than are other cities. In part, fiscal policy activism on the part of cities that do not experience such fiscal stress might be characteristic of cities that wish to avert difficult fiscal problems in the future. In other words, fiscal policy activism becomes a preemptive policy–although this is speculative and subject to further research.

Third, evidence suggests that fiscal policy actions are more likely to be realized when the longer-term measure of a city's fiscal health is utilized. If so, this means that fiscal shocks to cities will not elicit an immediate response. Only after ending balances are threatened and drawn down will more-than-normal fiscal policy activism be pursued.

This entry has presented cities' fiscal positions and their available fiscal policy actions at a high level of aggregation. Further research might disaggregate cities into a variety of city-types in order to assess whether, for example, reformed cities or home-rule cities or low-debt cities are more likely to adopt revenue or expenditure actions than other cities. Furthermore, cities that have reached their tax limits might approach their fiscal policymaking options differently than other cities, as might cities that have access to local option sales or income taxes. It is to these questions that research on how and why cities make budget adjustments and fill revenue gaps should turn.

MICHAEL A. PAGANO

BIBLIOGRAPHY

Apogee Research, 1987. *Financing Infrastructure: Innovations at the Local Level.* Washington, D.C.: National League of Cities.
Cyert, Richard and James March, 1963. *A Behavioral Theory of the Firm.* Englewood Cliffs, NJ: Prentice-Hall.
Gold, Steve and Sarah Ritchie, 1994. "State Actions Affecting Cities and Counties, 1990–1993." *Public Budgeting and Finance* (Summer) 26–53.
Herbert, Leo, Larry N. Killough, and Alan Walter Steiss, 1984. *Governmental Accounting and Control.* Monterey, CA: Brooks/Cole.
Mikesell, John, 1993. *City Finances, City Futures.* Columbus: Ohio Municipal League.
National Governors' Association/National Association of State Budget Officers, October of each year. *The Fiscal Survey of States.* Washington, D.C.: NGA/NASBO.
National League of Cities, various years. *City Fiscal Conditions.* Washington, D.C.
Nicholas, James C., ed., 1985. *The Changing Structure of Infrastructure Finance.* Boston: Lincoln Institute of Land Policy, Monograph #85-5.
Pagano, Michael A., 1988. "Fiscal Disruptions and City Responses: Stability, Equilibrium, and City Capital Budgeting." *Urban Affairs Quarterly,* vol. 23 (September):118–137.
———, 1994. "Prediction of Rebudgeting Outcomes in Cities." Paper prepared for presentation at the Association of Budgeting and Financial Management annual conference, Washington, D.C., October 14.
Pagano, Michael A. and Ann O'M. Bowman, 1995. *Cityscapes and Capital: The Politics of Urban Development.* Baltimore: Johns Hopkins University Press.
U.S. Advisory Commission on Intergovernmental Relations (Cited as ACIR). Various years. *Changing Pubic Attitudes on Governments and Taxes.* Washington, D.C.: U.S. ACIR.
U.S. Congress, Joint Economic Committee, 1979. *The Current Fiscal Condition of Cities: A Survey of 67 of the 75 Largest Cities.* Washington, D.C.: U.S. Government Printing Office.
———, 1983. *Trends in the Fiscal Condition of Cities: 1981–1983.* Washington, D.C.: U.S. Government Printing Office.
Wolman, Harold, 1983. "Understanding Local Government Responses to Fiscal Pressures." *Journal of Public Policy* 3 (August): 245–264.

BUDGET ANALYST.

Specialized analysts who work in the central budget bureaus of national, state, and local governments. Budgeteers are variously called budget analysts, budget examiners, budget and management analysts, or budget and policy analysts, depending upon the central budget bureau.

The Portrait of a Budgeteer

A portrait of the budgeteer is found in four categories of the literature. There are a few insider accounts, such as from Paul Appleby (1957), Percival Brundage (1970), John Burton (1943), Bruce E. Johnson (1984), Al Kliman (1990), Norman Pearson (1943), Herbert Persil (1990), Edward Rall (1964), and Paul Veillette (1981). There are some statistical descriptions from Robert D. Lee (1991), and Sydney Duncombe and Richard Kinney (1987). There are a few case studies, such as from Frederick Mosher (1952) and New York State (1981) for New York, Thomas Anton (1966) for Illinois, Irene Rubin and Lana Stein (1990) for St. Louis, and Kurt Thurmaier (1995b) for metropolitan Kansas City governments. Finally, there are a few works that study budgeteer influence in the budget process, such as James Davis's and Randall Ripley's (1969) work on federal Office of Management and Budget (OMB) examiners, James Gosling's studies of Wisconsin (1985) and other midwestern budget offices (1987), Katherine Willoughby's (1993a, 1993b) study of southeastern states, and Thurmaier's (1995a, 1992) works on state and local budget offices. Most budgeteers work in the context of an executive budget process, which defines their role as key gatekeepers in public budgeting.

Most states, nearly all cities with over 10,000 population, and the federal government use the executive budget model for their budget process. (Sokolow and Honadle [1984] describe alternative budgetary methods in small, particularly rural, communities.) The executive budget structures the budget process so that information and decisions flow through the chief executive's budget office (mayor's, governor's, or President's). The great bulk of the budgeting work in this process is done by the Central Budget Bureau (CBB) before the legislative body gets its first formal peek at the budget document. The document presented to the legislature is presented as the chief executive's budget, not an agglomeration of all agency requests.

The Gatekeeper Function

From its inception, the CBB was designed to serve a powerful gatekeeper function for the chief executive in the executive budget process. Spending requests flow into the budgetary process from endless tributaries, including citizens, interest groups, and program administrators (to name a few). Each agency (as a first-level gatekeeper "upstream") will select which proposals it will submit to the chief executive for inclusion in the executive budget. As program advocates, the agencies are not prone to cutting or denying funding requests of their clientele. Although most requests only seek continued funding of existing programs, agencies still have many ideas of how to expand programs and may request considerable increases in some programs.

Consequently, the CBB is flooded with spending requests. The chief executive (and the legislature) count on the CBB to hold back the spending flood by denying the bulk of the new funding requests. Only a small share of the budget decision items are actually decided by the chief executive in person. This may seem self-evident at the national level, but it also holds true to a great extent at the state and local government levels, too. Studies of local government budgeting suggest that most of the decisive determinations are made early in the process (Lehan 1981; Cowart and Brofoss 1978; Thurmaier 1995a). Chief executives do not have enough time to conduct a thorough review of all the budget requests. In all but the smallest jurisdictions, chief executives employ analytical budget assistants who report to the chief executive's office.

The proximity of budgeteers to decision events in the budgetary process makes them extremely influential budgetary actors. Once a budget demand is moving through the budgetary process, budgeteers have considerable control and influence over its destiny. They bear formal responsibility for a much larger set of specific decisions than the other actors in the budgetary process. To some degree, agencies try to influence the recommendations of the analysts with "new" information or favorable interpretations of current information, and this part of the process involves some degree of negotiation and bargaining. Agencies can also appeal the recommendations of the budgeteers and the budget director to the chief executive, but earlier participants in the budgetary process generally account for a greater share of approved decision items than do later participants (Gosling 1985). To a large extent, the CBB determines which matters shall be brought to the attention of the governor.

The controlling nature of the CBB is reflected in its bias against spending. And although the CBB has taken on many additional responsibilities over the century, at heart, the concerns of the CBB are fiscal. Naturally, some CBBs will be more powerful than others, some agencies will be able to bypass or mitigate changes recommended by the CBB, and some chief executives will be more dependent upon the CBB than others for information, analysis, and recommendations. But the central features of the process will be discernible.

Inside the CBB: A Look at the Budgeteers

The budget submitted to the legislature is an expression of the executive's policies. Within the CBB, fiscal and other policy considerations are considered, balanced, and coordinated to produce a policy instrument that assures responsive and responsible government. The budget is formulated through both a top-down and a bottom-up process. Generally, the top-down process sets the boundary of the budget and the bottom-up process involves negotiations of budget specifics within the boundary. Policies are communicated down to the agencies through the budget instructions distributed at the beginning of the executive budget process (top-down), and the policies are given expression in the flow of decisions on agency requests through the CBB and up to the chief executive (bottom-up).

The Budget Director

The management of the process within the CBB is the responsibility of the budget director. The structure of a common CBB is a flat organizational pyramid, with the cadre of budgeteers managed by the budget director on top. In between are policy area team leaders and one or more assistant directors, their numbers depending upon the size of the CBB. At the state level, the number of analysts can vary from small bureaus of 15 analysts (as in the State of Kansas) to over 100 (as in the State of New York). The office of Management and Budget for the City of New York has more than 100 personnel! Team leaders are first-level managers that supervise analysts who are collectively responsible for a particular policy area. For example, the education team might include analysts for K–12, vocational-technical, and university agencies.

The budget director is often viewed as the chief executive's financial right arm, and the influence of the CBB often reflects the strength of the relationship between the chief executive and the budget director. Appointed by the chief executive, the director is keenly aware of the executive's policy preferences as well as the financial and political "big picture." The chief executive relies upon the budget director to define the economically feasible alternatives to reach the administration's goals.

One of the director's principal responsibilities is to convey the policies of the chief executive to other members of the CBB staff and to the agencies. Seventeen of the state budget directors responding to a survey by Allen Schick (1971) preferred that their offices be regarded as "policy staffs" and seven regarded their offices as "management assistance operations;" none listed "control over expenditures." The responses showed that directors "view themselves as policymakers and want to eschew a financial control role (p. 174)."

Flows of Information

The budget director uses the top-down flow of information to define the fiscal and policy parameters within which agency budget requests will be considered by CBB staff. The director is heavily dependent upon the budgeteers to manage the bottom-up flow of agency requests to the chief executive. Following the major flows of information through the CBB illuminates the critical gatekeeper role played by the budgeteer within the CBB.

Top-Down: Budget Instructions. There are two components of the top-down stream of information: (a) policy guidelines that indicate the policy priorities and directions of the chief executive, and (b) revenue forecasts that set fiscal parameters. Both sets of information are contained in the budget instructions that are transmitted from the chief executive down to the agencies via the CBB.

Budget planning begins with the chief executive formulating goals and policies in accord with revenue and expenditure forecasts. The CBB advises the departments as to the chief executive's policies by issuing guidelines in the budget instructions. These policy guidelines may be general or may be tailored to specific agencies.

The formulation of the guidelines is of considerable importance. The guidelines often include a suggested range of expenditures to match projected revenues and areas in which some special considerations seem to be needed. They identify programs that need particular attention to meet developing problems, areas where there is room for improved efficiency, and programs that may require significant increases or decreases in expenditures—or even the entire elimination of programs because they are no longer required or must be dropped because of fiscal constraints. New programs are often under consideration to meet new needs that have developed. However, an important constraint on policies, especially new programs, is the availability of revenues.

The revenue forecast is an important piece of information for all actors in the executive budget process. Flowing from the top down, it provides fiscal guidance to the budgeteers as well as the agencies. It places an upper limit on total planned expenditures and thus helps to determine which and to what extent public programs and services will be funded. The forecast plays a particularly prominent role in the budget formulation processes of state and local governments, which, with few exceptions, are required to balance their budgets.

The initial revenue forecast is announced, to some degree, as part of the CBB's strategy to curb acquisitive spending by agencies. The instructions usually indicate a tight fiscal situation and some agencies may treat the forecast as a mere formality. Typically, initial revenue forecasts are refined as more current data become available to the CBB. Whereas it is a rare set of budget instructions that

urges agencies to "ask for the moon," the policy directive for a particular agency may "open the door" to consideration of larger-than-average spending increases for certain programs. The budgeteer must apply these top-down cues from the budget director—fiscal and policy—to the analysis of the bottom-up flow of agency requests.

Bottom-Up Process: Agency Requests. Executive budgets are formed in an iterative process that requires budgeteers to bring their judgment to bear on thousands of individual decision items. Information streams into the budget process from a multitude of sources, including agencies, interest groups, legislative representatives, and other interested persons. Important decisions are being made along these tributaries to determine what information finally flows into the agency budget requests. All of these requests, in turn, flow into the CBB, where they are held for analysis and recommendation by the budgeteers.

There are basically three types of decision items, with various levels of policy and technical considerations involved in the analyses. Type I decision items are for financing the budget base (current spending levels) and the costs to continue current levels of services (inflation adjustments), and are reviewed for technical issues such as whether the agency has applied the inflation rate allowed (if any) in the budget instructions. These requests form the bulk of the agency requests in terms of dollars, and are usually not subject to intense analysis by either the budgeteer or subsequent budget actors. Rather, the work is mundane and consumes considerable time. Budgeteers double-check mathematical computations because accuracy is important. If intergovernmental transfers are involved, the numbers included in the agency request need to be compared to the most current estimates available regarding their accuracy (especially in periods of declining intergovernmental transfers). Narrative descriptions for each request are edited to conform with prevailing guidelines issued in the budget instructions. More comprehensive analysis is reserved for decision items involving more significant changes to existing programs, whether increases or decreases.

A Type II decision item seeks to alter incrementally (or decrementally) the funding or number of positions for a certain program. Although these types of decisions involve only a fraction of the dollar value of the base budget, they usually constitute the bulk of the decision items in the agency request. The technical analysis required of these decision items often involves scrutiny of current workloads of existing staff in the agency or bureau, including comparisons of workloads over time. How have the changing workloads affected the output of the bureau's services? Are there indications that citizens have been receiving dissatisfactory services?

This type of analysis is often colored with political considerations. The budgeteer must recognize when a technical solution could create political problems. Whether the analysis is extensive or superficial depends in part upon (a) the priority the agency has placed on gaining the funding in this budget, and (b) whether the budgeteer thinks the chief executive (as initially represented by the budget director) will want to support the request or deny it. Both are political pressures that bear on the budgeteer indirectly from the executive's office and from the various departments. These types of analyses require sensitive judgments that incorporate economic and noneconomic considerations. A budgeteer may base an initial recommendation to the budget director on the policy decisions made from time to time during the past year, the latest interpretations from the director and deputies, and, if necessary, extrapolations from past decisions when timely policy guidance is not available for current issues.

Although each of the two previous types of budget decision items involve policy considerations at some level, a third type of budget request is dominated by policy considerations from the beginning. A Type III decision item involves a major change to an existing program, or the creation of a new policy or program. These types of decisions normally constitute only a small share of the total number of decision items in a given budget. But depending upon the budgeteer's policy responsibilities, there could be one or two such decision items in every annual budget. In these types of decisions, the analysis must include a full range of technical, economic, social, legal, and political considerations—if the budgeteer is to provide the budget director with a recommendation that is well reasoned and well supported with evidence.

The Budgeteer as Gatekeeper

The budgeteer is the archetypal figure in the CBB and is usually assigned responsibility for a group of programs or agencies. The principal source of the budgeteer's status as a gatekeeper within the CBB is that the budgeteer is the primary point of contact agencies have with the CBB. Departmental budget representatives rarely, if ever, see the CBB budget director, much less the chief executive. Their negotiations are with the budgeteers. The budgeteer is thus the principal information conduit between the assigned agencies and the budget director. The budgeteer is responsible for conveying budget directions, policy guidance, and other matters to the agencies, and for assisting the agencies in their fiscal and other management problems. Much of the formal communication that goes out under signature of the budget director has been written by the budgeteer.

The budgeteers use the execution phase of the budget cycle to improve their information base and thus enhance their gatekeeper positions. The CBB executes the budget by dispensing allotments of funds to agencies and insuring that appropriated amounts are credited to the appropriate agency activities. More importantly, this phase is a critical period when the budgeteer can gather information on agency goal performance, evaluate program performance, and identify potential issues for the next annual budget. Throughout the year, agencies approach their assigned budget analyst with ideas for program modifications and expansions, for help on technical budget issues, for advice (and sometimes consent) on legislative problems and initiatives, and other topics that fall under the purview of "budget and management" issues. As they assist agencies in fiscal, policy, and other management problems, the budgeteers are gathering information that will be useful in their analyses of the budget requests forthcoming in the next annual budget development phase. The bifurcation of the budget process and the ability of the budgeteer to gather information and analyze issues pertinent to assigned agencies plays an important part in allowing the analyst to make informed and justifiable recommendations during the hurried budget development period.

Experience gained through these wide-ranging responsibilities makes the budgeteer a key source of information for the budget director and the chief executive regarding budget and policy issues of assigned agencies. Consequently, the primary hurdle for agency requests to surmount in order to gain budgetary approval by the CBB is the CBB's own gatekeeper, the budgeteer. Granted, their decisions are subject to review at several points later in the process, both within and beyond the CBB. But experienced budgeteers realize they must justify and defend their recommendations at each review point, and they gain a "feeling" for the bounds of acceptable and reasonable recommendations.

Once the budgeteers reach their decisions and submit their recommendations, the question for subsequent actors is whether to accept or modify the budgeteers' recommendations. On some issues, their recommendations will fall to political agreements reached after their recommendations have been forged; that is part of the budget process. But in many (perhaps most) cases, their judgments will be affirmed. In part this is due to their tendency to deny agency requests for increased spending. But it is also due to their budgetary craftsmanship, that is, their ability to gauge whether a decision item has political support, whether it meets certain technical criteria, and whether it is compatible with the fiscal guidelines under which the budget process is proceeding. Most importantly, it is due to their ability to balance and weigh these factors in a recommendation that can be justified in repeated challenges throughout the remainder of the budget process.

Budgeteers do not have the same degree of influence on all issues. Though the budgeteers have "enormous power" over the small items, their influence over major issues is weaker. The variable influence of the budget office is a product of the conscious and unconscious "chain of delegation" of budgetary power by the elected officials—executive and legislative. Delegation of decisions to the CBB is more applicable to decision items that involve little or no policy change, or little or no fiscal effect, and less applicable to items involving major policy and fiscal change. And although legislative participants are much more inclined to amend recommendations for the most controversial budget decisions, budgeteers still exert their influence on a sizable portion of the budget.

Budgetary Perspective. As much as the budgeteers' responsibilities have branched out to policy formulation and program evaluation, the roots of budgeting remain in accounting and the control orientation. The assumption of new policy responsibilities as part and parcel of budget analysis has not entirely displaced that orientation. Even though an aggressive and imaginative budget division may advocate program approaches of its own, at bottom, the concerns of the budgeteer are fiscal with a bias toward economizing. Whether agencies inflate their budget requests or not, those reviewing the estimates approach them with healthy skepticism. Recognizing the built-in pressures to expand budgets, and believing these pressures to be reflected in budget requests, reviewing officials naturally see themselves as "cutters." The cutter perspective is diverse, widespread, and deeply ingrained in the CBB culture. One state budget director observed (in 1965) that the budget agency was created "to keep the rascals from stealing the capitol dome, and a whole set of attitudes and procedures was developed to carry out this job" (Cornett 1965: 172).

Yet the CBB staff have had to adapt their position and role in the process to meet changing and expanding management needs. They have come to realize that they cannot convey the impression that their analyses are restricted to the legendary "box of pencils" and expect to be invited to summit meetings on important policy and other management issues. Appleby (1957) maintains that "a budget organization that is always and wholly negative is something less than ideal. There are ways to save money by spending more. . . . Nor should budget personnel be so blind to values other than their own that they do not see imaginatively and sympathetically the public service values behind the figures they deal in" (p. 120).

The cutter perspective of budgeteers has broadened from that of an accountant to that of a manager. As accountability is no longer the primary goal of budget analysis, budgeteers have needed to be more than accountants. To assist proper political decisionmaking, budget analysis has required interpreting, identifying, and analyzing the policy ramifications of budget proposals. The ideal budgetmaker (preferably a generalist recruited from a public administration school) is viewed as "a good judge of the worth of things," combining a healthy respect for programmatic values with the tempered, critical mentality of a scholar (Lehan 1981: 4).

This broader perspective of budgeting is grounded less in the notion of scientific budgeting that the reformers had in mind at the beginning of the century and more aptly in the notion of budgeting as a craft. Rejecting the pretense of budgeting as having a scientific foundation, Lehan argued that "budgeting can be most accurately described as a craft-like activity involving analyses and judgments about the worth of things. The tools of this craft are the reflective values of evidence and logic. . . . Thus, to budget well is to practice a craft" (p. 4).

One of the more important aspects of the budgeting craft is the ability of the budgeteer to have strong and respected interpersonal relationships with the budget director, on the one hand, and the agency officials, on the other. Even a junior budgeteer in the CBB will deal with department secretaries and assistant secretaries, whereas the same grade analyst within an agency might not even see his or her own department secretary. This trust maintains the flow of information through the budgeteer and serves as a springboard for the analyst to explore fiscal and other budget policy ideas with CBB and agency officials.

Sydney Duncombe and Richard Kinney (1987) found that 44 percent of state agency budget officers in their survey defined "budget success" as including the maintenance of good relationships with the governor and executive budget staff. Good relations were helpful in getting an item included in the executive budget; an omission from the executive budget was seen to have "two strikes" against it. Smooth relations were also important for getting gubernatorial support behind the agency's requests during the legislative process, and to protect an item in the final state budget from an executive veto.

The experienced analyst develops a role concept, becoming a "realist" about what can and should be changed with respect to agency requests and a "buffer" between the chief executive and the budget director, on the one hand, and the assigned agencies, on the other. The experienced budgeteer does this while maintaining healthy interpersonal relationships with budget actors in the agency and the CBB. A former New York State budget director (Veillette 1981) noted that "sensitive judgment is required, as are close coordination and communication between the division and gubernatorial aides. Success of the total process insures democratic accountability by the governor to the people: the budget submitted to the legislature should leave few of a governor's policies to the imagination" (p. 67).

It should now be clear that whether as a civil servant or a political appointee, the central budget office budgeteer serves the chief executive. Al Kliman (1990) noted that it comes down to "do what the boss wants to do." The budgeteer's perspective in analyzing agency requests is thus biased toward denying increases and finding places to cut expenditures—but never outside the context of seeking to fulfill the chief executive's policy guidelines.

Budget Analysis as Policy Analysis

Budgeting is an integral part of the policy process, and discussions of policymaking invariably include fiscal considerations. It is a challenge to think of any government program that can be administered without money. Public funds are required for whatever the government does. As Paul Appleby (1957) wrote, "The budgeting function, like any other particular one, is a specialized way of looking at problems in decision making," with a premium value on "fiscal sense and fiscal coordination" (p. 119).

In effect, budget analysis is really just a special type of policy analysis. A budget analyst is particularly concerned with how different resource allocations will affect the content of policies and programs and the substantive consequences and outcomes they produce. They analyze how different resource allocations impact the means for moving toward a desired course of events or outcome. Budgeteers analyze how budget allocations within programs influence the ability to carry out executive policies.

At the heart of budget decisions, then, is a concern for the effect of different allocations of financial resources on the operations of various programs. Since financial resources are used to purchase many other types of program resources, and even the distribution of these resources within a program influences program outcomes, budget analysis must be concerned with the broader policy effects of budget allocation decisions. Thus it may be said that budget analysis is consonant with policy analysis and particularly emphasizes financial issues.

The role of budgeting in the policy process highlights the gatekeeper roles of the CBB and the budgeteers in budgetary decisions. Although the introduction of new programs and policies is the general responsibility of the agencies, the CBB is a critical part of the initial determinations of whether a proposed policy or program is feasible, and sometimes it even initiates important policy measures for the chief executive. During budget preparation, the budgeteer may be found negotiating with the agency on the reformulation of the program and policy as the agency seeks continued funding and the budgeteer seeks to insure that the program or policy is meeting some or all of its objectives.

John Kingdon's (1984) study of the policymaking process notes that the budget process is a predictable "policy window" in which policy actors have the opportunity to make significant changes to public policies and programs. His insightful analysis reveals that budgeteers are key actors in setting the public policy decision agenda. As gatekeepers, budgeteers almost exclusively play a reactive role in the budget and policy process. The alternatives they analyze have already been pruned by the policymaking process. The budgeteers normally choose their recommendation from among the main alternatives competing for the decision agenda. The other policy specialists have tried out their policy ideas on each other, refining and recombining as necessary to make sure their alternative solutions to problems are ready for the decision agenda when the time is right. The proposals that survive this "policy primeval soup" to the status of serious consideration meet several criteria, including technical feasibility, a fit with dominant values and the current national mood, budgetary workability, and a gauge of the political support or opposition they might experience. If elected officials are receptive to selected policy alternatives, then the specialists push their ideas. If not, they shelve the proposals and wait for a new administration or a new mood in the legislature.

Budgeteers, acting on behalf of the chief executive in the policymaking process, are key managers of the decision agenda. They take cues from political leaders as to what problems will be on the agenda, and then sift and prune the alternatives from the policy community to determine which alternative (or alternatives) will be promoted for consideration by elected officials. When items are not on the agenda, the budgeteers are informally delegated decision authority by the legislature and chief executive, and their instinctive response is to "just say no." When budgeteers receive cues that a policy area is on the agenda, they are critical gatekeepers who help determine the set of legitimate alternatives. Several options may emerge from the policy primeval soup, but the budget director wants the budgeteer to *recommend* an alternative, with a rationale that shows how the recommended alternative satisfies the political as well as technical feasibility criteria (i.e., who wins and who loses). Thus, other political actors in the decisionmaking structure are keen to get agreement from the CBB, thereby surmounting a major obstacle in the policymaking process.

The rationale is critical because it must also persuade elected officials. Kingdon (1984) observed that policy specialists discard many ideas because they "cannot conceive of any plausible circumstances under which they could be approved by elected politicians and their appointees. Some ideas are kept alive in the hope that the larger political climate will change, even though the ideas might not be currently in favor" (p. 146). Budgeteers are criticized only infrequently for making unpopular recommendations because they are sensitive and responsive to policy direction. Veillette noted that the sensitive judgment required of budgeteers incorporates the politics of the issue—even while maintaining standards of neutral competence: "One must have the discernment to avoid stretching a good principle to its breaking point."

As a collaborator in the policymaking process, the budgeteer is embroiled in the creation and modification of public policy. Consequently, budgeteers must be concerned with more than the traditional notion of budget analysis as fiscal analysis; they are inherently concerned with policy analysis. The involvement of budgeteers in policy analysis increases their personal influence in the budget process. Positioned astride the needs and desires of assigned agencies and the needs and desires of the chief executive, the budgeteer is aptly positioned to serve as the eyes, ears—and mouth—of the chief executive. Beyond merely reacting to agency requests during budget formulation, budgeteers can also act on behalf of the chief executive in formulating policies.

The active involvement and the prominent personal influence of the budgeteer introduces another factor into the budget process. Like all human beings, "decision makers tend to hear and interpret messages in such a way to confirm their preexisting beliefs about the world" (Hays 1985). The budgeteer's own ideology, attitudes, beliefs, and values will filter the information received in the budget process, and how the information is interpreted by the budgeteer plays an important role in the political process. Mainly, the ideology and policy orientations of the budgeteer will filter information received in the budget analyses, giving credence to certain interests and their policy-alternatives while discarding arguments of others. The ideological predispositions of the budgeteers provide them with an interpretive framework to understand the world and cues to evaluate policy outcomes. Consciously or unconsciously, the budgeteer's sociocultural perspectives work to eliminate some possible policy alternatives immediately.

Although policy experts often pride themselves by associating the products of their methods with such terms as "unbiased," "objective," or "nonpolitical," according to Chimerie Osigweh (1986) politics is inherent in all program evaluations. "The reality," he argues, "is that the art or science of evaluation exists neither in a pure, nor in a divine form. The belief that a program evaluation can purely produce hard, unadulterated facts, all the way, is therefore a fallacy—the *divine fallacy* of evaluation research" (pp. 93–94). No evaluation is free of assumptions upon which its objectives were formed, and these assumptions guide evaluators as to whether the program is achieving its goal, including which variables to focus on and which are determined to be relatively unimportant and ignored. "Within this context the evaluator must be a politician (p. 94)."

Even when dealing with "facts," the opinions and values of the budgeting "experts" count a great deal in the final judgments of the budget directors. But the influence is even greater when the decisions to be made are more complex than choosing an alternative to achieve a given end. This would include situations in which the policymaker may be uncertain about the nature of the problem or situations where the problem is well defined but there is no standard method for choosing an alternative. "In such cases, which are quite frequent in practice, it is appropriate to say that the analyst gives advice rather than instructions or prescriptions," as is the case when a decision is viewed as merely choosing the best program to achieve an end (Majone 1989: 26–28). And characteristi-

cally, the budgeteer *qua* advisor realizes that the advice is taken or left at the discretion of the budget director or chief executive. If the advice is not taken, the budgeteer retains the satisfaction of knowing that she or he made a cogent argument in favor of the recommended action, and that is the budgeteer's ultimate responsibility.

It is prudent to note here that the "stylized" version of budgeting painted in this entry is not found in all American governments. Governments that continue to treat budgeting as merely a control instrument to contain spending and restrict tax increases will likely find the role of the budgeteer as gatekeeper overstated. However, where budgeting has been expanded to incorporate broad program and policy management on behalf of the chief executive—where the budget has become the vehicle for clearly delineating executive policies—there will be a closer correspondence between the stylized picture just presented and budgeting in practice.

The newly independent local governments of democracies in central and eastern Europe are taking lessons from the U.S. experience with central budget office staff. Thurmaier (1994) noted that as Polish local government leaders try to use the budget as a policy decision tool, they are discovering that they need to rethink the role of the central budget office, and the personnel that staff it. The American experience provides them with an example of one road to follow to redirect budgeting to be useful for policymaking. As Polish local governments assume greater responsibilities for delivering public services, they find a need to focus their attentions and efforts on priorities to coordinate the diverse activities for which they have been responsible. They are experimenting with the American model of budgeteer to provide increased policy and management analysis, positioning the budget office staff to serve as the financial right arm of the city executive.

The portrait of CBB budgeteers is one of experienced craftspeople, skilled in the creation as well as execution of public policies, with great influence over the fate of budget decision items and, consequently, public policies. Budgeteers play a central gatekeeper role in the executive budget process because they are the central actors within the institutional gatekeeper, the central budget bureau. It is at the budgeteer level that the mixing of microeconomics and micropolitics takes place in a concentrated form and with a sustained effect.

KURT THURMAIER

BIBLIOGRAPHY

Anton, Thomas, 1996. *The Politics of State Expenditure in Illinois.* Champaign: University of Illinois Press.
Appleby, Paul, 1957. "The Role of the Budget Division." *Public Administration Review* 17 (Summer): 156–158.

Brundage, Percival Flack, 1970. *The Bureau of the Budget.* New York: Praeger.

Burton, John E., 1943. "Budget Administration in New York State." *State Government* 16 (October).

Cornett, Robert, 1965. "The Summing Up." Director of the Budget, Department of Finance, Kentucky, in *Budget Analyst in State Management.* Partial Record of the First Budget Institute, Lexington, Kentucky, held August 2–7, 1964, (February): 170–172. Chicago: National Association of State Budget Officers.

Cowart, Andrew T., and Karl Erik Brofoss, 1978. *Decision, Politics, and Change: A Study of Norwegian Urban Budgeting.* Olso: Universitetsforiaget.

Davis, James W., and Randall B. Ripley, 1969. "The Bureau of the Budget and Executive Branch Agencies: Notes on Their Interaction". 66–67. In James W. Davis, Jr., ed., *Politics, Programs, and Budgets: A Reader in Government Budgeting.* Englewood Cliffs, NJ: Prentice-Hall.

Duncombe, Sydney, and Richard Kinney, 1987. "Agency Budget Success: How It Is Defined by Budget Officials in Five Western States." *Public Budgeting and Finance* (Spring): 24–37.

Gosling, James J., 1987. "The State Budget Office and Policy Making," *Public Budgeting and Finance* 7 (Spring): 51–65.

———, 1985. "Patterns of Influence and Choice in the Wisconsin Budgetary Process." *Legislative Studies Quarterly* 10 (November): 457–482.

Hays, Allen R., 1985. "Perceptions of Success or Failure in Program Implementation: The 'Feedback Loop' in Public Policy Decisions," *Policy Studies Review* (August): 55–56.

Johnson, Bruce E., 1984. "From Analyst to Negotiator: The OMB's New Role." *Journal of Policy Analysis and Management* 3 (4): 501–515.

Kingdon, John W., 1984. *Agendas, Alternatives and Public Policies.* Boston: Little Brown & Co.

Kliman, Al, 1990. "A Successful Budget Process." *Public Budgeting and Finance* 10 (Summer): 110–114.

Lee, Robert D., 1991. "Developments in State Budgeting: Trends of Two Decades." *Public Administration Review* 51 (May-June): 254–262.

Lehan, Edward A., 1981. *Simplified Government Budgeting.* Chicago: Municipal Finance Officers Association of the United States and Canada (now GFOA).

Majone, Giandomenico, 1989. *Evidence, Argument and Persuasion in the Policy Process.* New Haven: Yale University Press.

Moak, Lennox L., and Kathryn Killian Gordon, 1965. *Budgeting for Smaller Governmental Units.* Chicago: Municipal Finance Officers Association of the United States and Canada.

Mosher, Frederick C., 1952. "Executive Budget, Empire State Style." *Public Administration Review* 12 (Spring): 73–84.

New York State, 1981. *The Executive Budget in New York State: A Half-Century Perspective.* Albany: New York State Division of the Budget.

Osigweh, Chimerie A. B., 1986. "Program Evaluation and Its 'Political Context.' " *Policy Studies Review* 6 (August): 93–95.

Pearson, Norman M., 1943. "The Budget Bureau: From Routine Business to General Staff." *Public Administration Review* 3 (Spring).

Persil, Herbert G., 1990. "The Profession of Budgeting." *Public Budgeting and Finance* 10 (Summer): 102–106.

Rall, Edward, 1964. "The Official Literature of Budgeting." Business Manager, Centre College, and Former Deputy Commissioner of Finance, Kentucky, in *The Budget Analyst in State Management, Partial Record of the First Budget Institute,* Lexington, Kentucky, held August 2–7, 1964, (February). Chicago: National Association of State Budget Officers.

Rubin, Irene S., and Lana Stein, 1990. "Budget Reform in St. Louis: Why Does Budgeting Change?" *Public Administration Review* 50 (July-August): 421–425.

Schick, Allen, 1971. *Budget Innovation in the States.* Washington, D.C.: Brookings Institution.

Sokolow, Alvin D., and Beth Walter Honadle, 1984. "How Rural Local Governments Budget: The Alternatives to Executive Preparation," *Public Administration Review* 44 (September-October): 373–383.

Thurmaier, Kurt, 1995d. "Execution Phase Budgeting in Local Governments: It's Not Just for Control Anymore!" *State and Local Government Review.* 27 (2) (Spring): 102–117.

———, 1995b "Decisive Decisionmaking in the Executive Budget Process: Analyzing the Political and Economic Propensities of Central Budget Bureau Analysts." *Public Administration Review* 55 (5): 429–438.

———, 1994. "The Evolution of Local Government Budgeting in Poland: From Accounting to Policy in a Leap and a Bound." *Public Budgeting and Finance* 14 (4) (Winter): 84–97.

———, 1992. "Budgetary Decisionmaking in Central Budget Bureaus: An Experiment." *Journal of Public Administration Research and Theory* 2 (4): 463–487.

Veillette, Paul T., 1981. "Reflections on State Budgeting." *Public Budgeting and Finance* 1 (Autumn): 62–68.

Walsh, John, 1975. "Office of Management and Budget: New Accent on the 'M' in OMB," pp. 185–193. In Robert Golembiewski and Jack Rabin, eds., *Public Budgeting and Finance.* 2d ed. New York: M. Dekker.

Willoughby, Katherine G. 1993a. "Patterns of Behavior: Factors Influencing the Spending Judgments of Public Budgeters,". In Lynch, Thomas D., and Lawrence L. Martin, eds., *The Handbook of Comparative Public Budgeting and Financial Management.* New York: Marcel Dekker.

———, 1993b. Decision Making Orientations of State Government Budget Analysts: Rationalists or Incrementalists?" *Public Budgeting and Financial Management* 5 (1): 67–114.

BUDGET PROJECTION, BASELINE.

In the United States, a projection of federal government receipts and outlays for one or more years, based on taxing and spending policies currently in effect. A baseline projection indicates what would happen if current budgetary policies were continued as is and serves as a benchmark for assessing possible changes in policy.

An organization—whether small or large—that makes a budget rarely does so from scratch. Although periodic calls are heard for reassessing every element of a budget from the ground up every year, zero-based budgeting has never taken hold anywhere for long. As a practical matter, the question always is: How does next year's budget compare to what is being done now? For a business or family, the starting point for budgeting is estimated income and spending for the current year. The current year's amounts are then adjusted for projected changes in salaries, tax rates, insurance costs, tuition, utility charges, and the like. The budgeting process for a government is similar but necessarily more complicated. The federal government's current commitments are extensive and are established by a host of laws and regulations. Different observers may define current policies in different ways. Baseline budget projections are also extremely sensitive to the economic and other estimating assumptions on which they are based.

History

The Congressional Budget Act of 1974 (Public Law 93-344) required the Office of Management and Budget (OMB) to prepare projections of federal spending for the upcoming fiscal year based on a continuation of the existing level of governmental services. It also required the newly established Congressional Budget Office (CBO) to prepare five-year projections of budget authority, budget outlays, revenues, and the surplus or deficit. OMB published its first current services budget projections in November 1974, and CBO's five-year projections appeared in January 1976. In her initial report, CBO Director Alice M. Rivlin observed, "The primary purpose of these projections is to provide a baseline from which the Congress can consider budget alternatives in its deliberations on the next annual budget."

Although the Budget Act gave no guidance concerning the basic philosophy or purpose of these long-term projections, CBO and OMB interpreted their mandates in much the same way. For tax revenues and entitlement programs, such as Social Security and unemployment insurance, they generally assumed that current laws would continue without change. (Certain programs of limited duration that were routinely reauthorized were assumed to continue.) The two agencies initially differed, however, on whether to adjust estimates of discretionary programs for anticipated changes in inflation. Until 1980, OMB's projections excluded inflation adjustments for programs controlled by annual appropriations, such as national defense and most routine functions of government. In contrast, CBO's projections assumed from the start that appropriations would keep pace with an appropriate measure of inflation, although CBO also published projections without these so-called discretionary inflation adjustments.

The reconciliation process—laid out in the 1974 act but not used fully until 1980—gave increased importance to CBO's multiyear projections of direct spending and revenues. In reconciliation, the congressional budget resolution contains instructions (termed reconciliation instructions) requiring the committees of the House and Senate to report by a given date legislation reducing spending for programs in their jurisdiction by specified amounts. The budget committees package these proposed spending reductions into a single reconciliation bill, which is considered under expedited parliamentary procedures. In developing the reconciliation instructions and in determining whether committees were in compliance with them, what yardstick was to be used for measuring spending reductions?—CBO's projections of spending under current budgetary policies. Sidney L. Brown, chief of budget review for

the Senate Committee on the Budget, gave these projections the name "baseline."

The Balanced Budget and Emergency Deficit Control Act of 1985 (popularly known as Gramm-Rudman-Hollings) provided the first legal definition of baseline. Gramm-Rudman-Hollings established a set of annual deficit targets, which were to culminate in a balanced budget by 1991. It also established a system of across-the-board reductions in spending (termed sequestration) that would be triggered if the deficit in the next fiscal year threatened to exceed the target. To determine the excess deficit and the amount of any reductions required in individual programs, a benchmark was again needed, and the baseline was again the answer. For the most part, the Balanced Budget Act defined the baseline in conformity with previous usage. If appropriations had not been enacted for the upcoming fiscal year, the baseline was to assume the previous year's level without any adjustment for inflation.

In 1987, unable to meet the original deficit targets, the Congress adopted a new set of targets extending through 1993. At the same time it amended the definition of the baseline to provide that discretionary appropriations would be adjusted to keep pace with inflation. The law specified that the nonpersonnel portion of each budget account would be adjusted by the projected increase in the gross national product implicit price deflator, and that the personnel portion would be adjusted by the amount of the federal pay increase scheduled under current law.

The Budget Enforcement Act (BEA) of 1990 abandoned fixed deficit targets, but it retained the sequestration process to enforce a new pay-as-you-go mechanism for revenues and entitlement programs and a set of statutory limits on discretionary appropriations. The BEA also made several technical changes to the definition of the baseline. It adopted the gross national product fixed-weight price index as the inflator for nonpersonnel spending and the employment cost index as the inflator for personnel amounts. It also provided that projections of the subsidized housing program should be adjusted to reflect changes in the number of assistance contracts up for renewal each year. The Omnibus Budget Reconciliation Act of 1993 extended the provisions of the BEA through 1998 and modified the calculation of the inflation adjustments for discretionary programs.

Current Issues

Baseline budget projections increasingly became the subject of political debate and controversy during the late 1980s and early 1990s. Some fiscal conservatives argued that baseline projections contributed to federal budget deficits by assuming that federal spending keeps pace with inflation, increases in caseloads, and other factors driving the growth of entitlement programs. Critics of the baseline concept also observed that entitlement spending continued to rise, even as eligibility rules were tightened and payment rates reduced. Changes that merely slowed the growth of federal spending programs, they argued, should not be described as cuts. It must be noted, however, that this objection has never been applied to the revenue baseline.

Another criticism of baselines is that they promote playing budgetary games. Through the judicious choice of baselines, the same policy may be described either as an increase or as a reduction. Although the baseline is defined in law for purposes of sequestration, the Budget Committees define the baseline used for preparing congressional cost estimates. Sometimes the Budget Committees will add items to the baseline in an effort to conceal increases in spending or maximize the appearance of deficit reduction. At other times they will do just the opposite.

Allen Schick (1995), a leading expert on the federal budget, argues that baselines also weaken the President's role in budgeting, because they provide a benchmark for congressional action that is independent of his recommendations. Indeed, the baseline has supplanted the President's budget as a point of reference for measuring the effects of policy changes on tax revenues and entitlement spending. The Appropriations Committees, however, still generally use the President's request as the starting point for marking up the annual appropriation bills.

In 1994 the House of Representatives passed a bill (H.R. 4907) that would have eliminated the adjustment for inflation in the baseline for discretionary programs and would have required the Budget Committees to use the current year's outlays rather than the baseline as the starting point for their deliberations; the Senate, however, took no action. When the Republican Party took control of the Congress in 1995, the House adopted a rule (Section 102 of H. Res. 6, Truth-in-Budgeting Baseline Reform) requiring cost estimates included in committee reports to contain a comparison of the proposed funding level for a program with the level under current law. In the Concurrent Resolution on the Budget for Fiscal Year 1996, the House adopted a provision finding that "the baseline concept has encouraged Congress to abdicate its constitutional responsibility to control the public purse for programs which are automatically funded under existing law." The resolution went on to declare, "It is the sense of the House of Representatives that baseline budgeting should be replaced with a form of budgeting that requires full justification and analysis of budget proposals and maximizes congressional accountability for public spending."

The critics of the baseline have had considerable success in changing the rhetoric of the budgetary debate, but they have been unable to stamp out such a useful concept. For example, although the defense budget is about the same in dollar terms in 1995 as it was in 1987, real cuts have been made: Troop strength has dropped, and there are fewer ships and planes. Similarly, proposed reductions in Medicare would mean that beneficiaries would have to pay more for medical services, or the providers of those services would be paid less. Even in the 1996 budget resolution, the reconciliation instructions are tied to the baseline levels.

PAUL N. VAN DE WATER

BIBLIOGRAPHY

Schick, Allen, 1995. *The Federal Budget: Politics, Policy, Process.* Washington, D.C.: Brookings Institution.

U.S. Congress, 1995. *Concurrent Resolution on the Budget for Fiscal Year 1996, Conference Report.* 104th Cong., 1st sess., H. Rept. 104–159.

U.S. Congressional Budget Office. Annual. *The Economic and Budget Outlook.* Washington, D.C.: GPO.

U.S. Office of Management and Budget. Annual. *The Budget of the United States.* Washington, D.C.: GPO.

BUDGET CONTROL.

Efforts by elected officials and other budget decisionmakers in government in an attempt to assure accountability with respect to the appropriate spending of taxpayer dollars. Controls are applied in both budget formulation and execution. Evidence suggests that, in some cases, the budget is both overcontrolled and out-of-control.

Introduction

Perhaps the most challenging task in budgeting is to execute a budget well, so that the best program outcomes are achieved with some degree of efficiency and a genuine concern for the proper use of public funds. Budget execution skill is required to respond to inevitable contingencies that arise to complicate the implementation of programs in the manner planned and according to the promises made in budget formulation. Accountability must be maintained, and at the same time uncertainty must be accommodated.

Budget execution typically is highly regulated to control what program managers may and may not do. Controllers are driven by the objective of insuring that budget appropriations, in total and by legally segregated accounts, are not overspent by programs (Anthony and Young 1984, chaps. 7–9). However, controllers also must be concerned with underexecution. Department and agency budget officers and program managers do not want to underspend and thereby lose claim to resources in the following year. Central executive budget office controllers do not want programs to be executed without good cause, so that money not used in the manner justified in budget formulation may be withdrawn from program managers. Executive controllers want to be able to withdraw funds from programs to protect the integrity of the appropriation process and to reallocate money to areas where it will be spent efficiently in response to client demand. For these reasons, budget execution typically is monitored and controlled carefully, both by agency budget staff and by central executive budget controllers. Execution also is often monitored closely by legislative oversight committees and their staffs, out of a desire to insure that legislative will is implemented faithfully and also to make sure that benefits are distributed to the clients targeted in the appropriation process (Anthony and Young 1984: 288). Because the electoral fortunes of legislators are tied to some degree to the public perception that they are solving the problems and meeting the demands of their constituents, legislators have considerable interest in budget execution control.

Among the techniques used to control budget execution, variance analysis is probably the most familiar. Controllers and budget officials in government program offices monitor the differences between projected and actual revenues and expenses in total and by account. They monitor revenue and expense rates against allotment controls by quarter, month, week, and day—temporal control generally is required by the allotment process. Other variables monitored are purpose of expense relative to budget proposal and appropriation rationale, and location of revenues and expenses by unit and, at times, by geographical location. Monitoring of actual revenue and expense rates, as well as program output and demand, where measurable, also is done to compare current spending to proposals made in the budget for the next year that are under negotiation at the same time as the fiscal year budget is expended. Comparisons are made to historical revenue and spending trends in some instances to better understand how current programs are performing. Budget execution monitoring and control is particularly important toward the end of the fiscal year for reasons stated previously, to avoid both over- and underexpenditure relative to appropriation.

The purpose of the analysis of budget execution control provided in the following sections is to improve understanding of control dynamics, incentives, disincentives, and behavior of the various participants in the budget execution process. The analysis focuses most closely in this regard on the roles of the central executive budget office controller and the program manager. The other purpose served by this analysis is to ask whether there is cause to change the budget execution process as it operates in most public organizations and, if so, what directions change might take. The analysis delineates alternative types of control applied in executing budgets and the rationale for employing these different methods. A distinction is drawn between budget execution control intended to influence the behavior and performance of managers of government programs from controls applied to affect independent private sector firms that contract to deliver goods or services to the public on behalf of government. The central theme

of this analysis is that budget execution control system design should fit the objectives of control and the nature of the entity to be controlled (Anthony and Young 1984:20).

Budget Execution Control Choices

Research in public finance has paid considerable attention to budget formulation, but has tended to ignore budget execution (Simon et al. 1954; Schick 1964, 1982). The reasons for this oversight are understandable: On one hand, government budgets are formulated in public, and the issues debated during this stage of the public spending process are dramatic and crucial. On the other hand, budgets are executed in private, and the issues raised in their execution are often mundane. Because of this selective attention, both observers and participants in the public-spending process understand program analysis far better than they understand controllership. Consequently, the conduct of program analysis has come to be guided by a fairly coherent set of professional standards. There is agreement on what is good analysis and what is good accounting practice. Although the design and operation of control systems can profoundly influence governmental performance, budget execution controllership is not guided by a coherent set of professional standards. Without appropriate performance standards, budget officers cannot be held accountable for performance of this function. Consequently, control systems are not designed to optimize the quality, quantity, and price of goods and services purchased with public money, but "to facilitate the controller's [other] work" (Anthony and Young 1984: 21).

The choice of whom to subject to controls and when to execute those controls is not easy. The control system designer has at least four options. First, the subject may be either an organization or an individual. Second, controls may be executed before or after the subject acts. The former may be identified as ex ante and the latter as ex post controls (Demski and Feltham 1976). Ex ante controls are intended to prevent subjects from doing wrong or to compel them to perform well. Necessarily, these controls take the form of authoritative commands or rules that specify what the subject must do, may do, and must not do. Subjects are held responsible for complying with these commands, and the controller attempts to monitor and enforce compliance. In contrast, ex post controls are executed after the subject decides on and carries out a course of action and after some of the consequences of the subject's decisions are known. Since bad decisions cannot be undone after they are carried out, ex post controls are intended to motivate subjects to make good decisions. Subjects are held responsible for the consequences of decisions, and the controller attempts to monitor consequences and rewards or sanctions accordingly. The control system designer may choose between four distinct design alternatives:

individual responsibility, ex ante or ex post, and organizational responsibility.

Purposes of Ex Post Controls

Ex post financial controls are used to reveal demand. They are executed after operating decisions have been made, after asset acquisition and use decisions have been carried out and output levels monitored. Their subject may be either a free standing organization, such as a private contractor or a quasi-independent public entity, or an individual manager subordinate to the controller, such as a responsibility center or program manager within a government agency.

In the first case, the structure of authority and responsibility within the organization is assumed to be an internal matter. The controller establishes a price schedule and specifies minimum service quality standards or a process whereby these standards are to be determined. This price or cost schedule may entail all sorts of complex arrangements, including rate, volume and mix adjustments, and default penalties. Where one organization can optimally supply the entire market, the controller may grant it a monopoly franchise, for example, in garbage collection for a small town or neighborhood. The significant characteristic of this approach is that a unit price cost schedule remains in effect for a specified time period (Goldberg 1976; Thompson 1984; Thompson and Fiske 1978). This means that the government's financial liability will depend on the quantity of service provided and not on the costs incurred by the organizations supplying the service.

If, for example, a municipality purchases gasoline at the spot-market price, or if states commit themselves to pay free standing organizations a fixed price for performing a specific service—such as paying a university a set price for enrolling students—or, for instance, if the Air Force buys F-16s for a fixed price, the controllers involved employ a budget control system design. They must rely upon interorganizational competition to provide sufficient incentives to serve suppliers, to produce efficiently, and to make wise asset acquisition and use decisions. If interorganizational competition is effective, those organizations that do not produce cost-effectively will not survive.

However, even where the declining marginal cost of the service in question makes monopoly appropriate, ex post controls can still be employed. This is done in businesses and businesslike public sector enterprise organizations by holding managers responsible for optimizing a single criterion value, subject to a set of constraints (Anthony and Young 1984). (The principal mechanism through which this control system design is employed at the federal level is the revolving fund [Bailey 1967; Beckner 1960].) For example, the manager is given the authority to make spending decisions to acquire and use assets, subject to output quality and quantity constraints determined by clients, and is held responsible for minimizing costs. Large private sector firms produce comprehensive operating reports describing the performance of responsibility centers and programs, but their budgets seldom are very detailed. The logic of ex post control is that the purpose of the budget is to establish performance targets that are high enough to elicit from the organization's managers their best efforts. Such budgets might contain only a single number for each responsibility center—an output quota, a unit-cost standard, a profit, or a return-on-investment target.

With this approach to budget control, the structure of authority and responsibility within the organization is of interest to the financial controller. The effectiveness of this design depends on the elaboration of well-defined objectives, accurate and timely reporting of performance in terms of objectives, and careful matching of spending authority and responsibility. Its effectiveness also depends upon the clarity with which individual reward schedules are communicated to responsibility center managers and the degree of competition between alternative management teams. Finally, with this approach, the financial liability of government depends on the costs incurred in providing the service and not merely on the quantity or quality of the service provided.

Ex Ante Control Objectives

In contrast to ex post budget controls, ex ante controls are demand-concealing. Their distinguishing attribute is that the controller retains the authority to make or exercise prior review of spending decisions. Ex ante financial controls are executed before public money is obligated or spent and govern the service supplier's acquisition and use of assets. Examples of ex ante financial controls include object-of-expenditure appropriations, apportionments, targets, position controls, and fund and account controls, which regulate spending by account and by the kind of assets that can be acquired by governmental departments and agencies. Such controls also govern the behavior of private contracting entities that supply services to government or to clients on behalf of governments.

Execution of ex ante controls requires assessment of the consequences of asset acquisition decisions. This consideration may be implicit, as it is in the execution of the traditional line-item budget and basic-research contracts, or explicit, as in the execution of performance and program budgets and systems development contracts. It is often influenced by information on current and past performance, but the consideration of the consequences of spending decisions is always prospective in nature.

The logic of ex ante control is that constraining managerial discretion is the first purpose of budget execution.

Since the degree of constraint will depend upon the detail of the spending plan, as well as the degree of compliance enforced by the controllers, these budgets need to be highly detailed. A department or agency budget must identify all asset acquisitions to be executed during the fiscal year and make it clear who is responsible for implementation.

Under ex ante budget control, service-supplying organizations must be guaranteed an allotment of funds in return for continually providing a service for a specified period. The service provider will assume some responsibility for managing output levels or delivery schedules, service quality, or price to the government customer. Government is directly responsible for all legitimate costs incurred in the delivery of services, regardless of the actual quantity or quality of the services provided.

Effectiveness of Ex Ante Controls

Where a manager seeking to increase his budget is subject to tight ex ante controls, the controller can enforce efficiency during the budget period by requiring affirmative answers to the following questions: (1) Will a proposed change permit the same activity to be carried out at a lower cost? (2) Will higher priority activities be carried out at the same cost? (3) Will proposed asset acquisitions or reallocations of savings support activities that have lower priority than those presently carried out? When operating managers are faced with these criteria, they respond appropriately. Controllers approve most changes in spending plans proposed by operating managers because only mutually advantageous changes will be proposed, in most circumstances.

However, when line-item or lump-sum appropriations have a comparative advantage, to say that ex ante controls are a necessary means of reinforcing the controllers' bargaining power should not imply that tight ex ante controls always must be administered by them. Under certain conditions, authority to spend money, transfer funds, fill positions, and so on, may be delegated to subordinate managers. The threat of reimposition of ex ante controls will be sufficient to insure that the manager's behavior corresponds to the controllers' and elected officials' preferences. In order for such delegation to take place, the following conditions must be present: (1) reimposition of controls must be a credible threat; (2) the gain to the manager from delegation must more than offset the associated sacrifice in bargaining power; the manager of an agency in the stable backwaters of public policy has little to gain from relief from ex ante controls if the price of such relief is a change in business as usual; and (3) controllers must be confident that their monitoring procedures, including postaudit, will identify violations of "trust."

Clearly, all long-term relationships with private contractors and government goods and service suppliers rely to some degree on ex ante controls. Even the operation of fixed-price contracts requires prior specification of product quality standards and delivery schedules. But flexible-price, cost-plus type contracts and appropriated budgets require considerably higher levels of reliance on ex ante controls and also on monitoring and enforcing compliance. And the cost of tightly held budget execution control is high.

At the very least, adoption of one of the budget execution control systems described herein means that controllers must take steps to ensure that suppliers fairly and accurately recognize, record, and report their expenses. This, in turn, requires careful definition of costs and specification of appropriate account structures, accounting practices and internal controls, direct costing procedures, and the criteria to be used in allocating overheads. Still, accurate accounting does not guarantee efficiency. Even where the service supplier's financial and operational accounts completely and accurately present every relevant fact about the decisions made by its managers, they will not provide a basis for evaluating the soundness of those decisions. This is because cost accounts can show only what happened, not what might have happened. They do not show the range of asset-acquisition choices and trade-offs the supplier considered, let alone those that should have been considered but were not.

Under line-item or lump-sum budgets and flexible-price contracts, asset acquisition decisions must be made by the contractor, but the contractor cannot be trusted completely to make them efficiently. Consequently, the contractor must be denied some discretion to make managerial decisions. The fundamental question is: How much must be denied? To what extent should government officials or their controller agents regulate, duplicate, or replace the contractor's managerial efforts?

This question must be addressed because oversight is costly, both in terms of monitoring and reporting costs, and also because of the benefits sacrificed due to failure to exploit the contractor's managerial expertise. The controller and the government official will very seldom be more competent to make asset acquisition decisions than the contractor. The answer to this dilemma is that controllers and officials should do the minimum necessary, given the incentives faced by and the motivations of the contractor. However, at times, the minimum necessary is a great deal. This decision depends on circumstance and the controller's skill in exploiting the opportunities created by the contractor's response to institutional constraints. In other words, all long-term relationships between government officials and contractors must rely on incentives, even those governed by lump-sum budgets and flexible-price contracts. The difference is that when these control system designs are employed, the incentives are deeply embedded in the process of budget or contract execution.

Budget Execution Control Dynamics in the "Real World"

Budget execution control should be matched to circumstances: Increasing costs and homogeneous outputs imply one kind of design, but decreasing costs and heterogeneous outputs imply another. What we observe in practice, however, is that this match is not always achieved. Controllers tend to rely on monopoly supply and ex ante controls (Thompson and Zumeta 1981; Pitsvada 1983; Draper and Pitsvada 1981; Fisher 1975). This combination cannot be appropriate for every service to which it is applied.

Evidence can be marshaled to show that a variety of services might be performed satisfactorily by competing organizations, including in air traffic controls (Poole 1982), custodial services and building maintenance (Bennett and DiLorenzo 1983; Blankart 1979), day care centers (Bennett and DiLorenzo 1983), electrical power generation (Bennett and DiLorenzo 1983), fire protection services (Poole 1976; Smith 1983), forest management (Hanke 1982), management of grazing lands (Hanke 1983) hospitals and health care services (Hanke 1985:106–107), housing (Weicker 1980), postal services (Hanke 1985:108), prisons and correctional facilities (Hanke 1985:108–109), property assessment (Poole 1980), refuse collection (Savas 1977; Bennett and Johnson 1979), security services (Hanke 1985:109–110), ship and aircraft maintenance (Bennett and Johnson 1981; Bennett and DiLorenzo, 1983:42), urban transit (Hanke 1985:110) and wastewater treatment (Hanke 1985:110). Furthermore, even when controllers eschew monopoly supply, they frequently fail to exploit fully the benefits of competition. In New York City, for example, the municipal social services agency acquires child care services for its clients from both public and private day care centers. But public centers are subject to the full panoply of ex ante controls associated with lump-sum appropriation budgets, and private centers are subject to those associated with flexible-price contracts.

To cite another example, Department of Defense (DOD) policy restricts the use of flexible-price contracts to situations characterized by considerable procurement risk (primarily R&D projects). In other contracts, the degree of incentive is supposed to be calibrated to the project's riskiness. The first ship in a multiship construction program is supposed to be constructed under a cost-plus-fixed-profit contract, while later editions are supposed to be built under fixed-price contracts on the assumption that experience permits the contractor to manage to a narrower range of cost outcomes and to assume a greater share of the risk burden.

It may be observed that although DOD generally makes the proper transition from cost-plus to award-fee contracts as it moves from design to prototype development, it may not make the transition to a fixed-price contract for downstream production. To be consistent with the logic advanced here, selection of defense system production suppliers should be reduced to a question of cost and price search. Acquisition should be based upon fixed-price contracts, awarded by competitive bidding.

Where production volume is sufficient, DOD should try to maintain long-term contractual relations with two or more producers, as multisourcing permits a price search at each renegotiation of the relationship between DOD and its suppliers. Nevertheless, winning a contract to develop a weapons system, in a high proportion of cases, continues to be tantamount to winning subsequent production contracts.

Finally, not only do controllers tend to subject government agencies and contractors to a wide array of ex ante controls, they often hold them to tight output, quality, and service delivery schedules. Performance targets that can be met all of the time are not very ambitious.

What accounts for mismatches between how budgets are controlled in practice and the approach advanced here? One explanation is ignorance of consequences on the part of the controllers and elected officials. Also, some of the empirical data required to employ the control criteria outlined here are often unavailable. The most critical gap in this knowledge is how costs vary with output. Definitions and measurements of service outputs and activities also are often inadequate. Insufficient effort has been made to correct this situation in most public organizations. Of the two tasks, getting knowledge about the shape of cost functions is the more difficult. But if we first answer the question, "Cost to do what?" this knowledge can be derived deductively in a manner similar to the methods used in cost accounting and conventional price theory. Cost and supply analysis can yield highly useful information about marginal and average costs. Finally, experimentation with funding and output levels will increase our knowledge of service supply and cost functions (Wildavsky 1975; Larkey 1979; Cothran 1981).

The kind of information called for here requires a high level of analytical sophistication, both in budget execution and in system design, skills that staffs responsible for executing budgets may lack. Indeed, even if controllers had good information on cost and service supply functions, some might not know how to use it. Their experience tends to orient them to the administration of the traditional line-item, object-of-expenditure budget. Effective administration of a lump-sum or line-item appropriation requires no more than a modicum of arithmetical ability, combined with a substantial amount of common sense and bargaining savvy. Nevertheless, matching control systems design to circumstances requires a practical understanding of applied microeconomics, and financial and managerial accounting. Controllers often fail to understand the ideas outlined here or how to implement alternatives to the line-item appropriations budget—where to exercise judgment and where to exercise specific decision rules. This is demonstrated by the persistent attempt of controllers to employ techniques devised for use within organizations, such as standard costs based on fully distributed average historical costs, to establish per-unit prices for public organizations such as hospitals and universities.

Budget Execution Reform Obstacles

Ignorance of options and objectives is not a satisfactory explanation for controller decisions to resist reform. Ignorance can be corrected, and incompetence may be weeded out. If a better match between control system design and circumstances would have a substantial payoff, why hasn't this situation been corrected? One answer regarding the implementation of reform is as follows:

A large part of the literature on budgeting in the United States is concerned with reform. The goals of the proposed reforms are couched in similar language—economy, efficiency, improvement, or just better budgeting. The President, the Congress and its committees, administrative agencies, even the citizenry are all to gain by some change. However, any effective change in budgetary relationships must necessarily alter the outcomes of the budgetary process. Otherwise, why bother? Far from being a neutral matter of "better budgeting," proposed reforms inevitably contain important implications for the political system, that is, the "who gets what" of governmental decisions. (Wildavsky 1961: 183–190)

If the controllers and elected officials empowered to determine the methods used in executing budgets are rational, this quote implies that they have a strong interest in maintaining the status quo. To explain the persistent mismatch between budget execution control system designs and practice it is necessary to determine who benefits from the status quo and, therefore, who will oppose the adoption of a more appropriate type of control (Zimmerman 1977). Members of Congress, state legislators, city council members, and any politician with a constituency worth cultivating would appear to lose as a result of reforms proposed. As the collective holders of the power of the purse, legislators clearly have the authority to order budgets to be executed in almost any way they like, including the power to delegate this authority to controllers. Efficiency implies an exclusive concern with the supply of goods and services to the citizenry, with some indifference as to the means used to supply the goods or even to the identity of the suppliers. However, legislators are frequently as concerned about where public money is spent and who gets it as they are with what it buys (Arnold 1979; Ferejohn 1974; Fiorina 1977; Shepsle and Weingast 1981). Line-item appropriations in general and object-of-expenditure budgets in particular are ideally suited to the satisfaction of legislative preferences with respect to how public money is spent, where it is spent, and who gets it.

L. R. JONES

BIBLIOGRAPHY

Anthony, Robert, and David Young, 1984. *Management Control in Nonprofit Organizations.* 3d. ed. Homewood, IL: Irwin.

Arnold, R. Douglas, 1979. *Congress and the Bureaucracy: A Theory of Influence.* New Haven: Yale University Press.

Bailey, M., 1967. "Decentralization Through Internal Prices," 337–352. In S. Enke, ed., *Defense Management,* Englewood Cliffs, N.J.: Prentice-Hall.

Barton, D. P., 1982. "Regulating a Monopolist with Unknown Costs." *Econometrica,* vol. 50.

Beckner, N. V., 1960. "Government Efficiency and the Military: Buyer-Seller Relationship." *Journal of Political Economy,* vol. 68.

Bennett, James, and T. DiLorenzo, 1983. "Public Employee Labor Unions and the Privatization of Public Services." *Journal of Labor Research,* vol. 4: 43.

Bennett, James, and Manuel Johnson, 1979. "Public Versus Private Provision of Collective Goods and Services." *Public Choice,* vol. 34: 55–63.

———, 1981. *Better Government at Half the Price: Private Production of Public Services.* Ottowa, IL: Caroline House.

Blankart, C. B., 1979. "Bureaucratic Problems in Public Choice: Why Do Public Goods Still Remain Public?". In R. Roskamp, ed., *Public Choice and Public Finance.* Cujas 155–167.

Breton, A., and R. Wintrobe, 1975. "The Equilibrium Size of a Budget Maximizing Bureau." *Journal of Political Economy,* vol. 83: 195–207.

Cheung, S. N. S., 1983. "The Contractual Nature of the Firm." *Journal of Law and Economics,* vol. 25.

Coase, R., 1937. "The Nature of the Firm." *Economica,* vol. 4.

Cothran, D., 1981. "Program Flexibility and Budget Growth." *Western Political Quarterly,* vol. 34: 593–610.

Demski, Joel S., and Gerald A. Feltham, 1976. *Cost Determination: A Conceptual Approach.* Ames: Iowa State University Press.

Draper, F., and P. T. Pitsvada, 1981. "Limitations in Federal Budget Execution." *Government Accountants Journal,* vol. 30: 3.

Ferejohn, John A., 1974. *Pork Barrel Politics: Rivers and Harbors Legislation, 1947–1968.* Stanford: Stanford University Press.

Fiorina, Morris P., 1977. *Congress: Keystone of the Washington Establishment.* New Haven: Yale University Press.

Fisher, Louis, 1975. *Presidential Spending Power.* Princeton: Princeton University Press.

Fox, J. Ronald, 1974. *Arming America: How the U.S. Buys Weapons.* Boston: Division of Research, Graduate School of Bus. Admin., Harvard University.

Goldberg, V., 1976. "Regulation and Administered Contracts." *Bell Journal of Economics,* vol. 7: 426–428.

Hanke, S., 1982. "The Privatization Debate." *Cato Journal,* 656.

———, 1983. "Land Policy," In R. Howill, ed., *Agenda 83.* Washington, D.C.: Heritage Foundation, 65.

———, 1985. "Privatization: Theory, Evidence, Implementation." In C. Howell Harris, ed., *Control of Federal Spending.* New York: Academy of Political Science.

Hofstee, G. H., 1968. *The Game of Budget Control.* London: Tavistock; Assen: Van Gorcum.

Holstrom, B., 1979. "Moral Hazard and Observability." *Bell Journal of Economics*, vol. 10.

Larkey, Patrick D., 1979. *Evaluating Public Programs: The Impact of General Revenue Sharing on Municipal Government.* Princeton: Princeton University Press.

Meyerson, R. B., 1979. "Incentives Compatibility and the Bargaining Problem." *Econometrica*, vol. 47.

Mirlees, J., 1976. "The Optimal Structure of Incentives and Authority Within an Organization." *Bell Journal of Economics*, vol. 7.

Mitnick, B., 1977. "The Theory of Agency: The Policing 'Paradox' and Regulatory Behavior." *Public Choice*, vol. 30.

Morgan, J., 1949. "Bilateral Monopoly and the Competitive Output." *Quarterly Journal of Economics*, vol. 63.

Peck, Merton J., and F. M. Scherer, 1962. *The Weapons Acquisition Process: An Economic Analysis.* Boston: Division of Research, Graduate School of Bus. Admin., Harvard University.

Pitsvada, B. T., 1983. "Flexibility in Federal Budget Execution." *Public Budgeting and Finance*, vol. 32.

Poole, Robert, 1976. "Fighting Fires for Profit." *Reason* (May).

———, 1980. *Cutting Back City Hall.* New York: Universe Books.

———, 1982. "Air Traffic Control: The Private Sector Option." *Heritage Foundation Backgrounds*, vol. 216.

Savas, E. S., 1977. "Policy Analysis for Local Government." *Policy Analysis*, vol. 3: 49–77.

Scherer, F. M., 1964. *The Weapons Acquisition Process: Economic Incentives.* Cambridge: Harvard Business School.

Schick, A., 1964. "Control Patterns in State Budget Executions." *Public Administration Review* 24: 97–106.

———, 1982. "Contemporary Problems in Financial Control," 361–371. In F. Lane, ed., *Current Issues in Public Administration.* 2d ed. New York: St. Martin's Press.

Shepsle, K., and B. Weingast, 1981. "Political Preferences for the Pork Barrel." *American Journal of Political Science*, vol. 25.

Simon, H., *et al.* 1954. *Centralization vs. Decentralization in Organizing the Controller's Department: A Research Study and Report.* New York: Controllership Foundation.

Smith, R. G., 1983. "Feet to the Fire." *Reason* (May): 23–29.

Stark, Robert M., 1983. "On Cost Analysis for Engineered Construction." In Richard Engelbrecht-Wiggans, Martin Shubik, and Robert Stark, eds., *Auctions, Bidding, and Contracting: Uses and Theory.* New York: New York University Press.

Stark, R., and T. Varley, 1983. "Bidding, Estimating, and Engineered Construction Contracting," 121–135. In Engelbrecht-Wiggans, *Auctions, Bidding, and Contracting.* New York: New York University Press.

Thompson, F., 1981. "Utility Maximizing Behavior in Organized Anarchies." *Public Choice* 36.

———, 1984. "How to Stay Within the Budget Using Per-Unit Prices." *Journal of Policy Analysis and Management*, vol. 41.

Thompson, F., and G. Fiske, 1978. "One More Solution to the Problem of Higher Education Finance." *Policy Analysis* vol. 34.

Thompson, F., and W. Zumeta, 1981. "Controls and Controls: A Reexamination of Control Patterns in Budget Execution." *Policy Sciences* 13: 25–50.

Weicker, J., 1980. *Housing.* Washington, D.C.: American Enterprise Institute.

Wildavsky, Aaron, 1961. "Political Implications of Budget Reform." *Public Administration Review* 21:183–190.

———, 1975. *Budgeting: A Comparative Theory of Budgetary Processes.* Boston: Little, Brown.

Wildavsky, A., and A. Hammann, 1956. "Comprehensive Versus Incremental Budgeting in the Department of Agriculture." *Administrative Sciences Quarterly* 10:321–346.

Williamson, Oliver, 1964. *The Economics of Discretionary Behavior: Managerial Objectives in a Theory of the Firm.* Englewood Cliffs, N.J.: Prentice-Hall.

———, 1975. *Markets and Hierarchies, Analysis and Antitrust Implications: A Study in the Economics of Internal Organization.* New York: Free Press.

Zimmerman, J., 1977. "The Municipal Accounting Maze: An Analysis of Political Incentives." *Journal of Accounting Research* 21: 107–144.

BUDGET CYCLE.

BUDGET CYCLE. Recurring (and overlapping) events in the budget preparation and execution process.

Both the state and federal constitutions (for example, Article 1, Section 1 of the U.S. Constitution) prescribe legislative and congressional responsibilities for budget decisions, including the appropriation of moneys. Federal and state laws also define executive and legislative branch responsibility relative to the preparation, presentation, and approval of budgets for the operation of government agencies and enterprises. Such constitutional and statutory requirements, along with other legal and regularized requirements for budgetary action (including dates of submission, presentation of recommendations, and the like), have created at all levels of government budget processes that are prescriptive, repetitive, and cyclical. The term "budget cycle" has evolved to describe the repetitive interactions of the two branches of government principally involved in the design, development, approval, and conduct of public programs.

The formalization of the budget cycle is designed to facilitate deliberate interaction between the legislative and executive branches of government during the budget approval and execution process. In all phases of the budget process, a regularized budgeting procedure insures that the major actors understand their roles and are fully integrated into the budget process. Though the composition and financing of budgets may change, the budget cycle normalizes the activities of the legislative and executive branches of government in making critical resource allocation decisions and helps to insure that policy and allocation decisions are made in a timely manner. In addition, the diversity of activities enclosed within the cycle insures that consideration is given to matters of efficiency and effectiveness in budget decisionmaking.

Because the phases of the budget cycle are continuous and recurring, an operating agency will typically be simultaneously involved in distinct phases of more than one budget cycle (for example, an agency could be involved in the preparation phase of the next fiscal year's budget while also being in the execution phase of the current fiscal year's budget cycle). These budget-year or fiscal-year phases serve as markers so that budget policy and allocation decisions can be made expeditiously, to facilitate smooth and effective government operations.

Fiscal-year periods for the various levels of government vary in the United States. For example, the federal fiscal year begins and ends on October 1, but all states except Alabama, Michigan, New York, and Texas operate on a July 1-to-July 1 fiscal year. (NASBO 1992). By convention, fiscal years are named after the year in which they end. For example, a fiscal year beginning on July 1, 1995, is referred to as the fiscal year 1996 (budget year).

Budget cycles vary, depending on whether a government entity has an annual or biennial budget process. An annual budget cycle typically spreads across the equivalent of one calendar year, with starting and ending dates normally not coterminous with a specific calendar year. Annual budgets are more "policy" flexible than biennial budgets, since adjustments can be made more frequently in response to economic and fiscal condition fluctuations. Biennial budget processes, however, encompass the equivalent of two calendar years and provide additional certainty for funded programs and policies, and allow more time for analysis and assessment activities. At the same time, state biennial budgets are more susceptible to "within period" budget changes due to unanticipated revenue fluctuations and associated expenditure reductions required to comply with state constitutional balanced budget provisions.

The federal government uses an annual budget process and cycle and approximately two-fifths of the states have biennial budget periods. Budget processes of biennial budget states are not entirely consistent. For example, states such as Arkansas, Hawaii, Indiana, Kentucky, Maine, Minnesota, Montana, Nebraska, Nevada, New Hampshire, Ohio, Virginia, and Wisconsin are biennial budget states that adopt two one-year budgets. By contrast, other biennial budget states adopt a single budget for the two-year period (North Carolina, North Dakota, Oregon, Texas, Washington, and Wyoming) (Mikesell 1995; ACIR 1994).

Since 1969, there have been 23 alterations in state budget periodicity, with seven states changing from biennial to annual periodicity (Kearns 1993). This fact suggests that there is not a single periodicity choice that is appropriate for all states at all times. Both annual budgeting and biennial budgeting processes have proponents and detractors in the executive and legislative branches. Legislative arguments in favor of annual budgeting include: (1) the increased time for legislative consideration of the budget; (2) the enhanced control that legislators have to manipulate intergovernmental transfers and to oversee agency activity; (3) the increased accuracy of revenue estimates; (4) the reduced power of the executive branch for discretionary spending; and (5) the elimination of many special sessions and supplemental appropriations. Some executive branch budget-makers prefer biennial budgeting because they believe that budget preparation costs are lower and that the opportunity exists for more long-term planning and program evaluation.

Among the critical elements of the budget cycle are executive preparation, legislative consideration, budget execution, and audit and evaluation. There are many differences in the preparation phase of the cycle across the spectrum of governments. The period of preparation may vary, as well as the degree of involvement of the chief executive. Though most governments have most of the elements of the cycle in some form, individual governments may condense or expand the cycle to meet their needs.

Budget Preparation

The first phase of the budget cycle involves a series of activities including: (1) the specification of executive branch priorities and policies, (2) the development and distribution of budget instructions, (3) the preparation of agency budget requests, (4) the executive branch budget office review of agency requests, (5) the forecasting of tax revenues, (6) the finalizaton of the executive branch budget recommendations, and (7) the transmission of the executive budget to the legislative branch for consideration by the date required by law or custom. The sequence of activities may vary due to convention, organizational structure, and legislative or executive branch agreements and requirements. However, these activities, in some form are normally involved in the budget preparation phase of the budget cycle.

The nature and content of budget instructions vary depending upon the budget process used (performance budgeting, zero-base budgeting, incremental budgeting, program budgeting, and the like); the type of data required by statute, regulation, or tradition; the information desired or required by the legislative branch review; and the degree of flexibility the chief executive may delegate to agency heads regarding program changes and initiatives. In most cases, budget instructions do include guidelines regarding the policy direction of the chief executive, the budget increase request limitations (in dollar or percentage increase terms), the form and content of the agency request, and the information required regarding program costs and expected outcomes. Budget requests may also require program justification, and agency heads may be allowed to recommend priorities and to make recommendations regarding changes in program activity structure and services provided.

The agency requests are forwarded to the executive branch budget office, which is responsible for reviewing the requests for consistency with policies and priorities of the chief executive, completeness and compliance with budget instructions or guidelines, and adequacy of justification and logical content. In some cases, agency heads may be asked to make presentations and to discuss their requests with the central budget office or with the chief executive, depending on the administrative and policy-making style. After budget request reviews and revenue forecasts are completed, the executive budget office and the chief executive finalize the executive branch budget recommendations and forward them to the legislative body for consideration, in accordance with dates and processes prescribed by law or convention.

Legislative Consideration and Approval

Upon receiving the executive branch budget recommendations, the legislative body begins budgetary reviews. The review process is initiated by the introduction of an appropriation bill (or bills) in the lower house of a bicameral legislature. (A unicameral system, of course, would only have one legislative review process.) The number of separate appropriation bills considered tends to depend on the size and complexity of the governmental unit (for example, Congress typically considers thirteen appropriation bills but some states adopt a single unified appropriation bill that covers all state appropriations). Budget and appropriation bill review processes, also, vary for Congress and the various states and local governments. For example, Congress passes a "budget resolution" early in the review process to provide guidelines for the appropriation review process. Some states' appropriation and revenue (budget) committees, however, provide "marks" or appropriation maximums to subcommittees charged with the review of specific program appropriation requests. Both of these processes are intended to provide discipline and to set maximum appropriation targets for the committees to use as they consider requests for funds within a broad appropriation area (cabinet or major policy areas such as transportation, agriculture, and the like) assigned to the review committee. The committees' challenge is then to consider request trade-offs, which may be required to match appropriation recommendations to available resources.

After the lower house has completed its review of appropriation requests and has passed the relevant appropriation bill or bills, it forwards the bill or bills to the upper house for consideration and review. After the upper chamber has passed its bill or bills, a joint conference committee is typically formed to mitigate the differences that might exist between the upper and lower chamber bills. The conference report or unified appropriation bill that emerges then returns to both houses for final approval and submission to the chief executive for signature or veto.

Veto authority varies across states and the federal government. Until 1996 the President could only veto or sign the entire appropriation bill. He did not have the authority to veto individual appropriation items as do the majority of state governors. However, in 1996 Congress gave him a limited line-item veto to take effect in 1997. All but seven governors either have the ability to exercise the line-item veto or to exercise similar options (NASBO 1992). When vetoes are exercised, the legislative body may de-

cide to attempt to override the veto (usually with a special majority vote) or it may revise its appropriation bill in order to obtain the signature of the chief executive.

Budget Execution

The budget execution phase of the budget cycle involves the expenditure of the appropriated funds for the purpose and intent defined by the appropriations bill. The agencies are charged with the responsibility of providing the services or constructing capital projects authorized by the legislative body and are normally required to limit spending in a manner consistent with the appropriations laws. As such, the approved budget or appropriations bill provides the legal basis for the expenditure of public funds and provides expenditure guidelines for government agencies. In addition to expenditure amounts and limits, appropriations bills may include specific language that clarifies legislative intent. During the execution phase, the executive budget office may impose control processes, such as allotments, which typically control expenditures by fiscal-year quarter, to guide and monitor the expenditure process. Such intra-fiscal-year expenditure control processes are important for state governments because the governments must be prepared to ensure that their budgets are balanced; as such, they may be forced to reduce the expenditures (or appropriations in cooperation with the legislative body) during the budget execution phase if unforeseen fiscal circumstances arise (such as revenue shortfalls).

Evaluation and Audit

The final phase of the budget cycle, the evaluation and audit phase, is intended to provide public officials and the general public assurance that (1) public funds are being used in accord with legislative intent and that (2) public agencies are carrying out programs and agency activities in the most efficient and effective manner, given legal and institutional constraints. The first type of audit, the audit of financial transactions, is referred to as a financial audit due to its focus on financial records, compliance with legislative intent and statutory authorization, and accuracy of financial practice and procedure. Such audits are typically carried out or supervised by "outside" auditors or audit agencies, such as elected or appointed "independent" state auditors, the General Accounting Office in the federal government, or by private accounting firms (a practice often followed by local governments). The public acceptance and credibility of such audits requires independence and professionalism in the auditing process.

The second type of audit (which focuses on outcomes of agencies and programs) is known as a "performance audit" due to its focus on determining whether the agency is conducting its programs in a manner consistent with laws and regulations applicable to the program and whether the agency has acted judiciously regarding the acquisition of and use of resources in performing the services for which it has statutory responsibility. The performance audit, by focusing on efficiency and effectiveness, can provide information to policymakers and managers regarding the means of enhancing program outcomes while minimizing resource requirements. Such suggestions are typically incorporated into the program or agency's strategic plan for the next budget cycle and can lead to statutory and regulatory adjustments as well as management decision changes.

It is noted that states with sunset laws typically require performance audits and reviews as part of the program reauthorization process. Such reviews provide policymakers insights regarding the effectiveness of programs in achieving desired outcomes, insights regarding factors that limit the effectiveness of programs, possible program duplications, and other information that may be relevant to the determination of whether a program should be reauthorized (a key requirement of the sunset law implementation) (ACIR 1976).

Although the budget cycle is common to all levels of government, the specific nature and character of an individual federal, state, or local government budget cycle will depend on the structure of the government, its budget process laws, and traditions affecting the budget process for that government entity. In some ways, however, the budget cycle elements of budget preparation–budget review (by the legislative branch), budget execution, evaluation, and audit–have become generic public budgeting activities. Individual governments may modify and expand the cycle to meet special needs and policy and management decision processes (for example, sunset law processes), including legal and statutory requirements. However, the regularized nature of the budget cycle has become an integral component of public policy development, implementation, and review. Moreover, the regularized process has facilitated executive and legislative interaction and has worked to enhance public policy making and public resource allocation.

Merl Hackbart

BIBLIOGRAPHY

ACIR 1994. *Significant Features of Fiscal Federalism: Volume 1: Budget Processes and Tax Systems,* June.

Advisory Commission on Intergovernmental Relations (ACIR), 1976. "Sunset Legislation and Zero Based Budgeting," Information Bulletin, (December), no. 76–5.

Kearns, Paula S., 1993. "The Determinants of State Budget Periodicity: An Empirical Analysis," *Public Budgeting and Finance,* vol. 13, no. 2 (Spring).

Mikesell, John L., 1995. *Fiscal Administration: Analysis and Applications for the Public Sector,* 42-49. Cincinnati: Wadsworth Publishing Company.

National Association of State Budget Officers (NASBO), 1992. *Budget Processes in the States 1992,* Washington, D.C.

BUDGET ETHICS.

A series of suggestions for the individual involved in the daily routines of budgeting to help establish what correct behavior should be for that individual. Some of these precepts may be applicable to all administrative life.

Introduction

This entry is normative and draws on what are, for budgeting, nontraditional sources. Of course, there are other ideas about budgeting ethics, but those that derive from great works of literature may also be of value to the budgeteer. In this instance, the ideas have been tested in the budgeting crucible and proven sound. The underlying philosophy of this particular entry is

> See thou character. Give thy thoughts no tongue,
> Nor any unproportion'd thought his act.
> Be thou familiar, but by no means vulgar.
> The friends thou hast, and their adoption tried,
> Grapple them to thy soul with hoops of steel.
> But do not dull thy palm with entertainment
> Of each new-hatch'd, unfledg'd comrade. Beware
> Of entrance to a quarrel; but, being in,
> Bear't that the opposed may beware of thee.
> Give every man thine ear, but few thy voice.
> Take each man's censure, but reserve thy judgment.
> Costly thy habit as thy purse can buy.
> But not express'd in fancy; rich, not gaudy;
> For the apparel oft proclaims the man;
> And they in France of the best rank and station
> Are most select and generous chief in that.
> Neither a borrower nor a lender be:
> For loan oft loses both itself and friend,
> And borrowing dulls the edge of husbandry.
> This above all, –to thine ownself be true;
> And it must follow, as the night the day;
> Thou canst not then be false to any man.

> —Shakespeare, Act I, Scene III
> *Hamlet, Prince of Denmark*

Budgeting Thinking

Being a good budgeteer is not necessarily based upon a particular degree or academic specialization. A great budgeteer could have a bachelor's degree in Romance Languages; a poor budgeteer could have a bachelor's degree in accounting and be a Certified Public Accountant. What distinguishes the two also seems generally to distinguish good budgeteers from bad ones.

First, a good budgeteer has character—in the sense of personal integrity, the capacity to know and defend one's work, thoughts, values, and beliefs in terms of professional and personal standards of the highest order.

Second, a good budgeteer is an excellent listener: one who hears and understands not only the words that are spoken but those that are not, the gestures that are made and those that are not; a "listener" who uses *all the senses* not just the ears. This listening aspect of budget thinking also means that a good budgeteer spends most of the time silent, seemingly detached but "listening" closely.

Third, a good budgeteer is inherently questioning. This budgeteer either mentally or vocally recalls H.L. Mencken's Six Friends: Who? What? Where? When? Why? How? Who is saying it? What are they saying? Where are they saying it? When are they saying it? Why are they saying it? How are they saying it, or How do they know it? Such questioning will soon lead the budgeteer to ascertain who and what can be relied upon. Just as numbers must be as accurate, precise, and verifiable as possible, so must assessments of people. It took one budgeteer about six months to learn which of her agencies' fiscal officers would only give her their agency's perspective rather than their professional judgment. She learned that the ones who would share their professional judgments also proved helpful when there was a need to test a policy idea.

Fourth, a good budgeteer is not unfriendly, but is cautious in human relationships. As a general rule, agencies do not like to tell their budget analysts bad news or give them a bad impression. Agencies seek to stay on what they perceive to be the "good" side of analysts. A story is recalled of a former budgeteer who moved to another career and became depressed at the lack of phone calls—a scenario that illustrates how tenuous budgeting "friendships" can be!

Fifth, a good budgeteer avoids emotional aspects of a disagreement so that emotions do not interfere with listening, subsequent analyses, and their reasoned judgments. However, a good budgeteer is prepared to defend an idea with reasonable assumptions, sound logic, and verifiable information.

Sixth, the good budgeteer is neither miserly nor extravagant in decisions, the results thereof, or in appearance (both personal and professional). The good budgeteer focuses thought and action on the three Es: Economy, Efficiency, and Effectiveness. A good budgeteer's words, written or spoken, are clear, concise, accurate, and cogently reasoned. It is difficult to take seriously a budgeteer's dictum for parsimony when he or she sits behind an expensive desk, wearing tailored pin-stripes. One senior budgeteer made a point of having a sparse office with an old, beat-up desk. It was an office that made an unspoken but visible statement about the importance to that budgeteer of the three Es.

Seventh, the good budgeteer is parsimonious with entrusted public resources: Although demands are elastic, resources are not. A good budgeteer *knows* that all problems are not solvable, even if given unlimited resources. This budgeteer also knows that there are usually alternatives, other than simply adding more resources. Since the opportunity costs of today's decisions may mean an inability to deal with tomorrow's problems, the good budgeteer is usually comfortable with the role of being a nay-sayer to many sound requests for more resources.

Eighth, the good budgeteer also knows the importance of reasonable uncertainty and its distinction from certain unreasonableness. Such prudent judgment enables the good budgeteer to be comfortable using simple tools to explain complex ideas; foregoing, for example, the use of a sophisticated model when simple percentages would better convey the meaning. Reasonable uncertainty also enables the budgeteer to be humane.

Ninth, the good budgeteer looks in the mirror and *knows* that the honest thing has been done. It means correcting errors of fact, calculation, judgment, or presentation, and saying, "I don't know but I'll find out" when such is the case. It is the headline test: Would I like to see this error with my name at the top of tomorrow's news?

Finally, the good budgeteer has a passion for excellence, accuracy, precision, and timeliness; a compassion for the variety of human conditions; and the wisdom to distinguish reality from the ideal in these feelings.

RICHARD E. ZODY

BUDGET FORMAT. The style, shape, and general layout of information selected for inclusion in a government's primary financial planning and forecasting document.

The format of a government's budget document is generally dictated by statute or ordinance, the entity's size and resources, the recommendations of its finance professionals, and the preferences and information needs of its elected officials and citizenry. The type of information included in a budget document varies considerably across governments and across funds within the same government. (For an excellent discussion of governmental fund accounting, see the article by Stephen Gauthier in *Local Government Finance,* a 1991 edited volume by John Petersen and Dennis Strachota.)

The trend is toward presenting a wider variety of information in a more "user-friendly" manner—encouraging decisionmakers and citizens alike to utilize budget documents to assess a government's priorities and performance. Affordable and easily usable computer technology and software have sparked this trend, along with the growing demands of the public to see precisely how government raises and spends taxpayer dollars. The emergence of professional association awards programs focusing on the style and content of public financial documents has also contributed greatly to the growing emphasis on budget formatting.

Budget formats differ considerably in the degree to which they promote control, management, planning, and accountability. Paralleling the evolution of budget processes, current-day formats tend to emphasize all these dimensions and typically contain at least some elements of line-item, program, zero-base, and performance presentation styles, along with a wide array of other information (organizational, procedural, environmental, political).

Line-Item Formats

This presentation style was devised around the turn of the twentieth century in response to growing corruption among governmental officials. Primarily focusing on the expenditure side of the budgetary ledger, this format presents spending data for various categories or objects of expenditures for the government as a whole (summary) and for individual departments and/or programs. (Table I is an example of a summary line-item object of expenditure format.) The emphasis is on what is to be purchased rather than on what outcomes or outputs those purchases will yield.

Typical categories or classes of expenditures include personal services, supplies, travel, utilities, equipment, contractual services, capital outlays, and so forth. These can, in turn, be broken down into subclasses (e.g., personal services can be disaggregated into wages, salaries, overtime, and fringe benefits) or very detailed categories identified by account code. (Table II is an example of a detailed account code line-item format for Personal Services.) Line-item formats may also classify expenditures by the "life" of a purchase: current, or annual, purchases (operating costs); long-term purchases lasting more than a year (capital outlays); and purchases made in the past but not yet fully paid for (debt service).

The biggest advantage of the line-item style of presentation is that it is easy to understand and use, especially when the information is presented by organizational units (departments, divisions) or free-standing programs. The line-item format promotes year-to-year comparisons, especially if a percentage change column is included. A change column calls attention to the new spending categories being proposed and the lines where the most dramatic increases/decreases are occurring. However, it tends to let categories with no or only incremental projected changes get by without much scrutiny. Some critics point to this as evidence of the line-item format's tendency to yield only

marginal, or incremental, changes in spending patterns from one fiscal year to the next.

Critics of line-item formats also attack them for their exclusive emphasis on inputs (dollars spent). The absence of output or outcome data makes it virtually impossible to reach conclusions about the efficiency, effectiveness, or equity of the spending or to hold government and its officials accountable for how government operates. Since the early 1960s, governments at all levels have experimented with different formats to remedy the shortcomings of the traditional line-item arrangement. But even during these periods of experimentation, most governments have retained some dimensions of the traditional line-item budget while supplementing it with data presented in newer formats.

Program Budget Formats

Program budget formats were designed to focus more on outcomes, rather than just inputs. This reform, which began at the federal level, was expected to yield better planning and management decisions. The planning-programming-budgeting System (PPBS) emerged in the early 1960s as an experiment by the Department of Defense. PPBS soon spread to other federal agencies and many state and local governments. PPBS as originally introduced required agencies to delineate measurable service objectives, to identify alternatives for achieving those objectives, and to use cost-benefit analysis to select the alternative to be funded. Projections were made on a multi-year, rather than an annual, basis, although they were updated annually.

Program budget formats, as they initially evolved at the state and local levels, cut across standard organizational (departmental) lines. Typically, a broad goal or objective was identified and labeled a program. The program was broken down into subprogram elements which were, in turn, broken down into various activities (outcomes), each viewed as a way to attain the broad goal the program was designed to address. Staffing and funding levels were reported for each program, subprogram, and activity, thereby permitting the calculation of an efficiency measure for each (although not an effectiveness measure).

Table III shows how budget information is presented for a Community Health and Safety program, comprised of four subprograms (Neighborhood Security, War on Drugs, Utility System Management, and Environmental Protection) and involving six departments. It further reports the 12 specific activities involved in one of the subprograms, Neighborhood Security. The exhibit shows that several departments are involved in more than one activity, thereby requiring that each department's total allocation be apportioned among the various activities in which it is involved. (What is not shown is that each department is

TABLE I. LINE-ITEM OBJECT OF EXPENDITURE FORMAT: SUMMARY (ALL DEPARTMENTS)

City of St Petersburg, Florida

ALL OPERATING FUNDS
SUMMARY OF EXPENSE BY OBJECT
($000 omitted)

	Actual 1990	Actual 1991	Budget 1992	Estimate 1992	Budget 1993
Personal Services	72,300	77,220	79,160	79,931	83,806
Employee Benefits	25,174	27,437	29,596	30,204	31,931
Services	63,722	67,869	72,340	69,914	70,940
Commodities	9,401	8,843	11,152	10,627	10,605
Capital Outlay	5,668	5,736	5,291	6,410	5,306
Transfers:					
Between Operating Funds	7,983	8,179	7,965	7,991	6,017
To Capital Project Funds	8,594	13,622	10,130	10,130	9,922
To Debt Service Funds	9,660	8,774	9,536	7,722	7,241
To Reserve Accounts	304	2,404	343	3,193	1,351
To Other Funds	2,490	1,879	2,235	1,969	1,841
Other	(306)	0	380	0	0
TOTAL	204,990	221,963	228,128	228,091	228,960

These definitions allow the reader to quickly identify types of expenditures presented in the table above without having to refer to a glossary.

DEFINITIONS:

PERSONAL SERVICES: Services rendered by full-time and part-time employees to support the functions of City departments. Costs include salaries, overtime, shift differentials, and other direct payments to employees.

EMPLOYEE BENEFITS: Contributions made by the City to designated funds to meet commitments of obligations for employee fringe benefits. Included are the City's share of costs for Social Security and the various pension, medical, and life insurance plans.

SERVICES: The requirements for a department's work program which are provided by other entities-either outside vendors and contractors or other City departments. Examples are the costs of repair and maintenance services (not materials); utilities; rentals; and charges from City Internal Service Funds.

COMMODITIES: Expendable materials and supplies necessary to carry out a department's work program for the fiscal year. Such items as repair and maintenance materials, chemicals, agricultural products, office supplies, small tools, and merchandise for resale are included.

CAPITAL OUTLAY: The purchase, acquisition, or construction of any item having unit cost of $100 or more, or a useful life of one or more years. Typical capital outlay items include vehicles, construction equipment, typewriters, computers, and office furniture.

Note: This summary presents expenditures by major objects as well as interfund transfers.

Source: Dennis Strachota, 1994. *The Best of Governmental Budgeting: A Guide to Preparing Budget Documents,* Chicago, IL: Government Finance Officers Association, Exhibit 3-13.

TABLE II. Detailed Line-Item Object of Expenditure by Account Format (Personal Services) All Departments

City of Sterling Heights, Michigan

% Change Column Focuses Attention on Lines With Bigger Changes

GENERAL FUND
EXPENDITURE SUMMARY BY ACCOUNT

Account Code →

Individual Line Items →

Object Category →

Account Number	Account Name	1991–1992 Actual		1992–1993 Budget		1993–1994 Budget	
		Dollars	%	Dollars	%	Dollars	%
	Personnel Services						
703000	Wages-Elected & Appointed	$50,616	0.10	$60,270	0.12	$66,150	0.13
704000	Wages & Salaries-Permanent	20,671,787	41.56	21,896,400	42.99	22,202,070	42.42
704001	Sick Time Buy Back	347,563	0.70	338,530	0.66	369,910	0.71
704718	Wage Reimbursement-WC	(1,493)	(0.00)	0	0.00	0	0.00
704721	Health Insurance Allowance	15,563	0.03	19,820	0.04	16,500	0.03
705000	Wages-Salaries-Temp/Part time	749,431	1.51	694,080	1.36	704,210	1.35
705001	Part Time/Temp - Non Permanent	63,096	0.13	68,720	0.13	29,500	0.06
706000	Wages-Salaries - Occasional	47,754	0.10	55,000	0.11	55,500	0.11
708000	Overtime	1,535,053	3.09	1,419,740	2.79	1,521,240	2.91
708001	Compensatory Time Buy Back	821,839	1.65	784,900	1.54	808,650	1.55
708795	Overtime - F. L. S. A.	0	0.00	0	0.00	30,000	0.06
710000	Longevity	653,648	1.31	592,890	1.16	620,150	1.18
711000	Holiday Pay	477,153	0.96	530,580	1.04	544,690	1.04
713500	Car Allowance	1,200	0.00	0	0.00	0	0.00
714000	Food Allowance	61,817	0.12	72,000	0.14	72,000	0.14
715000	Clothing Allowance	253,576	0.51	224,350	0.44	224,500	0.43
717000	FICA	910,232	1.83	929,660	1.83	943,930	1.80
717012	Medicare FICA	40,318	0.08	51,780	0.10	56,930	0.11
718000	Worker's Compensation	634,540	1.28	286,990	0.56	351,920	0.67
719000	Unemployment Compensation	12,098	0.02	13,570	0.03	14,520	0.03
720000	Pension-General Employees Retire.	525,931	1.06	698,400	1.37	822,830	1.57
720001	Pension-Police and Fire Retirement	3,174,410	6.38	3,300,540	6.48	3,691,610	7.05
721000	Hospitalization	2,316,780	4.66	2,803,630	5.51	3,217,010	6.15
721001	Hospitalization-Retirees	255,517	0.51	269,720	0.53	294,300	0.56
721002	Retiree Medical-Police & Fire	265,818	0.53	334,850	0.66	457,910	0.87
722000	Dental Insurance	371,687	0.75	420,970	0.83	403,930	0.77
723000	Life Insurance	106,173	0.21	116,350	0.23	85,270	0.16
724000	Eye Care Insurance	1,763	0.00	1,480	0.00	1,570	0.00
725000	Disability Insurance	238,275	0.48	278,880	0.55	293,350	0.56
	Total Personnel Services	34,602,145	69.56	36,264,100	71.21	37,900,150	72.42

Note: This City's budget contained four object categories: Personnel Services, Other Charges, Capital Outlay, and Transfers Out. Only one category is presented here.

Source: Adapted from Dennis Strachota, 1994. *The Best of Governmental Budgeting: A Guide to Preparing Budget Documents.* Chicago, IL: Government Finance Officers Association, Exhibit 3-14.

TABLE III. Program Budget Format: One Program (Community Health and Safety) and One of its Subprograms (Neighborhood Security)

City of Dayton, Ohio

Community Health and Safety Program

To protect the lives, health and property of all citizens and to take direct action and lead regional efforts to reduce drugs, crime, violence, and environmentally unsafe conditions.

Program	'92/'93 Staff	1992 Budget	1993 Budget	Bgt.% Chng.
Neighborhood Security	1,004.7/989.9	$52,921,200	$55,320,600	4.5%
War on Drugs	52/50	$3,209,900	$3,115,100	-3.0%
Utility System Mgmt.	412.5/428.3	$53,075,400	$55,018,600	3.7%
Environmental Protection	6/6	$17,286,100	$13,857,100	-19.8%
Total	1,475.2/1,474.2	$126,492,600	$127,311,400	0.6%

■ Community Health and Safety is slightly up 0.6% primarily due to adding capital resources for well field improvements.

Neighborhood Security

To protect the life and property of all citizens from physical disaster and criminal activity.

Operating Allocation Plan

Activity	Department	'92/'93 Staff	1992 Budget	1993 Budget	Bgt.% Chng.
1. Fire Suppression	Fire	316/320	$18,679,000	$19,844,100	6.2%
Reflects cost for 4 recruits.					
2. Hydrant Maintenance	Water	3/3	$259,100	$272,600	5.2%
3. Police Investigations	Police	80/62	$3,746,300	$3,416,000	-8.8%
Reflects 18 positions reassigned to other divisions.					
4. Arson Abatement	Fire	4/4	$233,100	$241,500	3.6%
5. Municipal Court	Courts	55.5/57.5	$2,393,100	$2,529,300	5.7%
Includes judicial review of criminal cases, small claims and traffic court. Also reflects budget increase for 2 new cars for capias program and 3 new cars for bailiffs.					
6. Prosecution of Criminal Cases	Law	8.1/8.1	$340,400	$358,700	5.4%
7. Human Rehabilitation Service	Human & Nbhd. Res.	131.8/129	$6,708,300	$6,670,100	-0.6%
8. Police Operations	Police	294/294	$14,831,900	$16,014,200	8.0%
Reflects 6 new police officer positions funded by DMHA.					
9. Clerk of Courts	Courts	55.8/55.8	$2,089,800	$2,160,300	3.4%
Includes judicial review of criminal cases, small claims, traffic court and management.					
10. Emergency Medical Services	Fire	50/50	$2,358,400	$2,507,900	6.3%
Reflects increase to purchase a paramedic unit.					
11. Prosecution of Traffic Offenses	Law	6.5/6.5	$294,800	$310,900	5.5%
12. City Jail	Human & Nbhd. Res.	0/0	$850,000	$850,000	0.0%
Operating Total		**1,004.7/989.9**	**$52,784,200**	**$55,175,600**	**4.5%**

Each budget category is subdivided into "programs" which provides the basis for the program budget.

The long-term goal or mission of the Neighborhood Security program is described here.

Information is provided for each activity within a program.

Notes are used to identify major changes from one budget year to the next.

Programs are subdivided into "activities." The department responsible for performing the activity is also listed.

"Totals" are presented in boldface type to highlight them.

Note: Program cuts across departmental lines. The subprogram detail is not presented for the War on Drugs, Utility System Management, or Environmental Protection sub programs.

Source: Adapted from Dennis Strachota,1994. *The Best of Governmental Budgeting: A Guide to Preparing Budget Documents.* Chicago, IL: Government Finance Officers Association, Exhibit 2-2.

involved in several other broadly defined programs besides Community Health and Safety. The jurisdiction whose budget is reported here has eight programs, most of which cut across more than on department.)

Proponents of traditional program budget formats applaud their emphasis on long-term planning and efficiency—the best ways of achieving desired outcomes. Critics attack the somewhat arbitrary assignment of expenditures to various programs and the difficulty of tracking those expenditures without a crosswalk. (A crosswalk is a document or spreadsheet detailing which account codes are combined to yield a program's budget actuals and estimates.)

Program budgets are perceived by many to be very "user-unfriendly" for reasons other than just the need for a crosswalk. First, when goals and objectives change, longitudinal analyses become noncomparable. Second, genuine cost-benefit analysis is frequently impossible due to limited time, resources, and expertise, not to mention disagreements over what is, and how to measure, a cost and a benefit. Some programs and activities are less amenable to cost-benefit analysis than others, namely those requiring the calculation of the value of a human life. For this reason, prevention-oriented activities are especially difficult to subject to meaningful cost-benefit analysis.

While it was officially terminated as the U.S. government's budget system in 1971, many federal, state, local and foreign government budgets still retain remnants of program budgeting, such as multi-year budgets and the analysis of major policy alternatives and tradeoffs using cost-benefit analysis, albeit in a rather limited fashion. A number of jurisdictions aggregate expenditure figures for broad community goals (e.g., cultural, library, and recreation) although they continue to present expenditure data by department in a more traditional line-item format. Table IV is an example of a popular format that creates broad program budget categories without splitting departmental allocations across programs. In general, program budgets, like line-item budgets, are perceived to promote incrementalism—a shortcoming zero-based budgeting aims to remedy.

Zero-Based Budget Formats

Zero-based budgeting (ZBB) followed PPBS at the federal level. President Carter brought it to Washington in 1977 from Georgia, where as governor, he had imported it to the state capital from the private sector. A ZBB process involves identifying decision units and their goals or missions, developing different decision packages for each unit, and ranking the alternative packages. A decision unit is identified by a program manager and can be defined as a program or activity, the basic requirement being that it is self-contained at least from a budgetary perspective. A specific decision package represents an alternative way of achieving the goal of the decision unit. Each package describes the outputs and outcomes of a specific level of funding and staffing. Ultimately, these alternative packages must be ranked by program managers, department heads, the budget office, and/or the chief executive. The amount of revenue available for allocation determines how many decision packages can be funded.

A ZBB format allows the comparison of outputs and outcomes which would be provided under different funding scenarios (e.g., cutback, no growth, growth). No department, agency, or program is permitted to propose a budget that merely calls for the status quo, reflecting ZBB's attack on incrementalism.

Table V demonstrates a ZBB format for a Community Policing program, or decision unit. The program goal is identified, along with six decision package alternatives. Each decision package projects the service level for a specific funding/staffing scenario. In this example, the department and the city chief executive rank-ordered these six packages. Packages 1 and 2 were ranked very high. Presuming that both would be funded, they would, in essence, reflect a marginal reduction from the previous year's funding and staffing levels.

ZBB proponents tout its attack on incrementalism, its attempt to weed out low-priority programs, and its efforts to force government officials to engage is more rational analyses of alternative service delivery mechanisms and levels. Supporters strongly endorse its contingency budgeting element requiring cost-benefit estimates for different budget parameters. Another positive attribute of ZBB is that it builds a budget from the bottom up rather than from the top down (in contrast to program budgeting).

ZBB opponents voice strong opposition to the time and resources it requires. To them, ZBB is a very unrealistic and inefficient way to present budget data to either government officials or the public at large. The sheer amount of paperwork for a single program's decision packages makes it highly improbable that all decision packages can be thoroughly analyzed and ranked by policymakers. ZBB also ignores the fact that certain programs or activities will never seriously be considered for elimination, while others have little or no chance of being funded. Opponents vehemently disagree with one another on its major premises, namely that past knowledge and information should be ignored to combat incrementalism. The difficulties involved in using a ZBB format have meant that very few governments use it in its purest form. However, some are using its hybrid—target-based budgeting.

Target-Based Budget Formats

Target-based budgeting (TBB) incorporates the most attractive elements of ZBB, namely the ranking of funding-service alternatives and the use of contingency budget parameters. TBB recognizes that certain programs are not

TABLE IV. PROGRAM BUDGET FORMAT CREATED BY CLUSTERING

City of Ft. Collins, Colorado

Program Area

Department/ Division Within Program Area

CITY EXPENDITURES BY SERVICE AREA (PROGRAM)

SERVICE AREA Department	ACTUAL 1991	BUDGET 1992	ADOPTED 1993	% INCREASE OVER 1992
ADMINISTRATIVE				
Administration	$149,138	$149,781	$155,748	4.0%
Employee Development	4,148,114	5,226,301	5,513,717	5.5%
Finance	5,781,688	5,953,984	6,344,255	6.6%
General Services	5,688,288	6,351,566	8,737,459	37.6%
Information & Communication Systems	2,810,260	3,011,117	3,365,212	11.8%
TOTAL ADMINISTRATIVE	18,613,488	20,692,749	24,116,391	16.5%
TRANSFERS TO OTHER FUNDS	(10,109,997)	(11,503,887)	(12,035,104)	4.6%
NET OPERATING ADMINISTRATIVE	$8,503,491	$9,188,862	$12,081,287	31.5%
CULTURAL, LIBRARY & RECREATIONAL				
Administration	$324,364	$324,088	$331,663	2.3%
Cultural Services & Facilities	1,303,519	1,470,435	1,695,228	15.3%
Library	1,556,474	1,475,955	1,652,838	12.0%
Parks & Recreation	7,418,029	7,886,439	8,850,856	12.2%
TOTAL CULTURAL, LIBRARY **& RECREATIONAL**	10,602,386	11,156,917	12,530,585	12.3%
TRANSFERS TO OTHER FUNDS	(324,751)	(345,298)	(343,949)	-0.4%
NET OPERATING CULTURAL, LIBRARY **& RECREATIONAL**	$10,277,635	$10,811,619	$12,186,636	12.7%
COMMUNITY PLANNING & **ENVIRONMENTAL**				
Administration	$164,844	$184,525	$186,808	1.2%
Building Permits & Inspections	614,477	647,587	684,840	5.8%
Economic Affairs	332,053	314,771	344,815	9.5%
Engineering	2,614,753	2,823,280	2,870,447	1.7%
Natural Resources	392,435	494,308	517,591	4.7%
Planning	678,307	721,942	801,939	11.1%
Transportation Services	1,363,529	1,282,486	1,516,715	18.3%
TOTAL COMMUNITY PLANNING **& ENVIRONMENTAL**	6,160,398	6,468,879	6,923,155	7.0%
TRANSFERS TO OTHER FUNDS	(1,101,501)	(70,969)	(65,904)	7.1%
NET OPERATING COMMUNITY PLANNING **& ENVIRONMENTAL**	$5,058,897	$6,397,910	$6,857,251	7.2%

Note: Existing departments are clustered under broad service area (programs). Departmental lines are maintained.

Source: Adapted from Dennis Strachota,1994. *The Best of Governmental Budgeting: A Guide to Preparing Budget Documents.* Chicago, IL: Government Finance Officers Association, Exhibit 3-11.

TABLE V. ZERO-BASED BUDGET FORMAT: DECISION PACKAGES FOR THE TEAM POLICING DECISION UNIT

City of Wichita, Kansas

Decision Unit

Decision Packages (reflect contingency budgets–different funding scenarios)

TEAM POLICING

ADAM AND BAKER TEAM POLICING
Budget Unit Goal: To protect life and property, prevent crime, respond to all calls for service from citizens, enforce City ordinances, State and Federal laws, investigate and follow-up assigned cases and improve response time.

Year 1978
Budget (000): 4,335.1 millions of $
Positions: 292

1979 Service level options

No.	Cost (000) S/L	Cost (000) Cum.	Positions S/L	Positions Cum.	Dept. rank	City rank
1.	3,878.6	3,878.6	262	262	1/60	2
2.	336.9	4,215.5	28	290	3/60	7
3.	27.2	4,242.7	2	292	16/60	148
4.	148.9	4,391.6	18	310	37/60	PSP
5.	163.4	4,555.0	12	322	46/60	343

Service level narrative
1. *Quality Reduction and Increased Citizen Risk,* Provides service to the citizens in emergency situations and the officers would respond to cases of a less serious nature. Response time will average 12 minutes per call. This level calls for 256 commissioned officers, 6 civilians, 66 marked (blue and white) vehicles, and 27 unmarked vehicles. These officers provide 24-hour police service to the citizenry. Investigative follow-up and crime scene processing is curtailed.

2. *Minimum Preventative Patrol.* Provides twenty-seven commissioned officers and one clerk typist, who are needed to provide beat officers to answer citizen request calls with a 2 minute per call reduction in the response time from 12 minutes to 10 minutes.

3. *Interaction with USD #259.* Provides for the reinstatement of two school liasion police officers who coordinate programs in the schools in two of the team policing areas. At this level, a school liason officer will be available in each of the six team policing areas.

4. *Adds Eighteen Police Officers to Reduce Response Time.* Adds eighteen police officers to provide coverage in the patrol function for vacations, emergency leave, in-service training, and back-up officers. At this level, response time for calls will be reduced from 10 minutes to 9 minutes per call. Positions are funded effective 1 April 1979 (9 months). Costs include $136,049 for salaries and $12,818 for initial uniforms and equipment.

5. *Improved Supervision and investigation.* Adds six detectives to insure more follow-up investigations, to accelerate the investigation process, and to improve clearance percentage; and six lieutenants to provide quality control through supervision and shortened span of control.

Note: S/L-Service level
Cum-Cumulative (including service levels below the line)
Dept. rank -Department head's rank of the service package/total number of service packages in the Police Services Department (all decision units combined)
City rank -Executive's rank of the service package out of all service packages forwarded by all City departments for their service units
PSP-Postponed; not ranked

Source: Adapted from Richard Aronson and Eli Schwartz, *Management Policies in Local Government Finance,* 2nd Ed. Washington, D.C.: International City Management Association, Figure 5-10, P 112.

likely to be candidates for drastic reductions or elimination (e.g., those affected by court rulings, entitlements, contractual obligations, or earmarking) and should be funded. Thus, each organizational unit is asked to develop two requests—one for the activities to be included in its target budget (funding level pre-established by the budget office) and another for activities it would like to have funded, money permitting. All items on the unfunded "wish" list are ranked first by the department/program, then by the chief executive before being passed to the legislative body. Target-based budget formats often incorporate performance data (past and projected).

TBB proponents see it as more flexible, realistic, and efficient than ZBB. The target-base can easily be shifted to reflect economic and political realities. TBB also reduces paperwork by eliminating the need to formulate decision packages for the sure-to-be-funded programs and activities. It also strengthens the role of program managers by permitting them to allocate resources in the way they best see fit. Opponents see TBB's flexibility as a major weakness whereby irresponsible managers are encouraged to protect pet projects from review by including them as part of the target-based budget request.

Some federal agencies use a variant of target-based budgeting, along with a wide variety of state and local governments. A number of experts also see a close parallel between TBB and Canada's envelope budgeting.

Performance Budget Formats

The need to know the effectiveness as well as the efficiency of a government's expenditures has been a high priority of constituents and elected officials for quite some time. Some track the emergence of performance budgets to the Hoover Commission report issued in 1949. This report called for budgeting reforms to improve the effectiveness of service delivery management. Others trace performance budgeting further back—to the mid-1910s in the case of New York City. A renewed interest in performance budgeting occurred in the 1990s at all levels, largely in response to scarce resources and greater public skepticism about the quantity and quality of government-provided services. The typical performance budget format incorporates elements of both line-item and program budgeting formats.

The first step in developing a performance-based budget format is for government administrators and policymakers to formulate goals and objectives for various activities or services provided by each department or organizational unit. The next step involves developing performance measures that are valid indicators by which to gauge whether goals and objectives have been met. Ultimately, a link between cost and output must be made, thereby permitting an evaluation of the efficiency and effectiveness of the endeavor and the development of management responses. Sometimes this link is only an indirect one whereby objectives, spending levels and trends, and performance outputs for a department or activity are reported in separate sections clustered together in a budget document.

Four types of performance measures are commonly reported in different sections of the performance budget format: demand, workload, productivity, and effectiveness. Mikesell (1995) in *Fiscal Administration* defines these as follows: "The *demand* section defines the expected operating environment for the budget year, with prior-and current-year levels for comparison. The *workload* section establishes how the operating unit intends to respond to expected demand by allocation of staff time. The *productivity* [efficiency] section presents cost per activity unit that emerges from the budgeted costs. The *effectiveness* section shows the unit's performance against criteria that indicate whether the unit is accomplishing its intended objectives" (p. 171).

Table VI is an example of how performance data are incorporated into the budget document for a Patrol Services program within a Police Department. In this example, performance objectives and data for the program follow sections reporting expenditure, personnel, and revenue data (past and projected). Demand, workload, efficiency, and effectiveness performance indicators are included.

Proponents of performance budget data are convinced their inclusion in a budget document promotes efficiency, effectiveness, and accountability, and ultimately improves management. Opponents complain that performance objectives are often arbitrary and selected purely because "good" data already exist, thereby minimizing the need to establish new, expensive data collection and analytic mechanisms. Another shortcoming is that some indicators selected are not valid measures of the outputs they are purported to capture nor are they comparable across organizational units. The tendency for the measures selected to emphasize quantity rather than quality is yet another shortcoming of performance budget formats, although more governments are including citizen satisfaction survey results to address the lack-of-quality-indicators criticism.

"Performance target," or "benchmark," formats are another popular variation of performance budgets. The federal government has enacted legislation establishing benchmarks in the educational arena. Many state legislatures have also enacted legislation mandating the establishment of benchmarks and the collection and reporting of target-related performance data in department or agency budget proposal packets. A 1991 survey found than 60 percent of the states require performance measures as part of their budget requests; some three-fourths of local governments collect performance data in their budgetary process. Besides elected officials and citizens, professional associations like the Government Finance Officers Association (GFOA) have promoted the benchmark principle.

TABLE VI. A PERFORMANCE BUDGET FORMAT

City of Fort Collins, Colorado

The program analysis highlights budget issues and changes in operations from the prior year. It includes information on a staffing reorganization.

Line-Item Format
Line-item expenditures and transfers are presented for three budget periods.

Personnel Format
Shows the mix of positions allocated to this program (e.g., hourly vs. volunteers).

Revenue Format
The source of financing for this program is also displayed.

Performance Format
These program objectives for the budget year tie to the performance measures presented.

Efficiency and effectiveness measures are presented for three budget periods.

Comments Section

CITY OF FORT COLLINS

PROGRAM	008301	PATROL SERVICES
FUND	101	GENERAL FUND
DEPARTMENT	800000	POLICE SERVICES

PROGRAM MISSION

To provide a full range of police patrol services, including crime prevention, trafffic enforcement, traffic and community problem solving.

PROGRAM ANALYSIS

We will continue using alternative response methods, allowing prompt and effective response to citizen demands for service in the most cost-effective manner. We will continue to emphasize problem-oriented policing whereby issues are addressed through application of problem-solving efforts. Patrol Services' Selective Enforcement Unit (SEU) will continue to concentrate on problem resolution within the community, and the Traffic Unit will continue to address traffic-related issues in 1993. In an effort to expand the application of problem-solving efforts the following changes will take place in 1993: The Records Lieutenant position will move to Patrol to coordinate problem-oriented policing efforts. In addition, the Crime Prevention Coordinator will move from Community Affairs to Patrol, and the Crime Analyst from Records to Patrol – both to be supervised by the Problem-Oriented Policing Lieutenant. For 1993, a DARE officer position has been added to this program.

EXPENDITURE	LAST ACTUAL 1991	CURR ADOPTED BUDGET 1992	REVISED BUDGET 1992	APPROVED BUDGET 1993
PERSONAL SERVICES	3,982,715	4,019,690	4,317,320	4,492,928
CONTRACTUAL	857,202	864,040	803,724	830,562
COMMODITIES	186,728	186,639	185,991	181,975
CAPITAL OUTLAY	12,446	0	26,772	0
TRANSFERS/OTHER	0	0	0	0
TOTAL	5,041,091	5,070,369	5,333,807	5,505,465

PERSONNEL				
CLASS/UNCLSS	82.00	84.00	84.00	88.00
SEASONAL	.00	.00	.00	.00
HOURLY	.00	.00	.00	.00
CONTRACTUAL	.00	.00	.00	.00
VOLUNTEER	.00	.00	.00	.00
TOTAL	82.00	84.00	84.00	88.00

REVENUE				
GENERAL FUND	5,024,206	5,070,369	5,321,015	5,505,465
GRANT	16,885	0	12,792	0
TOTAL	5,041,091	5,070,369	5,333,807	5,505,465

PROGRAM PERFORMANCE BUDGET

| PROGRAM | 008301 | PATROL SERVICES |

OBJECTIVES 1. To meet 100% of citizens' requests for service.
2. Continue to use alternative response methods to most effectively utilize sworn officers.
3. Maintain 1992 response times.

PROGRAM INDICATORS	1991 ACTUAL	1992 BUDGET	1992 REVISED	1993 BUDGET
DEMAND				
1. Total Incidents	71,186	55,395	76,716	80,550
2. Population Served	89,439	90,709	90,709	92,079
3. Incidents per 1000 Population	796	611	846	875
WORKLOAD				
1. Dispatched Calls Responded to	35,091	39,452	36,846	38,688
2. Dispatched Calls per Non-Supervisory Police Officer and CSO*	516	680	526	545
3. Dispatched Calls Taken by CSO*	6,667	7,200	7,369	7,738
PRODUCTIVE				
1. Per Capita Cost–Patrol	$54.58	$54.14	$57.04	$57.90
EFFECTIVE				
1. Response Times (minutes):				
Priority 1–Routine	17.00	19.86	19.00	19.00
Priority 2–Urgent	7.00	5.41	8.00	8.00
Priority 3–Emergency	4.00	4.00	3.00	3.00
2. % Calls Delayed (stacked) More than 5 Minutes	28.00 %	40.00 %	28.00 %	28.00 %
3. % Dispatched Calls Handled by CSOs*	19.00 %	20.00 %	20.00 %	20.00 %

COMMENTS * CSO is Community Service Officer

Note: In this city, the service format is used for all programs presented within the operating budget.

Source: Adapted from Dennis Strachota, 1994. *The Best of Governmental Budgeting: A Guide to Preparing Budget Documents.* Chicago, IL: Government Finance Officers Association, Exhibit 2-3.

TABLE VII. A SITE-BASED FORMAT

Savannah-Chatham County Public
Schools, Georgia

FY 1993 BUDGET - EXPENDITURES BY SCHOOL

SCHOOL ELEMENTARY	SALARIES & FRINGE	DISTRICT SUPPLIES	MEDIA MATERIALS	TEXTBOOKS	EQUIPMENT	FIELD TRIPS	OTHER SUPPLIES	SERVICES	STAFF DEVELOPMENT	SUBTOTAL	PROGRAM IMPROVE	TOTAL
BARTOW	$1,472,739	$39,299	$3,4472	$1,857	$0	$3,149	$18,505	$9,824	$5,711	$1,494,354	30	$1,494,356
BLOOMINGDALE												
BUTLER												
EAST BROAD												
ELLIS												
GADSDEN												
GARRISON												
GOULD												
HAVEN												
HAYNES												
HEARD												
HESSE												
HODGE												
HOWARD												
ISLANDS												
ISLE OF HOPE												
LAROO-TIBET												
LOW												
POOLER												
PT. WENTWORTH												
PULASKI												
O. SMITH												
SPENSER												
SPRAGUE												
THUNDERBOLT												
WHITE BLUFF												
WHITNEY												
SUBTOTAL												
MIDDLE												
SUBTOTAL												
HIGH												
SUBTOTAL												
TOTAL												

Note: Site-based budgeting is becoming more common among school districts. This particular summary presents major object of expenditure line-item data for each elementary, middle, and high school in the school district.

Source: Dennis Strachota, 1994. *The Best of Governmental Budgeting: A Guide to Preparing Budget Documents.* Chicago, IL: Government Finance Officers Association, Exhibit 3-15.

TABLE VIII. Capital Budget Format with Geographical Mapping Element

FY96 CAPITAL BUDGET/FY96-FY00 CIP PROJECT DETAIL

GENERAL PROJECT DATA:	COMPREHENSIVE PLAN INFORMATION:
Project Name: Caspersen Beach	Project Listed in CIE? Yes
Access	Comp. Plan Reference:
Functional Area: Traffic Circ.	
Department: Transportation	LOS/Concurrency Related: No
Location: BUS41 to County Park	

PROJECT NEED CRITERIA	
GROWTH	
DEFIENCY	X
OTHER	X

PROJECT SCHEDULE	FY96	FY97	FY98	FY99	FY00
	1 2 3 4	1 2 3 4	1 2 3 4	1 2 3 4	1 2 3 4
Proj. Mgt.					
Design/Arch					
Lanc./ROW	■				
Construct					

PROJECT DESCRIPTION, RATIONALE & OPERATING BUDGET IMPACT

DESCRIPTION:

Reconstruct 1.75 miles of two lane roadway with four foot wide bike lanes and sidewalks. The project involves reconstruction of portions of the existing roadways. Airport Ave. and Harbor Drive. Design (FY92) was completed in prior years. This project is being constructed as part of a dual tax settlement with the City of Venice. Right of way expenditures in FY96 are for payment of anticipated court-ordered right of way judgment cases.

RATIONALE:

The project is being provided as a by-pass to Caspersen Beach to avoid cut-through traffic on local and residential streets in Venice. It will also improve pedestrian and bicycle circulation and safety. The project is consistent with Comp. Plan Traffic Circulation Policy 1.1.1 as it relates to safety and efficiency of the transportation network and Policies as they pertain to pedestrian and bicycle safety.

OPERATING BUDGET IMPACT:

Construction of the roadway will add 3.6 lane-miles to the county's maintained roadway system. This will result in an increase of $12,250 in annual operations and maintenance costs.

	Prior	FY96	FY97	FY98	FY99	FY00	Prior-FY00
EXPENDITURE PLAN (000's)							
Project Mang.	30						30
Design/Arch	551						551
Land/ROW	54	38					92
Construction	1,711						1,711
Total Project Costs	2,346	38	0	0	0	0	2,384
FUNDING PLAN (000's)							
Surtax	2,090	38					2,128
Gas Tax	56						56
Other	200						200
Total Funding	2,346	38	0	0	0	0	2,384
OPERATING BUDGET IMPACT (000's)							
Personal Services		6	6	7	7	7	33
Non-personal		6	6	7	7	7	33
Operating Capital							
Total Operating	0	12	12	14	14	14	66

Planning Deptartment   Project # 85721

N. RIVER ROAD
VENICE AVE.
CENTER ROAD
U.S. 41

Source: Department of Budget, Sarasota County, Florida.

Geographical/Political Formats

The emergence of site-based and geographical information system (GIS)-based formats is a relatively new phenomenon that emerged in the 1990s. Typically used in conjunction with the more standard formats, these geographically based formats primarily focus on permitting some determination of whether spending equity has been achieved. They are also an outgrowth of the decentralization movement aimed at strengthening the involvement of constituents in the budget and policymaking processes.

A *site-based format* reports budget information for different geographical locations where a service/program/facility is provided. It is most commonly used by school districts. Each school site is treated as an organizational unit. This type of format permits comparisons of funding across object-of-expenditure categories for like types of schools (e.g., elementary, middle, secondary). Table VII is an example of such a format.

Site-based formats are quite popular with policymakers and constituents, who find them easy to understand and use for comparison. Critics attack these formats for promoting comparisons of schools that may not match, especially in terms of student or teacher profiles.

A *geographical information system (GIS) format* visually graphs budget information, most often capital projects, onto census tracts, planning districts, or neighborhoods located within a government's boundaries. Table VIII is an example of a capital budget format that includes a map showing where the proposed project will be located.

A less-common variant, a *geo-political format,* maps budget data onto elected officials' districts in jurisdictions where legislators are elected via single-member districts. In addition to the budget information, district socioeconomic characteristics are reported to show policymakers and constituents that the spending needs and the ability of residents to pay for services may differ considerably across a community, state, or region.

Critics of GIS-based formats, particularly those mapped onto political geographies, claim that rather than promoting equity, they do the opposite. Opponents charge that a district's representative and constituents tend to measure fairness as equal distribution of goods, services, and/or facilities across districts rather than in terms of comparative district need or ability to pay. However, proponents of GIS-based formats disagree and argue that policymakers and constituents alike are perfectly capable of making needs-based equity judgments.

Personnel Information Format

Rare is a government budget document that does not contain a personnel summary section since the biggest expenditure category for most governments is generally Personal Services. Consequently, policymakers and citizens alike often want more, not less, information on the number of employees and their cost to government.

At a minimum, a budget document will report the number of full-time equivalent employees for each organizational unit. Some personnel formats also report data on full-time versus part-time employees, permanent versus temporary employees, or filled versus budgeted positions. Some report the salary range for each position classification along with the number of employees in each classification. Table IX is an example of a format presenting the salary range and total number of full-time equivalent (FTE) personnel in each classification.

Often the personnel summary part of a budget document includes a comments section. This allows an organizational unit to indicate reasons for changes in its personnel levels and costs, ranging from court orders (e.g., more jail supervisors) to reorganizations or shifts in its customer or user base. Comments, or explanation, space is also often included in many other sections of a budget document (e.g., object of expenditure, performance, revenue).

TABLE IX. PERSONNEL SUMMARY: SALARY RANGE AND FTE FORMAT

DEPARTMENT STAFF: FIRE DEPARTMENT

Positions	Monthly Salary Range (1.0 FTE)	Approved Full-Time Equivalents (FTE)
Fire Chief	4,119–5,572	1.00
Assistant Fire Chief	3,612–4,884	1.00
EMS Officer	3,295–4,459	1.00
Captain/Shift Commander	3,295–4,459	3.00
Training Officer	3,295–4,459	1.00
Fire Prevention Manager	3,295–4,459	1.00
Lieutenant/Team Leader	2,480–3,534	12.00
Firefighter II/Paramedic	2,446–3,352	6.00
Fire Inspector	2,264–3,227	1.00
Firefighter I	2,264–3,227	18.00
Temporary Part-Time Firefighter	N/A	.50
Firefighter II Apprentice	1,835	3.00
Firefighter I Apprentice	1,698–1,766	6.00
Administrative Specialist	2,220–2,712	1.00
Accounting Specialist IV	2,010–2,457	1.00
Secretary II	1,639–2,002	1.00
FIRE DEPARTMENT TOTAL		57.50

NOTE: Salary ranges reflect FY 93–94 class and compensation schedules until final agreement is reached with all bargaining units. N/A includes city council appointee salary ranges and hourly/seasonal rates that vary by position.

SOURCE: City of Corvalis, Oregon, Annual Budget, fiscal year 1994–95.

TABLE X. Format Linking Capital Expenditures to Current Operating Budget

**New Castle County
Fiscal Year 1995 Capital Budget
Annual Operating Budget Impact**

Departmental Summary

The 1995 Capital Budget and the Annual Operating Budget Impact are summarized below. Additional information is available in the Departmental Profiles beginning on Page 131.

		Annual Operating Budget Impact			
FY'95 Capital Budget		Personnel Service Costs	Other Operating Costs	Debt Service Costs	Total
Department	Appropriations				
Public Works	$7,683,000		$2,000	$533,500	$535,500
Water Resources	730,000			63,875	63,875
Parks and Recreation	2,399,000	$36,000	20,000	185,000	241,000
New Castle County Airport	3,140,000		13,000	98,000	111,000
Administrative Services	2,689,000	(84,000)	35,000	560,000	511,000
Public Safety	915,000		6,000	146,000	152,000
Libraries	5,884,000	74,000	201,000	109,000	384,000
Community Development & Housing	500,000			43,750	43,750
Executive	410,000			36,000	36,000
Total	$24,350,000	$26,000	$277,000	$1,775,125	$2,078,125

Source: New Castle County, Delaware. *Fiscal Year 1995 Comprehensive Annual Budget Summary.*

Revenue Information Formats

Historically, government budget documents have included revenue summary information for the jurisdiction at large in a detailed line-item format. The drawback of relying exclusively on summary data became evident following the first round of federal budget cuts in the early years of the Reagan administration. Those cuts caught many state and local governments in the embarrassing situation of having to acknowledge to the press and citizenry that they did not know which departments, programs, or activities would be most affected by the reductions. Now it is common for revenue information to be presented for each organizational unit for which expenditure data are reported. Table VI is an example of a organizational unit's budget with a revenue source element.

The advantage of including revenue source data for each organizational unit is that it allows policymakers to gauge which units may be most adversely affected by sharp reductions in elastic revenues (intergovernmental, sales tax, income tax). A disadvantage is that calculations may be more precise for functions funded via an earmarked revenue (e.g., a gas tax for road improvements) than for general activities funded via unearmarked sources.

Capital Improvement Project Information Formats

Capital improvements are defined by the GFOA as "major construction, acquisition, or renovation activities which add value to a government's physical assets or significantly increase their useful life." Typically, these improvements are either funded by current operating revenues or the sale of government bonds. In either case, they are often multi-year in scope but have at least some impact on the current operating budget.

The trend has been to require organizational units to report some detail on the impact of proposed capital improvements on their operating budget. Such a requirement often follows a widely publicized incident whereby a capital project was completed midyear, but no funds were budgeted to permit it to go on-line.

Annual debt service costs (principal plus interest) must also be reflected in a government's operating budget.

TABLE XI. DISTINGUISHED BUDGET PRESENTATION AWARDS PROGRAM: AWARDS CRITERIA, GOVERNMENT FINANCE OFFICERS ASSOCIATION

The Budget as a Policy Document

1. The document should include a coherent statement of organizationwide financial and programmatic policies and goals that address long-term concerns and issues.

2. The document should describe the organization's short-term financial and operational policies that guide the development of the budget for the upcoming year.

3. The document should include a coherent statement of goals and objectives of organizational units (e.g., departments, division, offices or programs).

4. Mandatory: The document shall include a budget message that articulates priorities and issues for the budget for the new year. The message should describe significant changes in priorities from the current year and explain the factors that led to those changes. The message may take one of several forms (e.g., transmittal letter, budget summary section).

The Budget as a Financial Plan

1. The document should include and describe all funds that are subject to appropriation.

2. Mandatory: The document shall present a summary of major revenues and expenditures, as well as other financing sources and uses, to provide an overview of the total resources budgeted by the organization.

3. Mandatory: The document shall include summaries of revenues, and other resources, and of expenditures for prior year actual, current year budget and/or estimated current year actual, and proposed budget year.

4. Mandatory: The document shall describe major revenue sources, explain the underlying assumptions for the revenue estimates and discuss significant revenue trends.

5. Mandatory: The document shall include projected changes in fund balances, as defined by the entity in the document, for governmental funds included in the budget presentation, including all balances potentially available for appropriation.

6. The document should include budgeted capital expenditures and a list of major capital projects for the budget year, whether authorized in the operating budget or in a separate capital budget.

7. The document should describe if and to what extent capital improvements or other major capital spending will impact the entity's current and future operating budget. The focus is on reasonably quantifiable additional costs and savings (direct or indirect) or other service impacts that result from capital spending.

8. Mandatory: The document shall include financial data on current debt obligations, describe the relationship between current debt levels and legal debt limits, and explain the effects of existing debt levels on current and future operations.

9. Mandatory: The document shall explain the basis of budgeting for all funds, whether GAAP, cash, modified accrual, or some other statutory basis.

The Budget as an Operations Guide

1. Mandatory: The document shall describe activities, services or functions carried out by organizational units.

2. The document should provide objective methods (quantitative and/or qualitative) of measurement of results by unit or program. Information should be included for prior year actual, current year budget and/or estimate, and budget year.

3. Mandatory: The document shall include an organization chart(s) for the entire organization.

4. Mandatory: A schedule(s) or summary table(s) of personnel or position counts for prior, current and budgeted years shall be provided, including descriptions of significant changes in levels of staffing or reorganizations planned for the budget year.

The Budget as a Communication Device

1. The document should provide summary information, including an overview of significant budgetary issues, trends, and resource choices. Summary information should be presented within the budget document either in a separate section (e.g., executive summary) or integrated within the transmittal letter or other overview sections.

2. The document should explain the effect, if any, of other planning processes (e.g., strategic plans, long-range financial plans, capital improvement plans) upon the budget and budget process.

3. Mandatory: The document shall describe the process for preparing, reviewing and adopting the budget for the coming fiscal year. It should also describe the procedures for amending the budget after adoption. If a separate capital budget process is used, a description of the process and its relationship to the operating budget should be provided.

4. Mandatory: Charts and graphs shall be used, where appropriate, to highlight financial and statistical information. Narrative interpretation should be provided when the messages conveyed by the graphs are not self-evident.

5. The document should provide narrative, tables, schedules, crosswalks or matrices to show the relationship between different revenue and expenditure classifications (e.g., funds, programs, organization units).

6. Mandatory: The document shall include a table of contents to make it easy to locate information in the document.

7. A glossary should be included for any terminology (including abbreviations and acronyms) that is not readily understood by a reasonably informed lay reader.

8. The document should include statistical and supplemental data that describe the organization and the community or population it serves, and provide other pertinent background information related to the services provided.

9. The document should be printed and formatted in such a way to enhance understanding and utility of the document to the lay reader. It should be attractive, consistent and oriented to the reader's needs.

SOURCE: "Distinguished Budget Presentation Awards Program Guidelines" Annual, Government Finance Officers Association, 180 North Michigan Avenue, Suite 800, Chicago, IL.

Thus, newer capital budget formats project the debt service costs generated by proposed capital expenditures for that fiscal year. Table X is an example of a format projecting each department's planned capital expenditures for that fiscal year, along with their impact on the personnel service, other operating, and debt service components of the annual operating budget.

What Constitutes a Good Budget Document Format?

The GFOA created its Distinguished Budget Presentation Awards Program in 1984. Benchmarks were established by which to judge a budget document's effectiveness in four areas: as a policy document, a financial plan, an operations guide, and a communications device. Table XI lists the specific assessment criteria.

The popularity of the GFOA awards program helps explain why many state and local government budget documents are now constructed using a variety of budget formats—line-item, program, zero-based, performance, geographical, capital, personnel, and revenue. Budget documents are also likely to include a government's organizational chart, a wide range of very appealing graphics (pie charts, bar charts, line graphs), policy statements from key elected officials, community profiles, key economic assumptions, long-range forecasts, and debt summaries. Even the federal government's budget document is changing due to the Government Performance and Results Act of 1993 that requires several federal agencies to prepare budgets containing performance elements in addition to the more traditional elements.

The executive director of GFOA has best summarized the status of budget formats in the introduction to *The Best of Governmental Budgeting* (1994): "Most budgets are no longer captives of endless line-item detail with little or no policy discussion. Instead, the majority of budgets are replete with performance indicators and predictions of both short- and long-term policy implications. Moreover, budgets have become powerful communication tools with the advent of affordable desktop publishing and graphics software."

A government's choice of formats dictates whether the primary emphasis of its budget will be on control, management, planning, or accountability—or a combination of each. Format choices determine the usefulness of a budget document to program managers, elected officials, and constituents.

SUSAN A. MACMANUS

BIBLIOGRAPHY

Hennessy, Barbara R., 1991. "Communicating Financial Data to Nonaccountants: A Case for Popular Reporting." *Government Finance Review*, vol. 7 (October): 7–9.

Mikesell, John L., 1995. *Fiscal Administration: Analysis and Applications for the Public Sector*, 4th ed. Belmont, CA: Wadsworth.

Phyrr, Peter A., 1977. "The Zero-Based Approach to Government Budgeting." *Public Administration Review*, vol. 37 (January/February): 1–8.

Prenchand, A., 1993. "A Cross National Analysis of Financial Management Practices." In Thomas Lynch and Lawrence Martin, eds., *Handbook of Comparative Public Budgeting and Financial Management*. New York: Marcel Dekker: 87–99.

Rubin, Irene, 1991. "Budgeting for Our Time: Target Base Budgeting." *Public Budgeting & Finance*, vol. 11 (Fall): 9–14.

Schick, Allen, ed., 1980. *Perspectives on Budgeting*. Washington, D.C.: American Society for Public Administration.

Solano, Paul L. and Marvin R. Brams, 1987. "Budgeting." In J. Richard Aronson and Eli Schwartz, eds., *Management Policies in Local Government Finance*, 3rd ed. Washington, D.C.: International City Management Association: 118–157.

Strachota, Dennis, 1994. *The Best of Governmental Budgeting: A Guide to Preparing Budget Documents*. Chicago, IL: Government Finance Officers Association.

Tigue, Patricia and James Greene, Jr., 1994. "Performance Measurement: The Link to Effective Government." *The Government Finance Officers Association Research Bulletin* (April): 1–8.

Wildavsky, Aaron B., 1975. *Budgeting: A Comparative Theory of Budgeting Processes*. Boston: Little, Brown.

BUDGET GUIDANCE.

Instructions to agencies as to how they are to prepare their requests for the next budget year.

In most governments, building a budget begins in part with agencies preparing requests for the upcoming budget year. Major amounts of staff time are required to calculate what resources will be requested, and still more time is needed by higher-level authorities to review the agencies' budget requests. In this labor-intensive endeavor, some guidance is desirable, if not essential, in directing agencies as to how they are to proceed. Guidance informs agencies about the assumptions to be made in preparing requests. Without such guidance, agencies would be left to their own wits in deciding how much to request.

Budget guidance can be thought of as establishing the rules of the game for preparing budget requests. Certainly, in any game, the various players need to have some rules to follow. Preparation instructions typically include a standard set of budget concepts and definitions, such as what constitutes a capital expenditure or how employees and their benefits are to be counted. The instructions include supporting documents (paper forms and/or computer templates) that calculated how agencies will prepare and submit their requests. Circular A-11, issued by the Office of Management and Budget, accomplishes this task for the federal government.

Who Issues Budget Guidance?

Governments vary widely regarding who issues budget guidance. Budget reform since the early 1900s has emphasized executive budgeting. In these systems, the budget office, acting on behalf of the chief executive, issues guidance to agencies. Such guidance is seen as helping to mold requests that will eventually constitute an overall package that reflects the priorities of the mayor, governor, or president.

Many governments, however, do not have executive budget systems. In governments where the executive has limited budgetary powers, guidance may be issued jointly by the executive and legislative offices. Texas, for instance, has had a Legislative Budget Board that includes executive and legislative officers who together prepare budget instructions for the agencies. Kentucky has had a legislative-not executive–Budget Review Office that issues budget instructions.

Why Use Budget Guidance?

If for no other reason, budget guidance is needed so that requests or budget proposals have some degree of consistency from one agency to the next. Standardized forms are utilized so that information of a given type can be found in the same location on the request for Agency A as that for Agency B. When the time comes for compiling requests into a single budget proposal, such uniformity is essential.

Guidance is needed for uniformity from the standpoint of the assumptions made in calculating requests. Without some direction being provided, one agency might ask for a vast increase in funding, regardless of obvious financial constraints being faced by the government, while another agency requests minimal funding in recognition of those constraints.

Centrally provided guidance can instruct agencies how to anticipate possible price and wage increases in the coming budget year. Should prices be expected to remain largely stable or increase by 5 percent or even more?

In the interest of agencies being parsimonious in their use of staff time, preparation should avoid long hours of calculating requests that will be promptly rejected. Guidance issued by a mayor's budget office can be helpful in instructing agencies about what types of new initiatives are likely to be well received and which ones will not. The guidance can help mold the budget to the policy agenda of the political leadership and more generally encourage allocation of resources in ways that further the missions of agencies. In this manner, budgeting can be an integral part of strategic planning.

Types of Guidance

At least six forms of guidance are used, with the first being the use of a dollar ceiling. This method entails some set of calculations by a central unit, such as a governor's budget office. A typical concern is to forecast available revenues for the coming fiscal year and then derive a budget ceiling for each agency so that when compiled, the agencies' requests will be within bounds of expected revenues. The method is particularly attractive from the standpoint of producing requests that are politically realistic, namely would not require expenditure increases that could only be funded through higher tax rates. However, this form of fixed-ceiling budgeting has the distinct drawback of judging the merits of agencies' needs before hearing any evidence.

Current services guidance, the second type, has gained wide acceptance at all levels of government. Agencies are instructed to prepare budget requests that would allow continuation of services at current standards. For example, the state park system may have standards regarding the use of lifeguards at swimming facilities, and if beach attendance is expected to rise, then the number of lifeguards will need to be increased and budgeted accordingly. Some jurisdictions leave agencies largely to themselves in making such current services calculations, whereas others provide some central guidance, such as providing baseline figures regarding inflation, wage increases, and the like.

Governments that face severe resource constraints or that simply wish to find means of increasing the efficiency of their operations may utilize the third form of guidance—minimum services. This type of guidance indicates that agencies are to submit budget requests that will only allow for essential operations. The guidance presupposes that agencies will be required to indicate how major budget cuts might be made while maintaining minimum services. In a school district, for instance, nonessential support of various student activities, such as clubs, might be a target for budget cutting when a minimum services request must be prepared. Of course, it is arguable what constitutes "minimum." For a state welfare department required to comply with federal and state laws, "minimum" is providing a predetermined level of payments to all individuals who are eligible and apply for benefits. More ambiguous is the situation of a police department. If a city uses two officers in each patrol car, would "minimum" be reducing the number to one officer? Such a cutback might jeopardize the safety of both the officer and the vehicle.

Fourth, guidance can require that agencies separately budget program improvements. An agency's existing budget might be treated as its base, whereas program improvements are considered additions to the base. This form of guidance typically requires more detailed information for the recommended improvements than is required for the base budget. For instance, an agency would be expected to show (1) how each line-item was calculated, such as salaries for specific types of personnel to be used, (2) what results can be expected from the improvement, such as improvements in clients' conditions, and (3) the expected costs and results over a multi-year period, such as over the next five years.

The fifth form, which entails ranking proposed budget changes, expects agencies to show what items have higher priority in their requests. A state central budget office might expect its highway department to indicate rankings of proposed budget increases for road maintenance projects, road replacement projects, and new road design and construction. The ranking method has been used widely over the years and helps executive and legislative decisionmakers understand the relative priorities of the agencies. The rankings can help emphasize that some changes are needed immediately, whereas others are urgent and still others have merit but are less pressing. Of course, the rankings may be based upon a set of criteria that differ from those of the chief executive or legislators. What may be urgent to a federal agency may be of little priority to the president. Ranking systems may be subject to administrative politics, in which items known to be of high priority to a mayor, for instance, are placed lower on a ranking list than other items. If the expectation is that items will be funded according to their rankings, then an agency may attempt to have the mayor fund its pet projects that have been given high rankings. If the mayor chooses to disregard the rankings, then complaints will be voiced that the rules of the game are being disregarded: "We were asked for our priority rankings and then they were ignored."

The sixth method is that of policy guidance. Whereas the other forms of guidance are largely policy neutral, the sixth one gives direction to agencies as to what types of policies and programs will receive favorable treatment upon review and which ones will not. The guidance might be of an overall nature, as in the case of a governor's budget office indicating to agencies that environmental programs might have high priority. Such guidance would encourage a state department of environmental resources to submit program initiative proposals, but the same would be the case for a department of community affairs that worked with local sewer authorities and a department of commerce that worked with corporations on air-pollution abatement.

Guidance can be directed at specific programs. The Office of Management and Budget has issued policy letters to federal agencies indicating which of their programs could expect to be well received and which ones required special documentation to avoid severe budget cutbacks or even potential elimination.

Policy guidance can be provided formally through a paper document (or comparable e-mail system) or more informally. A budget office can call a meeting of key departmental officials and brief them on what to expect in the new budget cycle that commences with budget preparation. In such a briefing session, department officials quickly learn what types of policies and programs will receive favorable treatment. Other nonwritten guidance may be in the form of one-on-one meetings between, for example, the governor (or budget director) and individual department officials.

Multiple Approaches to Budget Guidance

These six methods of budget guidance can be used in combination with one another. Some governments have asked agencies to prepare both current services and minimum services budgets for the same upcoming budget year. This approach sometimes has been used under the rubric of zero-base budgeting. In other situations, departments are given dollar ceilings within which to budget but also a set of program priorities that include expectations that certain programs will be enhanced. Under such circumstances, a department's budget request would show how expected program improvements would be funded while staying under a fixed ceiling. The request would almost certainly indicate how "savings" would be achieved through budget reductions in other components of the department's budget.

Usage in State Governments

A long-term study of state government budget offices illustrates the extent of usage of these various practices and how usage has changed over time. All six forms increased in popularity between 1975 and 1990. As can be seen from Table I, more than half of the states in 1990 used current services guidance, program improvement guidance, ranking systems, and policy guidance. Rankings were most popular, with 89 percent of the states reporting usage. Only 11 percent of the states reported they used no form of guidance. Kansas and Vermont reported using all six forms of guidance, and nine other states reported using five forms (Arkansas, Connecticut, Kentucky, Louisiana, Montana, New Hampshire, North Dakota, Utah and Virginia).

Information Needed to Respond to Budget Guidance

One set of constraints on the use of multiple approaches to budget guidance relates to the ability to collect, manipulate, and comprehend information. As recently as the early 1980s, many government departments were severely constrained in their handling of data because of computer technology limitations. Recent progress in technology,

TABLE I. BUDGET GUIDANCE IN STATE BUDGET PREPARATION

	PERCENT USING GUIDANCE	
Type of Guidance	1975	1990
Dollar ceiling	18	45
Current services	17	61
Minimum services	0	24
Program improvements	26	65
Ranking	28	89
Policy guidance	42	60
No guidance	43	11

SOURCE: Surveys conducted by Robert D. Lee, Jr., Department of Public Administration, Pennsylvania State University.

however, allows agencies to submit budget requests in numerous formats.

What may not have changed, however, is the amount and quality of data collected by agencies. If all that is required is what can be called "resource" information, then compliance with multiple types of budget guidance is possible. By resource information is meant data regarding finances (revenues and expenditures) and personnel, which typically constitute the largest component of operating expenditures. Since computer information systems routinely record expenditures and revenues and personnel-related data, such as when people are hired, what they are paid, and the like, these computerized systems can be programmed to generate data needed in budget preparation.

A problem arises, however, with regard to program information or what is called "performance measurement." While there are numerous forms of measures, two critical ones are those that pertain to the work or activities performed by a program (often called "workload" and/or "outputs") and the resulting "impacts" on the program's target, namely clients or the environment (such as reducing water pollution caused by farm drainage into streams). Many governments have taken great strides in collecting such information, but others have not. In the latter situation, then, these governments cannot readily respond to guidance that asks for quantified programmatic information that might be called for in budget systems requiring the identification of program improvements or that provides for policy guidance. The federal government in the 1990s is attempting to upgrade its efforts in this area as it implements the Government Performance and Results Act of 1993.

In any government and within any department, wide variation exists over the quality of data being collected and compiled. Some data are quite reliable, while other data are largely worthless. Budget requests built on the latter are of little utility. Decisionmakers within the executive and legislative branches, then, must gain some sense of the quality of data, namely when to rely on agency data and when to file and forget them.

Even when program information is in abundance, problems remain. One problem is that of simply being able to digest what is available. Computers may be able to generate far more pieces of data and far more forms about departmental programs than the department staff can comprehend, and the problem is greater at the central budget office level, where the number of people may be quite limited in trying to examine agency budget submissions. Offices that issue guidance must be wary of having agencies submit budget requests in numerous formats that result in mountains of paper or masses of computer files that defy comprehension.

Guidance and the Quality of Decisions

While budget guidance has changed over time and governments make increasing use of multiple forms of guidance, left unanswered is whether budget guidance leads to improved budget preparation and whether better budget preparation improves the quality of decisionmaking. Certainly, budget requests can be no better than the systems upon which they are based. If agencies comply with the guidance provided them, then presumably budget requests are in formats that are more conducive to the needs of those who deliberate on budgets. Nevertheless, one must recognize that politics is a fundamental component of budgeting and that no budgetary technique, such as current services guidance or priority ranking, will circumvent political influences. The question, then, is whether these alternative techniques help political leaders in their quest for decisions that fit their priorities.

ROBERT D. LEE, JR.

BIBLIOGRAPHY

Clynch, Edward J. and Thomas P. Lauth, eds., 1991. *Governors, Legislatures, and Budgets: Diversity Across the American States.* New York: Greenwood.

Lee, Robert D., Jr., 1992. "The Use of Executive Guidance in State Budget Preparation." *Public Budgeting & Finance,* vol. 12 (Fall): 19–31.

U.S. Congressional Budget Office, 1993. *Using Performance Measures in the Federal Budget Process.* Washington: U.S. Government Printing Office.

U.S. General Accounting Office, 1992. *Program Performance Measures: Federal Agency Collection and Use of Performance Data.* Washington: U.S. Government Printing Office.

BUDGET PATTERNS. The non-legal aspects of the budget process; the informal budget tendencies that seem stable and predictable over time (see **agency strategies, Wildavsky, budget strategy**).

At the U.S. national level, agencies appear as advocates who ask for more, and reviewers in the parent department, the Office of Management and Budget (OMB), and Congress cut those requests. The period from the end of World War II until the early 1970s is sometimes referred to as the classic period in American budgeting. There was a recognizable budget process: Conflict over the budget among budget process participants was routinized and diminished by "informal understandings" between participants. These "informal understandings" included a balanced budget norm, even though budgets were never balanced and usually in a small deficit position (see **deficit**). There was agreement on the general outline of public policy. The economic climate exhibited sustained growth and this growth resulted in growing budgets and the sense that government could and should attack and solve many of society's problems. This ethos was particularly strong during the early 1960s. Thus budgetary growth became part of the political culture; budget claimants assumed that the next budget would be larger than the current budget and that the focus of budget discussion would be on the increment of change (see **incremental budgeting**), not the absolute size of the budget, and not on a complete and thorough review of every program starting from zero (see **zero-based budgeting**).

Theorists argued that it was rational to analyze budgets in increments and not rational to attempt to do comprehensive analysis of the total budget in each cycle; they argued that aggrieved parties would announce when something was done wrong and that this could be fixed either in the next budget process or by amendments to the current budget. In the main, the budget was made by experts, and most of budgeting was done in various venues in agencies, in the parent departments, in committees and subcommittees in Congress, all out of the public spotlight. Some observers argued that since budgets cast up decisions as just a matter of dollars, and not fundamental principals, compromise was easier to achieve and the result was generally a stable and predictable budget process.

Lance LeLoup and William Moreland (1978), in "Agency Strategies and Executive Review: The Hidden Politics of Budgeting," captured the essence of this period by describing the Department of Agriculture (DOA) budget process from 1946 to 1971 (pp. 180–192). Their focus was on the hidden politics of budgeting that take place within the executive branch between the agencies in Agriculture, the Agriculture Department Budget Office, OMB, and in Congress. To do this, they examined what agencies within the department asked for, how these requests were treated by the Department Budget Office, what the Office of Man-

agement and Budget did to the department recommendation (see **U.S. OMB**), and then what Congress gave and how this compared to the current appropriation. For example, budget changes are computed over the budget base (the appropriation for the current year): if an agency has an appropriation of US $100 million and asks for an appropriation (budget) of US $110 million, it is asking for a 10 percent increase over the base. If the department recommends US $107 million (a cut, but still an increase of 7 percent) and OMB suggests US $104 (a cut, but still an increase of 4 percent) and the final appropriation given by Congress for the budget year is US $103 million, this means that all reviewers cut the agency request, but compared to the current budget, the agency received an increase of 3 percent over its base. For LeLoup and Moreland, each of these steps would constitute a measurement point for an observation.

While the LeLoup and Moreland article illustrated how complex the budget process was, the reader is also struck by the regularity of the process. In examining 36 DOA agency requests over 25 years as they processed through the Department Budget Office, OMB, and then Congress (498 observations–not all agencies were extant in all years), LeLoup and Moreland reported the following findings:

1. The average outcome for all agencies was incremental; that is to say that the growth from one year to the next in the agency budget appropriation averaged 11 percent.
2. Reviewers–the Department Budget Office, OMB, Congress–tended to cut budget requests. On average, the department cut 4 percent; OMB cut 9 percent more, and Congress cut an additional 2 percent, but the final appropriations averaged an increase of 11 percent over previous appropriations over the whole period.
3. OMB always cut and cut the most, averaging 9 percent.
4. Those agencies who asked for the most, got the most, but also were cut the most. Those who asked for greater than 100 percent (36 instances) were cut 20.2 percent by the department, 16.2 percent by OMB, and 10.5 percent by Congress; however, for this group as a whole, their appropriations increased an average of 130 percent.
5. During this period, Congress was a marginal modifier: On average, it cut 2 percent from requests, and it cut less than 1 percent in 65 percent of the cases.
6. Agencies were varied in what they asked for. Some agencies asked for more than double their current year's budget (36 cases out of 498); others asked for less than they had in the current year (60 cases).
7. Those who asked for less than they had in the current year got cut; if these agencies thought being frugal

would cause others to give them money, they were in error. (Recently when asked about this tendency, an OMB analyst commented, to the author: "We are a 'kick them when they are down' agency; if they do not ask for money, we sure are not going to give it to them. We have too many other places that need money.")

8. The Department Budget Office appeared to balance the extremes; it cut a lot from those who asked for a lot, and it added money to those who asked for less than their current year appropriation. It is easy to picture the harried departmental budget officer trying to rein in the more aggressive agencies and encourage the less aggressive agencies, knowing full well that if they do not ask for enough money, it will probably be up to the departmental budget office to find it for them during the budget year, hence the adding back of money by the Department Budget Office. Nonetheless, those agencies that asked for less, received a cut of 21 percent in their appropriations and those that asked for a lot were cut a lot but were rewarded with increased appropriations averaging 130 percent.

Although the average of all outcomes was incremental (11 percent), the two largest groups of cases were mildly aggressive: 121 cases (24.3 percent) asked for increases of 10 percent to 24.9 percent and 103 cases (20.6 percent) asked for increases of 25 percent to 49.9 percent; however, these two groups received final appropriation increases an average of 1.3 percent and 4.6 percent respectively (LeLoup and Moreland, Table 2. p. 185). These are well within incremental boundaries, irrespective of the mildly aggressive aspirations of the agencies, and would seem to indicate the gatekeeping power of reviewers who guarded the power of the public purse during this period.

Recent Patterns

By the 1980s, the Department of Agriculture had become a potpourri of programs, ranging from direct provision of scientific information and advice about agriculture to crop forecasts to price stabilization programs to direct spending on welfare programs to a variety of credit programs. A majority of its budget consisted of what is called direct spending (because it is money that is sent directly to those who qualify and not used by the department to provide services), either mandated by entitlement programs or driven by changes in the economy which subsequently cause credit programs and price stabilization programs to change. In general, administrators have little discretionary control over these programs. They cannot ask for a lot to get a lot, and they cannot ask for decreases and let the programs die out. These programs are embedded in law and what happens to them is a product of what happens in the economy (see **entitlement**). Good budget analysis in these cases does not involve asking questions about administra-

tive travel patterns, personnel attrition rates, or the schedule of planned equipment purchases and their necessity, instead it involves estimating and forecasting what the economy is going to do and how this effects the number of people who will claim benefits. By the end of the decade these nondiscretionary accounts had grown to 81 percent of the Agriculture budget.

Figure I indicates what a historical profile looks like for four of the nondiscretionary entitlement accounts. (These programs were the child nutrition program, the special milk program, the food stamp program, and the food donations program.) It captures what the agency asked for, what the Department Budget Office recommended, what OMB decided, and what Congress gave. It is striking how closely the budget recommendations cluster around the final appropriation compared to the discretionary accounts in Figure II. They do this because the agency, the department, OMB, and even Congress have little room to cut or add money; the key variables here are estimates of how many people will be entitled and how much they will be entitled to get. Normally, the decision closest to the time the budget is executed would be the most accurate; this means that Congress should be the most accurate (using numbers from the Congressional Budget Office—see **Congressional Budget Office**) and the agency should be the least accurate because it must begin the budget process first and is farthest away in time. For fiscal years 1983 and 1985, the agencies were low in their forecasts, but for fiscal years 1981, 1984, and 1989, they were very close to the final appropriation. Over the ten-year period, the agency and department estimates for these four entitlement programs were identical just over half the time (on 22 out of 40 occasions). This probably indicates how difficult the estimation process is, although it may also indicate a policy preference to reduce or increase programs.

The discretionary budget accounts have room for value judgments at every step in the process, and participants can add or cut depending upon what they believe the program is worth and their estimate of the politics of getting support for their position by others in the budget process. Entitlements are different and this difference appears in Figure I. There should be little disagreement over these program estimates because each participant is obligated by law to try to estimate what the economy is going to do and how many claimants will be entitled to claim benefits or want to participate in a program (see **entitlement**). In other words, outcomes in these programs are not up to the discretion of administrators, budget analysts, or committee members and Congress, but rather driven by who has the best estimate. There is little discretion in these programs; the differences are due to differences in estimation or forecasting. Changing an entitlement program first requires changes in substantive law guiding who gets what benefits; in the 1980s changes to taxes and entitlement programs

FIGURE I. Four Entitlement Accounts FY 1980–89

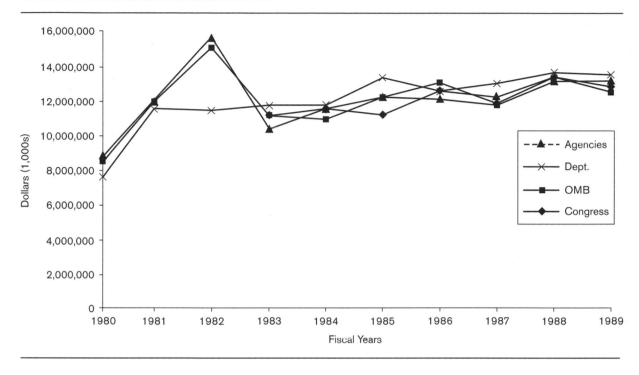

FIGURE II. Some Discretionary Accounts FY 1980–90

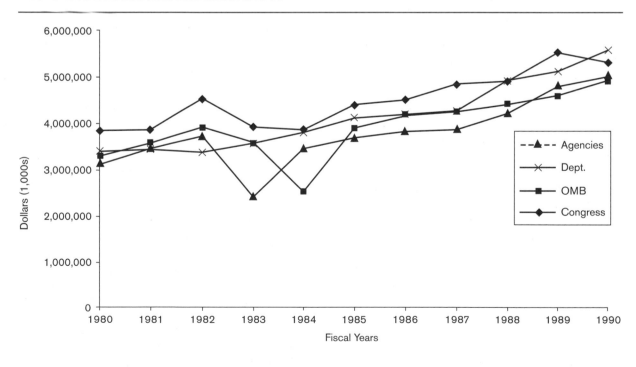

were sometimes accomplished by passing a separate legislative vehicle called a reconciliation bill (see **reconciliation**).

There is another trend in this profile that is interesting. To some extent, by the 1980s, farm programs were countercyclical programs. They cost more during times of economic stress, when more people depend more heavily on them; in the 1980s, these programs ranged from food stamps to child nutrition programs to increased subsidies for price supports to credit programs to crop insurance. When the economy gets better, the dependence of people on programs like these decreases and the programs cost less. For the four entitlement programs in Figure I this increase in dependence can be seen between fiscal years 1980 and 81, 1984 and 85 and 1987 and 88 by examining the final appropriation trend line (Congress). The decrease in need can be seen between fiscal years 1981 and 82 and 1985 and 86. When need is increasing rapidly, mistakes are made; for example, the huge increase in requests by the agency, the department, and OMB between fiscal years 1981 and 82 was a result of a misestimation of the cost of the food stamp program in a period when inflation and unemployment were rising rapidly.

Allen Schick has argued in *The Capacity to Budget* (1990) that the old agency-centered routines of OMB—and for that matter the Department Budget Offices—are no longer as relevant as they once were; that average paygrade of employees, attrition rates, spending on office supplies, and exorbitant travel profiles now mean less to budget analysts than do changes in GDP, inflation, and unemployment rates in the economy (pp. 86–87). Shifts in these numbers drive changes in the two-thirds of the federal budget that is now considered mandatory (payment on the national debt, other federal credit obligations, entitlements, contracts). Thus discretionary judgments and administrative expertise are no longer so important in budgeting as are the abilities to estimate growth and change in the economy and the number of clients or claimants who will be eligible for benefits and can make claims on the treasury. These estimates are sometimes called baselines. In some years budget baselines have become very controversial and budget reviewers have argued about who has the most accurate baseline. Figure I illustrates what these new politics of budgeting look like on the surface, but much of the real work seems to involve constructing and critiquing baseline forecasts.

Budgetary politics are not absent from entitlement accounts. Sometimes it is a politics of rhetoric whose purpose is to gain electoral advantage by, in effect, confusing observers over what has been done to the budget. Schick (pp. 95–101) calls this practice baseline alchemy. When there is an increase over the base (current year appropriation), but below the baseline forecast for the program adjusted for newly eligible claimants or inflation, supporters of the program can call the new number a cut (it is a cut from the baseline forecast) and opponents can call it an increase (it is an increase from the appropriation, but below what it will take to deliver the same program to all who are eligible).

Sometimes the politics of entitlements get even more confusing when budgets are sent to Congress that anticipate that substantive changes will be made in entitlement programs in laws to be passed later in the legislative session. For example, in 1982, the Administration, supported by the House, proposed funding for food stamps, child nutrition, and the Women, Infants, and Children (WIC) programs that were so low that funds would have run out before the end of the fiscal year. This meant the child nutrition program would have been funded for 10.5 months, WIC for 7.5 months, and food stamps for 9.5 months. The food stamp program would have been US $2.2 billion short in 1983. This was a way to reduce funding in these programs without first changing the substantive law that guided the programs. Advocates of this position suggested the substantive changes legitimizing these levels would be made later, and if they were not made, then a supplemental bill could always be passed to make up the full annual funding for these programs.

The Senate stood firm for full funding of the programs in fiscal year 1983. In December, the Administration gave in and sent the required budget changes to Congress, and House and Senate conferees agreed on funding the programs for the full year. This turbulence can be seen in the entitlement accounts for fiscal year 1983 in Figure I. Here the administration did not make a mistake in estimating what it would take to fund these programs; rather, it incorporated policy changes in its budget requests for the programs that it assumed would be passed into law later in the year (see the *Congressional Quarterly Almanac* for 1982, pp. 258–261), notwithstanding that it knew there was fierce opposition to these changes in the Senate.

Had the Senate acceded to this budget strategy but refused to pass legislation changing the substantive entitlement legislation (because it did not want to reduce these programs) and counted on passing a supplemental appropriation later in 1983 to fully fund these programs, it is highly likely that the House would have blocked the supplemental appropriation (because it wanted the programs reduced), and the programs would have remained partially funded despite the fact that there had been no change in the substantive legislation establishing entitlement criteria for these programs. In this case, aggrieved claimants could have sued after the money had run out, but redress of grievances through the courts is normally far too late to effect events within a given fiscal year. In sum, what appears to be a technical area where all that counts is the right formula or computer model turns out to be filled with subtle political rhetoric and actions. This is also an object lesson in political strategies; the Administration took the initiative by suggesting budget amounts which reduced entitlements without the necessary entitlement law changes. The Senate held firm to a blocking position, which was critical; it held its power. Had it given in, it would have been in the position of having to get a supplemental bill through the House. The outcome was that the Senate forced full funding and, in so doing, compliance with the then-current entitlement statutes governing these programs.

Agriculture Discretionary Expenditures

Department of Agriculture budget documents also allowed for analysis of some of the discretionary accounts during the decade of the 1980s. (LeLoup and Moreland did not divide their study into mandatory and discretionary accounts.) These accounts represented budget lines ranging from the Office of the Secretary to various libraries and statistical services to animal, plant, and grain inspection services and to the agricultural extension service. Some 19 accounts were followed over the 11-year period, from the agency through the Department Budget Office, through OMB, and through Congress; this provided some 228 observations. (These were mainly accounts that carried out the administrative work of the department; others included some information and inspection programs, some grant programs, and the supplemental food program.) Although these comprise almost two-thirds of the accounts in the Department of Agriculture budget structure during this period, they represent only about 19 percent of the funds. For example, according to the Congressional Budget Office Summer 1991 baseline, mandatory expenditures amounted to 81.3 percent of the Department of Agriculture budget. Nonetheless, the accounts collected and pictured in Figure II illustrate the hidden politics of budgeting as it existed in the 1980s for discretionary accounts, those accounts agency administrators, departmental budget analysts, OMB, and Congress had discretionary control over in the budget process.

In general, the profile for these discretionary accounts resembles the profile suggested by LeLoup and Moreland only to the extent that in most years these agencies asked for more than they were given. The year 1982 might be considered typical for the LeLoup-Moreland era: Agencies asked for a lot, were cut a lot by the Department Budget Office, were cut some more by OMB, and were cut substantially in the final appropriation. The years 1980 and 1981 show evidence of great agreement among reviewers (Department, OMB, Congress) about what these agencies should get; naturally, it was a lot less than they asked for.

The interesting aspect of this period lies in how different it was from the classic period. LeLoup and Moreland would have recognized 1982; here, the agency request was greater than the departmental recommendation, OMB's mark, and the Congressional outcome. However, the subsequent years were normal only in the sense that the agency request was greater than final appropriation. In-

deed, in 5 of the 11 years the final appropriation was closer to the Agency request than it was to either the Department Budget Office or OMB recommendation.

Part of the history of agriculture policy in this decade was an effort in cost containment by the President; this can be seen in the OMB recommendation in 1983 and the departmental recommendation in 1984; both suggested large cuts that were basically ignored by Congress. In 1983, OMB tried to cut rural water disposal grants by 40 percent and the supplemental food program by 100 percent; OMB suggested reductions in the Office of the Secretary of Agriculture of 12 percent, in departmental administration of 17.8 percent, the office of legislative liaison of 21 percent, in the cooperative state research service of 12 percent, in animal and plant inspection of 13 percent, and in the agriculture cooperative service of 14 percent. In addition, to Department Budget Office cuts, the office of legislative liaison would have been reduced by 54 percent, the cooperative state research service by 24 percent, and the soil conservation service by 33 percent. In 1984, the Department Budget Office made the most effort to cut programs, suggesting, for example, that the extension service be cut by 12 percent, rural water grants by 25 percent, the soil conservation service by 15 percent, and the supplemental food program by 100 percent. These were intentional efforts to decrease the size of the discretionary accounts within the department; they were generally rejected by Congress and suggested a battleground that would be played out the rest of the decade.

For most of the rest of the decade, Congress protected these discretionary agencies within the Department of Agriculture against the budget reduction efforts from both OMB and the Department Budget Office. When the President wants to reduce spending in a department or policy area, he can work through OMB or he can work through the head of the department, who is appointed by the President, and the department budget staff, who are responsible to that appointee. Figure II seems to suggest that both these approaches were attempted from 1983 on, but that support in Congress for the agencies within Agriculture was strong enough to offset executive branch pressure. Far from being a marginal modifier, Congress was an important supporter of these programs throughout most of this decade.

Some agencies asked for a decrease from their current year's base, just as they had in the previous study and with almost the same frequency. Part of the negative baggage of incrementalism was the implication that agencies always asked for more and that budgets always went up. The LeLoup and Moreland study was interesting because it seemed to suggest that there were instances (about 12 percent of the cases) where bureaucrats would ask for less than they had in the current budget. The difficulty with putting too much emphasis on this argument in the LeLoup and Moreland study was that these constituted such a small percentage of cases that over a quarter of a century they might well have represented instances of bureaus ratcheting down as their clienteles disappeared, of mandatory expenditures that declined, or of bureaus that were simply closed as budget lines only to appear as a component of some other function. This still may be true for that period.

In the 1980–90 study of discretionary accounts, 7 agencies asked for a decrease in a single year and 5 agencies asked for decreases in multiple years (24 instances total). For example, Animal and Plant Health Inspection requested a decrease from 1983 through 1986, the Agriculture Cooperative Service requested a decrease from 1983 through 1987, and the Agricultural Marketing Service requested decreases from 1983 through 1985 and in 1990. Administrators do sometimes ask for less. The Department Budget Office did not change the requests of these agencies in 12 instances. In 6 instances the Department Budget Office further decreased the request, but in another 6 instances, it increased or gave money back. This could be seen as the Department Budget Office balancing the extremes, just as it had done in the earlier period. OMB cut in 22 cases, but added money to 2, more than the agency asked for and what the department recommended. This is a somewhat different profile for OMB from the LeLoup and Moreland study, in which OMB appeared to always cut. Congress for its part added money to all but 4 of these requests, but just as in the earlier period, the final outcome was still below the current year budget in the majority of cases (19 of 24 instances).

Although Congress supported Agriculture's programs, it did not do so with blind enthusiasm; it seemed to know what it wanted and sent budgetary signals until the agency got it right. In 1988, advisory committees requested a decrease from the base of 6 percent and received exactly what they had in the current year from Congress (i.e., Congress restored the cut). Evidently taking this as a signal, advisory committees became wildly aggressive and asked for increases of 74 percent and 68 percent the next two years and received increases of 14 percent and zero respectively. Asking for a lot did not get them a lot. In fact, over the three-year period, this account grew 14 percent, and all of the increase was in 1989. In 1983, the Office of Public Affairs requested an increase of 99 percent over the previous year only to receive its current year's budget (no increase). The next year, it requested a decrease below the base, but was restored to the current year budget (no decrease). This would seem to indicate that Congress had an idea of the size of the budget it wanted public affairs to have and maintained its idea of that size despite the agency's efforts first to grow a lot and then to let things slide.

The 1980s were a turbulent period in budget history, marked by disagreement over policy, deficit reduction politics, continuing resolutions, appropriations passed well into the fiscal year and for the latter part of the decade by rather violent disagreement between Congress and the President over budget directions for the agriculture programs. It was also an era of divided government with the Republicans holding the White House and the Democrats holding at least one house in Congress. This further complicated the budget process. Allen Schick suggests that the 1980s were a period of improvisational budget procedures where budgetmakers had to deal with intense policy preferences and a budget process that did not work as it should have (pp. 159–196). Some of this turbulence can be seen in OMB's effort to reduce Agriculture's discretionary accounts only to have them restored by Congress. Moreover, while the hidden politics of budgeting still exist, for Agriculture at least, most of the budget was comprised of entitlements and credit programs where what matters is not what Agriculture managers, OMB, and Congress think about a program but what the law says and what the economy does, and careful budget analysis is less important than accurate estimation for programs whose structure is fixed in law, at least in theory. In practice, subtle and powerful political strategies are also employed in the entitlement programs.

JERRY L. MCCAFFERY

Note:

I would like to thank Capt. John Mutty, USN ret., holder of the Conrad Chair in Financial Management at the Naval Postgraduate School, for his helpful comments on this article. Data for the analysis in this essay were taken from the relevant years of the Budget of the United States. Additional data were provided by the budget office of the Department of Agriculture. The basis for suggesting which Department of Agriculture accounts should be considered discretionary and which mandatory (or direct) came from a Senate Budget Committee staff person who reviewed the research. I wish to express my gratitude to all of the above.

BIBLIOGRAPHY

Congressional Quarterly, 1982. *Congressional Quarterly Almanac.* Washington, D.C.: Congressional Quarterly Press.

LeLoop, Lance T. and William B. Moreland, 1978. "Agency Strategies and Executive Review: The Hidden Politics of Budgeting." *Public Administration Review*, vol. 38 (May-June).

Schick, Allen, 1990. *The Capacity to Budget*. Washington, D.C.: Urban Institute Press.

BUDGET REFORM. An effort to improve the operations of budget systems at any level of government with regard to the management, allocation, or control of public resources.

Budget reform has been an ongoing and consuming topic for budget scholars and practitioners for more than a century. The concern with reforming the budget process as a way to ensure accountability, promote management, or foster different budget outcomes dates from the early days of the progressive reform movement in the late 1800s but remains very salient today. In some sense, all "reforms" are the reactions to the excesses or shortcomings of the status quo.

Allen Schick has written that there are three functions of budgeting. The first is control of public resources. As an example of this, the earliest reform efforts were a reaction to the excesses that were perceived to exist in the machine cities of the late 1800s, or as efforts to bring business practices to government. The second is the management of public resources, mainly in the context of designing efficient means to arrive at agreed upon public ends. The third is planning for the future allocation of resources. Under this function of budgeting, budget reform aims to influence broad budget outcomes. In addition to these three functions, many more recent budget reforms—including most federal reforms of the past 20 years—have focused on the relationship between the executive and the legislative branches in the budget process or (particularly at the federal level) on devising procedural solutions designed to reduce spending or to control budget deficits.

Although it is difficult to precisely define historical break points between various types of budget reform, this entry will consider four periods that differ as to the emphasis placed on different functions of budgeting. The first began in the 1870s and continued until approximately the late 1930s. The second began at that point and ended around 1960. The third covered the period from around 1960 until 1985. The fourth continues to this day. A review of each of these periods can demonstrate the motives behind the various budget reforms.

Period One, 1873–1937

Prior to the late part of the last century, budgeting was characterized by weak executive power, little central control, and processes that were idiosyncratic. Beginning in states and local government, and later extending to the national government, budget systems were developed to increase the chief executive's power and control over the budget. The early reform movement was focused first and foremost on the effective control of budget accounts. It established economy and efficiency as the primary values of budgeting.

Budget reform began as early as 1873, following a sharp recession that occurred after the rapid expansion of government following the Civil War. Early on, budget reform was a tool used by people who wanted to bring sound business practices to government and who wanted to reduce demands from public departments and government constituencies; in other words, budget reform was about controlling costs. But other reformers had other motivations. The progressive reformers who started the Research

Bureau movement in New York City in 1906 had political motivations; they considered budget reform to be less about budget control and more about correcting the political excesses of machine politicians. Although these two sets of budget reformers—the business conservatives and the progressives—wanted to reform the budget for different reasons, they both advocated budget reforms that emphasized strong executives. The businessmen wanted to reform the budget process because they wanted smaller government. The progressives, however, supported a larger, but "cleaner" government. They also apparently had political motivations; many of them were interested in playing a larger role in running the postmachine governments.

In the federal government, the Taft Commission on Economy and Efficiency issued the earliest call for budget reform. In 1912, it recommended the establishment of a national budget. Under this plan, the president would review department estimates and transmit them in a unified document to Congress. The Taft Commission reformers were very much within the tradition of the probusiness conservatives, who sought smaller government and lower taxes.

The executive budget called for by the Taft conservatives did not become a reality, however, until the passage of the Budget and Accounting Act of 1921. The Budget and Accounting Act established the Bureau of the Budget (BOB) in the Treasury Department, and (for the first time) required the president to review department budget estimates and submit to Congress an annual budget proposal. In addition, the act provided an institutional capability for review and audit of executive branch programs through the creation of the General Accounting Office (GAO).

The Budget and Accounting Act of 1921 has had a lasting effect on the president's power over the budget. Perhaps one of the most lasting legacies of the passage of the Budget and Accounting Act is institutional. BOB, its successor agency, the Office of Management and Budget (OMB), and GAO have influenced the debate over budget policy. BOB/OMB has contributed greatly to the ability of the president to control and manage the budget. GAO has substantially increased the ability of the federal government to audit and evaluate the results of federal spending.

Period Two, 1937–1960

The orientation toward spending control embodied in the 1921 Act eventually gave way to a concern for the ability of the president to manage the affairs of the executive branch. The management focus was spurred by the challenges accompanying the increase in federal activities and expenditures after the adoption of the New Deal programs in the 1930s. The budget process was viewed for the first time to be the key process for determining the extent of public activities. Thus, it switched focus from an input-oriented process to one that is output-oriented. Perhaps most significantly, the influential President's Committee on Administrative Management (also known as the Brownlow Commission, after its chairman, Louis Brownlow see **Brownlow Commission**) in 1937 recommended that the Bureau of the Budget be transferred from the Treasury Department to the newly created Executive Office of the President as part of an overall effort to improve presidential management of the executive branch. This transfer was effected in 1939.

This emphasis on management had implications for budget reform. In response to the report of the First Hoover Commission (1949), a proposal was advanced to integrate more data into the budget process. This proposal, which was referred to as "performance budgeting," was designed primarily to allow managers to develop measures of workload and cost effectiveness. Performance budgeting indicated a shift from budgeting based on expenditure control to budgeting based increasingly on management concerns. The emphasis was not on making government-wide budgetary trade-offs; rather, it was on measuring workload on an agency basis. The focus was on the work to be done, not on the usefulness of the objectives themselves. Although performance budgeting was never adopted as a governmentwide budgetary process, it is significant because it emphasized the integration of program information and budgeting. This emphasis was to be continued in future reform efforts.

Period Three, 1960–1985

Beginning in the 1960s, reforms began to develop that focused on planning for the use of public resources. The predominant early reform of this type, program budgeting, had its federal heyday during the administration of President Lyndon Johnson. By contrast with performance budgeting, program budgeting was explicitly focused on budgetary choices among competing activities. Although performance budgeting was designed to discover which of several ways is the most efficient method of accomplishing a given objective, program budgeting treated the objectives themselves as variable. As such, program budgeting was not a management system, but a resource allocation system. It was a specific alternative to the traditional manner of making budgeting trade-offs, which focused on marginal adjustments to the status quo.

The important distinction between program budgeting and the previous reforms (control-oriented and management-oriented budgeting) is in its desire to fundamentally affect the process of resource allocation. As such, it is an effort to respond to the fundamental question of budgeting, first raised by political scientist V. O. Key in the 1940s. Budgeting, said Key, is about responding to the question, On what basis shall it be decided to allocate x dollars to activity A rather than activity B? Program bud-

geting attempted to respond to that question by making a specific effort to link program costs with the results of public programs.

Although program budgeting has been attempted at various levels of government (and elements of these systems remain in many budget processes to this day), the federal effort is embodied primarily in the mid-1960s effort by President Johnson to put into effect a planning-programming-budgeting system (PPBS) throughout the federal government. PPBS was based on a successful 1960s effort by Secretary of Defense Robert McNamara to put PPBS into practice in the Department of Defense (DOD).

Secretary McNamara saw the budget process as his primary vehicle for exercising control over the department. In DOD, the budget process would be divided into three phases: planning, programming, and budgeting. Of the three, the planning phase had the most global perspective; the programs designed in the programming phase would intend to carry out the mission embodied in the plan. The budgeting phase was limited to determining the costs associated with carrying out the first year of the program. The practical vehicle for carrying out PPBS was the Five Year Defense Plan, which projected costs and personnel according to missions and programs. This highlights a key characteristic of PPBS—it eschews organizational boundaries in favor of a mission-driven orientation that may cross organizational lines. The defense PPBS system still formally exists, although it has never lived up to the high hopes that Secretary McNamara had for it.

The early success of PPBS in defense led to its expansion to the rest of the federal government. In 1965, President Johnson ordered the Defense Department's system to be employed throughout the federal government. It was not nearly as successful elsewhere, however, as it had been in DOD. By 1971, requirements that agencies include the PPBS system data was suspended, and PPBS ceased to exist, at least explicitly, in the federal government.

Reports and evaluations indicate that the PPBS was much less successful in civilian agencies than in the Defense Department, particularly because it lacked administrative commitment to integrating it fully into civilian agency management systems. Although Secretary McNamara clearly was committed to putting PPBS into effect in the Defense Department, in most other cases the system was treated as an annual reporting requirement rather than as a management or budgeting opportunity. Several other arguments have been made for the failure of PPBS to catch on:

- It was introduced across the board without much preparation.
- It flew in the face of existing budgetary traditions and relationships; in particular, many people strongly objected to the suggestion that the budget process, which is inherently political, could be made "rational."

- It was not given adequate resources, and top managers were not entirely committed to it.

- Good analysts and data were in short supply, and they were necessary to produce the kind of information crucial to the success of PPBS.

- Because PPBS was intended to require a review of all activities in each year, the reform caused so much conflict that the political system was not capable of handling it.

- PPBS made a clear assumption that efficiency was the primary value to be considered in evaluating the usefulness of programs, which was not generally agreed to and is a difficult assumption to make in the case of a public program.

- PPBS was an executive budget system and largely ignored the role of the Congress in the budget process. The result was that Congress ignored the system in favor of its established procedures.

PPBS was unable to fulfill its promise as a budgetary reform. In particular, it did not change the budget process from one that focused primarily on making small incremental changes to one that could make comprehensive alterations. Federal budget decisions were still made largely at the margin. Like performance budgeting, however, PPBS increased the role of analysis in budgeting and led to better-informed budget decisions. This increase has continued long after PPBS has faded from view.

The administration of President Jimmy Carter brought its own model of budget reform to Washington in 1976 in the form of zero-based budgeting (ZBB). ZBB, which President Carter had used as governor in Georgia, was also designed to affect resource allocation and promote evaluation of effectiveness in that it would permit comprehensive review of the federal budget, as opposed to the traditional, more incremental approach. This comprehensive evaluation never caught on, however, and President Reagan abandoned the experiment in 1981.

In a "pure" ZBB system, instead of concentrating on budgetary changes at the margin, all programs are evaluated each year. The process of arriving at a budget is literally to start from scratch. At the federal level, that would require answering such questions as, What if we didn't have an army and navy? or What if Social Security did not exist? In practice, no government ZBB system, including the federal one, went this far. President Carter's Office of Management and Budget used a variant of ZBB in which agencies were asked to rank their programs within some funding limits. The question thus became, What if the Department of Defense only received 90 percent (for example) of the current year's funding?

The experience at the state and local levels was similar to that of the federal government. The "pure" form of ZBB never took hold, and was abandoned by virtually all governments. The reduced form of ZBB, however, does survive in many governments, particularly those who are forced to cut back on spending. Instructing agencies to submit budgets at prescribed target levels because of revenue constraints (called "target-based budgeting"), in fact, has become an established feature of many budget processes since the early 1980s.

Many other budget reforms since the early 1970s have focused less on control, management, or planning, and more on the relationship between chief executives and legislative bodies in budgeting. At the federal level, the resurgence of legislative budgeting is tied to the passage of the Congressional Budget and Impoundment Control Act of 1974. This act was passed in response to the perceived incursion of the executive branch on Congress's fiscal turf. In particular, Congress was disturbed by what it viewed as President Nixon's extreme exercise of impoundment power.

The 1974 Act attempted to strengthen the congressional role in the making of the budget by creating new committees (in particular the House and Senate Budget Committees) to coordinate the congressional consideration of the budget and by creating a new Congressional Budget Office (CBO) as a source of nonpartisan analysis and information relating to the budget and the economy. In trying to impose some order, the act laid out a specific timetable for action on the budget. The instrument created to coordinate various portions of the budget was the concurrent budget resolution, a form of congressional decision that can bind congressional action but does not require a presidential signature. The resolution was an opportunity for Congress to act on the budget as a unified whole, and it provided a general budget blueprint that the authorizing and appropriations committees were compelled to follow.

To curb the president's ability to circumvent Congress's allocative powers, the act also included a procedure for dealing with impoundments. Two forms of presidential cutbacks were permitted—rescissions (removal of budget authority) and deferrals (delay of budget authority). The president could propose both, but to be effective, the former needed explicit congressional approval and the latter tacit acquiescence. The deferral process has fallen into disuse, but the rescission process has been used frequently in recent years to make midyear reductions in spending.

Budget Reform After 1985

Budget reform remains a salient topic among government officials, academics, and the public. The scarcity of resources at all levels of government—illustrated most familiarly by the federal budget deficit—has promoted the use of the budget process once again as an instrument of federal budget control since 1985. In addition, the two themes that were active between 1960 and 1985—introducing more of an outcome orientation to budgeting and sorting out

Budget Control Again

As the federal budget deficit grew substantially in the wake of the passage of the Reagan economic program in 1981, Congress increasingly became aware that the budget process could not serve as a constraint against these large deficits. Frustration with large deficits and the inability to contain them ultimately led to the passage of rules to attempt to limit federal spending and the deficit. The first of these was the Balanced Budget and Emergency Deficit Control Act of 1985, popularly known as Gramm-Rudman-Hollings (GRH). GRH attempted to control the deficit through setting gradually declining deficit targets and was to result in a balanced budget by fiscal year 1991. If the deficit targets were not met, automatic across-the-board spending reductions, or sequestration, took effect.

The deficit, of course, did not come down as promised by the Gramm-Rudman-Hollings legislation. In fact, the fiscal year 1993 deficit (which would have been zero if the law, as revised in 1987, had met its goal) was actually US $225 billion. The act did put a premium on short-term budgeting; under GRH, all that mattered was the single year for which the projections were being made. These annual targets were complied with through short-term fixes and budget gimmickry, including basing the budget on optimistic economic and technical assumptions, selling assets, and shifting costs between fiscal years.

The successor to Gramm-Rudman-Hollings, the Budget Enforcement Act (BEA), was passed in 1990 and was designed to enforce the five-year deficit reduction agreement reached between the president and Congress in that year. The BEA effectively eliminated annual deficit targets, placed limits on the level of discretionary spending through fiscal year 1995, and established the pay-as-you-go (PAYGO) process to ensure that any tax or mandatory spending changes were deficit neutral. The original Budget Enforcement Act would have expired in 1995; the Omnibus Budget Reconciliation Act of 1993 extended both the discretionary spending limits and PAYGO until 1998.

Despite the progress in deficit reduction that occurred in 1990 and 1993, some policymakers advocate further budget reforms to force additional deficit reduction actions. Foremost among these proposals is an amendment to the U.S. Constitution to require a balanced federal budget. This proposal has been voted on several times since 1982, but only twice (in 1982 and 1995) has either house of the Congress been able to muster the needed two-thirds vote that would be necessary to forward the amendment to the states for ratification. Most proposed amendments would require the budget to be balanced at some specified point in the future (the amendment considered in 1995, for example, would have required a balanced budget by fiscal year 2002 at the earliest). None of these proposed amendments specify which spending is to be cut and which taxes are to be raised in order to comply with the provisions of the amendment. Even if such an amendment were to be passed, however, Congress and the president would need to fill in the budgetary details and establish mechanisms for enforcement.

Performance-Based Budgeting

Despite the failure of some past reforms (such as PPBS and ZBB) to transform budget decision making, the increased use of performance measurements in the budget process has remained on the agenda. The 1990s have seen a renewed call for "performance-based budgeting"; this generally describes a process by which more explicit connections are made between financial inputs and program results. The move toward performance-based budgeting has been advocated as a part of the "reinventing government" movement. Further, many state and local governments have allegedly made progress in developing budgets that tie dollars and outcomes.

In the federal government, the passage of two pieces of legislation—the Chief Financial Officers Act of 1990 and the Government Performance and Results Act of 1993—have spurred the effort to link budgets and results. In addition, Vice President Albert Gore's National Performance Review specifically endorsed the idea of performance-based budgeting. As of the date of this entry, it would be premature to evaluate the performance-budgeting effort. It is probably fair to say, however, that in an era of fiscal retrenchment, efforts to evaluate the results that are occurring from the expenditures of scarce public resources will continue to be of paramount importance.

Budgetary Power

Particularly at the federal level, reform efforts have been aimed at increasing the power of the chief executive in the budget process, either by promoting the president's budgetary choices or through offering more flexibility to him in carrying out the budget. In the former case, many reforms react to the power exercised by Congress since passage of the 1974 Budget Act. These include providing the president with the authority to veto individual line-items in appropriation bills. This is a power possessed in some form by 43 state governors. Another proposal would involve the president formally in the process of approving budget resolutions (currently these resolutions are approved only by both houses of the Congress and do not require the president's signature).

In the latter case, the most obvious example is the effort to move to a biennial budget process, which would require the enactment of a budget only every other year. One stated purpose of this change would be to permit federal agencies and the president to better manage the executive branch by providing for a greater degree of budgetary certainty. In addition, reforms have been proposed that would increase the flexibility of agencies in spending money by removing itemized controls.

PHILIP G. JOYCE

BIBLIOGRAPHY

Burkhead, Jesse, 1956. *Government Budgeting.* New York: John Wiley and Sons.
Fisher, Louis, 1975. *Presidential Spending Power.* Princeton: Princeton University Press.
Howard, S. Kenneth, Jr., 1973. *Changing State Budgeting.* Lexington, KY: Council of State Governments.
Joyce, Philip G., 1993. "The Reiterative Nature of Budget Reform: Is There Anything New in Federal Budgeting?" *Public Budgeting and Finance,* vol. 13, no. 3 (Fall), 36–48.
Key, V. O., Jr., 1940. "The Lack of a Budgetary Theory." *American Political Science Review* (December), 1137–1144.
Rubin, Irene S., 1991. "Budgeting for Our Times: Target-Based Budgeting." *Public Budgeting and Finance,* vol. 11, no. 3 (Fall), 5–14.
———, 1994. "Early Budget Reformers: Democracy, Efficiency, and Budget Reforms." *American Review of Public Administration,* vol. 24, no. 3 (September), 229–252.
Schick, Allen, 1966. "The Road to PPB: The Stages of Budget Reform." *Public Administration Review,* vol. 26, no. 4 (December), 243–268.
———, 1971. *Budget Innovations in the States.* Washington, D.C.: Brookings Institution.
———, 1973. "A Death in the Bureaucracy: The Demise of Federal PPB." *Public Administration Review,* vol. 33, no. 2 (March/April), 146–156.
United States Congressional Budget Office, 1993. *Using Performance Measures in the Federal Budget Process* (July).

BUDGET STRATEGY.

The tactics that participants in the budget process use as they perform the role of advocate on behalf of their programs and funding. Budget advocates develop strategies intended to enhance the likelihood that their programs will survive and receive adequate funding relative to demand for their services.

Introduction

Observers of the public budget process have documented use of strategy in budget advocacy (Wildavsky, 1964, 1988; Anthony and Young, 1984; Pfeffer and Salancik, 1974). A wide variety of ploys and maneuvers have been identified to be used in either justifying new budgetary resources or defending against proposed cuts, e.g., "foot in the door," "gold watch," and "Washington Monument."

Wildavsky has educated generations of students interested in budgeting on the ways in which government agencies determine how much to ask for in their annual department or agency budget proposals and how to support the need for additional funding. Generally, it is accepted in the budgeting literature that, other things equal, organizations with a plan or a strategy on how to approach budget decisionmakers with their proposals are better off than organizations without plans. The fact that external factors affect the allocation of resources in budgets must be acknowledged. Floods produce disaster relief funding, changes in national governments influence foreign aid, eligibility for social assistance produces transfer payments from entitlement accounts. If there is no obvious external factor to justify budget augmentation, however, it may be incumbent upon the creative government manager to develop a synthetic rationale for the organization's budget proposal. Similarly, after the budget has been appropriated some further ingenuity may be needed to permit the organization to spend the funds available to it for the priorities deemed to be highest by managers, somewhat independent of the priorities of budget decisionmakers in the executive and legislative branches of government. Budget executors appear to want to maximize their own discretion at the expense of decisionmakers so as to gain greatest efficiency in spending money to achieve organizational objectives.

Whether in budget formulation or budget execution, certain dynamics appear to apply in budgeting. For example, it is often noted that advocates for spending inflate their budget requests with the expectation that this strategy is likely to produce more nearly the amount of funding that is actually needed. This practice is countered by budget cutters who routinely reduce all budget proposals by some fixed percentage, using at times rather specious justifications. The manner in which the budgeting game is played informs participants that in order to be successful, they must play by a certain set of written as well as unwritten rules. In this case, the written rule is that budgets must be fully justified up to some constraint. However, the wise budget game player knows to inflate the request in anticipation of the standard reduction by budget analysts. As Wildavsky (1964) explains, much of budgeting is incremental and historical. What an agency is likely to gain in each annual iteration of the budget process is best predicted, other things equal, on the base of what it already has and on how long the agency has commanded such resources to serve a particular clientele.

Overstatement of requirements is an example of what may be termed strategic misrepresentation in budgeting, that is, the deliberate and systematic misstatement of fact to achieve organizational objectives in response to a set of incentives that are the result of rewarding deception as long as it fits in with the tradition and rules governing how the game of resource negotiation is played. The key to this definition is that misrepresentation is planned and executed carefully to exploit the full benefits provided within the rules the game in competition with other agents, when a total constraint exists on the amount of benefits to be distributed in any particular iteration of the game. Strategic misrepresentation in budgeting may be distinguished from lying or other forms of dishonesty that are in conflict with the mores and norms of the organization or society. In budgeting, as in some other forms of organizational competition and negotiation (e.g., labor contract negotiation), some degree of planned lying to gain competitive advantage is not only tolerated but expected.

Economic and psychological theories can be used to inform this discussion. From the perspective of the economist, the framework of the rules of the budget process systematically distributes rewards rather than penalties to those who lie well. Similarly, from an operant conditioning perspective there is a systematic rewarding of a specific set of behaviors (i.e., strategic misrepresentation in budgeting) and a withholding of rewards from individuals who do not exhibit these behaviors (Skinner, 1978). From either perspective rewards can be had if deception is practiced in response to some event.

Rewards in budgeting are not distributed solely on the basis of lying or cheating. Where a strategy of misrepresentation is used deliberately, it must be thoroughly documented and explained, and it is likely to be accepted only when it fits historically into a pattern of advocacy by mission, role, and performance record of an organization. This view leads to the hypothesis that different types of organizations misrepresent in different ways in budgeting. Evidence to test this hypothesis thoroughly is yet to be evaluated. However, it is evident that the various participants in budgeting play very distinct roles and use different tactics in performing these roles.

The example noted earlier in which program advocates or "spenders" inflate budget requests that are then countered by budget controllers or "cutters" who justify reductions based upon allegations of inefficiency or ineffectiveness demonstrates role differentiation. Both the inflated budget request and the reductions based upon alleged inefficiency are supported with justifying data. And in many, if not all, cases, data are chosen primarily on the basis of whether they support the argument made by the advocate or critic. This is an example of misrepresentation in negotiation that is accepted in the budget game—telling only one side of the argument with the expectation that the "opposition" in the game will engage in the same behavior but with different tactics. Such selective truth-telling leaves to decisionmakers and their staffs the role of sorting out relative truth and fiction in the various forums in which budgets are negotiated and enacted.

Budget Roles, Rules, and Controls

To understand the dynamics of representation in the budget process, it is necessary to fully comprehend the roles of the participants and the role differentiation that influences budget advocacy, examination, decision, and execution. The roles of budget process participants have been examined in some detail in the budget control literature (Jones and Thompson, 1986). To characterize strategic misrepresentation accurately, however, it is necessary to reach beyond role behavior to the incentive structure faced by clients, spenders, cutters, controllers, auditors, evaluators, and other budget process participants. Further, it is necessary to comprehend both the phases of the budget process in which specific strategies of misrepresentation are applied and the factors that stimulate the behavior in question. And, because much of budgeting is concerned with accountability and control within an organization's overall management control process, it is useful to differentiate between different types of control and the purposes of control in the budget process. In this light, ex ante controls applied before spending take place (generally in the preparation, negotiation, and enactment phases of the budget process) may be distinguished from ex post controls that are applied as spending occurs or after spending has taken place (after encumbrance, expense and disbursement).

The purpose of ex ante controls is to regulate what may and may not be done in a budget before spending takes place; for example, standard inflation indices can be applied across the budget in projecting it into future years or rules can prescribe the manner in which budget proposals must be justified. Standard unit cost estimating rules also fall into this category. Ex post controls are then applied after spending takes place to design and modify future budget and program performance. These rules result from observing how money is spent and evaluating trends to influence or direct future budget preparation and execution. Ex ante rules are enforced generally by budget analysts in the executive and legislative branches and by their political masters, the elected and appointed officials, as they review new spending proposals. Ex post controls are derived by economists, program evaluators, policy analysts, and auditors as they render the results of their examination of performance, accountability, efficiency, effectiveness, and cost/benefit after programs have been delivered to their clientele. It is important to differentiate between types of controls and their objectives because controls specify the rules by which the budget game is played.

We assume that strategic misrepresentation contributes to meeting organizational objectives within the context of a complex set of rules. Planned and systematic deception is unlikely to contribute to the overall effectiveness of the organization unless a system of rules and controls is in place and until a set of participants sanction the game in the distribution of resources as they play out their roles in the budget process. It is not assumed or argued that strategic misrepresentation contributes to efficiently meeting organizational objectives.

Strategic Misrepresentation and Phases of the Budget Process

The practice of misrepresentation has been reviewed in the budget and accounting literature (Anthony, 1985; Meyers, 1990). The examples provided earlier of inflating proposals and generalizing the justification of cuts are only tips of the misrepresentation iceberg. Other examples may be classified temporally, that is, according to when they occur for example, in the budget preparation instructions when executive analysts specify inflation adjustments below levels that are likely to be present in future budget years. On the one hand, this conditions program advocates to inflate their budget requests. On the other hand, budget proposals often attempt to hide new programs and costs within the base to avoid the exceptional scrutiny given such proposals in budget review.

Perhaps one of the most effective forms of misrepresentation in the budget formulation phase occurs when the executive, through his or her budget office, specifies new rules for the entire budget game. Thus, the installation of zero-based budgeting may be justified on the grounds that it will cause real program priorities to surface and allow the base to be examined with the same care as the increment. With this high-minded objective, a new set of rules is to give advantage to the rule makers at the expense of the rule learners. Program advocates are at a disadvantage in competition with budget examiners in that they do not fully comprehend how the game is to be played. Budget examiners take advantage of the predictable uncertainty wherever it occurs with the resulting effect of allowing the executive to target budget reductions at their discretion, for example, at programs that are ideologically or politically unacceptable but for which there are not sufficient grounds to reduce or eliminate on the basis of efficiency or ineffectiveness (Jones and McCaffery, 1989).

Another predictable ploy in budget formulation is for the executive or legislative branch to intentionally overestimate or underestimate revenues or expenditures. This is done to provide the excuse for budget cutting or to support the case that the proposed budget will be more in balance than is likely to obtain when actual revenues are received and expenses are incurred. In the federal government, the U.S. Congress has repeatedly accused the executive branch of overestimating revenues to minimize the annual budget deficit. The estimates of the Congressional Budget Office (CBO) have been regarded by Congress as much more reliable than those provided by the President's Office of Management and Budget (OMB). This is a result not only of Congress having more confidence in its own staff; ex post evaluation has in many, but not all, instances shown CBO to be more accurate since creation of the office in the 1974 Congressional Budget Impoundment and Control Act.

An example of misrepresentation in the politics of revenue estimation is available from California prior to enactment in 1978 of Proposition 13, the act which stimulated a wave of property tax reform and reduction across the nation (Levy, 1979). The Governor of California misinformed the public on the level of the state budget surplus in the apparent belief that if the actual size of the surplus were know, voters would choose property tax reform to retrieve the surplus. The governor's fears proved well-founded as property tax reform was approved by voters despite misrepresentation of the level of the surplus.

Analysis of the budgetary politics of negotiation and enactment permits the segregation of decision contexts and issues into macro- and microcategories. The macropolitics of the budgetary process typify the debate over high profile issues which command great public attention. Reform of the Social Security Tax or provision of aid to Contra forces in Central America are examples of macrolevel policy issues debated between and within the executive and Congress. The microlevel issues are just as political as the macrolevel issues, but they are negotiated between agency budget officers and executive and legislative budget analysts. The allowable inflation adjustment is one such issue, as is the attempt to conceal new programs in the base. Other similar ploys at the microlevel include intentional agency miscalculation of the budget or a failure to adjust downward on items as directed to put the onus of budget compilation and the rationalization of components to the whole on the backs of budget examiners. Computers have assisted budget examiners with the task of defining the base and incremental adjustments relative to a set of budget instruction parameters, but computers do not always catch cleverly disguised "errors" of this type.

Typical ploys in budget negotiation include inflating constituent group size and consequent demand for the program and use of organized lobby organizations to magnify the case for spending by applying pressure to the reelection calculus of elected officials. The age-old use of campaign funds and other types of benefits to trade for legislative votes providing employment in an elected official's state or district supports misrepresentation of client demand. Clientele groups with the best lobby typically are rewarded in the budget process wherein their effort is carefully coordinated with the program justification of the agency sponsor of the program. What is lamented by political scientists as the evil of pork-barrel politics is democracy in action from the viewpoint of many client groups.

Budget execution to some degree has a life of its own in most government organizations. The manner in which spending takes place and the services or assets acquired often do not relate directly to the proposals approved and promises made in budget formulation and negotiation. Agency and department program managers and budget officials typically reveal a strong preference for maximizing discretion in the application of resources to programs. They prefer to be as free as possible from the constraints applied by elected officials and controllers in the executive and legislative branches unless control provides necessary protection. Strong preference for discretion over the program for which managers are responsible is exactly what the precepts of management control recommend, that is, that managers be held accountable for the successes and failures of their programs relative to outputs achieved rather than to "political" variables (Anthony and Young, 1984; Euske, 1984).

A reward structure that emphasizes outcomes motivates managers to take ownership of their programs and to become more results-oriented. Budgetary discretion permits managers to apply resources where they are deemed to produce the desired mix of output. Output is contingent upon a technical core designed to solve problems that inhibit generation of output or block achievement of organizational goals. Program managers try to insulate and protect the critical technical cores of their organizations from interference, or political "noise," intruding from the resource decision environment (Thompson, 1967). Noise is reduced through the application of various ploys to gain budget execution freedom and to insulate against external interference.

Where a tight system of oversight, control, and audit is applied to budget execution and where program managers are strong protectors and supporters of their "technological cores" of problem solvers, pressure is placed on managers to misrepresent both factors of production and details of budget execution from oversight, audit, and program evaluation (Jones and Thompson, 1986). Motivation to behave in this manner typically is related legitimately to the desire to solve real problems (Euske and Euske, 1993).

Conclusion

Implicit in the argument made here is the assumption that the incentives for strategic representation and misrepresentation are not produced exclusively by the executive or the legislative branches of government or that they are the product of one or the other side of the political spectrum. And it should not be implied that strategic misrepresentation is engaged in only by budget and program advocates or budget controllers. Rather, strategic misrepresentation is a type of behavior in evidence across the board in the game of budgeting as a result of incentives established and reinforced by the dynamics of the public budgetary process.

Furthermore, it must be reiterated that all budgetary advocacy or control does not involve or require strategic misrepresentation and that all strategy in budgeting does not involve misrepresentation. Rather misrepresentation is a contingent strategy employed in response to a set of incentives present under specific circumstances. Implied in this analysis is that a democratic decision process then re-

form of the rules of budgeting is necessary to reduce or eliminate it.

L. R. JONES

BIBLIOGRAPHY

Anthony, R., 1985. "Games Government Accountants Play." *Harvard Business Review* (November–December) 161–170.
Anthony, R. and D. Young, 1984. *Management Control in Non-Profit Organizations*, Homewood: Irwin.
Euske, K., 1984. *Management Control: Planning, Control, Measurement, and Evaluation*. Reading, MA: Addison-Wesley.
Euske, N.A. and K.J. Euske, 1993. "Institutional Theory: Employing the Other Side of Rationality in Nonprofit Organizations" *British Journal of Management*.
Feldman, M. and J. March, 1981. "Information in Organizations as Signal and Symbol." *Administrative Sciences Quarterly* (June) 171–186.
Jones, L. and J. McCaffery, 1989. *Government Response to Financial Constraints*. Westport: Greenwood.
Jones, L. and F. Thompson, 1986. "Reform of Budget Execution Control." *Public Budgeting and Finance*, vol. 6, no. 1 (Spring) 33–49.
Levy, F., 1979. "On Understanding Proposition 13." *The Public Interest*, vol. 56 (Summer) 66–89.
Meyers, R., 1990. "Strategic Budgeting in the Federal Government." Paper delivered at the Annual Conference of the American Society for Public Administration, Los Angeles, CA, April 9.
Pfeffer, J. and G. Salancik, 1974. "Organizational Decision Making as a Political Process: The Case of a University Budget." *Administrative Sciences Quarterly*, vol. 19: 135–151.
Skinner, B. F., 1978. *Reflections on Behaviorism and Society*. Englewood Cliffs: Prentice-Hall.
Thompson, J., 1967. *Organizations in Action*. New York: McGraw Hill.
Wildavsky, A., 1964. *The Politics of the Budgetary Process*. Boston: Little, Brown.
———, 1988. *The New Politics of the Budgetary Process*. Glenview: Scott, Foresman.

BUDGET SUCCESS. Achieving one's objectives in one or more aspects of agency budgeting.

The term "budget success" has been used in statistical studies as a means of abbreviating a long description into a few words. For example, Ira Sharkansky (1968) has used "short-term budget success" to denote "the percentage of the agency's request for the coming budget period appropriated by the legislature." (p. 1222). He used a second measure, "success in budget expansion," to show the percentage of current expenditures appropriated by the legislature for the coming budget period. Using correlation analysis, Sharkansky came to a number of conclusions including, "A favorable recommendation from the Governor seems essential for agency budget success in the legislature" (p. 1230). Ira Sharkansky and August Turnbull (1969) and others have used these same techniques in analyzing budget increase in specific states.

Budget success has been used in a different fashion to describe the objectives that agency budget officials set for themselves and how they depict success in meeting these objectives. Sydney Duncombe and Richard Kinney (1987) interviewed 50 agency budget officials in 5 western states and asked them how they would define agency budget success. The criteria used by these officials in evaluating budget success were multifaceted and, in many cases, not easily quantified. The discussion that follows evaluates various means that might be used to measure agency budget success from the perspectives of the agency, the chief executive, the legislature, and their budget staffs.

Getting 100 Percent of Your Request Funded by the Legislature

Getting a high percentage of an agency's request funded by the legislature is obviously desirable and is easily measurable. However, this criterion of agency budget success, termed "short-term budget success" by Sharkansky, has its limitations. Some agencies add bargaining pieces to their budgets, expecting most of them to be cut, but hope to end up with a larger appropriation increase than other agencies that do not use this ploy. Agencies that use bargaining pieces will routinely show a lower percent of their requests funded than those who do not use this tactic. Moreover, the legislature may add to an agency's budget increases for new programs that the agency did not request or even desire. Agency budget officials interviewed in the Duncombe and Kinney 1987 study were reluctant to be evaluated by this measure of budget success and only 4 percent defined agency budget success in these terms.

Getting the Largest Possible Increase in Appropriations

It is relatively easy to calculate the percentage increase in an agency's appropriations over a prior year's expenditure or appropriation base. This measure is termed "success in budget expansion" in a number of statistical studies and merits full consideration. From an agency point of view, there are a number of problems in using this as a sole measure of budget success. A large percentage increase in appropriations depends, in part, on whether growth in tax revenues is sufficient to allow generous increases in agency appropriations without requiring a tax increase. In a 1986 study, Duncombe and Kinney found that 140 budget officials in 5 western states ranked revenue availability as the most important single factor affecting the appropriations of state agencies. In a study of the county budget process, Duncombe, Duncombe, and Kinney (1992) found that 84 percent of the budget officials in nearly 200 counties considered the amount of revenue available as very important

in influencing county budgets. While the federal government does not have constitutional requirements mandating a balanced budget, revenue availability also operates as a constraint on increases in agency appropriations at the federal level.

There are other reasons that agency officials are reluctant to have budget success evaluated on the basis of a percentage increase in their appropriations. The legislature may add large amounts to their budgets for an item of low agency priority and then make substantial cuts in ongoing agency programs. Moreover, too large an increase in appropriations provided by the legislature in one year could unduly stretch existing staff and not be effectively administered. A slow, stable increase in appropriations is often preferred by agency budget officials over rapid increases followed by declines. Furthermore, the process of exerting pressure through interest groups to gain a large percentage increase in appropriations may alienate the chief executive and the legislature. For these and other reasons agency budget officials in the Duncombe and Kinney 1987 study were very reluctant to define agency budget success in terms of percentage increases in appropriations.

Ability to Obtain Adequate Funding for Agency Programs

Agency officials tend to be "satisfiers" not "maximizers." Sixty percent of the agency respondents in the Duncombe and Kinney 1987 study volunteered that budget success is obtaining enough funds to meet agency needs and to maintain programs at current operating levels with a few improvements. They placed a higher priority on defending the agency base from reductions than they did on getting large increases for new programs. They were influenced undoubtedly by the fact that the study took place during a period of fiscal austerity. State agency officials are not alone in placing great emphasis on defending an agency's appropriation base. Aaron Wildavsky (1984) reported the same practice at the federal level.

Maintaining Good Legislative Relationships

Maintaining good relationships with legislature and its budget staff cannot be quantified, but it was so important to the respondents in the Duncombe and Kinney 1987 study that 60 percent included this as part of their definition of budget success. The key to good legislative relations was the credibility of the agency director and top staff. This credibility, once lost, took years to regain. As one Nevada official explained, "Credibility is my ability to say to the appropriation committee members in my own way, 'You've known me for years. I've never gone for the top dollar in requests. I need this request very badly.' Budget success is for the legislative committee to believe me and grant me this request" (pp. 32, 33). Aaron Wildavsky (1984) provides evidence that agency officials at the federal level also find it advisable to "play it straight" with the appropriations committee and develop a reputation for integrity (pp. 76–79).

Maintaining Good Relations with the Governor and the Executive Budget Staff

Maintaining good relationships with the governor and the executive budget staff was considered helpful both in getting an item in the executive budget and in persuading the governor to throw his or her full support behind the budget of the agency during the legislative process. Moreover, approval of the governor and/or executive budget staff was often needed to transfer amounts between programs or budget items during the execution stage of the budget. To maintain good relationships with the governor and the executive budget staff, state agency officials suggested keeping their executive budget analyst informed of new developments, being honest in presenting budget information, and being a good "team player." A good team player does not undercut the department director and governor by "grandstanding" to get the legislature to add back to the budget all amounts cut at the departmental and gubernatorial levels.

Success in Budget Execution

Agency budget officials recognize that success in budget execution is very important, not only for effective program administration but also to build a reputation for effective fiscal management. Respondents to the Duncombe and Kinney study (1987) felt that successful budget execution included living within legislative appropriations, carrying out legislative intent, allocating appropriated funds fairly within appropriations, and effectively managing cash flow. Successful budget execution was facilitated if restrictive language was omitted from appropriation acts, an agency was given the authority to carry forward appropriation balances into the next year, and the agency had flexibility to secure funds quickly in an emergency.

Conclusions

Agency budget success means achieving one's objectives in all phases of budgeting, not just success in achieving larger appropriations. Success is achieved in the budget execution stage when an agency has flexibility in the use of its

funds, is able to live within its appropriations, and allocates funds fairly to programs and subprograms. Agency budget success in the appropriation stage depends upon the availability of revenues and other factors such as support by the governor, key legislators, and influential interest groups. Agency success in gaining higher appropriations is hard to measure because the percentage increase in appropriations is affected, not only by revenue availability, but also by whether the legislature adds new programs of low priority to the agency. A better means of budget success is whether an agency has obtained sufficient funds to meet its needs with some additional funds for new or improved programs.

Maintenance of good relationships with the chief executive, the legislature, and their budget staffs is an essential part of budget success. These relationships hinge on the credibility, integrity, and honesty of agency budget officials in presenting their budget requests and in administering their budget. The reputation for integrity built by agency directors and agency officials over a period of years and the trust that this inspires play an important role in budget success.

SYDNEY DUNCOMBE

BIBLIOGRAPHY

Duncombe, Sydney and Richard Kinney, 1986. "The Politics of State Appropriation Increases: The Perspective of Budget Officers in Five Western States." *State Government,* vol. 59 (September/October) 113–123.
———, 1987. "Agency Budget Success: How It Is Defined by Budget Officials in Five Western States." *Public Budgeting & Finance,* vol. 7 (Spring) 24–37.
Duncombe, Sydney, William Duncombe, and Richard Kinney, 1992. "Factors Influencing the Politics and Process of County Government Budgeting." *State and Local Government Review,* vol. 24 (Winter) 19–27.
Sharkansky, Ira, 1968. "Agency Requests, Gubernatorial Support, and Budget Success in State Legislatures." *The American Political Science Review,* vol. 62 (December) 1220–1231.
Sharkansky, Ira and Augustus B. Turnbull III, 1969. "Budget Making in Georgia and Wisconsin: A Test of a Model." *Midwest Journal of Political Science,* vol. 13 (November) 631–645.
Wildavsky, Aaron, 1984. *The Politics of the Budgetary Process,* 4th ed. Boston: Little, Brown.

BUDGET THEORY. The conceptual structure which defines how observers think about, analyze, and explain the budget process and its outcomes.

Allen Schick (1988b) defines the core characteristics of budgeting as a collection of rules and procedures that allocates money among competing claims for scarce resources. Budget theory attempts to explain how the budget process operates and why some claims are honored whereas others are rejected. Budget theory can be approached from a variety of perspectives, from the analytic concepts of economics to the sociologies of human interaction, communication, and negotiation, but no set of budget theories is as compelling as the incremental synthesis of Aaron Wildavsky. Wildavsky melded elements from various fields mentioned above to construct a compelling vision of how the budgeting process works in government. The collection of behaviors came to be called incrementalism.

According to Wildavsky (1992, pp. 416–425), the norms of balance, annularity, and comprehensiveness keep an incremental system in place. Balance refers to keeping spending within available revenues. Annularity means budget reviewers can review, approve, or reject every spending item each year. Comprehensiveness indicates that the budget contains all spending items.

Incrementalism operates as a bottom-up process that focuses on microitems such as salaries, contracts, supplies, and activities performed by agencies. Spending units initiate the decisionmaking process with the development and submission of a budget proposal. Generally, agencies make the case for additional resources. As a group, proposed spending increases almost always outstrip available money. Requests go initially to the central budget office guardians, who analyze submissions. Central budget offices report to the chief executive, such as a mayor, governor, or president, who must submit a comprehensive budget to the legislature.

Both spenders and reviewers view budget proposals as consisting of the base, or last year's spending, and the increment, or request for new money. Budget reviewers focus on requests for new money and take the base as given. Traditionally, an agency's base consists of the dollars appropriated last year, and many governments still use last year's appropriation. However, some governments, including the United States federal government, view the "current services" baseline as the base. The baseline includes the money necessary to continue current activities. Thus, it encompasses the last appropriation plus additional resources needed to cover cost increases tied to inflation, such as escalations in utility costs. A current services baseline places a portion of new money in the base, and it reduces the amount of resources available to cover agency increments.

Incremental budget decisionmaking does not use articulated policy priorities to guide the review of proposals. In fact, analysts do not examine the budget as a complete document. Instead, a decentralized review process takes place in which individual reviewers specialize and concentrate on a limited number of agency requests. Usually, reviewers work with requests from the same agencies each year. Analysts react to agency proposals as autonomous items not impacted by decisions about other spending requests. Generally, spenders, through hearings or informal

interchanges, respond to the questions from analysts about the need for new money. For the process to function correctly, both advocates and guardians must carry out their prescribed roles. Agencies realize that cuts are coming, so budget proposals contain items that would be nice to have but are not necessary. Reviewers cut budgets under the assumption that agencies ask for noncritical things.

The central budget office bundles modified spending unit requests into a comprehensive budget and the chief executive sends it to the legislature. With the exception of small local governments, legislative consideration also operates as a decentralized process with specialists. Lawmakers unbundle the comprehensive budget and parcel out pieces to different appropriations committees or subcommittees. While lawmakers assume a guardian role, it is tempered by legislative desires to increase spending that benefits constituents and enhances prospects for reelection.

Once legislative specialists review and modify their segment of the budget proposal, the full membership accepts or modifies their work. In the United States Congress and 49 of 50 American state legislatures, budgets must pass the House and Senate in identical form. If the initial versions of the two chambers diverge, conference committees reconcile the differences. Once each chamber approves the conference report, spending bills are sent to the executive for signature or veto. Legislatures usually change spending bills to accommodate executive demands when veto overrides fail.

The incremental decisionmaking process depends on several mechanisms to simplify decisionmaking and reduce conflict among persons brought together each year to work on the budget. As a disjointed process with many decision points, budgetmaking allows a diversity of groups to impact decisions. Rather than a comprehensive and time-consuming effort to find the "best" way to divide new resources among the claimants, persons reviewing budgets seek acceptable outcomes that accommodate a variety of participant perspectives. The absence of clearly stated spending priorities makes it possible to avoid distinct trade-offs between programs and to avert dissension among budget players. Differences of opinion are resolved through bargaining and compromise at various points in the segmented process. Budget outcomes reflect a result that all parties find acceptable.

In *The Politics of the Budgetary Process,* Wildavsky (1964) argues that an incremental budget decisionmaking process produces incremental budget outcomes. When the review process is complete, the new budget looks very much like last year's product. Spending units receive small increases and each agency consumes about the same share of the budget pie as last year. As William Berry (1990) notes, incrementalism suggests that the decision making process determines allocation outcomes at the expense of external factors such as changes in the public attitudes, agency strategies to increase their share of new money, and declines in resources. In effect, the process causes the budget allocations to operate like a large ship. Over a period of time, changes in course may occur, but quick changes in direction are impossible.

The inability of the incremental budget process to accommodate large swings in spending in a short period of time favors the base, or existing claims on resources, over new claims. With only minor adjustments in spending, public officials avoid disruptions to government agencies and the accompanying negative political consequences. If minor changes in spending produce unintended consequences, corrective action in the next budget cycle can remedy the problem.

In essence, the two concepts of incrementalism embody a pluralist decisionmaking process that produces minor changes in spending policy. Participants carry out defined roles. The allocation process operates as a bottom-up mechanism with agencies initiating the action. Reviewers only look at parts of the budget rather than the whole document. Disjointed consideration minimizes conflict by avoiding explicit policy trade-offs. Differences of opinion are resolved through bargaining that produces small modifications in last year's spending.

Empirical Criticisms of Incrementalism

Several budget scholars such as Lance LeLoup (1988) and Irene Rubin (1988) suggest that incrementalism does not represent an empirical description of budget decisionmaking. Many deviations from incrementalism occur when governments depart from the norms of annularity, balance, and comprehensiveness.

Mandatory spending, also known as entitlement programs, represent a major divergence from each of the three norms supporting incrementalism. These programs define eligibility for government benefits and mandate that all eligible recipients receive payment. With mandatory programs, governments transgress annularity because laws setting benefits are not reviewed each year. Jurisdictions violate balance since these programs require payments to all eligible recipients without regard to government income. Comprehensiveness is breached since these programs allocate money outside the annual budget process. Currently, about 65 percent of United States federal government spending supports mandatory programs such as Social Security, Medicare, and agricultural crop subsidies. Minimum foundation formulas for public education in American states also operate as entitlements. Education committees outside the budget process develop formulas that funnel money to school districts based on the number of pupils and other criteria. State budgeters must set aside money to cover these financial commit-

ments unless the legislature alters the formula to lessen the financial impact.

Many jurisdictions violate the norm of comprehensiveness by using money allocating mechanisms outside the budget process. As Irene Rubin (1988) notes, actors who lack formal budget roles impact allocation decisions. These may include legislative committees that initiate spending directives that lock in future appropriations. For example American state legislatures sometimes approve pay raises that are phased in over several years. American state and local governments also operate with special funds. Often governments authorize spending from special funds outside the normal budget process. For instance, in many American states, transportation committees initiate highway projects paid with earmarked gasoline taxes.

Evidence also suggests that the environmental factor of fiscal scarcity threatens the norm of balance. The incremental pattern of marginal increases is disrupted when revenues decline or dollar increases fall below the level of inflation. Consequently, many spending units do not retain their share of the budget pie. As Marcia Whicker (1992) points out, Wildavsky first applied incrementalism to the budget process in the 1950s and 1960s when growing revenues made the distribution of the increment the focus of budget decisionmaking. By the 1980s, budget decisions for many governments around the world shifted from distribution of the increment to redistribution of the base among the claimants.

Wildavsky (1992) states that redistributive politics heightens ideological conflict and leads to a decline to accommodation. Whicker (1992) observes that the desire to control the redistribution of resources drives recent efforts to centralize budget decisionmaking. Barry Bozeman and Jeffrey D. Straussman (1982) report that tight money increased top-down executive leverage in the U.S. federal government during the late 1970s and early 1980s. As Richard Doyle and Jerry McCaffery (1991) point out, the federal government adopted caps on discretionary or nonmandatory spending in 1990. A budget summit between President George Bush's administration and congressional leaders worked out the details. Congress ratified the agreement. As Karl O'Lessker (1993) reports, President Clinton pushed a budget through Congress in 1993 that is intended to limit the size of the deficit over a five-year period. The plan caps domestic spending and raises taxes.

The phenomena of increased executive leverage over budget decisions is occurring in other countries. McCaffery (1984) describes the same phenomenon in Canada. Allen Schick (1986) studied five industrialized countries in the mid-1980s. He demonstrates that scarcity leads to an increase of centralized top-down budgeting.

When governments violate the norms of annularity, comprehensiveness, and balance, deviations from incremental budgeting occur. At the same time, many scholars such as Whicker (1992), Naomi Caiden (1986) and Edward J. Clynch and Thomas P. Lauth (1991) emphasize that the separation-of-powers system used by most governments in the United States limits the shift from incremental to top-down centralized budgeting. Constitutional constraints prevent executives from controlling budget decisions over long periods of time. From time to time, the electorate gives an executive a mandate for change that results in nonincremental budget outcomes. At the federal level in America, President Franklin Roosevelt in the 1930s, President Lyndon Johnson in the mid-1960s, and President Ronald Reagan in the early 1980s dominated budget decisionmaking. Within a few years, however, the preferences of legislative majorities made it difficult for these presidents to alter spending patterns in a meaningful way. Clynch and Lauth found that power over budget decisions in the American states ebbs and flows between governors and legislatures. If one of the actors starts to dominate budget decisions, the other reacts and claims a meaningful role in the budget allocation process.

Normative Criticisms of Incrementalism

Most budget scholars agree that incrementalism offers an incomplete description of budget decisionsmaking. Many writers also point to the existence of nonincremental budget outcomes. At the same time, however, incremental budget processes continue to function. Moreover, many, if not most, budget outcomes represent small changes from last year's spending. Given its staying power, incrementalism continues to attract both defenders and critics along normative dimensions.

Wildavsky and other supporters of incrementalism argue that the disjointed and sequential decisionmaking process allows input from a variety of community interests. The diversity of interests in most countries requires a budget allocation process that takes competing views of who gets what into account. Incremental budget decisionmaking allows give and take as decisionmakers reach the compromises represented by allocation outcomes.

The critics of incrementalism question that an incremental pluralist decisionmaking system serves as the best way to allocate scarce resources among competing claimants. One line of criticism by scholars such as Irene Rubin questions the assumption that incremental decisionmaking accommodates the views of all segments of society. In their view, multiple access points do not guarantee that every perspective will make its way into negotiations over budget outcomes. For instance, the less affluent segments of society lack the political resources to participate in a meaningful way. Additionally, groups advocating new programs experience limited success. They find it very difficult to gain a foothold since reviewers do not want to shift resources from the base of ongoing activities.

A second line of criticism concerns the desirability of a process that produces minor changes to last year's spending through bargained agreements. Instead, critics say that budget decisions should reflect the spending priorities of a majority of citizens. Rather than disparate independent actors who take part in a disjointed process that produces bargained decisions, reformers want budget decisions placed in the hands of elected executives who represent the entire electorate.

As Schick (1986) points out, the budget decisionmaking process determines the potency of agencies and executives. A change in the rules can alter the ability of each group to affect budget outcomes. Instead of an agency-initiated bottom-up process that focuses on unconnected microitems, budget decisionmaking needs to allow executives to consider the budget as a whole. This permits the president, governor, or mayor to dominate spending outcomes through top-down macrodecisions that set priorities. Executive priorities divide resources among major functions such as education, transportation, public health, and so forth. These preferences guide micro-agency requests. When budget requests reach central budget offices, reviewers recommend changes to agency proposals based on congruence with executive priorities. Once the budget reaches the legislature, this body only makes changes in microrequests. The division of resources among macro areas remains intact.

Majoritarian budget champions also advocate budgets prepared in a program format that ties spending to particular activities. This design enhances the ability of reviewers to judge if individual spending requests further executive goals. Majoritarians expect budget reviewers to go beyond determining the "fit" of microrequests into macropriorities, however. They also want budget mechanisms that permit reviewers to determine the efficiency and effectiveness of microlevel programs. To accomplish these goals, the programmatic budget format needs to include information suitable for analysis. Efficiency is measured by indicators that tie the cost of units of work performed and things purchased to unit of activity produced, such as the cost to service a client. Zero-based budgeting expands the information available by showing the consequences on program outputs when different levels of money are provided. Effectiveness is demonstrated by linking the costs of activities performed to units of results achieved, often with cost-benefit analysis. For example, effectiveness measures may determine the number of clients successfully treated with a given amount of money.

Analytical information allows scrutiny of specific programs, but reviewers may find it difficult to base budget decisions on the analytical conclusions. High-priority programs may receive increases even when evidence suggests inefficiency and ineffectiveness. Low-priority programs that work well may not be rewarded with above average increases. As Wildavsky notes in *The New Politics of the Budgetary Process* (1992a), decisionmakers use analytical results to justify politically acceptable budget outcomes while ignoring information that fails to support desired conclusions.

EDWARD J. CLYNCH

BIBLIOGRAPHY

Berry, William D., 1990. "The Confusing Case of Budgetary Incrementalism: Too Many Meanings for a Single Concept." *Journal of Politics,* vol. 52, no 1: 167–196.

Bozeman, Barry and Jeffrey D. Straussman, 1982. "Shrinking Budgets and the Shrinkage of Budget Theory." *Public Administration Review,* vol. 42 (November/December) 509–515.

Caiden, Naomi, 1986. "Comments on Bernard T. Pitsvada, 'The Executive Budget—An Idea Whose Time Has Passed.' " *Public Budgeting and Finance,* vol. 6 (Spring) 95–99.

Clynch, Edward J. and Thomas P. Lauth, eds., 1991. *Governors, Legislatures, and Budgets: Diversity across the American States.* New York: Greenwood Press.

Doyle, Richard and Jerry McCaffery, 1991. "The Budget Enforcement Act of 1990: The Path to No Fault Budgeting." *Public Budgeting and Finance,* vol. 11 (Spring) 25–37.

LeLoup, Lance T., 1988. "From Microbudgeting to Macrobudgeting: Evolution in Theory and Practice." In Irene S. Rubin, ed., *New Directions in Budget Theory.* Albany, NY: State University New York Press, 19–42.

McCaffery, Jerry, 1984. "Canada's Envelope Budget: A Strategic Management System." *Public Administration Review,* vol. 44 (July/August) 373–383.

O'Lessker, Karl, 1993. "The Clinton Budget for FY 1994: Taking Aim at the Deficit." *Public Budgeting and Finance,* vol. 13 (Summer) 7–19.

Rubin Irene S., 1988. "Introduction." In Irene S. Rubin, ed., *New Directions in Budget Theory.* Albany, NY: State University New York Press, 1–18.

Schick, Allen, 1986. "Macro-Budgetary Theory Adaptations to Fiscal Stress in Industrialized Democracies." *Public Administration Review,* vol. 46 (March/April) 124–134.

———, 1988a. "Micro-Budgetary Theory Adaptations to Fiscal Stress in Industrialized Democracies." *Public Administration Review* (January/February) 523–533.

———, 1988b. "An Inquiry into the Possibility of a Budgetary Theory." In Irene S. Rubin, ed., *New Directions in Budget Theory.* Albany, NY: State University New York Press, 59–69.

Whicker, Marcia Lynn, 1992. "Toward a Grander Budget Theory." *Public Administration Review,* vol. 52 (November/December) 600–603.

Wildavsky, Aaron, 1964. *The Politics of the Budgetary Process.* Boston: Little, Brown.

———, 1992a. *The New Politics of the Budgetary Process,* 2nd ed. New York: Harper Collins.

———, 1992b. "Political Implications of Budget Reform. *Public Administration Review,* vol. 52 (November/December) 594–599.

BUDGET TOOLS, COMMONSENSE. Techniques that skilled budget practitioners develop over time; these include the use of rounding, ratios, guesstimates, error-checking procedures, fishnetting, and matrix-drawing. Budgeting depends on numerical accuracy and some very sophisticated analytical concepts, like benefit-cost analysis, but budgeting also depends on a set of everyday commonsense tools.

Introduction

This entry is about some commonsense budgeting tools gathered from various sources, experiences, and ideas over the years. It is not intended to be inclusive: There are opposing ideas, alternative tools, and many more additional ideas and tools. It is intended to be helpful to those who aspire to membership in a worthy profession, budgeting. It is both normative and empirical.

Intuition Tool

Although budgeteers tend to rely on quantification, blind reliance on quantities and the results of rigorous numerical thinking can lead to disastrous results. Beginning budgeteers are particularly prey to the "law of the instrument," but senior ones are known to be victims, too. Budgeteers should "question" and be mentally open to "questions" about data and approaches to them. The value of the Garbage In, Garbage Out (GIGO) rule of automatic data processing is most evident in those having a blind faith in the results of a computer-assisted analysis, that is, spreadsheet jockeying. Unfortunately, the trend appears to be along the lines of emphasizing spreadsheet jockeying without the virtue of understanding what is behind the numbers, including a basic understanding of the operations that the numbers represent. It also means that if "something" about data or other documentation does not "feel" right, prudence dictates that a budgeteer should resolve the uncertainty before proceeding.

An agency was about to release a report of major importance. The agency director shared it with a visitor, suggesting that he read it as it would affect the results of their discussion. The visitor read the report. Something did not "feel" right about the report. Fortunately, the methodology of its calculations was in the report. The visitor acted upon personal intuition by doing some manual calculations of the data, using the prescribed methodology. The results were different; they led to different conclusions. Verifying the calculations, the visitor then contacted the agency head and asked if the report's data were correct. The response was, "sure, we used an X spreadsheet to do it." The visitor explained that manual calculations indicated errors in either the methodology or its results and suggested that before the report was made public, it should be rechecked. Not surprisingly, the reassessment found errors in the computerized formulas of the methodology. The larger lesson of this example is that intuition should not be ignored. It is a difficult precept for quantitatively oriented people to follow.

Budget Reading

In reading budgeting materials, regardless of whether they are quantitative or qualitative, the analyst should ask some fundamental questions:

What is said? What is not said?
What is shown? What is not shown?
What has been done? What has not been done?
Who is/What is affected? Who is/What is not affected?
What are the effects?
How are the effects known?
What are the larger, short- or long-term consequences, that is, does it have budgetwide implications?

In many instances, the latter question is not asked but should be. For example, a budget request may seem well-documented by a requesting organization and its circumstances, yet the request could be a significant, government-wide issue. Inflation, salary increases, and tuition and fee increases illustrate these types of sleepers. Another sleeper may often be found in "program experiments." For instance, a health organization may request funding for a pilot program with sound, ample documentation, except that nothing is mentioned about the costs if the program is successful and expanded through the jurisdiction in future years.

Matrix Tool

It is not uncommon for a budgeteer to be faced with the analysis of a largely unquantified problem. These problems are often found in narrative-heavy policy documents. Matrix thinking may help the analyst to address the problem. The lineage of the matrix approach is uncertain, although its parents are probably found in the philosophy of science, statistics, and quantitative research methodologies. The matrix tool is most useful in dealing with complex problems and, increasingly, with problems that initially appear very simple. The matrix tool is logically based upon the relationships between variables and their consequences.

The first step in the matrix approach is to tentatively identify all (given available time and resources) the variables ("variable" is here used in its broadest sense of exclusive entities, including "concepts"). Second, the analyst should then identify all the logically possible relationships and orderings. It helps to think singularly and in combinations. For example, consider two variables, X and Y. There are eight logical possibilities:

$$X, Y, XY, \overline{X}, \overline{Y}, \overline{X}Y, X\overline{Y}, \text{ and } \overline{XY}$$

It is most helpful to array the possibilities in a matrix format (hence the tool's name). After arriving at the logical

possibilities, the analyst then begins the third step of ascertaining factual possibilities. This analysis may also require additional consideration of both *relationships* and orderings. Some refinements of the variables usually occur at this stage through adding, subtracting, deleting, dividing, multiplying, combining, or synthesizing. As the specificity of the analysis proceeds, quantification, or the basis for it, frequently begins to emerge (although this is neither necessary nor sufficient). This seems true because of the constant searching for factual (but not necessarily quantified) information to sustain the generated logical information. Perhaps even more important, in dealing with unquantifiable problems such as frequently occur in policy analyses, the matrix approach can reveal gaps or variances between and among policies and their implementation strategies.

Fishnetting

There are a variety of quantitative techniques for dealing with uncertainty. Uncertainty is endemic to our world as are the risks or exposures associated with uncertainty. Risktaking may well differentiate the proactive budgeteer from the reactive budgeteer. If so, then the budgeteer needs some basis for taking risks. One basis for risktaking is to "fishnet." Fishnetting is based on the idea that one can exclude, by using nets with holes of different sizes, fish of a relatively specific size. Fishnetting for budgeting use simply means utilizing criteria to filter alternatives. Keep in mind that criteria are tests of preferredness and that preferredness can be valued in utility terms (e.g., quantified through cost-utility analysis). In nonquantified terms, preferredness may be ascertained by asking a related set of questions illustrated by the following questions (based on G. Odiorne, 1969, pp. 66–78):

1. Does it contribute?
2. What does it cost?
3. Will it work?
4. Is it timely?
5. What are the side effects and effects?
6. Will quantification lead to sounder predictions or assessments?
7. What are my preferences? Why?

Obviously, questions such as these should be asked in people, technical, feasibility, and other resource terms.

Equity Tool

Has everyone been treated equitably? is a not an infrequently asked question of budgeteers. The question is not a simple one, for its act or action regarding a policy proposal is not always clear. There are at least four definitions of equity (based in part on Levy, Meltsner, and Wildavsky, 1974, pp. 16–17):

1. *opportunity equity:* all receive the same level of service
2. *market equity:* all receive according to their apportionment
3. *results equity:* all are in the same condition after something is done
4. *criterion equity:* all are treated equally according to some standard

Under the first definition, the budgeteer would answer Yes if all received an identical allocation. For example, each receives an allotment of US $1,000 for travel. Under the second definition the budgeteer would answer Yes if the allocation was based on the portion that the receiver represents of some whole. For example, each receives an allotment based upon their portion of the total amount budgeted for travel. Under the third definition, the answer would be Yes if the allocation created equal results. For example, all employees are provided funds to attend one conference per year. The fourth definition would yield a Yes answer if the allocation is by a common standard. For example, travel funding will be based on the relationship of the travel to the strategic objectives of the unit. Each of these meanings of equality can result in widely different policy proposals, decisions, budget allocations, and political controversies.

Percentages

Percentages are among the most useful tools at the disposal of a budgeteer. They are often underused. Budgeteers are usually comfortable with relatively large arrays of precise values; most people are not, as evidenced by the decided tendency to skip over tabular data when reading. Thus, percentages can assist the budgeteer in conveying the importance of information to nonquantitatively oriented audiences, including many political decisionmakers.

Percentages enable the good budgeteer, and others, to assess the relative size of numbers by mathematical simplification and the use of a base 100. Percentages help the analyst focus on relative size rather than absolute size. The percentage ratio between two numbers is often a most revealing value. Percentages (increase/decrease or absolute) are particularly useful in making comparisons. However, the decision as to whether to make a percentage or absolute values comparison must be made on the basis of the nature of the data and their circumstances. In developing percentage tables, it is often analytically helpful to do both row and column percentages, even though the general rule

is to calculate percentages in the direction of "causality." While percentages above 100 percent are nonsense and can be very misleading, they are commonly used. It is an ill-advised practice. Zeisel's classic *Say It with Figures* (1957) is highly recommended for a thorough reading.

Visual Tool

The visual tool can be one of the most useful tools for the budgeteer if it is appropriately selected. While it is axiomatic that a picture is worth a thousand words, the tendency today is to rely on whatever an automated spreadsheet and supplemental graphics package and printer will produce. The key question to ask in creating a visual tool is, What do I want to effectively convey? (The obverse question—What is not being conveyed?—is useful for budgeteers when they are being presented visuals.) In some instances, drawing a rough picture of the results of an analytical effort can prevent needless subsequent efforts, for example, plotting the results of a linear relationship. Einstein understood well the inherent elegance of simplicity. Budget analysts are well-served by his example.

It may be wise to keep in mind the story of a professor who was busy working on his Monday lecture one Sunday. His six-year-old son kept interrupting his concentration with questions and other attention-getting behavior. Finally, the professor had an idea. He recalled a map of the world in the morning's paper. He found it, carefully cut it up into many different pieces, and gave it scrambled to his son to reassemble. He returned to his lecture preparation thinking that the map puzzle would keep his son occupied. However, his son soon returned to his father saying, "I did it, Daddy!" Puzzled, the father asked his son how he solved the puzzle so quickly. His son proudly said, "Look, Daddy, there's a picture of a man on the back of the puzzle, and when the picture is right, the puzzle is!" With some thought, complex data or data presentations can often be more easily understood by presenting a simple picture. Be mindful, however, that 80 percent of something still does not account for 20 percent of the something!

In another context, and recalling the prior illustration, a budget manager was consistently having trouble satisfying the information requests of a budget-knowledgeable, appointed official. Finally, after a number of instances in which the staff did very good jobs of seemingly responding to information requests only to discover it was not what the requestor wanted, the budget manager got an idea. The next time he met with the appointed official to get briefed on a request, he listened, drew a rough matrix of the request, with the column and row headers, as he understood the request, and asked the official, "Is this what you want when we're done?" The official paused and said, "No, damn it, this is what I want . . ." and proceeded to redraw the matrix and headers. He paused at various times, revising his initial drawing twice before he said, "This is what I want to know." It was what the budget manager wanted to know, too, and thereafter, he successfully used picture drawing in clarifying assignments.

Error Tool

Another old but useful tool is the rule of error: If a balance does not equal its parts by an odd number, then a recording transposition may have occurred; if the balance does not equal its parts by an even number, then the error may be one of addition.

Proof Tools

Proof tools are essential to the good budgeteer. Proof tools may involve formal logical (including mathematical) reasoning or rigorous informal reasoning. Discussion here focuses on some arithmetical proofs (based in part on *Smith's Arithmetic of Business, passim*). Although some of these tools now may be arcane, their logic is not.

Despite the use of automated spreadsheets, the old accountancy tool of "cross-footing" to verify sums remains a useful tool for budgeteers. For those unfamiliar with cross-footing, it is the process of summing the sums of the rows and summing the sums of the columns to assure that they are identical. Once a tedious but necessary task, it is something that should be a standard part of any spreadsheet's background template.

Addition verification may also be done by repetitive applications in the same or opposite direction (i.e., up or down, back or forth).

The "cashier's" method involves adding columns independently, placing the right-hand value of each under the second value of the total above it. The column totals are summed as follows:

	Verification
57	
38	
65	
43	
22	32
27	22
252	= 252

The "casting out" method uses some value, for example, 7. The first step is to cast out all 7s from the first values in the column. This is done by finding the highest multiple value of 7 in a particular row and subtracting that value

from the row value. Then, the same procedure is applied to the sum of the respective columns. If the resulting differences are identity, then the addition is probably correct:

213	3	(213 − 210 = 3)
654	3	(654 − 651 = 3)
389	4	(389 − 385 = 4)
731	3	(731 − 728 = 3)
442	1	(442 − 441 = 1)
2429	14	(2429 − 2429 = 0) = (14 − 14 = 0)

Subtraction verification may be handled similarly to the first addition verification tool. It also may be done by adding the subtrahend and difference. If the result and the minuend are identity, the subtraction is correct.

The "casting out" method can also be used in multiplication verification, in this instance, again using 7s:

653	2	(653 − 651 = 2)
× 239	1	(239 − 238 = 1)
156,067	2	(156,067 − 156,065 = 2)
		= (2 × 1 = 2)

Of course, multiplication verification can also be done by transposing the values and multiplying again.

The factor method of multiplication verification can be used when a multiplier can be decomposed into *two* factors. The product can be ascertained by multiplying the multiplicand by one of the factors, and multiplying the result by the other factor:

57		57
× 45	(45 = 9 × 5)	× 9
2,565		513
		× 5
		2,565

Ratios can be used in making gross estimates. For example, suppose a budgeteer knows that each increment of US $1.00 to a US $750 unit value represents an additional systemwide cost of about US $500,000. If a proposal is made "at the table" to increase the unit value by US $50, then it is known that additional systemwide cost will be about US $25 million. Good budgeteers take the time to ascertain significant ratios in their areas of responsibility.

Guesstimation Tool

Wise budgeteers are justifiably suspect of requests that contain a relatively large number of zeros to the right of a whole number(s). At best, these "neat" numbers represent high-order magnitude rounding; at worst, they may represent a crude guess-wish.

Rounding Tool

The convention in rounding is to round up with an integer of 5 or more and to round down when the integer is 4 or less. Accountants do not like rounding but budgeteers do. Some jurisdictions think rounding to the nearest US $100 is a lot of rounding, others round to the nearest US $100,000; the U.S. federal government rounds up well above these amounts.

Precision Tool

Much is written in the academic literature about false precision. That is not what the precision tool is about. The precision tool deals with the issue of how many integers should be calculated to the right of the decimal point. The precision tool holds that the number of integers to the right of the decimal point should be equal to the number of integers to the left of the decimal point plus one. The academic notion of false precision now enters this discussion: It is not usually necessary to present a large array of decimal-point-right integers to demonstrate how fine the calculations have been done. Normally, presenting more than two decimal-point-right integers is superfluous.

Comparison Tool

Data analysis, like efficiency, requires comparison to be meaningful. Comparisons may be made between, among, and within similar sets of information through or across time, location, entity, or resources, but they must be made if the budgeteer aspires to be more than a clerk. Comparison implies a standard. It often falls to the budgeteer to explicate the standard, whether it be a quantity or quality. Relatively few numbers have significance in isolation; the others become significant when they are placed against numbers from other, similarly based or related situations. The question is, What can this be reasonably compared with or against?

Fund Splits

Fund splits refer to any consideration of U.S. governmental funding allocations since its accounting is based on fund-accounting. It is common for governmental units to use a mix of funding sources in budgeting programs. It is critical for those with budget interests to be informed on relevant fund splits. Unfortunately, few people outside of budget and finance professionals understand the implications of fund splits. One governor, for example, was not shy in pronouncements of how his administration had increased higher education funding. In nominal dollars, his pronouncements were correct. What was not being said, however, was that he had increased the total funding by

reducing the general fund contribution and increasing tuition and fee requirements to more than cover the general funding reduction. The budgeteer must always think in terms of the funding splits of affected programs and the implications to these funding splits of policies. In some budget environments, fund splits are required as "match" requirements. True match requirements, however, normally refer to a funding source that requires a definite match of some magnitude from another, separate source. For example, a state program for localities may provide 60 percent of the funding subject to a locality contributing 40 percent of the funding either through direct or in-kind means. Although federal budgeteers rarely deal with funding issues except in intergovernmental transfers (getting the money is a Treasury function), they need to be cognizant of this state and local issue and its import to these jurisdictions.

Summary

This entry focused on a variety of commonsense tools of the craft, some old and some new. The tools range from qualitative to simple quantitative ones. They are tools that are rarely referenced in budgeting and finance work despite their value in the day-to-day efforts of budgeteers. It is not a definitive study of such tools, but a beginning.

RICHARD E. ZODY

BIBLIOGRAPHY

Levy, Frank, Arnold Meltsner, and Aaron Wildavsky, 1974. *Urban Outcomes: Schools, Streets, and Libraries.* Berkeley: University of California Press.
Odiorne, George S., 1969. *Management Decisions by Objectives.* Englewood Cliffs, NJ: Prentice-Hall.
Smith's Arithmetic of Business. I am unable to ascertain the publication particulars on this out-of-print, high school textbook published early in this century. My copy, much used by earlier owners, does not have a title page or other relevant information, and is missing the publisher's information as well.
Zeisel, Hans, 1957. *Say It with Figures,* 4th ed. rev. New York: Harper & Row.

BUDGETING. A process which matches resources and needs in an organized and repetitive way so those collective choices about what an entity needs to do are properly resourced. Most definitions emphasize that a budget is an itemized estimate of expected income and operating expenses for a given unit of government over a set time period. Budgeting is the process of arriving at such a plan. Once a fiscal year has started, the budget becomes a plan for disbursing resources to attain goals.

Political scientists and policy analysts tend to examine budgeting in terms of who gets what, who pays and who benefits, and under what conditions. Economists tend to examine budgeting from the perspectives of stabilization, distribution, and allocative efficiency. Stabilization refers to policies pursued through the budget to stabilize the economy. Distribution refers to policies that transfer income from one set of citizens to another through government action. Allocation refers to choices over which goods and services should be provided by government and which are better left to the private sector. Public administrationists are primarily concerned with how the budget is produced and how the information in it is presented and analyzed.

In the American context, the budget process begins in the executive branch of government, where the budget plan is developed, and proceeds into the legislative branch, where the budget plan is reviewed and amended. The process usually concludes in the executive branch, where the chief executive must sign the budget bill or bills into law. At the federal level, the chief executive may veto budget bills he does not like, but eventually he must sign some sort of compromise bill. The majority of state governors have an item veto which allows them to change bills in different ways, depending upon the precise nature of the veto power. The budget power is a shared power, developed under a system of checks and balances and the separation of powers, although the Constitution is clear that the taxing power rests with the legislature and, by inference, ultimately the spending power.

Parliamentary systems are different; here, the party that controls the legislature forms the government or cabinet composed of the prime minister and various ministers who control different departments and who are also elected officials who serve in the legislature. The budget represents the government's work plan; if the legislature does not approve it as submitted, a vote of no confidence may ensue, leading to the fall of that particular government and the calling of a general election. In general, the threat of a vote of no confidence holds the majority party together when the budget is in the legislature and prevents any changes except those that the majority party has decided to make itself. In the United States, Congress is free to put its own imprint on the president's budget. Although Congress generally only marginally modifies the president's budget in dollar terms, Congress can take a position that is very different from the president's in respect to any particular agency or program. This is particularly true when control of the congress and the Presidency is divided between the two parties. When one party holds the executive branch and the other party holds one or both houses in the legislative branch, the budget process can be both heated and extended. In the 1980s, there were several presidential budgets called "dead on arrival" when submitted to Congress; this might have led to a vote of no confidence and a

general election to elect a new government in a parliamentary system. Instead, these sessions usually led to late appropriations bills, summit meetings between leaders of the executive and legislative branches, and policy gridlock, sometimes followed by budget process reform efforts.

Once the appropriation bills have been signed, it is the function of the executive branch agencies to execute the budget as enacted. This is not as simple as it seems. Changing conditions may lead the executive branch to try to defer spending or rescind programs; sometimes emergency supplemental appropriations are sought to fund recovery from natural disasters, and there is a continuous traffic in reprogramming and transfers, some of which agencies can make on their own; others must be approved by Congress. In short, budgeting seems to be a never-ending activity. While the current budget is being executed, the budget for the next year might be under review in the legislature, and the budget for the year following that might be under construction by agencies in the executive branch. Some reformers have suggested that the federal government pursue a biennial budget process where budgeting is done every two years in order to put more planning and analysis into the budget process. Biennial budgeting is a form of budgeting found in 19 American states in 1990 (see **biennial budgeting**).

At its heart, the budget process is a planning process. It is about what should happen in the future. For agencies, this planning process might involve estimates of how many audits or accounts will be done in the next year; for welfare advocates, it might involve estimates of what it will take to provide a decent standard of living to the poor; for defense agencies, it might involve appreciations of foreign policy and defense resource planning about threat capacity and potential responses, involving everything from aircraft carriers to tanks. Although numbers give the budget document the aura of precision, it is still a plan; this is seen most clearly in budget execution when agencies struggle to execute the budgets they have prepared in an environment that is usually changed slightly from the one in which the budget was developed. Budget systems usually provide some capacity to modify the enacted budget during budget execution; these range from fund transfers and reprogramming to emergency bills and supplementals to emergency legislative sessions.

Budgets come in different types. Many, but not all, jurisdictions have a separate capital and operating budget. The capital budget is usually used for investment type functions, including buying park lands and constructing buildings and roads, whose consumption will span generations. Thus, these projects are usually paid for by issuing bonds whose principal provides the money for the capital budget projects. These bonds normally will be paid back over a time period that approximates the consumption of the asset—usually set at 30 years. Recently, jurisdictions have taken to issuing various bonds and notes, some for capital projects and others to fund shortfalls in their annual operating budgets.

The operating budget funds the annual operational needs of the jurisdiction. These may range from road maintenance to park and recreation supervision, tax collection, education, welfare, public safety, defense, and the like. If the capital budget allows for the construction of a state office building, it is the operating budget that allows for daily activities of government in and around that building. This includes hiring of personnel of different type and rank, equipping them with computers and office supplies, and providing them with telephones and heat and light and desks and chairs and all the apparatus of modern offices. It is also the operating budget that provides funding for education and corrections programs and transfer payments for retirement, health care, and welfare, and it supports institutions as diverse as the state university and the state prison system.

In the American system, there are some general budget patterns by level of government. The federal government concentrates on providing defense and entitlements like Social Security and Medicare and some Welfare programs; state governments tend to focus budget efforts on colleges and schools, prisons, and mental health institutions and highways, whereas local governments tend to provide police and fire functions, parks and recreation, and either provide or supervise water, sewer, and trash collection. Welfare may be funded across all levels of government in a system of shared payments and guiding regulations. All governments have regulatory functions; these tend not to cost much in direct funding, although their impact on citizens may be great and the cost to the private sector considerable. There are also many special districts created to provide services as diverse as flood control, libraries, and fire protection. Most of the drama in budgeting occurs around the priorities that are expressed in reviewing the annual operating budgets of this multitude of governments, as claims are raised, evaluated, and decided, concerning funding for the diverse bundles of goods and services these governments provide.

Operating budgets are produced and presented in various forms. The most basic type of operating budget form is the object of expenditure budget. This type of budget identifies, sometimes in excruciating detail, the items that will be purchased with budget funds. These objects of expenditure usually include personnel, supporting expenses, and minor capital outlay amounts for desks and office machines and the like. Personnel are usually listed by position type and position grade and perhaps by seniority, with a certain percentage added on to represent the cost of fringe benefits like vacation, sick leave, health, life and disability insurance, and retirement plan costs. Consumable items range from computer parts to telephone installations to pencils. A budget of this type is called a line-item budget because each item is presented on a separate line in the budget document. The

TABLE I. WHERE FEDERAL $ GOES

Function	Percent of Function from Federal Revenues: 1991
Defense	100
International affairs	100
Space programs	100
Postal service	100
Agriculture	87
Unemployment ins.	100
General retirement	96
Medicare	100
Welfare and social services	76
Health and hospitals	48
Medicaid (care for poor)	56
Natural resources, parks	38
Highways and streets	26
Transit and railroads	33
Higher education	15
Research and libraries	24
Civilian safety	8
Education, K-12	4

SOURCE: U.S. Department of Commerce, Bureau of Economic Analysis, National Income and Accounts Data. Expenditures by Function and Level of Government.

line includes the name of the item, the budgeted amount for the current year, and a requested amount for the next year. Many jurisdictions also include what was spent on that item the previous year. Most line-item budgets have some brief explanations of the reason for the change from the amount in the budgeted year to the amount requested. Revenue sources may be broken into equally excruciating detail, not only general taxes—for instance, sales, property, and income—but also revenue from fees, charges, and miscellaneous sources, including parking fines, dog and bicycle licenses, and garage sale permits.

Building budgets with this level of detail for large and complex jurisdictions quickly approaches information overload and reviewers have to struggle to avoid being trapped questioning inconsequential details about office supplies while major policy concerns are not fully addressed. Aaron Wildavsky's classic portrayal of the budgetary process (1964) suggested that the overwhelming complexity of the budget drove an incremental approach, where programs were reviewed a piece at a time, with different parts being reviewed in different places and reviewers relying on participant feedback to tell them if they had cut too much from one program or another. The complexity of the budget process dictated that some people must trust others in this process because they can only check up on them a small part of the time and because no one can be an expert in everything. Wildavsky saw man's inherent intellectual limits making an incremental approach a necessity. This view assumed constant making and remaking of the budget, with a heavy concentration of review on what is changed in the current year from the previous year. The picture of an incremental process with specific roles for budget participants dominated how people saw the budget process in the United States in the last third of the twentieth century (see **Wildavsky** and **incremental budgeting**).

Irrespective of the accuracy of this portrayal, much of the history of budget reform for the last 50 years involves finding ways to present budget information to decision-makers in a more meaningful way so that better decisions can be made about how to allocate scarce resources. These reforms have included performance budgeting, program budgeting, zero-based budgeting, planning-programming-budgeting and various systems focused on target or mission-based budgeting. Some reforms have focused on the budget process itself in the belief that better staff or a more timely process would provide a better budget process. Paramount among these sorts of reforms are the Budget and Accounting Act of 1921 and the Congressional Budget Reform and Impoundment Act of 1974.

Dissatisfaction with budget outcomes, usually in respect to growing deficits, has resulted in a different type of budget reform, basically attempting to mandate a balanced budget, one where spending does not exceed revenues. Examples of this kind of budget reform include the Gramm-Rudman-Hollings (GRH) Acts of 1985 and 1987 and the Budget Enforcement Acts of 1990 and 1993 and several attempts at a Constitutional Balanced Budget Amendment at the federal level. These efforts were not without some adverse consequences. Attempts to meet the GRH targets often involved optimistic estimates of spending and revenues and certain gimmicks like shifted paydays, which probably did more to damage the budget process than reform it, especially since few, if any, of the GRH targets were met.

Only nine times from 1930 to 1994 has the U.S. federal budget been in a situation in which revenues exceeded spending and a surplus is not predicted before the year 2000 (*A Citizen's Guide to the Federal Budget* 1996). The Great Depression of the 1930s and the intense effort of World War II appear to mark a turning point in American society; from that period on, policymakers appear to have committed to a larger role for government. In practice, this has meant that claims on the budget have exceeded available resources, and the federal government has usually been willing to go into debt to meet those claims. In 1995, the national debt stood at US $4.8 trillion, after quintupling from 1980, and annual payments for interest on the national debt were the fourth largest category in the federal budget. Rhetoric about the national debt and deficit reduction has provided a constant subtext to budget discussions from the mid-1980s onward.

Ultimately, budgeting always involves a rationing process. Allen Schick (1990) has argued that claiming and rationing are at the center of the budget process. Individuals and groups articulate demands on government for services. If the government can satisfy all demands, no budgeting process is necessary. Conversely, if government is so poor that it can satisfy no demands, then no budget process is possible, necessary, or feasible. History offers few examples of societies so rich that all demands can be accommodated and perhaps even fewer where the power-holders of that society wished to accommodate all such demands. The oil-revenue rich states in the Mideast in the late 1970s perhaps came as close as one can come in recent history to being able to satisfy all demands; even here, their status was helped enormously by the mix of an abundant natural resource base—oil—and a relatively low population base. At the other end of the spectrum, there do exist third world countries that have such a restricted resource base that they are able to meet few demands, and the resources they do raise seem to evaporate under the impact of inflation almost as soon as they are raised. In neither case does a true budget process exist. For budgeting to exist not only must demands be articulated as claims for government to meet, but government must have the capacity to satisfy some, if not most, of those claims. Most governments exist in a middle ground, able to meet many, if not most, claims and able to meet more in good years than bad years.

From a comparative perspective, countries differ in the amount of their wealth they make available to government for solving problems. What they choose to spend it on can also differ. For example while the United States chose to spend 18 percent of its budget on defense in 1995, the United Kingdom spent 9 percent; while the United States spent 22 percent on social security, the United Kingdom spent almost 35 percent. (*Citizen's Guide*, p. 2; *Budget in Brief*). The fiscal conditions surrounding the budget process may change dramatically; for example, the inflation rate in Chile was 12,000 percent a year from 1984 to 1985, but fell to 15 percent after draconian fiscal reforms in 1985 ("As Inflation Burns," p. 20.) The goals that a nation pursues can change over time. In 1962, the United States spent 50 percent of its federal budget on defense; this has fallen to 18 percent in 1995, and Social Security, which provides benefits to over 43 million retired and disabled workers, is the largest category in the U.S. budget, consuming 22 percent of all federal spending (*Guide*, p. 3). One of the conditions of modern budgeting is the rise of spending on entitlement accounts like Social Security, veterans pensions, medical care, and interest on the national debt. These are called mandatory accounts since they consists of bills the government must pay in the short run. Government may freeze spending on capital outlay or travel, but it cannot refuse to pay Social Security benefits; for their part, individuals who qualify for certain programs are "entitled" and may sue government to get their benefits, if it comes to that. Most governments consider paying interest to their bondholders an absolute must, else who will buy their bonds next time they need to offer them? In 1995, these mandatory accounts amounted to about 64 percent of the U.S. budget (*Guide,* p. 4). The necessity of paying for these programs limits the flexibility decisionmakers have to attend to new national needs through the budget. Even where nations make a similar commitment, the resourcing of that commitment can vary dramatically; spending on social protection in Western Europe ranges from about 20 percent of GDP in Greece to over 30 percent in Holland. Within this range, there appear to be four groups, with Germany, France, Belgium, and Luxembourg having insurance systems designed to maintain the income level of the sick, disabled, and unemployed; Britain and Ireland rely on general taxation not to sustain the previous standard of living but to provide adequate subsistence; Italy and Holland fall somewhere between these two approaches; and Spain, Portugal, and Greece are in a fourth group, where a high proportion of people are not eligible for benefits. Thus, the gap in benefits can be wide; a disabled person unable to work can receive benefits equal to 97 percent of the average industrial wage in Belgium, but only 30 percent in Portugal. An unemployed Belgian will receive 79 percent of his pay in the first year out of work while a Briton in the same circumstance gets 23 percent. In general, Western Europe's spending on health care and social security is nearly twice as much as Japan's and more than 60 percent greater than in the United States ("'Enlightened' Welfare-Seekers Guide to Europe," p. 57). This diversity in program is an outcome of the budgeting process.

Aaron Wildavsky (1964) has argued that the purposes of budgets are as varied as the purposes of men (pp. 1–3). The words and figures in the budget represent a prediction about the future, consequently budgets become links between financial resources, human behavior, and policy accomplishment. Once passed, a budget is also a contract about what government will do and who will benefit and who will pay. In this sense, a budget represents a series of goals with price tags attached.

Budget History

The word "budget" appears to be derived from the Middle English "bouget," or "wallet," which derives from Old French "bougette," meaning leather bag. This bag or purse was where the funds of the king were kept (Burkhead, 1956 p. 2.) In England, "budget" first meant the leather bag in which the government's plans for taxing and spending were carried to Parliament by the chancellor of the exchequer subsequent to the fourteenth century; eventually "budget" came to mean the plans themselves. This is perhaps the origination of the term "public purse."

Historically, the story of the budget process is part of the heritage of developing representative government. The birth of the budget power may be traced to the Magna Carta in 1215 when a group of barons forced the King of England to accept certain constraints on royal powers. One of these constraints shifted the power to tax from the King to the Council of the Realm, stipulating that no "revenue shall be imposed in the kingdom unless by the Common Council of the Realm." This so-called Common Council was basically composed of the highest level of hereditary nobility under the king; thus, it in no way resembles the electoral representation of current day elected common councils, but it did serve as a check on the absolute power of the king to raise tax revenues and subsequently to carry out policy. Without money, even kings are limited in what they can do. Interestingly, there are hints of this phrasing in the American Constitution, which states, in Article I, Section 9, that no money shall be drawn from the Treasury but in consequence of an appropriation made by law, and it requires a statement of all expenditures and receipts of public monies to be published from time to time. The power to originate tax bills was given to the House, which, elected directly, was a common council of the realm.

Consequently, two themes may be seen to pervade the history of budgeting. The first has to do with the use of the budget power as a means of constraining the power of the executive, be that executive king or president. In the United States, this has come to be translated into arguments over how much power the legislative or executive branch shall have to make policy choices and how they shall be modified to ensure that the desires of the various groups of citizens are represented. This is an issue involving who gets to make decisions and who shall modify those decisions. Items of discussion here involve total budget size, budget shares by program or function, the types and levels of taxation, the size of the annual operating deficit (if any), and what functions should be reduced or expanded, and the extent to which the budget should be used to implement countercyclical economic policy. Discussions frequently involve debate over inflation and unemployment numbers, revenue estimates, and rates of expenditure. During the budget year, these arguments continue over reprogramming and rescission issues, spending deferral, end-of-year spending patterns, and other legislative oversight issues. The question of the correct balance of budgetary power is an issue that will never be completely decided; in 1986, the first version of Gramm-Rudman-Hollings was invalidated by a Supreme Court opinion that a legislative agent—GAO—did not have the power to tell the executive branch when an across-the-board cut had to be made. The continuing business of government means there will often be arguments over details that involve the correct parsing of the budgetary power.

The second theme is concerned with the process of better budgeting. This has a more modern lineage, perhaps dating to the end of the 1800s, and arises as a part of the professionalization of government process, the quest for more efficient and effective means of carrying out policy, and the simple growth of the role of government in modern society, both as a direct provider of services and as a regulatory overseer whose task is to shape a roughly even playing field in society. This theme involves such issues as information management and budget process issues, and it is littered with terms like performance measurement, performance budgeting, executive budgeting, budget baselines, and congressional budget reform. At a certain level, both issues seem to join together; a movement toward a balanced budget amendment at the federal level may be seen as a prudent professional measure not to spend more than is available, but it may also be seen as a way of constraining the role of government by limiting the amount of money available to create policy. The federal government has had an operating budget deficit since 1969; only nine times since 1930 has the federal budget been in a surplus position. It appears that federal policymakers have a greater propensity to spend than to tax or, perhaps, that creating and funding programs is easier than raising taxes. Holding federal decisionmakers to a balanced budget holds down their program creativity or it makes them decide which old programs are no longer valid. Constraining decisions by constricting revenue availability may be said to rest implicitly in the Magna Carta. However, the historical development of the budget power in England was very different from the development in the United States: In England, the process involved a gradual diminution of the power of the king; in America, the process involved a gradual diminution of the power of the legislature.

Subsequent to the Magna Carta, the development of the budget power in England as a check on the power of the king was evolutionary. By the middle of the fourteenth century, the House of Commons had been established and was passing broadly phrased revenue acts; once the money was raised, the king's ministers could spend the money as they wished. The next step was for Parliament to insert appropriations language in supply acts, stating the particular purposes for which the money could be used. Rules were made for the proper disbursement of money and penalties imposed for noncompliance. Progress in setting up a budget process was not linear and a full-fledged system would have to wait hundreds of years. Aaron Wildavsky (1975) suggests that the appearance of a formal budgeting power may be dated from the reforms of William Pitt the Younger (p. 272). As Chancellor of the Exchequer from 1783 to 1801, Pitt was faced with a heavy debt load as a result of the American Revolution and continuing struggles with France. Pitt con-

solidated a maze of customs and excise duties into one general fund from which all the government's creditors would be paid. He reduced fraud in revenue collection by introducing new auditing measures and he instituted double-entry bookkeeping procedures to track both debits and credits in one system. Pitt established a sinking fund schedule for debt repayment, and he altered the basic schedule of taxes and customs to reduce the allure of smuggling.

Until the Revolution, the American colonies generally followed English practices, although they chafed under the environment of taxation without representation (McCaffery 1987). Colonial legislatures set the salaries of royal governors and other officers, but neither expenditures nor taxes were heavy. England could and did impose duties and customs intended to regulate trade and navigation. After the Revolutionary War, the colonies vested power in various legal arrangements in the legislative branch, to the initial exclusion of the executive branch. Under the Articles of Confederation, the central government was weak and the legislative branch of government carried out both the legislative and executive functions of government. The colonists had just waged a war to escape rule by a monarch, and they were not interested in substituting another strong executive in place of the king. Under the Articles of Confederation, Congress basically prepared all revenue and appropriation estimates, enacted them into law, and then attempted to execute what had been enacted. This system did not work very well. The revolutionary period was marked by a scarcity of hard coinage, various paper money schemes, a dependence on debt and letters of credit, an aversion to national taxes, and some degree of negligence, wastefulness, disorder, and corruption. George Washington's struggles with Congress over funding for the army are almost as well known as his struggles with the British.

In 1781, Robert Morris became the first superintendent of finance, charged with the oversight of public debt, taxing, spending, and developing plans for establishing order and economy in the expenditure of public money. This was an important first step, and Pitt's equivalent on the American scene was probably Alexander Hamilton, who, as the first Secretary of the Treasury (1789–1795) established the nation's credit, created a banking system and a stable currency, funded the war debt at full value, and developed a stable tax system based on excise taxes to fund the payment of debt and to provide funding for future appropriations.

Although the Constitution had created an executive branch, Hamilton saw the post of Secretary of Treasury as an agent of Congress. By 1792, Hamilton was turning increasingly toward the president for guidance, and Congress was increasingly specifying itemized appropriation bills in an attempt to ensure congressional control over the purse. Aaron Wildavsky suggests that one of the outcomes of this critical period in American history was an ideological commitment to a balanced budget as a norm that has basically been honored by politicians for over 200 years except in time of war or extreme national crisis.

During the nineteenth century, the federal budget was small and federal functions few, and the budget power was divided between the president and cabinet secretaries, with presidents and secretaries dealing with funding on an ad hoc basis. The Secretary of the Treasury was charged with making an annual report, and at the beginning of the year, he provided a book of estimates setting forth the budget requirements of the departments and agencies. This function was primarily clerical; as Burkhead says, the Treasurer did not criticize, alter, reduce, or coordinate the requests (1956, p. 11). For most of this period, the federal budget problem lay in deciding how to spend up the surplus produced by a system of protective tariffs. Departments and bureaus often did their best to make friends with Congress and, where they had popular programs, could conveniently spend up their appropriation and go back to Congress for more to finish out the year. This strategy was called a "coercive deficiency" and only worked for popular programs. There was no central agency to pull together the estimates of all departments, review and evaluate them, and present a budget proposal with totals for revenues and spending.

The development of an executive budget system would have to wait until the passage of the Budget and Accounting Act of 1921, which established the Bureau of the Budget and gave the president the power to submit a budget to Congress that would represent all the needs of the federal government for the coming year. The stimuli for passage of this act may be found in the deficits incurred in World War I and the various reform movements rising out of local governments and the Progressive Movement. It also had a national background. Irene Rubin suggests that some part of federal reform comes from efforts to oversee the railroads at the end of the nineteenth century. Railroads were big and important to the public for carrying goods and passengers. With the quick expansion of railroads and the consolidation of one railroad by another, it was not always easy to tell if a railroad was making a profit, or, indeed, if the railroad was solvent. This meant it was also difficult to tell if the rates that were set for freight and passengers were fair. Thus, in the 1880s, the Interstate Commerce Commission was put in the position of regulating rates, but to do this it had to develop better accounting tools in consultation with the railroads. Once these procedures had been implemented for railroads—considered the largest, most complex, and most sophisticated of private corporations—government was then urged to make similar improvements for its own operations (Rubin 1993, p. 440). These efforts were echoed by Frederick Cleveland at the New York Bureau of Municipal Research in the first decade of the twentieth century and by President Taft's Commission on Economy and Efficiency

in 1912. Long before the federal government had passed the Budget and Accounting Act of 1921, many American cities had passed local budget reform acts that prevented city councils from appropriating money outside the confines of a budget. As early as 1899, the National Municipal League drafted a model municipal charter, which incorporated a budget system under the direct supervision of the mayor. (Burkhead 1956, p. 13). In the United States, twentieth-century budget reform spread from the local level to state and national levels.

The Great Depression of the 1930s forced the federal government into countercyclical economic policies and the Full Employment Act of 1946 made the goal of obtaining full employment an official policy of the U.S. government. As the role of government expanded, various study commissions developed plans for better methods of doing budgeting; in 1949, the Hoover Commission (see **budget reform**) advocated performance and program budgeting as a way of making what government did more intelligible. Throughout this period of time, the Bureau of the Budget had gained great credibility for neutral professional expertise, but in its rise to power, it also sowed the seeds of its own destruction. The political staffs whom it served increasingly grew frustrated by the Bureau's nonpartisan array of solutions and sought for political options that would benefit the party in power. In 1970, the realignment of the Bureau into the Office of Management and Budget was partly to emphasize the managerial side of budgeting and partly to create political positions within OMB to allow for a more political direction to budget solutions. At the time, President Nixon said the intent of the reform was to bring "real business management into government at the very highest level" (Lee and Johnson 1989, p. 41). No sooner had this reform been accomplished than the excesses of the Nixon administration in impoundments and in Watergate raised new doubts about the ability of Congress to counter the strength of the new executive budget pattern. Partly in reaction to a series of impoundment decisions by President Nixon and partly to provide Congress with better budgeting tools, the Congressional Budget and Impoundment Act of 1974 was passed. This gave Congress a budget timetable, created Budget Committees to set overall totals for taxing, spending, and any operating deficit, and called for subtotals by functional area. This information was carried in a joint budget resolution passed by both houses of Congress. The numbers in this resolution would provide the benchmarks for scorekeeping as the budget process unrolled. Later, they would also provide targets for points of order when appropriation bills threatened to exceed the agreed upon total for a functional area. The premise of this reform was that better information on a more timely basis would make for a better budget process and ultimately better budget outcomes. This optimistic view of budget reform turned to brute force control of annual deficits with the Gramm-Rudman-Hollings reforms of the 1980s and efforts at spending control with the Budget Enforcement Act of 1990 and its subsequent revisions. These were less optimistic efforts to directly control the pace and pattern of spending at the federal level while coming to grips with seemingly out of control growth in the entitlement and medical care programs. These reforms mainly sought to stop the growth of the annual operating deficit and the national debt.

On the U.S. scene, there has been a healthy tension between federal and state and local governments over budget reform. In some cases, federal budget reforms led state and local budget reform. In other cases state and local practices helped shape federal practices. It is probably most true to say that, from 1890 to 1920, local budget reforms led federal reforms. It is probably most true to say that, from 1920 to 1974, the federal government led state and local governments in budget reform technique. Planning-programming-budgeting was a defense budget system that caused great excitement and some emulation in the 1960s but had little staying power in state and local governments by the end of the decade. This did not mean that the state-local scene was bereft of innovation. President Carter brought zero-based budgeting along with him from the state of Georgia, and the property tax limitation movement symbolized by the passage of Proposition 13 in California in 1978 may be seen as a precursor to the Gramm-Rudman-Hollings limitations in the 1980s at the federal level.

In the U.S. context, many of the issues in budgeting have been issues for a long time: These include the type and extent of taxation, how large the national debt should be, what the relationship should be between the executive and legislative branches and how budgets should be presented—in lump sums, itemized detail, or in some other format that might lead to better decisionmaking. These questions endure because they are important and not easily solved.

JERRY L. McCAFFERY

BIBLIOGRAPHY

"As Inflation Burns, Brazil Fiddles," 1994. *World Press Review,* vol. 41, no. 4 (April) 20.
Budget in Brief, December 1994. London: Ministry of Treasury.
Burkhead, Jesse, 1956. *Government Budgeting.* New York: John Wiley and Sons.
A Citizen's Guide to the Federal Budget. Fiscal Year 1996. Washington, DC: U.S. Government Printing Office, 1995.
"The 'Enlightened' Welfare-Seeker's Guide to Europe." *The Economist,* vol. 330, no. 7854 (March 12, 1994).
Lee, Robert D., and Ronald W. Johnson, 1989. *Public Systems,* 4th ed. Rockville, MD: Aspen.
McCaffery, Jerry, 1987. "The Development of Public Budgeting in the United States." In Ralph Clark Chandler, ed., *A Centennial History of the American Administrative State.* New York: Macmillan, 345–379.
Rubin, Irene, 1993. "Who Invented Budgeting in the United States?" *Public Administration Review,* vol. 53, no. 5 (September/October) 438–444.
Schick, Allen, 1990. *The Capacity to Budget.* Washington, DC: Urban Institute.
Wildavsky, Aaron, 1964; rev. ed. 1984. *The Politics of the Budgetary Process.* Boston: Little, Brown.
———, 1975. *Budgeting: A Comparative Theory of Budgetary Processes.* Boston: Little, Brown.
———, 1988; rev. ed., 1992. *The New Politics of the Budgetary Process.* Glenview, IL: Scott, Foresman.

BUDGETING AND POVERTY.

Public poverty implies that the resources available to support a government's budget are minimal—far more restricted than what is customary for other governments. Budgeting entails planning how resources will be used in some future period, typically the future budget year or what remains of the current budget year. Such planning assumes some degree of predictability of the future. The needs for programs are presumed to be known along with the amount of revenues that will be available to address those needs. In poor governmental jurisdictions, the future may be predictable, but it is a bleak one in which needs far outstrip expected revenues.

Comparing Poor U.S. Local Governments and Poor Developing Countries

Poor local governments in the United States and governments in developing countries often face similar financial conditions and as a result have similar budget processes. Both poor countries and poor local governments in the United States have little ability to control their destinies. Both types of governments are buffeted by trends in the world economy and changes in specific industries, such as the steel and automobile industries. A town in the United States may be thrown into chaos when a conglomerate corporation, whose international headquarters may be outside of the United States, decides to close the local plant. Similarly, a developing nation's economy and its government's budget can be devastated by foreign corporate decisions or by a single weather event, such as a freeze or drought that damages the country's main exporting crop.

U.S. local governments and those in developing nations, of course, are different in other important respects. U.S. cities and other local governments are subordinate to their respective states and the national government, whereas developing nations are sovereign states. These countries have responsibility for a complete set of policies and services, whereas local governments in the United States have responsibilities for a limited number of services. The latter lack responsibility for defense, foreign policy, freeways, and the like, and have only limited responsibility for such expensive programs as welfare benefits and health care for the needy. Poor countries, unlike U.S. local governments, must conduct their foreign affairs, including having embassies in many nations, but these poor countries also are eligible for grants, loans, and other support from the United Nations, the World Bank, and the International Monetary Fund. Many cities in the United States would undoubtedly welcome an opportunity to apply for aid to one of these organizations.

The degree of political instability and economic crisis is far more severe in some developing countries than in others and certainly far more severe than in U.S. local governments. Extreme cases exist, such as Bosnia-Herzegovina, Rwanda, and Somalia in the 1990s, which make almost ludicrous any notion of budgeting for the future. The conditions in those countries certainly defy comparison with even the worst of situations of any government in the Unites States. While budgeting for war, and even for civil war, is possible, the conditions in these and other countries are of a magnitude that would boggle the mind of any budgeteer anywhere.

The Characteristics of Poverty

Poverty must be considered a relative term, since what is poverty in one locale may not be in another locale. The abject poverty found in many developing nations may not exist to any extent in the United States, which enjoys a relatively high standard of living.

However, poor jurisdictions, wherever they are located, share some common characteristics. They often are nonindustrialized or are experiencing what has been called "deindustrialization." In modern times, manufacturing has been a major source of income, with nations exporting products in order to gain wealth. Manufacturing has been an important factor in the economic growth of U.S. cities and even now, in their decline. Today, many central cities have factories that are closed, that will never reopen, and will never generate jobs again. Developing countries rather than having unneeded and obsolete factories often have none at all and frequently have little prospect for industrial development. Both poor countries and poor cities in the United States, then, have weak economic bases, which translate into weak tax bases for their respective governments.

High levels of unemployment or underemployment are additional characteristics. Work simply is unavailable for able-bodied citizens. In developing nations, the work that is done may be of a subsistence nature, with people toiling long hours simply to raise enough food to support themselves.

The populations of poor nations and locales tend to be characterized by low levels of education and limited employment skills. Corporations are only attracted to these places when in need of inexpensive, unskilled labor.

Problems may be compounded by high birthrates coupled with improved mortality rates so that people live longer but with no better prospects for employment. U.S. local governments may have the additional burden of increased in-migration of low-skilled workers and out-migration of higher-skilled workers. Central cities in the United States tend to be the gathering points for immigrants, both legal and illegal, with limited education and job skills.

Fragile and deteriorating capital facilities are often characteristic of poor governments. Roads, water and sewer systems, school buildings, and the like may be rudimentary or, as is common in the United States, may be in varying stages of disintegration.

Budgeting in Poor Governments

Budgeting is commonly referred to as dealing with scarce resources. That is an understatement in poor governments, where the scarcity of resources can be overwhelming. Officials in a poor city government may be unsure how they can possibly cover the costs of operating the police department, the city sewer system, and the rest of city government, and then may be faced by the crisis caused when the city's water treatment plant breaks down.

Not only do poor governments have few resources but their plights are compounded by attendant uncertainty stemming from a variety of external sources. A developing nation with some oil reserves cannot be sure of projected revenue given the volatility of world oil prices. Foreign assistance may be uncertain in that what may be seemingly promised by another government or by an organization such as the World Bank may not materialize or at least not materialize as soon as expected. Poor U.S. local governments face many of the same types of problems, such as uncertainty over the amount and timing of intergovernmental financial assistance.

In these situations, "coping" may be a better word than "budgeting." Poor governments have limited ability to budget for the fiscal year, let along future years, and instead live from day to day coping with a seemingly endless string of small and large emergencies. Given this situation, governments engage in what has been called "repetitive budgeting," in which plans may be developed for a budget but are always being revised. All decisions must be treated as tentative, since no one knows what emergency will arise next. A city parks department in the United States might be given provisional approval to renovate a set of picnic shelters, but months may pass before approval is granted to commence the work. When approval is granted, an agency should commence work immediately lest another turn of events tempts decisionmakers to rescind their approval. Indeed, projects may be halted in midcourse due to an unanticipated shortage of funds.

This same kind of problem is prevalent in developing nations. A health department might win tentative approval to begin a program for birth control education in rural communities, but the effort might take years to be implemented due to a lack of resources.

Once programs and activities are under way in a government, problems continuously arise regarding what would be routine funding in governments with better financial foundations. Meeting this month's payroll in a poor U.S. central city may be a daunting task, and the problem will return again each month, when once again employees expect to be paid. A common practice may be to divert funds to cover immediately pressing needs. Monies intended for the purchase of equipment, for instance, may be used for operating expenses, but if general revenues coming into the government are inadequate, the equipment budget may be totally depleted. Federal and state agencies in the United States have found that sometimes financially pressed local governments have diverted grant monies for other needs. "Creative accounting" may have been used in an attempt to hide these transactions, and when brought to light, little can be done to correct the situation. Similar problems have arisen in connection with aid to developing nations.

Corruption and Incompetence

No nation, no state, and no local government is immune from corruption, but the effects of corruption on poor governments are more pronounced than on others. Similarly, incompetence may be endemic to all organizations–private and public–but the results of incompetence may be more devastating on poor governments than on wealthier ones. When resources are squandered on nonproductive projects, such as erecting elaborate monuments to the leader of a nation who has proclaimed himself to be permanent ruler, the total resources available for productive activity are necessarily reduced. When scarce funds are siphoned off for the personal gain of political leaders and their families, resources become even scarcer. Wasteful government contracting in which awards are made to politically connected corporations and at prices far above market levels has been found in poor local governments in the United States and in poor countries. Again, such wasteful and corrupt contracting is not found exclusively in poor governments, but the effects there are more dramatic on reducing the funds available for productive projects and programs.

Corruption and incompetence have debilitating effects on government workers and the citizenry. Ethical workers may become unethical when they see corruption all around them. Citizens may feel justified in cheating on their taxes when their government is considered illegiti-mate because of its corrupt practices. Alienation of the citizenry can lead to rioting in U.S. cities and to insurrection in poor countries.

What Options Exist?

The above discussion may be so discouraging that throwing in the towel may seem to be the only sensible option. However, if reform is desired, some options are available, although the would-be reformist must consider each with care and select only a few for implementation in the short term. Attempting to undertake simultaneously a large number of reforms probably would result in failure in most respects, since efforts would be spread over too many initiatives.

Addressing fundamental political issues, including corruption, most be high on any agenda for reform. The disintegration of Yugoslavia and the ethnic strife that followed is only one example of how long-standing hatreds can result in destructive behavior. Fine-tuning of budget systems and adopting the newest techniques in accounting will hardly strengthen the viability of a government, but governments may be more likely to engage in such tinkering, when seemingly intractable problems demand attention.

Revision of the revenue system and particularly taxes and intergovernmental aid can be an important part of addressing fundamental political issues. In poor countries, tax systems often need to be revised to make them more equitable. In the United States, local governments may need to have greater taxing authorities granted to them by the state governments and, perhaps more important, may need to have greater financial support from their state governments. Whether that is politically feasible is subject to debate. States faced with their own sets of priorities and financial problems frequently are unable or unwilling to address the financial needs of poor local governments.

Governments can undertake activities that increase their efficiency in the delivery of services. Bureaucracies may be rationalized to reduce duplication of services; for example, two or more city agencies that are responsible for inspecting and licensing restaurants could be consolidated. The rationalization of bureaucracies in poor countries would include examining whether semiautonomous corporations should remain such. The use of computers or expanded use of them can increase efficiency, although the problem immediately arises of finding the funds to buy the equipment and ancillary software. Budgets can be trimmed although some poor governments would contend that budget cutting has gone as far as it can. If that is the case, then an important option to consider is whether the outright elimination of some programs may be desirable in order to fund essential services at some minimal level.

Improved use of talented personnel is another important option. Poor countries and poor cities in the United

States may have difficulty attracting and retaining highly qualified personnel in large numbers, and therefore the need for optimal utilization of staff becomes apparent. Efforts can be made to take workers from nonproductive assignments and place them in productive positions.

An area that deserves special attention, particularly in poor countries, is the use of planning for development. If the future of these nations is as uncertain as described above, then efforts at comprehensive long-range planning are futile and are simply a waste of resources. Planners might be better utilized in shorter-range efforts and on projects of limited scope rather than economywide planning. The same approach can be taken with planning offices and planners in poor local governments, where such offices exist. Focusing upon short-term planning of a project nature may be more beneficial than wishful planning for 25 years from now.

The roles of development budgets in poor countries and capital budgets in poor local governments need to be evaluated. Often these budgets consist of wish lists that will not be funded in the near future, no matter how strong their merits. Since resources are extraordinarily scarce, local governments may find themselves approving capital improvement projects and adopting capital budgets for which funds simply are unavailable. The pressing daily problems of paying for operating expenses may make capital budgeting an empty exercise. Similarly, poor countries may prepare elaborate development plans that are visions of fanciful futures that will never become reality. Development projects may have better chances for being funded if they are seen as part of the overall budget rather than being an addition to the operating budget.

Decentralization and entrepreneurial management may be worthy of consideration. Some centralization may be necessary for helping to meet agencies' payrolls and other expenses, but decentralization may be able to reduce inefficiencies. When entrepreneurial management is added to the reform, the opportunity exists for agencies to be creative in how they manage themselves. Such an approach may include allowing agencies to be creative in how they generate revenue for projects, whether that means separate fund-raising activities or entry into partnerships with other entities, including private enterprises. Some central control, of course, is essential for insuring compliance with laws that regulate the powers and practices of governments.

No Panaceas

None of the above proposals singly or in combination with others forms a panacea for dealing with the harsh realities that challenge poor local governments in the United States and in developing countries, but the options do offer some hope for reform. Much of existing budget literature that discusses how budget systems operate and how they should operate are directed at systems with some degree of wealth and at governments that have some control over their fu-

tures. Poor governments, however, face conditions that defy budgeting in any traditional sense of the word.

ROBERT D. LEE, JR.

BIBLIOGRAPHY

Caiden, Naomi and Aaron Wildavsky, 1974. *Planning and Budgeting in Poor Countries.* New York: Wiley and Sons.
Johnson, Ronald W. and Syedur Rahman, 1992. "Improved Budgeting and Financial Management as a Tool for Enhancing the Performance of Local Government in Developing Countries." *International Journal of Public Administration,* vol. 15, no. 5: 1241–1261.
Lee, Robert D., 1992. "Linkage Among Poverty, Development, and Budget Systems." *Public Budgeting & Finance,* vol. 12 (Spring) 48–60.
Lee, Robert D., and Ronald W. Johnson, 1994. *Public Budgeting Systems,* 5th ed. Gaithersburg, MD: Aspen.
Rahman, Syedur and Khi V. Thai, 1991. "Context of Public Budgeting in Developing Countries." In Ali Farazmand, ed., *Handbook of Comparative and Development Public Administration.* New York: Marcel Dekker, 405–418.

BURDEN OF PROOF. A phrase denoting the duty of a party in a court proceeding to produce evidence and persuade the finder of fact in order to prevail on his or her claim or defense. The phrase "burden of proof" is ambiguous and refers to two distinct concepts—the "burden of production and the burden of persuasion."

The burden of production is the duty to introduce evidence in support of a party's legal position. Burden of persuasion refers to the need to persuade the finder of fact— the court or the jury—that the party's version of the facts is correct.

In order to satisfy the burden of production, a party must produce some evidence that indicates his or her legal claim exists and is supported factually. This is usually accomplished by introducing evidence as to those facts, which if proved would entitle the party to win the claim or prevail on the defense. If the burden of production is not satisfied, the claim cannot be considered by the finder of fact. In jury trials, the failure to meet the burden of production means that the court will grant directed verdict or motion for judgment made by the opposing counsel.

The term "burden of persuasion" refers to the proof needed to convince a jury of the existence and truth of the factual basis for the claim. In civil cases, generally, a party must establish the factual elements of its case by a preponderance of the evidence. This generally means that the jury is convinced that a fact is more likely true than not true.

In some civil cases, for policy reasons, a party may be held to a higher standard of persuasion. For example, cases seeking mental commitment frequently involve a higher standard of proof. In these cases, a party must establish its claim by clear and convincing evidence. This standard is satisfied when a party presents evidence that creates a firm belief in the mind of the jury or finder of fact that the party's proposition is highly probable.

In criminal cases, the prosecution is held to an even higher standard. The prosecution must prove "beyond a reasonable doubt" all of the elements that are necessary to prove the crime that the criminal defendant is charged with.

In cases before administrative agencies, the party challenging an administrator's action usually has the burden of proving that the administrator's action was wrong. In some cases, this may be tantamount to approving the administrator's actions, but it likewise gives the administrator or agency a range of discretion within which to operate. For example, in *Goldberg v. Kelly*, 397 U.S. 254 (1970), the Supreme Court held that a welfare recipient is entitled to notice and an opportunity for a hearing before welfare benefits are cut off. The recipient is entitled to show that the state's reasons are incorrect. In such a hearing, the burden normally is on the recipient to show that the proposed action is wrong, thus affording rights to the recipients while maintaining a presumption that the administrative agency is correct.

MICHAEL A. WOLFF

BIBLIOGRAPHY

29 *American Jurisprudence* 2d, § 155–183
31A *Corpus Juris Secundum*, § 103–110
Warren, Kenneth F., 1996. *Administrative Law in the Political System*. Englewood Cliffs, NJ: Prentice-Hall, 326–327.

BURDEN SHARING. The distribution of the financial and other costs of any joint or collective endeavor involving national governments or other public agencies (such as the provision of economic aid or of defense within an alliance)–and, as such, not only a matter for initial decision or negotiation but also frequently one of continuing dispute among participants.

No doubt evidence could be found to show that the burden-sharing issue arose among the tribes of ancient Gaul in their organization of a defense against the Romans, among the Christian monarchs who mounted the medieval crusades and among the states on both sides in the American Civil War. However, it was not until the first half of the twentieth century that the question began to appear regularly on the international political agenda: for example, when decisions were required on covering the outgoings of the League of Nations or administering specific functional ventures like the Universal Postal Union. It was not until the second half, with the proliferation of international institutions and increased sensitivity among coun-

tries about equity (fair shares) in bearing the costs of collective action, that the topic began to feature frequently in intergovernmental deliberations.

Currently, it is a subject that receives more or less constant attention–and occasionally produces acute disagreements–in a number of contexts. Prominent among these is the security domain, where the matter at issue may be (1) contributions to an alliance such as the North Atlantic Treaty Organization (NATO), (2) participation in particular coalition operations such as the 1990/91 Gulf crisis and conflict, or (3) involvement in peace enforcement actions or peacekeeping duties such as those now regularly mandated by the Security Council of the United Nations (UN). Another is the field of international finance, where questions arising for developed nations may include (1) who shall offer what through formal or informal development aid consortia, (2) who shall provide how much by way of relief funds for chronic debtor states, or (3) who shall accept what responsibilities for monetary crisis prevention in circumstances where no one state can be expected to serve as lender of last resort for the entire global payments system.

Decision or negotiation about burden sharing, in whatever context, is problematical because there are few generally accepted guidelines for the distribution of costs associated with international agreements. Certainly no universal burden-sharing formula has been devised for international organizations. In the absence of such a formula, participating states naturally follow their own self-interest. For all but the very largest states, this often dictates doing as little as possible–or at least no more than is necessary–in the joint endeavor: in short "free riding." Disputes about burden sharing arise generally because there are no guidelines and especially when "free riding" is observed (or suspected).

The root of the problem is the absence of any authority with the power to define and demand appropriate contributions from sovereign states, as national governments define and demand contributions from their citizens (through taxation) to obtain the money for financing public provision domestically. The principal reason for disagreements–leaving aside the technical matter of calculating subscriptions–is the lack of consensus about what constitutes equity in collective effort. It is broadly accepted that, even in voluntary affiliations, arrangements should be fair; but opinions differ on the meaning of fairness.

Both economists and political scientists have contributed to our understanding of the burden-sharing question: examining why and how it arises and considering what to do about it when it does. On the "why and how" aspect, Paul Samuelson's seminal work on public goods theory (1954) provided the basis for elucidating the "free rider" phenomenon. Put simply, whenever it appears that a leading nation or group is disposed to commit resources to a particular purpose from which others will benefit–deterrence, defense, development aid, debt relief, underpinning the global financial system, or whatever–it can be shown that those others will understate their interest in the provision and seek to minimize their own voluntary contribution(s) to sustaining it. Who pays what necessarily becomes, therefore, a matter of negotiation and compromise. Hence the interest in formulas for resolving the matter; or, more practically, criteria to be applied (or, even more loosely, relevant considerations to be taken into account) in the bargaining process.

Analytical work on "what to do about it" has accordingly focused on such criteria (and relevant considerations). The case has been made for uncomplicated tests like adequacy of effort, viz. in NATO, meeting agreed force goals, or, so far as economic aid is concerned, allotting an arbitrarily fixed proportion of the gross domestic product (GDP) to this purpose. Most discussion, though, has centred on achieving equity of effort–sometimes construed as equality of sacrifice–in collective provision. In principle, equity can be considered in real resource terms or in money terms. In either case the difficulties in devising criteria are daunting. However, they are somewhat less formidable if attention focuses on financial contributions, not least because there is scope then for looking to principles of taxation for guidance in the undertaking. In practice, therefore, this is the approach that has found favor with theorists and bargainers alike.

The taxation principles that lend themselves to adoption are the so-called benefit principle and the ability-to-pay principle (from each according to his/her capacity to contribute). In international "taxation" (burden sharing) there has been some application of benefit criteria. Contributions to the Universal Postal Union (UPU) are based on volume of postal traffic, area, and population. The administrative costs of the General Agreement on Tariffs and Trade (GATT)–forerunner of the World Trade Organization–were related to members' foreign-trade proportions. However, ever since the League of Nations abandoned the UPU system in favor of a method of determining subscriptions reflecting members' ability to pay (in the early 1920s), the primary emphasis in international burden-sharing negotiations has been on gauging equity in this way.

Within this framework, almost all expert studies and political discussion have assumed that contributions to international organizations should ideally be progressive, like most domestic income taxes. That is to say, it has been assumed that it should be possible to take a measure of each country's capacity to contribute (based on total or per capita GDP, or the one weighted by the other) and to compare that to each country's subscription to the relevant joint endeavor (defense, aid, etc.), and the countries with the higher capacities to contribute would be expected to pay progressively larger shares of the common expenditures. This is a theoretically sound approach, given that progressive impositions correspond to most countries'

own ideas of equity, as demonstrated by their internal income-tax systems. The major stumbling block that has prevented its widespread application is the difficulty of obtaining agreement on what rates of progression to use in the absence of any objective standards. (There are some exotic technical impediments too, e.g., the best guide to capacity to contribute is real national income and the significance in equity of progressive levies for international efforts is ambiguous unless taxes are actually assessed on individuals.)

Because of these practical obstacles to adoption of the ideal–or, rather, the least unsatisfactory–basis for calculating subscriptions, governments have tended to settle for the simpler concept of equi-proportional contributions to collective efforts. That is to say, they have argued for the same share of (say) GDP to be paid by each participating state regardless of the absolute level of its national income (as opposed to the progressively larger shares from richer states that the ideal requires). This approach retains the connection with ability to pay, albeit in a crude fashion. However, it can also be invested with something of the character of a progressive system by the straightforward expedient of specifying a sliding scale of lump-sum exemptions for individual countries–the poorer the contributor, the more generous the exemption. Subscriptions to the Organization for Economic Cooperation and Development (OECD) are assessed in this manner, and a modified variant applies throughout the UN system.

The United States has generally favored this proportional rule when assessing what the American share of the burden of collective activities should be and when judging the adequacy of partners' efforts. Thus, in NATO, it has regularly pressed its European allies to devote to the common defense proportions of GDP matching its own. In response to such pressure, the allies have typically countered with one of two main lines of argument (and often both). The first of these says that if financial sacrifice is to be the basis of assessment, then the progressive taxation guidelines ought to apply. It is entirely reasonable, therefore, that European defense/GDP proportions should be lower than the American figure; and for the United States to accuse its partners of "free riding" on this account is wrong. The second notes that defense spending is a measure of the value of a nation's inputs to the joint endeavor and argues that attention should also be paid to participants' military outputs–for example, the share of the alliance's front-line strength that each provides. Until the mid-1990s, such output measures invariably presented the European contribution in an altogether more favorable light than when expenditures alone were considered, partly because all the continental Europeans (except Luxembourg) maintained relatively low-cost conscript armies. Related to this second thesis is an additional argument that came to particular prominence in the U.S.-European defense burden-sharing disputes of the 1980s: namely, that there are many nonquantifiable aspects of an ally's contribution to a joint or collective security arrangement that should also enter the reckoning. Indeed, to take account of these–and, it must be said, in an effort to put an end to transatlantic exchanges that were becoming increasingly acrimonious–the alliance's international staff sought to shift the entire basis upon which member nations' contributions might be evaluated. The organization instituted an examination of how "roles, risks, and responsibilities" were shared and proposed the appraisal of allies' efforts in these terms. In short, it sought to promote equity of effort broadly defined as a basis of assessment in place of equality of sacrifice gauged exclusively in money terms.

This summary account of the NATO experience illustrates the fundamental truth about burden sharing. It is essentially a political matter, to be resolved by negotiation and compromise within a bargaining process to which many arguments may be admitted. There is general agreement among nations that the expenses of international activities should be fairly shared. Where it is simply a matter of specifying financial contributions, equity requires respect for each participating state's capacity to contribute and, to the extent possible, the application of principles of progressive taxation in this regard. Bargaining thus takes place with certain limits and disagreements may be confined to more or less technical matters. In more complex and costly undertakings, like alliance defense, it is harder to forge a consensus on what is equitable, especially if not only money costs (inputs) but also outputs and unquantifiables are to be taken into account. Bargaining is accordingly more complicated and the potential for divisive dispute, involving issues of principle, is correspondingly greater.

DAVID E. GREENWOOD

BIBLIOGRAPHY

De Strihou, Jacques M. V. Y., 1968. "Sharing the Defense Burden Among Western Allies." *Yale Economic Essays,* vol. 8 (Spring) 261–320.

Duke, Simon, 1993. *The Burdensharing Debate: A Reassessment.* London: Macmillan.

Kennedy, Gavin, 1979. *Burden Sharing in NATO.* London: Duckworth.

Kravis, Irving B. and M. W. S. Davenport, 1963. "The Political Arithmetic of International Burden Sharing." *Journal of Political Economy,* vol. 71 (August) 309–330.

Mason, Edward S., 1963. "The Equitable Sharing of Military and Economic Aid Burdens." *Proceedings of the Academy of Political Science,* vol. 27 (May).

Olson, Mancur and Richard Zeckhauser, 1968. "An Economic Theory of Alliances." *Review of Economics and Statistics,* vol. 48: 266–274.

Pincus, John, 1965. *Economic Aid and International Cost Sharing.* Baltimore, MD: Johns Hopkins Press.

Samuelson, Paul A., 1954. "The Pure Theory of Public Expenditure." *Review of Economics and Statistics,* vol. 36, no. 4: 381–389.

Singer, J. D., 1959. "The Finances of the League of Nations." *International Organization,* vol. 13: 255–273.

Volcker, Paul, 1993. *Financing an Effective United Nations.* New York: Ford Foundation.

BUREAUCRACY.

From "bureau" and "kratos": the power of the office. The bureaucracy is the administrative apparatus of the modern state; but also any organization or part of an organization with specifically modern characteristics. In business administration, the rationalized parts of the firm are bureaucratic.

Next to "charisma," "bureaucracy" is probably one of the most popularly used terms derived from sociology, specifically the sociology of Max Weber, and perhaps the most misused and misunderstood by layman and professional alike.

The popular use of "bureaucracy" refers to what a large part of clients in the late industrial welfare states perceive as the negative characteristics of the administrative apparatus: impersonality, slowness, oppressiveness, and rigidity. Closer examination shows these are the obverse side of neutrality, deliberateness, capacity to mobilize for projects of unprecedented magnitude, and predictability. These may be considered positive values of a civilization claiming legitimacy of its authority based on the rule of law and reason. In short, the negative side of the coin is not composed of deviations from an ideal bureaucracy but of necessary latent functions. (But, see Merton, 1936, and Selznick, 1949, who see unanticipated negative functions; and Goodsell, 1994, who minimizes them.)

The professional misuse of "bureaucracy" stems from the isolation of inner structural characteristics from external functions, as these were developed within the Weberian theory of knowledge that gave birth to the sociological concept. Especially nation builders, organizational consultants, and analysts tend to treat "bureaucracy" within the tradition of post-Platonic idealism, encouraged by Weber's use of the term "ideal type." Idealism suggests that once the component parts of a structure are perfected and connected, a bureaucratic structure will result. Weber's concept of the ideal type refers to something more earthy and quite different: an observer forms ideal types as pure mental constructs based on an empirically observed set of social orientations by which social actors typically orient themselves and their actions toward each other. Once an ideal type is constructed it is then possible for the analyst to operate with clear ideas that can be brought into logical relationships with each other (see **Max Weber**). Bureaucracy as an ideal type is not ideal in the sense of *desideratum.* It is a construct with admitted internal characteristics but whose outer meaning is determined by the context within which it was formed. In the case of Weber's concept, this context was the millenia-long development of the specific form of legal-rationalist culture, society and institutions that characterized Western Europe in the nineteenth and early twentieth centuries and which conquered much of the world.

Bureaucracy, then, cannot be allowed to be defined only by its inner characteristics but must be defined within the context of the growth of a civilization. To do otherwise has the result of setting up formal structures that imitate bureaucratic traits but whose actual operations are deflected from the legal-rational path by the prevailing indigenous culture, for example, those of Bangladesh or Oklahoma (for the latter, Elazar, 1972).

The inability to distinguish between popular, idealizing, and ideal-typical uses of the term is responsible for great confusion about what is being advocated or defended in the public administration literature. This is remedied by placing bureaucracy in its economic, cultural, and general civilizational context.

Bureaucracy in Its Context

Bureaucracy is the administrative apparatus of modern civilization, whether in the private or public sector. In the study of both business and public administration, this form of organization, however, has been caricaturized. In the typical textbook presentation, bureaucracy as modern organization is alleged to be present wherever six characteristics are present in an organization, stenographically: division of labor, hierarchy, written documents, staff of trained experts, full working capacity of the official, and the presence of general rules under which it operates. Attempts to modernize so-called underdeveloped or developing countries, however, show that instituting these characteristics does not produce modern business, modern government, or modern civilization in general. That such effects are expected shows that bureaucracy is still quietly conceived in the Western mind as not merely an administrative apparatus but as an engine of development as, indeed, it was by its first investigator.

Within modern Western civilization as a whole, bureaucracy is the means to assure the application of the authority of law conceived as a coherent system of rules for which rational grounds can be given. Legal-rationalism requires not only a rational legislative procedure but also an administrative procedure that follows and nurtures faith in the rule of reason: law must be transparent as to its justifications and apply to all alike. From the sociological point of view, all alike must be able to direct their behavior according to the expectation that the monopoly of force to which the state ultimately lays claim will be applied in a predictable manner.

Culturally, bureaucracy becomes an educator and enforcer of general, predictable, calculable values of living life.

Whatever the position given to economics in the generation of the modern state, culture, and society—whether as a substructure that carries the rest as superstructure (Karl Marx) or as a sector separate from politics (Adam Smith and the liberal economists)—the function of bureaucracy in the development and maintenance of modern economics becomes crucial as the context for understanding the meaning of bureaucracy. Weber subscribes both to a materialist and to an idea-oriented explanation for the generation and function of bureaucracy. This is crucial also for understanding the type of individual who can qualify to inhabit its structures and the kind of individual who can qualify to be served and ruled by them (Hummel, 1977).

Economically, bureaucracy is a response to modes of production that separate ownership and management of industry and business from the personal household. This, however, is achieved in Western civilization only once personal short-term interests are subordinated to a higher, long-term value resulting in an economic system of self-denial: "otherworldly asceticism" (Weber, 1930 [1904–1905]). This orientation makes it worthwhile for investors to reinvest the profits produced by an enterprise (Weber: reinvestment capitalism) because wealth is an indicator of future salvation.

Weber saw modern capitalism's material conditions and of the spirit that legitimated it as originating in separate developments of "elective affinity": the scientific and technical developments that made the modern mode of production possible and the rise of the "Protestant ethic," whose spirit legitimated the new economic attitudes and behaviors. Both the material procedures and the spirit, however, required conditions of the larger environment that could make them viable. Not only did Weber see bureaucracy as the governmental structure that evened the playing field for the rising industrial and merchant classes but he took it for granted that only a bureaucratic spirit compatible with the economy's entrepreneurial spirit could produce officials dedicated to applying law evenhandedly and predictably on the field of economic activity. A duty ethic would correspond to the entrepreneurial reinvestment ethic: the one originating with Luther, the other with Calvin (cf. also Bendix, 1962, pp. 312–313, fn. 13).

If this interpretation of the development of modern civilization is not taken into account, as it generally has not been in the narrow precincts of public administration, the spirit of officialdom needed in a truly modern bureaucracy cannot be understood. In short, the structures of bureaucracy also require the presence of people who will feel bound to the ultimate functional values of bureaucracy within the context of reinvestment-capitalist economic development. These values stem from a now-faded religious sense of God's way in the world (theodicy).

The entire symptomatology of complaints about latter-day bureaucratic dysfunctions is already contained in Max Weber's depiction of its founding functions. Say, for example, officials lack the duty ethic. This ethic requires that they consciously subordinate themselves to the economic spirit that requires stable markets and other legal constraints (such as the guaranteed enforcement of contracts and collection of debts). In the absence of the ethic, bureaucracy gets in the way of economic development. This applies to already established modern countries or countries still hoping to become modern. Alternatives originating in organizational structures of the past then threaten to be resurrected in the present and future. Without a neutral and reliable bureaucracy, for example, the present Russia and mainland China cannot produce the stable and predictable playing field that will encourage original capital investment, much less reinvestment. The six characteristics of bureaucracy plus one—the duty ethic is subordinate to something resembling the Protestant ethic (see Bellah, 1957)—must therefore be carefully read in the context of alternative history of future culture.

The Meaning of Bureaucracy's Inner Structures

Once the external functions of bureaucracy are held clearly in mind, the meaning of the structures of bureaucracy can be grasped by contrasting them against their most recent alternatives (although this does not exclude logical speculation about the constellation of future alternatives). We do so by following Weber (1968, pp. 956–958).

Division of Labor

In government, this refers to fixed official jurisdictional areas. These are contrasted against the vague, unsteady, and unsystematic splitting of tasks under previous patriarchal and patrimonial systems, clear obstacles against rational economic development.

Hierarchy

The principle of office hierarchy, levels of graded authority, a firmly ordered system of super- and subordination provides orderliness fostering internal control that can produce outward predictability. Where jurisdiction produces clear division between tasks at any given level, hierarchy produces a vertical division of levels concerned with matters of different scope and importance. Hierarchy is also the control mechanism that holds the division of labor together resulting in a unified policy and program structure. In contrast, with premodern organizations it is not reliably possible for clients to tell who is in charge of what, that is, whose commands are responsible or authoritative in relation to another's. Technically, hierarchical structure allows the creation of a massive administrative structure within which the higher-ups can at least claim abstract knowledge of what is going on below, even if millions are involved.

Written Documentation

Written documentation produces a third referent between disagreeing parties to a dispute, contrasting against word of mouth in which one party's claim is directed without further evidence against another. In contrast to the oral history of patriarchal or patrimonial authority, documentation provides bureaucracy with a memory independent of the minds and mouths of officials, enabling both internal controls and external controls by the political authorities. Documentation makes the actions of bureaucrats traceable and at least in principle inspectable by authoritative outsiders. This paper trail seen from the negative side is red tape.

Staff of Trained Experts

The separation of action from purely personal qualifications and the subordination of such qualifications to impersonal and general standards, is further advanced by the requirement for expert training of officials. This produces a culture and psychology amenable to standardized administrative rules and procedures. In contrast, earlier forms of administration tended to be personalistic and dependent on the luck of the draw in the assignment of a judge or official (rule by amateurs in the original sense of the word).

Full Working Capacity of the Official

This term is not understandable, or understandable only in ergonomic terms, except for a previous comprehension that the official is driven by a duty ethic that draws on the generalized work ethic of the modern civilization. Under this ethic, fulfillment of one's duties is naturally assumed to be of the highest priority before any personal needs, preferences, or wants. The duty ethic guarantees all clients probable fulfillment of their expectation that their legitimate needs will be taken care of with all possible human effort.

General Rules

In contrast to the prior publication and continuous imposition of general rules, premodern organization works under arbitrary, often unpublished ex post facto rules, the very opposite of predictable administration that the economy and law of a modern civilization require.

RALPH P. HUMMEL

BIBLIOGRAPHY

Bellah, Robert N., 1957. *Tokugawa Religion: The Values of Pre-Industrial Japan.* Glencoe, IL.: Free Press.

Bendix, Reinhard, 1962. *Max Weber—An Intellectual Portrait.* Garden City, N.Y.: Doubleday.

Elazar, Daniel J., 1972. *American Federalism: A View from the States,* 2nd ed. New York: Crowell.

Goodsell, Charles, 1994. *The Case for Bureaucracy: A Public Administration Polemic,* 3rd ed. Chatham, N.J.: Chatham House.

Hummel, Ralph P., 1977. *The Bureaucratic Experience.* New York: St. Martin's.

Merton, Robert K., 1936. "The Unanticipated Consequences of Purposive Social Action." *American Sociological Review*, vol. 1: 894–904.

Selznick, Philip, 1949. *TVA and the Grass Roots*. Berkeley, CA: University of California Press.

Weber, Max, 1930 [originally, 1904–1905; collected in 1920]. *The Protestant Ethic and The Spirit of Capitalism*. Tr. Talcott Parsons. New York: Scribner's. [*Die protestantische Ethik und der "Geist" des Kapitalismus*, 1904–1905; collected in *Gesammelte Aufsaetze zur Religionssoziologie*, vol. 1. Tuebingen: J. C. B. Mohr]

———, 1968. *Economy and Society: An Outline of Interpretive Sociology*. Eds. Guenther Roth and Claus Wittich; trs. Ephraim Fischoff *et al*. New York: Bedminster Press.

BUREAUCRAT BASHING.

A slang term meaning unjustified attack on government employees, used primarily in the United States and often in reference to career civil servants of the federal government.

While the word "bureaucrat" has a technical meaning in the sociology of large organizations, in lay parlance it is a pejorative term referring to any long-term government employee or civil servant. The bureaucrat in this sense is regarded as personifying the allegedly negative features of "bureaucracy," that is, being lazy, rule-minded, rigid, wasteful, and eager to retain power.

The verb "to bash" has had a number of slang meanings in the English-speaking world over the past two centuries. In this context, it means to strike with a crushing or smashing blow or to flog. Some etymologists believe the term is echoic, that is, an example of onomatopoeia, a word whose pronunciation imitates the sound of its referent. Other historians of language think the term may be a blend of the verbs "bang" and "smash" or, alternatively, a thickening of "pash."

"Bureaucrat bashing" probably entered the American political vocabulary in the 1970s. The expression has since spread to some other English-speaking countries, but seems not to be as popular there as in the United States. The term, on its face, would appear to be useful to those who are disgusted with government. Yet, those most likely to use it tend to have the opposite view, that condemnation of government employees is often unjustified and should itself be condemned. To them, "bureaucrat bashing" means an undesirable or unneeded flogging of public employees.

It is possible that the term was used this way for the first time during the 1976 presidential campaign of Jimmy Carter. Some observers, particularly journalists and academicians empathetic with federal civil servants or the existing political establishment, were dismayed by Carter's attacks on "the bureaucrats" as entrenched defenders of the Washington status quo. During his presidency, Carter continued this line of rhetoric from time to time, accompanied by small acts considered insulting by federal employees, such as levying parking charges and turning off the hot water in government bathrooms. Critics said he was "bashing" federal bureaucrats.

The term's use was reaffirmed in the following decade in the aftermath of the 1980 presidential campaign of Ronald Reagan. He attacked bureaucracy with renewed vigor, connecting the theme to his ideological conservatism. The federal bureaucrats, particularly those holding key positions in Washington, were depicted as contemptible loafers, incompetents, meddlers, and–above all–spenders. Once in office, he continued, like Carter, to sound the theme in speeches, giving the impression that a smaller and less interfering government would be possible only if the permanent bureaucracy could be beaten back. Also, as under Carter, a number of workplace practices further infuriated federal workers, such as monitoring phone calls, reducing office size, seeking antileak pledges, and sampling urine for drugs. The Administration's Private Sector Survey on Cost Control, otherwise known as the Grace Commission, heightened tensions further by conducting a campaign to save billions of dollars by investigating the supposedly wasteful practices of government with a view to replacing them with efficient business methods.

The administration of Bill Clinton, coming to power in 1993, did not "bash" bureaucrats overtly but did take the position that the federal government was "broken" and needed drastic overhaul. Its program, known as "reinventing government," was led by Vice President Gore and institutionalized by means of an organization and process called the National Performance Review (NPR). The problem with government, according to the NPR, was bad systems rather than bad people, yet many federal civil servants felt that the underlying objective was to lower federal expenditures and numbers of employees in preparation for Clinton's 1996 reelection campaign.

Since the mid-1980s, those disturbed by bureaucrat bashing have taken a number of steps to counter the practice. Paul A. Volcker, former chairman of the Federal Reserve, contended that a "quiet crisis" of lowered morale and recruitment attractiveness had emerged in the federal service. He hence organized the National Commission on the Public Service, or Volcker Commission, to promote respect and enhancement of the federal career service. The American Society for Public Administration launched a National Campaign for the Public Service and the Public Employees Roundtable, a coalition of pro-civil-service associations, sponsored an annual Public Service Recognition Week. Recognizing that all of these activities were directed at the national government, a National Commission on the State and Local Public Service, known as the Winter Commission, was formed to promote study, reforms, and renewed appreciation of government service at the state and local levels.

Yet, bureaucrat bashing will not come to a halt in the face of such bureaucrat boosting. Indeed, its further intensification can probably be expected in the years and decades ahead. The reason is not an objective inferiority on the part of America's public servants; they are among the most efficient, honest, and responsive in the world. The explanation lies, rather, in the simple fact that bureaucrats make a handy scapegoat for disenchantment with government. Elected officeholders can point to the bureaucrats to explain why their policies did not work as promised. Campaigning politicians can say that inefficient bureaucrats are a source of budgetary fat that can be cut in order to reduce taxes even while increasing programs.

Condemnation of government employees occurs in every country of the world, of course. In authoritarian regimes it is often deserved because of arbitrary and unfair conduct by officials. In developing countries it may be justified by corrupt behavior or inadequate levels of service quality or quantity caused by lack of funds. But in some nations, such as Western European states and the industrialized polities of the Pacific Rim, the public service has a dignified history and is sufficiently professionalized to enjoy substantial respect. The United States, with its individualistic culture and market-oriented economy, together with a tradition of limited and checked government power, does not possess the historical legacy or contemporary context required to support such a view. Hence bureaucrat bashing will continue to be a feature of its political landscape.

CHARLES T. GOODSELL

BIBLIOGRAPHY

Goodsell, Charles T., 1994. *The Case for Bureaucracy*, 3rd ed. Chatham, NJ: Chatham House.

Lane, Larry M. and James F. Wolf, 1990. *The Human Resource Crisis in the Public Sector.* New York: Quorum.

Wamsley, Gary L. *et al.*, 1990. *Refounding Public Administration.* Beverly Hills: Sage.

Wickwar, Hardy, 1991. *Power and Service.* Westport, CT: Greenwood Press.

Wilson, James Q., 1989. *Bureaucracy.* New York: Basic Books.

BUREAUCRAT, BUDGET MAXIMIZING.

A senior official of a government agency who is singularly interested in expanding its budget.

The theory of the "budget maximizing bureaucrat" was first presented by William Niskanen (1971) in *Bureaucracy and Representative Government*. Niskanen developed a model of government bureau behavior based on the simple assumption that bureaucrats are budget maximizers. The study is a classic in the field of public choice. Three factors are posited to influence the supply of government services: (1) objectives of bureaucrats, (2) characteristics of

bureaus, and (3) relations between bureaus and the environment (Niskanen 1971; 1975; 1991).

Objectives of Bureaucrats

Like most public choice analyses, the theory assumes maximizing behavior by the key participants in the service delivery process. What do bureaucrats maximize? "Among the several variables that may enter the bureaucrat's utility function are the following: salary, perquisites of the office, public reputation, power, patronage, output of the bureau. All of these variables except the last two . . . are a positive monotonic function of the total *budget* of the bureau during the bureaucrat's tenure in office" (Niskanen 1971, p. 38).

One of the most important criticisms of the theory questions whether bureaucrats are principally concerned with budgetary growth.

Migue and Belanger (1974) argue that rational bureaucrats seek to maximize the discretionary budget, defined as the difference between the budgetary appropriation and the minimum cost of producing agency output. Budget size alone may not provide bureaucrats with many opportunities to increase pay, power, and prestige if legislative committees restrict the larger appropriation to specific areas. Instead, because of the flexibility it provides to pursue a broad series of objectives, budgetary discretion, not size, is more likely to increase the power of a bureaucrat. Conceding to his critics, Niskanen (1991) has more recently argued that the budget maximization assumption "should now be dropped entirely in favor of an assumption that [bureaucrats] act to maximize the discretionary budget" (p. 28). (See also Blais and Dion, 1991, for a critical evaluation of Niskanen's theory.)

Characteristics of a Bureau

Government bureaus in the Niskanen model share two attributes: (1) owners and employees do not derive personal income from any economic profits of government activities and (2) much of the bureau's revenue stream is related to the provision of "collective goods" that are not sold at a per-unit rate. In brief, bureaus are nonprofit organizations that are generally financed by lump-sum appropriations or grants.

Environment of Government Bureaus

The most critical factor shaping a bureau's environment is the relationship with its sponsor. Sponsors are typically legislative committees responsible for bureau oversight. Because sponsors are dependent on a single bureau for services, and the bureau is dependent on a single sponsor for budgetary authority, Niskanen models the relationship as a bilateral monopoly. As such, a bureau offers a "promised set of activities and the expected output(s) of these activities for a budget" (Niskanen 1971, p. 25).

The bureau's characteristic "package" offer of a promised output for a budget has important implications for the behavior of bureaus: Under many conditions it gives a bureau the same type of bargaining power as a profit-seeking monopoly that discriminates among customers or presents the market with an all-or-nothing choice. The primary reason for the differential bargaining power of a monopoly bureau is the sponsor's lack of a significant alternative and its unwillingness to forego the services supplied by the bureau (Niskanen 1971, p. 25).

Bureaucrats have several advantages over sponsors in the budgetary process. First, bureaus enjoy a significant information advantage on the actual production costs and benefits of programs. Traditional budget formats such as the line-item budget do not link inputs to outputs and consequently advance informational asymmetries. Second, legislative committees (the sponsors) are composed of individuals that have a greater demand for the bureau's services than the average citizen. A congressional committee on agriculture, for example, oversees the operations of the Department of Agriculture and is likely to be comprised of "high demand" legislators from farm states. Last, bureaus have monopoly rights to supply specific services which increases their power because sponsors cannot shop around for the best budget package. For these reasons and others, the theory generally expects sponsors to be passive observers in the budgetary process.

Niskanen's theory predicts that these advantages taken together enable bureaucrats to supply a level of government services in excess of what is socially optimal. Alternatively stated, if the assumptions of the theory are valid, government bureaus will always produce output greater than competitive private industry operating under similar conditions. Several reforms can restrain the oversupply tendencies of budget maximizing bureaucrats.

One approach is to have bureaus that provide similar services compete with one another. The introduction of such "intragovernmental redundancy" can simulate a competitive marketlike environment. However, Niskanen (1971) notes that such competition is "generally regarded as undesirable or, at best, in deference to certain institutional traditions, as tolerable" (p. 195). A second reform is to competitively contract services to private producers (Miranda, 1994). City governments such as Phoenix, Arizona, and Indianapolis, Indiana, have allowed unions to submit bids for service production in competition with private sector firms. Yet, a third possibility, "gain sharing," would reward bureau managers and employees for producing surpluses between the annual agency appropriations and the minimum cost of producing services. Each of these approaches characterizes the "reinventing" brand of thinking in contemporary public administration.

Summary

Although empirical tests have yet to establish conclusive support for the theory, Niskanen's work has stimulated a considerable amount of scholarly work on bureaucracy in the fields of economics and political science. As a guideline for future inquiry, in a reflection on *Bureaucracy and Representative Government* 20 years after its publication, Niskanen (1991) suggests that "it will continue to be more useful to focus on the distinctive characteristics of bureaus and the political institutions and process in which they operate than to explain the behavior of bureaus in terms of the distinctive attributes of bureaucrats" (p. 28).

ROWAN MIRANDA

BIBLIOGRAPHY

Blais, Andre and Stephane Dion, eds., 1991. *The Budget-Maximizing Bureaucrat: Appraisals and Evidence.* Pittsburgh: University of Pittsburgh Press.
Migue, Jean-Luc and Gerard Belanger, 1974. "Towards a General Theory of Managerial Discretion." *Public Choice,* vol. 17: 24–43.
Miranda, Rowan, 1994. "Privatization and the Budget Maximizing Bureaucrat." *Public Productivity & Management Review,* vol. 17, no. 4: 355–369.
Niskanen, William A., 1971. *Bureaucracy and Representative Government.* Chicago: Aldine Atherton.
———, 1975. "Bureaucrats and Politicians." *Journal of Law and Economics,* vol. 18: 617–644.
———, 1991. "A Reflection on Bureaucracy and Representative Government." In Andre Blais and Stephane Dion, eds. *The Budget-Maximizing Bureaucrat: Appraisals and Evidence,* Pittsburgh: University of Pittsburgh Press.

BUREAUPATHOLOGY.

A sickness found in governmental organizations that reduces their effectiveness in meeting policy and program goals in an efficient, yet responsive manner.

Modern bureaucracy has been viewed by many observers as an efficient method of structuring large organizations that perform routine and complex tasks. The Weberian model of legal-rational authority as found in bureaucracy is believed to be an ideal that in practice may take varied forms. Nonetheless, certain features are considered most common: hierarchy, division of labor, adherence to written rules, record-keeping, objective and impartial decisionmaking, and full-time, expert career professionals. Bureaucracy as an efficient machine is a metaphor for its ability to perform tasks consistently, impartially, and economically.

However, modern bureaucracy has its critics in organization theory, as well as among the general public. Their criticisms range from the witty to the sophisticated. Several simple "laws" of bureaucracy draw attention to "dysfunctional," even "pathological," administrative behaviors, that is, behaviors that are considered pathological because they do not enable the organization to accomplish its goals. For example, Parkinson's Law is "work expands so as to fill the time available for its completion," and the Peter Principle states, "Employees tend to be promoted to their level of incompetence." These light-hearted jabs at bureaucracy point to the perceived inefficiency and incompetence of bureaucrats.

More serious criticisms of bureaucracy were written in the mid-to-late twentieth century by organization theorists who believed that seemingly desirable characteristics of bureaucracy can become dysfunctional or pathological for the organization. This can occur due to individual needs or because of the bureaucracy's structure and reward system.

An early critic, Robert Merton (1940), argued that strict adherence to rules can become an end in itself, resulting in "goal displacement," that is, where the organization's goals are replaced by conformity to rules. Often promoted by the bureaucratic training and reward system, this process in turn produces bureaucratic rigidity, red tape, and resistance to change.

Another pathology focuses primarily on the interpersonal behavior of bureaucrats, both in client and subordinate relationships. Victor Thompson (1961) defines "bureaupathology" as the behavior pattern of insecure people using their authority to dominate and control others. Personal anxiety and insecurity may be produced by certain personality traits but can also be encouraged by the bureaucracy's elaborate system of rules, oversight, and punishments. With employees, managers may develop a host of procedures, policies, and standards that govern even the most trivial decisions of subordinates. In trying to follow the rules to the letter to avoid reprimands, officials may make little accommodation for the exceptional case. As bureaucracies stress impartiality and impersonality in public contacts, bureaucrats may also adopt an arrogant, harsh, and domineering attitude toward those they serve.

A fascinating study of dysfunctional bureaucratic behavior in two French public bureaucracies was written by sociologist Michel Crozier (1964). He observed these characteristics: impersonal rules, centralization of decisions, ineffective communication between hierarchical levels, peer group pressures on the individual, and the development of internal power relationships. These resulted in an organization's inability to correct its behavior by learning from its mistakes. Crozier also argues that some observed behaviors may be exacerbated by society's culture, especially in his cases, the French reliance on formal (rather than informal) relationships, the isolation of the individual, and the lack of collective, cooperative norms.

Scholars in the 1970s and 1980s drew attention to the debilitating effects on individuals from a lifetime career in bureaucracy. Drawing on Max Weber and German

philosopher Jurgen Habermas, Ralph Hummel (1982) describes the bureaucrat as a "truncated" personality who is able to understand life only in the structured terms of hierarchy and technical competence. As a result, humanistic values are absent in one's personal and professional life, as well as in the organization. Technocratic and bureaucratic values are thus dominant within public organizations that should be held accountable by outside political and constituent forces but often are not.

More recent critics of bureaucracy have suggested that public agencies are inherently inefficient because they tend to maximize their own self-interest in a fashion that may be rational for managers and the agency, but pathological for the government and for the public interest. Bureaucrats are thought to seek budget growth, to expand the number of subordinates, and to control information flows in order to improve individual and organizational power and prestige. These behaviors are encouraged not only by the traditional characteristics of bureaucracy, but also by key economic factors—that is, the lack of market competition for public services and the nature of public goods that are usually supplied by government.

RUTH HOOGLAND DeHOOG

BIBLIOGRAPHY

Crozier, Michel, 1964. *The Bureaucratic Phenomenon.* Chicago: University of Chicago Press.
Hummel, Ralph, 1982. *The Bureaucratic Experience,* 2nd ed. New York:
St. Martin's.
Merton, Robert K., 1940. "Bureaucratic Structure and Personality." *Social Forces,* vol. 17: 560-568.
Parkinson, C. Northcote, 1975. *Parkinson's Law.* New York: Ballantine.
Peter, Laurence J. and Raymond Hull, 1969. *The Peter Principle.* New York: William Morrow.
Thompson, Victor A., 1961. *Modern Organization.* New York: Alfred A. Knopf.

BURNOUT.

"Exhaustion of physical or emotional strength." An earlier version of *Webster's Dictionary* defined burnout as "to destroy, obliterate, or to cause to fail, wear out, or become exhausted by making excessive demands on energy, strength, or resources" (Webster, 1987). Herbert Freudenberger, a clinical psychologist practicing in New York City, first used the term to describe the pathology of helping professionals who were worn out in their roles after several years in their professions. He defined burnout as a syndrome that included symptoms of exhaustion, a pattern of neglecting one's own needs, and feeling both intense internal and external pressures. Maslach and Pines took this further and identified the burnout syndrome as "a multifaceted state of emotional, physical, and mental exhaustion caused by chronic stress that occurs when members of the helping professions experience long-term involvement with other people in emotionally demanding situations" (Caputo, 1991, p. 3).

Stages and Symptoms

Key to understanding burnout is knowledge of the stress phenomena. According to Hans Selye (1956) stress is the nonspecific response of an individual, in terms emotional, physical, and behavioral, to the demands of life. Stress has three stages. The first stage is the alarm stage, in which the demands are made and the individual decision is made whether to respond to the demand. The second stage occurs when the individual responds to the demand and energy is expended to conquer or scare off the stressor; this is the resistance stage. The third stage is the exhaustion stage; this occurs when the energy levels of the resistance stage are maintained for long periods of time with no sign of relief. The result of the exhaustion stage is burnout and eventually death.

Caputo (1991) has concluded that burnout is a syndrome characterized by three types of exhaustion: emotional, physical, and mental. The results of this tri-dimensional exhaustion are totally overwhelming. Caputo then identified three major areas of burnout symptomatology: psychological, physical, and behavioral. Psychological symptoms include feelings of anger, anxiety, despair, helplessness, and apathy. They also include attitudes of cynicism, self-doubt, and indifference as well as disruptions in cognitive function. Physical symptoms can be mild or major in their occurrence. Possible mild physical symptoms include fatigue, headaches, weight changes, muscle tension, gastrointestinal problems, and insomnia. Major physical disorder can include heart attacks, strokes, high blood pressure, and ulcers. The behavioral symptoms are divided into four categories: interpersonal relations, work performance, substance abuse, and significant behaviors. Symptoms in the category of interpersonal relations include withdrawal, conflicts with family and friends, and blaming and criticizing of others. Work performance symptoms are absenteeism and tardiness, lowered productivity, workaholism, and obsessiveness. Substance abuse of alcohol, drugs, caffeine, and/or tobacco and suicidal or unnecessary risk-taking behaviors are also symptoms of burnout.

Types of Burnout

Burnout is not just an individual phenomenon. Organizations can also burnout. In fact organizational burnout can often be a precipitator of individual burnout, especially among its executive staff. Organizational burnout is not the result of accumulated individual burnouts. Simendinger and Moore (1985) have identified four characteristics of organizational burnout: bickering between employees and divisions, a sense of resignation especially among middle management, stagnation of the organization's decision-making and delegation of authority, and a lack of vision especially in terms of the external environment.

Intense long-terms stress is undergone by many individuals and organizations. However, not all of these develop burnout. According to Gold and Roth (1993) in their study of teacher burnout, there are several factors that contribute to the likelihood of burnout. One factor is lack of social support. Social support includes six functions: listening, professional support, professional challenge, emotional support, emotional challenge, and the sharing of social reality. Demographic factors that predisposed individuals to burnout indicated that single males teaching in higher grades in suburban or rural environments were most at risk. Low self-concept, lack of administrative support, difficult parents, isolation, and a high sense of role conflict and role ambiguity were all factors identified as contributing to the likelihood of burnout.

Prevention Strategies

Uris (1958) described seven "qualities of success" characteristics used by managers to avoid burnout. These were a high tolerance for frustration, encouraging participation of subordinates in decisionmaking, self-questioning, acceptance of the competitive internal and external environments, dealing calmly with both victory and defeat, self-identification with stable groups who were available as support systems, and realistic goal setting.

To reduce burnout the causal stress must be reduced, eliminated, or the individual must accept the fact that the stressor cannot be changed and therefore the individual must change. Techniques to reduce stress include setting goals, confronting others, saying no, using relaxation techniques, and building support systems. A possible method to eliminate stress is to take direct action by changing the work or personal environment or by soliciting assistance from a supervisor or trusted friend. Individual changes should concentrate on positive mental and physical health choices, assertive and upbeat attitudes, a perspective that recognizes that the world is imperfect and that life is often unfair, and the decision to seek professional mental health assistance if necessary (Caputo, 1991).

Organizational burnout can be reduced in a number of ways. Much of the information about reduction of organizational burnout has been obtained from a study of Japanese management. Organizational features that are thought to reduce burnout include an emphasis on product quality, long-term perspective and strategies, consensus-based decisionmaking, a lean organizational structure, a commitment to lifetime employment, and a people-sensitive management style based on the concepts of mutual responsibility and loyalty (Simendinger and Moore, 1985).

In order to deal effectively with burnout, one must be able to recognize its existence, accept responsibility for responding to it, develop effective coping strategies, and plan preventive strategies to discourage its return. There is no single effective cure or antidote. All the techniques described are time-consuming and require both commitment and diligence. Each individual or organization must take the steps that best meet its needs in the particular environment in which the burnout is occurring. Taking the first step of admitting the burnout exists is often the most difficult.

PATRICE ALEXANDER

BIBLIOGRAPHY

Caputo, Janette S., 1991. *Stress and Burnout in Library Service*. Phoenix, AZ: Oryx Press.

Gold, Yvonne and Robert A. Roth, 1993. *Teachers Managing Stress and Preventing Burnout: The Professional Health Solution*. London: Falmer Press.

Kurland, Roselle and Robert Salmon, 1992. "When Problems Seem Overwhelming: Emphases in Teaching, Supervision, and Consultation." *Social Work*, vol. 37, no. 3 (May) 240–244.

Poulin, John and Carolyn Walter, 1993. "Social Worker Burnout: A Longitudinal Study." *Social Worker Research and Abstracts*, vol. 29, no. 4 (Dec) 5–1.

Selye, Hans, 1956. *The Stress of Life*. New York: McGraw-Hill.

Simendinger, Earl A.. and Terence F. Moore, 1985. *Organizational Burnout in Health Care Facilities*. Rockville, MD: Aspen.

Truch, Stephen, 1980. *Teacher Burnout and What to Do About It*. Novato, CA: Academic Therapy Publications.

Uris, Owen, 1958. *The Effective Executive*. New York: McGraw-Hill.

Webster's Third New International Dictionary of the English Language, Unabridged, 1987. Chicago, IL: Encyclopedia Britannica.

BUSINESSLIKE MANAGEMENT.

The practice of applying private sector principles, norms, and procedures to the administration of government-run organizations. In the American public administration literature, this ideal may be traced back to early scholars such as Woodrow Wilson (1856–1924), Frank Goodnow (1859–1958), and Leonard D. White (1891–1958).

Woodrow Wilson, the political science professor who would later become United States president, first proclaimed that "the field of [public] administration is a field of business" in a paper written in 1887 entitled "The Study of Administration." Wilson, who went on to say that "it [public administration] is removed from the hurry and strife of politics" (1887, p. 202), helped pioneer the intellectual history of the discipline.

Frank Goodnow (1900) had written that politics involves policies or expressions and administration involves the implementation of those policies (pp. 10–11). Value neutrality and other businesslike principles that were applied to government administration all originated from the now disclaimed politics-administration dichotomy.

The dichotomy was the cornerstone of the early or classical period (1880s to 1930s) and its supporters, members of the Good Government Reform Movement, proclaimed a separation of politics from administration in their quest for a pure science of administration. Such a science would provide virtually no distinctions between government and private sector management.

White, a University of Chicago professor who wrote the first public administration textbook (1926), believed that the study of administration should be based in the affairs of management and the American Management Association rather than law and the decisions of the courts (p. viii). This belief was based on the notions of value neutrality and apolitical, neutral competence and provided the framework for early public administration theory.

Toward the end of the 1930s, scholars such as Luther Gulick (1892–1993) and Herbert Simon (1916–) challenged the notion that politics could be removed from the administration of government. Gulick, although desiring a pure science of administration, parted with his contemporaries of the classical era and argued that separation was impossible and undesirable because government should use the expertise of the administrator on matters of public policy (see Fry, 1989, p. 74).

Simon was a behavioralist, whose works appeared primarily after the classical era. In *Administrative Behavior* (1947), he proposed the fact-value dichotomy or the "factual" element of decisionmaking as the appropriate domain for constructing a science of administration (also see Fry, 1989, p. 182, and Simon, 1976, p. 51).

Present day scholars have long abandoned the idea of a science of administration. However, Gulick's and Simon's position on the politics-administration dichotomy is now the accepted school of thought and is supported by the fact that government administration operates in an environment permeated by politics; this makes government administration distinct from business administration. Such an environment includes, but is not limited to, the impact of government budgeting, lobbying, and citizen demands for government agency responsiveness.

Today's scholars conclude that the most successful government administrators are those who are the most politically skilled at handling the various pressure points (budgeting, lobbying, etc.) that the administrator confronts on a daily basis. These pressure points comprise an administrator's organizational or task environment, and the agency administrator or manager is forced to deal with them in the process of achieving organizational goals, presenting quite a different picture from business administration, where decisionmaking is primarily governed by the economic forces of supply and demand.

Currently there is a renewed interest in businesslike management in the United States. This stems in part from the popularity of privatizing or contracting out government services to the private sector in order to cut costs and increase productivity and efficiency. This reasoning is driven by the belief that the private sector performs more efficiently and effectively than government-run monopolies. The argument is that private sector competition and the need to make a profit drive down costs. Thus, privatization and contracting out make the delivery of government services more "businesslike."

Critics, however, argue that competition is not solely a private sector phenomenon but that government agencies may also adopt competition as a method to bring down the cost of service delivery. This approach has been taken in United States cities such as Charlotte, North Carolina, and Phoenix, Arizona, where city departments compete directly with the private sector and other outside vendors for the delivery of government services.

Supporters of this new wave of businesslike management are fully aware that politics and administration cannot be separated. This movement is enveloped by the need for greater efficiency without sacrificing the democratic ideal of responsive government. This is exemplified by the relatively new body of literature developing on ways to define and/or measure government efficiency as well as government productivity.

Since most government agencies do not produce tangible products that would enable one to directly measure productive output based on overall monetary cost, government productivity is usually defined as providing the same level of service for less cost or providing a higher level of service without a corresponding increase in cost. The literature that developed around the issue of (public sector) productivity first began to appear in the 1970s (see Holzer and Nagel, 1984).

Since businesslike management is associated with the politics-administration dichotomy and the Good Government Reform Movement, jurisdictions that felt the greatest impact from the movement may maintain more businesslike administrations. The council-manager system of government is one example.

In the early years, supporters of the council-manager form of government sought to separate politics from administration by placing a professionally trained administrator, rather than an elected politician, in the position of chief administrative office of the city. This nonpartisan appointee, usually chosen by and answerable to the city council, would therefore not be bound by any political favors and could make decisions and select appointments based on merit rather than political favoritism.

Dayton, Ohio, was the first major American city to adopt this system of government (in 1913). In examples such as Cincinnati, Ohio, local elections are nonpartisan as well and the office of the mayor is reduced primarily to ceremonial and/or advisory capacities. The person who assumes the position of mayor does so by receiving a plurality of votes in at-large city council elections. Examples of other major American cities with council-manager systems

of government include Dallas, Texas, San Diego, California, Phoenix, Arizona, and Miami-Dade County, Florida. This type of government is more numerous as well as manageable in small- to medium-sized cities and is found mostly in midwestern and western states.

Council-manager systems of government are less prevalent in states touched less by the Good Government Reform Movement. For instance, they are almost nonexistent in the historically populist state of Louisiana and in Mississippi, where the state constitution prohibits nonpartisan elections. In these and other nonreformed states, the administration of public policy is regarded as more highly political and less professional or businesslike.

It should also be noted that although the Good Government Reform Movement, with its emphasis on businesslike management, was the most popular at the state and local levels of government in the 1920s and 1930s, its emphasis on merit over politics in the recruitment, selection, and promotion of government employees played a major role at the national level in 1883 when Congress passed the Civil Service Reform Act (CSRA), or Pendleton Act. This legislation established the U.S. Civil Service Commission, and its passage signaled a victory for the merit principle over the spoils system.

Currently, there is disagreement over whether public and private sector administration are more similar or dissimilar. Scholars such as Michael A. Murray (1983, pp. 60–71) conclude that public and private administration are not inherently different as far as substance, procedure, and methods. By contrast, Graham T. Allison (1992) quotes Wallace Sayre (1905–1972) and suggests that although there are as many similarities as differences, "the differences are more important than the similarities" (pp. 457–475).

Common business or housekeeping practices such as computerization of records and inventory systemization may be applied with the same level of efficiency in both sectors. However, overall efficiency often suffers when the will of the public must be adhered to in decisions regarding whether to cut wasteful programs that provide a service the public demands. This led one businessman turned big city mayor to conclude that "the business of government is government, not business" (Cervantes, 1983, pp. 350–352).

There is also a discussion of the "blurring," or convergence, of the differences caused by a mixing of governmental and nongovernmental activities. This is most noticeable in areas of government regulation and contracting. Some private sector firms have taken on governmental attributes (e.g., budget cycle, government audits) due to their high level of dependency on government contracts. This allows businesslike management to be intermingled with governmental regulations in the delivery of government services.

Yet, the conclusion of scholars such as Hal G. Rainey, Robert W. Backoff, and Charles H. Levine (1983, 93–108) does not support the notion of either a widescale or an incremental convergence. They conclude that there is no empirical evidence to support the proposition that public and private sector management practices are converging.

JAMES D. WARD

BIBLIOGRAPHY

Allison, Graham T., Jr., 1992. "Public and Private Management: Are They Fundamentally Alike in All Unimportant Particulars?" In Jay M. Shafritz and Albert C. Hyde, eds., *Classics of Public Administration,* 3rd ed. Pacific Grove, CA: Brooks/Cole, 457–475.

Cervantes, A. J., 1983. "Memoirs of a Businessman-Mayor." In James L. Perry and Kenneth L. Kraemer, eds., *Public Management: Public and Private Perspectives.* Palo Alto, CA: Mayfield, 350–352.

Fry, Brian, 1989. *Mastering Public Administration.* Chatham, NJ: Chatham House.

Goodnow, Frank J., 1900. *Politics and Administration.* New York: Macmillan.

Holzer, Marc and Stuart Nagel, eds., 1984. *Productivity and Public Policy.* Beverly Hills, CA: Sage.

Murray, Michael A., 1983. "Comparing Public and Private Management: An Exploratory Essay." In James L. Perry and Kenneth L. Kraemer, eds., *Public Management: Public and Private Perspectives.* Palo Alto, CA: Mayfield, 60–71.

Rainey, Hal G., Robert W. Backoff, and Charles H. Levine, 1983. "Comparing Public and Private Organizations." In James L. Perry and Kenneth L. Kraemer, eds., *Public Management: Public and Private Perspectives.* Palo Alto, CA: Mayfield, 93–108.

Simon, Herbert, 1976. *Administrative Behavior,* 3rd ed. New York: Free Press.

White, Leonard D., 1926. *Introduction to the Study of Public Administration.* New York: Macmillan.

Wilson, Woodrow, 1887. "The Study of Administration." *Political Science Quarterly,* vol. 2 (June) 202.

BYLAWS. A document that provides direction and guidance for governing a nonprofit organization. The initial incorporators or their designee can write the bylaws to support the needs of the organization; however, states might require certain bylaw provisions as specified in their state laws on corporations.

Responsibility for preparation of the initial set of bylaws is usually assumed by the individual(s) filing the articles of incorporation. Presentation of the bylaws must be a primary agenda item at the first meeting of the Board of Directors, following the state's acceptance of the Articles of Incorporation. Without formally adopting bylaws, the board of directors would not have any defined powers for conducting its first official meeting, and there would be no rules and guidelines for supporting subsequent meetings.

Nonprofit corporations completing Form 1023—the application for seeking federal tax-exempt status—will dis-cover that the Internal Revenue Service (IRS) requires a nonprofit corporation to include a copy of bylaws in their application. The IRS is interested not only in the stated purpose of the organization but also how the board of directors plans to operate. Specifically, the IRS is interested in provisions that address the avoidance of conflict of interest and in a dissolution provision that provides for disposal or transfer of assets to other nonprofit organizations or governmental entities.

There are many possible provisions that can be contained in a set of bylaws. Inclusion of certain provisions is based on the organization's function, character, or methods of operation. The content of the provisions may also vary depending on the organization's primary tax-exempt purpose. The following are a representative list of bylaw provisions:

- organization name
- organizational purpose
- principal location of corporation
- enumeration of the duties of the board and its officers
- procedures for electing officers
- number of board members and officers
- annual meetings
- required notices of meetings
- frequency of meetings
- quorum requirements
- conditions for reimbursement for board members' meeting expenses
- procedures/rules for conducting meetings
- proxy requirements
- board terms of office
- nominating procedures
- election procedures
- procedures for filling vacancies
- attendance requirements
- membership and dues requirements (if established as a membership organization)
- causes for resignation and expulsion
- waivers of notice
- board liability
- standing committees
- process for appointment of committees
- requirements for corporate contracts
- requirements for signing checks
- requirements of distribution of funds (if a private foundation)
- indemnification
- requirements for keeping records
- fiscal year designation
- corporate seal designation
- procedures for amending the bylaws
- procedures for the dissolution of the corporation and disposal of assets

Many problems associated with an organization's bylaws can be attributed to board members' failure to use the bylaws as a tool of governance. A typical problem is found in the attendance provision, which outlines the expectations of attending board meetings and the consequences of non-attendance. Many boards overlook this rule and will ignore the difficult responsibility of removing a frequently absent board member.

Since self-perpetuating boards have the direct authority to add, remove, or revise bylaw provisions, it seems unreasonable for these types of boards to be out of compliance with their own operational rules. Also, membership organizations can seek their members' permission to similarly alter or remove bylaw provisions that are not a good organizational fit. When boards violate specific provisions in their own bylaws, they may be exposing themselves to liability for improper decisionmaking practices. For this reason, board members should periodically review their bylaws.

STEPHEN R. BLOCK

BIBLIOGRAPHY

Block, Stephen R. and Jeffrey W. Pryor, 1991. *Improving Nonprofit Management Practice: A Handbook for Community-Based Organizations.* Rockville, MD: OSAP/Public Health Service, U.S. Dept. of Health and Human Services.

Hopkins, Bruce, 1992. *The Law of Tax-exempt Organizations,* 6th ed. New York: John Wiley & Sons.

CABINET GOVERNMENT. A form of collective government in which the leader of government and a team of ministers, meeting in cabinet, determine policy as a group; they are collectively responsible to the legislature and reliant on continuing support there; that support is usually guaranteed by party discipline.

In 1884, Woodrow Wilson looked enviously at the system of cabinet government in Britain, wishing that the cohesion and discipline he saw there might be grafted onto the dispersed American system of government. His description (Wilson, 1884) and his diagnosis of what amendments might be required to transform U.S. government remain largely accurate, although the system he was describing has sometimes mutated as it was transferred to different countries. It remains, however, the antithesis to the separation of powers found in the United States.

Cabinet government now has many variations. In the Netherlands and Germany, for instance, proportional representation has led to the formation of coalition governments that have reduced the power of the leader to select or dismiss ministers. In the Netherlands, ministers are responsible to, but not members of, parliament. In Australia, Labor Party ministers are elected by the parliamentary party, and thus the leader, although significant in the selection of colleagues, is not the only person whose priorities are considered. In Canada demands for regional representation meant that the number of ministers in Cabinet once reached 40, a size too large for effective decisionmaking.

Yet, all these systems of cabinet government have as core requirements some basic factors: collective responsibility and reliance for survival on the continued support of the party in the legislature, guaranteed by the discipline imposed by party membership. The leader of the government is regarded as the head of a team whose opinions must be sought, and individual ministerial responsibilities must be given due scope for action.

Cabinet government has a number of advantages that can in part explain its longevity and popularity. It is infinitely flexible. The cabinet will include the senior members of the governing parties, but that does not preclude a range of formats to arrange the process of governing. In Germany and the Netherlands, tradition and even the German Basic Law require that ministers have full scope for action in their designated portfolios; the cabinet is therefore more inclined to consider broad strategic decisions or general directions. In those countries that have developed from the British model, the prime minister is ceded greater authority and is able to determine the rules and procedures by which Cabinet will be run and who will be involved in selected committees that may intrude on the activities of individual portfolios. To say that cabinet government exists is not to

define how government will be organized. Cabinet government refers not merely to the meetings of the full Cabinet but also to the substructure of committees and conventions that make it work. In practice, decisions may be made by ministers, by discussions between the minister and the prime minister, by decision of a cabinet committee, or after deliberation by the Cabinet itself.

Cabinet will play several functions at the same time. As the link between the administrative and political worlds, it may

- act as a clearing house for decisions made elsewhere and then reported to Cabinet as a fait accompli;
- act as an information exchange where information papers and memoranda keep colleagues informed of government activity in other portfolios;
- act as arbiter between ministers disputing over policy turf or between the treasurer and ministers over spending priorities; only Cabinet can decide who wins or loses;
- impose political priorities on the technical proposals presented by the nonpartisan career officials who support most cabinet governments. The elected representatives may put the partisan spin on the policies or proposals that may be electorally insensitive, even if operationally attractive;
- co-ordinate government to prevent the diverse functions of government, often expressed as ministerial ambitions, from too obviously overlapping or contradicting one another;
- manage crises when events are out of control, and it needs the most powerful and legitimate leaders of the government to put events back on track;
- behave as guardian of the strategy or party platform; government is broken into manageable policy arenas—only the Cabinet has the prestige to relate the particular to the general.

Cabinet does not consciously play each of these roles separately; and it may play some much better than others. Many critics complain that the Cabinet is not adequately fulfilling the function that they regard as crucial, whether it be setting strategy or making technically correct decisions, yet they are all essentially interlinked, demanding the attention of the most powerful people to determine issues that cannot be settled elsewhere. In practice, a Cabinet tends to consider items sequentially, as it settles the pressing issues of the day, and seldom considers the middle- or long-range issues; crises or immediate demands dominate. But the great benefit of a forum that brings together the leading figures of a government is that they will consider a number of angles of a proposal and will fulfill several of those listed functions at the same time. Several minds will come to better decisions than one.

Cabinet government also makes all the members of the government collectively responsible for the actions of their colleagues. The principle of collective responsibility demands that, having had the opportunity to argue the case in Cabinet, ministers must publicly support any decisions taken there or resign. It is not essential that they agree, but they must at least acquiesce in the conclusions of their colleagues. As a consequence, some ministers may be promoting a policy imposed on them by Cabinet. The convention is based on the idea that a government cannot survive or govern if its ministers are constantly squabbling about the best solutions to the problems they face. In coalition governments, the collapse of collective responsibility usually presages the departure of one of the partners from the coalition. In single-party Cabinets, individual ministers may resign or be jettisoned to maintain the public image of unity on which the survival of cabinet government depends.

Of course, the statement that government is collective still leaves scope for debate on the actual locus of power in a cabinet system. Even before Woodrow Wilson praised the benefits of the cabinet system, his contemporary, Walter Bagehot, was analyzing the reality of the parliamentary system. He had concluded that much of the authority in British government had moved away from the formal centers of power to the Cabinet; he described the former parts of the constitution as "dignified," but no longer real. Later observers, particularly Richard Crossman and John Mackintosh, have proposed that the Cabinet has become in its turn a "dignified" part of government as power has been shifted far more into the hands of the prime minister. Thus, a body that was initially an informal meeting of ministers to agree on what views they would put to the monarch has now become little more than a forum to endorse and legitimize decisions actually taken elsewhere.

It is true that the procedures of Cabinet have become more institutionalized, with Cabinet minutes now the vital currency of bureaucratic battle and with requirements that the agenda be carefully planned. The structures that have been created to support Cabinet have grown more sophisticated and the procedures for recording and circulating decisions more routine; but they are still open to manipulation by the prime minister.

Yet, the crucial component of the Cabinet cocktail is the approach of the prime ministers and their relations with their ministerial colleagues. Powerful prime ministers who are determined to get their own way, as Margaret Thatcher was, may choose to direct crucial issues to Cabinet committees where they are able to be sure of support. More consensual leaders like John Major will choose to take items to Cabinet and listen to the views of their ministers. Thus, the same machinery can be used for very different purposes without any formal change in the official procedures. That is partly because making the cabinet system work is one of the primary responsibilities of the prime minister but also because of the infinite flexibility of the Cabinet itself.

Coupled with internal flexibility is the capacity to exert great power over the machinery of government. Since the Cabinet can rely on the support of the parliamentary party to put its legislation through the Parliament and the nonpartisan public service to implement its plans, a united and determined Cabinet has a great capacity to control political events. At times, it is true, the Parliament may exert its will or the bureaucracy may alter the impact of the policies by the delivery of services. But the restraints on an effective Cabinet are few and only occasionally applied.

Doubtless, it was this capacity to exert the government's purpose that attracted Woodrow Wilson. Although there is a Cabinet in the U.S. system of government, it has none of the strength of direction of cabinet government. Its members will seldom meet as a group; their role is to advise the president, not to reach a common view of policy that will then be implemented. They have little ability to ensure that their programs are accepted by Congress, whether or not their party has a nominal majority. Cabinet membership refers to a rank more than to an ability to participate in the common function of governing.

At its best, cabinet government is able to exert a considerable direction to the work of government. By controlling the making and the implementation of policy, an effective Cabinet has few limitations on its ability to act. At its worst it may be secretive, ineffective, and factional, ensuring poor government and little ability for anyone else to intervene. That is both the strength and weakness of the concentrated power that parliamentary systems have ceded, not always intentionally, to Cabinet. Cabinet is a forum that must be judged by political, not managerial, criteria. It is a meeting of the most powerful political leaders, often settling the most intractable problems.

No wonder Woodrow Wilson was keen to insert such discipline and power into the fragmented, pluralist, and separated system in the United States. It may have made the position of president easier if the national leader could head a Cabinet that was collectively responsible and could lead and control the legislature. But it would also have imposed a system that was based on monarchical, unitary, and concentrated power on a government dedicated to the opposite objective of limiting power.

PATRICK WELLER

BIBLIOGRAPHY

Bagehot, W., 1963. *The English Constitution* [first edition 1867]. London: Fontana.
French, R., 1980. *How Ottawa Decides.* Toronto: Lorimer.
Hennessy, P., 1986. *Cabinet.* Oxford: Blackwell.
Mackie, T. T. and B. W. Hogwood, eds., 1985. *Unlocking the Cabinet: Cabinet Structures in Perspective.* London: Sage.
Mackintosh, J., 1977. *The British Cabinet,* 3rd ed. London: Stevens.
Weller, P., 1985. *First Among Equals: Prime Ministers in Westminster Systems.* Sydney: Allen & Unwin.

Wilson, Woodrow, 1884. "Committee or Cabinet Government." *Overland Monthly,* series 2, vol. 3.

CABINET OFFICE. The source of organizational support and advice that the Cabinet receives from its civil service in the United Kingdom; many of Britain's former colonies have, to some extent, adopted the same institutional practice. With the exception of the cabinet secretary (the head of the Cabinet Office), who is appointed permanently, staff are seconded from other departments usually for a period of about two or three years. This is designed to avert the possibility of the Cabinet Office developing its own agenda since it is expected to be politically neutral and organizationally supportive. Civil servants selected for Cabinet Office posts are considered high-fliers and will often make repeat appearances with the unit as they ascend the promotional ladder.

The terms "Cabinet Office" and "Cabinet Secretariat" cause problems; strictly speaking, the two are not synonymous but are commonly used interchangeably. Formally, the British Cabinet Office encompasses four secretariats and two additional sections. These comprise the four policy secretariats (foreign and defense, economic, home, the European Union); and these are complemented by two other staffs, the intelligence assessment staff and the science and technology staff. However, in common parlance, the terms "Cabinet Office" and "Cabinet Secretariat" are used interchangeably. Primarily, this is because the function of the Cabinet Office sounds like that of any secretariat. It is the unit for the provision of support and advice to the group of ministers who make up the Cabinet. In its simplest terms, the purpose of the Secretariat was laid down by the Haldane Report in 1918, which stated that a Secretariat should be permanently maintained "for the purpose of collecting and putting into shape [the Cabinet] agenda, of providing the information and the material necessary for its deliberations, and of drawing up the results for communication to the departments concerned" (p. 6). That description is as relevant today. The Cabinet Office is tasked to perform such functions for all Cabinet ministers but, in practice, tends not to be overly concerned with departmental ministers who have their own staffs. In short, it concentrates on the prime minister. In a radio interview in 1967, Harold Wilson, the former British leader, argued that in addition to its role as servicer of the whole Cabinet, "the Cabinet Secretariat is the private department of the Prime Minister" (BBC, 1967).

Development

The genesis of the Cabinet Office can be traced back to a statement in the Houses of Parliament in 1903. The House of Commons was told that a full record of meetings of the Committee on Imperial Defence should be kept, which would be a "full-blooded and detailed account of the reasons on which . . . conclusions come to be based" (*Hansard,* March 5, 1903). Such an edict necessitated at least one secretary to record the proceedings. However, by May 1904, this had been expanded into a fully funded secretariat; in 1912, it was headed by the man who has come to be viewed as something of a giant in the development of the Cabinet Office itself, Maurice Hankey. Despite the acquisition of such a formidable man, the Secretariat remained relatively informal until 1916 when the pressures of the war forced Lloyd-George to form a Cabinet Secretariat. This was initially achieved by simply co-opting the Secretariat of the Committee on Imperial Defence. Hankey thus became the first Cabinet Secretary.

In the immediate postwar years, there was considerable political antipathy toward the Cabinet Office because it was claimed that it had become unduly and unconstitutionally powerful. The clamor for its abolition was so great that during the run-up to the 1922 general election, Bonar Law threatened to do just that. After the election, however, no doubt recognizing its utility, he chose only to reduce its size. Bonar Law also ensured that from 1924 onward, the minutes of the Cabinet meetings would no longer be a record of the proceedings meeting but would instead be a record of the decisions and actions taken at those meetings.

Influence

Given its proximity to the prime minister, there has always been considerable potential for the Cabinet Office to exert influence. The level to which that potential is realized is almost entirely due to the relationship between the prime minister and the cabinet secretary; that in turn depends upon many factors, not least their respective characters.

The cabinet secretary attends all Cabinet meetings in addition to chairing many of the most important "official" Cabinet committees, that is, those committees staffed by nonministers, which shadow relevant "ministerial" committees. Since 1981, he has also been the head of the Home Civil Service, which by many accounts can take up as much as 30 percent of his time. As a result, a great deal of work previously done by the secretary has been devolved to the heads of the individual four secretariats. Although this can, to a certain extent, deprive the secretary of a "finger on the pulse" it can also allow him more time to cultivate his relationship with the prime minister. Harold Wilson was clear about the role of the secretary: the cabinet secretary was not only the Cabinet's servant "but he is also my Permanent Secretary. He advises me, briefs me, not only for Cabinet meetings and other Cabinet Committees over which I preside but on the general running of the government so far as policy is concerned" (BBC, 1967).

This comment could have applied to any holder of the office of cabinet secretary. To date, there have been only seven. The first was Maurice Hankey, who served from 1916 to 1938, working for five prime ministers in a variety of different types of government, including wartime coalition, Labour, and Conservative. Hankey, the consummate "Treasury man," having entered the civil service in the Treasury in 1919, set the secretarial style. A contemporary of Hankey's described him: "[He] progressively became secretary of everything that mattered. A Marine of slight stature and tireless industry, he grew into a repository of secrets, a Chief Inspector of Mines of Information. He had an incredible memory . . . which could reproduce on call the date, file, substance of every paper that ever flew into a pigeon-hole" (Vansittart, p. 164). Hankey epitomized the "knowledge is power" thesis and arguably proved it. The length of time he served allowed him, and his successors, to achieve the acme of influence by providing continuity of information across a series of prime ministers.

Hankey was followed by Edward Bridges, who might best be described as the archetypal civil servant—principled, apolitical, the gentleman amateur. He served three very different British prime ministers—Chamberlain, Churchill, and Attlee—during some of Britain's most crucial years. In fact, during the war Bridges' influence increased yet further as he supported Attlee, who effectively ran the home front while Churchill concentrated on the war effort. Attlee leaned heavily on Bridges' experience and, as such, Bridges drew great influence to himself and his office, very much in the Hankey mould.

Immediately after the war, Bridges was succeeded by his deputy, Norman Brook. Between 1945 and 1947, they had worked in tandem, with Bridges being also responsible for the Treasury. In 1947, Brook took complete control formally while Bridges remained at the head of the Treasury until his retirement in 1956. From that time, Brook took on the responsibility of the Treasury, thus maintaining the tight link between the cabinet secretariat and the Treasury, which remains one of the main axes of power in British politics. During this period, another "Treasury man" was working as Brook's assistant: Burke St. John Trend succeeded Brook in 1963, serving Macmillan, Home, Wilson, and Heath. Trend was a meticulous and intensely private man who conformed rigidly to the style of the British civil service, particularly in the preparation of briefs—deliberately neutral, setting out all the pros and cons and allowing the elected decisionmakers to do their job. It is said that Trend's rather dry approach irritated Ted Heath, who preferred the French model of policy advocacy.

In contrast to Trend's low-level conformist style, his deputy and successor, John Hunt, was dynamic, even pushy. He accrued great power to the Cabinet Office, both formally and informally. Formally, he was instrumental in garnering new contingency units, such as "devolution" and "European issues" to the Cabinet Office. Informally, he struck up a close relationship with the Central Policy Review Staff, further strengthening the powerful economic connection. Hunt's dynamism could have a Machiavellian bent, which meant that his stewardship was sometimes viewed with suspicion, but he undoubtedly enhanced the profile of the office. Hunt served the Heath, Wilson, Callaghan, and Thatcher governments from 1973 to 1979 and was succeeded by Robert Armstrong (1979–1988). Uniquely, Armstrong served only one prime minister, Margaret Thatcher. He was the antithesis of Hunt, not easily accessible, deferential, smoother, and less pushy. He was precisely what Mrs. Thatcher wanted, and as such, he was quietly influential. The reverse side of the coin, however, may have been that his character did not allow him to utilize the potential for influence that his post made possible. The cabinet secretary appointed in 1988, Sir Robin Butler, is an avuncular and accessible character and in style somewhere between the assertive Hunt and the passive Armstrong.

Conclusion

The influence of the British Cabinet Office derives primarily from the role that the cabinet secretary either chooses or is allowed to perform. In the bureaucratic milieu around the center of power, the Cabinet Office has many competitors for the prime minister's attention. These have included several think-tanks, defunct and surviving, and the large spending ministries. In addition, the No. 10 staff cannot be discounted: Among more mundane administrative tasks, it prepares presummit briefings; the press secretary can wield great power, as can the political secretary. All of these, in addition to informal "inner cabinets," compete to serve and influence the prime minister, but ultimately the prime minister will decide how much influence specific government units will have. Obviously, in its ability to manipulate agendas and slow or speed proposals, the Cabinet Office can have great influence but it can never impose. Perhaps it is all the more powerful an institution because of such subtlety.

CHRISTOPHER BRADY

BIBLIOGRAPHY

Attlee, Clement, 1956. *As It Happened.* London: Heinemann.
BBC Third Programme, April 6, 1967, Interview with Harold Wilson.
Gordon-Walker, P., 1972. *The Cabinet.* London: Heinemann.
Haldane Report, 1918. *Report of the Machinery of Government Committee.* London: HMSO.
Hennessy, Peter, 1986. *Cabinet.* Oxford: Blackwell.
Vansittart, Lord, 1958. *The Mist Procession.* London: Hutchinson.

CAMPAIGN MANAGEMENT.
The development, organization, and implementation of a strategy to win political office.

Development of the Campaign Strategic Plan

Campaign managers must figure out the most effective way to allocate their three most valuable and scarce resources—people, time, and money. Without people and money, campaigns cannot deliver their message to voters. With a fixed amount of time, campaigns must utilize their people and money carefully. The campaign plan serves as a roadmap for the campaign to plot its course. Bill Sweeney, a campaign professional, has argued that "a campaign without a plan is a journey without a map" (Sweeney, 1995). There are six essential elements in a successful campaign plan: (1) strategy, theme, and message; (2) candidate and opposition research; (3) fund-raising; (4) survey research; (5) media; and (6) field.

The most essential part of the plan is the development of a strategy, theme, and message. The strategy, theme, and message must explain which voters will support a candidate and why they support the candidate. The message needs to clearly communicate with voters, in one sentence, why a candidate is running for political office. When developing a strategy, campaigns do not exist in a vacuum. They occur surrounded by a host of other events to which they must pay close attention. Campaigns must consider economic and political conditions, not only in the campaign's specific city, county, or district but in the nation as a whole. A successful strategy will account for these factors when determining which voters a campaign will target.

A campaign strategy must also account for other factors such as the candidate, the constituency, the level of office being sought, rules of the electoral system, the financial resources available to the campaign, and the political trends of the year in which they are running (Thurber, 1995). All of these factors will play a role in the theme and message of the campaign, as well as how the theme and message are implemented.

The development of a campaign strategy, theme, and message must occur simultaneously with both candidate and opposition research. The campaign must be aware of the candidate's personal and professional history to make sure that a candidate's track record does not conflict with the message that the campaign is trying to disseminate. The campaign must also understand their opponent's history so that a clear and accurate contrast can be drawn between the candidate and the opponent.

Financing the Campaign

To implement a strategy and communicate a message, a campaign needs money. As the costs of campaigns have risen, fund-raising has become a daunting task for many campaigns. In 1994, the average cost of a winning campaign for the U.S. House of Representatives was US $564,013 (Federal Election Commission, 1995).

Campaigns raise money from a variety of sources using many different techniques. Candidates and finance committees solicit money directly from individuals and political action committees (PACs). Campaigns also organize events, such as breakfasts and barbecues, which range from low dollar fundraisers used to broaden the campaign's base of donors, to US $1,000 dinners where donors get a chance to meet the candidate. In addition, many campaigns solicit money from potential supporters using direct mail.

Once a campaign has money, its management can conduct more specialized survey research. Political polling and focus groups have become essential elements of a successful campaign. Pools allow campaigns to assess their position in the electorate and to evaluate which voters need to be targeted. Pools also assist the campaign in deciding where to most effectively allocate their people, time, and money by identifying specific groups that need to be targeted. Both surveys and focus groups give the campaign an opportunity to test their message and their television advertisements on a group of individuals representative of the voters in the district.

Media Coverage and Publicity

In the modern age of campaigns in which Americans rely on television to get their political information, the media have become a crucial means of voter contact. There are two basic types of media in a campaign, earned and paid. Media coverage of a campaign is called earned or free media because the campaign does not pay to produce advertisements. Instead, the campaign earns media coverage by holding an event that the press will cover. For campaigns that lack resources, earned media may be their only source of advertisement, and they need to work hard to get press coverage.

Depending on a campaign's financial status, it does not need to rely on the media for campaign coverage. Campaigns can hire media consultants who create paid advertisements for their clients. These ads have five basic functions: name identification, candidate image, issue development, attack, and defense (Bryant, 1995). Candidates will use their media to define themselves and their issue positions while attempting to define their opponent and defend themselves from attacks.

Election Day Strategy

The final part of the campaign plan is the formation of an election day strategy. The field organization, usually made up of volunteers, is crucial for getting supporters to the polls on election day. The more local the race, the less publicity the race receives and the more important the field operation becomes. Many campaigns overlook the role of the field organization. In a close race, the field team can make the difference between a winning and a losing campaign.

Summary

Campaigns are dynamic and complex organizations. No two campaigns are alike and campaigns need to be flexible and able to adjust to their external environment. Not all campaigns need, or can afford, all of the strategic elements discussed above. Depending on the campaign's resources, some elements of the plan will be emphasized over others. A campaign with little money but a lot of people will highlight their field operation and work to obtain earned media. Campaigns with substantial resources can afford to utilize survey research and paid media. With the proper strategy and a message that resonates with voters, even the most underfunded campaign can win.

MARNI EZRA

BIBLIOGRAPHY

Bryant, Jay, 1995. "Paid Media Advertising," In James A. Thurber and Candice J. Nelson, eds., *Campaigns and Elections: American Style.* Boulder: Westview Press, pp. 84–100.

Federal Election Commission Press Release, April 28, 1995, "1994 Congressional Fundraising Climbs to a New High." Washington, DC, p. 12.

Sweeney, William R., 1995. "The Principles of Planning." In James A. Thurber and Candice J. Nelson, eds., *Campaigns and Elections: American Style.* Boulder: Westview, pp. 14–29.

Thurber, James A., 1995. "The Transformation of American Campaigns." In James A. Thurber and Candice J. Nelson, eds., *Campaigns and Elections: American Style.* Boulder: Westview, pp. 1–13.

CANON LAW. Derived from the Greek word "kanon," which means "seal" and refers to the legal system of the Roman Catholic Church; therefore, a part of the larger concept "church law." This concept includes theoretically any legal system of any church. It must be said though that of all the ecclesiastical legal systems, the canon law of the Roman Catholic Church is by far the most extensive one and that it can rely upon a long tradition and history.

Origin and History

Canon law grew gradually and organically. During the Roman era, Christianity prospered amid a Jewish environ-

ment, with the strongly hellenized Near East in the background. The young church did not embrace a legal system of its own, but it accepted pragmatically the rules that were in force in the local communities, sometimes corrected by the Christian body of thought.

From the first half of the second century onward, a proper law started to develop in which liturgical definitions and rules of life, often strongly morally oriented, altered each other. The customary law was thus conceived.

A new impulse was given by the "councils." From the third century onward, in the Africa of Saint Ciprianus, they became significant, although their real importance must be seen in the following century. At the end of that fourth century, the first papal decretals emerged as well. In this way, the two main and most important sources of canon law, i.e., the papal decretals and the canons of the general, regional, and local councils were formed. When in 313 the Roman Emperor Constantine admitted Christianity, an exceeding mixture between the secular and the ecclesiastical legislation began to take place and continued, for instance, during the Merovingian and Carolingian period. Secular sovereigns enacted rules that influenced church life, rules that were sometimes opposing and sometimes corresponding with their own church principles. In the legislative sphere, all of this produced a disordered situation, which some private individuals tried to solve by creating their own personal legislation. This occurred from the fourth century onward and resulted in both systematical and chronological law collections. One of the problems of these unofficial collections was, of course, that a lot of issues, if not everything, depended on the compiler's preferences and procedures.

Gradually, the importance of canon law increased. A first factor in this growth was the feudal system that appeared in Europe after the treaty of Verdun (843). The secular power dissolved and Christianity became more and more the connecting link of the European civilization. A second factor to be mentioned was the growing power of the pope. From the middle of the eleventh century to the first decades of the fourteenth century, the pope enjoyed a very large prestige. The intellectual revival of the twelfth century was the third factor. It elucidated the rediscovery of Roman law and the bloom of the universities.

In this era of growth and development most of the popes were skilled jurists. The poor law collections from the past had to stand aside for the *Corpus Iuris Canonici.* This corpus was progressively established and is the assembling of different law collections, namely, the Decretum Gratiani (1140), the decretals of Gregory IX (1234), the Liber Sextus of Boniface VIII (1298), the Constitutiones Clementinae (1317), de Extravangantes of John XXII (1317–1324), and the Extravagantes Communes (1261–1484).

The appelation *Corpus Iuris Canonici* refers to the totality of canonical collections, which had developed slowly over time and which until recently formed the backbone of canon law.

In the fourteenth century, however, a decline occurred. In the profane-political sphere, centralizing tendencies began to gain the upper hand. The pope lost a fair amount of his power. In the sixteenth century, the Reformation (from 1517) enlarged the crisis even more. The creative expansion of canon law came to a dead end, since the legislation that was promulgated by the Council of Trent (1545–1563) intended to maintain primarily the traditional doctrine and rules in defense against the extending Reformation. The next and new council came only centuries later, Vaticanum I (1869–1870). By this time, the political secular power of the Vatican had finished. The unification of large European states such as Germany and Italy became a fact. In reaction to this, the church introduced its own politics of centralization, relying on the *societas perfecta* doctrine, which does not mean that the church was considered to be perfect but that the church believed to have all the qualities, even more than the newly formed states, to operate as a perfect society.

In 1904, Pope Pius X ordered the execution of a code for the Latin church. This code, primarily accomplished by the illustrious Cardinal Pietro Gasparri, was promulgated in 1917, during the pontificate of Benedict XV. The following year, it came into force. This new code, consisting of 5 books and 2,414 canons, replaced the former legislation and had a very juridical-technical complexion. According to some, the code had a much too positivistic character. However, it was not in use for very long. In 1959, Pope John XXIII declared his intention to summon a new ecumenical council and to achieve an *aggiornamento* of the ecclesiastic code. The Second Vatican Council took place from 1962 to 1965 and caused much theological modernization, seeing the church both as a religious community and a gathering of people. The new and modern ideas also influenced the code that was promulgated and came into force in 1983 and was applied in the whole Latin church. By way of curiosity, one could also mention the enactment of the code for the (small amount of) Catholics of the eastern rites in 1990, into force in 1991.

Canon Law Today: Foundations

What are the theoretical foundations of the presence of law in a church? Precedingly, one must remark that this question is in fact a question to be asked afterwards. Canon law has organically and gradually grown and its existence has for a long time just been taken for granted. As long as the social and public interest of the church, in particular its law, was beyond all doubt, a complicated justification was not under discussion. The maxim "*ubi societas, ibi ius*" (there where a society is, there is a law) was as comprehensible as simple clarification of the presence of law in a church.

It is only when the role of the church in society began to crumble away that the impulse for a thorough theoretical and theological foundation of the existence of canon law was given. Canon law is by many people today considered a theological discipline rather than a juridical one. This can, of course, be seen as a consequence of the strict borderline between church and state as it has been drawn today. In the past, this was not the case, since church and state belonged to one large unity, the *christianitas*, in which canon law submitted not only the ecclesiastical but also the common social relations to a specific regulation. The more theological approach, however, is also originated by the rather insufficient connection of canon law with the modern Western legal system. In canon law, there is, for instance, no separation of powers, and the law is—partly due to a scarcely elaborated jurisprudence, with the exception of matrimonial law—only to some extent enforceable.

In a rough outline of today's situation in connection with canon law, one could discuss five different schools. The main parameter in this division is always the relation between law, theology, and canon law.

The first school arose from the leading theological journal *Concilium*, in which the illustrious Dutch canon lawyer P. Huizing played an important role. The dejuridicizing of canon law was very important in this context. Huizing and his supporters did believe in a theological foundation of the legal rules, but they wanted to liberate the rules that were too pregnant with theological meaning in order to restore their flexibility.

The second school is that of the Italian lay canonists, where P. A. d'Avack and O. Giacchi are key figures. They adhere strongly to the old *ubi societas, ibi ius* theory. They confirm that one should not consider the church only in juridical terms but that the canon lawyer has to concentrate on these juridical aspects. The influence of theology on law reveals itself on a metajuridical level. Theology as well as history are thus applied only as auxiliary sciences in canon law.

The third school can be described as the school of Navarra. Many of its members came from the Opus Dei university of Navarra in Pamplona. Some canonists of today such as A. de la Hera, J. Hervada, and the late P. Lombardia relate to this approach. They also consider canon law a juridical discipline; nevertheless, they hold canon law subordinate to church authority. This last perspective is stronger in the school of Navarra than in the school of the lay canonists.

The fourth school is the school of München, of which Klaus Mörsdorf is the founder. Mörsdorf perceives ecclesiology, in particular, word and sacrament, as constitutive for the church. He denominates canon law in this way as a theological discipline with a juridical method. Some of his students carry the line of thought even further. E. Corecco, for instance, presents canon law as *ordinatio fidei*, an ordinance of faith. He considers canon law a theological discipline with a theological method.

The fifth school is more difficult to localize but has its representatives at the universities of Leuven, Strasbourg, and North America. This school holds a skeptic attitude toward an approach that might be too abstract and deductive and no longer believes in canon law as an organic reality. Much attention is paid to the role and utility of the humanities as auxiliary sciences and to the most recent developments in the sphere of juridical thought. Theology is still important, not that much as a theoretical background, but more as a criticical control measure of the quality that the legal system provides.

Which school is at this moment considered to be dominant? The question is of relatively limited importance, because one cannot always define rigid borderlines between the different schools. A widely separated line of thought in regard to the foundations of the system does not necessarily lead to a different practical approach. Still, one can acknowledge that today the school of München and Navarra take the lead. They influence directly or indirectly, implicitly or explicitly, the largest amount of practitioners of canon law.

Did they also affect to a large extent the church code of 1983? A reply to this question must be carefully differentiated. Some of the subdirectories of the code, such as the juridical position of the laity and the clerics, the church organization, the teaching office of the church, and the sacraments were strongly influenced by the new theological body of thought. Other areas such as penal law and process law, temporal goods, and a large part of the general norms are still governed by the elder approach. This means a fairly positivistic juridical policy without too many underlying questions, in short, an approach that relates more to the code of 1917 than to the one of the Second Vatican Council.

The Code of Canon Law of 1983

The code of 1983 consists of 1,752 canons, which is a distinct diminution in comparison with its predecessor of 1917. The canons are spread over 7 books.

Book I (can. 1–203) covers the general norms. It can be regarded as the counterstone of the system, because it hands out the techniques and instruments that are essential to every canon lawyer practicing the profession. It covers every question one might be confronted with. The first book thus contains definitions about ecclesiastical laws, custom, general decrees and instructions, administrative acts, persons, juridic acts, the power of governance and ecclesiastical offices.

A few basic options catch the eye: According to canon 11, for instance, one becomes a member of the Catholic Church when one is baptized in the Catholic Church or was received into it when baptized in another Christian church. When one has become a member, however, one can never leave. This position, although socially speaking, there are, of course, no actual consequences, does sound in our modern ears, used to freedom of religion, rather drastic. It is, in fact, based on the theological principle that considers baptism as an ineffaceable mark and regards baptism and membership as one.

Another basic option can be found in canon 129. The power of governance, i.e., the legislative, executive, and the juridical power, can only be executed by those who have received sacred orders. Lay members can only cooperate in the exercise of this power. Despite the more ample competence ascribed to lay members elsewhere in the code, this conception of principle expresses a fundamental restriction. The power of governance is exclusively assigned to the ordained, even if they would prove to be less competent than certain lay members. Again, however, a theological principle lies at the bottom of this basic option, namely, the unity—although historically not always respected—between the power of ordination and the power of governance.

Book II (can. 204–746) is of extreme importance within the code. With a rather conciliarly sounding title, *De populo Dei* (the People of God), the book opens with the status of the Christian faithful. It is remarkable how for the first time in the history of the Roman Catholic Church, human rights are acknowledged. The chapter that deals with human rights does not bear the heading "human rights," which would sound too revendicative, but the title "Obligations and Rights of all the Christian Faithful" (can. 208–223). Next to the principle of equality (can. 208), the carefully formulated principle of freedom of expression (can. 212 § 3), and the freedom of theological research (can. 218), there are other principles promulgated that are indispensable for the correct functioning of a modern constitutional state, such as the right to a fair process (can. 221 § 2) and the principle of legality—"no penalty without law" (can. 221 § 3). This positive evolution is present in this chapter but not always followed elsewhere in the code. Add to this that the description of the rights and duties of the Christian faithful are simply mentioned next to and between other statements throughout the book, it explains, for instance, their weaker formal superiority.

After this, one finds the statutes of the lay Christian faithful, the sacred ministers or clerics, the personal prelatures, and the associations. The church organization is the next subject in *Book II*. It is described on a universal and thus Roman level and on a private individual level, in which the diocese has a central place. It is remarkable how much attention the bishop receives in the line of the Second Vatican Council. He is offered numerous possibilities to promulgate private juridical norms in his own diocese, norms that, of course, should not be contradictory to the universal regulation of the church code itself. Altogether, one could state that with these points of view, the code moves clearly in the direction of an increasing decentralization. The church code still exists, of course, as it did in 1917, but the decline in volume (from 2,414 to 1,752 canons) combined with the more ample jurisdiction of the bishop shows the growing insight that in a vastly stretched out world church, only the basis regulation can be collective and universal. Nevertheless, today a fairly large amount of norms are still being considered to be the basis norm.

For the sake of completeness, one should also mention that *Book II* contains a part about the insitutes of consecrated life and societies of apostolic life.

Book III (can. 747–833) deals with the teaching office of the church, i.e., the subject matter of the preaching of the word of God, the catechetical instruction, the missionary actions, the Catholic education in schools and universities, and the instruments of social communication, specifically books and the profession of faith. It often concerns soft law, especially when only the general principles are elaborated.

Book IV (can. 834–1,253) embraces the office of sanctifying in the church, in which the sacraments hold a central place. On the one hand, it touches typical inside ecclesiastical problems, with little relevance on a governmental level. But on the other hand, it is clear that the practice of canon law is to a large extent directed by these matters, particularly by marriage law (can. 1,055–1,165). The Roman Catholic Church holds faith in the principle of indissolubility of the marriage, because due to theological reasons marriage is considered to be part of divine law in virtue of the sacrament. Its legal force was apparently derived from the gospel (Mt. 5: 32; 19: 9; Mc. 10: 11–12; Lc. 16: 1; 1 Cor. 7: 10–11). The combination of the concept of indissolubility and the hard reality of many broken marriages leads, not taking into account some rare exceptions, to only one conceivable solution: the declaration of nullity of the marriage. Therefore, one has to look for a deficiency in the consent from which then the nullity from the moment of the celebration of marriage onward results. In this code and in the line of Vatican II, the amount of legal grounds for the nullification has been augmented. Next to the traditional justifications such as, for instance, simulation (with the exclusion of children or the unity of marriage), force and fear, there are now introduced, i.e., in canon 1,095, grounds such as grave lack of discretion of judgment concerning essential matrimonial rights and duties

and also incapacity of assuming the essential obligations of matrimony due to causes of a psychic nature. Although on a Roman level, especially after two sermons of Pope John Paul II in 1987 and 1988, a too generous approach of nullification is repudiated; in many countries, the local courts of law hold their own and different approach.

Particularly in the United States, the number of nullifications is very high. In the European countries, the situation is rather distinct: Even in the same country, there can be a discrepancy between the several dioceses. Table I (from 1992) illustrates the situation.

When on a local level, in the first instance and in appeal the nullification is ascertained, one can no longer appeal to the Roman Rota. For the American files, this might be advantageous since not all of them are able to respond to the criteria applied at the Roman Rota.

Book V (can. 1,254–1,310) outlines the temporal goods of the church. Here the acquisition and administration of goods and also the contracts and alienation in particular are under discussion. The fifth book is rather concise. The reason is that a detailed regulation would be pointless because one has to take into account the legislation of the countries in question in which the church is active.

Book VI (can. 1,311–1,399) covers the sanctions in the church. This book appears to be equally concise if one considers the rich history of this subject the church holds. The most well-known sanction is undoubtedly the excommunication. It does not mean that the excommunicated is repelled from the church. The person remains a member of the church but is situated due to punishment in the outskirts of church life. This also results in the forbidden admittance to certain offices and sacraments.

TABLE I. CATHOLICS AND NULLIFICATION PROCESSES

Country	Number of Catholics in Million	Number of Nullification Processes	Number of Declared Nullifications
USA	55	103,562	59,030
Great Britain	5	3,756	1,512
Netherlands	6	994	406
Germany	28	1,735	869
Spain	37	1,819	758
Ireland	6	1,635	767
Italy	55	2,628	1,057
Belgium	9	277	169
Switzerland	3	84	42
France	47	741	330
Europe	288	18,224	7,050
World	958	142,035	78,829

Finally, *Book VII* (can. 1,400–1,752) deals with the procedural law in the church. The book consists of some general rules, a more thorough treatment of the contentious trial, and certain special procedures such as the matrimonial process, the procedure for annulment of sacred ordination, penal procedure, and ultimately some administrative procedures. In regards to the administrative jurisdiction, the code of 1983 lives up to the expectations that were created along the history of legislation. Eventually, the independent administrative courts on the level of the conference of bishops did not develop. But they did devise a mixed procedure. Against administrative orders, one can initially follow the way of the hierarchical appeal, after which the second section of the Apostolic Signatura in Rome can appear as the undeniable administrative court.

Next to the Code of Canon Law of 1983 and the Eastern code of 1990 exists also another important document of universal legislation. The Code of Canon Law after all does not hold a monopoly position. The apostolic constitution Pastor Bonus (June 28, 1988), for instance, is for the organization of the Roman Curia and the central administration in Rome the key document.

Particular Law

More than in the past, the current code of canon law of 1983 takes into account the local individuality. More space was given to particular law. But still the universal law continues to set stringent limits.

The code of canon law indicates, for instance, in canon 231 only a concise status for the laymen who would wish to work for the church. The private legislator has therefore some latitude, although certain definitions from the sacramental law have to be acknowledged, in which some actions are reserved for clerics only.

Another example is offered by canon 145, which gives the definition of an ecclesiastical office, which is any function constituted in a stable manner by divine or canon law to be exercised for a spiritual purpose. Private legislators can create such offices according to their own level. Of course, these offices may never be opposed to the fundamental structures of the church (with, amongst other things, parishes led by a pastor). Apart from that, there are many cases in which the private legislator not only can but must enact a law. The church code explicitly bestows the responsibility on the legislator to do so.

The individual color and taste the local churches attempt to attribute to their juridical organization, depend not only on the particular legislation. Multicoloredness can also be achieved via the customary law that gives legal force to customs on a local level, customs that live next to the existing law or go against it. The only objection is that

these manners should not be unreasonable or opposed to the rules that the church considers as belonging to the divine law.

Canon Law as an Academic Discipline

Canon law as an academic discipline is lectured at universities around the world. All in all, there are about 20 locations. Especially in Europe, more precisely in Italy and Rome, there are several training possibilities. If one wants to graduate in the English language, one has the choice of studying in Washington (Catholic University of America), Ottawa (St. Paul's), or Leuven (Katholieke Universiteit Leuven).

A licentiate or a doctor's degree are helpful or necessary for all sorts of inside church offices, both on the level of governance and jurisdiction. During and immediately after Vatican II, a crisis seemed to stand out. There was in any case a difficulty with the number of students: The new theological way of thinking made the more formal-looking canon law for many persons less necessary. But today, one can easily talk about a renewed focus on canon law as a discipline. Structural and organizational topics are again more appreciated.

Research takes place on a large scale, which is demonstrated by the (still growing) number of professional journals and interesting monographs. Because of its practical importance, marriage law is in this respect successful. But also the more delicate topics such as church organization, the role of the laity, the investigation of theologically justified structures that can also function in today's world are not left in the dark.

Church and State

The relationship between church and state is a field of study that has received more and more attention in the last years. The European and American points of view vary explicitly though. In the United States, the emphasis is on the freedom of religion and the principle of equality of religions. In Europe, each country has its own traditions in regard to the connection between church and state, which often leads to privileged positions of certain churches, with freedom of religion and free exercise as a minimum requirement.

In recent years, the practitioners of canon law have paid more attention to the legislation of the state that could directly or indirectly be of importance for the churches. Since the church is no longer exposed as a *societas perfecta* that lives in a crystal sphere, one is looking constantly for a successful method to integrate canon law into the existing profane legislation.

There is, for instance, the question of "labor relations" to be solved. How can one offer those who work in the service of the church a correct status on a labor law and at the same time create enough room for the own demands that canon law requires?

A problem of similar nature arises with respect to "public health legislation." Can one behold the Catholic identity of the institutions of the public health sector when one adds church juridical desiderata to the necessary profane juridical statute? Today there is a clear shift in this problem area in comparison with the church-state question of the nineteenth and early twentieth century. At that time, church and state were presented as two rivals, fighting to obtain the largest amount of authority. Now the church reveals a more modest character and takes advantage of the profane law to effectuate its own objectives. Of course, it goes without saying that in doing this, the church should always be able to benefit its own traditional autonomy.

RIK TORFS

CAPACITY BUILDING.
The facilitation of the development of adequate managerial, financial, and political skills within local governments for meeting local service delivery and policymaking responsibilities.

Local government capacity, according to Honadle (1981), is the ability to anticipate and influence change, to make informed decision about policy, to attract and absorb resources, to manage resources, and to evaluate current activities to guide future action. The institutional capacity of local government is of fundamental importance to community and economic development. Local governments are important direct providers of public services, and they implement important state and national government policies. Local governmental units are important in the communication linkages among citizens, all levels of government, and other institutions. Overall, local responsibilities continue to increase in the American political system.

Researchers have described and analyzed the lack of managerial and financial capacity of local governments, especially small rural local governments. Local government officials, who usually serve part-time on a volunteer basis, often lack the political will to make difficult decisions. While self-management of government affairs by local citizens is in the best traditions of democracy, there are growing disadvantages to local government performance.

Knowing what local capacity means is far different from knowing how to develop it. State governments, the national government, municipal and professional associations, foundations, and universities provide a variety of capacity building activities to local government officials to help improve local governmental performance. These include direct technical assistance, circuit riders, and the encouragement of intergovernmental and intersector cooperation. National and state programs and mandates on local governments increasingly incorporate the consideration of unique small and/or rural community needs in the policy or program development stages of new initiatives. Local governments are "creatures of the states." States can make statutory and constitutional changes to empower their local governments with greater structural authority, such as home rule, to decide on how they want to be organized to improve their performance. Similarly, the states can enable greater revenue flexibility to their local governments, thus permitting greater diversification of local revenue sources so that local governments can better adapt to change.

Technical assistance programs are usually by request. One trend is the provision of training programs for newly elected local officials to help them understand the specifics of local government. Circuit riders are personnel assigned to provide long-term technical assistance on an ongoing basis to a group of communities. Such programs are especially helpful in building the capacity of widely dispersed rural communities—in writing and managing grants, meeting regulations, budgeting, and financial management. Strengthening the voluntary sector as a means to improve service delivery also builds the general capacity of local government. Training in and the use of alternative dispute resolution techniques builds local capacity by improving local officials' skills and by reducing costs.

Encouraging intergovernmental and intersector cooperation and partnerships in planning, financing, and delivering public services also builds local government capacity. School consolidations and functional consolidations of specific services (e.g., regional police, 911 systems) and regional water system sometimes yield financial savings. Regional cooperation in other types of service delivery and in joint purchasing arrangements can achieve economies of scale. Joint service administration can lower overhead and improve quality by allowing the use of more specialized capital equipment or highly skilled technical personnel. Intermunicipal units such as voluntary organizations of local governments (COGs, or councils of governments) can be established to accomplish a set of agreed-upon activities. Their organization is often facilitated by a capacity builder, such as a state government agency. Beginning in the 1980s, a growing trend at the local level has been to privatize the delivery and/or the production of some local services. Contracting with the private sector is the most common privatization activity.

Local government capacity not only requires skilled elected and appointed officials, it also requires sufficient institutional and governmental authority to undertake existing and emerging roles. Adequate financing is necessary to implement governmental responsibilities. Thus, capacity building by state government encompasses the need to provide local governments more flexibility through diversifying the revenues available to those governments. Expertise, local management capacity, and good strong leadership are keys to ensuring that authority and resources are used wisely.

BEVERLY A. CIGLER

BIBLIOGRAPHY

Honadle, Beth W., 1981. "A Capacity-Building Framework: A Search for Concept and Purpose," *Public Administration Review*, vol. 41, no. 5 (September/October) 575–580.

Honadle, Beth Walter and Arnold M. Howitt, eds., 1986. *Perspectives on Management Capacity Building.* Albany: State University of New York Press.

CAPITAL BUDGETING.

Making decisions about investments having significant future benefits or costs for various entities and their stakeholders.

Capital budgeting is the backbone of financial economics. Related topics in financial economics include the time value of money, the meaning of net-present value, the determination and use of cash flows, accounting concepts consistent with present-value calculations, the rate of discount and uncertainty, the state-preference approach, the capital-asset pricing model, and option valuation techniques (see Bierman and Smidt, 1993).

In the public sector, the term is often exclusively associated with plant and equipment investments. It is more properly associated will all policy choices that have significant, long-term consequences, especially decisions about missions, programs, products, processes, or procedures.

There are standard solutions to several kinds of capital-budgeting problems: make or buy decisions, investment in working capital (especially inventories) decisions, maintenance-level decisions, project selection, the choice of mutually exclusive investments, and investments in plants with fluctuating rates of production. However, the same basic calculus of benefits and costs is supposed to guide all classes of policy choices of with long-term consequences.

Financial Theory

Financial theory teaches that in the presence of a capital market where funds can be obtained at a price, the welfare of an entity's stakeholders—a firm's stockholders, a not-for-profit's clients, a jurisdiction's citizens—will be maximized by the implementation of all policy choices that generate positive net-present values. This means, in part, that the timing of cash flows—future benefits or costs—accruing from the policy choice is generally of no importance, so long as benefits or costs are properly discounted.

This conclusion follows from the separation principle, often called Fisher separation, after its formulator, Irving Fisher. This principle states that an entity's operating decisions should be independent of the personal consumption decisions of its stakeholders. Where the entity maximizes net wealth, individual stakeholders can maximize utility by borrowing against this wealth or lending it, thereby timing cash flows to match their personal consumption preferences.

Many students of financial economics further assert that an entity's capital budgeting decisions should also be independent of the source of financing. This view is associated with the work of Nobel laureates Franco Modigliani and Merton Miller and derives from two distinct inferences: (1) the law of one price, which says that owing to the possibility of "homemade leverage" or "arbitrage" by investors, two similar assets must have the same price (i.e., must be priced to yield the same expected rate of return); (2) the irrelevance of capital structure, which says that under certain conditions, an entity's value will be the same regardless of whether it finances its activities with debt or equity—this conclusion is easily extended to debt and taxes.

Taken together, these two assertions imply that all capital-budgeting decisions should be governed by cost-benefit analysis, which says do it whenever benefits exceed costs. There is only one basic caveat to this rule: Delay may be justified when it will provide additional information about the true costs or benefits of a decision. As Avinash Dixit and Robert Pindyck (1994) explain, holding a decision opportunity that can be postponed is analogous to holding a call option; it gives you the right but not the obligation to exercise it at a future time. When an entity makes an irreversible decision, it "kills" its option to decide. That means that it sacrifices the possibility that waiting would provide information that would affect the desirability or timing of the decision. This "opportunity cost" (lost option value) should be included as part of the cost of the decision. Hence, where decisions are both irreversible and can be postponed, the net-present value rule should be amended to read, do it whenever benefits exceed costs by an amount equal to keeping the option alive.

Budget Processes

The institutional arrangements through which capital-budgeting decisions are made in the private sector are often analogous to the authorization/appropriations processes of the federal government of the United States. Indeed, Donaldson Brown, then chief financial officer of the General Motors Corporation, explicitly referenced the authorization/appropriations processes of the federal government when he created the first modern procedure for the allocation of capital funds between corporate divisions in 1923. Under Brown's system, appropriation requests had to include detailed plans of the buildings, equipment, materials required, the capital needed, and the benefits to be achieved from the appropriation. A general manager's signature was sufficient authorization for a request below a certain amount. However, all very large projects were subject to review by the Appropriations Committee and required the approval of both the Executive Committee and the Finance Committee (Chandler, 1962, pp. 146–147).

Prior to 1981, when the General Electric Corporation (GE) restructured and decentralized operations, capital budgeting at GE followed a similar procedure. First came strategic planning, which authorized organizational units to undertake various initiatives. This process produced tentative income targets for each business unit and allocations of capital from corporate headquarters to sectors, from sectors to strategic business units, and from strategic business units to divisions. Commitment was provided in the next step of the capital-budgeting process, which authorized sponsoring managers to encumber funds to carry out initiatives. Division managers could appropriate up to US $1 million for each initiative, sector executives US $6 million, and the CEO US $20 million; larger amounts had to be appropriated by the board of directors. The appropriator was supposed to ascertain that the strategic purpose behind the initiative was valid and then determine that the proposed initiative was optimally designed for its purpose (Anthony and Govindarajan, 1995).

Traditionally, detailed appropriation requests have served as operating budgets for capital projects in business—i.e., as a starting point for project control and variance analysis.

Differences Between Capital Budgeting Processes in Business and Government

Despite certain similarities, the differences between the way capital budgeting is done in the private sector and governmental budgeting are often great and in several respects decisive.

In the first place, most private entities employ multiple budgets: capital budgets, operating budgets, and cash budgets. Private-sector capital budgeting is concerned only with decisions that have significant future consequences. Its time horizon is the life of the decision; its focus is the discounted net-present value of the decision alternative. It is always distinguished from operating budgeting, which is concerned with motivating managers to serve the organization. In the operating budget, the relevant time horizon is the operational cycle of the administrative unit in question, perhaps a month or even a week in the case of cost and revenue centers, usually longer where investment and profit centers are concerned. Operating budgets focus on

the performance of the administrative unit, outputs produced and resources consumed—where possible, these are all measured in current dollars. Cash budgeting is concerned with providing liquidity when needed at a minimum cost. Most governments try to make one process do the work of three. Not surprisingly, that process usually fails to do any one thing very well. What governments do best is liquidity management, although, paradoxically, liquidity is rarely a serious concern to most national governments.

Second, private-sector capital budgeting is selective. It is usually concerned only with new initiatives, and then only with changes in operations that are expected to yield benefits for longer than a year. Despite powerful inclinations to incrementalism, governmental budgeting tries to be comprehensive. All planned asset acquisitions, including current assets as well as long-term assets, are typically included under the appropriations/authorization process.

Third, private-sector capital budgeting tends to be a continuous process. Most well-managed firms always have a variety of initiatives under development. The decision to go ahead with an initiative is usually made only once, when the initiative is ripe, and is usually reconsidered only if it turns sour. In contrast, budgeting in the government tends to be repetitive—most appropriations are reconsidered annually on the basis of a rigid schedule.

Fourth, an initiative's sponsor or champion within the organization is usually given the authority and the responsibility for implementing it. In government, the new initiative's champion is seldom assigned responsibility for its implementation; instead, that responsibility is usually given to someone else, sometimes even in an entirely different department (see Bower, 1970).

Another difference is that the objective of capital budgeting in the private sector is the identification of options with positive net-present values, since in the absence of real limits on the availability of cash or managerial attention, the welfare of a firms' shareholders will be maximized by the implementation of all projects offering positive net-present values. Although many government decisions are informed by cost-benefit and cost-effectiveness analysis (in the United States, federal water and power and state construction projects have long been required to pass a benefit-cost test; Congress has recently imposed similar requirements on mandates and regulations; and federal loan-guarantee and insurance programs are funded in present-value terms), appropriations requests rarely show all the future implications of current decisions in present-value terms. For example, in the United States, the federal government routinely reduces current outlays by delaying major acquisitions and maintenance efforts, often thereby increasing discounted costs 60 percent or more. This irrational policy is justified by the need to reduce the deficit and, thereby, avoids borrowing at interest rates of 7 percent or less at present.

The biggest difference, however, between budget authority in most governments and the capital budgets approved by top management in the private sector lies in their relationship to operating budgets.

Government Budgeting and Operational Budgeting

In the private sector, operating budgets are management control devices. They are a means of motivating managers to serve the policies and purposes of the organizations to which they belong. In the private sector, management control is not primarily a process for detecting and correcting unintentional performance errors and intentional irregularities, such as theft or misuse of resources. Operational budgeting comprehends both the formulation of operating budgets and their execution. In operating-budget formulation, an organization's commitments, the results of all past capital-budgeting decisions, are converted into terms that correspond to the sphere of responsibility of administrative units and their managers. In budget execution, operations are monitored and subordinate managers evaluated and rewarded.

The budgeting systems of some governments do this. But there are critical differences between programming and budgeting in most governments and standard practices in well-run firms: Operational budgets in government tend to be highly detailed spending or resource-acquisition plans, which must be scrupulously executed just as they were approved; in contrast, operating budgets in the private sector are usually sparing of detail, often consisting of no more than a handful of quantitative performance standards.

This difference reflects the efforts made by firms to delegate authority and responsibility down into their organizations. Delegation of authority means giving departmental managers the maximum of feasible authority needed to make their units productive—or, in the alternative, subjecting them to a minimum of constraints, Hence, delegation of authority requires operating budgets to be stripped to the minimum needed to motivate and inspire subordinates. Ideally, the operating budget of an organization contains a single number, or performance target (e.g., a sales quota, a unit cost standard, or a profit or return-on-investment target), for each administrative unit.

Responsibility budgeting is the most common approach to operational budgeting used by well-managed private organizations. The fundamental construct of responsibility budgeting is an account (or control) structure that is oriented toward responsibility centers. A responsibility center is an administrative unit headed by a manager who is responsible for its actions. Responsibility centers have purposes or objectives and they use inputs (resources) to produce outputs (goods or services). The outputs of a well-designed responsibility center will be closely related to its objectives.

Responsibility centers are classified according to two dimensions: (1) the integration dimension—that is, the relationship between the responsibility center's objectives and the overall purposes and policies of the organization; (2) the decentralization dimension—that is, the amount of authority delegated to the responsibility manager, measured in terms of the manager's discretion to acquire and use assets. On the first dimension, a responsibility center can be either a mission center or a support center. The output of a mission center contributes directly to the organization's objectives. The output of a support center is an input to another responsibility center in the organization, another support center or a mission center. On the second dimension, discretionary expense centers, which mimic the governmental norm, are found at one extreme and profit and investment centers at the other. A support center may be either an expense center or a profit center. If the latter, it "sells" its services to other responsibility centers and its "profit" is the difference between its expenses and the "revenue" it gets from the "sale" of its services.

In the context of responsibility budgeting, budget execution means monitoring a responsibility center's performance in terms of the target specified and rewarding its manager accordingly.

Effective delegation of authority is possible in the private sector in part because capital budgeting and operational budgeting are treated as related but distinct processes. An organization's operating budgets must reflect its long-term commitments. Thus, a decision to invest resources in a new initiative should be reflected in the operating budgets of all the responsibility centers affected. The process by which commitments are reflected in operating budgets is called programming or, in the case of discrete multiperiod projects, project budgeting. In programming, operating budgets are revised to reflect the benefit and cost flows that justified the decision to go ahead with a new initiative in the first place. Increases in performance expected of each administrative unit or responsibility center are specified, targets are revised to take account of anticipated improvements, and responsibility for realizing them is assigned.

Again, government budgeting often reflects the form but not the content of private sector capital and operating budgets. The United States Defense Department's (DOD's) planning-programming-budgeting system, for example, starts with strategic plans. These are then broken down by function into broad missions (e.g., strategic retaliatory forces) and are then further subdivided into hundreds of subprograms or program elements. Next comes the identification of program alternatives, forecasting and evaluating the consequences of program alternatives, and deciding which program alternatives to carry out. This exercise produces a plan detailing both continuing programmatic commitments (the "base") and new commitments ("increments" or "decrements") in terms of force structure (including sizes and types of forces) and readiness levels, inventories and logistical capabilities, and the development of new weapons and support systems. The consequences of the DOD's programmatic decisions are estimated in terms of the kind, amount, and timing of all assets to be acquired, including personal services as well as plant, equipment, and supplies, to be funded for each program package (assuming no change in commitments) during the next six-year period. These acquisition plans are expressed in terms of current U.S. dollars and arrayed by military department, object of expenditure, and function. These estimates constitute the financial management portion of the Defense Plan, the first year of which constitutes its budget proposal (Jones, 1991).

However, even in the United States Defense Department, government budgets do not really distinguish between deciding what to do and actually doing it. What Congress decides is what is supposed to be done—budgets are supposed to be executed the way they are enacted. For the most part, operating managers within the federal government may do only what their budget says they can do: buy things, e.g., personal services, materials and supplies, long-lived plants and equipment. Their budgets focus exclusively on assets to be acquired by individual administrative units and on the timing of those acquisitions—on objects of expenditure or line-items rather than performance targets, on many inputs rather than a few critical outputs or results. In other words, most operating managers in the federal government are treated like the managers of discretionary expense centers; they have no real authority to acquire or use assets; without this authority, they cannot be held responsible for the financial performance of the administrative units they nominally head.

Historical Development

That there are great differences between the budgetary process in government and the way capital budgeting is done in the private sector is hardly surprising. Governmental financial management has always been sui generis, unique unto itself. In the English-speaking world, its roots are to be found in a procedure that was established in the twelfth century involving a teller, a tally cutter, an auditor, a clerk of the pells, a scriptor talliar, and several chamberlains and survived more or less intact until 1826. Object-of-expenditure appropriation and accounting was introduced in 1666 to prevent Charles II from spending money from the navy allocation on his mistresses. This system, which has come to be known as fund accounting and evidently was inspired by the pigeonhole design of the roll-top desk (or bureau), assumed its present form in 1689. Thus fund-accounting dates from a time when double-entry book-keeping was generally unknown, few gentlemen knew Arabic numbers, and financial transactions involved an exchange of hard coins (specie) or personal IOUs.

This system was revised in 1829, but at that time the recommendations of the accounting profession were rejected in favor of the civil servants', which were against double entry and the shift from a cash to an accrual basis of accounts and which left intact the previous confusion between the balance sheet and the income statement and current and long-term assets and liabilities. Also during the nineteenth century, the English-speaking world adopted French budgetary norms—comprehensiveness, exclusivity, repetition, and annuality, which had already been introduced to most of the European continent along with other aspects of bureaucratic rationality by Napoleon's conquering armies.

The United States was a laggard in this area. Most of its financial management practices were improvised from whatever was at hand to deal with problems or needs as they arose. The result was neither pretty nor systematic, but on balance worked fairly well. The Progressives changed all this. As Irene Rubin (1993) explains, progressive officials and academics, those who favored expansionary, activist government, invented or imported modern public budgeting in the United States. The reformers were generally committed to making procedures more orderly and to increasing executive authority. They were not really interested in business practice, and business played almost no role in providing examples for government to follow, although business leaders often supported budget reform and funded its study and implementation.

Even where business and government use similar terms, they often refer to different things. For example, many state and local jurisdictions remove large-scale, lumpy investments in plants and equipment (highway construction, waste-management facilities, public housing, educational facilities, hospitals, etc.) from their operating accounts/budgets to a plant or fixed assets fund/capital budget. Often they borrow the cash used to make these investments and match repayment of principle and interest payments to the life of the asset. These payments are then charged to the operating fund. Lacking economically sound rentals, these payments more or less satisfactorily measure the consumption of the asset. Certainly, they are no less satisfactory than the straight-line depreciation schedules business often use for their general purpose financial statements and, in some cases, their cost accounts. Nevertheless, this procedure turns capital-budgeting practice on its head, i.e., instead of converting future flows of benefits and costs to present values, large, lumpy current outlays are converted into a stream of future payments.

In fact, differences between the institutional arrangements through which capital-budgeting decisions are made in government and in business were probably never greater than they are in the United States right now. This is the case for two reasons. First of all, business has reduced its reliance on tight capital controls. Businesses used to believe that capital was their most valuable asset and that the chief task of top management was allocating it to productive uses; now most realize that their most precious resource is knowledge and that management's most important job is ensuring that knowledge is generated widely and used efficiently. As Jack Welch, chairman of GE recently explained, the centralized capital-budgeting procedures it once used were "right for the 1970s, a growing handicap in the 1980s, and would have been a ticket to the bone yard in the 1990s" (quoted in Anthony and Govindarajan, 1995, Instructor's Guide).

Second, in 1974, in the Budget Impoundment and Control Act, Congress adopted the defunct Keynesian economics of the 1967 report of the President's Commission on Budget Concepts and now gives as much weight to outlays as to budget authority and sets ceilings (toplines) on both obligational authority and outlays (Doyle and McCaffery, 1991). This is deplorable, since outlays have little real economic significance, except insofar as the sources of government financing or the timing of payments influence long-term considerations arising from the level of savings or private sector investment.

Elsewhere, governments, starting with New Zealand but now including Australia, Canada, Denmark, Finland, Sweden, and Britain, have been adopting private-sector budgeting techniques.

New Zealand

Most of the attention given to New Zealand has focused on its efforts to improve the quality of external financial reporting practices: the adoption of accrual accounting and reporting on performance. New Zealand has become the first country to publish a rational set of government accounts that includes a balance sheet of its assets and liabilities and an accrual-based operating statement of income and expenses that is similar to the accounts of a public company. Accrual accounting provides a more accurate picture of a government's financial position because it keeps track of the changing value of assets and liabilities. Capital investment is depreciated over the life of the asset rather than being written off in the year when the money is spent, as is done under cash accounting. Likewise, future pension obligations count as a liability. All of these changes have helped to bring New Zealand financial reports into line with present-value calculations.

However, the changes made in the structure of the government of New Zealand designed to promote effective resource use and investment are perhaps even more significant than are the changes in its financial reporting practices (the following is based on Scott, Bushnell, and Sallee, 1990; Ball, 1994). First of all, New Zealand's Parliament

has privatized everything that is not part of the "core public sector." The residual "core public sector" includes a mix of policy, regulatory, and operational functions: military services, policing and justice services, social services such as health, education, and the administration of benefit payments, research and development, property assessment, and other financial services.

Second, Parliament has redefined the relationship between it and the department heads. Departmental heads lost their permanent tenure and are now known generically as "chief executives." They are appointed for fixed terms of up to five years, with the possibility of reappointment. Each works to a specific contract, the conditions of which are negotiated with the State Services Commission and approved by the prime minister. The State Services Commission also monitors and assesses executive performance. Remuneration levels are directly tied to this performance assessment.

Third, under the Public Finance Act of 1989, Parliament changed the way it appropriates funds for use by the government departments remaining. It has tried to link appropriation to performance, allowing Parliament to control the level of resource use and the purposes to which resources are put, but, at the same time, providing greater flexibility for department chiefs. The basis of appropriation depends on the department's ability to supply adequate information about its performance. Three modes of appropriation are possible, recognizing that some departments provide goods and services that are more "commercial" or "contestable" than others.

All departments started out in Mode A, but most have now progressed either to Mode B or C. Under Mode A, departments are still treated as discretionary cost centers. Parliament appropriates funds for the purchase of resources. Indeed, the only change from budget process in effect before 1989 (or, for that matter, the budgets used by most jurisdictions throughout the world) is that separate appropriations were provided for expenditures for plants and equipment. This mode remained in force until the department developed a satisfactory accrual accounting system and identified its outputs, both of which are needed for performance assessment.

Under Mode B, departments are treated like expense or quasi–profit centers. This mode is designed for departments that supply traditional, noncontestable, governmental services: the central control agencies, including the State Services Commission, most regulatory and police functions, and some justice services, i.e., policy agencies and activities that include an element of compulsion for the buyer. Under this mode, Parliament appropriates funds retrospectively to reimburse departments for expenses incurred in producing outputs during the period covered by the contract, whether for the government or third parties. Expenses are measured on an accrual basis; they include depreciation, but exclude taxes and the return on funds employed. Any increase in the level of the state's net-asset holdings in the department is also explicitly appropriated.

Under Mode C, departments are treated like investment centers. Appropriations pay for the outputs produced by the department and for any changes in the department's net assets.

Departments in Mode C are required to pay interest, taxes, and dividends and must establish a capital structure. The department is set up in a competitively neutral manner so that its performance can be assessed by comparison with firms in the private sector. The price paid for the outputs supplied the department is supposed to approximate the "fair market price." In general, this means that the department must show that it is receiving no more than the next best alternative supplier would receive for providing the outputs. Under Mode C, departments are similar to state-owned enterprises, but they are not permitted to borrow on their own behalf nor to invest outside their own businesses.

Each month, each department reports on its financial position and cash flows and resource usages and revenue by output. Variances are calculated and explanations provided. Under both Modes B and C, managers are free to make some decisions (most, under C) about investments in plants and equipment. The fact that their financial performance is one of the main bases upon which their performance is assessed helps to ensure that those decisions will be sound.

Government's key capital-budgeting decisions remain firmly in the hands of Parliament, however. The decisions that have the most significant future consequences for the government of New Zealand's stakeholders are clearly those which have to do with the kind, quantity, and quality of service provided by the citizenry. Under the existing system of appropriations and financial reporting, those issues must be explicitly confronted when cabinet enters into long-term contracts with departments, state-owned enterprises, and firms to deliver service outputs and its consequent liabilities must be stated in present-value terms. The fiscal outcomes of the government of New Zealand's decisionmaking processes are truly both mission driven and results oriented.

Implementing Mission-Driven, Results-Oriented Budgets in the United States

The locus of United States Congress's power lies in its power over the purse and the details of administration, as exemplified by item-by-item approval. More than any other institutional arrangement, item-by-item approval distinguishes congressional government from parliamentary systems, in which the legislature's power is largely a sham.

Can the kind of arms-length, quasi–transfer-pricing mechanism adopted in New Zealand under Modes B and C be adapted to the realities of congressional power, or, is it necessary to transform Congress to give meaning to the mission-driven, results-oriented budget concept? That a number of states have experimented with mechanisms like New Zealand's suggests that the American form of government, with its separation of powers, is not inherently inimical to the adoption of businesslike budgeting practices (see Barzelay, 1992). Indeed, it is possible that Congress could allow enough flexibility to make it work merely by increasing agency discretion to transfer budget authority between lines and through time, by treating budget authority as permissive (i.e., permitting but not requiring the obligation of funds), and by restricting its propensity to fund long-term investment programs on a one-year-at-a-time basis.

Robert Anthony (1990), for example, argues that this could be done by dividing the United States budget into an operating portion and a capital portion, much like some state and local budgets. The operating budget would be appropriated annually or biannually and would be expressed in terms of the amount of expenses authorized for the period in question. The capital budget would be directed to the acquisition of long-lived assets and would in essence be unchanged from existing provisions of obligational authority.

Anthony recognizes that responsibility centers cannot possibly meet all of their needs using spot-market transactions. They frequently need to enter into long-term, exclusive relationships with outside suppliers, and support centers have to make long-term commitments, involving highly specific assets, to supply other support and mission centers within government. Regardless of how mission centers obtain the use of long-term assets, directly from an outside supplier or indirectly through a support center, their employment will give rise to discrepancies between obligations, outlays, and consumption. The use of long-term assets and inventory depletion also give rise to intertemporal spillovers from one budget period to the next and, therefore, discrepancies between operating budget accounts and the Treasury's cash account. Reconciling these discrepancies under Anthony's proposal would necessitate the creation of an additional annual (or biannual) appropriation for changes in working capital. Presumably, too, Anthony would have Congress set up a capital fund to provide both mission centers and their suppliers in government with financing for the acquisition of long-term capital assets.

Elsewhere, however, I have argued that one could go still further toward making congressional budgeting even more like capital budgeting in benchmark businesses, that is, permissive, continuous, and selective (Thompson, 1994). What this means is that congressional budgeting should focus on all of the cash flows that ensue from its programmatic decisions (operating expenditures and transfers as well as acquisitions and construction), and for the life of the decision, not just the cash flows that occur in the initial fiscal year. New obligational authority should be expressed in terms of the discounted present values of those cash flows. Congress would also deemphasize the budget resolution, with its fixation on outlays, and reemphasize obligational authority. The core of congressional power lies in its authority to decide to go ahead with a program, activity, or acquisition, which is what the authorization/appropriations process has always been about. Its next step would be to throw away the comprehensive, annual executive budget. Executive branch agencies should be permitted to come forward at any time with proposals to change the scope, level, or timing of their operations.

Congress should consider proposals to try something new as soon as they are ready to be considered, but consider them only once. Once a project has been approved by Congress, it should be reconsidered only if circumstances change or the project goes bad. This means that obligational authority should be granted for the life of the project and should reflect the discounted present value of the project's cash flows. Standing appropriations should be continuously adjusted to reflect these important decisions.

Congress currently takes about the right approach to providing budget authority for the acquisition of long-lived assets, although the system of one-year-at-a-time authorization and appropriation that Congress has adopted in recent years is inimical to sound project management. Nevertheless, where plants and equipment are concerned, current costs are present values. In contrast, where ongoing activities are concerned, current costs greatly understate government's actual obligations.

The third step would be to make legislative budgeting more selective—this means that most federal budgeting would be more like the current process of authorization and appropriation for social security. Congressional budgeting should focus only on significant changes in operations, activities, and investments in fixed assets. Otherwise, congressional attention should not be necessary.

Most government departments/responsibility centers should probably operate under permanent authority. They should have to seek budget authority from Congress only when they wanted to make changes with significant future consequences and then only if the changes increased the Treasury's liabilities. If Congress wanted to reduce spending, it would have to enact programmatic changes that reduced permanent appropriations (although performance-based spending cuts could be built into those appropriations.)

Under this approach, most departments would still have to obtain congressional authorization to make major new investments or changes in their corpus. And Congress would probably still reconsider funding levels for research and development on an annual or biannual basis. Aside from these exceptions, however, all new obligational authority would be expressed in terms of discounted net cash flows—which would dramatically change congressional authorizations and appropriations for operating purposes. Congress would probably also have to acknowledge formally that obligational authority is permissive rather than mandatory.

Fiscal control under this approach to congressional budgeting would remain more or less as it is now. Presumably, the Office of Management and Budget's monthly apportionments to responsibility centers would remain at constant levels as long as Congress did not increase (or reduce) their budget authority. In addition, the Treasury should probably be authorized to buy and sell notes on behalf of agencies to provide it with short-term liquidity and to match cash inflows with the actual pattern of cash outflows.

There really is nothing new about any of these proposals. In essence, they merely would restore the congressional budget process that existed prior to the passage of the Budget Act in 1921, which established a comprehensive, annual executive budget for the federal government, created what has become the Office of Management and Budget, and, at the same time, restricted congressional power. Many of the constraints that Congress has built into the existing budget process can be interpreted as efforts to overcome those restrictions and to escape the procrustean bed imposed by the comprehensive, annual executive budget (maybe because a comprehensive, annual executive budget was a bad idea to begin with or maybe because it has now outlived whatever usefulness it once might have had).

In any case, congressional budgeting used to be much more like private-sector capital budgeting than it is now. It was once permissive, continuous, and selective rather than comprehensive and repetitive. Indeed, looking at policy choices in present-value terms is the only real difference between the congressional budget process that existed prior to the Budget Act and private-sector capital budgeting. But even appropriating on a present-value basis has a clear precedent in the congressional budgetary process. Congress currently funds the federal government's loan-guarantee and insurance programs in precisely that manner. Perhaps the time has now come to make congressional budgeting more like private-sector capital budgeting.

FRED THOMPSON

BIBLIOGRAPHY

Anthony, R. N. 1990. "The AICPA's Proposal for Federal Accounting Reform: It Should Focus on the Budget System, Not the Accounting System." *Management Accounting*, vol. 72, no. 1 (July) 48–52.

Anthony, R. N. and Vijay Govindarajan, 1995. *Management Control Systems*, 8th ed. Chicago: Irwin.

Ball, Ian, 1994. "Reinventing Government: Lessons Learned from the New Zealand Treasury." *Government Accountants Journal*, vol. 43, no. 3 (Fall) 19–28.

Barzelay, M., with B. J. Armajani, 1992. *Breaking through Bureaucracy: A New Vision for Managing in Government.* Berkeley, CA: University of California Press.

Bierman, H. and S. Smidt, 1993. *The Capital Budgeting Decision: Economic Analysis of Investment Projects,* 8th ed. New York: Macmillan.

Bower, J., 1970. *The Resource Allocation Process.* Boston: Harvard Business School Division of Research.

Chandler, A., 1962. *Strategy and Structure: Chapters in the History of Industrial Enterprise.* Cambridge, MA: MIT Press.

Dixit, A. and R. Pindyk, 1994. *Investment Under Uncertainty.* Princeton, NJ: Princeton University Press.

Doyle, R. and J. McCaffery, 1991. "The Budget Enforcement Act of 1990: The Path to No Fault Budgeting." *Public Budgeting and Finance,* vol. 11, no. 1 (Spring) 25–40.

Jones, L. R., 1991. "Policy Development, Planning, and Resource Allocation in the Department of Defense." *Public Budgeting and Finance,* vol. 11, no. 3 (Fall) 15–27.

Rubin, Irene S., 1993. "Who Invented Budgeting in the United States?" *Public Administration Review,* vol. 53, no. 5 (September/October) 438–444.

Scott, G., P. Bushnell, and N. Sallee, 1990. "Reform of the Core Public Sector: The New Zealand Experience." *Public Sector,* vol. 13, no. 3: 11–24.

Thompson, Fred, 1994. "Mission-Driven, Results-Oriented Budgeting: Financial Administration and the New Public Management." *Public Budgeting & Finance,* vol. 14, no. 3 (Fall) 90–105.

CAPITAL CAMPAIGN.

An organized fund-raising effort focused on generating resources necessary to construct new buildings, refurbish existing structures, increase endowments, or provide equipment and furnishings.

Traditionally, a capital campaign is a part of an overall development plan and strategy. While capital fund-raising is generally considered to be the easiest form of fund-raising activity, it often is also seen as the most fun. Donors and boards of directors seem to be able to relate much more readily to a new building or wing to be constructed than the programs or routine operating needs of a nonprofit organization. The capital campaign presents a special opportunity for an organization to attract support from larger donors or special one-time donors who only give to capital projects.

Advantages to capital campaigns are many. They provide an opportunity for high visibility projects that will enable nonprofits to create a more positive and established community image. Generally, the giving to a capital effort is in larger average gift amounts by major donors spread over multiple years. This helps create a high-end giving group to strengthen a nonprofit's donor family. These major donors are much more likely to provide ongoing or continuous financial support in future years, after they have fulfilled their campaign commitments.

The most significant reason a nonprofit conducts a capital campaign is to build a building or major renovation without having to put the organization in long-term capital debt. However, often the capital fund-raising effort can be used to lever the issue of tax exempt bonds or more favorable mortgage-loan terms when capital debt assumption is warranted.

Occasionally, charities will join capital and endowment campaigns into one effort. It takes a strong nonprofit to successfully implement this strategy. When this approach works, it is not uncommon for as much to be raised for endowment as capital. Some organizations have even established a fund-raising policy of "one dollar into endowment for each dollar into capital."

A capital campaign is great way to add new individual donors. People enjoy seeing the way a new building might look and are often interested in "naming" ideas for wings or special rooms. This creates the potential for larger individual gifts and a very loyal donor who is a high probability for a planned or estate gift in the future. If an organizational fund-development plan is well designed around the capital effort, substantial new program start-up grants can also be obtained.

There are some disadvantages to capital campaigns. The most often cited disadvantage is simply overbuilding. A building built by a campaign but sitting empty can be the "kiss of death" for a nonprofit. The additional cost of maintenance, cleaning, upkeep, and depreciation must be factored when considering a campaign. Overhead costs also many times are not factored realistically in agency-operating budgets. The size of capital gifts also can have a detrimental effect on other fund-raising efforts. Organizations that build a donor family based on capital gifts often must continue to conduct additional capital projects to keep donor support. Two negative capital campaign maxims are worth mentioning: "never turn a shovel of dirt until you know how you are going to make your goal" and "when the roof goes on, the campaign is over."

A capital campaign usually requires a separate campaign fund-raising committee. This affords an opportunity to bring in new volunteer leadership, and often very influential people can be recruited to head major components of the effort. The best campaign structure is for this committee to report to the nonprofit's governing authority and divide the work into subcommittees of major gifts, foundations, corporations, individuals, and special events. The board working with this committee and staff of the organization is the best team.

A good brief campaign case statement that lays out the need, reason for expansion, amount of campaign, and timeline for completion is essential. Don't forget the value of thank-you notes and letters. Don't underestimate the importance of celebratory events such as ground-breaking, ribbon-cutting, and open house. These case statements and events play a major role in establishing or enhancing a nonprofit's image.

The upcoming tough times for nonprofits may change the donor priorities, but a well-designed and successfully implemented capital campaign can create positive momentum for all fund-raising and development activities of the organization.

GARY BAKER

BIBLIOGRAPHY

Dove, Kent E., 1988. *Conducting a Successful Capital Campaign.* San Francisco: Jossey-Bass.

CAPITAL INVESTMENTS.

In the public sector defined as any type of government outlay that provides economic benefits beyond the current budget cycle.

Donald Axelrod says, "On one extreme some say only tangible assets such as capital facilities and major pieces of equipment qualify as capital investment. At the other extreme, not only tangible assets, but investments in human capital such as education and training programs, are included in definitions of capital investments" (1988, p. 100).

The United States General Accounting Office guidelines say an asset qualifies as a capital item if it has a service life longer than one year, is tangible, and represents a nonrecurring expenditure. The Office of Management and Budget, however, distinguishes between tangible and less tangible capital investments such as capital facilities, construction and rehabilitation, acquisition of major equipment, conduct of research and development, conduct of education and training, and loans and financial investments. All of these items are classified as capital investments (Axelrod 1988, p. 101).

Some states and local governments have included supplies, library books, and minor equipment as part of their capital investment policy; this is a political call. It was this type of capital-budget manipulation that helped precipitate New York City's virtual bankruptcy in 1975.

John F. Due and Ann F. Friedlaender (1973) provide an explanation of why government's capital investments are necessary. In the first half of the nineteenth century, individuals had insufficient capital to undertake many necessary capital improvements; there were some public goods that the private market economy could not provide. These goods had a basic quality: If made available at all, they had to be made available equally to all individuals. No one could be excluded from their benefits. Therefore, public goods could not be produced and sold on a profit-making basis. Capital investment in such things as national defense and transportation (highways and roads) is the most obvious example and has always been made by government. Reflecting on the history of capital investment, one must consider the corrective steps that society took through the passage of various acts, reports, and laws to ensure the appropriate handling of public goods (pp. 2–4).

According to Frederick C. Mosher (1976), 1 Statute 12 1789, adopted on September 2, 1789, outlined how and

why the Department of the Treasury, the secretary of the Treasury, the comptroller, the auditor, the treasurer, the register, and the assistant secretary of the Treasury were to be established. As described in the act, "the department's major responsibility was to prepare and report estimates of public revenue and expenditures, and execute services relative to the sale of the lands" (p. 36). Mosher also chronicles the *1912 Report of the Taft Commission on Economy and Efficiency* that required department heads to prepare annual expenditure reports for Congress that outlined expended appropriations by class of work including land, buildings, and other improvements (p. 76).

In 1921, the Budget and Accounting Act established the Office of the Budget and requested the president to transmit to the Congress of the United States an expenditures and receipts estimate. These estimates included expenditures for capital investments, identified as land, buildings, and other improvements. The president continued transmitting and reporting capital investments in the operating budget through the enactment of the Budgeting and Accounting Procedures Act of 1950, the Bureau of the Budget Bulletin No. 66-3, Planning-Programming-Budgeting (1965), and the Congressional Budget and Impoundment Control Act of 1974.

Until 1985, the federal government relied on a unified budget. The acquisition of capital assets was treated like any current operating expenditures. Beginning in January 1985, the Public Works Act of 1984 (PL 98-501) requires the president to include in the budget projections for major capital investment, assessments of the needs for capital investment, and estimates of capital facilities expenditures by state and local governments (Axelrod, p. 106).

Michael A. Pagano and Richard J. T. Moore (1985) say, "Investments serve three purposes; the first is a foundation for economic growth. The second is as an element of general capital formation and the third is to reduce the cost of production for firms, thus contributing to private capital formation" (pp. 6–7). The public sector's provision of infrastructure should be viewed as a vital and necessary aspect of capital formation and investment. However, there have been reports about the deteriorating quality of public capital stock at all levels of government (p. 3).

An explanation of long-term trends presented by Lansing (1995) says, "In the 23-year period from 1947 to 1969, non-military capital investment in the United States averaged 3.5 percent of GNP. From 1970 to 1992, however, the corresponding figure was only 2.5 percent, a decline of nearly one-third. Both sectors have decreased over time, leading some to conclude that the United States is currently underinvesting in public capital" (pp. 2–4).

Economic, land use, and population studies are used to evaluate the viability of capital investments. These studies are often grounded in Keynesian and neo-Keynesian policies, the economic approach of John Maynard Keynes, the British economist who emphasized the role of government in strengthening and providing stability for a free enterprise economy. In theory, the determination of worthwhile public capital investment is straightforward. A capital investment is desirable when its estimated flow of benefits, discounted at the community's cost of financing, exceeds or equals its cost. If the project meets this criterion, it is considered profitable, because it will earn more than the community's interest rate. If present value exceeds the outlay, the project should be acceptable to the community (Due and Friedlaender, pp. 79–84).

Rationalizing Capital Investment

J. Richard Aronson and Eli Schwartz (1987) explain how there are ways of rationalizing capital investment programs. They maintain that the standard "public good" argument says that the government should provide goods and services that would be underproduced by the private sector (pp. 401–406). The benefits of the capital investments are not always quantifiable because benefits can be intangible in nature. Their usefulness is social and not easily determined in monetary terms, although capital cost remains a theoretically correct criterion for investment in the public sector. This is why projects such as parks and recreation centers are left for the government to supply.

Capital investments serve many vital purposes such as financing the goals of operating programs; health, education, correctional services, housing and economic development; constructing and maintaining roads, bridges, waste disposal plants, mass transportation, water supply systems, airports, communication systems, and power generating plants. Capital investment programs (CIPs) are timetables that specify the projects selected for improvement or construction; the target dates for every phase of the project such as design, land acquisition, contract-letting, construction, installation of equipment, and operation; the estimated costs and methods of financing a multi-year program (Axelrod 1988, p. 108).

Capital Investment Programs

The CIP outlines government's capital priorities, choices, and fiscal strategies. Standards and criteria have been developed for virtually every type of capital facility. They serve as a basis for deciding capital investment needs and for decisions to maintain, improve, or replace existing structures. In capital investment what counts are the total costs of a facility or major piece of equipment over its estimated useful life and not just the acquisition cost or the cost of design and construction. This is called life-cycle costing (Axelrod 1988, p. 116).

Other significant costs are research and development, preproject planning, packaging bonds for sale, debt service, operation and maintenance, and the salvage value of discontinued equipment or facilities. This analysis gives a far better insight into the commitment government undertakes approving a capital facility rather the more limited appraisal of design and construction costs. When all costs are considered, a project with a high construction cost may turn out to be more economical than one built at a lower cost (Axelrod 1988, pp. 114, 116). For these reasons, the Office of Management and Budget requires life-cycle costing for capital investments.

State and local governments have been far more aggressive than federal governments in formulating annually updated CIPs. Usually, the states' capital-programming processes are mandated by statute, coming after years of citizens' dissatisfaction with capital projects' planning and financing. Many local governments, in the United States and elsewhere, pioneered urban planning. Urban planning proposes the construction and rehabilitation of capital projects through capital investment to strengthen the local economy. Almost all 50 state governments have a capital budget that reflects capital investment. The cities' investment in their infrastructures is a necessary ingredient in firms' decisions to locate or expand at specific sites. Faced with survival, cities are finding it's imperative to continue investments in existing and new public stock.

State and local governments rely on borrowing as a major source of funding for capital investment. In 1979, grants accounted for over 40 percent of total capital investments by state and local governments. Without this aid, governments would not have mounted high levels of capital investment in recent years. While the relative importance of federal aid varies among state and local governments, almost all of them rely on grants to fund their capital projects (Lansing, pp. 1–3).

Developing countries use capital investments as instruments of modernization for projects such as new ports and highway facilities (Pagano and Moore, p. 6). Peter Carty (1994) describes how industrialized nations may want to meet the needs of an ever-expanding service sector by providing better mass transit or communication service. More than 100 developing countries have multi-year economic and social development plans that include physical projects, as well as less tangible investments in human capital such as education, health, and training. India also focuses its capital investment on intangible assets—family planning, research and development, and training that advances economic development (pp. 34–36).

Among the advanced industrialized market economy countries, only France and Japan practice broad-scale planning. However, capital projects are mainstays of economic development. Most advanced countries provide detailed information on capital investments, although they do not have a separate capital budget. Examples include France and Britain (Axelrod 1988, p. 107).

A revolution in capital investment is taking place in Britain. Both major parties favor tapping private funds for infrastructure projects such as bridges and roads, normally financed with public monies. Historically, this is not new; up until the end of World War II, the British railroads were in private hands. Carty reports that Britain's intent is to improve the flow of capital investment in public services by attracting private sector capital into services such as nursing-home care, waste disposal, prison services, water and sewage infrastructure.

Sweden singled out capital assets with a life of three years or more and a predetermined monetary value for special attention.

The Soviet Union emphasized capital investments and classified them by construction and acquisition of equipment through five-year comprehensive plans.

Debt financing of capital investments is a global phenomenon. Governments typically turned to private banks and investors, nationalized banks, and even to higher levels of government for financing. In some countries, subnational governments depend on the central government for substantial loans. This is the case in Australia, Canada, and Britain. Conversely, several countries such as France and Denmark oppose such direct loans.

AUDREY L. MATHEWS

BIBLIOGRAPHY

Aronson, J. Richard and Eli Schwartz, eds., 1987. *Management Policies in Local Government Finance,* 3rd ed. Washington, D.C.: ICMA Training Institute, International City Management Association.
Axelrod, Donald, 1988. *Budgeting for Modern Government.* New York: St. Martin's Press.
Carty, Peter, 1994. "Private Funds for Public Profits." *Accountancy* (August) 34–36.
Due, John F. and Ann F. Friedlaender, 1973. *Government Finance: Economics in the Public Sector.* Homewood, IL: Richard D. Irwin.
Lansing, Kevin L., 1995. "Is Public Capital Productive? A Review of the Evidence." *Economic Commentary,* Federal Reserve Bank of Cleveland, (March) 1–4.
Mosher, Frederick C., ed., 1976. Report of the (*Taft) Commission on Economy and Efficiency: The Need for a National Budget (1912). *Basic Documents of American Public Administration 1776–1950.* New York: Holmes & Meir, pp.76–81.
———, 1976. Treasury Department 1 Statute 12 1789, adopted on September 2, 1789. *Basic Documents of American Public Administration 1776–1950.* New York: Holmes & Meir, pp. 36–38.
Pagano, Michael A. and Richard J. T. Moore, 1985. *Cities and Fiscal Choices: A New Model of Urban Public Investment.* Durham, N.C.: Duke University Press.

CAREER COUNSELING.
Facilitating individuals' choices of short-term and long-term goals for lifework.

Career counseling is a process involving two primary participants: a counselor who facilitates the process and a person who makes decisions related to individual development and work. Employees who are interested in finding opportunities to excel in more satisfying or more challenging jobs may seek a facilitator for career development or advancement. High school students deciding whether or not to attend college, college students selecting careers and appropriate major fields of study, and adults reentering the workforce also seek career counseling (see **career ladder**). There are four stages in the process: self-assessment, feedback, exploring career options in organizations, and goal setting.

Self-Assessment

Various assessment instruments may be used in the first stage of the process. The facilitator may need a license to administer some of them and should only choose those appropriate for each case. Any instruments that are administered should be used in an ethical manner. Results must be given to clients with respect for their rights to confidentiality and should not be used by managers as criteria for selections. For example, an employee who completes the instruments may choose to share results with a manager and solicit feedback about results, but the primary purpose of instrumentation is to give useful data to the employee making career decisions.

As part of the self-assessment, the Adjective Check List (ACL) may be used to quantify observations about personality. The instrument describes a person on 37 scales. Several of the scales have served as the basis for research concerning leadership: need for achievement, dominance, order, affiliation, autonomy, aggression, self-control, and self-confidence. Therefore, one application of ACL results is input for choices between careers in management or other career paths. Research in the United States, Ireland, and Italy verifies the benefits of this application (Mani, 1993).

Individuals who find work interesting will be satisfied in their jobs (Career Systems, Inc., 1987). The Strong Interest Inventory may be used to assess interests. This inventory may be used by qualified facilitators to identify the Holland codes, which describe an individual's career interests. The six codes are realistic (R), investigative (I), artistic (A), social (S), enterprising (E), and conventional (C). An individual who completes the Strong Interest Inventory learns the three-letter code that best describes his or her interests. For example, consider a nonmanagerial employee who is deciding whether or not to pursue a career in management, whose Holland codes are ESC. Those whose Holland codes include E (enterprising) and S (social) enjoy persuading, motivating, and leading people and aspire to manage service-oriented organizations or work in nonprofit settings. It is likely that this employee would find the work of a manager in the public sector interesting and satisfying (Mani, 1992).

The Myers-Briggs Type Indicator (MBTI) is also used by facilitators to help individuals identify their interests. One's type according to the MBTI is described by 1 of 16 four-letter combinations. Each of the four letters of one's type represents a preference on one of four scales: extroversion or introversion; sensing or intuition; thinking or feeling; and judging or perceiving. The use of the MBTI to facilitate students' and employees' career choices has been documented in Japan, Great Britain, Canada, and Australia (Myers and McCaulley, 1985). The MBTI results may help decisionmakers use knowledge of type to select careers congruent with their interests (Mani, 1993).

Career anchors are nonmonetary or psychological factors that individuals find important and rewarding to them over time: technical/functional and managerial competence, creativity, autonomy and independence, and security. These factors influence job satisfaction and decisions to stay or leave positions and organizations. A sixth career anchor may be appropriate in public administration–public service motive. Those with this career anchor will find positions satisfying if they provide opportunities to participate in the process of policy formulation, to serve the public interest, and to make a commitment to a mission of social importance (Barth, 1993). Positions in public sector organizations may provide opportunities to satisfy the public service motive or the security career anchors, as well as some others. It is important for employees who are seeking job satisfaction to assess these factors, for themselves and for positions they might set as career goals.

Some career counselors' clients have specific needs for self-assessment to meet requirements for organizations or special positions. Some sensitive positions require a psychological assessment. For example, a law enforcement official who is required to use firearms might seek a licensed facilitator to administer the California Psychological Inventory. One who seeks career counseling may also need to know intelligence quotient (IQ). A qualified career counselor may use the Otis-Lennon Mental Ability Test to assess IQ.

During the self-assessment, employees analyze prior experience and develop descriptions of skills developed and evident in prior positions. Working with computers, solving problems, analyzing financial statements are examples of skills. It is important to assess skills because individuals who possess skills required for a position should be able to perform satisfactorily in that position (Career Systems, Inc., 1987).

Soliciting Feedback

In the second stage of the process, the decisionmaker solicits feedback from others to analyze the accuracy of the self-assessment. The roles of the career counselor/facilitator and the decisionmaker's supervisor are critical in this

stage. Although supervisors should continuously give employees feedback to help improve performance, feedback that is part of the career-counseling process is most effective when dissociated from the performance appraisal process (see **performance appraisal**). As part of the career-counseling process, supervisors should help employees set realistic career goals, assess the accuracy of the employees' self-assessments, give feedback, that is, explain why they should do more, do less, or continue as they now do, and listen to employees' concerns.

Identifying Realistic Career Options in the Organization

The supervisor also plays an important role in the third stage of the process by helping the employee understand the organization and identify realistic career options. Knowledge of networks, organizational norms and structure, organizational goals and objectives, funding limits, dead-end jobs, and various career paths and options, influence career choices. For example, an employee might consider a goal to move from a technical position into management after learning the career anchors. However, many public agencies are "rightsizing" and eliminating managerial positions. In addition, "baby boomers" are now at the age where many of them are eligible and competing for the limited managerial jobs that remain. This knowledge might lead an employee to choose a different career path. What are alternative career paths? The traditional view of career development has been upward, that is, development equals promotion. Intermediary moves, such as downgrades, lateral moves, temporary assignments, assignments that enhance skills in the current position, or moves to other organizations also provide developmental opportunities and experience that may lead to promotions (Career Systems, Inc., 1987).

Individual Development Planning

In the fourth stage, employees set individual development goals, plan activities to accomplish the goals, and work to accomplish the activities in the development plan. The supervisor and the organization play important roles in this stage. The supervisor must refer employees to those who can provide developmental assignments, provide references and support, and adjust workloads to permit employees' release. The organization must provide accurate and timely information regarding structural changes, developmental opportunities, and funding.

Many public sector organizations—for example, the Internal Revenue Service (IRS)—implement internal career-counseling programs. The projected benefits of the program include improved morale, improvements in the quality of employees' work life, and enhanced recruitment and retention of quality employees. An agency-developed computer software, CareerPoint, an eight-hour, self-paced program, assists employees' in self-assessments. Managers may attend career-counseling workshops to learn their roles in employees' career development. In addition, career counselors are employed to facilitate the career development process and outplacement counseling, as well as organizational development and teambuilding initiatives, and to conduct career-development workshops and orientations for new employees.

BONNIE G. MANI

BIBLIOGRAPHY

Barth, Thomas, 1993. "Career Anchor Theory." *Review of Public Personnel Administration*, vol. 13, no. 4 (Fall) 27–42.

Career Systems, Inc., 1987. *Partners in Career Management: Training for Managers in Career Coaching Skills.* Silver Spring, MD: Career Systems, Inc.

Mani, Bonnie G., November 1992. *Developing Quality Leadership: Preparing to Meet and to Match Organizations' and Employees' Needs for Effective Leadership Skills.* Paper presented at the annual meeting of the Southern Political Science Association, Atlanta, Georgia.

———, "Progress on the Journey to Total Quality Management: Using the Myers-Briggs Type Indicator and the Adjective Check List in Management Development." *Public Personnel Management*, forthcoming.

Myers, I. B. and M. H. McCaulley, 1985. *Manual: A Guide to the Development and Use of the Myers-Briggs Type Indicator.* Palo Alto, CA: Consulting Psychologists Press.

CAREER DEVELOPMENT.

Sequence of job-related experiences and activities that create certain attitudes and behaviors in an individual in the pursuit of consecutive progressive occupational achievement.

Although careers have typically been defined in terms of upward mobility, recent definitions have enlarged the concept. For example, an individual can continue to acquire and develop new skills in the same job without moving upward in an organizational or professional hierarchy. Also, an individual may move among various jobs in different fields and organizations. In addition, contemporary career development practices recognize the diversity of individual choices and career alternatives, including newly emerging work and lifestyles.

According to Shafritz, Hyde, and Rosenbloom (1986) in *Personnel Management in Government,* there are four basic and sequential phases of career development as practiced in public personnel management. These phases are (1) the entry phase—a break-in time period when the new employee achieves a journey worker's level, that is, adequate working level of operational competence; (2) the specialist phase—a period when the employee concentrates on performing a set of specific work assignments involving technical and work skills; (3) the generalist phase—a period when specific technical skills are less important and more supervisory responsibilities are acquired; and (4) the management phase—a period when the employee assumes responsibilities for administering and directing work operations, managing the execution of programs, and formulating plans for future organizational action.

In the private sector, where employee empowerment is growing in acceptance, many organizations have adopted self-directed career-development programs giving employees the primary responsibility for their own career development. For example, the employees of British Petroleum Exploration (BPX) take advantage of a four-phase career-development program consisting of self-assessment, goal-setting, career-planning, and implementation phases. The program enables employees to have open, two-way communication with their supervisors throughout the four phases. To foster the sense of openness and trust, the career development program is voluntary. Nevertheless, to encourage participation, the organization gives recognition and supervisory support to employees who do enter the program. Employees use the program to improve their skills and job performance. Moreover, they use their career-development plans to market themselves within the organization. Throughout the process, BPX provides career-development opportunities, but it is up to the employees to take advantage of them.

Prior to 1970, the public sector, particularly state governments, lagged behind private industry in providing career-development programs and, with few exceptions, even failed to provide career-counseling services. By 1978, steps were being taken to improve career advancement in the federal government through the Civil Service Reform Act. However, the applicable provisions in this legislation were limited to the career development of senior executives.

Prior to the Civil Service Reform Act of 1978, the Federal Office of Management and Budget and the former Civil Service Commission only issued memoranda to federal agencies encouraging the initiation of programs to develop senior managers. There was little positive response to these memoranda. After the act in the 1980s, 54 agencies immediately outlined career development programs and over 600 candidates were selected from the ranks of middle management to participate. Agencies varied some of the features of their programs. The length varied from six months to two years, and the array of creative approaches included formal training courses, briefing sessions, developmental work assignments, internships with mentors, shadow assignments, and the like. All programs emphasized managerial rather than technical skills and included career-development plans for each participant.

Some state and municipal governments began to adapt aspects of the federal programs. Moreover, affirmative action goals prompted some employers to pursue career-development programs with their employees, not only for senior-management positions but throughout the organization. Recent studies on affirmative action have shown some progress for minorities and women. In a 1991 study of senior executive service (SES) women in the federal government, questionnaire data from 645 women covered issues of how executives learn, how they develop their careers, and what career-development choices were most critical in advancing to the highest ranks within their organizations. Results of the study revealed that there were common "key events" and "lessons learned" by these women in the process of shattering the glass ceiling in the federal government. Another common theme discussed by these women related to the influence of bosses and role models. The study concluded that these common factors needed to be accounted for as women with high potential for management are developed by their organizations.

Lee (1993) in *Public Personnel Systems* suggests that there are at least six types of job mobility in the context of career development. These six types are identified as intra-agency, interagency, interorganizational, geographic, occupational, and social-class mobility. Intraagency mobility involves movement from one job to another within an agency. Interagency mobility refers to movement from one agency or department to another within the same governmental level.

The third type of mobility, interorganizational, includes movements between different levels of government and between government and private corporations. Mobility between the public and private sectors is often associated with corporate interests in obtaining government contracts. Interorganizational and interagency mobility have been the center of continuous controversy. Some personnel systems are structured to discourage or even prohibit these forms of mobility, requiring that a person enter at a low-level position to be eligible for higher positions. These restrictions are said to encourage career-development and to guarantee that supervisors and managers are fully aware of operations at lower echelons. Because the federal government makes both career and noncareer appointments, particularly at the top levels, the term "career" in this context refers to the method of appointment, not to length of government service.

The fourth type of mobility is geographic. This form of mobility often occurs in association with another type of mobility, as when workers change employers or make intra- and interagency position changes. About half of all federal supergrade personnel (i.e., employees who have reached top levels in their designated job classification or career ladder) have at least once in their careers moved from one region to another.

Occupational job changes are the fifth type of mobility. These types of changes are likely to occur early in one's professional development, usually within the first ten years.

Because employees in this stage of their career development are at lower levels in their career ladder, position classification and qualifications standards greatly limit occupational mobility opportunities. Perhaps the most common type of occupational change is into administration.

Social-class mobility is the sixth form of mobility. Government employment has been an important route for persons to move from the working class to the middle class. Historically, the blue-collar workers in the United States in farm- or factory-related jobs in one generation became the white-collar workers in a government bureaucracy in the next generation. By the 1950s and 1960s, social-class mobility took place within the same generation and the move to government employment and subsequent career development was enhanced by increased formal education. At some point in one's career, promotions cease. Promotions are awarded to productive workers who are expected to be equally productive in positions of greater responsibility. Eventually a person is promoted to a position for which he or she is not well qualified, and further promotions are not forthcoming.

Organizational Improvement

Enabling and encouraging individual employees to set and achieve personal career goals are often consistent with improving an organization. Career development in the context of overall organizational improvement involves effective advancement through career stages along career paths. Career development usually involves career ladders for designated occupations or job classifications. In the case of the federal government, agencies usually employ various methods of training, education, and staff development to provide employees the opportunity to upgrade their skills to qualify for and/or compete for advanced sequential positions in the career ladder. The agency's use of career planning in advancing opportunities for each employee's mobility may also involve crossing from a position classification in a career ladder where opportunities for advancement are limited to another classification or ladder with more potential for upward movement. However, crossovers are rarely made in unrelated fields. Employees usually move to a job that can be done well almost immediately and that is part of a career ladder that the employee, with appropriate training and experience, would like to add or pursue.

At the end of a career is retirement, a subject that is attracting increasing attention. One concern is that employees are not psychologically prepared for retirement, which typically constitutes an abrupt change in lifestyle.

Employees engaging in career planning are, naturally, concerned about whether there will be positions available if they participate in a training program and/or switch from one career ladder to another. Employers who work with their employees in career counseling and development also have a concern. Both public and private employers recognize a risk in investing in an employee's growth and development only to see that employee leave and work for someone else. A policy issue that employers face is whether to limit their support of employee development to the jobs that their employees are currently performing or to allow for and support development that is more directly related to a career, rather than a job.

Over the past five to ten years and into the future, this policy issue has and will become even more critical with budget reductions and demands for reducing the size of government influence over career-development programs for employees in the public and private sectors. Career development for individual employees is closely linked to training activities.

Training

Training is an integral part of any organization's career development program. Prior to 1990, general skills training was only one of the main areas of training programs. Advanced basic skills training was and continues to be an important training area, especially as it pertains to career ladder positions. Training that focuses on management development and employee enrichment has been and still is important in career development. However, in the 1990s, general skills training is the type of training most often employed by chief administrative officers and most subject to massive organizational initiatives. If the public sector follows a pattern similar to the private sector, this trend will increase for the next five to ten years.

The most popular form of general skills training is Total Quality Management (TQM) training. Typically, many types of general skills training are integrated into the TQM programs.

Three major training areas can be identified in TQM programs. The first is introductory training programs, typically ranging from one to three days. Executive teams may participate in such training to decide how to design the overall quality infrastructure. Management teams may use the training to decide on what pilot programs to launch. Frontline employees may learn in the training that their role to innovate and cooperate in new ways will mean a redefinition of their jobs. Successful organizations usually target all employees for introductory training.

The second area is a major emphasis on "team technology," which combines the team concept with the need to meet the new challenges of technology. In a traditional authority hierarchy, ideas and decisions tend to flow through the organization from the top downward. TQM tries to reverse that tendency and to facilitate the flow of ideas and decisions upward from the workers directly involved in the work processes. Yet, to be successful, the

team technology of quality improvement must be studied, practiced, and improved like any other process. Outside facilitators are initially critical in assisting with the teaching of empowered team techniques and the shifting of the corporate culture. Implementing a quality infrastructure and instilling a corporate culture of empowered employees may take two to five years. This type of training will usually include special training for team leaders with senior executives and quality management process consultants.

The third area of quality training usually involves quality-control management and process-analysis methods. Examples of typical quality-control management methods that are studied include Pareto charts, checklists, statistical process-control techniques, various types of flowcharts, and nominal group techniques. Process-analysis techniques tend to consider the actual flow of the work from one worker and division to another. Workshops about process analysis and its tools vary in length from one to five days, with three or four days being the average for such a program. Typically, these programs are open to most or all employees. Large organizations with a mature TQM program may even have an advanced seminar in process-analysis tools.

By 1994, national leaders in public sector TQM training included almost all major federal executive agencies; the states of Arkansas, Colorado, and New York; the city of Madison, Wisconsin; Maricopa County, Arizona; and hundreds of other public sector agencies at the city, county, and municipal level that are just beginning serious TQM training initiatives.

ROSS PRIZZIA

BIBLIOGRAPHY

Dresang, Dennis L, ed., 1991. *Public Personnel Management and Public Policy,* 2nd ed. New York: Longman.
Lee, Robert D., Jr., 1993. *Public Personnel Systems.* Baltimore, MD: University Park Press.
Little, Danity M., 1991. "Shattering the Glass Ceiling." *Bureaucrat,* vol. 20 (Fall) 24–28.
Shafritz, Jay M., Albert C. Hyde, and David H. Rosenbloom, eds., 1986. *Personnel Management in Government—Politics and Process,* 3rd ed. New York: Marcel Dekker.
Tucker, Robert and Milan Moravec, 1992. "Do-It-Yourself Career Development." *Training* (February) 48–52.
———, 1993. *Handbook of Training and Development for the Public Sector.* San Francisco, CA: Jossey-Bass.

CAREER LADDER.

The sequential progression of jobs through which employees advance as they gain experience and seniority. Career ladders are often referred to as "career paths," indicating that they represent a route map for an employee's journey up the organizational hierarchy. As such, they perform a number of important functions within the staffing system.

For the individual worker, a clearly defined career path specifies promotion options and thus reduces some of the uncertainty and anxiety that often exist inside large and impersonal organizations. Because of this link to promotion and advancement, they are a critical component of motivation. One's progress up the career ladder represents a tangible measure of the person's worth to the organization; the mere fact that the next step in the ladder is perceived to be within reach may be sufficient to spur many workers to greater effort. However, should the path be blocked by real or imagined obstacles (favoritism or insufficient promotional opportunities, for example), then the task of motivating the worker becomes far more problematic.

For the organization's decisionmakers, career ladders provide critical information that informs many activities. Staffing specialists, for example, use them when articulating qualification standards for recruitment and selection. According to the conventional wisdom of personnel management, some entry requirements (educational level, most especially) should be set on the basis of the last (highest) job that a worker is likely to attain, not the first (entry level). Career ladders also make a significant contribution to the organization's planning activities, since they permit managers to forecast future personnel needs so that recruitment, selection, and training efforts can be adjusted accordingly. By studying the traits and abilities of the workers within any particular career ladder, managers gain insights that can aid such decisions as who has the greatest promotional potential; what types of training and experience will be required to assist the workers in reaching their full career potential; what skills are lacking, and how can the organization best remedy that deficit? In effect, then, career ladders are one of the essential building blocks of an organization's human resources system.

Historical Background

Contemporary approaches to career ladder design probably originated with the writings of Max Weber (1864–1920), the German sociologist who advanced the notion of an "ideal type" bureaucracy. In explaining why bureaucracy is the most efficient form of social organization, Weber emphasized the advantages of specialization, division of labor, a hierarchy of authority, recruitment and selection on the basis of merit, and jobs that constitute careers (i.e., workers are hired on the basis of their expertise and with an expectation of continuous employment as long as they perform up to a certain standard). These various components were used by Frederick Taylor (1856–1915) in the early 1900s to devise "scientific management," an effort to create a systematic theory of management based on the premise that there is "one best way" to accomplish any administrative task.

To Taylor, most characteristics that Weber identified converged in the concept of "position classification." In order to impose order and control on the organization, Taylor was intent upon classifying jobs into distinct groups on the basis of their characteristics and level of responsibility. Because salaries were tied to job classifications, this allowed the organization to ensure (theoretically, at least) the goal of "equal pay for equal work." Other advantages included a uniform job terminology, clearly delineated duties, and a hierarchy of positions that together constitute a career. In other words, the imposition of a position-classification scheme instantly created career ladders for the organization's employees. Workers were to be recruited on the assumption that they would remain in the organization indefinitely and that they would refine their skills over time. Thus, job classifications and career ladders are inextricably linked.

The public sector quickly embraced job classification as the basic raw material of personnel management. Beginning with the Classification Act of 1923, the U.S. civil service used formal job classifications as the basis for almost all personnel activities. Similar actions took place throughout most public jurisdictions for the same reasons that they were so attractive to the federal government: A personnel system based on "scientific" classifications gives managers a very high level of control over the staffing function. It also promotes expertise, which at the time was perceived as the best antidote to political manipulation of the civil service.

In regard to career ladders, the attraction should be evident. Job classes permit the grouping of positions for which the duties and qualifications are sufficiently alike to justify the same treatment with respect to pay, selection, and other personnel processes. "This contributes to efficient and cost effective management by reducing the number of categories for which it is necessary to separately recruit, examine, certify, train, and establish pay levels" (U.S. Office of Personnel Management, 1979, pp. 3–5). All the organization needs to do in order to create a career system is to assemble the various classifications into "class series." By stacking the classes on top of one another according to the experience and skill levels required to perform adequately, the system designers delineated the normal lines of promotion within an occupational field. In general, the hierarchy usually begins with one or more entry level classes, followed by the "experienced" levels (also called "journeyman"), the "advanced" level (also called "expert"), and ultimately the supervisory and/or administrative level.

This approach to career system management remains dominant today. The linkage of job classifications, pay grades, and career ladders—a career system termed "rank-in-job"—is a pervasive phenomenon in public personnel systems. Yet, despite their predominance, a relatively recent development indicates that public sector career systems may gradually be transformed. With the adoption of the Civil Service Reform Act of 1978, a more flexible style of career ladder was introduced to the highest reaches of the classified federal service. Workers in the Senior Executive Service (SES) are not confined to one explicit career track, but are eligible to compete for promotions with everyone else in the service. They constitute a pool of high-level executives who can be reassigned according to their talents and interests. If the system—known as "rank-in-person"—is working well (a debatable point, at best), then an employee's career track might involve any number of job assignments (and promotional opportunities) in different functional, programmatic, or even technical areas. This format is difficult to manage in that it requires much more effective selection and evaluation strategies than are ordinarily present in rank-in-job systems. Despite this fact, rank-in-person career ladders have proliferated in recent years and are likely to spread further as public managers gain experience with their operation and maintenance.

Types of Career Ladders

In addition to the rank-in-job/rank-in-person distinction, several other forms of career ladders exist in government and industry. The narrowest and most inflexible is the "functional" career path, in which the employee moves up the hierarchy within a single job specialty. Also called the "traditional" career ladder, it is most often found in clerical and technical fields. For example, engineers may start their careers as draftsmen, move through various grades (Engineer I, II, III, Master Engineer), and ultimately become an engineering supervisor or manager. The assumption in this arrangement is that each preceding job is essential preparation for the next higher level. Except in highly unusual circumstances, all engineers are expected to ascend the hierarchy step by step, without skipping any levels.

Obviously, the functional career ladder is highly effective at fostering skill acquisition and specialization. Its major disadvantage is that workers ascending a very narrow career ladder seldom accrue a broad understanding of the organization's total operation. As a consequence, they may be susceptible to "occupational myopia," a condition that impedes their ability to understand the perspectives of workers in different specialties.

Organizations that wish to give their workers a broader perspective often implement "network," or "cross-functional," career ladders. Under this approach, employees are allowed (or required) to move across functional departments; thus, their career paths contain both horizontal and vertical mobility. By gaining experience in a variety of different departments, the workers gain an appreciation for many specialties. The broader perspective that results from

this form of job rotation more accurately reflects the interdependence that prevails in modern organizations.

This technique is thought to be more conducive to employee development objectives, and some researchers argue that it enhances worker motivation due to the challenge and variety of the work performed. Moreover, cross-functional training produces workers who generally have a wider array of promotional opportunities than those groomed in a functional career ladder. The chief disadvantage is that employees may not become truly expert at any of the specialties ("jack of all trades, master of none"). Relatedly, network career paths are not as predictable as the traditional approach. The promotional path has more detours and potential dead ends, which can cause many workers a considerable degree of anxiety.

Employees who enter the workforce with advanced degrees often follow a career path that is neither functional nor cross-functional. The recipient of a Master of Public Administration degree (MPA), for instance, may enter the workforce as an assistant city manager. Future job movement may lead to a department head position in a larger city, elevation to the city manager's office, or perhaps to a line position in a state agency. This type of professional progression is known as a "radial" career path. The employee starts in a relatively high position with duties that may resemble an apprenticeship and then gradually accrues increased responsibility as knowledge and experience are gained. Employees who follow this type of career track usually develop a wide array of generalist skills that are applicable to high-level settings. The approach does not give a good perspective on how the bottom of the organization functions, and it may discourage the development of specialized knowledge.

A completely different approach to managing promotional opportunities is found in the "dual career ladder." This strategy was originally developed to accommodate technical and professional workers who need to be motivated and rewarded, yet who have no desire to move into managerial positions. In effect, two parallel hierarchies are established. One provides a managerial career path, whereas the other permits staff to progress hierarchically without having to assume administrative responsibilities. Scientists, computer specialists, and many categories of technical workers can thus receive increments of rank and salary that reflect their professional accomplishments. This helps the organization to retain their services and encourages the workers to remain up-to-date in their fields.

Although dual career ladders are very popular in both government and industry, they are not regarded as being especially successful at providing equitable rewards for workers in the two separate tracks. Pay and perquisites for the managerial track tend to exceed those of the technical workers. Advancement up the managerial career ladder also leads to positions of power and influence, whereas the knowledge workers' primary reward for career advancement is increased autonomy to practice their specialties. This is often an adequate trade-off for many professional and technical employees, but some become discouraged by their relative lack of organizational influence. Moreover, problems often result when the technical ladder is used as a dumping ground for displaced managerial personnel.

Problems with Public Sector Career Ladders

In recent years, the public management literature has devoted considerable space to the fact that career ladders in government are losing their appeal to prospective workers. Simply stated, job mobility and career advancement opportunities have become progressively more scarce. This phenomenon—termed the "career plateau"—is attributable to diminished job growth in the public sector, along with the demographics of the public labor force. A huge number of well-educated and ambitious "baby boomers" are locked in career tracks that do not offer much chance for promotion because of government's slow rate of growth (or even decline).

In 1990, for instance, there were 13 workers in competition for each high-level executive grade position in the federal government. Because most of these workers are reaching the plateau at an earlier age—the average age is now 42, down from 47 since 1980—most have little hope of making substantial progress up the career ladder. Similar situations prevail in other governmental jurisdictions, with the possible exception of those in prosperous or high-growth locations. As a consequence, public agencies everywhere are faced with attrition and attraction problems. In its lengthy discussion of this dilemma, the Volcker Commission (1990) listed compressed career ladders as a major impediment to the recruitment of college graduates to the public service. Study commissions in a number of states have issued identical warnings.

A closely related problem arises from the somewhat surprising fact that government career ladders are often quite short. Unless one is employed in a very large agency or one that goes to extraordinary efforts to provide cross-functional mobility, the number of potential promotions for most workers is severely limited. This problem is partly attributable to relatively flat organizational structures (a fact that should surprise many citizens), as well as the recent barrage of budget cuts. Because a single promotion tends to create several additional opportunities within the same career ladder, the elimination of any position exerts a negative multiplier effect on all potential career opportunities. Moreover, the highest level jobs are often reserved for political appointees, thus placing additional limitations on the public sector career ladder.

In addition to these specific dilemmas, a few generic factors complicate career management in government. Af-

firmative action and equal employment opportunity issues are highly relevant, especially considering the paucity of promotional opportunities. Tensions arising from social equity considerations are likely to heighten as increasing number of women and minorities compete for a diminishing choice of steps on the career ladder.

The fact that government operates relatively open career systems further increases occupational competition. Public sector personnel systems have long permitted and even encouraged lateral entry, the process by which employees can enter a career ladder at any level (as opposed to starting at the bottom and working one's way up). This is regarded as being a healthy recruitment practice, since it introduces "new blood" into the organization. Yet, workers who see an outsider hired into a position above them can become demoralized as their promotional opportunities decline.

These various factors indicate that the management of public sector career ladders will be a troublesome concern for many years to come. Declining promotional opportunities, compressed career ladders, and increased competition for the remaining slots will challenge public managers to develop creative ways to motivate and reward their employees. At a minimum, public agencies will need to devote more attention to alternative career paths, such as the cross-functional and dual approaches. Likewise, increased resources will certainly need to be invested in career-planning resources, so that civil servants will be better equipped to deal with the realities of the contemporary workplace.

STEVEN W. HAYS

BIBLIOGRAPHY

Feldman, Daniel C., 1988. *Managing Careers in Organizations.* Glenview, IL: Scott, Foresman.

Hall, D., 1976. *Careers in Organizations.* Santa Monica, CA: Goodyear.

Hays, Steven and Richard C. Kearney, 1995. "Promotion of Personnel—Career Advancement." In Jack Rabin, Thomas Vocino, W. Bartley Hildreth, and Gerald Miller, eds., *Handbook of Public Personnel Administration.* New York: Marcel Dekker, pp. 499–529.

Pergl, G., 1990. "Plateau Prevention." *Government Executive* (January) 40–43.

Schein, Edgar H., 1971. "The Individual, the Organization, and the Career: A Conceptual Scheme." *Journal of Applied Behavioral Science,* vol. 7 (Fall) 415–426.

U.S. General Accounting Office, 1990. *Recruitment and Retention in Government Employment.* Washington, D.C.: Comptroller General.

U.S. Merit Systems Protection Board, 1987. *Federal Personnel Policies and Practices: Perspectives from the Workplace.* Washington, D.C.: U.S. Government Printing Office.

U.S. Office of Personnel Management, 1979. *Position Classification: A Guide for City and County Managers.* Washington, D.C.: U.S. Government Printing Office.

Volcker Commission, 1990. *Leadership for America: Rebuilding the Public Service.* Lexington, MA: D. C. Heath.

Wolf, J., 1983. "Career Plateauing in the Public Service: Baby Boom and Employment Bust." *Public Administration Review,* vol. 41 (March–April) 160–165.

"Worldwide Executive Mobility," 1988. *Harvard Business Review,* vol. 66 (July–August) 105–123.

CASE STATEMENT. A document representing the rationale for supporting an organization or a fund-raising campaign for an organization.

According to the *Fund-Raising Dictionary* (p. 28), a publication of the National Society of Fund Raising Executives (NSFRE), a case statement is "a carefully prepared document that sets forth, in detail, the reasons why an organization needs–and merits–financial support. In the context that the 'case' is bigger than the institution, it documents its services, human resources, its potential for greater services, current needs and future plans."

Harold J. Seymour, author of *Designs for Fund-Raising* (1966, p. 33), a seminal work in development whose principles have been devoutly followed for nearly a half-century by practitioners, defines the case statement as "the one, definitive piece of the whole campaign. It tells all that needs to be told, answers all the important questions, reviews the arguments for support, explains the proposed plan for raising the money, and shows how gifts may be made and who the people are who vouch for the project and will give it leadership and direction."

George A. Brakely, Jr., in his *Tested Ways to Successful Fund Raising* (p. 14), talks about the case for support and its need to meet two criteria. "First, it should be 'bigger' than the institution; that is, it must relate the activities and needs . . . to larger social endeavors and issues. . . . Second, it is related to goals that are demonstrably valid, . . . presented with adequate documentation of their feasibility and efficacy, are urgent and . . . unique."

Current practice in development would indicate that what constitutes a case statement for a nonprofit can encompass anything and everything. A case statement may represent the ultimate reference piece for an organization–the place where staff and volunteer alike can seek answers to virtually any question relating to the organization. Some organizations refer to the campaign brochure as their case statement, because it provides the framework for the campaign or project for which funds are currently being sought.

The handout (#9) accompanying materials for the fund-raising "First Course" of NSFRE provides the following guidelines:

Format:
a. *Be brief:* A case statement should be no more than 2–3 pages for some markets; it may be up to 10–15 pages for others.

b. *Demonstrate success:* People give to successful organizations; want to be a part of that success.

c. *Be targeted to motivations of that market:* Different markets and market segments have different motivations for giving. You must know those motivations, through research.

d. *Describe how the contributor's investment will solve a specific problem:* Concentrate on the problem or problems that are of concern to the market. If yours is a multipurpose institution, do not attempt to address all of your programs in the case statement.

e. *Be compelling:* The purpose of your case statement is to persuade the prospective contributor to action in the form of a monetary gift.

Information:
a. *The organization's mission stated in one to two sentences:* The mission should be woven into all case statements; its slogan, if any, should also be used.

b. *History and track record:* Include a brief history of the organization, its track record, and why it should be entrusted to solve the problem presented.

c. *Goals, strategies, and specific objectives:* Detail major organizational goals and strategies and specific objectives related to each goal.

d. *Organizational resources:* State the resources the organization has at its disposal to levy against the stated problem–such as facilities, staff and other professional resources, and volunteers.

e. *Accountability:* Provide evidence of management competency and financial accountability, including most recent audited financial statements.

f. *Problems to be addressed:* Include a factual description of the problems the organization will address and the population to be served.

g. *Trends affecting the problem:* Describe demographic, social-economic, and other environmental trends.

h. *Future organizational plans:* Address relevant long-range goals of the organization to provide greater services to further deal with the problem.

Case statements, including recent award-winning and gift-getting examples, have contained other elements not cited above. These include "named gift opportunities," how to make gifts in tax-advantaged ways, stories about people who are helped, the articulated dreams of those involved, and challenges to be matched by other donors.

In essence, the case statement is what the nonprofit needs it to be to serve its purpose in addressing the audience that will be reading and using it. At the heart of it, the case statement is the printed message the organization wants the reader to receive most.

ROBERT W. BUCHANAN AND WILLIAM BERGOSH

BIBLIOGRAPHY

Brakely, George A. Jr., 1981. *Tested Ways to Successful Fund Raising*. Public Service Materials Center.

Levy, Barbara R., and R.L. Cherry, 1996. *NSFRE Fund-Raising Dictionary*. New York: Wiley.

Seymour, H. J., 1966. *Designs for Fund-Raising*. Rockville, MD: Taft Group.

CASE STUDY. A form of empirical inquiry that focuses upon a single, bounded social event within its holistic context. A case study researcher may use multiple data-gathering techniques, both qualitative and quantitative, to capture the event within its context, and the researcher may use the case study to describe phenomenon, test hypotheses, and create theory. The case study may also be used as a simulation tool for management instruction (Windsor and Greanias, 1983).

There are many types, and even different typologies, of case studies (Yin, 1994), yet they all tend to pivot on the degree of "complexity and duration" of the case analysis (Mitchell, 1983, p. 195). Indeed, a case study is typically constrained by both "structural (level of group), and historical (period of time) boundaries" (Stoecker, 1991, p. 98). In addition, the case study is particularly useful when the theoretical distance between the variable and the context of the variable cannot be unambiguously discerned (Yin, 1981). Consequently, because of the case study's emphasis upon contextual interpretation, it offers unique opportunities for the empirical examination of organizations (Stake, 1995; Sjoberg et al., 1991).

The case study is a frequently used (McCurdy and Cleary, 1984; Perry and Kraemer, 1986), though oft maligned (White, 1985; Bailey, 1992), form of empirical inquiry in public administration. Many of the most important theoretical insights we have in public administration have been developed through case study analysis, including administrative power (Caro, 1974), organizations (Kaufman, 1960), decisionmaking (Allison, 1971), agenda-setting (Kingdon, 1995), and implementation (Pressman and Wildavsky, 1984).

History

The case study predates most contemporary, particularly inferential, forms of empirical inquiry, and its roots lie in antiquity. At least one scholar attributes Thucydides' *History of the Peloponnesian War* as a form of systematic inquiry and considers it one of the first case studies (Fielding, 1993, p. 155). The case study would later become a tool for policy development during the period of British colonial rule, particularly during the late nineteenth century (Fielding, 1993.)

Still, the contemporary notion of the case study, even the term "case study," is derived from the fields of medicine and psychological research (Becker, 1970, p. 75). Indeed, much of the basis for modern psychoanalysis stems from Freud's, and his colleagues, case study research (Orum, Feagin, and Sjoberg, 1991, p. 6). Case-study analysis has been adopted by most social scientists including those in the fields of anthropology (particularly ethnography), sociology, and political science. The case study is also used extensively in basic and applied educational research. In addition, case-study analysis is used in the humanities by both literary critics (Stake, 1995) and historians (Runyan, 1988). Although the number of case studies conducted each year remains quite high, the case study has diminished in its importance as a form of empirical inquiry.

There are a number of reasons for the decline in approbation of the case study; some relate to concerns of methodology and practicality, discussed below, others relate to both the demand for case-study research and the increased availability of quantitative data. Case studies are typically written in a narrative style with an emphasis on detail and context, thus the findings of case studies may be difficult for researchers to communicate and for readers to fully comprehend (Yin, 1981, p. 64). Moreover, as the availability and accessibility of computers and computer software, coupled with advances in probability sampling, increased, the ability to do large sample size quantitative analysis using mathematical models increased (Mitchell, 1983). In addition, federal, state, and local governmental agencies, several prominent universities, and nonprofit organizations have aggressively expanded their data collection activities through censuses and surveys creating readily available quantitative data sets (Sjoberg et al., 1991). Consequently, researchers now have at their disposal both the tools, computers and software, and the raw material, packaged data sets, to conduct, more easily than ever before, quantitative research culminating with results that are easier to communicate and understand. By contrast, computer technology, particularly advances in software development that could support case study research, has lagged (Richards and Richards, 1994). The slower development of computer applications for case study research can be explained in part by the multiplicity of observational techniques involved in case study research and, most important, the case study's reliance on qualitative methods.

Observational Techniques

The case study is unique in that it is a form of empirical examination that can, and often does, employ multiple observational techniques (Trow, 1970; Yin, 1981, 1994; Lofland

and Lofland, 1995; Stake, 1995). Often a researcher will use multiple observational techniques to minimize threats to validity (Stake, 1995). I briefly describe a few of the techniques used in case study research; I categorize them as either qualitative or quantitative.

Qualitative

There are two basic forms of qualitative empirical techniques available: interviewing and participant observation.

Interviewing. Interviewing is a method of data collection. There are two basic types of interviewing techniques: structured and unstructured. The structured interview requires the researcher to ask a series of preconstructed questions and to record the responses. In many cases, the structured interview is similar in design and application to the survey questionnaire. To the extent that the structured interview resembles a survey questionnaire, it is a relatively easy form of data collection. By contrast, the unstructured interview is a deceptively simple form of data collection.

The unstructured interview is described as unstructured because it embodies a symmetrical communication between a researcher and an informant. The unstructured interview does not, however, imply a lack of methodological rigor. For the unstructured interview, the researcher carefully determines the area to be discussed with the informant (Lofland and Lofland, 1995). The researcher may even have a series of opening questions for these areas, yet it will be during the interview process that the researcher will attempt to understand the context and meaning of descriptive, conceptual, and theoretical issues pertaining to the area being examined.

There is controversy regarding whether a tape recorder should be used during an interview. Lofland and Lofland (1995) insist one should attempt to use the device to maximize data-gathering and minimize omission, yet Stake (1995) suggests one avoid using the device and instead rely on note-taking and immediate write-ups of the interview. Still, both agree the researcher should write up the results of the interview within a few hours of completion so as to retain as much of the data as possible.

Participant Observation. Participant observation is a form of data-gathering in which the researcher attempts to become associated with the event or phenomenon being studied. At one time, participant observation was so closely identified with case-study research that the two were considered synonymous (Becker, 1970). Indeed, Becker and Geer (1970) argue that participant observation is superior to merely utilizing unstructured interviewing. Many argue, however, that participant observation is merely one of many potential data-gathering techniques used in case studies (Trow, 1970; Yin, 1981, 1994; Lofland and Lofland, 1995; Stake, 1995).

The chief attribute of participant observation is the immersion of the researcher within the contextual environment of the phenomenon under investigation for a long period of time. The researcher may adopt one of two broad research roles: covert investigator or overt investigator (Lofland and Lofland, 1995). The distinction between the two roles is the degree to which the researcher's objective of investigation is disclosed to those being studied. The covert investigator adopts an inconspicuous identity; the overt investigator reveals the research and thus his or her identity. Lofland and Lofland insist the covert research role involves serious and far-reaching ethical issues, yet the overt role, though not devoid of ethical issues, involves strategic issues of research design (1995, pp. 33–37).

Data-gathering is done primarily through observation and interviewing and recording the observations in field notes. Field notes constitute the major source of raw data in participant observation. As with the interview, researchers are advised to keep detailed and accurate records of their field notes, and they are advised to record them, formally, as narratives of their observations. This is a time-consuming and laborious task, yet recent advents in computer technology, most notably software developments, have eased the analysis of qualitative data (Richards and Richards, 1994; Lofland and Lofland, 1995).

Quantitative Methodologies

Quantitative methodologies involve the enumeration of social phenomena and theoretical concepts to facilitate mathematical manipulation. This manipulation involves two basic forms of quantitative statistics: descriptive and inferential.

Descriptive Statistics. By far the most frequently used statistical form in the case study is the descriptive statistic. Descriptive statistics are used by researchers to illustrate, describe, and compare. The most commonly used form of descriptive statistics are frequencies, proportions, measures of central tendency, and measures of dispersion. Descriptive statistics may be employed for as many uses as there are case studies. For instance, Pressman and Wildavsky counted the number of decision points, a frequency, to illustrate the difficulty associated with inter- and intra-agency cooperation (1984, pp. 87–124).

Inferential Statistics. Inferential statistics are based on the notions of probability sampling and are used to generalize from a sample to a population using tests of statistical significance and measures of association (Knoke and Bohrnstedt, 1994, p. 22). Though much less frequently used, inferential statistics can be a powerful tool to illustrate and test propositions within case-study research. For instance, Schumaker (1991) effectively used inferential statistics in his case study examination of the urban power structure of Lawrence, Kansas.

Qualitative and Quantitative

Many case studies use both qualitative and quantitative statistics. Indeed, Becker advocates the use of field-note statistics in participant observation research (1970, p. 81). That is, enumerating observations drawn from field notes and analyzing the observations to demonstrate the frequency of a phenomenon. Moreover, most of the research noted above employs both quantitative and qualitative methods to illustrate, support, and embellish the ideas of theories embodied in each.

Critiques of the Case Method

Prior to World War II, the case study was the dominant form of empirical analysis. During the postwar era, however, many challenged the legitimacy of case studies as a form of empirical analysis. The objections can be classified into two broad categories: methodological and practical.

Methodological

Methodology is a form of epistemology (Babbie, 1983, p. 6), and epistemology is the branch of philosophy regarding the origin and nature of knowledge. One challenge of the case study has been its legitimacy as a source of scientific knowledge. Some consider the methodology of case studies different from that of the natural science method associated with experimental and quasi-experimental research (Sjoberg et al., 1991; Stake, 1995; Bailey, 1992), and much of the criticism of case studies is a criticism of the nature of its methodology.

The natural scientific approach is based on the logico-deductive framework of empirical positivism based in nomothetic research (Gilgun, 1994; Sjoberg et al., 1991; Stake, 1995). That is to say, the natural scientific approach is grounded in a methodology that minimizes the number of variables, separates the variables from their contextual environment, and uses mathematical procedures to attempt falsification of theoretically deduced propositions. By contrast, many case studies adhere to the tradition of hermeneutics (Smith, 1993; White, 1986) or the expansion of knowledge through explanation and interpretation (Habermas, 1971).

One of the most important distinctions between the two approaches is the interpretative role of the researcher. Proponents of the natural science method recognize that subjective factors enter into a researcher's decision calculus of topic and method, yet they reject the notion of subjective interpretation. Advocates of case studies do not reject the need for objective interpretation, yet they vigorously challenge the positivist notion that interpretation can be objective, particularly with a social phenomenon (Habermas, 1971). Moreover, some argue that case study researchers, particularly those using qualitative methodologies involving "thick description" (Geertz, 1994, p. 213), should strive to form empathy between the reader and the subject under investigation (Stake, 1995, p. 39). Indeed, it is the interpretative role of the researcher that often raises concerns of validation and replication.

Validation and Replication. Though the usage of the case study is widespread, it has been referred to as an "attractive nuisance" (Miles, 1979, p. 590). Campbell and Stanley leveled perhaps the gravest criticism claiming that case studies "have such a total absence of control to be of almost no scientific value" (cited in Campbell, 1975, p. 179). Though Campbell would later modify his position regarding the case study (1975), his and Stanley's initial reaction reflected a widespread belief of the general inferiority of the case study as a form of scientific inquiry.

Methodological critiques of case studies center around their idiographic design. That is, the case study is, typically, based on one observation point consisting of many variables. The critics charge that case studies are prone to difficulty in validation and replication of analysis.

There are two types of validation: internal validity and external validity. Internal validity is the ability of a researcher to make claims that an independent variable has a nonspurious, covarying influence upon a dependent variable. With experimental and quasi-experimental designs, researchers are able to determine nonspurious covariation through the use of careful design controls and/or statistical manipulation. External validity allows a researcher to generalize the results of an analysis to a larger population. Again, researchers using experimental or quasi-experimental designs attempt to do this using multiple observation points (e.g., individuals, organization, cities, nation-states) and through appropriate random sampling techniques.

Replication, in its simplest form, is the ability to reproduce the results of an experiment. In experimental and quasi-experimental research designs, the researcher carefully documents the study's procedures so that a separate and independent researcher can attempt to reproduce the original results. The reasoning behind the notion of replication is that it acts as a check on deceptive or slipshod scientific inquiry. Moreover, replication can lead to greater reliability of measurements and further the acquisition of knowledge.

The most frequent and specific critique of case studies is that they are vulnerable to researcher bias. Because the case study often involves interpreting data to fit conceptual models from, typically, one observation, the researcher may interject subjective interpretation upon the analysis, thus threatening both the validity and replicability of the study (Miles, 1979). There have been a number of recommendations to minimize the threats to internal and external validity, and to increase the replicability of case studies.

In regard to internal validity, a number of scholars suggest triangulation whereby the researcher attempts to find two or three different methods to substantiate findings (Stake, 1995, pp. 107–116). Campbell (1975) suggests still another method whereby the researcher matches case observations to important theoretical relationships. McClintock, Brannon, and Maynard-Moody (1979) advocate clustering cases whereby the researcher attempts to define the unit of analysis into discrete clusters thus increasing the number of observations. Finally, many scholars propose either the comparative case method or the case survey method as strategies to increase internal validity of case analysis (Stoecker, 1991; Yin, 1981, 1994).

External validity, the generalizability of a case study, is much more problematic. To a modest extent, the case survey method (Yin and Heald, 1975) and the case comparison method (Yin, 1994) increase the external validity by increasing the number of observation points from one. Still, Stake suggests generalizations differ and may be categorized by their scope and specificity (1995, p. 7). In addition, Yin points out that some case-study critics, and those conducting case-study analysis, should not confuse probabilistic inferences, or generalizations, made from a sample to a population with inferences from analysis to theory (1994, pp. 30–32).

Stoecker argues, however, that when the generalizability of case studies is challenged, proponents of case studies resort to challenging the generalizability of experimental and quasi-experimental research (1991, p. 93). Stake notes that the singular and qualitative nature of case studies are worthwhile and defining characteristics (1995, pp. 7–8). Yin echoes the point when he suggests that the use of case studies should be recognized as a distinct approach, comparable with experiments, to conducting empirical research (1994, pp. 18–19).

One of the chief issues involved with the external validity of case studies is whether what one studies is typical or atypical. Should case studies be conducted upon phenomena that are presumed to be typical or ordinary? For instance, case studies have the potential to uncover the nuance and intricacies embedded in the explained and unexplained variance of statistical analysis. Or should case studies focus on the atypical, the outlier, the exception? Case studies also have the ability to examine those instances that are outside the norm and reveal information that might otherwise be overlooked, even dismissed, in some natural science models of inquiry. There is no clear answer to these questions, yet they are instructive regarding the purposes case studies serve.

Still, Cronbach (1975) admonishes researchers to take care regarding the generalizations they make. He notes that most generalizations are time bound. Moreover, Cronbach notes that the more open and permeable the social phenomenon under examination is, the greater its contextual complexity, the shorter the duration and accuracy the researcher's generalizations will be (1975, p. 123).

Replication, the ability to repeat an analysis and duplicate its findings, is also possible with case studies. If one believes that symbol and meaning vary by individual experience, however, then replication is impossible. This is further confounded by the fact that case studies are intertwined with time and context. People, relationships, and places all change over time; this makes case study replication devilishly difficult. Still, Becker (1970) argues replication can succeed but only if the replicating researcher follows exactly the procedures of the original researcher. The dilemma is that too many case study researchers do methodologically careless research, poorly documenting time, place, and the context of data (Orum, Feagin, and Sjoberg, 1991). Yin addresses this by suggesting that case study researchers carefully develop research strategies that provide detailed documentation and storage of case study materials (1982, 1994).

Practical

Case study research, particularly comparative case study research, is a resource-intensive form of empirical inquiry. Case studies often take much more time than experimental or quasi-experimental research designs, particularly the cross-sectional research design. Indeed, the very definition of the case study, particularly case studies using participant observation, imply long-term devotion to the subject under analysis. Moreover, it takes more time to compile and interpret data. Becker suggests that researchers should use a method of examination in which analysis is an ongoing process throughout the research project (1970, p. 79) and, as noted above, increasing developments in computer software are easing the laborious tasks of sifting through qualitative data (Richards and Richards, 1994; Stake, 1995). Still, too frequently case-study researchers find themselves with insufficient financial resources to pay for trained and qualified staff. Because of these constraints, at least one set of authors argues that case-study research becomes a labor of love (Lofland and Lofland, 1995). That is to say, the researcher has an intense interest in the subject, and the researcher believes the research results can provide important theoretical contributions to scientific knowledge and of the human experience.

DAVID R. ELKINS

BIBLIOGRAPHY

Allison, Graham T., 1971. *The Essence of Decision: Explaining the Cuban Missile Crisis.* Boston, MA: Little, Brown.
Babbie, Earl, 1983. *The Practice of Social Research.* Belmont, CA: Wadsworth.
Bailey, Mary Timney, 1992. "Do Physicists Use Case Studies? Thoughts on Public Administration Research." *Public Administration Review,* vol. 52 (January/February) 47–54.
Becker, Howard S., 1970. *Sociological Work: Method and Substance.* Chicago, IL: Aldine.

Becker, Howard S. and Blanche Geer, 1970. "Participant Observation and Interviewing: A Comparison." In William J. Filstead, ed., *Qualitative Methodology: Firsthand Involvement with the Social World.* Chicago, IL: Markham, pp. 133–142.

Campbell, Donald T., 1975. "'Degrees of Freedom' and the Case Study." *Comparative Political Studies,* vol. 8 (July) 178–193.

Caro, Robert A., 1974. *The Power Broker.* New York: Alfred A. Knopf.

Cronbach, Lee J., 1975. "Beyond the Two Disciplines of Scientific Psychology." *American Psychologist,* vol. 30 (February) 116–127.

Fielding, Nigel, 1993. "Ethnography" In Nigel Gilbert, ed., *Researching Social Life.* London: SAGE, pp. 154–171.

Geertz, Clifford, 1994. "Thick Description: Toward an Interpretative Theory of Culture." In Michael Martin and Lee C. McIntyre, eds., *Readings in the Philosophy of Science.* Cambridge, MA: MIT Press, pp. 213–231.

Gilgun, Jane F., 1994. "A Case for Case Studies in Social Work, Research." *Social Work,* vol. 39 (July) 371–380.

Habermas, Jurgen, 1971. *Knowledge and Human Interests.* Beacon Press.

Kaufman, Herbert, 1960. *The Forest Ranger: A Study in Administrative Behavior.* Baltimore, MD: Johns Hopkins.

Kingdon, John W., 1995. *Agendas, Alternatives, and Public Policies,* 2nd ed. New York: HarperCollins.

Knoke, David and George W. Bohrnstedt, 1994. *Statistics for Social Data Analysis,* 3rd ed. Itasca, IL: F. E. Peacock.

Lofland, John and Lyn H. Lofland, 1995. *Analyzing Social Settings,* 3rd ed. Belmont, CA: Wadsworth.

McClintock, Charles C., Diane Brannon, and Steven Maynard-Moody, 1979. "Applying the Logic of Sample Surveys to Qualitative Case Studies: The Case Cluster Method." *Administrative Science Quarterly,* vol. 24 (December) 612–629.

McCurdy, Howard E. and Robert E. Cleary, 1984. "Why Can't We Resolve the Research Issue in Public Administration." *Public Administration Review,* vol. 44 (January/February) 49–55.

Miles, Matthew B., 1979. "Qualitative Data as an Attractive Nuisance: The Problem of Analysis." *Administrative Science Quarterly,* vol. 24 (December) 590–601.

Mitchell, J. Clyde, 1983. "Case and Situation Analysis." *The Sociological Review,* vol. 1 (May) 187–211.

Orum, Anthony M., Joe R. Feagin, and Gideon Sjoberg, 1991. "Introduction: The Nature of the Case Study." In Anthony M. Orum, Joe R. Feagin, and Gideon Sjoberg, eds., *A Case for the Case Study.* Chapel Hill: University of North Carolina Press, pp. 1–26.

Perry, James L. and Kenneth L. Kraemer, 1986. "Research Methodology in Public Administration Review, 1975–1984." *Public Administration Review,* vol. 46 (May/June) 215–226.

Pressman, Jeffrey L. and Aaron Wildavsky, 1984. *Implementation: How Great Expectations in Washington Are Dashed in Oakland,* 3rd ed. Berkeley: University of California Press.

Richards, Lyn and Tom Richards, 1994. "From Filing Cabinet to Computer." In Alan Bryman and Robert G. Burgess, eds., *Analyzing Qualitative Data.* London: Routledge, pp. 146–172.

Runyan, William McKinley, 1988. "A Historical and Conceptual Background to Psychohistory." In William McKinley Runyan, ed., *Psychology and Historical Interpretation.* New York: Oxford University Press, pp. 3–60.

Schumaker, Paul, 1991. *Critical Pluralism, Democratic Performance, and Community Power.* Lawrence: University Press of Kansas.

Sjoberg, Gideon, Norma Williams, Ted R. Vaughan, and Andree F. Sjoberg, 1991. "The Case Study Approach in Social Research: Basic Methodological Issues." In Anthony M. Orum, Joe R. Feagin, and Gideon Sjoberg, eds., *A Case for the Case Study.* Chapel Hill: University of North Carolina Press, pp. 27–29.

Smith, John K., 1993. "Hermeneutics and Qualitative Inquiry." In David J. Flinders and Geoffrey E. Mills, eds., *Theory and Concepts in Qualitative Research.* New York: Teachers College Press, pp. 183–200.

Stake, Robert E., 1995. *The Art of Case Study Research.* Thousand Oaks, CA: Sage.

Stoecker, Randy, 1991. "Evaluating and Rethinking the Case Study." *The Sociological Review,* vol. 39 no. 1: 88–112.

Trow, Martin, 1970. "Comment on 'Participant Observation and Interviewing: A Comparison'." In William J. Filstead, ed., *Qualitative Methodology: Firsthand Involvement with the Social World.* Chicago, IL: Markham, pp. 143–149.

White, Jay D., 1985. "On the Growth of Knowledge in Public Administration." *Public Administration Review,* vol. 46 (January/February) 15–24.

Windsor, Duane and George Greanias, 1983. "The Public Policy and Management Program for Case/Course Development." *Public Administration Review,* vol. 43 (March/April) 370–378.

Yin, Robert K. 1981. "The Case Study Crisis: Some Answers." *Administrative Science Quarterly,* vol. 26 (March) 58–65.

———, 1982. "Studying Phenomenon and Context across Sites." *American Behavioral Scientist,* vol. 26 (September–October) 84–100.

———, 1994. *Case Study Research: Design and Methods,* 2nd ed. Thousand Oaks, CA: Sage.

Yin, Robert K. and Karen A. Heald, 1975. "Using the Case Survey Method to Analyze Policy Studies." *Administrative Science Quarterly,* vol. 20 (September) 371–381.

CASH MANAGEMENT.

A set of activities directed toward achieving more efficient management of public funds including the mobilization and investment of tax receipts, user fees, and other funds collected by a government until needed for expenditures.

The processes and practices employed by public-sector cash managers were principally derived from the private sector. Historically, private companies have tried to minimize the opportunity cost of uninvested cash reserves by developing a series of cash management practices and procedures.

Active cash management by governmental entities began to receive greater attention in the 1970s, when high interest rates caused the opportunity costs of holding idle cash to rise significantly. In recent years, public managers have realized that a sound cash management system can became an important source of supplementary revenue, particularly in times when public funds have become constrained and agency responsibilities have broadened.

Conceptually, a governmental cash management program may be divided into four distinct components (Ramsey and Hackbart, 1993):

1. cash mobilization, or controlling the receipt and disbursal of funds;
2. cash forecasting, or estimating future net cash balances;

3. banking relationships, or the use of financial services provided by banks to implement an effective cash-management system; and

4. investment management, which involves the selection of portfolio assets and investment strategies.

Cash Mobilization

The cash mobilization component of a cash management program basically involves (1) accelerating the receipt of funds so that they may become available for investment and (2) managing the disbursal of funds so that they can be invested as long as is feasible. The processes and activities involved in carrying out these functions will depend on the fund being managed (including its source and use), the governmental/entity and geographical characteristics (concentrated or dispersed nature), and the nature and capabilities of the financial institutional support system available to implement cash-mobilization practices and procedures.

Revenue Acceleration

Revenue acceleration can be achieved by statutory or regulatory changes affecting revenue payment or by utilizing new and innovative practices to overcome receipt processing bottlenecks. For example, the receipt data for tax collections is typically specified in enabling statutes or ordinances and, therefore, may be beyond the current policy or operational influence of the cash manager. State and local government officials, however, may find that requiring taxpayers to remit payments more rapidly (sales taxes, corporate taxes, and the like) allows funds to be invested for longer periods, thus increasing investment income. In such cases, statutory or regulatory policies may be adjusted to permit the cash manager to accelerate revenue collections.

Bottlenecks and slowdowns have generally been described as "negative float." Negative float is the time delay between the disbursement of tax receipts by an individual or corporation and the availability of "good" funds by the state treasurer or appropriate financial official. Three types of negative floats are mail float, processing float, and clearing float.

Mail float is the lag between the time the taxpayer or other revenue source mails a payment and the moment at which the state or local government unit receives the payment. Processing float is the time lapse between the receipt of the tax payment or revenue source and the deposit of such funds in the appropriate banking institution. Clearing float is the time lapse that may occur between the deposit of the check in the bank and the time at which the bank recognizes the check as a legitimate source of funds. Government entities have developed three major methods, among others, to combat this "negative float": lock box systems, cash concentration accounts, and electronic funds transfers.

Lock box systems offer one technique for speeding revenue collections. Taxpayers mail payments to a local postal box. A bank or other third party in that city promptly empties the box, deposits checks, and transmits transaction details to the appropriate government treasurer or cash manager. Such third party actions significantly reduce the mail and processing time involved in accumulating revenues.

The second float reduction method, cash concentration accounts, involves placing all revenues received into a cash pool rather than into the particular accounts from which the checks will be written. As cash is needed to cover the various expenses, it is transferred to the specific account. In this way, monies received can be immediately invested in order to receive optimal return.

Electronic funds transfers involves the use of wire transfers of funds to replace the mail system to move funds. Most transfers are conducted by the Fed Wire. Using the Fed Wire, settlement occurs on receipt by the receiving Federal Reserve Bank, thus providing immediate funds availability. Furthermore, the Federal Reserve guarantees the wire transfer once it has been entered into the system.

Disbursement Management

While the mobilization of public funds is dependent on activities designed to accelerate the deposit of funds, it is also enhanced by practices that manage the disbursement of such funds. Among the disbursement management practices available to the public funds manager are (1) managing the authorization of the disbursement to coincide with vendor discounts (if available), (2) managing the check writing and disbursement process to take into account the time period between check issuance and the time that funds are released by the entity's depository bank (disbursement or positive float), and (3) managing the time that funds are invested so as to coincide with the time that the funds are required to pay vendors for services and products provided (Ramsey and Hackbart, 1993).

Disbursement float can be managed with a zero-balance account system. With such a system, a single general account is established with single clearing accounts for individual agencies or funds. The special clearing accounts are maintained with zero balances until checks are presented for payment. At that time, funds are transferred from the general account to the clearing accounts to cover the payment or payments scheduled for that time period. The funds in the general account are invested in relatively liquid securities, which can be converted to cash as the need arises (Ramsey and Hackbart, 1993).

Cash Forecasting

Cash forecasting is a key element of the cash management process as it provides the investment manager with information regarding patterns of revenue receipts and expenditures. The matching of investment time periods with receipt and expenditure patterns is the goal of the cash forecasting process. Cash forecasting accuracy is critical because if an asset is prematurely liquidated due to unanticipated cash flow needs, income from that investment may be severely reduced. Therefore, forecasting precision is critical to effective cash management.

Forecasts may be made by

1. subjective judgment or evaluations based upon past patterns of receipts and expenditures;
2. time series analysis which utilizes statistical equations to predict future cash flows based upon the supposition that past patterns best predict the future; and
3. economic analysis, which explains past cash flow relationships including tax and other revenues and expenditures and economic performance to predict future cash flows through mathematical and statistical equations.

Such forecasts can involve daily, weekly, or monthly assessments of cash flow patterns, depending on the scope of the investment period.

Bank Relationship

As suppliers of specialized services to state and local governments, banking institutions provide an integral component of the cash management process. Banks, due to their role within the federal reserve system, are unique among financial intermediaries. In addition to providing transaction services, banks facilitate investment activities and may provide an investment option for public-funds managers as a provider of certificates of deposit or repurchase agreements (Harrell, 1986).

Banking policy issues for state and local governments include such issues as method of payment for banking services and specific services to be provided by the banking institution. These issues are clearly important to the public-funds manager, as the management of the portfolio requires a huge number of different transactions. The inability of a bank to perform certain functions could seriously limit investment income of the government entity. Likewise, high transaction fees could negate some of the investment gains.

Investment Management

The final component of a comprehensive cash management program involves the investment of available funds. The investment of public funds is usually carried out pursuant to the achievement of three goals: safety, liquidity, and yield. The pursuit of these goals typically involves trade-offs or compromises.

For example, trade-offs exist between rate of return and risk (safety). In other words, certain investment assets contain a credit risk premium to reflect the probability that the original cash value may not be realized at the maturity of the investment assets. Since public-funds managers generally manage portfolios comprised of tax dollars, they generally opt for investments that are safe and therefore have a lower rate of return.

The term "liquidity" refers to speed and ease of conversion of an investment to cash. Liquidity is determined in the credit markets by the strength of the secondary market for the asset. As there is a very active secondary market for United States Treasury securities, they are considered to be highly liquid assets. Real estate, by contrast, has a less active secondary market and is, therefore, considered less liquid. Asset-liquidity characteristics are important to public-funds managers as they attempt to align cash inflows with required outflows.

Public-funds portfolio yield, typically, consists of both interest income and capital gains income. Interest income is achieved by holding an asset, which bears an investment rate of return. Capital gains income is achieved through an enhancement of the value of the investment. For example, a share of stock, bought at US $40 a share realizes a US $10 capital gain when sold at US $50 a share (Ramsey and Hackbart, 1993).

How public-funds portfolio managers balance the pursuit of these investment goals is reflected in their being classified as active, passive, or hybrid managers. An active manager assumes that credit markets are not efficient and that temporary price disequilibriums do occur in the markets. By taking advantage of these trading opportunities, the public-funds manager can increase portfolio yield through asset price appreciation. The active manager is willing to take a predetermined amount of risk in order to achieve a greater portfolio return.

A passive manager, by contrast, assumes that the credit markets are efficient and perfect information is transmitted instantaneously to an infinite number of buyers and sellers. The passive manager, therefore, buys and holds assets. The hybrid manager, as the name implies, uses elements of both strategies in pursuing investment goals. Each fund or account may be handled differently according to the goals and funding structure of each account (Ramsey and Hackbart, 1993).

Cash management, therefore, is a multifaceted set of activities including accelerating receipts and controlling expenditures that allows for cash reserves to be invested in order to earn interest income. Cash forecasting, bank relations, and investment goals and strategies are additional key elements of a comprehensive public-funds cash management program.

MERL HACKBART

BIBLIOGRAPHY

Harrell, Rhett D., 1986. *Banking Relations: A Guide for Government.* Chicago, IL: Government Finance Officers Association of the United States and Canada, pp. 221–222.
Ramsey, James R. and Merl M. Hackbart, 1993. "Public Funds Management: Current Practices and Future Trends," *The Handbook of Municipal Bonds and Public Finance.* New York: New York Institute of Finance, pp. 194–208.

CAUSALITY.   One variable's effect upon another, or the *independent variable's* effect upon a dependent variable. Causality refers to the relationship between a cause and an effect; whenever "X" occurs, there is a very high probability that "Y" will occur.

Despite making great methodological strides, public administrators and policy analysts are not able today to demonstrate that they have proven that a change in one variable "causes" another variable to change. Indeed, some social scientists argue that given the complexity in public life, it would be impossible to prove, with absolute certainty, that an independent variable "caused" the dependent variable to change. Researchers must spend a good deal of time examining whether other independent variables are involved in the relationship under study. If they are not, those variables could be eliminated as explanations for the change in the dependent variable.

Public sector analysts try to explain whether the outcome of an event (or program) produces certain desired (programmatic) effects. Observations of the effects produced by a cause can greatly assist analysts in developing and improving public programs. For example, observation and measurement might lead some to argue that eligible students who participated in a Head Start program (independent variable) will have a higher reading level (dependent variable) in the first grade than will eligible students who did not participate. The Head Start program was developed for preschoolers from disadvantaged backgrounds to give them an opportunity to be more prepared when they entered regular school. Isolating the Head Start program alone as the "cause" is, methodologically, extremely difficult to do.

Aristotle was less interested in the question, What causes Y? as he was interested in the philosophical question, What is meant by cause? He addressed four types of causes: efficient cause (process of change), final cause (the purpose for change), material cause (the entity or thing that changes), and the formal cause (the entity or thing into which something is changed). Later writers such as René Descartes and Sir Isaac Newton viewed causality within the framework of things arranged by God.

John Stuart Mill focused on understanding causality from the standpoint of discounting inadequate causal arguments. Based upon experimental observation, Mill wrote about methods of agreement, difference, and concomitant variation. Each contributes insight into causality.

Herbert Simon discussed causality within the context of hypothetical "models," recognizing the difficulties of discussing the subject with real word examples.

Generally, public administrators and policy analysts are most concerned with causality when attempting to develop explanatory research designs. Explanatory designs go beyond answering the question what happened, describing a set of events, toward answering the question why something happened. To demonstrate that two variables are causally related to each other four conditions must be satisfied:

1. covariation,
2. temporal precedence,
3. nonspuriousness, and
4. theoretical justification

In examining whether variable X causes an effect in variable Y, we look to see if there is a covariation between the variables. That means that as one variable changes, so too does another variable. If X increases, Y may increase or it may decrease. Similarly, as X decreases, Y may increase or it may decrease. If each time there is an observed change in X, there is an observed change in Y, we can say that X and Y covary with each other. If each time there is an observed change in Y, X neither increases nor decreases but remains the same, then we can say that X and Y do not covary.

To say that two variables covary is not the same thing as saying that one of those variables causes a change in the other variable. Covariation is a necessary condition for causality, but it is not sufficient. If two variables covary, it is important to see if a change in Y, the dependent variable, is always observed after there has been a change in X, the independent variable. This is what is meant by the temporal factor, or temporal precedence. X can only be said to cause a change in Y if each time a change is observed in X, a subsequent change in Y, in a particular direction, is observed. If a change in the dependent variable does not follow a change in the independent variable, then a statement saying that X causes a change in Y cannot be made.

Two variables may covary in the sequence of a change in X being followed by a change in Y and still not be causally related. There may be other "third" variables that intrude upon the hypothesized effect of X on Y. X and Y may not even be related but both may be caused by a third variable. This would be a spurious relationship. A spurious relationship is a relationship in which two variables, X and Y, appear to be related, but both are caused by a third variable, Z. The end of the arrow expresses the direction of causation.

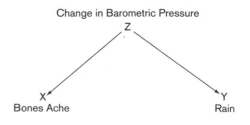

Change in Barometric Pressure

Z

X   Y
Bones Ache   Rain

For example, an individual might assert that his bones ache (X) and, therefore, predict that it will rain (Y), for each time the individual's bones ached in that way in the recent past, it did then rain. Bones aching cannot "cause" it to rain. Rather, bones aching and rain are both caused by a change in the barometric pressure (Z). There is no inherent link between the two. Similarly, an analyst might claim that whenever Iowa has a bumper crop of wheat (X), there are monsoons in southeast Asia (Y). In fact both are probably "caused" by the weather pattern (Z).

In order to demonstrate causality, the public administrator/analyst must be able to exclude all other possible independent variables as the explanation for changes in the dependent variable. One finding might be that there is an intervening relationship, that is, that X causes Z, which in term causes Y.

The Western Electric Company Studies, the "Hawthorne Experiments," illustrate an intervening relationship well. The company's stimulus, X (attention to lighting, to length of break times, and to other variables), created group cohesion, Z, which caused greater group productivity, Y. For a long time it was thought that the stimulus "caused" the "effect" of increased productivity. Further examination demonstrated the group cohesion that resulted from the workers being observed, and from that group cohesion greater group productivity resulted.

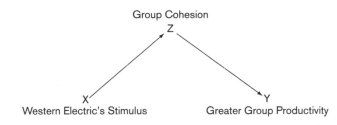

It is difficult to say that the Head Start program alone is responsible for early year educational successes. Perhaps a child's participation in the program caused some parents to read more to their children or to talk with them more. In other words, participation in the program (X) in some measurable ways changed some parents' interactions with their children (Z), which in turn caused educational successes (Y). The relationship then would be an intervening one rather than a direct cause and effect. It is instructive to see a chain of events through the interaction of a set of variables that explain a change in the dependent variable. In the Head Start example, other variables could most probably also be linked to X and Y.

At times, it is just not possible to control for all third variables. In conducting data analysis, it is easy to become paralyzed with thoughts about other variables that could be controlled if there was more time or more money. There are always compromises that public administrators/analysts may have to make to conclude research studies.

That is why it is so difficult to demonstrate causality in this field.

Assuming that the researcher is able to demonstrate covariation, the temporal sequence of change, and nonspuriousness, it is still not sufficient to say that there is a "cause" and "effect" relationship between X and Y. There must also be a theoretical or substantive justification for the relationship. At the most basic level, an affirmative response is required in answer to the question, Does the relationship make sense? There must be an inherent link between the two variables that justifies the conclusion that X causes Y. It is only with that inherent linkage, combined with the other three conditions, that causality can be said to have occurred.

Public sector systems are "open," meaning that it is extremely difficult, if not possible, to isolate all relevant "third" variables, or to control for the impact of those "third" variables on the relationship between the independent and dependent variables under study. Thus, even though techniques of analysis are constantly being refined, it may not be possible to demonstrate "cause" and "effect" relationships in the public sector.

BRUCE D. ROGERS

BIBLIOGRAPHY

Blalock, Hubert M., Jr., 1964. *Causal Inferences in Nonexperimental Research*. New York: W. W. Norton.
Blalock, H. M., Jr., ed., 1971. *Causal Models in the Social Sciences*. Chicago, IL: Aldine Atherton.
Campbell, D. T. and J. T. Stanley, 1966. *Experimental and Quasi-Experimental Designs for Research*. Chicago, IL: Rand McNally.

CAUSE-RELATED MARKETING. A term coined by the American Express Company in 1981 to describe partnership arrangements between business corporations and charitable nonprofit organizations that provide resources to the charity as a by-product of promoting the corporation's product.

The original American Express program linked credit-card usage to payments made by the company to the Statute of Liberty Foundation. Since its inception by American Express, different forms of cause-related marketing (CRM) have been adopted by many companies, including Scott Paper, Reebok, Ralston Purina, Nike, Ben and Jerry's Ice Cream, Proctor and Gamble, MasterCard, and many others. Many charities, including the National Coalition Against Domestic Violence, Amnesty International, the Humane Society, Boys and Girls Clubs of America, and the Special Olympics, have benefited from such arrangements (Giroud, 1991).

CRM programs take two basic forms—sponsorships and product promotions. Corporate sponsorships are usually linked to special events such as Live Aid, the Olympic Games, or other one-time or periodic nonprofit public purpose of fund-raising activities, or with programs on public radio or television. Under sponsorship arrangements, corporations help defray the costs of the event in exchange for being identified as the event's sponsor. In product promotions, the sales of particular products are tied to payments to specific charities. The latter programs may take the form of periodic (annual) promotional campaigns or continuing arrangements by which sales of a certain product generate payments to a charity (Giroud, 1991).

CRM is best understood as an approach to business marketing, not as a substitute for traditional corporate philanthropy (Gingold, 1993). It is "based on the premise that consumers will purchase products or services that offer an emotional bonus in the form of a contribution to charity" (Giroud, 1991, p. 140). However, CRM developed in an era when large corporations had been downsizing, corporate charitable contributions had stopped growing, and corporations had become much more strategic in their giving programs. Along with the development of corporate employee volunteer programs, in-kind gifts programs, and a more general shift of corporate-giving programs toward the strategic interests of the corporations, CRM is accurately described as one of several components in a long-term realignment of corporate-giving programs (Smith, 1994). Nonetheless, CRM has been described as a "win-win" arrangement through which corporate interests are served while charities benefit from the resources generated on their behalf.

Students of CRM have identified potential benefits of this practice as well as risks (Gingold, 1993; Giroud, 1991). The benefits to a corporation include increased sales of its products, improved ability to recruit employees, and better public relations for the corporation as a whole. The benefits to the charitable partners in CRM arrangements include new streams of flexible funding, increased long-term prospects from existing sources of funds resulting from greater public visibility received as a result of the corporation's promotional efforts, and access to valuable corporate resources such as professional marketing expertise.

Risks to the corporation from CRM include a loss of reputation if the corporation associates itself with a charity or cause that is viewed as controversial, disreputable, or ineffective, or if the arrangements by which consumer purchases translate into charitable contributions lack credibility or are not clearly disclosed. Such reputational losses presumably can lead to losses of markets for the company's products.

Risks to nonprofit organizations from CRM are twofold: risks to individual nonprofits that enter CRM arrangements and risks to the nonprofit sector as a whole as CRM grows as a form of corporate support. Risks to individual nonprofits include potential losses of other sources of support (sales revenues, charitable contributions, foundation or government grants) for either of several reasons: (1) The corporate sponsor may diminish the nonprofit's attractiveness if the corporation or its product is unpopular with the nonprofit's donors or service consumers; (2) the corporation may misrepresent the charity to its customers causing the latter to lose credibility; or (3) donors or other funders may view revenues from CRM as substantial substitutes for their own support (see crowd out). Another risk is the sensitivity of CRM arrangements to market conditions. If the nonprofit becomes dependent on CRM for a substantial portion of its revenues and the corporation's product sales diminish, the nonprofit may be left with a financial shortfall. In general, particular CRM arrangements depend on the ability of the corporate tie to charity to boost sales. If sales are not maintained, the corporation is likely to terminate the arrangement.

Possible risks to the nonprofit sector as a whole from CRM center on its potential reallocative effects on charitable resources. First, CRM is more likely to focus on popular and attractive causes that can boost company products and hence neglect important but unattractive causes that cannot do so. Moreover, given its direct tie to corporate sales, CRM may in the long run become a substitute for traditional forms of corporate philanthropy. In this contingency, nonprofits stand to lose support for worthy charitable programs that cannot meet the CRM market test.

Because of the potential for abuse of CRM, the business community has identified several areas of recommended ethical practice including clear disclosure of the amounts contributed to charity, informing consumers on what portions of purchases may be tax deductible, and avoiding deceptive practices such as false advertising claims and misrepresentation of the charity's mission or activities (Gingold, 1993).

Since 1981, the practice of CRM has grown rapidly in popularity and magnitude reaching a level of US $1.8 billion by 1988 and continuing to grow at a pace of 10 to 15 percent annually (Giroud, 1991). The immediate future promises more of the same: Corporations will continue to streamline and reorganize themselves in the face of international competition and technological advance while they seek strategic ways to maintain support for their communities. Nonprofits will continue to seek new sources of revenue as government funding constricts and philanthropic sources fail to respond apace. In this environment, cause-related marketing appears likely to enjoy increasing popularity.

DENNIS R. YOUNG

BIBLIOGRAPHY

Gingold, Diane, 1993. *Strategic Philanthropy in the 1990s.* Washington, D.C.: Diane Gingold and Associates.
Giroud, Cynthia G., 1991. "Cause-Related Marketing: Potential Dangers and Benefits." Chapter 11 in James P. Shannon,

ed., *The Corporate Contributions Handbook*. San Francisco: Jossey-Bass, pp. 139–152.

Smith, Craig, 1994. "The New Corporate Philanthropy." *Harvard Business Review* (May/June) pp. 105–116.

CENTRALLY PLANNED ECONOMY.

Refers to the economic systems prevailing in communist countries. Sometimes the term is used in a narrower sense to refer to one of the forms of the above economic systems, to the bureaucratic centralized one in contrast to the selectively decentralized planned economy. At the end of the 1980s, the Soviet-type communist system collapsed in Eastern Europe as did the form of centrally planned economy.

The idea of modern communism emerged as criticism and complete negation of the kind of capitalism that developed in the nineteenth and early twentieth century. The ideological founders of the communist system (most notably Karl Marx, Friedrich Engels, and Vladimir I. Lenin) wrote mainly about capitalism and gave only a few hints about how a socialist economy should function (socialism in their usage of the term meant the first phase of communism).

According to Marx, the capitalist system, after fulfilling its historical task to lay down the material foundations of an affluent society, would be replaced by socialism in the most advanced countries, and this would be achieved through social revolution. In his vision, the elimination of private property, the foundation of the capitalist system, would entail the abolition of commodity production and money, and they would be substituted by planning. Lenin had further developed the ideas of Marx, revising a crucial thesis of Marx, by placing the socialist revolution not into the most advanced but the weakest part of the capitalist world. He lead the Bolshevik revolution to victory in Russia in 1917 and created the first communist state.

Having no blueprint of socialism to rely on, the Soviet-type economy evolved through experience, amidst enormous internal and external political tensions. By the second half of the 1920s, Joseph V. Stalin emerged as the unchallenged leader of the Soviet Union, and under his strong influence, a very centralized and oppressive form of socialism emerged, often qualified as Stalinist or state socialism. After his death, that form of socialism has softened in most of the communist countries.

The general characteristics of a centrally planned economy are as follows:

- social (collective) ownership of the overwhelming majority of the means of production;
- ideological dominance of the Communist Party in all spheres of social life, including economic policy and economic life in general;

- market mechanism is largely replaced by economic planning, which is normally the responsibility of the Central Planning Authority. Resources are allocated primarily by administrative commands—such as production assignments, allocation orders, and rationing—rather than by markets and prices;
- socially equitable distribution of national income. Private consumption is supplemented with a comprehensive system of goods and services provided collectively by the state.

In the bureaucratic centralized model, economic processes are dominated by the hierarchical system of planning and management. Due to the economic circumstances its main objectives became rapid growth and structural change (industrialization). Economic growth, however, was not equally promoted in all economic sectors. The expansion of industrial sectors was stressed, leading to a chronic neglect of agriculture and the social sphere (education, health care) in most communist countries. As a result, the centrally planned economy became associated with several distinctive features such as a clear set of national priorities, detailed planning of production and distribution in physical terms, administrative plan assignments given to the enterprises, vertical rather than horizontal coordination of economic activity. Planning had gradually assumed a rather broad meaning. It became the complex system of the "planned management" of all economic processes involving production, trade, distribution, investment, and consumption.

In centrally planned economies, the market mechanism is superseded to a large degree by state planning. (In some areas, such as certain consumer goods and services, markets have, however, never completely disappeared.) The state exercises monopolistic control over the basic economic structure and resources of the country. It owns and operates large-scale industries, mines, power plants, railways, shipping, and various means of communication. It engages in farming through state farms, and it largely controls peasant agriculture through collective farming. It has an exclusive monopoly of banking and foreign trade, and it controls the domestic channels of distribution. It is the sole notable employer and as such dominates bargaining between itself and the employees. Although trade unions are allowed, their function is purely subsidiary to the interest of the state.

Central planning relies on a system of plans for different time periods. Long-term (15 to 20 years) plans are primarily concerned with problems of structural changes on the national scale, technological development, the training of labor force, and the like. The greatest role is played by medium-term (mostly 5 or 7 years) plans, concerned mainly with forming the sectoral production capacities. Short-term (annual) plans are concerned with balancing sources and uses of various products and funds.

The details of the plans are worked out by the Central Planning Authority following the instructions given by the Central Commission of the Party and in close collaboration with the different ministries. Central planning creates and relies on a huge informal planning machinery, involving thousands of experts. The National Plan is first examined by the Council of Ministers and then submitted to Parliament for formal approval. The plan becomes in this way a law. The plan targets and responsibilities are disaggregated and transmitted to various levels (ministries, branch associations, enterprises). The plan is put into effect by means of directives and indicators, administrative regulations, orienting guidelines, and incentives. In the extreme case of hierarchical planning, the plan is simply imposed from above by the central planning authority on the different administrative organs and individual units.

The internal consistency of the plan with regards to the distribution of resources is ensured by the extensive use of material balances or of interbranch balances (the "balance method"). The overall balances of the national economy comprise all the important economic variables. Although centrally planned economies use a monetary system and prices, the prices of goods and services and those of factors of production are not determined by markets and do not provide reliable guides for economic decisions.

The central banks combine the functions of both central and commercial banking. The basic monetary policy instruments are irrelevant; instead, monetary policy is a part of the financial plan and is concerned with controlling the amount of money in circulation and providing credit for enterprises. The state budget is the prime vehicle for the allocation of resources among various ends and is also a control mechanism because it provides a considerable proportion of the investment funds for enterprises. Enterprises are severely restricted to carry out investments outside of those specified in the plan.

Most enterprises operate under the direct control of the state. There is little place left for small private enterprises, but for the most part their operation is also closely monitored. Some organizations are left to local governments to operate. The bulk of industrial production comes from state enterprises, which are strictly subject to state planning and are managed by state appointees. The enterprise is obligated to fulfill the production and financial plans set down by the state, which specifies targets or success indicators to be attained. The enterprise's operating plan is only an elaboration of the targets set forth in the national plan. Agriculture is carried on by collective farms, state farms, and individual farmers. The state exercises a monopolistic control over the agricultural resources, too, through national economic planning, the control of the state budget and the banking system. Distribution at both the wholesale and retail levels is usually the responsibility of the state trading network or the cooperative trading network. Again, the cooperative network

operates under close state control and is subject to national economic planning.

The centrally planned economic management showed several advantages, especially in the period of major structural changes (socialist industrialization). Its special strength is that it allows the concentration of enormous resources on specific projects, a modification of the social structure, stabilization of prices and wages, and a reduction of the effects of changes in the world economy on the domestic economy, provided the cadres are fully committed to the fundamental objectives of the system.

The history of central planning has showed that it suffers from severe problems. It neglects efficiency at the microeconomic level, and it is unable to adjust quickly and flexibly to changes in the environment. Deficiency of central planning encourages selective violation of instructions and the working of the "second economy." The lack of economic thinking leads to decisions that cannot be justified by economic criteria, to excessive inventories, to a slow rate of technological innovation, to poor quality of output, and to the low productivity of labor and capital. The incentive structure and the official government policy of full employment lead to a large amount of hidden unemployment of labor and to underemployment of capital equipment and materials. The overcentralization and rigidity lead to cumulative shortages and informal bargaining. Central planning creates also a large bureaucracy and an elitist social structure.

As central planning proved to be less capable of securing economic efficiency, various waves of reforms were started in the socialist countries to move away from the bureaucratic, centralized planning to a decentralized model. In the latter model, market-type regulations are allowed for or simulated together with planning, some responsibilities are delegated to lower-level bodies and enterprises, the number of directive indicators is reduced, profitability is accepted as the main criterion of enterprise performance and therefore prices more closely reflect production costs. The ideal blueprint of this model is called "market socialism."

MIHÁLY HŐGYE AND ERNŐ ZALAI

BIBLIOGRAPHY

Borstein, M., ed., 1994. *Comparative Economic Systems: Models and Cases.* Burr Ridge, IL: Irwin.

Hare, Paul G., 1991. *Central Planning.* Chur, Switzerland: Harwood Academic Publishers.

Kornai, Janos, 1991. *The Socialist System: The Political Economy of Communism.* Princeton, NJ: Princeton University Press.

Wilczynski, J., 1970. *The Economics of Socialism.* London: George Allen & Unwin.

CERTIFICATION OF ELIGIBLES.

A process used by human resources offices to let hiring officials know which applicants may be offered a position. After applicants complete the process for consideration for employment for an organization, they are evaluated as to their eligibility for hire. In many personnel systems, the central personnel office develops a list of those who are found to be eligible for hire. The lists are usually rank ordered, and the agency doing the hiring usually has to hire from the top of the list. Many public-sector jurisdictions use a "rule of three" or some similar criterion in which the person doing the hiring must choose from among the top three (see **rule of three**). This permits a little discretion to the one actually employing the individual.

The concept of certification of eligibles was developed so that employers would choose the best, based on the evaluation process for applicants, and to limit the chances of abuse of discretion by agency managers. Critics claim that the evaluation processes do not really discriminate in meaningful ways among applicants. Thus, some new approaches have developed in which anyone above a certain score or in a given range of scores is eligible for hire.

Many jurisdictions use multiple lists. Individual lists usually exist for each class of position. In most cases, the list is in response to the recruitment for a particular position, but there are also lists for classes of positions such as clerical staff. Lists may vary by whether the individuals are currently employed and thus would be promotion lists, whether they have been employed before in the organization, or whether they are external applicants. Organizations have differing policies on whether any of these categories of applicants are given preference.

Once the hiring agency receives the list, it has the opportunity to do further review. Thus, the hiring official may check references and previous employment. An interview may be required as well. Once the hiring official makes a determination that a particular individual is the choice, arrangements are made to make a formal offer to hire.

N. JOSEPH CAYER

BIBLIOGRAPHY

Saso, Carmen D. and Earl P. Tanis, 1974. *Selection and Certification of Eligibles.* Chicago: International Personnel Management Association.

CERTIFIED FUND-RAISING EXECUTIVE (CFRE).

The title conferred on a development professional who meets certain criteria establishing professional competency.

The "CFRE" credential was established by the National Society of Fund-Raising Executives (NSFRE) in 1982 to enable fund-raising professionals to be recognized by their colleagues and employers as having reached a certain level of expertise and professionalism. There are four steps to certification:

1. submission of application;
2. evaluation and verification of professional and personal history;
3. examination of the candidate's knowledge;
4. approval of certification by the Society's Certification Board.

To be considered as a candidate for certification, the following criteria must be met:

- employment as a fund-raising executive;
- at least five years of experience;
- a pledge in writing that fund-raising activities are conducted in accordance with the NSFRE Code of Ethical Principles;
- information provided to the Board, attesting to professional experience, performance, education, and service to the profession;
- passing a 200-question multiple-choice examination.

Advanced Certified Fund-Raising Executive (ACFRE)

NSFRE introduced advanced certification in 1991 as the final step in establishing credentials to "identify superior mastery of the profession." To achieve ACFRE status, a candidate must

- possess the CFRE credential and have been renewed at least once;
- have 10 years or more experience;
- possess a B.S./B.A. or equivalent;
- adhere to the NSFRE Code of Ethical Principles;
- participate actively in NSFRE or other fund-raising organizations with "demonstrated service to other nonprofit organizations";
- have attended or instructed 24 hours of advanced-level development seminars and/or courses.

ROBERT W. BUCHANAN AND WILLIAM BERGOSH

CERTIORARI.

Comes in the form of either a writ or a petition. A writ of certiorari is a writ or an order from the Supreme Court to a lower court, calling the records of a particular case up for review. In practice, the Supreme Court does not issue writs without a petition for certiorari. Since a writ of certiorari is not granted without a petition, the burden is placed upon the petitioner. A petition for certiorari is a request to the Supreme Court for a higher court to review a decision made by a lower court. The petitioner is calling for a review because a federal court of appeals, a state supreme court, or an administrative agency has ruled against the petitioner. Since certiorari is a Latin term that means "to make more clear," a petitioner is requesting that a higher court clarify the record by resolving existing legal questions.

Certiorari is the usual avenue by which cases reach the Supreme Court. Although cases can come to the Supreme Court by appeal, a writ of certiorari is discretionary whereas an appeal is a matter of right. In practice, both modes of review involve discretionary judgment but chances for appeal are more likely through petitions of certiorari. Since 90 percent of these petitions are denied every year, the discretion involved is considerable. When a court calls up a case for review by granting certiorari, a minimum of four justices deem this case worthy of being heard. This practice has aptly been called the "rule of four," meaning that if only three justices believe a case is "cert-worthy," a petition is denied.

The Supreme Court has an elaborate set of rules and procedures for petitions of certiorari. The petition for certiorari and the opposing brief, or cross-petition, must be filed in a timely fashion. The petitioner has 90 days to file a petition and after receiving notice of this petition, respondents have 30 days to file their opposing brief, or cross-petition. Filing requirements for each include a US $300 filing fee and 40 copies of each petition or brief. Both the petitioner and the respondent must follow the same certiorari check list and ensure that materials carefully comply with an elaborate color code designed to facilitate the Supreme Court's reviewing procedures. Once the Supreme Court grants or denies a certiorari petition, the clerk of the Supreme Court will notify the lower court and the counsel of record. If a case is denied, a petitioner can file a petition for rehearing. This requires an additional US $200 filing fee and 40 copies of the petition. In this case, the respondent is not required to file a response unless requested. Following this, discretion is again left to the Supreme Court to grant or deny the petition for rehearing. In short, the petitioner must summarize the lower court's opinion, state the legal questions involved, and provide reasoning on why this particular case merits review by the Supreme Court.

Origin and Subsequent History

In response to an ever increasing case load, due to a growing population and increased amount of government activity, Congress created the federal courts of appeals in 1891 to alleviate the Supreme Court's load. Congress acted again in 1925 with legislation that has been referred to as the Certiorari Act. William Howard Taft, the only justice to serve on the Supreme Court after being president, was influential in shaping this bill. This bill relieved the Supreme Court from having to take almost all of the cases appealed to them. In effect, the Certiorari Act enlarged the Supreme Court's discretion over the cases it considers worthy of review. The source of the Supreme Court's methodology of granting review through the minimum of four votes is less clear. According to the testimony of Justice Van Devanter, the "rule of four" was designed to ensure that the viewpoints of large minorities get heard. Its practice can be traced back to common law tradition because it is not explicitly spelled out in the Certiorari Act.

The passage of the Certiorari Act has changed the relationship between the Supreme Court and the solicitor general. Although the solicitor general has statutory responsibilities to the executive branch of government, the person holding this position advises the Supreme Court on which cases should be granted certiorari. The dual solicitor general creates tension over the separation of power. On one hand the solicitor general serves on behalf of the president as the government's lawyer, but on the other hand, he or she provides an important service to the Supreme Court. The Supreme Court will ask the solicitor general to submit briefs on cases in which government is not a party, to assist the Supreme Court with complex legal problems, and to control a significant portion of the cases that come before the Supreme Court's docket. This close relationship between the Supreme Court and the solicitor general makes the role of the solicitor general highly influential. The power of the solicitor general is reflected by the number of petitions for certiorari filed by the Solicitor General's Office and the number of those petitions granted. It is noteworthy that out of 3,878 petitions for certiorari that came before the Supreme Court in 1983, only about 3 percent were granted for review. If the petitioner is the solicitor general, the probability that a certiorari petition will be granted increases significantly. Seventy-nine percent of all the petitions filed by the solicitor general are granted. It would make sense for petitioners outside of government to somehow get the solicitor general to write an amicus curae brief on their behalf. The key here is that the solicitor general is not only acting on behalf of government but also has the ear of the Supreme Court; therefore, petitions from that office have a strong chance of being heard.

Current Practice in the United States

The practice of granting and denying petitions of certiorari is one of three functions the Supreme Court performs. Justice Rehnquist (1987) in *The Supreme Court: How It Was, How It Is* states that the Supreme Court receives more than 4,000 petitions for certiorari a year, accumulating at a rate of 80 to 100 a week. In order to facilitate the review of these petitions, several justices began the practices of pooling their law clerks in 1987. This practice has allowed the Supreme Court to more efficiently select around 150 cases to review. Once the Supreme Court makes its selection, it must hear those cases, make a decision, and write majority and/or dissenting opinions.

The Supreme Court has made it a common practice not to elaborate on the reasons that certiorari is denied. This, in turn, makes it difficult for lower courts and attorneys to interpret what denial means. There are several reasons not to attach too much significance to a denial. Justice Felix Frankfurter cautioned that denial of certiorari is of little significance and that denial means nothing more than the fact that four justices were not able to agree that a specific case should be heard. In the words of Justice Stevens, "Denials have no precedential value" [*Illinois v. Gray*, 435 U.S. 1013, 1013 (1978)]. Regardless of criticism and conflicting interpretations over the meaning of the Supreme Court's denial, the practice of not stating reasons for granting or denying certiorari continues.

Rehnquist describes some of the subjectivity involved in granting writs of certiorari: "Whether or not to vote to grant certiorari strikes me as a rather subjective decision, made up in part of intuition and in part of legal judgement." Rehnquist (1987, p. 265) goes on to describe the factors considered in a certiorari decision: "conflict with other courts, general importance, and perception that the decision is wrong in light of Supreme Court precedent" (Rehnquist (1987, p. 266).

While Rule 10 of the 1990 Supreme Court rules (Title 28, U.S. Code, p. 544) provides some guidance on the standards applied in granting or denying petitions for certiorari, it includes a caveat that makes the standards hard to follow. Least useful for petitioners is Rule 10.1, which states that the guidelines given are "neither controlling nor fully measuring Supreme Court's discretion." The 1990 rules warn petitioners that a writ of certiorari is a matter of judicial discretion and not a right. It states that for certiorari to be granted there must be "special and important reasons." These reasons include "a decision in conflict with another decision of another U.S. Court of Appeals," or when an appeals court is in conflict with a state supreme court over a federal question, or when any court has decided a question of federal law that should be decided by the Supreme Court. These rules indicate that the Supreme Court is less interested in hearing diversity cases.

The significance of certiorari procedures has to do with the small ratio of cases granted certiorari. Certiorari can be used on state or national cases. This includes petitioner requests for certiorari to appeal decisions made by administrative agencies. Since more and more administrative cases are going to court, the Supreme Court's discretion in selecting cases to review can have a significant impact on administrative law cases. If Supreme Courts choose not to review administrative petitions, the administrative agency in question is consequently given more discretionary power.

K. KIM LOUTZENHISER

BIBLIOGRAPHY

Kaplan, Lincoln, 1987. *The Tenth Justice: The Solicitor General and the Rule of Law.* NY: Vintage Books.

Rehnquist, William H., 1987. *The Supreme Court: How It Was, How It Is.* New York: William Morrow.

———, 1994. "1993 Year-End Report on the Federal Judiciary." *American Journal of Trial Advocacy*, vol. 17: 571–580.

Salokar, Rebecca Mae, 1992. *The Solicitor General: The Politics of the Law.* Philadelphia: Temple.

Stern, Robert, Eugene Gressman, Stephen M. Shapiro and Kenneth S. Geller, 1993. *The Supreme Court Practice*, 7th ed. Washington D.C.: Bureau of National Affairs.

CHALLENGE GIFT.

Also referred to as a corporate challenge. The philanthropic process whereby individuals or companies seek to leverage their support for a philanthropic cause or nonprofit organization during a public fund-raising campaign by requiring that a specific amount be raised from the general public prior to making a sizeable donation. The gifts are usually announced to an attentive audience (often via Public Radio) and require that the nonprofit organization raise a general or specified amount from other contributors before the company will provide its support (Sheldon, in Rosso, 1991). While always time-bound, such challenges are individually defined but usually require that general contributors meet some pre-established deadline or collectively contribute some pre-established amount: "We have received a challenge gift offer from _____ and for every membership (or specific contribution, or call) we receive by the end of this hour, or broadcast, Company XX will contribute x dollars" or "Company XX will match the gift dollar for dollar." Or, for example, the challenge could be "if a certain amount is raised by the end of this broadcast [or hour], the company has pledged to contribute x dollars."

Challenge gifts are often tied to the desire of a local firm to present its image as a good corporate citizen. When nonprofit community organizations such as the local affiliate of National Public Radio or the Public Broadcasting Service seek individual donations during annual (biannual or triannual) fund-raising drives, they are often recipients (usually following solicitation at some point) of challenge gift offers. Using this particular challenge technique, the nonprofit revenues can be enhanced dramatically and the local corporation receives free publicity, enhancing its image as a firm committed to community service or betterment.

Research has tied this phenomenon of corporate citizenship directly to the concept of corporate enlightened self-interest. Companies desire to have an educated and healthy workforce, and it is often in their interest to support community services to enrich the lives of their employees (Sheldon, in Rosso, 1991, p. 230). By providing a challenge gift, the community is served through the enhanced strength of the nonprofit; simultaneously, the challenge gift serves to remind the community of the local corporation's presence and social consciousness.

ERNA GELLES

BIBLIOGRAPHY

Rosso, Henry A. and Associates, 1991. *Achieving Excellence in Fund Raising.* San Francisco: Jossey Bass Nonprofit Sector Series.

CHAOS THEORY.
Borrowing from the natural sciences, chaos theory posits that organizations and their associated systems contain self-ordering properties that can lead to enhanced capacitization and renewal if allowed to evolve.

Origin and Significance

Chaos theory has emerged from the natural sciences. Also referred to as nonequilibrium theory, biology, chemistry, and physics become reference points in considering the essential characteristics of chaos. From this perspective, traditional views concerning planning and management of organizations are turned on their head, with far-reaching implications for public policy and administration.

Public administration has been oriented to the achievement of stability within organizations, including the dynamic equilibrium associated with homeostasis. Symmetry and predictability are valued factors that are a part of the Weberian bureaucratic model. Chaos theory, by contrast, assigns value to chaos as a road to new order and vitality. The lack of stability found with chaos, while unpredictable and by definition dissipative, can at the same time shake systems off their existing plateau and cause them to reorder themselves. Rather than experiencing entropy, dissolution, and death, they can emerge in more complex and resourceful configurations.

Dealing with Paradox

The proposition of bringing order from chaos can be a difficult one to accept beyond the natural sciences. In terms of management and public administration, it means acceptance of unpredictability, shaping your future as you move forward rather than crafting long-term assumptions, and constantly intervening to shape outcomes. The natural sciences demonstrate that order and chaos are not dichotomous. As Ralph D. Stacey (1992) mentions, "The discovery that order can produce chaos and chaos can lead to new order should lead managers to think and act differently when considering how to develop and control a business" (p. 98).

Application to Public Sector

The question becomes how can chaos theory be applied in the public sector? What are the lessons to be learned? How can application of chaos theory be applied to public policy and systems? First, chaos theory suggests that substantive change is more likely to flow from a state of disequilibrium than one marked by stability. When operating in a steady state mode, changes tend to proceed incrementally.

In a rapidly changing environment, this can lead to a pace of organizational change insufficient, in an open system sense, to generate enough energy input to underwrite renewal. The strength of the organization ultimately dissipates.

L. Douglas Kiel (1989) talks about purposeful destruction of organizational symmetry in order to trigger forces of renewal. In some instances "Japanese business leaders intentionally destroy organizational symmetries. These efforts are aimed at 'liberating' employees from existing mind sets and regimens in hopes of generating organizational self-renewal" (p. 548). Similarly, General Electric (GE) talks of liberating employees and uses Organization Development (O.D.) strategies (e.g., approaches to employee empowerment) to break symmetry and arrive at what can be called a bifurcation point.

Connectivity of Order and Chaos

When a system becomes destabilized, it becomes unpredictable. As Margaret Wheatley (1992) suggests, "Chaos is the final state in a system's movement away from order. Not all systems move into chaos, but if a system is dislodged from its stable state, it moves first into a period of oscillation, swinging back and forth between different states. If it moves from oscillation, the next state is full chaos, a period of total unpredictability" (p. 122).

What occurs at the full chaos stage is a shifting of the pendulum. Some point in the disarrayed system, commonly called a "strange attractor," serves as a mobilization point in reshaping the overall system. In organizational terms, it may be a set of corporate values that serves as a navigation system in arriving at a new order. The new order, while perhaps fitted to corporate values, will tend to be unpredictable.

Lessons

The lessons to be drawn from chaos theory as applied to public policy and administration are also visible in evolving thought related to management and leadership. First, there is a need to let go and trust the process. This is not what has been at the heart of acceptable management practice, organizational theory, or styles of leadership.

To deal with chaos requires nonlinearity and intuition. Most systems today are predicated on linearity, including those that are process flow related. Unless backed by hard quantification—which can be particularly difficult in forecasting future events—changes tend to come in incremental fits and starts. The new focus is on use of creative insights, being open and ready to make major shifts that prove necessary, and constant transformation of the organization in relation to new realities. Stacey says, "Pro-action and reaction are replaced by continually creative interconnection."

In fact, it is the creative interactions and new networks—sometimes referred to as "virtual organizations"—that are both an earmark of chaos theory and the basis of organizational forms now gaining prominence. Emphasis is given to relaxation of boundaries within the organization, whether lateral or hierarchical, and maintaining close contact with the surrounding environment.

Colin Hastings (1993) says, "No longer can we rely on the false comfort of the neat and tidy relationships between functional and hierarchical roles displayed on the conventional organizational chart because this has shown itself to be too rigid, too slow, and insufficiently innovative" (pp. 8–9).

What also tends to be too slow is the style of leadership. Business schools still tend to produce individuals endowed with analytical and quantificative skills. These skills are often acquired by examination of past events and linear styles of evaluation. They are ill suited for the dynamics of an environment impacted by rapid and even violent change. The style of leadership coming into vogue is more value centered and less interventionist in application. Intuition and nonlinear thinking are valued. Leadership is transformative rather than incremental in character.

A Matter of Subtlety

When we deal with chaos theory, we deal with subtlety, because chaos is the doorway to order, and order can be the wellspring of chaos. Margaret Wheatley says, "Any time we see systems in chaos, our training urges us to interfere, to stabilize and shore up. But if we can trust the workings of chaos, we will see that the dominant shape of our organizations can be maintained if we retain clarity about the purpose and direction of the organization" (1992).

ROBERT L. DILWORTH

BIBLIOGRAPHY

Hastings, Colin, 1993. *The New Organization.* London: McGraw-Hill.
Kiel, L. Douglas, 1989. "Nonequilibirum Theory and Its Implications for Public Administration." *Public Productivity Review.*
Stacey, Ralph D., 1992. *Managing the Unknowable: Strategic Boundaries Between Order and Chaos in Organizations.* San Francisco: Jossey-Bass.
Tichy, Noel M. and Stratford Sherman, 1993. *Control Your Own Destiny or Someone Else Will.* New York: Doubleday.
Wheatley, Margaret J., 1992. *Leadership and the New Science.* San Francisco: Berrett-Koehler.

CHARISMA.
Literally, the gift of grace; denotes the extraordinary or even superhuman power of a leader whose orders are perceived as totally compelling by his or her followers on grounds of faith; it is the form of authority most opposed to bureaucracy and its legal-rational context.

The term "charisma" has a long history in the study of theology, Christian church history, and Church organization (hierocracy) whence it was taken and introduced to the social sciences by Max Weber, who credits Rudolf Sohm with being "the first to clarify the substance of the concept" (Weber, 1968, p. 216; cf. Roth in Weber, 1968, p. xc).

In general use, the term has tended to lose its religious content altogether, being applied not only to figures such as Jesus Christ and Gandhi but also to American presidents such as Abraham Lincoln, Franklin Delano Roosevelt, and John F. Kennedy, as well as to lesser figures such as Marilyn Monroe and the Beatles until further attenuation makes it nearly meaningless (Cf. Bendix, 1967).

Nevertheless, the term is used to refer to an experience of which all humans are capable in their search for meaning through the leadership of others. It is popularly used in secular society to celebrate anyone or anything that even slightly stands out from the legalistically and rationalistically based routines of the modern everyday. In its fullest sense, it deals with leadership exercised on behalf of saving or reestablishing the world as a meaningful totality (Weber, 1968, p. 450).

In social scientific usage, the term retains its fullest salience as part of the tripartite set of types of authority considered by Max Weber to be dominant in the development of Western civilization: charisma, tradition, and legal-rationalism. The sequence is visible in the history of Europe though with a caution: "But the idea that the whole of concrete historical reality can be exhausted in the conceptual scheme about to be developed is as far from the author's thoughts as anything can be" (Weber, 1968, p. 450).

Sociology's major contribution to the concept is the unfolding of its reality as a social relationship. Leaders and followers both constitute the charismatic relationship. This conceptualization provides critical and corrective insight into the simple, though profound, popular experience that all power emanates from the leader. It also corrects the psychological conception that emphasizes characteristics of the leader while ignoring the neediness of the follower who would totally submit his own life and fate to the charismatic leader.

Weber's own oft-cited definition may originally contribute to the trait theory of charisma: "The term 'charisma' will be applied to a certain quality of an individual personality by virtue of which he is considered extraordinary and treated as endowed with supernatural, superhuman, or at least specifically exceptional powers or qualities" (Weber, 1968, p. 241). The sociological emphasis is on the word "considered," not the purported qualities or powers, which—to borrow from psychoanalysis (which Weber did not do)—may be a function of projection. To quote Weber: "What is alone important is how the individual is actually regarded by those subject to charismatic authority, by his 'followers' or 'disciples'" (Weber, 1968, p. 242).

Charisma finally becomes unavoidably part of the theory of revolution that Weber repeatedly promised but was prevented from delivering by his early death. Arising out of the need of a population to find meaning in a world and time characterized by "anomia," charisma becomes the carrier both of a return to lost orthodoxy and to innovation. In *Ancient Judaism* (1952 [1921]), Weber demonstrates the rise of charismatic prophecy among the people of Judah and Israel at the time of the pre-exile invasions and under monumental economic, political, and social changes. Finally, turning to prophets acting as "political demagogues" at the city gates, a part of the populace there sought for an explanation of why their God had deserted them. The answer was both a condemnation and a promise of salvation: the people of Israel had broken God's law, all would be destroyed—except for a remnant. Their faith in their God resurrected through the charisma of the prophets, Israelites went faithfully forward into their uncertain future.

Attempting to turn the originally sacred concept into a value-neutral one that could be applied to understand both religious and secular leaders (Roth, Weber, 1968, p. xc), Weber established charisma as a revolutionary force that confronts tradition and reason. While charisma, with its origins in eros, is antagonistic to bureaucracy, with its origins in order, the two do not exclude each other in empirical situations. So, for example, legal-rational society, the home of bureaucracy, might require a charismatic president (Weber, plebiscitary leadership, 1968, p. 266–271), and a charismatic leader might require a bureaucratic administrative apparatus: "It was only by the rise of charismatic leaders against the legal authorities and by the development around them of groups of charismatic followers, that it was possible to take power away from the old authorities. It was furthermore only through the maintenance of the old bureaucratic organization that power once achieved could be retained" (Weber, 1968, p. 266). And, of course, traditional societies are typically headed by a leader partaking of at least inherited charisma: hereditary chieftainship or kingship.

Ultimately, the need to find total meaning in life gives way, once achieved, to more particular interests and "the routinization of charisma" ensues (Weber, 1968, pp. 246–249). Seldom does full charismatic authority survive the death of the original charismatic leader: It is at best carried on in the form of the office charisma of the successor or in another, attenuated form.

Transcending the limits of the Western charismatic experience, Weber distinguishes between ethical and exemplary prophecy as distinct carriers of charisma relevant to the West and the East respectively. The carrier of ethical charisma, the "ethical prophet" preaches "as one who has received a commission from God, [and] demands obedience as an ethical duty" (1968, p. 447). Of the "exemplary prophet," this: "On the other hand, the prophet may be an exemplary man who, by his personal example, demonstrates to others the way to religious salvation, as in the case of Buddha. The preaching of this type of prophet says nothing about a divine mission or an ethical duty of obedience, but rather directs itself to the self-interest of those who crave salvation, recommending to them the same path as he himself traversed" (1968, pp. 447–448). The prophet as a carrier of charisma is always characterized by "an effort to systematize all the manifestations of life," thereby "producing a 'meaningful' ordered totality" (1968, p. 451).

As is true of all of Weber's work, the concept of charisma, whether actualized as political demagogy or religious prophecy, takes its meaning only from the larger question he asks. This arises as the task for the sociology of religion: How did the way of life and institutions of modernity rise in the West and only in the West? The understanding of pre-exile Judaic charisma (*Ancient Judaism*) and its theory of revolution presents for Weber only a step in the direction of answering this fateful question.

Criticism of the charisma concept has included complaints that Weber's value-neutral term covers both "good" and "bad" leaders, lumping together widely disparate personalities and situations such as those of Jesus, Gandhi, Napoleon, and Hitler; orthodox analysts using the charisma concept will respond that it describes the social structure of all of these and more, and let the chips fall where they may.

Latter-day attempts to discover a separate and distinct charisma for leaders that meet moral standards, however, have created a more serious problem: the failure to consider the dark side of the force. So, for example, James McGregor Burns's (1978) concept of "transformational leadership" serves the purpose of raising this kind of leadership above the notorious give-and-take mundane transactions of American politics; but it does not take care of Weber's claim that all kinds of charisma involve exchanges, that even in the case of sacred charisma there is an exchange, in this case of soteriological (salvationist) goods. The distinction against transactional leadership raises transformational charisma to an exclusively positive force. Subsequent research suggests transformational leaders providing inspiration, emotional support, and intellectual stimulation (e.g., Bass, 1985); the last characteristic, however, contradicts the obvious regressive emotional effect of major political leaders that would fall within the transformational category, to say nothing of the vicious, if not deadly, scapegoating associated with the authoritarian personality.

The emphasis on the elevating, allegedly moral side of charisma has had the result of focusing only on factors such as the extraordinary behavior of a self-confident individual with a vision who is perceived as an agent for desirable change (typically, in the business administration literature). Such redefinition of charisma makes a value judgment of what is desirable. The concept is forced into the confines of the field of organizational behavior without taking due note of the constraining effects of the organizational structure and culture that, in modern times, would tend to keep leadership at least within formally rationalistic bounds. And the reformulation ignores historical events in which charismatic leadership led and still leads to extermination camps and within the corporate world to wholesale loss of livelihoods when organizational members followed prophets of excellence.

Perhaps no other term exposes the lability of the formulation of social science terms to the dominant interests of time and place as does the term "charisma," especially in the absence of balancing historical and cross-cultural concerns.

RALPH P. HUMMEL

BIBLIOGRAPHY

Bass, B. M., 1985. *Leadership and Performance Beyond Expectations.* New York: Free Press.
Bendix, Reinhard, 1967. "Reflections on Charismatic Leadership." *Asian Survey,* vol. 7: 341–352.
Burns, James McGregor, 1978. *Leadership.* New York: Harper & Row.
Sohm, Rudolf, 1892. *Kirchenrecht.* Cited in Weber, *Economy and Society,* p. 216 n. 1.
Weber, Max, 1952 [1921]. *Ancient Judaism.* [*Das antike Judentum.*] Trs. and eds. Hans H. Gerth and Don Martindale. New York: Free Press.
———,1968 [1922]. *Economy and Society: An Outline of Interpretive Sociology.* [*Wirtschaft und Gesellschaft: Grundriss der verstehenden Soziologie.*] Eds. Guenther Roth and Claus Wittich; trs. Ephraim Fischoff et al. New York: Bedminster Press.

CHARITABLE CONTRIBUTIONS.
A gift to a charity for charitable purposes without personal benefit to the donor.

United States

Economic Activity

Giving USA (published by the AAFRC Trust) reports that U.S. charitable contributions totaled US $126.22 billion in 1993, comprised of contributions from individuals (US $102.55 billion), foundations (US $9.21 billion), bequests (US $8.54 billion) and corporations (US $5.92 billion). Most contributions were made to religious organizations (45 percent), followed by educational organizations (12 percent), human service agencies (10 percent), health organizations (9 percent), arts organizations (8 percent), and a variety of other organizations (16 percent).

Although many charitable organizations rely exclusively on contributions for their support, many others generate most of their revenue from their exempt functions. Universities and hospitals, for example, generate much of their revenue from tuition and fees for services so that they are not as dependent on charitable contributions as other charities.

Gift Law

A charitable contribution is a gift rather than a contract. With a contract, each party gives something of value whereas with a gift the recipient benefits without having to give something in return. Consequently, a donor has not made a charitable contribution to the extent that he or she receives a financial benefit (e.g., paying tuition to a university).

Some courts require a donor to demonstrate that the gift was motivated by disinterested generosity, but most courts do not require this. For example, most courts would conclude that a donor would have made a charitable contribution by giving sufficient money to have a building at a university bear the donor's name, even though the donor was motivated only by ego gratification rather than charity. Recognition of a donor's contribution is not considered a personal benefit to the donor that would disqualify a contribution.

Although a person generally cannot enforce in court someone else's promise to make them a gift, a special exception allows charities to enforce a pledge that has been made to it. If a charity has relied on a pledge, it can require the pledger to pay the amount. For example, if a charity begins construction of a building based on a donor's pledge, a court could order the donor to fulfill the pledge.

Tax Law

When the Congress increased tax rates to pay for military expenditures for World War I, it enacted an income tax deduction for charitable contributions. It was concerned that people might otherwise curtail their charitable contributions to pay the higher taxes. Thus began the legacy that has made the United States the nation with the world's most generous income tax laws toward charitable contributions and charitable organizations.

What Is Deductible?   Only contributions of cash and property are deductible. There is no tax deduction for contributions of services, such as volunteer work of a doctor at a health clinic.

Who Are Eligible Recipients?   A donor can only claim an income tax deduction for a contribution to a U.S. charitable organization (see also **charitable organizations**): No income tax deduction is permitted for a contribution directly to a worthy individual nor for a contribution that is given to charity that is earmarked for an individual or a foreign charity. It is, however, possible to claim estate and gift tax deductions for contributions to foreign charities.

U.S. charities fall into one of two categories: public charities and private foundations. A public charity generally receives contributions and other revenue (e.g., ticket sales by a symphony) from many individuals. By comparison, a private foundation either receives contributions from only one family or business or receives substantially all of its revenue from investment income. A private nonoperating foundation is generally a grant-making endowed charity (e.g., the Ford Foundation) whereas a private operating foundation engages in a hands-on charitable activity (e.g., the Getty Art Museum). Private foundations are subject to special excise taxes, and donors to private foundations receive fewer tax benefits than donors to public charities (see below: "How Much Is Deductible?" See also **charitable organizations and private foundations**).

When Is a Contribution Deductible?   A contribution is deductible in the year that the property and its legal title have been delivered to the charity. If a donor instructs his or her agent to make a gift to a charity, then delivery is not complete until the agent delivers the property to the charity or to the charity's agent.

A special exception allows donors to claim a current income tax deduction for gifts of certain remainder interests, such as a contribution to a charitable remainder trust (see also **deferred giving**). For example, a donor can claim an income tax deduction for a contribution to a charitable remainder trust that will pay income to the donor for life and, upon the donor's death, will transfer the remaining assets to a charity. The deduction will be only a fraction of the total amount contributed: the present value of the remainder interest.

How Much Is Deductible?   For estate and gift taxes, there is an unlimited tax deduction for the amount of property transferred to a charity. For example, if a decedent's will provided that a parcel of real estate should be contributed to an environmental organization and if the property was included on the estate tax return with a value of US $1 million, then the estate can claim a US $1 million estate tax charitable deduction.

The general rule for income taxes is that a donor can claim an income tax deduction for the amount of cash or the value of property that is contributed to an eligible charity. For example, if an individual contributes clothing that was purchased for US $2,000 to a charity at a time when the clothing is worth US $300, then the donor can claim an income tax deduction of US $300.

There are two principal exceptions. The first is that the amount of the deduction may be reduced if the value of the property is greater than its cost ("appreciated property," discussed below). The second is that the income tax deduction for the year may be limited based on the amount of the taxpayer's income ("annual deduction limitations," discussed below).

The tax laws favor gifts of certain forms of appreciated property over gifts of cash. Whereas a gift of cash only produces one income tax benefit (a charitable deduction), a gift of appreciated stock produces two: a charitable deduction for the full value of the property plus avoidance of the income tax that would have been paid had the property been sold.

However, these benefits can only be obtained for gifts of certain types of property that are given to public charities. The property must be "long-term capital gain property" (property that, if sold at its fair market value at the time of contribution, would result in a long-term capital gain). Thus, the property must generally have been owned by the donor for at least 12 months and must qualify for a capital gain tax treatment, rather than ordinary income treatment, if it had been sold. For example, most gifts of stock and real estate qualify for capital gain treatment. In addition, the gift must generally be made to a public charity: a gift to a typical private foundation is not eligible for favored tax treatment.

Most of these technical laws were enacted as part of the Tax Reform Act of 1969. The laws restricted the tax benefits from many gifts of appreciated property in order to eliminate several abuses of the tax laws. At that time, it was possible to be wealthier by contributing appreciated property to a charitable organization than to sell the property and keep the cash (particularly if the property was "ordinary income property," described below). Under current law, the greatest tax benefits occur with gifts of appreciated stock, real estate, and, in limited circumstances, gifts of tangible personal property (such as gifts of paintings or historically significant artifacts to museums). Gifts of other forms of appreciated property, such as inventory of a business, do not provide substantial tax savings.

EXAMPLE: Ms. Donor purchased a highly successful stock many years ago for virtually nothing. Now the stock is worth US $100,000, and she thinks the time is right to sell. She also wants to make a charitable contribution of US $10,000. She will either give cash of US $10,000 or will give US $10,000 of stock.

The gift of stock is the best option. Her taxable gain will be only US $90,000 instead of US $100,000 since she will only have legal title to that much stock at the time of sale. In addition, she can claim a US $10,000 charitable deduction for the value of the stock that she gave to the charity. By comparison, if she gave the stock to a private nonoperating foundation, she would only be able to claim a charitable deduction for the cost of the stock rather than the value.

FACTS: Fair Market Value of Stock: US $100,000

Cost of Stock (near zero): US $ -0-

PC: Public Charity

PF: Private Foundation

	Gift of Cash to PC or PF	Gift of Stock to PC	Gift of Stock to PF
Sales Proceeds	US $100,000	US $90,000	US $90,000
Cost of Stock	-0-	-0-	-0-
Gain on Sale	US $100,000	US $90,000	US $90,000
Charitable Deduction	(US $10,000)	(US $10,000)	-0-
Taxable Income after sale and charitable gift	US $90,000	US $80,000	US $90,000

Ordinary income property is property that if sold at its fair market value, results in a gain other than a long-term capital gain. Ordinary income property includes inventory and works of art or literature created by the donor.

Whereas a taxpayer can normally claim a tax deduction equal to the value of the contributed property, the deduction for gifts of "ordinary income property" must be reduced by the amount of gain that would have been realized had the property been sold. The net effect is that the tax deduction is usually limited to the taxpayer's "basis" in the property (usually its cost). For example, assume a business contributes to a charity inventory that has a value of US $10 but was purchased for US $6. The US $10 tax deduction is reduced by the amount of ordinary income that would have been recognized had the property been sold (US $4) so that the net deduction is limited to the taxpayer's basis in the property (US $6).

Tangible capital gain property includes paintings, books, and personal autos but does not include intangible property such as stocks. In most cases, the deduction for gifts of such appreciated property will be limited to the donor's adjusted basis (usually the property's cost). If, however, the charitable organization uses the property for its charitable purpose, then the donor can deduct the full fair market value.

The classic example is a painting: If a donor contributed a painting to a college that used it for educational purposes by placing it in its library for display and study by art students, then the use was related to the college's charitable purpose. Thus, if the donor had purchased the paint-

ing for US $30,000 but its value was US $100,000 at the time of contribution, the donor could deduct the full US $100,000. However, if the college sold the painting and used the proceeds for educational purposes, the painting was used for an unrelated purpose and the donor's tax deduction would be limited to US $30,000.

The tax deduction for a gift of any type of appreciated property (either long-term capital gain property or ordinary income property) to a private nonoperating foundation is reduced so that the donor can only claim a tax deduction for the adjusted basis of the property. The principal exception is that a grant to a private operating foundation (e.g., an endowed museum) receives the same tax benefits as a contribution to a public charity.

How Much Can a Donor Deduct in Any Given Year on an Income Tax Return? Once a donor has determined the total amount of a gift that can be deducted under the rules listed above, there is a limitation of how much of that amount can be deducted in the year of contribution and how much may be carried forward and deducted in future years. This is called the "annual deduction limitation." The rules vary depending upon whether the donor is an individual, a corporation, a trust, or an estate. The rules are the most complex for individuals.

Partnerships are not subject to these rules. Instead, a partnership informs each partner about that partner's share of the partnership's charitable contributions. The partner then adds that amount to his or her other personal charitable contributions, and each partner then calculates whether he or she is subject to an annual deduction limitation.

As a general rule, if all of the charitable contributions cannot be fully deducted in the year of contribution, the excess can be carried forward and deducted over the next five years, provided that the total amount of charitable contributions do not exceed the annual deduction limitations in those years. If the taxpayer was unable to deduct the amounts in the year of contribution or in the succeeding five years, the deduction carryforward expires and the taxpayer will not be able to obtain a tax benefit from the charitable contribution.

Most corporations are subject to an annual deduction limitation of 10 percent of taxable income. For example, if a corporation with US $100,000 of taxable income makes a charitable contribution of US $30,000, it can only deduct US $10,000 in the year of contribution (10 percent of its US $100,000 of income) and it will carry forward the remaining US $20,000 and attempt to deduct that amount over the succeeding five years, assuming there is sufficient income to meet the 10 percent threshold in those years. The deduction expires after five years.

Estates and trusts are eligible for an unlimited income tax charitable deduction, providing that the contribution came from income rather than corpus and was made pursuant to the governing instrument (e.g., the will or trust instrument). For example, if a person's will provides that upon the person's death the estate should make a gift of US $50,000 to a university, the estate can claim a US $50,000 charitable tax deduction on the estate tax return. However, the estate cannot claim any income tax deduction on the estate's income tax return because such a gift is assumed to come from principal rather than income. One way to qualify for an income tax deduction is to specify in the will that to the maximum extent possible, the payment should be made from "income in respect of a decedent" (e.g., uncollected rent, pension-plan distributions, and other assets that produce taxable income to the estate). Under those circumstances the bequest will qualify for both an estate tax and an income tax deduction.

The annual deduction limitation for individuals depends on a complicated formula involving the individual's income, the type of property contributed, and the type of charity that receives it. More specifically, the amount of the deduction depends on (1) the amount of adjusted gross income ("AGI") shown on the individual's income tax return for that year, (2) the type of property contributed (either ordinary income or long-term capital gain property, described above), and (3) the nature of the charitable organization. Amounts that cannot be deducted in the year of contribution may be carried forward for five years.

The rules are generally as follows:

Type of Charity	Ord Inc Prop	CASH AND CAPITAL GAIN PROPERTY (Stock & Real Estate)
Public Charity	50% of AGI	30% of AGI
Private Nonoperating Foundation	30% of AGI	20% of AGI
Private Operating Foundation	50% of AGI	30% of AGI

What Evidence Must a Taxpayer Have to Claim a Charitable Income Tax Deduction? Congress and the IRS were concerned that many donors were improperly claiming charitable tax deductions when they received something of value from a charity. For example, if a donor paid US $100 to attend a fund-raising dinner where the value of the meal was US $30, the donor should only deduct US $70 rather than the entire US $100. In addition, the IRS determined that many donors who contributed property, such as real estate or art work, were claiming inflated values for their contributions. Consequently, in addition to the usual rules that require taxpayers to substantiate their income tax deductions, additional requirements must be met to claim an income tax charitable deduction.

1. *Receipt with Specific Language for Each Gift of US $250 or More.* A donor will not be able to claim a charitable income tax deduction for any single gift of cash or property of US $250 or more unless she or he can produce a "contemporaneous written acknowledgement" for that contribution from the charity.

To meet the requirements the acknowledgement (1) must contain certain information and (2) must be received within certain time limits. The acknowledgement should state (1) the amount of cash and a description (but not necessarily the value) of any property given and (2) whether the charity provided any goods or services in exchange for the property described in clause (if so, then it must give a description and state the value of the goods and services).

EXAMPLE: The acknowledgement for a typical contribution to a charity should state something to the effect: "You did not receive anything of value in exchange for your contribution of _____, so the entire amount of your contribution is deductible on your federal income tax return." If the acknowledgement fails to contain such a statement, then the donor cannot claim a charitable income tax deduction. Cancelled checks are not sufficient evidence. If something of value was given, a description of the benefit and an estimate of its value must be disclosed. For example, a US $100 ticket to a charitable fund-raising dinner should state the value of the meal (e.g., US $20).

2. *Donor Must Attach a List That Describes Contributions of Property.* If contributions of property (other than cash) to all charities exceed US $500 in a year, then the donor must attach IRS Form 8283 to the income tax return for that year. The donor must list the organizations and the property that was contributed.

3. *An Appraisal Must Be Attached to the Tax Return for Gifts of Property over US $5,000.* Because of numerous instances of overstated values, Congress instituted a requirement that donors who contribute property (other than publicly traded securities) valued at more than US $5,000 in any year must substantiate the value with "qualified appraisals" from "qualified appraisers." The rules generally prohibit a charity, a donor, or persons related to the donor from serving as the appraiser. The US $5,000 threshold is increased to US $10,000 in the case of nonpublicly traded stock.

A charity that receives such property must sign a copy of the appraisal report (IRS Form 8283–"Noncash Charitable Contributions"), which should then be attached to the donor's income tax return. Signing the report does not mean that the community foundation agrees that the value is correct: rather, it is more of an acknowledgement that the property was, in fact, received.

If a charity disposes of the property listed on IRS Form 8283 (through sale, noncharitable disposition, etc.) within two years of receipt, it must file a separate report with the IRS and disclose facts about the disposition. It must also send a copy to the donor. The

IRS's objective is to compare the amount of the tax deduction that the donor claimed with the proceeds that the charity actually received.

International

General

The amount of charitable contributions, and the laws governing such contributions, varies dramatically by nation and by culture. In nations such as the United States and Canada, charitable organizations have a history of depending on contributions from private individuals. Many such organizations are relatively independent of government. By comparison, many similar organizations in other nations, often referred to as nongovernmental organizations, or NGOs, receive most of their support from government or from fees that they charge (see also **charitable organization**). Whether they also receive charitable contributions depends to a large extent on the culture and history of the nation. In Japan, for example, NGOs are relatively new and rare, and the Japanese culture does not have the same history of charitable giving as exists in North America or Western Europe.

For example, the percentage of the population that contributes either money or services to charitable organizations varies among the following five western nations:

	USA	Canada	United Kingdom	France	Spain
Percentage of residents contributing cash	55%	62%	65%	27%	71%*
Average monthly cash contribution	$38	$43	$14	$8	$15
Percentage of residents contributing services	20%	25%	15%	10%	11%
Average monthly time contribution (hours)	2.2	5.2	1.8	1.6	1.6

*Spain's figure includes sales of lottery tickets issued by major national charities, which are purchased by nearly half of the adult population.

Tax Laws

The United States provides donors with the most generous tax benefits. This is probably a result of the entrepreneurial culture in the United States. U.S. charitable organizations depend significantly on voluntary contributions from individuals. The situation is different in other nations. By contrast, in western Europe many social welfare organizations receive most of their contributions and funding from the government. In other parts of the world NGOs are an emerging force.

This leads to wide discrepancies concerning the tax treatment of charitable contributions. For example, assume that an individual with US $100,000 of income opens a safety deposit box and removes US $60,000 at the end of the year and gives it to a single charity. The income tax deduction would be the following amounts in the following countries:

1. United States–US $50,000 (50 percent of income)
2. Canada–US $20,000 (20 percent of income)
3. Germany–US $5,000 (5 percent of income)
4. France–US $1,500 (1.5 percent of income)
5. Sweden–nothing
6. Switzerland–nothing
7. United Kingdom–US $900 (approximately)*
8. Russia–nothing
9. Bulgaria–nothing

The likely reason for this sharp discrepancy in tax treatment is probably the result of cultural differences (as explained earlier). Although a nation's culture is often reflected in the laws of that nation, the laws can also have an impact on the culture, particularly the culture's ability to support NGOs. The different tax treatment probably has a significant effect on the vitality and the economic strength of the NGOs in each nation.

CHRISTOPHER HOYT

BIBLIOGRAPHY

AAFRC Trust for Philanthropy, 1994. *Giving USA 1994*. New York: AAFRC Trust for Philanthropy.

CHARITABLE ORGANIZATION ("CHARITY").

A nonprofit organization that engages primarily in charitable activities, as defined in the tax code.

United States

Economic Activity

The IRS Statistical Bulletin reports that in 1991, there were 516,554 charities recognized by the IRS. This figure does not include the estimated 340,000 churches in the United States, since churches are not required to apply to the IRS for tax-exempt status. Each year, the IRS grants tax-exempt status to approximately 31,000 organizations from the 41,000 applications that it receives. It only denies a few hundred applications; many others simply abandon their

---

* There is, however, a method by which the entire amount can be deducted in the UK: If the gift is made under a "deed of covenant," then the entire amount can be deducted. Under a deed of covenant, the amount must be paid in cash installments over at least four years.

quest when the IRS asks for additional information. The IRS does not publish a record of the number of charities that fail or go out of existence every year.

Public charities in the United States received revenue of US $491 billion in 1991 (all data from IRS Statistical Bulletin). Nearly US $225 billion of this amount were received by hospitals for patient-care charges and US $189 billion were received by colleges and universities for tuition and fees. Approximately 18 percent of revenue comes from charitable contributions (see **charitable contributions**). The revenues and expenses of charities constitute 7 percent of the nation's gross domestic product. Public charities own assets worth US $778 billion (US $232 billion of which are owned by hospitals), and private foundations own assets worth US $158 billion.

Legal Requirements

Overview. The most important law that a charity must comply with is § 501(c)(3) of the Internal Revenue Code. By meeting the requirements of that statute, a charity will be exempt from income tax on its revenue (service fees, sales, investment income, and charitable contributions), and donors can claim charitable income and estate tax deductions for contributions to it (see **charitable contributions**). Consequently, the definition of a charity in the United States is dictated more by federal tax laws than by state statutes or court decisions.

For tax purposes, U.S. charities are divided into two categories: public charities and private foundations. A private foundation is a charity whose primary source of revenue is investment income or charitable contributions from only one family or business. A private foundation is subject to special excise taxes that public charities are exempt from (see **private foundations**).

A charity must be established for charitable purposes and must engage primarily in charitable activities. It may engage in some unrelated activities, such as lobbying for changes in the law or publishing a magazine for profit, but it will lose its charitable status if it engages in a substantial amount of noncharitable activities. Although charities are generally exempt from paying income tax, all charities must pay income tax on profits from unrelated business activities, such as selling holiday cards as a fund-raising program (see **unrelated business income tax**), and private foundations are subject to certain excise taxes. In addition, although most states and cities exempt charities from their income, sales, and property taxes, a few jurisdictions impose taxes on charities.

Requirements under § 501(c)(3).

1. *Charitable Purposes.* The statute specifically defines charitable activities to include religious, scientific, literary, and educational activities. The tax regulations expand the definition to include

relief of the poor and distressed of the underprivileged; advancement of religion; advancement of education or science; erection or maintenance of public buildings, monuments, or works; lessening of the burdens of Government; and promotion of social welfare by organizations designed to accomplish any of the above purposes, or (i) to lessen neighborhood tensions; (ii) to eliminate prejudice and discrimination; (iii) to defend human and civil rights secured by law; or (iv) to combat community deterioration and juvenile delinquency.

Additional activities that are not mentioned in the statute or regulation qualify as charitable activities. An organization will usually qualify as a charity if it can demonstrate that its activities will benefit the community. The principal area of controversy for the "community benefit" standard is whether the group that benefits from the organization is sufficiently large and diverse to constitute a community. Consequently, an organization that will beautify a large residential area can qualify as a charity whereas a homeowners association for a condominium development will not qualify because its benefits are limited to members. The community benefit standard has frequently been an issue for medical service providers such as hospitals. A common issue is whether the operation of a medical facility provides a benefit to an entire community or only to the few doctors and managers who operate the facility. Usually, the operation of a public emergency room is a sufficient community benefit to justify awarding charitable tax-exempt status to a hospital, even if the hospital generally limits admission to patients who have the ability to pay for services.

2. *Organizational Test.* The organizational test requires that the organizational documents (articles of incorporation, articles of association or trust instrument) state that a charity will be operated "exclusively" for charitable purposes. A nonprofit organization will not qualify as a charity unless its organizational documents expressly restrict its operations to charitable activities. Except for public charities that have annual receipts of less than US $5,000 and churches, an organization will not qualify as a charity unless it has first applied to the IRS on Form 1023 for tax-exempt charitable status and has submitted its organizational documents for approval.

3. *Operational Test.* The operational test examines whether the organization's actual activities are primarily charitable or not. The tax law permits charities to engage in unrelated activities, provided that the amount of these activities is not "substantial." For example, a symphony can raise money by selling clothes and other merchandise, provided that the revenue from that activity is insubstantial compared to the revenue generated from symphony ticket sales and charitable contri-

butions. By comparison, a greeting card store that does nothing but sell commercial merchandise but devotes 100 percent of its profits to charitable causes will not qualify as a charity because it is essentially a commercial enterprise that has dedicated all of its profits toward charitable gifts. Lobbying to change laws is also considered an unrelated activity.

4. *Private Inurement Prohibited.* Whereas a for-profit corporation is owned by shareholders who become wealthy with the success of the corporation, a charity is not permitted to have any shareholders or owners who benefit from the net earnings of the charity. Instead, all profits are held by the charity and are applied toward its charitable purposes in future years. A charity must serve public, rather than private, purposes.

Private inurement can also occur through indirect ways. Examples include excessive salaries to directors or executives, large unsecured interest-free loans and unwarranted reimbursements of personal expenses. The prohibition against private inurement usually prohibits individuals from having compensation formulas determined by a charity's net profits. For example, an arrangement where 50 percent of a hospital's net profits will be distributed to the principal doctors, in a manner similar to a partnership, would be a violation of the private inurement prohibition.

5. *Absolute Prohibition on Participation in Political Campaigns.* A charity can lose its charitable tax-exempt status if it ever participates in any political campaign. The prohibition applies to supporting or opposing any candidate who is running for, or who may be appointed to, public office. Congress did not want tax-deducted charitable dollars to be spent in political campaigns. However, Congress recognized that the sanction of losing charitable tax status is draconian and it permits the IRS to impose financial penalties on a charity rather than rescind its charitable status if the IRS finds this alternative sanction to be appropriate.

6. *Limited Prohibition on Lobbying.* Whereas there is an absolute prohibition for a charity to participate in a political campaign, there is only a limited prohibition on lobbying. The tax laws permit a charity to lobby, provided that lobbying does not comprise a substantial part of its activities.

Lobbying occurs if a charity attempts to influence legislation. Lobbying takes place if the organization (1) contacts, or urges the public to contact, members of a legislative body for the purpose of proposing, supporting, or opposing legislation or (2) advocates the adoption or rejection of legislation. The term "legislation" includes action by Congress, state legislatures, local councils, or similar bodies or by a vote of the public on a referendum, initiative, constitutional amendment, or similar change of laws.

For many charities, such as organizations that seek to assist youth, the elderly, or the environment, lobbying is an important method to accomplish the charity's objectives. Such organizations are concerned that their lobbying activities might jeopardize their charitable status. Unfortunately, the laws do not specify the amount of lobbying that is considered excessive. It is clear that an organization that devotes more than 50 percent of its resources to lobbying has exceeded the limit. Congress enacted §501(h), which allows a charity to elect a mathematical safe-harbor that will permit it to make lobbying expenditures of up to US $1 million or a fraction (maximum 20 percent) of its expenditures on its charitable activities, whichever is less. To date, only about 2 percent of the nation's charities have elected this option. The reason might be that many smaller charities do not have adequate accounting systems to allocate the resources spent between lobbying and exempt activities.

Many charities establish separate §501(c)(4) social welfare organizations to lobby on issues that they are concerned with. Although a social welfare organization is tax-exempt, donors to the organization generally cannot claim charitable tax deductions as they can for a contribution to a §501(c)(3) charity (see **social welfare organization**).

The IRS has discretion to impose penalties in certain situations for excessive lobbying rather than to revoke the organization's charitable tax-exempt status. If the IRS revokes a charity's tax status for excessive lobbying, it is prohibited from converting into a §501(c)(4) social welfare organization.

International

The international counterpart to a U.S. charity is referred to as a nongovernmental organization (NGO). NGOs constitute what is commonly referred to as the "third sector," the first sector being government and the second sector being business. The general perception is that the third sector addresses issues that are inadequately served by the other sectors (e.g., meager medical care, relief to the poor, and other social needs for which government and business support is inadequate). (See also **philanthropy**.)

The function of an NGO varies dramatically with each nation. For example, an NGO in Western Europe may receive most of its funding from the government to carry out the charitable purposes specified by the government. By comparison, an NGO in a third world nation might be established to provide basic services, such as water and roads, in a rural area where the government has not furnished, and does not intend to furnish, such services.

The operations of NGOs also vary dramatically with each culture. Whereas Western NGOs tend to conform closely to the operation of charities and social benefit organizations in the United States, NGOs in developing nations often engage in political activities, social movements, and mutual assistance. For cultural reasons, NGOs have only recently begun to emerge in Asia.

NGOs in Eastern Europe experienced spectacular growth during the early 1990s when the iron curtain fell. Until that time, NGOs were practically nonexistent because the state had discouraged the establishment of independent NGOs just as it had discouraged the establishment of for-profit businesses. Many laws were enacted in the early 1990s to grant favorable tax treatment to NGOs. However, most of those laws were repealed when numerous businesses claimed charitable status in order to exempt their commercial activities from taxation. Many Eastern European nations are expected to enact favorable tax benefits when a system of public disclosure and accountability for charitable activities is in place.

CHRISTOPHER HOYT

BIBLIOGRAPHY

Hopkins, Bruce, 1992. *The Law of Tax Exempt Organizations,* 6th ed. New York: John Wiley and Sons.

CHIEF FINANCIAL OFFICER.

Following the Chief Financial Officer Act of 1990, one of 23 persons who have responsibility by statute for the orderly improvement and operation of federal financial management practices and systems.

The chief financial officer (CFO) position was established by statute in 1990 to provide leadership, policy direction, and oversight of federal financial management and information systems, including productivity measurement and improvement, credit and asset management, cash management, and internal controls. The act established a CFO in the Office of Management and Budget (OMB), 22 CFOs in the major agencies, a reporting requirement to OMB and from OMB to Congress, including both an annual evaluation and a five-year plan, and a CFO council to provide a circle of advisers and a network to deal with problems and issues throughout the federal government. While some of this structure had been created by administrative directives prior to 1990, the passage of the statute gave this reform effort a statutory basis and a life beyond the particular policies of any particular presidential administration or Congress.

The CFO of the United States is appointed by the president, with the advice and consent of the Senate. As deputy director for Management in OMB, the CFO is charged to "provide overall direction and leadership to the executive branch on financial management matters by establishing financial management policies and requirements and by monitoring the establishment and operation of

Federal Government financial management systems." Essentially, the CFO is tasked to provide the framework and guidelines indicating how the government should implement financial management improvements. This is to be done by specifying the type and form of information that will be produced by the government's financial management systems, by identifying projects that will accomplish systems integration, and by estimating the costs of the plan. The act requires that OMB submit annual reports to Congress on the status of federal financial management.

Within individual agencies, CFOs report directly to the head of the agency regarding all financial management matters. CFOs oversee all financial management activities relating to programs and operations of the agency, and they develop and maintain integrated agency accounting and financial management systems, including those for reporting and financial controls. CFOs direct, manage, and provide policy guidance and oversight of financial management personnel, activities, and operations. They are also charged with monitoring the financial execution of the budget.

The chief financial officer of an agency is to be appointed by the president or designated by agency heads, as required by law. The U.S. General Accounting Office (GAO), in its report of September 1991, outlined agency CFOs' responsibilities as follows:

- developing and maintaining integrated accounting and financial management systems;
- directing, managing, and providing policy guidance and oversight of all agency financial management personnel, activities, and operations;
- approving and managing financial management systems design and enhancement projects;
- developing budgets for financial management operations and improvements;
- overseeing the recruitment, selection, and training of personnel to carry out agency financial management functions;
- implementing agency asset management systems, including systems for cash management, credit management, debt collection, and inventory management and control;
- monitoring the financial execution of the agency budget in relation to actual expenditures (*Chief Financial Officer Act: A Mandate,* 1991, p. 6; see also Jones and McCaffery, 1992 and 1993).

The CFOs are directed to prepare and annually revise an assessment of their department's progress. This is submitted to OMB for submission in the Five-Year Financial Management Plan (*Chief Financial Officer Act,* 1990, p. 2843). This submission includes a description and analysis of the status of financial management of the agency, annual financial statements, an audit report transmitted to the head of agency, a summary of the reports on internal accounting and administrative control systems submitted to the president and the Congress under the amendments made by the Federal Managers' Financial Integrity Act of 1982, and other information the head of the agency considers appropriate to fully inform the president and the Congress concerning financial management of the agency.

For the agencies, this five-year plan provides an intermediate term strategy to bring current systems into compliance with the provisions of the act, to eliminate duplicative systems, and to integrate existing financial management systems. Agencies must provide a plan for the annual preparation and audit of financial statements; they also must provide an estimate of the costs for implementing the proposed five-year plan. To fulfill their responsibilities, agency CFOs have been given significant authority to access all records, reports, audits, reviews, documents, papers, recommendations, or other material that are the property of the agency, that are available to the agency, or that are related to programs and operations for which the CFOs have responsibilities. Additionally, the CFOs may request such information or assistance as may be necessary to accomplish their duties.

Although there is no universal pattern for the chief financial officer position, in the private sector the CFO generally directs the accounting staff and works with department heads and top management including the chief executive and the board of directors in budgeting, in analyzing financial data, and in focusing strategic planning from a financial perspective. These responsibilities often include both oversight and "hands on" responsibility for external and internal reporting requirements, accounting systems, budget systems, and other negotiations that have financial implications. The chief financial officer is sometimes called a comptroller or controller, but current usage seems to indicate that the chief financial officer has a more strategic focus than the typical comptroller's office. In governments of any size, often the accounting and budgeting functions are separated, each with separate staffs and separate objectives and work cycles. Often the personnel function is separate from both due to the requirements of civil service systems. Consequently, it is often difficult to pull together the diverse elements of a government's fiscal life to do strategic planning, and this is further complicated by oversight requirements flowing from the legislature and various statutory audit agencies. Originally, this fragmented system was deliberately encouraged in order to provide checks and balances and prevent theft of public funds or misuse of resources. With the growth of government and the relegation of many of these systems to lessor priorities, these checks and balances invited inefficiencies of their own. The CFO Act seeks to remedy these defects in the name of strategic vision and efficiency and the prevention of fraud, waste, and misuse of resources.

Neglect of Financial Management

In some respects, entering the 1980s financial management was a neglected stepchild. Budget decisions held the center stage and the assumption was that whatever decisions were made would be expeditiously carried out, despite the fact that federal machinery for financial management was growing increasingly antiquated and the programs the budget funded were growing increasingly complex, with direct payments, third party payments, and various credit and loan guarantee programs.

Not only did the business of financial management get more complex, the growth in sheer size of the federal budget meant that more people were involved with spending dollars. In the federal government, financial management business is carried out by accountants, acquisition technicians, budget analysts, examiners, and officers, procurement officers, contracting specialists, controllers, and comptrollers. The Department of Defense is estimated to have 100,000 personnel in the defense procurement area alone, who produce 250 million hours of paperwork a year (Jones and Thompson, 1994, p. 101).

The size and complexity of federal financial operations is difficult to imagine. While the annual budget drama steals most of the attention, the management of a huge financial institution rolls along almost unnoticed by most citizens until some flagrant abuse of good financial practices occurs. When the CFO Act was being considered in the late 1980s, the Office of Management and Budget and the Treasury Department had the responsibility for oversight of spending annually an amount equal to about one-fourth of the gross national product; they managed a US $2 trillion cash flow, US $900 million in annual contract payments, a payroll and benefit system for 5 million civilian and military personnel, and a budget with 1,962 separate accounts; altogether, the federal government operated 253 separate financial management systems (Wright, 1988, p. 136). In testimony before Congress in May 1995, John Hamre, the DOD Comptroller, noted that each month the department processed 2.5 million invoices, spent US $9.2 billion, and issued 10 million paychecks: "So that's 10 million times to get things screwed up," he said, noting that his own pay had been miscalculated six times in 18 months (Lewthwaite, 1995, p. 11). Hamre observed that in 1994, the Pentagon was accountable for more than US $1 trillion in assets, and 3 million military and civilian personnel and its US $272 billion budget accounted for about half of the federal government's discretionary spending. The systems that budgeted and disbursed these funds included more than 250 accounting systems, including 6 systems for paying uniformed personnel and 10 for civilians. It also included a military travel voucher system that involved 40 transactions and cost the Defense Department US $0.30 for every travel dollar, while private sector travel costs averaged one cent per travel dollar.

TABLE I. FEDERAL FINANCIAL MANAGEMENT FUNCTIONS, SYSTEMS, AND APPLICATIONS BY AGENCY, 1994

Agency	Functions	Number of FM Systems	Number of FM Applications
DOD	B,F,S	274	283
DOT	F,I,P,PR,G	111	113
HUD	****	96	96
TREASURY	B,F,I,P,PR	38	118
USDA	B,F,I	23	102
HHS	B,F,I,P,PR,G	12	105
DOI	B,F,I,P,PR,G	52	57
STATE	B,F,S	50	54
AID	B,F,I,P,PR	48	48
SBA	B,F,I,P,PR,G	16	61
GSA	B,F,S	22	47
VA	B,F,I	24	44
COMMERCE	B,F,I,P,PR,G	28	28
DOJ	B,F,I,P,PR	11	41
EDUCATION	B,F,S	15	19
NASA	B,F,S	16	16
DOL	B,F,I,P,PR,G	13	13
FEMA	B,F,G,S	1	22
EPA	B,F,I,P,PR,G	11	11
OPM	B,F,S	5	10
NSF	B,F,G	6	6
NRC	B,F,I,P,PR	5	5
DOE	B,F,S	1	7
TOTAL		878	1306

Note: In the functions column are listed the functions over which the agency CFO has jurisdiction. (B = budget formulation and execution; F = financial operations and analysis; I = information resources management/financial systems; P = personnel; PR = procurement; G = grants management; S = financial systems only. **** = organization stipulated by HUD Reform Act of 1990. Information is from the 1994 OMB Five Year Plan.) The systems column identifies the number of systems the agency uses and the applications column identifies the number of applications in which the systems are employed. (For example, one system that was used for payroll, purchasing, grants management, and performance measurement would appear as a 1 in the systems column and a 4 in the applications column; in 1994, FEMA had 1 system used for 22 applications and DOD had 274 systems used for 283 applications.)

SOURCE: Federal Financial Management Status Report and Five-Year Plan. Washington, D.C.: OMB, 1994.

Frank Hodsoll, the first chief financial officer for the federal government under the 1990 legislation, observed that the political system was not interested in accounting, financial management, and internal controls, and as a policy and program official with 28 years of service, it had never occurred to him that there was anything wrong with financial management in the federal government. What a shock it was, he noted, to discover that many program administrators did not know the results of their outlays, the location and value of their inventories, the wear and tear on their buildings, the aging of their receivables, and the souring of their loan and loan guarantee portfolios. Should anyone think the amounts here are negligible, Hodsoll noted that on the OMB high-risk list were some US $14 billion in delinquent loans at the FHA, US $13.7 billion in Department of Energy contracting that was inadequately managed, and Medicare and Medicaid misestimates of US $21 billion and US $9 billion respectively. Hodsoll further observed that in some cases the financial numbers were not known on an auditable basis, that due diligence was not taken in extending the nation's credit and credit guarantees—a total contingent liability of a mere US $95,000 per family for all federal credit and insurance programs—and that the results of expenditures and investments often were not measured and when they were, there was little assurance that the measures were accurate and comparable across programs (Hodsoll 1992, pp. 72–74). In Hamre's May 1995 testimony, he acknowledged that the Pentagon had an accounting gap of US $28.8 billion, with US $15 billion attributable to a variety of bookkeeping shortcomings and an imbalance of US $13 billion between checks written over the previous ten years and the vouchers it could produce to account for those payments. Hamre suggested that a predisposition for error existed because the system was set up to expedite payment and to do the accounting later. This often resulted in situations in which defense contractors themselves frequently had to report back to the Pentagon that they had been overpaid.

In addition to correcting the obvious difficulties noted above, Hodsoll emphasized that nonbudgetary financial management was important because it could indicate if budgeted money had been spent for the purposes provided; whether those who received the money used it for the purposes intended; if the money owed in taxes, fees, or credit repayment had been collected; and because it indicated the condition of assets and their need for maintenance, repair, replenishment, or replacement. It could tell how many dollars were saved as a result of efficiencies and how efficiencies compared and allow for the measurement of the effectiveness of both our own performance and the outcomes of policies and programs and how those compared to others.

In August 1990, with little fanfare, the Chief Financial Officer Act was passed with bipartisan support and with unusual agreement between the executive and legislative branches that the time was now at hand to ensure that there would be a structure to keep the ongoing effort of financial management reform alive.

Provisions of the CFO Act

The CFO Act strengthened the financial management practices of the federal government in order to make government operations more efficient, effective, and accountable by improving accounting, financial management, and internal control systems to ensure the provision of reliable financial information to deter fraud, waste, and misuse of

Government resources. The specific steps taken by the Act included

- increasing financial management oversight responsibilities of the Office of Management and Budget (OMB) by creating a Chief Financial Officer of the United States for federal government financial management;
- creating Chief Financial Officers in 22 major federal departments and agencies;
- creating a CFO Council to advise and assist with implementation of the act;
- requiring agencies to submit a proposal for consolidating accounting, budgeting, and other financial management functions under their agency CFO;
- requiring the submission of five-year plans describing the implementation of the consolidation from each agency;
- mandating an annual audited financial statement;
- requiring annual management reports.

The CFO Act established a centralized financial management structure within OMB and in major departments and agencies. The act also created the Office of Federal Financial Management in OMB, headed by a controller who serves as deputy for the CFO. The CFO and controller preside over a network of agency CFOs located in the 14 departments and 9 major agencies of the executive branch (Jones and McCaffery 1992, p. 83).

History of Federal Financial Management Reform

Financial management reform can be traced to the creation of the Joint Financial Management Improvement Program (JFMIP) in 1948. This reform brought together the director of the Bureau of the Budget (now the Office of Management and Budget), the comptroller general of the United States, the secretary of the Treasury, and the director of the Office of Personnel Management to better coordinate disparate federal management functions. The JFMIP is credited with improving federal accounting, auditing, budgeting, financial management training, and education (Staats, 1981, p. 44), and cash management. As a result of the JFMIP efforts, federal auditing standards were set, offices of inspectors generals were established in federal departments and agencies, and accounting standards were evaluated.

Several Hoover Commissions and the 1967 President's Commission on Budget Concepts led to the creation of the unified federal budget in 1968 and important changes in the role of the Office of Management and Budget. The President's Commission also pressed for improvements in federal receipts and outlay accounting and reporting. Other efforts to improve federal financial management have been undertaken. For example, the General Accounting Office (GAO) and the Office of Management and Budget have worked over the past two decades to improve and

standardize federal accounting, auditing, reporting, and other financial management procedures. Efforts to improve internal auditing in federal agencies initiated in the 1950s also continue to the present.

The purpose for these and other efforts was summarized in 1981 by Elmer Staats, then the Comptroller General of the United States, who said that good financial management can help retain public confidence and trust, but that financial management was "often very low on the list of priorities of many top governmental managers. Financial management deserves its fair share of their time and attention" (p. 54), said Staats.

Financial management is about both little and big things. It is about paying vendors on time and for the right amount, about depositing money as soon as it is received, and about preventing vendors, employees, and others who receive or process federal monies from misusing federal funds and assets. These little sins add up on a federal scale. For example, in 1981, OMB concluded that federal financial management focused inordinately on budgeting to the neglect of cash, credit, and financial management systems. Excessive concentration on budgeting led, in turn, to other problems, including

- failure to establish federal credit policy for programs totaling more than US $50 billion in direct and guaranteed loan portfolios;
- absence of a governmentwide cash management system. The government could not receive or make payment by electronic funds transfer and 30 percent of federal payments to firms were late, while 45 percent were made too early;
- a proliferation of financial management systems. Almost 400 financial systems were in use and many were antiquated, incompatible, and redundant;
- insufficient awareness of the need for internal controls to prevent fraud, theft, diversion or misuse of funds and federal assets;
- little connection between budget and accounting data and very little management information available to measure the impact and benefits of spending (Wright, pp. 136–137).

In 1985, Comptroller General Charles Bowsher recommended a number of changes in federal financial management, suggesting that "for too long" financial management in the federal government had been practiced as a rather narrow function involving mainly accountants and budget analysts and that the idea of bringing management issues and analyses to bear upon budgeting and accounting questions had not "taken root" throughout the federal government, although some progress had been made in this direction during the previous two decades.

Bowsher called for a more comprehensive and consistent budget and budgetary accounting, better data on federal agency performance, improved planning for capital-investment decisionmaking, increased accountability for costs and results, and refined fund controls. Bowsher concluded, "Action along [these] . . . lines would provide the federal government with the tools needed for practicing pro-active financial management . . . this cannot be a short-term effort. Although policy makers should feel a sense of urgency about this. . . they have to realize that a full implementation would span several years" (Bowsher in *Improving Federal Financial Management,* 1989, p. 21).

The Department of Defense is a good case in point. Financial management problems in DOD tend to be both well publicized and rather large. For example, in 1993 DOD made overpayments to defense contractors in the amount of US $1.3 billion, which, once discovered, were recouped. With the conclusion of Desert Storm, DOD was still paying some 1,100 personnel after they had been discharged from the service. In September of 1993, DOD was unable to match US $19 billion in disbursements to specific requirements in acquisition contracts. This appeared to be the result of clerical data entry errors in keypunching, and DOD moved toward a systemic solution of this by designing a system to improve the accuracy of data entry.

While some financial management problems are easily seen and solved, others have historical roots. DOD Comptroller John J. Hamre suggests that some of DOD's financial management failures originate in the way the department was formally created and organized. When it was established in 1947, the Department of Defense retained the existing military departments with their vertical chain-of-command mode of operations. This vertical chain-of-command organization is essential for success on the battlefield, but it has distinct consequences for peacetime operations. For example, when computers came along and every organization sought to automate its processes, these organizations were not compelled to emphasize horizontal connections across organizations of like functions, such as pay or contracting. Financial management systems were designed within the chain of command to support the commander of that operation (Hamre, 1994, p. 1). Thus many of the problems that complicate financial management in DOD are systemic in nature and may take years of effort to solve. The Chief Financial Officers Act provides a structure and an emphasis to do this, both within DOD and its chief financial officer and from the general government perspective with a chief financial officer in OMB and with the annual reporting structure and the movement toward audited annual financial statements. It is widely recognized that it will take several years to see the results of the various initiatives undertaken by DOD to improve financial management (*Federal Financial Management Status Report and Five Year Plan,* 1994, p. 52).

However, DOD is not the only federal agency with financial management problems. In 1989, GAO and OMB studies of "high-risk" programs identified as many as 78 different problems that posed potential federal liabilities reaching into the hundreds of billions of dollars. Other problems identified by Congress included failure of the IRS to collect US $63 billion in back taxes, an alleged US $30 billion in unnecessary inventories bought by the Department of Defense, and losses at the Federal Housing Administration estimated at over US $4 billion (House of Representatives Report, p. 14).

Congressional Concerns Leading to Passage of the CFO Act

Congressional expectations for the act were clear. Senator Roth spoke of the act as a medium "to effect change and improve the fundamental problem in the structure and operation of the federal government." Senator Glenn stated that the act was "the single most important step. . . to reduce the risk in the high-risk programs." Representative Conyers commented that the act was "the beginning of the end of much fraud, waste, and abuse. . . . It will create a centralized and professional leadership structure"; for his part, President Bush, upon the signing of the act, stated "improving the government's stewardship over public funds is critically important" (Kent 1991 p. 26).

Testimony given before the Committee on Government Operations in the fall of 1988 focused on three problem areas for financial management reform legislation: management failures and inconsistencies, accounting systems and internal controls, and audited financial statements.

Management Failures and Inconsistencies. Testimony seemed to indicate that decisionmakers at all levels of the federal government were not getting the financial information they needed to make policy and management decisions with sufficient knowledge of the ultimate financial impact of those decisions. Too many important decisions were made based on rudimentary cash flow projection and "check book balancing" with insufficient consideration given to the qualitative nature of expenditures and future costs and liabilities (Congressman DioGuardi, in *Improving Federal Financial Management,* 1989, p. 38). An inevitable outcome of excessive concentration on outlays and cash management was executive and congressional struggle over short-term budget targets and outlay rates.

Accounting Systems and Internal Controls. Testimony also indicated that federal government systems had failed to keep up with a changing world and had become inadequate. "Once a leader in the early days of automation, the Government's financial systems and operations have eroded to the point that they do not meet generally accepted accounting standards" (Congressman Craig in *Improving Federal Financial Management,* 1989, p. 34). It was suggested that the federal government was managing today's financial challenges with yesterday's technology and that without modern accounting systems, financial managers could not perform their jobs well. Costs associated with servicing, upgrading, and replacing antiquated systems were estimated in the billions of dollars. While accounting systems and internal controls had been strengthened somewhat in recent years, continued deficiencies still had serious consequences. The Committee on Government Affairs concluded that the absence of timely, relevant, and comprehensive financial information and persistent internal control weaknesses compounded the difficulty of controlling government operations and costs.

Audited Financial Statements. The committee was impressed by testimony indicating that a key element of the reform would be strengthened, and it expanded financial reporting with the development of audited annual financial statements. Financial statements provide a scorecard for an agency. Moreover, subjecting them to the rigors of an independent audit would, it was argued, instill discipline in financial systems and strengthen accountability (Bowsher, in *Improving Federal Financial Management*, 1989, p. 68). There was some discussion of how the use of financial statements differed between private and public organizations and the difficulty of doing financial statements for certain types of government functions, but on the whole the argument for moving toward auditable financial statements was persuasive.

The Social Security Administration had published its 1988 annual report including audited financial statements that attempted full disclosure of financial information on agency administered programs. These financial statements attested to the financial soundness of the social security system. This was a good example for the committee. In another instance, audited financial statements were said to have proven their worth by detecting serious financial problems. When GAO audited the Federal Savings and Loan Insurance Corporation using accrual-based accounting, it showed a US $13.7 billion deficit. The cash-based position for the same period reflected a substantial surplus (Craig, 1988, p. 25).

OMB continues to argue that annual audited financial statements for federal agencies are crucial to the proper management of federal dollars. First, the process of preparing financial statements and subjecting them to independent audit establishes discipline in the federal financial management process. Second, an audited financial statement can provide an invaluable analytic tool for obtaining a deeper understanding of the federal agencies' financial condition and operations. Third, it can provide insight into the conduct of agencies' programs and the adequacy of their management practices while highlighting material management problems requiring attention. In 1994, OMB Director Leon Panetta commented: "It is true that most people's eyes glaze over at the mere mention of audited financial statements or plans for performance measurement pilots. But without proper attention to these

building blocks of government reform, efforts to restore faith in government inevitably will fail" (quoted in *Federal Financial Management Status Report and Five-Year Plan*, 1994, p. 36). OMB has devoted considerable effort to providing guidance for the form and content of agencies' annual financial statements and the process for auditing these statements.

Qualifications of the CFO

The multiplicity of responsibilities consolidated under the CFO requires that those who fill these positions have broad financial management experience. The CFO Act specifies the basic qualification standards, but it goes further by requiring that OMB develop and maintain additional qualification standards for agency CFOs and Deputy CFOs. The provisions of the act also make it advantageous for CFOs and deputies to be experienced as comptrollers or financial managers, to be skilled in financial management systems design, and to have working knowledge of procurement, human resource management, and regulatory policy. This is a formidable list of qualifications and not all of the early nominees for agency CFO met these criteria. In late 1991, Senator Glenn complained about nominees from Health and Human Services and the Department of Agriculture, "The enormous job of cleaning up the books and hauling the government into the modern financial management age cannot be undertaken by just any political appointee looking to polish a resume" (quoted in "Fixing Financial Management," 1992, p. 9).

In the 1992 Five-Year Plan, OMB emphasized that the skills that the CFO must possess include the knowledge and experience of a comptroller, a manager, and a skilled financial management system designer; a CFO must also be comfortable in the areas of procurement, human resources, and regulatory affairs. Specific standards cited included sufficient experience and knowledge of generally accepted accounting principles; of laws and regulations applicable to financial management and operations; of budget preparation, and execution; of the principles, preparation, and auditing of financial statements; of financial performance standards and measurement concepts; of internal and management control concepts; and of design, installation, and management of automated financial management systems (*Five-Year Plan*, 1992, pp. ii–vi).

Comptroller General Charles Bowsher has suggested that to carry out the broad mandates of the CFO Act, agency CFOs must have demonstrated capability as influential financial management leaders, as successful catalysts for bringing about change, and as accomplished managers at the top levels of an organization. Additionally, the CFO must be skilled at effectively communicating financial management objectives and issues to the agency head and other top level officials outside the financial management area and at applying sound judgment in planning, developing, and implementing financial management systems (Bowsher, 1991, pp. 5–6).

For the Future

The CFO Act is intended to provide for oversight of the ongoing modernization of the federal financial management function. First, it establishes a primary accountable official in the person of the statutory chief financial officers. Second, it puts a powerful financial management organizational structure in place with 22 CFOs reporting directly to the heads of departments and agencies and to OMB and Congress. Third, it requires agencies to develop financial management improvement plans and produce annual progress reports. It provides high level visibility with the creation of the chief financial officer of the United States in OMB and the creation of a CFO Council. Fourth, it sets the stage to move toward financial statements that more accurately represent the financial position of federal agencies and federal programs.

Full realization of the benefits of the CFO Act may take decades, and some experts argue that there are almost as many factors working against the success of the CFO Act as for it, ranging from the way Congress does business to the complexity of financial statements and the difficulty of their use in long-range financial decisions to the size of the investment that will have to be made to improve and maintain financial management systems (Jones, 1993, p. 87). Nonetheless, some important accomplishments have been made. Appointing the CFOs as financial management community leaders is important. Irrespective of what OMB chooses to emphasize, financial management reform can go forward in the agencies. For their part, the agencies have already made significant progress in their ability to produce financial statements that may be audited. In 1990, only five financial statements were prepared; three were audited and none received a clean bill of health. In 1992, 130 financial statements were prepared, 91 were audited, and 32 had no material weaknesses in accounting controls (Buckner, 1994, p. 46).

In 1991 Charles Bowsher, to whom much of the credit belongs for the structure of the CFO Act, observed that the CFO Act's requirement for producing annual audited financial statements, in particular, was "demonstrating its value in several important ways. First, a much clearer picture is emerging of the government's true financial condition. . . . Next, in addition to shedding light on the government's fiscal posture, audited financial statements have brought much needed discipline in pinpointing waste, mismanagement, and possible illegal acts and in highlighting the gaps in safeguarding the government's assets. . . . Third, CFO Act financial audits have identified actual and potential savings of hundreds of millions of dollars. . . .

Finally, the financial audits are also confirming just how little confidence the Congress and program managers can place in the information they now receive" (p.1). Although much has been done, there clearly remains much to do in the continuing struggle to modernize federal financial management.

JERRY L. MCCAFFERY

BIBLIOGRAPHY

Bowsher, Charles A., 1991. *The Qualifications for and Role of Agency Chief Financial Officers.* GAO/T-AFMD-91-7, June 7. Washington, D.C.: USGPO.
Buckner, Charles, 1994. "The Chief Financial Officers Act of 1990." Master's thesis, Naval Posgradute School.
The Chief Financial Officer Act: A Mandate for Federal Financial Management Reform, 1991. General Accounting Office Report, GAO/AFMD-12.19.4, September. Washington, D.C.: USGPO.
The Chief Financial Officer Act of 1990, Public Law 101-576, 1990. (104 Stat. 2838). Nov. 15.
Federal Financial Management Status Report and Five-Year Plan, 1994. Washington, D.C.: OMB, Executive Office of the President.
"Fixing Financial Management," 1992. *Government Executive,* vol. 24, no. 2 (February): p. 9.
Hamre, John H., 1994. *Statement of the Department of Defense Comptroller on Financial Management Reform.* Senate Committee on Governmental Affairs, April 12.
Hodsoll, Frank, 1992. "Facing the Facts of the CFO Act." *Public Budgeting and Finance,* vol. 12, no. 4 (Winter) 72–74.
House of Representatives Report, number 101-818, 101st Congress, 2nd Session, Part 1, Chief Financial Officer Act of 1990. Washington, D.C.: USGPO.
Improving Federal Financial Management, 1989. Washington, D.C.: USGPO.
Jones, L.R., 1993. "Counterpoint Essay: Nine Reasons Why the CFO Act May Not Achieve Its Objectives." *Public Budgeting and Finance,* vol. 13, no. 1 (Spring). 87–94.
Jones, L. R. and J. McCaffery, 1992. "Federal Financial Management Reform and the Chief Financial Officer's Act." *Public Budgeting and Finance* (Winter) 75–86.
———, 1993. "Implementation of the CFO Act." *Public Budgeting and Finance,* vol. 13, no. 1 (Spring) 68–76.
Jones, L.R. and F. Thompson, 1994. *Reinventing the Pentagon.* San Francisco, CA: Jossey-Bass.
Kent, Jill E., 1991. "Organization of the Agency Chief Financial Officer." *Government Accountant Journal* (Spring): 26.
Lewthwaite, Gilbert, 1995. "Pentagon Unable to Account for $28.8 Billion; Error Prone Payment System Cited." *Baltimore Sun,* May 17: p. 11.
Staats, Elmer, 1981. "Financial Management Improvements: An Agenda for Federal Managers." *Public Budgeting and Finance,* vol. 1, no. 1. (Spring) 43–54.
Wright, Joseph P., Jr., 1988. Testimony at: *Hearings on Improving Federal Financial Management, House of Representatives, Committee on Government Operations, Sub-Committee on Legislation and National Security.* 100th Congress, 2nd Session (September 22). Washington D.C.: USGPO.

CHILD LABOR.

The employment of minors in any gainful occupation. The concept of child labor is the result of the industrial revolution and is defined as the employment of youths under a certain age in jobs requiring physical labor, most notably factories, mines, or other potentially dangerous occupations. The derivation of the concept involves the social issue of children's welfare, the labor issue of replacing wage-earning adults, and the educational issue of what constitutes the minimum amount of schooling necessary. Even today there are debates concerning the juxtaposition of education as a function of schools and the need for work experience as an essential part of a child's experience and training.

History

From the earliest civilizations, children were an integral part of the labor force needed to sustain life. With the ensuing move to an industrialized setting and the need for a more literate population, the concept of working children began to change. The family was no longer isolated as a single economic unit with each member having a job to do as in an agrarian economy. With industrialization and the expansion of a middle class in the United States, the term "childhood" was being redefined, and children were depicted as innocent beings in need of protection. This depiction coupled with the emphasis on universal primary education led social reformers to denigrate using children as workers. The development of labor unions in the United States and the subsequent focus on job-related economic goals for wage earning adults also gave impetus to a censorious definition of child labor.

Legal History

Great Britain attempted to regulate child labor in the early nineteenth century, but it was not until the early twentieth century that the United States aspired to do the same. As part of the Progressive Movement, supporters of social legislation that was anti–child labor and pro-reform held the view that children would become the citizens and leaders of the future and thus deserved the protection of government. In 1912, Congress was encouraged to establish a Children's Bureau, which was to research, collect data, and produce reports on the welfare of children. The hope was that this would lead to legislation regulating child labor. In the 1920s, an unsuccessful attempt was made to pass a constitutional amendment that would halt child labor.

At the federal level, early attempts at legislation were struck down by the Supreme Court in *Hammer v. Dagenhart* (1918) and *Bailey v. Drexel Furniture Company* (1922). Many states passed strong laws before the federal government. Indeed, the argument against a federal child labor law was centered on the issue of states rights. It was not until the Fair Labor Standards Act in 1938 that child labor was successfully addressed by federal legislation.

Fair Labor Standards Act

Under the Fair Labor Standards Act (FLSA), the age and type of employment are defined. Children under the age of 14, except in certain cases, are prohibited from working. Youth between the ages of 14 and 15 are allowed to work for stipulated hours on school days, with slightly longer work hours permitted on nonschool days and in certain designated occupations. At age 16 and over, other provisions of the act, such as overtime, take effect. Many states have supplemented the FSLA with legislation that governs child labor.

Today and in the Future

Child labor remains a perplexing problem in the world today. In developing nations, children are still being exploited. Efforts are being made through trade policies and international human rights and labor organizations to attempt to find solutions that will balance the growing labor needs of a country trying to compete in the world market and, at the same time, protect the rights and lives of their youth.

In the United States, companies and organizations are still being fined for violations. Tom Lantos in an article in the *Labor Law Journal* (February 1992) notes that violations remain a serious problem. "The number of federal child labor law violations has risen sharply in recent years, up from 10,000 in 1983 to over 40,000 in 1990" (p. 68). The problem stems from the dichotomous relationship of education and work ethic. The rise in fast food outlets and the demand for a workforce willing to work at unskilled jobs for minimum wage is on the increase. The focus on child labor in the United States today has changed from one of protection to one of dealing with youth unemployment, on utilization rather than exploitation.

SHERRY S. DICKERSON

BIBLIOGRAPHY

Fuller, Raymond, 1974. *Child Labor and the Constitution.* New York: Arno Press.
Lantos, Tom, 1992. "The Silence of the Kids: Children at Risk in the Workplace." *Labor Law Journal* (February) 67–70.
Myers, William E., ed., 1991. *Protecting Working Children.* London: Zed Books.
Reubens, Beatrice G., ed., 1983. *Youth at Work: An International Survey.* Totowa, NJ: Rowman and Allanheld.
Trattner, Walter I., 1970. *Crusade for the Children: A History of the Child Labor Committee and Child Labor Reform in America.* Chicago: Quadrangle Books.

CHINESE ADMINISTRATIVE TRADITION.

The management practices and organizational culture in China from ancient times to the present. Chinese administrative tradition dates back over 2,000 years. It emphasizes rule by talented, moral men, but also uses complex administrative procedures. China is the only ancient world civilization that has maintained a continuous history to the present. Its administrative tradition has contributed to this continuity as well as to the formation of the strong, prosperous Chinese states which have controlled substantial empires during the last 2,200 years.

Pre-Imperial Antecedents

Although a Chinese cultural unity has existed for almost four millennia, China did not become politically unified until 221 B.C.E. In the five centuries prior to political unification, various Chinese states attempted to gain suzerainty. The states became more powerful as states became more bureaucratized, aristocrats lost control of political power and land to powerful families and farmers, the numbers of merchants increased as industry and commerce became freer, and military technology and warfare advanced. Larger states, each determined to unify China under its own aegis, began to "swallow" smaller states. The number of states declined precipitously from 170 states in c.600 B.C.E. to 20 states in c.400 B.C.E. and seven in c.250 B.C.E.

This warfare, which created misery and chaos, prompted the tremendous political, social, and economic changes mentioned above and stimulated a significant flowering of political thought concerning the ideal political system. While numerous schools of thought developed, three have particular relevance to the subsequent development of Chinese administrative tradition.

The Confucians believed society and government would function well if all men, especially the rulers, were moral. Confucius (c.551–479 B.C.E.) said, "If a ruler is moral, all will go well even without orders. But if he is not moral, his orders will not be obeyed" (*Lunyu [Analects]*, XIII, p. 6). A later Confucian, Mencius (c.372–289 B.C.E.), stated the most valuable component of a nation were its people, while the ruler was the least important (*Mengzi [Mencius]*, VIIB:14). Mencius also said the common people could rebel to overthrow a ruler lacking morality because a ruler lacking morality lacks the qualifications to be a ruler and hence is not a ruler (*Mengzi*, IB:8).

The Taoists (also romanized Daoists) believed man should be in harmony with the universe. Politically, the Taoists favored "nonaction" and expressed a lack of interest in material things. People would stay at home, live a simple life and have no concern over affairs in a neighboring village. Ironically, in succeeding centuries, many imperial Confucian officials became Taoists during the 27-month mourning periods for their parents, which Confucian ideology mandated. (These mourning periods served as a kind of sabbatical for officials.)

Unlike the Confucians, the Legalists eschewed morality. Rather they believed a state should have strict codes of laws and regulations with certain rewards and punishments for heeding or disobeying the codes. In Legalism, all subjects, including the highest officials, had to be absolutely loyal and obedient to the ruler.

Using Legalism as its underpinning ideology, the northwestern state of Ch'in (Qin) defeated its competitors and unified China in 221 B.C.E. The founder of the new Ch'in Dynasty (221–209 B.C.E.) proclaimed himself China's first "emperor" and established a strong bureaucratic state. Centrally appointed officials were sent to rule local areas while aristocrats were brought to the capital as hostages. The state unified weights and measures, built roads, and established a post system for communications (an essential requirement for a bureaucratic empire). Very severe punishments in the strict law codes and huge public works such as the unification and enlargement of fortifications, which became the Great Wall, caused great suffering. The severe punishments such as death for arriving late with a work detail despite bad weather actually created incentives to rebel. When the powerful first emperor died (210 B.C.E.), his son lacked the ability to provide the leadership required by the Legalist system and the dynasty fell of its own weight. In establishing itself, the succeeding Han Dynasty (206 B.C.E.–220 C.E.) used the Legalist framework, which the Ch'in Dynasty had created, but made Confucianism the predominant philosophy, especially during the reign of Emperor Wu (141–87 B.C.E.).

The Chinese Imperial State

The Chinese imperial state proved a marvel of human creation. It lasted—with some breaks—for over 2,100 years, from 221 B.C.E. to 1911 C.E. Such continuity of a political system is unparalleled in human history. Furthermore, the system ruled over more people than any other premodern system and controlled huge geographic areas. This marvel of human creation was truly successful. To ask "what went wrong" misses the fundamental success of the system. The system worked well and did not collapse under its own weight. Rather, the system fell under the impact of the huge population explosion in the eighteenth and nineteenth century (caused to some extent by the importation of New World crops such as Irish potatoes, sweet potatoes, maize and peanuts, which enabled the tilling of hitherto unused upland areas) and the intrusion of the aggressive and technologically superior Western imperial powers.

Naturally, like all political systems, the Chinese imperial state evolved. Although an imperial bureaucratic state during its first centuries, officials came mostly from powerful aristocratic clans. During the T'ang (Tang) Dynasty (618–906 C.E.), the imperial institution began to recruit officials through examinations, a change which widened the recruitment base. Aristocrats too had to pass the examinations to become officials. This weakened the aristocracy and increased the emperor's power.

The power of the emperor increased over time. T'ang Dynasty emperors sat with their high officials. During the Sung (Song) Dynasty (960–1279), the emperor sat on the throne while high officials stood. In the Ming Dynasty (1368–1644), the emperor forced high officials to perform the humiliating kowtow ceremony and even had them publicly flogged. Mongol rule, known in China as the Yuan Dynasty (1270–1368), which occurred between the Sung and Ming dynasties, hastened the processes of centralization and brutalization.

In theory, the Chinese emperor became extremely powerful. He was supreme political administrator, military leader, chief judge, and religious head. In the West, the church and aristocracies helped restrain the throne, but the Chinese emperor combined temporal and spiritual authority. There was no human agency above the emperor and no independent institution to which one could appeal. No Western political leader controlled such power.

Naturally, in practice some restraints did constrain the emperor. The Confucian belief system provided one important restraint. Confucianism required the ruler to be both moral and filial to his parents. As the Son of Heaven, the emperor owed his father, Heaven, obeisance. Every year the emperor had to kowtow to Heaven and to offer sacrifices to both Father Heaven and Mother Earth. The emperor's authority derived from the Mandate of Heaven, a mandate which could be withdrawn if the emperor performed poorly.

Basically, success determined whether or not an emperor had the Mandate of Heaven. If an emperor was not performing well, Heaven would deliver such portents as floods, droughts, and famines as well as eclipses and sightings of strange creatures. Such portents were not above official manipulation. For example, a study of the Han Dynasty found that during good times, officials often did not record actual eclipses while during bad times they recorded eclipses that astronomically could not have occurred. By contrast, portents such as floods were clearly related to the functioning of government because floods were much more likely when government neglected maintenance of dykes.

If an emperor neglected his duties (and the evidence we have is that the best rulers worked extremely hard) or performed poorly, aspirants could claim the Mandate of Heaven, arguing with Mencius that the emperor, lacking morality and not ministering to the needs of the people, no longer was qualified to be called a ruler. While most rebellions failed, some did succeed and led to dynastic change. In order to inculcate Confucian values, the sons of emperors studied the Confucian classics, and many became very good scholars.

The Confucian belief system also required officials to remonstrate with a ruler if they believed a matter needed the ruler's attention or if the ruler himself needed correction. In order to institutionalize this remonstration function, the imperial Chinese state established a censorate. Censors were supposed to bring shortcomings to the attention of the emperor without fear or favor. In fact, some censors paid the ultimate penalty, and the censorate did not always function well. However, it often did serve as an important check on errant officials.

The difficulty of administering the huge, complex Chinese empire also provided practical restraints on the emperor. No emperor could run everything himself. Furthermore, emperors required information and specialist advice. Many emperors closely followed weather reports and grain prices throughout the empire, work necessary to efficient running of the empire and the anticipation of difficulties. Some emperors became involved in such detailed administration as the engineering of proposed irrigation and flood control systems. Ultimately, however, even emperors who became involved in detailed planning and administration required specialist advice and options papers. Often the emperor and officials shared an interest in running the empire well. But bureaucracies also had their own vested interests, which were not necessarily identical to the emperor's interest. Thus, a tension also existed between the emperor and administration. The emergence of the Grand Council in the eighteenth century was one attempt by emperors to overcome their dependency on bureaucratic organizations.

The Chinese civil service recruitment of officials through an examination system gave the Chinese imperial state a cadre of eminently talented administrators during the late imperial period (1368–1911). (The Chinese system became the inspiration for civil service examinations widely adopted by Western countries in modern times.) The examinations, based on the Confucian classics, tested general rather than technical knowledge. Thus, prospective Chinese officials were not tested on their knowledge of hydraulic engineering, but in fact some officials later became quite proficient in such technical fields. In testing for general intelligence rather than specific knowledge, the Chinese system bore more resemblance to the British rather than the American civil service system.

The government carefully administered the complex examination system. The number of successful candidates was strictly limited by quotas. In order to obtain the lowest degree, one had to pass a sequence of three examinations held twice every three years. The number who could pass the lowest degree during any examination sequence in the nineteenth century ranged from 25,000 to 30,000. Thus, in a population of about 400 million, about 525,000 to 650,000 persons or 0.2 percent held this lowest degree at any time.

This small group of successful examinees formed an elite group within Chinese society, which Western scholars have called the Chinese "gentry," a group radically different from the English gentry. The Chinese gentry had a privileged legal status. They were not subject to corporal punishment. Commoners could not involve the gentry in lawsuits and commoners who insulted members of the gentry received more severe punishments than commoners who insulted other commoners. Unlike commoners, the gentry did not have to use submissive etiquette before officials. The gentry wore special clothing indicating their status, and commoners who wore such clothes were punished. Members of the gentry were exempt from official corvee labor service and from personal taxes such as the head tax. Only members of the gentry could perform certain ceremonies in Confucian temples. According to Chung-li Chang (1955) between 1 and 2 percent of the population in nineteenth-century China was gentry or gentry related.

Yet, within this small elite, the examination system selected an even tinier group from which officials were chosen. Only 1 to 2 percent of candidates passed the provincial examinations held once each three years. The triennial quota averaged about 1,500 and perhaps a total of 18,000 to 19,000 persons held the provincial examination degree at any one time during nineteenth-century China, less than one person in each 20,000. Those who passed the provincial examination could proceed to the capital for the metropolitan examination. Only 300 obtained the metropolitan degree in each triennial examination.

Despite its great geographic span and large population, the Chinese imperial state had relatively few officials, about 15,500 civil officials appointed by the government. (There were another 7,500 military officials chosen by a separate military examination system, but military officials had much less prestige and power than civil officials. Civilian control over the military was an important feature of the Chinese imperial state.) The leanness of the system is illustrated at the lowest level, the county or district, where the state sent one official, the county magistrate, to administer a population that averaged about 300,000 during the nineteenth century.

The complexity of the appointment procedures for county magistrate, detailed by John R. Watt (1972) illustrates the care devoted to the selection of Chinese officials. Counties were graded according to size, importance, and any special difficulties such as collection of taxes. Only experienced magistrates were appointed to especially important or difficult posts. Most county magistrate appointments were made on the 25th of each lunar month. The monthly quota of 23 to 26 appointments varied according to whether the month was odd or even. In even months, the quota included five metropolitan examination graduates, two new metropolitan examination graduates, five provincial examination graduates, two local educational officials who had completed six years of service, four qualified by financial contributions, three serving officials qualified for promotion and two sons of outstanding offi-

cials. In odd months the quota included four officials who had completed mourning and two officials who had requalified for office after having been impeached and dismissed.

In order to ensure the county magistrate represented central interests, the Chinese imperial state took several measures. First, it followed the "rule of avoidance," meaning magistrates could not be appointed to their native areas. Magistrates could not serve in their native province and had to serve at least 165 miles (265 kilometers) from their native county. Thus, a magistrate usually could not speak the local language or "dialect," was often unfamiliar with local customs, and frequently knew none of the local leaders. Second, magistrates served limited terms, normally no more than two three-year terms, in one place. Finally, magistrates were subject to repeated evaluations from their administrative superiors as well as from censors about such issues as the amount of taxes raised and public order.

Naturally, a magistrate could not run a county singlehandedly. Thus each county magistrate appointed an average of six private secretaries, each of whom was also a member of the gentry and from outside of the county, as well as a number of nongentry personal servants. The county office, the yamen, also employed native clerks and "runners," including messengers, police, guards, janitors, sedan-chair bearers, night watchmen, and grooms. In order to perform well in strange surroundings, most magistrates worked closely with the local gentry. This relationship was symbiotic in that both the magistrate and the local gentry wanted a well-run, peaceful county, but there were also tensions in the relationship because the magistrate had to extract resources from the locality, something the local gentry wished to minimize.

Despite the great expenses and risks, office-holding remained by far the most remunerative source of income in nineteenth-century China according to Chung-li Chang (1962). Being a private secretary, performing local services and teaching, provided gentry with much higher than average incomes, but these paled when compared to office-holding. Some merchants, especially those in government-protected monopolies like the salt business and foreign trade, earned good incomes. Land provided a secure investment, but returns were low. Thus, although wealth could improve educational opportunities and even purchase degrees and office, most of the time it was education and success in the examinations that made wealth possible. The examination system led to a remarkable degree of social mobility. According to Ping-ti Ho (1962), about half of those who obtained the highest metropolitan degree during the Ming Dynasty (1368–1644) lacked even one ancestor in the previous three generations who had attained a degree. Thus, half of those reaching the pinnacle of the examination system lacked any gentry background. This proportion was reduced to a still significant one-fifth during the Ch'ing (Qing) Dynasty (1644–1911), partly because the foreign Manchu rulers wanted to co-opt the Chinese elite. Of course, because each generation needed to pass the examinations and because estates were equally divided between sons, imperial China also saw considerable downward social mobility.

The People's Republic of China

After the last Chinese imperial dynasty fell during the Revolution of 1911, China entered a period of political division, a phenomenon common in Chinese history after dynastic change. The Nationalist Party (Kuomintang, Guomindang) achieved a partial unification of China after 1927. Although the Japanese occupation of Manchuria (Northeast China) in 1931 and the full-scale invasion of China Proper in 1937 contributed to the disintegration of the Nationalist government, a more fundamental reason for the Nationalists' failure was their inability to build such institutions as the party, government, and military. This made it impossible for the Nationalists to deal with Japanese imperialism, to solve economic and social problems, or to defeat their much more organized opposition, the Chinese Communist Party.

When the Chinese Communists proclaimed the People's Republic of China on October 1, 1949, they actually had substantial experience in practical government. Following the breakdown in the United Front between the Nationalists and the Communists in 1927, the Communists established a series of rural-based soviets in southern China with populations totaling two to three million people. These soviets fell when the Nationalists forced the Communists to embark on their Long March of 1934–1935, but after the Japanese invasion of 1937, a second United Front between the Nationalists and Communists as well as active organization behind Japanese lines enabled the Communists to develop several rural-based Border Region governments in which a total of about 80 million people lived. This experience undoubtedly helped prepare the Communists to rule all of China, although many Chinese scholars later criticized Chairman Mao Tse-tung (Mao Zedong) for continuing to use methods applicable to war when he should have been more concerned with peaceful economic development.

Despite these advantages, the Chinese Communists faced many problems. Large areas had lacked administrative structures for many years. The Communists sought to penetrate well below the county (to which the imperial state had sent officials) down to the township and village. The economy, which suffered from warlordism (1911–1927), the Japanese invasion (1937–1945), and the Civil War between the Nationalists and Communists (1946–1949), required repair and stabilization of a rampant inflation. The Communist leadership wanted to conduct social and economic revolution with land revolution and the socialization of industry and commerce. In addi-

tion, the Chinese Communists felt it necessary to send troops to the Korean War.

Furthermore, the Chinese Communists lacked adequate cadres to staff government. Although they initially relied on the "liberating" military forces to establish regional and local government, the rural-based revolutionaries had little urban experience and few educated cadres. According to a senior Chinese leader, in 1949 only 720,000 of the 4.5 million party members were even minimally qualified to staff the party, government, and mass organizations, about one-third of the number required. While some former Nationalist officials were also used, the Communists made many efforts to train their own people.

Although the Communists emphasized cadres who were "both red and expert," political reliability rather than skill took precedence. Cadres frequently had to undergo political study and thought reform (sometimes known as "brainwashing"). As Chairman Mao distrusted bureaucracy because he sensed it favored the status quo rather than revolutionary change, he frequently initiated "campaigns" or "movements" designed to shake up what he perceived as complacent leaderships and organizations. Yet, the harsh penalties for political "errors" led the bureaucracy to minimize risk taking and to accrete the very "bureaucratic" phenomena that Mao wished to eliminate. This background helps explain why many Chinese leaders urge bureaucrats to convene fewer meetings and do more work.

In some ways, the Chinese Communist system under Chairman Mao (1893–1976) appears quite different from the Chinese imperial state. The Communists penetrated deeply into society with both administrative and security networks. They exercised much more control over the economy. And in trying to "turn over" society in a revolutionary manner, they promoted people of poor educational background while eliminating intellectuals from political power (though "revolutionaries," including those of prosperous class background, remained at the top of the totem pole). Yet, Chairman Mao in many ways became a new emperor and, with the assistance of the powerful administrative and security networks, he had much more power and much more state-sponsored veneration than his imperial predecessors.

China's great size has created an important dilemma for the Chinese Communists about the appropriate degree of administrative centralization. In the early years of the People's Republic, the Communists established six regional governments under the administration of the military's field armies. In 1954, the Communists decided to centralize. Yet, regional variation, the huge size of China in area and population, and poor communications have always mandated a degree of decentralization. Thus, although the Chinese Communists have always maintained the People's Republic is a unitary state, compromise has led to a system of "dual leadership." Central party organs and ministries provide vertical leadership whereas provincial and local party committees and governments provide horizontal leadership. Chinese leaders argue these vertical and horizontal leaderships work smoothly together, but they often conflict. At times, the Chinese Communists have emphasized the precedence of vertical leadership whereas at other times, horizontal leadership prevails.

Since the death of Chairman Mao in 1976, China has undergone a series of economic reforms, which has affected China's administrative system. The government now plays a much smaller role in the economy. Enterprises have greatly increased autonomy, indicative planning has replaced detailed central planning, and the prices of many goods are no longer fixed. Private enterprise and foreign investment are playing ever increasing roles.

Unlike the Chinese imperial state, staffing of organizations remains rather chaotic. The party through its nomenklatura system controls key appointments and maintains extensive personnel files. Yet, the Chinese still have not passed a civil service law and Chinese specialists in public administration say there are no regularized procedures for appointment.

In one way, the Chinese Communist system has become more Chinese. The Communists now seek to appoint "talented people." In a manner reminiscent of the imperial state and similar to the Chinese states in Taiwan and Singapore, "talent" is often equated with university degrees, especially doctorates obtained in Western universities.

The high level of security consciousness in China has made it relatively difficult for Western scholars to study the decisionmaking processes of the Chinese administrative system. Generally, scholars agree that Chinese bureaucratic units have considerable autonomy in their areas of concern and that policy changes require considerable bargaining and consensus among all relevant units. Even when senior leaders express a preference for a new policy, bureaucratic units can drag their feet or even subvert the new policy. Significantly, even though the Chinese state on Taiwan has become much more democratic and open, bureaucratic units in Taiwan seem to have a similar autonomy.

J. BRUCE JACOBS

BIBLIOGRAPHY

Late Imperial China (1368–1911)

Bartlett, Beatrice S., 1991. *Monarchs and Ministers: The Grand Council in Mid-Ch'ing China, 1723–1820.* Berkeley: University of California Press.
Chang, Chung-li, 1955. *The Chinese Gentry: Studies on Their Role in Nineteenth-Century Chinese Society.* Seattle: University of Washington Press.
———, 1962. *The Income of the Chinese Gentry.* Seattle: University of Washington Press.
Ch'ü, T'ung-tsu, 1962. *Local Government in China Under the Ch'ing.* Cambridge, MA: Harvard University Press.
Ho, Ping-ti, 1962. *The Ladder of Success in Imperial China: Aspects of Social Mobility, 1368–1911.* New York: Columbia University Press.
Lunyu (Confucius), 1979. The *Analects.* New York: Penguin.
Watt, John R., 1972. *The District Magistrate in Late Imperial China.* New York: Columbia University Press.
Zelin, Madeleine, 1984. *The Magistrate's Tael: Rationalizing Fiscal Reform in Eighteenth-Century Ch'ing China.* Berkeley: University of California Press.

People's Republic of China (1949–)

Burns, John P., ed., 1989. *The Chinese Communist Party's Nomenklatura System: A Documentary Study of Party Control of Leadership Selection, 1979–1984.* Armonk, NY: M. E. Sharpe.
Harding, Harry, 1981. *Organizing China: The Problem of Bureaucracy, 1949–1976.* Stanford, CA: Stanford University Press.
Lieberthal, Kenneth G. and David M. Lampton, eds., 1992. *Bureaucracy, Politics, and Decision Making in Post-Mao China.* Berkeley: University of California Press.
Lieberthal, Kenneth and Michel Oksenberg, 1988. *Policy Making in China: Leaders, Structures, and Processes.* Princeton, NJ: Princeton University Press.

CHRISTIAN DEMOCRACY. A European social and political movement that gained momentum after World War II. It is based upon Christian principles and maintains that democracy is the best form of government in the contemporary world.

Christian Democracy is a social and political movement with origins in the nineteenth century, although it did not really assume an identity of its own until after World War I. It became a major political force in Europe after World War II and today is a political force in some 70 countries, mostly in Europe and Latin America, but with small groups in Asia and Africa.

It is not easy to define Christian Democracy, which, along with socialism, liberalism and conservatism, is one of the most important of the political families, each with its own international movement. An attempt was made by Michael P. Fogarty (1954), who wrote the first history of Christian Democracy in the English language. He defined it as "a movement of lay persons who, under their own responsibility, attempt to solve political, economic and social problems in accordance with Christian principles and who deduce from these principles and from practical experience that democracy is the best form of government in the contemporary world" (Fogarty 1954, p. 461).

Although substantially correct, this definition is too broad. The only effective way to understand what Christian Democracy is, is by examining the movement's identity and aims and the way these have been expressed in government. Subsequently, we shall look at Christian

Democracy in Latin America and Christian Democracy as an international movement.

History

To quote the historian Jean-Marie Mayeur (1980), an acute observer of this phenomenon, "The Christian Democrat parties—or, as they sometimes prefer to be called, democratic parties of Christian inspiration—have, together with the conservative and traditionalist parties, the liberal and anti-clerical democratic parties, the socialist and communist parties [the fascist and national socialist parties could also be added here] formed a part of the European political landscape in the 19th and 20th centuries" (1980, p. 5).

Much the same may be said of the Latin American Catholic and Christian Democrat parties since World War II.

Jean-Marie Mayeur talks of "Catholic parties" because it is not easy to find a Christian Democrat nucleus within the vast movement of different types of associations—social, cultural, etc.—and parties that were formed in Europe as a reaction to the French and industrial revolutions.

The French Revolution spread anticlerical liberalism, an often uncontrolled nationalism, and a rather abstract and individualistic conception of democracy—liberal, in fact—that admitted no hierarchies, associations, or "intermediate bodies" between the citizens and the state. Faced with these new tendencies, which threatened traditional religious institutions, from marriage to funeral, encouraged the secularization of society, and placed severe limits on Catholic and church interests, Catholic movements were formed in many countries, made up of associations and parties that reacted initially at a social level and then politically to liberalism and, at the same time, to socialism, which was beginning to play an important role.

The industrial revolution was a violent shock to agricultural society and culture, uprooting masses of people from the countryside and forcing them to live in urban poverty and misery, causing social divisions that are unthinkable today.

Socially involved Catholics reacted to these two revolutions in different ways. Some were intransigent counter-revolutionaries, pining for the *ancien regime*, some were liberals, hoping to reconcile Christian values and democracy, while others were more concerned with the social consequences of the industrial revolution, trying to alleviate the suffering it caused, at times joining forces with the intransigent Catholics in a call for a *societas christiana* to oppose both political and economic liberalism. There were even Christian socialists who called for a proletarian revolution. In some parts of Europe, such as Ireland, Poland, Belgium, and Catalonia, social demands were coupled with the desire for freedom from foreign cultural oppression, giving rise to irredentist Catholic movements.

The Catholic leagues and parties that were typical of the nineteenth century often embraced all or some of these tendencies. At first, Christian Democracy was just one of these, calling in particular for moral, religious, social, and political renewal in the church and in the Catholic world. Its first rumblings were heard in the 1830s, above all in Felicité de Lamennais' Paris journal *L'Avenir.* Although accepting the constitutional monarchy that came after the July revolution, the paper criticized some of its policies and called for political and governmental decentralization and freedom of teaching. Above all, it called for the separation of church and state, a demand that was too audacious for the Holy See, which condemned *L'Avenir* shortly afterward.

The first Christian Democrat movement in the true sense dates back to 1848, the year of national, liberal, and social revolutions in various European countries. It was precisely those liberal aspirations, coupled with social concern, that created a deep split with traditional and conservative Catholics. Christian Democracy now had a social and political meaning: democratic government inspired by Christian principles, under the banner "God and freedom." It aspired to a "new era," which was to become the name of the newspaper published in France by Antoine F. Ozanam and the Abbé Maret. However, the papal condemnation of Catholic liberalism in the Syllabus of Errors of 1864, together with the restoration of the monarchies, also put a stop to the development of Christian Democracy.

The second Christian Democrat movement was the brainchild of Leo XIII and his great political and social encyclicals, *Rerum Novarum* of 1891 in particular. This great Pope realized that with the end of the "Christian sovereigns," society could no longer be reconquered from above. Instead, he dreamed of the advent of a new Christendom to replace medieval Christendom. This would be brought about by the works of lay Christians according to a far-reaching program of social democracy. He believed, however, that it was essential for Catholics to remain united politically—a problem nonexistent in the Anglo-Saxon countries, where there are no anti-clerical parties—and in his encyclical *Graves de comuni,* he condemned any involvement by Christian Democrats outside the social field. Politically, in fact, the Christian Democrats would not have joined forces with the conservatives, and the result would have been a divided Catholic front.

It was not until the end of World War I, with universal suffrage, the consolidation of parliamentary institutions, and the advent onto the political scene of the masses, that the third Christian Democrat movement arose. In the 1920s, the so-called popular parties, the first real Christian Democrat parties, were formed, taking as their main model the *Partito Popolare Italiano* of Don Luigi Sturzo. These parties suffered the impact of fascist and communist totalitarianism and the crisis of civilization that was looming over

Europe in those years, and consequently political democracy and peace were central to their programs. The totalitarian regimes, however, and the outbreak of World War II, put an end to them, even though their ideals remained alive in the hearts of many people.

At the end of World War II, and sometime during the resistance against fascism, new Christian Democrat or Christian Socialist parties were formed in various western and central European countries. To general surprise, midway through the 1940s, the Christian Democrats became the majority parties in a number of countries, forming or taking part in governments, something that had rarely happened between the wars. Thus, they played an important role in the reconstruction of democracy and European integration.

Identity and Program

Within the various cultural and political traditions of Europe a political movement's identity has, at least until now, been of vital importance. This identity is bound up with its historical memory, its fundamental beliefs, its program, its party organization, and its government record as well as with its political leadership and its grassroots support.

Underlying Christian Democracy are three sets of relationships: first, between Christian values and the secular nature of politics; second, between these values and democracy; and third, between these values and the social teachings of the churches–Catholic and, since the end of World War II, also Protestant. The relationship between Christian inspiration and secular politics was soon settled by Christian Democrats as a distinction between levels– the political and the religious. Politics have their own autonomy, which is not, however, absolutely independent from ethical and religious values, for the purpose of politics is to serve humankind.

In the relationship between Christian inspiration and democracy–the fundamental contribution of Christian Democrats to the Catholic world in the 1930s and 1940s– the basis of democracy is respect for the person and a person's values. The result is an original conception of the relations between civil society and state that excludes all forms of state or party totalitarianism (including "clerical-fascist") and instead fosters cultural, social, and institutional pluralism and the bonding together of social democracy with political democracy. It is a democracy founded on the principals of the community (individuals are part of a community, not isolated monads) and subsidiarity, above all to protect the person and the family. At first Christian Democracy was to some extent dependent on the church's social teachings, but gradually it became increasingly independent, without falling into unrestrained secularization.

The party structure and program have also been particularly important in giving the Christian Democrat parties an identity. As the historian and political scientist Hans Maier (1988) says, the characteristic feature of the parties of the liberal era was not the social background of their supporters but their political beliefs–and, I would add, their indirect structure in the case of the conservatives. The socialist parties of the last century were the first parties based on class and program. Political beliefs became ideologies. They were the mass parties in embryo, parties able to unite and mobilize the masses on ideological and organizational levels, in antithesis to the conservative and liberal parties and competing within society with the Catholic parties (Protestant political organizations were of little importance and there were no equivalent movements in the Orthodox countries). These parties were not representative of any one class and their organization was similar to that of the conservative parties, with an indirect structure based on a wide network of associations, with a still rather indeterminate political policy and program. Often they were confessional. Generally speaking their position was center-right. Their models were the German *Zentrumspartei* and the Belgian *Union Catholique*.

Compared to these, the popular, or Christian Democrat, parties that appeared after World War I in a number of countries were a new phenomenon. Their structure was still indirect, but they showed much greater unity than the traditional conservative or Catholic parties. They were the first true mass parties founded on a political policy and well-defined program of social transformation–that is, based not on a religious confession but on a program and a social block. And they did not merely defend Catholic interests. On the contrary, they went on the offensive, attempting to embody Christian values in a program for the good of society as a whole, offering an alternative to both liberalism and socialism. They favored political independence, looking, unlike the traditional Catholic parties, not to the Catholic Church but to the secular state. Politics, not religious or social matters, were the most important thing. Instead of center-right, they were center-left. Although they had limited success, they were the first modern parties outside the Anglo-Saxon countries. Their model was the *Partito Popolare Italiano*.

After World War II, the Christian Democrat parties obtained an enormous and unexpected success. They were nonconfessional and wanted to break from the tradition of the Catholic parties, an aim partly achieved by the popular parties in some countries between the two wars. They shared with the latter the central importance of a political program, often a medium-term program of principles and a short-term electoral program. At first, they were usually center-left parties, but they evolved rapidly and, also because they were not class parties, moved toward the center or sometimes right of center. What was new was collaboration with Protestants in Germany and Holland. The most important parties were the German CDU/CSU, the Italian Christian Democrats, and the Belgian Social Christian Party. The Dutch Catholic Party remained in many ways a traditional Catholic party.

The main points of the first programs drawn up by the Christian Democrat parties after the war—and, in secret, during the war—were the following: inspiration of the temporal sphere by the spiritual one, hence a close link between ethics and politics; the consolidation and extension of social and political democracy; national economic planning, with more democracy in business and state ownership of strategic industries; farm reform; a fair redistribution of income; welfare services for all; a great effort in education and culture to promote the growth of a pluralist, well-ordered society; federalism and regional decentralization; regional integration and democratization of international life. The role assigned to the state, which was no longer an object of fear, was to create a just society, not simply to uphold the existing order.

Here the party takes on a special role. Society and the state carry out the program, the party formulates and promotes it. Much debate has taken place over the nature of the party. The traditional party of notables was no longer desirable, and a new party was needed. For some, this should be progressive, with its own ideology, whereas for others, it should be a national party including all social groupings. Some favored a labor party, closely linked with the Christian Workers Movement, and there were even those with an almost Leninist view who wanted strong leadership. Militant groups were also formed, belonging to movements that claimed to be "pure" and "strong" (the word "militant" is significant, for it evokes the idea of political volunteers; now it is out of fashion).

The idea of renewal, however, in spite of much resistance, was soon set aside, although this did not happen until after the Christian Democrats, together with the other political groupings that had fought against fascism, had embodied their ideas in constitutional charters, in some countries at least (France, Italy, the German Federal Republic). In practice, these new constitutions were regarded more or less as blueprints for a new society.

By the 1950s, the cold war had divided Europe into two opposing camps, and parties had to decide where they stood. The Catholic Church, prior to the Second Vatican Council, was not yet prepared to leave lay Catholics completely free to rebuild society. The Christian Democrat parties were moving steadily toward the center, as their electorate now grouped together all social classes with different political ideas, from liberal to progressive. Conservative forces were again taking the initiative. Moreover, government matters were prevailing over party matters—the parties, in fact, were gradually losing much of their independence and power. National reconstruction and European integration were therefore pursued according to a neocapi-

talist design that was different from the original Christian Democrat ideal of a Christian-inspired community, although they did make their own contribution toward creating a mixed economy, democratic planning, the welfare state, and so forth, often in partnership with social democrat and, sometimes, socialist parties. These were years in which even the Christian Democrat parties seem to have lost their innovatory thrust and the spirit of the antifascist resistance. Antiplanning tendencies appeared more and more frequently, almost as if to remind people that what had been, or was being, created was the best of all worlds—for some, if not for all.

From around the middle of the 1960s, the Christian Democrat parties rediscovered an interest in planning. Finding themselves in opposition for the first time since the war (with the exception of Italy, whose democracy was blocked because it had the strongest Communist Party in the West), shaken by student and social protest as well as by the great economic and social changes that were taking place and by the first openings of the Catholic church after Vatican II, they realized that new ideas were needed. Parties had to be restructured, policies that had remained unchanged since the war needed to be revised. However, faced with the need to change development mechanisms that were coming increasingly under attack for the distortions and injustice they were causing, the European Christian Democrat parties, theoretically underequipped and conditioned by what they had already achieved, were incapable of returning to their original ideals and pursuing, with creativity and courage, the *novum* demanded by a large part of society. All they could do was introduce corrective measures designed mainly to improve the redistribution of income. This was often done in collaboration with the socialists—in Italy, it was the time of the "center-left," in Germany the "grand coalition."

Subsequently, Catholic thought, reinvigorated by Vatican II, has been concentrating on how to reconcile moral and practical issues in an attempt to overcome the current fragmentation of the Catholic world.

What do the European Christian Democrat parties propose today? Is any effort being made to revise their basic beliefs and political aims? To what extent have they sought to replace the myth of unlimited growth, to which they have implicitly or explicitly paid tribute over recent decades, with a more human, sustainable growth based on fairness and the recovery of ethical and cultural values, the foundation stones of a society that was once supposed to be personalist and communitarian? To what extent has the collapse of their main adversary, communism, made them rethink their identity, in which anticommunism has so far been a dominant feature? And to what extent does triumphant free trade raise theoretical and practical problems for them in western and central Europe, as well as in the developing countries? Strategically, where do they stand today?

Government

As we have already seen, the Christian Democrat parties, which were minorities between the two wars, had an enormous and unexpected success immediately after the end of World War II in a number of countries: the MRP in France, the DC in Italy, the CDU/CSU in West Germany, the PSC in Belgium, the CHU, ARP, and KVP in the Netherlands, the PSC in Luxembourg, the Workers Party in Poland, the Popular Party in Czechoslovakia, and the Christian Democrat Popular Party in Hungary. Between 1947 and 1948, the central European countries were cut off behind the iron curtain. In the western European countries mentioned, the Christian Democrat parties were elected democratically and were often the leading government parties. It was mainly these parties that restored peace, rebuilt their countries, and took the first steps toward European integration.

Restoring peace at home, which meant reconciling citizens who had fought on opposing sides in what was often a civil war, not just a war of resistance against a foreign enemy, was carried out successfully, and the majority of the people, whose attitude for years had been one of "wait and see" without committing themselves either for or against the fascist regimes, joined the new democratic parties, where they were taught the meaning of democracy. The Christian Democrat parties were also the first to oppose the threat of Soviet communism in defense of Christian civilization.

As to reconstruction, in the immediate postwar years, the Christian Democrat parties started off with progressive policies, including an important state role in the economy, nationalization of companies to prevent private monopolies, encouragement of the trade unions, democratic planning, and so on. Gradually, however, their policies became more conservative. There were various reasons for this, such as the difficulty of making decisions in coalition governments, the pressure of the middle classes, who did not approve of the Christian Democrat parties' progressive tendencies, the influence of the Marshall Plan, which made western Europe part of a large western market.

There was probably another reason as well—the Christian Democrat parties' lack of government experience. This had been negligible between the wars, for even though their intellectual contribution had been considerable, especially in the case of the Italian Popular Party and the French Popular Democratic Party, most of the Catholic parties had done little but support corporative experiments. These limitations were overcome by adopting liberal (L. Erhard in Germany and L. Einaudi in Italy) or labor (New Deal, Keynes) theories.

Thus, the Christian Democrats were often the tributaries of the programs of other movements, especially in the theory of government and economics—two strategic sectors. We should not forget either that the Christian Democrat parties have always governed in coalitions and consequently have had to adapt their policies to the demands of other political forces.

The historian Jean-Dominique Durand (1995) identified four principles that have guided Christian Democrats. These are the redistribution of property, an economy at the service of humankind, improvement of capitalist models, and aid and cooperation for the Third World.

In the 1960s and 1970s, the Christian Democrats went into opposition in many countries, often being replaced by socialist or social-democrat parties or, alternatively, forming large transitory coalitions. The struggle against socialism, which was particularly strong in Germany and Austria—in the Benelux countries and Italy, they were often together in coalition governments—led steadily toward a polarization that eventually extended into the European Parliament, where the need for a stable majority induced the German Christian Democrats in particular to form increasingly close coalitions with the English Conservatives.

With the fall of the Berlin Wall and the collapse of the Soviet empire, the Christian Democrats lost the political enemy that had shaped their strategies and, ultimately, their identity. The risk now is that they will be swallowed up in this great neoconservative vortex, which appears to be victorious and ready to embrace the whole world. Within the Christian Democrat parties, too, the flow of ideas that they tried to implement in the postwar years seems to be drying up, and their policies have at times become neoconservative. Less and less is heard of the mixed economy, while virtually all parties have by now adopted the German formula of the social market economy, a formula which in reality is open to various interpretations but is basically a market economy that is less finance-dominated than the American one, that concentrates more on stable relations with civil society—the unions above all—and is able to correct disparities through social policies without structural reforms.

With regard to the European Community, the Christian Democrats, unlike the socialists, for example, have always been its main promoters and defenders—Robert Schuman, Konrad Adenauer, and Alcide De Gasperi were its founding fathers. The building of Europe has gone ahead steadily in spite of many difficulties, such as De Gaulle's nationalism and the perennial reservations of the United Kingdom. Today, there are fewer prospects of a true federation. Instead, the aim seems to be a more modest confederation, with precise powers, that embraces a greater number of member countries. Fortunately, the Christian Democrats are no longer along in facing this political challenge, which, though formidable, holds out great hopes for the future.

Latin America

The Christian Democrat parties of Latin America were born after the end of World War II, often imitating European models, in particular the French *Mouvement Républi-cain* and the Italian *Democrazia Cristiana*.

Unlike the European Christian Democrat groups, which arose out of local reactions to the liberal and industrial revolutions, the Latin American parties, which react above all against underdevelopment and undemocratic regimes, have also been encouraged from above, by the Christian Democrat Organization of America, which set itself the task in the mid-1940s of spreading Christian Democracy in Latin America. The continent's greater cultural and linguistic unity (Christian Democracy has never really taken root in Brazil) and its common personalist inspiration led to the growth of a more united movement than in Europe.

Notwithstanding this encouragement from above, the Christian Democrat parties have taken root in the souls of the people of many Latin American countries, more so than the socialist and communist parties. At the same time, even in the years of nonalignment, Latin American Christian Democrats did not adopt markedly Third World attitudes, and their links with Europe remained predominant.

What unites these movements is the idea of creating a new Christendom, nonconfessional—in the past, most bishops sided with the conservative parties—but lay, democratic, and pluralist, in keeping with the teaching of the philosopher Jacques Maritain. In concrete terms, the program of Latin American Christian Democracy is the creation of a mixed economy with a vast self-managing sector, the nationalization of strategic sectors, key products above all, prudence in admitting foreign capital, which often makes them dependent, and finally the adoption of democratic planning. At the institutional level, the role of the state is not merely to be the guarantor of civil society but also to act as a driving force for social and economic change. This involves continuous and active participation by the people. Culture and education play a fundamental role in developing the values of the community and the person within the community.

In the 1960s, in Chile, a Christian Democrat party won a general election for the first time, and Eduardo Frei became the first Christian Democrat president in the Americas. The United States looked on him as an alternative model to Castro, who dominated Cuba with his Caribbean communist regime.

Frei carried out a series of reforms in the name of the "Revolution in Freedom," which, in spite of difficulties raised by the right, was an important step in the country's democratic evolution. Farming and education were reformed, copper was nationalized, and regional integration was reinforced.

Soon afterward, the continent's second Christian Democrat president, Rafael Caldera, won the elections in Venezuela. Frei was no longer an exception. The Christian Democrats had shown that they knew how to win demo-

cratic elections and how to govern. Caldera's government was not so concerned with social justice, but it succeeded in restoring peace to the country—the communist guerrillas were persuaded to lay down their arms and take part in the elections—and in nationalizing the oil industry in spite of North American opposition.

A third case, Salvador, shows clearly how difficult it is to solve problems democratically in an underdeveloped continent. In the conflict between right-wing forces and the left-wing guerrillas, the Christian Democrats of President Duarte, who had been elected with the help of the United States, tried fruitlessly to impose peace. In the end, this was achieved by the right-wing government of President Cristiani.

Today the Christian Democrat movement in Latin America is not losing ground but does not seem to be making much further progress.

The Christian Democrat International

As we have seen, true Christian Democrat parties were formed between the two world wars, and of these the Italian Popular Party and the French Popular Democratic Party were the most important. It was these that, in 1925, promoted an International, often called "white" or "popular," that gathered together Christian Democrat, Catholic, and Christian Social parties from Western and Eastern Europe. Don Luigi Sturzo was the driving force behind the event.

As I wrote in my book *Don Luigi Sturzo e l'Inter-nazionale Popolare* (1995), the parties that attended the International had various interests, such as the struggle against fascism (PPI) and the desire for a forum in which to discuss Franco-German problems (PDP and the *Zentrumspartei*), but also, and more important, a common unifying factor: a longing for peace and a determination to influence international relations so that the horrors of World War I—the "useless slaughter," as Benedict XV called it—would not be repeated.

Exchanges between the traditional Catholic parties had been relatively rare because their confessional nature—in practice they were dependent on local bishops—and their lack of a true political program—their main purpose was to defend Catholic interests against liberalism—had not encouraged them to act on a more global level. After all, they already had the International *par excellence:* the Roman Catholic Church.

The *Secrétariat International des Partis Démocratiques d'Inspiration Chrétienne*, as the Popular International was called, took place, like the Liberal International and the International of the Peasants Parties between the two world wars, some 60 years after Karl Marx's first Workers International, which had been held in 1864. Why such a delay? In my opinion, the true reason is that the workers' movement was aware of the negative effects of the industrial revolution much earlier than the Catholics. There were individuals and Christian social groups who realized what was happening and reacted, but it was not until *Rerum Novarum* in 1891 that there was any official, coordinated Catholic reaction.

Rerum Novarum may rightly be called the Magna Carta of social Catholicism and Christian Democracy. In the last century, the church still confused the temporal and the religious spheres, preventing Catholics from taking important initiatives that were not explicitly religious unless they had been approved by the pope or the bishops. Let us not forget that class consciousness acted as a strong bond for workers' movements (although it was no stronger than nationalism: in spite of appeals by the Socialist International, German and French workers did not refuse to enlist in World War I). Another reason for the delay is that the Catholic movement tends to be regional rather than - international—for many years, in fact, regional identity has often been confused with ideology, especially in Latin America.

The importance of this first attempt to move onto the international stage was little more than symbolic and left few traces inside the Christian Democrat movement. The second, after World War II, had much longer lasting effects. In 1947, the *Nouvelles Equipes Internationales* (NEI) was formed (the name, proposed by the *Mouvement Républicain Francais,* was deliberately devoid of any ideological connotations so that non-Christians could also be accepted) and in 1949, the Christian Democrat Organization of America (CDOA) was founded.

It was not until 1961, at Santiago, Chile, that the NEI and ODCA, together with the Christian Democrat Union of (exiled) Parties of Central Europe (CDUCE), established the World Christian Democrat Union, which later changed its name to Christian Democrat International (CDI).

In 1976, members of the European Parliament were to be elected directly for the first time, and so the Christian Democrat parties of the European Community founded the European Popular Party, which, in spite of its limitations, was the first transnational political party—the liberal and socialist federations are not parties in the true sense.

With the fall of the Berlin Wall, the old and the new Christian Democrat parties and the CDUCE enjoyed a brief moment of glory. Above all, it was hoped that they would be able to regain the positions they had held between the wars, but this was not to be. Today the political field in Eastern Europe is dominated by conservatism and the return of former communists.

The CDI is more than the sum of its regional organizations. It is responsible for coordinating some 70 parties in all five continents, although these retain their independence. Its charter gives it rather limited powers: It has a voice at the United Nations and the UN agencies, it can hold congresses, introduce the movement into new coun-

tries, and so forth. However, it does have an important role in mediation to resolve political problems and tensions.

In the 1980s, in spite of political difficulties (due mainly to the attraction felt by some important Christian Democrat parties toward the Conservative International) and financial problems (partly connected to the previous problem), the CDI grew considerably. A great effort was made to reintroduce and strengthen democracy in Latin America, especially Chile and Central America. The same is true for the Philippines. Much has also been done along these lines in Africa and Eastern Europe.

Between 1990 and 1993, the number of members of the CDI rose from 53 parties to 67. The new members were from various continents, not only the former Soviet block.

The aim of the CDI—which was created by the Christian Democrat parties and not by the traditional Catholic parties—is not to create societies that are officially Christian, but societies inspired by the values of Christian humanism (or, better, personalism) in full collaboration with the values of other branches of humanism.

Today this Christian humanism is radically opposed to the social conservatism of the market economy in its current global domination, as we can see from the stances taken by many bishops, both Catholic and non-Catholic. Many Christian Democrat parties, however, refuse to do anything concrete to change the situation and tend to align themselves with right-wing forces. Although these alliances may often be merely tactical, they risk becoming strategic, which would be a total involution compared to the fundamental principles of Christian Democracy.

ROBERTO PAPINI
TRANSLATED FROM ITALIAN BY MICHAEL BEAVON

BIBLIOGRAPHY

Durand, Jean-Dominique, 1995. *L'Europe de la Démocratie Chrétienne.* Brussels.

Fogarty, Michael P., 1954. *Christian Democracy in Western Europe 1820–1953.* London.

Maier, Hans, 1988. *Revolution und Kirche. Studien zur Frühgeschichte der Christlichen Demokratie 1789–1850.* Freiburg.

Mayeur, Jean-Marie, 1980. *Des Partis Catholique à la Démocratie chrétienne XIX–XX siècle.* Paris.

Papini, Roberto, 1995. *Don Luigi Sturzo e l'Internazionale Popolare.* Rome.

CIRCUIT RIDER.

CIRCUIT RIDER. Personnel who travel to an assigned group of communities to provide technical assistance on a long-term basis.

Local government circuit riders bring a variety of technical skills to small and rural governments, including rural counties, that help ensure the delivery of vital public programs and services to local residents. Small rural local governments often lack the necessary managerial or financial resources to provide essential services to their constituents in efficient, cost-effective ways. The administrative costs of a circuit rider may be shared among two or more local governmental jurisdictions, enabling all to receive professional and technical expertise.

Local circuit riders include municipal managers, municipal finance directors, public works directors, public safety directors, recreation directors, code enforcement officers, zoning administrators, fire administrators, economic development officials, personnel directors, grant writers, and other positions. These administrators can have a significant impact in the communities they serve in terms of improved financial management practices, improved service delivery, efficient cost savings, and increased economic development.

While local circuit riders increase in use and popularity, circuit riding programs are somewhat difficult to administer at the local level. The same local governments that lack the technical and managerial expertise to hire full-time administrators must develop sound contracts that share administrative costs with other governments and then must monitor circuit rider performance.

Origins

The governmental use of circuit riders is generally tied to the legacy established by the circuit judge of the Old West, but circuit-riding lasted from the 1760s to the early twentieth century as a Methodist practice in Pennsylvania and points west to compensate for the shortage of formally educated ministers. The concept was originated in England by John Wesley. Circuit riders were a religious and moral force in the American frontier and in the rural South. Other denominations adopted this Methodist practice.

Today, in rural America, churches are turning once again to circuit riders as a cost-savings approach. Small congregations, with decreasing church attendance, make it difficult to finance a pastor's salary and living expenses. The receptivity of local church congregations to the circuit-rider concept may facilitate the acceptance and use of local government circuit riders.

Circuit riders have achieved prominence in other areas as well. A new type of medical specialist, an abortion circuit rider, for example, has evolved as antiabortion groups escalate personal attacks on doctors who perform abortions. Abortion clinics have turned to out-of-town doctors who are willing to travel extensively among clinics.

Current Practices

In the largely rural Southern Tier of New York State, the New York Main Street Alliance project manages a circuit rider, called a Main Street Manager, to work with towns and villages to increase the capacity of local community-based organizations to engage effectively in local development and commercial-area revitalization, including tourism and small business development. This program provides an information and technical assistance link to a statewide network of downtown revitalization practitioners. Each of the half dozen or so participating communities makes a small financial commitment (approximately US $4,000 per year) to the program and the circuit rider dedicates about one day per week to each community. What results is coordinated commercial-area revitalization among the communities, community-based short- and long-term marketing and business development strategies, and new opportunities for businesses in the area.

Beginning primarily in the late 1970s, some American states began to help fund (and sometimes administer) circuit-rider programs to build the managerial and financial capacity of their local governments. This is especially the case for financially distressed municipalities. The state programs generally pay the salaries and benefits of local circuit riders and often require a local matching of funds. University programs in public administration and planning offer circuit-rider internships to their students while helping local governments meet their service-delivery responsibilities.

An indication that the concept of local circuit riders is thriving is the emergence in the 1990s of federal and state government agency use of circuit riders to handle local technical assistance. The Ohio T2 Center Circuit Rider program, for example, provides free on-site services to Ohio villages, townships, cities, and counties. The program is jointly sponsored by the Federal Highway Administration and the Ohio Department of Transportation. Circuit riders help with road and bridge maintenance, road signs and traffic control, and safety standards for construction and equipment operations.

The circuit-rider concept is being used in Canada as well as the United States and other nations in a variety of policy areas for providing practical, hands-on training. In the mid-1990s, water treatment operators from 13 communities in northern Ontario participated in a pilot project that resulted in the recommendation of circuit-rider training as the primary method for training operators across Canada. The program is operated by First Nations organizations and serves Native American communities. Such programs now extend beyond Ontario to include communities in Manitoba, Alberta, Quebec, and British Columbia.

The State of Maryland's Office of Planning assists 25 Eastern Shore municipalities in implementing their Chesapeake Bay Critical Area Protection Programs. Circuit riders assist the small jurisdictions that are unable to support specialized staff to meet state mandated requirements. In addition to providing administrative support, the circuit riders review proposed development projects for compliance with local program regulations, assist in the monitoring of project compliance, prepare comprehensive reviews of program implementation, and prepare program amendments, studies, and regulations for local approval.

BEVERLY A. CIGLER

BIBLIOGRAPHY

Banisky, Sandy, 1993. "Abortion 'Circuit Rider' Accepts Risks: 'Stubborn' Doctor Defies Many Threats." *The Baltimore Sun,* September 7, p. 5B.
Cashnelli, Toni, 1995. "Circuit Riders Ministered to Ohio Frontier." *The Cincinnati Enquirer,* January 8, p. CO1.
Niebuhr, Gustav, 1995. "Modern-Day Circuit Riders' Split Ministry among Congregations: Rural Churches That Can't Afford Full-Time Pastor Share Preachers." *The Dallas Morning News,* April 2, p. 4A.

CITIZEN PARTICIPATION.

Citizens having enough information to participate in initial decisions on the allocation of resources and creation of institutions that will affect their lives (Edgar and Jean Cahn, 1968). Sherry Arnstein (1969) gives a more complete definition of citizen participation as

> a categorical term for citizen power. It is the redistribution of power that enables the have-not citizens, presently excluded from the political and economic processes, to be deliberately included in the future. It is the strategy by which the have-nots join in determining how information is shared, goals and policies are set, tax resources are allocated, programs are operated, and benefits like contracts and patronage are parceled out. In short it is the means by which they induce significant societal reform which enables them to share in the benefits of the affluent society (p. 216).

Citizen participation was one of the most hotly debated issues in urban politics in the 1960s. However, the issue is as old as democracy itself, surfacing during the era of the Greek city-states when it was believed that everyone should be allowed to participate in decisionmaking. This concept is sometimes referred to as "primary democracy" and is practiced in relatively small political jurisdictions where all the citizens can have a voice in decisionmaking. Except for the New England town meetings and citizen group associations, our government has never functioned as a primary democracy.

From the earliest days of the Republic, Americans have prided themselves on being an activist nation. This has usually taken the form of neighborhood and community associations actively seeking to influence the outcome of decisions affecting their communities. During the past 30 years, America's neighborhoods have become hot-beds of citizen participation.

This entry focuses on the recent growth of citizen participation from the War on Poverty programs of the Johnson administration to the recent changes in specific American cities. Attention is also paid to the different levels of citizen involvement, the expanded federal requirements, and the efforts in the 1970s and 1980s to institutionalize the citizen participation process in many of America's largest cities.

In the 1960s, white middle-class-dominated police departments, public school systems, county welfare agencies, and a whole host of public sector agencies were all charged with being insensitive to the needs of racial minorities. Citizen participation was one of the remedies proposed to cure the ills of a city government that had become overbureaucratized and remote. But disadvantaged residents were not the only persons who had a stake in citizen participation. Middle-class citizens found that they, too, needed new means to make city officials more responsive to their concerns and interests.

During the 1960s, serious doubts were raised in many urban areas as to just how well elected officials represented the diversity of needs and views in the city. This led to efforts to find new techniques for citizen involvement in the political and administrative decisionmaking process. By the 1970s and 1980s, citizen participation was being touted as an important tool that would both enhance democracy and improve the effectiveness of city government. Many local governments had already taken steps to institutionalize the process of citizen participation.

Citizen participation is as old as the Greek city-state and is practiced in many other democracies. Few Western democracies experienced the rioting and looting that occurred in the United States during its attempt to define the proper relationship between citizens and their local governments. One reason put forth for the heightened turbulence in America's cities was the population diversity in urban areas.

Most countries in Western Europe have more restricted immigration policies than the United States. As a result, there are fewer interest groups competing for resources in the urban political arena. In recent years, this pattern has been changing.

In France, Germany, and the United Kingdom, there have arisen large racial and ethnic groups seeking to use the local politics system to improve the quality of their lives. The issues that have generated the most citizen anger and involvement have been the quality of education, the availability of adequate housing, and the openess of the job market.

In Scandinavia, for instance, where the national governments have passed fairly restricted immigration laws, there has been far less multiculturalism in the population. This does not mean there is no citizen participation in Scandinavian cities, rather there is less diversity in the population and consequently more agreement on issues of importance to urban dwellers. In Scandinavia, citizens actively involve themselves in issues of planning, historic preservation, and housing.

Urban Riots, the War on Poverty, and Citizen Participation

In the 1960s, citizen participation became a rallying cry for many urban residents who sought to open up the whole structure of government and thereby redistribute power and authority. They sought to establish it as an ongoing component of the political process. Bureaucrats and city-wide officials, in contrast, viewed citizen participation as a more static concept. They did not necessarily wish to redistribute power. Local government officials often saw citizen participation as a tool to appease communities and satisfy federal guidelines.

The riots of the 1960s occurred during a democratic administration that was sympathetic to identifying new approaches and to undertaking new programs to assist the nation's poor. The culmination of this concern for poor people occurred during the Johnson administration's Great Society, with the passage of the Economic Opportunity Act, sometimes referred to as the War on Poverty. Title II of the Economic Opportunity Act called for the "maximum feasible participation" of local residents in the community action agencies. Problems often arose as these federally funded organizations developed programs that city officials opposed. In 1967, Congress responded to these concerns by passing the Green Amendment. The Green Amendment gave local government officials the option of taking control of community action agencies, provided that a third of the board members represented the poor. In this way, Congress hoped to eliminate some of the more distasteful programs and to return much of the responsibility for oversight to mayors and council members.

The Levels of Citizen Participation

Different actors have different definitions as to just what activities constitute citizen participation. A review of the literature seems to indicate that citizen participation runs along a continuum from voting to violence with a number of variations in between. These include letter writing, interest group activity, organizing community groups, testifying before the city council, lobbying, picketing, nonviolent demonstrations, and obstructionist tactics such as sit-ins.

Sherry Arnstein attempted to sort out the various meanings of the concept according to an eight-rung Ladder of Citizen Participation. The bottom two rungs of the ladder, which represent nonparticipation, were called "manipulation" and "therapy." The middle three rungs indicated degrees of tokenism and were labeled "informing," "consultation," and "placation." The top three rungs indicated degrees of citizen power including "partnership," "delegated power," and "citizen control" (pp. 216–244).

The Arnstein typology is important because it shows that not all forms of participation entail real power sharing among citizens and bureaucrats. Bureaucrats and city officials have been very willing to use those forms of participation toward the bottom of the ladder that enable the co-optation or manipulation of the citizenry. Citizens are brought into the process, given the illusion of decision-making power, and led to accept the agency's goals and plans as legitimate. In many cities, community action programs neutralized potential critics by giving activist citizen leaders positions on community boards or jobs with local action agencies. In other cities, however, citizen leaders determined that it was more important for them to remain outside the government in order to accurately reflect the views of community residents. In these later instances, the community leaders pushed, to use Arnstein's words, for greater "degrees of citizen power."

Desmond Connor (1988) suggested in an article in the *National Civic Review* that perhaps we now need a "new ladder" of citizen participation that would describe "a systematic approach to preventing and resolving public controversy about specific policies, programs, and projects" (p. 250). On Connor's ladder the bottom three steps—education, information, and feedback and consultation—are for use by the general public. The next three steps up the ladder—joint planning, mediation, and litigation—represent processes used by the public leaders. According to Connor, the hope ultimately is that the process will lead to the seventh step, resolution/prevention.

Writing from the vantage point of the late 1980s, as opposed to the turbulent 1960s, Connor concerned himself with identifying a cooperative and somewhat elitist means of consensus building. Still direct action, conflict, and confrontation are sometimes essential tools, in both suburban and central city communities, in getting municipal officials to address citizen needs.

Measuring the effectiveness of citizen participation is very difficult. Citizen participation under certain circumstances can be successful if large numbers of people attend meetings, regardless of the outcome of the issue. In other instances, a small number of knowledgeable and persistent individuals can be very effective in achieving desired results but will appear elitist to outsiders because large numbers of community residents are not participating. The vagueness of the citizen participation concept as well as the diverse nature of programs, localities, public officials, and citizens groups involved have made the task of measurement virtually impossible.

Citizen participation requirements were not always greeted enthusiastically by state and local government officials nor were they always vigorously enforced by federal officials. A combination of federal monitoring from above and neighborhood pressure from below was often needed to ensure that the rights of citizens to participate were not flagrantly violated.

As citizen groups became more sophisticated and learned about their rights under federal rules and regulations, they became more effective. Initially, they used protests to ensure their voice would be heard, occasionally bringing unwanted neighborhood projects to a halt. Later citizen groups learned how to mobilize legal teams, which in court were able to uphold the rights of citizens to be heard in the decisionmaking deliberations. Government officials who failed to comply with federal guidelines for citizen involvement often found the courts intervening on the side of citizens, with the end result being a work stoppage on the project until all violations of citizens' rights had been remedied.

Expanding Citizen Participation: Once Again the Federal Role

Even before the "maximum feasible participation" clause of the 1964 Economic Opportunity Act, several federal programs required citizen participation. Three of the most notable were the Urban Renewal Program, the Workable Program for Community Improvement, and the Justice Delinquency Demonstration Projects. The Model Cities Program called for "widespread citizen participation" in community action programs.

During the 1970s, citizen participation requirements in federal legislation began expanding at a rapid rate. In program after program the responsible agencies were required to "hold hearings," "involve citizens," or "seek consultation with affected parties" in implementing federally assisted programs. According to a 1979 Advisory Commission on Intergovernmental Relations report, 31 percent, or 155 out of 498, federal grants to state and local governments required some form of citizen participation.

The Institutionalization of Citizen Participation in the 1970s and 1980s

Citizen participation became less volatile and less conflictual in the late 1970s and 1980s. The 1980s were characterized by a more institutionalized pattern of involvement in the form of organized interest groups, citizen advisory committees on specific services, and individual citizen contacts with agencies.

In the 1980s, the federal rules on regulations governing citizen participation at the local level were also weakened. Ronald Reagan believed that local, elected officials were the duly chosen representatives of local populations. Federal rules that required special participation efforts and that gave an element of the citizenry new opportunities to challenge the decisions of local, elected officials were seen to undermine local democracy. In administering federal aid programs, federal bureaucrats during the Reagan era did not always pay close attention to monitoring local efforts at citizen participation.

Despite all these changes, citizen participation continued. As urban political scientist John Clayton Thomas (1986) showed in his study of Cincinnati, community organizations are regular participants in local politics. More recent work on citizen participation and community power by Scavo (1993) and Pecorella (1994) confirms both the growth and the formalization of institutional methods designed to increase citizen involvement in policymaking decisions.

The Changing Style of Citizen Participation: Frostbelt and Sunbelt

One city where citizen participation has been incorporated into the decisionmaking process for years is Dayton, Ohio, a city with a reputation for neighborhoods with active and assertive community leaders. As far back as World War I, Dayton began a strong citizen involvement campaign.

Other cities that have demonstrated the value of strong neighborhoods with active citizens in constant touch with city hall include Portland, Oregon, and St. Paul, Minnesota. Recently, a number of other cities have studied and adopted some of the citizen involvement strategies and tactics that have worked in Dayton over the past 80 years. Among the new converts are San Antonio; Phoenix; Indianapolis; Richmond ; Santa Clarita; California; and Minneapolis.

By the 1970s and 1980s, many groups that had earlier followed the confrontational tactics of social activist Saul Alinsky (1971) refined their approach to include a new focus on service delivery. Alinsky's classic writings made clear his confrontational approach. In the 1960s, the Woodlawn Organization (TWO) in Chicago successfully used Alinksy-style tactics to take on a number of targets. By the 1970s, TWO shifted its focus "from Protest to Programs," as its own slogan phrased it. Like a number of other Alinksy-style organizations, TWO become less concerned with protest activities and more concerned with providing services that would improve the life of community residents.

In the Sunbelt, newly emergent citizen groups have sought to challenge the hold on decisionmaking that local elites traditionally exercised in the region. In a number of Sunbelt cities, a new style of citizen participation has emerged as citizens resort to the referendum and initiative processes to check the power of government. Phoenix voters, for instance, repeatedly turned down proposals initiated by former Mayor Terry Goddard for development, expanded mass transit, and a new baseball park.

Carl Abbott (1987) believes that two distinct factors explain the recent rise of citizen action in the Sunbelt. First, new elements in the white middle-class community have pressed for environmentalism, good government, and home-owner concerns. The second source of community activism in the Sunbelt is new community groups formed to represent the demands of the region's minority populations.

In San Antonio, in 1974, Communities Organized for Public Services (COPS) was organized to protest the underprovision of infrastructure and other services on the city's west side. Organized to represent the needs of poor and middle-class west-side Hispanic homeowners, COPS used confrontational tactics to win new investment in street repair and drainage projects and the adoption of a system of ward-based elections that maximized Mexican American and black political power.

COPS's approach has been emulated in a number of other cities. In Houston, the Metropolitan Organization (TMO) used the pressure of a mass membership "accountability" meeting to convince Mayor Kathryn Whitmire to sign a compact agreeing to meet with TMO leadership on the average of once a month and to attend a large TMO meeting—promises Whitmire kept. In El Paso, a city with a 65 percent Hispanic population, EPISO (the El Paso Interreligions Sponsoring Organization) was formed in 1977 by Sister Eliza Rodriguez after the COPS experience convinced her of the success a church-sponsored grassroots organization might obtain.

What does a review of the activities of these community groups reveal? First is the continued vitality of community groups. Second is the continued importance of both conventional and unconventional participation strategies to people who would otherwise be excluded from urban decisionmaking. Third is the tendency for community groups to change their style over time as they gain acceptance from bureaucrats and the media and as they attempt to provide services to a larger organizational base. Finally, this moderation in approach has at times allowed poor people's groups to form coalitions with other citizen and neighborhood organizations. Still, experience shows that often these alliances prove quite unstable and likely can be pieced together only on an issue-by-issue basis.

The Continuing Debate over Citizen Participation

Citizen participation has secured a regularized position in city politics over the years. Mayors, county executives, and city managers have all become involved in helping to implement the process of citizen participation in their communities. Building a relationship of trust between citizens and government is an important factor in developing a successful citizen participation program. However, such

trust does not come easily. Increased citizen participation can pose a threat to bureaucrats who find the scope of their decisionmaking narrowed by citizen activism. Furthermore, as citizen participation opens up the process of government and gives neighborhood residents greater access to information about programs and policies, citizens are better able to discuss problems with bureaucrats and elected officials. Bureaucrats have come to recognize that they need to produce information that can be understood not just by other professionals but by lay people as well.

The major arguments advanced for developing a meaningful citizen participation program can be summarized as follows. Citizen participation

- is consistent with democratic theory;
- mechanisms help develop leaders in a community who might otherwise not emerge;
- mechanisms help create political and social networks essential to building a community;
- is psychologically rewarding for those who participate;
- makes local government appear more legitimate to neighborhoods and city residents as people believe they have access to government and that public officials are listening to their point of view;
- increases citizens' acceptance and enthusiasm for a program, thereby increasing the chances of successful service intervention.

The major arguments against citizen participation are that it

- tends to heighten parochial concerns to the detriment of citywide concerns;
- never is completely representative of the range of community interests;
- increases competition and conflict among community factions; and
- is lengthy and time consuming.

BERNARD H. ROSS

REFERENCES

Abbott, Carl, 1987, *The New Urban America: Growth and Politics in Sunbelt Cities,* rev. ed. Chapel Hill: University of North Carolina Press, pp. 215–218.

Advisory Commission on Intergovernmental Relations, 1979. *Citizen Participation in the American Federal System.* Washington, D.C.: ACIR, Chapter 4.

Alinsky, Saul D., 1971. *Rules for Radicals.* New York: Vintage Books.

Arnstein, Sherry R., 1969. "A Ladder of Citizen Participation." *Journal of the American Institute of Planners,* vol. 35 (July).

Babbit, Bruce, Former Arizona Governor, 1989. Address delivered to the annual meeting of the National Civic League, Denver, Colorado, October 25.

Bailey, Robert, Jr., 1979. *Radicals in Urban Politics: The Alinsky Approach.* Chicago: University of Chicago Press, pp. 61–62.

Berry, Jeffrey, Ken Portney, and Ken Thomson, 1993. *The Return of Urban Democracy*. Washington, D.C.: Brookings Institution.

Cahn, Edgar S. and Jean Camper Cahn, 1968. "Citizen Participation." In Hans B. Speigal, ed., *Citizen Participation in Urban Development*. Washington, D.C.: NTL and National Education Association, pp. 218–222.

Cahn, Edgar S. and Barry A. Passett, eds., 1971. *Citizen Participation: Effecting Community Change*. New York: Praeger.

Connor, Desmond M., 1988. "A New Citizen Participation Ladder." *National Civic Review*, vol. 77 (May–June).

Johnson, David R., John A. Booth, and Richard J. Harris, eds., 1988. *The Politics of San Antonio: Community Progress and Power*. Lincoln: University of Nebraska Press.

Langton, Stuart, ed., 1979. *Citizen Participation Perspectives*. Medford, MA.: Tufts University Press.

Pecorella, Robert, 1994. *Community Power in a Postreform City: Politics in New York City*. Armonk, NY: M. E. Sharpe.

Plotkin, Sidney, 1987. *Keep Out: The Struggle for Land Use Control*. Berkeley : University of California Press.

Reitzes, Donald C. and Dietrich C. Reitzes, 1987. *The Alinsky Legacy: Alive and Kicking*. Greenwich, CT: JAI Press.

Scavo, Carmine, 1993. "The Use of Participative Mechanisms by Large American Cities." *Journal of Urban Affairs*, vol. 15: 93–110.

Sekul, Joseph D., 1989. "The Free Rider Myth and Institutional Mobilization." Paper presented at the annual meeting of the Urban Affairs Association, Baltimore, March 8–22.

Silberman, Charles, 1964. *Crisis in Black and White*. New York: Vintage Books, pp. 308–355.

Stone, Clarence N., Robert K. Whelan, and William J. Murin, 1986. *Urban Policy and Politics in a Bureaucratic Age*, 2nd ed. Englewood Cliffs, NJ: Prentice-Hall, pp. 148–149.

Thomas, John Clayton, 1986. *Between Citizen and City: Neighborhood Organizations and Urban Politics in Cincinnati*. Lawrence: University of Kansas Press.

Villareal, Robert E., 1987. "EPISCO and Political Participation: Public Policy in El Paso Politics." Paper presented at the annual meeting of the Western Political Science Association, Anaheim, CA, March 26–28.

CITIZEN'S CHARTER. The British government initiative to improve public sector services and to make them directly and financially accountable to their users. Begun in 1991 under the sponsorship of Prime Minister John Major, the Citizen's Charter is a ten-year program administered from the Cabinet Office by the Citizen's Charter Unit. Annual reports give progress on improvements and increased accountability.

Following the large-scale privatization programs of the 1980s, the British government determined the need to establish principles of public service provision. The essential notion is to set benchmarks against which customers of public services can gain redress for an array of bureaucratic maladies held to be endemic in the sclerotic workings of a system still insufficiently exposed to the healthy circulation of commercial competition. These standards of performance are published in a series of charters covering all public services—such as schools and colleges, medical services, the rail system, local councils, the police, employment cen-

ters, the post office, roads, customs and excise, tax offices, and many more. In addition, the private utilities of electricity, gas, telephones, and water have their own charters. John Major has said, "The Charter is a radical program aimed at improving public services right across the board. Through it, the Government aims to give the citizen a better deal by extending consumer choice and widening competition. Whether the service is provided by the public sector or the private sector, the aim is to ensure that the citizen gets good service and value for money" (Citizen's Charter, 1992, p. 2).

Six principles have been developed in order to reform what has been called Britain's "sniff and snarl" tradition of public service (Dynes and Walker, 1995). These are

- the setting, monitoring, and publication of explicit standards for the services that individual users can reasonably expect;
- the provision of accurate information about how public services are run, what they cost, how well they perform and who is in charge;
- the availability of choice for consumers and consultation with them to define the standards to be delivered;
- the assurance of courtesy and helpfulness from public servants (who lose their traditional anonymity);
- the ready accessibility of a complaints review process to ensure that putting things right—apologies, full explanations, and a swift and effective remedy—is done properly;
- the validation of performance standards to ensure value for money in the public sector.

As the Citizen's Charter Unit reported in 1994, the principles are designed to maximize "efficiency and economical delivery of public services within the resources the nation can afford" (Citizen's Charter, 1994, p. 3).

The setting up of the Citizen's Charter is best understood as one of a number of initiatives taken by the British government from the mid-1980s onward to hold bureaucrats' feet to the fire. It belongs with market testing, privatization, and contracting out as a means by which the public sector is challenged by market-oriented government. Its establishment tacitly acknowledges the limited success of the ombudsman system. It reflects the changing understanding of ministerial accountability in a unitary state where power is held centrally but responsibility and accountability are being devolved downward and outward to the points of actual service provision (to local hospital trusts, for example, rather than the relevant secretary of state). Ministers will, therefore, face fewer parliamentary questions about the implementation of policy, whilst remaining accountable for policy itself. "The Charter is not about more state action. It is about the right of citizens to be informed and to choose for themselves" (Citizen's Charter, 1994, p. 3). Conceptually at least, the charter is designed to empower British citizenry within a constitutional system that acknowledges them only as subjects of the sovereign-in-Parliament.

Doubts about the Citizen's Charter have been expressed in three areas. The first is that it is no more than a public relations exercise: no extra resources are offered to departments of state to enable better services to be provided; the improvements have to be found through better systems of public management in a policy environment that favors less rather than more public spending. The second is that ways have not yet been found to reward the genuine efforts of public service employees to improve services before those improvements have manifestly worked their way through the system to consumers (Dynes and Walker, 1995). Finally, the Citizen's Charter may have created the preconditions for a growth of private and institutional litigation in what might be termed a reparations culture. Whether these doubts about the system are realized, or the extent to which it is developed and refined, depends on the extent to which future British governments share John Major's enthusiasm for enforcing consumer choice on the organs of the state and its agencies.

PETER FOOT

BIBLIOGRAPHY

The Citizen's Charter, 1992. *The Citizen's Charter: First Report 1992,* Cm2101. London: HMSO.
———, 1994. *Report Back 1994,* Dd8390141. London: HMSO.
Dynes, Michael and David Walker, 1995. *The New British State.* London: Times Books.

CITIZENSHIP ETHICS.

An approach to the ethics of public administration based on the nature of the citizens' role in a democratic society. According to citizenship ethics, the public administrator is more than an employee of a public organization; the public administrator is also a member of a political order and as such has a particular set of moral obligations in the performance of administrative duties.

In the history of Western political philosophy, citizenship appears in both weak and strong versions. The weak version, characteristic of classical liberalism, views citizenship as a legal status, one that entails a set of individual rights limiting the power of government: for example, the right to vote, the right to a fair trial, freedom of speech, religion, and association. Liberal citizenship connotes few if any duties, however. The citizen is left free to pursue private interests. Perhaps because of this lack of substantive content, the weak version of citizenship has not served as a major source of inspiration for ethical norms in public administration.

The strong model of citizenship views it as a set of activities and capacities that involve individuals in public life. The prototype is found in Aristotle's (1981) *The Politics,* which argued that citizens take turns ruling and being ruled. This version of citizenship includes four major elements: (1) the exercise of authoritative judgment about public affairs; (2) use of the public good rather than private interests as the guide to decisionmaking; (3) the idea that involvement in public affairs develops individual citizens' personal capacities for governance; and (4) the idea that participation in public-spirited dialogue and debate binds citizens together in a political community that can be formed in no other way. The strong model of citizenship entails the exercise of decisive judgment in the public interest, an experience that develops political and moral capabilities of individuals and solidifies the communal ties among them.

Development of Citizenship Ideas in Public Administration

The first appearance of the idea of citizenship in public administrative thinking came during the progressive reform era of the late nineteenth and early twentieth centuries. As middle-class reformers sought to purge municipal governments of machine bossism and to professionalize public administration, a key element in their campaign was an appeal to the notion of "efficient citizenship." The idea was that a more knowledgeable and active citizenry, in contrast to party hacks, could promote good government by understanding and supporting scientific and professional approaches to solving city problems. Early public administration was seen as a cooperative effort between citizens and professional administrators. Evidence of this link between professionalism and citizenship is found in the names of the first two schools of public administration: the Maxwell School of Citizenship and Public Affairs at Syracuse University and the University of Southern California School of Citizenship and Public Administration. Increasing emphasis on the scientific aspects of administration, however, led to a decline in emphasis on citizenship. Not until the 1980s did it reappear in the literature, in Frederickson (1982) and Frederickson and Chandler (1984), the latter a special issue of *Public Administration Review* that contained proceedings of a 1983 "National Conference on Citizenship and Public Service." At this conference, Terry L. Cooper introduced the idea that public administrators are themselves citizens and should use the citizen role specifically as an ethical anchor (Cooper, 1984), an idea he and others have expanded upon since then.

Ingredients of a Citizenship Ethic

The literature of public administration offers the following ethical guidelines, which are keyed to the four traditional aspects of strong citizenship in Western political philosophy:

Authoritative Judgment in Public Affairs

Because public administrators share the citizen role equally with other citizens, they should maximize horizontal authority relations both within agencies and externally with organizations, groups, and individuals. They should foster collaborative rather than chain-of-command decisionmaking and use what discretionary authority they have to develop a range of opportunities for direct citizen involvement in agency policy formulation and implementation, consistent with applicable laws and regulations.

Public-Spiritedness

Public administrators should put consideration of the widest possible interpretation of the public interest ahead of all other considerations, including efficiency, professionalism, or practical politics. They should strive for knowledge of what is right to do given the circumstances, cultivate an other-regarding or enlightened form of self-interest, and act as fiduciaries for the broad interests of citizens.

Development of Governance Capacity

Public administrators should educate citizens about important public issues and about the workings of government. They should create opportunities for substantive dialogue and cooperative activity among citizens and administrators.

Community

Public administrators should foster community: not only a sense of mutual covenant, friendship, and regard among citizens and administrators, but more widely, through a critical sense of which community interests are supported by or excluded from the work of their agencies. Within legislative or regulatory guidelines, they should use administrative discretion to foster equality among the members of a democratic community.

In summary, a citizenship ethic for public administration requires administrators to act as citizens, practicing in light of the above precepts, and to act with other citizens, viewed as equals in what is ultimately the common endeavor of governance.

CAMILLA STIVERS

BIBLIOGRAPHY

Allen, William H., 1907. *Efficient Democracy*. New York: Dodd, Mead.
Aristotle, 1981. *The Politics*. Translated by T. A. Sinclair. Harmondsworth, UK: Penguin Books.
Cooper, Terry L., 1984. "Citizenship and Professionalism in Public Administration." In H. George Frederickson and Ralph Clark Chandler, eds., *Citizenship and Public Administration*. Special issue of *Public Administration Review*, vol. 44: 143–149.
———, 1991. *An Ethic of Citizenship for Public Administration*. Englewood Cliffs, NJ: Prentice-Hall.
Frederickson, H. George, 1982. "The Recovery of Civism in Public Administration." *Public Administration Review*, vol. 42 (November/December) 501–508.
Frederickson, H. George and Ralph Clark Chandler, 1984. *Citizenship and Public Administration*. Special issue of *Public Administration Review*, vol. 44.
Stivers, Camilla, 1994. "Citizenship Ethics in Public Administration." In Terry L. Cooper, ed., *Handbook of Administrative Ethics*. New York: Marcel Dekker, pp. 435–455.

CIVIL LAW. The tradition of law that evolved from the Roman compilations of the Emperor Justinian. This great consolidation of Roman law came to be known as *Corpus Juris Civilis*. It was a collection of imperial enactments brought together as a code. Over its long history, Roman law was shaped by French, German, and Italian influences. The Roman law maintained its theoretical and systematic influence as European nation-states developed their legal and juridical systems. France and Germany generated five civil codes incorporating much of the theory of Roman law in the nineteenth century. Other European states such as Switzerland and Italy followed the codification technique. Today civil law is employed in the states of continental Europe as well as in some of their former colonies, such as Quebec in Canada and Louisiana in the United States.

In Louisiana, civil law is codified law that has been derived mostly from the Spanish law. The first civil code of Louisiana under the jurisdiction of the United States was proclaimed in 1808. The code is believed to be solely of Spanish origin, although some historians argue that there are parts of it that resemble the French Napoleonic Code. The criminal law of the state of Louisiana is derived from the common law tradition of the United States and U.S. legal precedents.

When the Seven Years' War ended, culminating in the Treaty of Paris of 1763, Quebec was brought under British rule. The British government moved to guarantee the private law of French Canada under the French-Canadian civil law which is based on the French civil code. So today the civil law codes remain the private law of Quebec. In August 1866 Quebec's private law was codified by legislative enactment as the *Civil Code of Lower Canada*. The only official revision of the code came in 1981 when it was proclaimed the *Civil Code of Quebec*.

Mixed Systems

Today in Quebec the widespread use of the case approach in federal and public law has diluted the purity of the civil law. The Quebec system is sometimes described as "mixed" or "hybrid" because of the powerful influences of the common law. It must be remembered that the Quebec Civil

Code predates the Constitution Act of 1867, and like the use of the French language, clearly illustrates the distinct character of Quebec society in the legal and linguistic landscape of Canada.

Canada's legal and judicial system comprises the practice and traditions of both the common law and the civil law, although the common law dwarfs the civil law in application. The civil law of France based on the *Code Napoleon* is still the historic model for jurisprudence in Quebec. Accordingly, the private law of Quebec is French-Canadian civil law. This functions in contrast to the Anglo-Canadian common law. But in public law matters, the common law is practiced in Quebec just as in the other provinces, as well as by the federal government.

In other parts of Canada as well as at the federal level legislators use the word "code" as just another name for an ordinary legislative act, such as a Highway Code or the Criminal Code. But in Quebec private law, the term "code" is used to mean a unified area of law: a great diversity of legislation that has been compiled and gathered in one place in order to facilitate consultation, as in family law. The code provides clear and precise solutions to practical legal problems in understandable language. But, unlike the more malleable common law, the codified written law brings the risk of rigidity. The codes face the possibility of not always responding to new social problems. Periodically they need extensive legislative overhauls to bring them up to date.

Civil Law Traditions

The private law of Quebec deals mainly with persons, corporations, civil status, marriage, property, ownership, co-ownership, gifts, wills, trusts, contracts, loans, rentals, and pledges. Unlike the common law, civil law applies abstract principles or doctrines of law to the settlement of disputes. The facts of each dispute are analyzed on principle, not in relation to prior judicial decisions that interpret the law. The civil law tradition is essentially "deductive" because it applies general rules to a particular case, whereas the common law tradition is essentially "inductive" because it builds its rules from particular cases and general principles. The civil law contains no formal notion of *stare decisis* (precedent) nor any other technique of binding case precedent. Unlike the common law system where judges exercise latitude and flexibility in the civil law system, primary responsibility for the interpretation of the law is left to experts. In fact, their role in giving final meaning to the codes tends to supercede that of judges. In the application of the civil law, judicial decisions are regarded as persuasive rather than as precedents that should be adhered to in future cases. For this reason, the writings of scholars and professors are given preeminent attention in the interpretation of legal doctrine.

Quebec's uniqueness as a legal culture was conserved not only by its governing provincial status but also in terms of federal public policy. For example, the Supreme Court of Canada is required by law to provide three judges from Quebec because it functions as a civil law court for private law appeals from Quebec and as a common law court for public matters across the country.

The influx of common law approaches through the federal and public law of Canada and the incidence of appeals to the Supreme Court of Canada have diluted the purity of civilian law in Quebec. Currently, the Quebec system of law might best be described as a "hybrid" or "mixed" system. But the differences between common law and civil law are still more than mere degree and are widely recognized as such by those who want to preserve the bicultural legal heritage of Canada.

It is very unlikely that a uniformity of law between Quebec and the other provinces will ever be achieved because both the civil law and common law systems have become so entrenched in Quebec's unique legal culture.

JAMES J. GUY

BIBLIOGRAPHY

Brierly, J. E. C., 1968. "Quebec's Civil Law Codification Viewed and Reviewed." *McGill Law Review*, vol. 14, 521–589.
Fitzgerald, P. and K. McShane, 1982. *Looking at Law: Canada's Legal System*. Ottawa: Bybooks
Gall, G. L., 1983. *The Canadian Legal System*. Toronto: Carswell.
MacDonald, R. A., 1980. "Civil Law–Quebec–New Draft Code in Perspective." *Canadian Bar Review*, vol. 53, 185–205.

CIVIL LIBERTIES. The rights possessed by individuals to be free from certain governmental restrictions. Sources of these rights include a few provisions of the Constitution written in 1787, such as the right of habeas corpus and prohibition of ex post facto laws. The major source of rights in the United States is the Bill of Rights—the first ten amendments to the U.S. Constitution. In general, the Bill of Rights is concerned with freedom of conscience in matters of speech and religion; rights of persons accused of crime; restrictions on law enforcement; and rights of fair procedure when life, liberty, or property is affected. The Bill of Rights was written to protect citizens from action by the government of the United States; after the Civil War, the Fourteenth Amendment was written to restrict state government. That amendment has been interpreted by the U.S. Supreme Court to give virtually the same protections to persons against state action that they have with respect to federal action. In addition to those rights specifically set forth in the Constitution and its amendments, the U.S. Supreme Court has interpreted the Constitution and its amendments to protect rights not specifically found therein, such as the right to privacy in certain personal areas, including birth control or abortion.

Civil liberties are often distinguished from civil rights, which are concerned with guaranteeing equal protection of the laws free from discrimination on such grounds as race and sex. They are also distinguished from political rights, such as the right to vote, which are guaranteed not to all persons but just to citizens. They are also often distinguished from economic rights, such as the right to engage in business. Finally, international human rights as expressed in United Nations documents that may include civil liberties may be broader, for example, by adding affirmative obligations on government, such as health care and minimum standard of living. In the United States, such affirmative rights are to be found in legislation passed by Congress. Civil liberties, in contrast, impose restrictions on what government can do, rather than imposing obligations on what government must do.

In the United States, the contours of civil liberties are developed through litigation in the U.S. Supreme Court in cases interpreting the Bill of Rights and the Constitution. What the Court has considered to be protected liberties has changed over time—for example, in the early 1900s, the Court held that the states could not interfere with the liberty to contract and run one's business and struck down state laws that set maximum hours employees could work and minimum wages they could be paid (for example, *Lochner v. New York*, 1905). Those decisions were overruled by the Court beginning in the late 1930s during the Depression.

The origins of civil liberties can be traced to ancient Jewish law, which prohibited the use of confessions to convict a person of a crime, and to Greek and Roman sources. Of great importance was the English Magna Carta of 1215, which guaranteed protections to the barons, putting the king under the law. It was the precursor to due process, a term first used in a statute passed during the reign of Edward III in 1355. Other important parliamentary documents to the development of civil liberties are the Petition of Right Act of 1628 and the Bill of Rights of 1689. The work of the English philosopher John Locke in his *Second Treatise on Government,* and that of the English jurist William Blackstone in his *Commentaries,* made important contributions to the idea that individuals were possessed of certain natural rights that could not be taken away by the government.

Important to the development of the U.S. Constitution and Bill of Rights were charters of the colonies, state constitutions predating the U.S. Constitution, and the 1776 Declaration of Independence, which stated that there were certain inalienable rights, including life, liberty, and the pursuit of happiness.

The sources of civil liberties, then, are both positive law—that is, statutes enacted by legislative bodies such as Parliament or state legislatures—and natural law and natural rights—that is, sources which stand independent of any governmental body and which exist in society without governmental action. It was to these sources that the Declaration of Independence referred. When the U.S. Constitution was enacted, members of the Supreme Court debated whether only the specifics of the Constitution, or natural law as well, are the sources of liberties. In the famous case of *Calder v. Bull* in 1798, Justice Samuel Chase asserted that natural law is a source of protection for individuals, while Justice Iredell said only the Constitution limits what government can do: "The ideas of natural justice are regulated by no fixed standard; [and] the ablest and the purest men have differed upon the subject."

To what degree are civil liberties protected from governmental infringement? The Supreme Court has never held that such rights are absolutely protected—for example, freedom of speech does not give a person the right falsely to shout "Fire!" in a crowded theater, said Supreme Court Justice Oliver Wendell Holmes. Additional difficulties occur when two liberties are in conflict, for example, when the press asserts its First Amendment right to publish information about a crime while a jury is being impaneled to hear the case and the news stories might make it impossible to choose a fair and impartial jury, which is required by the Sixth Amendment.

Civil liberties are most often threatened in times of crises. For example, during World War I, the free speech rights of persons who were pacifists or otherwise opposed to the war were abridged by laws attempting to suppress speech. During World War II, persons of Japanese ancestry were removed from their homes and put in relocation camps, even though there was no evidence that they were disloyal to the United States. In the 1980s and 1990s, the war on crime has resulted in court decisions that seem inconsistent with earlier decisions interpreting the Fourth Amendment's prohibition of unreasonable searches and seizures.

Civil liberties decisions are often unpopular because a decision to uphold a challenge to a law results in the will of the majority, as reflected in the law, being invalidated in behalf of a minority. Yet that is the inevitable consequence of a Bill of Rights that was written precisely to protect even a single person from the majority's decision to deprive others of certain basic rights. The father of the Bill of Rights, James Madison, initially opposed adding a Bill of Rights to the Constitution for fear it would indicate that the federal government could deprive persons of other rights not enumerated. Madison was also skeptical whether a mere "parchment barrier" could protect persons whose rights were denied by overbearing majorities. Despite his worries, the Bill of Rights has largely been effective in the United States and is the envy of many other countries whose constitutions are modeled after the United States—and most of which give many more rights—but whose courts have not been independent from the other branches of government, so that the rights are often there in name only.

The approximately 160 countries with constitutions modeled after that of the United States have similar protections of civil liberties but often add specific protections not present in the U.S. Constitution, for example, the right of asylum for political prisoners; the right to an education; family rights; the presumption of innocence; the right to rest and leisure; the freedom to strike; the right to join trade unions; and the right to work.

ROGER L. GOLDMAN

CIVIL SERVICE COMMISSION.

The authoritative governing body of a civil service employment system. Throughout the world when nations decide to implement a public sector selection system based on some merit standards, a governing body is necessary for day-to-day governance. This governing body is usually charged with establishing operational policies and procedures governing the administration of the civil service system.

Although civil service commissions have existed at all levels of government in the United States, the best known historically was the United States Civil Service Commission (USCSC) created by the Pendleton Act of 1883. The USCSC was composed of three commissioners appointed by the president and subject to presidential removal. Not more than two of these commissioners could be members of the same political party; thus, the USCSC was to be bipartisan in nature. The USCSC issued rules and regulations governing the federal civil service system between 1883 and 1978, when it was abolished by the Civil Service Reform Act of 1978. During this period of time the federal bureaucracy grew enormously and continually increased the number of its positions included in various merit systems.

Historically the USCSC was a body constantly torn, trying to be all things to all people. It was expected to be an adviser to presidents and their appointed officials, a part of the management team, advising administrators regarding personnel policy and procedures. At the same time the Commission was supposed to be a protector of the merit system from partisan political abuse. It was supposed to act as the police and keep elected officials from subverting the merit system by placing their own cronies into merit system positions by using less than merit-based procedures. Simultaneously, it was supposed to manage the implementation and expansion of the merit system. Mechanically it was supposed to develop procedures and instruments for written testing, for job studies, for classification systems, for evaluation systems, for systems of veterans' preference hiring, for the ongoing collective bargaining process for federal employees, and the list goes on and on.

Ultimately these countervailing strains led to the demise of the Commission following the revelation of complicity by commission staffers with the Nixon administration in undermining its own merit system procedures. After losing face and political support, the Commission was replaced by the Office of Personnel Management, the Merit Systems Protection Board, and the Federal Labor Relations Authority as a part of the Civil Service Reform Act of 1978.

At the state and local levels in the United States, civil service systems usually have some sort of civil service commission as their governing body. These are sometimes referred to as boards, panels, or by other names, but their function as the overall policy determining agency is generally the same. Typically at the state and local levels the members are chosen by some combination of elected officials from the executive and legislative branches. For example, the governor of a state might appoint one member, the speaker of the house might appoint one member, and the president pro tempore of the Senate might appoint one member. Recently there has been a trend toward having one position designated as an employee member and elected by employees working in the civil service system.

ROBERT H. ELLIOTT

BIBLIOGRAPHY

Heclo, Hugh, 1977. *A Government of Strangers: Executive Politics in Washington.* Washington, D.C.: The Brookings Institution.

United States Civil Service Commission, 1974. *Biography of an Ideal: A History of the Federal Civil Service.* Washington, D.C.: United States Government Printing Office.

Van Riper, Paul, 1991. "Americanizing a Foreign Invention: The Pendleton Act of 1883." In Frank Thompson, ed., *Classics of Personnel Policy.* Pacific Grove, CA: Brooks/Cole Publishing Company.

CIVIL SERVICE EXAMINATIONS.

Tests used to determine decisions regarding matters such as initial selection and promotion of employees within a civil service system. Today it is common for democratic regimes throughout the world to employ written examinations as a part of their public service selection systems. Civil service examinations are closely associated with the idea of a merit system and have traditionally been used as devices designed to measure the varying amounts of merit that candidates possess.

Historically, examinations have been an integral part of government service. Written testing for public service positions can be dated back to ancient China. In the United States examining programs for the service academies were initiated in the early 1800s, the Treasury Department developed and used written tests by the 1850s, and the Interior Department and the New York Customs House were using written tests during the Rutherford B. Hayes administration (1876–1880).

When the original merit system in the U.S. national government was established by the Pendleton Act of 1883, one of its essential components was that positions should be filled through "open competitive examinations" that would be "practical in their character."

Examinations may be assembled—all candidates assemble in one location and take the examination; or they may be unassembled—each candidate submits his or her credentials individually to the examining agency, where these credentials are then reviewed and graded. The latter of these two examinations is sometimes referred to as training and experience evaluation.

Whatever form the examinations take, they have traditionally been essential devices to measure candidates' relative capacities for civil service positions, and have been used to establish employment registers of eligible names that would be sent out to the hiring departments.

In the United States since the civil rights movement of the 1960s the courts have increasingly scrutinized civil service examinations used at all levels of government. This judicial focus has been brought about by charges made by minority groups that examinations contain cultural biases that make it more difficult for women and other minorities to attain acceptable scores. In a series of United States Supreme Court cases beginning with *Griggs v. Duke Power Company* (1970) and followed by *Albemarle Paper Company v. Moody* (1975) and *Washington vs. Davis* (1975), the Court made it clear that if an employer intends to use tests or other screening devices that might result in an adverse impact on minorities, the employer has a responsibility to demonstrate that the tests are scientifically valid (that is, shown to be directly related to the ability of the employee to perform the job in question), or to in some other way justify the test or screening device under federal law. Though there was some weakening of these job relatedness standards by the more conservative court by the end of the 1980s (*Wards Cove v. Atonio*, 1989), Congress reasserted the earlier *Griggs* standards in the Civil Rights Act of 1991. This act also allowed, for the first time in such Title VII cases, a right to trial by jury, and the awarding of punitive damages against private sector employers. Both these actions were seen as placing more pressure on employers to work diligently to ensure that their selection devices will meet judicial standards of job relatedness.

ROBERT H. ELLIOTT

BIBLIOGRAPHY

Albemarle Paper Company v. Moody, 1975. 422 U.S. 405.
"An Act to Regulate and Improve the Civil Service of the United States," 1883 (Pendleton Act). United States Congress, 22 Stat. 27.
Griggs v. Duke Power Company, 1971. 401 U.S. 424.
Sharpless, Jr., Norman R., 1968. "Public Personnel Selection—An Overview." In J. J. Donovan, ed., *Recruitment and Selection in the Public Service.* Chicago: Public Personnel Association.
Washington v. Davis, 1979. 426 U.S. 229.

CIVIL SERVICE REFORM.

Efforts made by individuals or groups to change the nature of government service. At times these efforts may have taken various shapes. They may have been efforts to overthrow a monarchy and establish a more democratic service; efforts within a communist system to modernize the public service and diminish Communist Party domination of all appointments; or efforts within an existing democracy to give previously disenfranchised groups more power through the public service. All these efforts share in common the desire to manipulate the nature of governmental service.

In the United States some of these reform efforts have been specifically focused, such as the reform efforts leading to the addition of veterans' preference points to the selection procedures of the federal government; others have been broad-based reforms aiming for fundamental change in the entire nature of the public service. Examples of civil service reforms falling into the latter category include the passage of the Pendleton Act in 1883 and the Civil Service Reform Act of 1978. The Pendleton Act was instrumental in minimizing the value of spoils as the basis for the system, and substituting other values such as merit, protectionism, and political neutrality. The Civil Service Reform Act of 1978 altered the structural features of the federal civil service by abolishing the United States Civil Service Commission (USCSC) and creating the Office of Personnel Management (OPM), the Merit Systems Protection Board (MSPB), and the Federal Labor Relations Authority (FLRA) in its place. The new Senior Executive Service was an additional creation of the 1978 reforms. These changes represented a new emphasis on values such as executive leadership, efficiency, and political responsiveness.

Historically our civil service systems have been torn between achieving any number of often incompatible societal values. Most reform efforts have been attempts to emphasize some values and de-emphasize others. Groups not benefiting particularly from government service have often been anxious to reform the civil service for their own group's benefit. Contrarily, groups traditionally benefiting have often sought to preserve the status quo. Thus political party officials and many elected officials who have benefited by the use of patronage-based appointments have resisted reforms designed to narrow the range of spoils-based appointments and the substitution of educationally based merit criteria. In the United States White Anglo Saxon Protestant males (WASPs) who traditionally benefited from the use of educationally based credentials have fought efforts by minorities to reexamine these traditional civil service selection devices. Line managers, not satisfied with the products of civil service hiring registers and unhappy with the range of managerial discretion in hiring and rewarding their employees because of what they perceive as overly restrictive civil service protections or union excesses, have sought reforms designed to increase the responsiveness of civil servants to their wishes in the name of greater efficiency. Career employees and union leaders often oppose reforms aimed at achieving greater managerial discretion based on the premise that discretion will be abused and the criteria of political party advantage and political loyalty will emerge as the true managerial criteria used in the selection and employee reward systems following such reforms.

Most reform of the civil service systems of the federal government in the United States has been incremental in nature, with successive pieces of legislation resulting in small changes in the overall system. Examples include the Position Classification Act of 1923, or the already mentioned Veterans' Preference Act of 1944. There have been very few fundamental landmark changes in the civil service system because, most of the time, presidents would rather work with or around the existing system than invest a considerable amount of their political capital trying to bring about change. For the most part, with competition from such issues as foreign policy and front burner domestic issues, civil service reform has seldom worked its way up high enough on the national agenda to achieve focused wide-scale national attention. The two major exceptions to this historical pattern were the Pendleton Act of 1883 and the Civil Service Reform Act of 1978.

ROBERT H. ELLIOTT

BIBLIOGRAPHY

"An Act to Regulate and Improve the Civil Service of the United States," 1883 (Pendleton Act). United States Congress, 22 Stat. 27.
Elliott, Robert H., 1985. *Public Personnel Administration, A Values Perspective.* Reston, VA: Reston Publishing Company.
Introducing the Civil Service Reform Act, 1978. Washington, D.C.: U.S. Government Printing Office.
Shafritz, Jay, Norma M. Riccucci, David H. Rosenbloom, and Albert C. Hyde, 1992. *Personnel Management in Government.* 4th ed. New York: Marcel Dekker, Inc.

CLASS ACTION.

A suit in which an individual or individuals sue on their own behalf and on behalf of all people who are in a similar situation. Class action proceedings originated in the English chancery courts in the body of law dealing with equity. Chancery courts emerged as mechanisms for providing remedies when there were no other alternatives available for doing so. Originally established as tribunals to deal with the Crown's dispensing of "grace," they gave some order to royal dispensation of justice separate from the courts of law. By the time of the American Revolution, the concept of equity had been well established and class action was one method of securing equity.

Traditionally, class action suits have been used in antitrust cases and by consumers who have been harmed by defective products. During the 1960s, class action suits proliferated as plaintiffs focused on school desegregation, legislative reapportionment, and voting rights. The decisions of the activist Supreme Court of the late 1950s and 1960s encouraged groups who felt they had no alternative to the courts in resolving their complaints regarding discrimination.

In recent years, class action suits have been used extensively in equal employment and affirmative action cases. For example, a female employee who has been discriminated against may seek remedy for the discrimination for herself and for all other females who have been discriminated against by the defendant in the case. Class action suits also are used frequently in environmental cases. Environmental pollution harms untold numbers of individuals now and in the future. Of course, some can demonstrate specific harm and those individuals can constitute a class for purposes of making monetary damage claims.

Class action suits are very complex because courts often require the plaintiffs to identify and contact all members of the class upon whose behalf they are suing. Not all such individuals can be found and many may be indifferent. In recent years, courts have been less rigid, especially if the litigants demonstrate a good faith effort to contact members of the class. If substantial numbers of the class do not participate in the suit, they can cause difficulty with any settlement. For example, in 1994, settlement finally was reached in a suit by women against a manufacturer of breast implants. The financial judgment in the case was to be distributed to members of the class. However, women not a party to the suit would still have the opportunity to sue on their own behalf. The manufacturer agreed to a settlement before going to trial, but a provision of the agreement was that it would be able to withdraw from the agreement if it appeared that too many individuals would not participate in the agreement and would pursue their own litigation.

Class action suits serve to resolve, in one proceeding, conflicts or claims of many people at once. Thus, they are a more efficient method of dealing with multiple parties who have the same claim. They also are helpful where there are limited resources against which claims may be brought. Thus, a class action suit may result in an equitable dispensation of the resources available for damages. Otherwise, those who are able to bring their actions first are likely to have their claims resolved and others may be left with no remedy.

N. JOSEPH CAYER

BIBLIOGRAPHY

Foster, Jr., G. W., 1974. *The Status of Class Action Litigation.* Chicago: American Bar Foundation.
Katzman, John and Steven Hodas, 1995. *Class Action: How to Create Accountability, Innovation, and Excellence in American Schools.* New York: Villard Books.
Yeazell, Stephen C., 1987. *From Medieval Litigation to the Modern Class Action.* New Haven: Yale University Press.

CLIENT ORIENTATION.

A managerial philosophy: the organizational culture required to develop and deliver user-centered public services.

History and Origins

The term is a variant of customer orientation, originating in management and marketing, which refers to organizations with superior skills in understanding and satisfying customer needs. The earliest proponent was the management specialist Peter Drucker (1954), who argued that creating satisfied customers is the only valid definition of business purpose. Thoedore Levitt's classic article "Marketing Myopia" (1960) highlighted the importance of anticipating and responding to customer needs. Tom Peters's and Robert Waterman's *In Search of Excellence* (1982) coined the pragmatic interpretation of "staying close to the customer." This best-selling book resulted in wide dissemination of the philosophy among business practitioners and consultants.

Ten years later David Osborne and Ted Gaebler's *Reinventing Government* (1992), with its prescriptions for entrepreneurial, customer-driven government, is having a similar influence, disseminating the philosophy among practitioners in government. Based on anecdotal experiences of government agencies in the United Sates, the authors call for a universal redefinition of clients of public services as customers.

Client or customer orientation is a central feature of the managerial approach underlying international public sector reforms, known as new public management. Governments in the United Kingdom, Australia, New Zealand, and more recently Canada and the United States have used different strategies, but a consistent and explicit objective has been to change the culture of public sector agencies from rule-based bureaucracies to service providers accountable for results. In the new model of public management client-oriented organizations define results in terms of outcomes for users rather than budgets for service providers. The objective is to increase accountability by making service providers more responsive to user's needs and problems. The practical effect has been to focus on specifying and measuring service quality and customer satisfaction. The language of business and consumer research techniques are being adopted by public managers.

Theoretical Foundations

Levitt's (1960) presciption that firms must anticipate and respond to the needs and wants of customers is universally accepted in marketing texts. The theoretical proposition, derived from microeconomics, is that as customers are the key stakeholders, market-focused firms will have superior performance. Frederick Webster (1992) distinguished the marketing concept as a philosophy from marketing strategy, recognizing the role of organizational culture in the successful implementation of strategy.

The fundamental assumption is a competitive market model where consumers are free to make rational decisions. Critics such as Christopher Pollitt (1993) argue that this model ignores the power of firms to influence consumer wants and assumes consumers know and can articulate their needs and how these should be satisfied. Applying the model to intangible public services where it is difficult to identify customers and needs is argued to be problematic.

United States Practice

In the United States, the Clinton administration's program for streamlining and improving federal government, documented in Vice President Al Gore's *National Performance Review* (NPR), is directed at changing the culture of government to results-oriented accountability. One of the four basic principles of the NPR is "putting customers first." This has been given practical effect in Executive Order 12862 (1993), requiring executive departments and agencies providing services directly to the public to define customer service standards.

International Practice

Strategies to achieve a client focus are a central feature of public management reforms in the United Kingdom, Australia, New Zealand, and Canada. Essentially there have been two approaches. The first seeks to change the culture of existing delivery systems by including service quality measures and evaluation of customer satisfaction as part of performance management. Examples are Canada's PS 2000 program and the Australian government's development of competency standards in client service for program evaluation. The second approach changes current delivery systems by structuring competition between providers to create choices for consumers. Formal agreements or contracts between funders and providers specify resources and services quality standards. Next Steps Executive Agencies and the Citizens' Charter in the United Kingdom are an example of this approach. Both reform strategies require identification of customers or clients and specification of service quality standards.

There is debate about the extent to which the rhetoric of customer orientation matches the reality, especially where changes are being made in the context of reductions in government funding. Proponents argue that focusing on customer needs will improve efficiency and service quality by concentrating resources to best effect. Critics argue that relationships between consumers and providers are necessarily more complex for public services and quality outcomes are thus difficult to measure and evaluate. The problem is identifying consumers and therefore priorities. There are at least two groups of customers with different priorities. Clients who use a service, but often do not pay directly for it, want effective outcomes that meet their needs. Citizens as taxpayers want efficient service delivery to minimize the tax burden. The problem for service providers is to reconcile the demand for greater efficiency with the expectation of being more responsive to clients. Critics of the reforms argue that efficiency or outputs which are more easily specified, rather than effectiveness or service quality outcomes, will dominate performance measures.

LINDA MCGUIRE

BIBLIOGRAPHY

Drucker, Peter F., 1954. *The Practice of Management.* New York: Harper & Row.
Levitt, Theodore, 1960. "Marketing Myopia." *Harvard Business Review* (July/August) 45–60.
Osborne, David and Ted Gaebler, 1992. *Reinventing Government: How the Entrepreneurial Spirit Is Transforming the Public Sector.* New York: Plume.
Peters, Thomas J. and Robert H. Waterman, 1982. *In Search of Excellence: Lessons from America's Best-Run Companies.* New York: Harper & Row.
Pollitt, Christopher, 1993. *Mangerialism and the Public Service.* 2nd ed. Oxford, UK: Blackwell.
Webster Jr., Frederick E., 1992. "The Changing Role of Marketing in the Corporation." *Journal of Marketing,* vol. 56 (October) 1–17.

CODES OF CONDUCT. Legislated behavioral requirements of a given entity, including federal, state, and local governments, that have been developed in an effort to prevent corrupt behavior and to set standards for appropriate conduct.

Codes of conduct in public administration exist as a part of legislated behavioral requirements of both government employees and clients or customers of public agencies. To help clarify the meaning of codes of conduct, the two words "codes" and "conduct" are defined separately. A "code" has been described, variously, as "laws, regulations, rules, standards, statutes." When "code" is written with "conduct," its meaning encompasses all these terms. A code of conduct is that specifically identified list of behaviors that have been deemed appropriate or inappropriate enough to have been incorporated into either laws or regulations or policy statements. "Conduct" is defined, generally, as "bearing, behavior, demeanor, and deportment." Thus, a code of conduct narrowly defines what one is to do in a given position or set of circumstances.

The terms codes of conduct and codes of ethics are frequently used interchangeably in common parlance. Therefore, one way to understand a code of conduct is to contrast it with a code of ethics. While codes of conduct provide a list of specific directions about what behaviors to exhibit under what conditions, codes of ethics provide a set of aspirational standards by which to live and work. In other words, codes of conduct contain specific, descriptive behavioral requirements about what one does and does not do in a given set of circumstances; codes of ethics provide idealistic, value-driven statements designed to inspire but not require appropriate actions.

Codes of conduct are typically enforceable by some set of legislated sanctions; people to whom they apply are required to know and abide by them. Codes of ethics are not usually enforceable except through some sort of censorship by the professional group that spawned them; proponents hope that people will know and abide them. Because both codes of conduct and codes of ethics are directed toward fostering what would be considered good and right actions, the meaning of the terms often blur.

In public administration, codes of conduct typically are a part of legislative action or policy statements. They contain a list of what kind of behavior is expected to occur under a given set of circumstances. Like codes of ethics, codes of conduct provide information about standards and limits of practice for members of the profession that issue them. Unlike codes of ethics, codes of conduct are related to the specific expectations about how one will behave while employed or being served by the organization or government entity that issues them.

Codes of conduct, however, do not represent professional assurances about high moral standards. Rather, they provide direction to those whose conduct they govern. Codes of conduct are minimalistic prohibitions against unquestionably subversive or criminal acts. They are designed to protect the government employee, the client, or the public at large.

Perhaps one reason for the confusion about what constitutes codes of conduct and what constitutes codes of ethics comes from the practice of labeling legislated standards of conduct "ethics laws" and from calling the agencies that enforce these laws "offices of government ethics." A close look at such "ethics laws," however, quickly shows that they contain enforceable behavioral standards.

To enhance understanding of the meaning of a code of conduct, the preamble and articles of the U.S. military code of conduct are shown in Exhibit I. The reader will note that it contains a contractual agreement between the U.S. government and the members of the armed forces whose conduct it governs, as well as an inspirational introduction. The reader should contrast its content with the noncontractual, nonspecific elements shown in the section on codes of ethics.

EXHIBIT I. MILITARY CODE OF CONDUCT

As a member of the U.S. armed forces, you are protecting your nation. It's your duty to oppose all enemies of the United States whether in combat or as a captive in a Prisoner of War (POW) facility. The code of conduct is a guide for your proper behavior. This code is the result of heroic lives, experiences, and deeds of Americans from the Revolutionary War through our most recent conflicts.

Your obligations result from the traditional values that underlie the American Experience as a nation. The United States constitution and Bill of Rights, which you have sworn to support and defend, emphasize these values. You have obligations to your country, service, unit, and fellow Americans. The code of conduct restates these obligations especially for military members.

Just as you have a responsibility to your country under this code, the U.S. government has an equal responsibility—always to keep faith with you and stand by you as you fight for its defense. If you become a POW, you may rest assured that your government will care for your dependents and will never forget you. Furthermore, the government will use every practical means to contact, support, and gain release for you and all other POWs.

To live up to the code, you must not only know its words, but the ideas and principles behind them. Our code of conduct is both an ethical and a moral guide. Its six articles deal with the chief concerns of Americans in combat. These concerns become critical when you must evade capture, resist while a prisoner, or escape from the enemy.

Experiences of captured Americans reveal that to survive captivity honorably would demand from you great courage, deep dedication, and high motivation. To sustain these personal values throughout captivity requires that you understand and believe strongly in our free and democratic institutions, love your country, trust in the justice of your cause, keep faithful and loyal to your fellow prisoners, and hold firmly to your religious and moral beliefs in time of trouble.

This courage, dedication, positive mental attitude, and motivation, supported by understanding, trust, and loyalty, will help you endure captivity, prevail over your captors, and return you to your family, home, and nation with honor and pride.

The Articles of the Code

The code of conduct for members of the armed forces of the United States was first published by President Dwight D. Eisenhower on August 17, 1955. In March 1988, President Ronald Reagan amended the code with language that is gender-neutral. The code, although first expressed in 1955, is based on time-honored concepts and traditions that date back to the days of the American Revolution.

Article I

I am an American, fighting in the forces which guard my country and our way of life. I am prepared to give my life in their defense.

Article II

I will never surrender of my own free will. If in command, I will never surrender the members of my command while they still have the means to resist.

Article III

If I am captured, I will continue to resist by all means available. I will make every effort to escape and aid others to escape. I will accept neither parole nor special favors from the enemy.

Article IV

If I become a prisoner of war, I will keep faith with my fellow prisoners. I will give no information or take part in any action which might be harmful to my comrades. If I am senior, I will command. If not, I will obey the lawful orders of those appointed over me and will back them up in every way.

Article V

When questioned, should I become a prisoner of war, I am required to give name, rank, service number, and date of birth. I will evade answering further questions to the utmost of my ability. I will make no oral or written statements disloyal to my country and its allies or harmful to their cause.

Article VI

I will never forget that I am an American, fighting for freedom, responsible for my actions, and dedicated to the principles which made my country free. I will trust in my god and in the United States of America.

SOURCE: AFP 50–34, vol 1. (November 1, 1992).

Origin and Subsequent History

Codes of conduct are part of a long tradition, traceable to the Babylonian Code of Hammurabi constructed in the eighteenth century B.C.E. In the same tradition are the Ten Commandments recorded in the Pentateuch (Deuteronomy 5:6–21) and codes of the Greek city-states, which began to be developed in the seventh century B.C.E. These ancient codes influenced the development of modern legal systems, as well as discrete situation-specific codes of conduct. They also influenced what might be called the first U.S. code of conduct, which identifies specific behaviors expected to be exhibited between members of the Massachusetts Bay colony. This code is contained in the 1630 sermon of John Winthrop, first governor of the Massachusetts Bay Colony (see Exhibit II). Like the present-day code of military conduct, this seventeenth century code contains a contractual agreement and an inspirational introduction.

EXHIBIT II. PURITAN CODE OF CONDUCT

We must entertain each other in brotherly affection; we must be willing to abridge ourselves of our superfluities for the supply of others' necessities; . . . We must delight in each other, make others' conditions our own, rejoice together, mourn together, labor and suffer together. . . . So shall we keep the unity of the spirit in the bond of peace, the Lord will be our God and delight to dwell among us, as His own people, and will command a blessing upon us in all our ways.

SOURCE: Miller, Perry. *The American Puritans.*

Underlying Theoretical Framework

No specific theoretical framework within public administration has been identified in regards to codes of conduct per se. They are in the legal framework of civil law. According to Karen Lewis, writing in the *Dickinson Law Review* (1990), codes of conduct "serve both proscriptive and prescriptive purposes. The proscriptive function is legislative in nature, and sets forth definitions for acts of professional misconduct that are legally punishable. In contrast the prescriptive function sets the standards to guide behavior and serves as a statement of moral order" (p. 933).

Such codes are necessary because of the presumed nature of humankind, described by Thomas Hobbes (1588–1679 C.E.) in his treatise *Leviathan,* which argues for the necessity of government. He argues,

> . . . the laws of nature, as justice, equity, modesty, mercy, and in sum, *doing to others as we would be done to* (italics in original), of themselves without the terror of some power to cause them to be observed, are contrary to our natural passions, that carry us to partiality, pride, revenge, and the like. And covenants, without the sword, are but words, and of no strength to secure a man at all. There- fore notwithstanding the laws of nature, which everyone hath then kept, when he has the will to keep them when he can do it safely; if there be no power erected, or not great enough for our security, every man will, and may, lawfully rely on his own strength and art, for caution against other men (Somerville and Santoni, 1963, pp. 148–149).

Thus, codes of conduct are constructed and given the power of law, so that each can rely upon each to act in ways that benefit them both.

Current Practice in the United States

Current practice in the United States varies only slightly between levels of government. *Standards for Ethical Conduct for Employees of the Executive Branch* provides a code of conduct for U.S. federal government employees. This code was published in the U.S. *Federal Register* (57 35006– 35067, August 7, 1992) with an effective date of February 3, 1993. As with the previous two examples, the code of con- duct for federal employees contains an inspirational pre- amble and a list of behavioral standards, called "principles of ethical conduct" (see Exhibit III).

The several states do not provide such a comprehen- sive list of required behaviors. Behaviors that are regulated generally come under the rubric of "ethics laws," and do not seem to appear in a discrete listing, like that of the fed- eral government. The *COGEL Blue Book* (Bullock, 1993) lists the substantive state restraints on conduct by state of- ficials and employees. In most states the following actions are prohibited: use of public position to obtain personal

---

EXHIBIT III. BASIC OBLIGATION OF PUBLIC SERVICE

(a.) Public service is a public trust. Each employee has a responsibility to the United States government and its citizens to place loyalty to the Constitution, laws, and ethical principles above private gain. To ensure that every citizen can have complete confidence in the integrity of the federal government, each employee shall re- spect and adhere to the principles of ethical conduct set forth in this section, as well as the implementing standards contained in this part and in supplemental agency regulations.

(b.) General principles. The following general principles apply to every employee and may form the basis for the standards contained in this part. Where a situation is not covered by the standards set forth in this part, employees shall apply the principles set forth in this sec- tion in determining whether their conduct is proper.

(1) Public service is a public trust, requiring employees to place loyalty to the Constitution, the laws, and ethical principles above private gain.

(2) Employees shall not hold financial interests that conflict with the conscientious performance of duty.

(3) An employee shall not, except as permitted by subpart B of this part, solicit or accept any gift or other item of monetary value from any person or entity seeking official action from, doing business with, or conducting activities regulated by the employee's agency, or whose interests may be substantially af- fected by the performance or nonperformance of the em- ployee's duties.

(4) Employees shall put forth honest effort in the performance of their duties.

(5) Employees shall not knowingly make unauthorized commit- ments or promises of any kind purporting to bind the govern- ment.

(6) Employees shall not use public office for private gain.

(7) Employees shall act impartially and not give preferential treatment to any private organization or individual.

(8) Employees shall protect and conserve federal property and shall not use it for other than authorized activities.

(9) Employees shall not engage in outside employment, or ac- tivities, including seeking or negotiating for employment, that conflict with official government duties and responsibil- ities.

(10) Employees shall disclose waste, fraud, abuse, and corruption to appropriate authorities.

(11) Employees shall satisfy in good faith their obligations as cit- izens, including all just financial obligations, especially those—such as federal, state, and local taxes—that are im- posed by law.

(12) Employees shall adhere to all laws and regulations that pro- vide equal opportunity for all Americans regardless of race, color, religion, sex, national origin, age, or handicap.

(13) Employees shall endeavor to avoid any actions creating the appearance that they are violating the law or the ethical stan- dards set forth in this part. Whether particular circumstances create an appearance that the law or these standards have been violated shall be determined from the perspective of a reasonable person with knowledge of the relevant facts.

SOURCE: U.S. Office of Government Ethics, *Standards of Ethical Conduct for Employ- ees of the Executive Branch.* Washington, D.C.: U.S. Office of Government Ethics, 1992.

benefit (41 states), providing benefits to influence official actions (42 states), use of confidential government information (37 states), receipt of gifts over a specified amount (35 states), representation of private clients before public authorities (34 states), financial conflicts of interest (35 states), nepotism (31 states), political activity by employees (20 states) outside employment or business activities (37 states) (pp. 158–167).

See **codes of ethics, standards of conduct**.

WILLA MARIE BRUCE

BIBLIOGRAPHY

Bullock, Joyce, ed., 1993. *COGEL Blue Book.* 9th ed. Lexington, KY: Council of State Governments.

Lewis, Karen, 1990. "Administrative Law Judges and the Code of Ethical Conduct." *Dickinson Law Review,* vol. 94, no. 4 (Summer) 929–963.

Miller, Perry, ed., 1956. *The American Puritans.* Garden City, NY: Doubleday & Co.

Somerville, John and Ronald Santoni, eds.,1963. *Social and Political Philosophy.* Garden City, NY: Doubleday.

U.S. Air Force, *AFP 50–34,* vol. 1 (November 1, 1992) 136–150.

U.S. Office of Government Ethics, 1992. *Standards of Ethical Conduct for Employees of the Executive Branch.* Washington, D.C.: U.S. Office of Government Ethics.

Winthrop, John, 1956. "A Model of Christian Charity." In Perry Miller, ed., *The American Puritans.* Garden City, NY: Doubleday & Co.

CODES OF ETHICS.

Published statements of the set of values and moral aspirations of a given profession, developed in an effort to prevent corrupt behavior as well as communicate professional behavioral standards to the public at large.

Codes of ethics in public administration exist as a part of the professional standards issued by many of the occupations that are considered a part of public administration. To help clarify the meaning of codes of ethics, the two words "codes" and "ethics" are defined separately. A code has been described, variously, as "laws, regulations, rules, standards, statutes." When "code" is written with "ethics," its meaning is narrowed considerably, to the one definition: "standards." In other words, a code of ethics is a set of standards for good and appropriate conduct. These standards indicate the kinds of behavior considered proper for a person in the profession for which that code was developed.

"Ethics" is defined, generally, as "ideals, morals, principles of right, mores, and scruples, and the rules or standards governing the conduct of a profession." At first glance it might seem that being ethical means "obeying the rules" or "living up to the standards of one's profession." And, that is, of course, correct. As those who work in government know, however, ethics in the real world is not so narrowly defined.

To put ethics into practical perspective, we can think of an ethical employee as one who does not engage in illegal behavior, and who consistently acts in ways that place the benefit of the government and the public above personal benefit. Codes of ethics challenge all workers to act as ethical employees. Indeed, "the central function of an ethics code is to prevent—rather than punish—unethical conduct . . ." (Lewis, 1993, pp. 142–43, citing the commission that drafted the ethics code for the City of Los Angeles, California).

Codes of ethics typically come from professional organizations. They contain a list of the social functions the organization exists to support and assurances that those functions will be carried out in accordance with high moral standards. Professional codes of ethics have two moral functions. They serve as a quality assurance guarantee to society and provide information about standards and limits of practice for members of the profession that issues them.

James Bowman, editor of *Ethical Frontiers in Public Management* (1992), identifies three characteristics of a successful code of ethics: it provides behavioral guidance; it is applicable to a variety of occupations within the same profession, and it has an effective mechanism to ensure compliance (p. 28). Most codes of ethics, however, do not contain sanctions.

When codes of ethics do include enforceable standards, they become more concrete and less ideal. They are no longer aspirational descriptions of what is good and right behavior. They become a list of clearly defined and enforceable legislated requirements. At the point a code of ethics becomes a list of required behaviors, enforceable under the law, it also becomes a code of conduct (see **codes of conduct**).

Two codes of ethics that represent the profession of public administration are those provided by the American Society for Public Administration (ASPA) and the International City/County Management Association (ICMA). Both of these codes have an enforcement process that encourages members to monitor and report one another, and which provides the accused with due process before any disciplinary action is taken. If an accused ICMA member is determined to be guilty as charged, the ICMA may cancel membership and either publicly or privately censor that member. If an accused ASPA member is determined to be guilty, that member will be expelled from the society.

Origin and Subsequent History

Lewis (1993) links codes of ethics in public administration to a long heritage. She notes that "Since Hammurabi, Moses, and Hippocrates, codifiers and executors have operated on a theory that it is easier to do the right thing when one knows what that is. As a result, codified standards of conduct have become a popular vehicle for clarifying minimum expectations about acceptable behavior" (p. 136).

One of the earliest codes of ethics is "The Athenian Oath," cited by Chandler (1983):

> We will never bring disgrace to this our city by any act of dishonesty or cowardice, nor ever desert our suffering comrades in the ranks;
> We will fight for the ideals and sacred things of the city, both alone and with many;
> We will revere and obey the city's laws and do our best to incite to a like respect and reverence those who are prone to annul or set them at naught;
> We will strive unceasingly to quicken the public sense of public duty;
> That thus, in all these ways, we will transmit this city not only not less, but greater, better, and more beautiful than it was transmitted to us (p. 134).

Codes of ethics in public administration are phenomena of the twentieth century. The International City Managers Association (now International City/County Managers Association) issued its first code of ethics in 1924. Plant (1994) provides a brief history from their genesis through the 1970s:

> Codes of ethics have been part of public administration since the International City Managers' Association promulgated the first major code in 1924. . . . The first codes were professional codes that bound public officials to standards of conduct defined by professional associations. In 1958, by a concurrent resolution, Congress enacted a code of conduct for federal executive branch employees. In 1961 President Kennedy strengthened the code by executive order. In the 1970s, the Watergate scandal triggered a wave of code-making, especially in state and local governments and the public service professions. . . . The Ethics in Government Act of 1978 reinforced the notion that ethical conduct was an aspect of public management (p. 222).

In 1981, after six years of deliberations, ASPA developed a set of moral principles that were finally incorporated into the society's first code of ethics in 1984. That code was revised in 1994, and is now published regularly on the back cover of every issue of *Public Administration Review*, the society's professional journal.

In 1989 a revised "Standards for Ethical Conduct for Employees of the Executive Branch" was published in the U.S. *Federal Register* (57 35006–35067, August 7, 1992) with an effective date of February 3, 1993. These standards provide a code of conduct, enforceable by law, to govern the behavior of federal employees. In regard to ethics codes developed by the various states, only four have codes that pre-date 1973, indicating that the influence of Watergate spread outward from Washington into other levels of government. The *COGEL Blue Book* (Bullock, 1993) lists the elements of the ethics codes of various states.

Underlying Theoretical Framework

The theory behind codes of ethics is an idealistic one, based on the somewhat naive belief that if people know what is considered inappropriate behavior in their profession, they won't display that behavior. Codes of ethics tend to be what Ralph Chandler (1983) calls "preachy," that is they tend to be somewhat vague, inspirational, and filled with platitudes.

Lewis (1991) suggests that "Codes are best associated with three general but realistic objectives: to encourage high standards of behavior, to increase public confidence, and to assist decisionmaking. . . . Different objectives lead to different models. Legislated codes provide legal penalties and protections as necessary and effective constraints on official power, public authority, and the potential for abuse of administrative discretion. Administrative standards and procedures assist decisionmakers and managers by providing an operational framework tied to workaday realities." Furthermore, when devising a code of ethics, "*a productive starting point is realistic managerial objectives: the internal, direct clients are the ethical managers and employees; the purpose is to assist them*" (p. 143, emphasis in original).

Codes of ethics may reflect either the "democratic ethos" or the "bureaucratic ethos," though they most often seem to represent the bureaucratic. The democratic ethos contains a set of assumptions that presume the ethical administrator should be evaluated on criteria such as upholding regime values, exhibiting good citizenship, serving the public interest, and promoting social equity. Codes that reflect this viewpoint encourage their adherents to value and promote service to the public. Value assumptions in the bureaucratic ethos presume that public administrators are technical experts with legal rational authority whose chief moral dilemma is how best to abide by and enforce rules and regulations (see **administrative morality**). It is possible to see both of these ethos represented in the codes of ethics for ASPA and ICMA members.

Current Practice in the United States

Ethics codes in the United States continue to be promulgated by both professional associations and government entities. The two codes of ethics exhibited here represent current professional practice in the United States. An examination of them will provide understanding about what values and standards the profession of public administration represents, and wants to communicate to its practitioners. Providing aspirational and representational statements of what is deemed good and ethical for a profession is necessary, and these codes do that well. Codes of ethics, however, are only as good as their ability to inspire adherence.

What happens in the United States seems to be a presumption that if a code of ethics is developed, people to whom it applies will understand it and act accordingly. That simply is not the case. Typically a code is developed

EXHIBIT I. AMERICAN SOCIETY FOR PUBLIC ADMINISTRATION CODE OF ETHICS

The American Society for Public Administration (ASPA) exists to advance the science, processes, and art of public administration. The society affirms its responsibility to develop the spirit of professionalism within its membership, and to increase public awareness of ethical principles in public service by its example. To this end, we, the members of the Society, commit ourselves to the following principles:

Serve the Public Interest

Serve the Public, beyond serving oneself.

Respect the Constitution and the Law

Respect, support, and study government constitutions and laws that define responsibilities of public agencies, employees, and all citizens.

Demonstrate Personal Integrity

Demonstrate the highest standards in all activities to inspire public confidence and trust in public service.

Promote Ethical Organizations

Strengthen individual capabilities and encourage the professional development of others.

Strive for Professional Excellence

Strengthen individual capabilities and encourage the professional development of others.

Enforcement of the Code of Ethics shall be conducted in accordance with Article I, Section 4 of ASPA's Bylaws.

In 1981 the American Society for Public Administration's National Council adopted a set of moral principles. Three years later in 1984, the Council approved a Code of Ethics for ASPA members. In 1994 the Code was revised.

---

or revised by a small, representative group from a profession. Their efforts are only fruitful when people in the profession they represent receive the education and socialization necessary to encourage their adherence to their code. Thus, while codes of ethics are important, they are not sufficient. They contain standards, but no guarantees.

Variations in Practice

Codes of ethics vary only slightly between public service professions, as is evidenced in Exhibits I and II. For a complete collection of professional codes of ethics, the reader should consult *Codes of Professional Responsibility* (Gorlin, 1990).

Codes of ethics promulgated by the different states vary somewhat. They seem as much codes of conduct as they do codes of ethics, though the states themselves tend to refer to their legislated standards of behavior as "ethics laws." As Jeremy Plant notes, "confusion over the three possible meanings (of ethics codes)—legal systems, moral systems, or symbolic means of communicating—is at the heart of the discussion of codes in public administration"

EXHIBIT II. INTERNATIONAL CITY/COUNTY MANAGEMENT ASSOCIATION CODE OF ETHICS

The purpose of the International City/County Management Association is to increase the proficiency of city managers, county managers, and other municipal administrators and to strengthen the quality of urban government through professional management. To further these objectives, certain ethical principles shall govern the conduct of every member of the International City/County Management Association who shall:

1. Be dedicated to the concepts of effective and democratic local government by responsible elected officials and believe that professional general management is essential to the achievement of this objective
2. Affirm the dignity and worth of the services rendered by government and maintain a constructive, creative, and practical attitude toward urban affairs and a deep sense of social responsibility as a trusted public servant.
3. Be dedicated to the highest ideals of honor and integrity in all public and personal relationships in order that the member may merit the respect and confidence of the elected officials, of other officials and employees, and of the public.
4. Recognize that the chief function of local government at all times is to serve the best interests of the people.
5. Submit policy proposals to elected officials, provide them with facts and advice on matters of policy as a basis for making decisions and setting community goals, and uphold and implement municipal policies adopted by elected officials.
6. Recognize that elected representatives of the people are entitled to the credit for the establishment of municipal policies; responsibility for policy execution rests with the members.
7. Refrain from participation in the election of the members of the employing legislative body, and from all partisan political activities which would impair performance as a professional administrator.
8. Make it a duty continually to improve the member's professional ability and to develop the competence of associates in the use of management techniques.
9. Keep the community informed on municipal affairs; encourage communication between citizens and all municipal officials; emphasize friendly and courteous service to the public; and seek to improve the quality and image of public service.
10. Resist any encroachment on professional responsibilities, believing the members should be free to carry out official policies without discrimination on the basis of principles and justice.
11. Handle all matters of personnel on the basis of merit so that fairness and impartiality govern a member's decisions, pertaining to appointments, pay adjustments, promotions, and discipline.
12. Seek no favor; believe that personal aggrandizement or profit secured by confidential information or by misuse of public time is dishonest.

(1994, p. 223). Thus there may be more variation in how one defines codes of ethics than in what professional codes contain.

WILLA MARIE BRUCE

BIBLIOGRAPHY

Bowman, James, 1990. "Ethics in Government: A National Survey of Public Administrators." *Public Administration Review,* vol. 50, no. 3, 345–353.
———, ed., 1992. *Ethical Frontiers in Public Management.* San Francisco: Jossey-Bass.

Bullock, Joyce, ed., 1993. *COGEL Blue Book*. 9th ed. Lexington, KY: Council of State Governments.

Chandler, Ralph, 1983. "The Problem of Moral Reasoning in American Public Administration." *Public Administration Review*, vol. 43, no. 1 (January/February) 32–39.

Gorlin, Rena A., 1990. *Codes of Professional Responsibility*, 2nd ed. Washington, D.C.: Bureau of National Affairs.

Lewis, Carol, 1993. "Codes of Ethics." In H. George Frederickson, ed., *Ethics and Public Administration*. Armonk, N.Y.: M. E. Sharpe.

——, 1991. *The Ethics Challenge in Public Service*. San Francisco: Jossey-Bass.

Plant, Jeremy, 1994. "Codes of Ethics." In T. Cooper, ed. *Handbook of Administrative Ethics*. New York: Marcel Dekker, 221–42.

CODE WORD.

CODE WORD. Euphemistic or politically acceptable word used instead of a less acceptable expression; a positive or inoffensive word substituted for a term with unpleasant or objectionable associations which is actually more precise. Also, a term given special meaning through wide usage different from customary connotations.

The use of code words is so common in the media that the public is often unaware of how messages are altered. While some uses of code words are appropriate to deal gently with sensitive issues, this type of vocabulary is used by government to disguise unpleasant facts. Code words may obscure reality so completely that only a few "insiders" comprehend the true significance of a message. The term "doublespeak" has been coined to describe this usage of code words. History records the use of code words from earliest times.

Code Words in the American Media

The American media's use of code words is pervasive. Code words become a part of everyday usage without conscious audience awareness. "Media code words" are words and phrases that call up pictures in the minds of the target audience which redefine concepts, groups, and ideas (Richardson and Richardson, 1993). The media's meanings often differ, not only from standard dictionary definitions, but from facts. The public's opinions on controversial issues are influenced by the media. The code expression "family values" suggests that there are "good" families and "bad" families. By inference a good family is one that comprises a mother, father, and children. Any other configuration is often considered a bad family. The code words "family values" imply that members of a "bad" family are abnormal or exceptional. In fact, there has never been a time in U.S. history when 100 percent of American families fit the "good family" pattern.

Code words are invented by the media as labels for people and events. They are also created by politicians and think tank scholars, and recycled by the media until they become part of everyday speech. During political campaigns the media may begin to label a candidate as the "front-runner"–the person in a political campaign the media identify as most likely to win. This label creates the impression that the person will win and improves fundraising opportunities. This ability to raise money allows the candidate to stay in the race longer. Media commentators may also influence a campaign by using code words to accuse an opponent of "negative campaigning." If the opponent responds to the media's allegations, the individual may then be charged with "press bashing." The media's use of code words may alter political situations.

Euphemisms and Doublespeak

"Doublespeak" is the use of code words by government to disguise reality. While euphemisms are often appropriate, doublespeak is less beneficial. A euphemism substitutes an agreeable expression for one that may offend. A word or phrase is used which is less expressive or direct but which is less harsh than another. Someone may say "he passed on to his reward" rather than "he died." "Remains" is more acceptable than "dead body" or "corpse."

While the use of euphemistic code words spares the feelings of others, the purpose of doublespeak is to mislead: to make the bad seem good, and to make the unpleasant appear attractive or at least tolerable. It is language that avoids responsibility. It pretends to communicate, but deliberately avoids what is tangible, real, and common. It is not the product of careless language or sloppy thinking–rather, it is language carefully constructed to appear to communicate when it does not.

The concept of doublespeak may have originated with English author George Orwell, who described it as words "designed to make lies sound truthful and murder respectable, and to give an appearance of solidity to pure wind" (Orwell, 1946). American author Randy Moore maintains that "our society is saturated with doublespeak" (1991, p. 324).

Doublespeak has a long history. The Greek historian Thucydides, writing in the fifth century B.C.E., noted that those in power altered the accepted usage of words: "Reckless audacity" was termed "courageous loyalty to party"; "prudent hesitation" was "cowardice"; and "moderation" was "spinelessness." The Roman emperor Julius Caesar described his brutal subjugation of Gaul as "pacification." "Where they make a desert, they call it peace," observed British tribal chieftain Calgacus of the Roman conquest of England (Lutz, 1990, p. 89).

The deliberate misuses of language are not unique to the United States. American author William Lutz, in his book *Doublespeak: From "Revenue Enhancement" to "Terminal Living"–How Government, Business, Advertisers, and Others Use Language to Deceive You*, includes examples from Canada, England, the Soviet Union, Japan, and South Africa. The English newspaper, the *Times* of London, carries letters to the editor that criticize the substitution of such phrases as: "Public Waste Reception Centre" for dump, "environmental hygienist" for janitor, and "environmental physicist" for plumber. In Canada, cutting down trees becomes "harvesting overmature timber."

United States citizens have special cause to detest corruption in language. The principles expressed in the passionate, exact language of the American Declaration of Independence are the cornerstone of democracy. Lutz warns of the doublespeak government uses to mask realities with words and phrases that, on the surface, sound justifiable, acceptable, or perhaps even inevitable. A lie becomes a "misspeak," killing becomes "pacification," stealing becomes "misappropriation," and censorship becomes "administrative control." The military does not kill civilians but inflicts "collateral damage." A president's budget message does not mention "taxes" but rather "new receipt proposals," "revenue enhancement," "user fees," or "tax base broadening." An economic recession is a "period of accelerated negative economic growth."

By using doublespeak, government officials avoid public understanding of nuclear power. Fire in a nuclear reactor is "rapid oxidation" or "an incendiary event," while an explosion in a nuclear plant is an "energetic disassembly" or a "rapid release of energy." A reactor accident is an "unusual event, " "an unscheduled event," an "incident," or a "normal aberration." An accident that occurs frequently is called a "normally expected abnormal occurrence." A nuclear meltdown is a "core disruptive accident." Mutual destruction by intercontinental missiles is a "nuclear exchange."

J. WALTON BLACKBURN

BIBLIOGRAPHY

Gruner, Charles R., Lara J. Travillion and Deborah E. Schaefer, 1991. "Testing the Effectiveness of Doublespeak." *Et Cetera*, vol. 48, no. 2 (Summer) 153–160.

Hasselriis, Peter, 1991. "All Toothpastes Are Equal (= Best): William Lutz's *Doublespeak*." *English Journal*, vol. 80, no. 2 (February) 91–92.

Lutz, William, 1989. *Beyond Nineteen Eighty-Four*. Urbana, IL: National Council of Teachers of English.

———, 1989. *Doublespeak: From "Revenue Enhancement" to "Terminal Living"–How Government, Business, Advertisers, and Others Use Language to Deceive You*. New York: Harper and Row.

———, 1990. "Doublespeak, the Invasion of Panama, and the Corruption of Public Discourse." *North American Review*, vol. 275, no. 2: 56–57.

Moore, Randy, 1991. "The Doublespeak of Science." *American Biology Teacher*, vol. 53, no. 6 (September) 324–326.

Orwell, George, 1946. "Politics and the English Language." *Shooting an Elephant and Other Essays*. New York: Harcourt Brace and Co.

Quarterly Review of Doublespeak.

Richardson, Willis and Gwenevere Daya Richardson, 1993. "How the Media Manipulate Us with Code Words." *Editor and Publisher*, vol. 126, no. 17 (April 24) 128, 116 ff.

COGNITIVE DISSONANCE.

A theory first postulated by Leon Festinger (1957), which holds that when an individual finds himself in a situation where he is expected to believe two mutually exclusive things, the subsequent tension and discomfort generate activity designed to reduce the disharmony. Festinger presents two basic hypotheses: (1) the existence of dissonance (inconsistency) is psychologically uncomfortable, which motivates a person to try to reduce the dissonance and achieve consonance (consistency); and (2) when dissonance is present, in addition to trying to reduce it, a person will actively avoid situations and information which would likely increase the dissonance.

Festinger further explains cognitive dissonance by defining the meaning of the two words "cognitive" and "dissonance." Cognition (the noun form of cognitive) is "any knowledge, opinion, or belief about the environment, about oneself, or about one's behavior." Dissonance is "the existence of nonfitting relations among cognitions" (Festinger, 1957, p. 3). Cognitive dissonance, then, can best be understood as an antecedent condition which leads to activity oriented toward reducing dissonance.

Festinger's concept of cognitive dissonance suggests that the human organism will always try to establish internal harmony, consistency, or congruity among his opinions, attitudes, knowledge, and values (i.e., a drive toward consonance among cognitions). He conceptualizes cognition to be decomposable into elements or clusters of elements. When confronted with some contradiction to a strongly held belief, people tend to try (either consciously or unconsciously) to find some element of the contradictory input with which they can identify.

For example, suppose that a career bureaucrat has loyally served the appointed agency head who hired him. The bureaucrat has enthusiastically supported the agency head's planning initiatives, policies, and programs. He is now faced with a newly appointed agency head affiliated with the opposite political party–an individual who campaigned on a platform that vehemently opposed the plans of his predecessor.

The career bureaucrat must confront conflicting inputs that create cognitive dissonance. He knows that the new agency head has been an outspoken critic of the plans that he developed and implemented. He knows that he has a few more years until he can earn full retirement benefits. He is not in a financial position to resign on a matter of philosophic difference. He is aware that other career bureaucrats in the agency are experiencing similar cognitive discomfort. Both individually and as a group, these bureaucrats must find elements of the new cognitive environment with which they can reestablish consonance. Individually and collectively they will conduct a cognitive cost-benefit analysis in order to resolve the internal conflict and to achieve consonance.

Gradually, the career bureaucrats will distance themselves from the policies of the past administration. Individual beliefs, values, and opinions will shift to accommodate the changing organizational environment. According to Miles's Law ("where he stands depends on where he sits"), people will adjust their cognitive positions to suit the circumstances (Miles, 1978). Career bureaucrats will grasp onto the elements of the new agency head's initiatives that they find cognitively palatable. They will minimize, avoid, and ignore those elements that generate personal cognitive dissonance. They will make cognitive adaptations until individual and organizational consonance is achieved.

Cognitive dissonance theory explains how and why human beings process and interpret contradictory information. Dissonance does not exist all by itself. It is a conflicting relationship between cognitive elements that causes people to try to eliminate or reduce the dissonance between what they observe and what they have held to be accurate knowledge, opinion, or belief in the past.

Since Festinger first presented the concept of cognitive dissonance in 1957, the phenomenon has been examined in both individuals and organizations. James G. March (1988) cites a number of studies that suggest that the conventional response to cognitive dissonance is to accept responsibility for the decisions (at least in the short run), deny disappointment, and behave as though the disconfirmations of expectations either did not occur or were unimportant. Charles E. Lindblom (1990) refers to individual preferences, wants, needs, interests, and choices as volitions. When faced with cognitive dissonance, he suggests that "people to some significant degree seek to adjust volitions to each other mutually or reciprocally, and in all directions" (p. 40). These internal cognitive adjustments are quite individualistic, not clearly defined, and not necessarily consistent. Individuals interacting in organizations inevitably generate cognitive dissonance within the group that must be resolved.

Cognitive dissonance theory has been examined in a wide variety of organizational studies. For example, a study of ethical conflicts in business found that cognitive dissonance theory is helpful in understanding the effect of ethical conflict on business decisions (Moser, 1988). Another study combined cognitive dissonance theory and standard economic models to conclude that the behavior of people in organizations can be explained by individual subconcious cost-benefit calculations based on individual perceptions of reality (Carter, 1988).

Cognitive dissonance theory will continue to play an important role in our understanding of both individual and organizational behavior. New information and change causes individuals to perform complex internal analyses, juxtaposing new data with existing cognitions. Elements that remain in conflict with existing cognitions are made consonant (i.e., made tolerable for the individual) through the cognitive dissonance process.

JOHN S. SHAFFER

BIBLIOGRAPHY

Bagby, R. Michael and James D. A. Parker, 1990. "A Comparative Citation Analysis of Attribution Theory and the Theory of Cognitive Dissonance." *Personality and Psychology Bulletin,* vol. 16, no. 2 (June) 274–283.

Carter, Richard, 1988. "Some Implications of Beliefs for the Public and Private Sectors." *Canadian Journal of Economics,* vol. 21, no. 4 (November) 775–784.

Festinger, Leon, 1957. *A Theory of Cognitive Dissonance.* Evanston, IL: Row, Peterson Company.

Lindblom, Charles E., 1990. *Inquiry and Change: The Troubled Attempt to Understand and Shape Society.* New Haven: Yale University Press.

March, James G., 1988. *Decisions and Organizations.* New York: Basil Blackwell.

Miles, Rufus, 1978. "The Origin and Meaning of Miles's Law." *Public Administration Review,* (September/October).

Moser, Martin R., 1988. "Ethical Conflict at Work." *Journal of Business Ethics,* vol. 7, no. 5 (May) 381–387.

COLLECTIVE BARGAINING.

The negotiations process that culminates with a written, binding contract between labor and management on the terms and conditions of employment, including wages, hours, and work rules. In the absence of collective bargaining, the terms and conditions of employment are generally set by the employer and individual employees. In its presence, union and management representatives negotiate wages, benefits, working conditions, and related matters. Collective bargaining occurred as early as 1799 in the United States, when cordwainers and master shoemakers formed a master trade agreement. Today around 16 percent of the United States's private sector labor force is covered by collective bargaining agreements, and nearly 40 percent of government workers. Generally, collective bargaining is much more extensively employed in Europe.

Collective bargaining differs between the private and public sectors in its environment, actors, and processes, but in either sector it requires the consent or at least the tolerance of government. The private sector environment for collective bargaining is driven by the profit motive and market forces. Government has few "products," and taxes and fees pay the costs of labor, not consumer purchases. The public sector bargaining environment also includes monopolistic, labor-intensive services. However, privatization has caused a restructuring of government "markets" and a rethinking of how government services should be provided. The environment of public sector collective bargaining remains suffused with politics and interactions between unions, management, citizens, elected and appointed officials, and the courts. Bargaining in government is a multilateral, multiparticipant affair.

The bargaining actors in the private sector have clearly defined roles and responsibilities. In government, a variety of models exist, most of them involving multiple participants with ill-defined roles and responsibilities and diffused authority. The elaborate system of checks and balances complicates government labor relations. For example, the federal system divides responsibility between the three levels of government, and complicates the legal framework for collective bargaining.

Finally, the bargaining processes, while ostensibly nearly identical, differ in the number of management participants and levels of politicization. Some elements of the bargaining structure are differentially emphasized as well. For example, impasse resolution techniques such as mediation and arbitration are used more frequently in the public sector, while the strike is more common in the private sector.

The major elements of collective bargaining include bargaining unit determination, the representation election, certification of the bargaining agent, and contract negotiations. Bargaining unit determination involves identification of the group of employees who will be represented by an employee organization for purposes of collective bargaining. The appropriate bargaining unit may be determined by a state administrative agency, statute, union preference, or case by case adjudication. The Federal Labor Relations Authority is responsible for unit determination in the federal sector. Among the factors that are taken into consideration in defining the membership of the bargaining unit are the community of interest (job factors held in common among members), history of previous relationships between the parties in the jurisdiction, extent of previous union organization, efficiency of agency operations, avoidance of fragmentation of units (a large number of small bargaining units presents a variety of problems for unions and management), and exclusion of supervisory and confidential employees. The goal is to derive a unit appropriate to the needs of both the union and the employer.

The tendency today is to consolidate existing bargaining units in state and local government into countywide or even statewide units, and to engage in multiemployer, multiunion bargaining. Ironically, the trend is the opposite in the private sector in the United States and in Europe, where collective bargaining is becoming much more decentralized. In Sweden, Australia, Germany, Italy, and the United Kingdom, as well as in the United States, private sector bargaining is decentralizing from the national level to industry levels, and within industries to the level of the individual firm.

After the boundaries of the bargaining unit are determined, it must be decided which union will represent the unit. This may occur through a representative election, a show of support by a majority of the members of the unit, or voluntary recognition by the employer if only a single union is active. The convention in the United States is to hold a representation election in which members of the unit vote on which union, if any, will represent their interests in collective bargaining. The use of a secret ballot is also usually required.

Once selected or designated, the bargaining agent is certified by the appropriate state agency, Federal Labor Relations Authority, or National Labor Relations Board (in the private sector) as the exclusive representative of unit members. Bargaining agents many be decertified if workers find them to be unresponsive to their demands, or for other shortcomings.

Contract negotiations between union and management representatives are the heart of the collective bargaining experience. Union representatives include a chief negotiator and negotiating team. The president or leader of the union is a major figure either at the table or behind the scenes. The union team must keep the rank-and-file membership in a supportive frame of mind, or risk losing their approval of final contract provisions.

The management team also comprises a chief negotiator and other team members. The variety of representation is nearly endless, but at the local level it typically includes an assistant city or county manager, legal officer, department head, and budgeting or personnel officer. Elected officials are usually not direct participants, but may operate behind the scenes. In jurisdictions where collective bargaining has been under way for a sustained period, it is increasingly likely that professional labor negotiators, usually labor lawyers, will be paid to represent the government. Gradually, authority for collective bargaining has been centralized in the executive branch of local and state government, with the legislative branch retaining final authority for approving the agreement.

In some jurisdictions the general public is involved in collective bargaining activities. Participation can range from active involvement at the bargaining table to simple public access to examine the final contract. Citizens may have the right to present formal comments on bargaining proposals, attend public hearings, or send representatives to observe negotiating sessions. Such citizen involvement is referred to as "sunshine bargaining" in states such as Florida, Minnesota, and North Dakota. The merits and problems of sunshine bargaining have been much debated.

Collective bargaining in government transpires within a highly charged political environment and generates outcomes that concern not only public employers and employees, but also taxpayers. The bargaining contest in the private sector is essentially economic, but in government it is predominantly political.

The internal politics of collective bargaining take place around the bargaining table. A critical aspect is preparation for negotiations, because the best-prepared party is most likely to emerge with more of what it wants than is the least-prepared party. Experience under the existing contract is carefully examined. Comparative wage and benefit data are collected and analyzed. Proposals are costed out (see **costing out**), often with the use of computer software. Prenegotiation conferences set rules of bargaining, an agenda of items to be considered is determined, and negotiating sessions are arranged.

The parties are required by law to bargain in good faith on mandatory subjects of bargaining (state statutory standards on good faith bargaining are closely patterned on those in the National Labor Relations Act).

There is an informal "script" for collective bargaining that is followed in most jurisdictions, with particular roles established and behavioral expectations largely complied with. For instance, the chief negotiator is the only member of the team who speaks at the table. The other members have various roles assigned to them, such as taking notes or watching the other team's facial expressions and body language. Grandstanding is common, for the benefit of union members, the media, and the citizenry. Expectations are usually that after initially staking out extreme positions a series of formal and informal discussions will eventually lead to compromise on the issues.

Interorganizational bargaining takes place within the ranks of each party, as some degree of consensus is sought in the positions brought to the table. Internal disputes within the ranks of management can facilitate "end runs" by the union to sympathetic individuals in the executive or legislative branch. Intraunion rivalries and conflicts can result in a negotiated contract that is rejected in a vote by the members of the bargaining unit.

The bargaining climate depends on a number of factors, including the history of the parties' relationship, economic and political conditions, and management and union attitudes. During the 1990s, concession bargaining became the norm in fiscally challenged jurisdictions. Confronted with demands for tax cutting, downsizing, and rightsizing, unions have found themselves fighting just to retain what they have won in the past, rather than seeking more. Reductions-in-force, furloughs, wage freezes, increasing copayments on health care benefits, and related "give-backs" have become important themes.

The power relations between unions and management have been a longstanding subject of research within the disciplines of economics, sociology, psychology, and political science. Role analysis and game theory are useful in understanding what transpires around and about the bargaining table and why the final outcomes appear as they do. Bargaining theory, as developed by Walton and McKersie, posits bargaining as either distributive or integrative. The former is characterized by conflictual interactions between the parties; the relationship is adversarial and outcomes tend to be zero sum. Integrative bargaining, which is less common but ultimately more desirable, exists where the parties perceive common interests and engage in mutual problem solving within a climate characterized by relative openness and trust. Outcomes are "win-win." Integrative bargaining is dependent on such factors as the personalities of the negotiating principals, the economic and political environment, and mutual trust and respect.

The most common depiction of integrative bargaining is Fisher's and Ury's "principled negotiations," as found in their popular book, *Getting to Yes* (1981). The basic points of principled negotiation include separating the people from the problem; focusing on interests, not positions; inventing options for mutual gain; and insisting on the use of objective criteria. Parties are urged to develop a best alternative to a negotiated agreement, which can be in the form of impasse resolution procedures for the total contract or narrower alternatives for specific issues. The Fisher and Ury formula has been applied in a wide variety of labor-management settings, with many favorable results reported. However, it is not a particularly helpful approach in situations where labor-management relationships are extremely adversarial and hostile.

Other theories of collective bargaining are less prescriptive. Chamberlain's and Kuhn's (1965) explication of bargaining power is intended to explain the possession and use of resources by the parties in a conflictual relationship. The dependence model of Bachrach and Lawler (1981) examines how a party's bargaining power grows as the opponent becomes dependent on the bargaining relationship to satisfy its needs.

External politics surround the activities that take place around the bargaining table, as various political and economic institutions and interest groups become involved. Lobbying activities by organized labor and business interests, among others, shape the bargaining process. Unions engage in electoral activities to help elect candidates favorable to the union agenda and to gain access in politics. Public opinion can be very important in shoring up support for management or union positions, and in establishing the parameters for what is and is not feasible in collective bargaining contracts.

Thus, the bargaining process is much more politicized in government than it is in the private sector, with politics pervading the labor relations environment. The effectiveness of public employee unions depends not only on what their representatives do at the bargaining table, but also on the effectiveness of their lobbying and electoral activities.

The impacts of collective bargaining may be assessed as directly monetary and personnel-related. Collective bargaining affects the budgetary processes of governments through its effects on operating accounts. Since 50 to 80 percent of government operating budgets is devoted to salaries and benefits, any bargaining settlement that drives up these costs must be met with revenue increases, productivity gains, or cost shifting. Moreover, the bargaining schedule often comes into conflict with the budget cycle. When negotiations or impasse resolution procedures run over into the next fiscal year, for example, the budget process and financial management are rendered less predictable.

Unions influence the level of pay and benefits through collective bargaining. Many factors are related to pay and benefit levels, including cost of living, the composition of the labor force, comparable pay and benefits, the fiscal capacity of the jurisdiction, and political variables such as the structure of government and partisan alignments. Certain decision rules play a role as well, including the prevailing rate rule, parity between two or more employee groups such as police and firefighters, and comparable worth.

Extensive empirical research indicates that collective bargaining is associated with higher pay and benefit levels. The relative effects of collective bargaining and unions in the private sector have ranged from 10 to 45 percent during the twentieth century, varying dramatically by occupation, place, and time. The union relative wage impact has diminished since the early 1980s, somewhat in tandem with the membership decline of unions. In government there is also much variation in the level of collective bargaining's impact, but generally it is much more modest than the private sector effects.

Results of empirical research on the economic effects of collective bargaining are somewhat suspect because of problems with research design, variable specification, and contaminating effects (e.g., the "threat effect"—employers in nonunion jurisdictions may raise pay and benefits to help prevent unionization of their work force). However, the general consensus is that the monetary effect is modest, ranging from 5 to 7 percent for teachers and police officers and about 8 percent for firefighters to only 4 percent for state employees. But as in the private sector, there is much variation across functional areas and time.

Although the research has not dwelt on benefits, it is clear that collective bargaining tends to drive up their costs through extending the scope of benefits and boosting their dollar value per employee. Retirement benefits tend to be much more favorable for employees who are represented by unions in collective bargaining than for unrepresented workers.

Productivity bargaining and gainsharing are two responses to the monetary costs of collective bargaining. The goal is to contain personnel expenses through jointly searching for and formalizing cost-saving opportunities, and sharing the savings. Some successes have been regis-

tered, especially where an integrative bargaining approach is utilized.

RICHARD C. KEARNEY

BIBLIOGRAPHY

Bachrach, Samuel B. and Edward J. Lawler, 1981. *Bargaining Power: Tactics and Outcomes.* San Francisco: Jossey Bass.

Chamberlain, Neil W. and James W. Kuhn, 1965. *Collective Bargaining.* 2nd ed. New York: McGraw-Hill.

Fisher, Roger and William Ury, 1981. *Getting to Yes.* New York: Penguin Books.

Kearney, Richard C., 1992. *Labor Relations in the Public Sector.* New York: Marcel Dekker.

Stevens, Carl M., 1963. *Strategy and Collective Bargaining Negotiations.* New York: McGraw-Hill.

Walton, Richard E. and Robert B. McKersie, 1965. *A Behavioral Theory of Labor Negotiations.* New York: McGraw-Hill.

COLLECTIVE RESPONSIBILITY. The fundamental principle of the British constitution and other Westminster-type constitutions that the government is accountable through its ministers to Parliament. Collective responsibility provides parliaments in Westminster systems with the means to hold the government as a body to account. Any government that is defeated in Parliament on an issue of confidence must resign together as a cabinet, and is usually expected to call a general election. Meanwhile individual ministers, whether members of the cabinet or not, take public responsibility for every cabinet decision even if they personally dissent from a particular decision. Every minister must be prepared to justify and defend cabinet decisions.

Like other conventions in the unwritten British constitution, collective responsibility is a principle that has been generalized from practical politics rather than from any abstract constitutional principles. Historically the notion of collective responsibility arose from the idea that the Crown is advised by, and its powers exercised on its behalf by, a group of ministers rather than a single individual. Although its origins date back to the eighteenth century, it was only during the mid-nineteenth century that collective responsibility became a major feature of British politics (Birch, 1964, pp. 135–136).

Ministers must be members of Parliament and are almost invariably, except during war-time or other emergencies, drawn from the ranks of the governing party. The prime minister appoints cabinet ministers (or strictly speaking recommends their appointment to the Queen or head of state), though in the case of Labour governments ministers in future will be elected by the parliamentary party while the prime minister will allocate portfolios (this procedure is already used by Australian Labor governments). Once appointed, ministers are individually and collectively responsible to parliament.

In contrast, "cabinet government" in the U.S. refers simply to a group of political appointees from outside the legislature who head the executive departments but simply advise the president or governor rather than share decisionmaking. Major government decisions are not made collectively in cabinet but by the president, who may or may not choose to involve the relevant cabinet secretary. Political responsibility for the executive remains solely with the president. Cabinet secretaries in the U.S. and similar presidential systems are only individually accountable to Congress, answering to Congress for the ways in which their departments spend money and interpret their legislative mandates.

In Westminster systems collective responsibility is reinforced by several other conventions. Cabinet documents are secret and ministers are obliged not to communicate any details of what occurred in cabinet except insofar as is required for the effective implementation of a decision. Ministers' personal views are not recorded in cabinet minutes, which record only decisions and necessary supplementary information. Ministers are expected to limit themselves to speaking only about their own portfolios and not to encroach upon other ministers' portfolios without their express permission. At the same time ministers are expected to refer major decisions within their portfolios to cabinet and keep the appropriate ministers informed of decisions outside their portfolios that touch on other ministers' responsibilities.

Collective responsibility as a constitutional principle does not require that every cabinet minister should be involved in the discussion of government policy for which he or she might be held responsible. Recent governments have concluded that a group of 20 or more people, many of whom are inevitably poorly briefed, is too cumbersome for effective decisionmaking, particularly as issues have become increasingly technical and complex in nature. In practice major policy decisions are often taken in cabinet committees and the cabinet as a body simply notes the decision. The important fact is that after the decision is made, ministers are bound to it regardless of their own involvement or lack of it.

The convention is important in contributing towards orderly government. Once a decision has been made in cabinet, the civil servants and others involved in implementing the decision know that every minister is in agreement and the decision is very unlikely to be changed. Cabinet decisions are also usually announced or defended by the minister most concerned; decisions are seldom announced simply as cabinet decisions. This is to avoid conveying the perception that there is a hierarchy of government decisions under which some decisions are less authoritative than others.

The convention also plays an important part in practical politics. Cabinet solidarity strengthens the cabinet in dealing with the opposition in Parliament, its own back-benchers, the media, and the civil service. The appearance at least of unanimity creates the impression that ministers are working together. The convention does not compel ministers to agree but simply enjoin them from publicly airing their disagreements. Similarly ministers are expected not to pursue their own political ambitions at the expense of the collective political well-being of the government. Even if the reality is different, the impression that ministers are working together encourages electoral and party confidence, as well as confidence in the government among foreign governments and financial markets. Cabinets that squabble gain a reputation for being indecisive and incompetent. Any differences among ministers are exploited by the opposition parties and such differences become very newsworthy.

Only in very unusual circumstances does collective responsibility, when the government fails to win a majority on a specified vote of confidence, provide effective public accountability. Thus its main roles are to ensure orderly government, to maintain the government in power, and to protect ministers, rather than to achieve accountability.

Collective responsibility is also used to justify secrecy. Until very recently the official view in Britain was that any disclosure of cabinet procedures weakened collective responsibility. Although the existence of cabinet committees was well-known, governments bizarrely persisted in denying their existence. Similarly collective responsibility is used to justify government's tight control of information.

However, changing styles of cabinet government–the claimed shift towards a stronger, presidential-type prime minister and the increased use of inner cabinets–has cast some doubts on the reality of collective responsibility in practice. In recent years ministers are becoming less willing to suppress their disagreements with cabinet policies; often these disagreements become well-known through leaks to journalists and through "coded" speeches. However, when these disagreements reach a serious level ministers are usually expected by the prime minister and their senior colleagues to resign.

MARTIN LAFFIN

BIBLIOGRAPHY

Birch, A. H. 1964. *Representative and Responsible Government.* London: Unwin and Allen.
Marshall, Geoffrey, ed., 1989. *Ministerial Responsibility.* Oxford: Oxford University Press.

COLONIAL LIBERALISM. A philosophy of comprehensive state action developed in a number of the British "settler colonies" from the late nineteenth and into the early twentieth century.

Toward the end of the nineteenth century several of the leading British settler colonies developed a distinctive blend of democratic politics, the comprehensive use of state power, the extension of industrial legislation, and the widening of suffrage, which became known as colonial liberalism. The comprehensive use of state power (sometimes termed colonial or state socialism by contemporaries), characteristically extended to the ownership of many basic infrastructure services and goods. Such extensive state involvement was also to become a feature of the postcolonial world in Africa and Asia. This process has been called "colonial developmentalism" to indicate both its strong economic character and to distinguish it from the more strongly democratic and egalitarian nature of colonial liberalism.

The former British settler colonies have had longer histories of government ownership of transport and communications facilities than Britain and most other advanced industrial democracies. Interestingly enough, the United States falls into the same historical camp as Australia in this respect. Particularly at the state level, governments were active providers of the infrastructure necessary to aid private investment (Broude, 1959). In the last quarter of the nineteenth century these activities were rolled back under the banner of free enterprise ideologies. In New Zealand and Canada, as in Australia, governments continued to play an active role in underpinning economic growth and expansion (Condliffe, 1920; Aitken, 1959).

In the nineteenth century, railway building and telegraph construction were the most significant forms of government involvement. They also marked ". . . the rise of government capital formation to a level matching that of private capital formation," according to economic historian Noel Butlin in his important chapter on "Colonial Socialism in Australia" (1959, p. 39). Government activism in those areas commenced in the 1860s and was intensified into the 1870s. As was the case in other former colonies, government stepped in after private capital had tried and failed. The peculiarity of the Australian case was that governments continued to play central roles in the provision of goods and services, even after private capital was in the position to undertake investment. In the meantime, social and political aims had been written into the charters of public enterprises.

Given the practice of early and extensive government ownership, laissez-faire ideas did not develop easily or naturally. Historians have deplored the lack of philosophically oriented debate in the colonies in this period (Loveday and Martin, 1967). Parliamentarians were obsessed with the rapid development of their colonies' natural resources almost to the exclusion of other matters. In Canada the origin of modern-style political parties was inextricably linked with political patronage and the development of the economy. The early parties were machines with dual roles:

the reelection of leadership coteries, and the provision of projects, jobs, and profits (Stewart, 1986, p. 57).

There had been some feeling concentrated in the middle of the nineteenth century that governments' extensive involvement was a necessary evil and a temporary expedient. Involvement by government was at least partly explained by the low level of economic development in Australia and New Zealand. This justification was used by adherents of the free trade perspective. Such views were never as strong in the world of the settler colonies as they were in Britain and the United States. The birth of the Free Trade Party in the colony of New South Wales, Australia, in the 1880s was quickly matched by the emergence of the Protectionist Party. This reflected the fact that the major political debate in the colonies was over free trade versus protection. It also indicated that political debate was rooted in the economic zone.

The settler colonies of Australia, Canada, and New Zealand contributed enormously to political practice, and saw the rapid development of modern-style political parties, early achievement of widespread suffrage for men and then universal suffrage; the Australian colonies pioneered the secret ballot (Crisp, 1985). However, it should be noted that those same colonies had rather poor records on the enfranchisement of their indigenous peoples. There were fewer original contributions to political theory during this period, but quite a deal of interaction between the "Old World" and the "New World." For example, Henry Parkes, the founder of the Free Trade Party of New South Wales and one of the leading figures of the federation movement in Australia, was made a member of the British-based free trade group, the Cobden Society.

After federation, Australia moved quickly towards the "workers' welfare state" (Castles, 1987). This was a peculiarly Australian version of the settler society phenomenon of *socialisme sans doctrine*. Socialism without doctrine was the European-based view that the early and rapid development of social reforms in those societies centered upon an active state was driven by necessity rather than doctrine, and/or it lacked strong theoretical underpinnings. Whereas in New Zealand governments themselves provided a variety of welfare payments, in Australia the "basic wage" (1907) was to provide for the worker and his family.

These developments in public policy provided fertile soil for the acceptance of the philosophy of "new liberalism." English-based, this perspective argued that the interests of the state and those of the individual were not inherently in conflict. T. H. Green was one of the leading exponents of this perspective (Richter, 1964). Developed and popularized in the last part of the nineteenth century, this philosophy not only justified state action to ameliorate harsh social conditions, it also provided a counterweight to the laissez-faire approach.

In its original British version, "new liberalism" had a strong emphasis on social welfare and urban reform. The versions of this doctrine in the settler colonies were clearly going to have different emphases. In the first instance, the "city problem" was not as advanced as in Europe and the United States. Second, there was much more social openness and economic inequalities were mediated by the absence of hereditary aristocracies and/or heavily entrenched sources of economic power. Thirdly, most sections of society had already compromised and accepted different kinds of government assistance. While there could be objections to the needy receiving government aid, any ideological objections would have a hollow ring.

At least by the early part of the twentieth century in the settler countries of Australia, Canada, and New Zealand, laissez faire objections were confined to a minority with the rising popularity of "new liberalism." In Australia and New Zealand even self-styled conservative politicians accepted the central role of the state in most aspects of economic life, especially economic development and infrastructure provision. Canada and Australia shared the emergence of rural-based parties characterized by "agrarian socialism." In Australia the phenomenon was called "tradecycle socialism" as the rural-based parties and pressure groups called on governments to socialize their losses, but allowed them to individualize their profits.

In Australia, a degree of local innovation in the general category of colonial liberalism (itself a coloration of "new liberalism," as was noted above) was provided by "Deakinite liberalism." Alfred Deakin, like Henry Parkes, had been a significant colonial politician, and subsequently went on to become—again like Parkes—a central figure in the federation movement. Unlike Parkes, the Cobdennite, Deakin was a Protectionist. In the early post-federation period in his role as the prime minister of the new Australian nation, he implemented the new protection policy (1904). Basically this policy reflected a negotiated agreement between capital and labor that in exchange for protection from overseas competition capital would support "fair" wages for workers. The state was to play a crucial role in negotiating the arrangement via two types of institutions, a centralized wage-fixing body and a board for setting tariff levels. Again the evidence supports the view that the settler colonies were innovators in terms of institution building, rather than in producing large tracts of theory.

MARIAN SIMMS

BIBLIOGRAPHY

Aitken, H. G. J., 1959. "Defensive Expansion: The State and Economic Growth in Canada." In H. G. J. Aitken, ed., *The State and Economic Growth*. New York: Social Science Research Council, pp. 79–96.

Broude, H. W., 1959. "The Role of the State in American Economic Development." In H. G. J. Aitken, ed., *The State and Economic Growth*. New York: Social Science Research Council, pp. 4–14.

Butlin, Noel, 1959. "Colonial Socialism in Australia." In H. G. J. Aitken, ed., *The State and Economic Growth*. New York: Social Science Research Council, pp. 35–46.

Castles, F. G., 1987. *The Working Class and Welfare*. Sydney: Allen & Unwin.

Condliffe, J. B., 1920. *New Zealand*. London: Victoria League.

Crisp, L. F., 1985. *Australian National Government*. Melbourne: Longman Cheshire.

Loveday, Peter and A.W. Martin, 1966. *Parliament Factions and Parties*. Melbourne: Melbourne University Press.

Richter, Merlin, 1964. *The Politics of Conscience: T. H. Green and His Age*. London: Weidenfeld & Nicholson.

Stewart, G. T. 1986. *The Origins of Canadian Politics: A Comparative Approach*. Vancouver: University of British Columbia Press.

COMBINED OPERATIONS. Military activities involving two or more forces from the same state or agencies from two or more allied states. In the context of the North Atlantic Treaty Organization (NATO), an allied operation could be one conducted by forces of a single member state under the aegis of the NATO alliance; it therefore may not be a combined operation. A coalition operation involves NATO forces together with forces of a state or states outside the alliance. Since two or more states are involved, it may therefore be a combined operation.

A combined operation is usually taken to mean one where the forces involved are linked operationally or tactically, rather than at the strategic level. Thus the operations of the German and Japanese forces in World War II, while concerted in that they were by allied forces against common enemies, cannot be described as combined. On the other hand, the British and French armies in the Crimea in 1855 coordinated their activities against the Russians in Sevastopol, and were therefore conducting a combined operation.

Relationship Between Combined and Joint Operations

The terms "combined" and "joint" have been used synonymously to mean operations involving two or more services or agencies (land, sea, air, or civil government departments) of one country. Indeed, Great Britain formed a Combined Operations Headquarters in 1940 to coordinate the efforts of her navy, army, and air force in specific operations. In modern NATO terminology, these were joint operations. The significant distinction to be drawn is that whereas joint operations have an interservice dimension, combined operations have an international one. It is of course possible, indeed normal, for modern combined operations to be joint as well.

History of Combined Operations

The history of combined operations is traceable back to the earliest beginnings of the modern nation state, the Greek "polis." The Greek city-states, although frequently at odds with each other, were quite capable of recognizing an overarching common purpose, and the fleet that defeated the Persian navy of Xerxes in 480 B.C.E. was two-thirds Athenian, one-third Spartan, under the unified command of the Athenian Themistocles.

Factors Affecting Combined Operations

A number of factors can serve to make combined operations more fraught with difficulty than those conducted by a single nation. Differences in training, doctrine, equipment, and language are all likely to militate against success, and need to be overcome or minimized. But experience has shown that if the question of command and control is resolved early, and unambiguously, solutions to the other issues will follow more readily. The requirement for one nation to subordinate its forces to a commander from another can raise difficult political issues, and may offend national sensitivities. But unless this is addressed, the commander of the combined operation may not be able to fulfill the mission. In a fast-moving conflict of high intensity, it is most important that the commander have the authority to deploy forces in the most appropriate way without delay. It therefore must be clear from the outset what degree of authority is held over troops of other nations so that the commander is not impeded by the requirement to seek and secure agreement from the nations involved. In World War I, in 1914, the commander of the British Expeditionary Force (BEF) was given secret orders which, while urging him to support and cooperate with the French army, also made it plain that his was an independent command, and in no case was he to come under the orders of any Allied general. The French, meanwhile, believed that the BEF was under the orders of their commander-in-chief. The misunderstandings that arose out these vague and contradictory orders generated much confusion, and laid unforeseen and gratuitous constraints upon the French commander, Marshall Ferdinand Foch, when he was trying to stem the eruption of the German army into northern France.

By contrast, the operation led by the American general Dwight D. Eisenhower to land on the Normandy beaches in June 1944 was a classic combined operation with one supreme commander. The United States, Britain, Canada, France, Poland, and other nations contributed forces, but because Eisenhower had the necessary authority from the beginning, he was able to take account of disparities in training, doctrine, equipment, and language in the planning process. He directed that the necessary training took place to ensure compatibility, saw to it that plans took account of different capabilities, and deployed the variety of troops and equipment to where they were best used.

A combined operation is most assured of success when there is sufficient commonality of political interest and unity of military purpose for one sovereign state to place its forces under the direct control of a commander from another. It is usual for the country with the greatest number of forces taking part to provide the overall commander. Thus, although U.S. troops were outnumbered in Normandy by British and Canadians, since the United States was the greatest single contributing country, the supreme commander was from the U.S.

Combined Operations and NATO

Forty years facing the Warsaw Pact gave NATO the stimulus that led it to develop the business of combined operations to a fine art. Levels of command and control were defined and agreed. For instance, "operational command" is the authority delegated by nations to NATO commanders, giving them authority to assign missions or tasks to subordinate commanders, to deploy units, to reassign forces, and to retain or delegate lower levels of command as deemed necessary. Lower levels of command such as "operational control," "tactical command," and "tactical control" specify further the limits by time, function, or location on the authority granted to a commander. Combined doctrine and standard operating procedures were devised, agreed, and practiced. Much equipment was made interchangeable. Standing multinational forces became a feature within the alliance. NATO was never called upon to operate against the adversary that precipitated its birth, but the expertise it developed in combined operations was used to good effect in the 1991 Persian Gulf War against Iraq, and it seems likely that any combined operation involving any NATO member in the future will draw heavily upon the work done in its name. Disparities between forces and national sensitivities can add substantially to the difficulties associated with planning and conducting combined operations. But the operation has the best chance of success if the nations involved can agree to unambiguous unity of command from its inception.

IAN R. GARDINER

COMMAND. The process by which a commander impresses his or her will and intentions on subordinates. Command normally only applies to military forces. It encompasses the authority and responsibility for deploying forces to fulfill their missions. Control is the process through which the commander, assisted by his or her staff, organizes, directs, and coordinates the activities of the forces allocated. Together, these two processes form a command and control system which the commander and staff use to plan, direct, coordinate, and control military operations. A commander exercises authority over subordinates by virtue of his or her appointment. That authority, which derives from law and military regulations, is accompanied by the acceptance of responsibilities that cannot be delegated. Implicit in that authority is the understanding that the commander is, in person, responsible for the actions of those under his or her command.

Levels of Command

The degree of authority given to a commander can be circumscribed in a number of ways. First, the nature of the appointment–commander-in-chief, divisional commander, platoon commander–will indicate the size of the force over which authority is exercised. Second, the scope of authority is likely to be defined. For instance, in the North Atlantic Treaty Organization (NATO), "full command" is the military authority and responsibility to issue orders to subordinates. It covers every aspect of military operations and administration, and is retained by national commanders. "Operational command" will be delegated by national commanders to NATO commanders, giving them authority to assign missions or tasks to subordinate commanders, to deploy units, to reassign forces, and to retain or delegate lower levels of command as deemed necessary. Lower levels of command such as "operational control," "tactical command," and "tactical control" specify further the limits by time, function or location on the authority granted to a commander.

The Relationship Between Command and Management

The distinction between command and management is a fine one. Both the commander and the manager deploy finite resources and assets–people, money, vehicles, stores, technology, fuel, and so forth–to achieve an objective within a given time frame. Both seek to get the best out of those resources within a competitive environment. There is no international consensus on the principles of command, or the principles of management, but there can be little doubt that there are strong similarities, and each can be made to apply to the other to a great degree. It is thus possible to dissect the functions of both the commander and the manager and conclude that the dynamics that affect them are the same.

The analogy can only be taken so far, because to take it further would be to suggest that war is essentially the same activity as commerce. What sets war apart from any other human activity is the potential for extremes implicit in conflict. Successful management may bring profit, prosperity, and good order. Failure can bring loss, unemployment, and bankruptcy. The province of the commander is war; and in war, governments and nations stand or fall on the results, and life itself is at stake.

This can place great responsibility on the shoulders of one person. For example, Winston S. Churchill wrote in his history of World War I, *The World Crisis* (1923), that Admiral John R. Jellicoe, the commander of the British fleet, "was the only man on either side who could lose the war in an afternoon." The battle at Midway in the Pacific in 1942 arguably had a significant effect upon the progress and duration of World War II. The result of the battle swung around the personal judgment of one man: Admiral Chester W. Nimitz. The commander of a submarine carrying nuclear ballistic missiles, usually a comparatively junior officer, carries an unparalleled burden on his shoulders. Thus, a commander may have staff providing support and advice, but the key decisions are made alone. Everything done within his or her command is done in his or her name. He or she by name is the victor, or the loser, of the battles, and alone is held answerable for the result.

The Relationship Between Command and Leadership

Command embraces all the functions of the manager in deploying resources to achieve an aim. Good commanders and managers seek to get the best out of their limited resources by using them in the most cost-effective way. Good leadership is the means whereby both will seek to get the best out of their human resources. The nature of leadership itself is a highly complex area not to be covered here, but in functional terms, it is a tool to be applied by the commander–and the manager–to his or her workforce. The commander and the manager both therefore need to be good leaders to achieve the best results.

War is an activity in which the motivation of people is an element that can far outweigh material factors. Napoleon observed that in war, "three-quarters turns on personal character and relations; the balance of manpower and materials counts only for the remaining quarter." History offers much evidence to support this. Napoleon himself, by leading a bayonet charge at the head of a column at the battle of Lodi in 1796, dislodged the Austrians from a bridge they were holding fiercely, and won the battle. The campaigns of Alexander of Macedon are characterized by his outstanding leadership. By his personal example in battle, notably at Granicus, and through his deep understanding of how to motivate men, he fired his army with an enthusiasm which played a major part in its consistent success, in spite of usually being heavily outnumbered.

Karl von Clausewitz wrote in *On War* (1823) that "war is an act of violence whose object is to constrain the enemy to accomplish our will." There are many instances where forces, outnumbered and outclassed materially, have succeeded because the force of will of the commander has led people to produce results quite out of proportion to their numbers, or other material circumstances.

Command and leadership, while separate concepts, are thus closely intertwined. A commander, however good he or she may be at managing his material assets, is unlikely to be successful unless he or she has the leadership qualities required to inspire and motivate people. And the best commanders are able to lead their people to exertions that defy reason.

The Commanding Officer

The singularity and authority of command is most apparent at the level of commanding officer of a unit: a ship or submarine, a battalion, or a squadron. The personality and example of the commanding officer has a direct and immediate effect on every aspect of unit performance. The quality of training, administration, and operational efficiency are usually a direct reflection of his or her professionalism. He or she personally will set the standards of performance and battle discipline within the unit. Moreover, the tempo of operations in which the unit is involved is often such that the commander will have to make immediate decisions affecting life and death based on incomplete and perhaps inaccurate information, in an atmosphere of exhaustion and confusion. Commanders in battle conduct their business in a far from calm environment. Depending on what type of battle is being fought, and by what service or arm, there will be noise, rain, heat, fog, snow, darkness, and many other stressful distractions such as the banging of guns, the roaring of an armored vehicle engine, or turbulence at sea, or in a vehicle or helicopter. He or she is also likely to be in a position of personal danger. For example, the British Fiftieth Tyne Tees Division lost all nine commanding officers of its infantry battalions to death, wounds, or capture in two and a half months in the battle for Normandy in 1944. Decisiveness, resolution, and courage are therefore crucial.

The composure and example of the commanding officer will have a fundamental effect upon the performance of every person under his or her command. This further tends to focus attention and weight upon the person of the commander, and places him or her in a unique position of authority. And implicit among the commanding officer's responsibilities is the ultimate duty: to persuade men and women to fight with him or her, if necessary, to the death.

Summary

In summary, command, management, and leadership are not synonymous. The manager and the commander have much in common, and this is especially so in peace. Both should be good leaders. Some managers, by their personality or the nature of their business, may from time to time find themselves in a position of great and direct personal responsibility, but this is not the norm. But war, the commander's business field, with its potentially momentous and irrevocable consequences, serves to place him or her in

a unique position of personal responsibility that few managers are ever likely to encounter.

IAN R. GARDINER

COMMERCIALIZATION.

A range of initiatives within contemporary public administration that aim to reorient government-owned organizations to norms and conditions associated with the traditions of commerce and markets. The concept conveys the idea of goods and services produced by publicly owned organizations being exchanged at a price, with the aim of cost recovery, as distinct from being provided free and funded by mechanisms such as taxation.

Strictly speaking, a move from nonmarket to market ("marketization") does not require a move from public to private or from the less competitive to the more competitive. Commercialization of public sector organizations in the 1980s and 1990s, however, has occurred within a context in which neoclassical microeconomic theory has dominated public policy discourse and has been further incorporated into the discipline of business management theory. Central to this economic and management theory have been the twin ideas that private is inherently more efficient and desirable than public and that competition is inherently more efficient and desirable than noncompetition (such as cooperation, bureaucratic authority).

The contemporary commercialization of public sector organizations has therefore involved two dimensions of change. First, it has involved change to the internal structure of public organizations—namely, restructuring them to emulate the actual or perceived characteristics of private commercial firms. Second, it has involved change to the organization's external relationships and environment—namely, exposure of the organization to conditions of external competition. Internal restructuring has tended to precede external change but only by degree: the two fields of restructuring soon become concurrent and interactive.

Over the past decade the public enterprise sector has been the prime focus of commercialization, the aim being to move the sector from quasi- to full commercialization. In the mid-1990s the focus of attention is switching to the core, tax-funded government sector, with even greater social implications than has been the case with public enterprise commercialization.

Institutional Forms of Commercialization

Commercialization initiatives can be grouped into two broad categories:

a. Emulating the accounting, pricing, personnel, and legal structures of private commercial firms;

b. Exposing public sector agencies to greater internal competition or to external competition from private commercial firms.

Emulating the Structures of Private Commercial Firms

Here some of the main initiatives have been:

Accounting Reforms. These have included cost-center accounting—refining financial management systems to show underlying cost structures more fully—and accrual accounting—moving to balance sheets that show assets and liabilities as they accrue (i.e., as they are earned or incurred, rather than when cash is received or paid).

User Charges and Cost-based Pricing. The former entails agencies increasing the range of goods and services for which they charge users. Like privatization (see below) user charges have a second rationale independent of fiscal constraint (i.e., the pressure to cap or reduce tax levels). Originating in neoclassical microeconomic theory, this rationale holds that the price paid by the customer reflects the value attached to the commodity or service purchased; suppliers therefore must find out what clients value or want.

Cost-based pricing seeks to align prices with costs, either in the form of full cost recovery or with a market-related margin for profit. It entails the elimination of cross-subsidies and the elimination of services that cannot be justified on commercial grounds. The only exemption acceptable is where the ultimate state authority designates that the loss entailed is outweighed by a community service obligation to provide the noncommercial service.

Personnel Recruitment from the Private Sector and Performance-Based Pay. This set of reforms seeks to emulate features of the recruitment and pay systems of the private sector. Features of this component include the establishment in some countries of a Senior Executive Service, the linking of these positions to performance-based contracts, wider private sector-style job evaluation of staff positions, and the beginnings of performance-related cash incentives for employees below as well as within the SES. These changes have often been accompanied by significant reductions in the number of in-house staff.

Corporatization. This reform involves the conversion of public sector entities from a statutory authority structure (established by legislation) or a departmental structure (established by executive government) to a company structure (in conformity with corporations law applying to the private sector). Under this restructure, capital of the agency is converted into share capital, with shares being held by various ministers. Corporatization often has the effect of freeing the restructured entity from the wider range of legislation and regulation governing noncommercial public sector bodies.

Privatization. Selling legal ownership of a public sector agency to private individuals or companies (for more information see **privatization**).

Exposing Public Sector Agencies to Greater Competition

Again, some of the main initiatives have been:

Internal Disaggregation. Creation of internal markets by break-up of integrated government business enterprises into competing units. Like corporatization, internal markets are often seen as a prelude to deregulation and privatization.

Deregulation. Allowing private sector firms to enter fields of commercial activity that previously were the legal monopoly of government enterprises.

Competitive Tendering and Contracting Out. Extending the point of competitive pressure to inside the public sector agency itself, by mandating that private bodies be able to tender for commercial or noncommercial services conducted by units within the public sector agency.

Purchaser-Provider Split and Separation of Regulatory and Commercial Roles. Ensuring that strategic policy and regulation fosters competition and is not distorted by the self-interest of public commercial bodies.

Shifting from Producer to Consumer Subsidies. Allocating public expenditure to entitled consumers in the form of cash vouchers rather than to established public or private providers.

Extent of Commercialization Internationally

By the mid-1990s public sector commercialization, along one or more of the lines described above, has without doubt become one of the most distinctive and influential developments in public policy and administration internationally. While components of commercialization may have initially been associated with particular countries such as the United Kingdom and New Zealand, by the mid-1990s at least some of the main components of commercialization have been initiated in many Organization for Economic Cooperation and Development (OECD) countries and in many other parts of the world.

While the precise extent and shape of commercialization appears to vary from country to country, the overall direction is very emphatic. Thus the contemporary norm is to introduce or increase user fees, not to move back to tax funding; to privatize, not to renationalize. Exceptions to this generalization can be cited—moves in some circumstances to partially reregulate after radical deregulation or to partially move away from competitive tendering—but these cases do not signal an end to the prevailing direction.

Thus, while commercialization reforms were implemented earliest and most swiftly in New Zealand and the United Kingdom, countries with centralist unitary constitutional systems, they have also taken root in federalist systems. Likewise, support for commercialization has tended to cross traditional political party boundaries. Neoliberal wings of pro-business parties have led the way but managerialist modernizers within parties of the labor and social democratic traditions have also facilitated reform when in office. Parties of both the right and the left have other, traditional constituencies consigned to ineffective opposition.

In the United States, the term "commercialization" may not have been widely used, but many elements of the commercialization program are being taken up under the banner of "entrepreneurial" or "competitive" government. Thus, more intensely competitive contracting out, new user charges (on business as well as consumer users), vouchers, and privatization—all these have shown up in the "Reinvention" movement and in the Gore National Performance Review Reports, most emphatically in the second round recommendations in late 1994.

Factors Responsible for the Growth of Public Sector Commercialization

The rationale underlying the spread of commercialization is that it provides the means by which the public sector can do more with less. Pressure to increase public sector efficiency and effectiveness intensified in the mid-1970s in response to a downturn in macroeconomic performance in many Western capitalist economies. The pressure to reduce public sector deficits by cutting costs and raising revenue took a further twist from the mid-1980s, this time in response to perceptions of globalization of capital markets and intensification of business competition across nation-state borders. Governments increasingly formed the view that their key strategic objective had to be the attraction of private capital by lowering costs and opening up profit opportunities.

From this has flowed many of the hallmarks of public sector commercialization: elimination of public enterprise cross-subsidies from business to consumers, removal of public enterprise monopolies in industries rendered more profitable by technology (especially important in telecommunications, electricity, and water), reductions in business regulation (regulatory review), as well as reductions in corporate tax rates.

These processes and policy outcomes can be seen, in part, as a manifestation of a shift in political power to private corporate and institutional capital, increasingly constituted in transnational forms. In addition to business sector lobbying, transnational forms of public institutions have also been important as catalysts and enforcers of public sector commercialization—institutions such as the OECD, the European Union, the World Bank, the International Monetary Fund, and GATT. Within both these power centers—business lobby organizations and transnational public apparatus—the role of neoliberal economists has been pivotal in providing an intellectual rationale for business interests.

The rationale for public sector commercialization has also drawn on notions of consumer-dominated capitalism—the notion that the market, not bureaucracy, is the natural instrument of consumer choice and empowerment. In part, these claims are congruent with rising educational levels in contemporary societies—and perhaps with wider social changes associated with postmodernism. But public sector commercialization is a program formulated and pushed by products of the disciplines of economics, accounting, and business management, not social science disciplines associated with citizen advocacy movements of the 1970s. These constituencies remain skeptical and hostile to the claims of the commercialists. They predict that commercialization will erode or destroy many of the social gains of the less well-off that these disciplines associate with the growth of the post-1945 social democratic public sector.

Commercialization represents an often profound break from legal and bureaucratic concepts and traditions of public administration. Controversy over its economic and social impact is likely to increase in the coming period.

MICHAEL J. HOWARD

BIBLIOGRAPHY

Alliance for Redesigning Government, 1994. *Competitive Government.* REGO Database Overview. Washington, D.C.: National Academy of Public Administration.

Duncan, Ian and Alan Bollard, 1992. *Corporatization and Privatization: Lessons from New Zealand.* Auckland: Oxford University Press.

Gore, Al, 1994. *Commonsense Government: Works Better and Costs Less.* National Performance Review Report, Appendix A and C. Washington, D.C.: U.S. Government Printing Office.

Kettl, Donald F. and John J. Dilulio (eds.) 1995. *Inside the Reinvention Machine: Appraising Governmental Reform.* Washington, D.C.: Brookings Institute.

Parliament of the Commonwealth of Australia (Joint Committee of Public Accounts), 1995. *Public Business in the Public Interest: An Inquiry into the Commercialization in the Commonwealth Public Sector.* Canberra: AGPS.

Organization for Economic Co-operation and Development, 1993. *Managing with Market-Type Mechanisms.* Paris: Public Management Studies.

Organization for Economic Co-operation and Development, 1991–1994. *Public Management Developments Update,* issued annually. Paris: Public Management Studies.

Whitfield, Dexter, 1992. *The Welfare State: Privatization, Deregulation, Commercialization of Public Services: Alternative Strategies for the 1990s.* Concord, MA: Pluto Press.

COMMITMENT, EMPLOYEE. The positive psychological involvement of an individual in his or her employing organization.

Employee commitment is an individual's positive psychological attachment to his or her work organization, which is manifested in a sense of personal investment, loyalty, and identification with the organization. Employee commitment is based on reciprocal relationships between employees and their work organizations. Organizations and managers must demonstrate commitment to their employees in order to get commitment from their employees.

Employees can develop psychological ties to the organization based on personal investments they have made in the workplace and on feelings of identification with and loyalty to important organizational values. Commitment ties based on investments and identification are not exclusive; they can be complementary. An employee can develop psychological ties based on investments or identification, or both. Or employees can fail to develop ties based on either. Investment-oriented ties are based on rational calculations of contributions and inducements. Identification- and loyalty-based ties are based on shared organizational values. Whether the employee's tie to the organization is based upon investments or shared values will depend upon what the employee wants out of work and what the organization has to offer its employees.

Investment-Based Commitment

Employees develop investment-oriented commitment to their employers when they feel they have invested a great deal in their work organization. The most common kind of investments are personal time and energy, such as an employee who has spent a number of years with one organization or who has worked long, hard hours for the employer. Such employees feel psychologically attached to their work organization because of their "sunk costs." Employees with an investment approach to their agencies care what happens to the organization because they have a great deal of time or energy invested in the agency. Investment-oriented employees make career decisions based upon whether they have more to gain by staying with the employer than by taking another job elsewhere.

Employees calculate their investments in an organization based on what they have put into the workplace and what they stand to receive if they remain. For example, an individual might hesitate to change employers because of the time and money he or she has tied up in the organization's retirement plan. Although retirement plans are the most obvious form of investment employees can develop in their employer, investments are not always in monetary form. Investments also can take the form of time devoted to a particular career track or cultivating work group and friendship networks. For example, an employee who has invested much time in a particular career track in one organization, say as a bank examiner for the U.S. Federal Deposit Insurance Corporation, may be hesitant to switch employers because of the "sunk costs" that would be wasted if he or she moved. If that same person took a new job as an auditor for the U.S. Securities and Exchange Commission, the employee probably would be able to transfer his or her knowledge and expertise but would have to start anew making other investments for the necessary career returns. New investments would take the form of the newly hired employee demonstrating abilities, building a work group network, and earning the confidence of his or her superiors.

Oftentimes employee investments are transferable within a particular level of government. For example, in the United States most federal employees can retain any accrued credits toward retirement, sick leave, and vacation time when they take a different job in another federal agency. This same circumstance typically also holds for most government employees who work under a unified personnel system. Investments in state-level retirement systems within the United States are usually portable among agencies of the same state; they can be transferred when the employee moves to another state agency job. While the employee may make a career shift, in the sense of undertaking a job that has an entirely new set of responsibilities and tasks and requires very different skills, he or she does not have to start at "zero" in the investments category.

Identification-Based Commitment

Employees who identify with and feel loyal toward their employer share the values of the organization and have a personal sense of importance about the agency's mission. One commonly shared value between government agencies and their employees is that of public service. Among public sector employees, identifying with one's employer can also be a way to fulfill a public service motivation. Shared values can be more narrowly tailored to the agency mission, too. For example, an employee who identifies with the U.S. Environmental Protection Agency would share that agency's values and personally feel the agency's mission of protecting the environment is important. Employees who feel loyal to the U.S. Civil Rights Commission share the agency's value of advancing the cause of civil rights. Similarly, employees who identify with a state highway department share that organization's values of building and maintaining safe and convenient roadways throughout the state. Sometimes these shared values are manifest in loyalty to and identification with an individual, perhaps a respected supervisor or a charismatic chief executive officer.

Employees who identify with their employers care what happens to their work organization because they share the organization's goals and values. In essence, employees with ties based on identification and loyalty are self-motivated to do their best for the organization because doing what is good for the organization is consistent with their personal values. Employees who identify with their agencies are likely to perceive that their employers expect them to feel loyal. Such employees also are likely to feel that their job responsibilities are compatible with their personal ethics, professional standards of performance, and personal values. Committed employees' family and friends are likely to support their affiliation with the organization.

Antecedents and Consequences of Commitment

Research on employee commitment has focused primarily on the antecedents and consequences of these psychological ties for individuals and employers.

Antecedents

Antecedents are those factors that increase the likelihood that employees will develop and sustain employee commitment. Individual levels of organizational commitment are influenced by personal characteristics, attitudes, employment experiences, and organizational factors.

Personal Characteristics. Gender, age, and organizational tenure are positively related to commitment. Women tend to have higher levels of employee commitment than men. Older workers tend to have higher levels of commitment than younger workers. And employees who have longer organizational tenure tend to have greater organizational commitment than those with shorter time in the agency.

Education is negatively related to commitment. The more education an individual has the lower the level of employee commitment he or she is likely to sustain. Presumably this relationship holds because more highly educated employees adopt more cosmopolitan views toward their work careers. Such employees are more inclined to develop commitment to their work careers (regardless of where they are employed) rather than to the work organizations through which they pursue their careers.

Attitudes. Individuals who have a strong work ethic, a sense of competence, and an achievement motivation tend to develop employee commitment. Employees who have higher levels of self-esteem and who feel they are important to their employer are more likely to sustain employee commitment than are those who do not share such feelings. Likewise, individuals who have positive attitudes toward their workplace and are socially involved in the organization's extracurricular activities are likely to have higher levels of commitment than those with negative attitudes and those who choose not to be involved socially.

Perceptions of agency effectiveness and perceptions of employer dependability are associated with higher levels of employee commitment. In other words, employees who think their work organizations are effective and who think they can depend upon their employers are likely to have higher levels of commitment to their employing agencies.

Work Experiences. The experiences employees have at work can influence the level of commitment they sustain to their employer. Employees who have had realistic job previews are likely to have higher levels of commitment than those who joined the organization with unrealistic expectations. Positive early work experiences contribute to higher levels of employee commitment. Furthermore, individuals whose expectations about work are fulfilled are likely to sustain higher levels of employee commitment.

Employee commitment is positively correlated with the scope of one's job. Individuals with jobs of broader scope (for instance, those that entail greater responsibility, complexity, and autonomy) are more likely to be committed to their employers than those with jobs of relatively narrower scope.

Work role conflict and role overload are negatively associated with employee commitment. Individuals who have jobs with conflicting expectations or jobs that have excessive demands assigned to them tend to have lower levels of commitment to their work organizations than individuals whose jobs do not entail role conflict or role overload.

Organizational Factors. Worker ownership and employee opportunities to participate in decisionmaking tend to be positively associated with employee commitment. Organizations that have cultures which encourage and demonstrate commitment to their employees and expect commitment in return are more likely to elicit commitment from their employees.

Consequences

Positive and negative consequences derive from employee commitment. In general, employee commitment, whether based on investments and/or shared values, has more positive than negative consequences for both organizations and individuals.

Positive Consequences. Organizational consequences of employee commitment include better performance and lower employee turnover. Employees with higher levels of organizational commitment are likely to be evaluated as better performers. Turnover is negatively related to employee commitment. Employees who feel commitment are more likely to remain with an employer and have better attendance records. Changing employers might mean employees have to start over on some key investments. Starting over is something that most employees with substantial investments in one work organization are hesitant to do. The greater the investment in a particular work organization, the greater the likelihood an employee will stay with that employer. And organizations with committed employees are perceived to be more attractive places to work by nonmembers, hence organizational recruitment is likely to be helped.

Other important benefits from employee commitment are much less tangible. With employee commitment, organizations and managers can harness the individual's conscience for the purposes of the agency. Committed employees do what is good for the agency because, in the process of advancing the interests of the organization, they are also advancing values that are important to them personally. Individuals who share the values of an organization are willing to perform "above and beyond" the call of duty to accomplish shared purposes or to promote common values. Employees who are committed to their workplace are more likely to make decisions consistent with the organization's best interests.

Individuals find employee commitment to be rewarding because working for an organization that promotes values they share provides employees with a sense of personal satisfaction. Committed employees develop a sense of belonging at work and are able to find worth and meaning in their work activities. Even if their particular jobs are not especially challenging and/or complex, committed employees can derive personal meaning from their activities because they value the organized effort of which they are a part. Employees feel an attachment to something bigger than themselves. They feel that the 40 hours (or more) of their work effort are for something meaningful. As a result, employees develop a sense of personal efficacy.

Research has demonstrated that employees can sustain high levels of work and personal commitments simultaneously. Time and energy constraints nonetheless create challenges for employees trying to accommodate both work and personal obligations.

Positive consequences of employee commitment result for work groups as well. Organizations with employees who feel committed to their employers have greater membership stability because turnover is diminished. As a result work group effectiveness and cohesiveness are enhanced.

Negative Consequences. There is the potential for employee commitment to generate some negative consequences for organizations and individuals. While high levels of commitment can reduce turnover, they also can diminish the infusion of new ideas and dampen levels of creativity.

Individuals who develop excessive levels of commitment, those whose identification and loyalty approach a level of zealotry, can overstep the boundaries of acceptable behavior in pursuit of organizational interests. Organizational zealots are so strongly committed to the organization that they are often blind to shortcomings in the organization and unwilling to entertain even constructive criticism of their employer. Examples of this can be seen in instances where individuals engage in illegal or unethical activities because they think it is in the best interests of the organization. Employee commitment can have negative consequences for individuals, too. By detracting from an individual's interest in employment elsewhere, employee commitment can reduce an individual's job mobility.

Cultivating Commitment

Employee commitment is a reciprocal relationship between employer and employee. Individuals need to experience commitment from their employers in order to develop and sustain a sense of commitment to their employers. Providing socialization experiences that communicate and inculcate pivotal agency values, building an organizational culture that encourages commitment, and meeting the expectations of employees are important factors in eliciting employee commitment.

Most employers seek to hire individuals who will "fit in" to the organization. That is, they seek individuals who can accept the basic assumptions and already hold key organizational values as their own personal values. Of course, most organizational selection procedures are imprecise and most employees need some assistance to become integrated into an organization's culture. Organizational socialization programs are especially important for this purpose.

The socialization process is important because employees must know what the values of the organization are before they can be expected to share those values. Once those values are clear, the potential for employee commitment is present. Employees cannot be expected to share the important values of the organization if they do not know what they are. Some people may choose to join an agency because they are predisposed to share the values of the organization. Others who lack a normative interest in agency programs may be attracted by investment opportunities. It is to be hoped that both groups of employees are candidates for commitment once they are employed by the agency.

The process of socializing employees into the pivotal values of the organization is an ongoing one. Usually the employment interview is the beginning of the organization's socialization program. It provides prospective employees with a glimpse of the employer's programs and values. Formal orientation programs typically follow. More subtle and deep-seated socialization continues through informal interactions with supervisors and coworkers.

Under optimal circumstances an organization's culture would not only allow commitment to develop but would encourage employees to feel committed to the organization. An agency's organizational culture must communicate to employees, through its artifacts, values, basic decisionmaking assumptions, and behaviors, that employees are valued by the organization. For example, an agency that uses layoffs or reductions in force only as a last resort demonstrates by its actions that it is concerned about the well-being of its employees. In contrast, an organization that gives little notice of staff cutbacks and fails to provide outplacement help for those released demonstrates little commitment and concern for the welfare of its employees.

Such an employer is likely to have a hard time eliciting and sustaining commitment among its employees—even among those who survive a substantial layoff.

Socialization into a supportive organizational culture is the beginning of the process for cultivating employee commitment. Employers must also devote attention to the question of whether the employees' expectations about work are met. Each individual develops a unique relationship with the organization where he or she works based on unvoiced expectations about the work experience. These expectations comprise a psychological contract.

Psychological contracts reflect unarticulated hopes and feelings about what the organization and employees each will give and get from the employment relationship. These expectations are referred to as psychological because they focus on more subtle aspects of the work relationships than those covered in explicit employment contracts. For example, employees usually have expectations about how much effort they must exert as a member of the agency. Individuals may accept jobs thinking that they will have to work extra hours just to do their assigned tasks; this is a common expectation of budget officers during the peak of the budget cycle. And in exchange for these long hours they typically expect job experiences that will help them to advance on their career ladder.

The terms of psychological contracts between employee and employer change over time. As needs and expectations change, psychological contracts must be renegotiated. Such renegotiations are most likely to occur during times of change for the organization or the individual. If the adjustment in expectations is not mutual, then there may be a feeling of betrayal similar to that of a breach of contract. Employees who feel this breach of psychological contract are not likely candidates for organizational commitment. Those who feel committed may begin to question their commitment in light of a breach of psychological contract.

Getting employees to feel commitment based upon a sense of investments in the organization is not very complicated. To foster investment-based commitment the organization has to offer opportunities and working conditions that are competitive with other prospective employers. Some of the more progressive corporations do this through liberal stock option and bonus plans. In the public sector typical investment factors include promotion prospects, development of work group networks, performance bonuses, and the accrual of vacation, sick leave, and retirement benefits.

Once employees have accrued investments in an organization, the employer need only remain competitive with alternative employers regarding the returns on investments offered to employees. But investment ties are oftentimes expensive to develop and maintain, requiring regular infusions of funds to underwrite promotions, bonuses, merit pay, and other returns on investment. Such resources are essential to sustain employees' sense that their investments are yielding a satisfactory return. Programs that nurture investment ties generally require great managerial care to ensure equitable administration. If employees perceive favoritism in the allocation of such programs, legal and morale problems are likely.

Without a competitive stance on investment opportunities, employers run the risk of losing investment-oriented employees who calculate that they have more to gain from changing employers than from staying where they are. Investment-oriented employees can be lured away by competitors who offer a higher "rate of return" in the form of higher salaries, greater promotion opportunities, more office perks, better bonus opportunities, and the like.

Having employees who only have an investment approach to their jobs can be a disadvantage to the employing organization. To the extent that an agency emphasizes investments as a tie for its employees, it is subject to the vagaries of the marketplace. As such, its ability to attract and retain qualified employees may be influenced by what its competitors offer employees. In essence, the employer's recruitment and retention patterns may be influenced by the investment opportunities available elsewhere—a circumstance beyond the employer's control.

Agencies that emphasize only investment ties among their employees also run the risk of giving employees an incentive to stay with the employer even if they have mentally "retired" on the job. This occurs among employees who take a minimalist approach to their jobs while they are waiting (sometimes several years) until they qualify for retirement. Such employees have more to gain by merely putting in their time until they can retire than by changing to a more challenging or interesting employer.

Psychological ties to one's workplace based on identification and loyalty are much less susceptible to influences from outside the organization (such as alternative employers) than are psychological ties based on investments. Once employees feel loyal to an agency they are much less susceptible to being lured away by competitors because the basis of the attachment is shared values, not self-interested investments. In contrast to investment ties, employee identification and loyalty requires fewer financial resources to sustain but greater managerial attention. In particular, managers must understand the nature of employee identification and loyalty and its importance for the organization.

Summary

Employee commitment—a sense of psychological investment in one's work organization—increases the chances that employees will perform well in the organization and stay with that employer. As we approach the world of work for the twenty-first century, the emergence of a global economy has profound implications for the prospects of employee commitment. The global marketplace brings with it greater opportunities and increased competition among groups which were heretofore too distant to influence each other's working conditions. Widespread marketplace restructuring, reorganizations, and organizational downsizing have dramatically eroded the prospects for employee commitment. The leaner and meaner employment climate of the global economy has eroded prospects for sustaining either kind of commitment. Ironically, because organizations have fewer slack resources than ever, this erosion in the prospects for employee commitment comes at the very time when agencies need this employee commitment more than ever.

BARBARA S. ROMZEK

BIBLIOGRAPHY

Allen, Natalie J., and John P. Meyer, 1990. "The Measurement and Antecedents of Affective, Continuance and Normative Commitment to the Organization." *Journal of Occupational Psychology*, 63: 1–18.

Amitai Etzioni, 1975. *A Comparative Analysis of Complex Organizations*. New York: The Free Press.

Caldwell, David F., Jennifer A. Chatman, and Charles A. O'Reilly, 1990. "Building Organizational Commitment: A Multifirm Study." *Journal of Occupational Psychology*, 63: 245–261.

Mowday, Richard T., Lyman W. Porter, and Richard M. Steers, 1982. *Employee Organization Linkages: The Psychology of Commitment, Absenteeism, and Turnover.* New York: Academic Press.

Perry, James L., and Lois R. Wise, 1990. "The Motivational Bases of Public Service." *Public Administration Review,* 50(3): 367–373.

Romzek, Barbara, 1990. "Employee Investments and Commitment: The Ties that Bind." *Public Administration Review,* 50(3): 374–382.

Rousseau, Denise M., 1989. "Psychological and Implied Contracts in Organizations." *Employee Responsibilities and Rights Journal,* 2(2): 121–139.

Simon, Herbert, 1976. *Administrative Behavior.* 3rd ed., New York: Free Press.

COMMON FOREIGN AND SECURITY POLICY (CFSP).

The policy by which the member states of the European Union coordinate some aspects of their foreign and security policy, define common positions, and adopt joint actions in international relations.

The Origins: "European Political Cooperation"

As a result of the failure to create a European Defense Community in 1954 and get an agreement on the Fouchet Plan in 1962, foreign policy and especially security and defense became a taboo in the process of European integration. As a part of the attempts to relaunch European integration in 1969–1970, the European Community (EC) member states accepted the "Luxembourg Report" or "Davignon Report," which established European Political Cooperation (EPC).

The Luxembourg Report emphasized "the need to intensify their political cooperation and provide in an initial phase the mechanism for harmonizing their views regarding international affairs." The purpose was "to cooperate in the sphere of foreign policy." First, the member states were to "ensure, through regular exchanges of information and consulations, a better mutual understanding on the great international problems." Second, they had "to strengthen their solidarity by promoting the harmonization of their views, the coordination of their positions, and, where it appears possible and desirable, common action."

These objectives indicate that European Political Cooperation, in contrast to the European Defense Community and the Fouchet Plan, did not have great ambitions and was not to restrict the national governments in defining their own foreign policy. European Political Cooperation was based on intergovernmental cooperation and was to operate beside and independent from the more supranational European Community, although EPC member states were the same as those of the European Community. This implied that the European Community's European Parliament, Commission, and Court of Justice were not involved in European Political Cooperation. The ministers of foreign affairs and the heads of state and government bore full responsibility for European Political Cooperation.

Practice revealed that European Political Cooperation could be influential when the main Western forum of consultation and policy harmonization–the North Atlantic Treaty Organization (NATO)–was less active. This was the case during the Conference on Security and Cooperation in Helsinki at the beginning of the 1970s, for example. When NATO or the United States as the main Western partner dominated, however, European Political Cooperation proved to be extremely weak (i.e., during the Middle East crisis in 1973–1974). Other crises, such as the Soviet invasion in Afghanistan in 1979 and the Poland crisis in 1980–1982, pointed to the inefficient procedures, the problems resulting from the noncommittal nature of European Political Cooperation, and the negative consequences of the artificial division between European Political Cooperation and the European Community as well as between the economic, political, and military aspects of security.

Subsequent adaptations of European Political Cooperation resulting from the Copenhagen Report (1973), London Report (1981), and Solemn Declaration of Stuttgart (1983) gradually widened the scope of European Political Cooperation and improved its procedures, though without fundamentally changing its original structure. Its weaknesses were not eliminated when the Single European Act of 1986 (which amended the European Community's founding Treaty of Rome) codified and institutionalized European Political Cooperation. The Single European Act linked European Political Cooperation with the European Community through its Title III:

"Treaty provisions on European Cooperation in the sphere of Foreign Policy." In this section, member states accepted for the first time the need to coordinate more closely their positions on the political as well as economic aspects of security. It recognized also some involvement of the Commission and the European Parliament, though without changing the intergovernmental character of European Political Cooperation.

The Establishment of Common Foreign and Security Policy

The fall of the communist regimes in Eastern Europe and the German reunification in 1989–1990 gave a new impetus to adopt European Political Cooperation. Negotiations in the framework of the Intergovernmental Conference of European Political Union resulted in the establishment of the "Common Foreign and Security Policy" (CFSP) as part of the European Union. This Common Foreign and Security Policy, established by the Treaty on European Union of February 1992 (Treaty of Maastricht), replaced the existing European Political Cooperation.

One of the objectives of the European Union, as defined by one of the common provisions of the treaty, is "to assert its identity on the international scene, in particular through the implementation of a common foreign and security policy including the eventual framing of a common defense policy, which might in time lead to a common defense."

The provisions of the CFSP are not included in the Treaty's Title II, which amends the provisions on the European Community, but are incorporated in a separate Title V. This lasting separation between the normal European Community provisions and the CFSP provisions symbolizes the fact that, as in the Treaty of Maastricht, foreign and security policy was considered as an intergovernmental affair that had to be handled separately from the more supranational process of integration.

This structure is in contrast with the provisions in the Treaty of Maastricht's introductory "Common Provisions," which mention that the European Union "shall be served by a single institutional framework" and that it shall "ensure the consistency of its external activities as a whole in the context of its external relations, security, economic and development policies." The Union indeed has one single institutional framework but, as will be seen, the institutions have different competencies in "community" matters (Title II) and CFSP matters (Title V). This lasting divide between the European Community and the CFSP with external economic relations and development policy falling under Title II and foreign and security policy under Title V, is one of the main reasons for the weakness of the European Union's external actions. The lack of a single decisionmaking center and a centralized political leadership, as well as the artificial division between the different dimensions of external relations, has inevitably had a negative influence on the European Union's external capabilities.

Scope and Objectives of Common Foreign and Security Policy

The scope of the Union's foreign action is widened to all aspects of security. The first article of Title V states that the "Union and its member states shall define and implement a common foreign and security policy covering all areas of foreign and security policy." This includes not only the economic and political aspects of security (as was the case in European Political Cooperation), but the military dimension of security as well.

The objectives, as defined in Article J.2(2), are: to safeguard the common values, fundamental interests and independence of the Union; to strengthen the security of the Union and its member states in all ways; to preserve peace and strengthen international security, in accordance with the principles of the United Nations Charter as well as the principles of the Helsinki Final Act and the objectives of the Paris Charter; to promote international cooperation; and to develop and consolidate democracy and the rule of law, and respect for human rights and fundamental freedoms.

It is important to emphasize that the objectives of the CFSP is to define a "common" policy, not a "single" policy. This implies that the policy of the Union is aimed not at replacing but complementing the foreign and security policy of the member states. It also partially explains why the CFSP has a policy toward only some areas in the world and toward only some security issues. This also indicates that there is no basis for high expectations about the scope of the CFSP. The discussion of procedures and institutional framework, too, indicates that there is no basis for high expectations about its effectiveness and impact.

The Treaty on European Union includes a provision that the CFSP, and in particular provisions on defense policy, may be revised on the basis of a report to be presented in 1996 by the Council of Ministers to the European Council. This provision is the result of the disappointment of a number of member states over the treaty provisions on CFSP. It is also included in view of the expiration of the Western European Union's Treaty of Brussels in 1998. A new Intergovernmental Conference in 1996–1997 can thus result in changes in the European Union's capability to act in the field of foreign affairs and security.

The Treaty of Maastricht provides several procedures to pursue these objectives.

Systematic Cooperation and "Common Positions"

First, the Union can pursue its objectives by establishing systematic cooperation between member states in the conduct of policy. Member states shall inform and consult one another within the Council of Ministers on any matter of foreign and security policy of general interest in order to ensure that their combined influence is exerted as effectively as possible by means of concerted and convergent action. Whenever it deems it necessary, the Council of Ministers shall define a "common position." Member states shall ensure that their national policies conform to the common positions. They shall coordinate their action and uphold the common position in international organizations and at international conferences.

The European Council defines the principles of and general guidelines for the Common Foreign and Security Policy. The Council of Ministers takes the decisions necessary for defining and implementing CFSP on the basis of the general guidelines adopted by the European Council. It ensures the unity, consistency and effectiveness of action by the Union. The Council of Ministers acts unanimously, except for procedural questions.

Any member state or the European Commission may refer to the Council of Ministers any question relating to common foreign policy and may submit proposals to the Council of Ministers. In cases requiring a rapid decision, the presidency, of its own motion, or at the request of the European Commission or a member state, convenes an extraordinary Council of Ministers meeting within 48 hours or, in an emergency, within a shorter period.

"Joint Action"

Second, the Union can pursue its objectives by gradually implementing "joint action" in the areas in which the member states have important interests in common. The procedure for adopting joint action in matters covered by foreign and security policy is the following.

The Council of Minsters decides, on the basis of general guidelines from the European Council, that a matter should be the subject of joint action. Whenever the Council of Ministers decides on the principle of joint action, it lays down the specific scope, the Union's general and specific objectives in carrying out such action, if necessary its duration, and the means, procedures, and conditions for its implementation. The Council of Ministers, when adopting the joint action and at any stage during its development, defines those matters on which decisions are to be taken by a qualified majority (with this qualified majority having as a supplementary requirement that at least eight member states vote in favor).

Joint actions commit the member states in the positions they adopt and in the conduct of their activity. However, in cases of imperative need arising from changes in the situation, and failing a Council of Ministers decision, member states may take necessary measures as a matter of urgency, having regard to the general objectives of the joint action. The member state concerned must inform the Council of Ministers immediately of any such measures. Should there be any major difficulties in implementing a joint action, a member state refers them to the Council of Ministers, which discusses them and seeks appropriate solutions. Such solutions must not run counter to the objectives of the joint action or impair its effectiveness.

Examples of joint actions are those decided immediately after the entry into force of the Maastricht Treaty. These joint actions concerned the dispatch to Russia of observers to monitor the parliamentary elections, humanitarian aid to Bosnia-Herzegovina, support of the democratization process in South Africa, and support to the Middle East peace program.

These first joint actions were considered as rather disappointing in view of their limited scope and the predominance of the national states in the implementation of some.

Delegation to the Western European Union

Special procedures are elaborated for defense matters. Article J.4 of Title V states that "The Common Foreign and Security Policy shall include all questions related to the security of the Union, including the eventual framing of a common defense policy, which might in time lead to a common defense." However, for these defense matters the involvement of the Western European Union (WEU) is foreseen: the Union requests that the Western European Union elaborate and implement decisions and actions of the Union that have defense implications. The Council of Ministers, in agreement with the institutions of the Western European Union, adopts the necessary practical arrangements. Issues having defense implications dealt with under Article J.4 cannot be subject to the procedures applicable to joint actions. This implies that the use of majority voting is excluded for decisions having defense implications. The Council of Ministers thus always acts unanimously.

These provisions concerning the security policy explicitly state that they do not prejudice the specific character of the security and defense policy of certain member states (such as the neutral status of Ireland). They respect the obligations of the member states of the European Union that are also members of the North Atlantic Treaty Organization (NATO), and they are compatible with the common security and defense policy established within that framework. The provisions in Article J.4 do not prevent the development of closer cooperation between two or more member states on a bilateral level (such as the Franco-German cooperation), in the framework of the Western European Union and the NATO alliance, provided such cooperation does not run counter to or impede that provided for in Title V of the Treaty on European Union.

Article J.4 is important because it establishes for the first time a link between the European Union and the Western European Union. In this sense, it can provide a basis for a closer relationship and give the European Union military instruments that are sorely needed to get the Common Foreign and Security Policy taken seriously (as was proved in the crisis in the former Yugoslavia). However, in practice, these provisions were not translated in an operational relationship that gave the European Union military strength, which implies that the European Union is still a "civilian power." This is partially the result of the lasting disagreement among the EU member states about the nature of the Western European Union. In the opinion of some member states, the Western European Union is in the first place an instrument which has to implement the Union's security policies and which should gradually be absorbed by the European Union. Other member states defend the idea that the Western European Union should remain an independent organization which is both the military arm of the European Union and the European arm of the NATO alliance.

The Intergovernmental Institutional Framework

The analysis of the procedures indicates that the Council of Ministers and European Council are the central actors in CFSP. These two institutions, both representing the member states of the European Union, make the decisions related to foreign and security policy. Moreover, nearly all decisions have to be taken by unanimity, which implies that there can be no agreement if one country objects. The possibility of making certain decisions by a qualified majority is indeed very limited. This possibility is limited to joint actions and does not apply to defense questions or to policy issues that the Council of Ministers does not explicitly designate as issues that may be the subject of joint action. Moreover, even for joint actions, the decision to make decisions by a majority can still be blocked by a single member state.

Nevertheless, the fact that the principle of majority decisions has been accepted for foreign policy and security, however limited it may be, is nevertheless important as it may be the basis for a future extention of this supranational feature in CFPS. The unanimity rule is indeed considered as one of the main constraints on the development of an effective and respected CFSP. It explains why the European Union is often unable to agree quickly on specific actions and often has to limit its interventions to vague declarations. In this sense, it can be considered surprising that the European Union was at all able to intervene in some important external developments and crises (such as the changes in Eastern Europe in 1988–89 and the first stage of the Yugoslav crisis).

The Role of Other Institutions of the European Union

The European Commission does not exercise the same power in CFSP it does in the normal decisionmaking procedures of the European Community (Title II), where it has an exclusive power of initiative and an important role in elaborating and implementing decisions. The treaty provision which notes that the "Commission shall be fully associated with the work carried out in the Common Foreign and Security Policy field" does not guarantee that the Commission is considered as an equal partner by the member states. The impact of the Commission is, however, larger than Title V might indicate. The CFSP often needs the use of European Community instruments to implement CFSP decisions (such as economic sanctions or financial and technical support), which implies the involvement of the European Commission. Moreover, the Commission is also given, together with the Council of Ministers, the responsibility for ensuring consistency in the external relations of the European Union.

The tasks the Commission has in community matters are partially executed in CFSP by the presidency (held in turn by each member state in the Council of Ministers for a term of six months) and by the Political Committee. The presidency represents the Union in matters coming within the purview of CFSP. It is responsible for the implementation of common measures and for expressing the position of the Union in international organizations and international conferences. In these tasks, the presidency can be assisted by what is called the "troika." This troika consists of representatives of the country that holds the presidency, together with representatives of the previous and next member states to hold the presidency.

A political committee, consisting of political directors of the different ministries of foreign affairs of the member states, monitors the international situation in all areas covered by CFSP. It contributes to the definition of policies by delivering opinions to the Council of Ministers at the request of the Council or on its own initiative. It also monitors the implementation of agreed-upon policies, without prejudice to the responsibility of the presidency and the European Commission.

The European Parliment plays no role at all in the decisionmaking procedures of CFSP, which is in contrast to normal European Community procedures.

Title V only contains the rather noncommittal provisions that the "Presidency shall consult the European Parliament on the main aspects and the basic choices of the Common Foreign and Security Policy and shall ensure that the views of the European Parliament are duly taken into consideration." The European Parliament may ask questions of the Council of Ministers or make recommendations to it. Despite the lack of powers under Title V, the European Parliament can indirectly bring influence to bear on CFSP because it is part of the EC's budgetary authority and because certain agreements with third countries or groups of countries require the assent of the Parliament.

The Court of Justice is not mentioned in Title V; its jurisdiction is not extended to this field. This also implies that the Commission, the European Parliament, or a member state cannot ask the Court to judge the noncompliance of member states with CFSP obligations. It is not the Court but the Council of Ministers that has to ensure that the member states "support the Union's external and security policy actively and unreservedly in a spirit of loyalty and mutual solidarity" and "refrain from any action which is contrary to the interests of the Union or likely to impair its effectiveness as a cohesive force in international relations."

STEPHAN KEUKELEIRE

BIBLIOGRAPHY

Regelsberger, Elfriede, Philippe de Schoutheete de Tervarent and Wolfgang Wessels, eds., 1997. *Foreign Policy of the European Union. From EPC to CFSP and Beyond.* Boulder/London: Lynne Rienner Publishers.

Edwards, Geoffrey and Elfriede Regelsberger, eds., 1990. *Europe's Global Links. The European Community and Inter-Regional Co-operation.* London: Pinter Publishers.

Ginsberg, Roy H., 1989. *Foreign Policy Actions in the European Community.* Boulder, CO: Lynne Rienner Publishers.

Hill, Christopher, ed., 1996. *The Actors in European Foreign Policy.* London: Routledge.

Holland, Martin, ed., 1991. *The Future of European Political Cooperation: Essays on Theory and Practice.* London: Macmillan.

Ifestos, P., 1987. *European Political Cooperation: Towards a Framework of Supranational Diplomacy.* Aldershot, Eng.: Avebury.

Laursen, Finn and Sophie Vanhoonacker, eds., 1992. *The Intergovernmental Conference on Political Union: Institutional Reforms, New Policies and International Identity of the European Community.* Maastricht, Neth.: EIPA.

Nuttall, Simon, 1992. *European Political Cooperation.* Oxford: Claridon Press.

Pijpers, Alfred, Elfriede Regelsberger and Wolfgang Wessels, eds., 1988. *European Political Cooperation in the 1980s.* Dordrecht, Neth.: Martinus Nijhoff Publishers.

Rummel, Reinhardt, ed., 1992. *Toward Political Union: Planning a Common Foreign and Security Policy in the European Community.* Baden-Baden: Nomos Verlagsgesellschaft.

COMMUNITARIANISM.

The belief that human beings nurture good character and meaningful lives primarily through fellowship or union characterized by personal intimacy, moral commitment, common and lasting bonds, fraternal love, and public-spiritedness. Some modern communitarians emphasize private aspects such as family and neighborhood, while others focus more on public aspects such as democratic participation and civic virtue.

Communitarianism has enjoyed a significant revival in the late twentieth century, especially in the United States. Its rejuvenation stems mainly from growing disenchantment with modern liberalism and its excesses.

Modern liberalism emerged as a distinct political philosophy during the sixteenth, seventeenth, and eighteenth centuries. Thomas Hobbes (1588–1679) and John Locke (1632–1704) are commonly identified as its principal expositors, though many others made very substantial contributions to its development as well. Included among its tenets are: (1) that human beings are estranged, isolated from one another because of hatred, fear, greed, avarice, and other divisive passions (Hobbes)—or at least because of frustrated acquisitiveness (Locke); (2) that individuals precede the existence of civil society, a mere artifact of human decision created for the sake of protecting each individual's "natural" right to life, liberty, and estate; (3) that such societies constitute aggregations of individuals who form, by "social contract," a governing order designed to maximize protection of individual rights; and (4) that human beings are driven by passion rather than reason. Reason serves only as an instrument of the passions. Thus, liberal politics is easily characterized as an interplay of competing, passionate interests. Governance amounts to management or manipulation of contending passions for the sake of preserving peace and protecting rights.

Liberal philosophy underpins the United States's Declaration of Independence (1776) and much of the Constitution of 1789. During the ratification process (1787–1988), those founders who opposed the new constitution (Anti-Federalists) often voiced concern that its liberal, economic premises would encourage vice and luxury, and thereby lead to the eventual corruption of society. They elicited grudging admissions from Federalist (nationalist) supporters of the Constitution that, at bottom, an enduring society must rely upon virtue in the people. The founding debate thus turned on communitarian criteria as well.

Twentieth-century communitarians have rejuvenated this debate. They believe that liberalism has been taken to excess. It has steadily engendered an American society dominated by economic acquisitiveness, effusive rights claims, and political cynicism. Over time, these factors have obscured deeper, communal dimensions of life, and left many in the United States in a rootless and impoverished state.

Communitarians blame excessive liberalism for many ills, including high divorce rates, escalating juvenile delinquency, suicide, greed, political corruption, erosion of public and private institutions, environmental degradation, and general moral decadence.

Although some communitarians despair of ever reversing these conditions, most offer at least some hope for the future. That hope lies in adoption of communitarian principles and practices that will counteract the excesses of liberalism.

At its base, communitarianism may be contrasted directly with the liberal tenets mentioned above. First, individuals are not fundamentally estranged and isolated. Rather, they abide together in close, intimate bonds. They are naturally drawn to each other, and ultimately shape their lives through a complex web of relationships.

Second, a good or meaningful life is defined largely through those relationships. An individual does not become a fully mature human being without them. In this sense community is a fundamental, natural phenomenon which precedes and nurtures individual life. Clarke Cochran, in his book *Character, Community, and Politics* (1982), argues that mature individuality cannot exist except against the background of "one or more sustaining communities."

> While individual moral autonomy, as long as it is properly understood, is essential to full humanity, we should observe that it is possible for an individual only after he has been educated and nourished by family, friends, teachers, and fellowships within a particular social and cultural context (p. 13).

Third, community transcends mere aggregations of strangers. It engenders specific, contextual, and ordered relationships. Not just any relationship will do. The notion of a social contract, therefore, represents an impoverished basis upon which to establish and sustain political society. Communitarians favor other metaphors, such as "covenant," for capturing the rich, character-forming milieu undergirding healthy political orders. Human beings require specific arrangements of family, friendship, civic association, religious affiliation, citizen responsibility, and so forth.

Communitarians often differ over which relations to include as essential, and over their order of priority. This reflects in part the diverse purposes they seek to fulfill through community life. Nevertheless, virtually all communitarians require much more than liberal tenets provide for civil societies.

Fourth, communitarians generally reject the liberal treatment of emotion and reason. The two are intimately rather than instrumentally connected. Reason can often temper and restrain passions, and passions may inform reason. The human process of interpreting meaning displays unification of reason and passion, not just within each individual, but socially as well. Hence, one's emotions are not solely private and irrational sources of value as liberals tend to assume. Emotions and values may be arranged in hierarchies of relation, which are established mainly through dialogical processes within communities. In short, some emotions and values are deemed more important than others, and are matters for community debate rather than sheer assertion by individuals.

As one might expect, communitarian politics takes on a very different cast from the liberal version. It emphasizes aspiration and public responsibility over the liberal's manipulation of contending selfish interests and protection of rights. Thomas McCullough (1991), argues that meaningful public life becomes possible only when, "as citizens, we hold one another accountable for what we know and value" (p. 79). Such "morally serious conversation about

the things that matter to us as human beings is what sustains a political community through the dissension and conflict that threaten its peace and even its existence at times" (p. 79).

This strain of politics entails some prudence about the problematic nature of the human condition, yet embraces a very positive faith that people can be other-regarding. They can define and achieve, however modestly, a unifying public good. Liberals today are generally too cynical to adopt this stance. Communitarians believe they create dangerous self-fulfilling prophecies as a result.

Despite these common features, substantial diversity exists in vision, structure, and emphasis among communitarians today. Some of the more dominant conceptions now influence political and administrative discussion, and therefore deserve brief description here.

Varieties of Communitarianism

Robert Booth Fowler (1991) surveys the breadth of communitarian thought emerging in the late twentieth century. He sees an "almost bewildering" array of images of community arising from diverse and "contesting" sources (p. x). This is a sign of communitarianism's strength and vitality, he argues. It is not likely to wither any time soon, and will have substantial influence on American political thought.

Fowler describes six significant images of community. The first is *community as participatory democracy*. This perspective focuses squarely on classical citizenship, which means active participation in rule of the community. It is sometimes referred to as "high citizenship" in order to distinguish it from the impoverished or "low" version that dominates in the United States. Low citizenship refers basically to the legal requirements of citizenship in the United States. There are very few. The U.S. Constitution emphasizes persons rather than citizens, and individual rights rather than citizen responsibilities. Thus, there is not even a requirement to vote, much less participate directly in daily governance.

Strong democratic norms in the United States, however, provide incentives for high citizenship. Participation advocates argue that direct, face-to-face self-governance promotes common purpose, self-esteem, and civic pride. These are prerequisites for community, and the moderation of liberal excess. Participatory models are therefore predominately local in their orientation. Some advocates argue, though, that substantial participation at this level will also improve the quality of national political life by supplying more responsible, civic-minded public servants to its halls.

Local participatory efforts have grown substantially during the 1980s and 1990s, and include groups with widely varying concerns. Some wish to emulate the spirit of 1960s communalism, while others represent religious, civic humanist, and feminist visions.

A second image is *community as virtuous republic.* Civic republicans focus more on appropriate models of political and administrative leadership, and upon the institutions that support community, locally and nationally. They are suspicious of direct democracy for fear of mob rule, even though they still embrace a robust citizenship as a key attribute of community. They want to improve the political institutions and discourse that give shape to community and character. Robert Bellah and associates (1991) argue that the culture of individualism in the United States dims understanding of the vital communitarian roles of institutions. They focus their analysis on more dominant political and economic structures because they exert such a pervasive influence upon modern society. Many civic republicans share their concern for national community and the U.S. character.

Despite many claims to diversity and individuality, U.S. citizens exhibit a common character that is easily identified by outsiders. Civic republicans strive to make this character admirable. They draw from many sources for appropriate models to emulate, but the most admired source is the founding era.

Civic republicans look to this era to show that communitarian principles and practices coexisted with liberal tenets. They often cite Gordon Wood's classic book, *The Creation of the American Republic* (1969), as a compelling confirmation of this point. They examine the influence of civic-humanist (from Roman civilization) and Puritan-covenantal thought on the founding generation. They gain much insight from historical exegesis, and also acquire some legitimacy for their models because of the great respect most in the U.S. hold for that era.

Civic republicans view the past as an important source of identity and character. Most of them are not reactionaries, hoping to return to the past. However, they believe the past should inform the current political culture. Robert Bellah and his co-authors (1985) define culture as an historical conversation in which individuals find rooted meaning for their lives. Individual life is enriched through social and political commitments engendered by this conversation. The authors believe most Americans today lack sufficient awareness of this public-spirited conversation, due largely to a blinding preoccupation with calculative (utilitarian) and expressive (therapeutic) forms of individualism. Politics, citizenship, and the common good will be greatly improved if more people are restored to a meaningful civic dialogue.

Fowler's third image, *community as roots,* concentrates more on private, traditional institutions such as family, neighborhood, school, voluntary association, and church. Many advocates stress family and tradition above all else. They lament the breakdown of family as the most basic institution for nurturing virtue. They view tradition in the Burkean sense of preserving ways of life that ennoble character. They are less interested in stimulating republican

debate, and more interested in fostering effective habits and dispositions through private institutions.

Advocates of traditional communities, such as Alasdair MacIntyre, Eric Voegelin, and Allan Bloom, criticize the U.S. penchant for embracing innovation and change over order and stability. This has led to rejection of the idea of human moral purpose in the world and universe. Emotivism and moral relativism reign, and act as a corrosive acid upon all collective and authoritative institutions. They call for a return to classical education, traditional religious practices, and family mores.

Other advocates are less interested in tradition, and more in reconceptualizing the basic institutions of society along more egalitarian lines. For instance, some wish to abandon the patriarchal aspects of family and community. Some feminist theorists, such as Adrienne Rich, Betty Friedan, and Jean Elshtain, strive to put motherhood and feminine aspects of community center stage, though not without a lot of criticism from other feminists who see them capitulating ultimately to male power.

Amitai Etzioni's recent book, *The Spirit of Community: Rights, Responsibilities, and the Communitarian Agenda* (1993), has become a widely read manifesto for a new communitarianism that reflects our egalitarian character. He argues that the liberal movement of the 1950s and 1960s stemmed from justifiable motives to reject authoritarianism and oppressive race and gender-based discriminatory practices. However, the liberal movement failed to provide adequate alternatives that preserve our common morality and the institutions that nurture it. His book, and a new quarterly journal (*The Responsive Community: Rights & Responsibilities*) which he and colleagues have recently established, call readers to join the communitarian movement and restore character-nurturing institutions such as family and school to a new vitality shed of some formerly oppressive characteristics.

The fourth image emphasizes survival through creation of a *global community.* This image grows mainly from fear of global annihilation through environmental degradation, nuclear war, economic exploitation, technological imperatives, and related types of abuse. Our only hope, they argue, lies in transforming societies into a global community that recognizes interdependence and harmony with nature. Some advocates invoke planning and environmental design through globally coordinated government policies. Others seek proliferation of local initiatives that will eventually coalesce into global changes. The global image is tinged heavily with naturalistic and sacral conceptions, and even borders on pantheistic tenets about earthly life.

Fowler identifies *religious community* as a fifth common image, and attributes its rise in part to "the unexpected and grudging growth of fascination with religion on the part of some intellectuals" (p. 2). It also stems from a variety of grassroots religious movements, most notably evangelical

Christianity. Religious communitarians present religion as the oldest and richest ground for communitarian life. Religion counteracts secularism by stressing wholeness and higher truths. It provides transcendent values born in relation to a deity, thus grounding community in a higher purpose.

In the United States, religious advocates have joined republican communitarians in excavating U.S. history for evidence of pervasive religious communitarian influence. The evidence is quite substantial. It is now employed in a variety of ways to lower, though not eliminate, the wall of separation between church and state, which was raised high through what many followers believe are erroneous constitutional interpretations. Many religious communitarians stress local initiatives and states' rights as a buttress for infusing religious tenets into public policy.

Fowler characterizes the sixth image as *existential community*. Its proponents call attention to the problematic nature of community given the frailties and paradoxes of the human condition. People are drawn together for the sake of nurture and consolation, and yet are simultaneously estranged. Advocates such as Glenn Tinder (1980) emphasize that we cannot escape such binds. People should strive for community, yet recognize that human failings make the goal unattainable. This approach highlights the virtue of prudence in human affairs above all else. Prudent people still aspire to a greater good, but take care to assess capabilities in realistic fashion. Existential communitarians bemoan the utopian moralism inherent in much communitarian thought, and provide a constant reminder that we live in a flawed world.

Communitarianism and Public Administration Theory

Communitarian thought, in these varied forms, enjoys growing influence in recent public administrative theory, especially in the United States. Public administration there has undergone a crisis of identity in political and intellectual life since at least the 1960s. Its role in U.S. society is subject to constant challenge and ridicule. A growing number of administrative theorists have begun exploring communitarian thought in hopes of constructing a more solid foundation for the profession and field.

Most of these theorists borrow eclectically from communitarian thought, and many would not consider themselves communitarians at all. Nevertheless, communitarian notions such as citizenship, common good, civic virtue, and democratic participation inform much of their work.

One example is Terry Cooper's work (1991). Cooper, as a former local community organizer and participatory activist, brings a wealth of insight and experience to the subject. He analyzes all aspects of citizenship in United States history, and crafts a theory of citizenship for public administrators. In the process, he resurrects the latent "ethical" or high tradition of citizenship in American politics.

Cooper argues that public administrators play a vital role in nurturing the "long term delicate process of building a sense of democratic political community in which self-interest rightly understood can be cultivated and maintained" (p. 197). He reminds officials of their duty to connect the liberal idea of self-interest to the communitarian notion of common good. This constitutes the U.S. version of civic virtue. Officials must not only emulate this standard, but protect and serve the infrastructure in which the many spheres of life thrive. Civic virtue arises though the conscious integration of these various spheres (personal, familial, fraternal, organizational, economic, political, and so forth) in individual lives.

The infrastructure comprises an array of private to increasingly public institutions. Some are government agencies, but many are extragovernmental, containing both public and private dimensions. Government, however, bears substantial responsibility for ensuring their balance and viability in the broader system. Cooper's administrators, therefore, are high citizens seeking to bring the public to the realization of their high citizenship as well. For Cooper this role makes democratic accountability and public life a meaningful reality.

Another example is John Rohr's work in constitutional history, theory, and interpretation. His book *To Run a Constitution* (1986) excavates the constitutional underpinnings of modern public administration, and posits a constitutional theory of administrative responsibility. In the process he accents republican thought in the founding era, and calls attention to Anti-Federalist criticism of the United States constitutional system. In another influential work Rohr (1989) critically analyzes some common approaches to administrative ethics, and then offers a dialogue-based method grounded in analysis of competing interpretations of values fundamental to the regime. In the early chapters he links his method to the ancient subject of civic virtue, especially to fostering prudence in public servants.

Though Rohr's work borrows from communitarian thought, he displays substantial ambivalence toward the concept as well. This is quite understandable given the obligation public officials have (in most cases by oath) to uphold a very liberal Constitution. Rohr seems committed to upholding both traditions, hoping to gain some good from both, while living with inevitably problematic consequences.

A final example is Camilla Stivers's work. She brings insightful feminist criticism to bear upon male-dominated conceptions of virtue, honor, leadership, participation, accountability, and responsibility as applied to recent administrative theory (Stiver, 1993). In offering her own feminist theory, she argues that attention to gender substantially modifies these concepts in ways that require much further exploration in order to meaningfully accommodate women's contributions to public life. For the most part she seeks to modify these concepts rather than eliminate them, and so in the end advances communitarian thought in public administration.

All three authors comprehend tensions in American political life between liberal and communitarian principles. Each seeks some balance among them for the sake of avoiding abuse through excess. Community can become as oppressive as liberalism if taken too far. After all, the liberal enlightenment grew largely in reaction to the abuses of communitarian-based regimes that had dominated the world scene since ancient times. Most administrative theorists who embrace communitarian ideas share this ambivalence. They also reflect the diverse images of community, differing over the purposes and processes attributable to this complex and essential feature of all political societies.

RICHARD T. GREEN

BIBLIOGRAPHY

A representative sample of works on communitarianism should include the following:

Barber, Benjamin, 1984. *Strong Democracy: Participatory Politics for a New Age.* Berkeley: University of California Press.

Bellah, Robert N., Richard Madsen, William M. Sullivan, Ann Swidler, and Steven M. Tipton, 1985. *Habits of the Heart: Individualism and Commitment in American Life.* Berkeley: University of California Press.

Bellah, Robert N., Richard Madsen, William M. Sullivan, Ann Swidler, and Steven M. Tipton, 1991. *The Good Society.* New York: Alfred A. Knopf.

Budziszewski, J., 1988. *The Nearest Coast of Darkness: A Vindication of the Politics of Virtues.* Ithaca, NY: Cornell University Press.

Cochran, Clarke E., 1982. *Character, Community, and Politics.* Tuscaloosa: University of Alabama Press.

Elshtain, Jean Bethke, 1982. *The Family in Political Thought.* Amherst: University of Massachusetts Press.

Etzioni, Amitai, 1993. *The Spirit of Community: Rights, Responsibilities, and the Communitarian Agenda.* New York: Crown Publishers, Inc.

Fowler, Robert Booth, 1991. *The Dance with Community: The Contemporary Debate in American Political Thought.* Lawrence: University Press of Kansas.

Hauerwas, Stanley, 1981. *A Community of Character: Toward a Constructive Christian Social Ethic.* Notre Dame: University of Notre Dame Press.

Heilbroner, Robert L., 1974. *An Inquiry into the Human Prospect.* New York: Norton.

MacIntyre, Alasdair, 1981. *After Virtue: A Study in Moral Theory.* Notre Dame: University of Notre Dame Press.

McWilliams, Wilson Carey, 1974. *The Idea of Fraternity in America.* Berkeley: University of California Press.

Pocock, J. G. A., 1975. *The Machiavellian Moment: Florentine Political Thought and the Atlantic Republican Tradition.* Princeton, NJ: Princeton University Press.

Norton, David L., 1991. *Democracy and Moral Development.* Berkeley: University of California Press.

Tinder, Glenn, 1980. *Community: Reflections on a Tragic Ideal.* Baton Rouge: Louisiana State University Press.

Wood, Gordon, 1969. *The Creation of the American Republic.* Chapel Hill: University of North Caroliva Press.

The following works represent more direct applications of communitarian ideas to public administration theory:

Cooper, Terry L., 1991. *An Ethic of Citizenship for Public Administration.* Englewood Cliffs, NJ: Prentice Hall.

Denhardt, Kathryn and Richard Green, 1984. "A Symposium on Character Ethics in Public Administration." *The International Journal of Public Administration,* vol. 17, no. 12 (December).

Frederickson, H. George and Ralph Clark Chandler, eds., 1984. "Citizenship and Public Administration." *Public Administration Review,* special issue, vol. 44 (March).

McCullough, Thomas E., 1991. *The Moral Imagination in Public Life.* Chatham, NJ: Chatham House Publishers.

Rohr, John A., 1989. *Ethics for Bureaucrats: An Essay on Law and Values.* 2nd ed. Lawrence: University Press of Kansas.

———, 1986. *To Run a Constitution.* Lawrence: University Press of Kansas.

Stivers, Camilla, 1993. *Gender Images in Public Administration: Legitimacy and the Administrative State.* Newbury Park, CA: Sage Publications.

Wamsley, Gary L., Robert N. Bacher, Charles T. Goodsell, Philip S. Kronenberg, John A. Rohr, Camilla Stivers, Orion F. White, and James F. Wolf, 1990. *Refounding Public Administration.* Newbury Park, CA: Sage Publications.

Wright, N. Dale, ed., 1988. *Papers on the Ethics of Administration.* Albany, NY: State University of New York Press.

COMMUNITY CONTROL.

The exercise of authority by the democratically organized government of a neighborhood-sized jurisdiction, according to Alan Altshuler, who wrote the classic work on the subject in 1970. His study analyzed the demand from African Americans for greater participation in city governance during the 1960s. Community activists have called for neighborhood self-determination as a means to redressing urban inequities. Neighborhoods in large U.S. cities excercise a variety of levels of authority, ranging from being part of the formal government structure to facilitating communication between neighborhood residents and city government.

Origin and Subsequent History

The idea of neighborhood governance has existed since the 1930s. The development of neighborhood or community-based governance went through an intense growth phase during the Model Cities program. In the 1970s, those community organizations that had developed workable structures and processes were strengthened by the Community Development Block Grant, but many declined with reduced incentives and fiscal support.

Community control of schools was attempted in New York City in 1967 in response to the demands of the city's

African American community. Three small districts were carved out of the citywide system, each with its board of neighborhood trustees. A labor dispute led to intervention by the state legislature, and the project was replaced by a citywide division into 31 areas, each with a local board that took citizen complaints but had no authority. In 1975, New York City revised its charter to create 59 community boards with advisory responsibility for local budget priorities, land use planning, and service monitoring. Washington, D.C., is the only other American city in which neighborhood structures are a formal part of city government.

While neighborhood empowerment was seen as an important component of urban revitalization efforts in the 1960s and 1970s, a retrenchment occurred in the 1980s that favored expert preferences, and neighborhood rebuilding rather than conservation. The national neighborhood movement is ideologically divided over the issue of self-reliance versus larger social structure change, and over the issue of whether neighborhood preservation leads to segregation.

In the 1980s, a new form of the community control spirit emerged under the acronym NIMBY (Not in My Back Yard). So-called NIMBY groups claim the right to prevent facilities they perceive as undesirable from being located in or near their communities, facilities ranging from hazardous or nuclear waste disposal sites to group homes for the disabled. NIMBY groups have prevented hundreds if not thousands of facilities from being constructed, and their potential strength has led to a crisis in finding new sites for many types of needed facilities, such as solid waste landfills. NIMBY groups tend to be middle class. Low-income areas, which tend to be less organized, have been found to bear a disproportionate burden of undesirable facilities.

Underlying Theoretical Framework

Altshuler traced the African American demand for greater participation in American city governance to several long-standing features of American politics, thought, and society. These included a high value on citizen participation, the long exlusion of African Americans from full membership in U.S. society, the persistence of ethnicity as a vital distinction in U.S. society, the preference for decentralized government, and an unwillingness to forego representation in dealing with public bureaucracies.

The value placed on citizen participation is evident in the historic expansion of various groups' rights to participate in government. Jacksonian democracy and Progressive reform in the United States, the French Revolution, and periodic unrest in Great Britain during the nineteenth and early twentieth centuries exemplified this trend. The civil rights movement of the 1960s witnessed a shift from seeking integration to seeking equality of power and in-

come as well as law. Community control was seen as a means to develop a political power base. Decentralization has been preferred on both the grounds that government should be close to the people, but also as a means for ethnic groups to achieve localized self-rule as minorities in the larger national system. Altshuler also cited studies showing U.S. Citizens, far more than citizens of other nations, prefer indirect political strategies (intervention by party or interest group representatives) to self-help legalistic strategies in dealing with bureaucracies. The demand for community control for urban African Americans, therefore, was understandable as an effort to shrink the political subunit to a scale where they might a gain a majority, and to decentralize authority for administrative decisions to that level.

There are several arguments in favor of community control. Neighborhood governance allows public services to be tailored to fit the needs of the neighborhood. It encourages more people to participate in governance, because they are not as intimidated by the distance to city hall or the size of the municipal bureaucracy. Residents have more direct control over neighborhood services, and those who feel that their needs are not met by the city-wide government because of prejudice benefit from a smaller political arena in which they might become the majority.

There is opposition to the idea of community control. Some object to what they see as more fragmentation of already divided metropolitan areas. Fragmentation could lead neighborhood governments to neglect the effects of their decisions on adjacent neighborhoods or the city as a whole, and might exacerbate racial and ethnic segregation. Low voting turnout might worsen if voters are asked to pay attention to even more candidates for public office. Finally, if neighborhood governments are required to be self-financing, poorer neighborhoods may have difficulties.

Frederickson (1973) argued that neighborhood control, to be effective in addressing urban problems, is separate from and should be combined with administrative decentralization and citizen participation. He contrasted the presumed values that each maximizes with some of their observed characteristics. His policy solution is to create a federated system of neighborhoods that enjoys the power and resources of the central municpal government and enables the necessary flexibility, equity, and excellence.

The idea of community control, like citizen participation in planning, is in tension with professional expertise. Planners and administrators are often concerned that neighborhood organizations, activists, and residents will fail to consider the broader view, the longer time range, and scientifically determined costs, benefits, and risks. Professionals are often reluctant to lose control of the decisionmaking process and its outcome, and a body of literature is available to assist them in surviving, designing, and even manipulating participation processes to achieve desire outcomes. Another school of thought calls on planners to welcome and nurture community-based initiatives, and in some instances to become advocates for underrepresented interests (White, 1991).

For specific programs and services, there is little doubt that neighborhood residents have experience and expertise needed for success. Block watch and neighborhood revitalization programs are very dependent on the meaningful involvement of area residents in needs assessment and service delivery. Neighborhood organizations help municipal officials by providing a focus for communication. Unorganized neighborhoods are at a disadvantage. Under fiscal constraints, municipal governments have reason to seek citizen assistance in meeting public needs.

Current Practice in the United States

Few cities have neighborhoods with formal powers, although there are thousands of neighborhood organizations in the United States. A large number of cities have neighborhood councils with some powers, little city halls, and neighborhood advisory boards. Neighborhood powers may involve whole or partial control over one or more services and programs. Generally, the more services and programs addressed by neighborhood governance, the less authority held by the neighborhood council. Little city halls may be branches of the mayor's office that administer some routine services and provide a neighborhood forum. Neighborhood advisory boards may also serve as a forum for residents, advising city officials on neighborhood issues and needs. Neighborhoods in Cincinnati, Ohio, and St. Paul, Minnesota, enjoy strong advisory capabilities to those city governments.

Portland, Oregon, and Pittsburgh, Pennsylvania, are among several cities that have citywide associations of neighborhoods that are formally recognized and supported by city staff. Other cities allow neighborhood organizations to influence city expenditures. The effectiveness of neighborhood organizations is often associated with the socioeconomic level of the residents.

A recent trend is for large cities to develop programs to accommodate neighborhood-based initiatives. Minneapolis, Minnesota, intends to restructure city departments, strategies, budgets, and policies around neighborhood-initiated action plans. Phoenix, Arizona, is also responding to self-organized neighborhoods as they develop, rather than determining boundaries to cover the entire city.

Variations in States, Regions, Cultures

Community control or influence does not vary by state or region, but rather by the unique circumstances of typically large cities' politics and needs. Neighborhood organizations

do vary in terms of their complexity, and have appeared to go through a life cycle similar to other organizations.

Variations in Regimes

In the more centralized welfare states of Western Europe, the movement for community countrol has been a grassroots strategy of the left, growing and succeeding when alliances overcame divisions among and between labor, students, and other groups. Experiments with various aspects of neighborhood control of housing, childcare, and open spaces have occurred over the years in London, Copenhagen, Brussels, and other cities. Rather than decentralize municipal government in response to citizen demand, these cities have often set up elaborate forms for citizen review of urban redevelopment and yet rarely have they accommodated changes in response to citizen demand.

In Israel, decentralized planning was incorporated into a five-year neighborhood rehabilitation project, primarily to gain citizen cooperation. In Tokyo, neighborhood service organizations called *chonokai* are semi-official and provide a variety of local services and a conduit for information between residents and large official jurisdictions.

Short of community control, neighborhood influence in municipal government varies in terms of formalization, whether it is general purpose or single purpose, and often depends upon the specific neighborhood's resources and abilities.

LISA S. NELSON

BIBLIOGRAPHY

Altshuler, Alan, 1970. *Community Control: The Black Demand for Participation in Large American Cities.* New York: Pegasus.
Frederickson, George, 1973. *Neighborhood Control in the 1970s.* New York: Chandler.
Nice, David, 1987. *Federalism: The Politics of Intergovernmental Relations.* New York: St. Martin's Press.
Silver, Christopher, 1985. "Neighborhood Planning in Historical Perspective." *Journal of the American Planning Association* 51 (Spring):161–174.
Simpson, Dick and Ann Gentile. 1986. "Effective Neighborhood Government." *Social Policy* 16:4 (Spring):25–30.
Susskind, Lawrence, Michael Elliott and Associates, 1983. *Paternalism, Conflict, and Coproduction.* New York: Plenum Press.
White, Jay D. 1991. "From Modernity to Postmodernity: Book Review." *Public Administration Review* 51:6 (November): 564–568.

COMMUNITY FOUNDATIONS. Legally independent, endowed public charities that receive donations from individuals, families, and businesses, and use them to benefit their community or region. The endowment is created from the gifts of many donors. These gifts are then pooled and invested. The interest (and sometimes the capital) is used to make grants for charitable purposes to nonprofit organizations, individuals, and governments. In 1992 there were approximately 350 community foundations that held $8.7 billion in assets and gave $638 million in grants and related expenditures.

The first community foundation was created as a community trust in Cleveland in 1914. Frederick H. Goff, president of the Cleveland Trust Company, conceived the idea for a combined fund that would aggregate the small gifts of many people to benefit the city of Cleveland. The major attraction of the community trust concept was that it was flexible enough to meet the needs that could not be anticipated when the donor gave his or her gift. Unlike the hundreds of private trusts languishing in banks and lawyers' offices, the community trust has a distribution committee to ensure that the funds continue to be disbursed for the community's benefit.

By the end of 1915 community trusts were formed in Chicago, Detroit, Minneapolis, St. Louis, Milwaukee, Boston, and Los Angeles. By 1924 there were 26 community trusts, half in the Midwest. Unlike the pattern for private foundations, the growth rate of community foundations did not accelerate until the 1970s and 1980s, when they became the fastest growing segment of the foundation field.

Community foundations are governed by distribution committees that include individuals appointed by trustee banks, elected officials and leaders of community organizations. Most community foundations employ staff to manage the grantmaking, operating programs, and development functions. Endowment investments are managed by banks and investment advisors.

Donors to community foundations have a variety of options. They may make a gift to the general fund or designate a field of interest such as the arts or healthcare. Under certain conditions a donor may name a fund and indicate the types of causes or organizations that the fund should support. Classified as public charities, 501(c)(3) organizations under the U.S. tax code, community foundations are exempt from taxes, and donations to them are eligible for the maximum charitable tax deduction, up to 50 percent of adjusted gross income.

As the private foundations, community foundations may play many roles in a community, region, or state. They can invest in planning and problem solving for their areas. Since they are not political entities, they are able to bring together community leaders to help explore and resolve local issues. Cities as large as New York City (The New York Community Trust with over $1 billion in assets) and as small as Flint, Michigan (Community Foundation of Greater Flint with assets of $34 million) have community foundations to serve their citizens.

As the concept of civil society takes root around the globe, community foundations are increasingly viewed as beneficial instruments of philanthropy and citizen participation. Community foundations have been created in Puerto Rico, the United Kingdom, Latin America, Portugal and elsewhere. See **foundations**.

ELIZABETH T. BORIS

BIBLIOGRAPHY

Hall, Peter Dobkin, 1989. "The Community Foundation in America, 1914–1987." In Richard Magat, ed., *Philanthropic Giving: Studies in Varieties and Goals*. New York: Oxford University Press, pp. 180–199.

Renz, Loren and Steven Lawrence, 1994. *Foundation Giving: Yearbook of Facts and Figures on Private, Corporate and Community Foundations*. New York: The Foundation Center.

COMMUNITY POLICING.

A philosophy and an organizational strategy based on a set of values emphasizing problem-solving partnerships between people and their police. It is based on the premise that both the police and the community must work together to identify, prioritize, and solve crime problems, toward the goal of improving the overall quality of life in the community.

Origin and Subsequent History

Community policing evolved from the social and political crises of the 1960s. The police were plunged into the center of the civil rights movement, urban riots, protests against the war in Vietnam, and a rising incidence of crime and drug use. As citizens and police officials alike watched the scenario of societal unrest unfolding, probing questions were raised about the apparent inability of the police to prevent—or at least control—such massive outbreaks. The situation called for decisive action and led to the formation of a number of commissions to examine the events surrounding the disorder and to develop recommendations for improving police operations.

Responding to rising public concern about crime, President Lyndon Johnson appointed the President's Commission on Law Enforcement and Administration of Justice in 1965. In 1967 the Commission published a report entitled *The Challenge of Crime in a Free Society*. The report called for the upgrading of police personnel through selection and training and specifically recommended that the police establish a better dialogue with the community and attempt to be more responsive to community needs.

The National Advisory Commission on Civil Disorders (Kerner Commission) was created after a nationwide series of riots in 1967. Its final report, published in 1968, included chapters on the role of police in the ghetto and police-community relations. The report found hostility between police and ghetto dwellers to be a primary cause of the disorders that raged across the United States between 1964 and 1968. The report concluded that traditional police tactics such as frequent stops and frisks often proved abrasive and aggravated community relations. The patrol car, meanwhile, removed officers from the street and alienated the police from residents.

While the commission reports of 1967 and 1968 were vital in drawing attention to the deficiencies in policing strategies and operations, the catalyst for change was the passage of the Omnibus Crime Control and Safe Streets Act of 1968. This marked the first time the federal government provided assistance for local criminal justice services. Although broad in its application, the act provided for extensive research that would challenge traditional policing assumptions and ultimately create the research base upon which community policing would be constructed.

The Research Base

The initial focal point of research was the value of the standard operating procedures that were an integral part of the professional policing model. These procedures evolved from several assumptions. A high value was attached to maximizing the number of police officers assigned to motorized patrol in the belief that random patrol was an efficient strategy for preventing crime. High priority was accorded to rapid response to calls for police service in the belief that speed was necessary to apprehend criminals and to assure citizens of the omnipresence of their first line of defense against criminal predators. Similarly, detective operations were organized so that all reports of crimes were followed up, in the belief this would contribute to their solution and thereby add to the atmosphere of deterrence the police were committed to creating.

Foremost among research studies conducted was the 1972 Kansas City Preventive Patrol Experiment sponsored by the Police Foundation. Three controlled levels of police presence were employed. One area received no preventive patrol, another area experienced twofold and threefold increases in police patrol presence, and a third area received the normal level of preventive patrols. In its final analysis of findings, published in 1974, the Foundation reported no significant differences in the level of crime, attitudes toward police services, fear of crime, police response time, or satisfaction with response time.

Other studies raised questions about the value of standardized operating procedures in which the professional model had placed great faith. A 1975 study by Peter Greenwood, under the auspices of the Rand Corporation, shattered traditional views about detectives. It found that follow-up investigations were frequently unproductive, in that most crimes were solved through information obtained by uniformed officers who were the first to arrive at the crime scene. A key source of information about crimi-

nal suspects was the public. A 1978 study sponsored by the Department of Justice disclosed that few calls to the police involved crimes in progress and, further, that most crime victims did not call the police immediately; victims often sought assistance and comfort from friends or relatives before calling the police.

The Flint Experiment

The developments, new insights, and research findings of the 1970s accelerated the growing awareness of the limitations of the traditional model of policing and stimulated experimentation with new approaches to reducing crime and improving police-community liaisons. In 1979 under the sponsorship of the Charles Stewart Mott Foundation and the evaluative stewardship of Robert Trojanowicz of Michigan State University, the Neighborhood Foot Patrol Program (NFPP) was launched in Flint, Michigan. The Mott Foundation provided a $2.6 million, three-year grant to put 22 foot patrol officers into base stations (many in schools) within 14 neighborhoods that contained 20 percent of the city's total population. The program was designed to alleviate three longstanding problems: (1) lack of citizen involvement in crime prevention, (2) depersonalization of interactions between officers and residents, and (3) lack of comprehensive neighborhood organizations and services. Among the program's ten basic goals were the decrease of crime and the enhancement of community awareness of crime problems and crime prevention strategies. The NFPP officers provided full law enforcement services as well as social service referrals.

In 1982 Trojanowicz and his associates conducted a three-year evaluation of the program. Highlights of the findings were that targeted crimes decreased almost 9 percent, citizens felt safer, crime reporting by citizens increased, and citizens saw foot patrol officers as more effective than motorized patrol officers in preventing crime and working with juveniles. Although the foot patrol experiment in Flint was ultimately disbanded in its original form due to extraordinary economic and political circumstances, the foot patrol effort in Flint was a remarkable success.

An important finding from the Flint experiment was that fear reduction was linked to the order maintenance activities of foot patrol officers. Subsequent experimentation in other cities, such as Newark, disclosed that tactics other than foot patrol that, like foot patrol, emphasized increasing the quantity and improving the quality of police-citizen interactions had outcomes similar to those of foot patrol, for example, fear reduction. The findings of foot patrol and fear reduction experiments, when coupled with the research on the relationship between fear and disorder, created new opportunities for police to understand the increasing concerns of citizens' groups about disorder and to work with citizens to effect solutions to crime problems.

Problem-Oriented Policing: Newport News, Virginia

Based on the concept of problem solving, as propounded by Herman Goldstein (1990), experimentation with alternate means of police responses to community problems evolved. Following a pilot test of the concept, the National Institute of Justice funded the Problem-Oriented Policing (POP) Program in Newport News, Virginia, during the mid-1980s.

The Newport News program was unique in that from the outset the objective was to make problem solving the focus of the daily operation of the entire agency. The department concentrated upon three major community problems: burglaries in a low-income, government-subsidized housing project; thefts from automobiles parked in downtown parking lots; and robberies related to prostitution in the downtown area. Additionally, it addressed chronic problems such as disturbances at convenience stores, drug dealing at specific locations, and robberies in the central business district.

In each case, the particular problem was solved not simply by solving the crimes and arresting perpetrators, nor by increasing levels of patrol (though both were done), but also by thoroughly analyzing the immediate conditions that were contributing to the offenses. The problem-solving approach viewed police incidents as symptoms of underlying problems, the resolution of which required disaggregating problems to identify their components in order to fashion a customized, effective response. Systematic inquiry into problems was a joint venture of the police and concerned community members.

The Development of Community Policing in Houston

Programs and experiments such as those implemented in the cities of Flint, Newark, and Newport News demonstrated that the community could be an important partner in dealing with the problems of crime, fear, and drugs, and that to build a partnership with the community the police had to find more effective ways of interacting with the community and responding to their needs. The experimental programs also revealed the realities of trying to operate community-focused programs within the context of organizations with administrative systems and managerial styles designed for traditional policing.

Upon the appointment of Lee P. Brown as police chief in 1982, the Houston, Texas, Police Department adopted a set of values that emphasized problem solving and collaboration with the community. Through a period of five years Houston steadily implemented changes designed to provide the public wih greater access to participation in policing efforts. Principal program elements included: (1) a police community newsletter, (2) a citizen contact program that kept the same officers patrolling the same beats to facilitate individual contacts with citizens in the area, (3) follow-up contacts with victims of crime in the days following their victimization to reassure them of a police presence, and (4) a police community contact center within which a truancy reduction and park program operated. Additionally, the department reconfigured its patrol beats to reflect natural neighborhood boundaries.

At the end of the five-year evolutionary period, the police department completed an organizational transition to become fully involved in a partnership with the community. Pursuant to this commitment, the department effected sweeping changes in its policing style to implement a fully interactive process between the police and the community to mutually identify and resolve community problems. The elements of this process, which embodied the essence of community policing, included the following: (1) an orientation toward problem solving and empowerment of beat officers to initiate creative responses to problems, (2) accountability to the community for crime control and prevention activities, (3) decentralization of organizational authority and structure, (4) responsibility for decisionmaking shared by the police and the community, (5) permanent beat assignments for officers, and (6) revised training and personnel evaluation practices to reflect a community policing orientation. Thus the Houston experiment represented an initial comprehensive program of community policing fully functioning within a major urban environment.

Underlying Theoretical Framework

Comprehensive research in this area has disclosed that community policing is based primarily on two social science themes: normative sponsorship theory and critical social theory. Normative sponsorship theory declares most people are of good will and willing to cooperate with others to satisfy their needs. It proposes that a community effort will only be sponsored if it is normative (within the limits of established standards) to all persons and interest groups involved. For a community to unite and actively support a program of community policing, the major groups in the community must agree that a project is worthy of undertaking in the context of their attitudes, values, norms, and goals. Robert Trojanowicz and Bonnie Bucqueroux (1994) cited the "Big Six" groups—police department, general community, businesses, civic officials, media, and public and nonprofit agencies—that must be identified and must work together to ensure the success of community policing efforts.

The community policing officer assumes a key leadership role in stimulating community groups to implement community policing. This frequently involves substantial information gathering, as the community policing officer must be prepared to inform the citizenry fully on the subject of local crime in order to encourage the formation of coalitions with shared social values to control and prevent criminality.

Critical social theory focuses on the process of community members coalescing to analyze the obstacles that prevent fulfillment of their needs, for example, public safety. The theory involves critically analyzing the problems of the community so that the citizens and community policing officers can be enlightened, and then empowered, and ultimately emancipated to become fully functional in working together to solve problems. Again, the community policing officer is the catalyst who brings together the community groups to engage in communication that will lead to some concensus of accepted action that will be implemented by the police-citizen partnership.

Problem-Solving Approach

A most important aspect of the community policing philosophy that derives from critical social theory is problem solving. In addition to the concept of formation of a partnership between the police and community, problem solving is the essence of community policing. After the partnership identifies and prioritizes problems, the next crucial step is problem resolution.

Herman Goldstein, in his classic textbook *Problem-Oriented Policing* (1990), identified the fundamental elements in orienting policing to a problem-solving perspective. Goldstein recognized that incidents requiring police response were often merely overt symptoms of underlying problems. Thus it is essential that relationships between incidents—for example, similarities in criminal behavior, location, involved persons—be recognized as well as conditions and factors that give rise to them. Examples of such substantive problems include chronic assemblages of disorderly persons in public parks, or recurring purse snatches at specific bus stops. Such problems are disaggregated systematically in the problem-solving approach in order to provide for effective, customized responses to discrete problems. This problem-solving policing is information intensive, requiring historical records and usable databases to facilitate careful and systematic inquiry.

Under the auspices of the Police Executive Research Forum, a national research association of police executives, John Eck and William Spelman (1987) developed a problem-solving methodology, the SARA Model, as a guide to problem solving. The SARA Model consists of four steps: (1) "scanning" to identify a problem, (2) "analysis" of the problem, (3) "response" in the form of a customized strategy, and (4) "assessment" to monitor the success of the response.

"Broken Windows" Concept

Discussion of the theoretical basis of community policing must include the contribution of James Q. Wilson and George L. Kelling, whose groundbreaking essay on the "broken windows" concept, published in the *Atlantic Monthly* (March 1982), revealed the extent to which daily incivilities disrupted neighborhoods. The point of the essay was that just as unrepaired windows signal to people that nobody cares about a building and lead to serious vandalism, untended disorderly behavior can also signal that nobody cares about the community and can lead to serious disorder and crime.

"Broken windows" gave voice to sentiments felt both by citizens and police. Police had believed that they should deal with serious crime yet were frustrated by lack of success. While citizens recognized serious crime was a problem, they were more concerned about daily incivilities such as youth gangs, drunks, and drug transactions occurring on neighborhood street corners. The notion of mobilizing community members to eliminate the environmental conditions that attract undesirable persons and in which crime breeds served the dual purpose of alleviating residents' nagging uneasiness while at the same time enabling police to gain footholds for halting the progression of criminal offenses, such as entrenched drug dealing and prostitution from abandoned houses and vehicles.

Current Applications in the United States

In its application, community policing encompasses as many variations as there are problems. As pointed out by Wesley Skogan in his 1992 cross-site analysis of community policing (award 92-IJ-CX-0008 from the National Institute of Justice), American police departments, under the rubric of community policing, are opening small neighborhood substations, conducting surveys to identify local problems, organizing meetings and crime prevention seminars, publishing newsletters, helping form Neighborhood Watch groups, establishing advisory panels to inform police commanders, organizing youth activities, conducting drug education projects and media campaigns, patrolling on horses and bicycles, and working with municipal agencies to enforce health and safety regulations.

Community policing has a variety of organizational styles in the United States. A survey of three cities' strategies points out the differing configurations.

New York City

The nation's largest city, with the largest police force, is committed to community policing as its prevailing operational and managerial philosophy. The New York City model was accomplished by establishing a separate community policing unit within each of its 75 precincts, while employing traditional strategies as the primary method of patrol. Thus, the Community Patrol Officer Program (CPOP) exists as a subset within the police department.

Under the CPOP model, specialists officers are given problem-solving "ownership" of specific areas within the city, usually employing foot patrol as their primary patrol method. The program involves more than 800 police officers, 75 sergeants, and 75 administrative aides. The beat officers solicit input from the residents and merchants in their beats in setting patrol priorities and in formulating solutions to neighborhood problems. The community police officers embody the law enforcement activities of traditional foot patrol officers, the outreach and coordinating activities of the community relations officer, and the tactical implementation activities of the police planner.

Madison, Wisconsin

The Madison, Wisconsin, Police Department community policing program is administered by a team of officers who are assigned to the "Experimental Police District" (EPD), a geographic region comprising one-sixth of the city. The EPD officers devise strategies for communicating with citizens, learning citizens' views on problems, and working with citizens to solve problems. The EPD provides three police functions: neighborhood foot patrol, motorized patrol and traffic services, and follow-up investigation services.

Community policing within the Madison Police Department evolved from a previous departmentwide commitment to the principles of "Quality Management." This management philosophy emphasizes the role of managers as facilitators, whose job is to improve systems, involve employees in decisionmaking, employ data-based problem-solving approaches, promote teamwork, encourage risk taking and creativity, and give and receive feedback from employees. Additionally, employees are viewed as internal customers and community members are viewed as citizen customers. Decentralization of department operations facilitates delivery of services to citizens. Madison was one of the first agencies to assert that there must be an internal foundation for the successful application of community policing.

Community policing efforts in Madison continue to evolve as successful organizational and community change occurs. Additional experimental districts will be added to bring the entire department gradually into the community policing philosophy.

Tempe, Arizona

The Tempe, Arizona, Police Department attained citywide implementation of community policing over a period of four years, beginning in November 1990 when the department received a Bureau of Justice Assistance grant for testing Innovative Neighborhood-Oriented Policing (INOP) in one of its beats. Contrasted with New York City and Madison, the Tempe INOP experience represents a successful, rapid implementation of community policing in a relatively small metropolitan police agency.

Problem solving is a significant part of the Tempe program, in fact, to the extent that the majority of the department's 15 beat teams intentionally established substations in locations identified as having crime and disorder problems. Additionally, the department formed problem resolution teams to address internal concerns related to deployment and communications and formed a crime-free multihousing pilot team to reduce the level of crime in multihousing structures through combined efforts of police and building managers.

Current International Applications

Community policing is a policing philosophy and strategy employed internationally. Its attributes are ubiquitous throughout the world. For purposes of comparison, three countries' styles of community policing are examined here.

Canada

In adopting community policing, Canadian police actually returned to their roots, the nineteenth century London model pioneered by the renowned Sir Robert Peel. The Canadian police had experimented with the professional model—reactive, motorized patrol—during the past few decades, but never really adopted it to the extent their U.S. counterparts had. The vast majority of Canada's police services accept community policing as the appropriate approach to their responsibilities for crime and order maintenance. Indeed, the Royal Canadian Mounted Police, the largest police force in Canada, contends that as a police force serving a predominantly rural and small town constituency, it has always been performing community policing.

At the municipal level, a number of police departments feature the central components of community policing. The Montreal Police Department has established storefront offices as well as a program for officers to visit all residences to establish positive community relations. The Toronto Police Department features community-based ministations and active participation by citizens in identifying local crime problems. The Edmonton Police Service features extensive foot patrols working out of storefronts strategically located in "hot spots" and a focused program of community involvement in problem solving.

England

Trevor Bennett (in Rosenbaum, 1994) describes developments in England. The shift toward community policing was an action in furtherance of restoring public confidence in the police, which had plummeted steadily in the years following the 1981 riots in Brixton, London. According to Bennett, however, the community policing philosophy has not become fully integrated into police thinking and beliefs, though it has been widely and publicly proclaimed as a central principle of policing in England.

The main development toward decentralization, a hallmark of community policing, has been sector policing. While this resulted in police command units small enough to provide a local police service, the restructuring of forces to enhance individual autonomy was only partially accomplished.

Community contact programs include foot patrols, police shops (substations), and Neighborhood Watch programs. The contribution of the community to crime prevention and problem solving is accomplished through consultations whereby they identify problems and provide the police with information that might assist them in their resolution, rather than engaging in joint actions with the police. The full potential of community policing has not yet been realized, and, as mentioned, its realization requires increased attention in the areas of the police culture and community liaisons.

Israel

Community policing in Israel is conducted through the Neighborhood Police Officer (NPO) program. According to Robert Friedmann (1992), "the NPO is a veteran police officer on patrol duties on the way to becoming a proactive police representative (an Israeli version of a mix between 'storefront' and foot patrol officer) who functions both as a law enforcer and order-maintaining official." The NPOs operate departmentwide and concentrate on public education, crime prevention, activation of volunteers, organization of community events, and searching for solutions to neighborhood problems.

Community policing is viewed as flexible in that it adapts to changing community needs and characteristics. It is by and large a police-controlled operation. The NPOs serve the mission of fortifying the community base the Israeli police already have. The NPOs operate under a centralized police structure, though they are rather autonomous. As pointed out by Friedmann, what is so interesting about the Israeli approach to community policing is that police are directing attention to the needs of the individual citizen in a country where for many years the citizens were expected to contribute their heavy share to the benefit of the collective.

MICHAEL K. HOOPER

BIBLIOGRAPHY

Eck, John E. and William Spelman, 1987. *Problem-Solving: Problem-Oriented Policing in Newport News.* Washington, D.C.: Police Executive Research Forum.
Friedmann, Robert R., 1992. *Community Policing: Comparative Perspectives and Prospects.* New York: St. Martin's Press.
Goldstein, Herman, 1990. *Problem-Oriented Policing.* Philadelphia, PA: Temple University Press.
Green, Jack R. and Stephen D. Mastrofski, eds., 1988. *Community Policing: Rhetoric or Reality?* New York: Praeger.
McEwen, Tom, 1994. *Evaluation of Community Policing in Tempe, Arizona.* Alexandria, VA: Institute for Law and Justice.
Moore, Mark H., *et al.*, 1988–1993. *Perspectives on Policing*, vols. 1–17. Washington, D.C.: National Institute of Justice and John F. Kennedy School of Government, Harvard University.
Rosenbaum, Dennis P., ed., 1994. *The Challenge of Community Policing: Testing the Promises.* Thousand Oaks, CA: Sage.
Sparrow, Malcolm K., Mark H. Moore, and David M. Kennedy, 1990. *Beyond 911: A New Era for Policing.* New York: Basic Books.
Trojanowicz, Robert and Bonnie Bucqueroux, 1990. *Community Policing: A Contemporary Perspective.* Cincinnati, OH: Anderson.
Trojanowicz, Robert and Bonnie Bucqueroux, 1994. *Community Policing: How to Get Started.* Cincinnati, OH: Anderson.
Walker, Samuel, 1992. *The Police in America: An Introduction.* 2nd ed. New York: McGraw-Hill.
Wilson, James Q. and George L. Kelling, 1982. "'Broken Windows': The Police and Neighborhood Safety." *Atlantic Monthly*, vol. 249 (March):29–38.

COMMUNITY POWER. A set of theoretical frameworks and accompanying methodological approaches that seek to comprehend and assess the nature and extent of leadership or influence within a predefined social context; also known by a number of similar terms, including community power analysis and power structure research. Recognition of community power as a discernable characteristic of public policy and administration in the United States stretches back to the turn of the twentieth century. Early muckrakers such as Lincoln Steffens expressed alarm over the disproportionate power exerted by private elites upon national and local community decisionmaking processes. Concerns derived from community power led to the municipal reform movement and related measures during the first several decades of the twentieth century.

From the late 1920s through the 1940s, the work of sociologists such as Robert and Helen Lynd and W. Lloyd Warner maintained an emphasis on the consideration of power relations within the framework of community studies. Not until the 1953 appearance of *Community Power Structure* by a disaffected social worker named Floyd Hunter was community power formally established as a distinct research area deserving of social scientific inquiry. Publication of C. Wright Mills's *The Power Elite* in 1956 and *Who Governs?* by Robert Dahl in 1961 not only provided a solid foundation for the new field, but set the stage for theoretical and methodological controversies that have become the hallmark of the subsequent literature.

Since the 1950s, a substantial number of community activists, organizations, social movements, and interest groups as well as academic social scientists have either conducted community power research, or utilized information gathered from such research. Knowledge of the dynamics of community power may assist citizens and various constituencies to better understand the decisionmaking process and the resultant policy outcomes. Such information may facilitate segments of the population becoming more involved in community affairs or local government. Public administrators and policymakers may also be able to deploy resources more effectively or otherwise become more proficient in the performance of their duties.

Power and Community

Various sources have defined power in a number of ways. A social dimension is requisite to an understanding of the fashion in which power operates. Exertion of influence on others may involve skillful persuasion or require the exercise of leadership. The ability to shape the decisionmaking process or influence its outcomes, as well as the authority to execute decisions, have also been described as attributes of power.

Community may be understood as any definable aggregation of individuals, interpersonal dynamics, or social structures, including cultural, political, or economic relations. Communities may be formal or informal, simple or complex, characterized by close personal ties or by highly codified bureaucratic relations. The community consequently provides the essential context for power; the locus of community power is the nature and extent to which power is exercised within a given community.

Orientations and Models

Community power researchers have predominantly been concerned with the national level or case studies of specific municipalities. The publication of the three landmark works by Hunter, Mills, and Dahl quickly established two camps into which most community power studies fall. The elite approach, as outlined by Mills, has primarily been associated with sociological researchers.

Elite theorists tend to view power as being held or exercised by a comparatively small and relatively cohesive group of individuals. Whereas the early work of the Lynds found a single family that dominated a local community decisionmaking process, Hunter and Mills depicted a circle of leaders or "power brokers" who played a central role. Mills described an interlocking triangle composed of business, civilian government, and military leaders who effectively controlled the policy process at the national level.

The rival camp, adhering to a pluralist perspective, is composed largely of political scientists. Some pluralists have held that power is diffused to such an extent that delineated lines of authority are not readily distinguishable. Others have argued that different sets of actors who largely do not overlap comprise leadership in diverse areas. Rather than a single identifiable elite, individuals or groups within a community may exert influence over fairly distinct policy concerns.

Elite theory has for the most part relied upon two methodological lines of investigation: assessment of the reputations of purported community leaders, or conversely, description of the positions that comprise the power structure. The reputational method involves identification of all persons within a community purported to wield power. A roster of knowledgeable experts is asked to rank these, and finally, to determine which are the most prominent.

The positional strategy seeks to identify which institutions or associations within a community may be the most powerful. Amongst those groupings, the most important positions are then identified. Finally, overlapping links between the positions within different organizations are established, providing the basis for the identification of an elite.

A decisional approach was created under the auspices of pluralism in which key decisions were seen as providing the basis for assessing the existence or strength of community influentials. The deployment of this strategy depends upon the identification of important community decisions. Several criteria have been articulated to ascertain the relative importance of decisions, including the number of people affected by the outcome, the types and amounts of the resources that may be distributed, and the fashion in which the outcome may offset preexisting patterns of distribution.

Theorists associated with the Marxist class analysis perspective have also engaged in community power research. A stratification variant of Marxist methodology may be considered as a form of elite theory, in which efforts are made to identify and describe a coherent elite organized around the ownership and operation of major economic institutions as a social class. A more conventionally class-based outlook argues it only makes sense to define a ruling class in opposition to the working classes. This approach contends that since Marxism is inherently a conflict model, the description of a socioeconomic elite in static terms constitutes an academic exercise.

New Developments

All of the models and orientations discussed above have been criticized, frequently by each other, for various deficiencies and shortcomings. The reputational methodology has been critiqued for a lack of empirical rigor, with its assumptions resting upon the assumptions of the researcher and the validation of experts nominated by that researcher. The positional strategy has been criticized for seeking to find a coherent elite where none may in fact exist. The decisional methodology has conversely been attacked for a failure to take into account the means by which elites may set and manipulate the policy agenda. The Marxist stratification approach has shared in the criticisms directed at elite theory. The conventional Marxist approach has functioned more to critique static interpretations of power structure rather than to contribute substantial new findings from a class-based perspective.

Since the 1960s, a number of advances in community power have begun to point the way beyond the elitist-pluralist divide. Sociologists Harvey Molotch and John Logan formulated a "growth machine" model, based on a common interest in the development and use of land as the core of a local power structure. From this standpoint, the principal role of local government is to promote growth. Political scientist Clarence Stone and others have elaborated a "regime theory" that seeks to incorporate change and examine power relations over a span of time. Regimes are seen as the product of coalitions that form in response to crises and opportunities.

Conclusion

Community power has enjoyed a renaissance in the last decades of the twentieth century. New models have emerged that promise greater sophistication in understanding the forms power takes in a community setting, and which may in turn contribute to an improved comprehension of decisionmaking, public policy, and administrative processes. Researchers in the mid-1970s expressed concern over the cynicism they observed as a result of the sense of powerlessness communicated by community power studies. Renewed interest in community power suggests the possibility that improved models and enhanced analysis may link to expanded opportunities for civic involvement on the part of all citizens.

JAY D. JURIE

BIBLIOGRAPHY

Dahl, Robert A., 1961. *Who Governs?* New Haven: Yale.
Hawley, Willis D. and Frederick M. Wirt, eds., 1968. *The Search for Community Power.* Englewood Cliffs, NJ: Prentice-Hall.
Hunter, Floyd, 1953. *Community Power Structure: A Study of Decision Makers.* Chapel Hill: The University of North Carolina.
Logan, John R. and Harvey L. Molotch, 1987. *Urban Fortunes: The Political Economy of Place.* Berkeley: University of California.
Mills, C. Wright, 1956. *The Power Elite.* New York: Oxford University.
Stone, Clarence N., 1989. *Regime Politics: Governing Atlanta, 1946–1988.* Lawrence: University Press of Kansas.
Waste, Robert J., ed., 1986. *Community Power: Directions for Future Research.* Beverly Hills: Sage.

COMPARABLE WORTH.

A reform effort to pay different job titles the same based on their value to their employer regardless of the gender predominance of those working in such titles; also called pay equity.

At the heart of comparable worth or pay equity is the fact that jobs traditionally done by women have been systematically undervalued in the marketplace. (By the same logic jobs traditionally held by minorities can be underpaid. This article, however, concentrates on gender salary disparities consistent with the focus of most of the pay equity reform). The net result is that jobs disproportionately held by women are paid less than comparable jobs with the same levels of skills and responsibilities but commonly held by males. This bias against women's work can

be demonstrated and subsequently eliminated by assessing the economic value of different jobs through the use of gender-neutral job evaluation systems. For example, secretarial and janitorial jobs can be compared on dimensions such as the education/training needed, the working conditions, the responsibility involved, and the effort required.

The worldwide diversity in political, social, economic, and labor market systems presents a challenge when writing about pay equity for an international audience. The attempt here is to focus on a common core of procedures that are the key ingredient of this reform in widely diverse political/social/economic settings. This key ingredient is the comparison of occupationally different jobs through the use of job evaluation (see job **analysis and evaluation**). The rare exception to the use of job evaluation to establish comparable worth or pay equity can be seen in Australia's 1972 elimination of the official markdown of female-dominated jobs. In that country, wages were set federally. Because gender disparity was clearly visible in the form of an official federal markdown for traditionally female jobs, pay equity could be approximated by merely deleting this markdown from the relevant policy documents. However, such instances are rare. Job evaluation is the principal ingredient for achieving pay equity in most settings. The emphasis of this article is on the use of gender-neutral job evaluation for creating equitable pay.

Definition of the Problem

Several discriminatory processes contribute to the wage gap between the average full-time working man and woman. Only one is addressed by pay equity: discrimination at the job title level (i.e., equal pay for job content of equal value). Groups of jobs—called job titles or classes—held primarily by women, such as clerical or nursing jobs, have been shown by pay equity studies to be paid less than jobs held primarily by men despite their equal skills, responsibilities, and effort requirements (see **discrimination, gender**).

Pay equity does not address other types of pay discrimination, such as discrimination at the individual level (i.e., unequal pay for equal work). This type of discrimination is illegal under laws that have been passed in many countries. In the United States it is prohibited under the Equal Pay Act of 1963. Nor does pay equity address discrimination at the firm or industry level. It may be that high technology industries are paid more because men predominate there, while service delivery industries are paid less because women predominate there. Likewise public sector institutions or firms may be paid less than those of the private sector because women are much higher proportions of the employees. These distinctions take on added significance in an international context. In countries such as Australia and pre-1990 New Zealand, where salaries are set centrally rather than by each employer, firm- and industry-based wage disparities may be minimized.

Pay equity job evaluation studies seek to differentiate legitimate wage differences from those that are solely a function of the sex of the typical job incumbent. Sometimes salary inequities are so blatant that advocates can simply offer them as evidence without providing job evaluation measures. For instance, a substantial proportion of school districts in the United States pay secretaries and teaching assistants considerably less than the cleaners. In Denver, nurses were found to make less than gardeners. In most cases, however, the process establishing the comparable value of dissimilar job titles from diverse occupational groups involves a complex process of job evaluation. Before we can understand how gender-neutral job evaluation can be used to establish gender-balanced salaries, we need to understand job evaluation's role in a conventional salary setting and how it contributes to gender bias in salaries historically.

Attaching Salaries to Job Content: The Traditional Systems

Most of us have very little understanding of how the salary we earn was established. We work in jobs that had fixed salaries assigned to them before we took them and, with the exception of longevity increments, will continue at the same relative salary for years. Employees and employers alike expect salaries to relate logically to job content including the level of skill, the length of training, and the degree of responsibility. Large employers in industrialized countries generally have systematic, ostensibly objective, institutionalized processes in place to relate the skills and responsibilities to salaries. Presuming that these systems are seen as valid by employees, they can minimize high turnover and/or low morale. Pay equity reform is directed at eliminating gender bias from the processes that link salaries to job content.

Certain assumptions underlie these processes, most notably, that jobs ought to be paid differently, that particular kinds of job content ought to be rewarded more than other job content, and that these kinds of job content, can be accurately measured. As Treiman (1979) notes, the fact that these beliefs are "taken for granted by most of the people professionally concerned with jobs and wages, and indeed probably by most Americans in general, does not make them any less value-laden" (p. 35).

The two primary processes systematically linking job content to salaries are called classification and compensation (see **position classification**). Classification involves the process of collecting job content information about individual positions. Based on common job content these individual positions are grouped into job titles/classes such

as Clerk Typist, Junior Accountant, Driver Messenger. Job titles, in turn, are categorized into job families or occupational groups and appropriate promotional tracks.

For the purposes of pay equity, the main thing to remember about the process of classification is that it collects information on job content and summarizes *job title/ class* content on a class specification. Unlike the position descriptions that define the job content of individual positions, class specifications define the job content that all the positions in a job/title have in common. The class specification is crucial because it is the primary source of job content information used in applying job evaluation systems. Job content not identified on the class specification will be rendered invisible to the job evaluation process and, therefore, will not contribute to salaries.

The second subdivision of the salary setting process, compensation, hierarchically ranks job titles based on a job evaluation process. The most common form of job evaluation used in conjunction with pay equity is point factor job evaluation. Point factor job evaluation identifies common denominator job content components (factors) that are used to compare different job classes. Most point factor systems are composed of nine to twelve factors that include:

> Job Knowledge (education and experience required)
> Managerial Skills (supervision)
> Accountability (responsibility for budgets, reputations, and so forth)
> Impact (range of bureaucratic influence)
> Freedom to Take Action (amount of supervision received)
> Problem Solving (amount of analytical reasoning required)
> Human Relations Skills (communication and interpersonal skills)
> Physical Effort (lifting weights, climbing, and so forth)
> Working Conditions Hazards (chance of injury or harm)
> Working Conditions Environment (exposure to discomfort)

Different systems give these factors different names. "Freedom to Take Action" may be called "Initiative." "Accountability" may be called "Results of Errors." "Problem Solving" may be called "Independent Judgment" or "Complexity/Judgment" or "Mental Demands."

The relative importance of each factor is established through factor weights. The simplest way to understand weights is that some factors get you more points than others. Each factor has steps or levels. The lower steps have fewer points attached to them than the higher steps. The increments between steps may increase as you go up the scale. For instance, if the job requires only a high school degree, it probably would be ranked on the lowest step on the "Education" factor and, thus, be assigned the points associated with that ranking, say, 87 points. If the job requires a postgraduate degree, it probably would be assigned to the highest educational step and be given the points associated with that ranking, say, 264 points.

Factors with more value or weight usually award more points even at lower steps. The increase in points as the steps go up is greater for the heavily weighted factors. In addition, the high value factors tend to have more levels than the factors with low value. Thus, high weight factors frequently account for more than 30 percent of the possible total maximum points. By contrast, low weight factors usually account for less than 5 percent of the total points.

The points assigned to a job title for each of the factors are summed to provide the total number of job worth points for that job title/class. For pay equity purposes this summary number provides the basis for comparing traditionally female jobs with those traditionally held by men. Jobs with comparable total points are considered of comparable worth and, theoretically, should receive equal pay.

Classically, however, job worth points are not directly translated into salaries. In most cases adjustments are made for the "market." Benchmark titles/classes are selected as representative of a particular job series or family. By surveying what other employers pay benchmark titles, the "fair market price" or competitive salary is established. If this salary does not approximate the one suggested by the job evaluation points, the point to pay ratio (the number of dollars paid for each job worth point) may be shifted up or down. This external market adjustment is generalized to all of the jobs in the job series or occupational group represented by that benchmark title. Since most job families and occupational groups are predominately male or female, this is one way that gender bias is perpetuated despite the use of point factor job evaluation systems.

No two salary-setting systems are exactly alike. Even salary-setting systems that use the same point factor job evaluation system differ in relation to organizational structure, size, external labor market constraints, union-management relationships, and legal and political considerations. What all salary-setting systems have in common is an image of being objective and impartial, gained mostly through appearing to be quantitative. But, at base, each point factor job evaluation system is a series of value judgments. Traditional job evaluation systems, which have been in widespread use since World War II, were constructed when gender bias permeated labor practices in many forms. It was perfectly acceptable to pay women substantially less for equal work, to lay them off for getting married, to exclude them from college and professional education, and to fire them to hire less competent men. Between 1979 and 1981, the National Research Council of the U.S. National Academy of Sciences studied the feasibility of using existing job evaluation systems for assessing gender equity in salaries. They concluded that the factors and weights in these systems tend to replicate existing wage hierarchies and, therefore, their use as a standard of job worth understates the extent of sex bias in salaries (Treiman and Hartmann, 1981).

Many U.S. pay equity assessments have ignored the U.S. National Academy of Science committee conclusions and used traditional job evaluation systems. In Minnesota and Oregon, the Hay management consultant firm's job evaluation system was used. This system was developed in the 1940s and early publications about its development indicate that gender pay disparity was embraced (Steinberg, 1992). Acker (1989, pp. 71–76) has provided us with an agonizing account of the struggles of the pay equity advocates on the Oregon Task Force to get Hay consultants to alter their Human Relations Skills factor. She notes that the consultants and the state management objected to the idea of adding two levels to this factor because this would reduce the salary differences between management and nonmanagement. This Oregon experience illustrates the dilemma of attempting to bring about change using a job evaluation system that was developed to keep things the same. Fortunately, some job evaluation systems have been developed, and are being developed, that allow for change (see Steinberg and Lawrence, 1992; New Zealand Department of Labor, 1991; Federation of Women Teachers Association of Ontario, 1990). There is a recognition that systems of job evaluation have been socially constructed and that they must be socially reconstructed (Steinberg 1990) to achieve gender balance in salaries.

Standards for Gender-Neutral Job Evaluation

Although some of the earlier work of developing methodological standards for implementing equal pay for jobs of comparable worth originated in the United States (see Treiman and Hartmann, 1981; Remick, 1984; Steinberg and Haignere, 1987), since the latter part of the 1980s, the bulk of the progress in this area has taken place in Canada. Five Canadian provinces, one territory, and the federal government have passed pay equity legislation. With the exception of the federal legislation, these Canadian laws specify that a gender-neutral comparison system (GNCS) must be used in establishing pay equity between male- and female-dominated job classes. Since the laws themselves do not define what constitutes a gender-neutral system, the implementation process has provided the world with some giant steps in the development of job evaluation systems that are socially reconstructed to remove gender bias in salaries. According to the 1991 Haldimand and Norfolk Decision of the Ontario Pay Equity Hearings Tribunal:

> The Act recognizes that gender biases have existed and the gender-neutral comparison system must work to consciously remove these biases. Gender bias can enter at different points in the process; in collecting information on job classes; in the selection and definition of subfactors by which job classes may be evaluated; in weighting of factors; and in the actual process of evaluating jobs. The Supreme Court of Canada has said when addressing programs designed to redress systemic discrimination in employment, that a system must be able to analyze and destroy systemic patterns and must include measures designed to break the continuing cycle of systemic discrimination (paragraph 16).

The importance of the above citation and the Canadian pay equity reform is that, in the U.S. and most of the rest of the world, pay equity or equal pay for comparable worth adjustments are taking place with no specific attempt to address and remove the gender biases embedded in salary setting systems.

The Ontario Pay Equity Tribunal's Haldimand and Norfolk Decision goes on to note, "The requirement to make women's work visible is a vitally important part of the requirements to accurately capture the work performed" (paragraph 28). In making this ruling the Tribunal recognized that a major way that traditional pay systems use to avoid properly valuing women's work is to ignore it. There has been a long history of work being invisible because of its association with what women do for free in the home. For example, the nineteenth century ideology that women were innately better teachers of small children did not mean that school boards paid women more because they were better teachers than men. Nor did it mean that they would employ a woman to teach small children, if a man were available. It meant that women could be used for superior service at half the price because their teaching talents were just extensions of their natural inborn nurturing qualities rather than job skills—and because their wages were just supplements to the real breadwinner (man's) income rather than a "living" wage.

This propensity to ignore and undervalue the job content, skills, and responsibilities that are extensions of women's home and family roles has broad implications. The vast majority of what we recognize today as female-dominated occupations and professional have evolved from women's family and nurturing roles. The historically approved women's professions of teaching and nursing are extensions of child care and sick care roles. Working-class jobs in food service, laundry service, domestic service, garment making, and prostitution are extensions of women's "home" work to the broader economy. At base, the whole of the service sector of most societies rest in fundamental ways on traditionally female home work expanded to the broader economy at minimum cost.

Collecting Uncontaminated Job Content (Cleaning Up Classification)

The conventional methods of collecting job content information capture gender differences along with job content. One reason is that the questionnaires commonly used to collect job content information rely heavily on open-ended questions. Questions like "List your major job activities and the proportion of your time spent doing each activity" capture gender differences in language usage. People in jobs with the same job content are likely to fill in these open-ended questions differently based on their verbal abilities, their perceptions of their jobs, their knowledge of bureaucracies, and their gender. Linguistic behavior, like other personal traits, is heavily influenced by what is overtly and subtly rewarded by those around us. As a result women speak and write more imprecisely using weaker verb forms ("feel" rather than "believe," "tell" rather than "inform") and qualifying adverbs and adjectives ("sort of") than men (Miller and Swift, 1977; Butturff and Epstein, 1978).

Research has documented the effect of gender stereotyping on both men and women. We know, for instance, that both men and women will judge artwork, literature, and resumés associated with women more harshly than those they associate with men. Both women and men have learned to characterize women's work as less important. Open-ended questions leave room for this socially learned gender bias to be incorporated into salaries. In this regard the Ontario Pay Equity Tribunal's Haldimand and Norfolk decision notes: "We find the Employer's proposal to use a closed-ended questionnaire a good one. A closed-ended questionnaire is one which frames the questions in such a way as to elicit more consistent and comparable responses, minimizing the impact of gender and linguistic differences" (p. 21, paragraph 63).

But closed-ended questionnaires must be constructed carefully so as not to overlook any important job content of either traditionally male or female jobs. Failing to collect information concerning traditionally female job content, and therefore rendering it invisible to the job evaluation process, is a primary way that gender bias in salaries has been perpetuated. The most direct way to be assured important job content is not being ignored is to ask the job incumbents, perhaps in focus groups, what they do in their jobs. You can find lists of frequently overlooked job content in Steinberg and Haignere (1987) or the Ontario Pay Equity Commission's publications *How to Do Pay Equity Job Comparisons,* as well as the Ontario Tribunal's

Haldimand and Norfolk Decision. Although it is not possible to provide an extensive list here, four categories of commonly ignored female-dominated job content that suffer from close association with the traditionally female roles must be mentioned. These are caregiving, exposure to communicable diseases, laundry and food services, and information management. Caregiving encompasses the classic bedside roles women are associated with in nursing homes and institutions, as well as caregiving to customers and the public (e.g., waitress, sales clerk, receptionist, motor vehicle clerk). Information concerning exposure to communicable diseases such as AIDS and hepatitis is likely not to be collected, while information concerning the possibility of falling off a ladder or being injured by a machine is collected. Job content collection instruments are also likely to ignore the skills, effort, and hazards involved in food and laundry service ("housewife" functions) and the skills of information management, such as filing, data entry, and record-keeping (clerical "office wife" order-keeping functions).

Although job incumbents are widely recognized as the people most familiar with the skills and requirements of their work, the job content information provided by job incumbents is usually "digested" by those who write the class specifications or otherwise transfer the information from the job content collection instrument to the job evaluation committee. These individuals are in a position to craft the information they are synthesizing in the direction of the existing salaries, which are likely to incorporate gender bias. If they are summarizing the information provided by 20 incumbents concerning their jobs, they can selectively choose excerpts consistent with bureaucratic, gender, and salary stereotypes. Studies have shown that knowledge of existing salaries may influence what is recorded about job content. Research has shown that, when a job was presented as having low pay, it was evaluated as less worthy on a series of compensable factors than when the same job was presented as having higher pay. Thus, those who have knowledge of current pay scales may be inclined to perpetuate these pay scales, complete with any existing gender biases. The work of the persons summarizing the job content information should be carefully reviewed for potential gender bias.

An example of how class specifications are shaped to be consistent with existing salaries was illustrated during an Ontario school board tribunal hearing. The classification analyst transferring the information from the job content questionnaires to the job evaluation committee indicated that teachers needed less than a month of experience to perform the job competently. However, according to the same analyst, the caretaker (janitor) needed a year or two of experience to competently perform his job and the maintenance foreman needed five to seven years. Similarly, Don Trieman (1979) found that the class specification

of a truck driver who drove a van or pick-up indicated 12 months was required for training. In the same system, a typist was judged to require one month of training.

Gender Balancing Measures of Job Content (Cleaning Up Compensation)

A school board in Ontario proposed to comply with the Ontario Pay Equity legislation through using a set of factors that did not measure (i.e., rendered invisible) the communication skills needed to provide instruction, responsibility for the welfare of students, skills needed to test and evaluate students, or responsibility for classroom management and supervision. Each of these ignored components of job content was, and is, central to the mandate of school boards. In the resulting Tribunal hearing, the Board's management consultant indicated that all these teaching skills and responsibilities would be measured by the Board's "Contact" factor. But the Board's "Contact" factor, like most "Contact" factors, was designed so as to measure the importance of the people contacted, rather than the skills and responsibilities involved. Community/school officials and mass media contacts were given greater value than contacts with the school's clients. In addition, routine contact with students was worth less than nonroutine contacts with the same people. This could mean that a principal applying discipline occasionally with a few students would get more credit on the "Contact" factor than a teacher who spends most of her or his working day in contact with many students. Students were not mentioned after level five of this nine level factor. Thus, regardless of the skill and training required, student/client contact could not bring a job class above level five. To reach level seven, the contacts needed to involve acting as a representative on behalf of the entire organization; and level nine could only be reached by those whose contacts were for the purpose of developing policy or formulating strategies that have organizationwide implications.

Most "Contact" factors are designed like the one described above. Rather than measuring related job content, they measure bureaucratic or managerial level as an extension of the importance of those contacted. Yet this was the factor that the Ontario school board claimed measured the teacher's job content. School boards, hospitals, and other service sector organizations serve clients/students/patients and their families. Contacts with these clients are crucial to the success of these organizations and their organizational missions. These interpersonal skills and responsibilities are rendered invisible by conventional "Contact" factors that primarily value the contacts of individuals high in the organization.

This type of gender bias is more evident if the factor addresses skills, for example, "Communication/Interpersonal Skill." If a particular job requires a specific level of interpersonal skill, it requires that level regardless of the importance of the people with whom the communication takes place. Indeed, it may take greater language, tact, and listening skills to persuade and influence and negotiate sensitive issues with an irate client/student/patient with poor verbal abilities than it does to deal with local politicians. Do those who negotiate contracts or speak with politicians or the media have greater communication skills than psychologists, chaplains, and counselors, who have years of training and education focused on listening, persuasion, and communicating skills?

Like the "Contact" factor described above, other traditional factors use the bureaucratic ladder to help those in primarily male and managerial job titles reach top levels. The Haldimand and Norfolk Decision draws attention to such factors:

> One example is the "Impact of Errors" subfactor, in which "loss to the Municipality's prestige" is two levels higher than "may result in serious injury to others." Another example is the "Outside Contacts" subfactor, in which contact with the media and publicity with respect to the image of the Municipality is seven levels higher than routine contact with patients. *The structuring of values is such that the jobs with formal managerial responsibility are to score at the highest levels* (p. 26, paragraphs 78 and 79, emphasis added).

Factors with a variety of titles, including "Decisionmaking," "Impact of Errors," "Creativity," "Planning," "Judgment," "Initiative," and "Problem Solving," among others, systematically exclude jobs from reaching the top levels unless they address, at minimum, departmental or branch procedures. The highest level is characteristically reserved for jobs impacting the organization as a whole, rather than those making decisions that require the most knowledge, planning, problem solving, or judgment. The most skilled scientific or professional job title—for example, one making decisions concerning the development of vaccines that could impact worldwide health—would be unlikely to obtain one of the top three steps of many Judgment/Problem Solving/Decisionmaking factors. That is unless, of course, this job title happened to also "direct activities fully impacting a department" or "the organization as a whole."

This is not to suggest that there should be no factors relating to the bureaucratic structure. Managerial and supervisory job content logically relates to bureaucratic levels. The higher levels of these factors may legitimately be reserved for those who coordinate more than one unit. Unfortunately, in many job evaluation systems, factors that favor managerial job content predominate. Moreover,

since they measure the same underlying dimension, these factors turn out to be strongly interrelated statistically.

If interacted/redundant factors disproportionately measure the job content of one gender and collect most of the weights, they magnify gender bias. The Ontario Pay Equity Commission's publication *How to Do Pay Equity Job Comparisons* correctly notes that redundant factors mean that "jobs containing this quality are getting double credit for it" (p. 26). If three or four factors are redundant, some jobs get triple or quadruple credit. Thus, a correlation analysis of redundancies provides important diagnostic information in deciding which factors can be dropped or combined. If two factors are highly interacted and both remain in the job evaluation system, their weights should be adjusted downward to minimize the "double credit" impact.

In many traditional job evaluation systems the problem of redundant factors is compounded by interacting two very similar types of job content on a grid. For example, "Supervisory Responsibility" is placed on one axis of the grid and "Number of People Supervised" is placed on the other axis. It is highly likely that jobs that supervise more people also have higher levels of supervision and vice versa. Any other combination of these two factors—low supervisory responsibility and high numbers of supervised or the opposite—is either illogical or tends not to occur. Even if there are only five levels on each dimension of the grid, this factor will have far more levels than any other; $5 \times 5 = 25$ cells. Thus, the purposeful interaction of two redundant factors on a grid can be used to give this factor much higher points (weight) than other factors.

Measuring Female Job Content

Factors that appropriately measure the job content of traditionally female job titles are rare or nonexistent. If, through focus group interviews or the published lists of the commonly overlooked job content of traditionally female jobs, you discover missing types of job content that are currently ignored, include them. It is better to encompass factors that may not be used than it is to fail to provide a factor to the job evaluators that represents important job content of either the male or female job classes. This assumes, of course, that the factor is not redundant to those already in the system.

There are two basic ways of incorporating previously unrecognized job content into a job evaluation system. The first is to edit an existing factor so that it recognizes and values job content it previously ignored. The second is to create new factors that measure these skills. Returning to the Ontario school district example, a traditional factor was recreated so that it would measure classroom management and client supervision. To do this each reference to "staff" in a traditional "Management/Supervision" factor was changed to "client/staff." Level four is provided below to illustrate how this factor could value the work of both educators and administrators.

> Work involves responsibility for client/staff management/supervision including scheduling, assigning, coordinating, and reviewing work. Duties include establishing work processes regarding routine situations where detailed procedures are established regarding a specific function or discipline or subunit. Job duties may involve responsibility for discipline and promotion.

To measure three other types of traditionally female school district job content—the skills of communication needed to provide instruction, responsibility for the welfare of students, and the skills needed to evaluate students—new factors had to be crafted, keeping in mind that they should be broadly applicable and not just apply to teachers' jobs or even just school board job titles. Therefore, in each case applicability was extended beyond clients and students to include staff. As a result the "Instruction" and "Evaluation" factors allowed anyone with responsibility for the instruction, training, evaluation, or testing of clients or staff to get credit for this job content. For example, level four of the "Instruction" factor reads: "Client/staff instruction involves diverse, occasionally changing subject matter from a specific discipline. Instruction is provided on a regular basis." Similarly, the "client/staff" phrasing was used in designing the factor measuring the responsibility for the "Physical and Mental Well-Being" of others.

The difficulty with creating new factors, as opposed to editing existing job evaluation factors, is that there are few guidelines as to how to weight factors that measure job content that has not previously been given a value. Weighting factors brings us face to face with our diverse cultural value systems (Haignere, 1991). Many of our monetary values conflict with our humanitarian values. Is responsibility for budgets or equipment more important than responsibility for safety and human lives? Is exposure to heat or cold a more negative working environment than exposure to the chronically ill or severely retarded? Despite the difficulty, weights are very important. All the bias elimination work that goes into the development of the factors can be negated in the assignment of weights.

To guide in assigning weights, there are two statistical correlation analyses (New Zealand Department of Labor, 1991). One assessment tests for the relationship of each factor to female and male job content. The other assessment tests for redundancy. Since these assessments cannot take place until points have been assigned to the job titles based on the factors, and yet they must be done before weights are permanently assigned to the individual factors, these diagnostic analyses should be planned ahead.

To examine which factors measure the work done by male- and female-dominated classes, it is necessary to calculate a correlation between the percentage of women in each job class and the score that each job class receives on a particular factor. A positive correlation (i.e., correlation greater than about +.3) indicates the factor is measuring job content more prevalent in women's jobs and a negative correlation indicates it is measuring job content more prevalent in men's jobs. Correlations around zero (−2 to +2) indicate the job content measured relates fairly equally to male and female classes. This information can then be used to advise equitable distributions of weight across factors relating to both male- and female-dominated jobs.

A statistical correlation procedure can also be used to check for factor redundancy. Factors that relate to pay tend to be related to each other; for example, jobs that require higher education tend to be those that involve higher responsibility and jobs that involve a high level of physical effort tend to have poor working conditions. However, there is a difference between some interaction and almost total redundancy. If two factors are interacted at .8 and above, consideration should be given to dropping one or merging these factors. If factors are correlated at the .5 to .79 levels, these interactions should be taken into account when weighting the factors involved. If both factors are given heavy weight then the common job content between the two will be getting very heavy weight. To avoid double or triple weighting, the degree to which factors in a system are redundant must be taken into account before deciding how much weight individual factors should receive.

Summary

Pay equity reform questions the long held cultural assumption that women are second class citizens and, by extension, their work is second class and can be paid accordingly. Given the pervasiveness of this cultural assumption throughout history and its thorough infiltration of traditional salary setting practices, it is crucial to develop gender-neutral job evaluation in order to successfully eliminate gender bias from salaries.

Most job evaluation studies are not pay equity studies. Most job evaluation studies are done to justify existing salaries. Too often so-called "pay equity" analyses are done using traditional job evaluation systems that ignore female job content and/or weight it too low. If a non-gender-neutral job evaluation system is used in making job comparisons, the result in all probability will be that job content that is disproportionately present in job titles where women predominate will be systematically ignored. This puts female job classes at a disadvantage, since all the important job content of men's job classes is included in the comparison while important parts of the job content of women's job classes are not included.

Lois Haignere

BIBLIOGRAPHY

Butturff, D. and E. L. Epstein, 1978. *Women's Language and Style.* Akron, OH: University of Akron.

Federation of Women Teachers Associations of Ontario, 1990. *Job Comparison System.*

Gunderson, M., 1994. *Comparable Worth and Gender Discrimination: An International Perspective.* Geneva: International Labor Office.

Haignere, L., 1991. "Pay Equity Implementation: Experimentation, Negotiation, Mediation, Litigation, and Aggravation." In J. Fudge and P. McDermott, eds., *Just Wages: A Feminist Assessment of Pay Equity.* Toronto: University of Toronto Press.

Haldiman-Norfolk Ontario Pay Equity Commission Tribunal Decision (29 May 1991) 0001–89 (P.E.H.T.) *Ontario Nurses' Association, Applicant v. Regional Municipality of Haldiman-Norfolk, Respondent.*

How to Do Pay Equity Job Comparisons, Ontario. Ontario Pay Equity Commission (undated).

Miller, C. and K. Swift, 1977. *Words and Women: New Language in New Times.* Garden City, NY: Anchor Press/Doubleday.

New Zealand Department of Labour, 1991. *Equity at Work.*

Remick, H., 1984. "Major Issues in *a priori* Applications." In *Comparable Worth and Wage Discrimination.* Philadelphia: Temple University Press.

Steinberg, R., 1990. "The Social Construction of Skill: Gender, Power, and Comparable Worth." *Work and Occupations* 17(4):449–482.

———, 1992. "Gender Instructions: Cultural Lag and Gender Bias in the Hay System of Job Evaluation." *Work and Occupations,* 19: 387–423.

Steinberg, R. and L. Haignere, 1987. "Equitable Compensation: Methodological Criteria for Comparable Worth." In C. Bose and G. Spitze, eds., *Ingredients for Women's Employment Policy.* Albany: Suny Press.

Steinberg, R. and W. L. Walter, 1992. "Making Women's Work Visible: The Case of Nursing, First Steps in the Design of a Gender-Neutral Job Comparison System." *Summary of the Proceedings of the Third Women's Policy Research Conference. May 1992.*

Treiman, D. J., 1979. *Job Evaluation: An Analytical Review, Interim Report to the Equal Opportunity Commission.* Washington, D.C.: National Academy of Sciences.

Treiman, D. J. and H. Hartmann, 1981. *Women, Work and Wages: Equal Pay for Jobs of Equal Value.* Washington, D.C.: National Academy Press.

COMPARATIVE PUBLIC ADMINISTRATION.

The subfield or perspective of public administration that contrasts and compares administrative practices in various countries and searches for theories broadly applicable to the practice of public administration in the world.

This article is divided into four sections: background, historical development of the subfield, methodological issues, and conceptual issues. The background examines the value of, types of, and the problems with comparison as a type of study. The historical development of the subfield reviews its historical rise in the 1950s and 1960s, its decline in the 1970s, and its reemergence as an important perspective in the 1980s and 1990s. Three prominent methodological issues—the proper definition, purpose of the subfield, and level of analysis—are next examined. Finally, a number of traditional and contemporary issues in comparative public administration are examined, such as the current challenge of transforming the administrative systems of former communist states to democratic and market-oriented systems with more flexible and smaller public sectors.

Background

The value of comparison is difficult to overstate. Robert Dahl, in laying out the three necessary elements for a science of public administration 50 years ago, eloquently stated that there must be a body of comparative studies that would allow for principles and generalities beyond national boundaries and peculiar historical experiences (Dahl, 1947). Therefore, public administration as a field cannot be a science unless it has a robust comparative element. There are other values in comparison as well. First, we gain a broad understanding by examining differences and variations, and tend to be better equipped to adapt to or initiate change. Second, the study of comparison leads to an appreciation of differences. Third, the study of comparisons vastly improves the ability to borrow and adapt selected ideas, practices, and innovations.

Comparative public administration is only one of a number of related studies including comparative politics, comparative public policy, sociology, and development administration. Comparative politics is the study of different political systems; political development is the term used for studies focusing on politics in developing countries (Mayer, 1989; Huntington, 1968; Weiner and Huntington, 1987). Because administrative systems are so affected by political systems, comparative public administration often overlaps this field a great deal, especially at the mid- and macro-theoretical levels. Comparative public policy "is the cross-national study of how, why, and to what effect government policies are developed" (Heidenheimer, Heclo, and Adams, 1975, p. i). Its major thrusts have been "environmental policy, education policy, economic policy, and social policy" (Heady, 1991, p. 47). Sociology has always had a comparative and broad thrust, including in its analysis cultural, historical, and even economic factors. Much of the theorizing at the macro or grand level in comparative public administration has been in the sociological tradition (Esman, 1968). Development administration (also known as technical assistance) broadly refers to the study of nation-building, which means that it can refer to wealthy and poor nations alike, but in practice has primarily applied to underdeveloped or developing countries. Development administration has generally been considered the applied half of comparative public administration, but has at times been considered a subfield in its own right (Gant, 1979; Hope, 1984).

The problems of rigorous comparison in public administration are numerous and very substantial, and can only be mentioned here. Five challenges for the study of comparative public administration will be identified. (1) Because public administration is a part of political systems, administrative variables are often dependent on complex political variables as well as numerous other economic, sociological, historical, and cultural variables. Sorting out independent, intervening, and dependent variables is a daunting task. (2) Data collection by noncitizens is immensely difficult because of: the size of public administration, language differences, the cost of travel, logistical hurdles, and access problems. Because most comparative research has been conducted by U.S. and European scholars, this has meant weaker coverage of former communist, authoritarian ruled, and underdeveloped countries. (3) Funding for the type of cross-national studies that link numerous experts in different countries to work on identical data collection strategies has been rare. (4) Because bureaucratic structures and governmental data categories vary so extensively, comparison is difficult without extensive interpretations or adjustments. (5) When an action orientation is applied, as in development administration, whose norms and values will be used in determining the prescription for change? Norms and values vary not only by culture, but also through time (see Aberbach and Rockman, 1988; Peters, 1988).

Historical Development of the Subfield

Politics and public administration have existed as long as humans have attempted to govern groups. However, while comparative politics traces its roots to Aristotle, comparative public administration is a "newcomer to the community of academic research and instruction" (Raphaeli, 1967, p. 1). It has its early scholarly beginnings in the eighteenth century German cameralists; in the nineteenth and early twentieth centuries, this commonly became the study of administrative law in Europe. Prior to World War II, most comparative work by U.S. scholars was related to technical aspects of administration such as personnel and financial systems.

The end of World War II dramatically shifted the course of comparative public administration as the United States assumed a disproportionately large role on the world stage for nearly 30 years. As the Cold War began in the late 1940s, the United States was called upon to help others rebuild (Europe) or redesign (Japan and Taiwan) their societies. The Point IV plan, the Marshall Plan, and Asian assistance were enormously successful and contributed to the powerful reputation of U.S. "know-how" and ability to help others. Unfortunately, the relative ease of reconstruction, as opposed to development, was poorly understood. The 1950s increasingly saw the development of technical assistance programs to underdeveloped countries, especially large infrastructure projects. Opportunities for comparative study increased as precursors to U.S. Agency for International Development funded development projects around the world at relatively high levels.

Scholars in the 1950s, however, did not limit themselves to technical topics as they had done in the past. Descriptive studies became more ambitious and midrange structural comparisons became more common. Probably the most identifiable beginning of the subfield was the Conference on Comparative Administration held in Princeton in 1952. Prominent scholars in the 1950s included William Siffin, Herbert Kaufman, Paul Meyer, Brian Chapman, Dwight Waldo, Ferrel Heady, and Fred Riggs.

Comparative public administration's "heyday" was from 1962 to 1971 (Heady, 1991, p.18). Most important in this period was substantial funding from the Ford Foundation to the Comparative Administration Group (CAG), which matches Heady's demarcation of the subfield's golden age. Ample funding encouraged an outpouring of work and specialized conferences, although the Ford Foundation was particularly interested in applied work. From 1969 to 1974 a journal called the *Journal of Comparative Administration* supported the subfield; this subsequently became *Administration & Society* and had a decidedly different focus. Also contributing to the enthusiasm of the period were continuing U.S. confidence in the value of disseminating the "American model," sustained high levels of foreign aid (USAID became an authorized agency under Kennedy), the acceleration of decolonization in Africa and Asia (which led the U.N. to call the 1960s the First Development Decade), and the reemphasis on Latin America with the Alliance for Progress after the Cuban revolution.

Scholarly work further expanded in the 1960s to include macrolevel theoretical treatises reflecting strong influences of the structural functionalism of comparative politics and the grand theorizing of sociology. Fred Riggs was especially prominent throughout this period, producing the single most important theoretical work, *Administration in Developing Countries* (1964), in reaction to the failure of explanatory power of the Weberian model outside the classic Western bureaucracies.

The early 1970s saw a sharp decline in the study of and courses in comparative public administration, with the loss of the Ford Foundation funding in 1971 and the journal in 1974. Events affecting the U.S. such as the fall of Vietnam, the oil shock of 1973, the domestic unrest stirred by Watergate, and increased cynicism about the effectiveness of government, also contributed to a more somber, isolationist mood in a subfield that had been largely dominated by U.S. scholars.

Critical, however, was the negative reaction to the voluminous work of the 1960s. At least five substantial strains characterized the critique. First, as was true for the general field of public administration, no paradigm or widely accepted model had evolved. Because of the extraordinary breadth to which comparative public administration had expanded, the lack of a focus made the contributions seem completely noncumulative and endlessly *ad hoc*. Second, the macrolevel studies, especially Riggs's, were heavily criticized as obscure and linguistically confusing. Third, those preferring a "normal science"-oriented discipline accused the subfield of being underdeveloped in terms of theory building and hypothesis testing (Sigelman, 1976). Fourth, those interested in the development side found most of the work detached from useful application. Fifth, it had become accepted that an ethnocentrism had pervaded much of the literature, due to the overwhelming influence and excessive confidence of U.S. scholars in U.S. ideals and models. In 1976, nearly a full issue of *Public Administration Review* was devoted to problems inherent in the subfield. While its leading adherents pointed to the overall impact on the field of public administration, which had lost much of its parochialism, they nonetheless had to admit that the subfield was likely to remain at a vastly reduced state for some time to come. More severe critiques called the subfield dead.

From 1976 to 1987, the distinctive identity of the subfield was much diminished, but comparative works continued at a substantial pace. A comprehensive study of the period noted: "Characteristics of recent journal literature include a significant practitioner component, a substantial orientation toward policy recommendations, a relative paucity of theory-testing studies, wide and mature coverage of a range of topics, and methodological practices that seem slightly better than the past but still far from ideal." The study further noted that the field as a whole "lacks features that give it a clear identity" (Van Wart and Cayer, 1990, p. 238). Probably the most important contribution to the field during this period was an annotated bibliography by Mark W. Huddleston in 1984, which complemented an earlier bibliography by Heady and Stokes (1962).

Both within the United States and around the world, the globalization of the economy and the insertion of the newly independent states into world affairs have brought a new dynamism to international topics and comparative interests. This has been reflected by a number of important works in recent years. Some of them include *Comparing Public Bureaucracies* (Peters, 1988), *Public Administration in Developed Democracies: A Comparative Study* (Rowat, 1988), *Public Administration in the Third World: An International Handbook* (Subramaniam, 1990), *Public Administration in World Perspective* (Dwivedi and Henderson, 1990), *Handbook of Comparative and Development Administration* (Farazmand, 1991), and *Public Administration: A Comparative Perspective, Fifth Edition* (Heady, 1995). Equally important, both management and policy texts contain far more comparative perspectives than in the past and the former ethnocentric tilt toward a perceived U.S. superiority has been replaced by a more balanced appreciation of innovations and successes from around the world (for example, Baker, 1994; Halachmi and Bouckaert, 1995).

Three Key Methodological Issues

Three of the persistent methodological issues of comparative public administration for the last 50 years are the proper definition of comparative (the minimum threshold); the proper purpose of the subfield—theoretical or applied; and the proper level of analysis.

At what point does a work qualify as comparative? At least four standards have been used, listed here from broadest to narrowest. (1) The broadest definition classifies any comparison as part of comparative public administration, even if the comparisions are intracountry. Although Goodsell proposed this definition (1981), it has rarely been adopted, and the term has connoted international comparison. (2) The next broadest definition is one that accepts as comparative any material that is useful to scholars who are interested in polities other than their own. This standard is used in the Huddleston bibliography (1984). (3) Sigelman and Gadbois (1983) offer a more restricted approach by including only the single-country case studies that have a comparative component. They suggest that single-country studies, which make up about two-thirds of the journal literature (Van Wart and Cayer, 1990, p. 245), can have a comparative component in three ways. First, while a single-country study may not compare two separate polities, it may compare levels of government within the polity. Second, a single-country study may be comparable by being conceptually or theoretically oriented, lending itself to comparative analysis. Third, a single-country study may test a hypothesis which also emphasizes potential comparability. (4) The strictest standard requires that two or more countries be overtly compared. Two major studies investigating the degree of comparison (Sigelman and Gadbois, 1983; Van Wart and Cayer, 1990) used found slightly under 30 percent of the comparative literature meeting this standard.

Another important methodological question is the degree to which theory building should be focused on scientific or pragmatic criteria. The debate over the importance of pure versus applied science is an old and continuing one, finding new expressions in different fields at different times. As noted before, development administration was the name given to the more pragmatically oriented literature, especially as it related to Third World country development. While some definitions of development administration have been broader, George Honadle's is truest to common use: "Development administration . . . has come to mean the study and practice of induced socioeconomic change in the low-income countries of the world. The image is transformational, directive, and cross-national . . ." (1982, p. 175). Content analysis of work in the subfield has indicated that slightly less than 15 percent is classified as development administration (Van Wart and Cayer, 1990), reflecting a long-term "academic" over "practitioner" interest (Henderson, 1969, p. 70). Nonetheless, boundary setting has at times (primarily in the 1960s and 1970s) nearly given development administration a separate status.

A third important methodological issue is the level of analysis. Should comparative studies focus on the technical level, should they focus on entire bureaucratic entities (especially as they interact the political system), or should comparative study seek to place public administration as a constituent part of a society along with the citizenry, political systems, economic system, and sociological norms that affect the component subsystems? As a shorthand, the first approach can be called an administrative model, the second can be called a bureaucratic model (also known as middle-range theorizing), and the third can be called a general systems model (also known as an ecological approach, a sociological approach, or grand theorizing). Standard topics in the administrative perspective include general descriptions of administrative systems and institutions, personnel administration, budgeting, private sector relations and activities, and policy administration. The bureaucratic perspective tends to focus on public administration as a policy player in the political-administrative system, especially where top-level civil servants interact with political bureaucrats and elected officials in the executive and the legislature. The general systems approach, strongly advocated by Riggs (1957, 1962, 1964, 1968, 1971, 1975, 1976), would emphasize cultural, historical, and economic factors in the analysis of administrative systems. In reality, all three approaches are valid and reflect the complexity in studying a complicated field. Today, less concern is expressed about the need for a single paradigm than the quality of analysis at any given level.

Conceptual Issues

Because of the great number of conceptual issues that have been tackled in comparative public administration, only a sampling can be rendered here.

One issue is to what degree is administrative apparatus (such as the number of employees or the specific types of structures) a function of a particular political polity or system? What is the range of public employment as a percentage of total employment among high-income democracies, among high- and low-income democracies, and among democracies and nondemocracies? What is the range of organizational structures that are used to execute what types of public policies in different polities?

A second issue is to what degree are administrative behavior and power a function of political systems? How does administrative behavior vary among presidential systems, parliamentary systems, and between these two types of democracy? How does administrative behavior and power operate in traditional elite regimes (e.g., monarchies), bureaucratic elite regimes (e.g., dictatorships), and various types of single-party regimes? Should organizational theory be specific to each country or cluster of related countries, or should organizational theory be broad enough to apply to all polities?

A third issue is the right balance between political and bureaucratic development. Until recently, this question was exclusively framed in the context of low-income countries trying to build public sector service capacities (everything from water provision to the ability to maintain order) and efforts to build private sector economies. Was a strong public sector needed to lead the way to economic development after which political development would catch up? Was a strong public sector highly prone to enshrine the economic status quo and lead to nondemocratic polities? Was development administration a friend of the forgotten masses in impoverished countries or a pawn of the national elite in the affected countries? More recently, the question of the proper balance of bureaucratic and political development is finding extensive consideration in the developed countries as the conservative revolution repudiates the excesses of the big government paradigm. There is much comparative interest in finding ways to reduce bureaucratic involvement in both service and regulatory functions and as a percentage of the national economy.

A contemporary issue of great concern because of the plethora of newly independent states is how to convert a centralized, state-run government economy to a more decentralized government with a robust market economy. Not only have large numbers of public administration specialists been visiting and assisting the new states, but so too have social and physical scientists from all disciplines as well as large numbers of practitioners. Specific issues being addressed include the setting up and regulation of private banking, lack of credit, tax policies, changing rigid bureaucratic mindsets to the new, more dynamic realities, dealing with failed projects and industries, financial management systems in government, and how to finance infrastructure development to support competition in the world economy.

Conclusion

Not since the decolonizing era of the 1950s and 1960s when the Cold War electrified the international arena have we seen such an interest in global affairs. The new global economy has given a new twist to old issues. Rather than concentrating on ways to increase governmental capacity to lead development, the question more frequently today is how to decrease governmental excesses and controls. Rather than concentrating on the transition from colonial bureaucracy to independent democracy (or other type of governmental framework), the concentration is on transition from a communist bureaucracy to market-driven economies in which central command structures are tremendously reduced. Finally, rather than implicitly determining how Western and U.S. models can be replicated throughout the world, the concentration is now on finding excellent practices and systems wherever they exist. Given the urgency of these issues, the resurgence of the subfield in the last decade is likely to gain further momentum.

HOWARD BALANOFF
MONTGOMERY VAN WART
KENNETH PRYOR

BIBLIOGRAPHY

Aberbach, J. D., and B. A. Rockman, 1988. "Problems of Cross-National Comparison." In D. C. Rowat, ed., *Public Administration in Developed Democracies: A Comparative Study.* New York: Marcel Dekker.

Baker, R., ed., 1994. *Comparative Public Management: Putting U.S. Policy and Implementation in Context.* Westport, CT: Praeger.

Dahl, R. A., 1947. "The Science of Public Administration." *Public Administration Review,* vol. 7 (Winter) 1–11.

Dwivedi, O. P. and K. Henderson, eds., 1990. *Public Administration in World Perspective.* Ames: Iowa State University Press.

Esman, M. J., 1967. "The Ecological Style in Comparative Administration." *Public Administration Review,* 27(3):271–278.

Farazmand, A., ed., 1991. *Handbook of Comparative and Development Administration.* New York: Marcel Dekker.

Gant, G. F., 1979. *Development Administration: Concepts, Goals, Methods.* Madison: University of Wisconsin Press.

Goodsell, C. T., 1981. "The New Comparative Administration: A Proposal." *International Journal of Public Administration,* 3(2):143–155.

Halachmi, A. and G. Bouckaert, eds., 1995. *The Enduring Challenges in Public Management.* San Francisco: Jossey-Bass.

Heady, F., 1991. *Public Administration: A Comparative Perspective.* 4th ed. New York: Marcel Dekker.

———, forthcoming, *Public Administration: A Comparative Perspective.* 5th ed. New York: Marcel Dekker.

Heady, F., and S. L. Stokes, 1962. *Papers in Comparative Public Administration.* Ann Arbor: Institute of Public Administration, University of Michigan.

Henderson, K., 1969. "Comparative Public Administration: The Identity Crisis." *Journal of Comparative Administration,* 1(1):65–85.

Heidenheimer, A. J., H. Heclo, and Adams, C. T. 1975. *Comparative Public Policy: The Politics of Social Choice in Europe and America.* New York: St. Martin's Press.

Honadle, G., 1982. "Development Administration in the Eighties: New Agendas or Old Perspectives?" *Public Administration Review,* 42(2):174–179.

Hope, K. R., 1984. *The Dynamics of Development and Development Administration.* Westport, CT: Greenwood Press.

Huddleston, M. W., 1984. *Comparative Public Administration: An Annotated Bibliography.* New York: Garland Publishing.

Huntington, S. P., 1968. *Political Order in Changing Societies.* New Haven: Yale University Press.

Mayer, L. C., 1989. *Redefining Comparative Politics: Promise Versus Performance.* Newbury Park, CA: Sage.

McCurdy, H. E., 1977. *Public Administration: A Synthesis.* Menlo Park, CA: Cummings Publishing Company.

Peters, B. G., 1988. *Comparing Public Bureaucracies: Problems of Theory and Method.* Tuscaloosa: The University of Alabama Press.

Raphaeli, N., 1967. "Comparative Public Administration: An Overview." In N. Raphaeli, ed., *Readings in Comparative Public Administration.* Boston: Allyn and Bacon.

———, 1962. "An Ecological Approach: The 'Sala' Model." In F. Heady and S. L. Stokes, eds., *Papers in Comparative Public Administration.* Ann Arbor, MI: Institute of Public Administration, University of Michigan.

Riggs, F.W., 1964. *Administration in Developing Countries: The Theory of Prismatic Society.* Boston: Houghton Mifflin.

———, 1968. "The Dialectics of Developmental Conflict." *Comparative Political Studies,* 1(2):197–226.

———, 1971. *Frontiers of Development Administration.* Durham, NC: Duke University Press.

———, 1972. "Agraria and Industria: Toward a Typology of Comparative Administration." In W. Siffin, ed., *Toward the Comparative Study of Public Administration.* Westport, CT: Greenwood Press (originally published 1957).

———,1975. "Organizational Structures and Contexts." *Administration & Society,* 7(2):150–190.

———, 1976. "The Group and the Movement: Notes on Comparative and Development Administration." *Public Administration Review,* 36(6): 648–654.

Rowat, D. C., ed., 1988. *Public Administration in Developed Democracies: A Comparative Study.* New York: Marcel Dekker.

Sigelman, L., 1976. "In Search of Comparative Administration." *Public Administration Review,* 36(6):621–625.

Sigelman, L., and Gadbois, Jr., G. H. 1983. "Contemporary Comparative Politics: An Inventory and Assessment." *Comparative Political Studies,* 16(3):275–305.

Subramaniam, V., ed., 1990. *Public Administration in the Third World: An International Handbook.* Westport, CT: Greenwood Press.

Van Wart, M., and J. Cayer, 1990. "Comparative Public Administration: Defunct, Dispersed, or Redefined." *Public Administration Review*, 50(2): 238–248.

Weiner, M. and S. P. Huntington, eds., 1987. *Understanding Political Development*. Boston: Little, Brown, and Company.

COMPARATIVE PUBLIC BUDGETING.

The systematic study of budgeting in a variety of contexts.

Efforts to compare public budget systems go back to the popularization of the budget concept during the nineteenth century, when proponents of the executive budget used international experience to bolster their advocacy and criticize departures from the norm. Since then, systematic study of budgeting has proceeded by fits and starts, and no single approach has emerged.

Purposes of Comparative Study

From a practical point of view, comparative study of budgeting combats parochialism and spreads knowledge of innovations. On a more ambitious level, comparative analysis is indispensable for development of general theory, since testing and verification of theories require empirical observation of a number of cases. On a middle level, comparative research seeks to relate institutions to environments, to classify types of budget systems, to explain how different environments give rise to the different types, and to elucidate how changes take place.

Difficulties in Comparing Budget Systems

Although budgeting is a virtually universal governmental function, and formal processes are similar, comparative study of public budget systems confronts formidable obstacles. Simple descriptions of formal processes and organizations yield little of real interest. In order to make comparisons meaningful and useful it is necessary to order the multitude of facts into a framework, to sift the significant from the inconsequential, and to explain the functions and dysfunctions of different arrangements. This process assumes underlying theories of budget effectiveness, purposes of public financial policy, institutional capacity, and organizational efficacy—all of which are contentious.

Other problems relate to the scope of budget systems. For example, do they include revenue raising or audit? Do they involve policy as well as administrative aspects? Should analysis embrace informal as well as formal processes, such as the interplay of administrative and political roles? How might the jumble of innumerable events, personalities, and relationships be categorized and compared?

A further problem lies in the level of generality. While a high level of generality might encompass a large number of cases, the theories derived from it may be overgeneral-

ized. Where the researcher abstracts features one at a time from different environments, contextual significance may be lost and comparisons may become mechanical and unrevealing. But the study of whole budget systems on a case-by-case basis may defeat comparisons altogether because of the unique complexities of each case.

There is thus no single approach to the study of comparative public budgeting. Some researchers have concentrated on a general, well-articulated model of budgeting, related to economic and fiscal theory. Others have taken budget modernization and innovation as a point of departure. A third approach, using both global comparisons as well as case studies, has examined how political, economic, and cultural influences have affected governmental expenditure and taxation policies and the processes by which these policies are made. Most recently, researchers have used comparative studies to elucidate specific questions, such as the capability of governmental budget institutions to cope with a growing imbalance between revenues and expenditures.

Comprehensive Budget Theory

One approach to the study of comparative public budgeting is to take fiscal policy as the major point of departure and to discuss different budgeting practices in the light of its parameters. One of the most comprehensive treatments of this kind is a volume published by the International Monetary Fund in 1983, *Government Budgeting and Expenditure Controls: Theory and Practice* by A. Premchand. The same general approach has been used by the World Bank and International Monetary Fund in advocating budget reforms in both developing countries and countries moving from command to free market economies.

In this approach, budgeting is seen primarily as an instrument of economic policy. It promotes macroeconomic balance by specifying appropriate economic growth rates, maximizing benefits from the allocation of revenues, equating the social benefits of expenditure and the social cost of resource withdrawal by the public sector, and financing deficits according to goals of growth and price stability. The focus of budgeting is on attainment of efficiency in the allocation of resources within the public sector, influenced at each stage by the goals of fiscal policy, seen as dealing with fluctuations in demand in industrialized countries, and with structural economic changes through development plans and economic, financial, and program analysis, as well as the functions of accountability, management, and economic policymaking.

This model has been employed in two main ways. First, it has been used as a benchmark for actual budget practices, which are often found wanting. Second, it has been used as an agenda for budget system reform. In both cases, emphasis is on macroeconomic budget frameworks, and the orientation of budgeting activities with centralized fiscal policymaking.

The advantages of this approach lie in the strength of the model of economic policymaking and the alignment of budgeting institutions and processes with it. Its drawbacks stem from practical difficulties: the clear outlines of the economic model seem to evaporate in arguments over appropriate fiscal policies and the utility of specific budget arrangements, which often require trade-offs and adaptations rather than straightforward applications. Recommendations are often overgeneralized, practices are abstracted from context, and there may be little guidance on implementation of reforms.

A similar approach has related changes in the role of government and basic budget processes and policies in developing countries. This approach, an adjunct to structural adjustment measures advocated by the World Bank and International Monetary Fund, has emphasized macroeconomic planning, investment programming and project preparation, budgetary comprehensiveness, more effective financial management information systems, transparency of documents, and budget implementation and control of expenditures.

Budget Innovations

Over the past 40 years or so, many governments have tried to modernize their budget systems through incorporation of such innovations as program and performance budgeting. Measurement of their efforts has provided a useful framework for comparative evaluation. Program budgeting aimed at rationalizing public expenditure through reformed budget classifications relating outlays to government objectives, and the use of analysis in budgetary decisionmaking to evaluate performance. The systems actually adopted differed both in details and in how far they actually moved toward these aims. There has been considerable advocacy for adoption of such systems, particularly in developing countries, where a simplified model was popularized through the United Nations *Manual for Program and Performance Budgeting* (1967).

Several short studies on implementation of program budgeting and its variants have been published. These illustrate the difficulties in using adoption of a normative budget system as a comparative framework. Lack of consistent definition hinders uniform criteria for judgment. Expectations differ: for some the glass is half full, for others half empty. Reports are not always consistent in the aspects they analyze. For some, formal program classifications are evidence of success. Others find difficulties in learning whether analyses are really performed or their results used in decisionmaking. Process changes satisfy some, but others wish to measure the reforms in terms of change in patterns of expenditure or allocational efficiency—

although opinions may differ and the new systems may not be responsible for the outcomes.

Comparative Theory

The normative approaches outlined above have generally either ignored actual budget processes, simply emphasized their shortcomings, or treated them as residual. An alternative approach analyzes existing practices in order to explain why they take the form they do.

By the 1960s, considerable information was available about the characteristics of public budgeting in developing countries in a number of official reports. In *Development Planning: Lessons of Experience* (Baltimore: Johns Hopkins, 1965), Albert Waterston noted a variety of common and persistent problems: prevalence of earmarked funds and special accounts; lack of budgetary planning; cost overruns and underspending; rejustification of estimates and poor estimating; recurrent expenditures driving out development funding. In *Planning and Budgeting in Poor Countries* (New York: Wiley, 1974; New Brunswick, N. J.: Transaction, 1980), Naomi Caiden and Aaron Wildavsky hypothesized that such behavior derived from characteristic conditions of poverty and uncertainty. In poor countries multiple uncertainties converged and built upon one another. In the absence of redundancy, central budget agencies remade the budget throughout the year in a process of "repetitive budgeting," while agencies adopted such strategies as padding, earmarking, and special funds to ensure their own survival.

This model has been identified in a number of contexts and served as a reference point for later work. There have, however, been few attempts to extend Caiden's and Wildavsky's analysis to establish systematic relationships between specific environmental conditions and methods of budgeting. Naomi Caiden (1974) explored prebudgetary patterns of financial administration in Western Europe, relating the interplay of accountability, revenue mobilization, and administrative control to particular historical conditions. In an ambitious attempt, Aaron Wildavsky built on the insights of the study of poor countries to construct a comparative theory of budgetary processes embracing experiences from diverse environments. In *Budgeting: A Comparative Theory of Budgetary Processes* (1975), Wildavsky hypothesized that while poverty and uncertainty generated repetitive budgeting (budgets are made throughout the year), rich countries with certainty practiced incremental budgeting (steady growth by increments); poverty and certainty yielded revenue budgeting (budgets constrained by available revenue); and rich and uncertain environments hypothetically gave rise to supplemental budgeting (budgets are supplemented as resources become available). Among rich countries, varied political institutions and norms governing elite relationships accounted for different budgeting styles.

The difficulties of this kind of endeavor are enormous—there are just too many variables once comparison goes beyond the basic categories. A comprehensive framework would require a typology of environments and a typology of budget systems, and then a means of establishing relationships between the two and accounting for change. One effort to establish a comparative framework of this kind was Fred Riggs's application of the prismatic society to financial administration (1965, pp. 1–46). Another was the encyclopedic work of Carolyn Webber and Aaron Wildavsky, *A History of Taxation and Expenditure in the Western World* (1986). They used the concept of political culture to identify different forms of regime and budgeting, where outcomes reflected the relative dominance of the respective cultures of sects, markets, and hierarchies. Wildavsky also used this typology in the second edition of *Budgeting: A Comparative Theory of Budgetary Processes* (1985). However, the difficulties of applying such generalized categories to the variety of actual experience has generated a different approach: the in-depth case study.

Case Studies

Full-length studies of foreign systems of public budgeting are relatively rare. In one sense, they are not comparative at all, as they deal with only one country, but since they shed light on a variety of budgeting experience, they are of considerable interest. They have the advantages of in-depth analysis, comprehensive coverage of topics, and capacity to relate process and context. But unlike the other approaches discussed here they do not employ a single comparative framework. In fact they ask quite different questions. During the 1970s, several case studies of this kind emerged.

Guy Lord (1973) analyzed how budget decisions were made. He saw the French budgetary process dominated by formal rules, centralization, advance commitment of most budgetary resources, and dominance of the higher civil service.

Heclo and Wildavsky (1974) sought to describe the operation of the expenditure process, illuminating the characteristic practices of British government, and accounting for both continuity and change. It was a kind of anthropology of the budget process, concentrating on the informal relationships of participants. British budgeting emerged as the product of a closed community whose games and rules were rapidly being overtaken by the harsh reality of the world outside.

John Campbell (1977) compared the Japanese budget process with those of other countries and related it to the broader Japanese political structure and purpose. He found budgeting to be historical and incremental, and relatively stable from year to year.

Richard Gunther (1980) asked the broader question whether differences in political regimes had effects on expenditure or taxation policies, or on decisionmaking processes. His analysis of Franco's Spain revealed a highly personalized style of economic decisionmaking, a high degree of spending ministry autonomy in setting intradepartmental priorities, the absence of any institutionalized systematic aggregation of interests, and the dominance of clientelistic criteria in the recruitment of political elites.

These case studies go beyond descriptions of formal systems or advocacy of budget models. They attempt to penetrate budgetary processes to determine how decisions are really made. They link politics and administration, informal behavior and formal rules, and budget policies and budget processes. Meanwhile, as economic conditions in Western industrialized countries deteriorated, the study of comparative budgeting focused on how budgeting systems cope with fiscal stress.

A Focused Approach

Ever since the late nineteenth century, there had been considerable interest in the growth of government expenditures, and a variety of theories were put forward to account for their expansion. By the early 1970s, governments of Western industrialized countries were trying to adjust to upward pressures on expenditures and inadequate revenues. There are now several studies of these adaptations.

The outlines of the predicament were set out in a collection of short case studies edited by A. Premchand and Jesse Burkhead (1984). The authors observed chronic deficits, growing inflexibility of government spending, and the prospect of stagnant or deteriorating economic conditions. While automatic mechanisms in budgets were generating large increments in expenditures, the weak economic situation and political resistance were simultaneously slowing the growth of revenues. Government responses varied, including medium term financial plans, multiyear budgeting, cash controls, and the Canadian "envelope" system.

A more ambitious attempt to compare contemporary budget systems in industrialized nations was reported in *The Control and Management of Public Expenditures* (1987). However, following a brief introduction, the material was presented on a country by country basis. Still, it represents one of the most comprehensive, if formal, descriptions available of Western European budget systems in the mid-1980s. A more analytical approach was summarized at about the same time by Allen Schick in two articles in *Public Administration Review* (1986, 1988). He found very similar practices: fiscal norms to restrain expenditures, use of ceilings and targets, baselines, multiyear budgeting, prepreparation of the budget, harmonization of macro and micro decisions, cutback budgeting, cash budgeting, changes in budget priorities, monitoring of government expenditures, and efforts to make managers more responsible for budget decisions in their jurisdictions.

Meanwhile powerful forces were at work to change the traditional roles and orientations of government. Spearheaded by the Thatcher government in Britain, a remarkably cohesive set of reforms was launched to cut back and privatize public services, improve efficiency and responsibility, and increase management responsibility. Accounts of these reforms are available in a number of sources, including A. Premchand (1990). But evaluative research on them has yet to appear.

The Elusive Comparison

There have been several approaches to the comparative study of budget systems. Where, then, is the cutting edge? While many studies exist, neither the scope nor agenda of comparative public budgeting has been fully defined. Normative approaches relate to a narrow ideological foundation and a preconceived institutional format, irrespective of context–industrialized democracies, developing countries, or nations in transition from command economies. Behaviorist studies either attempt to encompass all of politics and society (case studies), or capture only a simplified version of reality, forcing complexity into preconceived frameworks whose boundaries expand to the point of tautology. The major comparative movements–the Comparative Administration Group of the 1960s and 1970s and contemporary comparative politics and policy–have all but ignored the budgetary area. Comparisons as a means of improving our understanding of public budgeting remain elusive.

Yet the potential remains, and the surface has barely been scratched. Because public budgeting encompasses an interdisciplinary arena, it is surely a prime field for furthering that scientific study of society which supplies the antidote to careless assumptions, glib and unfounded theories, primitive prejudices, and fawning conformity to passing fads and fashions. The comparative study of public budgeting should be more than the listing of nomethetic processes and institutions, or the application and advocacy of neoclassical economic theory, or description of a set of untested reforms, or a generalized collection of governmental responses to fiscal stress. Rather it should seek to understand contemporary predicaments in the light of long-term societal trends, trace the consequences of institutional arrangements, illuminate alternative options, relate processes and policies, and evaluate the rapid change that is the defining characteristic of our age. There is no lack of opportunity for the avid researcher, who may explore budgetary decisionmaking in such relatively uncharted areas as the newly industrialized countries; the model of transformation from command economies; evaluation of decentralizing reforms and quasi-markets in industrialized countries; the present and future of the welfare state; the problems of micro-states; or the national-local relationship, to cite only a few topics.

Many of these areas have been studied by other disciplines. Often they present difficult and sensitive research issues. And there will be no definitive answers, for to study the ways in which a society chooses to allocate its resources is to study society itself.

NAOMI CAIDEN

BIBLIOGRAPHY

Caiden, Naomi and Aaron Wildavsky, 1974 and 1980. *Planning and Budgeting in Poor Countries.* New York: Wiley; New Brunswick NJ: Transaction.
Campbell, John Creighton, 1977. *Contempory Japanese Budget Politics.* Berkeley: University of California Press.
Gunther, Richard, 1980. *Public Policy in a No-Party State: Spanish Planning and Budgeting in the Twilight of the Franco Era.* Berkeley: University of California Press.
Heclo, Hugh and Aaron Wildavsky, 1974. *The Private Government of Public Money: Community and Policy Inside British Politics.* Berkeley: University of California Press.
Lord, Guy, 1973. *The French Budgetary Process.* Berkeley: University of California Press.
Organization for Economic Cooperation and Development, 1987. *The Control and Management of Public Expenditure.* Paris: OECD.
Premchand, A., 1983. *Government Budgeting and Expenditure Controls: Theory and Practice.* Washington, D.C.: International Monetary Fund.
Premchand, A., ed., 1990. *Government Financial Management: Issues and Country Studies.* Washington, D.C.: International Monetary Fund.
Premchand, A. and Jesse Burkhead, eds., 1984. *Comparative International Budgeting and Finance.* New Brunswick, NJ: Transaction.
Riggs, Fred W., 1965. *Administration in Developing Countries: The Theory of Prismatic Society.* Boston: Houghton Mifflin.
Schick, Allen, 1986. "Macro-Budgetary Adaptations of Fiscal Stress in Industrialized Democracies." *Public Administration Review* (March/April) 124–134.
———, 1988. "Micro-Budgetary Adaptations to Fiscal Stress in Industrialized Democracies." *Public Administration Review* (January/February) 523–533.
Stourm, René, 1909. *Le Budget.* Paris: Alcan.
United Nations, 1967. *Manual for Program and Performance Budgeting.* New York: United Nations.
Waterston, Albert, 1965. *Development Planning: The Lessons of Experience.* Baltimore: Johns Hopkins.
Webber, Carolyn and Aaron Wildavsky, 1986. *A History of Taxation and Expenditure in the Western World.* New York: Simon and Schuster.
Wildavsky, Aaron, 1985. *Budgeting: A Comparative Theory of Budgeting Processes.* Boston: Little, Brown.

COMPENSATION POLICY.

The established criteria and processes for paying employees for the work they do. Compensation includes both direct salary and wages and employee benefits. Most public organizations use formal compensation (pay) plans that attempt to base pay for a particular position on considerations of internal and external equity. Internal equity refers to other positions in the organization. Thus, the value or importance of positions relative to one another serves as a basis for establishing internal equity. External equity refers to how compensation for a position compares to what other organizations pay for similar positions. External equity is achieved through salary and wage surveys of other employers. To the extent that individuals perceive the compensation policy as fair and equitable, the policy helps in recruiting, motivating, and retaining employees (see **recruitment**).

Typically in the public sector, compensation plans array a number of pay ranges and steps within ranges across a table. For example, range 1 may have a yearly range from $15,000 to $18,000 in five steps, each with an increment of $750. Range 2 then might start at $16,500 with increments of $825.00. This pay plan reflects a 10 percent differential between ranges and a 5 percent differential between steps. Positions throughout the organization are placed in specified ranges. Compensation policy usually allows for hiring people at any step within the appropriate range depending upon qualifications and experience of the new hire.

In recent years, formal compensation plans have come under increasing criticism. Advocates for reform in compensation policy claim most public sector pay plans are too rigid and do not recognize performance differences, as employees move through steps in the plan based primarily on the time they remain in a position doing no more than meeting basic performance requirements. To recognize different performance levels, these critics suggest using merit pay or pay for performance, a very attractive notion to elected officials and citizens alike. Therefore, all levels of government in the United States have experimented with merit or performance pay systems. Canada has used performance-based pay successfully, but the experience in the United States has been mixed with very few examples of success. Performance-based pay systems seem to fail primarily because evaluation of performance usually results in very little documentation of differencies in performance levels among individual employees. Additionally, the rewards for meritorious performance usually have been so minimal they have not served as performance incentives.

The alternative to pay increases based on performance is the across-the-board increase, sometimes referred to as the cost of living increase since it usually is based on some percentage of the change in cost of living. The attractiveness of this approach is that there is little discretion involved in distributing pay increases except that employees usually must have acceptable or satisfactory performance to qualify for the increase. Theoretically, high performers find this system demoralizing because it does not recognize their contributions.

Pay equity is an issue that has been of major concern to public personnel management. Pay equity has two components—equal pay for equal work and comparable worth (see **comparable worth**). Equal pay for equal work was ad-

dressed in the United States by the Equal Pay Act of 1963, which requires the same compensation for people performing the same jobs, all other factors being equal. Comparable worth (now often called pay equity) focuses on paying work of equal value to the organization at the same rate even if the substance of the work is different. Job analysis is done to examine the various components of the job and their value to the organization (see **job analysis and evaluation**). The purpose of comparable worth policy is to eliminate pay differentials that are gender-based. Many local governments and some states have adopted comparable worth policies.

In the federal government, compensation policy also addresses disparities in cost of living across the country. Thus, locality pay allows for adjustment to the pay schedule to account for differences in living costs in different locations. A variation of locality pay would be the British system of hazardous duty or hardship pay, in which the employee is given pay adjustments for serving in some foreign locations.

Employee benefits also are part of compensation packages. Employee benefits include mandated benefits such as Social Security, unemployment compensation, workers' compensation, and family leave, and discretionary benefits such as health insurance, vacation leave, retirement pensions, and dependent care services. Public employees generally have enjoyed better benefit levels than private sector employees and the benefits, especially retirement pensions, usually have been more secure. The rising costs of health care and other benefits are causing close reviews of benefits offered. Flexible benefit plans, in which employees have a fixed dollar amount to apply to the benefits they choose, are becoming popular. Increasingly, benefits are factored into comparability studies when public sector compensation levels are based on what other organizations pay.

N. JOSEPH CAYER

BIBLIOGRAPHY

Cook, Alice H., 1991. "Pay Equity Theory and Implementation." In Carolyn Ban and Norma M. Riccucci, eds., *Public Personnel Management: Current Concerns–Future Challenges.* New York: Longman, pp. 100–113.
National Research Council, 1991. *Pay for Performance: Evaluating Performance Appraisal and Merit Pay.* Washington, D.C.: National Academy Press.
Perry, James L., 1986. "Merit Pay in the Public Sector: The Case for a Failure of Theory." *Review of Public Personnel Administration,* 7 (Fall) 57–69.
Siegel, Gilbert B., 1992. *Public Employee Compensation and Its Role in Public Sector Strategic Management.* New York: Quorum Books.

COMPETENCE. Having the knowledge, skills, and abilities to perform the duties of a particular job at some predetermined level of adequacy. Competence in public sector organizations comprises many facets, including technical competence, managerial and leadership competence, cultural competence, political competence, neutral competence, and constitutional competence.

Competence is not all-encompassing, in that it is possible to be competent in one domain and incompetent in another. Competence exists as a continuum; at the one end are those individuals who excel in that field or area and at the other end are those who are incapable of even basic action in that field or area.

Technical competence is having the ability to perform the work of some specialized area that may require distinctive training and/or education. Specialization is one of the anchors of a bureaucratic organization. In government, technical competence can be based on knowledge of the rules, regulations, and procedures of a particular program or agency as well as knowledge of a field of study such as nursing or accounting. Technical competence is the most transferable; that is, an individual who is skilled as a systems analyst can be transported from one environment to another and maintain competence in that area. Since the rules, regulations, and procedures tend to be agency-specific, competence in that technical area is not as transferable. However, once an individual masters the bureaucratic maze of one organization, it is relatively easy to apply what has been learned to other settings.

Managerial competence, although less transferable than technical competence, is also transferable, especially if we accept the distinctions proffered by Zaleznik (1993). Leadership competence is situation-specific, and although an individual can be a leader in a variety of settings, it is to be expected that adaptive behaviors will be utilized. Political competence requires adaptive behaviors and a commitment to a leader or a cause. In addition, it requires an individual to be an astute student of the changing nature of the citizenry or the changing environment within the organization.

Increasingly in organizations employees as well as managers are required to be culturally competent, that is, to understand the differences in the values and methods of communicating in various cultures. Although this has always been a pluralistic society, very little attention was paid to cultural differences. It was expected that everyone would adapt to the U.S. way of doing business. Due to the globalization of the economy, the private sector developed programs in this arena in order to assure their position in the marketplace. As the antidiscrimination laws began to be enforced and the workforce in the public sector began to change, the public sector recognized the need to be culturally competent, especially since it is evident that the workforce will become increasingly diverse by the twenty-first century.

According to Rourke (1992), neutral competence is the wealth of knowledge and skills possessed by civil servants and available in the corridors of bureaucracy that all elected officials, no matter what their political persuasion, could call upon for both useful information and disinterested advice in designing national policy.

Both Rourke (1992) and Rosenbloom (1993) argue the need for constitutional competence among public officials and administrators. Constitutional competence is understanding the framework of the Constitution in order to promote the public interest. As Rosenbloom (1993) states, the judicial involvement in public administration is so pronounced, and the legal approach so strong, that the need for public administrators to understand the Constitution is obvious.

In public sector organizations the various facets of competence coexist. Each agency has its technical experts—those who have been educated or have gained work experience in a particular technical field. Public administration as a profession is a difficult concept for some because there are numerous professions that comprise the work of government and these professionals generally have a strong allegiance to their technical field rather than to public administration. It is, however, these individuals who keep the system running year after year. The competent members of any field will keep abreast of the changes in the field and will recommend changes of a technical nature. However, they are not likely to recommend changes in the overall system.

Technical competence is generally easy to assess through various methods. It is also relatively easy to write performance descriptions for technical positions. Although tolerance for error is subjective, and therefore variation exists in ratings by supervisors, there exist some minimum standards for technical competence that are set either by a credentialing agent or an academic institution. Technical competence is often agency-specific. For example, in the Department of Human Services there are individuals who must be able to handle infectious diseases, blood-borne pathogens and psychotropic drugs, while individuals in the Department of Environmental Protection must be able to handle hazardous waste materials or measure the impact of development on the wetlands. Incompetence in these areas puts lives in jeopardy and, therefore, it tends to be monitored closely by various accrediting bodies. Deviations in procedures are dealt with strictly and generally swiftly. Although specific to these agencies, people with technical expertise could work for other organizations in the private or not-for-profit sectors, thus demonstrating that technical competence is often transferable. However, it is in this area of competence that public sector employees tend to fall behind their counterparts in the private sector. Due to budgetary constraints and a reluctance to invest in new technologies and in human resource development, the technical expertise of many public sector employees is outdated. As the world was moving to a

PC-based environment, public sector organizations were clinging to mainframes. Training budgets and staffs were cut in order to save millions of dollars, and expenditures on technology that would lessen or perhaps even compensate for the impact of the cuts were ignored.

Government-specific technical expertise, such as unemployment insurance regulations, though transferable from one state to another and between states and the federal government, does not hold the same possibilities for the private and not-for-profit sectors. However, there is a body of knowledge that workers must master in order to demonstrate competence in these areas, and there are mechanisms for detecting when someone has crossed over the line that delineates competence from incompetence.

Attempts at treating managerial competence in the same manner as technical competence have proven to be ineffective. The traditional paper and pencil examinations for managerial positions were as accurate as tossing a coin. Although there is a body of knowledge that comprises information managerial staff need, it is interpersonal and human relations skills that separate the effective from the ineffective manager, and these skills cannot be assessed through traditional mechanisms. Thus, in systems where selection for managerial positions is based on longevity in a technical position and/or the use of traditional examinations, the likelihood of promoting the most competent manager is significantly decreased. Although often viewed as a prerequisite for advancement, technical competence does not in and of itself bestow upon the individual competence at other organizational levels. In fact, the skills and competencies required for positions in a technical area or in other areas may be diametrically opposed to the skills and competencies required for positions at other levels.

The public sector, due to its attention to fairness and due process, is more prone to using longevity and technical expertise as the main criteria in promotions. The impact of this tendency has been decreased by the implementation of training programs such as the Certified Public Manager Program, which aims at improving managerial skills through a comprehensive, theoretical, and practical course of study.

In most systems, managers will be most interested in staying the course (that is, not making any changes to the way things are), thus preventing any major disruptions of service to the clients that are served by the agency. Therefore, they will initiate the necessary controls to ensure that the work is done in a predictably routine fashion. The strong desire to remain attached to the past way of doing business is for the most part based on the reward systems many organizations have in place, and not some inborn trait of those who chose public service as a career. Rewards are generally based on consistency, not change. Errors are scoffed at and the individual who makes the error is often made to feel less competent than his or her counterparts.

Risk taking is not rewarded; unlike the private sector, in which an error does not place one in immediate jeopardy of losing one's job, the message in the public sector, whether spoken or unspoken, is to avoid risk at all costs. The competent manager in the public sector does not make any waves.

Depending on the political administration, managerial staff may or may not be expected to lead their organizational units. For some, managerial competence is restricted to controls and accountability; for others, getting the staff to see and understand a vision of success is within the realm of the manager. Upper-level managers should spend an increasing amount of time formulating and disseminating the organizational vision, which is likely to transcend partisan politics.

As in all organizations, the public sector has both formal and informal leaders. Both will have a followership, and in some instances they will be working at cross purposes. In the public sector, there are leaders who are appointed by the party in power and who have gained the respect of not only the workers they are to lead but the clientele they are serving. They have done so by demonstrating competence in the field prior to their appointment. These individuals are likely to engender an *esprit de corps* within the organization, and they will encounter very little opposition from the informal leaders at various levels within the organization. On the other hand, in situations where the appointed leader is viewed as an interloper who has done nothing to gain the respect of any constituency, is seen as incompetent in the areas that relate to the work of the agency, and attempts to make swift and unexplained changes in the way business is conducted, turf battles and passive or active resistance will occur.

The clash that occurs in the public sector regarding competence to lead is one that results from a lack of clarity regarding what comprises political competence, the use of appointments to repay party faithfuls, and the role that those who possess political competence or who achieve an appointment should play in oganizational life. Political competence is an essential skill in any organization. It is that skill which allows an individual to survey the environment quickly and determine what type of allies are needed, what type of risks will pay off in the short term and the long term, or determine the mood of the clientele as well as the employees within an organization. Partisan affiliation—that is, campaigning for and contributing to a particular party, and thereby gaining entry to various public sector positions—is limited to the public sector. These are very different, although often confused. In every administration there is a mix of those who are politically competent and those who have used a connection in order to achieve a high position. The former knows when to depend on the careerists and how to elicit support; the latter is often like the proverbial "bull in a china shop."

Although there is a great deal of discussion regarding cultural competence in organizations and the number of diversity training programs has increased significantly, virtually no attempts have been made to incorporate into the performance appraisal and reward systems the ideas of working together and managing individuals from different ethnic backgrounds in an equitable fashion. In most instances, the emphasis is still placed on getting the newcomer to act more like the majority population.

Neutral competence had been the cornerstone of the public sector bureaucracy. Regardless of the administration, the career bureaucrat could be expected to give unbiased information and advice on matters of public policy. According to Rourke (1992), this is being questioned and the "declining faith in the neutral competence of civil servants threatens to undermine the legitimacy of bureaucratic participation in national policy making." (p. 539).

Those individuals who were brought into the system as appointees, and therefore without the scrutiny of the open-competitive process, were expected to leave after the tenure of that administration was over. Over the years, and particularly in recent years with the downsizing of private sector organizations as well as government, there has been a tendency to bestow upon political appointees civil service status. This practice is, in part, responsible for the tremendous growth in the size of government during the past decade. This attempt—a fairly successful one—to place one's allies in permanent positions before leaving office has eroded the credibility of a true meritocracy and therefore calls into question the neutral competence of the bureaucrat.

It would be inaccurate and unfair if we placed the blame for all of the problems facing the public sector today at the feet of the bureaucrats. The media, politicians, and others have gone on a virtual feeding frenzy at the expense of public sector employees. While it is fair to assume that (as in every other type of organization) there are those who are incompetent, and that not all of the incompetent individuals are "street level bureaucrats" or managers, some insights from Ott and Shafritz (1994) are appropriate here. There tends to be a need to find a scapegoat when things go wrong. Therefore, if an organization is not effective, there must be an individual or group of individuals who are responsible. Ott and Shafritz discuss the issue of organizational incompetence and state that "organizational culture is the issue, not the intelligence of individuals in the organization". "Organizational incompetence is changed by altering the organizational culture, not individuals" (1994 pp. 372, 375).

Thus, as important as training and development is to an organization, it can be rendered useless. In these rapidly changing times, if the intent of the training is to make individuals more effective and efficient at what they do and no time is spent helping them to rethink their organization, its culture, and its mission, organizational change will not result, incompetence will continue, and perhaps the ultimate result—organizational extinction will occur.

ALMA M. JOSEPH

BIBLIOGRAPHY

Ott, J. Steven and Jay M. Shafritz, 1994. "Toward a Definition of Organizational Incompetence: A Neglected Variable in Organization Theory." *Public Administration Review,* vol. 54, pp. 370–376.

Rosenbloom, David H., 1993. *Public Administration: Understanding Management, Politics and Law in the Public Sector.* New York: McGraw-Hill Inc.

Rourke, Francis E., 1992. "Responsiveness and Neutral Competence in American Bureaucracy." *Public Administration Review,* vol. 52, pp. 539–546.

Zaleznik, Abraham, 1993. "Managers and Leaders: Are They Different?" In William E. Rosenbach and Robert L. Taylor, eds., *Contemporary Issues in Leadership.* Boulder: Westview Press, pp. 36–56.

COMPETITION POLICY. A means to enhance efficiency and economic growth, through legislative, administrative, or regulatory programs to lessen monopoly and promote robust markets, thereby increasing economic efficiency.

Competition policy is the centrepiece of the microeconomic reform programs of many modern governments. It is based on the premise that by stimulating competition in both the private and public sectors, a higher level of efficiency will be achieved. In a climate of genuine competition it is argued allocative efficiency will be maximized, product diversification and research encouraged, and the range, quality, and price of goods and services available to the consumer increased. The key objective therefore is to create an integrated economy where there is competition for and access to goods and services in all markets (Hilmer et al., 1993, p. xvii).

Competition policy can be divided into two broad areas: regulation and deterrence of uncompetitive practices, and structural reform of markets to create greater access and competition. An early but limited manifestation of the regulatory approach was trade practices legislation. Instances are the Fair Trading Act (United Kingdom) and the Trade Practices Act (Australia). There have been problems with the "watchdog" regulatory approach. Regulation typically has been static and has not covered all anticompetitive practices; regulatory bodies have faced difficulty in monitoring market behavior; and often the legislative sanctions have been insufficient to discourage anticompetitive practices (Hilmer et al., 1993, p. xviii). More important, until recently such legislation failed to exclude regulation of anticompetitive conduct in the public sector and labor markets.

The second area of competition policy, the structural reform of public and private monopoly power, is receiving increased attention. In the U.S. the longstanding manifestation of this approach has been antitrust laws aimed at ensuring the existence of a competitive market structure. In many industrialized nations governments have been the sole providers of infrastructure such as power, transport, and energy. It has been argued that lack of competition in these industries led to inefficiency. Not only was this reflected in price and quality combinations offered to final consumers but also input prices. Structural reform of public monopolies aims to improve efficiency by creating competition or by providing access to monopoly resources to potential competitors.

Governments have undertaken structural reforms by privatizations and direct measures to increase competition, for example, the sale and break-up of the publicly owned electricity generation and distribution industry in the UK. There is a variety of forms of privatization, including complete sale of government enterprises, contracting out of management, and partial privatization. Privatization options have become increasingly popular worldwide, with sales of state-owned enterprises reaching US $200 billion in the 1990–1993 period (OECD, 1994, p. 48). An alternative to privatization is regulated competition by allowing privately owned companies to compete alongside a government-owned utility. In the United States where telephone companies traditionally have been privately owned a similar effect has been achieved by breaking up local monopolies. In Australia the government has recently opened the telecommunications industry to allow a private carrier to compete with the government-owned Telstra.

Where competition has been created in place of a publicly owned monopoly, it has been necessary to separate the regulatory and commercial functions. This separation is designed to ensure that public utilities do not enjoy a competitive advantage over the private sector companies operating in that industry. Effective competition also requires that potential competitors be ensured access to essential facilities; for example, a power generation company requires access to the electricity transmission grid.

Also crucial to competition policy is the continuing reform of existing regulations that are designed to or have the effect of hindering competition and that cannot be justified in the public interest. These areas include statutory marketing arrangements, product labeling, health and safety standards, and licensing arrangements for professions and businesses. The reform of the professions is a significant part of competition policy and in the United States, New Zealand, and the European Community the distinction between professions and other forms of trade has been removed (Hilmer et al., 1993, p. 136).

JULIAN TEICHER

BIBLIOGRAPHY

Bishop, M., J. Kay, and C. Mayer 1995. *The Regulatory Challenge.* Oxford: Oxford University Press.

Hilmer, F. G., M. Rayner, and G. Taperell, 1993. *National Competition Policy.* Canberra: Australian Government Publishing Service.

Organization for Economic Cooperation and Development, 1994. "Industrial Policy in OECD Countries." *Annual Review, 1994,* p. 48.

COMPETITIVE TENDERING.

A mechanism for introducing choice between alternative providers of publicly funded goods and services, through competition for supply contracts. In recent years it has become a significant instrument of public sector reform, used specifically to enhance efficiency (reduce costs) and effectiveness (increase quality) of public services.

Closely related to the concepts of "contracting out" and "outsourcing," competitive tendering has been interpreted by some critics as being simply privatization in disguise: a transfer of economic activity from the public to the private sector. Although competitive tendering often results in contracts being awarded to private sector suppliers of goods and services, the role of competition must be distinguished from that of ownership—whether suppliers are privately or publicly owned. International evidence suggests that competition has a distinct and powerful influence on economic performance, independent from that of ownership (see, for example, Domberger and Rimmer, 1994).

The Process

Competitive tendering is a means of introducing competition at predetermined intervals, by inviting competitive bids for the provision of goods or services of specified type and quality. In circumstances where it is not efficient to have more than one provider at a time, as for example with office cleaning, continuous or direct competition between suppliers will not be feasible. The public sector organization could, of course, produce its own services by setting up a cleaning division. Alternatively, it could invite competitive tenders from potential suppliers and appoint a contractor on the basis of price and/or other selection criteria.

The tendering process involves specifying the quantity and quality of services to be delivered, calling for bids from external providers and the in-house team if the client organization has its own provider, evaluating the tenders, appointing the preferred contractor, and managing the contract. Although the principle is straightforward, implementation is both costly and demanding of management time. Precise estimates of the costs of tendering are hard to come by, but they are likely to be higher for public sector organizations than for their private sector counterparts. The reason is that public sector accountability and transparency requirements lead to greater demands for information and adherence to due process. Conversely, formal tendering is often eschewed by the private sector in favor of direct negotiations of contracts in order to avoid the costs of tendering.

Scope of Use

The application of competitive tendering varies from country to country although it has generally been on the increase. In the UK, the Conservative administration that came into office in 1979 has deployed it extensively both at central and local government levels. In 1988 competitive tendering was made compulsory for all basic services such as street cleaning, refuse collection, and school meals provided by local authorities to their residents. Central government services such as cleaning, maintenance, security, and laundry now are also subject to competitive tendering.

In the United States, competitive tendering has been used in the transport and energy sectors since the beginning of the century. The federal government also purchases its defense supplies and prison services in this way. State governments use it for the provision of recreation services, training, and public transport, among others. At the local government level, road construction, waste collection, building maintenance, and other services are regularly subjected to such competition.

In Australia and Asia, the application of competitive tendering has grown rapidly in recent years. Recent surveys (see Farago and Li, 1993) suggest that state government expenditures on services in Australia are increasingly being allocated in this way. Central government is now subjecting defense forces' support services, equipment purchasing, maintenance, and legal services to competition.

Assessment

Competitive tendering has become a politically charged issue and is often treated with the same vehemence as privatization. In the UK, the introduction of compulsory competitive tendering for local authority services sparked a heated controversy on the merits of such policy. Early research by Domberger, Meadowcroft, and Thompson (1986) indicated that the introduction of tendering, even before it was made compulsory, was associated with savings in the region of 20 percent. Recent work by Szymanski and Wilkins (1993) confirmed these estimates and suggested that savings levels have not decreased since tendering was made compulsory. A recent survey of worldwide evidence on competitive tendering and costs concluded, "A review of the literature illustrates a broad

consensus that competitive tendering and contracting usually leads to substantial reductions in service costs. While the level of cost changes varies greatly, . . . average reductions of 20 percent are usually attained by its use (Domberger and Rimmer, 1994, p. 446).

On the question of quality the results are both sparse and equivocal due to the paucity of data. However, recent quantitative research by Domberger, Hall, and Li (1995) based on an econometric model of price and quality suggests that the introduction of tendering maintains or even enhances quality, notwithstanding substantial reductions in contract prices. The evidence seems to suggest that, provided contracts are well designed and implemented, competitive tendering can yield efficiency gains without sacrificing service quality.

Conclusion

Competitive tendering is not new. In France the rights to build and operate public transport and water distribution facilities were first put up to competitive tender in the early part of the nineteenth century. Interestingly, competitive tendering is on the increase in the public sector precisely at a time when outsourcing is gathering pace in the private sector. Could these two trends be related to each other?

The answer would seem to be in the affirmative. Three factors lie behind these developments. First, global competition in the private sector and fiscal restraint in the public sector have combined to make the quest for efficiency a much higher priority.

Second, the reappraisal of the role of government (Osborne and Gaebler, 1992) has shifted the emphasis in the public sector from the production of goods and services to the coordination and regulation of their supply. Finally, technological changes, particularly in the information technology industry, have made contractual solutions more attractive than hitherto.

All the evidence suggests that the use of competitive tendering will continue to grow. The challenge for public sector managers lies in designing and implementing efficient contractual solutions across the ever increasing variety of services that are being subjected to competition.

SIMON DOMBERGER

BIBLIOGRAPHY

Domberger, S., C. Hall, and E. Li, 1994. "The Determinants of Price and Quality in Competitively Tendered Contracts." *The Economic Journal*, vol. 105, in press.
Domberger, S., S. Meadowcroft, and D. Thompson, D. 1986. "Competitive Tendering and Efficiency: The Case of Refuse Collection." *Fiscal Studies*, vol. 7, 69–87.
Domberger, S. and S. Rimmer, 1994. "Competitive Tendering and Contracting in the Public Sector: A Survey." *International Journal of the Economics of Business*, vol. 1, 439–453.

Farago, S. and E. Li, 1993. "Contracting in NSW Government Agencies." *CTC Newsletter* no. 4, Graduate School of Business, The University of Sydney.

Osborne, D. and T. Gaebler, 1992. *Reinventing Government: How the Entrepreneurial Spirit Is Transforming the Public Sector.* Reading, MA: Addison-Wesley.

Szymanski, S., and S. Wilkins, 1993. "Cheap Rubbish? Competitive Tendering and Contracting Out in Refuse Collection 1981–88." *Fiscal Studies*, vol. 14, 109–130.

COMPREHENSIVE PLANNING.

An activity taken by a general purpose local government in order to direct future community growth and land use patterns. It is one of the major legal land use tools available to local government. The terms "general plan" and "master plan" are used synonymously with comprehensive plan.

Comprehensive planning is important as a process and as a legal document. The process is an opportunity to organize important demographic, economic, and physical characteristic data, to inform the community, and to engage the community in public involvement processes to shape a vision for the future. The resulting document includes statements of the community's goals and a map or set of maps with complete coverage of the community indicating the boundaries of zones for different kinds of land use or preservation, both at the present and in the future. References to related zoning, special district, subdivision, and other ordinances are included to guide the plan's implementation. In some states, zoning decisions must be based on and consistent with an approved comprehensive plan. Plans need to be continuously updated to reflect changing community needs and to keep the public awareness of community planning goals at a high level.

Origin and Subsequent History

In the United States, the Spanish heritage of the American Southwest includes city layouts fostered by Spain's colonial period "Law of the Indies," visible in cities such as San Antonio, Texas; Santa Fe, New Mexico; and St. Augustine, Florida. William Penn's Philadelphia had an initial planned layout that was overtaken and thwarted by rapid development during the nineteenth century. James Oglethorpe's layout for Savannah, Georgia, withstood development pressure well into the nineteenth century. L'Enfant's design for Washington, D.C., was a grand project of civic display that integrated streets, structures, and public spaces.

Midwestern and Western cities that developed during the nineteenth century used a rectangular pattern of long and wide primary streets crossed by short and narrow feeder streets. This pattern attended to commercial development needs but ignored natural terrain features and surrounding residential areas and their needs.

Modern planning and the development of the comprehensive planning process with its several different elements arose as a response to crises of various sorts: slum conditions, adjacent incompatible land uses, and the loss of aesthetically pleasing vistas. A movement of architects and engineers to promote urban design, known as the "City Beautiful" movement, came to fruition in the Columbian Exposition in Chicago in 1893. The exhibition was followed by a comprehensive plan for the city of Chicago in 1909. Although this plan contained fewer of the elements now usually associated with comprehensive planning, it was the first effort to plan for the future growth of a modern industrial city.

One of the elements of Roosevelt's New Deal in the 1930s was a Resettlement Administration organized to develop new towns. Only a few towns were planned and built before the program lost support, but the ideas of comprehensive design got some exercise. Another program provided funding for local and state planning, which did much to boost planning as a profession.

Municipal planning expanded after World War II, as urban renewal programs, the interstate highway system, and environment protection programs were initiated. All of these programs played a direct role in the plans cities developed. Federal influence in comprehensive planning is also felt in the requirements it attaches to federal aid. One such requirement has been for grant recipients to conduct citizen participation activities during the course of their planning.

Overall, planning in the United States has not enjoyed the political support that it has in other industrialized nations. Because of hostility toward the Soviet Union, planned economies and planning in general were suspect activities. Public planning imposes restrictions on private actions related to private property, and because there remain so many parts of the country that have not fully developed comprehensive planning processes, arguments over the legitimacy of the activity continue to be raised. In well-established urban centers and their suburbs, planning is solidly established as an appropriate public activity and concern.

Underlying Theoretical Framework

Purpose

The goal of comprehensive planning is to direct development in directions that will provide for maximum economic development while preserving quality of life and other values defined by the community. Although not all communities aim to accomplish the same goals with their planning processes, most states that require planning look for planning elements that protect health and public safety, ease circulation, provide and locate services and facilities, fit the community's fiscal resources, serve the community's economic goals, and protect the community's environmental quality. Some comprehensive planning also exhibits goals that are intended to redistribute wealth and influence more broadly in the community. For instance, some states require that local governments conduct planning with the maximum feasible participation of community residents.

Several examples illustrate various planning elements. Improving the circulation of traffic on a community's roads and streets is an important goal of comprehensive planning. Organizing street widths and types to separate through traffic from local traffic is a widely accepted principle. Designing and providing various forms of public transportation is an important component of comprehensive planning.

Legal Justification and Issues

The legal framework for comprehensive planning is the same as for other legal tools of land management: the state's police power to protect and enhance public health, safety, and welfare.

The concerns of planning and the controls that it may place on private landowners have led to a number of controversies, especially at times when urban growth or urban values has expanded into rural areas. Critics claim that land use planning and its related tools impinge upon private property owners' rights. Advocates claim that planning is necessary to make maximum use of limited resources rationally and to protect the interests of future generations. Some planning advocates have challenged the preservation of private property rights in light of the greater good of providing an adequate base for social and natural systems, but support for this position has not materialized in the United States.

Planning and the Provision of Municipal Services

From the point of view of municipal managers, planning is necessary to provide services such as sewers, traffic control, and fire and police protection in an orderly and efficient manner. Health measures in comprehensive planning include measures regulating residential density and assuring that the load on water and sewer facilities will not exceed their capacity. Typical public safety measures in planning ensure access for emergency vehicles, prohibit certain types of construction in floodplains, and locate schools so that children don't have to cross high-traffic streets. Finding optimum locations for facilities such as recreation areas, schools, hospitals, and other public functions is an important feature of the comprehensive plan.

Economic Planning

Communities often plan with an eye to the fiscal impact of various forms of development. Usually they seek to encourage development that will increase revenue rather than cost more than it provides in additional revenues. Communities may plan to limit future growth, even at some cost, in order to preserve existing community qualities. Such planning elements are difficult to implement if private landowners disagree with community values. Communities may also be especially interested in establishing areas that will lure industry and commercial activities, especially if community jobs are a concern. Communities can offer incentives and arrange to supply utilities to such sites.

Environmental Quality

Another important stream of planning thought comes from the work of Ian McHarg, who wrote *Design with Nature* in 1969. McHarg initiated the idea of looking at different aspects of the landscape (geology, soil, water, and hazards) which, when combined as separate overlay maps, give a good indication of which areas are appropriate for development and which are not. Computerized versions of this technique, known as Geographic Information Systems (GIS), are now commonly used by planners. Preservation of open space and ecologically important or fragile areas is increasingly an element of comprehensive planning.

Planning and Public Participation

Rational planning faces difficulties in a democratic political system. Technically elegant processes and results do not always conform with aggregate public preferences. "Reasonable minds can and will differ both about what constitutes a desirable future and about what means are best suited to achieve that future" (Kelly, 1993). Planners are often frustrated by the lack of support they receive from the public or from interest groups that have a different agenda. Planners may deal with this problem by developing political astuteness regarding area stakeholders and negotiating the results they desire, or by making a commitment to an open process in which the public is recruited and involved in setting the community's direction. Pragmatically, public involvement is seen as a way to build support for the later implementation of the plan.

Comprehensive planning blends the professional planner's training in urban form and function with the considerations of a particular community's financial, political, and sociological circumstances and preferences.

Current Practice in the United States

Methods of planning vary widely among local jurisdictions in the United States, partly as a function of government and professional capacity, but also as a function of the local community's perceived needs. Smaller jurisdictions often hire consultants to carry out the process. Some communities simply extrapolate current trends into the future, or develop plans in response to some crisis. Others may employ sophisticated modeling techniques. Despite these variations, these is a conventional process through which most comprehensive planning occurs.

Comprehensive planning commonly consists of five steps, which in practice overlap: a research phase, clarification of community goals and objectives, plan formulation, plan implementation, and review with revision (Levy, 1991).

The comprehensiveness of the research is in part determined by the community's goals and needs. Data relevant to comprehensive planning might include population forecasts, inventories of land use and environmental features such as soils and water, traffic projections, recreation surveys, and fiscal forecasts. The proportion of the public involved in the goal-setting process may vary, but the usual result is a short list of feasible goals. Public involvement in formulation is also critical to the plan's eventual support. Plan formulation typically involves developing alternatives to achieve stated goals and then evaluating the costs and benefits of each alternative, not just financially, but relative to each other in terms of how well each accomplishes the main goal and is complementary to other goals.

Ideally, implementation of the comprehensive plan is facilitated by consistency with other municipal planning activities, particularly the location, timing, and form of capital investments. In many cases this is difficult to accomplish because authority over expenditures is divided. The primary tools for implementing a comprehensive plan are capital improvement expenditures, subdivision regulations, and the enforcement of the zoning ordinance. Of these tools, capital improvement expenditures, once made, may have a much more significant impact on land use and development. Implementation problems, changing community goals, and outside changes all contribute to the need to update the plan periodically, adapting it to internal and external change.

Variations in State and National Planning

Overlaying the diversity of local jurisdiction planning is the complexity contributed by the uneven distribution of state and national land use planning. States own land for which they plan, and also set up the requirements for planning among local jurisdictions. The federal government owns approximately one-third of the nation's land, most of it concentrated in Alaska and eleven states.

Statewide land use controls began in Hawaii in the early 1960s, and Vermont followed in 1970. Several other states have since followed. In 1988 Vermont went beyond its growth management laws to set up comprehensive planning for the entire state, covering elements such as housing, transportation, and the environment.

Several federal agencies have jurisdiction over the use of federally owned land. Managers of the largest holdings include the Bureau of Land Management (BLM), the National Forest Service, the National Park Service, the United States Fish and Wildlife Service, and the Department of Defense. The Forest Service and BLM are re-

quired to carry out planning at the district and resource area level for resource development, recreation, and natural area preservation. Some areas are designated as wilderness, to be protected from development in perpetuity. Other areas are open to a variety of activities, including hard-rock mineral mining, oil, coal, and gas leasing, timber sales, grazing, and recreation uses. Federal agency managers are required to conduct their planning processes with public involvement and to coordinate with local and state officials.

Variations in Regimes

Western European countries have a more centrally organized planning approach and a longer tradition of urban design. The political culture in Europe expects certain services from government more than it expects government to stay out of where it is unwanted. Planning in Europe involves more and more aspects of society.

In Britain, central government departments must approve local land use policies and proposals. Local authorities have a great deal of discretion in determining whether individual actions are in conformance with plans, but often override local preferences for larger public interests that have been determined by the central government, such as providing or protecting agricultural land.

The French planning system is based on guaranteeing the rights of developers as long as they conform to a local area's planning provisions. The planning regulations are often elaborate, and developers often negotiate based on the particulars of their case.

The legal basis for physical planning in the Netherlands was established in 1965 (Vonk, 1983). Plans have the force of law, and compliance or noncompliance is the absolute grounds for development approval. Common practice is for municipalities to purchase land, provide service hook-ups, and then sell the land to developers. In some cases, perhaps because of the municipal interest in the success of development proposals, municipalities grant approval to a nonconforming proposal on the grounds that it is in compliance with the intention of a not yet approved plan revision.

Comprehensive planning and its implementation is a highly variable activity across and within regimes. In contrast to the United States system, which with some exceptions leaves planning to local jurisdictions, Western European countries employ a more top-down approach. British, French, and Dutch central policymakers state the policy and operational requirements and provide the funding, and the locality is responsible for execution. As the above examples indicate, while the planning laws may appear stricter in these countries, in practice they are made flexible by the participants (Cullingworth, 1994).

LISA S. NELSON

BIBLIOGRAPHY

Cullingworth, J. Barry, 1994. "Alternate Planning Systems: Is There Anything to Learn from Abroad?" *APA Journal* (Spring) 162–172.

Kelly, Eric Damian, 1993. *Managing Community Growth.* Westport, CT: Praeger.

Levy, John M., 1991. *Contemporary Urban Planning.* 2nd. ed. Englewood Cliffs, NJ: Prentice Hall.

McHarg, Ian, 1969. *Design with Nature.* New York: Natural History Press.

Ortolano, Leonard, 1984. *Environmental Planning and Decision Making.* New York: John Wiley and Sons.

Vonk, Franz, 1983. "Citizen Participation in the Netherlands: Some Comments." In Lawrence Susskind and Michael Elliott, eds., *Paternalism, Conflict, and Coproduction.* New York: Plenum Press, pp. 343–347.

White, Jay, 1991. "From Modernity to Postmodernity: Two Views of Planning and Public Administration." *Public Administration Review* 51:6 (November/December) 564–568.

CONFLICT MANAGEMENT. Systems for sustaining bounded relationships between states or in internal conflicts even if hostilities have occurred or are high probability policy options. In its contemporary usage, conflict management reflects a U.S. "engineering" approach to conflict. As an extreme example of this, some theories of nuclear deterrence have been based upon a mechanistic presumption that even the use of nuclear weapons can be controlled; thus a nuclear conflict can be managed and survived, and therefore rationally planned for.

More practically, conflict management finds a number of expressions. It could be, for example, the consequence of a dominant power or imperial system of international relations. At the zenith of its power, the Roman Empire possessed sufficient military means—through the legions and the auxiliaries and the political structures of Roman rule—to control conflicts among its subject peoples. More commonly, military alliances represent a much used instrument of state policy by which adversaries seek to either deter conflict, or share risks if conflict occurs, by seeking a balance of power.

By other, less direct practices than colonization, the major European colonial powers and the United States sought to manage conflict in various areas of the world. The Monroe Doctrine (1823), initially more by aspiration and restraint of other states such as Britain, and the "Roosevelt Corollary" (1904) more operationally, provided the United States with a rationale for asserting a dominant power role in Central and South America and the Caribbean. In a similar way, Britain, through the means of treaties of protection, controlled the tendencies to piracy, smuggling, and slave trading of the coastal states of South Arabia, from Aden to Kuwait. A general term used to cover this form of conflict management by dominant powers was "gunboat diplomacy."

In the period just after World War I, the League of Nations Covenant contained a general scheme of conflict management by means of collective security obligations. However, two other approaches to conflict problems are actually of more lasting significance. First, the schemes of arms control and disarmament in the period had very specific provisions related to conflict management. The naval arms limitation agreement (Washington, 1921–22) attempted both to satisfy national seapower strategies and prevent competitive warship building. In some of the disarmament schemes presented to the Geneva talks in 1933, there was a very clear attempt to divide weapons into defensive and offensive categories and to emphasize the provision of controls or reductions in the latter category. Thus fortresses were seen as more desirable than tanks.

Second, although equally unsuccessful, was the attempt within the Washington naval agreements to allow Japan regional naval superiority within the context of understandings on the peaceful pursuit of political aspirations in the region. As part of these agreements Britain and the United States agreed not to construct additional fortifications between Pearl Harbor and Singapore. This example has parallels with the 1972 SALT I agreements, which contained both political and arms control provisions.

During World War II, there was really only one example of conflict management, and that was the tacit state of mutual deterrence caused by the restraint of the belligerents with respect to the nonoperational use of chemical and biological warfare weapons. There were certainly preparations for the use of these weapons, including the earmarking of military units, such as the chemical warfare companies of the British Royal Engineers.

During the Cold War, the gradual development and deployment of nuclear weapons led states to place a high premium on conflict management. Amid the plethora of writings on nuclear deterrence can be found a clear strand of thinking on conflict management. Examples include Herman Kahn's "ladder of escalation," the studies of limited war in the nuclear age, and NATO's flexible response posture as an operational example. In the Korean War, there are several examples of national conflict management policies. The People's Republic of China took care to represent all the units of the People's Liberation Army as volunteers. The United States, under the United Nations auspices, took care to restrain the offensive zeal of General MacArthur and decided against the use of nuclear weapons. The eventual cease-fire was made more secure by the creation of a demilitarized zone between North and South Korea.

Probably the most significant feature of the post–Cuban Missile Crisis era in East-West relations was the wide range of conflict management approaches developed by the two sides. These included the Soviet-United States hot line, the trailblazing SALT I agreements, and the

NATO-Warsaw Pact attempts to negotiate a conventional arms Mutual and Balanced Force Reduction agreement. Although the latter did not succeed as such, it did lead to the successful Conventional Force Europe arms reduction agreements. In another approach, the Conference on Security and Cooperation in Europe agreement included in one of the "baskets" a series of "confidence-and-security building measures" (CSBMs), all designed to reduce the risk of conflict by promoting "transparency" in military affairs.

At the global level, the United Nations Charter represented an approach to conflict management based upon a form of legislation of "great power" global policing. At its inception, the Security Council was supposed to have available very large scale contributions of military forces (12 to 20 divisions, 60 to 1,200 bombers, and 4 to 6 aircraft carriers) so that preponderant global military power could be brought to bear on any aggressor state. After 1989, UN Secretary-General Boutros Boutros-Ghali sought to revise, in a more limited format, such an approach in his *Agenda for Peace* (1992). Referring to the conflict management task of restoring and maintaining a cease-fire, Boutros-Ghali recommended that the Security Council consider "the utilization of peace-enforcement units . . . " (1992, para. 44).

A very somber challenge is presented to advocates of conflict management techniques by the depth and complexity of some recent conflict situations: the former Yugoslavia, Rwanda, Somalia, Chechnya. The West seems to have relegated the Chechen problem to an almost nineteenth century understanding of spheres of influence. The prolonged conflict in Bosnia seems unmanageable by any of the available means, Rwanda was largely ignored, and Somalia has been abandoned to its fate.

FRANK GREGORY

BIBLIOGRAPHY

Bloomfield, L. P., ed., 1987. *The Management of Global Disorder: Prospects for Creative Problem Solving.* Lanahan, MD: University Press of America.

Boutros-Ghali, Boutros, 1992. *An Agenda for Peace.* New York: United Nations.

Carter, A., 1989. *Success and Failure in Arms Control Negotiations.* Oxford: Oxford University Press.

Halprin, M. R., 1963. *Limited War in the Nuclear Age.* New York: Wiley.

Kahn, K., 1960. *On Thermonuclear War.* Princeton, NJ: Princeton University Press.

CONFLICT MANAGEMENT, ORGANIZATIONAL.

An approach to conflict that emphasizes the need to manage it in ways that prevent it from escalating to higher levels. As such it is often differentiated from conflict resolution, which is seen as finding a way of resolving the conflict. Managerial approaches to conflict are often criticized for focusing on the symptoms of the underlying problems and simply trying to mitigate consequences rather than dealing with fundamental causes. Nevertheless, it is arguable that in many cases, resolution is impossible and conflict management is the only realistic alternative.

Twenty years ago, the advice in the management literature was to "resolve" conflict, to contain and neutralize its effects quickly and quietly. Now, the management literature uses the term we use as the title for this discussion, "Conflict Management." Conflict is inevitable, and often beneficial. For example, the leaders of many high-tech companies believe that disagreements foster innovation. Hence the saying, "Two heads are better than one only if they contain different ideas." Conflict is often a sign of tension among ideas and alternatives, not simply a battle of egos. But conflict, to be productive, must center on ideas, not on people. Unfortunately, disagreements quickly become personal, and are most often based upon misunderstandings.

In this discussion we will present some principles and tools used by practitioners to take groups and individuals beyond the gridlock of quarrels to the progress of reasonable argument and, in some cases, collaboration. The focus will be primarily on conflict within an organization; however, the principles can be useful in managing conflict *among* organizations and various parties.

Most organizations need a process for dealing with the inevitable tensions and frictions that arise when people disagree or begin resisting or resenting one another. This discussion will offer some principles that can be used to create a process for managing conflict. Roger Fisher, of the Harvard Law School's Negotiation Project, says, "There is a high cost in failing to distinguish between (1) What do I think is the best goal? and (2) How shall you and I best proceed when each of us has different ideas about what ought to happen?" (1994, p. 16).

When the driver of a cement truck backs into your car, you want a quick and fair settlement for the damages, not a supportive, long-term relationship with the driver. But this option of settling and walking away is not available to people who need to maintain a working relationship. When coworkers clash, and conflict becomes a significant barrier to performance, the people involved need to count the cost of escalating the conflict. Is either party willing to withdraw completely and leave the organization? Does either party believe any effort to settle the conflict would be hopeless? Is either party willing to destroy the other to make a point or settle the score? If the answer to any of these questions is yes, the parties need to talk about cutting their losses and considering litigation or exit. But in most conflicts, people are not willing to lose their jobs or risk antagonizing the other party to violence. There is usually

FIGURE I. SILENCE TO VIOLENCE

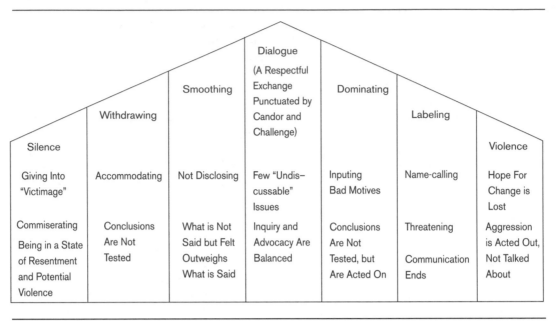

room for dialogue, and a good process will help the parties find that room and enlarge it.

Figure I is a modified version of a model used by the Praxis Group, a management consulting firm that specializes in facilitating organizational change. The diagram marks two extremes of behavior in human relationships: silence and violence. In the middle is dialogue, a process that allows people to create meaning and agreement. Behavior that draws the parties to either extreme is usually dysfunctional.

Notice that when we reach a state of silence and withdrawal, we are usually in a state of resentment, and even potential violence. Silence can be a useful tool in quelling conflict, but only as a temporary measure that one party uses in order not to return an insult for an insult, or one accusation for another. But silence and emotional withdrawal in an ongoing relationship are usually dysfunctional methods for managing conflict. Silence and violence are different points in the same circle.

People who retreat from disagreements may eventually withdraw into silence. They may continue to interact in the relationship and "get the work done," but most people divest from a relationship or situation psychologically before they withdraw from it physically. Avoidance and accommodation are usually not effective strategies, especially if they are used in ongoing relationships. Avoidance sets a pattern of relenting, giving up and giving in, encouraging the other party to take control, and falsely assuming the silent party is committed. But compliance is not commitment, and what is not talked out will usually be acted out in some way.

Violence in the Workplace

Reports of violence in the workplace are on the increase. Research by the National Safe Workplace Institute of Chicago indicates that there were 110,000 reported incidents of workplace violence in the U.S. in 1992, and that a conservative estimate of the attendant costs of these incidents is $4.2 billion (Bensimon, 1994, p. 27). The fastest growing category of homicide and critical injury in the workplace involves assaults against employers or former employers by employees who have been fired, laid off, or passed over for a promotion. Supervisors and human resource professionals are often the targets of the violence. Significantly, when consulting firms and external agencies are asked to intervene following a violent episode in an organization, they often find that a rigid and authoritarian workplace has contributed to the violence. Workers who become violent often contend that the incident that triggered their rage was not the fact that they were laid off, but the "dehumanizing" way in which the action was carried out (Bensimon, 1994, p. 30).

Far more common than deadly assault are outbreaks of physical violence such as fistfights and shoving matches, punctuated by bitter name-calling and labeling. The angry words often leave deeper scars than the physical fights themselves, and build bigger barriers between coworkers. A survey by the Society for Human Resource Management found that human resource professionals who were close to the conflicts cited "personality conflicts" as the major single cause of the friction in physical assaults. This category was cited more than twice as often as the next major cause, family and marital problems (15 percent), with other factors cited even less often—drug or alcohol abuse (10 percent), non-specific stress (7.5 percent), and firings or layoffs (7 percent) (Smith, 1994, p. 6). People who become violent in the workplace usually bring serious personal problems to the job with them; however, the evidence continues to grow that many of the volatile situations at work can be prevented by effective conflict management.

Organizations Need a Process for Managing Conflict

Organizational leaders can learn much from these extreme examples. Employees who turn violent to vent their rage or settle scores are in a tiny minority, but they sometimes represent frustration and unexpressed fear that reach much farther into the organization. People need to talk through frustrations. The "closed" organization that breeds too many "undiscussable issues" is probably moving toward some kind of breaking point. The investments organizations make in stress and conflict management, effective communication, and effective hiring and termination practices are well worth the costs.

But silence and withdrawal are, far more often than violence, the "coping strategy" of choice. Under the pressures of confrontation, most people in organizations will pull away, some eventually withdrawing into virtual silence. When asked why they do not confront the problem, most people will say that they fear recrimination, as in challenging a supervisor or boss. But often the fear of job loss or more subtle forms of punishment are not well founded. The real motivation behind the withdrawal and silence is the need to avoid the emotional discomfort of discussing the sources of tensions. We lack a method, a process, for handling disputes, and so we work around them. But organizations need a way of dealing with disputes just as they need a way of dealing with a workplace accident or a computer virus that threatens their information system.

The Structural Triggers to Conflict

Conflict has three characteristics: interaction, interdependence, and goal conflict (Jablin et al., 1987, p. 552). This means that conflict, to be considered a significant organizational phenomenon, must occur in relationships where people frequently and regularly interact; where people depend upon one another for information or resources or authority; and where at least one of the parties involved believes that their goals and purposes are somehow in conflict. Specifically, the parties involved in the conflict must be in a position to restrain or interfere with the goals of the other (Jablin et al., 1987, p. 552).

Some jobs seem almost designed to conflict, though the people in those jobs may be acting in good faith with high standards of professionalism, and have a great need to collaborate toward a mutual purpose. This pattern is so common it has been referred to as the "accidental adversaries" pattern of interaction (Senge et al., 1994, pp. 145–150). For example, in a human services agency in a large county government, members of various departments may all agree that they need to serve the needs of their client population. Each group's solution, however, may be a barrier to another group's success. The public information department may overwhelm the capacity of the service delivery units to respond to the commitments created by public information campaigns. Clients pour into the agency with high expectations for service, but are then frustrated when the services are late or inadequate. Service units may be frustrated when the financial or accounting unit places limitations on how services can be funded or delivered because of accounting issues or auditing regulations. Concerns over legal issues can constrain the process as well, creating the impression that the legal department "has no heart," or is more concerned about staying out of court than helping people. As Senge and his co-authors describe the process, relationships begin to disintegrate as each party imputes bad motives to the other.

> In general, at this stage, each partner [or group] has almost forgotten its original purpose in collaboration. It is much more aware of the things its purported partner— that traitor!—has done to block it. This makes the partner even more unlikely to talk, and it becomes even more unlikely that either side will ever learn the effect it is having on the other (Senge et al., 1994, p. 148).

When this condition settles in, the organization finds itself in gridlock. Gridlock occurs when actors "behave as if their behavior is independent of everyone else" (Senge et al., 1994, p. 169). Often, in an accidental adversaries situation, it is necessary for a third party facilitator to bring the involved parties into a room and have them describe their purposes in some detail, without interruptions or criticism from others. It usually becomes clear that each unit is acting rationally and responsibly from their local perspective; the accusations of heartlessness and stupidity can be put aside. But all parties need to understand how their policies or behavior are affecting the other units, and all parties need to be willing to make necessary changes.

Comprehending the Mind We Want to Change

Understanding the other party's map of reality or core purpose is one of the most powerful principles in conflict management. Roger Fisher, founder of the Harvard Negotiation Project, uses the example of a U.S. Army colonel who objected strongly to this principle during a seminar Fisher was teaching on conflict management. Fisher had told the participants in the seminar that they must be willing to see a conflict from the point of view of their adversaries. The officer bristled in disagreement and said,

> The better we understand their concerns and their ideas . . . the greater the chance that we will lose confidence in the rightness of our own cause (1994, p. 19).

But, as Fisher then pointed out, to understand does not mean to reach an accommodation with someone else. The goal is to comprehend, not necessarily agree with. "We would like a road map of territory we might want to invade—a clearer view of a target, *a better appreciation of a mind we would like to change*" (1994, p. 20, emphasis added).

Major disputes are usually not managed well by ever deepening recourse to the "facts." They are managed by dealing with what is going on in the heads of the disputants. We will never understand the roots of conflict without getting inside the heads of those who disagree with us. That is a principle few would argue with, but when emotions rage, it is a difficult principle to implement. The most important strategy of conflict management is thus: study the other party's position, feelings, and needs until you can describe them to the complete satisfaction of the other party. This principle is the beginning point. Without success here, it is usually fruitless to proceed. Often, a third party is required to take disputants through this process. But if one of the parties can at least attempt to describe how the other sees the issue, the chemistry of conflict can be changed to something more collaborative.

The Central Attribution Error

Why do so many people fail so often to understand how the other party sees the situation? A major reason is what social psychologists call the "central attribution error." We tend to see our own behavior as a reasonable response to a given situation, but we see the behavior of others as caused by a stable, negative trait, such as laziness, or a person's upbringing or training ("she's an engineer, what would you expect from that point of view?"). We can evaluate our own choices based upon our intentions, because we are in our "own skin." But we can evaluate other people's choices based only on the limited slice of behavior that we have access to. Our view of ourselves is from the inside; our view of others is from the outside. We judge ourselves by our intentions, but we judge others by our limited view of their actions. The limitations posed by the central attribution error require us to get inside the skin of the other party and at least understand, if not appreciate, that other party's view of reality.

Thomas and Pondy, in a study designed to examine how people attribute motives to others in conflictual situations, asked about 60 executives to describe a conflictual experience in which they had been involved as a principal party. They next had the executives describe the way in which they themselves had handled the conflict, and then the way the other party had handled it. The executives saw themselves as cooperative and reasonable, but the other party as motivated by competitiveness and unreasonable demands and expectations (1977, p. 1089).

Even in mild disagreements or irritations, we tend to impute bad motives to the other party. "Maria didn't finish the quarterly report because she's lazy"; "Terry's team won't let us use their training room because they're jealous of our team." The more intense the conflict, the less aware we are of how our own behavior is fueling the fire. Thus, a second key strategy in managing conflict is: impute good motives to the other side.

Part of imputing good motives is to assume the other person is acting consistently with what he or she believes to be the case. Coworkers, family members, and teammates can avoid pushing one another's buttons if they test conclusions before acting on them. For example, a frustrated member of a project team can put a legitimate concern on the table:

> The last time we had a major project thrown on us, the design unit didn't finish the estimates on time. Now, we seem to have the same problem in front of us again. I'm concerned about this becoming a pattern, but I may not understand what's going on. I'd like to hear how other people feel about this. Can we talk about it?

In this example, the person is testing the meaning of his observations by explaining what he is seeing and then inviting others to share their views. But most people draw a conclusion based upon a limited observation and then begin acting upon that unverified conclusion. This behavior will provide "data" (evidence, or proof) to other people which they will then act on—without testing their conclusions either. Soon the spiral of reacting to an action that we did not understand in the first place, and inspiring a negative response in the other party, is well on its way to a major conflict. This simple but powerful strategy of testing observations, if used consistently, would eliminate a significant percentage of conflicts. But this strategy requires the confidence and skill to "put things on the table" and to verbalize one's frustrations or misgivings. Chris Argyris (1994) calls these feelings that are thought and felt, but often unexpressed, "left-hand column issues." For example, if we tape-recorded a conversation between two people who are discussing a work-related topic, and then typed the conversation, word for word, the transcript of the conversation would provide the "right-hand column," the words actually spoken. But in the left-hand column we could ask the same people to record the thoughts and feelings that went through their minds, but which they did not express. Left-hand column issues typically emerge when people begin to feel frustrated. The root causes of many frustrations are such factors as the following:

- They believe they are not being treated fairly.
- They are frustrated about someone else's performance.
- They believe the wrong decision has been made or is about to be made.
- They believe they are not being listened to or given the respect that others receive.
- They do not trust the motives of a coworker or group of coworkers.
- They have a need or value which, though unexpressed, is important to them, and they feel it is being threatened.

The things people talk about—the right-hand column issues they discuss—will often not reveal these deeper concerns, so people work around their real frustrations without dealing with them.

The unspoken, left-hand column can reveal the real intentions and needs of the participants, and can also reveal the way in which the intentions of the other party are being interpreted (Argyris, 1994). The challenge is, though we all know we have left-hand column issues, how do we use them to clarify meaning and surface our deeper concerns? In some instances, this process requires the help of a facilitator, but if one of the people involved has the confidence and skill to share at least one left-hand column issue, a potential confrontation can be turned toward a problem-solving session.

Approaches to Conflict Management

Kenneth Kaye, a clinical psychologist and consultant specializing in conflict management, insists that every organization needs a conflict management system. Conflict, disagreements, and friction are inevitable in organizations. The challenge is to use them to help the organization learn by fostering better ideas and challenging existing practices. Conflict can be managed if people have the skill and will to do it. When conflicts flare, leaders should consider these responses.

- Focus on common goals: People conflict when they do not share an explicit, common purpose.
- Don't squelch differences: Organizations benefit from the tension of opposing ideas. Intellectual diversity is a resource, not a problem.
- Don't run away from emotions: Emotions are the footprints of values. We become emotional when we care deeply about something. Emotions should also

be considered "data points" and not just irrational "noise in the system."

- Don't tolerate the destructive, catastrophic, or wasteful kinds of disputes: People need to know that healthy disputes can be managed and benefitted from, but destructive conflicts will not be tolerated, period (adapted from Kaye, 1994, p. 22).

If you are required to facilitate a group that is in conflict, a good strategy is to begin with a simple task, such as finding common purposes, and then moving to another plan of intervention only if the easier plan fails, and the parties agree they want to move to the next one. The following advice on the stages of conflict management are adapted from Kenneth Kaye (1994).

Plan A: Look for Shared Goals and Win/Win Solutions. A conflict is no longer a conflict if a group is addressing problems together. The techniques and skills required to make Plan A work are active listening, positive framing, and speaking with candor while encouraging candor in others. People need to be trained to listen actively. They need to seek out the views of the other party, and feel reassured that they themselves will have a chance to talk. For speakers, two rules are helpful:

- First, do not yield the floor until you feel you have been accurately heard.
- Second, do not ask a question until and unless you are prepared to listen patiently to the response.

Listeners, on the other hand, must agree not to respond until the speaker is finished, and the listener must then check with the speaker to be certain the message has been understood before giving a response: "Can I tell you what I think I've heard so far, and then respond to that part before you go on to your next point?"

If the parties are already involved in a significant conflict, Plan A may require a facilitator who is mature and skilled enough to stand above the fray, help the group maintain a civil dialogue (point out and eliminate name-calling, insults, attributing bad motives to others, and drifting from the issue at hand). The group may need help in framing concerns and frustrations positively rather than negatively. For example, an agitated teammate can be invited to phrase a concern in this way:

I have the impression that every time we reach the end of a reporting period, and we're all under a lot of pressure, our need as evaluators to do the work quickly and in a way we're comfortable with conflicts with Carolynn's [the supervisor's] needs to make sure all the reports will be done on time with high quality. I begin to feel like I'm being micro-managed and not trusted. I wonder if I'm the only one who feels that way.

Instead of this way:

> All I know is that when Carolynn goes into her "I better watch you poor fools every minute so you don't make some stupid mistake" routine—which she does at the end of every reporting period—I just want to run out of the place screaming.

Helping people engage in a constructive dialogue carries benefits that go far beyond solving the problem at hand. The next time the group disagrees or conflicts, they will be better prepared to manage their own differences effectively, and perhaps improve the quality of their work in the process.

The main purpose of Plan A is to discover if the parties have significant reasons for working together. They can ask themselves, "What are our respective goals, and do these goals connect?" At this crucial stage, people need help in stating goals in concrete and coherent ways. They will often state perceived problems, assumptions, or judgments, even suspicions, as goals. For example, a person who feels that women are not being treated fairly by co-workers may suggest as a goal, "End male chauvinism in the department." This is a goal, but it needs clarification. It may be more helpful to say something like, "Create a working environment in which women's contributions and proposals are acknowledged as readily as men's" (Kaye, 1994 p. 25). A "goal" such as "Juan is not committed to the bond project," is not a goal, it's a judgment based upon some observations. With help, people can clarify these statements into goals. They then need to prioritize the goals, taking at most the top three or four, and developing a plan for accomplishment.

If an organization had nothing more than this kind of process in place, with two or three people capable of facilitating the shared goal discussion, that organization could deal quite effectively with the majority of its conflicts. Plan A is a good place to start, but most organizations do not have even the rudiments of a conflict management process in operation.

Plan B: Clarify, Sort, and Value Differences. The parties may need nothing more than Plan A. Some common goals may be listed and a feeling of mutual respect and understanding established. These parties do not have to be friends, but they need to be teammates. In Plan B, the parties have agreed they need to go further. They may have identified some common goals, but still be in serious conflict over other issues. Here we work on the goals and concerns that are *not* shared by all parties. Some of these differences are based on misunderstandings that can be cleared up. Some are created by differences in points of view, as between an evaluation unit and a service delivery unit, or between policy designers and implementers. Plan B also provides an opportunity to identify serious problems carried by individual people in the group, such as

FIGURE II. PLAN A. LOOK FOR SHARED GOALS

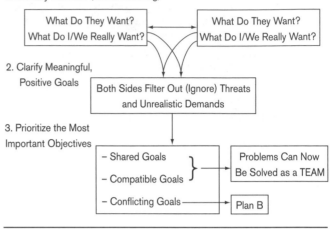

emotional instability, addictions, or antisocial behaviors that make it impossible to collaborate. These problems should be dealt with outside the group.

This process prepares the parties either to go back to Plan A and work on shared goals, or to move to Plan C and clarify what each party needs to change. Plan B is seldom a terminal process; it usually leads to Plan C or back to Plan A.

Plan C: Gain Commitment to Change. Plans A and B revolve around gaining a common focus (groups and people often conflict because they do not have a focus or purpose) and identifying some behaviors and barriers that cause friction. In Plan C the goal is to shift the energy of the group away from diagnosing problems and toward committing to change.

Are the parties able and willing to recognize their part of the problem? Without that commitment, the cycle of conflict will continue. If the parties can be drawn into a deeper commitment to change, and an understanding of why some of their behaviors need to change, the parties can return to Plans A or B. Obviously, in cases where the conflict is deeply rooted, the parties involved will need more than one work session to be successful.

Most conflicting parties are not equally willing to make such commitments. Someone usually has to lead the process. If you are one of the principal parties, take the lead in making some public commitments to change:

> The next time I have a question about an audit report, I'll call the auditor directly instead of bringing up the issue in a management team meeting. I realize now that I upset people when I do that because they feel I'm criticizing them without having the facts.

If you are acting as a facilitator, try to gain some simple commitments from the people you believe are most willing and able to make them. An effective way of gaining some commitment to change is to invite people to make their commitments public. Changes that are public, specific, and recognized by other people are far more likely to endure. At this point, if a person is not willing to make a public commitment, he or she should not be forced to do so. The commitment may come later.

Plan D: Analyze the Recurring Cycle. If parties get to this stage, the conflict has a mature history; it is a cycle. The parties need to analyze the cycle and examine how the cycle can be broken. If the process has reached this stage, and the conflict is still recurring, it is likely that people are not fighting about what they say they are fighting about (Kaye, 1994, p. 38). Conflicts that reach this stage should be facilitated, preferably by an experienced expert.

This stage requires stepping back from the details of the latest incident, and examining the pattern beneath the events. Somehow, the conflict ignites, then escalates, then subsides, allowing peace to "break out." But the same source of shared fear or anxiety or frustration remains that will lead again to conflict. This cycle should be examined carefully.

These recurring cycles of conflict are preplexing. Why do people, who claim to want to end this kind of cycle, continue to participate in it? Many social psychologists believe that the parties involved are actually working on managing the conflict by fighting on one level so they will not fight on another. The surface conflict becomes a way of not allowing the deeper source of conflict to erupt. It is usually not possible to get to these deeper issues, even if the parties admit that they exist. But examining the cycle, and identifying early warnings that the conflict is about to erupt, will help the parties mitigate, if not prevent, the cycle from recurring.

The creation of a conflict management process in an organization can be done by doing some fundamental training in effective interpersonal communication and then building on that experience. In most cases there are people within the organization who are excellent facilitators and role models, but these people might need some formal training themselves before they undertake to train others. In the process of these discussions, which should themselves be models of open and candid communication, a process for dealing with conflict can be developed and improved upon. The opportunity for employees to participate and talk through difficulties and frustrations should be one of the core purposes of this kind of training. Managers in the organization should also examine their own practices and policies to see if they are contributing to friction and resentment with hiring and dismissal procedures, as well as with their own leadership styles. If the leaders at the top of the organization are not managing their own conflicts well, they should assume that conflicts will be managed poorly elsewhere.

The core principles of understanding the perceptions of the other party, imputing good motives, testing assumptions, and using the skills of active listening are powerful tools for dealing with the inevitable conflicts in the workplace. For managers, perhaps the most important principle is to deal with conflict in a positive and open way, not to deny that it exists, or simply hope that somehow people will control the level of conflict in the organization without any tools or assistance from their leaders.

MICHAEL THOMPSON

BIBLIOGRAPHY

Argyris, Chris, 1994. "Good Communication that Blocks Learning." *Harvard Business Review* (July/August) 77–83.
Bensimon, Helen Frank, 1994. "Violence in the Workplace." *Training and Development,* vol. 48 (January) 27–32.
Fisher, Roger, Elizabeth Copelman, and Andrea K. Schneider, 1994. *Beyond Machiavelli: Tools for Coping with Conflict.* Cambridge: Harvard University Press.
Jablin, Frederic M., Linda L. Putnam, Karlene H. Roberts, and Lyman W. Porter, eds., 1987. *Handbook of Organizational Communication: An Interdisciplinary Perspective.* London: Sage.
Kaye, Kenneth, 1994. *Workplace Wars and How to End Them: Turning Personal Conflicts into Productive Teamwork.* New York: American Management Association.
Senge, Peter, Richard Ross, Bryan Smith, Charlotte Roberts, and Art Kleiner, 1994. *The Fifth Discipline Fieldbook: Strategies and Tools for Building a Learning Organization.* New York: Doubleday.
Smith, Bob, 1994. "Cease Fire! Preventing Workplace Violence." *HR Focus,* vol. 71 (February) 1–9.
Thomas, Kenneth W. and Louis R. Pondy, 1977. "Toward an 'Intent' Model of Conflict Management Among Principal Parties." *Human Relations,* vol. 30, 1089–1102.

CONFLICT OF INTEREST. Situations where public employees encounter opportunities to use their public office for the sake of their own private gain. Conflicts of interest present dilemmas in which a public servant must choose between serving his or her own self-interest or the interests of the public. An interest would include any influences, loyalties, feelings, or concerns that might dissuade administrators from making competent, reliable, impartial judgments in their capacity to serve the common good.

Hence, conflicts of interest pose clashes between various kinds of influences and the interests of the society that public officials are bound to serve. As trustees of the public interest, public administrators may jeopardize their fiduciary role by acting on behalf of their own interests, breaching the public trust, and creating a loss of credibility in the efficacy of government. Furthermore, some experts have emphasized that being in a potential conflict of interest is almost as serious as an actual conflict. The appearance of such conflicts can be sufficient to jeopardize the public's faith in the integrity of government.

Specific types of conflicts of interest have been viewed either narrowly, focusing exclusively on financial gain, or broadly, referring to anything of value. In terms of financial gain, the conflict of interest lies in a collision between a public manager's official duties and her or his own personal economic interest. For example, money or any valuable commodity used illegally to influence an official action constitutes bribery, thereby creating a conflict of interest. Viewed from a broader ethical perspective, conflict of interest entails not only personal financial gains, but other personal benefits, which might be psychological, social, or political. Hiring one's relative instead of objectively screening other qualified candidates (nepotism) may be done because of emotional ties or to secure more power in an agency. Regardless of the motive, the principle of fairness is violated for the self-serving purposes of the official and, consequently, a conflict of interest has occurred.

In other words, conflict of interest seen from a legal point of view is usually defined in economic terms and thus provides the minimal standard for acceptable conduct. A broader definition extending conflict of interest beyond financial interests to social, psychological, and political relationships implies that ethical principles, such as the rule of law, fairness, benevolence, and veracity, ought to be considerations for public administrators in helping them to understand their fiduciary obligations and avoid conflicts of interest.

In the broad sense, conflict of interest could be said to be a form of graft or political corruption. Although no consensus exists regarding the definition of political corruption, the concept, which has been equated with graft, could be described as the acquisition of money, gain, or advantage by dishonest, unfair, or illegal means through the abuse of one's public office. Thus conflict of interest could be likened to graft or political corruption.

Conflicts of interest can be classified into eight types:

1. Bribery is the illegal acceptance of money or other valuable considerations in exchange for special favors from public employees having to do with their official duties.
2. Influence peddling occurs when a public official attempts to influence a government decision in favor of a third party in which the employee has an interest.
3. Information peddling transpires when public officials who are privy to confidential information use it to their own advantage, monetary or otherwise.
4. Financial transactions can result in a conflict if the direct or indirect economic interests of a public employee collide with her or his responsible performance on the job.

5. Gifts and entertainment, as one particular type of bribery, create a conflict if these are perceived to influence a public servant's impartial discharge of duties.
6. Outside employment, which includes part-time jobs, contracting, consultations, or self-employment, can produce a conflict if the public employee uses his or her official status to enhance that private employment, if the job drains away or wastes energy necessary to complete an official's public duties, or if government equipment or services are used for private employment purposes.
7. Future employment can also create a "revolving door" syndrome if the public official intends to seek a future job with a private company with which she or he now transacts business.
8. Nepotism means public administrators may be a position to give preferential treatment to relatives in hiring, promoting, awarding contracts, or other public business.

Although a willingness to engage in a self-serving action and a conscious intention to deceive must be present in most cases, the appearance of these practices conveys an image of corruption to the public and reinforces a disillusionment with public officials and the political institutions they represent.

The origins of conflict of interest are rooted in the Western concepts of individualism and citizenship that have evolved in U.S. society. On the one hand, individualism has come to represent the notion that each person is the locus of political, economic, and social rights. Hence, satisfying one's own desires, acquiring wealth, property, and status are considered legitimate forms of conduct. On the other hand, the role of citizenship is also acknowledged as a legitimate obligation to act on behalf of the common good, which creates an inherent dilemma between self-interest and public duty, or between the acquisitive tendencies of private life and obligations of the public role.

In addition two other factors exacerbate the private and public dilemma. First, the structure and nature of modern society create multiple roles in which the individual must maneuver, thus compounding the complexity of sorting out private rights and public demands. Second, the assumptions of working in an organization mirror the same tensions between the individual and the collective. For example, one requirement of employment is working for the good of the organization, yet individual promotion and success is considered equally legitimate. How are they to be balanced?

Moreover, some critics of the individualistic ethic suggest that private interests have become dominant over public concerns. As a result the collective good is seen as a secondary priority in light of protecting one's rights or advancing one's position in life. The irony is that society demands that public officials live up to a higher standard of conduct than is expected of private citizens, namely serving the public interest over self-interest. It is not surprising that conflict of interest problems among public officials are pervasive in modern societies because of the fragmented notions of individualism and citizenship that create an irreconcilable split between private and public realms.

External and internal controls are the two approaches that have been characteristically used to maintain responsible conduct among public officials and prevent conflict of interest problems. External controls have to do with political and institutional devices such as ethics legislation and codes of ethics; internal controls such as ethics training are aimed at cultivating a moral sense within public employees to act rightly. Consequently, ethics legislation, codes of ethics, and ethics training have been combined to curb conflict of interest violations within American society.

The evolution of ethics laws represents the most pervasive means of dealing with conflicts of interest. Although conflict of interest legislation at the federal level began in the 1850s, its roots are discernible as far back as 1789, when an act to establish the Treasury Department was created that prohibited conflict of interest by stating that no public official should either directly or indirectly be involved in private business.

After President Andrew Jackson was elected to office in 1829, he made good his campaign promise to replace entrenched government employees with his political supporters. Patronage jobs were considered legitimate rewards for political party activity, since no laws existed covering standards for federal employees. The concept of professional public servants was nonexistent at the time. Fraud, waste, and abuse of public office escalated, leading to passage of the first conflict of interest laws (1853–1864) to deal with influence peddling, the selling of information, and the misuse of public funds for personal gains.

Periodic legislation followed to expand on the types of interest conflicts encountered, penalties for violations, and coverage pertaining to public employees. The Civil Post-Employment Statute of 1872 prohibited executive department employees from serving as counsel, attorney, or agent during the two years following their federal employment in the prosecution of any claims pending in the department while they were in office. Laws enacted in 1919, 1944, and 1948 extended coverage to all federal employees and prescribed criminal penalties for infractions. An outside compensation act, passed in 1917, forbade governmental employees from receiving salaries through any nongovernmental source.

One of the most significant events in the development of conflict of interest laws occurred when the Bar of the City of New York undertook an extensive review of ethics

legislation in 1955. In 1960 they proposed the Executive Conflict of Interest Act, which became the basis for the first codification of federal conflict of interest statutes passed during the administration of President John Kennedy in 1961.

President Lyndon Johnson extended these conflict of interest statutes when he signed the Presidential Order of Federal Ethics, which prohibited public officials from holding direct or indirect financial interests that conflict substantially with their duties as federal employees and established restrictions on outside income. Financial disclosure emerged as the primary mechanism for gaining compliance with these conflict of interest statutes. By filing a financial disclosure statement, public employees would become informed of potential conflicts and legal sanctions, thereby providing a vehicle for both prevention and enforcement.

Yet conflict of interest problems persisted due to an insufficient regulation of postemployment conduct, an inadequate process of financial reporting, and infrequently prosecuted cases. The response was the passage of the 1978 Ethics in Government Act under President Jimmy Carter which, among other things, established more specific financial disclosure provisions and postemployment regulations with subsequent penalties; created the Office of Government Ethics under the Office of Personnel Management, which assumed responsibility for implementing provisions of the act and recommending ethics legislation; and developed a means for appointing an independent counsel to investigate charges of violations by high-ranking executive officials.

The Ethics in Government Act has been amended numerous times since then to adopt broader and more stringent laws. For example, the 1988 amendments established the Office of Government Ethics as an independent organization with the authority to ensure that every federal agency develops procedures for evaluating financial disclosure information. Furthermore, under President George Bush the Government Ethics Reform Act of 1989 tightened up restrictions on public employees representing private interests before government agencies in which they were formerly employed, and provisions to cover the congressional as well as executive branch were extended to include gift and honoraria restrictions.

Consequently, at the federal level the Office of Government Ethics is the primary agency responsible for monitoring conflict of interest legislation through the use of ethics codes and agency training. Compliance is ensured by requiring every federal agency to have a designated agency ethics officer (DAEO), who is obliged to provide training and counseling on conflict of interest laws and financial disclosures matters. Cases of suspected violation can be adjudicated through the agency, the Justice Department, or the office of the Inspector General.

Codes of ethics have been a second essential device for determining conflict of interest restrictions on public employee conduct. At the state level, while most American states have enacted conflict of interest laws, little uniformity appears across jurisdictions. For example, ethics codes, developed primarily through the efforts of government-related associations such as the Council on Governmental Ethics Laws and the National Municipal League, define conflicts of interest exclusively in financial terms. However, an example of a liberal interpretation of conflict of interest has been incorporated into the commonwealth of Massachusetts' ethics law, which warns public officials to avoid even the appearance of conflicts of interest that might bias their judgments to advance their own interests.

As in the states, U.S. municipalities also vary considerably regarding the conflict of interest restrictions in their ethics codes. Only a few have comprehensive prohibitions that involve all eight types of conflict of interest. The most typical codes and statutes narrow conflicts to economic ones.

Besides legislation and codes of ethics, the third strategy used to combat conflict of interest problems in U.S. government involves ethics training. A compliance approach is used on federal, state, and local levels, in which public employees are instructed in the laws, the ethics codes pertaining to them, and the penalties incurred for violating them; case studies are utilized to teach how restrictions apply in practical situations. The compliance training model predominates because U.S. public administration is grounded in the law and because the rash of scandals in government and society at large since the 1970s has led the public to react by demanding more ethics legislation as the most obvious remedy for combating corruption. Thus, knowledge of and compliance with the law are conveyed by formal training.

How do other societies deal with conflict of interest problems in comparison with the United States? While this question can only be addressed in a limited way, a brief look at examples from industrialized and developing countries may suggest some patterns. In Western industrialized countries, conflict of interest is determined by the structure and functions of government under their respective constitutions. For example, Britain, France, and Canada each display somewhat different types of conflict problems in contrast to the United States.

In Britain the principle of ministerial responsibility prevails, which means that public officials are responsible for what takes place in their ministry. Parliament is sovereign and as a result ministers who lose the confidence of Parliament lose their offices as well. The British orientation can be juxtaposed with U.S. public administration, where the principle of separation of powers and the omission of public service in the Constitution leads to uncertainty as whether civil servants are ultimately responsible to Congress or the president.

While the French constitution also adheres to separation of powers, the role of French public administration is clearly placed under the authority of Parliament, and the constitution goes so far as to specifically define conflicts of interest for public officials. Not only are pursuits of economic interests banned, but outside employment is placed off limits. However, in practice enforcement is relaxed and consequently the French are relatively inattentive to conflict of interest problems.

The constitutional structures of Canada and the United States account for numerous differences in conflict of interest practices pertaining to public administrators in both countries. Two illustrations may elucidate this point. For example, in the Canadian parliamentary system, the cabinet dominates the legislature and has the authority to impose ethics standards on its public officials by nonstatutory codes, whereas the U.S. Congress has the prerogative to legislate conflict of interest laws. Characteristically, the legislature has imposed harsher measures on the executive branch than on itself.

Another example concerns postemployment regulations. The Canadian government is more flexible than the United States because high-ranking public officials are career politicians who, if forced to leave office, would find private employment difficult to secure. In the United States, executive appointees often come from the private sector and are likely to return to it, securing a more lucrative position than offered in public service. Other significant distinctions exist in the realm of conflict of interest; however, suffice it to say that the constitutional structure and functions of a nation provide the context for the nature of conflict of interest problems.

This thesis is also pivotal to understanding conflict of interest issues in developing states, as in Africa. Zimbabwe, for instance, emerging from a long legacy of colonial rule, has been preoccupied with fundamental political questions as to who will rule and on what basis. As a result administrative concerns by necessity have been relegated to a secondary level. Economic and social development is focused almost entirely through the state, since conditions in society at large are characterized by material deprivation. Employment by government is the chief means of material advancement. Moreover, elite groups in Zimbabwe, and for that matter Africa as a whole, derive their power from the public sector, not the private sector. Hence, it is not surprising that public office is fraught with patronage politics or "personal rule" as a means of maintaining political advantage. In such a context, conflict of interest stemming from a modern, industrialized, Western tradition makes little sense.

In other words, when a country is preoccupied with the political struggle of moving towards constitutionalism, issues such as conflict of interest are of secondary importance. However, once a particular constitutional regime is established, the necessity for implementing that political order elevates the role of the administrative state to one of primary importance. As a result conflict of interest problems arise based on the social, political, economic, and cultural history of a country and the nature of constitutional government that is established.

APRIL HEJKA-EKINS

BIBLIOGRAPHY

Association of the Bar of the City of New York Special Committee on the Federal Conflict of Interest Laws, 1960. *Conflict of Interest and Federal Service.* Cambridge, MA: Harvard University Press.

Beard, E., 1978. "Conflicts of Interest and Public Service." In J. T. DeGeorge and J. A. Pichler, eds., *Ethics, Free Enterprise and Public Policy.* New York: Oxford University Press.

Cooper, Terry L., 1990. *The Responsible Administrator: An Approach for the Administrative Role.* San Francisco: Jossey-Bass Publishers.

Friedrich, Carl J., 1990. "Corruption Concepts in Historical Perspective." In Heidenheimer, Arnold J., Michael Johnston, and Victor T. LeVine, eds., *Political Corruption: A Handbook,* New Brunswick: Transaction Publishers.

Hejka-Ekins, April, 1994. "Ethics in Inservice Training." In Terry L. Cooper, ed., *Handbook of Administrative Ethics.* New York: Marcel Dekker, Inc.

Kernaghan, K., 1975. *Ethical Conduct: Guidelines for Government Employees.* Toronto: Institute of Public Administration of Canada.

Lewis, Carol W., *The Ethics Challenge in Public Service: A Problem-Solving Guide.* San Francisco: Jossey-Bass Publishers.

Moyo, Jonathan N., 1994. "Administrative Ethics in an African Society: The Case of Zimbabwe." In Terry L. Cooper, ed., *Handbook of Administrative Ethics.* New York: Marcel Dekker, Inc.

Rohr, John A., 1994. "Constitutionalism and Administrative Ethics: A Comparative Study of Canada, the United Kingdom, and the United States." In Terry L. Cooper, ed., *Handbook of Administrative Ethics.* New York: Marcel Dekker, Inc.

Sennet, Richard, 1974. *The Fall of Public Man.* New York: Vintage Books.

Stark, Andrew, 1993. "Public-Sector Conflict of Interest at the Federal Level in Canada and the U.S.: Differences in Understanding and Approach." In H. George Frederickson, ed., *Ethics and Public Administration.* New York: M. E. Sharpe.

Tussman, Joseph, 1960. *Obligation and the Body Politic.* New York: Oxford University Press.

CONFLICT RESOLUTION.

The study and application of procedures that seek to identify the options for acceptable compromises and awards in response to conflictual interactions between at least two parties. To be successful it is necessary for the parties in conflict to be prepared to reexamine their relationship and the points of conflict in order to seek conflict-free solutions.

Because the analytical starting point for an examination of conflict resolution is the existence of a conflictual interaction in human relationships, a cautionary point is necessary. It has to be recognized that conflicts are rarely ever resolved in an absolute sense. For example, the potential for conflict between factions in Afghanistan seems endless despite many efforts at conflict resolution. Thus Rangarajan offers a view of conflict resolution, within a conflictual interaction: "An action which limits a conflict is one which, in all probability, and as far as one can predict, directs its future evolution away from a violent end towards the possibility of accommodation" (1985, p. 4).

In the field of international relations, studies of conflictual interactions and resolution frameworks and techniques cover diverse issue areas as well as situations of actual or potential armed conflict. Thus the literature covers obvious cases such as the Arab-Israeli wars and the less well-known cases, for example the international commercial problems handled by the International Chamber of Commerce.

The coverage of diverse issues is matched by the presence of a number of different intellectual starting points in the literature on techniques of conflict resolution. From mathematics, game theory has been used as an explanatory and predictive framework for approaches to conflict resolution, seeing conflicts in terms of bargaining situations. However, game theory's limitations are also well recognized, especially in relation to asymmetries in bargaining positions.

Using other intellectual perspectives, conflict resolution is approached from the field of psychology by a focus on people behaving aggressively; political science traditionally has concentrated on states at war but will now also address a broader range of conflictual relations within a framework of complex interdependence; the sociological perspective will take account of role-playing within political and bureaucratic structures. Thus the identification of different causal variables will lead to differences in the emphasis given to particular techniques of conflict resolution. For example, concern with the problem of the policies of states as dominant causal factors in conflicts can lead to searches for other paradigms such as the notion of "collective communities" (Azar and Burton, 1986).

In essence, conflict resolution can be seen as an application of some procedure whereby no party in the conflictual interaction emerges as either the winner or the loser. The general development of such procedures in the modern and postmodern international system is usually traced back to the first Hague Conference of 1899 and the drafting of the General Act for the Pacific Settlement of International Disputes. This encouraged third party involvement in dispute settlement.

Such third party involvement usually involves one or more of the following procedures: good offices, mediation, conciliation, arbitration, and adjudication. The third party can be provided from many sources: for example, a declared neutral state such as Switzerland, a representative of a "great power" (Cyrus Vance in Bosnia), a representative of an intergovernmental organization (an emissary of the UN Secretary-General), or the International Court of Justice. In some of these procedures it is necessary to distinguish between the passive and active roles of third parties. For example, under "good offices" the third party may merely convey messages between the parties in conflict; more actively, the third party may propose a plan for conflict resolution, as did Norwegian diplomats in the context of Israel's relations with the Palestinian Liberation Organization in 1992.

Adjudication and arbitration are usually more formalized procedures. The former is effectively restricted to examining a conflict in terms of international law and by reference to legal issues. However, states rarely see their conflicts as resolvable through the International Court of Justice, as all parties to a conflict will usually claim to be legally correct in their actions. On the other hand, the Antarctica Treaty (1959) is a good example of states using an instrument of international law to collectively place their conflicting sovereignty claims in abeyance in order to cooperate on scientific exploration. Arbitration offers a procedure under which other criteria as well as legal ones can be used to produce a settlement. A well-known dispute between America and Britain arising out of the American Civil War, the 1872 Alabama Arbitration, used this procedure.

In the twentieth century, the League of Nations represented a marked innovation in the development of international procedures for the peaceful resolution of international conflicts and disputes. Under the Covenant of the League, there was a collective obligation to intervene in international conflicts and member states were obliged to submit their disputes to procedures for peaceful settlement. This innovation and its principle, with some modifications, was carried forward by the United Nations. Alongside the universal international organizations, regional bodies such as the Organization of African Unity, Organization of American States, the European Union, and the OSCE have developed or are attempting to develop similar principles and roles.

UN Secretary-General Boutros Boutros-Ghali reaffirmed these global goals in *An Agenda for Peace* (1992). He stressed the role of the Security Council as "and a central instrument for . . . resolution of conflicts . . . " and identified UN aims regarding that role of the Security Council as:

- To seek to identify, at the earliest possible stage, situations that could produce conflict, and to try through diplomacy [good offices, mediation, etc.] to remove the sources of danger before violence results.
- Where conflict erupts, to engage in peacemaking aimed at resolving the issues that have led to conflict (Boutros-Ghali, 1992, para. 15).

Unfortunately these goals remain as difficult as ever to achieve in situations where the parties in a conflictual interaction have still to accept an alternative to victory or defeat. Thus, a resolution to the conflict in Bosnia is no nearer despite significant and continuing UN involvement and the UN has actually completely withdrawn from Somalia.

Conflict resolution is one of those human endeavors that seems always destined to proceed more on the basis of hope than expectation of success. This is because it addresses complex problems and identifies the need to build new relationships between parties in a conflictual situation, relationships which avoid structural coercion and in which the parties can fully appreciate their own position.

FRANK GREGORY

BIBLIOGRAPHY

Azar, E. and J. W. Burton, eds., 1986. *International Conflict Resolution: Theory and Practice.* Brighton, UK: Wheatsheaf.
Boutros-Ghali, Boutros, 1992. *An Agenda for Peace.* New York: United Nations.
Holsti, J., 1992. *International Politics.* 6th ed. Englewood Cliffs, NJ: Prentice-Hall.
Kriesberg, L., 1992. *International Conflict Resolution in the US-USSR and the Middle East Cases.* New Haven: Yale University Press.
Rangarajan, L., 1985. *The Limitation of Conflict: A Theory of Bargaining and Negotiation.* London: Croom Helm.
Reisman, W. M., 1992. *Systems of Control in International Adjudication and Arbitration: Breakdown and Repair.* Durham, NC: Duke University Press.

CONGRESSIONAL BUDGET OFFICE.

The fiscal support agency for the United States Congress.

The Congressional Budget Office (CBO) was established by Title II of the Congressional Budget and Impoundment Control Act of 1974 (PL 93–344). Its mandate is to provide economic and budgetary information to the Congress.

CBO was created during a period of tense budgetary conflict between the executive and legislative branches. Just after his reelection in 1972, President Richard M. Nixon impounded (that is, refused to spend) recently appropriated funds for a variety of domestic programs. This challenge to the Congressional "power of the purse" infuriated many members of Congress, and they responded by drafting legislation that would greatly limit the ability of the president to impound funds for policy reasons. This language became Title X of the Congressional Budget and Impoundment Control Act (CBA). The first nine titles were designed to deal with another problem—the difficulty Congress had in passing consistent budgets by the beginning of the fiscal year. This problem was due in large part to the extreme decentralization of the Congress—spending and taxing committees often passed separate bills without paying much attention to the budget totals.

The Act created House and Senate budget committees to coordinate these bills, a process of creating budget targets in budget resolutions, and enforcement mechanisms to help the Congress meet these targets. The Congressional Budget Office was established to support the new process. One reason was that each budget committee, like all committees composed of a partisan majority and a partisan minority, had the largely political responsibility of developing and enforcing budget resolutions. Given the difficulty of this task, the budget committees could not reasonably be expected also to provide technical information and advice to all members of Congress. The CBO was structured as a nonpartisan, professional agency that could fulfill this function.

CBO was also created to bolster the fiscal independence of the legislative branch. With the legislative fiscal agency's expertise, Congress would no longer have to depend on the executive branch for macroeconomic forecasts and budget projections. Though impoundments stimulated this drive for independence, the General Accounting Office, not the Congressional Budget Office, was given the main responsibility for overseeing impoundments.

Though the CBA was amended substantially in the two decades after its passage, the language governing the CBO was changed very little. Over this period, CBO quickly developed into a highly professional agency, and is respected across the country as the leading legislative fiscal office. It has frequently served as a model to legislatures in democratizing countries that have wanted to develop independent sources of reliable fiscal information. Despite this sterling reputation, there is remarkably little scholarly research on the CBO.

Functions, Products, and Clients

Though CBO's mission is the relatively narrow one of providing economic and budgetary information, this mission encompasses numerous functions and products for a variety of clients. Questions about the accuracy of these products are covered in later sections.

Macroeconomic Forecasts and Projections

CBO makes economic "forecasts" and "projections" for the major economic variables of gross domestic product, unemployment, inflation, and interest rates. The forecasts and projections are prepared on a semiannual basis, and released in two reports—"The Economic and Budget Outlook," typically released in January, and "The Economic

and Budget Outlook: An Update," typically released in August.

CBO makes two distinctions between the terms "forecasts" and "projections." Forecasts cover the next 18–24 months, and projections are for longer periods. Forecasts predict the likely cyclical fluctuations of the economy, whereas projections simply model long-run trends by applying historical trend rates to current conditions.

CBO uses standard econometric models to prepare forecasts and projections. It incorporates information from commercial economic forecasting companies, and receives advice from a distinguished panel of economic advisers. The goal of the process is to develop a consensus forecast that fits within the mainstream of the economics discipline.

Baseline Budget Estimates

The baseline is a projection of spending and revenues assuming there will be no changes in current policy. CBO prepares baselines biennially for the major reports described above. Since spending and revenues are affected by economic conditions, CBO relies on the aforementioned economic forecast projections to develop baselines. It also monitors actions by executive agencies and program beneficiaries to project how spending will likely change in the future. These assumptions are often critical inputs into complicated computer models that are used to develop baseline projections.

Cost Estimates

The Congressional Budget Act requires that each bill reported by an authorizing committee be accompanied by a CBO estimate of the five-year costs of the legislation. Cost estimates are also prepared for many draft proposals, floor amendments, and conference agreements. Following passage of the State and Local Cost Estimate Act of 1981, CBO began to project the costs of some federal mandates on state and local governments. Cost estimates are printed in the bill reports from committees; CBO has prepared an annual total of between 500 and 900 cost estimates in recent years.

Cost estimates on the spending side of the budget are prepared by CBO's Budget Analysis Division. Tax cost estimating responsibilities are shared by CBO's Tax Analysis Division and the Joint Committee on Taxation, a technically oriented staff that supports the House Ways and Means and Senate Finance Committees.

Cost estimates contain several sections. Most important are the numerical estimates of budget authority, outlays, receipts, and revenues, which are then used for budgetary scorekeeping. These estimates are almost always point estimates, even though there may be substantial uncertainty about their potential accuracy. Nearly as important, therefore, are the cost estimate descriptions of CBO's assumptions, data sources, and methodologies for preparing each point estimate. By fully describing the basis of the estimate, and occasionally including ranges that bound the point estimate, CBO indicates how sensitive a point estimate is to changes in assumptions or methodologies. Cost analysts collect this information from a variety of sources, including numerous phone calls to program administrators.

Scorekeeping

Scorekeeping is the process of keeping track of all fiscal legislation in order to determine whether Congress will meet its budget targets. While the parliamentarians in the House and the Senate have the final say on this matter, CBO plays a very significant role in the process. This work is coordinated by the Scorekeeping Unit of CBO's Budget Analysis Division, with input from the cost estimating units in this division. The Scorekeeping Unit provides frequent reports to budget and appropriations committees, who then advise the parliamentarians. Cost estimates include separate projections for discretionary and mandatory spending. Scorekeeping of discretionary spending is complicated by the tentative nature of authorizations of appropriations. These authorizations enable appropriations for certain purposes and may place a ceiling on amounts that can be appropriated, but do not require appropriations committees to provide any funds. Consequently, the scorekeeping process must follow all appropriation bills throughout the process, from subcommittee markup through conference committee agreement.

A critically important factor in scorekeeping is the calculation of "spendout rates." These rates show how quickly budget authority is converted into outlays; CBO derives the rates from analyses of historical data.

Another scorekeeping product is the sequestration report. Sequestration was established by the Balanced Budget Act of 1985 (popularly known as "Gramm-Rudman-Hollings"), and modified by the Budget Enforcement Act of 1990 and other laws. Sequestration requires that budgetary resources previously granted to agencies be cancelled in the event that enacted legislation would cause budgetary targets to be exceeded. Under the law, the Office of Management and Budget has the final responsibility for issuing sequestration reports. Given the suspicion that the executive branch might make politically inspired sequestration decisions, the law requires CBO to issue advisory sequestration reports.

Budget and Program Analyses

Some CBO products are not tied directly to steps in the legislative process, and instead provide analyses of budgetary options. For example, each February, CBO analyzes the president's proposed budget. This analysis takes the president's proposed policies and substitutes CBO's economic projections and technical assumptions for the president's, allowing Congress to compare presidential policies to the congressional baseline.

CBO also produces a report each spring entitled *Reducing the Deficit: Spending and Revenue Options*. This report lists over a hundred illustrative deficit reduction options, showing potential savings and describing the programmatic advantages and disadvantages of each option.

Finally, CBO releases published reports and unpublished memos on a wide variety of budgetary issues, which are usually prepared by CBO's program divisions. These analyses identify program and policy options for dealing with economic, national security, and social problems. CBO does not generally make recommendations to Congress in these reports. This policy was established in CBO's first year, when in response to the high profile taken by then Director Alice Rivlin, the appropriations committees warned CBO that it should not take policy positions.

In practice, however, there is one exception to this rule. CBO directors are often called on to testify about how well the budget process is working, and have felt free to suggest reforms to the process. Many of these recommendations have been in the area of budget concepts; a leading example is "credit reform," a 1990 change in accounting for direct loan and loan guarantee programs that CBO supported strongly. The Deputy Director of CBO has also served on the Federal Accounting Standards Advisory Board.

Clients

The Congressional Budget Act established a hierarchy of clients for CBO: first on the list are the budget committees; second are the other fiscal committees—appropriations, ways and means, and finance; and third are other committees and members. Though CBO works directly for Congress, its reports are utilized heavily by the media, interest groups, and the general public. By congressional directive, CBO reports are free of charge, and are widely distributed—about 250,000 copies are distributed to the public each year. CBO executives have always valued active and clear writing styles, which makes products readily understandable by both busy members of Congress and the general public.

Like most institutions, CBO occasionally faces workload peaks. These peaks occur during analysis of the president's budget, near deadlines for committee reporting of bills, during preparation of budget resolutions, and near the end of the legislative session. CBO staff work many hours of overtime to cope with these peaks, but CBO executives also have negotiated with clients over the completion of products. The statutory hierarchy has been the most important factor, but also important have been the time spent in the queue since the product was requested and the difficulty of the analysis. On occasion, members of the minority party have claimed that their requests are delayed, but this assertion is routinely denied by CBO staff.

Leadership, Organizational Structure, and Personnel

The director of the CBO is appointed by the Speaker of the House of Representatives and the president pro tempore of the Senate. Terms last for four years beginning on January 3 of the year after the congressional election that does not fall in a presidential election year (the so-called off-year election). Directors may be removed by a simple resolution passed by either the House or the Senate.

The CBO directors and their terms of office are as follows:

Alice M. Rivlin: 1975–1983
Rudolph G. Penner: 1983–87
Edward M. Gramlich (Acting): 1987
James L. Blum (Acting): 1988–89
Robert D. Reischauer: 1989–95
June O'Neill: 1995–

The Congressional Budget Act requires that each director be selected "without regard to political affiliation and solely on the basis of his fitness to perform his duties" (Sec. 201 (a) (2)). This admonition has been followed with regard to fitness, as all of the directors of the CBO have been extremely well-regarded fiscal analysts—for example, Rivlin, Penner, and Reischauer were drawn from high-ranking positions at, respectively, the Brookings Institution, the American Enterprise Institute, and the Urban Institute. When discussing potential candidates, elected officials have apparently placed strong weights on a moderate policy stance and an image of supporting "fiscal responsibility," interpreted as supporting deficit reductions. The position of CBO director has acquired an informal job description not unlike the expectations for Treasury Secretary and Chairman of the Federal Reserve Board of Governors (and unlike the more political role planned for director of the Office of Management and Budget).

However, political affiliation has certainly mattered in the selection process. When Rivlin—a Democrat—retired after two terms, the Congress was under divided control. The Republican Senate advocated Penner—a Republican—arguing that appointments as CBO director should alternate between adherents of the two major parties. When Penner retired after one term, there was a two-year impasse regarding his replacement. This resulted from a disagreement between the Senate and the House—both of which were controlled by Democrats—over which branch's preferred candidate should be appointed.

CBO personnel have been selected without regard to political affiliation and on the basis of their educational

and work backgrounds. According to 1990 data, 70 percent of the professional staff had completed advanced degrees. A majority of the staff were trained as economists, and a substantial minority had training in public administration and policy.

The nonpartisan personnel selection practice is not legally protected by the rigid constraints used in the executive branch. For example, pay is based largely on performance rather than on a time-in-grade system, and CBO analysts do not have civil service protection—they can be fired in short order. Despite the lack of these standard protections of the merit system, CBO executives have built a nonpartisan staff. The risk of this approach became apparent shortly after Republicans took control of the Congress in the 1994 elections, when unnamed senior Republican staff were quoted in newspapers suggesting that all CBO professional staff would be fired. However, while June O'Neill, the new director, did replace some senior staff, most professional staff were retained.

The Congressional Budget Act leaves CBO's internal organization entirely up to the director, and Alice Rivlin decided to use a model that she was familiar with from her previous service as the Assistant Secretary for Planning and Evaluation in the Department of Health, Education, and Welfare. Rivlin had been appointed to her job only after the Senate supported her view that CBO should do program analysis as well as support the budget process. She felt that demands for short-term question-answering tended to derive out long-term analysis, and that this could be prevented by separating CBO's budget process support and program analysis functions.

The organizational structure created by Rivlin has changed remarkably little since its creation, though the staffing ratio has shifted slightly towards the budget process support functions. Figure I is an organizational chart from a 1993 CBO publication.

The Budget Analysis Division is charged with almost all of the budget process support functions—cost estimating, projections, and scorekeeping. Four program divisions—for national security, natural resources and commerce, health and human resources, and special studies—have the main program analysis responsibilities. Two divisions—for tax and macroeconomic analysis—combine budget process support and program analysis responsibilities. And in practice, CBO is small enough and flexible enough that on major bills—for health care reform and farm program reauthorizations, for example—the budget analysis and program divisions have worked jointly.

Relationships with Other Agencies

CBO's relationships with executive branch line agencies are both cooperative and adversarial. Given that CBO's total staff only numbers about 220, CBO is highly dependent on

FIGURE I. ORGANIZATON OF THE CONGRESSIONAL BUDGET OFFICE

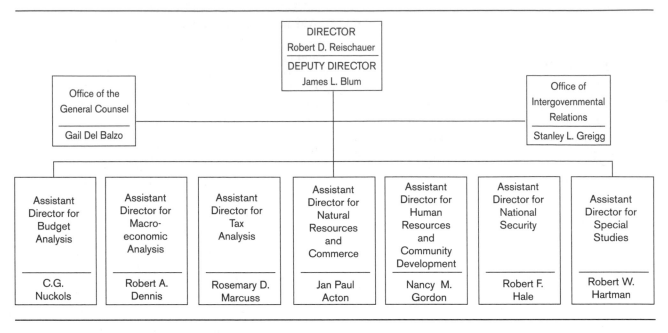

government agencies for information. These agencies are required by the Congressional Budget Act to provide budget figures and program data to CBO. Successful cost analysts develop close relationships with their counterparts in agencies, and sometimes negotiate informal understandings regarding technical assumptions, but the occasional CBO disagreement with an agency estimate can cause friction.

CBO's relationship with the Office of Management and Budget (OMB) is similar but more intense. Both agencies share a budgetary control orientation, and many analysts find it difficult to justify many spending programs and tax preferences. The staff of both agencies are also proud of their quantitative sophistication. Nevertheless, the politicization of the OMB, which affects technical decisions made by OMB examiners, creates a gap between these examiners and CBO analysts.

CBO has a narrower mission than two other congressional support agencies—the General Accounting Office (GAO) and the Congressional Research Service (CRS). The appropriations committees have required that the support agencies consult with each other to reduce redundancy in the studies they carry out, but this system has been generally ineffective. CRS, a division of the Library of Congress, provides professional research assistance to committees and members of Congress. GAO is the nation's auditor, and also conducts a great amount of program research. Both CRS and GAO have published budgetary studies— CRS notably in the area of budget process, and GAO on many topics, including long-run budget forecasts. GAO has also evaluated and criticized CBO estimating method-

ologies. CBO's relationship with the other support agencies has therefore been somewhat competitive. This was particularly true during the mid-1980s, when GAO Comptroller General Charles Bowsher strongly advocated moving towards accrual accounting in the budgetary process and abandoning the unified budget in favor of a structure that resembled state and local fund accounting budgets. CBO leaders viewed these actions as uncomprehending of the political difficulty of preparing budgets in the federal government, and as a challenge to the function of CBO from an agency with a staff 20 times its size. By the beginning of the 1990s, however, CBO and GAO had reached an accommodation on these issues, with each agency moderating its positions.

CBO Independence and the Accuracy of Its Estimates

President Harry Truman once confessed that he yearned for a one-handed economist—one who wouldn't give him advice in the form: "on the one hand, on the other hand." One of the bases of CBO's reputation for independence is that since CBO staffers are hired from disciplines that inculcate ideals of objectivity, they work in an organizational culture that places a high value on being "two-handed." The organizational importance of this ethic is shown by the appearance of the "on the one hand, on the other" slogan on the front of a CBO softball team T-shirt!

The institutional framework in which CBO operates also creates a demand for balanced analyses. Partisan and interest group conflict is rampant in the Congress, and advocates and opponents of almost any policy proposal quickly latch onto new information and use it in debates. Were the CBO to issue a report that advocated a particular position, it would be cited by the position's advocates. But this would likely upset the opponents, who would then claim bias and attack CBO's budget and staffing levels. The pragmatic response to this threat is to write analyses using a format that always displays several options. A frequent outcome is that different sides on an issue all quote from different sections of the same CBO report. This happened, for example, with CBO analyses of income distribution changes that were requested by various members of Congress.

Though CBO has been able to guard its independence, it has not been easy. Each CBO director has learned that part of the job is to listen to numerous threats and "suggestions" from members of Congress and powerful staff. In addition, CBO has the responsibility to bear bad tidings, and no one, especially a politician, likes to hear difficult news. CBO has successfully dealt with these challenges in part because it has been led by directors with large reservoirs of personal integrity and superb communications skills. In *The Agenda* (1994), Bob Woodward wrote that CBO Director Robert Reischauer "cultivated the air of the last sane man in a town gone crazy" (p. 148), a description that seems particularly apt to the whole agency.

On occasion, however, CBO has not been completely independent of political influence, particularly in the areas of scorekeeping and macroeconomic forecasting.

Scorekeeping practices have become remarkably complicated and tremendously influential. According to the Congressional Budget Act, CBO's scorekeeping products are only advisory to the budget and appropriations committees. Since changing a scorekeeping practice can produce major shifts in budget estimates, these committees have occasionally directed CBO to use assumptions that advantage or disadvantage different proposals. Following the passage of the Gramm-Rudman-Hollings Act, however, CBO and OMB began regular consultations with budget and appropriations committee staff and successfully resolved many scorekeeping controversies. In addition, a growing desire for an impartial arbiter of budgetary disputes has effectively granted CBO substantial authority to make scorekeeping decisions of great importance and to resist political pressure. Consider, for example, CBO's treatment of President Bill Clinton's health care plan, which proposed employer mandates to provide health care insurance and health care alliances to administer the plans. Opponents of the plan claimed that the mandates were equivalent to a tax and that alliances were equivalent to government agencies, and therefore all health expenditures should be placed on budget. After months of speculation and after political pressure from both sides of the argument, CBO agreed with this argument, though in its report

CBO stated that this decision was merely a recommendation and that Congress and the president should decide the question as a policy issue. The episode stimulated the Clinton administration to complain that CBO had too much power for a group of electorally unaccountable bureaucrats.

Political debate over CBO's macroeconomic forecasting techniques began several years after CBO was created, when some macroeconomists began criticizing CBO for failing to use "rational expectations" theory for its forecasts. Then, in 1981, CBO departed somewhat from its consensus economic model to move closer to the Reagan administration's "supply-side" forecast. At the time, CBO leaders felt that not doing so would make CBO vulnerable to substantial retributions from the Republican-controlled Senate.

At many other times, however, CBO has been criticized by Republicans for not projecting large responses to policy changes, particularly on the tax side of the budget. This debate became known as the choice between "static" and "dynamic" scoring. In the popular debate, CBO's static approach does not account for the effects of policy changes on behavior, and a dynamic approach does. In fact, CBO often accounts for behavior, at least in the first order. For example, if a new tax increases the price of a good and if demand is not totally inelastic, the revenue increase projection takes the price-induced demand reduction into account. What CBO's critics have in effect been arguing, therefore, is that CBO has assumed behavioral responses that are smaller than what the critics believe would actually occur. For example, some proponents of capital gains tax rate reductions have argued that these reductions would stimulate huge increases in personal savings and investments, causing aggregate revenues to increase rather than decrease. Because the consensus among economists is that the behavioral responses would not be so large, CBO has projected net revenue decreases from capital gain tax rate reductions.

CBO's estimates of individual policy changes are truly static, however, in the sense that any change is assumed not to affect the rate of growth of the economy and the revenues and spending that are tied to this economic growth. CBO justifies this convention using two arguments. One is related to the interaction of fiscal and monetary policy. Assuming that the Federal Reserve targets a certain rate of growth in the economy and that the Fed is skillful in responding to fiscal policy changes, any fiscal policy change will not have a significant effect over the short and medium terms. The other argument is based on the uncertain nature of second-order effects and the great difficulty of conducting general equilibrium analyses under time pressures.

Another criticism of CBO estimating practices—one accepted by CBO leadership—is that CBO errs on the side of procedural conservatism. That is, advocates of policy changes argue that CBO requires too much information before it will agree to score large budgetary effects. Designers of President Clinton's health care proposal, for example, lamented that CBO would not credit large savings from shifting to a system of managed care. CBO justified this decision by arguing that there was too little reliable information available, and that to do otherwise would expose the budget process to decisionmaking based on hopes and wishes, not fact-based analysis. This procedural conservatism is also due to uncertainty about which budget concepts are most appropriate for a highly charged political environment. CBO has tended to defend status quo concepts, even though scorekeeping based on these concepts may produce questionable numbers. For example, scorekeeping rules have sometimes produced inaccurate baselines for Medicare and Medicaid and for programs whose authorizing legislation is expiring.

Independent empirical studies of errors in CBO estimates have largely been restricted to macroeconomic forecasting. These studies usually show that CBO's short-run forecasts are generally accurate. Long-run CBO forecasts, in contrast, show a bias towards optimism regarding economic growth, though this bias is less than is present in executive branch forecasts. CBO's bias mostly reflects its unwillingness and/or inability to predict recessions. Some observers have argued that relying on the average of a set of private sector forecasts would be cheaper to the government and more accurate, since many private sector forecasters predict recessions and they are sometimes right! This proposal has not received much serious attention.

CBO does an annual analysis of the differences between actual spending, revenues, and deficits and the targets in the budget resolution, apportioning the causes of these differences between policy, macroeconomic, and technical factors. Policy factors account for the effects of legislation enacted after the budget resolution that was not assumed in the resolution, and macroeconomic factors are from incorrect projections of gross domestic product, unemployment, interest rates, and inflation. Technical factors are the residual after policy and macroeconomic factors, and therefore include many estimating assumptions that are to some degree economic–sectoral conditions in banking, agriculture, and so on. These analyses confirm the independent estimates of a bias in macroeconomic forecasting. They also show a comparable degree of inaccuracy in technical assumptions, though relatively little bias, since these inaccuracies tend to cancel each other out.

ROY T. MEYERS

BIBLIOGRAPHY

Blum, James L., 1990. *A Profile of the Congressional Budget Office*. Washington, D.C.: Congressional Budget Office.
Congressional Budget Office, 1995. "Budget Estimates: Current Practices and Alternative Approaches." January.
Kamlet, Mark S., David C. Mowery, and Tsai-Tsu Su, 1987. "Whom Do You Trust? An Analysis of Executive and Congressional Economic Forecasts." *Journal of Policy Analysis and Management*, vol. 6 (Spring) 365–384.
Kates, Nancy D, 1989. *Starting from Scratch: Alice Rivlin and the Congressional Budget Office*. Cambridge: John F. Kennedy School of Government, Harvard University.
Novak, Viveca, 1994. "By the Numbers." *National Journal* (February 12) 348–352.
Woodward, Bob, 1994. *The Agenda*. New York: Simon and Schuster.

CONGRESSIONAL BUDGET PROCESS.

The rules and procedures that affect the consideration of the federal budget, from the presentation of budget recommendations by the president to the enactment of laws affecting taxes and spending.

The federal budget process is not actually a single process. Rather, the term broadly refers to all the rules and procedures that affect presidential proposal and congressional consideration of spending and tax legislation. The Constitution does not establish any specific guidelines for a budget process, and budget procedures have been the subject of considerable debate and discussion throughout history. The majority of the major provisions that govern current consideration of the budget were adopted in the last 75 years. They result from two laws–the Budget and Accounting Act of 1921 and the Congressional Budget and Impoundment Control Act of 1974. In addition, the 1980s and 1990s have seen efforts to use the budget process as a tool for deficit reduction.

History of Congressional Budgeting

Congressional budgeting probably got its start in the late eighteenth century with the development of a standing committee system. In the House, a temporary Committee of Ways and Means was first created on July 24, 1789, to advise the House on matters of public finance. The establishment of a standing committee system in the Senate included a Committee on Finance in 1816 that had parallel jurisdiction over money matters. Control over both revenues and expenditures was centralized in a single committee in each chamber. This was the primary reason that the nation's finances could be coherently maintained even without a formal budget process.

The next major change in the budget process involved separating the authorization process from the appropriations process. This separation is neither mandated nor described in the Constitution. The origin of a formal rule mandating the separation of authorizations and appropriations dates to 1835 when the House discussed the increasing delays in enacting appropriations. Including legislative language in appropriation bills created many of these delays. As early as 1837, the Rules of the House were amended to prohibit legislating in appropriation bills. The Senate did not formally adopt a parallel rule until 1850 when it prohibited amendments proposing additional appropriations unless it was for the purpose of carrying out the provisions of an existing law.

This dispersal of appropriations was compounded by a similar lack of coordination in the executive branch. Executive departments submitted their requests for funds directly to the various committees with spending jurisdiction. Although the Treasury did begin compiling the requests of the various departments into a single "Book of Estimates" in 1878, there was no authority for the president to submit a single, coordinated budget proposal, or for Congress to consider one. The president was thus limited in his ability to influence or coordinate the efforts of cabinet members.

The watershed event in the development of an executive budget system was the passage of the Budget and Accounting Act of 1921. This act required the president to submit a single, consolidated budget proposal for congressional consideration each year. The act also established the Bureau of the Budget (predecessor of the current Office of Management and Budget) to provide the president with the resources necessary to produce such a proposal, and the General Accounting Office, to provide Congress with the resources to ensure accountability. The most important changes resulting from that legislation–the requirement for a presidential budget submission, a central budget office, and the General Accounting Office–remain to this day.

The consolidation of presidential budgets did not carry with it a comprehensive approach by the legislative branch. Congress reduced the portion of the budget under the direct control of the Appropriations Committees, instead using "backdoor spending" techniques that bypassed the annual appropriations process. This trend toward backdoor spending continues to this day. In 1974, discretionary spending represented 53 percent of all federal spending; by 1993, the Appropriations Committees controlled less than 39 percent of this spending. Backdoor spending can be created in several forms:

- Borrowing authority, which allows a federal agency to incur obligations and make payments to liquidate those obligations out of borrowed money;
- Contract authority, which allows agencies to enter into obligations in advance of appropriations and compels the Appropriations Committees to provide subsequent funds for the liquidation of the obligation; or
- Entitlements and mandatory appropriations, which establish an obligation for the federal government to make a payment in advance of appropriations. Many entitlements, such as Social Security and interest on the public debt, are provided by permanent appropriations.

Many observers of congressional budgeting became concerned that the failure of Congress to consider the whole budget (promoted by the proliferation of backdoor spending) was leading to irresponsible results. Irresponsible or not, however, members of congress generally agreed that this piecemeal approach to the budget constrained Congress's ability to make comprehensive policy. At the same time, President Richard Nixon challenged the spending priorities of the Congress by asserting that he had the authority to refuse to spend (or impound) funds appropriated by Congress.

These concerns prompted Congress in 1973 to create the Joint Study Committee on Budget Control. This committee sought to devise new methods to protect congressional budgetary prerogatives. The Joint Study Committee eventually reported two bills to standing committees of the House and Senate (the Joint Committee itself had no legislative jurisdiction). Ultimately, the move toward a congressional budget process culminated in the passage of the Congressional Budget and Impoundment Control Act of 1974. The act attempted to strengthen the congressional role in the making of the budget by beefing up and centralizing its budgetary capacity. It provided for additional committees and staff. The House and Senate Budget Committees were to coordinate congressional consideration of the budget, and the Congressional Budget Office (CBO) was established as a source of nonpartisan analysis and information relating to the budget and the economy. Indeed, perhaps the most important early role for CBO was to provide economic forecasts to Congress independent of those provided by the executive branch.

In trying to impose some order, the act laid out a specific timetable for action on the budget. The instrument created to coordinate various portions of the budget was the concurrent budget resolution, a form of congressional decision that can bind congressional action but does not require a presidential signature. This resolution, which the Budget Committees were to formulate by April 15 and Congress was to pass no later than May 15 each year, was an opportunity for Congress to act on the budget as a unified whole, and provided a general budget blueprint for the authorizing and appropriations committees. Once the resolution was passed, Congress reverted to its old procedures, but the committees were largely forced to live within the parameters set by the resolution.

To curb the president's ability to circumvent Congress's allocative powers, the act also included a procedure for dealing with impoundments. Two forms of presidential cutbacks were permitted–rescissions (removal of budget authority) and deferrals (delay of budget authority). The president could propose both, but to be effective the former needed explicit congressional approval and the latter tacit acquiescence.

There is general agreement that the Congressional Budget Act has led to a reassertion of the congressional role in budgeting, increased the attention of Congress to the whole budget (as well as to its disparate details), and resulted in the control of impoundments. But the attention to budget totals did not, nor was it intended to, result in achieving budgetary balance.

As the budget deficit grew substantially in the wake of the passage of the Reagan economic program in 1981, Congress increasingly became aware that the budget process could not serve as a constraint against these large deficits. Frustration with large deficits and the inability to contain them ultimately led to the passage in 1985 of the Balanced Budget and Emergency Deficit Control Act of 1985, popularly known as Gramm-Rudman-Hollings (GRH) after the sponsors of the legislation: Senators Phil Gramm (R-TX), Warren Rudman (R-NH), and Ernest Hollings (D-SC). GRH attempted to control the deficit through setting gradually declining deficit targets, and was to result in a balanced budget by fiscal year 1991. If the deficit targets were not met, automatic across-the-board spending reductions, or sequestration, took effect.

The passage of GRH represented a fundamental change in the focus of the budget process. For the first time, the budget process was used to specify a result to be achieved, rather than simply the rules to be followed to achieve any number of different budget outcomes. As such, it was a switch from a focus on rules governing decisions, timing, and priority-setting to rules that specify particular budget results, such as levels of spending and the deficit.

The deficit, of course, did not come down as promised by the Gramm-Rudman-Hollings legislation. In fact, the fiscal year 1993 deficit (which would have been zero if the law, as revised in 1987, had met its goal) was actually $255 billion. The act did put a premium on short-term budgeting; under GRH, all that mattered was the single year for which the projections were being made. These annual targets were complied with through short-term fixes and budget gimmickry, including basing the budget on optimistic economic and technical assumptions, selling assets, and shifting costs between fiscal years.

The successor to Gramm-Rudman-Hollings, the Budget Enforcement Act (BEA), was passed in 1990 and was designed to enforce the five-year deficit reduction agreement reached between the president and Congress in that year. The BEA eliminated annual deficit targets, placed limits on the level of discretionary spending through fiscal year 1995, and established the pay-as-you-go (PAYGO) process to ensure that any tax or mandatory spending changes were deficit neutral. Both the discretionary caps and the PAYGO process are enforced through a sequestration of spending in the offending category—discretionary or mandatory—only. The original Budget Enforcement Act would have expired in 1995; the Omnibus Budget Reconciliation Act of 1993 extended both the discretionary caps and PAYGO until 1998.

The importance of the BEA changes was that they shifted the process away from deficit targets to spending controls. By so doing, they focused attention on those actions that Congress and the president could control (spending and revenue actions), rather than those that they could not (primarily, the performance of the economy). As such, it has been described as a "no-fault" budget process. As long as budget rules are followed, the deficit can grow substantially without anyone being held responsible for the increase.

One of the most important developments to emerge from the 1974 Congressional Budget Act has been reconciliation, which developed into an important procedure for implementing the policy decisions and assumptions embraced in the budget resolution in a way that was unforeseen when the Act was written. Under the original design of the Act, reconciliation had a fairly narrow purpose. It was expected to be used in conjunction with a second budget resolution (since deleted) adopted in the fall, and was to apply to a single fiscal year and be directed primarily at spending and revenue legislation acted on between the adoption of the first and second budget resolutions. Congress has subsequently used the procedure to enact far-reaching omnibus budget bills, first in 1980, but most recently in 1990 and 1993.

The Congressional Budget Process Today

As the description of the evolution of the process suggests, the budget process currently in place has become a complex web of rules and enforcement procedures. The budget comes together as a result of myriad actions affecting revenues and expenditures. There is no single action that dictates all budgetary outcomes. Instead the congressional budget process includes consideration of the budget resolution, revenue measures (both temporary and permanent), appropriations bills (13 regular annual appropriations bills as well as any necessary supplemental appropriations bills or continuing resolutions), and authorizations (including entitlement legislation). In addition to these steps, the process periodically may involve other major decisions, such as the consideration of reconciliation legislation or increases in the statutory debt limit.

In practice, the budget process in Congress is normally initiated by presidential submission of the budget proposal each year, as first required by the Budget and Accounting Act of 1921 (31 U.S.C. 1105 requires the president to submit the budget by the first Monday in February). Congress, however, is not bound by any of the president's assumptions or recommendations, and may originate any budgetary legislation it chooses.

The process of developing a congressional budget formally begins when each committee submits its views and estimates to the House or Senate Budget Committee on all budget matters within their jurisdiction (currently required by February 25 each year). This information, as well as other information gathered or produced by the Budget Committees, is used to construct a concurrent resolution on the budget. The Congressional Budget Act provides a deadline of April 15 for adoption of the budget resolution, but final agreement is often not reached until later, often much later. As adopted, this resolution reflects budgetary priorities and assumptions about how the legislative branch expects to achieve its collective budgetary goals.

The Budget Committees also use baseline estimates prepared by CBO to prepare the budget resolution. The CBO baseline projections attempt to project the budget for the future based on current policy. In the case of revenues and mandatory spending, the projections estimate the conditions (economy, caseloads, etc.) that will be present and forecast what revenues and spending would look like if the laws were not changed. In the case of discretionary spending, baseline projections are done by adjusting current service levels for inflation (the exception is that, through 1998, the levels of discretionary spending are prescribed by the BEA). These baseline estimates, along with the CBO economic forecast, are to be presented prior to February 15 each year. They are updated in August or September. The law also requires OMB to do a mid-session review (the president's budget update) by July 16 of each year.

The budget resolution may, but does not have to, recommend changes in programs governing mandatory spending or revenues. Congress is in no way required to make changes in mandatory spending and revenues as a part of the annual budget process. In recent years, reconciliation has become an important procedure used by Congress to make changes in both entitlements and revenues. Reconciliation is triggered when the budget resolution includes instructions directing congressional committees to achieve savings in tax or spending programs under their jurisdiction. Congressional committees comply with these instructions by reporting to the budget committees proposed changes necessary to implement the revenue and spending targets in the budget resolution. The Budget Committees then package these responses into omnibus measures (called Omnibus Budget Reconciliation Acts, or OBRAs) which are then considered in their respective chambers under special procedures described in the Congressional Budget Act. As with the budget resolution, these provisions impose restrictions on both debate and amendments.

In many years, the focus of attention is on the fate of the annual appropriation bills. The passage of these bills is the only budgetary action absolutely required by Congress each year. Both the Senate and the House subdivide appropriations action into 13 separate bills, considered by appropriations subcommittees with jurisdiction over funding for specific portions of the government. After passage by the House, each bill is then referred to a Senate Appropri-

ations subcommittee with jurisdiction parallel to its House counterpart. (By custom, the House considers all appropriation bills first). The overall level of funding in appropriation bills is constrained by the amount allocated to the Appropriations Committee (as well as suballocations and applicable spending cap restrictions imposed by the Budget Enforcement Act) under the budget resolution.

In addition to the budget resolution limits and Appropriations Committee activity, appropriations for individual programs or agencies may also be influenced in various ways by the authorization process. An authorization is legislation establishing a government entity (such as a department or agency), activity, or program. As substantive law, authorizations are permanent unless otherwise specified. By itself, an authorization generally does not permit any funds to be obligated; it only allows appropriations of such funds to be made. In current practice, authorizations establish government programs, agencies, and duties, as well as use statutory language explicitly to authorize the enactment of appropriations, often specifying specific limits or conditions for appropriations. These authorizations of appropriations serve as ceilings on expenditures, rather than floors.

Overarching all of these procedures for enacting budgetary legislation are the procedures for enforcing budgetary discipline. These procedures are currently codified in the Budget Enforcement Act, as enacted in 1990 and revised in 1993. The Act enforces budget discipline through the dual system of discretionary spending caps and the pay-as-you-go process. If Congress appropriates in excess of a spending cap, a sequester order will be issued by the president to reduce budget authority to the required limit. Revenues and mandatory spending are restricted by pay-as-you-go, which would require that the net effect of new mandatory spending and revenue legislation be deficit neutral. Although the level of mandatory spending and revenues can change due to economic or technical factors, Congress is constrained from making changes that would worsen the deficit. If the net effect of congressional actions would increase the deficit, a sequester order would be issued to reduce nonexempt mandatory spending to the level necessary to bring revenues and mandatory spending back into the required balance.

Budget Process Reform Proposals

Despite the numerous reforms described above, there are various other changes to the congressional process that have been proposed in recent years. Some of these proposals are relatively marginal ones, such as those that would allow limited amounts of additional (above the caps) discretionary spending if they were offset by tax increases or reductions in mandatory spending, or those that would tighten the wide latitude that now exists with the emergency

495

designations. (Under this classification, virtually any spending increase or tax cut can be exempted from the discipline of the BEA if the President and the Congress agree to label the action an emergency.) But others involve more fundamental changes to the existing process. The most frequently discussed of these would amend the Constitution to require the federal budget to be balanced or to grant the president item veto authority. A number of other proposals have been considered as well, including capital budgeting and biennial budgeting.

Balanced Budget Amendment

Amending the Constitution to require a balanced budget would create an ultimate constraint against pressures for spending to outpace revenue. Numerous such balanced budget proposals have been introduced in recent sessions of Congress. Both the House and the Senate defeated proposed balanced budget amendments during 1994. In 1995, the House passed a proposed amendment, but the Senate fell one vote shy of the number needed to send the amendment to the states for ratification.

On the one hand, a balanced budget amendment would almost certainly prove a more restrictive limit than Gramm-Rudman-Hollings or the BEA. Such an amendment, however, would have to be implemented through legislation that established the necessary procedures and enforcement mechanisms. There is no particular reason to expect that these processes would not fall prey to the same sorts of gimmicks to which GRH was subject, including short-term fixes and movements to off-budget financing. The fixed deficit targets of the GRH Act have illustrated how such subterfuges can be induced by a rigid standard.

Further, a balanced budget rule could constrain the ability of the federal government to use fiscal policy to manage the economy. The traditional tools of fiscal policy–tax cuts and increases in expenditures–would be much more difficult under a balanced budget constraint and more reliance would be placed on the Federal Reserve to stabilize the economy. Denied the ability to pursue their objectives through spending policies, policymakers may resort to mandates on states, localities, and businesses; expanded regulatory efforts; and tax incentives that distort economic decisions. Such a response could undercut economic efficiency and reduce the visibility and controllability of federal policy.

Line-Item Veto for the President

The line-item veto has been sought by many presidents since Ulysses S. Grant but has never gained much favor in the halls of Congress. At the state level, 43 of the 50 governors currently have such authority to reduce or eliminate specific items in an appropriation bill. The president has only two options–either to sign or veto a bill in its entirety. Proponents argue that the line-item veto would empower the president to reduce low priority spending–so-called "pork-barrel" projects–thus leading to a reduction in the deficit. They argue that the president, as a representative of the general interest, should have the power to strike provisions that focus only on a narrow interest.

The line-item veto, however, could involve a significant shift of power between the branches, since the president could use the threat of such a veto to keep Congress in line with his or her wishes. Research on state experiences with the line-item veto suggest little impact on the level of state spending. Many governors, however, have used the line-item veto for partisan political purposes.

In 1996, the Congress passed, and the President signed, the Line Item Veto Act (P-L-104–130), which is intended as the statutory equivalent of an item veto. This Act faces an uncertain future however, since the U.S. District Court struck it down as unconstitutional in April of 1997.

Capital Budgeting at the National Level

Much of the federal budget consists of expenditures that are long-term in nature. Some people have argued, therefore, for separating the budget into capital and current operation, and removing the capital component from calculation of the deficit. This is the approach taken by most state and local governments. An argument in favor of this change in budgetary treatment of capital spending is that it might promote more spending on capital investment activities. These types of spending may currently be disadvantaged because their costs are front-loaded relative to the benefits that flow from such projects.

Alternatively, the creation of two categories of spending may increase budgetary game playing. There is no clear definition of a capital expenditure. The content of the capital budget, then, depends on subjective assumptions concerning what capital is and how it is to be measured. The tendency may be for proponents to seek protected status for their favorite "investment" activities.

Biennial Budgeting

There have been proposals to go to biennial budgeting, enacting the budget (budget resolution, appropriation bills, and other legislation) every two years, instead of annually. This is a practice currently followed by 19 states. In fact, in 1993, both the vice president's National Performance Review and the Joint Committee on the Organization of Congress recommended that the federal government move to a biennial budget process.

The federal government has experimented in a haphazard way with multiyear budgeting–the 1987 summit agreement represented a two-year budget and the agreements of 1990 and 1993 set budget parameters for five years. A more systematic approach would have two-year budget agreements which could be reached in the first year of each Congress–that is, in odd-numbered years. Proponents have argued that biennial budgeting would free up Congress to concentrate on nonbudgetary issues during the nonbudgetary year. Biennial budgeting, however, might also make agreements more difficult to achieve, since the stakes would be higher. Although some might argue that biennial budgeting would add stability to agency and program planning, uncertainty would increase as well; the ability to forecast budgets for future years is notoriously weak in biennial states. Others have asked whether it is desirable to confront budget decisions less frequently at a time when budget deficits are still at unacceptable proportions.

Conclusion

The creation of a congressional budget process has unquestionably led to a reassertion of the congressional role in budgeting, and has also increased in importance as the federal budget and deficit have moved to center stage. It will probably continue to engender controversy and calls for reform, for two main reasons. First, the many changes that have already been made have made the process much more time-consuming and complicated, and many continue to advocate a simpler set of rules. Second, since the process has been used as a means to attempt to reduce federal deficits and spending, it will continue to be criticized by those who do not approve of budget outcomes.

PHILIP G. JOYCE

BIBLIOGRAPHY

Doyle, Richard and Jerry McCaffery. "The Budget Enforcement Act of 1990: The Path to No-Fault Budgeting." *Public Budgeting and Finance,* vol. 11, no. 1:25–40.
Fenno, Richard, 1966. *The Power of the Purse.* Boston: Little Brown.
Fisher, Louis, 1987. *The Politics of Shared Power: Congress and the Executive.* 2nd ed. Washington, D.C.: Congressional Quarterly.
Hanushek, Eric, 1986. "Formula Budgeting: The Economics and Analytics of Fiscal Policy Under Rules." *Journal of Policy Analysis and Management,* vol. 6, no. 1.
Ippolito, Dennis, 1981. *Congressional Spending.* Ithaca: Cornell University Press.
Joyce, Philip G. and Robert D. Reischauer. "Deficit Budgeting: The Federal Budget Process and Budget Reform." *Harvard Journal on Legislation* 29:429–453.
Lee, Jr., Robert D. and Ronald Johnson, 1989. *Public Budgeting Systems.* Rockville, MD: Aspen Publishers.
LeLoup, Lance, 1980. *The Fiscal Congress.* Westport, CT: Greenwood Press.
Meyers, Roy, 1994. *Strategic Budgeting.* Ann Arbor: University of Michigan Press.
Schick, Allen, 1980. *Congress and Money.* Washington, D.C.: The Urban Institute.
———, 1990. *The Capacity to Budget.* Washington, D.C.: The Urban Institute.
———, 1995. *The Federal Budget: Politics, Policy, Process.* Washington, D.C.: The Brookings Institution.
Stith, Kate, 1988. "Rewriting the Fiscal Constitution: The Case of Gramm-Rudman-Hollings." *California Law Review,* vol. 76, no. 3 (May).
Wildavsky, Aaron, 1988. *The New Politics of the Budgetary Process.* Glenview, II: Scott Foresman.

CONGRESSIONAL GOVERNMENT.

A term applied to the United States government dominated by the legislature (Congress), most descriptive of American government in the nineteenth century, except during periods of war.

In the nineteenth century, the functions of the national government were generally limited and reflective of a largely agricultural and rural economy, but one that was geographically expanding and moving towards industrialization. Consequently, Congress focused on basic nation-building legislation that addressed such issues as tariffs, public lands, treaties, and national currency. During this period, Congress also established administrative agencies and directly interceded in administrative agency operations, including agency budgets and the appointment of officials. As the United States grew in physical size, population, and complexity, however, the inherent weaknesses in government by a fragmented legislative body became increasingly apparent. In his classic work *Congressional Government* (1885), Woodrow Wilson (political scientist and U.S. president, 1913–1921) judged the government to be far too divided and unwieldy for an efficient, responsible, and prompt system of government. Instead, Wilson argued that the legislature, as the representative arm of government, should be the originating force of government, setting broad standards, with administrative issues, "the clerical part of government," best left to the executive branch (p. 273).

The United States Constitution establishes a system of checks and balances that divides, yet blends and shares, power among the three branches of government: legislative, executive, and judicial. Based on their English heritage and colonial experience, the framers of the United States Constitution designed a system of government that gave primary responsibility for policymaking to the legislature. Although recognizing the need for an effective executive branch, the framers were more concerned about protecting against an overreaching executive than in assuring administrative efficiency. The competition for ascendancy among the three branches often creates institutional conflict and inefficiencies, especially at times of ideological and policy conflict. At the same time, the checks and balances system of government enables the system of government to respond to competing pressures within the polity. Other systems of legislative-executive arrangement developed successfully in other democratic countries, for example, the British Parliament and cabinet form of government, have been viewed favorably by critics of the checks and balances system, especially when the political system experiences significant conflict and fragmentation.

As twentieth century reformers pressed for a public administration based on scientific principles and focused on efficiency, the executive model of government became firmly established. Overwhelmed by the immensity of administrative detail and a federal budget that needed to be managed, Congress yielded power to the president to control administrative agencies, most significantly by establishing the executive budget system in the Budget and Accounting Act of 1921. Although yielding its ascendancy over administrative agencies, Congress continues to compete with and to exert its influence over the executive branch through the exercise of its government financing, appropriation and budgeting, and oversight powers. Political scholars continue to debate the appropriate balance between the lawmaking and representational functions of Congress and the appropriate degree of Congressional control necessary to oversee the executive branch. Although Congress has increasingly yielded administrative power to the presidency, Congress retains all its constitutionally derived powers to reassert its administrative influence whenever it is sufficiently provoked.

JOY A. CLAY

BIBLIOGRAPHY

Davidson, Roger H. and Walter J. Oleszek, 1994. *Congress and Its Members.* 4th ed. Washington, D.C.: Congressional Quarterly Press.
Schick, Allen, 1976. "Congress and the Details of Administration." *Public Administrative Review,* vol. 36 (September/October) 516–528.
Wilson, Woodrow, 1885. *Congressional Government: A Study in American Politics.* 2nd ed. Boston, MA: Houghton Mifflin.

CONSOLIDATION (AGENCY LEVEL). Occurs when several similar government agencies are brought together into one administrative unit. This organizational restructuring usually occurs in an attempt to eliminate duplication of efforts, reduce administrative overhead, lessen the paperwork requirements, and potentially result in the saving of tax dollars. Why has consolidation become such a buzzword in the public sector of the U.S., why are its praises being sung worldwide, and are its potential impacts financially, socially and politically all as positive as they appear on the surface? This article will discuss some of the reasons consolidation is occurring in government agencies throughout the world, how it is occurring, and its potential impacts on the consumer.

The current government focus on agency consolidation has arisen due to a number of different political and budgetary pressures. These political and budgetary pressures are being felt to some degree by many countries throughout the world. In the United States, political pressures have been created by a taxpayers' revolt that resulted in the election of many Republican candidates, an ongoing drive by the Clinton administration to downsize government, and a call to return certain government functions to the private sector. These various political currents are due to social, economic, and demographic trends that can be expected to continue to shape U.S. government policy well into the twenty-first century. Perhaps the most compelling of the new currents affecting many countries was created by the major shift in the world's political balance of power that occurred in the late 1980s.

One of the first changes that strongly affected the movement toward more agency consolidation and lent it strength in both the United States and Europe was the breakdown of the Soviet bloc and the end of the Cold War. The U.S. found itself with a large standing army but without a major enemy.

Future defence requirements will be focused on small policing actions, which require the creation of a fairly small, highly trained, highly mobile fighting force. As a result of this shift in defence needs, the Department of Defense (DOD) has found itself the center of consolidation efforts by the government. In November of 1993, U.S. Deputy Defense Secretary Perry announced changes that would result in a contraction of about 50 percent in almost all defense-related industries. Through various internal consolidation efforts the Department of Defense expects to decrease its employees by over one million people and expects to see across-the-board budgetary savings. Along with the more highly publicized base closings and military force reductions, DOD is also downsizing its data centers from 428 centers to 52 centers in its first phase of consolidation. When its consolidation efforts are complete, DOD intends to have consolidated all of its base level data centers into five bases. In Europe, the decreasing Soviet threat and the reunification of West and East Germany has resulted in increasing costs for social programs designed to help the newly emerging nations gain self-sufficiency while maintaining Europe's political stability. As increased spending for peacetime efforts in both European nations and the U.S. is occurring, there has been a decrease in spending on defense-related items such as military forces, bases, and hardware. For many defense-oriented government agencies both in the United States and in Europe, consolidation and downsizing have become almost synonymous terms.

In the United States one of the major reasons that consolidation and downsizing have become so closely tied together stems from efforts by Vice President Al Gore's National Performance Review (NPR), which began functioning in 1991. The main purpose of NPR is to overhaul existing government programs, to cut costs, and to downsize or consolidate the various federal agencies. Cost-cutting efforts and agency consolidation by the government have become essential tools in its attempts to control the burgeoning government budget deficit. As of the fall of 1994, the NPR has successfully eliminated over 71,000 federal workforce positions. As a result of these position eliminations and other cost-cutting efforts, NPR had achieved a savings of approximately $47 billion and has launched efforts in nine federal agencies aimed at further streamlining government and decreasing costs.

The Department of Veterans' Affairs (VA) was one of the nine agencies targeted by the NPR in its early cost-cutting efforts. The VA developed a plan intended to consolidate dozens of medical facilities and to make about 5,000 personnel cuts by fiscal year 1995. These initial changes are only a part of the efforts the Department of Veterans' Affairs will be taking in order to meet the NPR staff reduction requirements. If fully implemented, the NPR requirements will force the VA to cut up to 25,000 full-time equivalent positions over the next five years. Additional cuts and consolidations in medical facilities are also being made by the VA to reduce predicted budget shortfalls in 1995. Thus, current consolidation plans by the VA, in response to both the budget shortfalls and NPR's cost-cutting efforts, will impact 50 facilities nationwide. This move appears to have the support of the Disabled American Veterans group, who feel that the consolidations make sense.

Along with the impact of worldwide political changes on the United States Department of Defense are the problems posed by a dramatically increasing budget deficit. Many members of the American public find themselves in a situation wherein they perceive that the future of their children is being mortgaged to support the day-to-day functions of the current government. This fact has led to a taxpayers' revolt calling for decreased government spending even more than for decreased taxes. The public wants to see duplication eliminated and costs controlled. Examples of this public pressure can be seen in editorial calls for the elimination of the multiple intelligence agencies that exist in the United States. Currently, the Central Intelligence Agency, the Drug Enforcement Agency, the Federal Bureau of Investigation, the Department of the Treasury, the National Security Agency, the Defense Intelligence Agency, the Department of Energy, and the State Department all receive funds from the National Foreign Intelligence Program to conduct classified intelligence gathering operations. These funds account for approximately $16 billion of the 1995 fiscal budget, and little administrative oversight exists as to how these funds are spent due to the classified nature of the various activities being undertaken. Elimination and consolidation of these various activities is seen as a means of eliminating costly duplication of intelligence activities.

Other attempts to consolidate functions at the federal level can be seen in the Job Training Consolidation Act of 1994. The focus of this act is to consolidate federally sponsored job training and employment programs and to create a public-private partnership intended to promote this end. The bill's sponsors, Senator Nancy Kassebaum (R-KS) and Senator Robert Kerrey (D-NE), want to consolidate the numerous federal job programs and reduce duplication. According to Kassebaum, the legislation would place primary responsibilities for job training with the states and local communities in order to implement job training programs that are designed to meet local needs. Estimates as to the cost of the Job Training Consolidation Act suggest that its implementation will not cost the taxpayer more than the existing plethora of federal programs, but it also may not cost less. The proponents of the Act hope that by consolidating departments, shifting the design of training programs to the local levels, and involving the private sector in the training process, the program participants will learn useful technical skills that will enable them to compete successfully in a rapidly changing job market. Thus, consolidation efforts at the federal level are not always strictly intended as cost-cutting aimed at lowering the budget deficit, but are also intended as a means of improving government efficiency and forming cost-effective cooperative efforts with the private sector.

Experience suggests that cost savings are possible at the federal level through the use of agency consolidation. Federal agencies that appear to be the most successful when consolidating are defense-related, fiscal, and information-based.

Shifting demographics within a number of states have also led to the need for consideration of agency consolidation in various regions, states, counties, cities, and villages. As the size of the elderly population increases throughout the United States and young workers move to areas that offer increased economic opportunities, various state and local governments have found themselves with shrinking tax bases with which to support existing programs. The simplest answer to this loss of tax revenue is to eliminate some of the government services being offered. However, the simplest answer is not always the best or the most politically acceptable answer. Local governments are faced with an increasing demand for certain types of services due to the aging of their local population. This demand is compounded by the fact that although most voters don't want to pay more taxes they also don't want fewer government services. The answer may lie in part in consolidation of agencies both within local governments and across various governmental lines. This cooperative approach to service provision may be carried out through regional approaches such as is being done in Massachusetts or between villages and town, as in Ossining, New York.

Massachusetts is currently working on plans to regionalize services in a consolidation effort to promote cost-effective strategies aimed at allowing them to continue to deliver needed services to areas with decreasing fiscal bases. Some of the regional efforts are occurring between communities, while others are more formal arrangements carried out by regional planning agencies. In 1992, Massachusetts's Executive Office of Communities and Development began offering technical assistance to communities that were in the process of developing regional agreements. The question facing local government planners in areas considering this type of regionalization is whether or not these attempts to consolidate agencies result in any measurable benefits for the various political entities.

In Ossining, the local village and town combined their fiscal functions into one department. The result of this effort was a fiscal savings of $75,000. Although this sum may seem rather small when viewed at a federal level, for small local governments this amount can be rather substantial. The village of Ossining is also proposing to go beyond the consolidation to elimination, by shifting all governmental functions to the town of Ossining and doing away with the village government altogether. Other local government agencies have also explored this type of intergovernmental agency consolidation. But not all types of agencies may lend themselves to successful consolidation due to the types of services they perform. Services that are labor-intensive, such as public health delivery, may not comfortably lend themselves to consolidation, or if they do, may not result in cost savings.

Agency consolidation efforts are not always going to serve the needs of the public or of the budget planners. No matter how creative the planners become, consolidation has its limits in terms of cost savings. A certain base workforce must exist if services are to be delivered. Once an agency's personnel level goes below the number needed to provide a base level of service delivery, the public must and will suffer. So unless entire agencies are eliminated, the use of consolidation as a cost-cutting tool has some natural limits created by the need to deliver service to a politically aware and often demanding population.

The voting populace have made it clear that they want responsive and accessible services from more cost-efficient government agencies. These agencies may have achieved this increased cost efficiency by consolidation and workforce cuts. However, agency consolidation may result in an increasing tendency to centralize services, and thus, in time, result in decreasing responsiveness and access. For example, consolidation efforts are being carried out in state universities and colleges throughout the U.S.; educational consumers have found that in universities with consolidated programs, service delivery has sometimes suffered because fewer classes and fewer programs are being offered. Yet educational demands have not decreased and in fact are projected to increase in the early portion of the next century given the mini-baby boom of the last few years. Social services agencies are being consolidated, and meanwhile increasing service demands are being made by a large

and growing population of elderly upon a decreasing government workforce.

Attempts to consolidate social and educational agencies and departments may result in increased voter dissatisfaction, and in some cases already have. Washington state passed legislation in 1995 intended to break up its state social services and health delivery department due to public complaints about the lack of responsiveness and the inaccessibility of the agency created by its large size. Thus, as seen in Washington state, consolidation of many small agencies into one large agency is not always the best answer when attempting to make government more accessible and responsive to public needs and demands. Obviously consolidation of agencies must be undertaken with care; some agencies may lend themselves to consolidation efforts, while others, due to the type of services they offer, may not be able to function at a level demanded by the public.

Consolidation may not be the answer to all of the world's budget or program delivery problems. However, early attempts indicate that in certain instances and with proper consideration consolidation may result in a cost savings and increased efficiency. The challenge facing public planners and decisionmakers is to identify which services can best benefit from consolidation efforts and which would suffer.

ROE ROBERTS

BIBLIOGRAPHY

Anonymous, 1994. "Consolidate U.S. Intelligence Operations." *Aviation Week and Space Technology* (November) 74.
Anonymous, 1994. "Legislation Calls for Collaborative Job Training Reform." *Industrial Engineering* (October) 9.
Koven, Steven and Don Hadwiger, 1992. "Consolidation of Rural Service Delivery." *Public Productivity and Management Review*,. vol. 25, no. 3 (Spring) 315–328.
Miller, Glenn, 1993. "Are There Too Many Governments in the Tenth District?" *Economic Review*. Federal Reserve Bank of Kansas City (Second Quarter) 67–77.
Ormond, Derry, 1993. "Improving Government Performance." *The OECD Observer*, no. 184 (October/November) 4–8.
Rubin, Irene, 1994. "Early Budget Reformers: Democracy, Efficiency, and Budget Reforms." *American Review of Public Administration*, vol. 24, no. 3 (September) 229–252.
Weissenstein, Eric, 1994. "VA Considers Options to Reduce Personnel." *Modern Health Care*, vol. 24, no. 24 (June) 34.

CONSTITUTION OF THE UNITED STATES.

The document drafted in Philadelphia in 1787 that came into effect two years later; since then it has provided both the fundamental structure of U.S. government and the fundamental safeguard of the individual rights of U.S. citizens.

Although the word "administration" does not appear in the text of the Constitution of the United States, its framers gave careful attention to questions that today would be clearly recognized as administrative. This is abundantly clear in the famous *Federalist Papers* where "administration" and its cognates appear more frequently than either "Congress," "President," or the "Supreme Court." Essays 68–77 in the *Federalist Papers* may well be considered the first formal treatise on public administration.

Many of the distinctive features of public administration in the United States can be traced to the text of the Constitution. Chief among these is the perennial problem posed by the dual accountability of high-ranking administrators to both the president and Congress, an accountability which is at once a cause and an effect of what has come to be known today as gridlock.

The second article of the Constitution vests "the executive power" (presumably all of it) in the president of the United States. And yet the same article adorns Congress with the traditionally executive power to create offices and the power to vest the no less executive power of appointment in the heads of the executive departments and in the courts of law as well as in the president. The Senate enjoys the extremely important constitutional power to "advise and consent" to presidential nominations to the highest offices in the land.

Throughout U.S. history these constitutional texts have served as invitations to presidents and Congress to struggle for control over the administrative apparatus of the state. Consequently, administrators have often found themselves caught between plausible competing claims of two constitutional masters. In recent years, a third constitutional master, the federal judiciary, has become increasingly aggressive in asserting its claims over the burgeoning administrative state.

In addition to these structural considerations, the Constitution of the United States and the tradition it has created provide normative guidance to federal administrators who take an oath to uphold it. Because of the preeminent place assigned to individual rights within the U.S. constitutional tradition, administrators are constantly reminded of their duty not to sacrifice the rights of individuals on the alter of managerial efficiency and effectiveness. These reminders come not only as authoritative commands from courts of law, but as ethical standards as well. The latest edition of the Code of Ethics of the American Society for Public Administration states that its members are expected to "[r]espect, support, and study government constitutions and laws that define responsibilities of public agencies, employees, and all citizens." Furthermore, they are committed to "[p]romote constitutional principles of equality, fairness, representativeness, responsiveness and due process in protecting citizens' rights."

JOHN A. ROHR

CONSTITUTIONAL FRAMEWORK.

The main rules and principles for the structure and operation of government and relations between citizens and the state usually, but not always, contained in a written constitution with superior legal status.

History

Written or unwritten rules of a constitutional kind are as old as the limits on governing authority. An early example in the Anglo-Saxon tradition is the Magna Carta under which King John (1215) and, later, Henry III, accepted limitations on their powers, one of the most famous of which is trial by jury. Constitutions in their modern form, however, began to emerge in the late eighteenth century, often in response to revolutionary movements, as in the United States, Poland, and France. By the end of the twentieth century, a written constitution has become the norm. Almost every country has one, acquired to mark self-government, independence, or major regime change, and assumed to be a necessary concomitant of nationhood. One notable exception is the United Kingdom, where circumstances which elsewhere have caused the introduction of a written constitution have not so far arisen. In that country, the constitutional framework is derived from other sources instead: statutes, principles of the common law, and constitutional conventions.

Scope and Content

Most constitutions provide for the basic elements of a system of government. They identify persons or bodies with governing authority and outline their powers. In a liberal democracy, they usually prescribe the composition and powers of each of the three branches of government: the legislature, the executive, and the judiciary. Most modern constitutions also deal with relations between individuals or groups and the state, through guarantees of particular rights and freedoms. Federal constitutions, and others which attach significance to the decentralization of power, specify relations between levels of government as well. Typically, constitutions also provide for the manner of amendment unless, unusually, the normal lawmaking procedure is to be used.

Constitutions have no fixed scope, however. Frequently, a constitution will include other matters deemed particularly important by the country concerned generally, or at the time that the constitution was framed. Thus, for example, the constitution of Canada protects language rights, the constitution of Japan prohibits the maintenance of an armed force, and the constitutions of several countries, including South Africa and Fiji, make provision for the position of traditional chiefs. Similarly, constitutions vary greatly in length, from the relatively concise constitutions of the United States and Australia to the much longer and more prescriptive instruments in India or Germany. No constitution attempts to prescribe all framework rules, but different countries make different judgments about the extent to which matters of important detail can be left to judicial decision, legislative enactment, or political practice.

As a general rule, shorter constitutions are likely to be supplemented more extensively by extraconstitutional sources of this kind. The United States Bill of Rights, for example, is less explicit than the Canadian Charter of Rights and Freedoms and therefore more dependent on judicial interpretation to identify the scope and application of the rights prescribed. The Australian Constitution relies on constitutional convention to delimit the actual role of the head of state, which is set out more explicitly in other countries in the same tradition, including India, Singapore, and Eire. These differences are matters of degree, however. In fact, extraconstitutional sources make an important contribution to the constitutional system of all countries, and no account of a constitutional framework is likely to be complete without them.

Inevitably, the substantive content of constitutions varies between countries, depending on the system of government for which they provide. Government decision-making structures might roughly be divided between three categories labeled presidential, parliamentary, and mixed presidential/parliamentary, but within each there are wide variations. A similar degree of diversity can be found between federal models, with the vertical allocation of powers used in the United States Constitution and the largely horizontal division of powers used in Germany representing the extremes on which many variations have been wrought. There may be greater similarity in the core content of Bills of Rights, drawing now on international norms, but real differences exist also in the additional rights protected and in the nature of the protection offered. The right to bear arms in the Constitution of the United States is a product of its time and circumstances and is not included in other, more recent lists of protected rights. One procedural innovation in recent years, which may spread elsewhere, is the Canadian "override" provision, which enables the Canadian Parliament or a provincial legislature to override a particular right for a limited, but renewable, period.

While the constitutional framework is likely to influence the structure and function of public administration, it usually makes only limited direct provision for it. As an example, the checks and balances in relation to the executive and the legislature in the Constitution of the United States dictate the essentials of public administration in that country, although there is very little explicit reference to administration in the Constitution. Similarly, the adoption of a parliamentary system under the Australian Constitution automatically incorporates the principal assumptions and practices of public administration that normally accompany that model, despite the almost total absence of any constitutional provision to that effect. The principal justification for this apparent indifference of constitutions to public administration is pragmatic. Flexibility in public administration within broad outer limits is a useful quality, allowing adaptation to new, practical needs and theoretical perspectives.

The constitutions of most countries have superior legal or, at least, political, status. This is likely to be manifested in the way in which they are amended and in their relationship to the rest of the system of law and government.

In most cases superior status, in turn, is a product of the circumstances or procedures or both by which the constitution came into effect. In the latter part of the twentieth century, familiar procedures for the drafting and enactment of constitutions include the use of a constituent or constitutional assembly or approval by special parliamentary majorities, often followed by direct popular ratification. Earlier in the century, some constitutions derived their force from other sources: the former colonizing power, as in the case of Australia and Canada, or agreement of the occupying forces, as with Germany and Japan.

Amending procedures also vary, but almost always differentiate constitutional amendment from other legal change and usually have some connection with the way in which the constitution originally was brought into effect. Common procedures include special majorities in the legislature and popular approval at referendum. For countries with a federal structure, some agreement by the constituent units is likely to be required as well. The United States is a case in point, where amendments initiated by special congressional majorities require approval by three-fourths of the state legislatures before they come into effect.

Interpretation and Application

In most liberal democratic systems, the superior status of the constitution requires other laws and public actions to comply with the procedural and any substantive requirements the constitution prescribes. Inconsistency with the constitution usually will make an action invalid, if so declared by an appropriate court performing its function of judicial review.

The practical impact of a constitution may differ between different regimes. A contrast often drawn is with constitutions for communist or socialist regimes, which tend to be aspirational rather than prescriptive, partly as a matter of style but partly also in practical consequence of party leadership and rejection of the doctrine of separation of powers. Even in these countries, however, a constitution will have special significance, albeit, perhaps, for different reasons. The Constitution of the People's Republic of

China, for example, was replaced or substantially amended seven times between 1954 and 1994 to reflect new political conditions, although constitutional rules are not enforceable through the courts as fundamental law.

While judicial review for the interpretation and enforcement of liberal democratic constitutions is the norm, it is not universally used across all such systems, or even within them. Many countries do not accept that decisions of courts can override enactments of democratically elected legislatures, although they might nevertheless rely on courts or other tribunals to ensure compliance with the constitution by executive government and other public sector agencies. The United Kingdom, with its constitutional tradition of parliamentary sovereignty, is in this category, leaving aside for the moment the complications of adherence to the European Union. Many countries in the civil law tradition are in this category as well for different reasons, having earlier rejected the dominant role for courts which judicial review implies. These countries deal with questions raised about the constitutionality of legislation in a variety of ways. Thus New Zealand, in the same parliamentary tradition as the United Kingdom, attempts to ensure that Parliament itself carries out a monitoring role in enforcing a legislative bill of rights. Consistently with its traditions of direct democracy, Switzerland recognizes challenges to federal legislation only through the popular initiative and referendum, rather than through judicial review. And France has pioneered review of the constitutionality of legislation before enactment, by a council especially constituted for the purpose.

The countries that accept judicial review of the constitutionality of legislation are numerous, however, and increasing. They include constitutional systems as diverse as the United States, Canada, Australia, Germany, India, Japan, and South Africa. Even in these countries, however, the courts will not necessarily adjudicate on the constitutionality of all disputes. The Supreme Court of the United States, for example, will not determine political questions, which typically involve aspects of the relations between the other two branches of government. The Australian High Court is reluctant to interfere with the normal legislative process, even where the letter of the Constitution has not been followed, on the grounds that the issues are not properly "justiciable." Parts of some constitutions deliberately are drafted as directives to governments or legislatures and therefore are not amenable to judicial review. The directive principles of the Constitution of India are an example.

Typically, in common law countries, constitutional adjudication is carried out through the ordinary court system, with the highest appellate court having significant, but usually not exclusive, constitutional jurisdiction. The United States, Canada, and Australia are examples. Countries from other legal traditions often use a specially designated constitutional court, as in South Africa, Germany, and Taiwan.

Issues for the Future

The phenomenon of internationalization, defined to include rapidly growing numbers of international arrangements, the gradual acceptance of international norms for a wide range of purposes, including human rights, and emergence of new supranational regional institutions are beginning to add new dimensions to the way in which constitutions work and the role they play. Most obviously, international arrangements may extend a constitutional framework to incorporate international norms or to allow new avenues of redress for citizens at an international level. An example of the former is the Netherlands, where international human rights commitments have superior force in domestic law, even though the constitution does not provide for judicial review of the constitutionality of legislation. Examples of the latter are increasing, as countries subscribe to international protocols that enable their nationals to approach international committees directly to complain of breach. While decisions of the committees are not binding, they are likely to have a significant influence on the national government's response.

The challenges presented to national constitutional systems by supranational arrangements are more novel. The form which some, at least, will take, is suggested by the experience of the European Union, so far the most sophisticated supranational arrangement although others, including the North American Free Trade Agreement (NAFTA), the Closer Economic Relationship (CER) between Australia and New Zealand of 1983, and regional arrangements elsewhere in the world may not be far behind. There is growing acceptance that the agreements on which the European Union is based have characteristics of constitutions as well as of treaties. In due course it may become natural to conceive of such instruments as a new form of constitutional framework, for polities which are neither national nor, in the usual sense of the term, international. This development in turn may be accompanied by pressure, already witnessed in the EU, for traditional public law principles and values to apply to decisions made under supranational agreements, including a right of public access to information, opportunities for scrutiny of executive action, and greater democratic legitimacy for decisions that are taken than is the case at present.

In any event, the impact of supranational arrangements on domestic constitutions is extending the range of matters for which a modern constitution might prudently provide. Supranational agreements shift decisions to forums in which national representatives, elected by national majorities, have neither the sole nor final voice. Assumptions about executive authority to enter into international commitments tend to distort the balance between the legislature and the executive as the range of international activity increases. These changing circumstances should be taken into account in designing or amending modern constitutions, to ensure that the constitutional framework suits the circumstances of the present, rather than of the past.

CHERYL SAUNDERS

BIBLIOGRAPHY

Beer, Lawrence W., ed., 1992. *Constitutional Systems of Late Twentieth Century Asia.* Seattle: University of Washington Press.

Bobbitt, Philip, 1991. *Constitutional Interpretation.* Blackwell.

Bogdanor, Vernon, ed., 1988. *Constitutions in Democratic Politics.* Gower Publishing Company.

Brazier, Rodney, 1988. *Constitutional Practice.* Oxford: Clarendon Press.

Dehousse, Renaud, ed., 1994. *Europe After Maastricht.* Munchen.

Ely, John Hart, 1980. *Democracy and Distrust.* Cambridge, MA: Harvard University Press.

Fisher, Louis, 1988. *Constitutional Dialogues.* Princeton, NJ: Princeton University Press.

Jowell, Jeffrey and Dawn Oliver, eds., 1994. *The Changing Constitution.* 3rd ed. Oxford: Clarendon Press.

Zoethout, Carla M., Ger van der Tang, and Piet Akkermans, eds. 1993. *Control in Constitutional Law.* Martinus Nijhoff Publishers.

CONSTITUTIONAL LAW.
The branch of public law comprising of court decisions interpreting provisions of a nation's constitution. In constitutional democracies, the provisions of constitutions and the legal decisions that rest on constitutional principles—whether written or not—are regarded as superior to the law based on statutes or case law.

Constitutional democracies rest on the dual principles of democracy and constitutionalism. The basic democratic principle is that duly elected officials are empowered to make law. The second, and sometimes conflicting principle of constitutionalism, restricts the powers of democratic governments. "The notion that the people should govern through those whom they elect sometimes blends lumpily with the notion that there are critical limitations on both what government—however democratically chosen—may validly do and on how it may carry out its legitimate powers" (Murphy *et al.,* p. 23).

Article VI of the United States Constitution states that the Constitution "shall be the supreme law of the land." This means that any statute, lower court decision, or government action at any level found by a court to be inconsistent with a provision of the Constitution is "unconstitutional," or invalid. While the ultimate power for interpreting the U.S. constitution rests with the U.S. Supreme Court, only a very small number of potential constitutional questions ever reach the Court. The Supreme Court is not required to hear appeals, and, on average, accepts only 1 to 3 percent from among the thousands of petitions filed. The justices generally agree to hear cases from the highest state courts and the federal courts of appeals that raise significant questions of constitutional law or federal law. Because there are twelve separate federal courts of appeals, they often reach opposing interpretations of the Constitution. Resolving these conflicts among the circuits is one of the criteria that determine whether a petition to the Supreme Court will be accepted for decision. Nonetheless, where the Supreme Court chooses not to hear a case, the lower federal and state court interpretations of the Constitution represent "constitutional law" until such time as the Supreme Court takes action. These lower courts, therefore, contribute significantly to an ever-changing body of constitutional law.

The U.S. Constitution sets forth the structure of the government, defines the powers of the legislative, executive, and judicial branches of the federal government, and allocates power between the federal government and states. The Bill of Rights then limits all government by its explicit protection of particular individual liberties. The body of constitutional law consists of court decisions about how the language of the Constitution is to be applied to an endless array of factual situations concerning how the government is to be managed and what rights citizens will have.

Beyond defining and limiting powers, constitutions, and the body of constitutional law derived from them through court interpretations or, as in the United Kingdom, the actions of Parliament, represent the fundamental political goals and values of a democratic society. Constitutional provisions rarely do more than "command the courts to *care* about basic political and governmental values without specifying with any precision the values or the problems to which the provisions apply" (Carter, 1994, p. 185, emphasis in original). A constitution provides the language and the framework for an ongoing political dialogue about what kind of society a nation seeks to become and what values it seeks to give priority in particular circumstances. Constitutional principles serve to frame debate over fundamental political and moral questions. Yet, as Alexander Bickel points out, "No good society can be unprincipled; and no viable society can be principle-ridden" (1962, p. 64). It is the principles embodied in constitutional law to which Bickel's insight refers.

Because the purpose of constitutions is to provide general guidelines and fundamental principles for the management of the government and its relationship to the citizenry, the language of constitutions is often vague and the appropriate applications open to considerable dispute. Constitutional law, therefore, involves interpreting what the general language of the constitution "means" and what actions it dictates in particular situations. In the United States, there is an ongoing debate over how the courts should interpret the constitution. Robert Bork (1990) and other supporters of the "jurisprudence of original intention" argue that courts should not invalidate the decisions of duly elected legislatures except in cases where specific constitutional principles have been violated. Judges, in this view, are not empowered to disregard existing principles of constitutional law or to enact new ones. This view is sometimes termed the "strict constructionist" or "interpretivist" approach.

The opposing position, sometimes termed the "activist" or "noninterpretivist" approach, urges judges to identify the basic principles of the Constitution and apply them to current issues according to the justice's own moral or political vision. Noninterpretivists feel comfortable looking outside the Constitution itself for guidance in particular cases so long as they remain consistent with the general values embodied in the Constitution. Former Supreme Court Justice William Brennan, for example, argues for a broad style of interpretation that relies on the Constitution's general commitment to "human dignity" as a basis for making decisions relevant to the current time. Over time, judicial activists and strict constructionists have been allied with different political philosophies, sometimes emerging as political liberals and other times as political conservatives.

In the United States, questions of constitutional law are raised and decided in only a small percentage of court cases, but these constitutional issues often deal with the most controversial and politically significant issues facing American society. These issues frequently concern either the relative powers of the states versus the federal government or the liberty of individuals versus society's need for order.

An example of the former is seen in the 1995 Supreme Court decision (*United States v. Lopez*) wherein the Court struck down the Gun-Free School Zones Act, in which Congress had attempted to outlaw the possession of a gun within 1,000 feet of any school in the country. The Court ruled that Congress lacked the authority to legislate on this issue because the Constitutional grant of power to regulate interstate commerce does not extend to regulating the mere possession of guns in a particular place. In the view of the majority, while selling or importing guns affects interstate commerce, mere possession does not. Prior to this decision, the Commerce Clause had not been used to strike down an act of Congress since 1936.

Examples of constitutional issues requiring the Court to balance the competing demands for liberty and order are cases in which the Court balances the rights of criminal defendants versus the need for effective law enforcement, "affirmative action" to correct race discrimination versus "reverse discrimination," a woman's right to control her own body versus the state's right to regulate abortion, and a plethora of issues balancing different aspects of First Amendment issues concerning freedoms of speech, religion, and assembly.

Constitutional law, as expressed through the decisions of the Supreme Court in the United States or the Parliament in the United Kingdom, ultimately rests on political acceptance by other institutional actors and by the people.

The Constitution in the United States may be called our "civil religion" (Levinson, 1988, p. 9) representing the "center of one's (and ultimately the nation's) political life" (Levinson, 1988 p. 4).

LEE S. WEINBERG

BIBLIOGRAPHY

Bickel, Alexander M., 1962. *The Least Dangerous Branch*. Indianapolis: Bobbs Merrill.
Bork, Robert H., 1990. *The Tempting of America*. New York: MacMillan.
Carter, Lief H., 1994. *Reason in Law*. 4th ed. New York: Harper Collins.
Levinson, Sanford, 1988. *Constitutional Faith*. Princeton, NJ: Princeton University Press.
Murphy, Walter F., James E. Fleming, and William F. Harris, 1986. *American Constitutional Interpretation*. Mineola: The Foundation Press.

CONSTITUTIONAL REFORM.

The means by which changes to existing constitutional arrangements are developed and implemented.

Origins and Subsequent History

All forms of civil society have systems of government that undergo evolution or more deliberate change from time to time. Constitutional reform in the sense in which the term now tends to be used, however, is associated with the emergence of distinct constitutional frameworks for governance, centered usually on a written constitution.

Constitutional change, which is a tangible manifestation of constitutional reform, may be effected in a variety of ways. The first and most obvious is constitutional amendment. Constitutions subject to interpretation and application by courts are likely also to change in meaning through judicial review. And all constitutions are affected to a greater or lesser extent by political practice, where particular practices become established as the norm by long use and are not, sometimes because they cannot be, challenged in the courts.

While this article deals primarily with formal constitutional amendment, the significance of these other techniques should not be overlooked. It can be illustrated by reference to United States experience. Many constitutional principles with considerable impact on the rules affecting government have developed from judicial interpretation rather than constitutional amendment, including the application of the Bill of Rights to the states, acceptance that the Constitution mandates one person/one vote, and privacy rights. Similarly, the practical operation of the Constitution has been altered through political practice, of which fluctuations in presidential power over certain forms of international agreements and the deployment of United States armed forces are an example.

The United States is not the only constitutional system in which less formal techniques for constitutional change are effective. In Australia, for example, a variety of current constitutional principles can be attributed to judicial review, ranging from the constitutionally protected freedom of political communication, derived from the requirement of representative democracy, to the inability of the Australian states to impose taxes on goods, as a consequence of a broad judicial interpretation of the exclusive federal power over duties of excise. The political process also has had an impact on the constitution in action, with the effective transfer of income taxing powers from the states to the Commonwealth, initially under wartime arrangements, as a prominent, continuing example.

The extent of constitutional change that can and should be achieved by these means is a matter of dispute. The protagonists would agree, however, that a degree of constitutional change through informal processes is inevitable. While constitutions vary in detail and length, most are written in somewhat general terms, as befits a framework document. Words are inherently ambiguous in any event, and open to different interpretations by courts and others as circumstances change. And where courts are not the final constitutional arbiters, in practice or by design, compliance with constitutional requirements depends on governments, legislatures, and other public bodies, which also may vary in their interpretation of the rules or may reach agreement on a mutually satisfactory interpretation that differs from that which applied before.

Framework for Formal Constitutional Change

Both the written constitutional text and considerations of democratic legitimacy place limits on the degree to which constitutional change can be effected through informal means. Formal change significant in extent, departing from existing constitutional provisions, or radically adding to them requires amendment of the text of the constitution itself. The procedures for change are likely to be incorporated in the constitution and are likely to differ from the ordinary lawmaking procedures. The mechanisms chosen usually will seek to recognize the special status of the constitution and its enduring character, while ensuring that it is not unduly rigid and is able to be amended as genuine need occurs.

There is a wide variety of mechanisms for constitutional change. As a generalization, they might be divided into three categories, involving special procedures in the legislature, a direct vote by the electorate, or a recommendatory or determinative decision by a constituent or constitutional assembly, specifically selected for the purpose. These mechanisms are not necessarily mutually exclusive: they may be combined, or prescribed as alternatives, or used for different purposes within the same constitution. The actual mechanism chosen may depend on a variety of factors: history and constitutional tradition; the procedure by which the constitution originally came into effect; in some cases, on the form of government for which it provides; and on the balance sought to be achieved between flexibility and rigidity.

Again, the point can be illustrated by reference to the United States, where the two alternative procedures for change to the national Constitution reflect both history and the federal character of the system of government thus created. The procedure generally used involves a two-thirds vote in each House of the Congress followed by ratification of the amendment by three-fourths of the state legislatures or by state constitutional conventions. The alternative procedure involves a constitutional convention, convened by Congress on the application of two-thirds of the state legislatures, followed by state ratification. The Constitution has proved to be relatively rigid. Since acceptance of the first ten amendments, almost contemporaneously with the Constitution itself, only 15 amendments have been adopted, two of which, concerning the prohibition of alcohol, canceled each other out.

Elsewhere, the factors identified earlier have resulted in a variety of different forms of amending procedures. Most federal countries employ a formula that reflects their federal structure in some way. Thus the Canadian Constitution, which before 1982 could be amended only by the United Kingdom Parliament by which the British North America Act originally was enacted, now can be amended by votes in the Canadian Parliament and a proportion of provincial legislatures, or, in the case of some amendments, a unanimous provincial vote. In Australia, the initiative lies also with the Commonwealth Parliament but ratification is required by popular vote, in which an overall national majority is achieved, as well as majorities in a majority of states. In Germany, by contrast, constitutional change can be effected by the federal legislature alone, involving, however, approval by the Bundesrat, directly representing the governments of the Lander.

Future Directions

In the last decade of the twentieth century, some interesting trends can be seen as emerging in constitutional reform.

The first is a tendency for new constitutions, or major changes to existing ones, to be submitted to popular vote. In some countries, of which Switzerland and Australia are examples, this is a formal requirement for constitutional change. In others, popular approval is sought for reasons of political necessity or judgment. Thus the Charlottetown proposals in Canada were put to referendum in 1992 and rejected. In 1994 the New Zealand electorate was asked to vote on major changes to the electoral system, ultimately approving a change to mixed member proportional representation that is likely to have a major impact on representative democracy in that country.

A second development is the willingness of the courts of some countries to recognize features of the constitution which are not able to be amended at all. So far, this has occurred in countries where the constitution is able to be amended by an incumbent legislature, through procedures which are relatively easily met. The leading example is India, where certain basic features of the constitution, including federalism and human rights, have been held by the Supreme Court to be immune from change. Other countries in the region have followed suit, however, including Bangladesh and Nepal. As a variation on the theme, some constitutions themselves prescribe particular principles as enduring, and not subject to change. Germany is an example, where amendments that would alter human rights principles or the federal character of the constitution are expressly prohibited.

A third development concerns the procedures that precede formal amendment, particularly where substantial change is being sought. Some countries, of which Canada, Australia, and Switzerland are recent examples, have experimented with expert, popular, or multipartisan processes to identify proposals or packages of proposals for change. Few of these in fact have had significant results. On the contrary, experience tends to suggest that constitutions are resistant to sweeping change, particularly where the formal amendment procedure involves the electorate at large.

CHERYL SAUNDERS

BIBLIOGRAPHY

Ackerman, Bruce, 1991. *We the People: Foundations.* Cambridge, MA: Harvard University Press.
Kammen, Michael, ed., 1986. *The Origins of the American Constitution.* Penguin Books.
Linder, Wolf, 1994. *Swiss Democracy.* Macmillan Press Ltd.
McRoberts, Kenneth and Patrick Monahan, eds., 1993. *The Charlottetown Accord, the Referendum, and the Future of Canada.* University of Toronto Press.
Saunders, Cheryl. "The Australian Experience with Constitutional Review." *Australian Quarterly* vol. 66 (3).
Suksi, Markku, 1993. *Bringing in the People.* Martinus Nijhoff Publishers.

CONSTITUTIONALISM. A central concept in Western political thought. Derived from the Latin verb *constituere* (to set up, to establish, to put together,) a constitution is primarily the instrument by which a system of governance is established. The "ism" suffix, however, belies the word's etymology and has come to stand for the principle that governments should be limited in their powers. Thus, a constitutional monarchy is one in which the king or queen has certain limited powers which are well understood and may even be stated explicitly in a written charter of government, that is, in a constitution.

The interaction between constitutionalism and public administration has been rich and varied. In England, it has led to the cardinal principle of ministerial responsibility and its administrative corollary of civil service anonymity. In British constitutional theory, ministers alone are responsible to the sovereign Parliament for whatever happens in their ministries. The same theory confers anonymity upon civil servants whose transgressions must be explained to Parliament by the responsible minister. The realities of the modern administrative state put considerable pressure upon the tidy notions of parliamentary sovereignty, ministerial responsibility, and civil service anonymity. One need not have watched the delightfully satirical television series "Yes, Minister," to realize that in the United Kingdom, as in every other developed country, civil servants play an exceedingly important role in national governance. Recent innovations such as the investigative functions of "select committees" of Parliament signal an important step toward making British civil servants more directly accountable to Parliament and to certain of its committees.

In the United States, the famous politics-administration dichotomy of the civil service reformers at the end of the last century foundered on the shoals of the bedrock American constitutional principle of separation of powers. Although the dichotomy has been discredited on empirical grounds for half a century, the more fundamental point is that even in theory it never made any sense within the confines of the U.S. constitutional tradition. To say that a U.S. administrator is to carry out the will of his or her political superior simply begs the question of which superior he or she is to obey when there are three of them—legislative, executive, and judicial—and each one is independent of the others.

In France, constitutional traditions have been profoundly influenced by administrative institutions and practices, whereas in England and the United States the causal nexus has flowed in the opposite direction, that is, from constitutional principles to administrative practices. This is because France has seen at least 13 constitutions since the Revolution of 1789. French political culture, marked by constitutional instability, has relied upon administrative institutions to stabilize the life of the nation as monarchies, empires, and republics have come and gone with distressing regularity. Chief among these has been the prestigious *Conseil d'Etat,* which has distinguished itself by introducing legal principles to safeguard individual rights in what might otherwise have been an oppressive administrative state.

Despite the remarkably different administrative traditions in France, the United Kingdom and the United States, these three countries and many more like them share a common drive to tame power by limiting it, that is, by sharing a common heritage of constitutionalism.

JOHN A. ROHR

CONSTRUCTIVISM.

The view that "reality" is a social construction devised by humans in their communities and groups. The hard science view that theory statements may be confirmed by objective facts is dramatically modified in constructivism. In constructivism, any claim that a statement is a description of objective fact is a suspect claim, since all statements contain presuppositions. Theory statements are themselves conditioned by context and prior perceptions.

Constructivism owes its name to the influential book by Peter L. Berger and Thomas Luckmann, *The Social Construction of Reality* (1966). The thesis of their book is that humans actively partake in creating the categories that signify our understanding of the world. A significant quality of constructivism is that it avoids reifying categories. Whereas other views of reality may assume, say, the rationality of human nature, or the concreteness of organizations, or the consensus around organizational goals, or the solidity of any human category, constructivism sheds these assumptions. The constructivist understanding is that the categories we use in daily discourse are often reifications. Reified categories are those that are injudiciously bestowed with autonomous force by their creators (humans). Reified categories are presumed to exist independently of human social interaction. Thus constructivism has its own view of reality, with a unique approach to making clams about truth. Philosophically, constructivism is grounded in phenomenology.

Phenomenological Roots

The word "phenomena" may be traced back to the philosophy of Immanuel Kant. Kant distinguished between physical reality, what he called "noumena," and the human perceptions about that reality, called "phenomena." Many philosophers have argued about whether there can be a one-to-one correspondence between physical reality and our perceptions of it, and phenomenologists tended to concentrate on our perceptual capabilities. The distinction between noumena and phenomena has also been expressed as the distinction between things-in-themselves (noumena) and things-for-themselves (for whom noumena become phenomena). Things-for-themselves have perceptual capacities, intentionalities, and consciousness while physical things-in-themselves do not perceive. Perception and consciousness are the endowment of things-for-themselves. Perceptions are the creations of things-for-themselves. There is a kind of unbridgeable gap between things-for-themselves and things-in-themselves, in that perception and consciousness cannot be proven to correlate precisely with the things-in-themselves that are the objects of perception. There is no basis for asserting that, through our capacities to percerve, we have faithfully reproduced the reality of things-in-themselves. Things-in-themselves cannot ultimately be known from their own points of view, as they do not have any. Knowledge, it follows, is on the phenomenal (things-for-themselves) and mind side of this ontological bifurcation between mind and matter. In that sense all phenomenology is Kantian or neo-Kantian. So too is constructivism.

Phenomenology has advanced since Kant, and has developed into a school of thought in philosophy. The generally acknowledged founder of modern phenomenology is Edmund Husserl (1859–1938). Husserl's project was to find an infallible foundation for philosophy and science within the structure of consciousness. Husserl's particular doctrines are not very influential today because he kept shifting and revising them and because they are often obtuse. Philosophers influenced by Husserl include Martin Heidegger, Maurice Merleau-Ponty, Jean-Paul Sartre, and Alfred Schutz. Phenomenology today connotes a loosely connected set of themes derived mostly from Husserl. Three themes are particularly important to constructivism: intentionality, bracketing, and nominalism. Each is an alternative to what constructivists regard as the naive, dogmatic, or ideological premises of mainstream thought, what Husserl called the "natural attitude." The natural attitude is the uncritical acceptance of given conventions.

Phenomenologists and constructivists agree that consciousness is intentional. Consciousness is consciousness of . . . something. In other words consciousness can never be found empty, it is always consciousness of something. Human subjectivity is the active spark in all this: the agent of intention. Our human subjectivity is evoked from the larger physical and cultural situation in which life is experienced.

But we are not thereby determined by that larger environment, as if we were nothing but the net result of external stimuli. Our movements are not determined by the calculable total effects of all the billiard balls (external stimuli) that knock us this way, then that way. In this conception, the external stimuli are the privileged causal agent of perception. Stimulus causes response. In organizational theory Taylorism and derivatives such as expectancy theory or behavior modification carry the residues of the natural attitude assumptions. This natural attitude was the operative standpoint in the early stages of the famous Hawthorne studies, where illumination was altered to measure its effects on worker productivity.

Intentionality depicts human consciousness and perception quite differently. Intentionality offers a more purposeful perspective of human motility. Understanding (that is, perception and consciousness) is not just for idle contemplation, but for action. We can dodge billiard balls if we want to, once we understand their movements. That is to say, agency resides in humans, not in the external physical environment. That agency is attributed elsewhere, inappropriately, is a frequent complaint of constructivists. Individuals with projects are agents; the organization, often thought to be an autonomous agent, is not. Organizations are often, inappropriately, presumed to have causal force. Of course organizations do not possess autonomous force at all, but are perceived that way because they are reified. Reification is the tendency of humans in the natural attitude to take malleable products of human culture as fixed and immutable, as alienated other. Reification is to "thingify." Harbingers of reification might be "the bureaucracy believes . . . ," "corporations do . . . ," and "the role requires." Phenomenologists and constructivists have a way of dealing with reifications. Bracketing, in the context of phenomenology, may be seen as the process of accessing the flow of consciousness in order to transcend or subtend reifications.

Phenomenologists are ever vigilant to bracket, or put in suspension, reifications such as bureaucracy, corporations, and roles. Experiences of the lifeworld (*lebenswelt*), as free as possible from reified categories are the emancipatory corrective. Phenomenology, then, privileges interpretation of the lifeworld over the so-called empiricism of collecting facts taken as discrete, atomistic entities and adding them up by means of some formal calculus. Interpretation of the lifeworld is commonly called phenomenological description and may be cast in the first person singular. In practice, social scientists influenced by phenomenology tend to utilize research approaches such as case studies, open-ended interviews, participant observation, focus groups and ethnomethodology.

Bracketing to overcome or avoid reification entails nominalism. Nominalism is an ontological stance specifically opposed to realism. Realism presupposes the independent objective reality of facts or things. As a corollary, it also often assumes that there is a one-to-one correspondence of symbols (words) to facts. Conversely, nominalism holds that facts are the product of human intentionality. Moreover, names have no dependent relationship to facts. Names are provided by humans—categories are socially constructed things—and one name is as good, which is to say as arbitrary, as any other.

The Uses of Constructivism

Adopting a constructivist standpoint on reality does not predetermine subsequent theorizing: a number of possibilities are consistent with it. Minimally, constructivism may

only interfere with realism and help one to avoid its excesses or the excesses of logical positivism. Constructivism can also be found in important works. The idea of paradigms, for instance, as popularized by Thomas Kuhn's *Structure of Scientific Revolutions* (1970) may be regarded as constructivist. Science was seen not as a direct apprehension of truth, but as a nexus of agreement negotiated and maintained by a particular generation of scientists. The very concept of having a sociology of knowledge informed by constructivism deprives scientific knowledge of universal validity. Scientific-fact realism, along with all other thought systems, fails to transcend its own particular social formation.

Two ambitious constructivist attempts to develop full blown theories of public administration are Michael M. Harmon, *Action Theory for Public Administration* (1981) and Charles J. Fox and Hugh T. Miller, *Postmodern Public Administration: Toward Discourse* (1995). In both of these, proactive administrative discretion is promoted once reified organizational imperatives have been exposed for what they are. Harmon looks to the integrity of face-to-face encounters as the appropriate means to organizational and personal health. Alternatively, Fox and Miller attempt to update constructivism. They move away from the extreme subjectivism implied when intentional consciousness is seen as primarily an activity of minds. To move away from excessive mentalism, they appropriate the concept of body-subject from French phenomenologist Maurice Merleau-Ponty. By locating consciousness in the nexus between body-subjects and the situation in which those body-subjects find themselves, a material grounding for human consciousness is introduced. The body-subject is simultaneously physical and mental, incorporating both objectivity and subjectivity. Because consciousness occurs in bodies—which possess capacities similar to other bodies of the species—there is the possibility of collective will formation, an important requisite to a discursively democratic government.

If constructivism can be summed up simply, it is that reality is socially constructed. This would be true for any political or administrative institution, including organizations. Because organizational reality is not imposed upon public administrators by some material force outside of human groups, it is amenable to adjustment. What we usually take to be "the organization" turns out to be nothing but habitual behavior, which is to say, recursive practices which have their foundation in material human bodies. Recursive practices may be adjusted, but not without first thwarting some set of sedimented habits that have been reinforced by social practice. Yet whatever the difficulty in altering these recursive practices, they are indeed social constructions.

CHARLES J. FOX
HUGH T. MILLER

BIBLIOGRAPHY

Berger, Peter L. and Thomas Luckmann, 1966. *The Social Construction of Reality.* Garden City. New York: Viking.

Fox, Charles J. and Hugh T. Miller, 1995. *Postmodern Public Administration: Toward Discourse.* Newbury Park, CA: Sage.

Harmon, Michael M., 1981. *Action Theory for Public Administration.* New York: Longman.

Husserl, Edmund, 1962. *Ideas: General Introduction to Pure Phenomenology.* London: Collier.

Kuhn, Thomas, 1970. *Structure of Scientific Revolutions.* Chicago: University of Chicago Press.

Schutz, Alfred, 1967. *The Phenomenology of the Social World,* trans. by George Walsh and Frederick Lehnert. Evanston, IL.: Northwestern University Press.

CONSULTANTS. Persons or firms who, pursuant to a contract, provide specific, often complex or technical reports, research, or services to government agencies.

The idea of "buying" technical assistance or other services from private or not-for-profit companies has been a common practice in government for many decades. The premise behind this activity is that certain information can be assembled more economically with the use of nonemployees. The consultant is hired on the basis of the firm's technical capacity and on the basis of the limited time frame associated with the specific task. This means that the government does not have to use the lengthy and expensive personnel search process for a person or persons with unique or specialized credentials and for whom there will be no work beyond a certain period of time. The definition of consulting used by the United States government was codified in U.S. Office of Management and Budget Circular A-120 in 1980. That definition reads in part, "those services of a purely advisory nature relating to the governmental functions of agency administration and management and agency program management. . . . These services are normally provided by persons and/ or organizations who are generally considered to have knowledge and special abilities that are not generally available within the agency" (OMB, April 14, 1980).

Consulting contracts have become virtually universal and indispensable for effective operations in every government around the world. The consultant becomes an adjunct to agency operations, performing important tasks which, nonetheless, would not necessarily get done in the absence of that consultant. The consultant, ideally, makes a positive contribution to the operating effectiveness of the government agency.

Depending on the level of government and the nature of the services required, consulting arrangements may represent a few days of a single individual, or they could represent several person-years of effort from a large firm. The common thread is in the use of contracts to purchase services, not in the nature of those services, nor in their scope. Consulting has much in common with the ideas of contracting out and privatization. What most distinguishes consulting is the emphasis on supporting governmental activities, rather than replacing them.

The practice of using consultants has never gained the public support that privatization and contracting out has found. The level of distrust this practice engenders is best exemplified by the sobriquet applied to the consulting firms of the Washington, D.C., area—"Beltway Bandits." Deserved or not, the public image of the consultant is that of an overpriced and underworked dilettante with few marketable skills, and fewer scruples. Expectations are low. Few see the product of the consultant as relevant or necessary. Like the image of the "bureaucrat" this image is made up of equal parts myth, misunderstanding, distrust of government itself, and the occasional, but well-publicized, bad contract. What is most telling is that many consulting firms work for both government and the private sector, but only earn distrust when under contract to a government agency.

Several issues are important to an understanding of the consulting arrangement. Those include:

1. The character of the work itself;
2. The absence of in-house "experts";
3. Contracting as a legal and managerial concept;
4. The perception of the need for "distance" from agency personnel;
5. Cost of work; and
6. Timeliness.

The Work Itself. Certain types of work activities lend themselves to the use of consultants. Studies to establish benchmarks for performance, the use of consultants to investigate work changes as in a managerial audit, and activities for which specialized equipment are required are three examples of work for which a consultant might be hired. The question to be asked is, are the skills required for this work of such a nature that permanent, full-time employees could do the work equally well? Often the answer is no, and therefore a consultant could be brought in to do the work. The rule of thumb is, if this work would not get done without outside support, then the assistance of a consultant would aid overall performance. In addition the consultant serves in an advisory capacity. It is not the responsibility of the consultant to establish agency policy. The consultant, therefore, works within known and well-defined parameters. Control remains in the hands of public managers.

This is possibly the most significant way that the use of consultants differs from the idea of privatization. The concept of privatization takes control of operations out of the hands of public managers and passes it on to the new program operators in the private sector. Furthermore, a consultant is used to enhance or supplement agency performance (if only by pointing out weaknesses in current practice, as may be the case in a managerial audit). Privatization represents the choice to use others because of the inferior performance of the public sector employee. It is not lack of competence, merely a lack of capacity that triggers the use of a consultant. In the latter case the outsider enhances performance; in the former the actual workers are replaced by presumptively superior private sector workers.

Lack of In-House Expertise. Closely related to the above idea is the use of consultants for specific, often technical work. Over the last two decades it has been common for government agencies, particularly at the state and local levels, to hire programmers to create new and unique software to help process paperwork. In a unique process for providing technical consulting services for cities in the U.S., Public Technology, Inc. was created, in part with funds from the National Science Foundation. PTI served as a clearinghouse for information on emerging technologies and provided consultants to help communities adapt those technologies to their needs. The underlying assumption in the creation of this nonprofit organization was that there was no other way for even relatively large cities and counties to obtain or share information on technological breakthroughs. For a relatively modest fee the community gained access to the consulting services and information resources of PTI (Rehfuss, 1989; Bingham and Felbinger, 1989). Without access to consultants, agencies would need to expand staffs to perform work that may be both nonroutine and intermittent. A little noticed, but frequently used practice in local governments is that of using executive search firms to screen and recommend candidates for city manager and other local government positions. The search firm has information about candidates and knowledge of screening techniques well beyond those available to a city council.

Legal and Managerial Issues. The use of a consultant presents a number of problems for the public manager. The basic problem is in monitoring performance. The work of a consultant is useful and effective only if it serves the ends desired by the public agency that hired the consultant. Particularly if the consultant is hired because of highly specialized skills, the ability to judge performance can be problematic. Rehfuss notes that a public manager may be skilled at directing agency operations, but ill-prepared to define performance standards for a contractor. In other words, how do you know if the consultant is doing a good job? The skills of contract negotiating and contract monitoring are vital, yet they may be beyond the ken of even very senior agency officials (1989, pp. 46–47). Donahue goes so far as to suggest that unless clear performance measures are defined and agreed to before a contract begins, then the work should remain in-house (1989, p. 83).

"Distance." Certain activities must be done by persons outside an agency to avoid even the appearance of unethical or conflicted behavior. The use of auditors to review the "books" of an agency is one such example. Similarly, program evaluations are frequently done by consultants. The other time when the use of outside assistance is useful is when developing elaborate management change strategies, such as strategic management or total quality management. Both of these strategies emphasize participative management in the development and implementation of those efforts. Many employees may regard the process as "stacked" if the manager's "team" is in charge. The use of an outside facilitator can avoid the appearance of bias, and signal an open process of change. The neutral consultants can be far more effective in communicating both the good and the bad of an impending change effort. Stated simply, an outsider is likely to have more credibility in such a process, and that credibility is a necessary prerequisite for successful implementation. The presence of the consultant could well be a critical factor in the ultimate success of the change effort.

Cost. The most common explanation offered for the contracting out of services is that it lowers the cost of government. Yet, as Hanrahan (1983) explains, the use of consultants and contractors may only add to the cost of government. One study of U.S. government found that 40 percent of federal programs that had a commercial content (i.e., ones which competed directly with the private sector, as defined in OMB Circular A-76) cost less than if the program were contracted out. Also, as noted above, contract monitoring costs must be considered when making cost comparisons. Nevertheless, cost is a critical factor in the decision to hire consultants and contractors. Where the alternative is that the task will not be performed with existing personnel (either because of hiring restrictions or because of skills required for the job), then the use of consultants represents a cost savings both in the short run and over the long run (since there are no costs for personnel accrued beyond the life of the project). Lastly the successful consultant has done the job—improved overall performance—and that in itself represents a cost savings.

Timeliness. One of the critical factors in choosing a consultant over in-house staff is the ability to direct the energies of a consultant to a specific task more quickly than may be possible if relying on agency personnel. The International City/County Management Association (Bingham and Felbinger, 1989, p. 13) cites a number of time-based factors, among others, as reasons for using contractors to provide government services. For example, even if in-house staff has the capability to perform the same work as a consultant, that work may need to be done at a time when that staff is not available. Work such as program evaluation cannot be set aside until staff can get to it; it is work that must be done during the operation of the program. A consultant hired for the task of program evaluation is available when needed.

The pitfalls in the use of consultants are many. The International City/County Management Association offers a checklist for ensuring that a community will have a successful relationship with a contractor. While a couple of these items are more directly pertinent to the more complex process of privatization, they remain valid for consulting contracts. The issues and concerns are as follows:

1. Is the elected body in favor?
2. Is contracting less expensive?
3. Do local employees have the expertise necessary to prepare bids and contract specifications?
4. Can the service quality and level be defined to a satisfactory level?
5. Do sufficient suppliers exist to ensure competition?

It is in answering these questions that the problems of using consultants can be avoided either by the decision to stay in-house or by careful contract monitoring. Questions three and four are the heart of the problem. Hanrahan, a former reporter for the *Washington Post,* found that abuse of consulting arrangements in U.S. government agencies were often the result of the uncertainty and even ignorance of the personnel in the agency paying for the consulting services. Agency personnel had little idea of the level of work effort necessary to complete the contract and, therefore, could not properly monitor progress. In such circumstances contracts would be renegotiated while in progress to accommodate task changes; costs inevitably rose (pp. 52–63). Sometimes such cozy arrangements are the product of corrupt practices, but more likely no one was available to monitor the work. The dilemma in this situation must be noted. It is accepted as good management practice to seek technical and specialized consulting support. But, by definition, these are precisely the circumstances when agency personnel are least knowledgeable. The best way to stay on top of the consultant is to know as much about the task as the consultant, but if agency personnel are that expert, that is probably the time to stay in-house and not use a consultant. That is why the concerns raised by the ICMA about contract specifications and procedures are so vital to a successful relationship.

The use of consultants is a practice of governments around the world. The advantages in using consultants are the same; lowering the cost of government operations, gaining access to unique or specialized knowledge nowhere else available, avoiding the appearance of bias in decisionmaking, and improving government operations. But it must equally be said that the problems are also universal; difficulty in defining tasks and costing that work, problems in contract monitoring, and overcoming the suspicion that the whole process is some kind of "boondoggle." Consultants play a positive role in improving govern-

ment productivity and therefore their use will continue, but, because of the suspicion that pervades their use, particularly in Washington, D.C., greater emphasis on training in contract monitoring and contract negotiating will be demanded.

RAYMOND W. COX III

BIBLIOGRAPHY

Bingham, R. D. and C. L. Felbinger, 1989. "Professionalism, Innovation and Entrepreneurship." In H. George Frederickson, ed., *Ideal and Practice in Council-Manager Government.* Washington, DC: International City/County Management Association.
Bryson, J. M., 1988. *Strategic Planning for Public and Nonprofit Organizations.* San Francisco: Jossey-Bass.
Donahue, J. D. 1989. *The Privatization Decision.* New York: Basic Books.
Hanrahan, J. D., 1983. *Government by Contract.* New York: W.W. Norton.
Machester, L. D. and G. S. Bogart 1988. *Contracting and Volunteerism in Local Government.* Washington, DC: International City Management Association.
National Academy of Public Administration, 1989. *Privatization: The Challenge to Public Management.* Washington, DC: National Academy of Public Administration.
Rehfuss, J. A., 1989. *Contracting Out in Government.* San Francisco: Jossey-Bass.
U.S. Office of Management and Budget, 1980. Circular A-120. Washington, D.C.

CONSUMER PRICE INDEX (CPI).

A measure of the change in minimum expenditure over time required for the consumption of a fixed market basket of goods and services, based on average price levels of the market basket bought in some comparison period by urban wage earners and clerical workers and by all urban consumers compared to the average price levels in a reference period.

History

Introduced in 1921, the first CPI was based on an expenditure survey of 12,000 workers in 92 cities conducted by the Bureau of Labor Statistics in 1918–1919. Subsequent revisions were based on expenditure surveys from 1934–1936, 1950–1952, 1960–1961, 1972–1973, and 1982–1984. In 1972, the survey was extended to other urban locations, and in 1978 and 1983 the methodology was revised significantly (see various U.S. Bureau of Labor Statistics publications for details). Currently, the measure is based on monthly price information and on quarterly expenditure surveys, which are used to change the weights of the goods and services in the market basket.

Theory

A true cost of living index would provide an answer to the question: how much would it cost the average household in the comparison period to be as well off as an average household was in some reference period? Since a true cost of living index is based on the concept of satisfaction or utility, it is difficult to retrieve from available data. A Konus, or "true" cost of living index, K, would be of the form:

$$K = \frac{e(p', u^\circ)}{e(p^\circ, u^\circ)} = \frac{e(p', u^\circ)}{\Sigma p^\circ x^\circ}$$

where e is expenditure, p' is the price vector in the comparison period, p° is the price vector in the reference period, u° is the level of utility or satisfaction in the reference period, and x° is the vector of goods in the market basket.

The Laspeyres index answers the question: what would it cost in the comparison period to buy the same bundle of goods that was purchased in the reference period? Using the notation described above, the Laspeyres ratio is of the form:

$$L = \frac{\Sigma p' x^\circ}{\Sigma p^\circ x^\circ}$$

The Laspeyres is the ratio of the cost of buying a market basket of goods in a comparison period to the cost of buying that market basket of goods in some reference period. There is wide consensus that the Laspeyres index overstates inflation through time, making it an upper bound of a true cost of living index.

A Paasche index answers the question, what could the consumer buy at the comparison period prices, if the expenditure from the reference period were available? The Paasche ratio is of the form:

$$P = \frac{\Sigma p' x'}{\Sigma p^\circ x'}$$

The Paasche index is a lower bound to a true cost of living index, and when $P > 1$, the consumer is better off in the comparison period. The Laspeyres is an upper bound to a true cost of living index, and when $L > 1$, the consumer is worse off in the comparison period. It is not the case that the true cost of living index lies between these two measures, nor is it necessary that Laspeyres be greater than the Paasche. Under certain restrictive conditions the indexes can be equal to the true cost of living indexes (see Pollak, 1989, for a technical discussion of these cases).

Current Practice

Based on data from the Consumer Expenditure Survey (CES) conducted by the Bureau of labor Statistics (BLS) and the Point of Purchase Survey conducted by the Census Bureau, the Consumer Price Index (CPI) is compiled and reported by the BLS. The CES tracks the prices of over 95,000 consumer goods and services, and the CPI is an aggregation of over 9,000 indexes.

A Laspeyres-type index, the CPI is widely used as a cost of living index, but it is far from a perfect measure of the effect of changes in consumer prices. As theory suggests a true cost of living index would take into account the substitution of goods in the presence of a price change. Commodity substitution bias refers to the errors in the CPI that result from the use of fixed weights for the index. While economists generally agree that the substitution bias exists, estimates of its magnitude vary. When prices change, consumers are likely to substitute one good for another (for example, coffee for tea or chicken for beef). Yet the CPI is unable to detect such shifts since it is based on the market basket of the reference period.

Seller substitution effect and outlet substitution effect refer to the errors possible in the CPI estimate due to consumer choice of producer. In the presence of price increases, consumers might do more comparison shopping, or shop at wholesale outlets or join cooperatives, foregoing the convenience of retail shopping in order to obtain the same market basket.

The CPI includes both durable and nondurable goods. Nondurable goods such as food and fuel are extremely volatile in price, giving rise to violent fluctuations in the monthly CPI. Prone to misinterpretation, the CPI is sometimes "annualized" in media reports (monthly CPI times twelve), which produces suspect and inflammatory estimates of inflation. The CPI includes import prices, which makes it sensitive to the influence of fluctuating exchange rates.

The CPI is calculated gross of direct taxes. The CPI does not include any information about taxes, which can be interpreted as the "price for publicly provided goods and services." This can produce some curious results when one considers the various uses for which the CPI is employed—income deflation, wage escalation, setting the poverty line.

Weighting shelter expenditures has been problematic. Home ownership is partly consumption and partly investment, but the CPI is a measure of consumption patterns. Recently, BLS has incorporated home ownership costs based on rental equivalence. To the extent that the index is used to represent current consumption, BLS sought to incorporate only the consumption aspects of housing, not the investment component of home ownership. This argument could be extended to the inclusion of some other durable goods, since consumers in all likelihood purchase durable goods during relatively affluent periods.

The CPI is a Laspeyres-type index, but does not necessarily provide an upper bound to the true cost of living index. The CPI takes into account the appearance and disappearance of goods from the market basket; the declining cost of new goods brought about by improvements in technology also must be incorporated into the CPI. This changing market basket prevents the CPI from being a true Laspeyres index.

Much attention is paid to the measurement error inherent in calculation of the CPI. However, detractors are unable to find an alternative measure that is preferable, especially when computation costs are taken into account. Despite its theoretical shortcomings, the CPI shows no sign of being displaced as the accepted cost of living index in the U.S.

Other industrialized nations confront the same questions, and the issues are strikingly similar. Culture seems to dictate which measurements or theoretical issues are perceived as the most problematic (Turvey, 1989).While the U.S. CPI is calculated gross of taxes, Denmark, Sweden, Finland, Ireland, and the Netherlands account for taxation in their indexes. New Zealand considers the appropriate treatment of interest on household debt and insurance in the CPI calculations, Australia the treatment of automobiles and fuel.

Variations

The Producer Price Index (PPI) measures the effect of changes in wholesale prices for raw materials and intermediate factors of production. The CPI and PPI do not necessarily move in the same direction. Because the CPI has a huge service component, and service prices are rising faster than the price of goods, in some recent periods the two indexes have run in opposite directions with the CPI increasing and the PPI decreasing.

PAULA S. KEARNS

BIBLIOGRAPHY

Braithwait, Steven D., 1980. "The Substitution Bias of the Laspeyres Index: An Analysis Using Estimated Cost-of-Living Indexes." *The American Economic Review*, vol. 70:64–77.

Pollak, Robert A., 1989. *The Theory of the Cost-of-Living Index*. New York: Oxford University Press.

Turvey, Ralph, 1989. *Consumer Price Indices: An ILO Manual*. Geneva: International Labour Organisation.

U.S. Bureau of Labor Statistics, 1992. *BLS Handbook of Methods*, Bulletin 2414.

Varian, Hal, 1978. *Microeconomic Analysis*. New York: W.W. Norton & Co.

CONTINGENCY PLANNING.

The strategies and policies that allow an organization to anticipate crises and emergencies and to provide a rapid response.

The Importance of Contingency Planning

The military and law enforcement have long recognized the importance of contingency planning in their overall planning activities. Outside of the military and law enforcement, however, contingency planning has been in widespread use only since the 1970s, with the number and variety of organizations using this technique growing significantly over the years to include business, industry, and some government agencies.

Benefits

The main benefit of contingency planning is that it allows an organization to recognize and prepare for a contingency well in advance of being substantially affected by it. The organization can thus better prepare to anticipate critical events, even if the contingency does not occur exactly as expected. Simply going through the exercise often broadens the perspective of an organization and makes it more adaptable.

Like the related technique of scenario development planning, contingency planning anticipates future events and incorporates alternative plans. But while scenarios usually cover a wide range of possibilities within an organization's environment, contingency plans focus on a particular event over a relatively short period of time, generally one that demands quick action and a rapid response. Along with scenario development planning, contingency planning eliminates the need to scramble for a response. With a thorough, yet malleable, response plan, orderly and timely decisionmaking can be made more effectively. In addition, contingency planning identifies early warning signals, giving an organization speed and flexibility in reacting to events, as well as that most precious commodity, extra time. Finally, because responses are thought out in advance, resources and personnel can be allocated effectively to mitigate losses and to take advantage of opportunities.

Although contingency planning has been used in many fields, it is most frequently associated with emergency preparedness, disaster response planning, and military planning. Police, fire, and rescue units, as well as government agencies at various levels, have established plans for dealing with events such a hazardous materials and transportation accidents, hurricanes and earthquakes, and the disruption of water or energy supplies.

Components of Contingency Plans

As with scenario development planning, there are vast numbers of subject areas for which contingency plans can be developed. Recognizing that it is impossible to predict the nature or magnitude of all events that could possibly occur, organizations tend to focus on circumstances which are likely to have a substantial impact on their basic welfare. There is no rigid format for the contingency planning process, but generally it would include the following:

Contingent event identification. Listing the events that could occur, and if they did, would have a critical significance for the organization.

Impact assessment. Identification of how the contingency will affect the organization's ability to pursue its mission or goals.

Trigger point specification. Analysis of the stage at which a contingent event becomes a reality, and when the contingency plan should be implemented. Development of an early warning system that identifies any signals which might indicate when the event is likely to occur.

Strategy and tactic development. Preparation of an optimum and a backup response for each event. The response document generally assigns individual responsibilities, along with actions to be taken, timing, and resource and priority needs.

Evaluation. Assessment of how much the contingency plan will capitalize on or offset the contingency. A testing of the feasibility of plan implementation, often through a simulation exercise. All of this will determine the value of the plan and help the organization establish resource allocation and funding priorities.

While most traditional planning techniques focus on one set of assumptions about the future, contingency planning assumes various contingencies that may not normally be considered. It helps organizations plan to deal effectively with a limited range of dramatic, significant events that necessitate a rapid, coherent, and generally coordinated response. It makes it possible for organizations to position themselves quickly and strategically to minimize the effects of negative events, and to take advantage of opportunities arising out of positive events.

Contingency planning raises an organization's awareness as to what could happen, and incorporates response systems to help the organization react successfully. Simply put, contingency planning allows organizations to cope effectively with the uncertainty of dramatic and powerful forces.

MICHAEL J. BLOOM

BIBLIOGRAPHY

Cline, Ray S., 1951. *Washington Command Post: The Operations Division.* United States Army in World War II. The War Department, Washington, DC: Office of the Chief of Military History.
Drabek, Thomas E. and Gerard J. Hoetmer, eds., 1991. *Emergency Management: Principles and Practice for Local Government.* Washington, DC: International City Management Association.
Fink, Steven, 1986. *Crisis Management: Planning for the Inevitable.* New York: AMACOM, American Management Association.
Ford, Kristina with Banes Lopach and Dennis O'Donnell, 1990. *Planning Small Town America: Observations, Sketches and a Reform Proposal.* Chicago: Planners Press.
Perla, Peter P., 1990. *The Art of Wargaming: A Guide for Professionals and Hobbyists.* Annapolis: Naval Institute Press.
Watson, Mark S., 1950. *Chief of Staff: Prewar Plans and Preparations.* United States Army in World War II. The War Department, Washington, DC: United States Army Center of Military History.

CONTRACT ADMINISTRATION.

The application and management of terms and conditions of employment as provided for in a collective bargaining contract. The contract represents the "law of the workplace." Contracts vary in length from ten to 100 pages or more (long-term collective bargaining relationships tend to be associated with lengthy contracts).

Contracts identify job standards, work rules, the rights of workers, and, more specifically, such matters as position descriptions, staffing sizes and assignments, wages, benefits, management rights, union security arrangements, grievance procedures, promotion standards, layoff or reduction-in-force procedures, the role of seniority, and the length of time the contract will remain valid.

The primary conceptual model for contract administration is industrial jurisprudence, in which the activities and relationships of the workplace, like democratic government, are enforced through laws that protect each party's rights. Practical enforcement of the contract usually is through negotiated or statutory grievance machinery. In some instances, unfair labor practice complaints are filed in state labor boards or other authorities, alleging a breach of contract by one of the parties (see **unfair labor practices**). Contracts may also be enforced through court proceedings, in lawsuits filed against the union or the employer in federal or state courts, or, in the case of federal workers, in actions filed before the Federal labor Relations Authority (FLRA).

Contract administration is a form of continuing negotiations throughout the life of the contract, as inconsistencies, vague language, departures from past practice, and other issues are clarified. As such, it represents a true test of the nature of the relationship between management and the union.

Written labor contracts first appeared in the United States private sector in 1930s. By the 1970s, they were common throughout the public sector as well. Typically, such contracts contain provisions that are fixed and provisions that are contingent. The fixed provisions usually remain unchanged during the life of the agreement (e.g., composition of the bargaining unit, management rights, union security provisions). Contingent provisions deal with activities likely to be characterized by change (e.g., layoffs, promotions, work assignments, work scheduling). The dispute resolution techniques found in the grievance machinery (see **grievance machinery**) are designed to resolve conflicts arising from the interpretation and application of the agreement, especially of the contingent provisions. A no-strike clause is in effect during the life of the contract, with grievance machinery usually culminating in binding arbitration.

The initiative in contract administration and dissemination resides with management, which is expected to abide by the language in the contract. The union role is to enforce the contract by reacting to management actions. However, union stewards also have responsibility for knowing the terms and conditions of the written agreement and for instructing members of the bargaining unit on their rights and responsibilities.

The union, as exclusive representative of the members of the bargaining unit, is charged with the duty of fairly representing all members of the bargaining unit, whether they belong to the union or not (see **duty of fair representation**). This responsibility includes representing grievants and helping them process their complaints. Refusal of the union to represent a member of the bargaining unit, as well as inept representation, may constitute a breach of the union's legal responsibility under the contract or the law.

Management has a duty to notify and to bargain with the union before making any changes in the pay, benefits, working hours, or working conditions of employees within the bargaining unit. If the employer does make a unilateral change in the terms of employment without the consent of the union, the FLRA or state public employee relations board may order the employer to negotiate with the union, return to the status quo, or even award employees back pay if they have been adversely affected by management's unilateral action. Employers under certain circumstances may make unilateral changes in the terms and conditions of employment during collective bargaining, and in some cases involving items not covered by the contract. When a contract expires, its provisions usually remain in effect until a new contract is negotiated and signed.

RICHARD C. KEARNEY

BIBLIOGRAPHY

Bowers, Mollie H., 1976. *Contract Administration in the Public Sector.* Chicago: IPMA.
Kearney, Richard C., 1992. *Labor Relations in the Public Sector.* 2nd ed. New York: Marcel Dekker.

CONTRACT FAILURE. An economic theory that helps to explain the existence of nonprofit organizations in a market economy. It is a particular aspect of the more general economic theory of "market failure" that specifies conditions under which unfettered competition among profit-making firms fails to provide particular goods or services efficiently.

The condition of contract failure is said to occur where consumers feel unable to judge competently the quality or quantity of services they are receiving (Hansmann, 1987). In this circumstance, consumers will be reluctant to purchase the goods and services they need, for fear of being cheated. Hence, markets composed solely of unregulated profit-making firms will fail to allocate economic resources to their most highly valued uses.

The basic source of contract failure is a condition called "information asymmetry" where producers have more accurate knowledge of the quantity, quality, and cost of services delivered than do consumers. There are three basic causes of information asymmetry. First, certain goods and services may be inherently complex or their quality may be difficult to judge. The technical and multifaceted natures of medical care or higher education illustrate this case. Second, the consumer himself or herself may simply not be competent to evaluate the services he or she is receiving. Preschool care or services to the mentally ill or the impaired elderly are examples of this type. Third, certain services may not be purchased by the same individual that consumes them. In this instance, the purchaser does not experience the service directly and may not be in a position to obtain good information from the consumer. Again, day care for young children purchased by parents, or nursing home care purchased by children of elderly parents, illustrates this condition. Another example is international relief services financed by donors in one country to help victims in another country distant from the first. (Note, for purposes of this discussion, donors can be considered one variety of consumer of nonprofit organization services.) One or more of these conditions may characterize a particular service, creating conditions of contract failure that inhibit the efficient functioning of normal markets because consumers may fear the possibility of exploitation.

The utilization of nonprofit organizations is just one possible remedy to conditions of contract failure. Other potential remedies include licensing and regulation of profit-making providers such as in the case of automobile repair; standards of practice and oversight by professional associations or accrediting bodies as in dentistry or teaching; or purchasing control by expert third parties, such as doctors who behave as consumer proxies for hospital care or insurance companies that oversee medical care purchases.

There is no clear-cut theory for determining which of the latter solutions best fits each circumstance of contract failure or when the participation of nonprofit organizations provides the best remedy. However, some sense of the latter can be discerned from the premises that underlie different theoretical approaches to the question of why participation of nonprofit organizations serves as a correction to contract failure. There are basically three streams of thought that purport to explain how nonprofit organizations help overcome the problems of contract failure and hence provide particular services more efficiently than profit-making firms. The most prominent explanation, developed by Hansmann (1980), is that the nondistribution constraint governing nonprofit organizations creates a disincentive for nonprofit organizations to exploit their customers or patrons. In essence, the nondistribution constraint prohibits those who control the organization (managers, trustees) from distributing financial surpluses (profits) for their personal benefit. If this constraint is effectively policed, for example by government authorities, then nonprofits will allocate all of their resources to the promulgation of their missions, and will have little incentive to cheat those who finance or consume its services. In this context, consumers and donors will find nonprofit organizations "trustworthy" and will exhibit less reluctance to utilize and pay for their services.

A second stream of theory, advanced by Young (1983) and Hansmann (1980), postulates that nonprofits become trustworthy by a different mechanism: the selection and screening of leaders. In this framework, executive leaders of organizations come to their positions with a variety of different motivations ranging from self-interested income and power seeking to the pursuit of personal beliefs and public ideals (see **nonprofit entrepreneurship**). The differences between profit-making and nonprofit organizations, including the presence of the nondistribution constraint for nonprofits, cause the pool of potential leaders to sort itself out among the sectors according to motivational differences, with the public service-oriented executives going into the nonprofit sector and the more wealth-seeking executives clustering in the profit sector. The result of this motivational sorting is to make the nonprofit sector more trustworthy by virtue of the kinds of people attracted to it, providing consumers and supporters with the confidence they require to overcome contract failure.

A third line of theory focuses less on the nondistribution constraint and more on other structural aspects of the nonprofit form that allow consumers and supporters to have greater control over service provision. Easley and O'Hara (1983) postulate that a nonprofit firm is distinguished from a for-profit firm by the fact that its managers accept a fixed amount of compensation and promise to devote all other resources to the costs of producing its services. In contrast, a for-profit firm contracts only on the basis of producing a given output for a given price. In this model, although the output of the nonprofit organization is difficult to measure, its expenditures on executive compensation and other inputs can be monitored and policed, helping to assure that the organization delivers what it has promised.

Ben-Ner (1986) takes still another view of nonprofits, arguing that they are distinguished by the fact that their donors and consumers play a more intensive role in gover-

nance of the nonprofit organization than they would in a for-profit organization. In this view, the nonprofit is a kind of consumer cooperative in which production and consumption of a service are integrated within the organization. This resulting close control by consumers overcomes information asymmetry by giving consumers an insider's view.

Each of these strands of theory suggest that under conditions of information asymmetry, the nonprofit form will serve consumers by promising that such organizations behave in more trustworthy fashion. Weisbrod (1988) elaborates on how more trustworthy behavior should manifest itself. In particular, he makes the distinction between "type 1" and "type 2" attributes of a good or service. A type 1 attribute, such as the physical appearance of a nursing home, is easily observable; a type 2 attribute, such as the caring nature of the relationship between attendants and elderly nursing home patients, is difficult for the outsider to observe. Weisbrod argues that if contract failure theory is correct, nonprofits should be superior to for-profits in the provision of type 2 attributes, but no different than for-profits in providing type 1 attributes. He points out, however, that verifying this hypothesis through research is intrinsically challenging: "Gathering data is difficult. If differences in type 2 dimensions of behavior persist across institutions, they must be difficult to discern—for analysts as well as consumers" (p. 147).

Nonetheless, empirical research has been carried out with some success (Steinberg and Gray, 1993). For example, surveys provide some evidence that people do distinguish between nonprofit and for-profit institutions and that they express more confidence in nonprofits. Studies of behavioral differences between nonprofits and for-profits within particular industries also provide some verification. For example, Weisbrod (1988) studied long-term care facilities for elderly, mentally handicapped, and psychiatric patients, finding that nonprofits were more likely than for-profits to provide family members with detailed information, less likely to sedate their patients heavily, and more likely to achieve higher levels of expressed satisfaction by patients' families. He interprets these data cautiously to suggest that nonprofits, especially those that are religiously affiliated, offer a more trustworthy alternative to for-profits in industries where type 2 attributes prevail.

While providing a powerful framework for understanding why nonprofits exist in certain areas of the economy, the theory of contract failure is not a comprehensive theory and leaves some unanswered puzzles (Steinberg and Gray, 1993). Most obvious is the fact that the theory does not fully distinguish between private, nonprofit organizations and government agencies, which are also technically nonprofit in a financial sense and which presumably should also engender greater trustworthiness than for-profit firms. Thus, a separate segment of theory has developed to explain why private nonprofits exist alongside government and are more efficient than government in some circumstances (see **government failure, third party government**). However, an interesting sidelight to this question is the issue of governmental contracting with nonprofit organizations for the provision of public services.

Here the question also arises as to whether the government should utilize the services of for-profit firms or restrict its contracting to nonprofits (Smith and Lipsky, 1993). If government as consumer/contractor also suffers the problem of information asymmetry, then the theory of contract failure can provide insight on its selection of nonprofit verses for-profit suppliers under various circumstances (Brodkin and Young, 1989). For example, if a service such as garbage collection is primarily of a type 1 variety, there is less reason for the government to prefer nonprofit contractors. However, for services such as children in foster care, contract failure provides a stronger rationale for nonprofit contractors. Moreover, the governmental choice of contractors is presumably influenced by the mechanism through which government chooses to finance privately supplied public services. If that mechanism is direct contracting with a few suppliers, government officials may be more able to police contractor behavior, whether profitmaking or nonprofit. But if the mechanism is subsidy of consumers who must make the choice of suppliers and monitor the services they receive, but are limited in their abilities to do so, the theory of contract failure suggests a preference for utilizing nonprofits.

Another lacuna in the theory of contract failure is that it does not directly address the puzzle of why we observe "mixed industries," such as day care for children or nursing homes for the elderly, in which profit-making and nonprofit organizations coexist. If nonprofits are more efficient in certain industries characterized by information asymmetry, why do they not drive for-profits in those industries out of business? While this question is unresolved, contract failure theory contains within it one source of explanation: If consumers vary in their levels of understanding and information about service quality, they might choose to utilize a variety of types of institutions. Well-informed consumers, confident in their ability to discern whether or not they were receiving a good bargain, might choose a for-profit provider, especially if it were cheaper or provided a variety of service closer to their personal preferences. A less competent consumer, or one who didn't have the time to gather sufficient information, might prefer to rely on a nonprofit organization in which he or she could place greater trust.

A related puzzle, however, is that if nonprofits enjoy greater trust in certain situations, why wouldn't some for-profit businesses disguise themselves as nonprofit organizations in order to exploit consumers' fears and drain away resources for their own benefit through various indirect means such as inflated salaries and sweetheart contracts

with suppliers? Clearly the answer to this question depends on the effectiveness with which the nondistribution constraint or other structural aspects of the nonprofit form are assumed to police such behavior. If "for-profits in disguise" can successfully infiltrate the nonprofit sector, analysts have shown that this could seriously undermine confidence in nonprofits in general, destabilizing mixed industries and driving nonprofits out unless other means were implemented to ensure the survival of honest nonprofits (Steinberg, 1993).

Contract failure is not just of interest to theorists, or to policymakers wishing to discern within what areas of the economy nonprofits should be encouraged to operate. This concept also highlights an important principle for managers and trustees of nonprofit organizations: the essential currency of nonprofit organizations is trust. When that is undermined, nonprofits lose an important reason for their existence and the confidence of those who support them or utilize their services.

DENNIS R. YOUNG

BIBLIOGRAPHY

Ben-Ner, Avner, 1986. "Non-Profit Organizations: Why Do They Exist in Market Economies?" In Susan Rose-Ackerman, ed., *The Economics of Nonprofit Institutions.* New York: Oxford University Press, pp. 94–113.
Brodkin, Evelyn Z., and Dennis Young, 1989. "Making Sense of Privatization: What Can We Learn from Economic and Political Analysis?" In Sheila B. Kamerman and Alfred J. Kahn, eds., *Privatization and the Welfare State.* Princeton, NJ: Princeton University Press, pp. 121–154.
Easely, David, and Maureen O'Hara, 1983. "The Economic Role of the Nonprofit Firm." *Bell Journal of Economics,* 14:531–538.
Hansmann, Henry, 1980. "The Role of Nonprofit Enterprise." *Yale Law Journal,* 89:835–901.
Hansmann, Henry, 1987. "Economic Theories of Nonprofit Organization." In Walter W. Powell, ed., *The Nonprofit Sector: A Research Handbook.* New Haven: Yale University Press, pp. 27–42.
Smith, Steven R., and Michael Lipsky, 1993. *Nonprofits for Hire.* Cambridge, MA: Harvard University Press.
Steinberg, Richard, 1993. "Public Policy and the Performance of Nonprofit Organizations: A General Framework." *Nonprofit and Voluntary Sector Quarterly,* 22:13–32.
Steinberg, Richard, and Bradford H. Gray, 1993. "The Role of Nonprofit Enterprise in 1993: Hansmann Revisited." *Nonprofit and Voluntary Sector Quarterly,* 22:297–316.
Weisbrod, Burton A. 1988. *The Nonprofit Economy.* Cambridge, MA: Harvard University Press.
Young, Dennis R. 1983. *If Not For Profit, For What?* Lexington, MA: D.C. Heath and Company.

CONTRACTARIANISM. An approach to political theory that views the relationship between citizens and their government as a form of contract in which citizens agree to give government leaders the power and authority to coerce them in return for certain benefits and protections.

Government, in contractarian theory, is established on the basis of at least the implicit consent of the governed. Contractarian political writers examine the logic of political constitutions by essentially asking the question, "What sort of constitution for government would a community of rational individuals agree upon?" The contractarian approach has its intellectual roots in the writings of Thomas Hobbes and John Locke and is also implicit in much of the argument contained in the *Federalist Papers*. It has been employed more recently by contractarian political economists such as James Buchanan and also by political philosophers such as John Rawls. The contractarian approach has been applied in recent years to an analysis of institutions of public administration and their role in U.S. constitutional governance. Discussion here will focus on the latter application of contractarianism and discuss the purpose, assumptions, and implications of the contractarian approach in this regard, and also criticisms of this approach.

The Purpose of the Contractarian Approach

The purpose of a contractarian approach in general is not to describe or to explain the history of constitutions but rather to render some sort of normative judgement about the desirability of the constitutional "rules of the game" by which government policies are formulated and implemented. These rules include not only those formally stated in terms of a written constitution, but also various customs and conventions relating to political behavior which have evolved over time. Constitutional rules and institutions are judged to be desirable or undesirable, from a contractarian point of view, according to whether or not they could command the unanimous support of a hypothetical community of rational individuals.

This agreement or consensus among a hypothetical community becomes the normative criterion against which constitutional rules and institutions can be evaluated in contractarian terms. The use of agreement here as a norm for constitutional analysis reflects an "individualistic" or "subjectivist" view of political values by contractarians, in that political values are seen as rooted in the desires and aims of individuals rather than in any set of transcendental ethical political values such as "social justice." James Buchanan makes clear the ethical stance of the contractarian in his book *What Should Economists Do* (1979) when he argues that, "If we reject the notion that there must exist a public interest or general interest apart from that of the participants, we are necessarily led to the conclusion that only upon unanimous consent of all parties can we be absolutely assured that the total welfare of the group is improved" (p. 153).

The Checking of Power

Key to most contractarian discussions since John Locke is the idea that a community of rational individuals would never agree to allow government officials to exercise unrestrained discretionary power but rather would seek limits on the use of power to protect them from harm by government officials. To use Locke's words, contractarians believe that "nobody has an absolute arbitrary power over himself, or over any other to destroy his own life, or take away the life and property of another." The necessity of checking power stems from what contractarians see as the inevitable fallibility of human nature. According to the contractarian argument, government officials are, like us, fallible men and women, and can be expected sometimes to pursue their own selfish interests and passions even when it is at our expense. Therefore, we must recognize that in the absence of any checks on their discretionary power, they will have little incentive to take account of the costs which their actions may impose on us. In other words, from a contractarian perspective, the activities of government are potentially beneficial but are also potentially exploitative of citizens. Given the potential costs to us of such exploitative actions, checks on the discretionary power of government officials are seen as necessary.

The role of a constitution from a contractarian perspective is, therefore, to limit the costs which governments can impose upon citizens by checking the use of discretionary power by government officials. In this sense, the term "constitution" is synonymous with the checking of government power and reflects a Whig or classical liberal understanding of the meaning on constitutionalism. Constitutions are seen as checking power by rules which seek to prevent government officials from taking particular actions against citizens (for example, the Bill of Rights) or by sharing political power among different political institutions so that each can exercise a power of veto over the actions of others (for example, federalism and the separation of powers among legislative, executive, and judicial branches of government).

The argument that government must be checked because government officials can be expected to pursue their own interests at the expense of citizens is central to the analyses of the political process undertaken by contractarian political economists such as James Buchanan. These economists see constitutional rules and institutions as limiting the external costs which self-interested government officials can impose upon citizens. However, this argument for constitutional checks on power is also consistent with those of eighteenth century British political writers such as David Hume, Adam Smith, Adam Ferguson, and Edmund Burke, all of whom held a somewhat pessimistic view of human nature and saw human behavior as driven by interests and passions. David Hume, for example, argued that "in contriving any system of government . . . every man ought to be supposed a knave" and that "the particular checks and controls" provided by a constitution "should have the effect of making it in the interest, even of bad men, to act for the public good." This argument was also essentially the one advanced by James Madison in *Federalist 51* when he noted that because of the "defect of better motives," it is necessary for a constitution to provide for "opposite and rival interests" so that ambition can "be made to counteract ambition."

Limits of Majority Rule

It is important to emphasize here that, while democratic elections provide, from a contractarian perspective, a necessary and desirable check on power, most contractarians do not see elections on their own as providing adequate protection for citizens against potentially exploitative governments. Majority rule, according to the contractarian view, can become a device by which individuals and groups seeking to advance their own interests and passions can form majority coalitions and take actions that benefit them at the expense of other citizens. The majority decision, from a contractarian perspective, is not an expression of the "will of the people" so much as the outcome of political coalition-building directed at majority exploitation of the minority. From a contractarian perspective, therefore, it is necessary to check even the power of democratically elected governments. In this respect again, the arguments of contractarians bear certain similarities to those of eighteenth century British political thinkers and to those made by the framers of the U.S. Constitution, all of whom, while supporters of representative democracy, were critical of notions of unlimited majority rule and advocated limits on the exercise of majority rule. Madison, for example, argued in *Federalist 51* that "a dependence on the people is no doubt the primary control on government; but experience has taught mankind the necessity of auxiliary precautions."

Implications for Public Administration

If one accepts the argument that power even when exercised democratically must be checked, then according to the contractarian approach certain implications can be drawn for the role of public administration in a constitutional system of government. In particular it is argued here that administrative discretion, so long as it is exercised within the law, may be seen as desirable as a check on the misuse of political power by elected officials. The contractarian approach argues that administrative discretion can serve as a check on power because it enables public administrators to modify, delay, or resist the directives of political leaders in a lawful manner. The exercise of administrative discretion can be seen here as limiting the ability of political leaders to use public administrators simply as instru-

ments of exploitation and, in doing so, limiting the costs that political leaders can impose on citizens.

According to the contractarian approach, the role of the administrator in checking political power is enhanced by the constitutional separation of powers among different branches of government. This, it is argued, is because such a separation of political power allows public administrators, where there is policy disagreement among different branches of government, to exercise discretion in regard to which branch's policy is carried out. Public administrators can thus check political power by choosing among their different political masters. Also, a career civil service is seen as helpful in that it limits the ability of political leaders to bring political pressure to bear on public administrators and so increases the discretion available to administrators.

Consistent with its emphasis on checking power, the contractarian approach to public administration does not, however, argue that public administrators should be permitted to exercise unrestrained discretionary power. Rather, it advocates the checking of administrative discretionary power through the use of administrative rules and procedures or red tape, which limit the ability of public administrators to enrich themselves at the expense of citizens and which limit the arbitrary treatment of citizens by administrators. Such rules and procedures are argued to be necessary here because administrators, like political leaders, are assumed to be motivated by their own interests and passions and so may engage in actions which exploit citizens. What is seen as desirable from a contractarian perspective, therefore, is a system of "constrained discretion," which allows administrators to exercise significant discretion in following the directives of political leaders but, at the same time, constrains the use of that discretion through administrative rules and procedures.

The contractarian approach to public administration differs from the traditional "instrumentalist" view of public administration taken by writers such as Herman Finer, who see public administration as exclusively an instrument of the will of elected officials and are critical of any independent role for administrators in the policymaking process. From a contractarian perspective, such an instrumentalist view of public administration conflicts with the idea that all political power, even the power of democratically elected leaders, must be checked, and implies that public administration should be simply a tool for use by exploitative political leaders. However, the contractarian argument also differs from arguments made for increased administrative discretion by "discretionist" writers such as Carl Friedrich, in that it emphasizes that the exercise of administrative discretion itself may be harmful to citizens and so should also be checked through rules and procedures. In this respect, the contractarian approach can be seen as an attempt to avoid the problems of abuse of power associated with either a purely instrumentalist or a purely discretionist view of public administration.

Criticisms of the Contractarian Approach

Given its sharp break from traditional public administration thinking, the contractarian approach to public administration has not surprisingly provoked controversy and has been criticized on a number of grounds (see the forum on "Public Administration and the Constitution" in the May/June 1993 issue of *Public Administration Review*). First, some writers see the contractarian emphasis on the role of self-interest in the political process as overly pessimistic and as ignoring the role that the public interest and public values play in the process. Second, it has been argued that the contractarian approach is overly abstract and gives insufficient weight to the role that political history and traditions have played in shaping the U. S. Constitution. Third, critics have argued that the emphasis of the contractarian approach on the constitutional checking of power provides too narrow a view of the role of a constitution and overlooks its role in creating institutions. Finally, the contractarian argument that public administrators should use their discretion to check the abuse of power by elected leaders has been argued to be inconsistent with democratic principles of elected majority rule.

Despite these criticisms, the strong parallels between the contractarian argument and the founders' argument for checking power do suggest that the approach has some potential value in redirecting attention to the founders' political philosophy and its possible relevance in thinking about the role of public administration. In this respect, the contractarian approach may be seen as part of a broader effort by John Rohr and others to explore the implications of the founders' thought for the modern administrative state. Furthermore, while it is undoubtedly too early to judge the impact of the contractarian approach, its major contribution may be that, despite its abstract character, it may help rekindle interest in the relevance of eighteenth-century British and American classical liberal thought for public administration. Certainly, it is my own view that an argument for "constrained administrative discretion," based on contractarian logic, can be rendered more powerful when set in the context of the founders' thought and the broader political philosophy of which it is a part.

MICHAEL W. SPICER

BIBLIOGRAPHY

The Contractarian Approach in General:

Buchanan, James M., 1975. *The Limits of Liberty: Between Anarchy and Leviathan*. Chicago: University of Chicago Press.
———, 1979. *What Should Economists Do?* Indianapolis, IN: Liberty Press.
Locke, John, 1939. "An Essay Concerning the True Original, Extent and End of Civil Government." In Edwin A. Burtt, ed., *The English Philosophers from Bacon to Mill*. New York: The Modern Library.

The Contractarian Approach to Public Administration:

Spicer, Michael W., 1990. "A Contractarian Approach to Public Administration." *Administration and Society*, vol. 22 (November) 303–316.
Spicer, Michael W., 1995. *The Founders, the Constitution, and Public Administration*. Washington, D.C.: Georgetown University Press.
Spicer, Michael W. and Larry D. Terry, 1993. "Legitimacy, History and Logic: Public Administration and the Constitution." *Public Administration Review*, vol. 53 (May/June) 239–245.
Spicer, Michael W. and Larry D. Terry, 1993. "Advancing the Dialogue: Legitimacy, the Founders and the Contractarian Argument." *Public Administration Review*, vol. 53 (May/June) 264–267.

Criticisms of the Contractarian Approach to Public Administration:

Lowi, Theodore, 1993. "Legitimizing Public Administration: A Disturbed Dissent." *Public Administration Review*, vol. 53 (May/June) 261–264.
Rohr, John A., 1993. "Toward a More Perfect Union." *Public Administration Review*, vol. 53 (May/June) 246–249.
Stivers, Camilla A., 1993. "Rationality and Romanticism." *Public Administration Review*, vol. 53 (May/June) 254–257.
Wise, Charles A., 1993. "Public Administration Is Constitutional and Legitimate." *Public Administration Review*, vol. 53 (May/June) 257–261.

CONTRACTING OUT. The process through which a government or public agency ceases to provide a specific activity or service through directly employing its own staff and instead purchases that service or activity from a private corporation or nongovernmental agency. The description derives from the fact that the purchase is on the basis of a contract between the public agency and the private or nongovernmental agency. A widespread illustration internationally is contracting out with private companies by local councils or other municipal bodies for garbage collection services.

All governments historically have purchased materials, goods, and services from private corporations and nongovernmental agencies, so contracts and contracting are conventional in government. In the sense in which it is defined here, however, contracting out is a form of privatization, in that the task of providing a service on a day-to-day basis moves from the public or government sphere to the private or nongovernment sphere. The increasing interest in and use of contracting out by governments and other public agencies is closely associated with attempts in the 1980s and 1990s to control or restrict levels of public expenditure. It is therefore historically linked with those parties and governments with reform agendas emphasizing the importance of controlling or restricting the role of government, such as those of Ronald Reagan in the United States and Margaret Thatcher in the UK. But it has also been increasingly advocated as a reform program by international agencies such as the International Monetary Fund and World Bank as one of a number of options for achieving privatization.

Contracting Out, Competition, and Commercialization

Contracting out is often undertaken by governments inviting bids or financial offers from various outside agencies before deciding how a particular service or activity will be provided. Of these procedures, know collectively as market testing, the most widely used is competitive tendering. Governments use competitive tendering by inviting a number of organizations to bid for the right to provide the service specified, such as garbage collection, providing information technology (IT) services, and so forth. Those invited may include the agency's own staff or department currently providing the service. The government then selects a preferred bidder or tenderer on the basis of the relative prices to be charged, how they will offer the service, their track records, the resources and skills they will bring to the work, and any other relevant criteria. If a private or nongovernmental agency is successful and a contract is awarded to it, competitive tendering will result in contracting out of the service. Where the government or public agency's employees or internal departments are allowed to bid and are successful, the activity will continue to be provided by them. In this instance competitive tendering is said to introduce market mechanisms and competition into the service arrangements of government, since the public agencies will have had to review and possibly revise their administrative, staffing, and organizational arrangements in order to bid successfully. More extensive use of competitive tendering is thus a component of the increasing marketization or commercialization of government activities.

Contracts with governments provide a potentially vast international market for corporations. The increasing use of and interest in contracting out from the 1980s is associated with the development of markets and private corporations in areas in which they have not previously existed. The potential scale of these markets and their international character has resulted in the development by international government bodies of regulations for the conduct of competitive tendering and contracting out. These include the European Union's Public Procurement Directives, which by 1994 governed tendering by any government or public body for all goods and services, and the Government Procurement Regulations of the General Agreement on Tariffs and Trade (GATT), which cover all government contracting in the U.S., Canada, European Union, and a number of other countries.

Contracting Out as a Political Process

In some instances, proposals to contract out services or to introduce more extensive competitive tendering are politically contentious and publicly contested in political debate. In others, they are deemed to be largely technical questions to be decided by the appropriate managers of the government agencies. The political significance and response depends on a number of factors which include: whether the administrative reform agenda is associated with a single political party or government; the extent to which governments have developed their own internal services or use outside contractors and agencies to deliver services (thus, local governments in the UK have tended to use their own employees for a wider range of activities than have local governments in the United States and or some parts of Europe); the nature, extent, and character of the potential competition; and the change to overall levels of public employment and service levels likely to be associated with the move to contract out.

Contracting out can be viewed at the "micro" level as a facet of the management of public organizations and governments. With this focus the important questions will be whether or not a specific government service should be contracted out, what the costs and benefits would be, how the process should be conducted, how decisions should be made between different tenderers, and so forth. It can also be analyzed at the "macro" level as part of the overall assessment of changes in forms and types of governance over time or between different social and political structures. So it has been suggested that the move by governments in North America and northwest Europe to divest themselves of nonessential activities and provide them through contracts with external bodies may be seen as the accommodation of government to a "post-Fordist" socioeconomic structure. Also, contracting out is one of the mechanisms propounded by the reinventing government movement associated with the book of that title.

The Consequences of Contracting Out

In the academic and public policy literature, particular concern has been paid to the consequences of contracting out in the following areas.

Costs of Services and Activities

Since contracting out is closely associated with an agenda to restrict or control government expenditure, much academic and political debate has focused on the financial savings which result. Empirical research in the U.S. and Australia has estimated average savings of around 20 percent in a number of services. Findings for services in the UK indicate a lower figure, averaging 6 percent. And a number of methodological issues have been raised about the possibility of being accurate in these estimates. While it is commonly asserted that contracting out produces financial savings to government, the level of these savings has been difficult to assess in a comprehensive or definitive way. For many political assessments, these financial savings are more than counterbalanced by the nonfinancial costs.

Employment

Contracting out is associated with reductions in the overall levels of employment in the governments and agencies in which it occurs and with changes in the character of public sector employment. There is also a potential equity dimension of concern to governments with equal opportunity legislation and policies, in that many of the activities which are contracted out employ disproportionate numbers of women or people from disadvantaged social positions.

Quality of Services

The impact of contracting out on the quality of government services is contested between those who propose its further extension and its critics. The difficulties in measuring quality, given its strong component of subjectivity, have resulted in little academic research in this area.

Accountability

With its strong emphasis on the cost of services, contracting out has been said to enhance the financial accountability of government. However, issues have been raised about its implications for accountability in a broader public policy sense. In some instances, contracting out removes clarity as to who takes ultimate responsibility for a government service or activity. Furthermore, the introduction of tendering and other procedures can lead governments to regard information that has previously been made publicly available as confidential because of its potential use in a commercial context.

MICHAEL PADDON

BIBLIOGRAPHY

Ascher, K., 1987. *The Politics of Privatization: Contracting Out Public Services.* London: Macmillan Education.

Osborne, D. and T. Gaebler, 1993. *ReInventing Government: How the Entrepreneurial Spirit Is Transforming the Public Sector.* Reading, MA: Addison-Wesley.

Whitfield, D., 1992. *The Welfare State: Privatization, Deregulation, Commercialization of Public Services: Alternative Strategies for the 1990s.* London and Concord, MA: Pluto Press.

CONTRACTORIZATION. The policy of transferring public sector support functions traditionally conducted in-house by directly employed personnel to private firms. Contractorization may result from a bidding process (see **market testing**) or from placing work with a private firm in the absence of competition. Importantly, contractorization differs from "privatization" in that the function remains accountable to government officials or other public authorities.

Origins and Subsequent History

Public organizations in most industrially developed states contract for support services to a lesser or greater extent. While it has attracted attention in North America and Europe, the most systematic and extensive application of contractorization policy has been in the United Kingdom since 1979. British government attempts to "roll back" the state, or reduce the size of the public sector, coupled with the view that private firms are inherently more efficient than public organizations, have generated large-scale contractorization. Contractorization currently affects a range of support areas throughout central government, local government, the National Health Service, and the defense sector.

Underlying Theoretical Framework

Proponents of contractorization cite potential benefits from private provision of public sector support requirements. Public organizations have various "make or buy" options. At one extreme they could maintain across-the-board in-house capability (vertical integration). At the other, they could buy ancillary services—a strategy common to large commercial organizations while concentrating in-house personnel on "core" organizational tasks. The economic case for contractorization arises when, provided service quality levels are specified and maintained, it is cheaper to substitute contractors for internal capacity.

Costs of private provision may be lower for three main reasons. First, a contractor can reduce unit costs by driving down the price of inputs, or increasing the intensity of their use. Examples here include: using regional rather than nationally defined pay scales; substituting part-time for full-time workers; or introducing incentive schemes. Second, firms may be more technically efficient through superior management or improved technology. Third, the contractor may improve productivity (output/input ratios) by operating with a more appropriate factor mix between, for example, capital and labor.

A further allocative efficiency justification for contractorization is optimizing the use of trained personnel. As advocates have claimed, contractors can relieve public sector managers of peripheral duties, enabling trained staff to concentrate on "essential tasks" (Ministry of Defense, 1989, p. 35). Within constrained public budgets, contracting out is thus assumed to have organizational benefits:

enhanced output without a corresponding rise in personnel (Ministry of Defense, 1990, p. 46).

Despite the *prima facie* efficiency gains from contractorization, the policy has remained controversial (Uttley, 1993). Critics have identified potential dangers from private provision of public services that include, among others: the loss of direct control and flexibility in the use of staff; the risks of contractor exploitation when in-house units are disbanded; and the longer-term effects of "deskilling" on areas contracted out. As the United Kingdom Audit Commission has pointed out, " it would be unwise to assume that all the benefits of enhanced competitiveness will be realized by handing over the problem to the private sector" (Audit Commission, 1987, p. 5).

Prospects and Developments

In the United Kingdom and elsewhere, contractorization has evolved from limited application to ancillary activities (e.g., catering, cleaning) to managerial functions (e.g., legal work, training) throughout the 1980s and 1990s. Evidence suggests that where considerable scope for cost savings are associated with private provision, contractorization will continue as an important public sector management technique.

MATTHEW R. H. UTTLEY

BIBLIOGRAPHY

Audit Commission for Local Authorities in England and Wales, 1987. *Occasional Paper: Competitiveness and Contracting Out of Local Authorities' Services,* Number 3.
Ministry of Defense, 1989. *Statement on the Defense Estimates, 1989.* HMSO: London.
Ministry of Defense, 1990. *Statement on the Defense Estimates, 1990.* HMSO: London.
Uttley, M.R.H., 1993. "Competition in the Provision of Defense Support Services: The UK Experience." *Defense Analysis,* vol. 9, no. 3:271–288.

CONTROL (INTERNAL CONTROLS). The measuring and monitoring of actual performance in comparison with predetermined parameters (objectives, plans, norms, standards, budgets), and the taking of any corrective action requested. Internal controls are the methods and practices used in the control process (system).

Some control activities are automatic, as in automation. These types of controls are used in automatic technological devices, such as manufacturing systems where operations are performed without direct involvement of humans. The idea of automatic control is based on the cybernetics principle of feedback: comparing inputs and outputs of a system with preestablished standard parameters, detecting deviations that occur, and then automatically generating corrective actions through feedback mechanisms. Principles of cybernetics and systems theory in the last decades were also applied to the methods and practices of internal controls in organizations and social systems (Beer, 1974). These principles are widely used in computer-based managerial technologies supporting controlling functions such as management information systems.

Within organizations, controls are used to ensure that behaviors and performance of employees confirm to an organization's objectives, plans, and standards. They are performed within an administrative system with the purpose and function of checking, regulating, restraining, or correcting, or otherwise exercising authority and power. To most people, this interpretation of controls as an administrative function has negative connotations of restraining, forcing, delimiting, watching, or manipulating. Most U.S. employees resent such practices because of their widely shared values of individualism and democracy. Methods of administrative managerial control are often the focus of controversy and power struggles within organizations (Alexander, 1991).

Together with planning, organizing, and coordinating, controlling is one of the basic managerial functions. Only by implementing systems of control can organizations ensure the successful achievement of their goals. Controls are an integral part of every organization's structure, forming the basis for measuring its performance and success. Controls are a feedback mechanism that enables management and staff to monitor how effectively they are delivering products and services, or fulfilling operations. Controls focus attention on a particular process or outcome, reduce variation, and add to the probability of success (Caldwell, 1994).

Controls in organizations are applied both to technical systems and social systems. Management controls both operations of an organization (technological processes, sales, marketing, and so forth) and employees who are performing these operations.

Two basic types of controls are preventive controls and corrective controls. Preventive controls are aimed at reducing errors and mistakes in order to eliminate or minimize the need for corrective action. The idea of preventive controls is to make sure that rules, regulations, and standards are being followed and are working. It is assumed that if everybody is following these restrictions the organization will achieve its goal without wasting additional time and money correcting errors and mistakes.

Corrective controls are used to change undesirable behavior (or performance) that deviates from established norms and standards, and to bring it back to initially introduced guidelines. Corrective controls may also include modification of the norms and standards themselves if they prove to be out of date and no longer correspond to the organization's goals. Using corrective controls, managers can detect and correct deviations from an organization's goals, plans, and standards. The corrective control process may be subdivided into several steps (Lowe and Machin, 1987):

1. Defining the control objects and subjects—Any production process, operation, activity, unit, group of employees, or individual within an organization may be treated as an object of control. Subjects of control are managers at different levels; organizational units supervised by such managers; and groups and individuals controlling different processes, operations, and activities. The CEO controls the whole organization, the product manager controls material flow, the controller controls money flow, the worker controls the machine, and so forth. The main task of this step is to define who controls what.

   The major subjects or sources of control are stakeholders, the organization itself, groups, and individuals. Stakeholders exercise different forms of external control. For business organizations stakeholders are stockholders, banks, customers, or regulating governmental agencies. Stakeholder control for public organizations refers to the same types of outside sources, with the exception of stockholders, although the role of the government is substantially different. If fact, governments are responsible for both external and internal controls in public institutions.

   All branches of the government—executive, legislative, and judiciary—have their own responsibilities and tools for external control of public organizations. The major subject or agent of internal control is an agency or organization head who is appointed by the government. Besides, there are numerous informal controls (and this partly refers to private sector as well): external, such as interest group representation, citizen participation, and the media; and internal, such as professional codes or ethical principles. The variety of controls makes control systems in public organizations more complex from the political point of view, as they are subjected to greater external pressure and a greater number of subjects of control than private businesses.

2. Identifying important parameters to be measured—It is important to identify from the very beginning what type of information is really needed to control a particular process or operation. This information should be selective, which means both sufficient and at the same time free of unnecessary data to avoid wasting time and money. There are always a limited number of characteristics that have a major impact upon the outcomes.

3. Setting standards for each parameter to be measured—Standards may be both qualitative and quantitative. Preselected parameters are evaluated against them as criteria. Qualitative standards of performance are of great importance for the public sector, as the performance of public organizations is rather difficult to measure in monetary terms (profit, loss, or sales). Following guidelines established by the "Reinventing Government" initiative, such standards were developed for federal agencies. For example, the most important customer service standards for the Social Security Administration are described in a report from the National Performance Review (1994, p. 14):

   - If you request a new replacement Social Security card from one of our offices, we will mail it to you within five work days of receiving information we need. If you have an urgent need for the Social Security number, we will tell you the number within one work day.
   - When you make an appointment, we will serve you within ten minutes of the schedule time.
   - We will provide you with our best estimate of the time we need to complete your request, and we will fully explain any delays.
   - We will clearly explain our decisions so you can understand why and how we made them and what to do if you disagree.

4. Collecting factual information—In order to compare actual performance with established norms and standards, information should be collected either by people or by automatic means. If it is collected by groups or individuals whose performance is to be measured, its validity must be checked. People tend to distort or conceal information if negative results will be used to criticize or punish them.

5. Making comparisons—This step means finding out whether there is any difference between what is really happening and what should happen according to the preestablished norms and standards. The basic idea is to concentrate on controlling deviations or exceptions. Otherwise the object under control may continue to operate without any corrective changes.

6. Analyzing and correcting problems—At this step the types, amounts, and causes of deviations from norms and standards are analyzed. The last task is to develop proper measures to eliminate those deviations. Response time for such corrective actions is also of crucial importance. If they are late and/or improper, the situation may become irreversible. Computer-based management information systems often help to overcome such inadequacies.

In order to be effective, controls should meet several criteria or requirements:

- *Linkage to desired objectives and goals*—Controls should be based on realistic goals and fact-driven objectives. They should help an organization to achieve desired results, such as stable performance or maintenance of the quality of products and services.
- *Linkage to objective norms and standards*—Controls should be based on predetermined norms and standards set up as evaluation criteria for an organization's performance. In this context, objectivity is the degree to which controls are impartial and cannot be manipulated by employees for personal gain. For example, the Financial Accounting Standards Board (FASB) and several U.S. federal governmental agencies are developing standard principles and practices to ensure that financial statements more objectively and accurately reflect reality.
- *Completeness*—Controls should be appropriate for the functions and operations that are supposed to be measured. The controls or control system should cover all major behaviors and results important for successful performance of an organization.
- *Timeliness*—Controls should provide information when it is needed most.

Overall, information should easily be understood in order to identify deviations from standards immediately and to take corrective actions. The controlling process begins during strategic planning when leadership establishes the organization's vision and goals. As management translates the strategic plan into action, the controls become more than just objective measurements; they become part of the managerial culture.

On the organizational level, there are several procedures of control exercised by different categories of managers:

Planning and scheduling. This process predetermines operations and their completion dates in accordance with customer or client requirements of internal norms. The results of this process are operational plans adopted in a form of directives and executive orders.

Managerial control. This activity transforms top management strategic decisions into everyday practices. Strategic plans are broken down into logical tasks and goals supported by allocations of funds to meet them. Specific individuals and units are assigned to carry out each task and goal, and management monitors the assignments to assure that they are carried out satisfactorily. Managerial control has as its objects the performance of employees and units.

Ongoing control. Procedures of this type are used to control the functional activities of an organization, as well as certain characteristics. Ongoing control is of less strategic character than the previous two types, but the results of these control mechanisms can be input for planning and managerial control. They include:

- *Operational control,* which determines the specific personnel, equipment, and material necessary to accomplish tasks and goals of the plan, and to make specific assignments for the work. Operational managers keep close supervisory contact, compare current operational results with plans, and take corrective action as required.
- *Inventory control,* which is the process of planning and maintaining a proper balance among the required kinds and amounts of items and materials so that within the organization the optimum combination of the major related costs is attained.
- *Quality control,* which is the systematic control of the variables that affect the conformance of the outcome to established quality standards. It involves real-time control of quality in addition to after-the-fact inspection and separation of substandard items. Quality control in mass production and service operations is based on statistically developed norms and standards, and the variety of methods set up to eliminate deviations.
- *Loss control,* which represents the techniques used to reduce an organization's loss frequency and/or severity arising from a loss exposure. Loss control involves a wide range of activities, including human safety, crime prevention, asset protection, product safety, and fleet management, encompassing both human and property exposures to risks.
- *Cost control,* the major goal of which is optimizing total costs through the identification, analysis, and control of the major cost components (labor, materials, supplies, maintenance, repair).
- *Financial control,* which is a very important part of any control system. Financial controls include a wide range of methods, techniques, and procedures. They are intended to prevent misallocation of financial resources, such as misuse or abuse of financial funds.

The monitoring aspect of financial controls is performed by external auditors and/or internal auditing departments (such as accounting, controller, and treasury). For public organizations, appointment of a controller (or comptroller) is the main vehicle of financial control. This office assures accountability of public organizations to the government, monitors execution of budgets, and makes sure that financial practices are in conformity with generally accepted accounting principles and special norms and regulations established for public organizations.

Among the most essential instruments of financial control are budgeting, comparative financial analysis, and cost-benefit analysis.

Budgeting is a key process for public organizations, as the budget is the resource basis for their operations. Budgets categorize proposed expenditures and link them to goals. They express the monetary costs of various tasks and resources. Budgeting is used for both corrective and preventive control. In the first case the emphasis is on identifying deviations from the budget and analysis of such deviations. Depending on the causes of deviations, practices may be changed.

Use of a budget for preventive control is based on viewing it as a set of norms and standards for an organization. Following budget guidelines is treated as meeting these normative requirements.

There are different types and forms of budgets. Their variety in the public sector reflects evolution of budgetary controls and the adjustment of the budgetary process to changing requirements and environments. The most simple approach to budgeting—line-item budgeting—is still most widely used by different levels of government, especially at the local level. Controls over financial administration is a predominant orientation of this type of budgeting. The intentions of governmental decisionmakers are defined as to how much will be spent on what activity. This, in turn, provides control over work by casting expenditures along departmental lines and characters of expense. Other forms of budgeting used by governments are: performance budgeting; program budgeting; planning-programming-budgeting system (PPBS); zero-based budgeting; and balanced-base budgeting (Miller, 1992).

Comparative financial analysis is used to evaluate an organization's financial conditions for two or more time periods, or to compare it with similar organizations in order to control competitive financial performance. In most cases ratio analysis is used for this purpose. It involves selecting two significant figures, expressing their relationship as a proportion or fraction, and comparing its value for two periods of time or with various ratios of other organizations. The most common types of such ratios used by organizations are profitability or rates of return, liquidity, activity, and leverage.

Cost-benefit analysis is an important instrument of strategic planning as the initial point-of-control process. Public organizations cannot usually identify profits; therefore, they cannot develop ratios where profit is one of the two components as measures and standards of their performance. Cost-benefit analysis, however, provides valuable criteria for establishing financial norms and standards, as it is based on the calculations of economic efficiency for suggested projects and programs. Unable to assign monetary values to certain outcomes of public programs, public sector organizations often use cost-effectiveness analysis (e.g.,

calculating cost for the saved lives) for analysis and control. Though economic efficiency and allocation and control criterion often conflicts with equity, which is a significant factor to be taken into account in the public sector, it provides economic estimates for the activities and operations of public organizations as measures and controls of their economic performance.

Controls provided by cost-benefit analysis for public organizations are somewhat of a replacement for market control; in businesses, market control occurs when price competition is used to evaluate the output and productivity of an organization. Businesses use a monetary value as an effective standard of comparison because managers can compare economic indicators to evaluate the efficiency of their organizations.

Customer monitoring is another important method of control. It consists of systematic efforts to obtain feedback from customers concerning the quality of goods and services. Customer monitoring is being used increasingly both in the private sector and recently in the public sector for corrective control, in an attempt to assess or measure customers' perceptions. Based on this assessment, managers make corrections within the organization before business is lost, or before complaints of customers' dissatisfaction ruin the reputation of a public organization.

Traditionally, controls have relied heavily on historical performance measurement, such as operating budgets, profit and loss statements, sales volume, and adherence to specifications and technical standards. They have included such elements of a closed or bureaucratic organization as extensive rules and procedures, top-down authority, tightly written job descriptions, and other formal methods for preventing and correcting deviations from desired behaviors and outcomes. These traditional, basic types of controls establish accountability for results.

Although they remain valuable measures, today's rapidly changing environment requires more dynamic controls that measure performance in multiple dimensions. The controls used in organizations based on an open (i.e., organic, dynamic) model include flexible authority, looser job descriptions, group and individual self-controls, and other methods for preventing and correcting deviations. In order to be successful, organizations should measure performance not only by today's norms, standards, and operational requirements; their controls must be also based on estimates of the future. The highest probability of success is based on concentration of resources on those products, services, and operations which will tend to be most important and attractive in the future. This requires special analytical forecasts based on the measures of consumer or customer response to current products, services, or activities, fast tracking and reaction to changes of consumer needs and acceptance, development of more complex and updated measures, and definitions of quality. An important parameter to be controlled is the timeliness of creating a new product or service, or redesign of an old one, as a response to customers' changing requirements. The essence and outcome of such a control system are continuous improvement of products, services, and operations.

Responsiveness of employees to correcting variations should become one of the most important measures of their performance to be continuously monitored. But rather than administrative controls by the organizational head and managerial hierarchy, group controls and individual self-controls should be given highest priority. As a result of training and cross-training of employees in new procedures and technologies, people should be able to better control the situation themselves as individuals or self-managed teams. They are much more effective in controlling performance if emphasis is placed not only on extrinsic rewards, such as wages, but also intrinsic rewards, such as meaningful work.

Such an approach requires reconsideration of the organizational culture, which must be seen as a way of integrating organizational, group, and individual objectives for greater overall control.

The "new generation" controls will use highly automated decision support models that are analytical and predictive in nature. That will allow organizations to correct variations almost immediately. Such organizations will be "flatter" in order to provide broad participation in design and use of controls (Caldwell, 1994).

PAVEL MAKEYENKO
VATCHE GABRIELIAN
MARC HOLZER

BIBLIOGRAPHY

Alexander, J. A., 1991. "Adaptive Change in Corporate Control Practices." *Academy of Management Journal*, vol. 34.
Beer, Stafford, 1974. *Decision and Control: The Managing of Operation Research and Management Cybernetics*. 5th ed. New York: John Wiley & Sons.
Caldwell, Alethea O., 1994. "Establishing Controls." In John J. Hampton, ed., *AMA Management Handbook*. 3rd ed. New York: AMACOM.
Dalton, G. W., and R. P. Lawrence, eds., 1971. *Motivation and Control in Organizations*. Homewood, IL: Irwin.
Euske, K. J., 1984. *Management Control: Planning, Control, Measurement and Evaluation*. Reading, MA: Addison-Wesley.
Lawler III, E. E., and J. G. Rhode, 1976. *Information and Control in Organizations*. Pacific Palisades, CA: Goodyear.
Lowe, T., and J. L. Machin, 1987. *New Perspectives on Management Control*. New York: Macmillan.
Miller, Gerald, J., 1992. "Productivity and the Budget Process." In Marc Holzer, ed., *Public Productivity Handbook*. New York: Marcel Dekker, Inc.
National Performance Review, 1994. *Putting Customers First. Standards for Serving the American People.* Washington, D.C.: U.S. Government Printing Office.
Nystrem, P. S., and W. H. Sturbuck, eds., 1981. *Handbook of Organizational Design*. New York: Oxford University Press.
Sord, B., and G. Welsch, 1964. *Managerial Planning and Control*. Austin, TX: University of Texas Press.

COOMBS COMMISSION.

The Royal Commission on Australian Government Administration (RCAGA) appointed by the Australian government in 1974, and chaired by Dr. Herbert C. Coombs, to review Australia's national public sector.

The Royal Commission on Australian Government Administration (1974–1976) conducted the only comprehensive review of Australia's national public sector. Since creation of the Commonwealth of Australia in 1901, external review of national administration had been relatively rare. There had been two royal commissions on the public service at the end of World War I whose recommendations formed the basis for the Public Service Act of 1922. Apart from parliamentary inquiries into the post office and defense administration in the early years of the federation, the major reviews had been into aspects of the promotions and recruitment systems in 1944 and 1957–1958 respectively.

The RCAGA was appointed in 1974 by the Whitlam Labor government. That government, elected after 23 years of conservative rule, adopted a policy favoring an activist and expansionary public administration. There was a sentiment in the ministry that the public sector had failed to respond to the requirements of the government. This consideration, combined with the government's general policy of subjecting all parts of the national administration to external, expert review, led to establishment of the RCAGA.

It was headed by Dr. H. C. Coombs, a long time government official and former head of the central bank, and composed of four other members: Peter Bailey, a senior career official in the Department of the Prime Minister and Cabinet; Professor Enid Campbell, a distinguished public lawyer; Dr. J. E. Isaac, a former professor of economics and then a member of the Conciliation and Arbitration Commission; and Paul Munro, a leading public sector unionist.

The RCAGA came late in the procession of postwar reviews of major public services (Hoover in the United States; Priestley and Fulton in the UK; Glassco and Heeney in Canada; McCarthy in New Zealand) and its methodology accordingly combined the procedures of a traditional royal commission with the research base of later bodies as well as innovations of its own designed to improve public access to and participation in its activities.

Thus there was a general invitation to public bodies and members of the public to make submissions. A nationwide series of public hearings was held on the basis of submissions. These were supplemented by less formal public meetings with bodies and individuals representing, generally, the beneficiaries of social programs. Industry perspectives were channelled through Business Advisory

Groups based in Melbourne and Sydney. Particular matters such as administration at the regional level, science in government, administration of policies for Aborigines, the making of economic policy, and promotion of efficiency in government were addressed by task forces led by various commissioners.

RCAGA itself sponsored a comprehensive research program including a statistical survey of public officials, the execution of which was handled by the Commission's staff of more than 50 and a range of consultants mainly drawn from universities.

The major recommendations of the RCAGA were directed to more orderly, systematic, and integrated allocation of public sector resources by processes which allowed a larger role for ministers; greater flexibility for departments and agencies in utilization and deployment of resources, combined with more structured monitoring of performance; more positive personnel management; and a stronger orientation to public ("client") expectations of government agencies. This last orientation in the recommendations owed much to the innovative influence of its international consultant, Professor B. B. Schaffer of the University of Sussex.

The Fraser government established an interdepartmental task force with a full-time supporting staff, both drawn from the central agencies of the public service, to advise the cabinet on implementation of the RCAGA's recommendations. In formal terms the RCAGA's influence was relatively slight and this led one leading analyst to describe it as a classic case of nonimplementation.

There are a number of reasons why this was a plausible view in the short and even medium term. An implicit assumption of the RCAGA was an active, expansionary public sector. The government to which it reported favored restraint and reduction in the range of administrative activity and was aided in pursuit of its public sector goals by its own Administrative Review Committee headed by another lifelong official, Sir Henry Bland. Moreover, the economic climate of the mid-1970s was not sympathetic to expansion of either the public sector or public expenditure (although the campaign for reduction had only indifferent success).

Second, many of the mainstream tasks of public sector reform that formed important elements of proposals of international counterparts of the RCAGA had, in fact, been addressed in Australian government administration by the Public Service Board, especially during the remarkable chairmanship of Sir Frederick Wheeler (1960–1971). These included rationalization of classification structures; competitive pay policies; mechanization (computerization) of routine administrative tasks; graduate recruitment for general administration; enhancement of staff development and training; and dedicated staffing for policy development.

From a perspective of two decades the influence of RCAGA can be seen more strongly. Integrated allocation of resources has been achieved in an era of restraint, ministerially through the cabinet's Expenditure Review Committee, and administratively through the Department of Finance, carved out of the Treasury in 1976, and termination of the Public Service Board's role in this field in 1984. Subsequent dismemberment of the Board in 1987 has brought greater agency autonomy. The growing range of evaluation activities has its origin in RCAGA proposals that reduced control should be accompanied by more review of performance. And even in a period when business practice is seen so much as the model for the public sector, the accent on customer service and satisfaction has a clear lineage from RCAGA's innovative interests in the public's perspectives on provision of public services.

Great changes of the past two decades, barely evident in the RCAGA report, are the effective end to staff tenure, institution of active redundancy procedures, extensive curtailment of staff appeal rights, and considerable circumscription of union influence, which may be attributed to the less propitious economic circumstances since the end of the generation-long postwar boom.

The RCAGA generally ignored revenue and costing matters and hence increasing use of user fees and contracting out mechanisms owe practically nothing to RCAGA influence.

In terms of ideas about public administration, the RCAGA until the dismissal of the Whitlam government was very much an open-house experience. It had neither the formality nor the discipline of counterpart inquiries, both a strength and a weakness reflected in its report and research output.

Subsequently there have been several public service inquiries, both governmental and parliamentary. RCAGA was a major artifact of a brief public inquiry/public participation era in Australian government. It has been succeeded by an era symbolized by the management consultant, more expensive, more expeditious, more secretive, less public, less participatory, and more attuned to immediate client needs. There have thus far been no signs of any aspiration to revive RCAGA style.

JOHN R. NETHERCOTE

BIBLIOGRAPHY

Hazlehurst, Cameron, and J. R. Nethercote, eds., 1977. *Reforming Australian Government.* ANU Press/RIPA (ACT Group).
Kouzmin, Alexander *et al.*, eds., 1984. *Australian Commonwealth Administration 1983.* CCAE/RAIPA (ACT Division).
Report of the Royal Commission on Australian Government Administration (Chair: H. C. Coombs), 1976. Canberra: AGPS.
    Four appendix volumes containing research reports
Smith R. F. I., and Patrick Weller, eds., 1978. *Public Service Inquiries in Australia.* University of Queensland Press.
Wilenski, Peter, 1986. *Public Power and Public Administration.* Hale & Iremonger/RAIPA.

CO-OPTATION. As defined by Philip Selznick in his classic work, *TVA and the Grass Roots: A Study of Politics and Organization* (1949): "the process of absorbing new elements into the leadership or policy-determining structure of an organization as a means of averting threats to its stability or existence" (p. 13). Selznick derived this term from co-optive theory; Saward (1992, p. 6) describes Selznick's functionalist approach as but one of several ideological approaches to co-optive politics.

Selznick, a sociologist, is known for his works on the behavior of organizations. His publication on the Tennessee Valley Authority (TVA) examines the relationships between a regional public corporation (TVA) and the "grassroots participation" of local institutions. The Tennessee Valley Authority was established by Congress in 1933 in response to President Franklin D. Roosevelt's request for a federally owned corporation combining the advantages of the powers of a government organization with the flexibility and initiative of a private organization. The TVA was designed to oversee the development and proper use of the natural resources of the Tennessee River drainage basin and its adjoining territory, which would have social and economic impact on the growth and welfare of the nation. Selznick describes the uniqueness of the TVA not only as a government-owned power business or conservation agency, but also in terms of an implied sense of social responsibility for the unified development of the resources of the Tennessee Valley. Selznick examines the TVA as a living social institution impacted by its social environment due to its official commitment to a democratic relationship with the local organizations and due to the unique management issues it faced as an "outsider" organization regulating the activities of established local organizations. In an attempt to analyze the special relationships between the TVA and the grassroots organizations and how these relationships affected the TVA's commitment to grassroots democracy, Selznick utilized the concept of co-optation as a means of examining the effects of the institutional environment on the structure, leadership, and policies of an organization.

Formal Co-optation

Selznick specifies a difference between formal co-optation—the public absorption of new elements through the establishment of explicit, written relationships—and informal co-optation.

The process of formal co-optation is utilized by an organization to reestablish the stability of formal authority when the legitimacy of the authority of a governing organization has been questioned. An organization formally incorporates those essential elements of the governed in order to gain or maintain their consent. In addition, formal co-optation is often necessary for an organization when those being governed are needed to participate in

self-government activities. This form of formal co-optation serves to enhance the legitimacy of established authority through the sharing of responsibility between the governing organization and those being governed. Usually, the use of formal co-optation does not involve the actual transfer of power, but serves to preserve political and administrative legitimacy by by openly involving the governed in the decisionmaking process. In the context of Selznick's publication, formal co-optation is involved in his analysis of the TVA and its establishment of voluntary associations to assist with the administrative functions of the organizations.

The use of formal co-optation was especially prevalent in the utilization of individual local citizens as well as voluntary associations. In 1939 there were nearly 900,000 citizen members participating in national agricultural programs such as the Agricultural Adjustment Administration, the Bureau of Agricultural Economics, the Farm Security Administration, and the Soil Conservation Service. This pattern of co-optation of farmers in the administration of national agricultural programs was a means of establishing a democratic partnership between the government and the people in order to promote the ideal of grassroots democracy. However, this method of co-optation can be viewed as a deviation from democratic ideals since there are concerns about the lack of representatives of the "common person" by those citizens and associations chosen to participate in the process, as well as by the government agencies' tendency to control those local representatives. This lack of representatives is further subject to criticism because this process is oriented toward a top-down management approach in problem solving and decisionmaking, rather than the ideal process of a bottom-up management approach more appropriately associated with grassroots democracy. Rather than viewing this as any organized effort by the government to manipulate local citizenry, Selznick concludes that this is a natural phenomenon in organizations when it becomes more politically expedient for the needs of administration to dominate and impinge upon the process for democratic participation.

Informal Co-optation

In contrast to formal co-optation, informal co-optation is the process by which an organization responds to the political pressures of established interest groups or individuals by allowing these outside elements positions of leadership and policymaking within the organization. There is no open acknowledgment of such an arrangement, as it might result in the undermining of the organization's position of legitimacy with the public. Selznick cites as an example of informal co-optation the inclusion of private interest groups, namely the agricultural community leadership, within the policymaking structure of the TVA. While this inclusion of external power structures into the internal power structure of the organization is adopted to eliminate or appease the opposition of these external forces, the formal organization's policymaking authority is compromised since the organization must adapt to the interests of the coopted groups. Taking a broad view, Selznick finds that an outcome of this "hidden" accommodation of outside interests results in a power shift within the organization in order to enhance the chances of survival for the formal organization.

In contrast to the openness of the process of formal co-optation, the covert nature of informal co-optation challenges the concept of democratic participation and raises public suspicion concerning whether the organization is actually serving the public interest through its policymaking authority. Current usage of the term co-optation by the media tends to view this process as politically manipulative and antidemocratic and is indicative of the prevailing climate of distrust of government organizations. The negative implication of this concept of co-optation is apparent in frequent news reports on union members decrying the demise of once powerful labor unions which are now being "co-opted" by management in the course of contract negotiations. This negative view of co-optation is also prevalent during election campaigns when each political party accuses the other of allowing its political platform to be "co-opted" by the agenda of various special interest groups. This common usage of co-optation promotes the notion that democratic participation is denied to those who are represented by the co-opted organization.

BRENDA L. BOYD

BIBLIOGRAPHY

Saward, Michael, 1992. *Co-optive Politics and State Legitimacy.* Brookfield, VT: Dartmouth Publishing Company Limited.
Selznick, Philip, 1949. *TVA and the Grass Roots: A Study of Politics and Organization.* Berkeley, CA: University of California Press.
———, 1948. "Foundations of the Theory of Organization." *American Sociological Review,* vol. 13 (February) 25–35.

COPRODUCTION. The involvement of citizens in the delivery of public services, either through direct collaboration with government or indirectly, by the actions of individuals, households or groups which contribute to or accomplish similar ends as governmental service production.

In the late 1970s, declining federal revenues and taxpayer revolts produced a fiscal crisis in cities throughout the United States. In an effort to manage with declining revenues (while service demands remained the same or even increased), local governments began to explore alter-

native means of delivering services. Although privatization of services, either contracting out or shedding responsibility altogether, was the most discussed alternative, cities also examined approaches which sought to involve citizen volunteers in a greater service delivery capacity.

The volunteer is certainly not a new idea to any community, in the United States or elsewhere. Parents have long volunteered time in their local schools and many rural areas depend entirely upon volunteers for fire and other emergency services. But coproduction, which this new interest in volunteerism was termed, represented a concerted effort in many fiscally stressed communities in the United States to have citizens perform service roles that had previously been the responsibility of government. The hope was to maintain current service levels while keeping public expenditures in check or even lower through substitution of volunteer labor for paid staff. This review is an examination of the evolution of the concept of coproduction. It begins with an analysis of the early definitional efforts followed by a presentation of the different theoretical schools of thinking which emerged. The final section is a discussion of the central issues in the study of coproduction, especially those investigated through empirical research.

Definitions of Coproduction

The concept of coproduction is often viewed within the broader notion of volunteerism in society. While coproduction is a voluntary act, it does differ (contingent upon the definition) from volunteerism.

Volunteerism is an action taken by a person to involve himself or herself in the community. It can be as simple as a householder making the decision to help his/her neighbor. Serving on the board of a local nonprofit is an example of volunteerism occurring within an organizational context. Volunteerism also is a type of collective action when, for example, residents band together to form a neighborhood watch group, working with police to lower the crime rate.

Depending upon the definition of coproduction, these examples of voluntary action would or would not be considered coproduction (see Brudney and England, 1983). Where definitions of coproduction differ most is the scope of the activity, whether it should be broadly construed to include any actions of citizens that impact upon service delivery, or more narrowly, just those set of interactions that include residents in an active and collaborative role with city government (see Warren et al., 1984). In the latter case, coproduction is not synonymous with volunteerism and is more appropriately understood as a specific form of voluntary action.

A consensus does exist on what coproduction means in terms of the labor mix in service production. Producers are divided into two categories: regular and consumer.

Central to this distinction is that a coproduced output depends upon a service transformation act by citizens (historically, the consumer), not just government acting monopolistically as the sole provider.

A lack of definitional agreement on what constitutes coproduction behavior has significant empirical implications. If a broader definition is utilized, the prevalence of coproduction is higher since a wide variety of activities are counted. Behaviors which would be included in this type of definition are citizen requests for governmental assistance and individual homeowner acts like the installation of deadbolts to prevent theft. A narrower conceptualization (coproduction as collaboration between government and citizen) results in lower prevalence levels. The consequence is that research based on definitions of varying specificity produce quite disparate conclusions about the extent of coproduction behavior. Greater preciseness in definition is needed, especially if empirical data are used by local jurisdictions for the purpose of planning or evaluating coproduction as a service delivery alternative.

Perspectives on Coproduction: Economic, Political, and Organizational

In a review of the literature, Brudney and England conclude coproduction is a multifaceted concept (1983, p. 61). It is not only an economic theory of production, but encompasses a different political theory of the role of citizens in the community as well as a new way to organize local government. These perspectives—economic, political, and organizational—are described below.

Coproduction as an Economic Process

As a theory of public organization, coproduction represents a basic reconceptualization of the producer-supplier relationship in the delivery of public services. Instead of government in the monopolistic position as the sole deliverer of services, the system is decentralized with local residents and/or neighborhood organizations engaged in the production process. Economists have long understood the role that consumers play in service production. Many services (e.g., the patient following the doctor's orders regarding a prescription) require joint action between producer and consumer for a successful outcome.

A public choice perspective has shaped thinking about coproduction as an economic relationship (Parks et al., 1981). It is premised on the advantages of nonhierarchical forms of service production. Coproduction offers a labor mix to governments, increasing their options in the delivery of services. Services can be individually defined in terms of the optimum mix of regular staff and volunteer labor. Cities can avoid increased labor costs due to slack labor by employing volunteers on an as needed basis.

Coproduction as Political Participation

When citizens take coproduction actions beyond the normal activities of daily life, these steps contribute to an increase in democratic participation.

Some forms of coproduction are so basic to everyday living, such as obeying traffic signals, that they do nothing to change the relationship of citizens to government. Traffic enforcement depends upon the voluntary compliance of people who use the roads, but obeying these laws is not an act of citizenship, but one of necessity (avoiding the chaos that would occur if no one paid attention to the law and the potentially negative incentive of being issued a ticket).

But other types of coproduction place the citizen in a role where he/she is interacting with government. Participating in the building of a local park with city assistance, for example, makes citizens more active members of their communities. From this perspective, coproduction is a training ground for democratic citizenship (Levine, 1984). The participatory values underlying coproduction are linked to Rousseau's concept of the democratic society (Bjur and Siegel, 1977). Participation allows for a type of social learning whereby the citizen becomes more experienced in and knowledgeable of government.

Coproduction as Governmental Organization

A theme throughout the literature on coproduction is the type of organizational arrangement it reflects. Several authors differentiate coproduction from the bureaucratic model, which is variously referred to as the "dominant approach" (Sharp, 1980), "Taylorian scientific model" (Bjur and Siegel, 1977) "Professional bureaucracy" (Levine, 1984), and "closed system" (Clary, 1985).

These distinctions reflect a basic perspective in organizational theory on the extent to which organizations are open to their environment. Classical theory pays little attention to the organization-environment interface. Coproduction is an example of the "open systems" perspective where the boundaries of the organization are seen as permeable. Task accomplishment occurs through the use of an environmental factor outside the immediate organization, the citizen, who crosses the system boundary and becomes a producer, not just a consumer of public goods.

Attention is also given to the organizational context or framework within which coproduction is most likely to occur. Several authors argue that coproduction requires decentralized political arrangements where the control of the professional bureaucracy is deemphasized (see Levine, 1984; Bjur and Siegel, 1977). Since coproduction is a form of citizen participation, the same circumstances that facilitate citizen input also benefit coproduction (especially in a collaboration between government and citizens). Rich concludes that neighborhood-based organization is an effective framework for coproduction (1979, p. 81). Other neighbors (functioning in coworker roles) are effective sources of encouragement for residents to engage in coproduction, neighborhoods can serve as "grassroots" infrastructures for service delivery, and neighborhood associations perform a liaison function with city hall.

Issues in Coproduction Research

Over the history of coproduction research, a number of issues are dominant. They are: the question of who participates in coproduction and for what reasons, the constraints of bureaucratic organization, the impact coproduction has upon a community, and whether it is really a form of privatization. These issues are considered in the following sections.

Participation in Coproduction

Conclusions from the research on the actual level of citizen participation of coproduction are far from definitive. No data are available on the proportion of services in communities which are coproduced and the type and extent of citizen involvement. The majority of the existing research is in the criminal justice area, which places limits on its generalizability (see Warren et al., 1984; Rosentraub and Harlow, 1983; Rosentraub and Sharp, 1981; Pennell, 1978). Participation rates differ depending upon the definition used: passive versus active, individual versus collective, direct versus indirect (see Brudney and England, 1983).

Nonetheless, the available research indicates fairly high levels of participation in selected service areas. A number of survey research studies are based on representative community and state samples so they can provide an idea of the magnitude of involvement within these contexts. Although the researchers in one criminal justice study consider household actions such as the purchase of locks, alarm systems, and weapons as parallel production (noncollaborative with government), which they distinguish from coproduction, almost 80 percent of the households engaged in this type of activities (Warren et al., 1984). Other survey investigations find similar levels of citizen participation for criminal justice-related behaviors (Pennell, 1978). In the area of health, preventative actions such as doctor visits are common (an example of parallel production), ranging from 61 percent for groups with income in the $6,000 range to 93 percent for those in the over $30,000 category (Rosentraub and Sharp, 1981). Survey research has also been used to measure the level of citizen involvement in household recycling. One study indicates a participation rate of almost 50 percent in 109 American communities with some form of recycling program, an activity which meets most of the criteria in definitions of what constitutes a coproduced service (Folz, 1991).

A number of empirical studies investigate the reasons behind a person's choice to coproduce. Most often, demographic factors are used as explanatory variables (Sundeen, 1988; Warren et al., 1984; Rosentraub and Sharp, 1981). A frequent conclusion is that participation is positively correlated with income and other measures of social status. The relationship raises the question of whether there is a class bias to coproduction. As an alternative form of service delivery, does it potentially benefit affluent areas more because of the greater likelihood of citizen involvement? Cities that are considering the adoption of coproduction strategies need to ascertain the capacity of low-income neighborhoods to participate and the potential for service delivery inequities to occur (Sundeen 1988; Warren et al., 1984).

Not all researchers on coproduction agree that it is most likely to benefit communities or parts of cities that already have resources. Because many coproduction activities do not require specialized skills and need limited funding, such as a neighborhood clean-up campaign, they may be quite appropriate for low-income areas (Rich, 1979, p. 89). Additionally, some studies question the importance of status variables in the prediction of coproduction behavior. Research on household participation in an energy conservation program finds that it is heavily contingent upon attitudes and knowledge, particularly commitment to environmental protection (Neiman, 1989). In another study, citizens who were most likely to engage in coproductive behavior evidenced the greatest concern about crime (Pennell, 1978, pp. 66–69). Further, analysis on household recycling behavior indicates that the community context is important: whether a local government has made the decision to initiate a program or not (Folz, 1991).

Citizen attitudes, community setting, and variations across policy domains require more investigation in predicting coproduction. Sundeen (1988) does examine participation within a variety of service areas in his secondary analysis of survey data, providing an example of how this type of research can be conducted. Research by Ben-Ari (1990) in Japan suggests the reasons people participate in household recycling are different than in the United States, evidence for the importance of context in the decision to coproduce.

Another predictor of participation is motivation. Studies of its effect on the decision to volunteer has been widely investigated and a multiplicity of motives have been identified. In the coproduction literature, this question has been less studied, but research on volunteers in emergency medical services indicates they possess a variety of motives (which is the same conclusion that can be drawn from the general research on volunteerism). The traditional value of social responsibility is a motivating factor, but personal and skill development are significant factors as well (Anderson and Clary, 1987).

Motivation is an important factor for local governments to take into account in designing coproduction systems. The willingness of citizens to engage in collaborative coproduction is not a given. Local government cannot assume a ready group of potential coproducers. Incentives are critical to the building of this labor pool (Brudney, 1990).

The one area of motivation that receives substantial examination in the coproduction literature is the "free rider" problem. The decision to coproduce services is not a mandatory activity. Many services are not easily divisible in terms of the separation of beneficiaries. A community watch program that succeeds in reducing the crime rate benefits everyone, even if only a small number of residents actually participate. For those neighbors who play no role, they are receiving a service for which they do not have to pay in the form of an in-kind contribution, their labor. With the existence of free rider payoffs, there is a strong incentive against participation since benefits are received regardless of the level of personal involvement (Rich, 1979, p. 82).

Organizational Constraints

Coproduction is often a more attractive service option to citizens and elected officials than to those who work in city hall. If proponents advocate it as a way to replace regular staff, a process which economists refer to as labor substitution, city employees rightly feel threatened. When the use of volunteers is not perceived as consistent with professional norms or values of particular service delivery activity, staff resistance occurs.

For example, the latter problem was evident in a survey of police officers' attitudes toward coproduction (Rosentraub and Harlow, 1983). While the police supported law enforcement activities traditionally associated with good citizenship, such as reporting crimes, they were resistant to citizen involvement that duplicated core functions such as police patrols.

Cities in the United States, when faced with fiscal constraints in delivering services, have not engaged in wholesale replacement of regular staff with volunteers. More typically, they have cut back services, privatized them, or supplemented existing city workforces with volunteer labor. In the latter case, getting citizens and regular staff to work together is a significant issue, especially when the workforce is unionized. Several factors militate against the successful employment of citizens as coproducers: lack of clarity regarding differing role responsibilities, the frequent attitude of paid, professional staff that citizens lack necessary knowledge and experience, and the absence of incentives to get staff to work with volunteers.

Coproduction forces administrators to define their roles in new and different ways. When working with a citizen workforce, administrators lack "command and control" prerogatives and must function as brokers, facilitating relationships between the city and its citizen and/or neighborhood coproducers (Sundeen, 1985, pp. 397–400). Training for employees is also necessary to educate staff to the value of citizen volunteers, how to design appropriate tasks for them, and how to provide necessary administrative oversight.

Cities must also avoid treating citizens as "free goods." Effective citizen involvement depends upon the existence of supports that regular staff have. Depending on the service, they need training, appropriate equipment, and adequate administrative supervision. In making the decision to coproduce a service, local governments have to balance these costs against lower staff expenditures due to the willingness of citizens to work without renumeration (Clary, 1985).

The incentive question is important as well. City governments generally have not utilized incentives as a way to motivate coproduction. In a national survey of municipal jurisdictions in the United States, just 31 percent employed incentives to increase participation. However, among those cities that used incentives, many creative approaches were evident, including stipends, discounts on municipal fees, social activities, prizes, and different types of public recognition (Buckwalter et al., 1993). These survey data indicate cities do have options so that incentives are not beyond the ability of local governments to provide.

A final point that cities must consider in fostering coproduction is the perceptions of citizens. As discussed earlier, coproduction is a form of citizenship building. Involvement in public affairs can increase expectations about governmental responsiveness (Pennell, 1978, pp. 70–71). Coproduction is not a one-way street. It not only holds the promise of a more committed citizenry, but local government must meet expectations about its role as a partner in service delivery. Awareness on the part of public administrators toward the special implementation issues raised by coproduction is critical for effective collaboration.

The Impact of Coproduction

Few empirical studies systematically assess the actual impact of coproduction on a community. Much of the research is descriptive, case studies which rely on anecdotal evidence. Most empirical work is a documentation of the types and frequency of coproduction. The focus is on the input side, the supply of labor. Less is known about the output dimension, especially in terms of service criteria such as efficiency and effectiveness. Nevertheless, the existing research does provide abundant evidence for the existence of coproduction in many service areas. Examples of the research documenting coproduced services include: criminal justice (Warren *et al.*, 1984; Rosentraub and Harlow, 1983; Rosentraub and Sharp, 1981; Pennell, 1978), emergency medical services (Anderson and Clary, 1987), energy production (Neiman, 1989), and waste recycling (Floz, 1991; Ben-Ari, 1990).

The available data, while limited, indicate coproduction can have an impact upon service delivery. For example, waste recycling is one service area where coproduction has a direct effect. Recycling programs depend upon the willingness of households to participate; they cannot be effective without the service being coproduced. In a survey of 109 American communities, almost a majority of households participated (49 percent), demonstrating the existence of a substantial labor pool for this activity (Folz, 1991, p. 101). A second example indicates that volunteers serving as emergency medical personnel were able to respond to calls, a critical component in the effectiveness of first response services, in less than half the time required under state statute (Anderson and Clary, 1987). On the other hand, questions have been raised about the contribution that individual households can make to energy conservation even when supported by residential conservation programs (Neiman, 1989).

Since coproduction is frequently listed as a form of privatization, a key issue is the extent to which it can produce cost savings. A review of the research on this question reveals that cost savings do occur with coproduction (Brudney, 1990, p. 40). However, it is argued that large reductions should not be expected and, in fact, expenditures may even grow. Significant organizational constraints militate against large cost savings. The most important are resistance to the substitution of citizen for staff labor, the necessary expertise to do tasks (which volunteers may lack), and the indirect costs which result from administrative oversight of volunteers and coordination with neighborhood organizations.

Brudney (1990, p. 37) thinks its advantages relate more to the ratio of inputs to outputs than a decline in inputs as measured by tax dollars or other fiscal indicators. The economic value of coproduction is its potential to increase the scope or coverage of services while allowing costs to be held constant or minimally increased.

Analytic studies conducted in small cities do indicate that cost savings can accrue from coproduction. Job analysis applied to a municipal workforce, a city with a 50,000 population and 50 percent of the budget in labor costs, indicated a potential existed for a savings of 19 percent (Bjur and Siegel, 1977, p. 144). Cost analysis of municipal fire protection showed volunteer departments had significantly lower costs compared to all-paid or mixed paid/volunteer departments. On the other hand, the level of effectiveness was higher for paid departments, even given the more difficult fire prevention environments in which they functioned (Brudney and Duncombe, 1992).

Given the focus of this research on modest-sized cities, a question is whether similar findings would result from analysis conducted in larger urban areas. The poten-

tial for cost savings may be less due to the sizable low-income population. The negative correlation between coproduction behavior and income indicates that for cities which have a significant number of residents at the lower end of the economic scale, coproduction behavior will occur less frequently (see Sundeen, 1988). Consequently, generalizations about cost savings in smaller communities or suburbs may have limited applicability to the large, central city.

For generalizable research on the impact of coproduction, comprehensive theoretical frameworks are required. Examples of this type of inquiry are limited. One useful model is in the criminal justice area (Koven, 1992). Coproduction in neighborhood law enforcement is conceptualized as having a multiplicity of effects, both positive and negative, on the crime rate. The impacts range from nothing at all (status quo) to the displacement of crime to another area of a city in response to effective neighborhood coproduction (default displacement). The value of the approach is that it organizes these impacts under a general theory of displacement of crime behavior, providing a set of testable hypotheses regarding the effects of coproduction.

Is Coproduction Privatization?

In one sense, coproduction is a form of privatization because it changes the monopoly role of government in service delivery. At the same time, it is a power sharing relationship quite different from contracting, where exclusive operational responsibility falls to the successful bidder. Privatization usually is seen as a reduction in the role of government. Alternatively, coproduction can be an enlargement through "negative entropy," importing resources (i.e., the citizen) from the environment. In the process, government may actually become larger as measured by staff levels and other related indicators even if the traditional resource base provided by taxes and other revenues declines.

Whether it is appropriate to label coproduction as a form of privatization is the subject of some debate. Morgan and England (1988) view privatization from two perspectives: as a means to achieve cost efficiencies, but also the extent to which it reflects and enhances important values of citizenship and community building. They posit five potential models of privatization: contracting with for-profit organizations, a competitive market for public goods, city contracts with neighborhoods, self-help arrangements, and vouchers. Only the latter three offer the possibility of moving the citizen from the passive role of consumer to active participant in community affairs. They conclude it is questionable to include these types of initiatives under the label of privatization.

In contrast, Savas (1987, p. 81) lists coproduction under the heading of "self-service." In his formulation, coproduction represents the purest form of privatization because the family or household is both the producer and consumer of a service. This definition is quite narrow since it does not encompass other forms of coproduction, most prominently individual/family/household collaborative production with a formal governmental authority.

In conclusion, this debate underscores the importance of broadly conceptualizing coproduction as a form of alternative service delivery. If viewed only with the context of privatization, the emphasis is on the cost savings side, downgrading or even ignoring its significance as a way to enhance citizen participation in the community. It can actually increase the scope of government, through the expansion of citizen involvement in service delivery. Since citizen producers are part of the public government serves, the change in the monopolistic role of government as a service deliver is substantially different than privatization alternatives that shift day-to-day administration and operation away from government to another sector of society.

BRUCE B. CLARY

BIBLIOGRAPHY

Anderson, Jolene and Bruce Clary, 1987, "Coproduction in Emergency Medical Services." *Journal of Voluntary Action Research*, vol. 16 (July-September) 33–42.
Ben-Ari, Eyal, 1990. "A Bureaucrat in Every Japanese Kitchen: On Cultural Assumptions and Coproduction." *Administration and Society*, vol. 21 (February) 472–492.
Bjur, Wesley E. and Gilbert B. Siegel, 1977. "Voluntary Citizen Participation in Local Government: Quality, Cost and Containment." *Midwest Review of Public Administration*, vol. 11 (June) 135–149.
Brudney, Jeffrey L., 1990. *Fostering Volunteer Programs in the Public Sector*. San Francisco, CA: Jossey-Bass.
Brudney, Jeffrey L. and William D. Duncombe, 1992. "An Economic Evaluation of Paid, Volunteer, and Mixed Staffing Options for Public Service." *Public Administration Review*, vol. 52 (September-October) 474–480.
Brudney, Jeffrey L. and Robert E. England, 1983. "Toward a Definition of the Coproduction Concept." *Public Administration Review*, vol. 43 (January-February) 59–65.
Buckwalter, Doyle, Robert Parsons, and Normal Wright, 1993. "Citizen Participation in Local Government: The Use of Incentives and Rewards." *Public Management*, vol. 75 (September) 11–15.
Clary, Bruce B., 1985, "Designing Urban Bureaucracies for Coproduction." *State and Local Government Review*, vol. 17 (Fall) 265–272.
Folz, David H. 1991. "Recycling Solid Waste: Citizen Participation in the Design of a Coproduced Program." *State and Local Government Review*, vol. 23 (Fall) 98–102.
Koven, Steven G., 1992. "Coproduction of Law Enforcement Services: Benefits and Implications." *Urban Affairs Quarterly*, vol. 27 (March) 457–469.
Levine, Charles H., 1984. "Citizenship and Service Delivery: The Promise of Coproduction." *Public Administration Review*, vol. 44 (March) 178–186.
Morgan, David R. and Robert E. England, 1988. "The Two Faces of Privatization." *Public Administration Review*, vol. 48, (November-December) 979–987.
Neiman, Max, 1989. "Government Directed Change of Everyday Life and Coproduction: The Case of Home Energy Use." *The Western Political Quarterly*, vol. 42 (September) 365–389.
Parks, Roger B., Paula C. Baker, Larry Kiser, et al., 1981. "Consumers as Coproducers of Public Services: Some Economic and Institutional Considerations." *Policy Studies Journal*, vol. 9 (Summer) 1001–1012.
Pennell, Frances, 1978. "Collective versus Private Strategies for Coping with Crime: The Consequences for Citizen Perceptions of Crime, Attitudes Toward the Police and Neighboring Activity." *Journal of Voluntary Action Research*, vol. 7 (January-June) 59–74.
Rich, Richard C., 1979. "The Roles of Neighborhood Organizations in Urban Service Delivery." *Urban Affairs Papers*, vol. 1 (Fall) 81–93.
Rosentraub, Mark S. and Karen S. Harlow, 1983. "Public/Private Relations and Service Delivery: The Coproduction of Personal Safety." *Policy Studies Journal*, vol. 11:445–457.
Rosentraub, Mark S. and Elaine B. Sharp, 1981. "Consumers as Producers of Social Services: Coproduction and the Level of Social Services." *Southern Review of Public Administration*, vol. 4 (March) 502–539.
Savas, E. S., 1987, *Privatization: The Key to Better Government.* Chatham, NJ: Chatham House.
Sharp, Elaine B., 1980. "Toward a New Understanding of Urban Services." *Midwest Review of Public Administration*, vol. 14 (June) 105–118.
Sundeen, Richard A., 1985. "Coproduction and Communities: Implications for Local Administrators." *Administration & Society*, vol. 16 (February) 387–402.
———, 1988. "Explaining Participation in Coproduction: A Study of Volunteers." *Social Science Quarterly*, vol. 69 (September) 547–567.
Warren, Robert, Mark S. Rosentraub and Karen S. Harlow, 1984. "Coproduction, Equity and the Distribution of Safety." *Urban Affairs Quarterly*, vol. 19 (June) 447–464.

CORPORATE FOUNDATIONS.

Legally independent charitable grantmaking entities created by profit-making businesses. They provide a vehicle for corporate social responsibility. Corporate foundations are private foundations under United States law. They are required to make grants for charitable purposes and obey the regulations pertaining to private foundations. In 1992 there were approximately 1,900 company-sponsored foundations in the United States that held assets of $6.59 billion and gave $1.57 billion in contributions. They account for 5 percent of U.S. foundations, but give away 15 percent of grant dollars.

Some companies create a foundation so that they can contribute gifts of cash, stock, or property to the foundation's endowment in profitable years and use the foundation's endowment as a source of charitable revenue in years when the corporation cannot afford to make contributions because of lower than normal profits. In recent years corporate foundations have drawn down their endowments by paying out in grants more than they have received in gifts from their companies.

Most corporate foundations do not have large endowments; they receive yearly gifts from the company to conduct their grantmaking program. Gifts made to a corporate foundation may not be reclaimed by the corporation; the funds must be used for charitable purposes. There are, however, 50 corporations that have substantial endowments that range from $27 to $268 million in 1992 figures. The five largest are the Alcoa Foundation ($268 million); General Motors Foundation ($125 million); Prudential Foundation ($125 million); AT&T Foundation ($124); and Metropolitan Life Foundation ($102 million).

Many business corporations create both a foundation and a separate direct contributions program. The contributions program often makes small, but visible gifts that promote the company's image. Contributions programs also make "in-kind" gifts of equipment and services like printing and office space. The corporate foundation, however, usually has a more focused and strategic grantmaking program. It usually includes a variety of interests including education, the arts, health, and social services. Matching gift programs for contributions of company employees are also popular. Analysts agree that corporate giving from both foundations and direct giving programs is dedicated to projects that serve the corporation's "enlightened self-interest."

The board of directors of a corporate foundation usually includes management level officials from within the corporation but may also include persons who are not affiliated with the corporation. Corporate foundations are often staffed by employees of the company who may have additional corporate responsibilities such as community relations and managing the direct giving program. In the smaller corporate foundations, staff salaries and the foundation's other administrative expenses may be paid by the sponsoring company rather than by the foundation's investment earnings.

In addition to being a visible, organized expression of social responsibility, corporate foundations are useful to multinational corporations because tax-deductible gifts to foreign recipients can only be made through a foundation.

ELIZABETH T. BORIS

BIBLIOGRAPHY

Freeman, David and The Council of Foundations, 1991. *The Handbook on Private Foundations.* Rev. ed. New York: The Foundation Center.

Renz, Loren and Steven Lawrence, 1994. *Foundation Giving: Yearbook of Facts and Figures on Private, Corporate and Community Foundations.* New York: The Foundation Center.

CORPORATE FUNDERS.

Business corporations that make philanthropic contributions to benefit the public, usually through qualified nonprofit organizations. Most corporate funders have organized contributions programs or corporate foundations that are managed by company staff. Known as corporate philanthropy, contributions, donations, or giving programs, the current terminology favors Corporate Community Involvement and extends to a variety of direct and indirect activities.

Early corporate philanthropy was legally limited to activities that were of direct benefit to the company. Partly as a result of beneficial activities undertaken by corporations during World War I, the tolerance for corporate social involvement expanded. The concept of corporate trusteeship gained ground so that by 1921, legally permissible corporate philanthropy included activities that benefited employees. The direct benefit concept was completely overturned in a challenge decided in 1953 by the New Jersey Supreme Court (*A. P. Smith Co. v. Barlow* et al., 1953). Corporate contributions were affirmed as an obligation of good citizenship and freed from the need to demonstrate a link to the company's economic benefit.

Enlightened self-interest is the dominant motivation for corporate contributions. Corporate funders generally prefer to make contributions in the communities where they do business or have plants. Contributions tend to enhance the company's visibility and promote its image as a responsible community citizen. Often, corporate funders provide scholarship programs for students, and support university research programs in areas related to their interests. They also sponsor arts and cultural programs that provide a maximum of visibility for the company name.

Under law, corporate funders may only receive a charitable deduction for contributions up to 10 percent of their taxable income. In reality, corporate contributions average about 1 percent of corporate income, which varies somewhat with profit levels and the health of the U.S. economy.

Contributions may be cash grants, gifts of appreciated property such as stock or real estate, in-kind donations of equipment, or services such as printing, public relations assistance, or use of facilities.

Employee volunteer programs and matching grant programs are also significant.

ELIZABETH T. BORIS

BIBLIOGRAPHY

Fremont-Smith, Marion R., 1972. *Philanthropy and the Business Corporation.* New York: Russell Sage Foundation.

Heald, Morrell, 1970. *The Social Responsibilities of Business: Company and Community. 1900–1960.* Cleveland: The Press of Case Western Reserve University.

Shannon, James P., ed., 1991. *The Corporate Contributions Handbook.* San Francisco: Jossey-Bass.

CORPORATE MANAGEMENT.

The coordination, control, and motivation of relatively autonomous organizational sub-units through systematic managerial techniques, in order to bring about their conformance to corporate goals. Corporate management is therefore distinguishable from management within subcorporate units, and constitutes a distinctive repertoire of managerial techniques, mainly derived from the private sector, for balancing centralized control with decentralized autonomy. The term also refers to the group of top managers who carry out these activities.

Theoretical Framework

Conceptually, corporate management is an intermediate model between classical bureaucracy and interorganizational contracting. The former is a unitary form, in which activities are structured in functional groups, administered by specialists and controlled through processes and procedures. The latter is a decoupled form, entailing contractual relations between separate organizations, each oriented to particular outputs. Corporate management entails elements of both. Each division or business unit within the organization is responsible for particular products or markets, and has relatively autonomous control over most of the functions necessary for handling them. Corporate headquarters sets organizational objectives and strategies, appoints divisional managers, monitors divisional performance, and allocates resources. Performance is monitored by post hoc measurement against prescribed output standards (e.g., sales revenue or investment return), and often related to incentive-oriented remuneration for divisional managers. Finally, recruitment and development for top corporate and divisional posts emphasizes generalist management skills. Thus corporate management is intraorganizational like its bureaucratic counterpart, but adapts devices such as output groupings, performance monitoring and incentive remuneration from organizational contracting.

At the level of the individual organization, the public sector conception of corporate management typically structures divisions by programs, responsible to the chief executive for particular outcomes. Senior managers form part of a governmentwide corps (such as the U.S. Senior Executive Service) whose expertise is in general management rather than functionally specialized. At whole-of-government level, each ministry or department is analogous to a division, and central agencies such as that servicing the head of government or finance and personnel offices play the headquarters role. In this notion, central agencies minimize transactional controls and hold line agencies accountable for results.

Origin and Subsequent History

Corporate management evolved in the United States after World War I in large business enterprises, such as Du Pont and General Motors, which had to find ways to coordinate the diverse activities that had proliferated in their organizations as a result of vertical and horizontal integration. As Chandler explained in *The Visible Hand* (1977), these companies' activities were "too large, too numerous, too varied, and too scattered" to be controlled through a single centralized functional organization (p. 460), so they developed decentralized multidivisional structures. By the 1960s, most of the largest U.S. corporations had adopted similar structures and control systems.

In addition, administrative experiments in the U.S. federal government elaborated supporting managerial tools. In the 1930s, the Social Security Administration introduced a form of performance measurement related to organizational goals, while the first Hoover Commission (1948) advocated performance budgeting. Program management was introduced in the California State Training Office in the mid-1950s. In the early 1960s Defense Secretary Robert MacNamara (a former Ford Motor Company president) introduced the Planning, Programming, Budgeting System (PPBS), which sharpened the focus on outputs and on corporate-level priority-setting. Related to this was Zero-Based Budgeting (ZBB), developed in the Agriculture Department in the late 1960s.

At the same time, some writers—in addition to Chandler—began to theorize and extend these developments. Important forerunners were Ridley and Simon, who emphasized orienting activity measurement towards defined objectives (*Measuring Municipal Activities,* 1937). Foremost was Peter Drucker, who in the 1950s crystallized the idea of "management for results" and the related technique of "Management by Objectives" (MBO), later embraced by the Nixon administration. Also important was the work of Christensen, Andrews, and others at Harvard Business School who elaborated the notion of general management and its characteristic devices.

Current Practice

The application of corporate management techniques in government in the U.S. has been patchy, tending to vary with the level of government, the elected administration, and the type of agency. PPBS has only selectively implemented in agencies other than the Department of Defense, and even there its salience has been intermittent. In the late 1970s Carter tried ZBB, but this was also a shortlived experiment. The Reagan, Bush, and Clinton administrations have selectively applied some corporate management techniques, but tended to submerge them within a concern for budgetary savings and a preference for contractualizing some government activities, typified by the 1982 Grace Commission and the 1993 National Performance Review. State and local governments have adopted corporate management to a greater extent, but again patchily.

The limited application of this model in U.S. governments reflects their structural character. The ongoing political contest arising from the division of power between the legislature and executive, and the related influence of interest groups, makes it difficult to establish one precondition for effective operation of corporate management: objectives which are internally consistent, easy to state clearly, and relatively stable.

By contrast, parliamentary regimes, especially of the Westminster variety, have enthusiastically adopted corporate management systems. The UK introduced the Financial Management Initiative (FMI) in 1982. This was more broadly managerial than its title suggests, as was its namesake in Australia, the Financial Management Improvement Program (FMIP), begun in 1984. Similar initiatives were seen in New Zealand and in Canada's Increased Ministerial Authority and Accountability scheme from the mid-1980s. Since the end of the 1980s, however, the UK with its "Next Steps" initiative and New Zealand with its introduction of market-based government have moved on to a more contractualist model, driven to some extent by ideology.

These governments, and other parliamentary regimes such as Sweden, were able to adopt comprehensive managerial reforms because the domination of their legislatures by their executives facilitates the establishment of more stable, consistent program objectives.

However, corporate management has made little headway in other large industrialized democracies such as France, Germany, and Japan. Although their political executives have been relatively strong, the greater interdependence of the public and private sectors in these countries has militated against another important condition for this model: the work in each program needs to be able to be independent of the actions of external parties, to make post hoc performance measurement meaningful.

In summary, corporate management tends to require particular conditions, such as clear goals and self-contained programs. The extent to which these conditions are present varies according to the type of activity, the political context, and the constitutional circumstances.

JOHN ALFORD

BIBLIOGRAPHY

Caiden, Gerald E., 1991. *Administrative Reform Comes of Age.* Berlin: Walter de Gruyter.
Chandler, Alfred D., 1977. *The Visible Hand: The Managerial Revolution in American Business.* Cambridge, MA: Belknap Press, Harvard.
Drucker, Peter F., 1955/1989. *The Practice of Management.* Paperback ed., Worcester, UK: Heinemann Professional Publishing.
Hood, Christopher, 1991. "A Public Management for All Seasons?" *Public Administration,* vol. 69 (Spring) 3–19.
Learned, Edmund P., C. Roland Christensen, William D. Guth, and Kenneth R. Andrews, 1965. *Business Policy: Text and Cases,* Homewood, IL: Richard D. Irwin.
Pollitt, Christopher, 1990. *Managerialism and the Public Services: The Anglo-American Experience.* Oxford, UK: Basil Blackwell.

CORPORATE PLANNING. A systematic approach toward clarifying corporate objectives, formulating corporate strategy, making strategic decisions, and checking the achievement of objectives, often manifested in an explicit corporate planning process and corporate plan.

The Meaning of Corporate Planning

The process of planning has been described (Argenti, 1972) as "anticipatory decisionmaking," that is, carefully and deliberately deciding what is to be done before an action is taken. There have always been circumstances in public sector organizations where planning is needed—in military operations, in infrastructure development, in urban and regional development, in production and distribution processes, and so on. Plans are the instructions resulting from the planning process that make it clear what is to be done, when, and by whom.

Corporate planning emerged in management literature in the 1960s—and in the management practice of some large private corporations before that—as a process by which anticipatory decisionmaking could be systematically undertaken at the level of the entity or corporation as a whole. Hence corporate planning is a structured process of anticipatory decisionmaking for the total organization, the purpose of which is to rationally choose the direction to be taken (defining objectives); choose the preferred means of getting there (strategy choice); make key decisions (strategic decisionmaking); express instructions clearly (through a strategic plan); and monitor and evaluate outcomes (review). Corporate planning is thus a rational management approach, rather than one which emphasizes incremental or unpredictable elements in management.

Those in the incrementalist tradition of Charles E. Lindblom question the extent to which rational processes such as corporate planning can be applied in the incrementalist world of public policymaking, while others see rational planning as describing only a portion of the decisionmaking universe.

Important Theorists of Corporate Planning

The first comprehensive treatment of the subject was H. Igor Ansoff's *Corporate Strategy* (1965), while other important pioneers were Russell Ackoff's *A Concept of Corporate Planning* (1970) and John Argenti's *Systematic Corporate Planning* (1972). All these treatments had in common the sequence of objective setting, strategic choice, strategic decisionmaking, and strategic review and evaluation. Ansoff's work is perhaps the most fundamental, drawing on his work with the General Electric Corporation.

More recently, corporate planning has become subsumed in more general studies of strategic management. Some recent writers, such as Mintzberg, in his book *The Rise and Fall of Strategic Planning* (1994), have contrasted the need for management to set strategic directions with the failure of attempts to overemphasise the rationality of management processes and to place undue emphasis on the role of back room planners and the formal plan document. Moreover, the advent of more decentralized organizations in the public and private sectors has placed greater emphasis in many organizations on planning at lower levels such as business units rather than at the level of the corporation as a whole, though the two are not mutually exclusive.

Application of Corporate Planning to the Public Sector

During the 1970s and 1980s corporate planning was adopted by many public sector organizations. This frequently required the appointment of a corporate planner and the establishment of a corporate planning section. Corporate plans setting out objectives, programs, milestones, and responsibilities became familiar in thousands of public sector organizations, especially independent government business organizations, infrastructure organizations, and local governments. Corporate planning rarely took hold in the central policy departments of government, where short-term decisionmaking and political influences together with the heterogeneous nature of the functions being pursued did not readily fit the corporate planning framework.

Business Planning

One response to the heterogeneous nature of some public organizations was the development of business unit structures and business planning as an offshoot of corporate planning. Business planning is typified by a relatively short time frame, a single business focus and an economy of consultation and written expression. Taut, focused business plans now form the focus of the planning process in many government business enterprises, although a global corporate plan drawing together the whole of the organization's intentions may also exist. Reorganization into business units, each with a coherent business plan, can sometimes be a preparation for privatization or market testing.

Corporate Planning Processes

Corporate planning processes typically begin with the statement, clarification, or restatement of the organization's objectives. This involves the application of the concept of management by objectives at the whole organization level, frequently accompanied by a statement or restatement of the organization's vision and/or mission. Corporate planning processes often involve scanning the organizational environment, consulting stakeholders, and utilizing various participative processes at this stage. In government, the issue of the clarification of objectives is frequently linked to the program of the elected administration at the time; government organizations can rarely adopt or restate their objectives unilaterally. On the other hand, elected representatives may at times enact in the legislature or otherwise impose new or revised objectives on a government body, that may use this as a starting point for a corporate planning process. A government body that seeks to act alone in its corporate planning risks the possibility that elected representatives will not endorse what is proposed. Thus stakeholder involvement has a special requirement in the public sector as to the primary involvement of elected representatives in the process of stating or reviewing organizational objectives.

In the public sector, there can be merit in elected representatives explicitly formulating the objectives to be pursued by a public organization and including this statement in legislation or in a nonstatutory statement of corporate intent. To do so may greatly assist the public organization to avoid confusion as to its mandate, and to lessen the extent to which it later becomes involved in contradictory activity. One the other hand, legislators must be careful not to burden the body with an inadequately framed set of objectives that may unreasonably handicap the efficiency or competitiveness of the body in carrying out its normal functions. It may be prudent for a legislature to conduct a participative process at the formative stage of a new public body to ensure that its objectives are well framed.

Strategy choice too may require government organizations to conduct their corporate planning in a participative manner. It may be necessary or desirable to define alternative strategies by which a policy goal can be achieved, and to publish options papers or conduct a process of public consultation to assess the public acceptability of alternative strategies. This again distinguishes many processes of public sector strategy making from their private sector counterparts, where strategy choice is more usually conducted as commercial analysis in confidence.

Public organizations frequently choose or are required to publish or make available to the public their strategic planning document. This then may form part of the process by which the public organization is held accountable, as well as part of the process by which it is managed.

Finally, the process of review and evaluation of the work of public organizations is frequently conducted by public processes, including the work of public auditors. Again, the extent to which objectives proposed in the corporate plan were achieved and with what degree of efficiency and effectiveness are likely to perform part of the external audit process, in addition to the extent to which they will form part of the internal process of control and review.

Conclusions

Corporate planning processes form an important part of the arrangements of many public sector organizations, especially government business enterprises. Larger government business enterprises and local governments will frequently also produce and rely on business plans, budgets, and other overview documents in charting their directions. Processes of corporate planning in the public sector environment, while similar in structure to private sector counterparts, often require significantly greater public involvement components, which can require skillful management in themselves.

E. W. RUSSELL

BIBLIOGRAPHY

Ackoff, Russell, 1970. *A Concept of Corporate Planning.* New York: Wiley.

Ansoff, H. Igor, 1965. *Corporate Strategy.* New York: McGraw Hill.

Argenti, John, 1972. *Systematic Corporate Planning.* Van Nostrand Reinhold UK.

Beringer, Ivan, George Chomiak and Hamish Russell, 1986. *Corporate Management.* Sydney: Hale and Iremonger.

Mintzberg, Henry, 1994. *The Rise and Fall of Strategic Planning.* Englewood Cliffs, NJ: Prentice Hall.

CORPORATIZATION. The act of making a public body, particularly a public enterprise, have the same accountability and management structures as a private company, in all aspects other than ownership.

Corporatization began in the UK and New Zealand in the early 1980s. Enterprises were corporatized as a preliminary step for the eventual privatization of public enterprises to make them suitable for sale by improving their efficiency, shedding surplus staff, and making a clearer relationship between enterprise and government.

Control and accountability are particular problems for public enterprises, which are deliberately set up to be relatively independent of direct political control. Setting control at a satisfactory level has been a perennial problem both for governments and their enterprises. If control is too tight, there is no advantage in having them set up as entities with a significant degree of independence. If government control is too loose, an enterprise may not be accountable to its owners, the public, raising a question as to why it is in government hands at all. One of the arguments for privatization is that public enterprises cannot be effectively controlled and that accountability is inferior to that of private companies. In the absence of important disciplines and rewards that commonly apply to private firms, the incentive for efficient management of public enterprises is reduced.

Corporatization aims to create an environment in which public enterprises can pursue commercial objectives in a competitive environment. Corporatization is designed to improve accountability by imitating the private sector in management and accountability as far as possible. A program of change to the management and structure of public enterprises to make them more like private sector firms in all things except ownership, it includes commercialization and administrative reform, but is a more consistent and comprehensive program than either.

Corporatization requires some combination of the following points. First, corporatization requires clear and nonconflicting objectives, such as the achievement of a commercial performance similar to that achieved by private sector organizations with similar risk characteristics. Second, it requires managerial responsibility, authority, and autonomy. Accountability for achieving objectives cannot be attained unless the board and management of a corporatized public enterprise have sufficient authority and autonomy to make the required decisions. Third, effective performance monitoring by the owner-government is required. Performance criteria and monitoring arrangements are aimed to compensate for the absence of market force sanctions, such as takeovers and bankruptcies. Fourth, it requires effective rewards and sanctions related to performance, so that managers are aware of a suitable system of rewards and penalties. Fifth, competitive neutrality in input markets is required so that a corporatized public enterprise is exactly like private companies it its external relationships. In other words, there should be no benefits or penalties resulting from the fact of government ownership. Sixth, competitive neutrality in output markets means that any protective barriers must be removed by taking away statutory barriers to entry and allowing competition in the industry. Seventh, there should be effective natural monopoly regulation in those industries prone to natural monopoly, with such regulation carried out by an independent body and not by the enterprise.

There are undoubtedly some benefits to corporatization. Accountability would be improved, mainly because of the setting of clear objectives which are purely commercial, so that failure to achieve them is quite transparent. The problem of efficiency should also be addressed. Providing incentives–both positive and negative–will be beneficial, as will being able to measure performance.

However, there are problems that will make it hard for the program to succeed. Corporatization has been rather slow to implement, even where both government and enterprises are agreed it should occur. The experience of natural monopoly regulation has not been particularly happy, especially in the UK. Also, there has been strong political opposition to corporatization.

From one perspective corporatization can work; a public enterprise which carried out such a program should be as efficient as a privately owned company. Whatever is done, public enterprise is still just that–public and enterprise–and from this stems the endemic problems of accountability. Even after corporatization, public enterprises remain untouched by a number of market disciplines that apply to private enterprises, such as the ability of private shareholders to trade in the equity capital of the enterprise; the requirement to compete for debt capital on commercial terms; the exposure of investment and/or borrowing programs to continual monitoring by the capital and share markets; the sanctions of takeover or merger for inferior performance arising from, say, the under-utilization of capital; and the risk of insolvency. From this perspective, the accountability of even a corporatized enterprise is likely to be inferior. Ownership does matter so that, even if corporatization is an improvement, it is not as good as privatization, meaning that every enterprise that can possibly be returned to the private sector should be.

Corporatization is most likely to be only be an interim step on the path to privatization. If corporatization is carried out properly, a government will receive little if any political benefit for its continued ownership. One purpose of public enterprise in the past was to carry out public functions, which can mean political functions such as rewarding supporters. Successful corporatization means that this political function is taken away, so that the government gains no political benefit from its ownership, other than income which has never been substantial and can be better obtained by other means. In other words, for a government the old public enterprise model is better in the sense that it could be used for winning votes, where the corporatization model cannot. For the public enterprise, or rather its management, privatization is better. They complain of government interference and look enviously at the private sector counterparts. Government ownership and monitoring is seen by them as a liability, restricting their ability to compete. For both parties to an agreement, corporatiza-

tion is an unsatisfactory compromise, satisfying neither. Either way, then, corporatization may prove to be simply a transition step on the path to privatization.

OWEN E. HUGHES

BIBLIOGRAPHY

McKinlay, Peter, 1987. *Corporatization: The Solution for State-Owned Enterprise?* Wellington, NZ: Victoria University Press.

CORRECTIONS ADMINISTRATION. The executive level management of any facility housing lawfully detained and/or incarcerated persons. There are operational distinctions between facilities housing pretrial detainees (jails and remand centers) and facilities holding persons serving court-imposed periods of incarceration (prisons, penitentiaries, and correctional institutions). In the United States, responsibility for corrections is shared among levels of government (i.e., federal, state, county, and local levels) and across jurisdictions and agencies within each level of government. Most European and Asian countries have centrally administered corrections systems that are responsible for prisoners awaiting trial, convicted but unsentenced inmates, and those serving court-imposed sentences. The centralized model assumes responsibility for corrections administration at all levels under national jurisdiction. The administrative responsibilities of the executive level managers of these various facilities, however, are essentially the same. Their primary objective is to ensure that persons charged into custody are incarcerated until their offensive behavior is corrected or until they are otherwise lawfully released.

Historical Background

The concept of incarceration in order to correct aberrant behavior is generally regarded to have its roots in the Pennsylvania Quaker laws established by William Penn in the United States in 1682. Prior to that time, incarceration was generally used for short-term detention pending the imposition of some fine or the execution of some corporal punishment. Incarceration was not the punishment. It was simply a means of detaining an offender until the punishment could be carried out. There was no pretense at rehabilitation. The Quakers, however, believed that the criminal was a perverse moral agent and that criminal behavior could be corrected through hard work and religious penitence. They founded what they referred to as a "house of correction" or "penitentiary" on these principles.

European roots to corrections are generally credited to Pope Clement XI and his architect Carlo Fontana, who constructed in 1704 an institution in Rome for delinquent boys known as the Hospice of San Michele. In addition to the principles of hard work and penitence, the Italian model included an absolute prohibition against communication—the entire sentence was served in complete silence. This correctional model assumed that the criminal could be rehabilitated and returned to society as a productive citizen. The European prisons that preceded the Hospice of San Michele, in contrast, were intended solely to incapacitate offenders until the punishment was executed—and frequently, the punishment was execution!

In the latter part of the sixteenth century, England had established the first "workhouses." In 1773, the *maison de force* (workhouse) concept was adopted in Flanders (Holland), primarily for housing and disciplining vagrants and beggars. These workhouses were founded on the principles of incapacitation, retribution, and deterrence—principles that still bolster the foundation of contemporary correctional models (Barnes and Teeters, 1947).

The underlying theory of incarceration is deterrence. The deterrence theory posits that a rational person will avoid criminal behavior if the severity of the punishment for that behavior and the perceived certainty of receiving the punishment combine to outweigh the benefits of the illegal conduct. If deterrence is to be effective, it must be swift, certain, and severe. The nature of the contemporary criminal justice system in the Western world is anything but swift, certain, and severe; thus the deterrence principle is significantly diminished. Criminals tend to believe that they will not get caught. Criminal conduct reinforces this notion each time they commit an offense and get away with it.

The retribution theory is another explanation for incarceration. Incarceration is a mechanism for social revenge against people who do not conform to societal standards. The retribution theory is grounded in the Biblical concept of *lex talionis,* which is commonly translated as "an eye for an eye and a tooth for a tooth" (Exodus 21:24). In its purest form, the punishment is matched to the offense. If an offender blinds his victim, then his punishment is blindness. Clearly, this concept cannot be literally applied in contemporary society. Society cannot condone raping a convicted rapist, or burning down the house of a convicted arsonist. While the death penalty is grounded on the "eye for an eye" principle, the number of murders committed would cause one to question its deterrent effect. It is generally acknowledged that the only real effect of the death penalty is incapacitation, which can also be accomplished through incarceration.

Incapacitation is the most fundamental theory of incarceration. If deterrence is not effective, and if retribution is not satisfying, incapacitation, at the very least, ensures that the violator will not have the opportunity to reoffend

during the period of incarceration. The cost of incapacitation is significant both in financial and human terms. In the fiscal year ending June 30, 1990, the total U.S. state and federal expenditure for correctional facilities was nearly $11.4 billion (Maguire and Pastore, 1994). In human terms, lengthy prison terms can be demoralizing and counterproductive if the ultimate goal is to return the offender to the community.

Three Models

The challenge for the contemporary corrections administrator is to maintain the inmate population in a safe, secure, and humane manner. John J. DiIulio (1987) describes three correctional administrative models: (1) the control model, (2) the consensual model, and (3) the responsibility model. The control model was in vogue in the 1950s and early 1960s. It emphasized a paramilitary style of discipline, obedience, work, and education. The consensual model emerged in the late 1960s and continued through the 1980s. It was a mixed model that embraced the paramilitary aspect of the control model, yet it was also characterized by an elaborate inmate grievance mechanism. The 1990s ushered in the responsibility model, which is often characterized by a decentralized unit management philosophy. Interestingly, the responsibility model also has a strict control feature founded on behavior modification principles. The responsibility model de-emphasizes paramilitary operations, and inmate classification and grievance systems are characteristic. The inmate is responsible for his or her own behavior and institutional privileges are earned through compliance and lost through misconduct.

DiIulio (1987) also offers three indices for measuring the conditions of confinement in a correctional facility: (1) order, (2) amenity, and (3) service. He defines the order index as the absence of individual or group misconduct as measured by the quantitative variables: assault rates, murder rates, disturbances, and riots. The amenity index is measured by the availability of things that enhance inmate comfort. These features are measured more subjectively; however, they are observable if present, and conspicuous if absent. These factors include such things as good food, adequate environmental/sanitation conditions, and access to recreational equipment/facilities. The service index is measured by the availability of things that may improve the inmates' life prospects. These would include educational programs, vocational training, decent health care, and unrestricted access to the courts.

Corrections administration is a dynamic field of public administration. There are significant changes occurring as a result of mandatory sentencing guidelines and conditions of confinement litigation. Inmate-initiated litigation is causing the courts to impose changes that impact on correctional policy, operations, services, environmental conditions, and physical plants. Ensuring order, amenity, and service standards in light of these challenges will require trained leaders in the future.

Leadership

Corrections administrators are the executive level managers who establish the standards for their facilities. They serve as role models for subordinate staff and facilitate the internal communications necessary to a vital organization. The strong correctional leader must be able to articulate a vision for the institution and instill a sense of teamwork and organizational commitment.

Recent research (Whitmore, 1994) suggests that correctional administrators have six principal areas of responsibility:

- to manage change within the institution;
- to provide leadership for the organization;
- to manage organizational performance;
- to conduct inspections and tours;
- to manage liability exposure; and
- to maintain a professional staff.

Managing change within the institution is a critical task. By their very nature, inmates and prison personnel are resistant to change. Change in one area frequently has some ripple effect in another. The integrated style of unit management that is the current correctional management model of choice is particularly sensitive to change. The impact of change must be carefully considered before implementation, and closely monitored and evaluated after implementation.

Leadership is another important area of responsibility for the corrections administrator. In times of crisis (e.g., in a riot or a hostage situation), the correctional leader assumes a centralized decisionmaking role over the life and death decisions that have to be made. During more routine operations, the corrections administrator serves as a symbol of security and control, while decentralizing decisions to lower levels of the organization. Well-run prisons have a "collapsible" organizational structure—and leaders that are capable of commanding a rigid, top-down paramilitary organization in times of crisis, yet comfortable managing a matrix structure for day-to-day operations.

Corrections administrators are charged with the responsibility of monitoring organizational performance. This requires an established mechanism for monitoring and evaluating key correctional indicators. The conditions of confinement indices proscribed by DiIulio (1987) (i.e., order, amenity, and service) encompass the critical indicators that enable corrections administrators to monitor prison conditions and to ensure organizational vitality.

The single most important feature of the monitoring mechanism is an effective communications network. Performance standards and measurement instruments must be developed. The monitoring mechanism must be complemented by a meaningful evaluation process that includes input from managers, supervisors, counselors, psychologists, medical staff, food service and maintenance personnel, corrections officers, and inmates.

Conducting inspections and tours is a formalized version of the technique that DiIulio (1991) refers to as management by walking around. A corrections administrator must maintain a presence inside the facility. That presence has both practical and symbolic significance. From a practical perspective, there is no substitute for direct observation and information gathering. Regular inspections and tours are symbolic in that they demonstrate commitment from the leadership of the organization. Identification with the correctional administrators by subordinate staff instills the organization with a sense of team membership and *esprit de corps*. Relationships develop and internal communications are enhanced.

Managing exposure to liability is emerging as a significant aspect of corrections administration. Litigation avoidance has become increasingly important as prisoner rights develop and court-ordered reforms are imposed. On June 30, 1993, 30 of the 50 U.S. states and the federal Bureau of Prisons had at least one or more adult prisons operating under court order (Maguire and Pastore, 1994). Managing the external environment is critical to managing liability exposure. Corrections administrators must educate themselves about and take a proactive approach toward the economic, social, and political influences affecting the corrections environment.

Maintaining a professional staff is important to effectively managing a correctional facility. A culturally diverse staff that is representative of the incarcerated population is the ideal foundation upon which to build a professional corrections staff. Recurrent training is required in order to maintain a professional identity. A management development program that grooms staff for promotion from within facilitates the team-building effort and encourages organizational commitment.

The executive level management of any facility housing lawfully detained and/or incarcerated persons requires multidimensional management experience. Corrections administration has evolved considerably over the past 300 years. Contemporary corrections administration requires the ability to recognize order and security as paramount concerns, while balancing the internal and external demands for prison amenities and services. Competent corrections administration requires extensive familiarity with institutional operations, correctional treatment theories, and current legal issues.

Current Trends and the Future of Corrections Administration

The cyclical prison reform movements that have periodically emerged over the years continue to present new challenges to corrections administrators. A current "back to basics" movement is calling for the elimination of recreational programs, televisions, and other inmate amenities. A greater emphasis is placed on work and basic education.

"Three strikes and you're out" laws are gaining great popularity in the U.S. These laws require mandatory life sentences for offenders convicted three times of certain violent offenses. These and other mandatory sentences will contribute to prison overcrowding.

The average age of the inmate population will rise as inmates begin serving longer sentences with less chance of early release. The higher health care costs of the elderly, along with the increasing incidence of hepatitis, HIV (human immunodeficiency virus), and TB (tuberculosis) in the correctional system will drive up both medical and operational costs.

Prisons and jails have recently become the target of privatization efforts. Some jurisdictions have resisted privatization on sovereignty issues (i.e., only the state can deprive a citizen of liberty, and this responsibility should not be delegated to a for-profit entity). Prison labor unions have also fought the nonunion private corrections corporations. Many state and local corrections agencies haven chosen to maintain the custody function, while privatizing inmate medical care and food services. These current correctional trends will certainly provide interesting administrative challenges for correctional administrators in the future.

JOHN S. SHAFFER

BIBLIOGRAPHY

Barnes, Harry Elmer and Negley K. Teeters, 1947. *New Horizons in Criminology.* New York: Prentice Hall, Inc.

DiIulio Jr., John J., 1991. *No Escape: The Future of American Corrections.* New York: Basic Books.

———, 1987. *Governing Prisons: A Comparative Study of Correctional Management.* New York: Free Press.

Maguire, Kathleen and Ann L. Pastore, 1994. *Sourcebook of Criminal Justice Statistics–1993.* Washington, D.C.: U.S. Department of Justice.

National Institute of Justice, 1991. *Crime File Study Guide, Death Penalty.* Washington, D.C.

U.S. Department of Justice, 1994. *Profile of Inmates in the United States and in England and Wales.* (October).

Whitmore, Robert C., 1994. "Correctional Administrator Task Assessment." *The Researcher,* Pennsylvania Department of Corrections, Planning, Research and Statistics Division (November).

CORRUPTION. Unsanctioned, usually condemned influence for some type of significant personal gain. Arnold Rogow and Harold Lasswell (1958) suggest that corruption can occur without any financial gain or incentive. It can include social, political, or ideological remuneration (Peter deLeon). Joseph Nye (1967) suggests that corrupt behavior includes acts of bribery (use of a reward to pervert the judgment of a person in a position of trust); nepotism (bestowal of patronage by reasons of descriptive relationship rather than merit); and misappropriation (illegal appropriation of public resources for private use).

Alexis de Tocqueville, a young French judicial official and author of the classic *Democracy in America* (1832), noted corruption as a potential component of the U.S. government and the dangers of and to its democratic society. Even before de Tocqueville, Niccolo Machiavelli studied the concept and role of corruption in political and social life. In his writings, Machiavelli knew corruption existed in Italian politics and would cause the demise of its ability to govern. Machiavelli defined corruption as the "process by which the virtue of the citizen was undermined and eventually destroyed" (Freidrich, 1989, p. 18). Even before Machiavelli, the act of bribery, a form of corruption, can be traced back to the government of the Roman empire in 74 B.C. (Bonadeo 1973; Noonan, 1984), and beyond.

John Peters and Susan Welch (1978) argue that "no matter what aspect of American politics is examined, the systematic study of corruption is hampered by the lack of an adequate definition." It goes beyond the simple personal greed that most people are inclined to think of. It can also include institutional and systemic forces that tolerate, condone, and in some cases actually encourage corrupt activities (deLeon, 1991).

David H. Bayley (1989, p. 935–952) defined corruption as follows: "while being tied to the act of bribery, (corruption) is a general term covering misuse of authority as a result of considerations of personal gain, which need not be monetary." Benson et al. (1978 p. xiii) modified Bayley's definition: "Political corruption is a general term covering all illegal or unethical use of government authority as a result of considerations of personal or political gain." James Scott (1972) suggests that there are three bases in order to define corruption: legality, public interest, and public opinion.

Theodore Lowi (1981) distinguishes between Big Corruption and Little Corruption. Big Corruption, or "Big C," refers to the "corruption that contributes to the decomposition, dissolution, or disorientation of the Constitution," which is "widely, though needlessly, feared." Those that are "Big C" go beyond the individual effects of corruption and "put the state itself at risk." Little Corruption, or "Little C," focuses on the private mores and "reflects or contributes to individual moral depravity." such as scandal. In their comparative text of political scandals around the world, Markovits and Silverstein (1978) identify scandal as a manifestation of liberal democratic rule and the industrial state. Only in a democratic state can scandal exist, they profess.

However, economists argue that in a pure world of free market competition, opportunities for corruption would not exist. Corruption exists because scarce resources aligned with allocation mechanism are open to political choice. Political choices, subject to the whim of those actors who govern, afford the opportunity for corruption. Therefore, according to Susan Rose-Ackerman (1978p. 1–2), in a true case of free market, these opportunities do not exist. She summarizes the economic-political definition of corruption as the:

> market system in which wide inequalities of income are taken for granted, [and a] democratic political system that grants a formal equality to each citizen's vote. . . . [P]olitical decisions that are made on the basis of majority preferences may be undermined by wide use of an illegal market as the method for allocation.

Her definition of "allocative mechanism" emphasizes corruption as a systemic problem. Because of the economic-political nature of the U.S. government system, corruption resides in the dividing line between market and nonmarket government allocation methods. Thus, due to the lack of clarity between the rules and expectations of the public and private sectors, the system is more susceptible to corruption.

Peters and Welch (1978 p. 976), in their search for a definition, argue that in an act of corruption there must be relationships between the parties present. The actors participating are corrupt depending on what officials, favors, payoffs, and donors are involved:

> We believe this process can meaningfully be partitioned into the "public official" involved, the actual "favor" provided by the public official, the "payoff" gained by the public official, and the "donor" of the payoff and/or "recipient" of the "favor" act.

To Peters and Welch, corruption does not exist in isolation and should be judged as a manner of degree.

Similarly, Arnold Heidenheimer (1989 pp. 161–163) places the definition of corruption on a color scale as 1) black: "which a majority consensus of both elite and mass opinion would condemn and would want to see punished on grounds of principle," 2) white: "the majority of both elite and mass opinion probably would not vigorously support an attempt to punish a form of corruption that they regard as tolerable, and 3) gray: which "indicates that some

elements, usually elites, may want to see the action punished, others not, and the majority may well be ambiguous." However, this leaves us with the dilemma of defining those corruptive acts that fall within the "gray" area.

Likewise, Johnston (1982), noting the difficulty in defining corruption, summarizes, "we should not expect to find a sharp distinction between corruption and non corrupt actions. Instead, we will find fine gradations of judgment, reflecting a variety of equivocations, mitigating circumstances, and attributed motives."

Corruption can take many forms, but how does the public sector deal with corruption? Anechiarico and Jacobs (1994) provide several eras of corruption control and the "visions" reforms: antipatronage, Progressive, scientific management, panoptic, and revisionist. These reforms are important not only to the definition of corruption in the political sense, but to the field of public administration as a measure of control.

The first vision, antipatronage, operated roughly between 1870 and 1900 during the civil service reform era, when it was believed that the strategy for good government was to focus on personnel systems. The cause of corruption, according to civil service reformers such as Carl Schurz and Leonard White, was the partisan control of personnel. It was believed that patronage would tear the moral fiber of American government. To the reformers, those devoted to public service should hold the highest principles and have outstanding credentials. Antipatronage movers like Julius Bing (1868) saw civil service reform as essential to save the government from "evil." He noted, "At present, there is no organization save that of corruption; no system save that of chaos; no test of integrity save that of partisanship; no test of qualification save that of intrigue."

The reformers' strategy targeted credentials, competency testing, and the merit system as key policy initiatives. As for public administration, corruption controls were more concerned with peer enforcement of norms and personal controls rather than organizational or managerial reforms.

During the Progressive movement for corruption control, the emphasis was professionalism in public administration and management. Progressives found the "key to rooting out corruption was complete reform of the political system, not just personnel policy. Corruption control was necessary for government efficiency and democratic accountability" (Anechiarico and Jacobs, p. 467). Woodrow Wilson, one of the most prominent of the Progressives, professed integrity in government and a corruption-free administration, but fell short of a plan. The questions of governance would be answered by merging the morals of U.S. democracy with the European administration's scientific superiority; the result: an honest, democratic, and scientifically sound administration (Nelson, 1982, p. 121).

The solution, posed by Frank Goodnow (1900), was a dichotomy of public administration and politics; managing government would be regulated by a set of standards and conduct, free of political intervention. Policy reform would turn to electoral reforms, independent regulatory commissions, administrative expertise, and politics-free administration. Here the implications for public administration would be enforced by standards of efficiency.

The Progressive movement toward corruption-free government found itself obsolete in terms of the scientific management vision. This era emphasized bureaucratic control over more general reforms. Inadequate design and control of organizations were presumed to be the problem behind corrupt acts, rather than political interference and public mores. Leonard White and Frank Goodnow were in the forefront of bringing scientific management principles to the public sector. Although scientific management was more goal oriented toward efficiency and rationality, out of it came a belief that administrative integrity could be achieved through systemic control. External control, stressed by Luther Gulick, was the strategy of anticorruption reform. Goodnow and Harold Seidman (1941) argued for external control as a necessary condition of an efficient, and therefore corruption-free, public administration. William Herlands, a central figure in the anticorruption effort, and those like him, expanded the definition of corruption to include appearance of conflict of interest, failure to fully disclose all financial interest, misstatements on job applications, unauthorized use of government telephones, leaving work early, accepting favors and gifts, and entering into public contracts with morally tainted private companies.

Anechiarico and Jacobs argue that "a new, panoptic vision of corruption control now influences and shapes public administration." They trace this new vision as an outgrowth of the previous anticorruption reforms. Pointing to the Watergate scandal, Anechiarico and Jacobs (1994) describe a panoptic era that began in the 1970s and continued into the 1990s, which focuses on the enforcement of laws against corruption as a means of administration. Its strategy is based on strong law enforcement to combat the lack of monitoring in the public sector.

Today, the public sector is often perceived to be corrupt, and therefore all public employees are suspect. Public perception regards "public officials, politicians, managers, and rank and file personnel as seekers of corrupt opportunities and . . . government as an organizational form that generates abundant opportunities for corruption" (Anechiarico and Jacobs, p. 468).

Despite progress, there has not been agreement on methods of control. These reforms and theories take on many forms. Banfield (1995) sums up the rationalist's perspective on government: "corruption is thought of (when it comes under notice) as something that must be eliminated 'no matter what the cost.'" Benson et al., (1978)

call for more education in the schools, churches, and even from the media in the area of ethics and civics. They also suggest funding from the federal and state level to "create" honest government in the law enforcement and judicial arena.

It is often thought that deregulation, by putting more decisions in the private sector, will reduce corruption. However, Rose-Ackerman (1978 p. 207), an economist, theorizes: "Deregulation may simply mean the substitution of a corrupt private official for a public one. It is not at all obvious that this is much of an achievement." The author suggests that perfect competition of all markets will prevent corruption. However, reaching that goal of deregulation under U.S. government is not possible.

DeLeon (1991) offers an examination of the "systemic conditions and incentive structures that incubate and inculcate corruption." Altering conditions so that opportunities are less available will reduce graft, bribery, and other crimes of corruption. His suggestion: a mixture of "embracing both the individual and systemic causes of political corruption because individuals are the operating units of the system." He recognizes that a total elimination of corruption would be politically and socially unacceptable. He rejects the traditional measures of more law and regulation, but suggests amending current laws with more deterrent penalties. "The key to change would be to write regulations and laws with genuine deterrent power, that is , one whose penalties, when (not if) enforced, would exceed by significant amounts the marginal value of the corrupt activities. The expected value of the illegal transactions must be sufficiently lowered (by raising either the fine or the risk of discovery) so that they are no longer seen as sustainable, worthwhile 'investments'."

In addition, deLeon suggests more "sunshine"-type legislation and regulation in additon to a sustained public attention to the policy process. By allowing more public access to the public decisionmaking processes, citizens, whether through the media or self-participation, keep a closer eye on potential attempts at corruption. He continues: "The good news is that there are policies that can be executed to reduce the incidence of political corruption. The bad news is that the easy remedies (usually ascribed to individuals) are not effective and the hard ones (dealing with systemic issues) are difficult to implement."

Reform is necessary. It requires a middle ground between the personal and the institutional structure that allow corruption to happen. DeLeon suggests that this type of reform may be politically costly and therefore more difficult to implement by elected officials.

In his review of the literature, deLeon (1991) notes, "many scholars would look upon corruption as simply another unavoidable, but relatively minor, cost of doing business," while others "declare corruption to be an integral, functional activity of government." He states that, if corruption is a part of the economics of running government or just a part of the structure that runs government, then by accepting this position there is no need to call for reform, just an acceptance of "what is there." Although he believes reform is necessary, he notes the opposing view:

> By much the same argument, if we find that corruption extracts such a relatively small price from the body politic and is as difficult and expensive to exercise as American history would convincingly demonstrate—that is, if the costs of tolerating corruption were perceived as less than the benefits of eradicating it—then best leave it be. The remedy game would simply not be worth the criminal candle, hence rendering a similar conclusion.

Garment (1991 p. 289) notes the present day efforts of corruption control: "We have invented a machine that will spend tens of millions of dollars to try to put Oliver North in jail while it strenuously ignores the systemic sores that caused the worst of the Iran-Contra scandal and they continue to fester."

As early as 1904, Henry Jones Ford recognized that an anticorruption goal could conflict with the goals of efficiency and effectiveness. He stated:

> It is better that government and social activity should go on in any way than that they should not go on at all. Slackness and decay are more dangerous to a nation than corruption. . . . The graft system is bad, but it is better for city government to lend itself to the forces of progress even through corrupt inducements than to toss the management of affairs out upon the goose-common of ignorance and incapacity, however honest. Reform which arrests the progress of the community will not be tolerated by an American City (pp. 678, 682–683).

Even during the 1950s, theorists noted that organizational controls over corruption had their costs. Nigro, in 1959, noted:

> [W]aging this type of battle[against corruption] becomes a habit and tends to continue long after the enemy is routed or voluntarily retires. Since civil service appropriations tend to be limited in the first place, concentrating resources on combating an imaginary foe means neglecting the development and expansion of urgently required or highly desirable activities such as more vigorous recruiting, personnel research, and training.

Not only would costs be a factor in anticorruption efforts, but the effectiveness of a public manager to administer also would diminish. Sayre and Kaufman (1965), in their study of New York City government in the 1950s, recognized the limiting effect on the discretion of the public official due to the increased volume of formal rules. In *The Politics of the Administrative Process* (1991), political scientists

James Fesler and Donald Kettl recognize the tangible and intangible costs of "control systems":

> Excessive controls can disrupt consistent administration and produce inequities. Excessive controls multiply requirements for review of proposed decisions, increase red tape, and delay action. So much energy can be spent attempting to control administrative activities, in fact little time is left to do the job at hand. Excessive controls, therefore, may dull administration's responsiveness to its public (p. 321).

Interestingly, contemporary rational choice theorists will argue that corruption is sometimes efficient. It is sometimes used for barter of political influence for cash that can produce social benefits. They argue that the costs of the unethical behavior must be weighed against the social benefit derived.

According to Naomi Caiden (1979 p. 295), "everyone knows what corruption is, and heart-searching over marginal cases is not worthwhile." This leaves us with the feeling that in certain cases, which we recognize as "marginal cases," some sort of corruption is accepted and not worth addressing. In fact, according to Theodore Lowi's (1982) definition, Big C is often justifiable. Johnston (1982 p. 186) proposes a "strategy of accommodation, a way perhaps to allow us to worry (and to get angry) a bit less."

More recently, in *Reinventing Government,* David Osborne and Ted Gabler (1992) argue that too much attention is being paid to minor acts of corruption and the idea of a corruption-free government. They recommend fewer corruption controls and more latitude for public managers.

JOSEPH DeIORIO AND KEITH CARRINGTON

BIBLIOGRAPHY

Anechiarico, Frank and James B. Jacobs, 1994. "Visions of Corruption Control and the Evolution of American Public Administration." *Public Administration Review,* 54(5): 465–473.

Bayley, D., 1989. "The Effects of Corruption in a Developing Nation." In A. J. Heidenheimer, M. Johnson and V. LeVine, eds. *Political Corruption: A Handbook,* 935–952. New Brunswick, NJ: Transaction Publishers.

Banfield, Edward C., 1995. "Corruption as a Feature of Governmental Organization." *The Journal of Law and Economics,* vol. xviii, no. 3: 587-605.

Benson, George C. S. et al., 1978. *Political Corruption in America.* Lexington, MA: D. C. Heath.

Bing, Julius, 1868. "Our Civil Service." *Putnam Magazine,* New Series, II, no. 8 (August) 233–236.

Bonedeo, A., 1973. *Corruption, Conflict, and Power in the Works and Times of Niccolo Machiavelli.* Los Angeles: University of California Press.

Caiden, Naomi, 1979. Shortchanging the Public." *Public Administration Review,* vol. 39, no. 3 (May-June) 294.

deLeon, Peter, 1993. *Thinking About Political Corruption.* Armonk, NY: M. E. Sharpe.

De Tocqueville, Alexis, 1946. *Democracy in America.* Vol. 2. New York: Alfred A. Knopf.

Fesler, James W. and Donald F. Kettl, 1991. *The Politics of the Administrative Process.* Chatham, NJ: Chatham House.

Ford, Henry James, 1904. "Municipal Corruption." *Political Science Quarterly,* 19 (December) 678, 682–683.

Friedrich, C.J., 1989. "Corruption Concepts in Historical Perspective." In A.J. Heidenheimer, M. Johnson and V. LeVine, eds. *Political Corruption: A Handbook,* 15–28. New Brunswick, NJ: Transaction Publishers.

Garment, Suzanne, 1991. *Scandal: The Culture of Mistrust in American Politics.* New York: Random House.

Goodnow, Frank J., 1900. *Politics and Administration.* New York: Russell and Russell.

Heidenheimer, Arnold J., 1989. "Perspectives on the Perception of Corruption." In A.J. Heidenheimer, M. Johnson and V. LeVine, eds. *Political Corruption: A Handbook,* 149–163. New Brunswick, NJ: Transaction Publishers.

Johnston, Michael, 1982. *Political Corruption and Public Policy in America.* Monterey, CA: Cole.

Klitgaard, Robert, 1988. *Controlling Corruption.* Berkeley: University of California Press.

Lowi, Theodore J., 1981. "The Intelligent Person's Guide to Political Corruption." *Public Affairs,* series 81, Bulletin No. 82 (September) 2.

Markovits, A. and M. Silverstein, 1978. *The Politics of Scandal.* New York: Holmes & Meier.

Nelson, William, E., 1982. *The Roots of American Bureaucracy: 1830–1900.* Cambridge, MA: Harvard University Press.

Nigro, Felix A., 1959. *Public Personnel Administration.* New York: Henry Holt.

Noonan, John Thomas, 1984. *Bribes.* New York: Macmillan.

Nye, Jr., Joseph S, 1967. "Corruption and Political Development: A Cost-Benefit Analysis." *American Political Science Review,* vol. 61, no. 2: 417–427.

Osborne, David and Ted Gaebler, 1992. *Reinventing Government.* Reading, MA: Addison-Wesley.

Peters, John G., and Susan Welch, 1978. "Political Corruption: A Search for Definitions and a Theory." *American Political Science Review,* vol. 72, no. 3 (September) 974–984.

Rogow, Arnold A. and Harold D. Lasswell, 1963. *Power, Corruption and Rectitude.* Englewood Cliffs, NJ: Prentice-Hall.

Rose-Ackerman, Susan, 1978. *Corruption: A Study of Political Economy.* New York: Academic Press.

Sayre, Wallace S. and Herbert Kaufman, 1965. *Governing New York City: Politics in the Metropolis.* New York: W.W. Norton.

Scott, James, 1972. *Comparative Political Corruption.* Englewood Cliffs, NJ: Prentice Hall.

Seidman, Harold, 1941. *Investigating Municipal Administration: A Study of New York.* New York: Institute of Public Administration, Columbia University.

COST ACCOUNTING. The gathering and processing of cost information for external reporting and internal decisionmaking.

In the past, cost accounting indicated providing information for external financial reporting. Many accountants and managers saw the purpose of cost accounting as distinct from managerial accounting. Cost accounting information was used for external reporting and managerial accounting was used for internal management. Other accountants and managers did not see such a strong distinction. They acknowledged a relationship between cost and managerial accounting; however, they saw managerial accounting playing a supporting role to cost accounting. Over the last ten years, the role of cost accounting has been expanding. Today, many managers are using cost accounting information for decisionmaking on internal matters. A major purpose of cost accounting continues to be to provide information that meets the requirements for external reporting in the public and private sectors. However, managers have realized that the requirements for identifying and measuring costs for the external financial reporting of an organization's activities may be less stringent than what is necessary for making decisions inside the organization. Increasingly, cost accounting is seen as having the dual purpose of providing useful cost information for decisionmaking and the required information for external reporting.

The change in perspective in the private sector can be attributed to a number of factors such as:

- shorter product life cycles;
- globalization;
- rapidly changing technology;
- an increasing emphasis on a customer focus;
- value-chain analysis;
- a general interest in continuous improvement.

Cost accounting information is being used in a similar way in the public sector. The expanded use of cost accounting information in the public sector can be traced to any number of influences such as:

- the need for greater efficiency because of shrinking resources;
- an increasing emphasis on accountability;
- the view that lots of good information for decision making is worthwhile;
- the belief that if it is good for the private sector, it must be good for the public sector.

The new perspective emphasizes costs beyond those that have been traditionally captured within the cost accounting system. In addition to traditional cost information, defined as a measurement of the sacrifice of specific resources that were purchased for some financial consideration, there is a recognition of long- and short-run costs that may be more broadly defined as psychic costs and social costs. Regardless, all of the costs accounted for involve some tangible or intangible sacrifice (such as harming the organization's public image) and have some value (either monetary or nonmonetary). In a sense, the cost accounting view has moved from a profit-maximizing to a wealth-maximizing perspective.

The new emphasis on the use of cost accounting information can be seen in two popular techniques: activity-based costing and strategic cost management. Each of the techniques is discussed below. They are important because each represents a way to expand the use of cost accounting information. Although neither one represents new thinking, they do help to refocus the attention of the information generator (the accountant) and the user (the decision-maker) in organizations.

Activity-based costing, or ABC, is used to trace the tasks of the organization (activities) to their causes (drivers) and, subsequently, to the services or products offered by the organization. Although over the years managers and accountants have been trying to do this with cost systems, the accountants and managers in some cases have not been successful because the systems have not accurately modeled the underlying processes. Altering the existing cost systems to provide a better model of the processes is difficult because of vested interests and tradition. As Euske has argued in a chapter in *Implementing Activity-Based Costing* (1991), possibly activity-based costing's most significant contribution is that it challenges the inflexibility of costing systems that are in place in organizations, by providing an alternative way to discuss cost flows. Challenging this inflexibility threatens the established order in organizations, which in turn makes the implementation of activity-based costing systems difficult.

Three key terms in activity-based costing are activity, driver, and process. An activity is a task performed in the organization that can be assigned a cost (e.g., labor hours of task times cost per hour = cost of task). Examples of tasks include entering an order entry, machining a part, and purchasing supplies. A driver generates a cost or an activity. A driver can be thought of as an event or decision; it is not an activity. In the ABC framework, activities do not cause activities. Examples of drivers are a delivery deadline, a management decision, new legislation, a missed schedule, or a material shortage. Activities are associated with drivers and then costs are associated with each driver. A process is a chain of drivers (e.g., a customer deadline leads to an order placed, which leads to a material order, which leads to a production decision). ABC, like most popular management techniques, has generated its own lexicon and literature. The Consortium for Advanced Manufacturing–International (CAM-I), a nonprofit research consortium, has published a glossary of ABC terms. *An ABC Manager's Primer* (1993) by Cokins, Stratton, and Helbling is an excellent introduction to ABC.

Strategic cost management emphasizes the use of cost information for strategic decisionmaking and management. Quite simply, the core argument of strategic cost management is: do not use cost data myopically, but use them in the strategic analysis of your processes and manage accordingly. Strategic cost management emphasizes that cost accounting information is extremely valuable and should be used to its fullest benefit to the organization. As Shank and Govindarajan argue in their book *Strategic Cost Analysis* (1989), "Accounting exists within a business primarily to facilitate the development and implementation of business strategy" (p. xi). Although Shank and Govindarajan focus on the private sector in their writings, strategic cost management is equally applicable in the public sector. Management can use the data to help formulate strategies, communicate the strategies, develop and carry out the tactics associated with the strategies, and develop and implement appropriate controls.

In the federal government, cost accounting is probably most readily identified with Cost Accounting Standards and the Cost Accounting Standards Board. The standards are an attempt to standardize cost accounting techniques across contractors to the federal government. The standards are needed because in many cases the government does not operate in a competitive market. Hence, the price for goods purchased by the government is not set by many buyers and sellers. This situation opens the door for potentially unfair practices by the federal government or contractors. Therefore, to generate a baseline for fair pricing, cost accounting standards are used. When the federal government is purchasing commodities that have prices set in a competitive market with many buyers and sellers, requiring the use of the Cost Accounting Standards may make the total cost of competitively priced products ultimately more expensive to the government. The first Cost Accounting Standards Board (CASB) published standards during the 1970s. It issued 19 statements numbered one to twenty (one statement was written but not issued). In 1980, Congress eliminated the Cost Accounting Standards Board, but not the standards. After 1980, problems concerning the standards arose and the executive branch of the federal government tried to address the problems. However, the legality of the attempts was questioned because only Congress had the power to change the standards. The end result was a new Cost Accounting Standards Board created by Public Law 100-679 (1988). Hubbard in an article in *Management Accounting* (1990) presents an interesting analysis of the history of the Cost Accounting Standards Boards.

Sourwine, in a *Management Accounting* (1991) article, groups the cost accounting standards created by the Cost Accounting Standards Board into three general categories: fixed assets, deferred compensation, and cost allocations. The standards *per se* are generally not considered controversial. However, interpretation of the standards is another issue. That is, few professionals have difficulty in understanding and accepting the standards; they have considerable difficulty agreeing on how the standards should be applied. For instance, one of the standards requires that certain types of costs be accumulated in homogeneous cost pools. Collecting costs in homogeneous groupings is not controversial. Deciding what particular costs belong in a given pool, however, has been contested by contractors and the government's representatives.

KEN J. EUSKE

BIBLIOGRAPHY

Cokins, Gray, Allen Stratton, and Jack Helbling, 1993. *ABC Managers' Primer.* Arlington, TX: Institute of Management Accountants and Consortium for Advanced Manufacturing–International.

Euske, K. J., 1991. *Activity Costing: A Historical Perspective.* In F. Collins, ed., *Implementing Activity Based Costing.* New York: Executive Enterprises, Inc.

Hubbard, Robert B., 1990. "Return of the Cost Accounting Standards Board: New Procurement Problems Called for New Solutions." *Management Accounting* (October) 56–59.

Shank, John and Vijay Govindarajan, 1989. *Strategic Cost Analysis.* Homewood, IL: Irwin.

Sourwine, Darrel A., 1991. "Cost Accounting Standards: Putting the Pieces Together." *Management Accounting* (July) 44–49.

COST OVERRUNS.
Broadly, whenever realized costs exceed the prior cost estimates. This, in turn, is almost inevitable whenever uncertainty is present.

Background

Cost overruns are not new and they appear in both private and public sector projects. In fact, the following illustration shows that cost overruns have been prevalent throughout history. In the beginning of the Christian era, the Roman Empire decided to build an aqueduct for the town of Troas in Asia.

Costs started to outrun the estimates as soon as the construction began. According to the historian Edward Gibbon, "the young magistrate, observing that the town of Troas was indifferently supplied with water, obtained from the munificence of Hadrian three hundred myriads of drachmas for the construction of a new aqueduct. But in the execution of the work the charge amounted to more than double the estimate, and the officers of the revenue began to murmur." The complaint of the revenue collectors was silenced by the generosity of the wealthy Julius Atticus, who met all of the extra cost out of his pocket. Since no Julius Atticus lives today, the taxpayer and the public treasury foot the bill, be it a civil or military project. (Nocic, 1970).

In the more recent past, we have seen cost overruns abound on major construction, pioneering energy projects, and in military procurement where uncertainty is widespread. The New Orleans Superdome, which had an initial cost estimate in 1967 of $46 million, was completed in 1975 at a final cost of $175 million. The Alaskan pipeline had an estimated cost of $900 million in 1970 and a final cost of $7.7 billion in 1977. Rancho Seco Nuclear Unit had an estimated cost of $142.5 million in 1967 and was completed at a final cost of $347 million. The M1 tank had an initial unit cost estimate of $765,000 in 1973 but by 1982 was estimated to cost $2.7 million.

All of these cost numbers are expressed in nominal dollars including the effect of inflation, and they also reflect changes in schedule and design. Many of the projects were organized, funded, and supervised by government agencies, which might help to account for the extent of the cost overruns observed. However, the history of cost overruns on nuclear power plants, the vast majority of which were built by privately owned electric utilities, indicates that cost overruns (cost underestimation bias) is not purely a government contracting phenomenon. Table II shows the extent of cost overruns after subtracting the effect of inflation. For example, in the 1950s 55 weapons

TABLE I

Project	Initial Cost Estimate	Final Cost	Unadjusted Cost Ratio: Final/Initial Cost Est.
New Orleans Superdome	$46 million (1967)	$175 million (1975)	3.8
Alaskan Pipeline	$900 million (1970)	$7.7 billion (1977)	8.6
Rancho Seco Nuclear Unit	$46 million (1967)	$175 million (1975)	3.8
M1 Tank Unit Cost (1973)	$765 thousand (1982)	$2.7 million	3.6

Costs are all expressed in nominal terms including inflation (Quirk and Terasawa, 1986; Gates and Midler, 1985).

TABLE II

Items Estimated	Adjusted Cost Ratio: Actual/Initial Est.[a]	Number of Projects	Deviation
Weapons, 1950s	1.89	55	1.36
Weapons, 1960s	1.40	25	.39
Public Works:			
Highway	1.26	49	.63
Water Project	1.39	49	.70
Building	1.63	59	.83
Ad hoc	2.14	15	1.36
Major construction	2.18	12	1.59
Energy process plants	2.53	10	.51[b]

[a]Actual cost is in real terms and adjusted for inflation.
[b]It is unknown how the standard deviation is affected by using the ratio of the last available estimate to the first available estimate instead of actual to originally estimated costs. (Merrow *et al.*, 1979, p. 73).

projects cost, on the average, 1.89 times more than the initial estimates, while 10 energy process plants cost 2.53 times more than their initial estimates.

Causes of Cost Overruns

Empirical Approach

The causes of cost overruns (or cost understimation), in a sense, could be empirically determined by comparing the initial parameters used for the estimation with actual experience. The Department of Defense, for example, uses the Selected Acquisition Reports (SAR) to explain cost variances from the baseline in terms of one or more of the following categories:

Economic change. A change due only to the forces of the economy, such as rising inflation rates.

Quantity change. A change in the quantity of the item to be procured.

Schedule change. A change in the contractor's completion date, or other intermediate time line changes for development or production.

Engineering change. A change in the physical characteristic of an item.

Estimating change. A change in the program cost due to a correction in the cost estimate, not attributable to the above categories.

Other. A change in cost due to unforeseen contract incentives, or other unpredictable matters.

Support change. Cost changes associated with training, training equipment, and so forth.

A criticism of this "factual" approach is that although it inevitably produces varied factors correlated with the cost overruns, it often fails to identify the underlying casuality.

The observed factors may merely represent a symptom of the cost overruns. This SAR approach often remains relatively limited in its predictive ability of the cost overruns.

Analytical Approach

Selection Bias and Cost Overruns. Recent literature points out that a truly unbiased cost estimation procedure can generate data consistent with an *observed* cost underestimation bias. This arises because cost estimates are not only estimates of the costs of completed projects, but also are used by decisionmakers involved in planning and overseeing a project. There is an observed estimation bias when, on average, observed cost estimates differ from the realized costs of completed projects (as adjusted for inflation). A selection bias is introduced into comparisons between observed cost estimates and observed final costs of projects because certain projects are rejected or abandoned on the basis of cost estimates.

To illustrate, suppose there is a project with its unknown cost distributed as a normal distribution with a mean $M = \$100$ million and a standard deviation of $\$S$ million. Let $P = \$100$ million be the decisionmaker's break-even cost, the maximum cost over which the project becomes rejected. Under this circumstance, the project is initiated only when estimates are below \$100 million. In other words, the project commences when the estimates drawn are from the left side of point A in Figure I. This means that, on the average, the cost estimate for the initiated project is lower than \$100 million, the true mean of realized cost. Average estimates for this example are $E1 = \$92.1$ million when the standard deviation is $S = \$10$ million, and $E2 = \$84.3$ million when the standard deviation is $S = \$20$ million. The "underestimation" corresponds to 8.6 percent and 18.6 percent cost overruns, respectively.

FIGURE I

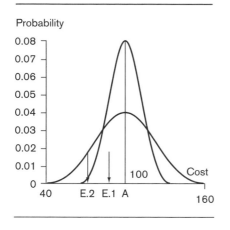

The figure shows that the greater the uncertainty, the larger the cost underestimation and corresponding cost overrun. Table III also shows that when the decisionmaker's break-even cost (P) becomes more ambitious (i.e., smaller), the overrun grows larger. For example, when the break-even cost is set at $P = \$88$ million, the average cost estimates for the two distributions become $83.2 million and $76.1 million, respectively.

The illustration demonstrates three salient aspects of cost overruns:

- the presence of uncertainty creates observed cost overruns;
- the greater the uncertainty, the greater the overruns;
- the more ambitious the project goals, the greater the cost overruns.

These phenomena are consistent with an unbiased cost estimation procedure and consistent with the actual experience of overruns.

Contact Type and Cost Overruns. So far, we have discussed a situation where there are no incentive problems in making estimates and executing a project. This, however, may not be the most common situation. The objective and the information available between the procurer and the contractor are not always the same. This creates what economists call an asymmetric information environment and creates incentive (principal/agency) problems. To investigate incentive problems, we will study cost overruns in the following three major contract environments: firm fixed price, cost-plus, and incentive fee contract.

Firm Fixed Price Contract. If all projects are contracted using a firm fixed price contract (FFP) with no renegotiation, then we would expect few cost overruns due to incentive problems. Under FFP, contractors will be paid a fixed sum of money irrespective of cost outcome. Since the contractors will bear the entire cost consequence, they will have no incentives to pad costs or to shirk effort in reducing costs (moral hazard behavior). Moreover, under FFP, contractors are less likely to reveal their cost estimates or realized costs. Consequently, the public will rarely observe cost overruns. However, when a contractor is more risk averse than the procurer, the procurer may pay more under the FFP contract than under other contracts.

Cost-Plus Contract. In other contract types where cost consequences influence the payment amount, such as cost-plus, or a price/cost-incentive contract, cost overruns due to incentives are more likely. In a cost-plus contract, a contractor is paid realized accounting costs plus a fixed-fee. In such contracts, the contractor has little incentive to invest in cost-reducing activities. Under this contract, a lower cost estimate enhances the probability of winning the contract without reducing profit, so cost underestimation becomes the preferred strategy and cost overruns become more prevalent.

Incentive Contract. The incentive contract is an "intermediary" contract between fixed price and cost-plus contracts. In this contract, the contractor is partially responsible for cost consequences. If a project has cost over-

TABLE III. Average Cost Underestimation Bias as a Function of Uncertainty and Breakeven Cost

	Smaller Uncertainty with $S = 10$	Greater Uncertainty with $S = 20$
No Cost Selection Criteria	$100 million (zero cost overruns)	$100 million (zero cost overruns)
Less Ambitious Plan ($P = 100$)	$92.1 million (8.6% overruns)	$84.3 million (18.6% overruns)
More Ambitious Plan ($P = 88$)	$83.2 million (20% overruns)	$76.1 million (31.5% overruns)

The computation is based on normal distribution with a mean of $100 million. The overrun percentage is computed by the ratio of the mean over the estimate.

TABLE IV

Procurer's Overrun share, a	Expected Fee, Contractor $F(a)$	Expected Cost, E(C)	Expected Cost Overruns, E(C − B)	Procurer's Expected Payment, E(P)	Expected Contractor Utility, E(U)
0.00	2.25	5.00	0.00	7.25	1.00
0.10	2.20	5.11	0.11	7.21	1.00
0.20	2.14	5.22	0.22	7.183	1.00
0.30	**2.07**	**5.36**	**0.36**	**7.179**	**1.00**
0.40	2.00	5.51	0.51	7.20	1.00
0.50	1.91	5.69	0.69	7.26	1.00
0.60	1.81	5.92	0.92	7.36	1.00
0.70	1.68	6.20	1.20	7.53	1.00
0.80	1.53	6.61	1.61	7.82	1.00
0.90	1.33	7.30	2.30	8.41	1.00
1.00	1.00	16.51	11.51	17.51	1.00

Contractor's utility function is given as $U = U(\pi) = \pi^{0.5}$. The profit function is given as: $\pi = \{F + B + a(C − B)\} − C − E$, where $C = 5 + X − \ln(E)$. The X in the cost function represents a random variable and takes the value 1 or − 1 with an equal probability of 0.5. The profit-maximizing effort level becomes $E = (1 − a)$ in this formulation. The fee is computed to keep the contractor's expected utility constant.

runs (i.e., the cost estimate [bid] is less than the realized cost), then the contractor becomes responsible for some fraction of the cost overrun. If there is a cost underrun, then the contractor is rewarded by being allowed to keep a portion of the underrun. If we represent a as the procurer's cost-sharing ratio for overruns, then the payment to the contractor is given by:

$$\text{Payment to the Contractor} = (\text{Fee} + \text{Bid}) + a(\text{Cost} − \text{Bid})$$

The profit to the contractor is the payment minus the cost of production and the cost of nonreimbursible effort. The profit formulation here incorporates the general case where not all efforts to reduce costs may be observable or reimbursible. Some management efforts or a new innovative production method may fall into this category. We can express the contractor's profit as follows:

$$\text{Profit} = \text{Payment} − \text{Cost} − \text{Effort}$$

$$= \text{Fee} + [1 − a] \cdot [\text{Bid} − \text{Cost}] − \text{Effort}$$

Optimal Cost Share (a) to the Procurer—A procurer might be interested in finding the sharing ratio, a, that minimizes the expected payment for a given bid. The bid reflects the prevailing level of competition in the industry. This is because a contractor's cost share $(1 − a)$ is positive to prevent cost padding. With the positive $(1 − a)$, bidders receive a higher profit with a larger bid, as long as they are the contractor selected. A high bid, however, reduces their chance of selection. Contractors must balance these two factors in setting their bids. The choice of the cost share

depends on the contractor's risk preference as well as the contractor's ability to reduce costs. Most people are risk-averse. They prefer a certain outcome to a gamble with the same expected return. For example, they prefer a sure gain of $50 to receiving a 50 percent chance of $100 and a 50 percent chance of nothing, even though the gamble's expected return is the same (0.5 * $100 + 0.5 * $0 = $50.) Anyone who is indifferent to a certain outcome and a gamble with the same expected return is risk-neutral. When the contractor is risk-neutral, the best contract is an FFP contract that leaves all the risk to the contractor ($a = 0$). This is because the agent will maximize the cost-reducing effort without imposing any risk premium on the price to the procurer. If, on the other hand, the contractors are risk-averse, then the procurer must compensate them for bearing risk. A higher fee must be paid with a higher contractor's sharing ratio $(1 − a)$, to maintain the same expected utility for the contractor. With a risk-averse contractor, an FFP may become too expensive for the procurer. The optimal contract, in this case, must balance the opposing effect of an increased risk premium and the reduced production cost associated with the increased contractor sharing ratio, $(1 − a)$. The total payment is now expressed as a function of a as shown below:

$$\text{Payment} = F(a) + B + a[C(a) = B]$$

where

$$F(a) = \text{Fee as a decreasing function of } a$$
$$B = \text{Bid}$$
$$C(a) = \text{Cost as an increasing function of } a$$

FIGURE II

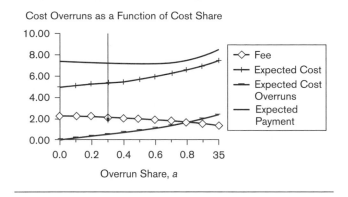

Cost Overruns as a Function of Cost Share

Overrun Share, *a*

Table IV illustrates a numerical example of the previous equation. The table is constructed assuming that the contractor's bid is B = 5 and the cost can be either low or high with an equal probability. For the different sharing ratios shown in Column 1, an effort level is chosen to maximize the contractor's expected utility. Fees are also chosen so that the contractor's expected utility remains constant. For example, if the procurer's overrun share ratio is zero, so all the risk is borne by the contractor, then the procurer will only pay the sum of the bid (B = 5) and the somewhat larger fee (F = 2.25). The procurer's total payment in this case becomes 7.25 irrespective of the cost outcome.

If, on the other hand, the procurer's overrun share is 1, so there is no cost risk to the contractor, then the procurer must pay the sum of the bid (B = 5) plus a smaller fee (F = 1) plus the full share of cost overuns. The cost overrun can either be low, 10.51, or high, 12.51, with the expected cost overrun equal to 11.51. The expected total payment becomes 17.51 = 1 + 5 + 11.51. The table also shows that a larger *a* increases the expected cost overruns. Although the expected cost overruns are minimized with *a* = 0, such a contract may not be optimal from the procurer's point of view. In fact, when the average cost overrun is 0.36 as in *a* = 0.3, the procurer's expected payment is minimized.

This example illustrates that the magnitude of cost overruns is influenced by the type of the contract and the cost overrun sharing ratio. It shows that cost overruns, *ceteris paribus*, become more likely and pronounced with a lower cost overrun sharing ratio for the contractor, (1 − *a*). This does not, however, necessarily mean that we will observe higher cost overruns associated with a contract with a higher *a* value. In reality, we only observe an overrun value such as 0.36 that corresponds to payment minimizing *a* for a given project. For other projects, the observed *a* could be lower with a higher cost overrun number. Such situations could easily occur with lower uncertainty and a lower bid reflecting higher competition. For example,

with X = 0.8 and Bid = 4.5, we have *a* = 0.2 and the expected cost overruns of 0.72. Although within each project, the expected cost overruns do increase with an increase in *a*, as shown in Table IV, we may never observe directly from the actual data that an increase in *a* magnifies the cost overruns.

Since cost overrun is defined as an excess of actual cost over bid, cost overrun, *ceteris paribus*, becomes more likely with a lower bid. Because a contractor's profit always increases with a higher bid for a positive share ratio, a contractor's incentive to submit a lower bid stems from increased bid competition. We would expect a greater cost underestimation tendency when bid competition becomes more intense.

Katsuaki L. Terasawa

BIBLIOGRAPHY

Gates, William and J. Midler, "Cost Growth in Major Army Weapon System Acquisitions: A Synthesis of Five Case Studies," Arroyo Center Research Report AC-RR-85-004, Jet Propulsion Laboratory, Pasadena, CA, January 1985.

Gibbon, Edward, *The Decline and Fall of the Roman Empire*, edited by D. M. Low, Harcourt, Brace and Company 1960.

Merrow, E., S. Chapel, and C. Worthing, *A Review of Cost Estimation in New Technologies*, RAND Report, R-2481-DOE, RAND, July 1979.

Nocic, David. "Are Cost Overruns a Military-Industry-Complex Specialty?" RAND Report AD-703861, March 1970, Rand Corporation, Santa Monica, CA.

Quirk, J. P., and K. L. Terasawa, "Sample Selection and Cost Underestimation Bias in Pioneer Projects, "*Land Economics*, Vol. 62, No. 2, May 1986.

COST EFFECTIVENESS. A means whereby an object or program is measured to determine whether it is economical, in that benefits are accured in a proportional relationship to the amount of money or effort spent to produce them.

Cost effectiveness, as a budgetary approach intended to measure program usefulness and viability, has been debated by government reformers since the late 1800s and the early 1900s. The Progressive reformers of the early 1900s favored the development of a responsive, expanding government that would focus its budgetary controls on assessing the cost effectiveness of individual programs. Progressives felt that government's job was to create programs that met the needs and demands of a knowledgeable, educated public. In contrast, the Taft Conservatives of that era focused their budgetary efforts on restriction of government growth, cost-cutting, and benefit analysis. This approach is similar to the one currently espoused by the Republican party's "Contract with America." The Taft Conservatives felt that the public lacked the education needed to understand and control government agencies, and that a natural elite would better serve the needs of society than the mob. Recognizing the political drive to downsize government, and do away with programs that are not cost-effective, questions facing decisionmakers when examining the applications of cost-effective measures to enacting reform include: what constitutes cost effectiveness; how does one measure it; and what is the balance between the resources allocated to a program and the benefits of that program?

The first step in understanding cost effectiveness as a concept is to distinguish its analytical approach from that used in a cost-benefit analysis. Both of these analytical approaches can be used to understand the allocation of program resources and are frequently employed in Planning, Programming, and Budgeting System studies. However, the similarities in these two approaches often leads to a confusion in the correct application of these two terms, as can be seen in the recent literature exporing current reform efforts and in the rhetoric of politicians.

A shared aspect of cost-effectiveness and cost-benefit analysis that may serve to foster confusion as to which approach is more appropriate for a given program is the fact that both approaches examine the cost of a program or project in much the same way. Both approaches examine the costs of the existing program and the costs of alternative approaches to achieve the same program results, and compare the numeric costs to establish the cost efficiency of the current program. Understanding which analytical approach to program analysis is the most appropriate to use, cost-effectiveness or cost-benefit, for a specific program requires that one recognize that all government services have certain costs and result in certain types of output. The real difference between cost-effectiveness and cost-benefit analysis lies primarily in the way in which each approach seeks to analyze the output of the program.

A key consideration, when attempting to understand the differences between cost-effectiveness and cost-benefit approaches to program analysis, and thus being able to choose which approach is more appropriate for the analysis of a particular program, is to identify what output it is one is trying to measure. Can one identify all of the outputs of a particular program and can one put a definitive price tag on each of the outputs in question? An example of a program with outputs that cannot always be assigned an economic value would be Aid to Families with Dependent Children (AFDC). The impact of a healthy diet, clean clothes, and shelter in the lives of poverty-stricken children may produce many outcomes in terms of the child's social integration and psychological status that may not be clearly defined or measured in economic terms. When it is not possible to assign a price tag to these program outcomes, then the best approach for understanding the budgetary and social implications of a program is to perform a cost-effectiveness analysis. Many

government programs can only be measured by cost-effectiveness criteria due to the intended aims of the policymakers who created them. Public policy has resulted in many programs that serve to promote equity issues, which are not clearly definable as outputs in strictly numeric terms. For example, attempts to promote the general welfare via governmental policies (such as Head Start) and their resulting programs often are aimed at producing outcomes that may include such ephemeral objectives as "making certain groups of disadvantaged people feel more positive about themselves."

Cost-effectiveness studies demand that the output created by a public program be specifiable, but the outcomes may not necessarily have to be measurable. For example, a successful program designed to increase condom use among at-risk teenage populations may find it difficult to translate increased condom usage and its potential reduction of pregnancy and sexually transmitted diseases into strict economic terms that could then be defined as a cost savings created by the program. A cost-effectiveness study also requires an understanding of the results of a program and the process that achieves the result. This process may itself be considered as a part of the valuation of the program's cost effectiveness. For example, an increase in condom uuse among at-risk teenage males may result from an increased sense of responsibility and self-worth created by the program in its attempts to change the behaviors of the young men. Although measuring the value of an increased sense of self-worth and responsibility is difficult, it is reasonable to argue that these emotions do have value and can have a positive impact on the individual and society. Thus, the process used in achieving the program output also has a value that must be recognized when assessing the cost effectiveness of the program. Also, a cost-effectiveness approach to program analysis does not require that budgetary decisionmakers understand how much, or how many, results are produced, since program analysis is not based on the number of units produced by the program. Measuring the numbers of units produced by a program may be one way to decide on the efficiency of a program, and in fact may be a reliable means of analysis in the private sector, but in the public sector not all outcomes are equal or even measurable. How can one compare the program value of increased condom use and enhanced self-image to a program designed to fill in the potholes in a city street? Both of these outcomes have a value to society, but they are so different from each other that comparing them to estimate which is more valuable seems intuitively unacceptable.

The growth of the U.S. budget deficit has resulted in national efforts to downsize government. Conservative political groups are demanding that some type of value be attached to the results of public service programs so that the budgetary assessments can be carried out in strictly numeric terms. This demand in part may also foster the current confusion between a cost-effectiveness and a cost-benefit approach to program analysis. Recognizing that most government programs produce results that are not easily quantifiable, the use of a cost-effectiveness approach to analyzing the value of public projects is essential. In the past, any attempt to measure the cost effectiveness of a particular program assumed that the service provided has some public benefit whether directly measurable or not. Now, given the economic and public pressure to downsize and consolidate government programs, the public and the legislators may not be as willing to assume that existing government programs do produce results that can be considered valuable. Approaches to analyzing the results of cost-effectiveness analysis of public programs based on specific criteria were first designed in the early 1960s by the Defense Department (DOD). These two methods are "constant-cost" and "least-cost" analysis.

The two methodologies designed by the DOD, constant-cost studies and least-cost analysis, are among the most commonly used methods for assessing the cost effectiveness of a program. Once the cost of a program has been established and its output specified, either of these methods can be used to establish which program is most cost effective. Planners can then choose between competing alternative programs when budgetary constraints exist for the decisionmaker.

Constant-cost studies examine the potential output of a number of different policies and assume that the cost of each of these policies is the same. For example, planners might compare a public safety policy designed to increase seatbelt use versus a stop-smoking program aimed at inner city high school students, programs which will cost $25,000 to enact. The planner will make no attempt to justify the merits of one policy or program over the other; he or she only attempts to provide the decisionmaker with the most return on investment in terms of the numbers of lives saved. Constant-cost studies are most useful when it is not possible to accurately define the exact number and nature of the outputs produced by a program.

Least-cost analysis attempts to compare different approaches based on their cost and the desired program output. An example could be the desire by the county to ensure that road repairs are carried out over the next four years. Least-cost analysis is most useful as a measure when the decisionmaker can identify the type (road repair) and number of outputs (four years) produced by a program and its cost. Approaches to achieving the program objectives might include hiring a private firm to perform the road repair or hiring public road repair crews. This ability to identify the types and numbers of outputs of a program may allow the opportunity costs to be assessed as well. For example, opportunity costs would stem from the fact that the money for the project is committed to it, and

thus cannot be used for other projects that might potentially return more value to the county. Opportunity costs may affect the final analysis of how cost effective a program is when weighed against any opportunity costs its existence creates.

The two methods used by the DOD in analyzing a program's cost effectiveness each use a different measurement approach. One method, constant-cost, assumes all costs are the same and the difference lies in the output, while the other method, least-cost, assumes all outputs are the same and the true difference lies in the cost. Both of these approaches have obvious problems created by the fact that it is not always possible to place a value on the individual program output. Also, in times of government cutbacks, decisionmakers may be forced to choose between two programs that produce different outputs. This choice can pose an enormous problem for the budgetary decisionmaker regardless of the criterion used to establish the cost effectiveness of a particular program. Thus, using a cost-effective approach to decisionmaking may mean that the values of the decisionmaker ultimately affect the program choices that he or she makes. The political realities of downsizing, and the personal values of the decisionmakers, may drive the budgetary system more than any other force when deciding which programs are most cost-effective and thus have more value to society.

The cost effectiveness of a program is defined in part by the value of that program to society, which in economics is termed its marginal social value. The marginal social value of a program is determined by assessing the private value and external marginal value placed on a specific commodity by an individual. The difficulty with this assessment is of course in the attempt to define the output of a program in terms which are easily understandable to, and which can be assigned a numeric value by, the public at large in terms of the worth of the project to them personally and its worth to them in terms of others having access to the project. These assigned values become the program's marginal value (MV). An individual may place a high private value on having a road from his home to his job (MV_{self}), but he must also place a value on the fact that the individual on the other side of town also has a road from her home to her job if a program is to have an external social value as well (MV_{other}). Now assuming that one does indeed place a value on others having roads for their own use, what is the value of having other roads for use by others to you? The marginal social value of a road may be determined by first assessing the value of the road to the other consumer plus the value you place on the other consumer having the road. So, $MV_{other} + MV_{self}$ equals the marginal social value of having the road. The difficulty in assessing the social value of the existence of roads can be seen when one tries to assign a numerical value to an individual's access to a road and the individual's belief in the value of others having access to a road. What one is willing to pay for having access to a service and what one is willing to pay for another's ability to have access to a similar service may differ widely. At what economic point does one decide that the cost of a program or service is too high and thus exceeds the marginal social value of that service? What is the marginal social value of poverty programs such as Medicaid or Aid to Families with Dependent Children (AFDC) to those citizens who do not currently need these services and who often perceive the recipients of these services as being somehow undeserving of the tax dollars spent in the delivery of these services? If the marginal social value assigned to these social services (AFDC) is judged to be very low, are these programs then to be assumed to not be as cost-effective as road building and thus subject to elimination in the next round of budget cuts? In a world governed by hard numbers and financial difficulties, can the need to cut costs negatively affect public policies designed to promote equity? Can equity issues, which are often undefinable in numeric terms, be considered as one measure of cost effectiveness?

History has not proven that conservative political and budgetary realities can find a comfortable fit alongside issues relating to equity and marginal social value. The Taft Conservatives found no need to endorse efforts to provide relief to groups that suffered from inequities. The achievement of equity was not seen as a measure of program effectiveness, while Progressives of the Taft era (and of today) felt that the need for equity assurance was essential. Although the winners in the early budgetary and programmatic battle were the Taft Conservatives, it would appear that overall the inheritors of the Taft Conservatives' legacy have again won the political and budgetary battle.

In the budget-conscious—and thus number-conscious—political climate of the 1990s, unmeasurable concepts such as marginal social value and equity may not be comfortably incorporated into an economic model that seeks to measure the cost effectiveness of a program in strict numeric terms. Yet the marginal social value and the equity attainments of a program must be recognized as a dimension of program effectiveness and counted into the mix when attempting to assess the cost effectiveness of public programs. If social value and equity issues are not accounted for in some fashion, then is the cost effectiveness of a program truly being measured or only its cost benefits?

ROE ROBERTS

BIBLIOGRAPHY

Cochran, A., 1972. *Effectiveness and Efficiency.* New York: Oxford Press.
Jacobs, Philip, 1991. *The Economics of Health and Medical Care.* 3rd ed. Gaithersburg, MD.: Aspen Publishers.
Rubin, Irene, 1994. "Early Budget Reformers: Democracy, Efficiency, and Budget Reforms." *American Review of Public Administration,* vol. 24, no. 3 (September) 229–252.
Singer, Neil, 1976. *Public Microeconomics: An Introduction to Government Finance.* Boston: Little, Brown.

COST OF LIVING ADJUSTMENTS (COLAs).

A mechanism for protecting workers or beneficiaries of governmental programs from the effects of inflation.

Most individuals know cost of living adjustments as COLAs, or those additions to their salaries designed to help compensate them for rising or inflationary prices. COLAs are a specific type of income compensation that is written into some labor contracts in both the private and public sectors pegged to the Bureau of Labor Statistics' consumer price index. COLAs are written expressly to guarantee workers full or partial compensation to help make up for the worker's loss of purchasing power as a consumer.

In 1977 some 61 percent of private sector workers under collective bargaining agreement enjoyed COLAs. The decline in COLA protection increased as of 1984, and by 1994 the percentage enjoying COLAS dropped to 28 percent. The percentage of public sector workers enjoying COLAs increased from 2 percent in 1984 to a high of 10 percent in 1991. As of 1994, 8 percent of public sector workers have COLAs. Retirees enjoy COLA protection to a much greater extent than workers.

Starting with the early 1960s with civil and military service retirement programs becoming indexed for inflation, COLAs have expanded to include efforts by governments to protect certain beneficiaries of governmental support programs against inflation. Governmental concerns with macrobudgeting targets have, it could be argued, introduced the importance of cost of living adjustments when it comes to calculating the correct inflation rate for the coming year and what governments will spend. Overall, the importance of COLAs to public policy is found in the issues of economic inflation, budgetary deficits, and social equity concerns.

Historical Development of COLAs

Not all salary or wage increases involve COLAs. In the common usage of the term, COLAs are salary, wage, or benefit adjustments made to compensate people for rising prices. Official cost of living indexes or consumer price indexes make possible the efforts of some people to protect themselves against the possible loss of purchasing power caused by inflation. These individuals could, based on statistical information about price changes, begin to pressure either private sector management or government for protection against rising or inflationary prices. Whether it be the CPI in the United States, the price index of living in Germany, or the general retail price index in France, a particular country's index for the cost of living has considerable symbolic and political importance when it comes to gauging the effectiveness of a government's economic and wage policy.

The first real effort in the United States to link wage adjustments with objective efforts to measure an increase in the cost of living occurred with the establishment of the Shipbuilding Labor Adjustment Board in 1917. The Board was created, in similar fashion to an earlier effort in Great Britain, to meet demands by shipbuilding workers regarding inadequate wages to compensate for the rapidly increasing prices of a wartime economy. This was not to be the last time that COLAs and wars were to become closely intertwined.

The 1917 effort helped to establish the basis for developing better indexes for measuring consumer prices in order to facilitate better informed wage negotiations. The ability of governments to supply an objective analysis of price changes did not go unchallenged by labor leaders, who in World War II challenged the objectivity of the Bureau of Labor Statistics' ability to effectively measure the true cost of the worker's cost of living.

The Bureau of Labor Statistics Search for a Valid CPI

The consumer price indexes of the Bureau have also been challenged by presidents, as recently as Jimmy Carter, in the context of the adequacy of the Bureau's efforts to estimate price changes correctly when it comes to the inflation rate for shelter. Methodologically and politically, the Bureau has faced problems in attempting to create a cost of living index or even a consumer price index since World War II that is acceptable to all parties when it comes to wage negotiations.

The earliest of efforts by countries to measure increases in the cost of living focused on determining only changes in the price of food. Starting first in Europe came efforts to devise a representative budget for workers so as to measure the cost of goods and services they needed for a certain designated standard of living. The Bureau of Labor Statistics in 1919, for example, tried to measure the expenditures of a governmental worker in Washington, D.C., if the worker were to maintain a healthy and decent life. The search for the actual cost of a hypothetical welfare budget, with time, gave way to the Bureau's present focus on measuring consumer prices for a designated "market basket" of goods and services purchased by urban workers.

The Bureau today produces two major national consumer price indexes based on the use of consumer expenditure surveys, intricate statistical sampling and weighting techniques, and periodic updates of their sample populations, market baskets, and points of purchase. The oldest is the CPI-W, which covers urban and clerical workers or most blue-collar workers, roughly 30 percent of the population. The second is CPI-U, in existence since 1978, which covers all urban workers, or some 80 percent of the population.

After heavy criticism during World War II, the Bureau changed the name of their major index from a cost of living to a consumer price index. By design consumer price indexes are used to help determine the size of COLAs to be negotiated and are not supposed to measure increases in the prices associated with a person's own changes in her or his standard of living over a given time. The purported standard of living represented in the base or index number for a consumer price index should reflect only those goods or services common to the very first or initial standard of living in the designated base year. Consumer price indexes do not measure the changes in a worker's standard of living that are different from the one in the designated base year. Consequently, consumer price indexes only approximate a cost of living index that would be the best measure of what a worker would need in extra income if she or he were to fully pay for her or his changing lifestyle. This fact and other problems individuals and organizations have in measuring the true cost of living make the Bureau's CPI-W limited in the very goal it was designed to accomplish in the first place.

There are other methodological problems inherent in trying to measure the cost of living needed for negotiations as to COLAs for a future contract or year. Consumer price indexes measure changes in prices over time for a certain market basket. Over time, the Bureau updates that market basket to reflect changing consumption habits, changing points of purchase, changing demographics, and so on. To ensure that the Bureau only measures changes in prices, it needs to hold constant the quality of goods and services being measured. The Bureau and others have a hard time isolating changes in prices due to quality upgrades or downgrades (such as airbags in cars and increased health care coverage, or a decrease in quality of goods, as during World War II). The purchases noted in a consumer price index constitute a large part of the true cost of living in a year, but not all the changes, especially any changes in quality. COLAs, as cost of living adjustments, are adjusted only to changes in a CPI, not to price changes reflected in a higher quality of life or better consumer goods.

The Bureau of Labor Statistics' CPIs have been citicized for having other biases. They are criticized for being more reflective of the expenditures of the wealthier, for their percentage of total consumption is weighted more heavily in the calculations of the CPIs. Labor, for this reason, has long fought to keep CPI-W as the correct CPI for all wage and COLA negotiations. Other groups, especially the elderly, have successfully pressed for a special CPI to reflect their special situation or special purchases. As composite indexes, the two main or most comprehensive CPIs may hide the different and higher prices paid by special groups. To the degree that they do, these groups would be benefited by a CPI that would support their own perceptions of their "higher" costs of living. Hence they challenge the use of the CPI-U or any other CPI that would mask their own particular vulnerability to certain higher prices.

CPI-W and CPI-U are only reflective of taxes that constitute a part of the consumption of goods and services, such as sales and property taxes. They do not include income and Social Security taxes, thereby underestimating the extent to which government may increase the cost of living.

These and other problems raise questions as to the accuracy and adequacy of any CPI to serve as a mechanism for determining any COLA to be part of a labor contract or to be added to the income given to the beneficiaries of governmental programs. Small incremental differences in a CPI index when it comes to COLA calculations make for major differences in the long term as to the growth of federal budget expenditures. This possibility can be seen in the different expenditure forecasts of the Office of Management and Budget and the Congressional Budget Office, which have significant macro expenditure and policy implications.

Reasons for COLA Protection

There are many mechanisms for the making of adjustments to a worker's wages or salaries. The case for COLAs as an appropriate way of making adjustments for rising or inflationary prices begins with an understanding of the political economy of inflation policy. Ideological differences help account for different views as to how serious a problem inflation is, its origins, and how it is to be solved, if at all. Some countries have made fighting inflation a higher priority than others. To the degree that inflation rates are kept down through monetary and fiscal policy, there is less of an urgency to rely on COLAs to compensate workers or citizens for any increases in their costs of living or the consumer prices they pay. In inflationary times, COLAs become more valuable and sit atop many a political agenda. In countries such as Brazil and Israel where inflation has historically been more rampant, there has been a rather long and comprehensive use of COLAs to protect their citizens, usually in the name of political stability. In the United States, the use of COLAs has been more limited, but the highly selective use of COLAs in both the private and public sectors signifies a politics of indexing.

To a large degree, the demand for and supply of certain workers help to account for the differences in certain workers becoming better protected against inflationary price increases than others. Workers in the primary labor market have fared far better than workers in the secondary labor market. Furthermore, lack of competition from both domestic and foreign competition may account for a firm's or industry's willingness to give COLA guarantees to its workers, believing that prices can be passed along to consumers.

Thanks to the work of R. Kent Weaver (*Automatic Government*, 1988), a lot more is known about the politics of indexing and which workers and beneficiaries receive or do not receive cost of living adjustments. Politicians, he suggests, vote for COLAs both for reasons of credit claiming and blame avoiding. Politicians find in COLAs a way of avoiding blame for failing to fight inflation. But, the granting of COLAs for retirees, for example, allows them to claim credit for their positive actions on the retirees' behalves. COLAs, it could be argued, have their political legitimacy because inflation is commonly viewed as a greater problem than unemployment. As a problem that is persistent, inflation is always in need of a solution. As public policy, compensation for inflation is sometimes perceived to be more feasible than curtailing inflation rates and incurring additional political problems and criticism.

In terms of the self-interest of workers, COLAs are preferable anytime they appear to be larger than any ad hoc salary or wage increase. On the other hand, the politically influential, when it comes to Congress, may favor ad hoc arrangements for their wage adjustments rather than relying on COLA protection as a less risky political strategy. For example, it is argued that labor unions favor COLAs the most only after their wage demands have been previously secured.

In the United States, any imbalance between firms' and industries' market power and the political influence of those would-be recipients of government COLA protection helps account for the presence of an unequal access to COLAs and a resulting inequality in protection against inflation. As a hidden tax, inflation is viewed often as having unfair negative impacts on certain people more than others. COLA protection makes some clear winners in the politics of inflation policy.

COLAs as Public Policy

The attractiveness of using COLAs for government, in theory, is greatest when there are inflationary times and deficit problems are minor. Economic growth is such that inflation is a problem, but governmental budgets are also being rewarded (presupposition of no indexing of income taxes, or the pre-1981 period in the United States). Second, COLAs are also feasible if inflation rates are low, but deficits are also low. COLAs may not be as needed, but governments can afford them. However, in the case of high deficits, but low inflation, a third possibility, COLAs are the least acceptable given the primary goal of deficit reduction. However, as evidenced by Gramm-Rudman-Hollings and the Budget Enforcement Act of 1990, Congress and politicians can continue COLAs despite expressed concern about the country's deficit problems. The politics of deindexing, it could be surmised, could result in so much blame and conflict that the deficit problem is of secondary importance for those wishing to be reelected. Finally, high deficits and high inflation suggest the situation where more pressure for COLA protection would create even greater problems for all politicians wanting to hold the line against greater budgetary deficits. Action to destimulate the economy should, in this case, be more apparent, but the important question is whether or not increased taxes to help pay for increased COLA protection would be forthcoming. In the end, any determination of the political legitimacy of COLAs requires analysis of the nature of economic, political, and budgetary contexts.

As of 1995, new COLAs are not presently being created, but they are not being drastically eliminated in any great numbers in the private and public sectors. COLA increases or decreases increasingly demonstrate an incremental type of decisionmaking and politics. COLAs are extended as contracts are extended but for longer periods of time. There are delays in phasing in COLAs in order to save money. And, there is increasingly only partial indexing for inflation. Increased efforts to select a lower CPI for government spending yields debates as to the correct CPI for budgetary policymaking. Decremental budgeting and small cuts and delays in phasing in COLAs are closely intertwined.

As public policy, COLAs and some entitlement programs may have, as the mid-1990s indicate, seen their better days. However, so long as inflation remains a problem to be reckoned with, COLAs remain a pivotal policy option for adjusting and compensating for inflationary prices. If governments cannot solve the inflation problem without unduly deflating the economy, COLAs as a policy of compensation can be viewed, in some quarters, as a favorable option. This would appear to be true for all who see retirees as especially vulnerable to inflation but with political influence. The willingness of Republicans and Democrats to doubly index Social Security benefits for inflation in the 1970s is good evidence of the political value of assuring protection for the elderly and the retired when it comes to inflation. The role of double indexing Social Security benefits for inflation, however, also points

out a long-running criticism of COLAs. COLAs, it is argued, exemplify a willingness to give up the fight against inflation so much so as to provide the accelerator for even more deficit worries for all the entitlement programs that are indexed for inflation.

For economists on the left, COLAs present a danger to workers, for many are not protected while only a selected few are. COLAs increase inflationary pressure with time as they increase protection for more and more people and programs. Robert Heilbroner and Lester Thurow (*Explaining Economics,* 1994), for that reason, favor wage and price controls as the better method of dealing with inflation. Wage and price controls, in turn, have been criticized for being rather selectively enforced and for being only, at best, successful in the short term. The policy value of COLAs increases to the degree that wage and price controls and other anti-inflation policies do not work.

As "good" public policy, COLAs need to be evaluated in terms of social justice and fairness. The selectivity of their presence, at first glance, signifies that some people receive more inflation protection or compensation than others. And because they do, those who do not gain protection suffer twice, for they also pay higher prices because of the compensation that selected workers receive. Ideally, in terms of social equity considerations, when it comes to inflation, all or none should be protected. In practice, not all are protected. In the case of federal entitlement programs, COLAs have become more or less a right, just as the entitlement programs have themselves.

For Aaron Wildavsky (*The New Politics of the Budgetary Process,* 1992), the precepts of the Budget Enforcement Act of 1990 dictate that entitlement could be viewed as only quasi-entitlements if they are to be subjected to the pay-as-you-go criterion in the Act. The same could be true for COLAs for those same programs. As of 1995, there appears to be added willpower to deindex some of those programs when it comes to inflation. The powerful, influential and the most vulnerable maintain their COLA protections for now, despite a Republican-controlled Congress concerned both with budget deficits and with tax reductions for families and businesses.

If COLA protection is not possible for all, who should be protected against price inflation? Empirical evidence supports the view that retirees should be, for they are reasonably well protected. Governmental protection against inflation, as a safety net, makes sense only if the protected really do lose to inflation. In the case of AFDC recipients, they receive protection against inflation when it comes to federal benefits, but do not in the case of state benefits, for states do not index for inflation when it comes to their AFDC supplements. The AFDC case helps make the argument for COLAs being needed for reasons of social equity and financial need; without the federal COLA, some of the most vulnerable would become a lot more vulnerable over time.

In times where deficit problems call for sacrifices, COLAs become a possibility for cuts, but the normative policy question to be asked is whether it is fair to cut those who are the most vulnerable. Macrobudgeting decisions and who controls the two legislative branches of government dictate the parameters of how much money there is to spend each year for COLAs for federal programs and how much willpower exists to cut COLAs for those most favored by past congressional and presidential support. The public policy importance of COLAs, at the federal level, will depend upon the future level of support for increased restraints on increased spending, continued political acceptance of COLAs already written into legislation dictating governmental spending levels, and definition of COLAs as part of the budgetary base for next year's federal budget.

In theory and practice, workers, both private and public, and the recipients of governmental income desire more than COLA protection. They may settle for adequate protection against inflation in economic hard times. Increasingly, however, COLAs' most immediate competition, when it comes to acceptable adjustments in one's increased cost of living, are those ad hoc adjustments that can be made when it comes to one's wages. In good times or times of budgetary surpluses, governments will try to make up for recent losses in purchasing power due to cutbacks. Lump sum quasi-COLA catch-ups are one way of helping public sector workers regain some degree of purchasing power. There are also cases where, through collective bargaining agreements, workers have negotiated for a certain share of any productivity gains and budgetary surpluses to be set aside for cost of living adjustments. Such arrangements guarantee some protection, but a protection that is far more vulnerable to economic and budgetary problems outside the control of workers and governments.

Conclusion

Future research in regard to COLAs will center more on the strategies and successes some have in maintaining their COLAs or even modified levels of protection against inflation. Newer strategies such as "cafeteria plans" may be viewed as prototypical of increasingly indirect and ad hoc efforts of public workers to protect their standards of living in budgetary dark times. A more direct campaign for more formalized and expanded COLA protection awaits new efforts to restimulate sluggish economies and improvement in the cases of the problems of unemployment and underemployment.

GEORGE FREDERICK GOERL

BIBLIOGRAPHY

Ahoroni, Yair, 1981. *The No-Risk Society.* Chatham, NJ: Chatham House.
Amble, Nathan and Ken Stewart, 1994. "Experimental Price Index for Elderly Consumers." *Monthly Labor Review,* vol. 117 (May) 11–16.
Cogan, John F., Timothy J. Muris and Alan Schick, 1994. *The Budget Puzzle.* Stanford, CA: Stanford University Press.
Davis, William, 1994 "Collective Bargaining in 1994." *Monthly Labor Review,* vol. 117 (January) 3–19.
Derthick, Martha, 1979. *Policymaking for Social Security.* Washington, D.C.: The Brookings Institution.
Douglas, Dorothy W., 1937. "Cost of Living." In Edwin Seligman, ed., *Encyclopedia of Social Sciences,* vol. 3. New York: Macmillan, pp. 478–483.
Fixler, Dennis, 1993. "The Consumer Price Index: Underlying Concepts and Caveats." *Monthly Labor Review,* vol. 116 (December) 3–12.
Goldberg, Joseph and William Moye, 1985. *The First 100 Years of the Bureau of Labor Statistics.* Washington, D.C.: Governmental Printing Office.
Kagan, Robert, 1978. *Regulatory Justice.* New York: Russell Sage Foundation.
Peretz, Paul, 1983. *The Political Economy of Inflation in the United States.* Chicago: University of Chicago Press.
United States Department of Labor, 1992. *Bureau of Labor Statistics Handbook of Methods.* Washington, D.C.: U.S. Government Printing Office.
Weaver, R. Kent, 1988. *Automatic Government.* Washington, D.C.: The Brookings Institution.
Wildavasky, Aaron, 1992. *The New Politics of the Budgetary Process.* 2nd ed. New York: Harper Collins.

COSTING-OUT.

Quantitative estimates by employee organizations and employers of the costs of proposed changes in wages, benefits, and working conditions that are associated with collective bargaining. The purpose is to determine the potential financial impacts of each item in the labor agreement.

Proposals involving ostensibly noneconomic items are also costed-out, including vacation schedules, staffing changes, time off for union business, and sick leave. Indirect costs that might result from the sacrifice of a management prerogative are also estimated. For example, a municipality might purchase a new garbage truck that requires one less sanitation employee. But if the sanitation union wins a contractual right to veto shift allocations or the purchase of new technology, there is a hidden cost to the municipality.

Elements of a proposed contract must be examined with comparative economic data in mind. Examples include trends in wages, benefits, and working conditions in similar functions or jurisdictions. Salary and benefit surveys may be used by labor and management to collect specific information from nearby firms or government jurisdictions that face similar market and economic conditions. National and regional economic data are often collected and analyzed as well, such as cost of living differentials. Changes in federal and state law that potentially influence personnel costs should also be weighed, such as policies on worker disabilities, healthy care insurance, or AIDS. Information on members of the bargaining unit is also useful, including average years until retirement, seniority patterns, and gender.

The most common methods of costing-out involve total annual cost of labor and management demands, annual cost of demands per employee, cost of demands in dollars per hour, and cost of demands as a percentage of payroll. Benefits present a special challenge because of future cost implications and the need to discount to present value. When costing-out procedures are based on the assumption that past conditions will prevail in the future, estimates can be seriously flawed.

The ready availability of personal computers and national databases make costing-out much more sophisticated today than a decade ago. Estimates that once required tedious pen and pencil calculations can now be completed in seconds with the proper software package. Graphic presentations and statistical analyses help present aggregate data in a form that is relatively simple to understand. Present value considerations are also easier to compute, so that the future value of a dollar is taken into account. And roll-up costs, which occur when wage increases lead to cost increases for certain employee benefits (for instance, a wage increase hikes the costs of vacation pay and sick leave), are much easier to calculate with modern computer technology. However, computers should not be relied upon to the exclusion of common sense and good judgment of political conditions and personalities.

Costing-out has benefits for unions, management, and the process of collective bargaining. The union can formulate more accurate and sophisticated contract proposals and improve its ability to appraise the potential economic effects of management proposals. Management can do a better job of defending its proposals and fending off union demands. The bargaining process benefits from a mutual understanding of contract costs both immediately and in the future.

RICHARD C. KEARNEY

BIBLIOGRAPHY

Leap, Terry L., 1991. *Collective Bargaining and Labor Relations.* New York: Macmillan.

COST-EFFECTIVENESS ANALYSIS.

A quantitative technique that examines alternative ways of achieving public (organizational) goals by systematically comparing benefits of the project to costs (expenditures) for the purpose of identifying the alternative yielding maximum net benefits; also known as cost-benefit analysis; risk-benefit analysis; benefit-cost analysis.

In cost-benefit analysis, benefits are usually expressed in monetary values, while in cost-effectiveness analysis benefits are measured in nonpecuniary units (e.g., human lives saved). Costs are generally expressed in monetary values, although they can also be measured in units of a scarce resource (such as labor).

In risk-benefit (also risk-cost-benefit) analysis the benefits are measured against possible risks (usually technological) that each alternative strategy achieving the stated end bears.

The private sector uses cost-benefit analysis for examining alternative investment opportunities, make-or-buy decisions, and so forth. It is called cost-volume-profit analysis.

Micro cost-benefit analysis examines efficiency on the scale of the individual project—relating direct benefits of a particular project to its direct costs—while macro cost-benefit analysis also takes into account externalities, or indirect costs and benefits (for instance, environmental pollution and increased employment will be, respectively, indirect cost and indirect benefit for a decision to build a chemical plant at a particular location, while direct costs will deal only with, say, rate of return for the investment).

Analysts trace the modern, institutionalized use of cost-benefit analysis in the United States back to the U.S. Flood Control Act of 1936, which required that the benefits "to whomsoever they may accrue" of federal navigation improvement and flood control projects should exceed costs (Hatry 1982, p. 167; Fuchs and Anderson, 1987, p. 25). By the 1950s, it became an established feature of water resources policy. Cost-effectiveness analysis gained momentum in the Department of Defense in the beginning of the 1960s, when Secretary of Defense Robert McNamara appointed Charles Hitch of the RAND Corporation (where cost-benefit analysis was very popular in the late 1950s) as comptroller of DOD. It was a part of a Planning, Programming, Budgeting System (PPBS). In 1965 President Johnson ordered the use of PPBS for all executive agencies (it was officially terminated in 1971). In the 1960s and 1970s there was a considerable growth of regulatory activities, and at the urge of industry, beginning in the 1970s, cost-benefit analysis was being applied to new federal regulations of economic activity. Under the Nixon administration, there was an effort to contain costly Environmental Protection Agency (EPA) regulations by bringing them within the scrutiny of the Office of Management and

Budget under a process called "Quality of Life Review." The Ford administration concentrated on fighting possible inflation in government's regulatory activities. President Carter wanted to regulate, but was wary of the costs of regulation. In January 1978, he established the Regulatory Analysis Review Group (RARG), and later issued Executive Order 12044, which required new regulations not to exceed $100 million in impact on the economy and not to cause a major price increase for an industry, level of government, or geographic area. President Reagan, on his second day in office, created the Presidential Task Force on Regulatory Reform (TFRR), and later signed Executive Order 12291, which essentially repeated the provisions of Executive Order 12044, adding a new restraint—regulation should not have an adverse economic impact on competition, innovation, and productivity. Because of the political nature of government policies, cost-benefit analysis never was fully institutionalized. As Fuchs and Anderson (1987, p. 32) argue, however it brought more systematic presidential oversight of regulatory activities and an increased agency concern for policy analysis. In many cases cost-benefit analysis was also incorporated into legislation. Some observers argued that cost-benefit analysis was used politically in the 1980s to prevent agencies from acting (Meier, 1984).

While the rhetoric of cost-benefit analysis is employed by virtually every government throughout the world, because of the inherent political nature of government's decisionmaking, the practice is never comprehensive in any country. Centralized economic planning theory in communist countries had efficiency as one of its commandments. Because of heavy military-political influence in the economic decisionmaking process and weak financial restraints for enterprises (a factory could operate with a loss for years), however, often the practice of cost-benefit analysis was ignored.

Cost-benefit and cost-effectiveness analyses are considered to consist of the following principal steps:

Identification and description of alternative projects. Programs should be as specific as possible, with listings of all crucial parts. The definition of alternative programs and the main parts of programs are preferably achieved through consensus between implementing managers and legislators, in order to make measurements of benefits and costs for each program more precise and nonoverlapping.

Operationalization of effectiveness and benefits. The determination of what exactly we want to measure (the precise concept or criteria) and how we do it (i.e., quantification of both benefits and costs).

- *Listing all the impacts.* Both positive (benefits) and negative (costs), both in the present and in the future.

Costs and benefits can be classified by: (1) internal and external effects; (2) tangible and intangible effects; (3) direct and indirect effects (Sylvia et al., 1991, pp. 53–55). Impacts should also be listed by specifying groups of people they affect, and how they affect various groups. For cost-effectiveness analysis, although effectiveness is not expressed in pecuniary terms, it must be clearly quantifiable.

- *Making monetary estimates for cost-benefit analysis.* Derived from welfare economics, benefits an individual or group of individuals receive from a project are valued according to their willingness to pay for that project in a voluntary transition. Thus, impacts are estimated based on: (1) market prices; (2) shadow prices, which are usually calculated for externalities—effects that accrue to outsiders (e.g., pollution)—and public goods—goods that are consumed collectively (e.g., clean air). Although there is no general agreement on methodology, there are a few methods for calculating shadow prices. For calculating the value for the most controversial incommensurable (effect for which there is no market)—human life—up to 12 different approaches are suggested (Thompson, 1982). Among them are the price an individual is willing to pay to avoid the risk of a negative consequence; the individual's possible lifetime earnings are often used as an estimate.

- *Future costs and benefits.* Future impacts in cost-benefit analysis are discounted in order to incorporate the effect of time. This is calculated by the following formula:

$$\text{Present Value} = \frac{\text{Future Value}}{(1 + \text{Discount rate})^{\text{time}}}$$

The rate used in this analysis should be a rate at which society will trade its present costs and benefits for future costs and benefits—it is often called the social discount rate. There is no agreement on what precisely the social discount rate should be, but there are a few suggested measures for it: market interest rates for government bonds, marginal productivity of investment, government borrowing rate, and corporate discount rate, among others. In the past, the federal government has recommended a discount rate of 7 percent for water projects and 10 percent for all others. Currently, the discount rates for government programs are tied to the Treasury Department's long-term borrowing rate (Sylvia *et al.*, 1991, p. 64).

- *In risk-benefit analysis, the first step is risk assessment.* Risk assessment essentially consists of: 1) hazard identification; 2) assessment of human exposure to the hazard; 3) modeling of the relationship between exposure and adverse impacts; and 4) estimate of overall risk (Fischer, 1995, p. 39). In a second step, the benefits are measured against nonmonetary assessment of risks that the project bears (e.g., deaths per million people).

Comparison of benefits and costs—The comparison requires:

- *Mathematical expression of effectiveness (performance, benefits) as differentiated from costs.* This allows decisionmakers to see trade-offs between costs and effectiveness for each alternative. For example, if there are five competing vendors for a certain product or service, each of whom can deliver products of differing quality at a given time, we will have five curves for each vendor, where quality (benefit) is a function of time (cost). If the time is constant and the service has to be delivered by a certain date, this substep is not necessary. But if time is a flexible resource, it may help us decide the desirability of each vendor at a specific time (the best vendor now is not necessarily the best one in the future—the curves for two vendors can intercept). This substep may be a luxury if each curve has only a couple of meaningful points (e.g., each vendor can supply either satisfactory or excellent products, all the other points on the curve are meaningless) and it may be easier to discuss these possibilities as separate choices than to draw a curve of all theoretical possibilities.

- *Methods of comparison.* Projects may be compared to each other based on: (1) net present value (NPV); (2) benefit/cost ratio; or (3) internal rate of return (IR). Net present value is the total discounted benefits minus total discounted costs. It is calculated as the sum of the present value of the project for all the years of the project. Positive NPV means the project will not bring losses. The project with higher NPV is preferred. Sometimes (rarely in the public sector) a cutoff period is established for cost-benefit analysis, when benefits are not accounted for over a certain period. Benefit/cost ratio is the result of dividing net discounted benefits by the net discounted costs. The project with the highest ratio should be favored, although it is often criticized as a criterion of efficiency that ignores effectiveness (the project with highest benefits for unit of cost can deliver the lowest net benefits). Internal rate of return (IRR) is a calculation that equates net costs of investment with net future benefits (discounted back to current values) that the investment will yield. According to this criterion, an investment is worth undertaking only if the IRR is higher than the established discount rate.

In analyzing public programs, the issue of distributional effects of the project is more important than in the private sector. It is important to take into account the impact the program is going to make on different groups of the population. Some analysts argue for using equity as one formal criteria for cost-benefit analysis, although they acknowledge the lack of a generally accepted formalized technique for incorporating equity into decisionmaking.

When dealing with a case where multiple criteria should be satisfied, or multiple constituencies should be served by the project, analysts propose two basic techniques of reconciling competing claims: (1) the criterion of Pareto optimality, or (2) the Kaldor-Hicks criterion (Miller 1992:255). The Pareto criterion, named after a nineteenth-century economist, favors a project where at least one person (or indicator of a particular impact) is better off and nobody (no indicator) is worse off as a result of a program. The Kaldor-Hicks criterion softens this requirement: a project is favored if those who are better off compensate the ones who are worse off, and the beneficiaries are still better off than in the case of the status quo.

Finally, because many estimates are uncertain, very often analysts perform sensitivity analysis. Sensitivity analysis shows the boundaries within which certain conditions can change, but the preferred solution will still be the same. For example, the net present value of Project A will be higher than the net present value of Project B if the discount rate (say, currently at 10 percent) is lower than 15 percent, but Project B will be preferable if the discount rate is more than 15 percent.

Making choices and presenting the results of cost-benefit analysis. The essence of cost-benefit analysis is a systematic, methodological approach to the problem at hand. Its purpose is to present the problem to decisionmakers in an organized and clearly defined manner, linking different courses of action to different consequences and stating why some consequences are more preferable than others. To the extent possible, original data should be collected and analyzed. Every presentation of the problem should include: (1) a description and consequences of the status quo—what will result if no action is taken; (2) an explicit depiction of constraints and assumptions of both goals and means of each alternative—legal, managerial-administrative, ethical, technological, budgetary (or resource); (3) the decision criteria—both the method (e.g., net present value) and particular characteristics (e.g., the value of discount rate); (4) the areas where there are possible effects, but which are not considered because of lack of time, expertise, money, and so forth (Sylvia et al., 1991, p. 68).

It is generally agreed that cost-benefit analysis is introducing systematic deliberation into the decisionmaking process, turning it into a more rational enterprise. Cost-benefit analysis is also often criticized on the basis that it extends economic logic to spheres where it does not belong, that not everything can be measured in monetary terms, and that many things that can be measured in non-monetary terms cannot be compared (e.g., human lives with something else). Steven Kelman (1990) attacks cost-benefit analysis because it stems from the moral philosophy of utilitarianism, and because it puts market prices on incommensurable things. His opponents argue that cost-benefit analysis is a pragmatic tool rather than a stretched extension of utilitarianism; that too much emphasis on incommensurables prescribes "entitled" rights to individuals that do not exist in nature and society (e.g., a zero-risk environment); that even if certain things are not measured in monetary terms, they are certainly affected by economic factors; and finally, that the government in real life very often has to make tough choices and that ignoring this fact by claiming inapplicability of cost-benefit analysis is not solving the problem at all (DeLong, 1990). They also argue that utilitarianism is not a simple hedonistic calculus and has moral imperatives (e.g., liberty), and that the list of incommensurables is very limited (Nisbet, 1990). Others argue that while cost-benefit analysis is good and useful in some spheres, on a larger scale it is a technocratic "extension of economic reasoning and its criteria into social and political realms governed by very different kinds of judgmental criteria and process of reasoning" (Fischer, 1995, p. 45).

Others agree upon the systematic effort, the efficiency-oriented nature of cost-benefit analysis, and the fact that it very often works, but mention that there is no "pure" economic efficiency in real life—it is blended with political rationality, especially at the higher levels of administration (Wildavsky, 1966), and find that other criteria, such as managerial feasibility and susceptibility to fraud, are often more heavily weighed (Miller, 1992).

Cost-effectiveness analysis is a quantitative technique that brings systematic perspective to decisionmaking. It has a wide range of applications in public policy, but also has its limitations. Decisionmakers should be aware of assumptions (ethical, political, technological, etc.) underlying each policy option under consideration.

VATCHE GARBRIELIAN

BIBLIOGRAPHY

Delong, James D., 1990. "Defending Cost-Benefit Analysis: Two Replies to Steven Kelman." In W. Michael Hoffman and Jennifer Mills Moore, eds., *Business Ethics: Readings and Cases in Corporate Morality.* 2nd ed. New York: McGraw-Hill, pp. 97–99.
Fischer, Frank, 1995. *Evaluating Public Policy.* Chicago: Nelson-Hall.
Fuchs, Edward P. and James E. Anderson, 1987. "The Institutionalization of Cost-Benefit Analysis." *Public Productivity Review,* no. 42 (Summer) 25–33.

Hatry, Harry P., 1982. "Cost-Benefit and Cost-Effectiveness Analysis." In Carl Heyel, ed., *The Encyclopedia of Management.* 3rd ed. New York: Van Nostrand Reinhold Company, pp. 197–171.
Kelman, Steven, 1990. "Cost-Benefit Analysis: An Ethical Critique." In W. Michael Hoffman and Jennifer Mills Moore, eds., *Business Ethics: Readings and Cases in Corporate Morality.* 2nd ed. New York: McGraw-Hill, pp. 90–97.
Meier, Kenneth J., 1984. "The Limits of Cost-Benefit Analysis." In Lloyd G. Nigro, ed., *Decisionmaking for Public Administrators.* New York: Marcel Dekker, pp. 43–46.
Miller, Gerald J., 1992. "Cost-Benefit Analysis." In Marc Holzer, ed., *Public Productivity Handbook.* New York: Marcel Dekker, 253–279.
Nisbet, Robert A., 1990. "Defending Cost-Benefit Analysis: Two Replies to Steven Kelman." In W. Michael Hoffman and Jennifer Mills Moore, eds., *Business Ethics: Readings and Cases in Corporate Morality.* 2nd ed. New York: McGraw-Hill, pp. 99–100.
Sylvia, Ronald D., Kenneth J. Meier and Elizabeth M. Gunn, 1991. *Program Planning and Evaluation for the Public Manager.* Prospect Heights, IL: Waveland Press.
Thompson, Mark S., 1982. *Benefit-Cost Analysis for Program Evaluation.* Beverly Hills, CA: Sage Publications.
Wildavsky, Aaron, 1966. "The Political Economy of Efficiency: Cost-Benefit Analysis, Systems Analysis, and Program Budgeting." *Public Administration Review* (December) 292–310.

COUNCIL OF ECONOMIC ADVISERS (CEA).

Created by the Employment Act of 1946; provides economic analysis and advice to the president of the United States and helps develop and implement national economic policies.

The president appoints two members and the chair of the Council. The chair guides the Council and exercises ultimate responsibility for directing the members and the professional staff. The professional staff, in recent years, includes around 20 senior and junior economists and a few statisticians. The senior economists, in most cases, are on leave of absence from other institutions, predominantly faculty positions at academic institutions. Their tenure with the Council is usually limited to one or two years. Junior economists generally are graduate students who spend one year with the Council and then leave to complete their dissertations.

The Council's annual report, jointly published with the Economic Report of the President, is the principal medium through which the Council informs the public of its work and its views. The typical 300-page report discusses monetary and fiscal policy, growth and employment, international trade, and contemporary special topics. In recent years, these special topics have included airline deregulation, global environment issues, health care, and regulatory reform. The report also contains over 100 pages of economic data including national income, production, price, and business and government finance data. The Council also assumes primary responsibility for developing the monthly Economic Indicators, which are issued by the Joint Economic Committee of the Congress.

The Council Chairs and Their Dates of Services.

Edwin G. Nourse (Truman)	1946–49	Herbert Stein (Nixon)	1972–74
Leon H. Keyserling (Truman)	1950–53	Alan Greenspan (Ford)	1974–77
Arthur F. Burns (Eisenhower)	1953–56	Charles L. Schultze (Carter)	1977–81
Raymond J. Saulnier (Eisenhower)	1956–61	Murray L. Weidenbaum (Reagan)	1981–82
Walter W. Heller (Kennedy, Johnson)	1961–64	Martin Feldstein (Reagan)	1982–84
Gardner Ackley (Johnson)	1964–68	Baryl W. Sprinkel (Reagan)	1985–89
Arthur M. Okun (Johnson)	1968–69	Michael J. Boskin (Bush)	1989–93
Paul W. McCracken (Nixon)	1969–71	Laura Tyson (Clinton)	1993–

KATSUAKI L. TERASAWA

COUNCIL OF EUROPE. An international organization of 40 European states committed to intergovernmental cooperation on the basis of multilateral conventions in virtually all policy areas with the exception of military defense.

The statute establishing the Council of Europe was signed by ten countries on May 5, 1949, and came into effect on August 3, 1949. The idea for such an organization sprang from a speech given by Sir Winston Churchill at Zurich University of September 19, 1946, when he called for a "kind of United States of Europe" with a Council of Europe being the first step. Subsequently in 1948 a Congress was held in The Hague in the Netherlands, which was convened by an international Committee of the Movements for European Unity. The Hague Congress, as it became known, comprised approximately 750 delegates. Two political forces or schools of thought were evident at the Congress: on the one hand there were the continental federalists and on the other there were the mostly British European Unionists who envisaged European states forming a looser, more intergovernmental type of organization. The statute adopted by the Congress, which was presided over by Churchill, provided for an intergovernmental organization whose aims were to "achieve a greater unity be-

tween its members for the purpose of safeguarding and realizing the ideals and principles which are their common heritage and facilitating their social and economic progress." The Council sets out to promote European unity by protecting and strengthening pluralist democracy and human rights; by seeking solutions to the problems facing European society (including such issues as minorities, xenophobia, intolerance, environmental protection, bioethics, AIDS, drugs); by promoting awareness of a European cultural identity; by providing a political anchorage and serving as a guardian of human rights for Europe's postcommunist democracies; and by assisting Central and Eastern European countries with their political, legislative, and constitutional reforms.

The range of activities of the Council of Europe is extensive, covering human rights, media, legal cooperation, social and economic questions, health, education, culture, heritage, sport, youth, local and regional government, and the environment. The conventions of the Council form the basis on which member states amend and harmonize their domestic legislation. The earliest and best known of the Council's 150 conventions is the European Convention of Human Rights, signed in Rome on November 4, 1950, and coming into force on September 3, 1953, under which participating states have in effect a contractual obligation to protect certain human rights and freedoms of individuals. The European Commission of Human Rights and the European Court of Human Rights were established in 1954 and 1959 respectively in Strasbourg to help guarantee that the civil and political liberties of the individual set out in the Convention are respected in the member states. Another major convention of the Council of Europe, the European Socal Charter (signed in 1961, coming into effect in 1965, together with an additional protocol adopted in 1988) aims to complement the Convention on Human Rights by promoting and protecting certain basic social rights such as the right to work, the right to form or join a trade union, the right to strike, and so on. The European Cultural Convention promotes intergovernmental cooperation in the areas of education, culture, heritage, sport, and youth. Similar conventions and agreements exist in such diverse areas as transfrontier television, data protection, wildlife and natural habitats, prevention of torture, suppression of terrorism, spectator violence, and regional and minority languages. In terms of promoting the functioning of local and regional democracy and the participation of local and regional authorities in the process of European unity, the Council established in 1994 the Congress on Local and Regional Authorities of Europe. It comprises 286 members and 286 substitutes who are elected representatives of local and regional authorities. In addition, the Council of Europe encourages links with nongovernmental organizations by granting consultative status to over 350 such bodies.

Institutional Structure

The Council of Europe's main institutions are the Committee of Ministers and the Parliamentary Assembly, which is assisted by a secretariat. The Committee of Ministers, the executive body of the Council, composed of the foreign ministers of the member states, meets at least twice a year. Ministers' deputies or permanent representatives meet each month and act as plenipotentiaries having the same decisionmaking powers as the ministers. The chair of the Committee of Ministers rotates every six months. Articles 15 and 16 of the statute empower the Committee to conclude conventions on policy areas within the scope of the Council, to make recommendations on the implementation of policies, and also to issue declarations stating solemn principles such as the Declaration of Freedom of Information of 1982. Decisions of the Committee of Ministers are forwarded to member states' governments either as recommendations or as the basis of European conventions, which are legally binding on those states that choose to ratify them. Most decisions require a two-thirds majority of the votes cast, while important recommendations addressed to governments require unanimity. The texts of conventions and agreements are prepared by committees of governmental experts. The Committee of Ministers acts as a permanent forum in which participating states may discuss political matters of common concern.

The Parliamentary Assembly is the deliberative organ of the Council of Europe and comprises 286 members and 286 substitutes who are appointed or elected by the national parliaments. The representatives sit in alphabetical order in transnational political groupings according to their political outlook. There are five political groupings including the Socialists, the European People's Party, the European Democratic Group, the Liberal, Democratic and Reformist Group and the Group of the European Unitarian Left.

The Assembly elects its own president, who together with the 15 vice presidents constitute the Bureau, which sets the agenda and schedules debates. The Assembly also elects the Secretary General of the Council of Europe, the Deputy Secretary General, and the judges of the European Court of Human Rights. Article 22 of the statute empowers the Parliamentary Assembly to debate all matters within the scope of the Council of Europe, while Article 23 empowers it to make recommendations to the Committee of Ministers and to pass resolutions on topical issues of mutual interest. Its annual session is divided into four weeklong parts. All debates are open to the public. The Assembly has an established system of committees dating from the 1950s.

The modus operandi of the Assembly involves first, a recommendation or a resolution with the support of members being referred by the Bureau to the appropriate specialist committee. The reporter of the committee produces a report, which is referred to the Assembly where it is debated and then voted on. For a resolution the procedure ends there, while a recommendation to the Committee of Ministers is taken up by either the Committee or their deputies and referred to one of its specialized committees. Joint Committee meetings are held between the Committee of Ministers and the Parliamentary Assembly to decide how best to bring the recommendations into effect.

The secretariat of the Council of Europe comprises an international staff of 1,300 officials. Article 36b of the statute provides for the Secretary General and Deputy Secretary General to be appointed by the Parliamentary Assembly on the recommendation of the Committee of Ministers. The Secretary General, who has a five-year renewable term of office, coordinates and directs the Council's activities.

The role of the Council of Europe has become increasingly important in post–Cold War Europe as is evidenced by the increase in its membership, particularly in recent years given its emphasis on promoting political, social, legal, and cultural cooperation on a pan-European scale. Its membership in July 1997 included: Albania, Andorra, Austria, Belgium, Bulgaria, Cyprus, Croatia, the Czech Republic, Denmark, Estonia, Finland, France, Germany, Greece, Hungary, Iceland, Ireland, Italy, Latvia, Liechtenstein, Lithuania, Luxembourg, the former Yugoslav Republic of Macedonia, Malta, Moldova, the Netherlands, Norway, Poland, Portugal, the Russian Federation, Romania, Slovakia, Slovenia, San Marino, Spain, Sweden, Switzerland, Turkey, the Ukraine, and the United Kingdom. These are currently five nascent democracies which are accession candidates, namely Armenia, Azerbaijan, Belarus, Bosnia-Herzegovina, and Georgia, while Israel has observer status.

The Council of Europe has two official languages, French and English, with the Parliamentary Assembly also using Italian and German as working languages. Its headquarters are in Strasbourg, France, in the Palais de l'Europe building, which also hosts the plenary sessions of the European Parliament of the European Union for one week each month. The Council of Europe has a budget financed by direct contributions from its participating states amounting to approximately £162 million in 1996.

MARGARET MARY MALONE

BIBLIO1GRAPHY

Archer, Clive, 1990. *Organizing Western Europe*. London: Edward Arnold.
Council of Europe, 1980. *Manual of the Council of Europe*. Strasbourg: Council of Europe.
———, 1992a. *The Council of Europe: Achievements and Activities*. Strasbourg: Council of Europe.
———, 1992b. *The European Social Charter*. Strasbourg: Council of Europe.

———,1992c. *The Council of Europe and Protection of Human Rights*. Strasbourg: Council of Europe.

———,1993. *The Council of Europe: Facts and Figures*. Strasbourg: Council of Europe.

Fletcher, I., 1980. "The Council of European Human Rights." In K. J. Twitchett, ed., *European Cooperation Today*. London: Europe.

Lipgens, W., 1982. *A History of European Integration*. Vol. 1, 1945–47. Oxford: Oxford University Press.

Robertson, A. H, 1961. *The Council of Europe: Its Structure, Functions and Achievements*. 2nd ed. London: Stevens.

COUNCIL ON FOUNDATIONS.

A nonprofit membership association of philanthropic grantmakers dedicated to promoting and strengthening organized philanthropy. Formed in 1949 as the National Council of Community Foundations, it was formally incorporated in 1957 with Wilmer Shields Rich as the first executive director. It was reorganized in 1964 as the Council on Foundations.

The Council on Foundations has as members more than 1,300 independent, operating, community, public, company-sponsored, and international foundations and corporate giving programs. It is governed by a board of directors that represents all types of grantmakers. Members are encouraged to be effective, accessible, and accountable to the public. Self-regulation rather than government regulation is promoted.

Following the adoption of the Tax Reform Act of 1969, the framework of regulations for private foundations, the Council on Foundations was reorganized to strengthen its ability to represent grantmakers and their interests to Congress, the Internal Revenue Service, the media, and the public. In 1979 the Council moved its offices from New York City to Washington, D.C., to facilitate its ability to represent foundations in the process of refining and implementing the regulations resulting from the Tax Reform Act of 1969.

The Council on Foundations subsequently conducted research to illustrate the impact and unintended consequences of various provisions of the Tax Reform Act of 1969 and successfully negotiated many modifications. By demonstrating the contributions of philanthropic foundations and promoting understanding of their operations, the Council contributed to a more favorable legislative climate. The legislative function is one of its most important roles.

Members of the Council on Foundations are required to subscribe to a set of principles and practices for effective grantmaking, a guide for ethical grantmaking. The Council also provides technical assistance and educational opportunities. It holds conferences and educational seminars, publishes books, and publishes *Foundation News and Commentary,* a bimonthly magazine with articles about current foundation and nonprofit issues. It also publishes a bi-weekly newsletter, *Council Columns,* that covers Council activities.

The *Foundation Management Report* published every two years, provides administrative information, including salary, board, investment, and other issues based on a survey of members.

Council members hold over $100 billion in assets and give more than $5.5 billion for programs in education, human services, health, scientific research, and the arts. Members pay dues to the Council based on their assets (or grants amount if they do not have endowments). In addition to dues, the Council raises money from its members for special projects, and receives income from publications and conferences.

The Council plays a leadership role in the nonprofit sector both nationally and internationally. It is involved in national level efforts to promote philanthropy and voluntarism, and works closely with Independent Sector, the national umbrella organization for nonprofit and philanthropic organizations. The Council works internationally in cooperative efforts, with the European Foundation Center in the formation of Civicus: World Alliance for Citizen Participation, and for the promotion of organized philanthropy around the world.

The Council collaborates with more than 30 regional associations of grantmakers that serve foundations and corporate grantmakers in many areas of the country. It also works with more than 25 special interest affinity groups, which form an infrastructure of grantmaking that promotes exchange of ideas, support, and collaboration.

ELIZABETH T. BORIS

BIBLIOGRAPHY

Freeman, David and The Council on Foundations, 1991. *The Handbook on Private Foundation*. Rev. ed. New York: The Foundation Center.

Hall, Peter Dobkin, 1992. *Inventing the Nonprofit Sector: And Other Essays on Philanthropy, Voluntarism, and Nonprofit Organizations*. Baltimore: Johns Hopkins University Press.

COUNTY.

An administrative subdivision of a U.S. state.

The U.S. county is an important unit of local government that was originally created by states for the purpose of delivering state services such as tax assessing and tax collecting to a widely dispersed citizenry. Since the county was first imported to the colonies from England in the seventeenth century, it has undergone vast changes in role, function, and scope of authority. This essay provides an introduction to U.S. county government, summarizing its historical development, the quest for local autonomy, governmental structure, roles played in the intergovernmental system, and how counties exercise political influence.

Origins of County Government

County government's lineage can be traced to the English shire of a thousand years ago. The English shire played two roles that influenced the development of the U.S. county: the shire as an administrative arm of national government and the shire as a traditional local government. Primitive counties delivered the principal services of the royal government through justices of the peace who were appointed by the king, but local officials, particularly the sheriff, were also important. Early responsibilities of the county included judicial, military, and public works functions. While the English county remained the leading unit of local government, the parish and borough also became providers of local services. Parishes were formed in small rural areas as a unit of the church and civil government to furnish elementary education, poor relief, and highways; boroughs were established in more urban areas to provide police and judicial services.

Early settlers in the future United States crafted a host of adaptations to conform to their own particular economic and geographic needs. In Virginia, initial jurisdictions were modeled after the parish, but because the colony was agricultural and its population widely dispersed, larger areas were called for: the colony created eight counties to serve as election, judicial, and military districts. These first counties were governed by a plural executive form called the county court, a model of government that was later replicated extensively in other counties, and especially in the South.

Local governments springing up in Massachusetts also served as models for later colonies. The small parish was considered more suitable for Massachusetts' clustered communities, an adaptation that evolved into a tradition of powerful cities and towns and weak counties. Massachusetts was eventually carved into four counties, each administered by a court of justices, a sheriff, and a treasurer appointed by the governor; county government, however, never attained the stature of its counterpart in the South.

New York and New Jersey adopted a third form of local government. These states were divided into counties, but elected township officials automatically became members of the county board of supervisors, and a penchant for large county governing boards commenced. In Pennsylvania the county became the primary unit of local government because of its widely dispersed population, and county governing bodies, called boards of commissioners, were elected at large.

While the form of county government reflected a diversity of needs among colonies, the dual tradition of the county as administrative arm of the state and as local government persisted. Virginia's strong county form was modeled throughout much of the South. Massachusetts' form, which provided fewer services, spread throughout New England. The county supervisor form originating in New York and New Jersey surfaced in parts of Illinois, Michigan, and Wisconsin. And Pennsylvania's county commissioner form was transported to many Midwestern and Western states.

Following national independence in 1776, early state constitutions conceptualized county government as an administrative arm of the state, often describing them as "nothing more than certain portions of the territory into which the state is divided for more convenient exercises of the powers of government."

By the Civil War in the 1860s county government was assuming more responsibilities. Many states fashioned counties into election districts, paving the way for their becoming significant political units for political party machines and placing them in the center of the "spoils system," a term connoting graft and corruption. County governing bodies also were gaining more elective positions, and the potential for corruption was increasing along with the expansion in their political power; thus were planted seeds that would later grow into a "deeply tarnished image" for county government—and subsequent cries for reform by the late 1800s.

Following the Civil War, populations grew and both cities and counties began experiencing greater demands for urban services. After World War I, three trends merged to strengthen the role of counties as units of local government: (1) population growth, (2) suburbanization, and (3) the movement to streamline governmental structure. By World War II trends toward urbanization and the desire to professionalize county government were bringing changes that broadened the role of counties further: changes in organization and structure, more automony from the state, a greater number of intergovernmental linkages, more resources and revenues, better political accountability, and a "cleaner image." Newer services joined the more traditional ones, such as responsibility for libraries, airports, hospitals and health services, planning and zoning, and fire protection.

County Home Rule

By the early 1900s county governments began pushing for greater local autonomy, particularly in personnel and structural matters. As part of a wave of Progressive reforms, counties sought to streamline their "plural executive" form of government and centralize authority for greater acountability. California launched the home rule movement for county government in 1911 when voters approved a constitutional amendment permitting counties to frame and adopt their own charters. The home rule movement began very slowly, picked up steam in the 1950s, and peaked in the 1970s. Home rule for counties, however, has remained an attractive alternative in the 1990s. In 1992 Arizona became the twenty-sixth state to grant counties charter authority, and in 1994 Idaho became the thirteenth to give counties "optional forms" of home rule. Thirty-nine states now authorize counties some discretionary authority through charter government or optional forms of home rule. Nine states are still considered "non-home rule" states. A chronology of state grants of home rule powers to counties appears in Table I. Optional forms of home rule permit county governments to chose among several structural forms (see Table II).

Charter Home Rule

Charter home rule permits counties to frame and adopt their own charters, or "little constitutions." Charter home

TABLE I. CHRONOLOGY OF COUNTY HOME RULE AUTHORITY

Year	Charter	Year	Optional Forms, Other
1911	California	1970	Illinois
1915	Maryland	1972	South Carolina
1933	Ohio[1]	1973	Minnesota
	Texas[2]		Utah
1945	Missouri		North Carolina
1948	Washington	1974	Arkansas
1958	Oregon		Kansas
	Minnesota[3]		Kentucky
1959	Alaska	1975	Indiana
	Hawaii	1976	Georgia
	New York[1]	1978	Iowa
1960	Louisiana	1985	Wisconsin
1963	Michigan[1]	1994	Idaho
1968	Florida		
	Pennsylvania[1]		
1970	Colorado		
1972	Montana[1]		
	New Jersey		
	New Mexico[2]		
1974	South Dakota[2]		
1977	Maine		
1978	Tennessee		
1985	North Dakota[2]		
	Virginia		
1986	New Hampshire		
	Massachusetts		
1988	Iowa[1]		
1992	Arizona		

[1]Optional forms also.
[2]Considered a non-home rule state.
[3]Lacks enabling legislation.

SOURCE: Tanis J. Salant, "County Governments: An Overview." *Intergovernmental Perspective* (Washington, D.C.: Advisory Commission on Intergovernmental Relations, Vol. 17, No. 1): 7.

rule generally conveys broader authority than optional forms; it has the potential to convey more discretion to county governing boards in personnel matters, ordinance powers, revenue generation, and structure (e.g., electing an executive; appointing a professional manager; appointing or consolidating some elective constitutional offices, such as treasurer, assessor, recorder). Since the first charter was adopted by Los Angeles County in 1912, approximately 134 counties have succeeded in adopting a charter out of the roughly 1,320 counties that are eligible. Charter home rule seems to be more appealing in urban counties and in those areas with reform-minded constituencies. Referenda on county charters, however, tend to fail more often than they succeed. Some reasons for failure include the absence of a compelling need to change, little interest among voters in reform issues, or the opposition of county constitutional officers, whose elective positions are often changed into appointive ones, consolidated with other offices, or eliminated altogether. Charter adoption, however, continues as an appealing option with which to govern counties; since 1990, about 32 charter referenda have been held, and 10 have passed.

County Government in the 1990s

There are roughly 3,042 county governments in the United States. There are another 22 city-county consolidations and 44 "independent cities," those located outside of county areas that administer functions commonly performed by counties. Forty-eight states are divided into functional county government (counties are called "boroughs" in Alaska and "parishes" in Louisiana). Connecticut and Rhode Island are divided into "unorganized county areas" only for the purpose of elections. The number of counties per state ranges from 3 in Delaware to 254 in Texas. Eight states have fewer than 20 counties and 7 have 100 or more; the average number of counties per state is 64. Counties range in area from 26 square miles to 159,099 square miles, and the average county area is between 400 and 599 square miles. Further, county populations range from as low as 164 in Loving County, Texas, to 8 million in Los Angeles County; the average county population is between 10,000 and 25,000 residents.

Structure of County Government

With few exceptions the county governing body and most line officers (constitutionally based department heads) are elected locally. Reform efforts have focused primarily on altering the form of county government. The most common form (and the "least reformed") is the commission form, or plural executive, in which the governing body and constitutional officers are all elected. The commission-manager form, in which a professionally trained manager is hired to oversee executive functions of the board, is gaining in popularity; about 786 counties now appoint a manager or administrator. Table II presents the basic forms of governmental structure.

Governing Boards. All functional county governments are governed by locally elected legislative/executive bodies. The composition and title vary greatly across states and sometimes within, but the board of commissioners or board of supervisors, with three to five members, is the most common. There are about 17 different titles for the governing board, and board size ranges from 1 member to over 50 members. In most counties, board members serve in both legislative and executive capacities, though the trend of hiring professional managers or administrators heightens their policymaking role. Boards have overall fiscal responsibility for the county, approving the budget and

TABLE II. Basic Forms of County Government

1. **Commission Form.** An elected county commission or board of supervisors, which is the most common form of county government, has legislative authority (e.g., to enact ordinances, levy certain taxes, and adopt budgets) as well as executive and administrative authority (e.g., to administer local, state, and federal policies, appoint county employees, and supervise road work). Typically, however, administrative responsibilities are also vested in independently elected constitutional officers, such as a county sheriff, treasurer, coroner, clerk, auditor, assessor, and prosecutor.

2. **Commission-Administrator.** There are three basic types of this form, some of which also have additional, independently elected constitutional officers. About 786 counties have one type of this form.

   A. **Council-Manager.** The county council or board, which is the legislative body, appoints a county manager who performs executive functions, such as appointing department heads, hiring county staff, administering county programs, drafting budgets, and proposing ordinances.

   B. **Chief Administrative Officer.** The county board or commission, as the legislative and quasiexecutive body, appoints a chief administrative officer to supervise and coordinate county departments, but not appoint department heads, and to prepare budgets, draft ordinances, and oversee program implementation.

   C. **County Administrative Assistant.** The county board or commission, as the legislative and executive body, appoints an administrative assistant to help carry out the commission's responsibilities.

3. **Council-Executive.** A county executive is independently elected by the people to perform specific executive functions. The county board or commission remains the legislative body, but the county executive may veto ordinances enacted by the commission, with the commission having override power by an extraordinary majority vote. The county executive's authority and responsibilities are much like those of a mayor in a strong mayor-council municipality. About 383 counties have this form.

SOURCE: Tanis J. Salant, "County Governments: An Overview," *Intergovernmental Perspective* (Washington, D.C.: Advisory Commission on Intergovernmental Relations, Vol. 17, No. 1): 9.

setting the property tax rate as well as levying other types of taxes.

County Constitutional Officers. A county constitutional officer is an elected county official—exclusive of county governing board members, elected county executives, and judges—whose duties and responsibilities are prescribed in state constitutions and statutes. County constitutional officers operate independently of county governing boards except in budgetary matters.

The number, type, and titles of county constitutional officers vary across the 48 states with organized county governments. Few states have exactly the same mix of constitutional officers. Despite their varied nature, certain types of constitutional officers tend to predominate. The major ones and their common functions are as follows:

- Assessor maintains property lists, determines assessments, and administers the general property tax.
- Auditor examines and approves bills and claims made against the county.
- Clerk of the board serves as secretary to county governing boards and sometimes functions as chief executive officer.
- Clerk of the court handles administrative duties associated with the court operation, especially the collection of revenues.
- Coroner holds inquests into violent, unlawful, and/or unattended deaths.
- County/Prosecuting attorney enforces state law and represents the county in civil matters.
- Recorder/Register of deeds issues titles to real estate, maintains property and other records, and may oversee certification of professions and corporations.
- Sheriff keeps the peace, executes court orders, and maintains jails.
- Surveyor surveys lands, drainage ditches, and county roads.
- School superintendent generally has administrative, judicial, supervisory, and inspection powers over school districts in the county.
- Treasurer receives, maintains, and disburses county funds.

County constitutional officers who perform essentially the same duties and functions often have different titles in different states. This variation can cause confusion when attempting to identify and classify them. For example, clerks of the court are also known as clerks of the circuit, district, superior, judicial, chancery, common pleas, orphan, or criminal court, or as prothonotaries. Assessors are also called property appraisers or property valuation administrators. Recorders and registers of deeds tend to perform the same functions, but in some states they are known as registers in chancery, registers (or recorders) of wills (or deeds), or registers of probate.

County Managers/Administrators. A trend among county governments is to hire professional managers or administrators to oversee the executive functions of the governing board. County administrators tend to have broad powers, particularly if the county operates under a charter. The position of county manager often brings with it personnel merit systems, broader local and regional functions such as economic development, and a higher number of professional department heads.

County Executives. The county executive–comparable to municipal mayor–is elected on a countywide basis rather than appointed. Elected executives are a popular option, particularly in New York and Maryland, and they are state-mandated in all counties in Arkansas, Kentucky and Tennessee. The number of elected county executives is about 382.

Roles of County Government

County government in U.S. political thought has traditionally been conceptualized as an administrative arm of the state. A more recent view gives county government a dual role, that of local government and administrative arm of the state. This duality is an outgrowth of urbanization and dwindling federal support to states and localities, where county government is called upon to deliver more services both within and outside of municipal boundaries. Contemporary scholars would hold that county government now serves a quardrople role, one that reflects a growing importance in intergovernmental affairs. This quadruple role is described as follows:

Administrative Arm of the State. County government delivers services that are state programs. The level of service provided is typically client- or formula-driven and beyond the control of counties. Health care to indigents is one example.

Traditional Local Government. Traditional functions are also state-mandated, but counties often have discretion in the level of service provided. Traditional functions include those provided by the offices of assessor, recorder, treasurer, prosecutor, and courts and, in unincorporated areas, law enforcement. Other services can include the county hospital and public works.

Local Government. These functions can be divided into three categories: municipal-type services in the unincorporated area, such as planning and zoning, libraries, parks and recreation; services provided jointly with cities and towns through intergovernmental agreements; and responding to individual requests by county residents.

Regional Government. This is the fastest-growing role and includes such functions as transportation, air quality, conservation, siting landfill and toxic disposal locations, and economic development. These functions are typically quality of life issues that address long-range problems and are not user-oriented (except for mass transit). Rural and midsize counties also play this role, especially in the areas of waste management, land use, and economic development.

In addition to traditional duties and other programs mandated by the state, counties perform a growing list of optional services once largely the domain of municipalities. Despite the limits and controls imposed by the state, many counties now enjoy a large measure of autonomy. Traditional government roles still claim the greatest portion of county budgets today, particularly in view of escalating expenditures for law enforcement, corrections, and courts, but newer roles as "local" and "regional" governments are growing rapidly. Urban problems are no longer confined to communities with population concentrations. Environmental concerns and the shift of indigent populations from inner cities to outlying areas have superimposed urban problems on rural structures. Urban, suburban, and rural counties alike are grappling with common concerns. Affordable housing, solid waste management, clean air, water quality, refugee resettlement, juvenile justice, hazardous material transportation, energy alternatives, cable TV, and management of natural disasters are just a few of the concerns of county officials–concerns that reflect intergovernmental complexity and a greater role for county government in societal problem solving.

Political Influence of County Government

While a majority of states now permit home rule, counties are nevertheless dependent on states for fulfilling their multiple roles: on constitutional and statutory home rule and other latitude in structural, functional, and fiscal areas; on state court rulings over jurisdiction in local matters; on the governor's attitude toward local control; and on state agency actions. County officials have long argued at state capitols that they get increasingly more responsibilities but not the commensurate authority and resources to carry them out. In spite of the degree of local autonomy, all counties are obligated to perform traditional state services, and their original role as administrative arm of the state remains intact. Moreover, the practice of states mandating to counties without adequate funding is a particular irritant that has galvanized county officials across the country.

The Mandate Issue

State mandates without adequate funding are a major problem for counties. The National Association of Counties (NACo) defines a mandate as "any responsibility, action, or procedure that is imposed by one sphere of government on a subordinate government through constitutional, legislative, administrative, executive, or judicial action as a direct order or as a condition of aid under threat of civil or criminal sanctions." County officials have long complained about bearing the fiscal burden of carrying out state priorities or pet legislative programs, but until the late 1980s, counties typically responded to mandates by scrambling to comply. In recent yeares, a trend toward county activism has emerged, and some significant victories against mandates have been won by county officials and state associations. New York county commissioners, for example, instituted a successful lawsuit in 1990 against an administrative mandate involving county nursing homes that would have cost counties $27 million. Colorado counties helped get a mandate reimbursement law passed in 1990. Wisconsin county officials worked aggressively to get an advisory referendum passed to prohibit the state from mandating without funds.

County and other local officals, working individually or through associations, may have considerable influence on the development of state and federal policies affecting them, on the distribution of state and federal funds, and on the extent to which state and federal policies are implemented. Further, the influence of NACo and other local government lobbying groups in Washington has culminated in both houses of Congress passing a bill to prohibit the federal government from mandating without funding; the mandate issue shot to the top of the national political agenda when the 104th Congress was elected in 1994: the "Mandate Bill" was one of the first pieces of legislation to pass in both houses in early 1995.

County Associations

Counties interact with the legislature and attempt to influence the course of legislation affecting county government through professional associations, lobbyists, and on a one-to-one basis. General legislation affecting counties statewide is tracked by the county association. Forty-seven states have county associations or something similar. Associations are governed by an exective committee of elected county officials and headed by an executive director appointed by the governing board. The major activities include lobbying the state legislature, interfacing with the executive branch, providing services to county officials such as training, information, and insurance pools, and facilitating the lobbying efforts of county officials themselves. Associations also assist single counties or groups of counties in obtaining, altering, or squashing proposed local legislation. County elected (and sometimes appointed) officials regularly contact members of their legislative delegation or others holding key leadership positions, and single counties also hire lobbyists. The executive directors of county associations, though, serve as the principal lobbyist and are generally in the best position to understand a broad array of county issues and concerns.

Though states retain ultimate authority over county governments, counties have whittled away at state su-

premacy and are asserting themselves through a variety of strategies and institutional arrangements. As county governments seek creative ways to finance and deliver ever-expanding services, they steadily gain statutory authority from states and rearrange old structures, especially in the finance domain where it is needed most. State courts also appear more amenable to upholding greater levels of authority, particularly as counties seek relief from unreasonable state dominance. Recently, state courts have been more willing to protect county home rule powers and fend off costly state mandates. The spread and success of county home rule and the emerging activism of county officials to challenge state actions in court have influenced a growing number of judicial rulings in favor of county governments.

Intergovernmental Relations

Over the past several decades county governments have assumed greater importance in both the horizontal and vertical dimensions of the intergovernmental system. Many counties are now "full service governments" that are deeply engaged in important service delivery activities. This is especially true in metropolitan areas where counties provide a number of urban services, often on a countywide basis, and in midsize counties experiencing growth. But rural counties also find themselves grappling with complex issues, including those of solid waste management, economic development, and environmental mandates, which necessitate more interaction with local, state and federal governments. Rural counties as well are a more active and sometimes dominant actor in regional and intergovernmental settings. The sheriff of a small rural county in Arizona, for example, won a court battle in 1994 challenging the federal government's right to mandate to local offficials to run handgun checks (i.e., handgun control in the Brady Bill). County legislators are well integrated in intergovernmental activities. They sit as members of multi-county agencies, maintain contact with a variety of state departments, and regularly attend meetings with other county officials. Organizations such as NACo and county associations on the state level not only further the policy objectives of county legislators but also provide forums through which county legislators and managers from different states or regions network, exchange ideas and information, and work out solutions to common problems. U.S. county governments are no longer dismissed as "the forgotten governments."

TANIS JANES SALANT

BIBLIOGRAPHY

Berman, David R. and Tanis J. Salant, 1996. "The Changing Role of Counties in the Intergovernmental System." In Donald C. Menzel, ed., *The American County: Frontiers of Knowledge.* Tuscaloosa: University of Alabama Press.
Bureau of the Census, 1994. *1992 Census of Government,* vol. 1, no. 1 (March), Government Organization. Washington,

D.C.: U.S. Department of Commerce, Economics and Statistics Administration, Bureau of Census.

Cigler, Beverly A, 1991. "The County-State Connection: A National Study of Associations of Counties. Paper presented at the annual meeting of the American Political Science Association, Washington, D.C., August 29–September 1.

DeSantis, Victor. "County Government: A Century of Change." In *The Municipal Yearbook 1989.* Washington, D.C.: International City Management Association, pp. 55–85.

Fairlie, John A., and Charles Mayard Kneier. 1930. *County Government and Administration.* New York: The Century Company.

Jeffrey, Blake R., Tanis J. Salant, and Alan L. Boroshok, 1989. *County Government Structure.* Washington, D.C.: National Association of Counties.

Marando, Vincent L. and Mavis Mann Reeves, 1993. "County Government Structural Reform: Influence of State, Region, and Urbanization." *Publius,* vol. 23 (Winter) 41–52.

Salant, Tanis J., 1989. *County Home Rule: Perspectives for Decision Making in Arizona.* Tucson: University of Arizona, Office of Community and Public Service.

———, 1990. "County Governments: An Overview." *Intergovernmental Perspective,* vol. 17, no. 1 (Winter) 5–9.

———, 1993. "Shifting Roles in County-State Relations: From Servant to Partner?" In David R. Berman, ed., *County Government in an Era of Change.* Westport: Greenwood Press.

Salant, Tanis J. and Lawrence L. Martin, 1993. "County Constitutional Officers: A Preliminary Investigation." *State and Local Government Review,* vol. 25, no. 3:164–172.

COUNTY SUPREMACY MOVEMENT. A

series of legal and symbolic actions undertaken by United States county officials in the early 1990s asserting county control over public lands within their borders.

The county supremacy movement is distinguished by two factors: resistance to United States federal government land management policies, especially those that restrict resource-based uses such as grazing or logging; and involvement by elected county commissioners. Estimates are that as of 1995 over 300 counties have considered county supremacy ordinances. At least 40 counties have passed ordinances or resolutions supportive of county supremacy ideals.

Most county supremacy activity has taken place in the Western United States because of the predominance of federal land ownership in that region. The movement is also primarily a rural phenomenon, since rural counties are most likely to be reliant on natural resource industries and have a higher percentage of federal public lands than urban counties.

A focal point of the county supremacy movement is a land use ordinance passed by Catron County, NM, in 1989. The ordinance asserts county supremacy over federal lands, and utilizes language in the National Environmental Policy Act (1978) to claim that federal land agencies must adhere to local customs and culture in implementing land use actions. Counties utilizing the Catron County model then adopt ordinances asserting that the resource-based in-

dustries upon which their economies are reliant represent their custom and culture. "Wise Use" movement groups, such as the National Federal Lands Conference based in Utah, distribute copies of these ordinances at conferences for county officials interested in Wise Use issues.

Other strategies that are part of the county supremacy movement include an outright rejection of the legitimacy of federal land ownership, sometimes referred to as the "equal footing" doctrine. The reasoning is that since the original 13 states had no public lands, and all subsequent states entered the union with "equal footing," the states retain ownership and control over federal lands in their borders. Other actions have included designating trails on public lands as county roads, to avoid wilderness designation.

The level of conflict between county officials and federal land managers has risen. Some county supremacy ordinances include the threat to arrest any federal official attempting to enforce land management policies. In 1995, an Idaho county sheriff asserted that federal land managers would now have to register with him before having the legitimate right to enforce federal land policy. Also in 1995, a Nye County, Nevada, county commissioner bulldozed a closed United States Forest Service road to open it while federal employees looked on.

Because of its opposition to environmental protection laws and its rejection of federal legitimacy over public lands, the county supremacy movement is often linked to the Sagebrush Rebellion (1979–1981) and the Wise Use movement.

STEPHANIE L. WITT
LESLIE R. ALM

BIBLIOGRAPHY

Arrandale, Tom, 1994. "The Sagebrush Gang Rides Again." *Governing,* vol. 7 (March) 38–42.

Erm II, Rene, 1993–94. "The 'Wise Use' Movement: The Constitutionality of Local Action on Federal Lands under the Preemption Doctrine." *Idaho Law Review,* vol. 30: 631–670.

Reed, Scott, 1993-94. "The County Supremacy Movement: Mendacious Myth Marketing." *Idaho Law Review,* vol. 30: 525–553.

COURT OF JUSTICE OF THE EUROPEAN COMMUNITIES. The Court which has to ensure

that the law is observed in the interpretation and application of the treaties establishing the European Communities and of the legal texts adopted for the implementation of the treaties.

Introduction

The Court of Justice was created by the Paris Treaty of April 21, 1951 which established the European Coal and Steel Community (ECSC). Its seat is in Luxembourg, which is also the seat of the ECSC institutions. On March 25, 1957, when the two Rome Treaties established the European Atomic Energy Community (EAEC) and the European Economic Community (EEC), it was decided that there would be one single European Court of Justice (ECJ) for the three Communities.

On February 7, 1992, the Maastricht Treaty established the European Union. This was founded on the three existing Communities and on complementary provisions establishing a common foreign and security policy plus cooperation between the member states in the field of justice and home affairs (which are referred to as the new "pillars"). However, the jurisdiction of the ECJ was not extended to these two new pillars, as it is the court of the European Communities only. The conditions under which a case may be brought before the Court sometimes vary depending on which of these Communities is concerned. However, in practice, nearly all cases brought before the Court concern the European Economic Community (which since the Maastricht Treaty has become the European Community). Therefore, as regards legal remedies and rules of procedure, only the provisions applicable in the EC framework will be considered.

In 1988 a Court of First Instance of the European Communities (CFI) was added to the ECJ to relieve it of part of its work. The CFI is not a separate institution; for instance, it does not have its own services but uses those of the ECJ. Nevertheless, it makes completely independent decisions, but the party which has been unsuccessful in whole or in part before the CFI may appeal to the ECJ. Such appeals may only relate to points of law, as the ECJ has no jurisdiction to question the way in which the CFI has assessed the facts.

The Court of Justice and the Court of First Instance interpret and apply Community law, that is, the treaties and the legal texts adopted by virtue of these treaties by the Community institutions (Council of Ministers, European Parliament, and European Commission). However, this is a task they share with the national courts of the EC member states—they are really the ordinary courts for the application of Community law. In fact, the entry into force of the treaties led to the jurisdiction of the national courts being extended to all litigation questioning the application of Community law, while the Court of Justice and the Court of First Instance only have jurisdiction in legal processes explicitly reserved for them.

The Different Legal Processes

Among the different actions that can be brought before the ECJ and CFI, traditionally a distinction is made between direct actions, those in which a litigant brings a case directly before one of these two courts, and referrals for a preliminary ruling, by which a national court, in the context of a case on which it has to give a ruling, asks the ECJ

for its opinion on the interpretation or to assess the validity of specific pieces of Community law. Direct actions are heard before the CFI if brought by natural or legal entities (it is not necessary to be a national of a member country to bring an action) and before the ECJ when they are brought by a Community institution or a member state. Requests for a preliminary ruling are always submitted to the ECJ.

Direct Actions

The Action for Annulment. This enables a member country, a Community institution, or a natural or legal entity to request the ECJ or the CFI to annul an act adopted by the Community institutions. The annulled act is then regarded as being null and void. Any act can be the subject of such an action, as long as it has binding effect. For instance, an action can relate to a directive issued by the Council of Ministers or the European Commission that imposes objectives on member countries although it leaves them free to choose the means whereby they achieve these objectives; or it can relate to a regulation whose provisions apply immediately throughout the European Community without member countries having to intervene; or it can relate to a specific decision which the Council or the Commission has addressed to a state or individual.

The member countries, the Council of Ministers, and the European Commission can challenge any act which has binding effect—this can be an act with general application (regulation, directive) or an act with individual application (decision)—without having to justify their interest in bringing the proceedings. The European Parliament may only challenge acts adopted in violation of its rights—for instance, if the act has been adopted without the European Parliament having been consulted or involved in the procedure. Companies and individuals can only challenge decisions addressed to them or acts of direct and personal concern to them, which means that they have to be in a particular situation distinguishing them from the other companies and individuals to which the act applies. For instance, this is the case with a regulation fixing import duties on products from a country outside the European Community with the aim to fight dumping practices. Although such a regulation has general application, it may be challenged by companies accused of dumping practices.

The act will be annulled if its originator did not have the power to adopt it. For instance, this is the case if the Commission adopts a regulation pursuant to a provision of the treaty which provided for Council jurisdiction, or if a Community institution adopts a directive outside the jurisdictional scope of the European Communities. However, an act can also be annulled if the rules of procedure for its adoption (e.g., consultation of a certain body) have not been followed or if the reasons it is being adopted are not stated clearly.

Finally, an act may be annulled because its substance is contrary to the provisions of the treaty or to the general legal principles derived by the ECJ. For example, an act would be annulled if it conflicted disproportionately with property rights or the freedom to carry out commercial transactions, or if it did not adequately respect certain rights already acquired by members of the business community and companies.

The Action for Failure to Act This is the counterpart of the action for annulment, as it allows the Council of Ministers, the European Parliament, or the European Commission to be punished for their failure to act, which would be contrary to Community law. As in the case of the action for annulment, the Community institutions may bring a case before the ECJ without having to justify their interest in bringing proceedings, while individuals may only bring an action if the act which they consider should have been adopted would have been of individual and direct concern to them. An action for failure to act is rarely undertaken because it is not often the case that a Community institution must act. However, an example is an action brought by a company that reproached the European Commission for not investigating a complaint it had made concerning an infringement of EC competition rules by another company.

The Action for Default The aim of this action is to have the Court find that a member country has failed to fulfill its obligations arising from Community law. For example, this would be the case if a member country infringes the EC treaty by introducing import duties on goods from other member countries or it fails to implement, within a set deadline, a directive adopted by the Council of Ministers of the EU. The infringement may involve any public body: government, administration, Parliament, courts, local authorities. However, the proceedings are always against the member country itself and it cannot argue that the infringement has been committed by another body over which it does not have any jurisdiction, such as a local authority.

Only member countries and the European Commission may bring actions for default. However, in practice member countries never exercise this right as they prefer settling their disputes with other member countries through political channels. Individuals do not have the right to bring an action for default, but they can of course always lodge a complaint with the European Commission should they believe that national legislation is in conflict with Community law by asking the Commission to institute proceedings against a country before the ECJ. In practice many actions for default originate from the complaints received from individuals or companies. However, the European Commission always has the power to assess whether the proceedings would be expedient: even when the infringement of Community law appears to be established, the European Commission can still decide not to bring an action without having to state its reasons for

doing so–these may be, for example, political considerations or the probability that the infringement will have minimal consequences.

In the context of the action for default, the referral of a case to the ECJ is preceded by an administrative procedure in which the country against which proceedings are being undertaken has the opportunity to explain in detail the charges against it and, if necessary, end the infringement. Frequently the European Commission stops its proceedings at the administrative phase, either because it is convinced by the member state's explanations, or because the latter has taken the necessary measures to fulfil its obligations. However, if this does not happen, the Commission will bring the case before the ECJ, which will establish the default or dismiss the application. If the ECJ establishes the default, its judgment will only have a declaratory effect, which implies that the infringement is not automatically terminated. If, for instance, the infringement is due to a national law, the Court's judgment will not result in this law being annulled but only in an obligation being imposed on the national legislator to amend the law. If the authorities concerned do not implement the judgment, the country may be sentenced to pay a penalty.

The Action for Damages This enables individuals and companies to obtain damages when a Community institution has acted illegally, thereby causing them damage. An example would be if the Commission were suddenly to abolish a subsidies system for the export of certain products without providing any transitional measures for the businesses that had already concluded export contracts under the previous system. Such a modification is likely to infringe the principle of legitimate exception, a general legal principle which every Community institution is obliged to observe, and this infringement obliges the Community to make good any damage suffered by the companies concerned.

References for a Preliminary Ruling

As stated above, it is the national courts which primarily apply community law. In fact, the drafters of the treaties did not want to set up a special judicial body for questions of Community law, preferring to entrust its proper application to the judicial systems already existing in the member countries, but to give certain specific complementary tasks to the ECJ and the CFI. In this respect the subsidiarity principle is applied; another example of subsidiarity is that national administrations are generally responsible for implementing Community policy.

However, there is one risk in this system: the way in which one member state applies and interprets Community law may differ from the way in which it is applied and interpreted by another member state. Of course, such a risk exists within each state and is usually limited by a supreme court whose interpretation of the law is binding upon all the other courts. With respect to Community law, the risk is even greater in view of the differences in legal culture existing between the member countries and the special nature of the concepts used, which usually have no equivalent in national law. But rather than place a supreme court above the courts of the member states, the drafters of the treaties preferred to set up a system of cooperation within which national courts ask the ECJ for its opinion when they are not sure about the meaning or validity of a Community provision, without having to relinquish jurisdiction in the case.

Unlike an appeal or cassation system, the request for a preliminary ruling is not used by a party wishing to challenge a judgment that has already been handed down, but by a court before it settles a dispute. The question raised may concern the interpretation of any Community law text or may be on the validity, from the viewpoint of the treaties or general legal principles, of an act adopted by the institutions. The ECJ itself never applies Community law to the facts of the case at hand; it merely gives an interpretation *in abstracto* of the text on which it has been asked to give its opinion or to rule on its validity. Of course, this interpretation or assessment of validity is binding both on the court which asked for the Court's opinion and then has to settle the dispute, and on any other court which has to apply the same text.

For instance, a case is brought before a member state court by a national of another member state with the complaint that the administration has refused to grant him or her access to a job as a public servant on the grounds that he or she is a foreigner. If the court involved is not sure whether the provisions of Community law on freedom of movement for workers also apply to public servants, it will have to ask the ECJ for its opinion. The Court's reply will concern the scope that should be given to the provisions of the EC treaty on the freedom of movement for workers and it will then be up to the national court to decide, taking this reply into consideration, whether the application should be granted.

The reference for a preliminary ruling is an original legal action enabling national courts to carry out their work without significantly jeopardizing the unity of Community law. However, it is also a useful complement for the direct actions. In fact, as stated earlier, the action for annulment is only open to individuals under restrictive conditions so that an illegal regulation against which litigation was not considered opportune by the member countries or the institutions might be applied to them. However, this risk is limited by the possibility they have to indicate the invalidity of a regulation during a national procedure and to urge the national court to ask the ECJ to assess the validity. As already stated, individuals can neither bring an action for default nor force the Commission to bring one. However, if they believe that a national legal text is in breach of Community law, they can invoke this breach before the national court in charge of applying it and, pursuant to the principles of precedence and direct effect, the latter will have to suspend the national text considered to be contrary to Community law after having perhaps requested the ECJ for a preliminary ruling.

From this point of view the legal actions that can be brought before the ECJ and the CFI form a very coherent whole enabling the two courts to fulfill their fourfold function: First, they are administrative courts, responsible for seeing that the Community institutions do not go beyond the confines of their powers and that they make good the damage they cause as the result of illegal behavior. This function is fulfilled in the framework of the action for annulment, the action for default, and the action for damages. However, the action for annulment, when used by the institutions or the states, also gives the ECJ the function of a constitutional court whose task is to see that each Community institution respects the powers of the other institutions and those of the member countries. By means of the action for default, but also indirectly through the preliminary ruling proceedings, the ECJ acts as an international court ensuring that the member states fulfill the obligations to which they subscribed when they ratified the treaties. Finally, the ECJ ensures the uniform interpretation of Community law in all member states and acts, in this respect, as a court of cassation. It performs this task mainly by way of the preliminary ruling proceedings but also by way of all other actions, since the interpretation given during these other actions must be taken into consideration by all the national courts.

Composition, Organization, and Procedure

The functioning of the ECJ and the CFI will be made difficult if the European Union admits new members since, in terms of composition, a place is reserved for each member country. There will not be such a problem with regard to the rules of procedure.

Composition and Organization

Since the accession of Austria, Finland, and Sweden to the European Union, the Court of Justice and the Court of First Instance have each been composed of 15 judges appointed for periods of six years by common agreement of the governments of the member countries. Their term of office is renewable and, in fact, the term of office of most judges has been renewed at least once. The judges of the ECJ must be "chosen from persons whose independence is beyond doubt and who possess the qualifications required for appointment to the highest judicial offices in their respective countries or who are jurisconsults of recognized competence."

The judges at the Court of First Instance should likewise be persons whose independence is beyond doubt and who "possess the ability required for appointment to judicial office." No condition of nationality is stipulated but, in practice, each member state appoints a judge to the Court of Justice and another to the Court of First instance. In view of the wide freedom of choice enjoyed by each state, the members of the Court of Justice originate from the most varied professional backgrounds: judges, professors in law, politicians, lawyers, diplomats. This diversity is clearly a source of enrichment for case law. Such diversity can also be seen among the judges of the Court of First Instance, although they are younger and often former associates of members of the Court of Justice.

The judges of the Court of Justice and the Court of First Instance sit in plenary session or may form chambers consisting of three or five judges, depending on the importance of the case.

The judges of the ECJ are assisted by eight advocates-general (this figure has temporarily been increased to nine due to the current workload) who are appointed under the same conditions as the judges. In practice, each of the five larger states permanently fills a post of advocate-general, with the other posts being shared among the small states in rotation. The role of the advocate-general is, "acting with complete impartiality and independence, to make, in open court, reasoned submissions on cases brought before the Court of Justice, in order to assist the Court in the performance of the task assigned to it." These submissions, given at the end of the verbal procedure, comprise a complete analysis of points of fact and of law, a study of the applicable texts, legal literature, and case law and, at times, a comparative study of the various national laws. In the submissions, the advocate-general also proposes to the Court a legal solution for the dispute. The advocate-general, who represents the "general interest," does not receive any instructions and does not assist in the Court's deliberations.

There is no permanent advocate-general at the Court of First Instance. However, this Court can, should the nature of the case so require, appoint one of its members to carry out this function. The judge thus appointed therefore does not take part in the deliberations on the case; but recourse to this option is very rare.

The judges of the ECJ appoint the president of the Court of Justice from among their number for a period of three years; the term of office is renewable. The judges of the Court of First Instance elect their president in the same way. The presidents of the Court of Justice and the Court of First Instance supervise the work of their respective courts and divide the cases among their various chambers. They appoint a judge-rapporteur for each case and establish the time limits for the proceedings and the date of the hearings and deliberations. Furthermore, they give rulings in a summary procedure by means of a reasoned order on applications for interim measures; this decision can nevertheless be referred to the plenary court.

The members of the Court of Justice (judges and advocates-general) appoint the Court's registrar for a renew-

able period of six years. The registrar of the Court of First Instance is appointed under the same conditions by the judges of that court. The registrar is responsible for receiving, transmitting, and keeping all documents and notifications and draws up the minutes for each hearing. The registrar is furthermore the head of the administration of the court, who manages the budget and supervises the functioning of the services. A certain number of officials assist in these various tasks.

The Court of Justice has its own linguistic service that translates the written statements, submissions from advocates-general, and judgments of the Court of Justice and the Court of First Instance into the 11 official languages of the Community. Apart from their knowledge of languages, the officials working in this service have all had extensive legal training. A specialized department provides interpreting services for the hearings. The Court of Justice also has a library and documentation service on the state of legislation, caselaw, and legal publications at both national and Community level.

Procedure

With respect to the rules of procedure, a distinction should be made between direct actions and preliminary ruling procedures. For direct actions, a written application must be submitted to the Court specifying the subject matter of the application and the grounds on which it is based. These grounds cannot be altered during the proceedings. On receipt of the application, the President of the Court designates a judge-rapporteur, who will have the task of monitoring the progress of the case very closely. The defendant is then notified of the application and has one month in which to lodge a defense. The applicant has the right to lodge a reply within a new period of one month and the defendant can then lodge a rejoinder within a renewed period of one month.

After this written procedure has been closed, a decision is taken on the prior report of the judge-rapporteur and after hearing the advocate-general as to whether the case requires preparatory inquiries, the parties to appear, documents to be requested, witnesses to be heard, expert reports to be drawn up, and so forth, and whether the case should be heard by a chamber or the full court. After carrying out any preparatory inquiries, the judge-rapporteur summarizes the alleged facts and arguments of the parties in a "report for the hearing." The case is then heard by the judges and advocate-general in open court who, on this occasion, put numerous questions to the parties. Several weeks later, the advocate-general presents his or her opinion. The judges then deliberate upon the basis of a draft judgment drawn up by the judge-rapporteur. The decision is taken by majority. The deliberations are carried out in private and no dissenting opinion may be expressed.

Within the framework of the preliminary ruling procedure, an application is referred to the Court of Justice originating from a national court or tribunal, without any formal requirements. The registrar has the application translated, then notifies the parties to the proceedings before the national court, the member states, the Commission and, if necessary, the Council, of the application. They have a deadline of two months within which to present written submissions, which they can then set out at an open hearing. The procedure is similar to that for direct actions.

Effect of the Court of Justice's Work

Due to the fact that it has placed considerable emphasis on the importance of Community law, the Court of Justice has played an important role in European integration.

Creating an Autonomous Legal System

The Court of Justice has made a contribution to incorporating the European Communities within a legal system of their own that can be distinguished from both national and international law. The sources of this Community legal system are clearly not national as they originate from the treaties, the Conventions agreed by the Communities with third countries, the general legal principles drawn by the ECJ, and the acts adopted by the institutions. But this legal system can also be distinguished from international law—the majority of its rules are not applicable there. In this way, the traditional principle according to which the party injured by the non-fulfillment of obligations which are incumbent upon another party may be exempt from fulfilling his or her own obligations, is inapplicable if it is an obligation based on Community law. For example, a member state cannot rely upon the noncompliance of other member states with a directive in order to justify its own failure to act in this respect. In the same way, even though international law leaves it up to the states to choose the means with which they intend to incorporate the provisions of the treaties into their national system (transposition of a treaty provision or adoption through national legal measures), Community law itself contains rules governing its relationship to national laws.

Two aspects of the case law of the ECJ deserve special attention in this respect, as they show both the originality and the power of the Community legal system. One relates to sources of Community law and the other to its nature.

General Legal Principles. The Court of Justice is gradually deriving general legal principles, it considers to be superior to acts adopted by the Community institutions, forming an unwritten source of Community law. In concrete terms, any Community regulation, decision, or directive must comply with the general legal principles, failing which they will be declared null and void by the Court of Justice. Furthermore, the Court of Justice considers that these principles must likewise be respected by the member states when they implement Community law.

Although the Court of Justice is supposed to apply these principles and not create them, the prior findings which the Court has to make are in fact to a large extent of a creative nature and it enjoys great freedom in this respect. Formally, they are "principles common to the legal systems of the Member States." But in reality, the principles derived by the Court are not always known in all the member states, sometimes not even in the majority. The Court effectively reserves the right not only to select from among the various solutions offered by the national laws (hence the principle of "legitimate expectation," which it regularly applies, is only recognized in German and Belgian laws), but also to declare void common principles that would be incompatible with the Community requirements.

Furthermore, the Court of Justice applies—whenever it has the opportunity to do so and by way of general legal principles—the provisions of the European Convention on Human Rights, while at the same time sometimes giving a different interpretation to that held by the European Court of Human Rights, which carries out its activities within the framework of the Council of Europe. This recourse to the provisions of the European Convention on Human Rights makes it possible to compensate for the fact that the European Communities do not have their own catalogue of fundamental rights.

The Court of Justice has derived many principles. Some refer to the protection of individuals against the acts of states or Community institutions: property rights, freedom to carry out economic activities, the right to respect one's privacy and family life. However, these rights are in themselves not absolute prerogatives and can be subject to restrictions compatible with the social function of protected goods and activities. In this way, the Court of Justice acknowledged that property rights could be restricted by a regulation banning the planting of new vines, as this regulation did not conflict with the very essence of the right but only with its exercise, and it was justified by the need to reduce the amount of wine produced in the Community territory.

Other principles relate to guaranteeing legal security: nonretroactive effect, challenging of acts which have not received sufficient publicity, legitimate expectation, rights of the defense. This last principle requires that the adversary nature of the procedure be respected not only before judicial bodies but also before administrative bodies, even if they are purely of an advisory nature, as soon as a person's interests "are perceptibly affected by a decision taken by a public authority."

Finally, the principle of equality requires that comparable situations should not be treated differently and the principle of proportionality requires that any burden imposed on the person to whom the Community rules are applied be confined to the extent strictly necessary to achieve the required objective and that as few sacrifices as possible be demanded of the companies and individuals to which it is applied.

Principles of Direct Effect and Precedence. These principles relate to the nature of Community law. Saying that a provision has direct effect means that any individual may request that it be applied by the national courts so as to draw a subjective right from it. The drafters of the treaties had intended for Community regulations to have such an effect—by definition, they are directly applicable in the member states. But the Court of Justice extended this capacity to certain articles in the treaty as well as to certain directives, since the provisions concerned are quite precisely defined and unconditional. Extending this to directives is all the more significant because these directives require, by definition, that measures be implemented on the part of the member countries. Therefore, they can only have direct effect if they have not been transposed within the deadlines and their direct effect can only be invoked against a state and not against a private individual.

As Community law is directly applicable in the member states, it is likely to conflict with national rules. This conflict is settled in favor of Community law by applying the precedence principle. All national rules contrary to a rule of Community law must be discarded whatever their respective priority may be *vis-à-vis* one another. A national constitution cannot be set against a Community regulation that is contrary to that constitution.

By virtue of these principles of precedence and direct effect, the national courts must, as far as possible, interpret national legal texts in a way that conforms with Community legal texts. If it proves impossible to interpret the national text in such a way, the courts must set aside the national texts that are contrary to Community law. In this way, a criminal court must discharge a defendant prosecuted on the basis of a national text that is contrary to an article of the Treaty. But it can sometimes occur that simply discarding national texts is not sufficient to give effect to the Community text. This is the case, for example, when a directive provides that the states will have to adopt certain measures in favor of individuals. If the directive is not implemented by the states, the mere fact of discarding the national law will not be sufficient. It is therefore necessary for the national law to be actually replaced by the provision of Community law (substitution effect). Finally, according to the Court of Justice, the national courts must compensate individuals who have been injured due to an infringement of Community law by a member state and order national administrations to reimburse them with the amounts they had to pay by virtue of national texts recognized as being contrary to Community law.

An Essential Contribution to European Integration

The establishment of a Common Market is the essential economic aim of the Community, and the Customs Union is its basic expression. It extends to all trade in goods and involves the prohibition among member states of customs duties and quantitative restrictions on imports and exports as well as the adoption of a common customs tariff in relations with third countries. In order to prevent the prohibition from being indirectly distorted, the drafters of the treaty have made a point of also prohibiting measures with the same effect as customs duties or quantitative restrictions. However, this provision has not prevented member states from introducing numerous charges for administrative services, health dues, statistical tariffs, and so forth aimed at penalizing imports. Due to a broad interpretation of the concept of measures having equivalent effect, the Court of Justice has managed to counter these attempts at misuse and, to a large extent, ensure the disappearance of fiscal and customs barriers.

However, the Common Market is also based on the principle of free and fair competition. There is likewise a ban on agreements between companies, decisions by associations, and concerted practices, as well as on the abuse of a dominant position likely to affect trade between member states. It is primarily incumbent on the Commission to verify that the rules are respected and to adopt, depending on the matter involved, coercive measures to act against the offending parties. These measures are, however, always subject to monitoring by the CFI and the ECJ and their case law has allowed barriers to competition to be limited considerably. Thus, the Court has considered a concerted practice to be a form of coordination between undertakings which, without an actual agreement being concluded, allows them to avoid complete exposure to the competition rules. In similar fashion a contract is an illegal competitive restriction when it imposes on the buyer the obligation to make use of the goods supplied for his or her own needs and not resell the goods in a specified region.

As regards the provisions of the treaty that prohibit aid being granted to certain companies by the member states when such aid has the effect of distorting competition, these provisions have been interpreted by the Court of Justice in such a way that they not only apply to direct subsidies but also forbid indirect aid, such as tax exemption, relief from social security charges to be paid by a company, or loan guarantees under conditions more favorable than those of the market.

In another field, the provisions of the EC treaty give the right to the workers of each state to apply for employment offered in the other member states under the same employment and working conditions as those offered to nationals. The Court of Justice has interpreted in broad terms the concept of employment and working conditions, integrating in them, for example, the conditions for access to housing and house ownership.

The Treaty of Rome also provides for the possibility for Community nationals who are pursuing a professional activity in a self-employed capacity to establish themselves in another member state or to provide services there under the same conditions as the nationals of that member state. The Court of Justice has proved to be very vigilant as regards the respect for these freedoms; it condemns not only discrimination on grounds of nationality but also discrimination which, while being based on an apparently neutral criterion, has in fact the same result. Thus a national rule that requires that persons pursuing certain activities reside in the territory of that member state has the practical effect of being unfair to the nationals of other member states, even though in legal terms it applies to nationals as well as nonnationals. It is therefore prohibited. Moreover, the ECJ has also handed down many judgments on the equality of access to public contracts.

Finally, the abundant case law of the Court of Justice on the principle of equal treatment of men and women has given this principle a scope for application that was certainly never anticipated by the Community legislators. Created originally so that companies in the different member states would be covered by equal conditions of competition, and limited in the EC treaty to equal pay, this principle has been extended by directives to working conditions and access to employment as well as social security. The Court of Justice has interpreted the concept of discrimination on grounds of sex very broadly by criticizing not only rules which make a distinction, explicitly and without justification, between men and women but also those rules which, while making use of other criteria, have the same result. It is particularly the case with all the rules that treat part-time workers unfairly, since it has been observed that this type of work is undertaken more by women than by men. But, above all, the concept of the direct substitution effect has found here a considerable field of application because it permits national courts to grant directly to the unfairly treated category the advantages that are granted to the favored category, whether these advantages are provided by a law or by a collective agreement.

Conclusion

One cannot stress enough the contribution which the judges of the ECJ have made to European integration. By permitting citizens to assert the subjective rights conferred on them by the Community legal texts before the national courts, the Court of Justice has placed in their hands the power to ensure indirectly that the member states are respecting their obligations. This decentralized control, emanating from the members of the business community and companies which have the greater interest in seeing integration continue, has proved to be extremely effective. This has been strengthened by the interpretations the Court of Justice has given to the Community provisions, interpretations which have always been guided by the wish to give the maximum effect to the provisions of the treaties, regulations, and directives, by referring to the objective being pursued rather than to the letter of the legal texts.

Spyros A. Pappas and
Christophe Soulard

BIBLIOGRAPHY

Publications of the Court of Justice

Selected Instruments Relating to the Organization, Jurisdiction and Procedure of the Court. This work contains a selection of the provisions concerning the Court of Justice and the Court of First Instance to be found in the treaties, in secondary law, and in a number of conventions. It is available in the eleven EC official languages from the Office for Official Publications of the European Communities, L-2985 Luxembourg.

Reports of Cases before the Court of Justice and the Court of First Instance. These reports are published in the eleven EC languages, and are the only authentic source for citations of decisions of the Court of Justice or of the Court of First Instance. The final volume of the year's reports contains a chronological table of the cases published, a table of cases classified in numerical order, an alphabetical index of parties, a table of the Community legislation cited, an alphabetical index of the subject matter, and a systematic table containing all the summaries with their corresponding chains of keywords for the cases reported.

Proceedings of the Court of Justice of the European Communities. A weekly bulletin of information on the judicial proceedings of the Court of Justice and the Court of First Instance containing a short summary of judgments delivered by the two Courts, brief notes on opinions delivered by the advocates-general, and a list of new cases brought during the previous week. Application to subscribe to this publication should be sent in writing to the Information Service of the Court, L-2925 Luxembourg, specifying the language required. It is supplied free of charge.

Books

Brown, L. Neville and Tom Kennedy, 1994. *The Court of Justice of the European Communities.* 4th ed. London: Sweet & Maxwell.
Hartley, T. C., 1994. *The Foundations of European Community Law.* 3rd. ed. Oxford: Oxford University Press.
Lasok, D. and J. W. Bridge, 1991. *Law and Institutions of the European Communities.* 5th. ed. London Dublin Edinburgh: Butterworths.
Schermers, Henry G. and Denis Waelbroeck, 1992. *Judicial Protection in the European Communities.* 5th. ed. Deventer, Netherlands: Kluwer.

Journal Articles:

Arnull, Anthony, 1990. "References to the European Court." *European Law Review,* vol. 375.
Due, Ole, 1991. "Legal Remedies for the Failure of European Community Institutions to Act in Conformity with Treaty Obligations." *Fordham International Law Journal,* vol. 14:341.

Harding, C., 1992. "Who Goes to Court in Europe? An Analysis of Litigations Against the European Community." *European law Review*, vol. 17:105.

Slynn of Hadley, Lord, 1993. "What Is a European Community Law Judge?" *Cambridge Law Journal*, vol. 52:234.

Vesterdorf, Bo, 1992. "The Court of First Instance of the European Communities After Two Full Years in Operation." *Common Market Law Review*, vol. 29:897.

COURT ORDER.

A command, mandate, or direction of a court either granting or denying the request of the party for some affirmative relief. A court order may be given verbally or in writing.

A court order has often been distinguished from a judgment in that a judgment involves the final adjudication of an issue and a court order involves a ruling on a preliminary or collateral issue. Practically speaking however, a judgment is a court order which has finality and from which an appeal can be taken. Ex parte orders are court orders which benefit only one party and which are entered without notice to the other party and without an opportunity to be heard. These court orders are entered when statutes or rules allow and where exigent circumstances exist.

A court order entered by a court lacking jurisdiction over the parties or subject matter or lacking the inherent power to enter a particular order is void and usually does not have to be obeyed. On the other hand, if a court order is erroneously entered based on a mistake of law or a mistake in the application of legal principles, the order is not void and must be obeyed until it is vacated or reversed.

Enforcement of court orders involves contempt proceedings and either threatened or actual punishment. If a party individually or acting on behalf of an agency or entity willfully disobeys a court order, the court may enter additional orders which involve imprisonment or fines or related orders to gain compliance of the individual with the original order. A finding of contempt of court can only be based on a valid order and there must be a showing of a willful violation of the order.

Court orders are as varied as the types of issues that come before courts and can range from a simple direction by a judge during a hearing to the issuance of a written order having a specific statutory or common law basis such as the well-known traditional or extraordinary writs. These writs (orders) generally enable a party to seek review in a higher court of actions taken by an inferior court, tribunal, or agency, when normal appellant review either is not available or does not afford a speedy and adequate means of review. These writs are quite frequently utilized by courts in administrative review actions.

The most commonly issued writs are the writ of habeas corpus (allowing a challenge to alleged illegal confinement or detention unrelated to a criminal procedure), writ of mandamus (utilized to compel or direct an inferior tribunal, person, officer, or agency to do an act which the law requires of them), writ of prohibition (utilized to prevent courts, officers, or persons from exercising jurisdiction with which they are not invested by law), writ of quo warranto (allowing a challenge of a person alleged to be usurping, intruding into, or unlawfully holding any office), and writ of injunction (utilized to compel or restrain action by individuals or officials to prevent some immediate harm resulting from their performance or nonperformance of an action). In addition, federal courts are now empowered under the All Writs Act, 28 U.S.C.S. §1651 (1948, 1949), to issue any type of writ necessary and appropriate to aid their jurisdiction and to afford an appropriate remedy in any given case.

STEPHEN J. WORRELL

BIBLIOGRAPHY

All Writs Act, 28 U.S.C.S. §1651 (1948, 1949).

2 American Jurisprudence 2d, Administrative Law, §548–553 (1994).

56 American Jurisprudence 2d, Motions, Rules, and Orders, §§29–46 (1971).

Black's Law Dictionary, 1968. Rev. 4th ed. St. Paul, MN: West Publishing Company.

COVENANT OR RESTRICTIVE COVENANT.

A promise or agreement between contracting parties in the conveyance of real property which stipulates benefits or burdens attached to that property. Covenants that run with the land bind successive owners to the terms of the original agreement. All original covenanting parties must agree on the duration and type of the covenant in order for it to be legally binding. Covenants must also touch and concern the land and be held reasonable to be enforced.

There are several important terms associated with the discussion of covenants. Expressed covenants are those which are written in deeds, declarations, plats, or other documents associated with the land. Implied covenants are those which are oral, or otherwise expressed by the original covenanting parties. Negative covenants are those which attach restrictions to a parcel of land and prevent the owner from engaging in an activity. Affirmative covenants are those which require the owner to perform an act or render a service.

Covenants attach burdens and benefits. A burdened or servient parcel of land is one in which the owner is restricted from action (negative covenant) or required to render service (affirmative covenant). The benefited or dominant parcel of land is one which gives the owner the right to sue for legal remedy. Benefits received in connection with the ownership of a benefited parcel are said to be held in appurtenant. Benefits required by covenant and received by persons who do not own the benefited parcel are benefits said to be held in gross.

The origins of covenants can be traced to the ancient law of promises, in which agreements pertaining to real property were expressed in deeds. The first legal enforcement of covenants occurred in the English common law and equity courts. In Spencer's Case (1583), the English common law courts recognized at law enforcement of covenants by holding that agreements pertaining to the use of land between the original owners were binding upon successive owners. These covenants attached to property were said to run with the land and became known as running covenants.

In 1848, the plaintiff in the case of *Turk v. Moxhay* sought an injunction against the owner of a parcel of land previously designated through covenant as the permanent site for a small park. The new owner wished to build a residence upon the land and the neighbor brought suit. The English Chancery (equity) court granted the injunction, which set the precedence for equitable remedy or equitable servitude. These two legal principles were transferred to the U.S. court system, and became generally known as real covenants.

Real covenants in the United States have been historically used to restrict the sale or rental of property to ethnic minorities. In the landmark case, *Shelley v. Kramer* (1948), the Supreme Court found all such discriminatory covenants in violation of the Equal Protection Act of the Fourteenth Amendment.

Currently, real covenants are used most widely in subdivisions and urban developments to restrict land use and building construction. Some covenants require parties to maintain drainage systems, bridges, and roadways.

Residential community associations and homeowners' associations also use covenants to require fees and assessments.

KIM L. MURPHREE

BIBLIOGRAPHY

Berry, C. P., 1915. *Digest of the Law of Restrictions on the Use of Real Property*. Chicago: George I. Jones Publishing.

Korngold, Gerald, 1990. *Real Estate Series: Private Land Use Arrangements: Easements, Real Covenants, and Equitable Servitudes*. Colorado Springs: Shepards/McGraw-Hill, Inc.

Siegel, Stephen A., 1988. *A Student's Guide to Easements, Real Covenants, and Equitable Servitudes*. New York: Mathew Bender & Company.

Sims, Henry Upson, 1901. *A Treatise on Covenants Which Run with Land Other Than Covenants for Title*. Chicago: Callaghan & Company.

Vose, Clement E., 1959. *Caucasians Only: The Supreme Court, the NAACP, and the Restrictive Covenant Cases*. Berkeley and Los Angeles: University of California Press.

CREDIT RATINGS. Summary of the risk of default on bonds. Organizations issue bonds to obtain capital and are required to obtain a bond rating to attract investors, who use the rating to asses the risk they are taking and what interest rate the bond issue should carry.

Borrowing money requires the ability and willingness to repay the party lending the money. Otherwise, the lender has no incentive to enter a voluntary transaction. A lender gains added comfort from having a third party assess a borrower's probability of nonpayment on a loan. It also offers borrowers, especially the stronger ones, a chance to bargain for better lending terms, such as lower rates. Individuals are used to having their credit history tracked and reported to prospective lenders, and so too are organizations, both private and governmental. Besides, credit quality may improve, deteriorate, or stay stable during the loan's duration. As a result, a credit rating process has evolved to summarize default risk, and specialized firms have emerged to provide these credit rating assessments. These ratings influence the costs of borrowing and, therefore, public policy.

Organizations issue bonds to obtain capital but must obtain a bond rating to attract investors. Several firms provide credit assessments upon application and payment of a fee based on the size of the proposed debt issuance. The two most prominent firms are Moody's Investors Service, Inc. and Standard & Poor's Corporation. These firms, and issuers of debt, seek to have a credit rating assigned before selling bonds. If the issuer does not apply for a rating, but a rating is in effect for outstanding parity issues (bond issues of equivalent rank), the ratings on the outstanding parity bonds may be withdrawn. Furthermore, the new issuance may be rated even without the issuer's application for one. A rating holds for the life of the bonds unless there is a change in repayment ability.

All the ratings firms use alphabetical symbols to show the relative investment quality or creditworthiness of the bonds they rate. Bonds are rated investment grade or below investment grade, with several subgrades in each category, as shown in Table I. The importance of receiving an investment grade rating is that many institutional investors (e.g., commercial banks, insurance firms, and mutual funds) can retain only investment grade bonds in their investment portfolios.

Ratings depend upon a review of the credit backing a proposed debt issuance. To start its review of an issuer's risk of default, ratings firms assign analysts (individually or in a working group) to assess the issuance. A detailed review occurs, focusing on the particular features associated with the proposed issuance and general aspects of the borrower. This detailed review may involve site visits and many exchanges of information between the analyst and the debt issuer. Furthermore, credit rating firms have access to other data collectors and their own extensive data files. Analysts review their recommendations with their supervisors, and

TABLE I. BOND RATING CATEGORIES

Rating Description	Moody's*	S&P*
Investment Quality		
Best Quality	Aaa	AAA
High Quality	Aa	AA
Good Quality	A	A
Medium Grade	Baa	BBB
Speculative Quality		
Speculative Elements	Ba	BB
		B
Little Assurance	B	CCC
Poor Standing	Caa	CC
	Ca	C
	C	
In Default	–	D

*The above rating scales can be further subdivided into classes such as A1 and Baa1. For example, A1 is higher than A.

the resulting proposal is presented to a rating committee of senior executives in that firm. This committee assigns the bond rating. After notifying the applicant, public distribution occurs. While an applicant may appeal the rating decision, it seldom results in any change.

Credit assessment firms maintain an active surveillance over debt issuers and ratings. These firms expect issuers to stay in close communication with them, sending financial documents and alerting them to relevant developments. Failure to provide information can result in withdrawal of a rating. This is a severe signal to the market that will compel some investors to sell the bonds whatever the price. Suspension of a rating can occur if "new or material circumstances arise, the effects of which preclude satisfactory analysis" (Moody's Investors Service, Inc., 1991, p. 45). Information on changed issuer policies is often required for clarification; in the interim, ratings remain suspended. Short of a suspension, but worrisome still, is when a rating service places an issuer's bonds on "credit watch"–meaning credit conditions are uncertain.

It is noteworthy, however, to find that trading activity and market values of seasoned bonds anticipate ratings' changes (Marks, Raman and Wilson 1994). This means that ratings firms' announcements lag market information about changes in credit quality.

A rating is a subjective result, meaning that different analysts may arrive at different conclusions. While the ratings firms rely on similar information to base their judgments, they emphasize different features. As a result, ratings may differ by firm. Academic researchers have tried to duplicate the bond rating process, at least in the state and local government market sector. The results have not been particularly successful (Aronson and Marsden, 1980). Models that try to predict the rating of municipal credits

based upon fiscal variables (e.g., debt per capita, assessed property value per capita) record limited predictive power. One explanation is that the ratings firms rely on many variables, some nonquantifiable, in arriving at their committee decision.

Market rates reflect credit quality. Investors receive a lower return on higher rated bonds since there is presumably less risk of default. Higher market returns, in contrast, accrue to investors willing to accept the alleged weaker credit risk associated with lower rated bonds. From the issuer's standpoint, the interest cost to borrow money generally increases in inverse relationship to the bond rating. Thus, lower bond ratings impose higher borrowing costs. It is, therefore, in the financial interest of borrowers to take all available steps to obtain a high credit rating.

Credit rating firms are clear in the narrow purpose of ratings. A credit rating is not a recommendation to purchase, sell, or hold a security since it does not consider other factors such as market price and risk performance of the investor. These firms seek to provide potential investors with all the information possible, but a rating is not a purchase recommendation. Quality determines the rating, not the reverse.

Most investors demand a rating before making an investment in bonds. This means that business and government borrowers alike have to obtain bond ratings. Of particular interest are two categories of government borrowers: sovereign governments and "municipals" (a term that includes state and local governments).

Rating Sovereign Governments

Prevailing practice in the world's financial markets considers the debt incurred by the United States of America default-free. U.S. Treasury securities set the standard for measuring the default risk of all other debtors. Still, the major industrialized countries possess sterling reputations and receive top ranked assessments.

Many sovereign governments issue debt both in their domestic currency market and in foreign currency. In the past, a bond rating was sought only on foreign currency offerings. With international capital now flowing into domestic obligations there is demand for bond ratings on all sovereign debt (Cantor and Packer, 1995).

Lenders of funds to sovereign governments are often external investors, and by implication less able to bring legal action in that country to enforce the repayment of funds. Besides, there may be a bias to fulfill domestic needs over foreign debt. As a result, ratings on foreign currency bonds never exceed, and are often lower than, the ratings for domestic currency obligations.

Assessing a country's willingness to pay is a major factor in making sovereign credit judgments. Investors remember several sovereign defaults during the Great Depression. Today, repudiation of debt is a severe action by a sovereign country interested in engaging in the global financial and trading markets.

Credit quality is based on many factors, but some important criteria for a sovereign borrower include (Standard & Poor's Corporation, 1979):

- Political stability: Includes political traditions and institutions, with attention on the stable transfer of power.
- Economic growth and diversification: Focuses on balanced and stable growth, including a strong export economy.
- Economic management: Examines fiscal and monetary policy and the institutions created to foster economic growth and diversification.
- External debt burden: Measures the amount of outstanding debt in relationship to gross domestic product and exports.
- International liquidity: Assesses the ability to meet timely cash needs using reserves and access to the financing of international organizations (such as the International Monetary Fund) to cope with unanticipated events.
- Balance of payments flexibility: Relates to economic policies fostering a balance of imports and exports, or making any needed adjustments.
- Economic outlook: Looks at a country's economic prospects.

The two dominant firms frequently disagree on specific sovereign ratings. This is especially the case in categories below investment grade, where there is greater uncertainty. Qualitative country risk factors (stability of political institutions, social and economic cohesion, etc.) make ratings assessments of sovereigns a unique field.

As reflected in market yields, sovereign debtors face a pessimistic market. The bonds trade at higher yields than comparably rated U.S. corporate bonds. Moreover, the gap widens as ratings quality declines. Simply stated, international investors expect a premium for investing in most foreign bonds.

Sovereign ratings influence the ratings on all borrowers within that country. Rating firms generally do not assign ratings to public or private sector issuers that are higher than their home country's sovereign rating.

Rating Municipal Securities

U.S. state and local governments borrow in a domestic "municipal" securities market (Hildreth, 1993). This market has evolved out of its unique status codified in the national income tax laws. Specifically, most investors in these securities do not have to pay U.S. income tax on the interest earnings from lending money to state and local governments, or for purposes issued on behalf of those governments. By definition, elimination of this tax-advantaged investment option (as with adoption of a "flat rate" national income tax) would negatively affect the existing market.

State and local governments issue two types of securities, depending upon the collateral pledged: general obligation bonds and revenue bonds. They require different rating perspectives.

General Obligation Bonds

Bonds issued by a subnational political jurisdiction backed by a broad collateral pledge are full faith and credit, or general obligation, bonds. For example, states enjoy access to a wide range of revenues, with most having both sales and income tax structures. This allows a state to offer a pledge to adjust taxes to meet its debt obligations. Local governments, including municipalities, counties and school districts, pledge the property tax. This is in effect a tax lien on every taxable land parcel (and improvements thereto) in the jurisdiction. Due to the nature of the full faith and credit guarantee, general obligation bonds traditionally enjoy higher ratings, and lower interest costs to the borrower, than debt backed by a single dedicated revenue source.

Assessing the credit quality of general obligation bonds requires an analysis of many factors (Moody's Investors Service, Inc., 1991) including:

- Economy: Analysis of tax base with particular emphasis on its diversification, resilience, and growth prospects.
- Financial: Reviews recent and projected finances in the context of professional tax administration, balanced budgets, financial flexibility, and accountability standards.
- Debt: Examines the security, structure, and amount of outstanding indebtedness, including debt on local taxpayers placed by other taxing jurisdictions.
- Government: Evaluates the ability to deliver services, the quality of management, and the history of political support to make prudent fiscal policy, with special attention on the willingness to honor debt obligations.

General obligation pledges are considered the most secure obligations of state and local governments. However, in recent years analysts have given renewed attention to the "willingness to pay" idea. Testing "ability to pay" is easier, many feel, than detecting the willingness of taxpayers to stand behind a legal pledge to repay borrowed funds.

Revenue Bonds

Another specialized form of credit analysis is for revenue-backed debt. Unlike general obligation debt backed by the full faith and credit of the government's taxing power, revenue debt has as security a dedicated source of funds. If that particular flow of funds ends, so too does the value of the bonds. While subnational governments in the United States rely greatly on this form of debt, this is not so elsewhere. For example, provinces and municipalities in Canada do not have the same experience.

A wide range of services depend upon revenue bonds for capital. In this group are many services: water supply and distribution; sewer systems; waste disposal operations; electric generation and distribution systems; public garages; civic centers; toll roads and bridges; university housing and restaurants; and economic development projects, among others. Any of these could receive financing through general obligation bonds. Modern management practice (and political necessity typically) suggests that these enterprises should rely upon the users as ratepayers, not as taxpayers, to pay for capital. Revenue bonds allow borrowing against the resulting rates. Earmarked tax revenues, such as from a local sales tax, can serve as the pledge for revenue bonds. In such a situation, investors are subject to revenue flow uncertainties from a single tax.

Credit analysts must carefully examine the particular features of bonds backed by pledged project revenues. The types of factors include (Moody's Investor's Service, Inc., 1991; Standard & Poor's Corporation, 1979):

- Demand: Examines the economic stability of the revenue-producing stream (e.g., the demand for a monopoly water service is more stable than for a parking garage).

- Feasibility: Tests the reasonableness of the demand forecast and projected revenue streams, the physical and engineering aspects of a project to produce as expected, and the methodologies and assumptions used in studies touting a project's benefits.

- Revenue: Questions the viability of the project, and its management, to meet its long-term revenue needs, and addresses the legal security of those pledged revenues.

- Coverage: Looks for the flexibility and resilience to produce more than enough revenue to cover basic operations and debt service.

- Debt levels and structure: Compares the reliance on debt financing on the enterprise's assets.

- Management and operations: Examines executive abilities to plan, direct, and carry out strategic actions in a political and regulatory environment to meet demand and maintain adequate operations.

- Bond covenants: Reviews the legal protections afforded bondholders and the provision of covenants that specify certain rules of enterprise operation, provisions to avert bankruptcy or default, and remedies for an issuer's default.

- Economics: Focuses on competitive services, management's ability to encourage economic activity, the sensitivity to local economic cycle, and local wealth and employment.

Influence of Ratings

Credit rating firms influence the borrowing behavior of municipal issuers. Without a rating, inexperienced or inadequately qualified issuers are effectively barred from entering the market. Some issuers, recognizing their own negative market qualities, rely upon local investors (e.g., local banks) instead of the broad market of investors. If, however, an issuer desires or needs access to the national or even regional, public market of investors, then an investment-quality rating is necessary.

It is difficult for all but the smallest issuers of debt to avoid the credit review process. According to Palumbo and Sacks (1987), small and rural governments face systematic adverse market assessment of creditworthiness. One reason is that the fee to obtain a bond rating is a cost of issuance that may be difficult to recover through interest savings. Besides, high bond ratings are associated with larger and more diversified cities. By one count, although a quarter of all municipal bonds were unrated, the total dollar volume of such bonds made up less than 10 percent of the entire municipal bond market (Petersen, 1989).

A rating by two different firms is the norm. While retail investors may have little appreciation for two credit assessments, institutional purchasers need them. Thus, while issuers might like to pay for only one rating, market demand requires otherwise. More important, a second rating lowers an issuer's borrowing cost, even if the ratings are different (Hsueh and Kidwell, 1988).

An issuer can avoid a direct credit rating by leasing the credit of a higher-rated institution. In this arrangement, a third party offers to guarantee the debt service. One form is an insurance policy. The issuer pays a one-time premium to a specialized insurance firm at the time of sale to provide investors with protection in case that issuer defaults. A second form of guarantee is a letter of credit. This is a form of preauthorized draft on a stock of funds at a highly rated financial institution. Both added protections are attractive to risk-averse investors. Plus, lower-rated issues receive clear economic benefits by buying bond insurance (Quigley and Rubinfeld, 1991). For these reasons, credit enhancement has become a widely accepted practice for investment quality borrowers to gain an added level of security for their investors. While a third-party guarantee can lead to an automatic "Aaa" rating, it does not guarantee that the issuer will borrow at levels commensurate with that rating (Bland, 1987; Reid, 1990). Despite renting the top-ranked credit of a third-part guarantor, the market recognizes that the underlying natural credit is much less.

Issuers attempt to influence the raters by adopting effective fiscal policies. Ratings firms broadcast the types of fiscal policies considered important for achieving and maintaining credit quality. High credit quality actions include tight financial controls, protection of fund balances, adoption of generally accepted accounting principles (GAAP), adherence to strong financial disclosure practices, and maintenance of political consensus. Strong fiscal management, however, will not offset the negative credit implications of the lack of strong economic activity and diversification (Loviscek and Crowley, 1990).

Public debt issuers stay in close contact with the ratings firms. This derives from the fact that borrowing costs decline with higher credit ratings. Most political leaders recognize the importance of the rating process. Credit ratings serve not only as a fiscal signal, but also a political one. Election results may turn on credit quality labels. Thus, credit ratings are an important public policy issue.

W. BARTLEY HILDRETH

BIBLIOGRAPHY

Aronson, J. Richard and James R. Marsden, 1980. "Duplicating Moody's Municipal Credit Ratings." *Public Finance Quarterly*, vol. 8:97–106.
Bland, Robert L., 1987. "The Interest Cost Savings From Municipal Bond Insurance: The Implications for Privatization." *Journal of Policy Analysis and Management*, vol. 6: 207–219.
Cantor, Richard and Frank Packer, 1995. "Sovereign Credit Ratings." *Current Issues in Economic and Finance*, vol. 1 (June).
Hildreth, W. Bartley, 1993. "State and Local Governments as Borrowers: Strategic Choices and the Capital Market." *Public Administration Review*, vol. 53 (January-February) 41–49.
Hsueh, L. Paul and David S. Kidwell, 1988. "Bond Ratings: Are Two Better Than One?" *Financial Management*, vol. 17 (Spring) 46–53.
Loviscek, Anthony L. and Frederick D. Crowley, 1990. "What Is in a Municipal Bond Rating?" *The Financial Review*, vol. 25 (February) 25–53.
Marks, Barry R., K. K. Raman and Earl R. Wilson, 1994. "The Effect of Municipal Bond Rating Change Announcements on Seasoned Bond Prices." *Municipal Finance Journal*, vol. 15 (Fall) 17–35.
Moody's Investors Service, Inc., 1991. *Moody's on Municipals.* New York: Moody's Investors Service.
Palumbo, George and Seymour Sacks, 1987. *Rural Governments in the Municipal Bond Market.* Washington, D.C.: Economic Research Service, U.S. Department of Agriculture.
Petersen, John E., 1989. *Information Flows in the Municipal Bond Market: Disclosure Needs and Processes.* Washington, D.C.: Government Finance Officers Association.
Quigley, John M. and Daniel L. Rubinfield, 1991. "Private Guarantees for Municipal Bonds: Evidence from the Aftermarket." *National Tax Journal* XLIV (December) 29–39.
Reid, Gary J., 1990. "Minimizing Municipal Debt Issuance Costs: Lessons from Empirical Research." *State and Local Government Review* (Spring) 64–72.
Standard & Poor's Corporation, 1979. *Standard & Poor's Ratings Guide.* New York: McGraw Hill, Inc.

CREDIT REFORM. As currently used in the budget process of the United States government, most commonly refers to the requirements of the Federal Credit Reform Act of 1990 (Section 13201 of Public Law 101-508).

In order to understand the significance of the Federal Credit Reform Act and the associated changes, it is necessary to delve into the evolution of the treatment of credit activities in the federal (national) budget.

"Credit," in the sense used in the credit reform act, refers to either of two actions:

1. Issuance of direct loans by the federal government. A direct loan is defined as a disbursement of money (or the sale of property or other assets on credit terms) by the federal government to a nonfederal borrower—to individuals, corporations, state or local governments, foreign governments, or others.
2. Issuance of loan guarantees by the federal government. A loan guarantee is defined as a guarantee or insurance by the federal government of loans made by nonfederal lenders to nonfederal borrowers. Under loan guarantees, the federal government assumes some or all of the credit risk of the loans, and it may or may not charge a fee for assuming that risk.

Credit, as such, is a commercial-type activity. Borrowers agree to pay interest in exchange for the use of lenders' money (or agree to pay insurance premiums in exchange for loan guarantees). Lenders agree to make the loans or guarantees in order to make profits. The amount that lenders charge is normally intended to cover all costs plus profits.

In contrast, federal credit programs have normally not operated with the objective of making money. Indeed, they frequently embed the objective of losing money (i.e., granting subsidies). These subsidies may be in the form of loans to high-risk borrowers or of guarantees of high-risk loans. They commonly involve making loans or guarantees at below-market rates.

Prior to credit reform, federal budgetary usages regarding credit were unsatisfactory, largely because they failed to capture this difference in motivation. Instead, they were structured to appear as if they were commercial credit activities (frequently programs that were designed to lose money were labeled "banks" or "insurance funds"), but they lacked the driving elements of commercial credit activities.

Background

In the United States, both governments and businesses engage in commercial-type activities, but there commonly are fundamental differences in motivation. Additionally, there are important differences between the powers and responsibilities of the federal government relative to those of lower levels of government, and these differences significantly increase the likelihood that the federal government will mislabel (and, thus, hide or obfuscate) the provision of subsidies through what are ostensibly business activities.

Motivation

Businesses exist to make money. When they conduct an activity, including making or insuring loans, they normally do so to make a profit. In contrast, when governments engage in commercial activities, they do so primarily in order to provide services or subsidies to the public.

Budgetary Accounting

State and local government commercial-type activities are frequently excluded from the regular government budgets (i.e., the programs are financed through funds that are required to be self-supporting). In federal budget practice, when commercial-type funds were created, they were outside the general fund, but most commonly they were included within the budgetary totals, and they were reported along lines that were superficially similar to business-type accounting. However, there was no requirement that such funds be, in fact, self-supporting (after all, if the operation is fully commercial, a question always exists about why the government is doing it in the first place), nor that they accurately report their losses. Since the essential elements of business accounting norms are to record profitability and track the equity of the entity, the combination of the sovereign powers of government and their tendency to operate "commercial" programs for noncommercial objectives creates a risk that the budgetary accounting may misinform the public about the financial operations of the entity.

Supervision and Powers

Additionally, the greater the size and complexity of the unit of government, the greater the opportunity for subsidies to be embedded (in a manner that obfuscates their costs) in ostensibly commercial activities.

Lower levels of government are always subject to greater constraints then the federal government. They frequently are subject to supervision by higher levels of government, by market tests (i.e., their ability to sell bonds), and by their proximity to taxpayers and voters.

Since the federal government is the largest, most complex, and most autonomous governmental entity in the United States, it has the greatest potential for gaps to develop between the form and substance of what it is doing when it engages in what are ostensibly commercial operations.

It is the combination of these factors that facilitated complex, confusing, and misleading reporting for credit in the federal budget prior to adoption of credit reform.

Budgetary Treatment of Credit Activities Prior to Credit Reform

Federal budgetary practices for credit activities evolved significantly over the past several decades. To a large extent this evolution was because of the inadequacies of the budget concept norms (i.e., the rules governing the way that transactions are recorded in the budget) and because of the political and bureaucratic incentives to spend money while obscuring the cost thereof. That is, the political incentive is to spend money in the near term on things that the public wants, without recording the cost of the spending at the time when the cost can be controlled.

Timing Basis for Recording Budgetary Transactions

Since its origin, the federal budget has been primarily on a cash basis. That is, income is recorded as receipts when the money is received, and the outlay (spending) is recorded when the payments are made. In contrast, the financial statements for business firms (whose model was ostensibly used to report commercial-type activities in the federal budget) is on an accrual basis (a basis that tries to match the cost of operations with the revenue derived from those operations).

In the main, the cash approach to federal budgeting reflects the nature of what the government does—it levies taxes to finance spending, and there is little match between the taxes and the spending. Even for earmarked taxes (i.e., taxes levied to finance a specific spending program, such as Social Security Benefits), one cannot match the income from operations with the cost of operations in the business sense, because the receipts are not closely related to the provision of specific benefits and services.

While the cash approach to measuring and controlling federal budgetary transactions is driven largely by the tax and spend nature of the great bulk of what the government does, it has had important consequences with regard to the way credit transactions have been recorded in the budget.

Direct Loans and Loan Repayments

Prior to reform, direct loan disbursements were recorded as federal spending (outlays) when the loans were made. In the early years of the budget most loan repayments were recorded as budget receipts (i.e., income), but some were recorded as offsetting collections (i.e., reductions in spending).

This had two primary results: (1) It overstated the budgetary cost of lending, since the cost is only the losses (or subsidies) on the loans, not the full amount of the disbursements. (2) It overstated the size of federal receipts and spending, because it recorded loans as spending and loan repayments as receipts (i.e., loan repayments were accounted for in the same category as taxes).

These imperfections provided strong incentives for the political process to devise approaches to recording federal loans. They greatly stimulated the creation of loan revolving funds (i.e., programs in which the loan repayments and interest income were offset against outlays within the associated expenditure accounts rather than being recorded as federal receipts; see offsetting collections.) Additionally, during the 1930s and early 1940s the government created a number of major loan programs that, by law or practice, were simply not counted as part of the federal budget. These exclusions were generally justified on the grounds that the programs were of an "emergency" nature or that the funds in question constituted self-supporting corporations rather than true spending by the government (even though they were not necessarily operated on a self-supporting commercial basis).

Most, but not all, federal credit programs were reincorporated within the budget during the Truman administration, but the practice of financing many—but not all—federal loans through revolving funds became firmly entrenched in budgetary practice.

The expanded use of revolving funds to finance loan programs weakened congressional appropriations control over the lending. As long as the revolving fund had unspent balances (such as from loan repayments), new loans could be made without annual appropriations of money to finance them.

The use of revolving funds also resulted in loan repayments being recorded as offsets to spending rather than as budget receipts—an approach that is generally consistent with current budget concepts. However, the budgetary incentives to record lower near-term spending (and deficits) soon led to the practice of selling loan assets. The proceeds of loan sales were treated the same way as loan repayments—as income (or offsets to outlays) when the money was collected.

A major motivation for loan asset sales was not to save the government money, but to reduce the near-term recorded size of the budget. Frequently the government lost money when it made the loans, and then lost additional money when it sold the loan assets. In addition, by the mid-1960s the efforts to maximize near term collections from the "sale" of loan assets led to devising packages of financial assets that were essentially indistinguishable from federal borrowing.

Loan Guarantees

For loan guarantees, the budget did not record any cost (other than administrative expenses) unless or until the government was required to disburse cash as a consequence of the guarantees. (This generally occurred as a result of loan defaults.) Indeed, if the government charged a guarantee or insurance premium, the budget recorded offsetting collections (i.e., reductions in budget outlays) on the front end when the premiums were collected, even though the government would probably have subsequent costs in order to honor the guarantees.

Credit Transactions Under the Unified Budget: Initial Stages

In the mid-1960s the credibility of the federal budget became undermined, largely as a result of the manipulations by the administration to finance the Great Society and the Vietnam War simultaneously without resorting to higher general taxes. This approach eventually failed, and one result was that President Lyndon Johnson created a commission to review federal budget concepts and recommended changes in those concepts. That commission issued a report in 1967 that provided the basis for many of the budget concepts still in effect.

The commission said that its most important single recommendation was that the federal government should operate using a "unified budget," which would include all fiscal activities of the government, no matter how financed. Under this rule, all federal credit activities should be included within the budget—they should not be spun off into nonbudgetary accounts.

However, another key recommendation of the commission was that the budget should distinguish between the subsidy cost of federal direct loans and the nonsubsidized cash flows. The commission recommended that budgetary spending be segregated into an "expenditure account" that would include most federal outlays, including the subsidy cost of federal loans, separate from the "net lending" (i.e., the unsubsidized portion of the loans).

The commission recommended that the expenditure account plus receipts be considered to be "the budget" for comparing spending to receipts in order to measure the fiscal policy impact of the federal budget. On the other hand, the sum of the expenditure account and net lending, plus receipts, was to constitute "the budget" used to measure the financing requirements of the government (i.e., the amount of borrowing or other financing that would be needed to finance any excess of spending over receipts).

The commission did not thoroughly review the way loan guarantees were recorded in the budget, but it recommended that the issue be studied in the future in anticipation of possible changes based on similar logic.

While the commission was able to enunciate a logic for separating the subsidy cost of federal loans from the nonsubsidized flows, the executive branch did not implement the commission's recommendations in this regard. Doing so would have required legislative approval, and the president implemented the unified budget through executive action rather than through legislation. Additionally, such action would have required major changes in budget and accounting systems, and neither the president nor Congress was anxious to make such changes at that time.

Starting with the 1969 budget, the budget included a separation between the expenditure account and net lending, but the net lending was recorded on the basis of cash disbursements and repayments and the expenditure account did not include the subsidies (i.e., the subsidies were included as part of the net lending). As a result, nobody paid much attention to the distinctions; they merely complicated the budgetary presentation without improving budgeting for credit. Within a few years the division was eliminated without any protest.

Experiments with Credit Reform: The Credit Budget

One of the key defects of traditional federal budgeting for credit was that most of the cost of credit programs was outside of the normal spending controls. The budget outlays did not even measure, much less control, the cost of credit subsidies. The bulk of federal credit was extended through revolving funds that made the loans or guarantees available automatically to anyone who qualified. Frequently the programs financed by these accounts were designed to lose money. While the losses (i.e., subsidies) had to be financed eventually, they were uncontrollable sunk costs by the time Congress had to appropriate money to cover the losses. Estimated credit subsidies were published in the chapter on federal credit programs in the special analyses document, but the estimates were based on limited information and at best served as a source of information entirely unrelated to budget allocation and control.

Eventually the Office of Management and Budget (OMB) sought to develop a credit control mechanism that would give the president and Congress some control over the credit activities before the losses became sunk costs. This approach left the existing budgetary system intact, but superimposed a new control system (the "credit budget") that would allow the president to recommend, and Congress to enact, controls on the levels of new loan and guarantees at the time that the government entered into obligations or commitments for the loans and guarantees (and, hence, could control their levels).

The credit budget was used for a number of years, and credit budget targets were included in the congressional budget resolution process, but eventually this approach was deemed to be a failure. There were three major reasons why the credit budget was a failure:

1. Part of the failure was due to the government's unwillingness to actually control the program levels for most federal credit programs—the authorized amounts were set high enough that they did not really bind, or if they actually came close to binding, it was found easier to raise the ceilings than to force constraints on activity.

2. Another major reason was that the credit budget was separate from the regular budget control process. Decisionmaking on the regular budget could go forward with no consideration of its impact on the credit budget.

3. However, the most important reason why the credit budget failed was that it was focused on the wrong measure of control—it sought to control the gross level of loan obligations or loan guarantee commitments rather than the cost of the program to the government (i.e., the subsidies).

The Federal Credit Reform Act of 1990

In the late 1980s a general consensus developed among budget technicians and their political leadership that further reform was needed. Indeed, the OMB (working for the president) and two major legislative branch staff agencies—the Congressional Budget Office (CBO) and the General Accounting Office (GAO)—all recommended enactment of credit reform legislation, and in the fall of 1990 Congress included the Credit Reform Act within the Omnibus Budget Reconciliation Act of 1990.

The most important elements of the Credit Reform Act are as follows:

1. The act specified the method for estimating the subsidy cost of new direct loans and loan guarantees. The cost is based on the cash flows to and from the government and the time value of money. (That is, the subsidy cost is essentially the present value of estimated future defaults and the effects of any interest differentials between what it cost the government to borrow and what the government charged lenders.)

2. It provided for a separation between the new loans or guarantees and the subsidies. The loans or guarantees themselves are to be made by "financing accounts" that are separate from the program (i.e., the subsidy) accounts, and the subsidies must be paid to the financing accounts to reimburse them for the losses due to the subsidies. The law specified that the financing accounts are to be outside of the budget (i.e., as components of the "means of financing" in the budgetary presentation). As a result, budget outlays include the subsidy cost to the government, but do not include the unsubsidized cash flows of the financing accounts.

3. In most cases, agencies are not authorized to enter into direct loan obligations or loan guarantee commitments (i.e., legally binding agreements to make direct loans or loan guarantees) without new appropriations of budget authority for the amount of the subsidy cost.

4. The combination of the requirement for appropriated subsidies, the separation of the subsidies from the

financing, and other control elements in the Budget Enforcement Act make it difficult for Congress to enact legislation that would vitiate these requirements.

5. The law provides permanent budget authority to correct any errors in the subsidies. At the time the loans or guarantees are made, the recorded subsidy costs are estimates of future payments and collections. When subsequent experience demonstrates that the subsidy amounts are either too large or too small, payments must be made from the program accounts to the financing accounts or vice versa to correct for any errors. Thus, the financing accounts should never have a permanent gain or loss as a result of the subsidies.

6. Since at the time the loans or guarantees are made the subsidy cost is inherently an estimate, there is always the danger of errors or bias in the subsidy calculations. The law authorizes OMB and CBO to coordinate the development of more accurate data. Any changes in the estimating approach are not to cover the cost of past errors—those are financed from the authority to correct for errors—but are intended to make the current estimates as accurate as feasible as a measure of the anticipated cost of current subsidies.

7. The act prohibits agencies from modifying post-credit reform loans or guarantees at any point after they have been made, unless the agencies calculate the subsidy cost of the modification and receive a subsidy appropriation adequate to cover that cost. The cost of modifications is treated in the same fashion as are new loan or guarantee subsidies.

8. Loans or guarantees previously outstanding were not subject to credit reform, since it was too late to control the subsidy levels in those transactions. However, any modifications in those loans and guarantees are to be treated the same as new loans or guarantees (i.e., the subsidy cost has to be financed through new appropriations).

9. The law required that credit reform begin on October 1, 1991, so that the budget was required to include estimates on a credit reform basis for all years subsequent to fiscal year 1991.

Credit reform is complex, and its implementation has not been easy or smooth. (See **credit reform implementation**).

THOMAS J. CUNY

BIBLIOGRAPHY

Congressional Budget office, 1989. *Credit Reform: Comparable Budget Costs for Cash and Credit*. Washington, D.C: Congressional Budget Office (December).
Cuny, Thomas J., 1991. "Federal Credit Reform." *Public Budgeting & Finance*, vol. 11, no. 2 (summer), 19–32.
Office of Management and Budget, *Budget of the United States Government*, various years. Washington, D.C.: Government Printing Office. In particular, see the *Special Analyses* document issued as part of the 1990 budget, pp. F-2 to F-18, for a discussion of the credit budget; see the 1988 budget supplement, part 3b, for the original OMB credit reform proposal; see the 1991 budget, pp. 243–246, for a discussion proposing a revised version of credit reform; and see the 1992 budget, pp. 223–226, for a discussion of credit reform as it was enacted.
Wattlesworth, Michael A., 1993. "Credit Subsidies in Budgetary Lending: Computation, Effects, and Fiscal Implications." In Mario I. Blejer and Adrienne Cheasty, eds., *How to Measure the Fiscal Deficit*. Washington, D.C.: International Monetary Fund, pp. 147–174.

CREDIT REFORM IMPLEMENTATION.

As currently used in the budget process of the United States government, the actions taken since enactment of the Federal Credit Reform Act of 1990 (Section 12201 of Public Law 101-508) to put into effect the terms of that law (see **credit reform**).

Credit reform is the current phase of a decades-long effort to improve the budgeting for credit activities in the federal (national) budget. The federal budget treatment of credit activities has long been unsatisfactory, and credit reform is an effort to remedy as many defects as possible. However, it should be noted that even though credit reform has significantly improved budgeting for credit (especially through increasing presidential and congressional control over, and public reporting on, the cost of credit subsidies), credit reform is complicated and requires a great deal of complex budgeting and accounting to make it work. This complexity results largely from the constraints that limited the government's ability to adopt a simple approach to credit reform.

The simplest approach to credit reform would have been for the government to cease making direct loans and issuing loan guarantees. Congress could simply appropriate subsidies for whatever purposes it chooses, and allow (or require) the recipients of the subsidies to do their borrowing on their own. Thus, for example, the student loan program could be abolished, with Congress appropriating direct subsidies for those students who meet specified qualifications. Those students could then use the combination of the subsidies plus their own resources to finance their education. A fundamental policy constraint that guided those who designed credit reform was that the president and Congress were unwilling to take this approach, so a more complex form of credit reform was the only available option.

The next simplest form of credit reform would have been along the lines of credit reform as it was adopted, but using market validation of the subsidy estimates. That is, the federal government could continue to make direct loans and loan guarantees, with the requirement that the subsidy amounts be estimated and financed through appropriations along the lines that were ultimately embedded in credit reform. However, the direct loan financing accounts would have sold all or a representative sample of the new loans in order to determine the market value of those loans, and treated the difference between the par value of the loan and the market value as the subsidy amount. Similarly, the loan guarantee financing accounts could have issued new loan guarantees, but could have been required to reinsure either all or a cross section of the guarantees in order to provide a market test of the differential between the insurance premiums actually collected and those that would be required by the market for similar insurance. This approach was proposed in the 1988 budget, as the administration's initial credit reform plan, but with the expectation that it would not be applied to every credit program.

Neither of these approaches was politically feasible. In part this is because the government had a series of credit institutions in place, and there was no inclination to abolish or radically change them. Furthermore, the market would have valued the subsidies at a different (and costlier) level than the valuation under credit reform as enacted (and, hence, the budget would have been forced to record higher subsidy costs than those that are required under current credit reform calculations). For example, the market would have required a higher discount for risk than credit reform requires; it would have required a premium to cover the cost of administering the loans (the Credit Reform Act excluded the government's administrative costs from the subsidy computation); and it would have required a premium designed to yield a profit margin. The political leadership was unwilling to accept any approach that would have required higher subsidy computations, so this approach was also ruled out.

These and other constraints had a major impact on the final design of credit reform and on its implementation. Specifically:

1. Even though credit reform implementation was known to be tremendously complicated, and even though it was known that it would take years for the agencies to fully conform to be requirements, the law required early implementation of credit reform (rather than leaving two or three years for the agencies to gear up). Part of the reason for this early implementation was the desire to embed the cost of credit subsidies within the constraints of the Budget Enforcement Act (the Federal Credit Reform Act and the Budget Enforcement Act were part of the same legislation—the Omnibus Budget Reconciliation Act of 1990). The sponsors did not want to wait for a later Congress or possibly another administration to put this new budgeting approach into effect. Partly this was due to a concern that if credit reform was not started quickly, subsequent legislation might be enacted that would exempt important segments of federal credit programs

from credit reform coverage. Additionally, there was some feeling that if the agencies were given an extended time in which to prepare for credit reform, they would simply concentrate on other pressing matters, and in the end they would be no better prepared than if it were implemented at an early date.

2. A major constraint flowed from the decision to move the financing accounts outside the budget while assuring that they would never have gains or losses. This meant that the credit programs had to track groups of loans through their entire life on both a cash and a credit reform basis so that the agencies could validate the previous subsidy estimates or could compute re-estimates of the amounts needed to compensate for errors.

3. A third constraint was that Congress retained the power to modify the terms of loans or guarantees, as long as it also appropriated subsidies adequate to cover the cost of the modifications. The ability to track both the original loan or guarantee plus the modifications added substantially to the complexity of credit reform accounting.

Credit reform is now in effect. Budgets have been formulated, appropriations enacted, and budgets executed (carried out) for several consecutive years under credit reform concepts. Admittedly, the execution is imperfect, since the accounting is still being developed. However, this was anticipated at the time that the legislation was enacted, and the government is still moving forward to improve the accounting. The Office of Management and Budget (OMB) and Treasury Department developed and issued extensive instructions, and they have modified the instructions in various ways (such as allowing for the use of weighted average interest rates) to maintain the substance of credit reform while simplifying the implementation.

Federal accounting for credit is improving. The Federal Accounting Standards Advisory Board has developed accounting standards for direct loans and guarantees based on credit reform, and those standards have been approved by OMB, the General Accounting Office, and Treasury, so that the credit agencies are now required to account for credit along these lines. This aligned federal accounting requirements with budget concepts in an unprecedented manner and gave accounting support to budget implementation. Agency accounting systems have been changed to accommodate credit reform requirements, and further changes are being made to improve the accounting and reporting system.

Perhaps most importantly, policy decisions have been affected. Congress now appropriates the credit subsidies, and has to trade off credit subsidy appropriations against other forms of spending within the budgetary constraints under the Budget Enforcement Act.

This is not to say that credit reform is working perfectly. Examples can be cited of "gaming" of credit reform; examples can be cited of breakdowns in agency reporting under credit reform; examples can be cited of accounting that is not up to standard; the treatment of administrative costs remains a problem when comparing alternative ways of operating a program; and, most certainly, agencies can cite the burden of additional accounting requirements that flow from credit reform (requirements that would not have been necessary if Congress had been willing to chose a simpler form of credit reform). Despite these reservations, there appears to be general agreement that budgeting under credit reform is significantly enhanced over pre-credit reform norms.

THOMAS J. CUNY

BIBLIOGRAPHY

Congressional Budget Office, 1992. *Budgeting for Administrative Costs Under Credit Reform*. Washington, D.C.: Congressional Budget Office (January).
General Accounting Office, various reports. The GAO issues reports on a wide range of topics, including implementation of various aspects of credit reform. Four recent reports on this subject are as follows:
Federal Credit Programs: Agencies Had Serious Problems Meeting Credit Reform Accounting Requirements. GAO/AIMED-93-17, January 6, 1993.
Federal Credit Reform: Information on Credit Modifications and Financing Accounts. GAO/AIMED-93-26, September 30, 1993.
Credit Reform: Speculative Savings Used to Offset Current Spending Increase Budget Uncertainty. GAO/AIMED-94-36, March 18, 1994.
Credit Reform: Case-by-Case Assessment Advisable in Evaluating Coverage and Compliance. GAO/AIMED-94-57, July 28, 1994.
Individuals interested in these or any other GAO reports can call the GAO publications office (202) 512-6000 and request copies. Individuals can call and identify specific reports that they want or they can identify subject areas of interest, and the publications office will perform a computer search for the relevant documents and provide copies upon request.
Office of Management and Budget, 1992. *Administrative Costs of Credit and Grant Programs*. Washington, D.C.: Office of Management and Budget (May).
———, 1993. *Accounting for Direct Loans and Loan Guarantees* (Statement of Federal Financial Accounting Standards Number 2). Washington, D.C.: U.S. Government Printing Office (August 23).
———, various years. *Budget of the United States Government*. The budget contains a chapter on credit, under different titles in different years, which discusses credit programs and has an appendix with summary estimates of data. The chapter in the 1995 and 1996 budgets was in the *Analytical Perspectives* document.
———, various years. *Budget of the United States Government: Federal Credit Supplement*. The supplement contains detailed tables on subsidy rates and amounts, the assumptions underlying the subsidy estimates, credit transactions, and other data. The supplement is available from OMB upon request.

CRIME CONTROL POLICY.

An agenda linking criminology, governance, law, and politics initiated to prevent and control crime. Citizens should perceive this policy as fair and just; government should fund the service providers who will implement this policy; and public safety should be enhanced because crime is decreased. This policy impacts on citizen morale, public health, public safety, diversity, global communitarianism, and economic viability.

Theoretical Origins

Criminology is the study of the nature of crime and of those groups who are affected by crime. Early criminologists often directed the analysis that enlightened societies should take pertaining to deviance. A chronological review of criminology provides a perspective for understanding present crime control policies.

Cesare Beccaria (*On Crimes and Punishment* 1764) and Jeremy Bentham (*Moral Calculus* 1789) altered the penal policy of the times by asserting that people choose to commit crime by rationally analyzing the risks associated with apprehension and punishment. They contended that corporal punishment and excessive executions were incompatible with a government's responsibility to be fair and reasonable. As jurists, Beccaria and Bentham supported the belief that the state had a responsibility to initiate policies that would control crime. Such policies would assure severe, certain, and swift punishment for criminals and this efficiency would prevent crime in society.

The issue of rational choice and analysis of risk are believed to indicate the principles of deterrence and incapacitation associated with the contemporary philosophy of choice theory. This theory alleges that criminals scrutinize the risk of arrest and the potential for imprisonment as punishment, then decide whether to commit a crime. The appropriate punishment is central to the control of crime in choice theory. Criminology sought to investigate why criminals would not or could not analyze the risk and make the rational choice to be law-abiding.

Research into the biological, physical, genetic, and mental factors within the criminal were studied from approximately 1810 to 1940 and then from 1968 to the present. Crime was considered a consequence of evolution whereby certain biological and mental traits made individuals crime-prone. Criminals were viewed as lower on the evolutionary ladder or not fully developed because of biological factors. Cesare Lombroso's (1863) work initiated the study of individuals, behavioral traits, and familial histories (i.e., genetics) by his contemporaries. When the biological aspects of individuals were found inconclusive in the explanation of criminality, criminologists searched for visible signs of abnormality as a possible explanation. Questions concerning physical anomalies and characteristics were researched to explain crime.

The psychological theories focused on mental aspects of crime, intelligence, personality, and criminal behavior. Crime was viewed as behaviors indicative of faulty thinking or learning that potentially developed into criminality. The nexus between biological and psychological theories of crime is furthered by the discipline of psychiatry.

Criminology became labeled "radical" when Willem Bonger (1916) developed conflict theory from Marxian principles. The conflict perspective theorized that crime is not of biological origins but of social ones. In every society there are those who have the power to set policies and they control society. According to conflict theory, in a capitalist society, both the desire to control segments of society and the desire to fight that control produce criminal activity. The control of those considered disadvantaged may be imposed based on age, race, gender, or economic status. The disadvantaged, however, are the only ones to be labeled as criminal.

Social conflict provided a foundation for the sociological theory introduced by Emile Durkheim in 1893 and refined by The Chicago School (1930) as it initiated the study of crime in the urban setting. Social structures theories furnished society with the potential for policy development. The Chicago School advanced theories directed at families, juveniles, and community development. They studied conflicts within a juvenile's family and peer group that can result in deviance. The Chicago School promoted community involvement to increase the well-being of juveniles, to decrease juvenile delinquency, and to promote social stability within the urban setting (Kobrin, 1959).

Criminologists explored the theoretical origins of deviance. After 1980, however, the politicization of the criminal justice system became the dominant configurative factor for crime control. Juveniles were no longer viewed as the victims of social conditions; rather, they were increasingly seen as the predators within society.

Development of Policy Agenda

Criminology was the model for theorizing about crime, but it became apparent that criminologists had neglected to grasp fully the importance of developing policy and evaluating measures which interrupted delinquency and crime. The policies of the 1980s were premised on the idea that theoretical endeavors of the past were unsuccessful in controlling crime and that offenders should be held responsible for their criminality (Wilson, 1975, revised 1985). The subjective and descriptive work of criminologists had failed to formulate a foundation for crime control directives citizens demanded in the 1980s. Crime control bureaucracies became interdisciplinary; economists, psychologists, political scientists, and medical researchers advanced alternative theories about the causes and solutions for criminal activity.

Economic analysis, pioneered by Jeremy Bentham, offered an explanation for the commission of the crime, the appropriate punishment, and the extent of that punishment. Psychologists studied the irrational criminal act from the analysis of behavior. Learning theory, adaptive behaviors, and symptoms of physical, sexual, and emotional abuse became the basis for insanity pleas. Paranoia, schizophrenia, bipolar mental illness, and psychosis caused behaviors labeled "mental illness" by psychiatrists and "criminal" by law enforcement and the courts.

Medical researchers ascertained the impact of fetal alcohol syndrome on adolescent criminality, the complexity of attention deficit disorder as it related to frustration tolerance, the legacy of drug-addicted infants, the challenge of multiple personality disorder, and the power of pharmacology to control criminal behavior.

The conflict between law and alternative theoretical interpretations for criminality is a consistent challenge to formulating crime control policy. In the late 1980s the Centers for Disease Control and Prevention, the National Center for Health Statistics, the National Institutes of Health, the American Medical Association, the American Academy of Pediatrics, and the National Pediatric Trauma Registry began to view violent crime as a major health threat. The medical field publicized the escalation of medical care necessitated by existing crime control policies (Rosenberg and Fenley, 1991).

In the 1990s, crime control policy is limited, not by research or theoretical development, but by political rhetoric. Fear of crime stimulates policies that emphasize incarceration, the death penalty, and long mandatory sentences. These have not lessened crime or the fear of crime but reflect society's increasingly punitive attitude toward criminals.

Necessity for Crime Specific Policy. Effective laws are dependent on formal and informal social controls supported by citizens within a community. When a cohesive community exists, there is little need for crime control policies. The increasingly fragmented U.S. society requires expanded legislated justice and criminal sanctions, however. A tension emerges when there are concurrent needs to be fair to all segments of society, to maintain public order, and to protect individual rights. Crime interferes with the way society progresses, threatens considerable harm to society, affects social policy agendas, and often defines the foundation of political campaigns.

Concern over crime control was pronounced during the 1960s when violent crime increased rapidly. Compared to the homicide statistics of other nations for the period 1955 to 1967, the United States ranked well above other countries (Uniform Crime Report, 1990). The politicization of crime control was initiated during the 1964 United States presidential campaign of Lyndon B. Johnson. Perceptions were of ineffectual policies and an inadequate commitment to a crime control agenda. The criminal justice system was scrutinized in terms of resources, programs, and administrative philosophies.

In 1968, the Omnibus Crime Control and Safe Streets Act was passed by Congress and the Law Enforcement Assistance Administration (LEAA) was established to initiate preventive measures for crime control, to improve institutional responses to crime through education and training, and to enhance the effectiveness of the courts. Although a popular period within the evolution of crime control policy, after the programs were evaluated, the results were seldom relevant for policy.

Violent crime and drug activity continued in the 1970s as rehabilitation and community treatment, which supported the philosophy that the criminal could be reeducated while in prison or community treatment, were devalued. Criminology and the social programs of the 1970s had not successfully addressed increased criminality or formulated policies that addressed recidivism; more crime was being committed and often by the same individuals. The tolerant crime control policies of the 1970s, coupled with escalating funding of the criminal justice system, had likewise failed to decrease criminal activity. The media used terms such as "soft" or "hard" on crime to intensify political campaign rhetoric.

Contemporary Policy Issues. Reformists highlighted the abuse of bail since offenders were often rearrested within hours of release from jail. Crimes were often violent and society began to demand protection from repeat offenders. Politicians were held responsible for providing a society safe from any criminal act by citizens who demanded safe streets, safe cities, and protection from crime in their homes. The crime-specific programs of the 1970s were adequately funded under a congressional mandate; however, there was no indication that a comprehensive and systematic strategy had been initiated for crime control. While U.S. crime control policy sought to decrease violent crime and drug activity, every other industrialized country continued to experience notably lower violent criminal activity. In 1980, President Ronald Reagan took a perspective sought by victims of crime and those who feared crime. Criminals would, presumably, fear being punished for their crimes in an atmosphere of punitive policy.

Prevailing Policy. Crime control policies in the 1980s focused on punishment. Punishment was to make the criminal suffer for the crime they had committed. If punishment failed to deter the criminal from further crime, incapacitation of the criminal in prison removed the criminal from society, thus protecting society and preventing further individual criminality (Wilson, 1975). The media publicize the crime committed by the offender, report the apprehension of the offender, summarize the finding of guilt, report the punishment and, thus, enhance the principles of deterrence. The 1980s emphasized swift and certain punishment with criminal justice no longer focused on the social characteristics of the criminal, but on the crime initiated.

State and Federal Changes. States initiated more exacting penalties for crime and criminal activity. Mandatory prison sentences were legislatively increased. Maine was the first state to abolish parole in 1977 and federal parole was abolished in 1987 in favor of supervised release. Supervised release negated the necessity of a parole board in favor of legislative mandates. Law enforcement and prosecution agencies received the moral and political support of citizens and politicians. Judges comprehended the frustration and fear of society caused by a small number of criminals who continued to commit the majority of the crimes. Appellate legal decisions justified the actions of the criminal justice system rather than supporting the constitutional rights claimed by criminals.

The Comprehensive Crime Control Act of 1984 established federal policies similar to the punitive attitudes of the states toward crime. Federal parole was abolished because recidivism had not been stemmed by its methods. The initiation of preventive detention and the denial of bail to arrestees offered protection to the community from further violence and the assurance of appearance of individuals such as drug kingpins at trial. The burden of proof was shifted to the defense to prove a defendant's insanity. Intricate computer data systems were funded through federal and state cooperation to track serial murderers, drug activity, laundered monies, fingerprints, and criminal histories.

The difficulty presented by drugs to effective crime control policy necessitated the technology and power of the United States military. In 1988, the preventive program of interdiction–the effort to seize drugs, drug couriers, and drug kingpins on their way from their country before entering the United States–had questionable success given the billions of dollars appropriated. Inadequate interdiction was thought to be one of the causes of an increased cocaine supply and falling prices when the use of United States troops to disrupt the production of drugs as a cash crop became policy (Reuter, 1985). The U.S. "War on Drugs" (1988) was the vehicle for interjecting the domestic drug control policy of the United States into the sovereignty of South and Central Latin America and the Caribbean.

International Crime Control

Crime control policy remains internationally consistent for two criminal issues: sale of weaponry for criminal activity and illegal drug activity. The export of the U.S. crime control policy toward drugs has increased the jeopardy to law enforcement and legal institutions in other countries. Where drugs are produced, sophisticated weaponry and radar are part of the drug producer's technology. Drug agents and the military are fighting the drug war in terrain that is known primarily to the drug producers. Proof of the extensiveness of the risk is seen in the increased murders of ministers of justice, elected officials, drug agents, and members of their respective families (Cardenas, 1990).

With the demise of the Soviet Union, the United States offered and engaged in collaborative development and initiation of drug control policies with the Eurasian region and Moscow. These policies reflect the realities of increased health risks and the threat of organized criminal activity within the region. Technology, military assistance, and federal law enforcement offered expertise in the preparation of training for the implementation of crime control policies.

The threat of terrorism to international governments by drug activity and weapon sales mandates increased vigilance if control is to be achieved. The United States had remained primarily untouched by radical terrorist activity until February 1993. When the New York World Trade Center became the target of an attack, the availability of arms and explosives and the money to fund such activity reinforced the need for intelligence activity and policy development directed toward international crime control (Federal Bureau of Investigation, 1993). In the Middle East, the use of drug activity to support terrorism requires consistent monitoring. The impact of religious philosophy on international terrorist activity is essential in comprehending state-sponsored terrorism that is religiously sanctioned and domestic religious cult activity that may be initially protected by the Constitution (Federal Bureau of Investigation, 1993).

Environmental Justice Policy. Environmental crime, a subset of white-collar crime, is a contemporary development within criminal behavior and crime control policy. Some criminologists believe environmental crime is an activity of organized crime; others argue that it is reflective of economic reasoning. The disposal of hazardous waste is an economic concern for legitimate business. The purveyors of environmental crimes rarely are sentenced to prison even through there is considerable cost to society.

Policy formulation for environmental crime has been unable to benefit fully from technology since victimization often is without borders or time limits. Some environmentalists charge that the disposal of hazardous wastes often occurs in communities populated by those with less political and economic power. However, communities may benefit from electing to be a disposal site for such waste. Environmental pollution is often a byproduct of technology and the solutions for this pollution require multifaceted policies. Initiating a policy agenda to control and prevent such crime requires a balance between economic self-interest and ethics.

Environmental justice is also a concern for international crime control policy and has serious ramifications for future generations. Contamination of water, air, and soil is impervious to borders. The currents of rivers, the airstreams, and the contaminants that fall on soils require

environmental policies that are international. Finding sanctions that will coerce countries to support fair environmental policies is a global challenge.

Political Conflict The crime control policies of the 1990s center around the politicization of law enforcement, legal institutions, and correctional facilities. The use of weapons, guns in particular, is primarily associated with the United States and guaranteed by the Second Amendment to the Constitution, which declares the right to keep and bear arms. Initiating policies directed at the ownership of guns is arduous because of political risk and constitutional protection in the United States. The incidence of death and serious injury related to the use of handguns during criminal activity is often judged to be insufficient for promoting sweeping gun control policies. The use of guns is no longer limited to the police, the military, or to sports enthusiasts. Research indicates that 12-1/2 is the median age of first-gun ownership in the United States and it is usually a male relative who bestows the gun as a gift. The number of available firearms is an aggravating factor responsible for the finding that guns are involved in more than 75 percent of adolescent killings. For instance, under President George Bush, 43 models of military-style semi-automatic rifles were banned in 1989 for "importation" into the United States. Within a year, clarification prohibiting the "assembly" of the semiautomatic style weapons in the United States from imported parts had to be added because the law was vague (Orrick, 1994).

The availability of firearms is a major concern to those who believe gun control should be depoliticized as a factor within crime control policy. The Bureau of Alcohol, Tobacco, and Firearms (ATF) reports that there are 211 million firearms owned by private citizens in the United States, that 71 million are handguns, that 225,000 firearms are reported stolen every year, and that a new handgun is produced every 20 seconds (Uniform Crime Report 1993). The international community often views these statistics as evidence that the United States is not committed to the control of gun violence.

Crime control policy is presently a primary factor within the educational environment where gun usage, violence, and drug activity present substantial challenges. Some U.S. schools resemble the fortified terminals of international airports where students pass through weapon detectors, are scanned for metal objects, have their personal belongings searched, and pass through halls where security officers and video cameras guard against violence. The participation of juveniles in increasingly serious criminal activity has escalated.

Two issues were evident during the 1980s. One, criminals were not concerned with the age or status of their victims, and two, adolescents did not commit crimes that should be solely characterized as juvenile. For every 1,000 adolescents between the ages of 16 to 19, 60.9 are assaulted. This a higher victimization rate that for adults (Orrick, 1994). The Uniform Crime Reports, compiled annually by the Federal Bureau of Investigation (FBI) show that in 1993, murder committed by those 14 years and under increased by 94 percent while the overall murder rate increased by 3 percent (Uniform Crime Report 1994).

Rape, sexual assault, and domestic violence against women in the United States is the leading cause of injury to women ages 15 to 44, including the combined total for automobile accidents, muggings, and cancer deaths. These violent acts are not limited by race, class, age, or ethnicity (Orrick, 1994; United States Department of Justice, 1994).

The control of violent crime has tempered U.S. prevention policies. School curricula are required to educate children about substance abuse and sexual abuse. Education about the impact of drug activity on health, academic progress, and the school environment are important aspects of crime control policies. Preventive programs are supported by bipartisan advocacy but their efficacy is undetermined. Offering youth alternatives to drug activity is viewed as another positive means of increasing the safety of society. Extracurricular activities such as athletic and academic activities after school are accepted as influential in assuring community security.

Current crime control policies that emphasize prevention offer a different approach. Child welfare and drug abuse specialists call for viewing drug addiction as a chronic, relapsing disorder that requires sustained familial and individual support. Opponents to this philosophy believe it to be a geographical problem of depressed inner city communities, but research indicates that drug abuse cuts across race, class, and ethnicity and ranges from experimentation to dependence. Many argue that crime control policy should be directed at increasing the periods of drug abstinence, decreasing the emotional and physical damage to children, and formulating long-term child welfare policy (Besharov, 1994). Kinship care—the care of children with drug-involved parents by other relatives—is considered more reflective of intervention and prevention and could result in less criminality. The use of large congregate institutions, the term for orphanages in the 1990s, is considered an alternative linked to the quality of parenting provided to the children. It is difficult to preserve the political advocacy that promotes such services, often because of perceptions based on race and class.

The politicization of crime control policy became magnified in the 1990s. The Crime Bill of 1994, signed by President Bill Clinton, is evidence of the conflict between preventive action and punitive reactions to crime. The crime statistics for the United States compared to other industrialized nations indicate that the expectation of crime control, the political promises, the resources allocated, and the punitive attitudes have been relatively inadequate.

Global Differences Toward Control. Compared to other industrialized nations, controlling for the differences in reporting, the United States is more criminal and more punitive in reaction to criminal behavior. For instance, trends in crime rates for the years 1960 to 1987 for the countries of Japan, the Federal Republic of Germany, Great Britain, and the United States show the U.S. with the overall highest crime rate for homicide and larceny. A 1989 Japanese White Paper on Crime published by the Ministry of Japan indicated not only lower rates but actual declining rates in Japan. Larceny is more commensurate with U.S. crime patterns in Britain and Germany. Japan and the U.S. stand at the opposite ends of the continuum for violent and property crimes (Hamilton and Sanders, 1992).

In the 1990s, the violence within the United States continues to be significantly higher than for other industrialized countries and the reason is often associated with the use of guns. The FBI, foreign embassies, and foreign crime reporting agencies report that in 1992, handguns were used to kill 36 people in Sweden, 97 in Switzerland, 60 in Japan, 128 in Canada, 33 in Great Britain, 13 in Australia, and 13,220 in the United States (Department of Justice, 1993). Ten U.S. men die by criminal violence for every Japanese, German, or Swedish man; 15 for every English or Swiss man; and over 20 for every Dane. Over 150 countries have lower murder rates than the United States. An individual is five times more likely to be robbed in New York than in London and 125 more times more likely to be robbed in New York than in Tokyo. Crime control policy of the 1980s was considered punitive, but did little to stem the spiralling number of arrests for drug activities and drug related violence (Cole, 1993; Orrick,1994).

The Criminal Justice System. Government and members of society formally empower a criminal justice system by framing crime control policies. A system of criminal justice seeks out responsibility and punishment for those who commit crimes. Law enforcement is responsible for arrest, investigation, and detainment of the accused. The courts are accountable for the process of judgment. Corrections is responsible for carrying out the sanctions that result from the judicial process. Crime control policies do not bridge the system; instead, individual discretion within the system prevails as the linking factor since formalized rules, statutes, and prison sentences can be ignored or altered. An example is the ability to ignore formal guidelines. Such protocol is not limited to the United States. Police are not required to make an arrest in all circumstances, prosecutors may choose not to prosecute or they may decide to plea bargain, judges may ignore plea bargains, and correctional officials may release prisoners who were sentenced to life in prison.

The racial disparity within the war on crime has escalated since the 1980s. Vigorous crime control appears directed toward the peasants of Latin America who cultivate drug-producing crops and the lower classes and minorities of the cities who buy the drugs. Discretion within crime control policy often serves to maximize political preferences that may be personal or institutional, and may minimize effectiveness. Discretion may be directed at race and class as a basis for various analytical approaches to crime control formulation (Wilson, 1985; E. Currie, 1993).

Numerous commissions have scrutinized the conduct of law enforcement (the Knapp Commission, 1973) and corrections (the Attica Commission, 1971), but the court link of the criminal justice system within the United States remains primarily autonomous. Crime control policy is relatively ineffective in fully influencing this disjointed segment of the system. Through the courts, judges and attorneys use procedural and substantive laws to seek out justice. Common law, case law, and legislative law have diluted or enhanced the roles of the officials within the adjudicative process.

An attempt to control judicial discretion is the use of mandatory sentences. The politicization of the sentencing process was redefined when prosecutors and victim groups pressured legislators to alter sentencing alternatives because of discretionary judicial conduct. During the 1980s and early 1990s, legislators determined the sentences for serious crime by revising the penalty sections of criminal statutes in response to the perception of judicial leniency. Determinant mandatory sentencing gradually increased prison sentences as well as the number of crimes that mandated prison. At the time of sentencing, because of these legislative changes, judges simply read the penalty from the statutes rather than deliberate over possible sentences, community alternatives, and treatment.

The legislative policies requested by crime victims have not fully controlled the discretion of prosecutors, however. *Nolle prosequi* is a privilege of the prosecutor to choose not to prosecute or to dismiss a case, often regardless of the victim's cooperation, testimony, or wishes. This action may occur inside the office of a prosecutor and outside the knowledge of a judge.

Prosecutorial discretion remains difficult to control since the courts and Congress have yet to establish a methodology for evaluating the full impact of this privilege. Recent "three strikes and you're out" legislation may significantly add to the overcrowding of penal institutions (i.e., the prison capacity deficit). The legislation is an attempt to imprison repeat violent offenders for life after the third conviction for a violent offense; however, offenders may avoid such a conviction if allowed to plead to a nonviolent charge. Another example of prosecutorial discretion is found in crimes of sexual violence. Whether the victim is a child or an adult, the FBI Uniform Crime Report reveals that in 1993 only 38 percent of reported rapes resulted in an arrest, and 16 percent of those reported rapes resulted in convictions (Uniform Crime Report 1994). The low conviction rate is often a result of a state's selective prosecution. Only 11 percent of reported sex crimes are prosecuted because of the difficulty in pursuing this type of crime and the political risk associated with prosecuting such cases.

Crime control policy in the United States is often a campaign issue. The increased violence of the crimes, the randomness of some crimes, and the perception that criminals are pampered while in prison are included in political platforms.

Differing Regimes' Views of Policy. Crime control policy is associated with the functions of arrest and imprisonment. The act of imprisoning an individual for criminal activity becomes a political promise because society is believed to value such action. Although President Reagan and President Bush were associated with conservative crime control policies, other conservative leaders questioned the efficacy of their policies. During Prime Minister Margaret Thatcher's government in Great Britain, a 1990 White Paper asserted that the principle of deterrence may be simplistic when describing the decisionmaking activity of a criminal. The White Paper further suggested that crime might be an issue of victim facilitation in which a crime is made attractive because of a victim's carelessness. The criminal who seizes the opportunity to commit a crime is engaging in impulse rather than a rational thinking process. Should sentencing policies then be constructed on a tenet that offenders weigh the consequences of their behavior far in advance of the criminal act (Home Office 1990)?

In 1987, Canada began to search for an empirical justification to the use of extensive imprisonment as a basis for criminal sanctions. By 1993, Prime Minister Brian Mulroney's government published *Crime Prevention in Canada: Toward a National Strategy.* This proposed abandoning the U.S. crime control policy that centers on imprisonment by initiating the European crime control policy, which focuses on prevention. The Canadian policy argued that, if imprisonment resulted in safer societies, then the harsh policies of the United States should produce the safest country in the world (Canadian Communication Group 1993). In 1994, a comparison of inmates among the United States, England, and Wales indicated that in 1991, inmates in the United States received longer sentences for similar offenses than inmates in the other countries. Further, the adult inmate population for the United States was 1.2 million or 640 inmates per 100,000 adults and 45,900 for England and Wales or 199 inmates per 100,000 adults (Lynch et al. 1994).

Research Agenda. The future of crime control policies rests with efforts to overcome the pressures associated with formulation and implementation. Qualitative and quantitative evaluations of crime control policies and programs are not always among the goals and strategies on policy agendas. Crime control policy directives often politicize research funding and agendas. Government formulates the research agenda for the future, determines the resources to be allocated for research, and indicates preferences in methodology. Research funds are filtered to universities and various institutes but the political constraint may be significant. In the United States funding comes primarily from the Department of Justice. The National Institutes of Health and the Department of Health and Human Services have, however, increased their role in setting the research agenda.

Crime control policy can support and fund small scale local programs that are specific to a community's needs, often including aspects of prevention. Strategies from one neighborhood to another may differ, while appropriate culture, ethnicity, and class attributes are preserved.

Crime control policy reflects the national character of a society. It includes interdisciplinary expertise to decrease the need for its own existence and an understanding of what can be done with the freed resources when crime is no longer a domestic crisis.

M. A. Toni DuPont-Morales

BIBLIOGRAPHY

Books:

Beccaria, Cesare, 1764. *On Crimes and Punishments.* 6th ed. Trans. by Henry Paolucci, 1977. Indianapolis: Bobbs-Merrill.

Bentham, Jeremy, 1789. *Moral Calculus.* In Mary Peter Mack, ed., *A Bentham Reader,* 1969. New York: Pegasus.

Besharov, Douglas, editor, 1994. *When Drug Addicts Have Children: Reorienting Child Welfare's Response.* Edison, N.J.: Child Welfare League.

Bonger, Willem, 1916. *Criminality and Economic Conditions.* Abridged ed., 1969. Bloomington: Indiana University Press.

Cole, George F., ed., 1993. *Criminal Justice: Law and Politics.* Belmont, CA: Wadsworth.

Currie, Elliott, 1994, *RECKONING: Drugs, the Cities, and the American Future.* New York: Hill and Wang.

Hamilton, V. Lee and Joseph Sanders, 1992. *Everyday Justice: Responsibility and the Individual in Japan and the United States.* New Haven, CT: Yale University Press.

Lombroso, Cesare, 1863. *Crime, Its Causes and Remedies,* trans. by Gine Lombroso-Ferrero, 1972. Montclair, NJ: Patterson Smith.

Reuter, Peter, 1985. *External Hope: America's International Narcotics Efforts.* Santa Monica, CA: Rand Corporation.

Rosenberg, Mark and Mary Ann Fenley, 1991. *Violence in America: A Public Health Approach.* New York: Oxford University.

Wilson, James Q., [1975] 1985. *Thinking About Crime: Revised.* New York: Basic Books.

Journal Articles:

Cardenas, Cuauhtemoc, 1990. "Misunderstanding Mexico." *Foreign Policy,* no. 78 (Spring) 113–130.

Kobrin, Solomon, 1959. "The Chicago Area Project—25-Year Assessment." *Annals of the American Academy of Political and Social Science,* vol. 322:20–29.

Orrick, Sarah, ed., 1994. "The Federal Role in Crime Control." *Congressional Digest,* vol. 73 (June-July) 161–192. Washington, D.C.: The Congressional Digest Corporation.

Government Reports:

Federal Bureau of Investigation, 1993. *Terrorism in The United States.* United States Department of Justice. Washington, D.C.: U.S. Government Printing Office.

Home Office, 1990 White Paper. *Protecting The Public.* London: H.M. Stationary Office.

Lynch, James P., Steven K. Smith, Helen A. Graziadei, and Tanutda Pittayathikhun, 1994. *Profiles of Inmates in the United States and in England and Wales, 1991.* United States Department of Justice. Washington, D.C.: U.S. Government Printing Office.

Standing Committee on Justice and the Solicitor General, 1993. *Crime Prevention in Canada: Toward a National Strategy.* Ottawa: Canadian Communication Group.

Federal Bureau of Investigation, 1990, 1991, 1992, 1993, 1994. *Uniform Crime Report.* United States Department of Justice, Washington, D.C.: U.S. Government Printing Office.

CRISIS INTERVENTION.

As defined by Slaikeu (1984), "A helping process aimed at assisting a person or family to survive an unsettling event so that the probability of debilitating effects (e.g., emotional scars, physical harm) is minimized, and the probability of growth (e.g. new skills, new outlook on life, more options in living) is maximized." According to Klein and Lindemann (1961) a crisis is "an acute and often prolonged disturbance that may occur in an individual or social orbit as the result of an emotional hazard." These definitions are based on the understanding that a crisis is a turning point in one's life that has the potential for both positive and negative outcomes. These outcomes will be affected by the severity of the event, the personal resources of the individual, and the social resources and assistance that are available at the time of the crisis. Negative outcomes are generally characterized by a breakdown in an individual's problem-solving capabilities.

According to Baldwin (1978) there are six major types of emotional crises:

- *Dispositional:* Distress resulting from a problematic situation in which the individual lacks the information and encouragement to solve a problem in a nontraditional manner.

- *Anticipated life transitions:* Anticipated and normative life transitions over which the client may or may not have significant control.

- *Traumatic stress:* Emotional crises as the result of unexpected and uncontrolled external stressors or situations that are totally overwhelming.

- *Maturational/developmental crises:* These crises are the result of a struggle to achieve emotional maturity by resolving an interpersonal issue that had not been resolved adaptively in the past.

- *Crises reflecting psychopathology:* Emotional crises that occur as the result of preexisting psychopathology that impairs a person's ability for adaptive resolution.
- *Psychiatric emergencies:* A crisis situation wherein the person is incompetent or unable to assume personal responsibility as a result of severe impairment of a person's ability to function in a normative manner.

All of these crises are candidates for crisis intervention activities. The process of crisis intervention has two phases: first-order and second-order intervention (Slaikeu 1984). The first phase is known as psychological first aid. It is offered upon first contact with the crisis victim by a wide range of community service provides and helpers. The second phase occurs when crisis therapy, aimed at the psychological resolution of the crisis, is provided over a significant period of time, by trained mental health professionals. Four generic crisis intervention principles have been identified by Sandoval (1988). These interventions may take place in or outside of the actual counseling setting. These principles are as follows:

- Facilitate the reestablishment of a social support network;
- Engage in focused problem solving;
- Focus on self-concept;
- Encourage self-reliance.

History

The history of crisis intervention can be described as occurring in four phases. The first phase began in 1942 when 493 people died in a fire at the Coconut Grove in Boston, Massachusetts. Erich Lindemann and his colleagues from Massachusetts General Hospital were instrumental in working with both the survivors and the families of the victims. His work on the psychological symptoms of survivors, and Lindemann himself, became integral parts of the foundation of the field of crisis intervention. The second phase was characterized by the examination of the significance of life crises in adult psychopathology. Gerald Caplan's work focused on critical life crisis intervention in a preventive effort to minimize psychological impairment. The third phase began with the growth of the suicide prevention movement in the 1960s, which was based partially on Caplan's crisis theory. Suicide prevention centers, staffed primarily by volunteers, initiated twenty-four-hour, seven-days-a-week telephone counseling hotlines. Their roles often expanded over the years to include community outreach, on-site interventions, and ongoing case management. The fourth

phase also began in the 1960s with the emergence of the community mental health movement and the passage of the Community Mental Health Centers Act of 1963. The act was in a large measure the result of the efforts of President John F. Kennedy, whose interest in mental health had been generated by the mental retardation of his sister Rosemary and his family's efforts to come to terms with her condition. Among the mandated services of the mental health centers established by the act were crisis intervention and emergency services (Slaikeu, 1984). In many mental health centers crisis intervention services are placed within emergency services programs.

Focus, Goals, and Process

Crisis intervention has a preventive focus and is a process that takes place after critical life events have occurred. it generally takes place after a crisis, when a person is in a state of severe psychological, and often physical, disorganization. Crisis intervention is usually short-term and time-limited therapy whose goal is to assist people in regaining their equilibrium. Sandoval (1988) has identified five goals for practitioners who are providing crisis intervention services:

- Establish the meaning and understand the personal significance of the specific situation.
- Confront reality and respond to the requirements of the external situation.
- Sustain relationships with family members and friends as well as with other individuals who may be helpful in resolving the crisis and its aftermath.
- Preserve a reasonable emotional balance by managing upsetting feelings aroused by the situation.
- Preserve a satisfactory self-image and master a sense of competence and mastery.

In this case short-term means four to eight weeks and is more limited in scope and duration than traditional counseling. It is also far more directive, with the counselor taking a significantly more active role in providing information and suggesting strategies.

Crisis intervention activities can be provided in a number of settings by a variety of nonprofessional and professional providers. A relatively new innovation has been the development of mobile crisis programs that have increased the accessibility of these services by going directly to persons in-need (Zealberg et al., 1993). These services may be performed by specially trained mental health professionals, organizational psychologists, employee assistance professionals, school counselors, health care professionals, ministers, and volunteers. A key point to remember is that when the person in crisis is not responding, referral to a mental health professional for further intervention and counseling is the recommended course of action. The goal is to avoid further trauma and psychological impairment.

The impact of crisis intervention can be financial as well as psychological. A study in 1993 documented significant savings as the result of inpatient admission diversion to community-based treatment when crisis intervention techniques were used (Bengelsdorf et al., 1993). Both costs and readmission rates were reduced when crisis intervention and a strong medical orientation were emphasized in a partnership between a large HMO and a fee-for-service acute inpatient hospital (Olden and Johnson, 1993). Many of the principles of crisis intervention have been incorporated into Critical Incident Stress Debriefing (CISD) activities. CISD techniques are used with law enforcement, fire and rescue, and military personnel after high stress disasters have taken place.

PATRICE ALEXANDER

BIBLIOGRAPHY

Baldwin, B. A., 1978. "A Paradigm for the Classification of Emotional Crises: Implications for Crisis Intervention." *American Journal of Orthopsychiatry,* vol. 48:538–551.
Bengelsdorf, Herbert, John O. Church, Richard A. Kaye, and Barbara Orlowski, 1993. "The Cost Effectiveness of Crisis Intervention: Admission Diversion Savings Can Offset the High Cost of Services." *Journal of Nervous and Mental Disease,* vol. 181 (12) (December) 757–762.
Klein, Donald C. and Erich Lindemann, 1961. "Preventive Intervention in Individual and Family Crisis Situations" In Gerald Caplan, ed., *Prevention of Mental Disorders in Children.* New York: Basic Books, pp. 283–306.
Olden, Kevin W. and Michael P. Johnson, 1993. "A "Facilitated" Model of Inpatient Psychiatric Care." *Hospital and Community Psychology,* vol. 44 (9) (September) 879–882.
Sandoval, Jonathan, ed., 1988. *Crisis Counseling, Intervention, and Prevention in the Schools.* Hillsdale, NJ: Lawrence Erlbaum Associates.
Slaikeu, Karl A., 1984. *Crisis Intervention: A Handbook for Practice and Research.* Newton, MA: Allyn and Bacon.
Zealberg, Joseph J., Alberto B. Santos, and Richard K. Fisher, 1993. "Benefits of Mobile Crisis Programs." *Hospital and Community Psychology,* vol. 44 (1) (January) 16–17.

CRITERIA/ALTERNATIVES MATRIX. A

technique for comparing the relative merits of alternative policies, programs, or projects by calculating their level of achievement of agreed criteria or organizational goals; also known as Goals Achievement Matrix.

The criteria/alternative matrix (CAM)—often known as the Goals Achievement Matrix (GAM)—was first evolved in transportation planning in the U.S. in the 1960s. Its clearest exposition and extended development came in the work of Hill (1968) and the Department of Environment

in Great Britain (1973). The technique was used in a variety of contexts by the early 1970s, but most often in land use planning (Boyce, 1970; Lichfield et al., 1975) and, by the late 1970s, had largely supplanted cost-benefit analysis in transportation planning in metropolitan areas in the UK (CIPFA, 1978). At the same time, it has aroused a great deal of opposition from proponents of alternative evaluation techniques, particularly cost-benefit analysis. These arguments are very cogently summarised in Lichfield et al. (1975). In more recent years, this technique, in modified form, has become the central matrix in the Japanese "house of quality" approach to Quality Function Deployment and is now widely used in quality management, with customer requirements used as the criteria and substitute quality characteristics used as the alternatives (Oakland, 1993).

The technique is based on a scoring of all alternatives against agreed criteria. A very simple format for such an analysis is shown in Figure I. The alternatives may be options for policies, programs, projects, services, or schemes. The criteria may be organizational goals or objectives, performance indicators, or other criteria agreed to by the decisionmakers. Often the criteria are weighted to reflect their relevant importance. The scores of each alternative against each criterion are calculated and multiplied by the weight given to that criterion. The sum of all these weighted scores is the "points score" for the alternative: alternatives can be ranked in order of desirability by comparison of their scores.

Figure I shows how this might be applied in the simple case of evaluation of the alternatives for a traditional swimming pool (rectangular, divided in lanes, with a shallow end and deep end) and a modern "leisure pool" (with "beach area," irregular shape, whirlpool, wave machine, waterslides, etc.). The three criteria are the total number of users attracted (in thousands per week), the utility of the pool for teaching of swimming (on a subjective scale between 0 and 10), and the number of out-of-town visitors attracted to the area by the facility (in thousands per week). These criteria have been given weights of 5, 3, and 1 respectively. The leisure pool emerges with the highest points score, essentially because the traditional pool has

FIGURE I. A CRITERIA/ALTERNATIVES MATRIX FOR APPRAISING OPTIONS FOR A NEW SWIMMING POOL

Criteria	To provide enjoyment	To improve skills in the water	To attract tourist visits	
		Weightings		Total Score
Alternatives	x5	x3	x1	
Traditional Pool	4	7	2	43
Leisure Pool	8	3	9	58

much lower scores except on the teaching criterion, which has the lowest weight.

This example immediately highlights some of the key choices that have to be made by the decisionmaker using a CAM. Clearly, the results will depend critically on the definition of the alternatives and the criteria, on the weights given to the criteria, and on the measurement scale used for scoring against each criterion.

Furthermore, the technique is capable of considerably greater sophistication. Under each criterion or objective, subcriteria or subobjectives can be specified (as in a hierarchy of objectives). Again, separate itemization of "benefits" and "costs" might be undertaken, so that a cost/benefit ratio for each criterion or objective could be computed (e.g., under criterion 3, the income from total spending of tourists attracted to the area could be counted as benefits and the total cost of consequent publicity and tourist information services could be counted as costs). At an even greater level of complexity, separate CAM analyses might be carried out for each stakeholder or affected interest group—or, if preferred, the benefits and costs under each criterion could be scored separately for each identified group, and then summed by means of a weighting given to the different groups (which would make explicit the decisionmaker's "social welfare function", in cost-benefit analysis terms).

In assessing the value of CAM, cost-benefit analysis is chosen here as the comparator, since it is the most developed of the alternative techniques in the literature. The strengths of CAM compared to cost-benefit analysis are:

- It ties evaluation to the objectives of the organization or the agreed criteria for a project, making evaluation much more politically sensitive;
- It is less technically complex to undertake and easier to explain to nontechnicians (although this would not necessarily be true of the more sophisticated applications mentioned above);
- It can directly incorporate qualitative judgments on the achievement of objectives or other criteria in areas for which tangible benefits and costs are not readily calculable;
- It can even operate with purely ordinal assessments of alternatives;
- It does not require monetary valuation of the achievements of the alternative considered;
- Nevertheless, it permits monetary evaluation of criterion achievement and even an itemization of benefits and costs under each criterion, if the analyst so desires and is able to supply the appropriate information—it can therefore be made formally equivalent to cost-benefit analysis;
- It can include and highlight equity objectives in a clear way.

The main weaknesses of CAM are:

- The difficulty of finding clearly expressed and explicitly agreed criteria (particularly if it is desired that these be the organizational objectives, expressing desired ends), the achievement of which can be measured;
- The even greater difficulty of getting weights for this set of objectives, given political reluctance to reveal such information, even where any consensus might exist;
- The problems attached to devising a measurement scale for each objective (or for each performance indicator that is to be aggregated into an index of achievement for a given objective);
- The dangers in aggregating scores based on different measurement scales, both in the calculation of indices of achievement for each objective and in the computation of the total points score across all objectives—perhaps necessitating the statistical normalization of scores;
- The difficulty of including the time stream of achievement measures in the framework without complicating it greatly;
- The danger that choices on each of the above issues will be made by analysts without any basis of legitimation (which in cost-benefit analysis would come from the use of preferences and valuations revealed in market or quasi-market behavior), which is tantamount to dressing up and systematizing their own prejudices—although it can be seen as an advantage of the technique that it allows decisionmakers to see the implications of varying their basic assumptions;
- The danger that both benefits and costs will be double counted within different objectives and that the distinction will be lost between the overall achievements of each alternative and the overall costs of that alternative;
- The danger that starting from agreed objectives will render the analysis incapable of recognizing and highlighting significant impacts on the welfare of certain groups in the community, which lie outside the purview of the specified objectives.

In addition, of course, there are many problems that are common to most evaluation techniques, such as the likelihood that only some stakeholders will have a voice that is heard in the evaluation process, that each stakeholder would use a different set of starting assumptions in the analysis, that much of the information is subject to selective measurement and reporting, that a key success factor for any alternative may be how well it fits into and creates synergy with other ongoing activities (rather than simply its intrinsic merits), that the most successful alternatives will "emerge" rather than be deliberately planned, that the evaluation framework and the fundamental parameters (such as the weights on the objectives) will be reworked until the final results emerging conform to the "desired" final rankings, that little attention will, in any case, be paid to the results by decisionmakers.

Nevertheless, the simplicity of the technique, its intrinsic plausibility, and its flexibility mean that it continues to find favor in a wide variety of evaluation contexts.

TONY BOVAIRD

BIBLIOGRAPHY

Boyce, David E., 1970. *Metropolitan Plan-making: An Analysis of Experience with the Preparation and Evaluation of Alternative Land Use and Transportation Plans.* Philadelphia: Regional Science Research Institute.
CIPFA, 1979. *Assessing Priorities. Output Measurement Working Party Report.* London: Chartered Institute of Public Finance and Accountancy.
Department of Environment, 1973. *The Use of Evaluation Matrices for Structure Plans. Structure Plans Note 8/72.* London: Department of Environment.
Hill, Morris, 1968. "A Goals-Achievement Matrix for Evaluating Alternative Plans." *Journal of the American Institute of Planners,* vol. 34:19–29.
Lichfield, Nathaniel, Peter Kettle and Michael Whitbread 1975. *Evaluation in the Planning Process.* Oxford: Pergamon Press.
Oakland, John S., 1993. *Total Quality Management: The Route to Improving Performance.* 2d ed. Oxford: Butterworth Heinemann.

CRITICAL THEORY (OF PUBLIC ORGANIZATIONS).

A theoretical framework with which to explore why public organizations tend to deemphasize citizen participation, and more significantly, promote the "scientization" of policy issues (the conversion of political issues into exclusively issues of management).

Since the early 1970s, there has been a growing interest in critical theory as applied to public organizations. This interest, in part, has been due to what many have argued is the deleterious influence of instrumental rationality (the technical emphasis on efficiency, expediency, and calculation of ends) that has penetrated the very core of how public organizations operate. According to David Ingram (1990), critical theory's "primary aim is not the discovery of statistical patterns enabling the prediction and control of social and political processes but the proffering of critical enlightenment regarding the justness and goodness of social and political institutions" (pp. 21).

From this perspective, critical theory is an inquiry into both the prevailing rationality residing in organizations as well as the examination of the bureaucratic domination over the polity. Concomitantly, critical theorists attempt to offer new suggestions of how to achieve a more democratic society in the face of an increasingly instrumental value system in political institutions.

Critical Theory and the Frankfurt School

By and large, the major influence of those impacted by critical theory has come from the works associated with the Institute for Social Research at the University of Frankfurt, Germany, that was created in the 1920s. These thinkers—who have included the likes of Max Horkheimer, Herbert Marcuse, and Eric Fromm (to name just a few)—attempted to combine the theoretical insights of Karl Marx, Georg Hegel, and Max Weber into a powerful critique of modern life that examined, among other things, the ubiquitous impact of technical (or instrumental) rationality on the social sciences, the family, bureaucracy, technology, and the legal system. However, it is the works of Jurgen Habermas (1971, 1973, 1979) that have generated the most interest in applying critical theory to the role of public organizations.

Habermas's thinking (which is representative of the second generation of the Frankfurt School), while complex in its scope, is predicated upon the notion that substantive issues (ethical issues) cannot be acknowledged, or fully understood, by instrumental reason alone. Instrumental rationality, claims Habermas, is too pedantic and myopic in that it excludes the normative discourse needed to explore the priorities of society. For Habermas there is a direct linkage between language and rationality that determines the substantive meaning of social and political life. According to Habermas, instrumental rationality has subordinated traditional structures of society in conformity to this pedantic mindset. Human action itself has become limited to the dictates of instrumental rationality, or what Habermas calls "purposive-rational" action. In short, instrumental rationality by its very nature tries to control human action, thus reducing action to a mere technique devoid of any moral purpose.

As harsh as this may sound, Habermas discusses another kind of rationality he calls "communicative reason"—a rationality based upon symbolic interaction. This communicative reason tries to develop a consensus in the form of argumentative speech. It is a rationality that fosters nondistorted communication in which an individual can freely participate in ethical deliberation, dialogue, and debate in order to reach a consensus as to what substantive ends to pursue.

If we apply Habermas's argument concerning communicative reason to public organizations, this would imply that such organizations must become a public forum for discourse dealing with the normative purposes and implications of public policy. It should be noted that Habermas does not explicitly state that administrators should completely disregard instrumental rationality in the performance of certain tasks, but rather that communicative reason has an equally important role to play in decisionmaking. Furthermore, Habermas argues that administrators cannot, and should not, base their claims merely on the "facts," but concomitantly on the normative and interpretative beliefs that can disclose the claims of appropriateness and ethical content.

Without such a critical view, Habermas stresses that administrators may only contribute to the depoliticization of the public sphere (which he also has termed the refeudalization of the public sphere), leading to increased public disenchantment and citizen apathy to political affairs. Habermas reiterates that critical theory raises such issues as social justice, political power, and human freedom—issues that can never be realized by an instrumental rationality prevalent in organizations. To Habermas this is due to the reason that instrumental rationality is inexorably subordinated to technical rules only, while communicative reason (or action) is free of external compulsion, and thus truth claims can be freely debated and discussed. The implication of this point is clear: the modern public organization, as a result of its grounding in instrumental rationality, promotes a distorted communication that hinders the individual's ability for ethical autonomy and critical self-reflection. What is occurring in modern society, Habermas insists, is the growing corruption of language that divorces speech from its ethical and moral character. Under these circumstances, communication itself becomes merely a tool to legitimize a particular configuration of power. This trend is particularly troubling given that instrumental reason strives to achieve "objective truth," as if it represents the preeminent mode of rationality. Given this proclivity, it is no wonder that citizen participation is confined to those who communicate only in an instrumental language that public organization can understand and appreciate. Such an instrumental language, Habermas fears, will only depersonalize administrative processes and lead to further citizen alienation.

Habermas's analysis, while only briefly outlined here, has had a salient influence on certain scholars' theory in public administration. For example, Robert Denhardt (1981) has argued that critical theory, especially as articulated by Habermas, has provided a new approach in addressing the schism between theory and practice in public administration. Critical theory, Denhardt states, goes beyond the mainstream literature in public administration (and public policy) in addressing the present legitimacy crisis of public organizations and the dominance of instrumental rationality that only leads to the alienation of the citizens from government. Denhardt also contends that a critical theory of public organizations forces us to examine—and expose—the power and domination of public organizations over citizens' lives. Thus critical theory, if taken seriously, raises the issue of the bureaucratic limitations that restrict communicative practices so important in promoting discourse and open communication.

Some Contemporary Perspectives on Critical Theory: An Organizational Perspective

In a similar manner, Ralph Hummel (1994) analyzes what he refers to as a critique of life in modern organization. Although Hummel calls himself a phenomenologist, he openly draws upon Habermas's ideas. Like many in the Frankfurt School, Hummel depends heavily on Max Weber's analysis of bureaucracy, especially Weber's distinction between "social action" (which refers to human action in terms of its subjective meanings and attachment of its meaning to others as well as to the individual) and institutionally commanded action (action that is externally imposed by others and when human action becomes completely socialized). Hummel's central point is that because bureaucracies are so embedded in instrumentally commanded action, they not only distort our language and thinking processes, but they inevitably replace politics itself with bureaucracy. Echoing Habermas's theme of the depoliticization of the public sphere, Hummel goes on to argue that what is needed is a new political imagination that can confront the power of bureaucratic thinking over the citizenry's lives. Such a political imagination—and here he is most influenced by the German philosopher Martin Heidegger—necessitates a fundamental reformulation of science, technology, and bureaucracy. However, Hummel also outlines a "postbureaucratic politics" that is based upon what he so aptly calls "process politics." Hummel points out that process politics acknowledges the role of instrumental rationality, but not as an end in itself. In the next breath, Hummel tells us that process politics is a manner in which each participant can contribute knowledge and viewpoints into the definition of the policy problem. In this respect, the political goals become not the desire to uphold instrumental values, but the pursuit of ends suited to promote the public interest. Yet, he admits this process politics may not be enough in satisfying—and facilitating—what he calls the "politics of care."

In sum, Hummel's critical approach to public bureaucracies is a critique based upon an existential criticism of the plight of the individual in a modern world increasingly being controlled by an instrumental value system that systemically prevents the person's "potential to be," as he calls it. The cost of this depersonalization, he articulates, is much too high and needs immediate attention by students of public organizations.

Another perspective of the relevance of critical theory to public organizations has come from the urban planning theorist John Forester (1983). While closely related to these other views, he advocates that critical theory can actually provide an empirically based and interpretive process in understanding the powerful forces shaping our social and political existence. He emphasizes that critical theory, unlike other traditional approaches to studying public organizations, is a form of transformative praxis (practice) that can be helpful in revitalizing these organizations to be more congruent to the public interest. Forester continues to push this point even more by arguing that critical theory can make a contribution to policy analysis. This contribution stems from its emphasis on philosophy and ethics and the concern critical theory has for imagining new possibilities for public action—actions that are often left off the policy agenda. Forester maintains that critical theory represents an advance in our study of public organizations because it focuses our attention on the concept of power rather than on efficiency. In other words, critical theory emphasizes that it is pursuit of democratic social relations that must always take priority over the instrumental concerns of achieving organizational effectiveness.

It is also worth noting that other scholarly works about critical theory include William Dunn and Bahman Fozouni's (1976) book, and, more recently, Jay White's (1990) article exploring the meaning of administrative rationality. While these works and others discussed have contributed much to our understanding of the instrumental rationality prevailing in public organizations, it has been argued that critical theory—as interesting as this theoretical approach may seem—hardly offers a blueprint for administrative reform. It is interesting that even Habermas does not address the need, or even the desire, to redefine public administration into a discipline based on communicative reason. Instead, Habermas believes that public (and private) bureaucracies are merely powerful institutions to be resisted always by the general public. Habermas put his faith in social movements such as environmentalism that can redefine a new role for the citizenry in its relationship to public organizations.

On the other hand, one of the most important practical issues that critical theory raises is the growing functional complexity of large organizations and the commensurate decline of citizen involvement in the policy process. A critical theory of public organizations, in the practical sense of the word, must somehow address this vexing imbalance (Barber, 1984).

Although it is true that many of the thinkers discussed here have relied, in varying degrees, on Habermas's conceptualization of critical theory, other prominent scholars have also taken a critical view, drawing their insights from other intellectual sources. One such important public administration scholar is Alberto Guerreiro Ramos.

Ramos (1981) posits that any critical theory of public organizations must ultimately confront the one-dimensional thinking prevailing in contemporary organizational design and analysis. Put simply, Ramos contends that organizational theory has become captive of a market ideology—an ideology that legitimizes a utilitarian mindset that converts the good into the functional and the ethical into the a-ethical. Ramos pulls no punches in his analysis of functional (or instrumental) rationality in public organizations: it strips reason of any normative role in shaping social and political affairs. Ramos argues that what has been lost in modern society is "classical (or substantive) reason." Substantive rationality, Ramos emphasizes, looks at such issues as the nature of the good society, the good individual, and social justice, to mention a few. In the words of Ramos, substantive rationality "is a force active in the human psyche which enables the individual to distinguish between good and evil, false and genuine knowledge, and accordingly, to order one's personal and social life" (1981, pp. 4–5).

Like Habermas, Ramos does not believe it is possible to formulate a critical theory without first demonstrating the normative weakness of instrumental reason. Any critical theory, Ramos reminds us, must be constructed on the basis of substantive rationality. Yet, according to Ramos, current organizational theorists do not understand, or fail to understand, that substantive and instrumental rationality belong to two distinct and different spheres of human existence. What Ramos is hinting at can now be more directly stated: formal bureaucratic organizations are not cognitively structured to incorporate—or tolerate—such concepts as self-actualization, nondistorted communication, love, and so forth. In short, bureaucratic organizations are simply not the appropriate setting for the introduction of such concepts when such organizations are so deeply embedded in the instrumental goals of efficiency, effectiveness, and calculation.

Similarly, Ramos is making another controversial point: organizational theorists often try to justify their approaches by uncritically incorporating normative concepts into their analyses. To Ramos this is nothing more than a form of theoretical deception that induces others to interpret reality in a manner that obscures rather than clarifies the realities of modern bureaucracies. A critical theory must, he contends, delimit the pervasive influence of the market ideology on political life and create new social spaces that reflect the differing substantive needs and activities of the individual.

Ramos aptly calls this new critical approach a "paraeconomic paradigm." This paradigm, as he describes it, is the designing of a variety of social enclaves that have specific requisites unique to their own setting. Ramos specifies that these design requirements include the factors of space, time, cognition, technology, and size. For example, Ramos states that if one is to design a social enclave emphasizing full participation and consensus there must be a sensitivity given to size. One cannot have a workable participatory democracy if the social enclave is too large. Thus critical theory, Ramos concludes, cannot have validity if it is divorced in any manner from a multidimensional view of human existence. Contemporary organizational theory, he surmises, has sadly ignored this basic point, which is why it is both uncritical and in a constant state of theoretical bewilderment.

Virginia Hill-Ingersoll and Guy Adams (1992), to some extent, build upon the analysis of Ramos's critical perspective on organizations. They introduce two terms central to their examination of public organizations: metapatterns and metamyths. In regards to the former term, they state "we are thinking of patterns themselves as recurring in a relationship, sequences that can often be expressed as a theme" (1992, p. 2). Conversely, metamyths are shared beliefs or meaning structures. Their purpose in using these two themes is to explore the underlying assumptions of action as they take place within an organizational setting—assumptions or meanings that stand behind the scenes, but which inform the action on stage. Taken together, these two concepts examine what they state is the tacit dimension of organizations.

They present an interesting critical view, but with a slight twist: they posit that organizational theorists have been guilty of what Ramos has termed a "misplacement of concepts." This misplacement of concepts refers to the way theorists have borrowed concepts (such as learning and culture) outside their proper experiential context, and, more importantly, inappropriate to their original meaning. For instance, Hill-Ingersoll and Adams indicate that those who use the concept of culture often do so without understanding the difference between subcultures and culture, and usually leave untouched any discussion of how our modern age is a culture of technical (or instrumental) rationality. Their argument, if taken seriously, implies that what passes for organizational theory, to a large degree, is merely an ideological set of assertions that reinforces the technical-rational system of organizations. Their central theme is that organizations are nested in the broader culture of modernity and we are often unaware of the instrumental lifeblood that runs through the veins of our modern organizations. Finally, they declare the need for a "postempirical" approach that can study (and uncover) how metapatterns and metamyths shape our "meaning maps"—that is, the meaning we make of organizations and the manner in which we fit work into one's larger self-definition.

From a somewhat different theoretical angle, William Scott and David Kirk Hart (1979, 1989) have constructed a powerful critique of modern bureaucracies based upon what they refer to as the "organizational imperative." The organizational imperative, they explain, is predicated upon the unquestioned belief system that whatever enhances the health of the organizations is also, by inference, beneficial to the individual and society. The organizational imperative, when taken to its logical conclusion, essentially drains the moral content from managerial decisionmaking due to

its emphasis on pragmatism and prudence. Moreover, the organizational imperative implies that whatever is good for the individual can only be achieved through modern, functional organizations. Taken together, these assumptions of the organizational imperative reduce individual values to the prevailing values of the organization.

While Scott and Hart have employed the concept of the organizational imperative to critique organizations, Michael Harmon (1981) has developed another critical view he refers to as an action theory for public administration. Although his analysis of "action theory" is deeply influenced by interpretive theorists (Alfred Schutz, Peter Berger, and Thomas Luckmann), Harmon's approach is not all that different from Habermas's communicative reason, a point he acknowledges. The key to Harmon's analysis is the criterion of "mutuality."

Here Harmon suggests that mutuality involves processes of social interaction and that action is important in itself because it is a way to articulate the individual's freedom and autonomy. Action cannot, therefore, be reduced to instrumental values, according to Harmon. In fact, it is only through action that the quality of social relations is realized and prevents individuals from being treated as a means to some instrumental end. Not surprisingly, Harmon stresses the need for face-to-face encounters as the appropriate decision unit (what he calls disaggregated decisions) over that of aggregated decisions, which apply decisions uniformly to social collectivities. What Harmon finds especially attractive about disaggregated decisionmaking is that it is sensitive to the unique and specific nature of individual problems. Although he is quick to point out that this approach is time-consuming and can rarely, if ever, be applied to public goods (e.g., national defense), it does serve as a counterweight to the treatment of citizens in an impersonal and abstract manner.

Harmon's argument does not stop here. He proceeds to mount a strong criticism against the concept of hierarchy. He contends that hierarchy is but one of five possible decision rules that govern authority in public organizations. Besides hierarchy, the other decision rules are: (1) voting (majority rule); (2) contract (voluntary agreement to a decision that is binding); (3) bargaining (a market rule in which individuals trade or exchange with one another to reach a noncoercive decision); and consensus (the integration of differing views that are acceptable to all parties). Harmon's point here is that the selection of decision rules becomes, in essence, the normative framework in assessing the structure of modern public organizations. He proceeds to formulate several criteria for the selection of these decision rules. Yet Harmon is clear in his preference: the consensus decision unit. Consensus, he suggests, is the most congruent to his idea of disaggregated decisionmaking and it is this decision unit that emphasizes discussion and debate free of organizational coercion. In sum, Harmon has conducted a critique of public organizations in order to re-focus attention on the substantive meaning of action and how it can reveal new purposes and goals for the public organization.

On the other hand, Curtis Ventriss (1987a, 1987b) has conducted research on the substantive meaning of the public. He argues that public administration theorists, for the most part, have accepted the role of managerialism as a given in public organizations and have never questioned in any serious manner the relationship of public organizations to the role of the state. Ventriss argues that managerialism "can be defined as an epistemological and philosophical belief system specifying that because public administration is primarily a utilitarian and pragmatic field devoted to managing public affairs, its greatest contribution is the application of managerial strategies to solve public problems" (1987a, p. 27).

With respect to the former point, Ventriss states that public administration has historically tried to emulate the perceived efficiencies of business administration. It is no wonder, he concludes, that public administration as a field has tended to believe that its greatest contribution to public organizations is in devising managerial strategies to solve public problems. This assumption is reflective of what he states is a "modern rationalist liberalism" that displaces political problems into managerial issues. Furthermore, it is manifested in the belief that to deal successfully with public problems the solution always becomes an issue of changing this or that administrative procedure, or organizing and reorganizing parts of the administrative state, or applying supposedly new managerial approaches, without ever considering that it may be the body politic itself that needs revamping and revitalizing.

What we are seeing, according to Ventriss, is not only the scientization of politics, but the growing role of public organizations to provide some kind of technocratic order to a ritualistic democracy based on constant political bargaining. What bothers Ventriss is that the incessant emphasis on managerialism tends to divert public attention away from other issues such as the structure (and distribution) of power in society and how some of the most pressing political problems may just indeed reside in the economic and political fabric of society itself.

The latter point is something he feels that public administration scholars have almost completely ignored. The relationship of public organizations to the state, he surmises, raises some of the most controversial questions facing public administration: do public organizations tend to legitimize the role of the state through the application of their technical knowledge and expertise? Or, put another way, do public organizations displace issues from the political fabric of society, thus elevating process over purpose? Ventriss reminds us that public organizations are, after all, agents of the state. Ventriss further argues that our

understanding of public organizations in relationship to the state is uncritical because scholars have fallen into a Hegelian trap that the "real is the rational" and that examining the state critically is tantamount to calling into question the very purpose and goals of public organizations in performing state functions (i.e., its legitimacy). He does not address what the role of the state should be; rather Ventriss concentrates on the idea that this relationship warrants more systematic analysis by those trying to develop any viable critical theory of public organizations (and the state).

Saying this, his critique of public organizations hinges on the belief that so far scholars in public administration (and policy) have been unable to formulate any meaningful theoretical linkages to the meaning of the public. Ventriss proposes that to address the meaning of the public we need to develop a public language, a public social science, create new public spaces for citizen involvement, and experiment with new public learning models. Furthermore, he maintains that public administration theorists must free themselves from the dangerous (and erroneous) assumption that the public and the state are somehow one in the same. A critical theory of public organizations, therefore, is an integral part of a critical theory of the public.

Even though a wide variety of critical views on public organizations has been discussed, such perspectives have not gone uncontested. Perhaps more than any other thinker who has taken strong exception to this kind of criticism is the widely regarded American public administration scholar Charles Goodsell (1994).

Goodsell argues that within the United States the role of public bureaucracies has been unfairly castigated by an array of scholars ranging from public choice theorists (those advocating market-oriented approaches to policy issues) to critical theorists. These criticisms can be categorized into three broad categories: (1) the oppression of individual autonomy; (2) the misuse of political power; and (3) the poor delivery of public services. Goodsell forcefully argues, using an array of polling results, that these criticisms are merely perpetuating misleading myths about public organizations. For instance, empirical evidence demonstrates that in the United States the clients of public organizations are actually quite satisfied with the overall performance of public organizations. Goodsell goes on to claim that public organizations can—and do—serve as agents of social change, in that government is often called upon to encourage change through public policy. In total, public organizations are simply criticized for the wrong reason and we forget that these organizations are more representative (in terms of who works in them) of the general public than any other institution of U.S. government. Goodsell's main argument against the critical theories of public organizations merits mentioning: critical theorists attack public organizations when their real purpose is a critique of the forces of modernity on political and social life. Those adhering to critical theory have overstated their case against public organizations and have ignored other empirical evidence that directly contradicts their hypercritical analysis. Goodsell's polemic view is that the U.S. administrative state not only plays a positive role in society, but it deserves to be supported as a legitimate force in shaping public affairs.

Conclusion

In conclusion, the various approaches presented here on critical theories of public organizations, while controversial in nature, are really an endeavor to redefine the civic purpose of public organizations and to construct, or help to construct, new intellectual avenues in understanding and acting upon those powerful forces that may be undermining the goal of a more democratic society. If nothing else, a noble calling.

CURTIS VENTRISS

BIBLIOGRAPHY

Barber, Benjamin, 1984. *Strong Democracy.* Berkeley: University of California Press.
Denhardt, Robert, 1981. "Toward a Critical Theory of Public Organization." *Public Administration Review,* vol. 41:628–635.
Dunn, William N. and Bahman Fozouni, 1976. *Toward a Critical Administrative Theory.* Beverly Hills, CA: Sage.
Forester, John, 1983. "Critical Theory of Organizational Analysis." In G. Morgan, ed., *Beyond Method: Strategies for Social Research.* Beverly Hills, CA: Sage, pp. 234–46.
Goodsell, Charles, 1994. *The Case for Bureaucracy.* 3d ed. Chatham, NJ: Chatham House Publishers.
Habermas, Jurgen, 1971. *Toward a Rational Society.* Boston: Beacon Press.
———, 1973. *Legitimation Crisis.* Boston: Beacon Press.
———, 1979. *Communication and the Evolution of Society.* Boston: Beacon Press.
Harmon, Michael, 1981. *Action Theory for Public Administration.* New York: Longman.
Hill-Ingersoll, Virginia and Guy Adams, 1992. *The Tacit Organization.* Greenwich, CT: JAI Press.
Hummel, Ralph, 1994. *The Bureaucratic Experience.* 4th ed. New York: St. Martin's Press.
Ingram, David, 1990. *Critical Theory and Philosophy.* New York: Paragon House.
Ramos, Alberto Guerreiro, 1981. *The New Science of Organizations.* Toronto: University of Toronto Press.
Scott, William and David Kirk Hart, 1979. *Organizational America.* Boston: Houghton Mifflin.
———, 1989. *Organizational Values in America.* New Brunswick, NJ: Transaction Books.
Ventriss, Curtis, 1987a. "Two Critical Issues of American Public Administraion." *Administration and Society,* vol. 19: 25–47.
———, 1987b. "Toward a Public Philosophy of Public Administration: A Civic View of the Public." *Public Administration Review,* vol. 49:173–179.
White, Jay, 1990. "Images of Administrative Reason and Rationality." In H. Kass and B. Catron, eds., *Images and Identities in Public Administration.* Newbury, CA: Sage.

CROSSWALK. A matrix chart used to show the direct correspondence between two different classification schemes for expenditures in a budget document in which one set of expenditure categories differs from another, such as when the categories used in the budget are different from those in the authorizing legislation, or the categories in the appropriations act differ from those of the organizational structure, the congressional or legislative committee structure, the accounting system, or a previous year's budget. Crosswalks may also be used for other organizational purposes when it is necessary to show correspondence between two different classification schemes.

Crosswalks were first developed for use in budgeting when budget reforms began to require use of expenditure classification schemes different from the traditional budget format that was familiar to legislators, members of Congress, and agency officials. Traditionally, government budgets in the U.S. and many other countries were presented in the line-item object of expenditure format. Usually these budgets were prepared by organizational units and then aggregated to form the agency or department budget. Budgets of this type used only one classification scheme, object of expenditure, and therefore did not require crosswalks to relate multiple classifications. In the mid-1960s with the adoption of Planning, Programming, Budgeting (PPB) in the U.S., crosswalks began to be needed because the program structure of PPB did not necessarily correspond to the organizational or appropriation structures of the budget.

The program structures used in PPB often were based upon policy and program categories that were different from and did not directly correspond to the government's organizational structure. These PPB program structures often crossed organizational lines and combined similar policy areas without regard to existing appropriations' categories or current agency structures. Since most appropriations acts and accounting systems were based upon the existing organizational structure and traditional object of expenditure classifications, this use of alternative, policy-based program structures caused problems in both budget development and subsequent presentations of the budget to decisionmakers. If government organizations had been restructured to match the new policy-oriented program structures, there would not have been a conflict with the traditional budget categories. In most cases, however, reorganizations did not immediately (or ever) follow the new program structures. As a result of these differences between the PPB program structures, traditional budget categories, and organization structures, crosswalks were needed to show how the new structures corresponded to the traditional ones. Although PPB eventually was modified and replaced by other budget formats, crosswalks have continued to be used whenever it is desirable to show the direct correspondence between the different budget classifications or categories.

Technically, a crosswalk is a matrix that shows one classification scheme on the vertical axis and the other classification scheme on the horizontal axis. These two sets of categories could be, for example, the appropriation structure of the budget and the object of expenditure categories of the accounting system for a government. Budgeted expenditure amounts are shown in the crosswalk according to both classification schemes simultaneously. Each column represents a category in one scheme, and each row a category in the other scheme. Rows and columns are summed to show the total for each category. The grand total in the bottom right corner is the sum of either all columns or all rows. This demonstrates that the total expenditure amount is the same regardless of the set of categories used. Figure I illustrates a crosswalk showing the correspondence between line-item object of expenditure categories on the vertical axis and programmatic expenditure categories on the horizontal axis. In this hypothetical example of a county budget, expenditures add to the same total according to either classification, and decisionmakers are provided with information that allows them to compare budget proposals according to the two sets of categories.

Crosswalks such as the one in Figure I are developed by calculating the expenditure amount that corresponds to each cell in the matrix. For example, the first cell in column one, row one is the personal services total for the public works and facilities department. This amount would be calculated from available budgetary information and entered into the crosswalk. Similarly, the cell at the intersection of row two and column one is a calculation of the amount of fringe benefits budgeted for the public works and facilities department. Each cell would be calculated similarly until the crosswalk was complete and could be reconciled to both classification schemes. Calculation of cell entries may require sophisticated analyses of the components of particular budgetary categories or may be as simple as copying budgeted amounts from two different spreadsheets and adding across and down to reconcile them.

Crosswalks are useful tools for budgeting in any situation in which it is desirable to use more than one expenditure classification scheme. Crosswalks allow budgets to be developed according to one set of categories and to be presented in another, since anyone wanting to compare the two sets of categories may use the crosswalk for that purpose. Crosswalks are especially helpful in complicated budgets such as the U.S. federal budget, in which the public document and even the appropriations bills use highly aggregated information in a broad program format that eventually has to be allocated to specific agencies and divisions and spent according to legal expenditure categories. Similarly, crosswalks allow the accounting system to use object of expenditure classifications to track expenditures for control purposes, for example, while providing deci-

FIGURE I. Crosswalk Example (in 1000s)

	EXPENDITURES BY PROGRAM							
Expenditures by Line Item	Public Works & Facilities	Public Safety & Judiciary	Health	Libraries	Social Services	General Government	Capital Improvements	TOTAL
Personal Services	16,625	105,460	128,975	10,575	65,550	33,880		361,065
Benefits	4,655	22,321	36,113	2,961	18,355	9,487		93,892
Operations & Maintenance	560	25,046	62,105	1,853	26,823	12,422		128,809
Contractual Services	6,720	320	15,020	8,400	125,000	12,050		167,510
Public Assistance			120,400		185,200			305,600
Equipment	21,040	2,650	22,000	32	4,000	2,400		52,122
Capital Outlay	40,546	475					78,556	119,577
Debt Service	12,040					25,136		37,176
TOTAL	102,186	156,272	384,613	23,821	424,928	95,375	78,556	1,265,751

sionmakers with programmatic information for policy decisionmaking. In public budget documents prepared by governments that use multiple classification schemes for their budgets, crosswalks may be prepared and included in an appendix to help citizens and other users of the budget understand how funds are allocated.

Crosswalks are robust tools for presentation and analysis of complex information in a simple, easy to understand format. In addition to their use in the budget process, crosswalks may also be used in other situations in which using more than one classification scheme is desirable, including personnel classifications, matrix project management, and many others.

GLEN HAHN COPE

BIBLIOGRAPHY

Axelrod, Donald, 1988. *Budgeting for Modern Government.* New York: St. Martin's Press, Inc..

Lee, Robert D., Jr. and Ronald W. Johnson, 1994. *Public Budgeting Systems.* 5th ed. Gaithersburg, MD: Aspen Publishers, Inc.

Lynch, Thomas D., 1979. *Public Budgeting in America.* Englewood Cliffs, NJ: Prentice-Hall, Inc.

Mikesell, John L., 1995. *Fiscal Administration: Analysis and Applications for the Public Sector.* 4th ed. Belmont, CA: Wadsworth Publishing Company.

Schick, Allen, 1971. *Budget Innovation in the States.* Washington, D.C.: The Brookings Institution.

CROWD-OUT. A term used by economists to describe the potential of one revenue source to reduce proceeds from another source in the financing of a governmental or nonprofit sector service. In the context of the nonprofit sector, studies of crowd-out have been primarily concerned with the question: Does government spending reduce private contributions to charitable organizations? Some attention has also been given to the question: Does sales revenue generated by a nonprofit organization reduce charitable donations?

The phenomenon of crowd-out is important to policymakers and governmental and nonprofit sector managers for several reasons. Policymakers should know the impacts of increases or reductions in government spending on the ability of nonprofit organizations to deliver promised social services. For example, if government funding results in commensurate reductions in private support, such spending will be useless as a means to increase resources for service delivery. Alternatively, if private donors fail to compensate for government cutbacks in funding to nonprofits, policymakers must expect consequent reductions in service output.

Similarly, nonprofit sector managers must understand how the receipt of government grants or the generation of earned income through sales of services will affect the organization's ability to raise donated funds. For example, crowd-out has potential implications for how nonprofit managers price their services (Young and Steinberg, 1995). If higher prices or the realization of profits from sales results in reduced donations, the nonprofit manager must design pricing policies that account for both sales and donor revenue implications.

Economists have developed theories of crowd-out based on the characterization of charitable giving as a public or a private economic good (Abrams and Schmitz, 1986). If charitable giving were a "pure public good" in the sense that donors were only interested in the amount of public service output produced by the recipient charity, then donors would be indifferent between having the charitable output financed by government or financed through voluntary giving. In this case, as increase in government contributions would be expected to result in a dollar for dollar decrease in charitable donations. However, if charitable giving were more like a private good and donors received some personal benefit from the act of giving itself, then an increase in government funding would be expected to result in less than a dollar for dollar reduction in private giving. That is, donors would likely continue to want to "purchase" some of the private benefit from giving. This situation has been called "impure altruism" by economists, and the private benefit associated with giving has been called the "warm glow" effect (Andreoni, 1989).

Researchers have also identified other factors that may influence whether government grants, under some conditions, may result in "crowd-in" of private donations, that is, an increase in donations as a result of government funding (Rose-Ackerman, 1986; Steinberg, 1993). Factors that might cause crowd-in include matching provisions that effectively lower the price of giving to charity (e.g., if matching is one-to-one it will cost the donor only 50 cents to give a dollar), conditions attached to grants that make the nonprofit's services more attractive to donors (e.g, regulations affecting quality, management practices, or eligibility for services), and information revealed in the grantmaking process that makes the charity more appealing to donors. For example, the receipt of government funds may be seen as a "seal of approval" for donors seeking reputable charities for their largesse.

Empirical studies of crowding out of donations by government grants tend to support the impure altruism model. According to Steinberg (1993), "estimated crowd-out ranges from 1/2 percent to 35 percent per unit of government spending" (p. 105). However, this is a summary perspective. Individual studies reveal a wide variety of results in different contexts.

Relatively little research has been done on the question of crowding out of charitable contributions by sales revenues, although this is an increasingly important issue given the nonprofit sector's growing dependence on earned income sources (Hodgkinson and Associates, 1992). Kingma (1995) investigated two models of how sales and donations interact within the context of local chapters of the American Red Cross. He found preliminary evidence of a large crowd-out effect, on the order of 90 cents of donations lost for every dollar earned in sales revenues from health and safety services. He also found that chapter managers appeared to have discretion in adjusting prices and quality of services, making them cheaper and of higher quality so that profits were reduced as donations were received (a reduction of approximately 26 cents in profits for a dollar of donations).

The issue of crowd-out is also of special public policy interest in the contemporary context of federal reductions in spending on social welfare services (Salamon and Abramson, 1994). The effect of federal reductions on revenue ultimately received by nonprofit service agencies is determined by three interacting factors–the level of reduction in federal payments to state and local government, the reactions of state and local government to the federal reductions, and the reactions of private donors to changes in overall government support for nonprofits. Steinberg (1993) calls the simultaneous adjustment of local government and private donors to changes in federal spending "joint crowd-out." The nature of joint crowd-out is important because, as Steinberg (1993) observes, if joint crowd-out is total (federal reductions or increases are matched by private donations and local government combined) then it would be best for the federal government to stay out of the financing of local services. On the other hand, if there is joint crowd-in, perhaps as result of federal matching requirements, then it is efficient for the federal government to be involved in service financing. In a theoretical analysis, Steinberg (1987) concludes that: "whether donations rise or fall in response to an exogeneous federal cutback, it is likely that the total of donations and local government expenditure will rise, but only by some fractions of the cutback. One should not count on the local and private sectors to replace the federal government's role in social service provision" (p. 32). Empirical research seems to support an even less optimistic conclusion since state expenditures appear to magnify changes in federal spending (crowd-in). According to Steinberg (1993), "Whereas donative crowd-out reduces the effectiveness of federal grants, state government reactions more than make up for this, so that overall, targeted federal grants are quite effective instruments for raising total expenditures on a specified good or service" (p. 117). If these results may be interpreted symmetrically for federal reductions, state reductions can be expected to magnify federal cutbacks and not be fully compensated by increases in private giving.

Overall, the leadership of nonprofit organizations may be expected to react to government spending reductions both by seeking more charitable contributions and by increasing sales revenues (Steinberg, 1993). While crowd-out effects of reduced government funding may increase donor contributions in this scenario, an increase in commercial sales may have the opposite impact. Further empirical research is needed to determine the net effects on donations and total revenue in this situation.

DENNIS R. YOUNG

BIBLIOGRAPHY

Abrams, Burton A. and Mark D. Schmitz, 1986. "The Crowding-Out Effect of Governmental Transfers on Private Charitable Contributions." In Susan Rose-Ackerman, ed., *The Economics of Nonprofit Institutions*. New York: Oxford University Press, pp. 303–312.

Andreoni, James, 1989. "Giving with Impure Altruism: Applications to Charity and Ricardian Equivalence." *Journal of Political Economy* 82:1063–1093.

Hodgkinson, Virginia A. and Associates, 1992. *Nonprofit Almanac: 1992–1993*. San Francisco: Jossey-Bass, Inc.

Kingma, Bruce R., 1995. "Do Profits Crowd-out Donations or Vice Versa?" *Nonprofit Management and Leadership* (Fall).

Rose-Ackerman, Susan, 1986. "Do Government Grants to Charity Reduce Private Donations?" In Susan Rose-Ackerman, ed., *The Economics of Nonprofit Institutions*. New York: Oxford University Press, pp. 313–329.

Salamon, Lester M. and Alan J. Abramson, 1994. "The Federal Budget and the Nonprofit Sector: FY 1995." A report to the independent sector. Baltimore: Institute for Policy Studies, Johns Hopkins University.

Steinberg, Richard, 1993. "Does Government Spending Crowd Out Donations: Interpreting the Evidence." In Avner Ben-Ner and Benedetto Gui, *The Nonprofit Sector in the Mixed Economy*. Ann Arbor: The University of Michigan Press, pp. 99–125.

Steinberg, Richard, 1987. "Voluntary Donations and Public Expenditures in a Federal System." *American Economic Review*, 77:1 (March) 25–36.

Young, Dennis R. and Richard Steinberg, 1995. *Economics for Nonprofit Managers*. New York: The Foundation Center.

CROWDING OUT.

"The proposition that government spending or government deficits reduce the amount of business investment." (Samuelson and Nordhaus, 1992, p. 733). Recently, however, discussions of crowding out have been broadened to encompass reductions in any of the private sector components of aggregate demand resulting from government spending or government deficits.

While fiscal expansion can occur with an increase in government spending, G, or a reduction in taxes, T, or with some combination of these two that increases $G - T$, it is helpful to focus on the effect of an increase in government spending to clarify the issue.

As will be seen, the nature of the crowding out that occurs depends on the situation. A classical view of a closed economy operating at full employment with fixed private saving emphasizes the effect of increases in government spending on reductions in investment. However, when saving responds to changes in the interest rate and full employment national output is obtained, increases in government spending reduce both investment and consumption.

In contrast, a Keynesian outlook emphasizes the effect of a fiscal expansion on national output when the expansion occurs during a recession. Increased government spending can have no effect on investment, or can decrease investment, depending on the assumptions.

Finally, with international trade playing an increasingly important role in the U.S. economy, the modern approach emphasizes the effect of the increase in government spending on the current account. At first, however, the discussion of crowding out is best understood if international transactions are ignored.

Classical View

If prices are sufficiently flexible to keep the economy at "full employment" output, Yf, and there is no government sector, private saving, Sp, which includes saving by both households and businesses, must just equal investment, I. This is because private saving is that part of national output not devoted to consumption and the only other spending activity besides consumption is investment.

When a government sector is added that includes both government spending and taxes, private saving must be used either to purchase investment goods or the government bonds used to finance the federal deficit, $G - T$. Therefore

$$Sp = I + (G - T)$$

In this situation, if private saving equals a certain proportion of disposable income, $Yd = Yf - T$, and the economy remains at full employment output, increases in G will necessarily reduce I on a dollar for dollar basis. This is an example of complete crowding out of investment from the specified fiscal policy expansion.

In practice one might imagine the government going to the capital market to borrow funds to finance the additional spending. When government demand is added to investment demand, the interest rate would rise and investment would be reduced. If private saving is not responsive to the changes in the interest rate, there would be complete crowding out of investment.

However, if private saving is responsive to higher interest rates, Sp would rise and consumption would be reduced. If this occurred, the effect of the government

spending would be to crowd out both investment and consumption.

Keynesian View

Keynesian analysis emphasizes the role of the government when national output is less than the full employment level. The early Keynesian perspective focused on the multiplier effect of increases in G. The initial increase in G resulted in a first round change in income, part of which was consumed and part saved. The part consumed led to a second round change in income, with the process continuing so that the increase in national output was some multiple of the change in G. As long as this process did not raise the interest rate, say, because the money supply was also adjusting, investment would not be affected. There would be no crowding out.

An expanded Keynesian view, however, analyzes how this process raises the interest rate. The increase in national income increases the transactions demand for money. Then, the smaller quantity of money available for precautionary or speculative purposes is rationed out at a higher interest rate. In turn this higher interest rate reduces investment. On net, however, while some investment is crowded out, aggregate demand rises by more than the increase in government spending. Specifically, consumption rises by more than the decline in investment.

Crowding Out in an Open Economy

When one adds international transactions to the analysis, it is helpful to begin with the fact that private saving can be used either for domestic investment, financing the federal deficit, or foreign investment. Foreign investment occurs in response to a current account surplus in which exports, EX, are greater than imports, IM. This is because foreigners must pay for the U.S. current account surplus by borrowing from the United States.

One therefore obtains

$$Sp = I + (G - T) + (EX - TM)$$

This relationship clarifies the connection between the twin deficits. A trade deficit occurs when exports minus imports are negative. There is a government deficit if government spending is greater than the taxes collected. Suppose that Sp, I, and T are constant proportions of full employment national output. Then increases in G at full employment output will necessarily decrease $EX - IM$. As a result, a dollar increase in the government deficit would result in a dollar increase in the trade deficit. The current account would be crowded out.

Interestingly, the same result occurs with a permanent fiscal expansion when a more complete analysis of the economy is employed (Krugman and Obstfeld, 1994, pp. 458–460). First of all one would expect national output to be at the full employment level in the long run, where this level is determined by supply side considerations. Only at this output level would the aggregate price level be constant.

There would also be a very close relationship between U.S. and foreign interest rates determined by the long-run interest parity relationship. Therefore, neither the full employment output level nor the U.S. interest rate would be affected by the permanent change in government spending. Investment, therefore, would not change.

As the permanent increase in government spending is a change in relative demand for U.S. products, there would be an expected long-run appreciation of the dollar. This expectation would cause the dollar to appreciate immediately in order to maintain parity between the interest return on a dollar deposit and the expected dollar return on a foreign deposit. As a result, net exports, $EX - IM$, would decline, and the effect of the permanent increase in government spending would be to crowd out demand for domestic products. National output would remain at the full employment level assumed to be in effect before the permanent fiscal expansion.

Conclusion

While there was early emphasis given to the trade-off in the long run between government spending and investment, the recent focus has been on the trade-off in the long run between government spending and the current account. In the short run, there may be some crowding out of investment if the fiscal expansion begins at an output level less than full employment. However, overall aggregate demand in this Keynesian scenario can be expected to rise in response to the rise in government spending.

GREGORY G. HILDEBRANDT

BIBLIOGRAPHY

Krugman, P. R. and M. Obstfeld, 1994. *International Economics: Theory and Policy*. 3d ed. New York: Harper Collins.
Samuelson, P. A. and W. D. Nordhaus, 1992. *Economics*. 14th ed. New York: McGraw-Hill, Inc.

CULTURAL BIAS. A predisposition toward favoring particular social values and practices. In the generally accepted meaning of the term, culture is defined as a shared design for living or the ideas, customs, and thoughts of a given people in a given period. Culture is based on the values and practices of a society (a group of people who interact together over time). An eclectic definition of culture is explained as a learned system of symbols with shared values, beliefs, ideals, and practices. According to Kim and Gudykunst (1988), culture is conceptualized as applying to all aggregates or categories of people whose "life patterns discernibly influence individual communication behaviors" (pp. 12–13). As we approach the twenty-first century, the term cultural bias, cultural one-sidedness, or cultural partiality is one of the most widely used terms in any discussion of the value of multiculturalism and the appreciation of world views.

Historically, the culture of any group is the result of collective living, institutions, and other structured forms of behavior that come into existence and in turn influence the behavior of individuals. Cultural bias is usually transmitted from generation to generation as a positive social value similar to nationalism, religion, and proper etiquette and manners.

In sociology the term cultural bias refers to any unfavorable or negative feeling or attitude directed toward any person or group on the basis of some assumed characteristic(s). Cultural partiality and discrimination are related concepts, but they are not the same. Cultural bias is a belief or attitude, whereas discrimination occurs when negative thoughts are acted upon. Ultimately, discrimination involves behavior that excludes all members of a group from certain rights, opportunities, and/or privileges.

Essentially cultural bias is not always a negative concept. Currently there are approximately 100 different ethnic groups in the United States. This diversity of talents has allowed the U.S. to flourish at home and in the global economic and political sphere. Various ethnic enclaves are scattered throughout the nation. For example, New York City as well as other metropolitan cities represents a microcosm of diversity. In New York alone, several distinct units of cultural ethnicity exist such as Chinese in Manhattan's Chinatown, West Indian and Italian in Brooklyn, Jewish on Long Island, Irish on Staten Island, and African American in Harlem, to name a mere few.

To another extent, cultural bias becomes an obstacle when a group becomes enamored of its own culture to the extent or extreme that its members believe their group to be superior. When the group attempts to exclude or deny the value of other groups, cultural bias becomes a costly dysfunctional malady. Ironically, when this happens, "discriminatory taste" becomes less palpable.

Cultural prejudice is generally an attitude toward a minority held by a person from the majority group. Although prejudice frequently occurs in both minority and majority groups, the social, political, and economic consequences of bias are more detrimental when held and acted upon by members of the majority group. It would be incorrect, however, to assume that the majority group has a monopoly on prejudice. While cultural bias is a group characteristic reflecting certain psychological needs, it reflects the values of society.

Theories of Cultural Bias

Historically, no other nation has embraced so many different races, cultures, and religions in such a brief period as has the United States of America. On one hand the U.S. philosophy of welcoming all immigrants is overshadowed by the chaos and frequently overt hostility directed toward the "new immigrant." On the other hand, within relatively short periods various European ethnics were able to assimilate and to acquire economic, political, and social mobility.

Over the years sociologists, historians, economists, demographers, political scientists, and psychologists throughout the world have made a number of attempts to understand the relationship between the formation of prejudicial attitudes and their persistence over time. Given the complexity of U.S. ethnic and racial cross section symbology and the socialization process in the United States, it is clear that the explanation of cultural bias would also have to be complex. According to Sarbaugh (1988), the extent of cultural differences present in a given interaction depends on the degree of heterogeneity in the worldviews of those interacting, as well as in their belief systems, overt behaviors, verbal and nonverbal code systems, relationships, and intentions. Various theories clearly illustrate that U.S. cultural biases stem from a combination of unique social, economic, political, and geographical practices and experiences.

To make clear the multifaceted aspects of cultural biases, an attempt will be made to classify some of the major underlying theories. This will be accomplished according to their significance and relationships to the development and process of beliefs, patterns of thought, and behavior. The major underlying theoretical frameworks are the exploitation theory, scapegoating theory, authoritarian personality theory, structural/ecological theory, linguistic theory, and self-hatred paradigm.

Exploitation Theory

The exploitation/Marxist theorists view racial subordination in the United States as a manifestation of the class system inherent in capitalism. In the nineteenth century this theory of economic and class bias was greatly advanced by Marx and Engles in such works as the *Communist Manifesto* and *Das Kapital*. From the Marxian perspective, prejudice is used to keep certain groups in subordinate positions, and to justify their exploitation. For example, the exploitation of slave labor found strong support and justification among white landowners. The view that blacks were inferior to whites served as justification for the institution of slavery. The role of class conflict and the exploitation of labor continued to occur at various points in U.S. history. After the turn of the century class conflict and exploitation of labor continued with the arrival of new immigrants such as the Korean, Filipino, and Mexican aliens who provided labor to California. Today the prejudice toward undocumented Mexican aliens ensures employers of a continuous source of cheap labor.

Another example of the exploitation theory is illustrated in the internal colonial model, where strong prejudicial attitudes are used as justification for the subordination and exploitation of ethnic and racial groups throughout the world.

Scapegoating Theory

The exploitation theory of cultural bias is a persuasive theory. John Dollard (1937) developed the "frustration-aggression" hypothesis to explain the psychodynamics of scapegoating. A review of the literature reveals that the term "scapegoating" derives from a practice of the ancient Hebrews, who once a year symbolically placed all of the sins of the tribe on a goat and drove the animal off into the wilderness. This purification ritual served to rejuvenate the moral and religious health of the Jewish community.

Scapegoating occurs when a person or group is blamed irrationally for another person's or group's problems or difficulties. For example, Hitler used the Jews as the scapegoat for all of the social and economic ills of prewar Germany. He was able to focus the attention of the German people on a common source of frustration, the Jews, and to use the Jews as the scapegoats of German society.

As another example, when Japanese Americans and Chinese Americans first arrived in the United States they experienced little overt prejudice, but when they began to enter the job market and compete with whites in the workplace, they encountered blatant acts of prejudice and discrimination. Lastly, the enslavement of African Americans and the removal of indigenous Indians was to a significant degree economically motivated.

Authoritarian Personality Theory

Some scholars have argued that prejudice is an isolated trait that anyone can have. The personality approach was introduced in Germany during the early 1930s; it was not, however, systematically studied until the end of World War II, when psychologists and social scientists became particularly interested in understanding the origins of prejudice at the individual level. *The Authoritarian Personality* by Theodore Adorno and his associates at the University of

California appeared in 1950. This classical study examined the psychological underpinning of prejudice.

It is important to note that the social psychologist must allow for the social context in which attitudes are formed. For example, critics contend that this form of bias exists in radical individuals and under extreme conditions. This personality trait develops from an early childhood of harsh discipline; a child with an authoritarian upbringing obeys and later treats others as he or she was raised. The authoritarian personality is the psychological construct of a personality type likely to be prejudiced and to use others as a scapegoat.

Structural/Ecological Theory

Morton Deutsch and Mary E. Collins are acknowledged for their pioneering research in the structural/ecological theory in 1951. This ideology espouses that cultural bias is influenced by societal norms and situations that serve to encourage or discourage tolerance of minorities. Proponents of this view who advocate that the immediate social environment contributes to the development of prejudicial attitudes subscribe to the ecological theory of prejudice. A social system may consist of a family, a group, a labor union, or a nation. For example, according to Frasier (1968), individual behavior is determined by the various collectives or systems of social relations. Frasier further explains that the collectives—labor unions, property associations, and other ecological organizations—define the objectives of individuals and determine the roles they play in different situations.

Another concept of the ecological theory points out that cultural bias is influenced by such factors as climate, geography, and demography, and—perhaps more important—by the type of economic exploitation.

Linguistic Theory

Edward Sapir, an anthropologist, and Benjamin Whorf, a student of linguistics, conducted pioneering research in this area. The linguistic theory is based on the idea that language and our cultural environment have a strong influence on our way of thinking and on the development of our ideas and opinions. For example, Ossie Davis pointed out that the dictionary has approximately 120 negative connotations describing "black" as soiled, lacking light, wicked or evil, gloomy, and other dismal meanings, whereas the word "white" has many positive connotations such as purity, innocence, freedom from evil intent, and harmlessness. Others terms include, but are not limited to, a "white lie," which is often interpreted to be something unimportant or harmless as when told to spare someone's feelings.

The Sapir-Whorf hypothesis advances the idea that the connotations of words become a part of the cultural environment. If such is true, attitudes and opinions are affected by particular words used to describe certain groups or by association of specific words with negative characteristics or experiences.

Self-Hatred Paradigm

Usually when we think about cultural bias we consider cultural prejudice to be one group hating another group. However, leading authorities in the area of self-negation (Mead, 1934; Cooley, 1956; Sullivan, 1953; Erikson, 1968; Essien-Udom, 1962) agree that an individual's self-concept arises through his or her interaction with other members of society such as parents, peers, teachers, and other societal representatives.

Many proponents of this thought describe the self-hatred paradigm as being uniquely confined to the masses of black colonization and class subordination. This form of self-negation occurs when a group hates itself. Members of groups held in low esteem by society may, as a result, have low self-esteem themselves, particularly when a group experiences prejudice, discrimination, and economic failure.

A persuasive argument that supports advocates of the self-hatred paradigm was presented in the landmark 1954 Supreme Court decision *Brown v. Board of Education*. The justices were persuaded in part by the testimony of social scientists. The most famous research presented was that of Kenneth and Mamie Clark, who had conducted an experiment in which schoolchildren from Arkansas and Massachusetts were shown four dolls: two brown dolls with black hair and two white dolls with blond hair. Kenneth Clark asked each child to indicate which doll the child liked "best," which looked "bad," and which had "a nice color." Clark also asked the children to identify the dolls by race. This study showed strong awareness of race. More than 90 percent of the seven-year-old African American children correctly identified the races of the white and brown dolls. The majority of the black children referred to the white dolls as the ones they liked "best" (Clark, 1955).

Many social scientists and psychologists believe that members of minority groups hate themselves or, at least, have low self-esteem. African Americans, for example, frequently are still aware of their racial subordination even when they have superficially achieved equality through economic success.

In summary, the development and process of cultural biases are derived from various aspects of one's environment, history and tradition. An individual's cultural bias or views can influence ideas, feelings, and behavior in positive and negative ways, as we tend to behave according to our degree of awareness, insight, and knowledge of the cultural context in which we live.

Cultural bias, cultural one-sidedness, or cultural partiality influences our relationships to others, which is exemplified by facts, opinions, traditions. The cultural bias paradox emerges from our ability to live by our self-defined ethnic values, while conforming to those of the common or wider society.

TAMU CHAMBERS

BIBLIOGRAPHY

Allport, Gordon W., 1954. *The Nation of Prejudice*. Reading, MA: Addison-Wesley. (Also New York: Anchor Books, 1958.)

Brigham, John and Weissbach, eds. 1972. *Racial Attitudes in America: Analyses and Findings of Social Psychology*. New York: Harper and Row.

Clark, Kenneth B., 1955. *Prejudice and Your Child*. Boston: Beacon Press.

Cooley, C. H., 1956. *Human Nature and the Social Order*. New York: Free Press.

Deutsch, Morton and Mary E. Colins, 1951. *Interracial Housing*. Minneapolis, MN: University of Minnesota Press.

Deutscher, Irwin, 1973. *What We Say/What We Do: Sentiments and Acts*. Glenview, IL: Scott, Foresman.

Dollard, John, 1937. *Race and Class in a Southern Town*. New Haven, CT: Yale Universtiy Press.

Erickson, E. H., 1968. *Identity, Youth, and Crisis*. New York: Norton.

Essien-Udon, E. U., 1962. *Black Nationalism*. New York: Dell.

Frazier, Franklin E., 1968. *On Race Relations*. Chicago and London: The University of Chicago Press.

Gonzales, Juan L., 1990. *Racial and Ethnic Groups in America*. Dubuque, IA: Kendal/Hunt Publishing Company.

Kim, Y. Y. and W. B. Gudykunst, eds., 1988. *Theories in Intercultural Communication*. Newbury Park, CA: Sage.

Mead, G. H., 1934. *Mind, Self, and Society*. Chicago: University of Chicago Press.

Miller, Arthur, *et al.*, 1982. *In the Eye of the Beholder: Contemporary Issues in Stereotyping*. New York: Praeger.

Pettigrew, Thomas F., George M. Frederickson, *et al.*, 1982. *Prejudice*: Cambridge, MA: The Belknap Press of Harvard University Press.

Schaefer, Richard T., 1990. *Racial and Ethnic Groups*, 4th ed. Glenview, IL: Scott, Foresman/Little.

Schuman, Howard, Charlotte Steeh and Bobo Lawrence, 1985. *Racial Attitudes in America: Trends and Interpretations*. Cambridge, MA: Harvard Univ. Press.

Sullivan, H. S., 1953. *The Interpersonal Theory of Psychiatry*. New York: Norton.

Williams, Robin M., Jr. 1994. *Strangers Next Door: Ethnic Relations in American Communities*. Englewood Cliffs, NJ: Prentice Hall.

CULTURAL IMPERIALISM. The process by which a dominant nation, country, or culture extends its degree of influence or control over other nations, countries, or cultures by the promotion of those skills, arts, or means of communication that can be transmitted across its boundaries and imposed on others. Languages, ways of thinking, styles, fashions, and forms of art are transferred from the dominant to the subordinate.

Cultural imperialism therefore presupposes degrees of inequality. words used to describe the influence employed, such as *rayonnement cultural* or *mission civilisatrice*, may imply a single center of enlightenment. Those dependent on a dominant culture cannot expect their own cultural artifacts to be considered of equal value with those from the imperial power. This subordination is expressed in various metaphors of "cultural humility" and "cultural cringe," the psychological condition of valuing only that which comes from the dominant set of influences. That condition may exist within an empire or within a single country. Some Australians used to feel subordinate to British culture; some U.S. citizens of black slave origin used to feel inferior to those descended from white settlers.

This sense of subordination might entail certain ironies, particularly in circumstances where the servants appear to know the masters better than the latter know themselves. The acculturation of the elite in colonized countries may lead to interesting parodies of the dominant culture. The Irish learned how to mock English manners; Indians found ways of seeing their British rulers as moral inferiors.

A major feature of cultural imperialism is the cultural construction of the emotions: people feel anger, love, loyalty, or resentment according to the context of their upbringing. Frantz Fanon (1968) stressed that the colonial power's greatest weapon was the imposition of its own images of worth. The decolonization of the mind therefore entailed fighting for a changed self-image. Many explanations of cultural humility involve the disciplines of social psychology and linguistics, because attitudes to cognition and language seem to have played a major part in defining and sustaining cultures. Nevertheless cultural imperialism is normally regarded as an international and political phenomenon, the power of one culture to compel imitation by others.

In contrast, international cultural cooperation rests upon mutual respect between cultures and upon a willingness to learn from the transmission of knowledge and skill across boundaries. That transmission normally takes place independently of governments. Religions, the arts, and the sciences have long been regarded as capable of natural dispersal. When governments are engaged in these transmissions they usually sponsor bilateral programs for the exchange of people or multilateral associations for regional or worldwide application. The United Nations Educational, Scientific, and Cultural Organization (UNESCO) was established as the principal international body charged with responsibility for cultural exchanges.

As an international phenomenon cultural imperialism has been linked to notions of "informal empire." There is no need to have the institutions of empire in order to transmit cultural influence. Many have regarded cultural imperialism as an essentially U.S. method of extending the power of the United States without undertaking the costs of imperial administration. U.S. popular culture in film, music, and dance was its own ambassador. Movies from Hollywood are distributed throughout the world. The U.S. occupation of Germany and Japan after World War II constituted a form of direct administration. But the concepts of cultural imperialism have often been developed where U.S. products are sold as much as where U.S. military forces are present. U.S. films create demand for certain products, because film-makers accept money from advertisers for "product placing." The availability of U.S. products led to the coining of such terms as "coca-colonization"—a reference to the worldwide sale of the drink Coca-Cola. The French Communist Party, for example, in the late 1940s sponsored a campaign against *civilisation transatlantique*.

The term "cultural imperialism" did not come into general use until the 1960s; it has polemical connotations. Its popularity stemmed in part from the "cultural nationalism" that coincided with the decolonization after 1945 of the empires belonging to the major European colonial powers. The later granted or conceded independence to former dependencies which then became new states. Cultural nationalism is a reaction against cultural imperialism; it means a release from the psychological condition of subordination and a renewed devotion to indigenous forms of expression. This often entails a revival of native languages and a cultivation of local literature. It may also entail a sense of resistance to modernization and a desire to return to more traditional forms of identity and status. The main forces of cultural imperialism have often been seen as those of advanced capitalism, and of the industrialization and social change which it brings.

For this reason some commentators have refused to define what cultural imperialism means. John Tomlinson (1991), for example, argues that "the concept of cultural imperialism is one which must be assembled out of its discourse." This approach encourages a concentration on the media—television, film, radio, print journalism, and advertising. These means of communication are considered the principal vehicles of cultural transmission because they all cross the boundaries between nations and cultures. The term "media imperialism" is sometimes employed. International broadcasting—beaming radio and television towards foreign audiences—is a particularly important phenomenon. A dispute within UNESCO was provoked by discussions before and after the MacBride Report (1980), which examined the accusation that information transmitted across the world was biased in favor of the dominant Western nations. The developing countries represented in UNESCO wished to see the creation of a New World Information and Communication Order (NWICO). The development of the Internet and other electronic highways in

the 1990s revived this debate in a new form. Space satellites and optic fiber cabling concentrate "transborder data flows" in certain parts of the world, particularly the countries of the Organization for Economic Cooperation and Development. Measurements of the flows in telephony, for example, can be used to delineate this concentration of wealth.

The interest in media imperialism has focused attention on the notion of cultural products and on resistance to their dispersal outside their region of origin. International broadcasters, for example, are accustomed to governments "jamming" their programs with noise placed on the wavelengths they are using. Governments also sometimes ban the use of satellite reception dishes. They may also regulate the import of films or books by imposing a quota. The Canadian government, because of the proximity of the United States, has long considered ways of preserving the Canadian content in all kinds of media. Governments may also from time to time declare an interest in a particular cultural product that lies outside their control. A lively area of controversy in international law is the repatriation of works of art. The Uruguay Round of negotiations to revise the General Agreement on Tariffs and Trade touched on the deregulation of cultural imports.

This stress on the media has spilled over into historiography. Since the 1960s a great deal of ethnography, anthropology, and history has been rewritten to take account of contemporary interests in cultural transmission. The terminology of contact between cultures, used initially to describe European expansion and settlement overseas or the encounters between settlers and indigenous inhabitants, has been adapted to comply with fresh interpretations of cultural exchange. There has been a revival of interest in the concept of a frontier, which is treated less as a border or boundary and more as a zone of interaction between different cultures. Books on the notion of the Western Hemisphere or on distinctions between civilization and savagery seem both Eurocentric and ethnocentric. Historians are less interested in the impact of European settlers on indigenous peoples and more concerned to understand how the latter manipulated the newcomers. World history is being rewritten with many different kinds of frontier in mind; U.S. history has been revised by scholars in the New Western History to emphasise the influence of Native Americans.

Similar revisions have taken place in the study of comparative literature. The latter used to be practiced by scholars interested in similarities of expression between different writers from different national cultures using different languages, and therefore in the sources of influence from one culture to another. They identified cultural colonialism whenever literature written by the colonizing group was given a higher value than that written by natives. With the widespread recognition of postcolonial literatures, the emphasis has shifted towards contacts between colonizer and colonized, and towards the function of translation. Ethnographers have used the term "transculturation" to describe how groups subject to the influence of a metropolitan culture select and invent modes of expression from the material transmitted to them. This process can now be examined in reverse. Perceptions of the world by those in a former metropolis may have been shaped by those on a former periphery.

At the heart of these kinds of revisionism is the problem of cultural commensurability: can cultures be measured or ranked? World order seems to depend on a choice between some general global culture in which everyone has both local and global identities, and some limited forms of mediation between cultures to build up sufficient mutual respect for international cooperation. Cultural imperialism seems to be one way of building upon the idea of a common humanity; resistance to it an affirmation of the truth that all cultures worthy of the name are specific and not general.

MICHAEL LEE

BIBLIOGRAPHY

Carony, M., 1974. *Education as Cultural Imperialism*. New York: McKay.

Fanon, Frantz, 1968. *The Wretched of the Earth*. New York: Grove Press (French original 1963).

Fondazione, Lelio Basso, 1979. *L'Imperialismo Culturale*. Milano: Franco Angeli Editore.

Kaplan, Amy and Donald E. Pease, eds., 1993. *Culture of United States Imperialism*. Durham, NC: Duke University Press.

MacBride, Sean, 1980. *Many Voices, One World*. Paris: UNESCO.

McPhail, Thomas L., 1987. *Electronic Colonialism: The Future of International Broadcasting and Communication*. Beverly Hills, CA: Sage.

Nandy, Ashis, 1983. *The Intimate Enemy:Loss and Recovery of Self Under Colonialism*. New Delhi: Oxford University Press.

Pagden, Anthony, 1993. *European Encounters with the New World: From Renaissance to Romanticism*. New Haven, CT: Yale University Press.

Said, Edward W., 1993. *Culture and Imperialism*. New York: Knopf.

Schiller, Herbert I., 1976. *Communication and Cultural Domination*. New York: International Arts and Sciences Press.

Tomlinson, John., 1991. *Cultural Imperialism*. Baltimore, MD: Johns Hopkins University Press.

Weber, Daniel J. and Jane M. Raushch, eds. 1994. *Where Cultures Meet: Frontier in Latin American History*. Wilmington, DE: Scholarly Resources Inc.

CUTBACK MANAGEMENT.
The management of the decline in resources associated either with a reduction in programs, activities, or personnel, or with a view to reducing the size and cost of government and/or to improving efficiency. It signifies the process through which retrenchment—the actual contraction in organizational activity and the cutting of costs—is achieved.

In the wake of fiscal stress and the perceived failure of government to solve economic and social problems, the need to reduce the size of government has become accepted wisdom across much of the political spectrum. This phenomenon is observable in both the developed and developing world, as well as the economies in transition. Considerable attention is also being given to improving efficiency and cost effectiveness—"doing the job with less."

Approaches to cutback management can range from top-down (prominent recent examples of this approach in the United States are the balanced budget constitutional amendment and the Republican approach to the fiscal year 1996 budget and to achieving a balanced budget by 2002) to bottom-up; from across-the-board to item-by-item; from focusing on personnel to focusing on whole programs and agencies. The approach, speed, and depth of cutbacks will depend on the nature and severity of any crisis confronting a government; the philosophy of the government; and the management of the (perceived) political fall-out.

Politically, across-the-board cuts and cutting personnel and capital spending are often seen as more appealing routes. The former because they seem to involve some element of fairness—sharing the burden—and the latter because they tend to have less immediate impact on the community. As more attention is given to the management dimension of cutback, the issue of the place of institutional mechanisms in forcing or facilitating cutbacks becomes more important. These range from the balanced budget amendment to the very effective independent commission established in the United States to recommend which defense bases should be closed. A common characteristic of all such approaches is greater transparency.

The purpose of this article is to identify retrenchment policies and cutback management strategies that have been adopted in order to reduce the size of government or to improve the efficiency of the public sector. A major thesis of this article is that cutting back government has overemphasized reducing employment and "doing more with less" and underemphasized attention to the role of government—fundamentally questioning what it is that government should take responsibility for. What government should actually do itself, and how it should do it, are separate and second order questions. This is closely related to the Peter Drucker argument that the "first reaction in a situation of disarray is always to do what Vice President Gore and his associates are now doing—patching. It always fails. The next step is to rush into downsizing. . . . The result is always a casualty." What is required, argues Drucker, is that organizations rethink themselves. A few organizations have done this as "they knew that the way to get control of costs is not to start by reducing expenditure but to identify the activities that are productive, that should be strengthened, promoted, and expanded" (Drucker, 1995, p. 54). In the public sector, the organization just happens to be the whole of government.

The article will also address the circumstances that have brought about the need for retrenchment and cutback management strategies and will draw on experiences ranging from the United States to developing countries.

Origin and Background

The post–World War II decades saw an unprecedented expansion in government in the developed world and, subsequently, in the developing world. Many factors contributed to this expansion, including the economic and social consequences of both world wars; the Great Depression; the rise of Keynesian economics, the political ramifications of which meant that the role of the state in economic activity was greatly enhanced; the spread of socialism; and the growth of foreign aid.

The theories of John Maynard Keynes lent respectability to the view that government had a responsibility to correct for market failure through macroeconomic policy. At the micro level the high-expenditure approach to the improvement of living conditions and as a solution to the problems of, for example, urban life became a significant component of government policy.

The growth in government, whether measured in terms of expenditure as a percentage of GDP or the size of public sector employment, has been on an upward trend for most of the twentieth century. The high expectations of the general public in Western countries in the post–World War II period helped entrench the welfare state across the political spectrum, the difference being the extent of the welfare state. The mood of the period is reflected in some of the literature of the time such as John K. Galbraith's *The Affluent Society* (1958) and Robert E. Lane's article on "The Politics of Consensus in an Age of Affluence" (1965), in which the underlying assumptions were based on the continuous improvement of the economy with the only question being what to do with the "fiscal dividend."

With the first oil shock of 1973 and its impact on economic performance, many governments saw this as a reason to step up government intervention. In the developing world, the early postindependence years saw a great enthusiasm for government as the engine of development. For many governments, however, economic crisis quickly engulfed them. Whereas prior to the 1970s cutbacks, where they were required, were more in the form of reducing the rate of growth of expenditures, the 1970s saw the emergence of a need for real reductions in expenditures and hence retrenchment policies.

It is not surprising that fiscal crisis first emerged at the local level. Specifically, the case of New York City was to become the critical event in urban fiscal stress, and the earliest

example that brought attention to the question of cutback management. In 1974–1975 the near bankruptcy of the city forced its administration to balance its budget by a combination of debt refinancing and cutting back its bureaucracy. Although the city was not typical in terms of its size, socioeconomic base, and political culture, it nevertheless became the symbol of retrenchment in U.S. government. Six years of economic decline—the result of a combination of factors from middle-class migration and the departure of business to lower class and minority concentration—saw revenues drop due to a weaker tax base. Institutional arrangements that encouraged operational expenditures to be classified as capital expenditure had helped fuel the rapid growth in expenditure. In their book *The Politics of Retrenchment* (1981), Levine, Rubin, and Wolohojian pointed out that "New York City's fiscal crisis proved to be a theoretical watershed in the literature on urban fiscal stress. For the first time, scholars began to devote attention to the *responses* to fiscal stress as well as the *causes* of such stress" (p. 12). Prior to this case, any contractions or closures in government departments were seen as isolated cases that did not merit concern from public management scholars.

Beginning in the 1980s pressure on governments from fiscal stress was compounded by an increasing view that government interventions were part of the problem. Conservative governments at the national level, such as those of Thatcher in the United Kingdom and Reagan in the United States, talked about rolling back the state, reflecting the view that economic growth was the preserve of the private sector. In the case of left of center governments, such as Australia and Sweden, there was a recognition of the need to make government work better.

The change in political ideology represented an attempt to return to the market in the wake of the perceived greater ill than market failure, namely government failure. This was the questioning of the "what" of government. The neoconservative argument, especially in the U.S. and the UK, with regards to government failure was that it should be met with cutbacks and the use of the private sector as the alternative for the operation of certain functions. Significantly, in Australia, it was the Labor Party that implemented reforms and cutbacks. The most radical reforms of all, in New Zealand, were begun by a Labour government. In its first two years the Clinton administration made some progress with deficit reduction but its health reform efforts led to it being accused of "(big) government as usual." Its reform efforts were particularly focused on the "how" of government through the National Performance Review (NPR)—make government work better at a lower cost. With the 1994 Republican landslide the "what" of government was under close scrutiny. Cutbacks and retrenchment were in the air and the question was whether there will be sufficient weight given to policy issues and the management of cutback. At the local level, New York, along with many U.S. cities, was again confronting fiscal crisis in 1995.

TABLE I. TOTAL GOVERNMENT OUTLAYS AS A PERCENTAGE OF GDP IN SELECT OECD COUNTRIES, 1970–1991

COUNTRY	1970	1975	1980	1985	1991
Australia	27	34	34	39	40
Austria	38	44	47	50	49
Canada	35	40	41	47	51
Finland	30	36	36	41	49
France	40	45	47	53	52
Germany	39	50	49	48	49
Greece	22	27	31	44	48
Japan	19	27	32	32	32
Norway	41	46	48	46	57
Switzerland	21	29	29	31	32
United Kingdom	40	47	45	46	43
United States	32	35	34	37	39

SOURCE: OECD/PUMA

Table I outlines the change in government expenditure as a percentage of GDP from 1970 to 1991 for some countries of the Organization for Economic Cooperation and Development (OECD). Despite the rhetoric, all countries show a higher percentage in 1991 than in 1970. Only the United Kingdom has been able to reduce its government expenditures in 1991 to a lower level than 1980 (it should be noted that 1991 was a recession year in many OECD countries). Some experienced stabilization during the 1980s. For example, the figures for Australia disguise the fact that between 1985 and 1989 the ratio of federal spending to GDP declined from 30 percent to 24 percent. This highlights the fact that cutting back is not a once-and-for-all exercise but requires a disciplined approach year in and year out.

Theoretical Framework

Why there is a need for cutback and retrenchment has found theoretical underpinnings in public choice. What should be cutback has the theory of public goods to support it. The theory of public goods gave the expansion of government theoretical respectability and acceptability and focused the debate on the type of goods and their amount. The theory of public choice, however, has provided an explanation for the continuous expansion of government based not on the provision of public goods but rather on the incentives for a self-expanding bureaucracy. In the years of expanding government, the definition of what constituted a public good expanded along with it; in the current environment, former public goods are suddenly found to be no longer public goods. The point is that argument over what is, and is not, a public good, plays

only a relatively small role in government decisionmaking. The concept of path dependence, now taken up as a key part of the theory of institutional economics, reminds us that we should be wary of claims of radical change, including in the area of cutback.

The theory associated with the management of cutbacks and retrenchment is not well developed. At the broad level, the debate is essentially about the efficacy of creating institutional mechanisms to constrain government (e.g., constitutional requirements to balance the budget). Generally speaking, recourse to such mechanisms is an admission of the failure of existing institutions to discipline the decisionmaking of government.

At the organizational level, the management of cutback is inextricably linked with the theory of organizational performance. The bulk of work in this field has been in the private sector. There is increasing consensus around the need to integrate cutbacks with clear articulation of the purpose of the organization—the bringing together of the why, the what, and the how. Arbitrary cuts in personnel are being increasingly questioned on theoretical grounds.

The general theme is that large and complex organizations can function more by reorganizing their processes and reforming their structures and relationships. This argument stems from the evolving theory of new institutional economics and principal-agent theory, as well as the experience of the private sector. The latter was articulated in Peters' and Waterman's book *In Search of Excellence* (1982). The experience of the private sector since the economic decline of the 1970s has been to trim down their size leading to leaner and more efficient organizations. The same arguments are being applied to government bureaucracy. The competitive nature of the private sector has also spilled over to the public sector, which has made regular cutbacks a reality in the latter. Drucker's argument, noted above, that the real issue is clarity of the role and purpose (which may lead to cutbacks) is a powerful one.

This theory has also focused on management per se and the notion that managers in the public sector should be allowed to manage and not simply to administer. Whereas administrators are seen as focusing on sets of guidelines and rules in the conduct of government activity, managers actually manage for results and have authority to make decisions that affect policy and its implementation. They are then held accountable for results and the proper use of the authority at their disposal. Associated with this perspective is the view that day-to-day decisions associated with restraint should be left to managers.

Cutback Management in the United States

Since the United States has a federal system of government, there are three main levels of government—federal, state—and city—that need to be addressed in order to provide an outline of the practice of cutback management.

Cutback Management at the Federal Level

At the federal level various institutional mechanisms have been tried in an effort to control the expansion of government, particularly as manifested in the deficit. Given that the climate is hostile to tax increases, this places the burden on expenditure restraint and cutbacks.

Examples of these mechanisms include the Balanced Budget and Emergency Deficit Control Act of 1985 (the Gramm-Rudman-Hollings Act [GRH]), the Budget Enforcement Act of 1990 (BEA), and the proposed balanced budget amendment to the Constitution.

The BEA was passed in an effort to control spending and to provide steadily declining deficit targets that had to be met in order to avoid across-the-board cuts. The ultimate target was a balanced budget. However, the legislature was able to avoid such drastic measures by employing bookkeeping gimmicks and thus failed to meet the optimistic objectives.

The BEA produced significant changes in the budget process but at the end of the 1991 fiscal year, the deficit stood at $268.7 billion, the largest in U.S. history. Perhaps the ultimate success of the act was to allow the government to function without the threat of sequesters, but it avoided the real goal of reducing the deficit.

National Performance Review.

Essentially, the National Performance Review (NPR) (1993) is an attempt at making government work better and cost less. The proposed target of 279,200 staff reductions over five years soon dominated the discussion of NPR in Congress and the fact that these reductions were meant to flow from a reengineering of federal agencies (NPR, 1993, Appendix B, p. 156) was lost sight of. The impressive aspect of the NPR is that, despite this, much innovative work is being undertaken at the agency level to do more with less.

The Bureau of Reclamation at the Interior Department provides an example of such initiative taking. It reduced staff by 1,348, or 18 percent, and the budget by $90 million, or 10 percent, over one year. The Bureau has been able, however, with the initiative of its top level managers and the approval of the Secretary of the Interior, to reinvent its functions, transforming itself from a construction bureau to a water resource management organization, and also to reengineer its operations. In other words, the management of change received at least as much attention as did cutback.

By the end of fiscal year 1994, approximately one year after NPR was launched, the Office of Management and Budget (OMB) estimated that 71,000 full-time positions had been eliminated. There was complete confidence in the target of 279,200 being achieved (although it is not clear how many times the savings generated have been applied to proposed new expenditures). The big issue is whether the tide that is likely to reduce significantly the

scope and size of the federal budget will also sweep away efforts to reform whole organizations and programs, as well as approaches to service delivery.

Cutback Management at the State Level

With more limited flexibility than the federal government, most state governments were forced to confront the need for cutbacks earlier in order to cope with economic realities. The requirement that states balance their budgets has had some effect on restraining expenditure, although it has probably done as much to encourage creative accounting. To the extent that state governments have observed the balanced budget constraint, it probably reflects a longstanding political tradition and the more immediate pressure of credit ratings. The 1991 recession saw 23 states not giving workers salary increases, 17 states cutting welfare benefits, and many cutting funding for higher education. In this latter context, the rapid increase in tuition fees has been a part of a very significant tide in favor of requiring users to pay for government services. In addition to these constraints and crises, many states have had to deal with a tax revolt. Nowhere has this been more evident than in California.

California's Proposition 13.

Passed on June 7, 1978, the proposition's key elements were the imposition of a 1 percent ceiling on the property tax rate that any local government could impose; limitation of the assessed value of any property to its 1975 value; and the stipulation that local governments cannot impose new property taxes without the approval of a two-thirds majority. It was a resounding statement against what was seen to be California's heavy property tax burden. The California Taxpayer's Association has calculated a cumulative $228 billion tax reduction during the proposition's first ten years.

One year after the vote, California's electorate passed Proposition 4, aimed at putting more pressure on the state government to reduce expenditures by putting a constitutional limit on spending increases. The combination of both propositions had the effect of reducing the state's revenues, which meant that cutbacks had to take place. Whereas the case of New York represented a deteriorating economic situation that led to the search for cutbacks, California was perhaps a voter-imposed method of ensuring cutbacks. Within five years, the state's surplus became a short-lived deficit and in 1987 California was up against the spending ceilings imposed by Proposition 4.

In a 1988 survey, a majority of Californians noticed a deterioration in some government services and a decline in the quality of the state's public schools. The decline in California's defense industry marks a further erosion of the economic and therefore revenue base of the state, which will call for more cutbacks to be made in order to reduce the state's deficit.

Cutback Management at the Local Level

New York City. The case of New York City, as mentioned above, represents perhaps the best known example of cutback management at the city level in the U.S. When the crisis first hit, there was an initial period of denial and delay whereby officials denied the existence of a fiscal problem, while manipulating the budget and hoping for an improvement in the city's revenues. Delays in maintenance costs were also used as a tactic, which contributed to subsequent problems, such as the collapse of the West Side Highway.

By 1975, New York City was on the brink of default, which practically led the financial markets to close their doors to the city government. A particularly interesting feature of this period was the resort to institutional mechanisms that reduced the autonomy of the city government. The state government's first response was to set up the Municipal Assistance Corporation (MAC) to reform the city's borrowing practices and constrain the city's autonomy. More autonomy was taken away with the creation of the Emergency Financial Control Board (EFCB), which was to control all the city's revenues, after the deficit proved to be four times larger than expected. The EFCB consisted of the mayor, the governor, the state and city comptrollers, and three other people appointed by the governor. Decisionmaking was virtually taken away from the city.

During 1975–1978, substantial cutbacks were carried out, reaching a total of over 60,000 positions. Those were mostly conducted by attrition in addition to seniority redundancies (last in first out). The reductions were comparable across agencies, as most of them were cut by 16–19 percent over the three year period. Education, however, was cut by 30.4 percent while Housing and Community Development was cut by 79.6 percent. These cuts proved to be insufficient, which led the new mayor (Ed Koch) to put forward new cuts in 1978 across all agencies, including the hospital system but excluding the police. The proposal was for a decrease of 13,000 positions by attrition and layoffs, half of which were to come from the school system, including 4,000 teachers. The plan set the course for the recovery from 1978 to 1982, producing a balanced budget in 1981.

From the three approaches to cutback management mentioned, it can be seen that the city applied the top-down across-the-board approach whereby the cuts were clearly imposed from the top levels of government, not just the city government but that of the state. However, the personnel reductions were mostly by attrition and seniority until the use of outright layoffs during the second period. There was little effort to redefine what it was that the government could afford to be involved in. When economic recovery occurred in the 1980s most of the people who had lost their jobs appear to have been rehired. The result is that in the mid-1990s, New York City is again battling with fiscal crisis. The institutional mechanisms to descipline decisionmaking on an ongoing basis are weak at the city level. Perhaps the lessons will be learned as Washington, D.C. is forced to deal with its fiscal crisis.

Cutback Management in Other Developed Countries

As in the United States, the economic realities of the 1970s that spilled over into the 1980s made their mark on practically every country. The need to reduce the role of government and cut spending became apparent elsewhere. In a study of deficit reduction experience in six countries, the GAO found that Australia, Germany, Japan, Mexico, and the United Kingdom moved from fiscal deficits as high as 16.9 percent of GDP to balance or surplus in the 1980s or early 1990s. The fact that four of these countries subsequently slipped back into deficit is partly to do with cyclical factors but, to the extent that there are structural elements (which there appear to be in all four), it reminds us that budgetary restraint is an ongoing discipline required of government.

The United Kingdom

All the elements that have influenced the need for and approaches to cutback are exemplified in the experience of the United Kingdom over the past 20 years—beginning with the 1976 intervention of the International Monetary Fund and then the election of the Conservative Party under Mrs. Thatcher in 1979.

The government of Margaret Thatcher came into power promising cuts in government expenditure as well as a reduction in the civil service. Both a ban on recruitment and real staff reductions were implemented upon assuming power. Cuts covered all departments and had a significant across-the-board component. Central government civil service staff numbers stood at around 735,000 in 1979 and by 1986 it was down to under 600,000, a 20 percent reduction.

During the first months, ministers undertook studies of their departments in order to determine where the staff cuts could be achieved, which functions could be improved or were no longer needed, which departments should be closed, and so on. The use of new technology was widely encouraged in order to improve performance and to reduce the reliance on personnel.

The Thatcher government's other achievement in terms of cutback strategies was the program of privatizations that was undertaken, which has subsequently become a blueprint for other countries to follow. This could mean either transferring whole industries and utilities to the private sector, or contracting government services to the highest bidding private firm. The early political motive was to reduce the power of the public sector unions as well as a firm ideological belief that government should not be involved in business. As the success of the program mushroomed after the highly popular and oversubscribed privatization of British Telecom in 1984, the program became a method of raising revenues and spreading share ownership across the country.

The capital investments required for the public sector industries were having an adverse effect on the public sector borrowing requirement, which the government promised to reduce in its cost-cutting drive. By privatizing those industries, the government was able to remove a huge investment burden. At the same time, transferring those industries to the private sector meant that approximately one million jobs were also transferred to the private sector, relieving the Treasury of another burden associated with public sector industries.

Ultimately, total central government expenditures were not greatly reduced as Table I illustrates. The "savings" from the civil service reductions and the privatization were largely eventually spent elsewhere. To a significant extent, there was a failure at the policy level—to reduce government (the reality rather than the rhetoric).

Another component of the UK reforms was the creation of semiautonomous agencies to deliver services. As of the late 1990s, these agencies encompassed some 90 percent of central government civil service staff. The main purpose was to improve the quality of service delivery (subsequenty reinforced by the Citizens' Charter). The associated pressure for increased efficiency contributed significantly to the reductions in the central civil service. For the public sector as a whole, between 1979 and 1992 employment was reduced by 26 percent to 4.9 million. The category that was most affected was that of blue-collar workers, which is not surprising given the emphasis on privatization. Proportionately, four times as many industrial staff were laid off as nonindustrial staff.

Australia

Whereas the cutback policies and management reforms in the United Kingdom and the United States have generally been associated with neoconservative governments, it was the Labor government of Bob Hawke in Australia that championed government reforms during the 1980s. The reforms emphasized policy as well as structure and process (the way in which the affairs of government were conducted), as opposed to clear-cut staff reductions. Naturally, one ultimate aim was to produce savings, reduce both the country's federal budget deficit and tax burden, and make government work better and meet its objectives with the available resources.

The establishment of a framework for the control of expenditure has proven to be a success, as a deficit of $8 billion during 1983–1984 was turned into a surplus of $9 billion in the 1989–1990 budget. As noted above, this was largely achieved by reducing the share of GDP passing through the budget of central government (from 30 percent to 24 percent). Driven by a crisis in the balance of payments, a more strategic approach to decisionmaking, reinforced by the evolving institutional framework, contributed to an approach to cutback management that judiciously combined a redefinition of the why, what, and how of government.

The framework was based on a system of three-year forward estimates that depicted the minimum cost of continuing all existing policies and programs. This reduced the creeping incrementalism that characterized budget growth when departments and agencies provided a bottom-up evaluation of their needs, with strong incentives to exaggerate their needs. By 1985, the forward estimates were firmly linked with the budget estimates. The Department of Finance was then given sole responsibility for changing the estimates taking into account government decisions, the economic situation, and other technicalities.

This has allowed government ministers to concentrate on matters of policy, as they no longer have to deal with the details of developing baseline estimates. Program appraisals and department evaluations could now be conducted. A decisionmaking structure was established that meant the cabinet would deal with strategic decisions; individual ministers and their junior ministers would make decisions concerning programs at the ministry level; and department managers would be given the authority over, and take responsibility for, management decisions. These changes were reflected in the machinery of government (MOG) changes of 1987, which reduced the number of ministries from 26 to 16.

It is noteworthy that the minister of finance, during the late 1980s when Australia was making major cutbacks, provided some rules of thumb for restraining expenditure. One of these was, "If making wide-ranging cuts or withdrawals, announce them in one hit, not in dribs and drabs. If everyone is squealing, nobody is listening" (Walsh, p. 23).

The government established the Running Costs System (RCS), also in 1987, which, after requiring an efficiency dividend of 1.25 percent each year, basically allowed departments to retain whatever savings they were able to produce and to introduce user fees for services provided. This provided managers with the incentive to improve management and efficiency as well as to pay attention to the quality of service.

The case of Australia provides an example of the application of structural and decisionmaking reforms as a means towards achieving cutbacks. The objective was to make government work better with the available resources, which by implication means fewer resources, thus eventually achieving savings and reductions in both the size of government and the expenditures of government. What Australia may have done more effectively than most reforming OECD countries, with the notable exception of New Zealand, is to create new institutional mechanisms which are more likely to sustain a discipline on decisionmaking. This is particularly the case with the full range of reforms associated with the published forward estimates (see Keating and Rosalky 1989). New Zealand has taken this even further with its Fiscal Responsibility Act of 1994, which requires governments to report regularly to Parliament on their longer-term fiscal objectives (against a set of benchmarks relating to debt levels) and regular fiscal disclosure. Thus transparency enhances accountability, better information enhances decisionmaking, and greater certainty enhances performance in both the private and public sectors. It is noteworthy that the pervasive value of discipline has contributed to an institutional framework in Germany and Japan which has limited, to date, the need for cutbacks.

Cutback Management in Developing Countries

The economic realities of the 1970s and 1980s had an even greater effect on developing countries. Unemployment and inflation, although prominent in the affairs of developed countries, were much greater in most developing countries. There has been a growing realization that reforming the public sector, and developing viable institutions that would be capable of managing the public sector effectively, are essential to the success of their efforts.

As a result of the continued economic decline of the 1980s in some countries, and the growing realization that many developing countries could no longer afford to maintain the government structures that they had built up

during the previous two decades, the World Bank began to include public sector reforms as part of its structural adjustment programs. A major focus was on privatization. Reforms also included the improvement of the management of public expenditure, civil service reforms, and improvement of the performance of public enterprises.

The World Bank supported reforms in employment and pay as well as long-term management reforms. The even greater focus on reductions in civil service employment reflected the fact that, in many developing countries, government had become the employer of last resort. The welfare state in many of these countries was symbolized by bloated bureaucracy rather than by the social welfare programs of the developed world. Table II illustrates reduction techniques and totals in selected countries.

Employment reforms were focused on reducing the numbers of workers. A first priority was to establish information about who was employed and where by conducting a civil service census, and then to maintain the new information base. The technique identified temporary staff, assisted in the enforcement of the statutory retirement age, and identified the ranks of "ghost" workers, defined as salaries being paid to workers who have died, retired, or never existed, or even simply not turned up for work.

Recruitment freezes were used in many countries to stop personnel expansion while at the same time altering the expectations of future graduates with regards to public sector employment. Additionally, voluntary retirement payouts were made, and retraining instituted to ease the transition of retrenched workers. However, such payouts, as in developed countries, have often led to the loss of the best employees.

The payroll reforms that were implemented included reducing the proportion of nonwage benefits and allowances by monetizing all forms of compensation and cutting fringe benefits. The decompression of the wage

TABLE II. EMPLOYMENT REDUCTION MECHANISMS FOR SELECTED COUNTRIES, 1981–1990

Country	Ghost Removal	Early Retirement	Voluntary Departure	Retrenchment (reg. staff)	Retrenchment (temp. staff)	Other	Total
Cameroon	5,830	5,000	-	-	-	-	10,830
Congo	-	-	-	-	-	2,848	2,848
The Gambia	-	-	-	919	2,871	-	3,790
Ghana	11,000	4,235	-	44,375	-	-	48,610
Guinea	1,091	10,236	1,744	-	-	25,793	38,864
Guinea Bissau	800	945	1,960	921	-	-	3,826
Laos	-	-	16,890	-	-	-	16,890
Senegal	497	747	1,283	-	-	-	2,527
Sri Lanka	-	30,000	-	-	-	12,000	12,000
Uganda	20,000	-	-	-	-	-	20,000

SOURCE: World Bank (1991).

structure was also important in order to minimize the flight of professionals from the higher levels of government as a result of pay erosion. The retrenchment of excess staff often had as a key objective the production of savings that could be used to increase wages and salaries, as well as a dividend towards deficit reduction.

Another feature of reform has been the effort to link budget realities and personnel management decisions. Computerization is playing an increasing role in this work. The particularly gray area in many countries is the relationship between the policies and program priorities of government and staffing levels. The former are often not well articulated and the latter are often based not on program needs but on patrimonialism and the employer of last resort principle. This makes efforts at basing retrenchment on what is needed to deliver programs efficiently and effectively particularly challenging.

As for long-term reforms, functional reviews of organizations and government agencies were conducted in order to determine the level of staff, skill, and funds required for the effective performance of the organization. Civil service exams were proposed but not implemented except in Guinea where the results, however, were not acted upon. Incentive schemes have been carried out in some countries in order to improve recruitment of personnel and to retain existing ones.

It seems that the direction of reform in developing countries is similar to that of the developed countries. The need to search for and then achieve cutbacks in spending and staff has prevailed and the differences have been the methods used in the management of those cutbacks. For the developing countries, the reforms are a part of an entire restructuring process. The challenge is to draw on existing institutions, or create new ones, which discipline decision-making, and to ensure that resources are used to best effect in development.

MALCOLM HOLMES

BIBLIOGRAPHY

Brecher, Charles and Raymond D. Horton, 1985. "Retrenchment and Recovery: American Cities and the New York Experience." *Public Administration Review*, vol. 45 (March-April) 267–274.

Curtis, Jr., Russell L., 1989. "Cutbacks, Management and Human Relations: Meanings for Organizational Theory and Research." *Human Relations*, vol. 42 (August) 671–689.

Davis, J. Tait, 1991. "Institutional Impediments to Workforce Retrenchment in Ghana's State Enterprises." *World Development*, vol. 19 (August) 987–1005.

Doyle, Richard and Jerry McCaffery, 1992. "The Budget Enforcement Act After One Year." *Public Budgeting & Finance*, vol. 12 (Spring) 3–15.

Drucker, Peter, 1995. *The Atlantic Monthly* (February).

Dunsire, Andrew and Christopher Hood, 1989. *Cutback Management in Public Democracies*. Cambridge, UK: Cambridge University Press.

Governance, 1990. Special Issue on Managerial Reform, vol. 3 (April).

Joyce, Philip G., 1992. "The Budget Enforcement Act and Its Survival." *Public Budgeting & Finance*, vol. 12 (spring) 16–22.

Keating, M. and D. Rosalky, 1989. *Rolling Expenditure Plans: Australian Experience and Prognosis*. International Monetary Fund Seminar.

Kettl, Donald F., 1994. "Beyond the Rhetoric of Reinvention: Driving Themes of the Clinton Administration's Management Reforms." *Governance*, vol. 7. (July) 307–313.

Lane, Robert E., 1965. "The Politics of Consensus in an Age of Affluence." *American Political Science Review*, vol. 59 (December).

Larkey, Patrick D., Chandler Stolp and Mark Winer, 1981. "Theorizing About the Growth of Government: A Research Assessment." *Journal of Public Policy*, vol. 1 (May) 157–220.

Levine, Charles H., 1978. "Organizational Decline and Cutback Management." *Public Administration Review*, vol. 38 (July-August) 316–325.

Levine, Charles H., Irene S. Rubin and George G. Wolohojian, 1981. *The Politics of Retrenchment*. Beverly Hills, CA: Sage Publications.

Musgrave, Richard A., 1986. *Public Finance in a Democratic Society*, vols. I & II. New York: New York University Press.

National Performance Review, 1993. *Creating a Government that Works Better and Costs Less*, Washington, D.C. USGPO. Also see subsequent Annual Reports.

Niskanen, William A. 1971. *Bureaucracy and Representative Government*. Chicago, IL: Aldine.

Peters, Thomas J. and Robert H. Waterman, 1982. *In Search of Excellence*. New York: Harper and Row.

United States General Accounting Office, 1994. *Deficit Reduction, Experiences of Other Nations*. Washington, D.C.

Walsh, Peter, 1991. "Australian Fiscal Policy in the 1980s," to the Symposium on "Budget Enforcement: Where Do We Go from Here?" sponsored by The Committee for a Responsible Federal Budget, Washington, D.C., February 22, 1991.

World Bank, 1991. *The Reform of Public Sector Management: Lessons From Experience*. Washington, D.C.: World Bank.